THE
PATRIARCH

THE
PATRIARCH

*The Remarkable Life and Turbulent Times
of Joseph P. Kennedy*

DAVID NASAW

THE PENGUIN PRESS

New York

2012

THE PENGUIN PRESS
Published by the Penguin Group
Penguin Group (USA) Inc., 375 Hudson Street, New York, New York 10014, U.S.A. ·
Penguin Group (Canada), 90 Eglinton Avenue East, Suite 700, Toronto, Ontario,
Canada M4P 2Y3 (a division of Pearson Penguin Canada Inc.) · Penguin Books Ltd,
80 Strand, London WC2R 0RL, England · Penguin Ireland, 25 St Stephen's Green,
Dublin 2, Ireland (a division of Penguin Books Ltd) · Penguin Group (Australia),
707 Collins Street, Melbourne, Victoria 3008 Australia (a division of Pearson
Australia Group Pty Ltd) · Penguin Books India Pvt Ltd, 11 Community Centre,
Panchsheel Park, New Delhi – 110 017, India · Penguin Group (NZ), 67 Apollo
Drive, Rosedale, Auckland 0632, New Zealand (a division of Pearson New
Zealand Ltd) · Penguin Books, Rosebank Office Park, 181 Jan Smuts Avenue,
Parktown North 2193, South Africa · Penguin China, B7 Jaiming Center,
27 East Third Ring Road North, Chaoyang District, Beijing 100020, China

Penguin Books Ltd, Registered Offices:
80 Strand, London WC2R 0RL, England

First published in 2012 by The Penguin Press,
a member of Penguin Group (USA) Inc.

Copyright © David Nasaw, 2012
All rights reserved

Photograph credits appear on page 869.
Frontis photo © Bettmann/CORBIS

Library of Congress Cataloging-in-Publication Data

Nasaw, David.
The patriarch : the remarkable life and turbulent times of Joseph P. Kennedy / David
Nasaw.
p.   cm.
Includes bibliographical references and index.
ISBN 978-1-59420-376-3
1. Kennedy, Joseph P. (Joseph Patrick), 1888-1969.   2. Ambassadors—United States—
Biography.   3. Politicians—United States—Biography.   4. Businesspeople—United
States—Biography.   5. Kennedy family.   I. Title.
E748.K376N37   2012
973.9092—dc23
[B]
2012027315

Printed in the United States of America
1   3   5   7   9   10   8   6   4   2

DESIGNED BY MICHELLE MCMILLIAN

CONTENTS

Cast of Characters   ix

Introduction   xix

Part I: East Boston to Cambridge to Brookline   1

  One: Dunganstown to East Boston   3

  Two: School Days   16

  Three: Starting Out   32

  Four: War   47

  Five: Making a Million   58

Part II: Hollywood   83

  Six: "My Own Master in My Own Business"   85

  Seven: Hollywood   105

  Eight: Gloria and Rose   128

  Nine: Last Exit from Hollywood   149

Part III: Washington   165

  Ten: On the Roosevelt Train   167

  Eleven: Waiting for the Call   185

  Twelve: To Washington   204

  Thirteen: Reelecting Roosevelt   238

  Fourteen: Maritime Commissioner   254

Part IV: London   281

  Fifteen: A Plainspoken Ambassador   283

  Sixteen: A Rather Dreadful Homecoming   312

  Seventeen: Munich   323

  Eighteen: The Kennedy Plan   348

  Nineteen: Sidelined and Censored   371

  Twenty: "This Country Is at War with Germany"   399

  Twenty-one: The Lives of Americans Are at Stake   408

  Twenty-two: Defeatist   427

  Twenty-three: The Fall of France   444

  Twenty-four: The Worst of Times   457

  Twenty-five: There's Hell to Pay Tonight   473

Part V: Washington, but Briefly   487

  Twenty-six: Home Again   489

  Twenty-seven: The Man Who Out-Hamleted Hamlet   505

Part VI: Palm Beach and Hyannis Port   523

  Twenty-eight: A Forced Retirement   525

  Twenty-nine: War   538

  Thirty: "A Melancholy Business"   570

  Thirty-one: The Candidate's Father   591

  Thirty-two: Family Matters   610

  Thirty-three: "The Great Debate"   632

  Thirty-four: The Next Senator from Massachusetts   652

  Thirty-five: Retirement   671

  Thirty-six: Making Money and Giving It Away   692

  Thirty-seven: The Catholic Candidate   709

  Thirty-eight: Electing a President   726

  Thirty-nine: "He Belongs to the Country"   749

  Forty: "No!"   775

Acknowledgments   789

Notes   793

Bibliography of Works Cited   829

Index   835

CAST OF CHARACTERS

Joseph Patrick Kennedy (1888–1969, m. 1914)
Rose Elizabeth Fitzgerald Kennedy (1890–1995, m. 1914), wife of
  Joseph P. Kennedy

Children and Children's Spouses
Joseph Patrick Kennedy, Jr. (1915–1944)
John Fitzgerald Kennedy, "Jack" (1917–1963, m. 1953)
Jacqueline Bouvier Kennedy (1929–1994, m. 1953), wife of
  John Kennedy
Rose Marie Kennedy, "Rosemary" (1918–2005)
Kathleen Agnes Kennedy Hartington, "Kick" (1920–1948, m. 1944)
William Cavendish, Marquess of Hartington, Billy Hartington
  (1917–1944, m. 1944), eldest son of the 10th Duke of Devonshire,
  husband of "Kick" Kennedy
Eunice Mary Kennedy Shriver (1921–2009, m. 1953)
Robert Sargent Shriver, "Sargent Shriver" or "Sarge" (1915–2011, m.
  1953), husband of Eunice Kennedy
Patricia Kennedy, "Pat" (1924–2006, m. 1954)
Peter Lawford (1923–1984, m. 1954), husband of Patricia Kennedy
Robert Francis Kennedy, "Bobby" (1925–1968, m. 1950)
Ethel Skakel Kennedy (1928–, m. 1950), wife of Robert Kennedy
Jean Ann Kennedy Smith (1928–, m. 1956)

Stephen Edward Smith, "Steve" (1927–1990, m. 1956), husband of
    Jean Kennedy
Edward Moore Kennedy, "Ted" (1932–2009, m. 1958, 1992)
Joan Bennett Kennedy (1936–, m. 1958), first wife of Edward Kennedy

Joseph P. Kennedy's Parents
Patrick Joseph Kennedy, "P.J." (1858–1929, m. 1887), father of
    Joseph P. Kennedy
Mary Augusta Hickey Kennedy (1857–1923, m. 1887), mother of
    Joseph P. Kennedy

Joseph P. Kennedy's Paternal Grandparents
Patrick Kennedy (ca. 1823–1858, m. 1849), grandfather
Bridget Murphy Kennedy (1821–1888, m. 1849), grandmother

Joseph P. Kennedy's Parents-in-Law
John Francis Fitzgerald, "Honey Fitz" (1863–1950), father-in-law of
    Kennedy, mayor of Boston (1906–1908 and 1910–1914)
Mary Josephine Hannon Fitzgerald, "Josie" (1865–1964),
    mother-in-law of Kennedy, wife of John Francis Fitzgerald

Dean Acheson, assistant secretary of state (1941–1945),
    under secretary of state (1945), secretary of state (1949–1953)
Robert S. Allen, journalist, co-columnist with Drew Pearson,
    "Washington Merry-Go-Round"
Joseph Alsop, Washington columnist
Nancy Astor, Lady Astor, member of Parliament (1919–1945),
    Cliveden set
Waldorf Astor, Lord Astor, politician, newspaper owner
Bernard Baruch, businessman, financier, Democratic Party adviser
Lord Beaverbrook, Max Aitken, newspaper owner, minister
    of aircraft production (1940–1941), minister of supply
    (1941–1942), Kennedy friend
Anthony Joseph Drexel Biddle, Jr., "Tony," ambassador to Poland
    (1937–1943), ambassador to governments in exile (1941–1943),
    U.S. Army in Europe (1944–1955)
Kirk LeMoyne Billings, "Lem," JFK friend

John Boettiger, husband of Anna Roosevelt, editor of *Seattle Post-Intelligencer*

Benjamin C. Bradlee, journalist and editor of *Washington Post, Newsweek*

Louis Brandeis, Supreme Court justice (1916–1939), Roosevelt adviser

Bart Brickley, Boston lawyer, Kennedy friend

William Christian Bullitt, Jr., ambassador to France (1936–1940)

John Burns, law professor, Massachusetts judge, SEC general counsel, Kennedy attorney and friend

Rab Butler, under-secretary of state for foreign affairs (1938–1941)

James Byrnes, senator from South Carolina (1931–1941), Supreme Court justice (1941–1942), Economic Stabilization Office (1942–1943), secretary of state (1945–1947)

Sir Alexander Cadogan, permanent under-secretary for foreign affairs (1938–1946)

Sir James Calder, head of Distillers Company, Kennedy friend

Boake Carter, radio commentator, Kennedy friend

Father John Cavanaugh, president of Notre Dame (1946–1952), Kennedy friend

Neville Chamberlain, prime minister (1937–1940)

Winston Churchill, first lord of the Admiralty (1939–1940), prime minister (1940–1945)

Count Galeazzo Ciano, Italian minister of foreign affairs (1936–1943), Mussolini's son-in-law

Clark Clifford, Washington lawyer, head of JFK transition team

Ralph Coghlan, editor of *St. Louis Post-Dispatch*, JFK campaign adviser

Benjamin V. Cohen, attorney, New Deal adviser

Duff Cooper, first lord of the Admiralty (1937–1938), minister of information (1940–1941)

Thomas Gardiner Corcoran, attorney, Felix Frankfurter protégé, New Deal and Lyndon Johnson adviser

Robert Coughlin, collaborator, ghostwriter for Rose Fitzgerald Kennedy's *Times to Remember*

James Michael Curley, mayor of Boston for several terms, representative from Massachusetts (1911–1914, 1943–1947), governor of Massachusetts (1935–1937)

Guy Currier, Massachusetts legislator, lawyer, lobbyist

Archbishop Richard Cushing, archbishop of Boston (1944–1970), cardinal (1958–1970)

Mark Dalton, JFK campaign manager (1946, 1952)

Russell Davenport, managing editor of *Fortune* magazine

Marion Davies, actress, mistress of William Randolph Hearst

Eddie (E. B.) Derr, Kennedy business associate

Paul A. Dever, candidate for lieutenant governor of Massachusetts (1946), governor of Massachusetts (1949–1953)

Thomas E. Dewey, governor of New York (1943–1954), Republican candidate for president (1944, 1948)

Joseph Dinneen, journalist with *Boston Globe*

Herbert von Dirksen, German ambassador to Great Britain

William J. Donovan, "Colonel Donovan" or "Wild Bill," lawyer, intelligence officer, Roosevelt adviser

William O. Douglas, law professor, SEC commissioner, Supreme Court justice (1939–1975), Kennedy friend

Morton Downey, singer, Kennedy friend

Allen Welsh Dulles, director of the Central Intelligence Agency (1953–1961)

Dwight D. Eisenhower, supreme commander of Allied forces in Europe (World War II), supreme Allied commander (1951–1952), president (1953–1961)

Henri, Marquis de la Falaise de la Coudraye, Gloria Swanson's husband

James Farley, postmaster general (1933–1940), Roosevelt adviser

James Fayne, Kennedy classmate, business associate

Robert Fisher, Harvard roommate and Kennedy friend

John J. Ford, "Johnnie," business associate, Fore River, Maine and New Hampshire Theatre Company, New York City office

James Forrestal, secretary of the navy (1944–1947), secretary of defense (1947–1949)

Felix Frankfurter, Harvard Law School professor, Supreme Court justice (1939–1962), Roosevelt adviser

Count Enrico Galeazzi, Rome liaison to Knights of Columbus, Vatican adviser, Kennedy friend

Ann Gargan, Rose's niece, chief caregiver after Kennedy stroke

John Nance Garner IV, representative from Texas (1903–1933),
Speaker of the House (1931–1933), vice president (1933–1941)

Robert L. Ghormley, vice admiral, Roosevelt military adviser

Arthur Goldsmith, Harvard classmate, Kennedy friend

Dr. Frederick Good, family doctor and obstetrician for Kennedy
children

Edmund Goulding, "Eddie," movie and stage director, screenwriter

Lord Halifax, E. F. L. Wood, foreign secretary (1938–1940), British
ambassador to the United States (1940–1946)

William Harrison Hays, Sr., "Will," president of the Motion Picture
Producers and Distributors of America

William Randolph Hearst, publishing magnate, head of Cosmopolitan
Pictures

Nevile Henderson, British ambassador to Germany (1937–1939)

Luella Hennessey, Kennedy family nurse

Father Theodore Hesburgh, president of Notre Dame (1952–1987)

Sir Samuel Hoare, Conservative Party politician, home secretary
(1937–1939)

Herbert Hoover, president (1929–1933), chair of Hoover Commission
(1947–1949, 1953–1955)

J. Edgar Hoover, director of the Federal Bureau of Investigation
(1935–1972)

Harry Hopkins, Roosevelt adviser, New Deal agency administrator

Arthur Houghton, manager of Fred Stone, Hollywood executive,
Kennedy friend

Louis McHenry Howe, Roosevelt adviser

Cordell Hull, senator from Tennessee (1931–1933), secretary of state
(1933–1944)

Harold L. Ickes, secretary of the interior (1933–1952)

Lyndon Baines Johnson, representative from Texas (1937–1949),
senator from Texas (1949–1961), Senate minority leader
(1953–1955), Senate majority leader (1955–1961), vice president
(1961–1963), president (1963–1969)

Joseph Kane, Kennedy cousin, family political representative in
Boston

Estes Kefauver, senator from Tennessee (1949–1963), Democratic
nominee for vice president (1956)

John Kennedy (no relation), "London Jack," journalist, publicist for Kennedy

Frank Kent, Baltimore columnist, New Deal opponent

Tyler Kent, U.S. embassy (London) code clerk, convicted of stealing documents

Philip Kerr, Lord Lothian, British ambassador to the United States (1939–1940)

Robert Kintner, co-columnist until 1942 with Joseph Alsop

Louis Kirstein, David Sarnoff friend, Boston department store owner, investor in FBO

Harvey Klemmer, Maritime Commission, attached to U.S. embassy in London (1938–1940)

Frank Knox, publisher of *Chicago Daily News*, Republican nominee for vice president (1936), secretary of the navy (1940–1944)

Arthur Krock, Washington bureau chief of *New York Times*, Kennedy family adviser

Ferdinand Kuhn, Jr., journalist with *New York Times*

James Landis, law professor, SEC commissioner, Kennedy lawyer, friend, adviser

Alfred M. Landon, "Alf," Republican candidate for president (1936)

Harold Laski, London School of Economics, tutor to Joe Kennedy, Jr.

Jesse Lasky, Hollywood producer and executive

General Raymond E. Lee, military attaché at U.S. embassy in London

Missy LeHand, secretary to President Roosevelt

John L. Lewis, labor leader, CIO organizer

Charles Lindbergh, aviator, opposed United States entry in World War II

Ronald Lindsay, British ambassador to the United States (1929–1939)

Walter Lippmann, Washington-based syndicated columnist

Henry Cabot Lodge, Jr., senator from Massachusetts

Breckinridge Long, ambassador to Italy (1933–1936), special assistant secretary of state (1939–1940), assistant secretary of state (1940–1944)

Clare Boothe Luce, actress, playwright, wife of Henry Luce, representative from Connecticut (1943–1947), ambassador to Italy (1953–1956)

Henry Luce, "Harry" (1898–1967), publisher of *Time, Life,* and *Fortune* magazines

Louis Lyons, journalist with *Boston Globe*

General Douglas MacArthur, UN commander in Korea (1950–1951)

Malcolm MacDonald, colonial secretary (1938–1940)

Torbert Macdonald, JFK classmate, politician, friend

George Marshall, secretary of state (1947–1949), author of Marshall Plan

Joseph McCarthy, senator from Wisconsin (1947–1957), Permanent Subcommittee on Investigations (1953–1955)

John McClellan, senator from Arkansas (1943–1977), Permanent Subcommittee on Investigations (1955–1973)

John W. McCormack, representative from Massachusetts (1928–1971), House majority leader

Colonel Robert McCormick, anti–New Deal publisher of *Chicago Tribune*

Timothy McInerny, Boston newspaper editor, family friend

Jeremiah Milbank, banker, associate of Elisha Walker

Jay Pierrepont Moffat, State Department's Western European division (1937–1940)

Raymond Moley, New Deal "brain trust," Roosevelt adviser, newspaper editor

Edward Moore, "Eddie," Kennedy friend, business associate, surrogate parent to Kennedy children

Mary Moore, wife of Eddie Moore, family friend

Henry Morgenthau, Jr., secretary of the treasury (1934–1945)

Francis Morrissey, "Frank," JFK campaign aide, nominee for federal district judge

Frank Murphy, governor of Michigan, Supreme Court justice, Kennedy friend

Paul Murphy, manager of operations, New York City office

Cardinal Eugenio Pacelli, Roman Catholic cardinal, secretary of state for the Vatican (1930–1939), Pope Pius XII (1939–1958)

Cissy Patterson, newspaper editor and owner of *Washington Times-Herald*

Joseph Patterson, editor of New York *Daily News*

Drew Pearson, syndicated columnist

Ferdinand Pecora, chief counsel, Senate Committee on Banking and Currency (1933–1934), SEC commissioner

Frances Perkins, secretary of labor (1933–1945)

Arthur B. Poole, business associate, accountant, Pathé, Hearst Corporation

Dave Powers, JFK adviser

Sam Rayburn, representative from Texas (1913–1961), Speaker of the House

James Reston, London journalist with Associated Press, chief diplomatic correspondent for *New York Times*

Paul Reynaud, prime minister of France (1940)

John J. Reynolds, Kennedy real estate adviser

Joachim von Ribbentrop, German ambassador to London, minister for foreign affairs (1938–1945)

Anna Roosevelt, daughter of President Roosevelt

James Roosevelt, "Jimmy," son of President Roosevelt, secretary to the president

Carroll Rosenbloom, Baltimore businessman, Palm Beach friend

George Rublee, director of the Intergovernmental Committee on Refugees

Louis Ruppel, journalist with *Chicago Times*

Howard Rusk, director of the Institute of Physical Medicine and Rehabilitation

Leverett Saltonstall, governor of Massachusetts (1939–1979), senator from Massachusetts (1945–1967)

David Sarnoff, RCA executive, founder of RKO

Joseph Schenck, Hollywood executive

Arthur Schlesinger, Jr., founder of Americans for Democratic Action, historian of JFK presidency, Robert Kennedy biographer

Sir John Simon, chancellor of the Exchequer (1937–1940)

George Smathers, representative from Florida (1947–1951), senator from Florida (1951–1969)

Al Smith, governor of New York (1919–1920, 1923–1928), Democratic presidential candidate (1928)

Theodore Sorensen, "Ted," speechwriter, chief adviser for JFK

Francis Joseph Spellman, Roman Catholic auxiliary bishop of Boston

(1932–1939), archbishop of New York (1939–1967), cardinal (1946–1967)

Adlai Stevenson, governor of Illinois (1949–1953), candidate for president (1952, 1956)

Henry L. Stimson, secretary of war (1940–1945)

Galen Stone, Kennedy mentor, founder of Hayden, Stone & Co.

Gloria Swanson, film star

Herbert Bayard Swope, editor of *New York World,* Democratic Party adviser, Bernard Baruch friend

Robert A. Taft, senator from Ohio (1939–1953)

Myron Charles Taylor, industrialist, represented United States at Évian Conference, president's representative to Vatican

Eugene Thayer, Boston and New York banker, Kennedy friend, business associate

Fred Thomson, film star

Joseph F. Timilty, "the Commish," Boston police commissioner, Kennedy friend

Walter Trohan, journalist with *Chicago Tribune*

Max Truitt, Maritime Commission, Kennedy friend

Harry S. Truman, president, 1945–1953

Arthur H. Vandenberg, senator from Michigan (1928–1951)

Elisha Walker, Wall Street investment banker, business associate

Henry A. Wallace, vice president (1941–1945), secretary of commerce (1945–1946)

David I. Walsh, senator from Massachusetts (1919–1925, 1926–1947)

Chaim Weizmann, Zionist leader, first president of Israel

Sumner Welles, under secretary of state (1937–1943)

Burton K. Wheeler, senator from Montana (1923–1947)

Thomas J. White, associate of and financial adviser to William Randolph Hearst

Wendell Willkie, Republican candidate for president (1940)

Horace Wilson, adviser to Neville Chamberlain

Stephen Wise, Zionist leader, American Reform rabbi

John Wright, Archbishop Cushing's secretary, bishop of Worcester, Massachusetts (1950–1959), bishop of Pittsburgh (1959–1969)

Darryl F. Zanuck, Hollywood producer

Adolph Zukor, Hollywood executive

INTRODUCTION

Joseph P. Kennedy was a man of boundless talents, magnetic charm, relentless energy, and unbridled ambition. His life was punctuated by meteoric rises, catastrophic falls, and numerous rebirths, by cascading joys and blinding sorrows, and by a tragic ending near Shakespearean in its pathos. An Irish Catholic from East Boston, he was proud of his heritage but refused to be defined by it. He fought to open doors that were closed to him, then having forced his way inside, he refused to play by the rules. He spoke his mind—when he should not have. Too often, he let his fears speak for him. He was distrustful, often contemptuous of those in power—and did not disguise it. His anger and his hatreds were legendary, especially at those whom he believed had betrayed him.

For the last thirty years of his life—and for more than four decades since his death—Joseph P. Kennedy has been vilified and dismissed as an appeaser, an isolationist, an anti-Semite, a Nazi sympathizer, an unprincipled womanizer, a treacherous and vengeful scoundrel who made millions as a bootlegger and Wall Street swindler, then used those millions to steal elections for his son. Tales of his immoralities, his mischiefs, and his criminal associations have multiplied, one on top of the other, until they have pushed into the background every other aspect of his and his family's remarkable story. That there is some truth to these allegations is indisputable, but they tell only part of a larger, grander, more complicated history.

Joseph P. Kennedy grew up the pampered son of a powerful and respected East Boston ward leader and businessman, then crossed the Inner Harbor to Boston Latin, where he led a near charmed life as a star athlete, class president, and boyfriend of the mayor's very pretty daughter. On graduation, he crossed another body of water, to Cambridge and Harvard College, where, as an Irish Catholic, he found himself for the first time in his life the odd man out.

There were no tortuous journeys of self-exploration. By the time Joe Kennedy left college, he knew who he was: the smartest man in the room, the one who would come out ahead in every negotiation he entered into. His ambition was to secure a place in a major Boston bank or financial house, but such positions, he discovered on graduation from Harvard, were reserved for "proper Bostonians," not the sons of East Boston Irish Catholic ward leaders. He made the best of the situation by getting a civil service job as an assistant bank examiner. At age twenty-five, he was named president of the East Boston bank his father had helped found. He could have remained there and made a healthy living for himself and his rapidly growing family, but he wanted more and had to leave Boston to find it.

During the 1920s, he was a major player in the nation's fastest-growing industry, moving pictures, and one of the few Irish Catholics to own or run a studio. The Hollywood he encountered was not a dream factory. It was a town and an industry focused on raising money to finance the transition to sound and organizing itself to repel attempts at censorship. Kennedy arrived as the head of a minor debt-ridden studio and positioned himself as a non-Jewish white knight who would rescue the industry from those who questioned its taste and its morals. He promised to apply a banker's good sense to making pictures: to cut production costs, raise studio profits, and boost share prices. His rise was meteoric, but he reached too far and traveled too fast. After only a few years in the industry, he retired—with Gloria Swanson as his mistress and millions of dollars in stock options.

Trusting no one, with no allegiance to any industry or firm or individual or place, he made a fortune in Hollywood, then in New York, buying and selling options, stocks, and bonds in the companies he managed or with which he was associated. Recognizing that the market was oversold, he anticipated the crash of October 1929, shifted the bulk of his fortune into safe havens, then made millions more by selling short into a falling market.

A multimillionaire by the age of forty, his outlook on the world was transformed in the early years of the Depression from one of hopeful expectation to an almost unshakeable pessimism. His fears for the future of capitalism should the Depression deepen prompted him to abandon the private sector in 1932 to campaign for Franklin Roosevelt's election as president. A conservative banker and stock trader with no experience in national politics, he was the odd man out on the campaign trail and, later, in New Deal Washington. But he forced his way inside. Few government appointments have been as universally condemned as was President Roosevelt's choice of Joseph P. Kennedy, a Wall Street operator, to be the first chairman of the Securities and Exchange Commission in 1934. And few were as universally acclaimed as Kennedy's was within months of his assuming his post. His years in Washington as chairman of the SEC, then chairman of the Maritime Commission, were marked by triumph, his reputation as a nonpartisan, truth-telling miracle worker enhanced to the point where he was prominently mentioned as a possible presidential candidate.

He was rewarded for his service in Washington with appointment as ambassador to the Court of St. James's. The first Irish American to be named to London, with no experience whatsoever to prepare him for the post, he was an outsider again, but this time he reveled in it. His grand successes in business and in government had boosted his already considerable confidence in his own judgment and his understanding of global economics. He would speak the truth as he saw it—and be saluted for it. He would, he was sure, triumph in London, as he had in Hollywood, on Wall Street, and in Washington. He was wrong. Driven, nearly obsessed, by fears that the war on the horizon would, if not prevented, deepen the depression, weaken capitalism and democracy, endanger the fortune he hoped to hand over to his children, and threaten the lives of a generation of young men, including his older boys, and convinced that no one in Washington understood the extent of the danger or how to deal with it, he set his own diplomatic agenda, violated State Department directives with impunity, and dedicated himself to preserving the peace—single-handedly, if necessary.

Already an outlier, he courted new criticism in Washington and London, first as a toady for Prime Minister Neville Chamberlain and the Cliveden set, then as a defeatist, a loud-mouthed Cassandra who believed the Nazis would easily conquer Europe and Great Britain. He returned to Washington in disgrace. He tried to be of service to his country after Pearl Harbor, but there was no place for him in the Roosevelt administration that he believed worthy of his talents.

He took little joy at the cessation of hostilities—his family's sacrifices had been too great. In the postwar period, his pessimism became more corrosive still, as did his conviction that he had been right all along to oppose the war against the dictators. He stridently, proudly, renewed his calls for appeasement, this time of the Soviet Union, and for isolation from rather than engagement in the world outside the western hemisphere, and did all he could to provoke a "great debate" on the wisdom of fighting a cold war that, he feared, might turn hot at any moment.

Had Joseph P. Kennedy not been the patriarch of America's first family, his story would be worth telling. That he was only adds to its drama and historical significance. His primary goal, as a younger man, was to make so much money that his children would not have to make any and could devote their lives to public service. He accomplished that much before he was forty. He took his role as the parent of nine seriously. He was an active, loving, attentive, sometimes intrusive father. He pushed his children forward, gave them advice whether they solicited it or not, gently chided them to do better, taught them to rely on one another, that family was sacred. He raised them to be as confident and as stubborn as he was, and as relentlessly optimistic as he was pessimistic—and, for the most part, they were. They understood his virtues and his vices, adored him for who he was. And they learned to push back, to make their own decisions, including ones he disagreed with.

The Kennedy children would complete the journey from Dungans-town, Ireland, to East Boston to the pinnacle of American political power and social prominence that their father had begun. He would glory in their political and personal triumphs. But the sorrows he endured as a father were as intense as the joys. All his life, he feared for his son Jack, who nearly died of scarlet fever at age two, was continually ill as a child and young man, and was debilitated by pain as an adult. And he feared for his eldest daughter, Rosemary, who, despite the best care his money could buy, never found her way. In the fall of 1940, recognizing that there was no cure for her retardation but advised that a simple operation might make it easier for her to live with it, he arranged a lobotomy that went horribly wrong. In August 1944, almost four years after Rosemary's operation, he suffered the greatest tragedy of his life when his eldest son and namesake, Joseph P. Kennedy, Jr., was incinerated in a bombing mission off the coast of England. In the spring of 1948, his second daughter, Kick, was killed in a plane crash in France. A decade and a half later, after he had been rendered speechless by stroke, he lost two more sons, this time to assassins' bullets.

When Ambassador Jean Kennedy Smith and Senator Edward Kennedy, on behalf of their family, asked me to write a biography of their father, I agreed to do so, but only if I was granted full cooperation, unfettered access to Joseph P. Kennedy's papers in the John F. Kennedy Presidential Library, including those closed to researchers, and unrestricted permission to cite any document I came across. The family accepted my conditions. No attempts were made to withhold information or to censor this book in any way.

I have spent six years in libraries, archives, and private homes in New York, Boston, Washington, Chicago, London, Los Angeles, Austin, Palm Beach, and Hyannis Port, studying thousands of documents, many of them never seen before by any researcher: unpublished diaries, telephone transcripts, diplomatic dispatches, interviews, oral histories, letters and cables, business memoranda, balance sheets, financial reports, FBI investigations, German diplomatic records, and the secret British Foreign Office "Kennedyiana" files. Research assistants located additional materials for me in Rome, in the Central Zionist Archives in Jerusalem, and at dozens of libraries and archives on three continents. I interviewed Joseph P. Kennedy's children, grandchildren, relatives, friends, employees, and business associates.

After reading newspaper and magazine accounts and the secondary literature on Joseph P. Kennedy and his family, I put it all aside, and started over again, taking nothing for granted, dissecting every tale and rumor, discarding anecdotal second- and thirdhand observations that I could not substantiate. Because this is the first biography based entirely on the historical evidence and because much of the material that was opened to me has been seen by no one else, the portrait I paint may bear slight resemblance to the ones that have appeared up to now in print or on film.

My goal in *The Patriarch* has been to narrate the life story of a remarkable man and the history of the turbulent times he lived through, the events he participated in, the men and women with whom he came into contact. We too often write our histories from the viewpoint of the insiders, of the winners. In consigning to the dustbin the views, the ideas, the sorrows, hopes, and fears of those who were forced or chose to remain on the outside, we diminish our pasts, robbing history of its density, its richness, its vitality. In reexamining the life of Joseph P. Kennedy, we relive our recent past and discover in it much we did not know was there.

This is the story of an outsider who forced his way into the halls of power and became both a witness and participant to the major events of the past century: booms, busts, wars and cold war, and the birth of a new frontier. Every biography is at one and the same time the portrait of an individual and of an era. In telling the story of Joseph P. Kennedy, we retell the history of the twentieth century.

PART I

East Boston to
Cambridge to Brookline

One

DUNGANSTOWN TO
EAST BOSTON

The Kennedy saga, like that of so many American families, begins with an ancestor's escape from poverty and oppression. Sometime in 1848 or 1849—we are not sure when—Joseph P. Kennedy's grandfather Patrick emigrated from Dunganstown in County Wexford, in flight from crop failure, famine, and the near genocidal effects of British colonialism.

The potato had been both the salvation and the curse of the Irish. By the 1840s, some million and a half survived on potatoes alone; for another three and a half million (out of a population of eight million), the potato constituted the major source of nourishment. When the harvest was late or the previous year's crop eaten up—as it often was by late summer—people went hungry. When the harvest failed, people died.

Had the British authorities been more attentive or humane, the potato blight of the 1840s might not have led to such devastation. But Parliament provided insufficient relief for a distant and despised people and then, in June 1847, passed the Irish Poor Law Extension Act, which mandated that already destitute communities raise their own tax moneys for poor relief, not one farthing of which was to go to heads of household renting a quarter acre or more of land. To qualify for relief, starving tenants had to abandon their farms. Those who remained were

evicted for failure to pay their taxes. The newly landless who could afford passage off the island emigrated. Large numbers of those who remained behind perished. From 1845 through the early 1850s, more than
a million died and two million more, about one quarter of the population, departed for North America.

Mass migrations are made up of individual journeys, and while Patrick Kennedy carried with him many of the same scars as did his
compatriots, he differed from them in significant ways. The Kennedys
were from County Wexford, on the southeast coast of Ireland, a region
"well served," Irish historian David Doyle has written, "by banks and
trade networks . . . and by schools." Population densities were relatively
low, land more fertile, agriculture somewhat diversified, landholdings
larger and costlier, and the percentage who emigrated smaller than that
from other Irish counties. While in the poorer north and west small
farmers divided their land among their sons, in the southeast the family farms were held intact and passed on from father to oldest son.[1]

As the third son and fourth child in his family, Patrick would have
no inheritance—and he knew it. The Kennedy leasehold would be
passed on to his older brother; additional resources would go toward a
dowry for his older sister and a second leasehold for brother number
two. Patrick could, had he chosen, have remained on the family leasehold as a landless laborer. Instead, he left the family farm at Dunganstown and walked the six and a half kilometers north along the River
Barrow to New Ross, the nearby, still thriving port town, where he
found employment at a cooperage.

There was a decent living to be made as a cooper, or barrel maker.
As the commercialization of Irish agriculture proceeded apace in the
1830s and 1840s, more land had been dedicated to the production of
wheat and barley for export off the island or to local breweries and
distilleries. Whatever form it took, grain or liquor, the barley and wheat
were transported in wooden barrels, which were handcrafted by New
Ross coopers.

In good times, there had been more than enough work for coopers
like Patrick Kennedy, formerly of Dunganstown. But these were not
good times. By 1848 or 1849, the effects of blight, famine, and depres-

sion had reached into every corner and occupational strata (undertakers excepted). Patrick Kennedy, already one step removed from the family farm, had little to detain him in Ireland.

There are several young Patricks, Pats, and P. Kennedys in the passenger lists of ships arriving in Boston in the late 1840s from Liverpool or New Ross. We cannot be sure which was our Patrick. But we can be certain that whether he left from New Ross or Liverpool, he was six weeks on a "coffin" ship, so called because for so many it would be a final resting place. With little edible food and a minimum of potable water, hundreds of men, women, infants, and the elderly were locked together in darkened, unventilated ships' holds for weeks on end, hatches battened, with no room to stretch, no decent air to breathe, and no escape from the accumulating human waste, the scourge of seasickness, hunger, and thirst, the stench of decay, disease, and dying, and the endless boredom, broken only by fits of panic when storms rocked or fire threatened. Only the strongest survived the passage with body and soul intact.

Patrick was one of these.

He arrived in East Boston (or Noddle's Island, as it was still known) and remained there for the remainder of his life.

East Boston was everything that New Ross was not. The population was growing, jobs and housing were available, and no one, not even the poorest of the poor, starved to death. East Boston had been annexed to Boston in the 1630s but remained virtually ignored and uninhabited until 1833, when William Sumner, a large landowner, joined forces with a few partners and, incorporated as the East Boston Company, raised sufficient capital to subdivide the land into a grid of streets and squares, sell off the most promising sites for vacation homes, build wharves, and arrange for regular ferry service across the harbor to Boston. By 1835, the population on the island was up to 604 from 24 just ten years before. Four years later, the partners' wildest dreams were realized when Samuel Cunard, who had been granted the right to transfer mail from England to North America, chose East Boston as his American terminus. By 1840, Cunard ships from Liverpool were arriving with regularity every fortnight, carrying not just the mail but every variety of English manufacture. East Boston prospered because it provided transatlantic shippers with a deepwater port, newly constructed and well-maintained piers, and easy access to warehouses and rail lines. It was also hundreds of miles closer to English, Irish, and Scottish ports than were Philadelphia or New York.[2]

By the time Patrick Kennedy walked down the gangplank after his six weeks at sea, East Boston was well on its way to becoming, as William Sumner declared in a letter to a business associate, so prosperous and populous that it could be accounted "a second Brooklyn." There were jobs aplenty for unskilled laborers and skilled artisans and mechanics unloading, repacking, and reshipping goods arrived from across the Atlantic and, after midcentury, supplying California's ballooning mining population, which, until the transcontinental railroads reached the West Coast, had to be fed, clothed, housed, informed, and entertained by eastern goods carried in clipper ships built in and sailing out of East Boston. "Ploughs and printing-presses, picks and shovels, absinthe and rum, house-frames and grindstones, clocks and dictionaries, melodeons and cabinet organs, fancy biscuits and canned salmon, oysters and lobsters; in fact everything one can imagine went through Boston on its way to the miners and ranchers of the white man's new empires."[3]

All of this and more—grain, rum, sugar, and salted fish—was shipped in wooden barrels, crates, and casks, fashioned by coopers such as Patrick Kennedy. Because he brought with him a marketable skill for which there was growing demand, Patrick Kennedy was one of the more fortunate Irish immigrants. The coopers were not the best-paid artisans, but they were offered higher daily wages and steadier employment than unskilled day laborers. We don't have statistics for Boston, but we know that coopers in New York in 1855 earned an average of $1.42 a day, almost 50 percent more than teamsters, cartmen, ditch diggers, and day laborers, the positions in which unskilled Irish immigrants predominated.[4]

With steady work on the horizon, Patrick Kennedy was able to marry Bridget Murphy, another recent emigrant from County Wexford, in September 1849 and buy a house. East Boston, though pockmarked with cheaply built shacks and permeated by the stench and smoke of shipyards and workshops, was not a bad place for first-generation Irish American parents to start a family. The population density was lower than in Boston; there was space to start a garden; rents and house prices were more affordable. Those who wished to attend Mass could do so in the meetinghouse of the Maverick Congregational Church, which in 1844 had been purchased and converted into a Catholic church dedicated to the patronage of St. Nicholas.[5]

Bridget and Patrick's first child, Mary, was born in 1851, followed by a second daughter, Joanna, in 1852; a son, John, in 1854 (he died at twenty months of cholera); a third daughter, Margaret, in 1855, and Patrick Joseph Kennedy in January 1858, nicknamed "P.J." so as not to be confused with his father. The family prospered as long as Patrick was able to bring home his paycheck. Regrettably, one of the disastrous by-products of steady work as a cooper was exhaustion. While most unskilled laborers—and the majority of skilled artisans—worked about sixty hours a week, coopers were expected to put in twelve hours a day, six days a week. Few could survive such a grueling pace for long. Patrick Kennedy did not. He died in November 1858, ten months after the birth of his son. The direct cause of death was cholera, but eight or nine years of seventy-two-hour weeks in the cooperage had no doubt weakened him to the point where he could neither resist nor survive the infection.[6]

Irish-born males of Patrick Kennedy's generation had a particularly high death rate in Boston, leaving unimaginably large numbers of second-generation Irish Americans like P.J. to be raised by their mothers. The four Irish Americans who in the years to come would dominate Boston politics—Martin Lomasney, John Francis Fitzgerald, James Michael Curley, and P. J. Kennedy—all lost their fathers in childhood.[7]

Patrick Kennedy, dead at thirty-five, with four young children, could not have picked a worse time to leave his family without its chief breadwinner. The financial panic of 1857, which directly affected both shipbuilding and international trade, swept through East Boston like the plague. The Kennedys were among the fortunate few who had the minimal resources necessary to keep the family intact, perhaps because Patrick had earned better wages as a skilled artisan than the mass of unskilled Irish laborers. On June 25, 1860, a little more than one and a half years after Patrick's death, Assistant Marshal Cyrus Washburn, the census taker for Boston's second ward, reported that Bridget Kennedy had personal effects worth $75, not an insignificant amount compared with those listed for her neighbors. Identified on the census records as members of her household were her four surviving children and two boarders, Mary Roach, eighteen, and six-year-old Michael O'Brien. In return for room and board, Mary Roach may have looked after the three Kennedy daughters and two-year-old P.J., while Bridget left the house looking for employment.[8]

Kennedy lore has it that Bridget Kennedy worked as a housecleaner and hairdresser before becoming the owner of an East Boston notions shop. Because her shop was located near the ferry, she began selling groceries and liquor to workingmen and -women returning to East Boston from jobs across the Inner Harbor. The 1880 census lists her occupation as "bakery," so we can assume she added baked goods to the wares. Her assets continued to grow through the decade. When she died in 1888, she left an estate valued at $2,200 (the equivalent of almost $54,000 today in purchasing power), with $375 of furniture, $825 in stock and fixtures in her shop, and $1,000 owed her from the mortgage she had financed for a Johanna Mahoney of East Boston.[9]

P.J., the only male in a household of women, was the privileged prince of the brood. Bridget made sure her boy got a proper education—at the Sacred Heart parochial school in East Boston. We don't know how long he stayed in school, probably into his early teens. The 1880 census records tell us that he was employed as a brass fitter; family lore tells us that he worked briefly as a stevedore, loading and unloading cargo at the docks. In his middle twenties, with his own earnings and no doubt a loan from his mother, he was able to buy ownership stakes in a few East Boston barrooms, then move into the liquor import business. While the census records list his occupation as "liquor," he did not spend much time behind the bar. His true vocation was politics, an allied but more respectable calling for a second-generation Irishman in East Boston. A quiet, private man who shied away from conflict, P. J. Kennedy had scant interest in kissing babies or making bombastic speeches. He preferred to remain in the background in the ward offices, where the real power lay, where candidates were chosen, votes gathered, and patronage dispensed. Good-looking, but not spectacularly so, with a broad, well-groomed handlebar mustache and a sturdy physique, he possessed a natural charm combined with quick intelligence, a head for numbers, roots in the community, and talents as a mediator, all of which inspired confidence. From the moment he was old enough to vote—probably earlier—P. J. Kennedy made the business of ward two in East Boston his own. At twenty-two, in 1880, he was named a delegate to the nominating convention for city "councilors." The next year, he represented ward two at the state senators nominating convention. In 1884, at twenty-six, he was appointed precinct officer, then temporary secretary of his ward.

It was the best of times for Irish politicians. Emigration from Ireland had not ceased with the recovery of the potato crop in the early 1850s but continued through the 1870s and 1880s. Where in the 1840s immigrants and their children had constituted a tiny proportion of Boston's population and electorate, four decades later the Irish had become "not merely the largest of the foreign nationalities but . . . the largest single element in the city." By 1895, there were more Bostonians with Irish-born parents than with American-born ones.[10]

Massachusetts law permitted immigrants to file naturalization papers after five years' residence, provided they could read and write English, which 90 percent of the Irish could. The Irish became citizens at a higher rate than any other immigrant group and, once naturalized, were more likely to exercise the franchise. Two thirds of Irish immigrants to Boston in 1885 were naturalized, compared with under 55 percent for the English-born and 16 percent for the Italians. Sixty percent of Irish-born citizens of Massachusetts (and no doubt a higher percentage of Bostonians) voted in the 1885 elections, compared with 33 percent of those born in Great Britain and 9 percent of the Italian-born. And almost all of those Irish votes went to Democratic candidates.[11]

State and city Democratic Party leaders, recognizing their growing dependence on Irish Americans, made sure they were repaid for their loyalty. In 1882, an Irish American, Patrick Collins, was nominated and elected to a congressional seat from Boston. Two years later, in 1884, Boston Democrats nominated and voters elected their first Irish-born mayor, businessman Hugh O'Brien. He would be reelected for three additional one-year terms. In 1885, P. J. Kennedy of ward two in East Boston was elected to the house of representatives of the Massachusetts General Court. He would serve five consecutive one-year terms.

P.J. was only twenty-eight on January 4, 1886, when he ferried across the Inner Harbor to take his seat at the general court. On November 23, 1887, he wed Mary Augusta Hickey, the daughter of a well-to-do

Irish-born contractor. Nine months and two weeks later, on September 6, 1888, their first child, Joseph Patrick Kennedy, was born. P.J. moved his family into a solid but undistinguished house at 151 Meridian in East Boston's commercial district. Francis Kennedy was born in 1891 but died a year later; Mary Loretta arrived in 1892; Margaret Louise was born in 1898.

Taking full advantage of the opportunities that came his way, P.J. accumulated a large fortune in East Boston. His political connections were invaluable in securing state licenses for his two retail liquor stores, Kennedy & Quigley at 81 Border Street and Cotter & Kennedy at 12 Washington, and, later, state charters for the Columbia Trust Company, of which he was a founding incorporator, board member, stockholder, and president, and the Sumner Savings Bank, of which he was a director. He also made money in real estate, profiting again from insider, advanced intelligence gathered in ward offices and legislative halls. By his early thirties, he was a pillar of the local community: ward boss, elected representative, businessman, banker, real estate developer, founder and officer of the Suffolk Coal Company, founding member of the local Knights of Columbus chapter, active in the Elks, the East Boston Yacht Club, the Holy Name Society of Our Lady of the Assumption Church, and the Noddle Island Antique Association, which sponsored the annual July Fourth parade.

The political success of the Irish in Boston did not, of course, go unnoticed by Yankee Protestants. In 1888, the year of Joseph Kennedy's birth and the third year of his father's tenure in the Massachusetts General Court, several anti-Catholic organizations and individuals, including the Committee of One Hundred, composed of wealthy Protestant businessmen, launched a hysterical campaign to remove every Catholic and Democrat from the elected Boston School Committee. Their fear was that the Irish, with political control of the city government and the school committee, would funnel money from public to parochial schools. The Irish and the Democratic Party mobilized their voting population (including women, who were permitted to vote in school committee elections) but were badly outvoted. Protestants won every one of the contested seats for the school committee, the Republican candidate for mayor defeated incumbent Hugh O'Brien in his bid for a fifth term, and Republicans took eight of twelve seats on the board of aldermen. The following year, 1889, the electoral results were every bit as disastrous.[12]

It was not simply Protestant rabble-rousers or the unlettered or those who worried about a papist conspiracy to destroy the public schools who joined the anti-Irish cause. As early as 1891, proper Bostonians such as Henry Cabot Lodge were already pressing for literacy tests, which they expected (perhaps wrongly) would end in the exclusion of large numbers of immigrants, including the Irish. In 1895, five young Boston "blue bloods," all with significant pedigrees and Harvard degrees, formed the Immigration Restriction League to carry the fight forward.[13]

Boston's Irish Catholic Democratic Party leaders, recognizing that they would no longer be able to elect Irish Catholic, Irish-born mayors as they had during the 1880s, shifted their support in the 1890s to Yankee candidates, and the Democrats won eight of the next nine mayoral elections. At the same time, they solidified their hold on the city's immigrant wards. In 1891, the year his son, Joseph, turned three, P.J. was elected chairman of ward two and moved from the state house of representatives to the senate. "An unwritten law of democratic [party] politics," the *Boston Daily Globe* would later report in a story about Boston's ward bosses, was "that to become a recognized leader in the higher councils of the party a man must have proved his political strength. The best way in which this test can be applied is by election to the state senate."[14]

P. J. Kennedy served his requisite two two-year terms in the state senate alongside his future in-law, John Francis Fitzgerald. His major assignment was to the "joint standing committee on street railways," where he did all he could to get East Boston connected by bridge or tunnel to the Boston streetcar grid. After two terms, he willingly stepped aside "in the interest of harmony" to support a Democratic candidate from a neighboring ward. He had never had much interest in being a candidate or officeholder; his forte was as ward boss.[15]

Ward two was one of the more contentious in Boston, with several factions and clubs competing for patronage and nominations for elective office. P.J.'s skill in handling the ward with minimal acrimony was near legendary among Boston's Democratic Party operatives. So was his near constant attention to his constituents. P.J.'s youngest daughter, Margaret, remembered the continuous flow through the house of well-wishers, favor seekers, and old pols and friends in need. "We never sat down to supper but what the doorbell would ring and it would be some-one down on their luck, coming to Papa for help."[16]

Joseph P. Kennedy was a lucky boy, the son of one of East Boston's most prosperous, respected, and powerful politicians. He was an at-tractive child, with short reddish brown hair. Years later, commenting on a childhood photograph of him wearing what looks like a dress—"a rather striking costume," he called it—Kennedy half jokingly asked his son, Ted, "to observe . . . the sharp piercing eyes, the very set jaw and the clenched left fist. Maybe all of this meant something!" Even wear-ing a dress as a four- or five-year-old, he looked tough—or tried to. He was not, like his grandparents who had landed in the New World forty years before his birth, a stranger in a strange land, but an American boy who spoke with a Boston, not an Irish, accent, whose paternal roots extended back two generations—a long time by East Boston standards, and whose mother came from one of the town's more prosperous fami-lies. The Hickeys were every bit as well-known in East Boston as the Kennedys. Joseph's maternal uncle Charlie Hickey was elected mayor of nearby Brockton; Uncle Jim was a Boston police captain; Uncle John was a doctor in Winthrop.[17]

Joe Kennedy grew up in a neighborhood where everyone, it seemed, knew and respected his family and his people. In the four decades since the first Kennedy had arrived in East Boston, the Irish had become the old-timers, the establishment, the majority, the insiders. The local bank-ers, landlords, shopkeepers, and politicians were more likely than not to be Irish and Catholic, as he was. It was the newly arrived southern Italians and Eastern European Jews who were struggling for a foothold, crammed into the unsanitary, overcrowded wooden tenements built to receive them, forced to send their children to work instead of to school.

As the oldest child in the family and the only male, Joseph Kennedy was the prince of the household, the successor who would inherit the family name, fortune, property, and the responsibility of looking after his sisters should they not find husbands. He was given a healthy allow-ance, dressed well, offered music lessons (which came to naught because he refused to practice), and at age six sent off to the parochial school at

Our Lady of the Assumption, a three-quarter-mile walk from his home, where he was taught by the Sisters of Notre Dame until he was old enough to be handed over to the Xaverian Brothers.

P. J. and Mary Augusta had, some years before, moved their family from the dusty flats of Meridian Avenue in the business district to 165 Webster Street, an elegant, tree-lined, almost suburban-looking avenue, where the wealthiest men and most powerful public officials in East Boston made their homes. Webster Street was within walking distance of the shops and the ferry terminal, but high enough above the "factories, shipyards, docks, piers, fish-curing establishments, oil works, coal depots, and grain elevators" to provide a bit of protection from the foul air and smoke that lingered below.[18]

The Kennedy house was not the grandest on the street, but it was large and imposing, at the top of the hill, on a double-wide lot, with a deep, wide backyard that sloped down to the water. Mary Augusta put in a garden with her "precious apple trees" but allowed her boy almost free rein in the backyard. Joe was, already by age eight, the leader of his pack. He organized the ball games, supplied bat, ball, and gloves, and in a large playhouse in the backyard (possibly converted from an old barn), rehearsed his friends and occasionally his sisters in plays performed—at no charge—for the other kids in the neighborhood. As was befitting the son of a ward boss, he organized his own July Fourth pageants and, on Decoration Day, assembled his gang to march in line to the cemetery for the official ceremonies.[19]

From his backyard, Joseph could look across the Inner Harbor to Boston proper, a faraway city that was not his own. East Boston might share a name, mayor, and board of aldermen with the larger city across the channel, but it had a feel, an identity, a being, all its own. Home for Joe Kennedy was not "over there," a ferry ride away, but "here" in East Boston, where his grandparents had arrived, lived, and died, where his parents had been born and raised, where he and his sisters went to church and school.

We know little of his boyhood in East Boston in part because Joseph P. Kennedy had no interest, as an adult, in looking back on his childhood, other than to recall on occasion in conversations with close friends how much he admired and adored his father. He had loved nothing more than accompanying the handsome, black-haired, mustachioed ward boss to torchlight parades, picnics, and outdoor rallies. He had almost nothing to say of his mother, Mary Augusta, a handsome, white-haired woman who, as she aged, grew rather stout. In the years to come, he would make little mention of his two adoring sisters, Margaret and Loretta, though he would remain in touch by letter and phone and support them financially.

Part of the reason for Kennedy's reluctance to recall his childhood may have been a desire to give himself full responsibility for his financial success. While he never professed to be either a "self-made" man or a child of poverty, he did not want to call attention to the obvious advantages he had enjoyed growing up as a member of one of East Boston's first families. He preferred to emphasize the ways he had made his own way and his own money by doing odd jobs in the neighborhood and organizing sandlot baseball games to which he charged admission.

Joseph P. Kennedy grew up in a Democratic ward in a Democratic city, controlled locally by Irish ward bosses such as his father and superintended by a citywide "board of strategy," a shadowy, extralegal, irregular caucus that met at the Quincy House Hotel, behind City Hall, to choose nominees for office, dispense patronage, and try to maintain some semblance of party discipline. When in November 1899 the *Boston Daily Globe* ran a preelection exposé on the "board" and the handful of bosses who controlled the Democratic Party in Boston, it identified P. J. Kennedy of East Boston as "the silent man" of the group, the only one who was not a strong stump speaker. "He is classed among politicians as a man of extremely good sense and sound judgment, an unselfish man, whose work is almost always directed to serving some friend rather than himself."[20]

In the fall of 1899, after Mayor Josiah Quincy announced that he would not run for reelection, the "board of strategy" nominated former congressman Patrick Collins to replace him. For P.J. and his fellow ward bosses, Collins—who had returned to Boston from London, where he had served as President Grover Cleveland's consul general for four years—was a dream candidate. The son of Boston and of County Cork,

Patrick Collins never forgot his roots but never flaunted them. He had gone to Harvard Law School, been a successful businessman and diplomat, dressed and spoke from the stump like a Boston gentleman, and identified himself as an American and a Democrat first, then an Irishman. There would not be another Irish Catholic, Harvard-educated candidate for office like him for another forty years—and his name would be John Fitzgerald Kennedy.

Joseph Kennedy was eleven years of age and at the Assumption school when Patrick Collins ran for mayor. Collins easily carried the Irish Catholic wards but did not do well enough to offset an unusually heavy Republican Protestant vote elsewhere in the city. Two years later, Patrick Collins ran again and this time was elected. P.J., who had, in 1899 and 1901, returned a heavy majority for Collins in the East Boston wards, was rewarded with patronage positions, first as an election commissioner, then as a wire commissioner, positions that paid handsomely but required almost no work.[21]

The Kennedys of East Boston would enter the new century with P.J. guaranteed a $5,000 salary from the city, equivalent to more than $135,000 in purchasing power today, and healthy incomes from his many business concerns. When Joe Kennedy left home that fall to attend school across the Inner Harbor, he did so as the privileged son of one of East Boston's wealthiest, most powerful, and most respected men.

Two

SCHOOL DAYS

On September 12, 1901, Joe Kennedy walked down Webster Street to the East Boston slip at Lewis Street, where, with several other East Boston boys, including his childhood friends Joe Sheehan and Joe Donovan, he paid his penny fare and boarded the ferry for Boston and his first day at Boston Latin, the oldest, best-known, and arguably most academically rigorous public school in the country. It was not uncommon for Catholic boys to go to public high schools in Boston. Joe's future father-in-law, John Francis Fitzgerald, had been a graduate of Boston Latin, as had many prominent nineteenth-century Catholics.[1]

While Boston Latin was the "elite" among the city's public schools, every male student who had graduated from a public grammar school or taken the entrance exam was entitled to entry—as long as he brought with him a "written statement from parents or guardians of their intention to give such candidates a collegiate education." This requirement drastically reduced the list of eligible applicants to those whose parents could afford to pay college tuition and forgo the four years of wages their boys might have contributed to the family income.[2]

Boston Latin, founded in 1635, boasted among its former students (and boast it did) Cotton Mather, Samuel Adams, John Hancock, Henry

Ward Beecher, Charles Sumner, Ralph Waldo Emerson, and Charles W. Eliot, Harvard's president from 1869 to 1909. The school had been the pre-Harvard training grounds for boys from Boston's oldest and most distinguished families until the mid-nineteenth century, when the Adamses, Cabots, Eliots, Lowells, and Everetts opted for newer, more exclusive private boarding schools. The blue bloods' places were taken by boys who were just as smart or smarter, but whose Boston ancestry did not extend back as far, a significant number of them Jewish and Catholic.

The curriculum remained a classical one, in large part because Boston Latin cherished its historic role as primary feeder school for Harvard College. From the moment they entered until graduation, Boston Latin students were drilled, trained, and prepared for the Harvard entrance examinations. There were no electives. Every student was required to take six years of Latin, centered on translation, memorization, writing from dictation, and reading metrically from Caesar, Ovid, Cicero, Sallust, and the *Aeneid,* six years of science, six years of mathematics, six years of English, five years of history (including a year of Roman history and a year of Greek history), four years of French, and three years and two months of Greek.[3]

Boston Latin's reputation as the "hardest" school in Boston was well earned. As Joe recalled in his 1935 speech at the school's tercentenary, even those who did as poorly in the classroom as he did regarded the school as "a shrine that somehow seemed to make us all feel that if we could stick it out at the Latin School, we were made of just a little better stuff than the rest of the fellows of our own age who were attending what we always thought were easier schools. . . . It seemed that everyone knew that we were the best 'prep' school in the country. The public officials and the City of Boston which maintained and supported the Latin School for us, must have felt the same way, for after all, were we not the only public school graduates who received actual sheepskins? Our diplomas . . . were printed on parchment whereas every other public school diploma was printed on paper." Getting that parchment was no easy task. The school showed little hesitation in asking those who did not meet its standards to transfer. Of the 116 members of Joe's sophomore class, only 79 would be promoted to their junior year and fewer still to their senior.[4]

In September 1905, during Joe's junior and most difficult year at Boston Latin, Boston's political world was turned upside down when the beloved mayor, Patrick Collins, died suddenly and unexpectedly at age sixty-one. P. J. Kennedy and the ward bosses on the "board of strategy" mourned their fallen hero but did not allow their grief to distract them from the task of choosing someone to replace him. In past years, their candidate would have been guaranteed the nomination, but in 1903, the Republican-led general court had passed a law mandating direct primary elections, hoping that this might reduce the power of the bosses and/or encourage strife among them. It succeeded in doing just that. Before the "board of strategy" had had a chance to nominate one of their own, John Francis Fitzgerald, former state senator, congressman, boss of ward six, and newspaper publisher, declared his intention to run for mayor.

"Honey Fitz" or "Little Johnny Fitz" or "Fitzie" or "young Napoleon" or "the little General," as he was variously referred to, was a small man with a large, round face, blue eyes, dark hair neatly cut and parted in the middle, and the build of a slightly over-the-hill welterweight. He was, in many ways, a strutting, singing, fiercely ambitious repudiation of everything Patrick Collins and P. J. Kennedy stood for. Fitzie reveled in his Irishness, refused to rein it in, and made it clear he had no use for Yankee politicians of any sort, Democrat or Republican. He was loud, brash, unrestrained on the stump, an indefatigable backslapper and hand shaker, who refused to bow to party discipline or accept the dictates of the "board of strategy." A decade earlier, at thirty-one years of age, he had run for Congress and defeated the "acceptable" Irish candidate whom P.J. and the other ward bosses had backed. Now, he campaigned for the mayoralty "from the back seat of an open touring car," speaking in every one of the city's wards and declaring to his Irish audiences that it was high time they elected a real Boston Irishman.[5]

The campaign for the nomination between quiet, dignified Ned Donovan, whom P.J. and the "board of strategy" backed, and the renegade Fitzgerald was as heated as any in Boston's past. On October 25, three weeks before the primary, the *Boston Daily Globe* announced on page one that East Boston's Democrats had endorsed Ned Donovan.

"The friends of Hon. P. J. Kennedy, wire commissioner, will now take off their coats and help along the Donovan campaign on Noddle Island."

It didn't much matter. Fitzie was too energetic, too outspoken, and too frenetic a campaigner to be ignored—and his message, that the Irish needed a loudmouthed fighter to battle the Yankees, resonated with voters. Ned Donovan carried only four wards on primary day; P.J.'s was one of them.

P.J., for whom loyalty to the party trumped all else, did not oppose Fitzgerald in the general election, but neither did he go out of his way to support him. When Honey Fitz came to East Boston and spoke at the ward two meeting hall, P.J. was conspicuous in his absence. Fitzgerald didn't need him. In December 1905, John Francis Fitzgerald, still a few months shy of his forty-third birthday, was elected to a two-year term as mayor.

While P.J. spent the fall of 1905 campaigning for Ned Donovan, his son struggled through his junior year at Boston Latin. "It is said that Winston Churchill was near the foot of his class," one of Joe's classmates later recalled, "and I think Joe must have tried to emulate that other great man, for scholarship was not a field in which Joe sought or obtained success." A near failure in the classroom, Joe was a star outside it. At Boston Latin, as in most institutions attended by adolescent males and watched over by men who fondly recalled their adolescence, athletes were accorded more than their fair share of respect. Joe was quite an athlete. He managed the football team in the fall, played basketball in winter and baseball in the spring, and was captain of the tennis team. He also became adept at military drill, one of the high-prestige activities at Boston Latin, where students were required to spend two hours a week. Joe, a natural athlete with perfect posture and obvious leadership skills, won his first prize at drill in his sophomore year and was named corporal of Company A. In his junior year, he was promoted to sergeant; in his senior year, to captain.[6]

In the fall of 1906, Joe invited the mayor's daughter, Rose Fitzgerald—without question the most famous and surely one of the prettiest Catholic girls in the city—to the first Boston Latin regimental dance of the year. Rose was petite, poised though vivacious, with shining black curly hair and a twinkling smile. The two had met in the summer of 1895 at a picnic at the Boston politicians' favorite summer resort, Old Orchard Beach, Maine. Joe was seven, Rose five. Eleven years later, they met again, but only briefly. "He was tall and thin and had sort of reddish hair and wore glasses," and, more important, he had made a name for himself at Boston Latin. "He was a very good baseball player. . . . He didn't drink and he didn't smoke and that impressed me as a girl . . . and then he was a very good polite Catholic . . . that made an impression too."[7]

Rose had to turn down her first invitation from Joe Kennedy. Her father, the mayor, "refused to let me go. He disapproved of a girl of sixteen going around to dances in strange places and meeting people who might cause trouble." Rose was, she remembered, struck by the illogic in her father's reasoning. There was nothing strange about Boston Latin, Honey Fitz's alma mater, and Joe Kennedy was not a boy who caused trouble. "He knew Joe and the Kennedys, and besides it was an afternoon dance, so I would be home before dark." Still, she had to have been aware that her father was not terribly fond of P.J., who was from East Boston, and had on two separate occasions backed his opponents. "Temperamentally," Rose Kennedy recalled in her memoirs, putting the best possible spin on their mutual enmity, "they were opposite, and I suppose they must have grated on each other's nerves at times."[8]

Undaunted by her father's refusal to let her go to the dance at Boston Latin, Rose asked Joe to a dance at her school, Dorchester High. While "regular dating was taboo and 'going steady' was completely out of the question," Rose and Joe spent a good deal of time together during the 1906–1907 school year. Rose attended "lectures in German and French and music at the Lowell Institute in Boston and they used to take place in the afternoon." Joe would meet her after the lecture, and "we would quite regularly walk miles towards home." Their relationship was a secret only to her father—and not much of a secret even to him. Her girlfriends, Joe's friends, and even her father's chauffeur knew all about it and did what they could to assist the young couple. "It took teamwork and conspiracy, because we needed reliable allies. Some were girlfriends of mine in Dorchester. . . . They gave more 'drop in' parties—well planned ahead—than they would have otherwise. . . . During that last year at Dorchester High, and the following year, when I was commuting to Sacred Heart, Joe and I managed to see each other rather often. Less often than we would have liked, but more often than my father was aware of."[9]

When Joe graduated in the spring of 1908, his class book "prophecy" predicted, with a world-class bad pun, that he would "earn his living in a very round-a-bout way. He will run the flying horses at 'Severe' beach [a reference to the carousel at Revere Beach]; on every horse there will be a pretty Rose—that is where the Rose Fitz."[10]

S ometime in the spring of 1907, in what he thought was going to be his last year at Boston Latin, Joe and his parents were informed that he was going to be held back. Even for a boy with his inexhaustible energy and drive, his out-of-the-classroom activities—the romance with Rose, sports and military drill and baseball on the weekends, and the commute back and forth every day—had taken its toll. Although his grades were in the passing range, the faculty had concluded that he needed at least another year to prepare for the Harvard entrance examinations.

His second senior year would be marked by one triumph after another. In September, the *Boston Daily Globe* noted Joseph Kennedy's reelection as manager of the football team with a large photo. That same month, his classmates voted him senior class president. In October, he was reelected captain of the baseball team. In December, at "Exhibition Declamation Day," he was awarded "the beautiful silver cup offered by Mayor Fitzgerald to the one attaining the highest batting average on the Latin School base-ball team." That spring, his photo appeared yet again in the Boston papers, this time in full military uniform, with his cap artfully askew, after the second Boston Latin regiment that he commanded swept the citywide "drill" competition at Mechanics Hall. Six weeks later, he was in the paper again, this time with a baseball cap on his head, having been selected as the starting first baseman on the Boston Interscholastic Nine.[11]

Sated, feted, and celebrated, Joseph P. Kennedy—colonel, allscholastic first baseman, and class president—had just one more task to complete.

On June 22, he sat for the first of four days of Harvard entrance examinations. He received Cs in elementary and advanced Greek and in French, a D plus in algebra, Ds in English, Latin, and geometry, a D minus (still passing) in history, and Fs in elementary physics and advanced Latin. Because two "advanced" examinations and one in science were required for admission—and he had failed his advanced Latin and elementary physics tests, he was admitted with "conditions," which were removed in his freshman year when he retook and passed the exams with Ds.[12]

And so it was on to Harvard in the fall of 1908. At age twenty, Joe was older than many of his classmates, more physically and emotionally mature and strikingly handsome—tall, trim, with the build of an athlete, burning blue eyes, a freckled face, brownish red hair still cut short, and gleaming white teeth. Academically, Harvard held no fears for Joe Kennedy and the Boston Latin boys. At Latin, they had had to take a rigorous diet of ancient languages; at Harvard, where the elective system was still in force, there were no required courses, no need even to choose and build a major. The result, as Van Wyck Brooks wrote in 1908, the year he graduated and Joe entered Harvard, was to encourage undergrads to follow "the line of least resistance" and take courses they knew they could pass with minimal effort. Joe took no math or science, but four years of economics and government; three years of German, English, and history; two half-year courses in comparative literature; a year of Latin; and half-year courses in education, social ethics, and public speaking.[13]

In 1908, as in preceding years, Boston Latin sent more students to Harvard than any other public or private high school, twenty-five, half the graduating class. The majority of Harvard undergraduates were "proper Bostonian" Protestants, but there were more public school graduates, more Jews, and more Catholics than at Princeton or Yale. About 9 percent of Kennedy's entering class was Catholic, enough to support a healthy St. Paul's Catholic Club, which Joe joined at once.[14]

Joe Kennedy did not disguise the fact that he was an Irish Catholic and a Democrat (a risibly small minority at Harvard), but neither did he emphasize it. He intended to make his mark, as he had at Boston

Latin, not as a Catholic or an Irish descendant or the son of a Democratic ward leader, but as an athlete who played that most American of games, baseball. Early in the first semester of his freshman year, he invited Bob Fisher, a star football player who had graduated from public school, then spent a year at Andover, to share his Perkins Hall rooms. He also befriended Tom Campbell, an Irish Catholic athlete from Worcester who lived off campus. Campbell and Fisher formed the nucleus around which Joe constructed his social network. "He had tremendous charm," Campbell recalled, "and as one friend described it 'he could charm a bird out of a tree.'" It was impossible to resist him once he decided that he wanted you in his corner. He was attentive, generous, loyal, fun to be around. "Joe led a model life" at Harvard. He attended Mass every Sunday and was a first Friday communicant as well. "He never drank, smoked or gambled at cards—off color stories were taboo."

In his senior year, Campbell, Joe, and Bob Fisher were invited to dinner with Professor Charles Copeland, one of the few professors who socialized with undergraduates. "When the coffee was served Joe apologized and said he never drank coffee. Later 'Copey' passed around his cigarettes." Everyone but Joe took one. "Not believing that anyone could spend four years at Harvard without some bad habits 'Copey' stared at Joe with mock severity and said, 'Young man, do you drink?' to which Joe replied, 'No sir.' 'Copey' then shook his finger at Joe and said, 'Young man, I suspect you of some great crime.'"[15]

There were several Harvards: the Harvard of the Adamses, Saltonstalls, Thayers, Cabots, Lowells, Lodges, and their elite clubs; the Harvard of the intellectual strivers such as Van Wyck Brooks and George Santayana and Walter Lippmann; and the Harvard populated by the public school graduates who spent their four years in dormitories or commuting to Cambridge from home. Joe was firmly situated in the public school sector. In his freshman year, he was an active member of the group that sought, unsuccessfully, to elect a public school boy as class president. He also volunteered for and served as a member of his finance committee of the Class of '12. As a sophomore, he helped plan the class smokers, the only events on campus that attempted to bridge the chasm between the "proper Bostonians" and the public school boys. As a junior, he was a principal organizer of the class dinner and junior prom. When, in his senior year, the men of '12 voted to wear a class button, it was Joe Kennedy who volunteered for the committee to design and distribute it.[16]

In February 1909, he tried out for the freshman team, made the final cut to twenty in April, and started at first base when the season began. In the most important game of the year—against Yale—he got two hits in four times at bat and stole two bases. As a sophomore, he expected to graduate to the varsity but didn't make it. He played instead for the sophomore class team. In his junior year, he was invited to make the trip with the varsity to Annapolis for spring training and started at first base in a practice game against Navy on April 18, but, as the *Boston Daily Globe* noted a week later, neither he nor his chief competitor for starting first baseman seemed to "be measuring up to the work." A Harvard classmate and rival, Ralph Lowell, later described him as "an ice wagon . . . slow and heavy. He couldn't run very fast at all."[17]

He didn't get into a varsity game until the very end of the season, when he played in four and came to bat seven times. Fortunately, one of those was the final home game against Yale, which earned him his Harvard letter and the game ball, which he pocketed. The story of Joe taking the ball for himself instead of giving it to the pitcher and team captain would decades later become a staple of the Joe Kennedy literature, early evidence of his unquenchable ambition and ruthless disregard of others. Kennedy's surviving teammates, when asked about the incident, denied that Joe had done anything wrong. He had, after all, made the final putout, and as Arthur Kelly, who played second base, recalled, it was the custom "then and now" for the man who made the final putout to keep the game ball.[18]

Joe did not try out for the baseball team as a senior, probably because he did not want to suffer the humiliation of not making it or of spending the season on the bench. Instead, he moved to the sidelines and coached the freshman team, a position that paid him a salary and brought with it some distinction. That summer, he concluded his career as a ballplayer in the semipro White Mountain League, organized by resort owners as free entertainment for their guests.

For an Irish Catholic public school graduate from East Boston, Joe Kennedy would do quite well socially at Harvard. He began with a cadre of friends from Boston Latin, added to it athletes he thought might be future teammates, and reached out to a few men (such as Arthur Goldsmith, a New York City Jew) who were neither Catholic nor Irish nor from Boston. In the fall of his sophomore year, he was selected with 128 other members of his class of 500 for the Institute of 1770, an honorary association that existed solely to differentiate the members of the class from one another. Harvard social hierarchy was so carefully calibrated that it mattered not just if one was selected for the institute, but in what rank order one was selected. Institute members were chosen in groups of ten; the first seven or eight tens were initiated into yet another secret society, DKE, also known as "Dickee" or "Deke" or "Deeks." DKE had no club rooms and no eating facilities. All it bestowed was honor—and a week of cruel hazing. Arthur Kelly, who lived in the Holyoke dorms, was in the room when "Joe returned from his initiation into the Delta Kappa Epsilon Fraternity. After observing his back I was not impressed with fraternities."[19]

In the winter of his sophomore year, the next act in the drama of Harvard social life was played out when the "final clubs" (so called because students, once initiated, would remain with these clubs until they graduated) chose their members. His friends Bob Fisher, the football star who had spent a year at Andover, and Bob Potter, another athlete who had come to Harvard from a private school, were swept into the top clubs. Joe, with his classmates from Boston Latin, and Irish Catholic Tom Campbell, from Worcester, were not. He had to have been disappointed not to get into Fly or Porcellian or A.D., though not as much as when he failed to make the starting baseball team. Joe Kennedy was, even at age twenty-one, too sure of himself to suffer for long because a group of Republican Episcopalians preferred not to live and dine with him. In his junior year, he was inducted into Hasty Pudding and invited to serve on the junior prom committee. In his senior year, he moved into Hollis Hall, the oldest and **grandest Harvard** dormitory, and along with Robert Benchley, from Exeter, and several of the better-known men of his year, was tapped for Delta Upsilon, a worthy (if not top-rank) Harvard club.

East Boston was only a few miles distant but worlds apart from Harvard Yard for everyone but Joseph P. Kennedy. His father had been tied to the Democratic Party since before he was born; he had grown up campaigning with his father and watching as he soothed tempers at ward meetings and catered to his constituents. The Democratic mayors, Irish Catholic and Yankee alike, had rewarded P.J.'s loyalty and political talents with high-paying, no-responsibility patronage jobs. These regrettably came to an end in 1907 when Honey Fitz, after a two-year term marked by scandal and charges of graft that were hard to refute and impossible to escape, was defeated for reelection. With a Republican now mayor, the only way P.J. could work his way back onto the municipal payroll was to run for office. And so, in the fall of 1908, at age fifty, after three decades in politics, he announced his candidacy for street commissioner, an elected, nearly no-show position that paid $4,000 a year. P.J.'s opponent in the primary was Captain Dunn, an unknown, untried, unaffiliated Spanish-American War veteran from South Boston. In years past, a ward boss with P.J.'s impressive and lengthy record of service to the party would have been swept to victory. But P.J., a cautious man who would not have put himself forward if he imagined the possibility of defeat, was caught unknowingly in the trap that had been set years before when renegade Democrats launched their attack on members of the "board of strategy" for being undemocratic "bosses."

When the votes were counted, Captain Dunn of South Boston had 380 more than his opponent. The only possible explanation for the upset, the *Boston Daily Globe* concluded, was that "the democratic voters of Boston [had grown] weary of bossism. . . . Mr. Kennedy, who is a good party man, was defeated because he was favored by bosses, whereas his opponent, Capt. Dunn, without any political leaders at his back, was elected."[20]

That was the official explanation. The unofficial one was that though

Honey Fitz and his supporters had publicly endorsed Kennedy, they had privately betrayed him by keeping down the vote in their wards. P.J. had supported Fitzgerald for reelection in 1907, but that had not been enough to undo the enmity he had engendered by opposing him in earlier elections.

P.J. graciously accepted defeat but was so humiliated by it that he pulled up stakes and, after a lifetime of service to and residence in East Boston, moved the family to Winthrop, Massachusetts. He was far from destitute and would continue for the rest of his life to live well on the income he received from his coal, real estate, liquor importing, and banking businesses. The new family house in Winthrop was spacious and attractive, and Joe would visit there often with his Harvard classmates and, in the years to come, with friends and family. But Winthrop was not and would never be his home.

Patrick Joseph Kennedy would not publicly complain about his fate, nor would his son in future years allow himself to feel sorry for his father. But P.J.'s defeat—in a primary for street commissioner—soured the son on local electoral politics forever. That an unscrupulous buffoon such as Honey Fitz could succeed where a man of dignity, discretion, and decency such as Patrick Joseph Kennedy could not was simply unacceptable. Joe Kennedy, like his father, would remain a lifelong Democrat, but not a very regular—or particularly loyal—one. Forty years later, when his son ran for public office, he would help him put together his own campaign organization, rather than trust his fate, as his grandfather had, to party leaders.

While his father's political career had come to an abrupt halt, his future father-in-law, John Francis Fitzgerald, ran for mayor again in 1910. Successfully dodging questions about the outsized amounts his administration had paid contractors to crush stone for the city's streets and supply it with coal, electricity, and other vital services, Fitzgerald campaigned around the clock, traveling by motorcade through every ward of the city, never failing to remind potential voters that his Republican opponent was a rich, spoiled, Harvard-educated Protestant businessman with no sympathy—and perhaps a bit of animosity—toward Irishmen, Catholics, and working people in general. Holding the attention of audiences with the skill of a seasoned vaudevillian, Honey Fitz told stories, made jokes, "called for 'Manhood against Money,' and promised his supporters 'A Bigger, Better, Busier Boston.' Before he left each gathering, he would sing 'Sweet Adeline' at the top of his voice, to the delight of his partisan supporters." He was narrowly elected to a four-year term.[21]

Though Fitzgerald never let potential voters forget that he had fathered six children, he had sent his oldest daughters out of the country after his 1907 defeat to protect them from the personal attacks and often well-founded accusations that their father was a grafter, boodler, payroll padder, liar, and crook. Rose and her sister Agnes spent a year at the Sacred Heart Convent in Holland, far from the reach of the Boston dailies. When Rose returned from abroad, she was sent away again, this time to the Sacred Heart Convent school on 133rd Street in upper Manhattan. Only after her father's election in January 1910 and her graduation from Sacred Heart in June was she permitted to return home to Boston. She was immediately thrust onto the public stage as she accompanied her father, the mayor, on official trips and appeared at his side at public ceremonies, substituting for her absent mother. The long-suffering wife of a politician who was never at home for long and known for his skirt chasing, Mary Josephine Hannon Fitzgerald, called Josie, was a quiet, dignified, deeply religious woman, the family disciplinarian, who took no pleasure in appearing in public with her husband. "For reasons not only of temperament but of time," Rose would later explain, "Mother had a limited capacity for the official social whirl. She also had young children at home who needed her." In her absence, Rose became her father's "companion, hostess, and assistant on a good many of the trips he took."[22]

In January 1911, Rose Fitzgerald celebrated her coming of age—with a spectacular formal debut at her parents' mansion of a home before an admiring claque of five hundred of her father's friends and political associates, every Democratic politician of note in the city and state, and a few out-of-town luminaries, including William Randolph Hearst and his wife, Millicent. As the papers dutifully reported the next morning, young Rose had looked gorgeous in her delicately embroidered white chiffon gown.

Despite P.J.'s lukewarm support of the mayor and his virtual exile in Winthrop, he and his family were invited to the event. "They were," Rose later remembered, "around at a lot of the festive gatherings that the politicians had." After the main reception, the older generation, including P.J. and his wife, Mary Augusta, returned to their homes, while Joe and his Harvard friends and roommates, Bob Fisher and Thomas Campbell, joined the younger set at a sit-down dinner and dance.[23]

That spring, Joe invited Rose to his junior prom at Harvard, "and to make it easier for me to get my parents' permission . . . arranged for one of his college roommates to invite a girl who was one of my best friends." Rose accepted, then had to decline when her father announced that he needed her to accompany him on a visit to Palm Beach. "I didn't argue with my father . . . I wouldn't have dreamed of doing so; but I was visibly upset, downcast, teary, and melancholy. . . . I sniffled a bit and submitted and boarded the train for a trip of some twelve hundred miles, each of which I heartily regretted." Rose not only missed going to the junior prom with Joe but was separated from him that summer, after her father demanded that she accompany him on a European tour.[24]

Despite her semiofficial duties as the mayor's daughter, Rose saw Joe regularly during his final two years at Harvard: at friends' houses, in Harvard Yard, and "in clandestine meetings" at locations like the Christian Science church in Boston, where no one would ever imagine looking for them. They made sure to attend the same formal dances, and there were a number of them, sponsored by Irish Catholic social clubs and voluntary organizations, some at Harvard, some in Boston. Rose, sparkling, witty, pretty, and the mayor's daughter, always enjoyed a full dance card, which she was obliged, as were all the girls, to show her parents after the event. To disguise the fact that she spent far too much time with one boy, Joe Kennedy, she and he conspired to "fix" her card, with Joe signing it with a variety of aliases. "He would put on 'Sam Shaw'—that was a favorite—SS—Sam Shaw."[25]

Honey Fitz didn't argue directly against Joseph Kennedy as a current boyfriend or potential husband, but he did caution his very eligible young daughter not to close her eyes to other suitors. "He pointed out that I was fortunate enough to have unusual advantages and opportunities. Therefore, I shouldn't say yes to the first man who fell in love with me and wanted to marry me. I should take my time and look around. This theme was often repeated and endorsed by my mother."[26]

Joe spent his last summer before graduating trying to make some money for himself. In partnership with Joe Donovan, his friend from East Boston, Boston Latin, and Harvard, he bought a decrepit-looking bus for $600, to be paid on the installment plan, painted it cream and blue with MAYFLOWER written in bold black letters on the side, used his contacts at City Hall to get a license to pick up passengers at South Street station, and went into the sightseeing business. Donovan drove the bus, while Joe handled the megaphone. "Passengers didn't take the ride just for fresh air or the thrill of motor driving. They were interested in history, and I let them have it. I made special studies of Paul Revere, dug up every record I could find in the Boston libraries."[27]

He returned to Harvard in September 1911 with money in his bank account, but not nearly enough to propose to the mayor's daughter. Having given up on Harvard baseball and with no real interest in his classes (he had passed all ten he took as a junior, with five Cs and four Ds), he was anxious to graduate as soon as he could and intended to double up on his coursework in the fall and exit a semester early. On September 30, 1911, a Mr. Cram from the Harvard dean's office wrote P. J. Kennedy in Winthrop. Cram had no doubt that Joe could, if he chose, take six courses in the fall semester and pass them, "but educationally such a plan is, I believe, deplorable, if not injurious. . . . I have urged him strongly to stay for the whole year . . . I hope that you will approve of his doing this. I don't think that he will waste the year here; he is not that type of fellow. Furthermore, for the sake of his College and class I should like to have him here. He is associated with men who are helping good causes, and I shall value his assistance much."[28]

After successfully petitioning the dean's office to reduce his senior workload because he was "engaged in business in Boston: building a garage and running a sightseeing car," Kennedy remained at Harvard through the spring semester. He graduated in June 1912, having completed the equivalent of seventeen full courses, the minimum required. His final record was heavy with Cs and Ds, a sprinking of Bs, but not a single A. In the end it didn't matter. He had his Harvard degree, several lifelong friends, and a number of "proper Bostonian" contacts he could call on in the future."[29]

Three

STARTING OUT

Why Joe decided to go into banking and finance after Harvard was a bit of a mystery, even to Rose, who recalled in her autobiography how difficult a road he had set himself. "The financial institutions of Boston were controlled by 'proper Bostonians.' They sat on their fortunes like broody hens on fertile eggs, and intrusions into their henhouses were met with resentful cluckings. I remember my father telling of an encounter he had with one old-line Boston banker. 'You have plenty of Irish depositors,' he commented. 'Why don't you have some Irishmen on your board of directors?' The banker replied, 'Well, a couple of our tellers are Irish.' 'Yes,' said my father . . . 'and I suppose the charwomen are too.'"[1]

The only answer to Kennedy's choice of vocation is that he had always aimed high and almost always succeeded. He was good with numbers, had a Harvard degree, and had made some contacts at Harvard with the "proper Bostonians" whose families controlled Boston's financial institutions. "Banking ranked as high as any commercial profession," he would explain to a reporter in 1928. "It was the basic business profession." And it offered a career "ladder with more than one rung. . . . Banking could lead a man anywhere, as it played an important part in every business."[2]

Boston had never been much of an industrial center. It had no steel mills and no large factories; its shipbuilding and maritime industries had long before entered into a state of permanent decline. What it had was capital, which had for more than a century been profitably invested in trade, textiles, and railroads. Regrettably for Joseph P. Kennedy of East Boston, Boston's banks and financial institutions were, in the early twentieth century (as they had been since the founding of the first bank in Boston in 1784), tightly controlled by the scions of old-established Brahmin families, none of which had any interest in offering a decent position to an Irish Catholic from East Boston. Thirty-five years after Joe Kennedy graduated from Harvard, John Gunther visited Boston while researching *Inside U.S.A.* and found that not much had changed. "Only one small Boston bank is Irish-owned, and only four out of thirty directors of the Chamber of Commerce are of Irish descent. There are few dominating Irish figures in . . . finance."[3]

Joe's classmate and friend Bob Potter had on graduation been offered a position at the National Shawmut Bank, a relatively new institution, but one controlled by the old Boston families. (In less than a decade, he would be promoted to vice president.) Kennedy received no such offer from any Boston firm. His Harvard diploma could not erase and did not compensate for the fact that he was an Irish Catholic from East Boston. With no entry-level position at hand, he decided to take a different route into the Boston banking establishment. He would sit for the civil service examination for assistant state bank examiner.

He spent his first summer after graduation studying for the examination under the tutelage of Alfred Wellington at the Columbia Trust Company, the tiny bank his father had helped found in East Boston. At the end of the summer, he took and passed the examination and secured an appointment, perhaps with some help from his father's and/or his future father-in-law's political friends. The job paid little—$1,500 annually (less than $35,000 in purchasing power today)—but offered an invaluable hands-on banking education from the inside and the opportunity for Kennedy to introduce himself to the trustees and directors of the state's larger banks.

Kennedy traveled across the state, poring over the books and records of savings banks and trust companies, compiling reports on their liabilities and their assets, and learning about bonds and stocks, mortgages, demand loans, time loans with collateral, overdrafts, foreclosed real estate, and currency and specie. Dressed impeccably in his three-piece suit, starched white shirt, rounded collar, and shining shoes, with his red hair carefully slicked down, he already looked the part of the prosperous young banker. He had anticipated that after a short time as assistant examiner, he would be offered a position by one of the bank officers whom he had impressed with his newly acquired knowledge of the banking business. But no such offer was forthcoming.

Keeping his options open, he invested his profits from his tour bus company and whatever earnings he could put aside (he lived cheaply, in his parents' house in Winthrop) in a real estate company, Old Colony Realty, with his friend Harry O'Meara. O'Meara ran the day-to-day business, Kennedy watched over the books. They had some successes and a few failures. Kennedy did not put much energy or time into the business. Real estate was not a profession worthy of his full-time attention.[4]

Writing her autobiography, Rose tried to recall precisely when, where, and how Joe had asked for her hand. She could not. It had been taken for granted, without questions asked or answered, that they would marry as soon as he was able to support a family. At Harvard and after graduation, Joe remained faithful to Rose in the way that men of his generation and class remained faithful to their best girls. He did not court other marriageable women, but neither did he remain chaste awaiting his wedding day.

His Harvard classmate and good friend Arthur Goldsmith remembered young Joe as quite "a ladies' man." On one occasion, while they were still students, the two took a couple of chorus girls from *The Pink Lady*, which was playing at the Colonial Theatre, skating at a Boston roller rink, where they came upon Rose. According to Goldsmith, Joe, arm in arm with his "charmer," was able to talk "himself out of that one." How, we do not know.[5]

The farther he got from Boston, the safer Joe was from such embarrassments. That may have been one of the reasons he visited Goldsmith, who graduated a year before him, in New York as often as he did. In April of his senior year, Kennedy had telegraphed Goldsmith from Baltimore, where he was probably at spring training with the freshman baseball team, which he was coaching: "Will arrive Wednesday in New York. . . . Notify Hazel if you can. . . . Leave for Boston on midnight Wednesday night. I've got to move quickly."[6]

Kennedy visited Goldsmith in New York City regularly after graduation. "I expect to go over on the five [o'clock train] Thursday. There's a chap named John Riley, our city's Real Estate Expert, [taking the train to New York] on Saturday. Do you think you could get Evelyn to get him a nice looking girl? He's a damned good fellow and I know you'll like him. Let me know however, how you're fixed right away. I'm looking forward to a hell of a time. I'll leave everything to you including my fair name."[7]

One of the perks of working for the bank commissioner's office were vacations so frequent and lengthy, even the governor publicly complained about them. In the summer of 1913, Joe was able to take enough time off to sail to Europe with a few Harvard friends on the *Kaiserin Auguste Victoria,* a whale of a ship that, when launched by the Hamburg-American Line in 1906, had been the largest in the world. In a photograph taken as they boarded ship, Joe looks every bit the "proper Bostonian" aristocrat, dressed elegantly in white slacks, black waistcoat, long black jacket, and starched white shirt with high collar.[8]

The *Kaiserin Auguste Victoria*—which on the way to New York from Hamburg and Southampton had brought with it a steerage-hold full of German and Eastern European immigrants—was returning to Hamburg with a complement of 652 passengers in first class, another 500 in second and third class, and 1,842 in steerage. The boys had saved enough to purchase first-class berths, but on their first day out, Joe realized they could do even better. He sought out and befriended the purser, who offered to move them into the imperial suite for an extra $50 apiece. When his friends balked—they had had a difficult enough time raising the money for the first-class passage—Joe stalked off angrily, then returned a few minutes later with a better deal: $100 total. According to his traveling companion Joe Merrill, Kennedy had been so insistent on the upgrade because he needed it to impress and "win the girl that he had set his heart on, the one that he wanted. . . . Your Dad's girl," he later wrote Ted Kennedy, who was collecting reminiscences about his father, "was Ruth Rea who was traveling with her father and mother. Her father was then President of the Pennsylvania Railroad." Ruth, Merrill remembered, was "very much" like Rose Fitzgerald, "about the same size, very good looking with a wonderful complexion. She was the retiring sweet type."[9]

Later that fall, Joe invited Ruth—and her father—to be his guests at the Harvard-Princeton game. "Think I will take a girl from Phila to Princeton game," he telegraphed Arthur Goldsmith in New York City. "Will give you particulars later." "Mr. Rea," Joe Merrill later recalled, "came up [from Philadelphia to Princeton] in his private car and Joe put on a great show for him." Merrill claimed that Joe's pursuit of Ruth was part of his larger strategy to convince Honey Fitz that he was a suitable husband. "If Joe Kennedy was good enough for the daughter of the Pennsylvania Railroad, he was good enough for his daughter." Whatever his ultimate motives, Kennedy had no intention and no hope of marrying Ruth Rea, who was a practicing Presbyterian and out of bounds as a wife.[10]

Rose was his girl, and it was Rose he was going to marry. The mayor had by now bowed to the inevitable. His acceptance of young Kennedy as a future son-in-law had probably been helped along by P.J.'s change of heart—and allegiance. In January 1913, P.J. returned from Winthrop to East Boston to greet the mayor, who was being honored—we don't know why—at a bowling tournament sponsored by the East Boston Literary Association. P.J. captained one of the teams, then, when the frames were rolled, sat with Fitzie at the "head table" for a "Dutch supper." In April, P.J. joined the mayor again for an event at the Somerset Hotel. In October, he appeared with Fitzie, his wife, and his daughters on the receiving stand for the Columbus Day parade.[11]

In the first week of December 1913, Joseph Kennedy resigned his position as assistant bank examiner, but not because he had been offered a position at any of the major banks or investment houses in the city or state. He returned home, instead, to East Boston and the Columbia Trust Company, which his father had helped found decades earlier and which was now threatened with takeover by several large Boston banks.

His resignation coincided with his future father-in-law's announcement that he was going to run for reelection. As the *Boston Daily Globe* reported on December 24, 1913, Patrick J. Kennedy's son, mistakenly identified as "Patrick J. Kennedy, Jr. . . . a Harvard man," had been selected as chairman of the newly formed "young man's nonpartisan league," which, while claiming it stood for "clean municipal government," endorsed John Francis Fitzgerald for another term.

This time around, Honey Fitz was going to need all the help he could get. He had made the near fatal mistake of procrastinating too long about whether to run for reelection, thereby opening the door to James Michael Curley, who, after serving two undistinguished terms in Congress, was ready to return home. Like Honey Fitz, perhaps even more so, Curley was a dynamo of a campaigner, a fiery speaker, and unscrupulous in attacks on his opponents. Unlike the mayor, who seemed always to be smiling, there was a churlish edge, a bitterness, to Curley's politicking. He wasn't content with merely getting more votes than his opponents; one sensed he wanted to eat them alive. On the stump, his language was laced with sarcasm, invective, belligerence. He presented himself as the only man of the people; those who dared oppose him or question his tactics or his motives were either boss-controlled and corrupt, such as Honey Fitz, or Irish Catholic–hating Yankee Protestant bigots.

The campaign of 1914 was hard-fought but short-lived. Honey Fitz, who had entered the race only six weeks before the primary, campaigned vigorously for a few weeks, then withdrew after Curley threatened to expose his relationship with a cigarette girl named Toodles, who was his daughter's age. Though the story would be kept out of the papers—for a while, at least—it reverberated throughout the Fitzgerald household. The revelation that Curley knew about Toodles, and was ready to let the whole world know, was followed by a second calamity when Honey Fitz injured himself inspecting a decrepit lodging house that had caught fire. Frightened at the prospect of being humiliated as a fifty-year-old who chased cigarette girls, unable to campaign as usual because of his injury, and recognizing the distinct possibility that he might be defeated in the primary, Honey Fitz announced his retirement. Miss Rose Fitzgerald, quoted the morning after her father's withdrawal, expressed only delight in his decision: "O, we feel ever so happy now that he had made up his mind to retire from the campaign, for we will soon have him with us all the time." Patrick J. Kennedy, also cited in the papers, agreed that the mayor had done right by leaving the race to protect his health. "Because of the constant strain and the fact that he worked so hard I have felt for some time that the Mayor was in need of a rest and, from my own viewpoint, I am glad to learn of his retirement. For several weeks past I have urged upon the Mayor's friends to have him retire because of the condition of his health."[12]

On Christmas Eve, five days after Fitzgerald's withdrawal, the Young Men's Nonpartisan League of Boston threw its support to Thomas Kenny, now Curley's chief rival. On January 4, Patrick J. Kennedy endorsed Kenny as well, but it was too late now to head off Curley. On January 14, James Michael Curley was elected mayor of Boston.

The disappointment experienced in the Kennedy household was quickly eclipsed by rather spectacular good news. On January 21, Joe Kennedy's photograph appeared in the Boston papers over the caption "Youngest in the State. Joseph P. Kennedy Elected President of Columbia Trust Company at Age of 25." This was the goal Kennedy had set for himself on resigning as assistant bank examiner.

Columbia Trust had been founded in 1895 and controlled since then by a small group of East Boston stockholders, P. J. Kennedy among them. When in late 1913 the largest of the stockholders died, the founders were faced with the choice of either raising the money to purchase his stock or becoming minority owners of their own bank. Joe volunteered to help raise the funds. He successfully borrowed from family members, including his relatively well-off uncles on his mother's side, and Eugene Thayer, who was president of the Merchants Bank of Boston, and used these loans to purchase bank stock, much of it in his own name. With control of more bank shares than anyone else, he had himself elected bank president and promoted family friend and mentor Alfred Wellington to the position of treasurer and vice president. He then brought in two new directors whom he could count on to support him.[13]

Joseph P. Kennedy was on the move. He had, he wrote Arthur Goldsmith in New York, been "one of the busiest little 'cups of tea' in the world . . . running a real estate office, getting ready to assume my bank duties, running a campaign for mayor and last but not least looking after the dearest girl in the world." He expected to get to New York in the next month or so. In the meantime, he asked Goldsmith for help in buying "stick [tie] pins," and "rather good" ones, for Mr. Thayer, Wellington, and a number of others "who were so kind to me on my bank proposition."[14]

Six days after becoming a bank president, Joseph P. Kennedy was appointed by his future father-in-law, the lame duck mayor of Boston, to the board of the Collateral Loan Company, founded decades earlier as the Pawners' Bank to provide loans to the poor. The position was unpaid, but it put Joe's name in the headlines again and added an important line to his résumé.

On February 2, James Michael Curley was inaugurated and almost immediately set out to distinguish himself from the free-spending Honey Fitz by vowing to cut back on public expenditures and instead raise money privately for what he called his "Boom Boston" fund. To curry favor with the new mayor, Joe Kennedy donated $200 to the fund. He knew full well where his $200 was going—into a glorified James Michael Curley slush fund—but he didn't much care. The same day that Kennedy's contribution was announced, his fellow bank president Allan Forbes, of the State Street Trust, foolishly announced that he had decided not to donate the $1,000 he had pledged the day before. Mayor Curley responded by withdrawing all city deposits from the State Street Trust. He could not in good conscience, he declared, deposit city funds in an institution "whose officers are so devoid of public spirit" that they declined to contribute to his economic development fund.[15]

Kennedy proved himself a more than able bank president. Almost immediately upon taking office, he injected new life into a trust company that in the last twelve months had lost 1 percent of its assets, while Boston's other trust companies had increased theirs by 3 percent. Commuting on the Boston, Revere Beach, and Lynn Railroad to the bank on 20 Meridian Street from his parents' house in Winthrop, he arrived early and stayed late, making full use of every family connection the Kennedys had acquired since the first Patrick Kennedy had arrived in East Boston. By June 1914, after six months on the job, he had increased Columbia Trust's holdings by some 27 percent to $920,204.[16]

Now a bank president and a successful one, even if his bank was among the smallest in the city, Kennedy was finally in a position to marry Rose Elizabeth Fitzgerald.

On June 20, 1914, the now ex-mayor and his wife announced the engagement of their daughter to Joseph P. Kennedy.

Joe and Rose, if we are to believe her account, spent a heavenly summer together, going to the Boston Pops, eating ice cream (Joe was a sweets addict), attending small soirees at friends' homes, and, whenever they could, attending tea dances with an orchestra "at one of the clubs or good hotels . . . we always had good times at these little soirees, partly because I loved dancing and Joe was such a good dancer. He always knew all the current steps," including the turkey trot and tango, which her father, the mayor, had declared to be morally injurious and banned from the city's public dance halls in October 1913.[17]

Just one week after the announcement of the Kennedy-Fitzgerald engagement, Austrian archduke Franz Ferdinand was assassinated in Serbia.

On July 28, Austria declared war on Serbia.

On August 1, Germany declared war on Russia.

On August 3, Germany declared war on France and on Belgium.

On August 4, Great Britain declared war on Germany.

Like newly engaged couples everywhere, Joseph Patrick Kennedy and Rose Elizabeth Fitzpatrick tried their best to hold the world at bay, but that was not easy. "The summer of 1914 was, of course a time of high drama and the crisis in Europe. . . . Nevertheless, we were young and in love and the Atlantic lay between us and that tragedy. President Wilson declared America's neutrality. We could assume that the war would be settled by somebody, and somehow fairly soon . . . with peace restored, before it could possibly affect our own life together in any direct way."[18]

Though Columbia Trust was very much a local bank, not even Joe Kennedy could protect it from the financial panic set in motion by the declaration of war, the British announcement that they would no longer exchange pounds sterling for gold, and the decision of European banking houses to cash in their American stocks and bonds for gold. To prevent wholesale disaster, the New York Stock Exchange closed its doors on July 31, 1914, and did not resume bond trading until late November or equity trading until mid-December. The nation's financial problems were compounded by a virtual cessation of international trade. For port cities such as Boston, the economic hardship was considerable. Citizens and businesses alike hoarded their capital and put off taking out new loans or mortgages. In the six weeks between September 12 and October 31, 1914, Columbia Trust's assets fell more than 5 percent.

Rose and Joe were married on October 7, 1914, in the middle of the financial downturn. The ceremony took place in Cardinal William O'Connell's private chapel. Honey Fitz gave the bride away; Joe Donovan, Joe's oldest friend and his partner in the sightseeing bus, was the best man. Rose's sister Agnes was her maid of honor. Though it was a wedding for family only, the groom wore a top hat, stiffly starched white shirt and collar, and tails; the bride was dressed in a full-length elaborately embroidered white dress. Following the ceremony, the wedding party gathered for a breakfast for fifty or sixty family and close friends at the Fitzgeralds' home. "I had a great many parties, receptions, and festivities while my father was mayor," Rose recalled. "So I preferred to have a small wedding, when it was time to be married." It was also possible, of course, that the Fitzgerald family, following Honey Fitz's still puzzling withdrawal from the mayoral campaign, felt it best to keep a low profile.[19]

The wedding might have been a simple affair; the honeymoon was not. The first stop was New York City, where the honeymooners stayed at the Hotel Belmont, had luncheon at Claridge's, went for a ride in Arthur Goldsmith's new automobile, then dined with him and watched the latest Douglas Fairbanks play, *He Comes Up Smiling*. The next morning, Honey Fitz and Rose's brother John showed up in New York City and took the train with the honeymooners to Shibe Park in Philadelphia for the first game of the 1914 World Series between the Boston Braves and the Philadelphia Athletics. After two days and two games in Philadelphia, both of which the Braves won, Rose and Joe left Honey Fitz behind and traveled south to The Greenbrier in White Sulphur Springs, West Virginia, where they spent the next ten days riding, playing tennis and golf, and meeting and dining with some very "distinguished people." Then it was back on the train to Atlantic City for a promenade on the boardwalk, "bathing" in the ocean, a formal photograph, and a night at the theater, where the celebrated actress Alla Nazimova was appearing in a new play.

The honeymoon ended where it had begun, in New York City. Rose and Joe saw another play on Friday and on Saturday managed to get tickets for *Chin Chin,* a musical comedy extravaganza starring Fred Stone and David Montgomery that the *New York Times* had five days earlier declared "far and away the biggest show of its kind . . . that has ever come to Broadway." They spent their final honeymoon evening dining at the Biltmore, then returned to Boston and moved into their new house on Beals Street in Brookline.[20]

Joe had spent everything he had on the purchase of the outstanding stock in Columbia Trust the year before and was left with only $500. Unfortunately, the house he and Rose had picked out cost $6,500; fortunately, he had no problem borrowing $2,000 from his family and getting a $4,000 mortgage from his own bank.

The Kennedy house was located at 83 Beals, the last one on the street. There were three bedrooms on the second floor and two more on the third, suitable for servants. It was a pleasant-looking house with a gabled roof and a very large balustraded porch and deck, which appropriately barricaded would be perfect for toddlers. Next door and across the street were vacant lots. Beals Street had sidewalks and sewers and telephone connections; the houses were large and comfortable, but not ostentatiously so; St. Aidan's Roman Catholic Church and the Edward Devotion public school were nearby; the trolley into Boston was in a short walk away. It was a solid, though rather lower-middle-class neighborhood, on the way up, the perfect place for a family with ambitions but not much cash. Though there was a Catholic church nearby—as there was almost everywhere in the Boston area—it was not an Irish Catholic community. Located at a reasonable distance outside the Boston city limits, Kennedy had the perfect excuse to stay out of the electoral politics he had come to loathe after his father's unconscionable defeat seven years earlier.[21]

Rose, the daughter of a prominent politician who had served as both congressman and mayor, had grown up in large, spacious, overdecorated late-Victorian splendor. Now married to an up-and-coming bank president, she intended to replicate, though in better taste and less ostentatiously, perhaps, the homes she had lived in as a child. There was much to do. She had to choose the color schemes for upstairs and downstairs, buy the furniture and the rugs, and arrange the wedding presents so that they could be seen but would not clash. With a decorator's help, she placed the marble statue of Napoleon, mahogany candlesticks, bronze ornaments, Venetian vases, banjo clock, pillows, pictures, and Oriental rugs in the parlor; and the silver nut set and bread tray, gold cup and saucer, tea napkins, platters, bon-bon dishes, and cut glass in the dining room. Copies of Turner, Hals, and Rembrandt paintings were hung on the walls of the parlor, which was furnished with the new baby grand the couple had received as a gift from her uncles, a matching sofa and armchair, and her husband's red lounge chair. The upstairs guest bedroom, boudoir (which would later be converted into a nursery), and master bedroom with its twin beds, bureau, dressing table, and chiffonier were furnished more plainly, as they would not be on display for guests.[22]

Everything having to do with the furnishing of the house or its management was left to Rose. Joe never asked about or questioned her decisions. And she, in turn, never inquired or was told anything about his business outside the home. She had been "brought up that way" and was convinced it was for the best. "Your husband worked hard and he had a good many difficulties during his business day and when he came home he wanted to have comfort and peace and love and affection," she later recalled. "He didn't want to be bothered and he didn't want a cocky wife or a complaining wife."[23]

By the fall of 1914, Columbia Trust's assets were beginning to stabilize. This would have been cause for mild celebration in the Kennedy household had Joe not been drawn into the midst of a financial scandal that, though not of his doing, reflected poorly on him. In early December, it was reported that the Collateral Loan Company, of which he was a director, had been robbed by its president of tens of thousands of dollars in a scheme whereby pawned objects and mining stock certificates had been taken from the vaults, then pawned again. One particular diamond ring, it appeared, had been pawned twice a week for twenty consecutive weeks. Questions were raised, and legitimately so, about the quality of oversight by the directors, young Joe Kennedy included. Kennedy cooperated fully with the district attorney, testified before the grand jury, and waited for the incident—and his name—to vanish from the newspapers. It did. But when his term expired, he was not reappointed.[24]

Fortunately, by late 1914 the economic situation in Boston and the nation had begun to brighten. The Wilson administration had, a bit reluctantly, accepted and adjusted to the inescapable reality that the British were going to retain control of the seas. In concrete terms, this meant that while bowing in the direction of neutrality, Americans would renew trading with the British and the French, protected by the British fleet, while allowing that same fleet to blockade trade with Germany.

American loans and credits flowed freely toward the British Isles, financing purchases of homegrown raw materials and nonmilitary commodities. European gold crossed the Atlantic in the opposite direction. As the domestic money supply expanded, so did credit and investment opportunities for American banks and businesses.

Columbia Trust rode high on the new wave of prosperity. Between October 31, 1914, and May 1, 1915, its assets rose by almost $46,000, an increase of more than 5 percent in six months.[25] Joseph Kennedy's personal fortune increased as well. He continued his association with Old Colony Realty, which now billed itself as the "Largest Operator in Boston Suburban Residential Properties." Did his real estate customers get preferential treatment when applying for mortgages from his bank? Probably. Was he breaking any laws? No.

Joe Kennedy was learning how to skate along the edges without falling in. As president of Columbia Trust, he had immediate access to capital and credit, which he used not only to finance his mortgage and real estate dealings, but to purchase stocks. As the economy righted and then boomed in early 1915, his fortunes soared. His former Harvard classmate and friend Tom Campbell remembered Joe telling him that every stock he "bought zoomed. It was such an easy way to make money that I wondered why more people did not know about it. I was afraid the market would close before I had all I wanted."

Then came May 7, 1915, the German torpedoing of the *Lusitania* and the deaths of more than a hundred American civilians. In the war scare that followed, the spectacular four-month stock market rise was halted, then reversed, "wiping out all [his] profits" and, according to Tom Campbell, knocking his "dreams of easy money . . . into a cocked hat." Fortunately for the nation and the Kennedys, fears that the *Lusitania* tragedy would lead to war were unfounded. The Germans pledged that there would be no more attacks on passenger liners, no more American civilian deaths. And with that, the economic boom generated by the Allies' need for American foodstuffs, commodities, and credit to pay for them shifted into higher gear. The stock market pushed forward again, climbing in almost a straight line from a low of 65 in June 1915 to 110 in November 1916. Joseph P. Kennedy jumped back in, wiser now, a bit more cautious, but convinced that having made a killing once, he could do it again.[26]

On November 2, 1915, short of capital to invest, he borrowed $55,000 from National Shawmut, where Bob Potter was now an officer. It was a short-term six-month loan, backed by some stock certificates, life insurance policies, and real estate. In the months and years to come, there would be other sizable loans from National Shawmut, Merchants Bank of Boston, and State Street Trust, some of them secured by notes backed by real estate, a few by Columbia Trust stock. He never borrowed more than he thought he could repay, and only at preferential rates; and he never defaulted, though occasionally he was forced to take out a new loan to pay off an older one.

His ability to juggle numbers and accounts was remarkable. So too his capacity to profit from a booming market. Later in life, Kennedy would confess to being a bear in all things, including the market, and take great pride in the money he had made betting on stocks to go down. But that was certainly not the case in his twenties, when he was convinced that no matter how violent the short-term swings, the American economy was strong and would only grow stronger.[27]

Joseph P. Kennedy, still in his middle twenties, was well on his way to becoming a wealthy man, but only on the way. Rose remembered her thrill "the day my husband drove home in our very own brand-new, gleaming black Model T Ford." It was not the most expensive automobile on the market and much less grand than the ones her father owned, but it was new and it was theirs. "Immediately after supper, in the summer twilight, off we went heading towards a neighborhood shopping center." Preoccupied with steering his new automobile, the first he had owned or, perhaps, driven, Joe Kennedy didn't notice the kerosene lanterns on the road or the excavation they marked. Rose "shouted a warning, [but] it was too late and into the ditch we went. . . . Neither of us was hurt except for a few black-and-blue bruises. And our beautiful car was relatively undamaged. They made tougher springs in those days." Joe gunned the car out of the ditch, with "no loss of nerve."[28]

Four

WAR

J oe Kennedy had to have wondered whether the Harvard Class of '12 reunion committee was congratulating or ridiculing him when they included in the schedule of events for their third reunion a mock "Bank-Presidents Verein [German for association or society]: Meet in J. P. Kennedy's room at 7:30. . . . The Federal Reserve Board will sing and the Controller of the Currency will read a paper on 'Our Boy President, or Risen from the Bank.'"[1]

Still, whether or not his classmates considered Columbia Trust of East Boston a fitting landing place for a Harvard graduate, he was a bank president and rather proud of it.

H e rose early seven days a week, did calisthenic exercises with his Indian clubs, ate breakfast, and set off for work or, on Sundays, for Mass at St. Aidan's. On those nights he came home after work, he and Rose had a formal dinner in the dining room (with their fine china and silverware), after which he retired to his big red lounge chair in the parlor to read the *Boston Transcript,* then his detective novel, and listen to classical music on the Victrola. On those nights he did not come home, Rose did not question where he had been—or why. "Joe's time was his own," Rose recalled in her memoirs, "as it had been and always would be."[2]

In marrying Rose Fitzgerald, Joe Kennedy had pledged to faithfully love and support her—and the children they might have together; to keep them safe and secure and well sheltered; and to do everything in his power, to work day and night, six days a week, fifty-two weeks a year if necessary, to provide for them. What he did not intend to do was give up being a "ladies' man." And we do not know if Rose expected him to. Her father had most certainly been with other women during his marriage. So had, and would, a large number of Joe's friends. Like them, he successfully demarcated his life into two parts, one of which he shared with his wife, the other spent apart from her, because he wanted to avoid situations that might cause her embarrassment or force her to confront the fact that he enjoyed the company of other women, hundreds of them over his lifetime: actresses, waitresses, secretaries, stenographers, caddies, models, stewardesses, and others.

The Kennedys were outsiders in Brookline and preferred it that way. They did most of their shopping and socializing in Boston and spent their summers at the seashore in a rented house on C Street in the Waveland section of Hull on the Nantasket Peninsula, about twenty-five miles away. It was there, in Hull, that their first child, Joseph P. Kennedy, Jr., was born on Sunday, July 25, 1915, nine months, two weeks, and four days after his parents' wedding. Rose, as was the custom, gave birth at home, with a squadron of doctors, attendants, and her housemaid. Joe waited in the next room; Honey Fitz was outside on the beach. When the doctors announced that it was a boy, a blue-eyed, big, healthy one, Honey Fitz rushed inside, greeted his grandson, daughter, and son-in-law, then contacted his friends in the Boston press to report how happy he was to be young (fifty-two), healthy, and a grandfather. Though Joseph P. Kennedy was not mentioned in the newspaper reports, the baby was named after him, not his famous father-in-law or father.

The Joseph P. Kennedys, now numbering three, returned to Brookline that fall. Columbia Trust continued to do well, riding the waves of prosperity set in motion as Great Britain and France, now entering their second full year of war, increased their purchases of American food and manufactured goods, much of it funded by credit from American financial institutions. Joe Kennedy was entering a new stage in his banking career, no longer a novelty, but on his way to becoming a respected, if decidedly minor, member of the business community. In May 1916, Eugene Thayer, president of the Merchants Bank of Boston, appointed him to the board of directors of a recently established "credit union" for workingmen. Serving with Kennedy on the board were a number of distinguished Boston businessmen and bankers.

By early 1917, Kennedy was making enough money to hire a full-time trained nurse to stay with Rose through her second pregnancy. The boudoir was turned into a nursery. Though the house had only one staircase—for the use of family and servants alike—it was large enough to accommodate three full-time servants on the third floor: nurse, nursemaid, and maid. The laundress who came in twice a week to do the family's wash, supplemented now by diapers, worked in the basement.

That spring of 1917, the tidy little world Joe Kennedy had created for himself in Brookline and in East Boston was threatened by forces beyond his control. On April 2, President Woodrow Wilson had gone before a joint session of Congress to ask for a declaration of war. On April 4, the Senate approved Wilson's declaration. On April 6, the House concurred and Secretary of War Newton Baker submitted legislation authorizing the drafting of a "National Army" of half a million men.

Kennedy was determined, from the moment war was declared, to do everything he could to remain out of uniform and stateside. As an Irish Catholic, he had no great love for the English and no desire to risk his life to protect the British Empire. As a young father, whose second son, John Fitzgerald Kennedy, had been born on May 29, 1917, he believed his first responsibility was to his family. As an ambitious young banker, he did not want to interrupt his career to spend time in the trenches. Kennedy did not advertise these views. His decision not to enlist or allow himself to be drafted was a private one, based on practical, not moral, choices. He was not opposed to all wars, just to Americans getting involved in this one. He resisted entirely the claims of the British propagandists and their American allies that the fight against the Huns was a fight for civilization.

Years later in a conversation with Doris Kearns Goodwin, Rose recalled how upset her husband got when, at a weekend gathering, his Harvard classmates applauded the daring and deadly British offensive at the Battle of the Somme in July 1916. "As Rose remembered the conversation at the house, at first Joe just listened to the enthusiasm of his friends and didn't say much. 'He merely shook his head with sadness.' And then, he counter-attacked. 'He warned his friends [that] by accepting the idea of the grandeur of the struggle, they themselves were contributing to the momentum of a senseless war, certain to ruin the victors as well as the vanquished.'"[3]

President Woodrow Wilson would have preferred to fight the war with an all-volunteer army, but resisted doing so in large part because of the British experience. The problem with a volunteer army, the British had learned, was that the wrong men volunteered for the battlefield, leaving the home front—which would have to supply the soldiers with armaments—bereft of skilled workers. The United States would prevent that from happening by organizing a "selective service" system to scientifically distribute the nation's young men, as needed, to the various branches of the war effort. Millions would be sent to the battlefield; others would be directed into munitions factories and the shipyards, where they too would fight the war against the Hun. To forestall the divisions, chaos, and occasional riots that marked the conscription process during the Civil War, the Selective Service Act of 1917 mandated that there were to be no substitutions, commutations, or abbreviated terms of service, no way, in other words, for wealthy businessmen such as Joseph Kennedy to buy their way out of the draft.[4]

On June 5, 1917, Joseph P. Kennedy reported as directed to his local polling place and filled out his registration card. The Brookline registrar certified that he was tall and stout, with blue eyes, brown (really brownish red) hair, and no lost limbs or disabilities. Line 9 affirmed that he had a "wife and 2 children" who were "solely dependent on [him] for support."[5]

That was not going to be enough, however, to get him the exemption he wanted. In the second week of August, the provost marshal general's office in Washington and the state director of military enrollment in Massachusetts issued what the *Boston Daily Globe* referred to as "sweeping orders" to reduce "exceptions of married men."

Honey Fitz, never one to sit out a battle, especially one as clear-cut as this, jumped into the controversy, his mouth wide open, demanding that the Republican governor of Massachusetts and the Republicans on local draft boards petition Congress to spare married citizens and draft aliens in their place. Though he may have had the best interests of his daughter and son-in-law in mind, he did them no favors by intimating that Republican draft board members, including the three in Brookline who would hear Joe's case, were less interested than he was in keeping American families intact.[6]

In late October, the provost marshal general declared unequivocally that "married men who have independent incomes . . . where the support of the dependents in their absence was assured" would be denied exemptions. Each case would be heard on an individual basis. To secure his "dependency" exemption, Kennedy would have to prove—which he could not—that his three dependents were fully "dependent" on him for support, that no one else, not even his rich father-in-law, would be able to provide for them.

Fortunately, there were other categories of deferment. At the same time that he moved to restrict "dependency" exemptions, the provost marshal general, in response to a petition from a committee of shipbuilders, authorized large numbers of "industrial" exemptions for "shipworkers of military age" with specialized skills. A number of those exemptions went to employees of the Fore River Shipbuilding Company of Quincy, Massachusetts, just ten miles from downtown Boston, which in 1913 had been acquired by Bethlehem Steel. Bethlehem had been contracted by the government to build forty-five destroyers at Fore River and been given $9 million of government money to construct a ten-bay shipyard at Squantum in Dorchester Bay.[7]

Joseph P. Kennedy was not a shipbuilder; in fact, as he admitted in a letter to his draft board, he had "absolutely no technical knowledge of shipbuilding." But he was young, smart, ambitious, disciplined, and well connected; he knew how to negotiate a contract, read a balance sheet, and get things done in Boston. He was, it appeared, a perfect candidate for a management position at Fore River—and the "industrial exemption" that would come with it.

In mid-October, three high-level executives of Fore River—J. W. Powell, the general manager, who had been promoted and was about to be transferred to Bethlehem headquarters in Pennsylvania; Samuel Wakeman, whom Powell had chosen to succeed him; and Guy Currier, the company's lawyer and chief lobbyist—met with Joseph Kennedy at Young's Hotel in Boston and offered him the newly created position of assistant general manager.[8]

For Kennedy, this was a golden opportunity. The pay was decent: $4,000 a year, equivalent to about $68,000 in purchasing power today, with a bonus based on total manufacturing profits at the plant. He would get an "industrial exemption" from the draft and the opportunity to associate himself with Bethlehem Steel, one of the nation's most dynamic corporations, led by two of its most respected businessmen: Eugene Grace, president, and Charles M. Schwab, chairman of the board.

The Fore River project was going to be huge. Thousands of new jobs were going to be created, bridges and roadways built, docks extended, and tons of building materials transported to Quincy and Squantum to construct an industrial city populated by tens of thousands. Every state and city politician, businessman, contractor, manufacturer, real estate promoter, and banker would want a piece of the multimillion-dollar project that Kennedy would now have a hand in managing.

On the morning of October 15, 1917, Joseph Kennedy got into his Ford, said good-bye to Rose, two-year-old Joe Jr., and five-month-old John, and drove the fourteen miles from Beals Street in Brookline to the Fore River plant.

Kennedy's first assignment was to help design and oversee the company's employee insurance programs. He was also asked to manage construction of the transportation infrastructure required to get twenty-six thousand workers to, from, and between Boston, Quincy, Fore River, and Squantum. He secured from the state the right to build and operate a privately owned Bethlehem shipyard railroad to connect the Fore River and Squantum shipyards. To get workers to Fore River, he negotiated with public and private authorities to rebuild the Neponset Bridge from Dorchester to Quincy and have the streetcar rails double-tracked and extended from downtown Boston to Quincy Square and on to Fore River. All this required endless meetings with the Boston Elevated Railway, Edison Electric, the Bay State Street Railway, the navy, the Emergency Fleet Corporation, the United States Housing Corporation, and state and government officials as to who would pay for what and when.[9]

As the new shipbuilding facilities went on line, the number of workers commuting to the shipyards increased to the point where the Bay State Street Railway, which was owned by Massachusetts Electric, was asked to add new trains for the morning commute. The railroad requested that the company instead stagger the hours for its morning shifts to relieve overcrowding. Kennedy had been named a trustee of Massachusetts Electric in May, but that didn't stop him from supporting the railroad's request. He persuaded the plant managers to agree to change their work shifts, thereby saving the Bay State Street Railway and Massachusetts Electric the cost of paying additional crews to run additional trains to and from the plant. Union representatives pointed out the obvious conflict of interest, but Kennedy did not back down. Still, he had learned his lesson. When, in the fall of 1918, he was offered a directorship of the Citizens' Gas-Light Company of Quincy, he turned it down. "My short experience . . . has taught me that the attitude of labor to-day towards management in charge of enterprises is not improved much by having labor think that there is too close a connection between the employers and those that sell them the commodity that they use."[10]

Kennedy quickly became a victim of his own competency and exceptional stamina. His workload increased exponentially as new duties were added to old ones. When it became apparent that the government would have to construct temporary housing for shipyard workers, he was assigned to negotiate with government officials on how to spend the funds quickly and efficiently. He was also asked to oversee the feeding of the tens of thousands of men who now worked at the shipyards. He brought in outside contractors to set up a self-serve cafeteria at Squantum that served 1,380 meals in fifteen minutes. Seeing the opportunity to make a handsome profit for himself, he organized a privately held company, the Fore River Lunch Company, and contracted out to it the task of feeding the Fore River employees.[11]

In the midst of all this activity—on insurance, transportation networks, housing, and lunchrooms—and to his (and his employer's) great surprise, Kennedy received a 1-A draft classification from the Brookline draft board in mid-February 1918. He appealed immediately to the district draft board for a "deferred classification on industrial grounds" and accompanied his appeal with a long letter in which he detailed his responsibilities at Fore River. J. W. Powell, vice president of Bethlehem Shipbuilding, sent an additional letter and then, a week later, followed up with a note to the Emergency Fleet Corporation executive in charge of securing exemptions for shipyard workers. The letters did the trick. Kennedy would never receive any official deferment, but neither would he be called for the draft. He would spend the remainder of the war at Fore River.[12]

Well aware that sending conscripted young men to risk their lives in European trenches would be met with significant opposition at home, President Wilson had, from the moment the nation declared war, focused his attention—and that of his newly created Committee on Public Information—on winning the battle for public opinion. In April 1918, Washington launched its third "Liberty Loan" campaign to raise money for the war and remobilize the home front. The opening of the drive in Boston, as elsewhere, was marked by a massive patriotic parade. Kennedy, assigned the task of publicizing and celebrating Bethlehem Steel's contribution to the war effort, conceived the brilliant idea of putting three hundred Fore River workmen on floats to demonstrate how they were aiding the war effort by "riveting a bulkhead of a destroyer, riveting a copper condenser-head and other work." The demonstration was such a success that Kennedy arranged for "two gangs of riveters [to give] an exhibition of their daily toil" at B. F. Keith's vaudeville theater to the accompaniment of "We're Building a Bridge to Berlin."[13]

While Kennedy was putting on shows in vaudeville theaters, his friends and classmates were serving in the armed forces, most of them still on this side of the Atlantic. Arthur Kelly, Tom Campbell, and Joe Sheehan were stationed at Camp Devens, about forty miles from Boston; Bob Potter was in Washington, D.C. Joe visited and wrote them regularly. He was neither ashamed of nor guilty about evading military service. Though not in uniform, he believed he was doing his part for his nation, working sixty-five to seventy hours a week, occasionally spending the night in his office.

When, in mid-April, the officers and foremen at Squantum held their first "get-together banquet," Kennedy was one of the six company executives invited to sit at the head table. In August, he was among the three Fore River executives delegated to greet Eugene Grace, the president of Bethlehem Steel and Bethlehem Shipbuilding, on his visit to Quincy.[14]

Still, he was decidedly middle management, an assistant general manager who remained in the background, doing research, running numbers, reviewing contracts. He would later boast loudly and often of having negotiated a deal with Assistant Secretary of the Navy Franklin Delano Roosevelt on a matter involving Argentine dreadnoughts that had been built at Fore River and returned for repairs. There is, however, no evidence and little likelihood that he ever dealt directly with Roosevelt or any decision makers in Washington, Boston, or Bethlehem headquarters in Pennsylvania.

The closest he came to managing anything was in the spring of 1918, when, reportedly on instructions from Charles Schwab, Bethlehem Steel organized a Steel League of baseball teams made up of steelworkers and shipbuilders, with as many major leaguers as could be "enlisted." Perhaps because he had won his Harvard "H" in baseball, a fact of which he was inordinately proud, Kennedy was recruited as general manager of the Fore River team.

On May 19, Fore River opened its 1918 Steel League season against Wilmington and won 4–2. Samuel Wakeman, Fore River's general manager and Kennedy's boss, "threw out the first ball and presented a silk flag to the team of his company," the *Boston Daily Globe* reported the next morning. "Before the game there was a parade to the grounds, headed by the Fore River Band and Fore River Guards. . . . A number of players of former big league fame were in the lineups" for both teams.[15]

Plant managers from Lebanon and Steelton, Pennsylvania, to Sparrows Point, Maryland, and Wilmington, Delaware, to Fore River, Massachusetts, competed for big leaguers with offers of generous salaries, minimal work in the yards, and guaranteed exemptions. Shoeless Joe Jackson, perhaps the best player in the major leagues, on receiving word from his Greenville, South Carolina, draft board that he had been classified 1-A and would be called to serve between May 25 and June 1, left the White Sox for the Bethlehem shipyard in Wilmington, Delaware. Two weeks later, on June 15, Boston Red Sox star Dutch Leonard arrived at Fore River. Kennedy offered him a salary of $250 a month, $200 from the plant and $50 from his own pocket, "thinking," as he wrote Eugene Grace's assistant at Bethlehem Steel, "that with the acquisition of this man it would make the pennant sure" for Fore River. Leonard pitched his last game in the major leagues on June 20, but then, instead of relocating to Fore River to pitch on June 21 or 22 as he had promised, he tried to get a better deal on the West Coast, playing for a naval reserves team. When the West Coast deal fell through, he returned to Fore River to pitch a game against Steelton on June 29, then a second against Bethlehem, with eighteen strikeouts, on July 4. Leonard continued to pitch until the end of August, when he lost his exemption—as did many other ballplayers—after a brief investigation (what took so long?) determined that he had signed on at Fore River "for no other reason than to 'duck the draft.'" Fore River ended the 1918 Steel League season in last place.[16]

Kennedy's final assignment at Fore River was to manage, as best he could, the influenza epidemic that hit Boston with sudden and deadly effect in the fall of 1918. On September 6, the *Boston Daily Globe* reported that the epidemic had begun to spread from sailors and soldiers to the civilian population. Eleven days later, it declared that the city was in the vortex of a "grippe epidemic." City officials closed the theaters and dance halls, forbade public gatherings, and advised churchgoers to remain home on Sundays. By September 21, more than two thousand cases of influenza had been reported at Fore River and Squantum alone. Kennedy was given the task of converting shipyard dormitories into infirmaries in the hope that isolating the sick might help stop the spread of further contagion. He spent days at a time at Fore River, unable and perhaps, given the fear of spreading contagion, unwilling to return to his wife and three children in Brookline. He was not worried for Joseph Jr., who was impossibly healthy and had always been so, but he feared for the health of John Fitzgerald, who had been sickly since birth, and his first daughter, Rose Marie (or Rosemary, as she would later be known), who was born on September 13, 1918, in the midst of the epidemic crisis. "She was," her mother remembered, "a very pretty baby and she was sweet and peaceable and cried less than the first two had, which at the time I supposed was part of her being a girl."[17]

Kennedy and his family would survive the epidemic intact, though according to Rose, the pressures on her husband were so great that he developed an ulcer, the first manifestation of the stress-induced stomach problems that would plague him all his life.

In late October, the epidemic crested. And that was good news. A month later, the war was over. In Quincy, the coming of peace was marked by a parade of fifteen thousand workmen carrying "shovels, picks and other tools," marching behind the Fore River Band from the plant to the city square. Kennedy was not among them. He had collapsed earlier, from overwork, lack of sleep, and stomach pains, and been sent away to recuperate at a "health farm."[18]

It was a different Fore River that Kennedy returned to after his convalescence. The months of feverish activity, the ceaseless construction of new roads, bridges, and dormitories, the nonstop expansion of plant and workforce: all this was over. Much of the work that remained was on government contracts signed during the war. No one knew what would happen when these were fulfilled and the ships currently under construction were sent to sea. Kennedy remained at Fore River through the winter and the spring of 1919, waiting for a new assignment. But none was forthcoming. The boom in shipbuilding did not survive the coming of peace. Bethlehem shifted its focus away from Fore River, Squantum, and shipbuilding in general and back to its core business, steel.

On June 30, 1919, bowing to the inevitable and, no doubt, both restless and anxious to move on after twenty months in the same place, Joseph P. Kennedy, assistant general manager, tendered his resignation.

Five

MAKING A MILLION

As an Irish Catholic from East Boston, Kennedy had always known that he would have to forge his own path into Boston business and banking circles. He chose his mentors carefully, suffering no fools along the way. His first and most important contact may have been Guy Currier, a former Massachusetts legislator who had studied law, gone into business, and made a fortune for himself as lawyer, lobbyist, and liaison between businessmen and legislators. It was Currier who introduced Kennedy to the Fore River executives who hired him as assistant general manager and probably to Galen Stone, his next employer.[1]

Stone was the co-owner, with Charles Hayden, of a brokerage firm with offices in Boston and New York. Hayden, Stone was a relatively small player in Boston finance, with nowhere near the assets or the influence of Kidder, Peabody or Lee, Higginson. Still, Galen Stone knew everyone who was anyone in Boston and in New York, served on dozens of boards, and appeared to be both well liked and well respected as a broker.

Kennedy accepted a position as manager of the brokerage department at the firm's Boston office. Though a newcomer to the business,

Kennedy had been investing in stocks on a fairly large scale since graduating from Harvard, perhaps even before. He had an account at Richardson, Hill & Co., one of the more prestigious Boston houses, through
which he bought and sold the stocks of companies he had some connection with or some insider knowledge of: Massachusetts Electric, of
which he was a trustee; Shawmut National Bank, where his former
classmate Bob Potter was an officer; Fairbanks Company, where one of
his banking mentors, Eugene Thayer, president of the Merchants Bank
of Boston, was a director; and Waldorf System, a company that ran
lunchrooms like the one he operated at Fore River.

While employed by Hayden, Stone, he continued, as he had since
graduation, to make money on the side by buying and selling real estate
through Old Colony Realty and a new entity, Fenway Building Trust,
which he had set up with Eddie Moore, his father-in-law's former secretary, who had also worked for Honey Fitz's successors, mayors James
M. Curley and Andrew Peters. Kennedy owned 98 percent of the new
company, Moore 1 percent, and a third investor the remaining 1 percent. Through a complicated set of arrangements, Moore had become
the agent for two women who owned property in Boston. The women
sold their holdings to Fenway Building Trust and received "notes" in
return, which somehow or other found their way back to Kennedy and
Moore, who used them to secure bank loans to buy more real estate and
stock. It was, at base, a shell game of sorts, but a legal, profitable one.[2]

This was Kennedy's first business transaction with Edward Moore,
who would become his best friend, constant companion, and most
trusted partner in business and politics. Moore and Kennedy had worked
together—on selected deals and projects—at Fore River. Sometime
in the early 1920s, as Kennedy's outside business interests grew, he hired
Moore as his full-time adviser, secretary, and chief of staff. "Joe," his
wife, Rose, later recalled, "had a rugged individualist's need for privacy; there were very few men he liked, trusted, and could relax with
entirely. . . . Eddie Moore became his closest friend, someone he trusted
implicitly in every way and in all circumstances. His wife, Mary, became an equally great friend, confidante, and unfailing support for
me. They were older than Joe and I, and we felt the full affection and
confidence and unquestioning mutual acceptance that might be felt of a

beloved aunt and uncle. They had no children; so they turned to ours" and became surrogate parents to all of them. "When our ninth child, and fourth son, was born, we named him Edward Moore Kennedy."[3]

Eddie Moore was the perfect complement to Joe. He respected him, followed his instructions, kept his mouth shut, appeared to enjoy playing second fiddle, and got the job done. The two would work together in Boston, Hollywood, New York, Washington, and London for the next thirty years. Wherever Kennedy would set up headquarters, there was an office for Moore. Moore was genial, placid, dignified, never lost his temper, never glowered or frowned, and was universally adored by those who came into contact or did business with him. Unlike Kennedy, who was imposing, handsome, and tall, Eddie was rather small, nearly bald, and entirely nondescript looking. Gloria Swanson, who didn't get along with many of the men in the Kennedy entourage, adored Eddie. "Slender, blue-eyed, and gentle, he had a very dry humor, which he employed only rarely and when he was certain of achieving the proper effect with it. He was Mr. Kennedy's chief brain, his auxiliary memory. He kept track of everything that went on."[4]

Joseph Kennedy's appointment at Hayden, Stone in June 1919 solidified his identification with the Boston business community. He lived in a suburb, dressed in tailored suits, wore custom-made shirts, and drove to the office instead of taking the streetcar. He gave up baseball for golf and in the summer of 1919, simultaneously with accepting his new position, joined the Woodland Golf Club in nearby Auburndale. In September 1919, when 1,117 of Boston's 1,544 policemen went out on strike, Kennedy publicly supported Republican governor Calvin Coolidge's decision to call out the militia and signed a solicitation for funds to assist the strikebreakers.

The largely Irish police force had voted to join the American Federation of Labor and been granted a charter in August. The Brahmin, Harvard-educated, "proper Bostonian" police commissioner appointed by the governor immediately suspended the union organizers. When the policemen threatened a strike if their leaders were disciplined, the commissioner called for volunteers to replace them. Large numbers of

Harvard students stepped forward as potential strikebreakers. Democratic mayor Andrew Peters was in favor of negotiating a settlement with the policemen, but he was overruled by Coolidge. Kennedy, instead of staying silent or supporting the policemen and the Democratic mayor, allied himself firmly with Governor Coolidge, Guy Currier, Harvard president Abbott Lowell, and the rest of the blue bloods and Republicans who cheered on as the strike was broken, the policemen fired, and "order" restored.

That fall, Kennedy continued his move toward respectability by filling out an application for membership in the Middlesex Club, the oldest Republican club in New England. When, only weeks after he had filled out his application, Governor Coolidge removed an Irish American as clerk of the court in East Boston and replaced him with a Protestant, Kennedy abandoned any further thought of becoming a Republican. "People like myself," he wrote the club president, Louis Coolidge, "must be made to feel that there is a chance in the Republican party to at least see that Irish-Catholics are not discriminated against just because they are Irish-Catholics."[5]

On February 20, 1920, Kathleen Kennedy, like her brother Jack and sister Rosemary before her, was born in the twin bed nearest the window in the upstairs master bedroom at Beals Street. Kennedy was not there for these births, as he would not be for the five that would follow. "The idea," Rose recalled with a bit of pride in her tone, "was [that giving birth] was something the woman had to do and the less bother she gave to anybody else including her husband the better it was, and the easier it was."[6]

Joseph P. Kennedy was a good father and a caring one, but he had seen little of his family during his years at Fore River. "He was under such pressure," Rose recalled, "that, except for Sundays, he came home just long enough to sleep." That pattern did not change significantly with the end of the war and his first year at Hayden, Stone.

Only days after Kathleen's birth, Jack, three months shy of his third birthday, was diagnosed with scarlet fever. He had been sickly since birth and "always thin," dangerously so, Rose thought. At dinner, she would always make sure that he was given "the extra juice from the steak when it was carved. . . . I had to build up his health." Jack had been feeling poorly for a few days when the doctors made the diagnosis of scarlet fever, which, Rose recalled in her memoirs, "was a dreaded disease, fairly often fatal, quite often crippling in aftereffects; heart, eyes, ears; there were various possibilities that were awful to think about. . . . And with that very contagious disease in that small house on Beals Street, there were fears that Joe, Jr. and Rosemary would get it, and that the new baby might also, and so might I. And yet there was no place in Brookline where Jack could be taken—the [local] hospital wouldn't admit patients with contagious diseases."[7]

The first imperative was to get Jack out of the house. But where? The Boston City Hospital had a special unit, the South Department, for infectious childhood diseases, and the physician in charge, Dr. Edward Place, was the nation's leading expert on measles and scarlet fever. The problem was that the Kennedys lived in the city of Brookline, not in Boston. Either through Honey Fitz or other contacts, Kennedy got in touch with Democratic mayor Andrew Peters, who arranged for Jack Kennedy, though not a Boston resident, to be admitted to Boston City Hospital.

"By the time he got there," Rose recalled, "Jack was a very, very sick little boy." Because Rose was adhering to her usual and prescribed regimen of remaining in bed for three weeks after childbirth, watched over by her own nurse, Kennedy took over the care of his dangerously ill second son. For the next two months, he rose earlier than usual, went to Mass, then to his Hayden, Stone office, then to the hospital, where he spent the late afternoon and evening at Jack's bedside.

He was devastated by his son's illness but suffered silently, never complaining or sharing his fears with anyone, certainly not with Rose. Only when it became clear that Jack was going to recover did he acknowledge his pain. Thanking Dr. Place "for your wonderful work for Jack during his recent illness," he confessed that he "had never experienced any serious sickness in my family previous to this case of Jack's, and I little realized what an effect such a happening could possibly have on me. During the darkest days I felt that nothing else mattered except his recovery."[8]

While his son was in the hospital, Kennedy had pledged to himself that if Jack was spared, he would give half his fortune to the church. When his son did recover, he made out a check for $3,740 (equivalent to more than $47,000 today), half of his liquid assets, to the Guild of Saint Apollonia, which had been organized in 1914 to provide free dental care to Boston's Catholic school children.[9]

On being discharged from Boston City Hospital, Jack, accompanied by a full-time nurse, was driven to Mansion House, a resort hotel in Poland Spring, Maine. Dr. Place had found "abundant clinical evidence" that contagion could "persist . . . for many weeks, as long as twenty at least," and the Kennedys, with three children under five at home, were taking no chances. Jack did not return to Brookline until his third birthday, some three months after he had been taken away. During this entire period, it was his father, not his mother, who visited him, cared for him, and watched over his recovery.[10]

Jack Kennedy would spend the rest of his life suffering from one malady after another, whooping cough, measles, chicken pox, colds and coughs, unexplained fevers. "His father was heartbroken at different times, when [Jack] was ill [but] he was with him. He went to the doctors, he made the decisions or he gave him the advice or he decided what he would do or where he would go." With each illness, accident, operation, and convalescence, the bond between father and son grew stronger and more resilient. Rose was left out of the loop because, she thought, her husband did not want to upset her and doubted she would have anything useful to add to the discussion. "A good many times I was not consulted . . . because I didn't know enough of all the circumstances and I was busy with the other children. We had eight other children to consider so we each had our own particular sort of department."[11]

In mid-March 1920, a month after Kathleen's birth and during Jack's convalescence in Maine, the Kennedys sold their Beals Street house to Eddie Moore and his wife and moved into a new one at the corner of Abbottsford and Naples roads in one of the wealthier sections of Brookline. Their Beals Street house was large, but not large enough for four children and three full-time servants. It was also situated in one of the lower-middle-class neighborhoods in Brookline, where the majority of families rented rather than owned their homes. The new home was, appropriately enough for Kennedy's status as a broker with Hayden, Stone, older, more elegant, and, with twelve rooms on one acre, much larger. It was, in fact, almost "reminiscent of Rose's girlhood home on Welles Avenue in Dorchester. . . . Designed in the Queen Anne Style that was fashionable in the late nineteenth century . . . the architecture incorporated turrets, tall chimneys, decorative windows and numerous varied decorative architectural elements, which mimicked in an abstract way a small castle." It cost $16,000, more than double what Kennedy had paid for the one on Beals Street.[12]

Kennedy could afford it, though barely. He was making $10,000 a year, a 150 percent increase from the $4,000 he had been paid as assistant general manager at Fore River, but he needed more, not just to provide for his growing household, but to prove to himself and his wife, family, friends, and ever-present father-in-law that the great expectations placed on him were justified. In East Boston, he was still P.J.'s boy; everywhere else he was known as Honey Fitz's son-in-law. He had taken the position at Hayden, Stone not because he wanted to spend his life trading stocks, but because it was the only one offered him. The big money, he knew, was not in brokerage per se, but in assisting businessmen in financing start-ups, expansions, and mergers, then managing their stock and/or their companies from the inside. This was the path Charles Hayden and Galen Stone had taken to becoming millionaires. In Kennedy's first twelve months at the firm, they and their associates had organized financing and floated new issues of stocks or bonds for sugar refiners, mining and petroleum corporations, and a few utilities. Kennedy had not been invited to take part in any of these deals for the simple reason that he knew neither the corporate executives nor the industries involved. If he was to succeed at Hayden, Stone or elsewhere, he would have to demonstrate a thorough understanding of an emerging business sector that none of the officers in the Boston banks or brokerage houses were paying attention to. Fortunately, there was such a sector—and it was thriving.

From childhood, when he put on patriotic pageants in his backyard, through Harvard, where he and his classmates spent as much time as they could at the theater—and with actresses and chorus girls after the theater—to Fore River, where he put together a vaudeville act starring ship's welders, Kennedy had always, it appears in retrospect, been drawn to show business. He was blessed to have grown up in Boston, a great theater town. It was in Boston that Benjamin Franklin Keith and Edward Albee had opened their first high-class vaudeville theater in 1885 and to Boston that every Broadway show decamped for months in a row.

In the fall of 1917, while working at Fore River, Kennedy had been introduced to Arthur Houghton, the manager of musical comedy star Fred Stone, whose last show, *Chin Chin*, Joe and Rose had taken in on the first night of their honeymoon in New York City. "It was," Houghton recalled years later, "in the lobby of the Colonial Theatre in Boston. After the introduction and discovery that we were part of two East Boston families who were close friends . . . we decided to take a stroll and talk over the East Boston family matters. . . . Our walk ended at St. James' Church where Joe left me to go inside to say some prayers suggested by his mother, and I being the manager of a New York musical show with 24 beautiful chorus girls, decided to take a raincheck on that visit but with a firm promise to meet soon again, which indeed we did, that very night."[13]

Kennedy would see a great deal of Houghton and Fred Stone during their frequent trips to Boston in the coming months. Stone, an accomplished song-and-dance man, acrobat, comedian, and tightrope walker, had become one of the highest-paid performers on the musical comedy stage. In the summer of 1918, he had gone to Hollywood and shot three films in ten weeks. The first, *The Goat,* was released in September 1918 to uniformly bad reviews and minimal box office. The second did just as poorly. The third, released in March 1919 while Stone was performing at the Colonial Theatre in Boston, was also a failure. Stone and Arthur Houghton blamed the bad reviews on the studio that had produced and marketed the films. Kennedy suggested they organize their own production company and produce their own films. He secured financing through Daniel Gurnett, a Boston investor, organized Fred Stone Productions Company, Inc., and made himself treasurer at the healthy weekly salary of $100. When the company ran out of capital after two years, Kennedy arranged for a $150,000 loan from Columbia Trust, backed only by the negatives of two as-yet-unreleased films.[14]

Kennedy had found the perfect vehicle for his ambitions as a banker and financier, the picture business. In the fall of 1919, he volunteered his services to put Boston's favorite son, Babe Ruth, in front of moving picture cameras. On September 5, 1919, the same day Ruth broke the major league record for home runs, he signed a movie contract with Henry Taylor, the former owner/manager of the Hollis Street Theatre, who promised him $10,000 to appear in a film to be shot in Boston as soon as the baseball season was finished. Taylor, who had no experience in the picture business, assigned the Ruth contract to Kennedy, who tried to interest the Fox Film Corporation in the project and in a distribution deal for future Fred Stone pictures. Fox turned down both proposals. Ruth refused to do any acting until he had been paid and gave Kennedy three weeks to come up with the money. When the three weeks were up, he pulled out of the agreement.[15]

Kennedy learned quickly from his misadventures as a producer that, for aspiring businessmen with large ambitions but limited capital, it made more sense to distribute and exhibit moving pictures than to make them. In November 1919, he organized his own film distributing company, Columbia Films, Inc., and secured the franchise to distribute Universal's films in New England. He paid himself an annual salary of $4,000 to manage the company.[16]

Although he had decided to concentrate on exhibition, he was not prepared to give up entirely on producing his own pictures. That winter, he tried and failed to finance a film starring Captain Robert Treman, a war hero whose major claim to fame was that he was the second husband of dancer and movie star Irene Castle, whose first husband, Vernon, also a war hero, had died in a plane crash in 1918. Kennedy asked E. B. Dane, the president of Brookline Trust, to contribute $10,000 to produce and distribute Treman's pictures and got a commitment for the full sum; then, deciding the deal was too risky, he returned the money, and backed out of his agreement with the captain.[17]

He worked both independently and as a representative of Hayden, Stone. When Frank Hall, the president of Hallmark Pictures, which produced and distributed low-budget pictures such as *The Heart of a Gypsy, A Dangerous Affair,* and *Impossible Susan,* approached Hayden, Stone for financing, Kennedy advised Charles Hayden against putting the firm's money or name behind the company, but suggested that it "would be a very good gamble for an individual who might care to put some money in . . . realizing that the future of an independent company might be developed into a real proposition." Six months later, after extended negotiations with Hall, Kennedy followed his own advice and bought one third of the company's stock. Hallmark would go bankrupt within the year, with debts of over $1 million, including $68,500 owed to Kennedy. Fortunately, he had not put his own money into Hallmark, as he would not into any of his other moving picture ventures.[18]

K ennedy had never intended to stay at Hayden, Stone forever, but the lackluster performance of the stock market through the winter and spring of 1920 reinforced his wish to move on sooner rather than later. In April 1920, when Assistant Secretary of the Treasury Russell Leffingwell announced his intention to resign, Kennedy asked Eddie Moore to organize a word-of-mouth lobbying campaign to get him appointed to the position. Boston mayor Andrew Peters, who had been the assistant secretary until he resigned to run for office in Boston, wrote David Houston, Wilson's new secretary of the treasury, on Kennedy's behalf, praising Kennedy as an "active and energetic" thirty-one-year-old Harvard graduate who had "shown marked ability" at Fore River and Hayden, Stone. Peters reminded the new secretary of the treasury that 1920 was a presidential election year, Republican governor Calvin Coolidge was riding high after breaking the police strike, and the appointment of an Irish Catholic native Bostonian might help the Democrats win Massachusetts. Secretary Houston replied politely that he had already chosen someone else for the post.[19]

Kennedy remained in place at Hayden, Stone as the stock market declined further, buffeted that summer of 1920 by the spectacular fall of Charles Ponzi, the dapper young man in the straw hat who had been jailed for bilking thousands of investors of millions of dollars. The Hanover Trust Bank, which Ponzi had taken over, fell with him.

One of the stocks that declined steadily that summer was Eastern Steamship Lines, a company organized and controlled by Hayden, Stone. As a protégé of Galen Stone, Kennedy had acquired a great deal of insider information on Eastern Steamship, and he had bought large quantities for his own account and for family and friends. Trading on insider information was not illegal—and would not become illegal until Kennedy, as the first chair of the Securities and Exchange Commission (SEC), made it so in 1935—but it was also not failure-proof. In mid-August 1920, Chris Dunphy, a friend from Boston who was currently manager of the Mount Pleasant Hotel in Bretton Woods, New Hampshire, and who, on Kennedy's recommendation, had purchased Eastern Steamship stock, wrote to confirm that he had secured reservations for "your gang arriving here on September 3," but joked that if Kennedy didn't do something to "curb the tactics of Eastern Steamship [and get the price up again], there will be no manager here to receive [you]. What I want to have you do is to give me the real dope on this stuff as I am in good and plenty and the boys are hollering for margin and I have no margin to give them. I am way down now and it will take a depth bomb to bring me back." He signed his letter, "Yours in desperate straits," then tacked on as a postscript, "You may rest assured that Miss Edling and Miss Bliss will be well taken care of during their stay at the Mount Pleasant." We don't know who the two misses were, though we can be sure Dunphy wouldn't have mentioned them had there been no connection to Joe.[20]

Kennedy responded the very next day. "Eastern may look tough but it's better than I ever told you it was. Keep up your courage. Some day you will make plenty on that." Ten days later, he wrote Dunphy that he had decided to leave for vacation on Thursday instead of Friday and wanted him "to kindly find out if they have Mass on First Friday morning, and if so, whether they hear confessions before Mass? I do not suppose you, in your ignorance and lack of religion, know the first thing about this yourself, but perhaps you can get one of those pious girls who go to the mountains to find out." His reference to Mass and confession in the first sentence, followed by his mention of the "pious" girls—was he referring to Miss Edling and Miss Bliss?—reveals, if ever a single document did, the complexity of the man and the ease with which he had juggled the sacred and the profane.[21]

In late August, just before he departed for his New Hampshire vacation, Kennedy was contacted by Rufus Cole, a partner in Robertson-Cole, an American company financed by London bankers.

Robertson-Cole was engaged in two disconnected businesses: making and distributing moving pictures in the United States and exporting to Great Britain and "the Orient" American trucks, pleasure cars, and the "Motalarm," a $3 device that was attached to a radiator cap and whistled when the water got low.

Like other small and medium-sized film companies, Robertson-Cole suffered from cash flow problems. The company, which had built a solid business distributing independent films, had decided to produce its own and purchased land from the Hollywood Cemetery Corporation to build a studio on Gower Street near Melrose, in the process accumulating some $5 million of debt. Cole contacted Kennedy in the hope that he would, through Hayden, Stone, take on his company as a client, secure new financing, and/or restructure his debt to his London bankers. Kennedy put him off. "I had a talk with Mr. Stone today," he wrote Cole on August 30, 1920, "with the idea of trying to get over to New York tonight, but it is just as I told you over the telephone, we are frightfully busy, due to a fight for control of the Mathieson Alkali Works—which management we control today, and it is taking all of the time of Mr. Stone and his lieutenants."[22]

On September 16, during a brief trip to New York for a stockholders meeting of Todd Shipbuilding, one of his Hayden, Stone clients, "he felt a concussion" on exiting the subway "and found himself on the ground. He got up in a dazed and stupefied condition and ran back to Wall St. where he saw clouds of glass flying and men and women with their heads split and blood streaming down their faces. Numbers were crying in agony and fear," he told a reporter from the *Boston Daily Globe,* who identified him as the "son-in-law of Ex-Mayor Fitzgerald." The House of Morgan at 23 Wall Street had been bombed a few seconds after noon, by whom we still do not know, though politicians, police, and the public assumed that it was the work of anarchists, socialists, or some other species of foreign-born radical assassins. Broken glass fell like hail on bankers and brokers at the stock exchange, the Bankers Trust Company, the Morgan offices, and nearby office buildings. The streets filled with smoke and were soon crowded with thousands of onlookers, more curious than frightened by the blast and falling debris. While none of the principals at Morgan were killed or badly wounded, thirty of Wall Street's "little people"—stenographers, messengers, and porters—were killed on their way to lunch. Another ten would die later of their injuries.

Hayden, Stone, probably on Kennedy's recommendation, decided not to take on Robertson-Cole as a client. The company was over-leveraged, the moment inauspicious for throwing new stock on the market, and the industry in the early 1920s "attended by too much uncertainty and hazard." While a few bankers (who were not coincidentally immigrants)—including Otto Kahn of Kuhn, Loeb and the Giannini brothers of the Bank of Italy in San Francisco and the Bowery and East River National Bank in New York—had begun to invest in moving pictures, they were the exceptions.[23]

Kennedy concurred with Hayden, Stone's decision not to do business with Robertson-Cole. Still, he was not about to let go of the opportunity presented by an increasingly desperate Rufus Cole, whom he led on a merry chase in the weeks and months to come. "As to the propositions which you so very kindly offer me," he responded to Cole's proposal that he invest in the company or solicit others to do so, "as I told you, my experience in the picture business with my own money, and, in some instances, with that of my friends, has been very disastrous, due, very likely, to our ignorance of the business and our childlike simplicity in taking any stock in anybody in the motion picture business. For that reason, I am very loath to try and interest any of my friends in the picture proposition, except in a small way. . . . At the same time, the banking situation [in the aftermath of the Ponzi scandals] has contributed to make the raising of money just a bit more difficult."[24]

He offered Cole a counterproposal. He would take over distribution of Robertson-Cole films in New England. "I have talked with my managers here regarding the possibility of a contract," he wrote Cole from Boston on November 19, 1920. "They verify, absolutely, every word I say: that we can increase the business and can show you much better return than you are getting today. Won't you, please, think out some basis on which you would be interested, and drop me a line?" He was, he insisted, doing Cole a favor by going into business with him. "I am spending considerable time with my people here, in order to come to some arrangement . . . that would be satisfactory and profitable to both your concern and mine. . . . Our past record with companies here gives me confidence that we can more than make good to you, and I am sure that I would not be so anxious to obtain this exchange if I did not feel that it would be profitable all round."[25]

Cole signed the distribution deal. Kennedy incorporated yet another new company, the Robertson-Cole Distributing Corporation of New England, issued $100,000 in preferred stock, and purchased $60,000 for himself. The remaining $40,000 remained "unbought" in the "treasury." He did not put any of his own savings into the project but got $20,000 from Honey Fitz, who borrowed it from the National Shawmut Bank with collateral supplied by Kennedy. He also borrowed $5,000 from his mother's account, took $5,000 out of his own, and arranged for a sweetheart loan of $20,000 from Columbia Trust. On December 23, 1920, he wrote Ethel Turner, the assistant treasurer of Columbia Trust, who acted as his personal secretary and accountant, outlining the parameters of the deal "so that your records may be clear." The financial manipulations were so complicated and the terms of the $20,000 loan from Columbia Trust so shaky that he asked Miss Turner to "kindly destroy the letter" after she had read it and executed his instructions.[26]

In the years to come, Kennedy's biographers, in attempting to find out how he financed his early ventures, would leap to the conclusion that his investment capital came from bootlegging operations. This, as we shall see later, was not true. Columbia Trust, which the Kennedy family would hold on to until 1945, was his primary source of investment capital in the early years. Kennedy also funded his investments with loans from Shawmut, where Bob Potter was vice president; from Brookline Trust, where E. B. Dane was president; and from Chase National in New York City, where Eugene Thayer had been named president. His initial loan from Chase National was $85,000 for three months, which he renewed every three months for the next year. When Thayer left Chase National in early 1921, after what appears to have been a breakdown of some sort, Kennedy still owed $77,500 on his loan. Thayer visited the loan officer and "asked him to put the soft pedal on for you, and I think they will." With Thayer's help, Kennedy got another two months to pay off the three-month loan he had taken out fifteen months earlier.[27]

Relying on the coffers of Columbia Trust and borrowing from other banks was a risky way to do business—and Kennedy knew it. As long as he was able to juggle collateral and loans, moving paper from one account to another, one bank to another, he could survive. His experience as an assistant bank examiner was invaluable in this regard. He knew precisely how far he could go without calling attention to himself or his bank.

It was never easy to keep all these balls in the air without dropping one or another, especially in a down market. "I really ought to be ashamed of myself," Kennedy wrote Chris Dunphy in Palm Beach on New Year's Eve 1920, "for not acknowledging your great kindness in sending us the grapefruit and oranges, but, to be truthful, I have spent most of the days scheming how to keep my friends and myself out of the hands of the ever watchful creditors. The days have been dark and dreary in more ways than one, but it looks now as if the worst were over. At any rate, we hope it is."[28]

One of the sources of cash he had relied on to pay the interest on his loans was the Fore River restaurant concession that as assistant general manager he had subcontracted to a company he owned. After leaving Fore River, he had managed to hold on to the concession and in May 1920 signed a new two-year contract. When, that fall, he was notified that the contract was being canceled, he fought back by asking Eugene Thayer, who was on the Bethlehem Steel board, to intervene on his behalf with Eugene Grace, the president.

On December 30, 1920, Grace wrote Kennedy to apologize. "I have, naturally, heard of your bitter feelings toward Bethlehem, occasioned, I understand, by the manner in which relations with you were severed." Grace invited Kennedy to meet with him in New York. After a few rounds of negotiation, Kennedy accepted a cash settlement he regarded as reasonable and a new two-year contract for $15,000 a year to provide "the management and the food" at Fore River.[29]

In January 1921, Kennedy's new firm, the Robertson-Cole Distributing Corporation of New England, opened for business at 39 Church Street in Boston. Kennedy enlisted Honey Fitz, still Boston's most accomplished promoter/performer, to help him promote his first film, a big-budget adaptation of *Kismet* starring Otis Skinner, opening at the Majestic. "There are countless ways you can suggest that we could get publicity, and all that means money in our pocket. . . . Your influence with the Boston newspapers would help us in getting a lot of things that we otherwise could not."[30]

Despite Kennedy's promises and Honey Fitz's promotions, the distribution deal he had offered Rufus Cole had done nothing to solve Cole's cascading financial problems. In late March 1921, Cole was visited in New York by the company's chief stockholders, Sir Erskine Crum and Sir Cecil Graham of Graham's of London, and a representative of Cox and Co. Kennedy boarded a train for New York, where he pulled off the first act in what amounted to a brilliant but ethically dubious double cross by suggesting to Crum that he rid himself of Cole and his debts by selling the company. Sir Erskine was entranced by the young Boston banker, as Cole had been. He asked Kennedy to keep their negotiations confidential until a plan had been worked out that he could present to his London partners.[31]

Kennedy broke Crum's confidence the next day when he boasted to Eugene Thayer that he was "practically representing Cox's Bank of London and the Grahams of London." Here was his big chance to break into the picture business—and he was not going to forfeit it. "I remember that you have spoken to me several times," he wrote Thayer, "about your interest in the Goldwyn Company. As you know, I have made a particular study of this motion picture business, with the idea that sooner or later the motion picture companies would need someone from the banking business who was familiar with the picture business. The time has now arrived . . . to my mind the only thing that can save all of the companies is consolidation of some kind." The consolidation he had in mind was of the Goldwyn and Robertson-Cole interests. "Of course, the whole thing would have to be confidential as news flies in the picture business. . . . If, however, you think it of any value at all, let me know and I will come to New York and discuss it with you or the men who are financially interested."[32]

Kennedy played his cards well. He sought and received permission from Galen Stone to act as Sir Erskine Crum's confidential adviser. On Kennedy's recommendation, Crum wrote down Robertson-Cole's outstanding debt, reorganized it as an American corporation, put Kennedy on the board of directors, and offered him an exclusive option to sell the company. He was to receive $1,500 a month for his efforts and a brokerage fee of $75,000 if he sold the business for $1.5 million or more.[33]

As exclusive agent for Sir Erskine Crum and Graham's of London, Kennedy was able to arrange meetings with every major financial player in the picture industry. He met with William Randolph Hearst of Cosmopolitan Productions, Joe Godsol of Goldwyn Pictures, James Hurd of Vitagraph, and later that year, W. W. Hodkinson, the former head of Paramount who operated his own distribution company. He proposed to each of them that they could cut costs and boost profits by merging with Robertson-Cole or, if that was not possible, consolidating their distribution networks.[34]

The logic of his position was sound, but Robertson-Cole was too small and too burdened with debt to be worth "consolidating with." In July 1921, with no offers forthcoming, Kennedy recommended—and the London bankers agreed—that instead of selling the company at a loss, they would hold on to it, make more pictures, and hope that finances would improve to the point where they could attract a buyer. Rufus Cole was removed as president, and Pat Powers, an experienced producer who had previously been Carl Laemmle's partner at Universal, was hired to replace him. The company was renamed the Film Booking Offices of America, FBO for short.

Powers and his second in command, Joe Schnitzer, invested a great deal of their own money in FBO and tried to get Kennedy to do the same. He declined. "Frankly, between you and me," he wrote Schnitzer in the summer of 1922, "I am all through with putting money in the picture business. Everything I have touched up to date has been very disastrous, and the local exchange up to date still owes me money. In addition to that, I am altogether too familiar with the R-C [Robertson-

Cole] situation to be willing—for the present at any rate—to put very much money in as an advance."[35]

He preferred, for the time being, at least, to focus his attention on distributing and exhibiting pictures, not making them. That spring, he tried to flatter his way into a business arrangement with Sidney Kent, who was in charge of distribution for Adolph Zukor's Famous Players–Lasky Corporation. "Personally if I intend to spend any further time in this industry I would like very much to make some kind of a tie up with your organization, because I feel that at the end of a couple of years the industry will be almost entirely in your hands, and I think an unwillingness to tie up the situation here shows an absolutely lack of foresight and vision."[36]

No one knew how to play the angles as well as he did. Though still a relative newcomer to the business, with no ties to Hollywood or Broadway, Kennedy had figured out how to use his outsider status to his advantage. The movie business was going through another of its periodic censorship panics. The causes were several, as they always were. There were too many racy films with racy titles like *Luring Lips, The Restless Sex, Short Skirt;* too many Hollywood scandals like the one involving Fatty Arbuckle, accused of rape, molestation, and the murder of a young starlet; and too many local and state censorship boards—with more on the way—stirred up by accusations, sometimes explicit, more often implicit, that the industry was not to be trusted because it was controlled by unscrupulous, money-hungry, immoral Jews.

For Kennedy, the crisis was a godsend because it gave him the opportunity to ride to the rescue as a white knight of sorts. True, he was not a midwestern Protestant Republican like Will Hays, the former postmaster general who had been hired to represent the industry as president of the Motion Picture Producers and Distributors of America at the outrageous annual salary of $150,000, but he was a Harvard graduate, a Boston businessman and banker, a family man, a practicing Christian, and decidedly not a New York City Jew.

In 1922, censorship bills were introduced in thirty-two of the forty-eight states of the Union. The key battle was in Massachusetts, where a state referendum had been called for election day in November. Kennedy offered his services—and political connections—to Will Hays, who was coordinating the campaign against the referendum. "Everything passed off very satisfactorily in Springfield," Kennedy wrote Hays after the Massachusetts State Democratic Convention had reaffirmed its commitment to the First Amendment. "From all indications," he continued, "we will have little trouble here in Massachusetts."[37]

At the same time he was assuring Hays that there would be "little trouble" in Massachusetts, he was using the censorship threat to frighten Famous Players–Lasky into selling him, a native Bostonian and politically connected banker, the Paramount Theater in Lowell, Massachusetts. "As you know, in New England practically no political or banking influence is behind any phase of the picture industry. I have been trying to interest people of both banking and political influence in houses, in order that they may see that it is an industry that should be supported, and get all the help that it could." Though his proposal to buy the Lowell theater was turned down, he was able to buy smaller theaters elsewhere. He purchased one in Stoneham, Massachusetts, for $15,000 and bought a 50 percent interest in the company that owned and operated two theaters in New Hampshire.[38]

Kennedy was now spending more evenings in Boston, where the theater district was still vibrant, thriving, and expansive, entertaining and being entertained by the actors, actresses, managers, theater owners, and aspiring picture producers he hoped to do business with. Rose sometimes accompanied him. "It was all," she remembered a half century later, "a completely new and different environment, gay, exciting and quite different and quite breath taking to me, who was a convent bred girl. I had heard that chorus girls were gay, but evil, and worst of all, husband snatchers. But nothing shocking happened. The people whom we met all seemed to have their own personal problems in which they were deeply involved, so we enjoyed the fun and excitement and novelty of the life in musical comedy. We even went to a skating party in the Boston Arena to celebrate the first birthday of [Fred Stone's *Jack O'Lantern*] show, and we skated around quite naturally with all the lesser and greater luminaries of the stage."

More often, however, Rose stayed home with the children and the servants while her husband went out. She claimed, again in retrospect, that she had no problem with any of this. "One characteristic of my life with Joe was that we trusted one another implicitly. If he had occasion to go out with theatrical people, he told me he was going and he went. There was never any deceit on his part and there was never any doubt in my mind about his motives or behavior." His socializing, she believed, was always in the interest of concluding one or another business deal. Still, she noted that Joe was becoming more and more attracted to "the life that revolved around Arthur Houghton" and to lots of show people he did not introduce her to.[39]

One of his new acquaintances was Vera Murray, producer Charles Dillingham's secretary, whom he had met through Arthur Houghton, Fred Stone's manager. Learning that Murray would be in Boston with Dillingham on August 15, 1921, for the opening of a new comedy at the Colonial Theatre, Kennedy telephoned, then wrote to ask her for tickets and to invite her to dinner with him, Eddie Moore, and a third friend. "At this dinner at 7 o'clock you might state what is your pleasure for the balance of the evening and the three Boston youths will try, insofar as they can, to make things pleasant for you during your stay. . . . Not knowing what the functions are of the right-hand man [Vera was Dillingham's chief assistant on the road] to the powers that be, I don't know how close you will be obliged to stick to your boss tonight. I know how close you would have to if I were your boss."[40]

In a similarly jocular tone, he wrote Arthur Houghton, who was moving to Boston for the winter with Fred Stone and his latest show, *Tip Top*, that he hoped "all the good-looking girls in your company [were] looking forward, with anticipation, to meeting the high Irish of Boston, because I have a gang around me that must be fed on wild meat lately, they are so bad. As for me, I have too many troubles around me to bother with such things at the present time. Everything may be better, however, when you arrive."[41]

The stock market, which had been in the doldrums since war's end, in mid-1921 began the steady upward climb that would continue until late 1924, when the great bull market took off toward the stratosphere. Kennedy remained heavily invested in the stocks of companies controlled by Hayden, Stone. As they increased in value, so did the amount of money he could borrow, with those stocks as collateral. Every transaction was remarkably complicated. On August 16, 1921, to cite but one example, Kennedy sold one thousand shares of Eastern Steamship for $77,500, which he then used to pay off some bank debts and the money he had borrowed to purchase his Todd Shipbuilding stock. At the end of the day, he would owe $37,500 at Hayden, Stone and thousands elsewhere, but he now had nine hundred shares of Todd Shipbuilding free and clear, which could be used to collateralize additional loans and purchase more stock.[42]

The juggling of his own accounts was enough to keep any ordinary investor occupied full-time, but Kennedy was also trading stocks, evaluating and overseeing investments, buying and selling real estate, and securing and monitoring mortgages and loans for friends, family, business associates at Columbia Trust, and influential investors like Matthew Brush, whom Kennedy had met when he was president of Boston Elevated and who had since moved to New York to become president of the American International Corporation, a large investment house. "I know of no pool operating in either stock," Kennedy wrote Brush from Boston in response to a query about two stocks Kennedy had insider information on, "but I have no doubt at all but what both of them will sell much higher. Let me know if you take any on, so that I can keep you posted on development." He was quite generous with advice and material assistance to those he considered his friends. Arthur Houghton got help in renting an apartment and in selling his mother's house. When Eugene Thayer was "forced to take a vacation as a result of poor health," Kennedy offered to lend him $50,000 to $75,000 on seventy-two hours' notice, if needed. "I would consider it a great favor if you feel that this can be of any service to you whatsoever."[43]

His closest friends remained his Harvard classmates. Since graduating in 1912, he had kept in touch with several of them, including Bob Fisher, who had been named Harvard football coach. According to Rose, "he and Joe would talk by the hour about the different maneuvers which Bob would make with respect to the team and respect to his own plans, as several people wanted to oust him."[44]

In June 1922, Kennedy celebrated his tenth college reunion. Opening night was marked by a formal dinner at the Pilgrim Hotel out-side Plymouth. The evening's entertainment consisted of a series of speeches, hopefully humorous ones, but as Oscar Haussermann, one of the reunion organizers, recalled, "our abundant supply of good pre-Prohibition liquor was beginning to create confusion long before the coffee was served. To calm things down, Joe said to me, 'Let's call off the speaking, turn out the lights and show the movies.' This we did. The movies, all furnished by Joe, consisted of a bathing scene from 'Kismet' and the Dempsey-Willard and Dempsey-Carpentier fight films. Viewing in the dark such films without any further alcoholic intake had a sobering effect on one and all. Joe both made and saved the day!"[45]

It should have been but was not a "dry" celebration. The Eighteenth Amendment, ratified in January 1919, and the Volstead Act, passed over President Wilson's veto in October, had together made illegal the manufacture, sale, barter, transport, import, export, delivery, furnish-ing, or possession of liquor. That didn't matter much to the men of Harvard. In preparation for the reunion, the "entertainment commit-tee" had purchased 180-proof alcohol. Kennedy, in his one and only venture into bootlegging, got in touch with a Mr. Dehan, who had le-gally "blended" liquor for P.J. in the days before Prohibition and "who really is one of the best men on this in this part of the country." "The stuff," Kennedy wrote Matt Brush after the event, "turned out very well indeed, and was perfectly satisfactory to all the fellows in the class who are, of course, used to the best—and the worst." Kennedy offered Brush some of the leftover gin. "Twenty-five dollars is the actual cost of the stuff, and I would be very very happy to have you have it, if you think it would be satisfactory."[46]

Outside of his sale—at cost—of leftover Harvard reunion gin to Matthew Brush, Kennedy neither imported nor sold any liquor during his years in Brookline or at any time during Prohibition. His father had been an importer and part owner of several stores, and Kennedy had helped him move his unsold supplies to his cellar in Winthrop, reserv-ing ten cases of very expensive French wine and the best champagnes for his own entertaining needs, but there was nothing illegal about any of this.[47]

Not only is there no evidence of Kennedy's being a bootlegger, but it flies in the face of everything we know about him. As an East Boston Irish Catholic outsider struggling to be allowed inside, he was willing to take financial risks, but not those associated with illegal activities such as bootlegging.

The charge that Joseph P. Kennedy was a bootlegger appeared only once during Kennedy's lifetime. In October 1960, the *St. Louis Post-Dispatch* reported that "in certain ultra-dry sections of the country," Joseph Kennedy was being referred to as a "rich bootlegger" by those out to derail his son's campaign for the presidency. Most of the stories about bootlegging originated in unsubstantiated, usually off-the-cuff remarks made in the 1970s and 1980s by Meyer Lansky, Frank Costello, Joe Bonanno, and other Mob figures not particularly known for their truth telling. Their revelations provoked journalists, reporters, and amateur historians to seek out additional stories that were used to buttress conspiracy theories connecting John Fitzgerald Kennedy's assassination to organized crime. "Eyewitness" accounts delivered decades after the events they purportedly described placed Kennedy at Sag Harbor, on the docks at Gloucester, at Cape Cod, and at Carson Beach in South Boston, unloading or supervising the unloading of liquor shipments from Nova Scotia or England or Ireland. Other stories linked Kennedy to Al Capone and an operation that brought liquor into the country from Canada through Lake Michigan. Evidence for this operation was supplied by a piano tuner who claimed that while tuning Capone's piano, he overheard Kennedy and Capone striking their deal. Despite the stories, there is no evidence, no mention, not even a report, of any rumors of bootlegging in any of Kennedy's FBI files or those that reference him. No allegations surfaced during his three confirmation hearings for SEC chairman, Maritime Commission chairman, and ambassador to Great Britain in the 1930s or in the four investigations conducted in the 1950s after he was recommended for presidential commissions.

The only seemingly credible evidence that has ever been offered to tie Kennedy to illegal liquor trafficking is a 1931 Canadian Royal Commission on Customs and Excise investigation that references a Joseph Kennedy Ltd. as engaged in the illegal export of liquor from the province of British Columbia. The Joseph Kennedy of Joseph Kennedy Ltd.

was not, however, Joseph P. Kennedy of Brookline, but Daniel Joseph Kennedy of 1119 Nelson Street, Vancouver.[48]

With or without evidence, the rumors of Joseph Kennedy's bootleggers remain part of his story. As Daniel Okrent, who spent years researching bootleggers and bootlegging and found no sign that Kennedy ever trafficked in liquor, reminds us, "One cannot prove a negative."[49]

For the summer of 1922, befitting his rise in the world and enhanced bank account, Kennedy rented a vacation home in Cohasset, a summer resort town thirty miles from Brookline, a much more appropriate location for a Hayden, Stone executive than Nantasket, the favored resort of Irish Catholic politicians, where the family had been summering. The big remodeled two-story house with a garage, overlooking the ocean at 25 Sheldon Road, was almost the same distance from the water as the East Boston house he had grown up in and the Hyannis and Palm Beach houses he would raise his children in.

Several of Kennedy's business acquaintances and Harvard classmates, including Bob Fisher, his former roommate and now the coach of the Harvard football team, rented or owned homes in Cohasset and belonged to the golf club there. Fisher volunteered to help Kennedy with his application to the club and asked Dudley Dean, who knew Kennedy and had been a club member for eighteen years, to sponsor him. In early May, Dean reported to Fisher that he had "had a chat" with Hugh Bancroft of the selection committee, who had "emphasized that a great many of the members regarded the outfit as a rather close corporation in a social way because of long acquaintance and not very heavily on the gold end per se. In other words, those having that special regard wanted to see old faces, continually. I want you both to know that it looks as tho it wouldn't be as easy sailing as I imagined when you broached the matter. . . . Wish to heaven I could turn over to him for this summer my family membership."[50]

The committee would never formally turn down Kennedy's application, but by not acting on it before the summer was over, they made their wishes known. Kennedy biographers and family historians would later make much of the fact that he had been denied admission to the

Cohasset golf club. Kennedy never did. Neither did Rose, who told her ghostwriter that she had taken it in stride. She had long since learned that in Boston and its environs, there were certain places Irish Catholics did not venture. The Cohasset golf club was among them. There were other places for Joe to play. He was already a member of the Woodland Club in Auburndale and the Braeburn Country Club in Newton.[51]

The Kennedy family would return to Cohasset for the following summer, further evidence that the rejection had not meant much to Joe or his family.

PART II

Hollywood

Six

"MY OWN MASTER
IN MY OWN BUSINESS"

There were now seven Kennedys in Brookline. Eunice Kennedy, fifth child and third daughter, had been born on July 10, 1921. The newspaper announcement again referred not to Kennedy, but to his more famous wife, whom the *Boston Daily Globe* jokingly described as "an ardent follower of the Roosevelt doctrines and . . . dead set against race suicide."[1]

Eunice's older brothers and sisters were doing well, though Jack, as thin and sickly as ever, continued to catch every childhood disease that came his way. In January 1922, he took ill with what may been whooping cough. Once again it was his father, not Rose, who took care of him, directing his secretary to call W. W. Hodkinson, the former head of Paramount, and tell him that "that Mr. K. could not get to New York because his boy is ill, and that he can't go over until the boy is a great deal better, which he hopes will be in a few days, but can't say definitely." Fortunately for all, Jack recovered as quickly and miraculously as he had taken ill, allowing his father to resume his normal routine. In September 1922, Jack would join his big brother, Joe Jr., at the Devotion School, the local public school named for Edward Devotion, a Brookline founding father.[2]

As the Kennedy household grew in size and complexity—with Joe Jr.

and Jack now in school and two toddlers and an infant at home, cared for by nursemaids and governesses, cooks, maids, and laundresses— Rose struggled to keep her head clear and above water. Kennedy, except for moments of crisis, was seldom around. When he wasn't traveling to New York or Washington or to one of his New England theaters, he was doing business or entertaining potential clients in Boston. He didn't even vacation with the family.

Years later, in an interview with Robert Coughlin, who worked with her on her memoirs, Rose explained that the idea of separate vacations had been hers. Her husband wanted to go to Palm Beach every winter to play golf. She did not. "I thought that was a terrible waste of money, to be always coming to the same place, but he used to say he worked hard during the year and he wanted to come and rest someplace. He didn't want to have to be coming to Europe where'd he have to wait around for customs and changing planes, but anyway I said that I'd like to go to California and that was before he was in the motion pic-ture business. So he said all right why don't you go with your sister. . . . He took care of the children while I was gone."[3]

Kennedy took his two-week Palm Beach vacation in early January. In April, Rose took a two-month trip to California with her sister. In her diary entry for April 3, 1923, the day she left on her vacation, she noted that as she walked out of the house, "Jack said, 'Gee, *you're* a great mother to go away and leave your children all alone.' "[4]

From California, she wrote Joe regularly, keeping him fully abreast of her adventures away from home. In Hollywood, she and her sister watched "Gloria Swanson taking a scene and it was so long to prepare and everything . . . it was tiresome. We met Owen Moore [another movie star] outside but he was bored to extinction and told us to go riding, etc. I guess we really have had all the thrills—that is we have not let anything go by that we could nab. But my dear, please do not let me ever go away again for so long. And how are you, anyway? . . . All my love, dear, and I do wish I were coming home sooner so as to see you all."[5]

"It really seems months since I have seen you and the children," she wrote a short time later. "I do hope you all are OK. I know you would not tell me if anything were wrong anyway—I shall be glad when we get started home again—the trip is just half over now and it really seems ages. . . . Please do tell me the minute anything is upset— There is no need of you shouldering too much too long and I shall gladly leave for home and go directly if you have the slightest wish in the matter."[6]

Kennedy replied in telegrams to California, which, though terser, were every bit as cheerful and chatty as his wife's letters. "Rosa dear, I still maintain a reputation as the greatest manager in the world," he telegraphed on April 8, at the start of her trip. "The children are fine. Jack is sleeping every noon and is greatly improved. . . . Joe is great and the little girls look fine. We go out Friday nights so the cook is great and all in all we are doing nicely. . . . I hope you are having a real good time because you richly deserve it. Please do not think too much about us and spoil your party. I am not lonesome because I find myself very happy in the thought that you are enjoying yourself."[7]

A week later, he attended his sons' parent/teacher conferences. Joe Jr. was in first grade; Jack was in kindergarten. "Saw school teachers. They report big improvement."[8]

He visited Winthrop often that spring. His mother, ill for some time, had been hospitalized. She died on May 20 and was buried on May 23. Rose returned to Brookline four days later. Five days after her return, she and the children left for Cohasset for the summer. For the next three months, she would see Joe only on weekends.[9]

In November 1922, Galen Stone announced that he was retiring from the company that bore his name. Kennedy, having lost his mentor and chief advocate in the firm, left soon afterward. "I knew the time had arrived for me to do at thirty-four what I had been determined to do at twenty-four—be my own master in my own business. So I took a bold step and announced that I had launched my own private banking business." He rented a small office at 87 Milk Street, the building that housed Hayden, Stone.[10]

In early 1924, taking advantage of the conversion of legitimate theaters from live to mixed live and moving picture entertainments, Kennedy incorporated and financed a new company, Columbia Advertising, with Eddie Moore as its nominal president, to sell advertising space on theater curtains placed over the back walls of the stages on which live performers crooned, joked, tap-danced, whistled, somersaulted, or did whatever they did before and after the moving pictures were shown.[11]

Curtains were installed, for the cost of about $1,000 each, in Boston, Newark, Brooklyn, Buffalo, Atlanta, Birmingham, and Memphis. Kennedy tried to interest the National Shawmut Bank in Boston, where Bob Potter was now a vice president, in advertising their savings accounts and safe deposit banks on the curtains. "I have already talked to them," he wrote Steve Fitzgibbon, who had worked with him at the Fore River restaurant and was his chief salesman, "about the idea and it is within the realm of possibility that we might sell them the two curtains. Of course if we did that, there would be no question about selling the remaining spaces." They did not get the Shawmut contract— or many others. The business failed, one of the few failures Kennedy would experience in his life. By March 1925, thirteen months after he had incorporated the company, Kennedy closed it down.[12]

After leaving Hayden, Stone, Kennedy continued to trade stocks in his own account and for his friends. Although he did quite well in the baby bull market of 1923, by December 1923 he was convinced that the market was running out of steam and it was time to get out or at least stop buying. "Unless your friends in New York strong-arm this market and elect Calvin Coolidge president, I think we are in for it," he wrote Matt Brush in New York.[13]

His first big score came in the spring of 1924. Walter Howey, the Hearst newspaper editor who had moved from Chicago to Boston, visited Kennedy in his offices on Milk Street and asked him to go to New York to rescue his friend John Hertz, the Chicago businessman who owned companies that manufactured and rented out Yellow Cabs. Howey claimed that Hertz, who had just listed his companies on the stock exchanges, was being attacked by "bears" who were selling his stock "short" and driving down the price precipitously. Short sellers operated by borrowing shares of high-priced stocks from brokers, dumping them onto the market, and spreading rumors that shareholders (actually the short sellers themselves) were getting rid of the stock because it was near worthless. When the share price fell low enough, the short sellers paid back what they owed in shares that cost less than the ones they had borrowed and sold. They pocketed the difference, which could be considerable.

On Sunday, April 13, 1924, Kennedy and Eddie Moore took the train to New York City to set up shop in a Waldorf-Astoria suite out-fitted with telephones and a ticker-tape machine. Their mission was to use money Hertz had borrowed in Chicago to buy as many shares of his Yellow Cab Company and its subsidiaries as necessary to push the price back up and frighten away the bears. Although he tried his best—and made use of the considerable resources behind him—Kennedy was not able to significantly raise the share price, though he might have stabilized it somewhat. He was paid $20,000 for his efforts. In mid-June, he invested $25,000 in Hertz's new "Drive-Ur-Self System," the precursor of Hertz Rent-A-Car, and told one of Hertz's chief lieuten-ants that he was "going to work along with it, not to the exclusion of my other business however, and see how it turns out." Regrettably for Kennedy, who was still looking for his main chance, Hertz wanted noth-ing to do with him.[14]

Though a staple of the Joseph P. Kennedy story, the Yellow Cab Company incident was more of a detour than a turning point. Either because he had operated under the Wall Street radar or because his triumph was not as spectacular as he would later claim, the Hertz job did not open the door to other work as a freelance stock specialist. Still, it had yielded him a $20,000 paycheck, the equivalent of more than a quarter of a million dollars today, and a story he would tell again and again.

At age thirty-six, Joseph Kennedy was not yet a millionaire, but he was making enough money at his various enterprises to exchange his Ford for a Rolls-Royce, hire a chauffeur, encourage Rose to do more shopping for more expensive clothing—in New York as well as in Boston—and move his boys from the local public school to the rather exclusive and expensive Dexter School on Naples Road in Brookline. Dexter served as the lower feeder school for Noble and Greenough, one of the private schools that had come into being and prospered in the late nineteenth century as an alternative pathway to Harvard for parents who preferred to have their children detour around Boston Latin and its growing Irish, Jewish, and immigrant student populations. Its alumni and present student body included boys named Lowell, Saltonstall, Appleton, Coolidge, and Storrow. Kennedy appeared to be the only Irish name on the register.[15]

All six Kennedy children—Joe Jr., Jack, Rosemary, Kathleen, or Kick as she was called in the family, Eunice, Patricia, or Pat, who was born on May 6, 1924—appeared to be prospering in their new home in Brookline. Joe Jr. had had some problems in kindergarten but was now doing well in the classroom and on the ball fields, where he was showing promise as a pitcher. Jack's health seemed to have stabilized. Only Rosemary appeared to have any trouble in school. "She was slow in everything," Rose recalled in her memoirs, "and some things she seemed unable to learn how to do, or do well or with consistency. When she was old enough for childish sports, I noticed, for instance, that she couldn't steer her sled. When she was old enough to learn a little reading and writing, the letters and words were extremely difficult for her; and instead of writing from left to right on a page, she wrote in the opposite direction. She went to kindergarten and first grade at the usual ages, but her lack of coordination was apparent and as time went on I realized she could not keep up with the work. In the Brookline school system intelligence tests were given to all the children very early. I was informed that Rosemary's I.Q. was low, but that was about all the concrete information I received, and it didn't help much." Rose consulted and would continue to consult for the next twenty years with everyone she could locate who professed some expertise: her own doctors, specialists in Boston, psychologists at Harvard, and a priest from Washington, D.C. "When I said, 'What can I do to help her?' there didn't seem to be very much of an answer. There were no classes in the public schools. There didn't seem to be any private schools, and I was really terribly frustrated and heartbroken."[16]

Though he was away most of the time, when at home Kennedy spent every minute he could with his children. His returns from business trips were moments of joyous pandemonium. "He would sweep them into his arms and hug them, and grin at them, and talk to them, and perhaps carry them around. Also, as each one became old enough to talk . . . he would want that child in bed with him for a little while each morning.

And the two of them would be there propped up on the pillows, with perhaps the child's head cuddling on his shoulder, and he would talk or read a story or they would have conversations." On weekends, when he was in Brookline, he piled the older kids into the automobile for the trip to Winthrop to visit his father, who had eased comfortably into retirement. He had grown a bit stouter, but he bore the weight well. His hair had grayed, but his mustache was still well groomed, and he was as handsome and imposing a presence as he had been as a young man. Honey Fitz was also thriving, as was his wife, Josie. They too spent time with their grandchildren, who adored their raucous granddad as much as they did their more restrained one.[17]

Kennedy had been on his own for two and a half years now and was making money from his various enterprises. But nothing had worked out quite as he had hoped: in banking, at Fore River, at Hayden, Stone, or as a private broker/banker. He was nibbling at the edges, still on the outside, with no chance, he knew, of ever being invited into one of the major financial firms in the city. He had gone about as far as he could in Boston. It was time to look beyond the city and focus his considerable talents on an industry the "proper Bostonians" had ignored: moving pictures.

In the spring of 1925, Kennedy decided to bid on FBO, the film company he had been instrumental in founding and then walked away from. Pat Powers, whom the London bankers had brought in to run FBO, had after two years succeeded only in piling new debt on old. Kennedy guessed that the long-suffering British bankers might now be willing to sell the company at a bargain price, and he prepared an offer for them. He had no intention of spending his own money—he never did—but he had friends and business associates who might be willing to. Guy Currier, the well-connected lawyer/businessman who had gotten him his job at Fore River, helped him secure investors and may have put in some money of his own.[18]

In preparation for his leap into the movie business, Kennedy paid off several of his outstanding loans, took back the stock that had been held as collateral for those loans, and deposited in his Columbia Trust safe deposit vault thousands of shares worth tens of thousands of dollars in

Eastern Steamship, the Yellow Cab Company, and the Maine and New Hampshire Theatre Company. This was to be his and his family's safety net should all go wrong. "It was at this time . . . that he established the trust funds for the children," Rose recalled later, "because he did not know how his venture would turn out and he did not know what would happen to his health and he wanted the children to have some money laid aside in case anything happened to him. Of course, it was a very small amount of money that was put aside then, but as the years went by gradually it increased in value."[19]

The summer before, in 1924, after two seasons at Cohasset, Kennedy had rented the Malcolm cottage, a large clapboard house at the end of Merchant Avenue in Hyannis Port. Unlike Cohasset or Bar Harbor or Newport, Hyannis Port was not one of the more luxurious summer resorts for Boston's elites. But it provided the Kennedys with everything they required. It was accessible by rail, there was a golf club that would be eager to have Kennedy as a member (unlike the one in Cohasset), a beach club for the children, a Catholic church, and the Wianno Yacht Club in Osterville, where Joe Jr., Jack, and the other children, as they grew older, could learn to sail and race, and there were no "proper Bostonian" families to look down their noses on the arriviste Irish Catholic from East Boston.

After spending much of his summer assembling the proposal for the London bankers who owned FBO—and the capital behind it—Kennedy left Hyannis Port for New York City in mid-August. On August 17, a few days before sailing, he wrote Rose from the Harvard Club with final instructions and his contact information in London and Paris: "Rosa dear, I am getting ready to go now & when you get this I will be on my way, but I will be coming back soon so please don't be too lonesome & have a great time. I just want you to know that going away on trips like this makes me realize just how little anything amounts to except you as years go on. I just love you more than anything in the world and I always wonder whether I ever do half enough for you to show you how much I appreciate you. Well dear this is just a little love letter from a husband to wife married 11 years."[20]

Kennedy wrote again from the ship, filling Rose in on the entertainment on board—"Carl Fisher of Vienna Opera Co. & Sophie Tucker, the American coon shouter"—and his traveling companions, theater producer Jack Potter, his father, who was the former manager of the Philadelphia Phillies, and his mother, "a splendid type, of fine family gone absolutely broke." On this and subsequent travels, he sent personalized greetings to each of his children. "You must learn French and come over here," he wrote Jack, the child who always needed coaxing to do well in school. "The little French boys roll a hoop instead of playing football."[21]

Kennedy, who abhorred being by himself but had had to leave Eddie Moore behind to look after their businesses and the Kennedy family in Hyannis Port, was miserably lonely, or so he wrote Rose: "I know it's terrible to tell you in every letter how homesick I am but it is terrible. I can't seem to shake it off at all. I think of you and the children all the time and almost go silly. All I have done all week is shop and visit a few churches. I really have had terrible luck as a shopper because I can't seem to get anything really cute especially for the children but I'll bring something home. I have received one letter from you but I suppose the others are in England. It was bread from heaven. I went to Communion Friday and went to an English Priest for confession. When I finished he asked me if I were a priest (how do you like that old darling). . . . The Potters are really very nice to me but I can't get along without you, Rosa. It may be nice to travel but only with you. . . . I haven't sent any cards or written to anybody so on the whole I'm a great kid."[22]

In London, Kennedy tendered his offer of $1 million to the consortium of banks, now led by Lloyd's, that owned FBO. His proposal was turned down, then months later, after he had returned to America, accepted. According to the story Kennedy later told Terry Ramsaye of *Photoplay*, he was on his way from the Harvard Club to Grand Central to catch the *Havana Limited* train to Palm Beach for a winter vacation with his friends when "a page boy dashed out as the taxi started. 'Phone call for Mr. Kennedy—they say it's important.'" According to Ramsaye, Kennedy "stopped the cab and went back into the club. A few minutes later he emerged and addressed his waiting companions. 'Sorry, but you fellows will have to go on to Florida without me. I'm going to Boston tonight. I seem to have bought a motion picture company.'"[23]

On February 6, 1926, the deal was finalized and FBO sold to a consortium of investors, organized and headed by Joseph P. Kennedy. The price was $1.1 million, $200,000 due on signing, the remainder to be paid down over the next three years. Congratulations and advice, solicited and unsolicited, flowed in from old friends and newer business acquaintances. Kennedy thanked William Gray of the Maine and New Hampshire Theatre Company for his "bible of good common sense" and took the occasion to apologize for having run roughshod over him in recent business dealings. George Byrnes, a friend from Boston, wrote to wish him "a world of luck and prosperity. . . . Anyway as South Boston used to say to Boston Latin (that's going back some)—If you put the ball near the plate for Joe Kennedy he'll kill it. Well, I see by today's paper that somebody put the film ball near the plate and you have socked it—and how!" Kennedy responded with his usual mixture of self-deprecation and self-confidence. "I am in a new game and will probably be tossed around a bit but I may have some fun and may get away with it."[24]

Within hours of signing the final agreement, Kennedy and Eddie Moore moved into the FBO offices at 1560 Broadway, off Twenty-fourth Street in New York City. All the major film executives had offices nearby, including Adolph Zukor and Jesse Lasky of Famous Players–Lasky; Marcus Loew (until his death in 1927), then Nick Schenck of MGM; Carl Laemmle of Universal; Harry Warner of Warner Brothers; and William Fox of the Fox Film Corporation. While the movies were produced in Hollywood—and the executives who worked there got most of the headlines and the glory—it was in New York City that the major decisions were made.

"After having sat in your chair for the past four days, and using your office and your efficient secretary, I am beginning to think I am a 'picture' man," Kennedy wrote Joseph Schnitzer, who ran the FBO studio in Los Angeles. "I brought over with me from Boston an expert accountant and we have been going over the financial situation, trying to familiarize ourselves with it." He had discovered that the cash flow problem was even worse than he had imagined. But that could be remedied by cutting per picture production costs and studio expenses and reducing the price of borrowing money to finance new pictures.

In the old days, when pictures were shorter and cheaper, the studios had been able to raise money internally to finance new production. In recent years, they had borrowed the money. Kennedy found a better way. He organized a new company, the Cinema Credits Corporation, raised money to fund it from the Boston investors who were investing in FBO, and used this separate corporation to finance his films at better rates than were available elsewhere.[25]

The movie business, he was convinced, was rife with inefficiencies. He instituted new accounting procedures, shifted control over expenditures from studio executives in Hollywood to New York City, and fired overpaid studio executives in New York and Hollywood. "The trouble with many concerns like my own," he explained in 1928 to a journalist, "was that employees occupying positions parallel to positions in other lines were vastly overpaid. It was not an uncommon thing for accountants to receive $20,000 a year, when in other business they graded from $5,000 to $10,000. My first problem was to change that, which was easy."[26]

He was interested not in making artful or even good pictures at FBO, but in making a profit by producing cut-rate "program pictures," low-budget westerns, stunt thrillers, and action melodramas and distributing them to independently owned and operated small-town theaters that could not afford to pay premium prices for expensive pictures.

A month after taking charge of the New York offices, Kennedy and Eddie Moore boarded a train to Los Angeles. "I imagine you will have quite a time out at the Coast," William Gray, his New England associate in the distributing business, wrote him. "If I were fifteen or twenty years younger, I would like to go out with you." Their every expense charged to their new company, the two Boston businessmen checked into the town's premier hotel, the Ambassador. Neither had ever been in Los Angeles before.[27]

Having entered a new business, Kennedy set about making new friends, working his charm on future business associates, and ingratiating himself with the members of the trade press, who would be critical to raising the reputation of FBO and its new chief. One of the first—and most influential—was Martin J. Quigley, a devout Catholic, owner and publisher of the picture industry trade journal *Exhibitors Herald* (later to merge with *Moving Picture World*), and because of his connections with the church hierarchy, a powerhouse in Hollywood on matters regarding censorship. "They say a man's lasting impressions in a new country, a new situation, or even a new business are formed by the first people he meets," Kennedy flattered Quigley in a letter written soon after they had met in Los Angeles. "I may say truthfully that if this old idea is true and one wants to like the film business he should first meet Martin Quigley. I know I feel this way because no one could have been kinder to me or launched me more successfully on the waves of the film industry."[28]

Kennedy also made the acquaintance of and initiated a lifelong friendship with Sime Silverman, the editor of *Variety,* who in return for financial favors over the years to come, including favorable loans from Columbia Trust, would supply him with the current Hollywood gossip. He introduced himself as well to the editors of the *Los Angeles Examiner,* owned by William Randolph Hearst.[29]

He was already on good terms with FBO's major (perhaps its only) asset, cowboy movie star Fred Thomson, whom he had advised on his career years before, when Kennedy was a consultant to the bankers who owned the studio. "We were at the end of our rope (one might call it lasso)," Frances Marion, Thomson's wife and a very successful screenwriter, recalled in her memoirs, "when we heard of a new man in the game . . . who was a great admirer of athletes and did not scorn horse operas. . . . Accustomed to the squinty-eyed appraisal of those in power who sat behind big desks and merely grunted or nodded when you entered their offices, we were rather taken aback by Kennedy's sudden leap from his desk, his warm handshake, and his friendly volubility. . . . He's a charmer, I thought, a typical Irish charmer. But he's a rascal; he knows exactly why we're here."[30]

By early 1925, Fred Thomson was a full-fledged Hollywood star. He was not a particularly talented actor or a strikingly handsome man, but he was a good horseman and stuntman, and with his rugged, athletic body and a cowboy hat on his head, he looked the part of the clean-cut boyish hero. His biography was custom-made for the publicists: he didn't drink, smoke, or use profane language; he had played football, been a track star, studied for the ministry at Princeton, and served as an army chaplain. Thomson's success was so remarkable that by the time Kennedy purchased FBO, he and Silver King, his horse, were being wooed by Joe Schenck at United Artists and by other studio heads who were prepared to pay him a higher salary and put him in big-budget features instead of the "B" westerns he was shooting for FBO. Kennedy, figuring that Thomson had become too expensive to continue at FBO, advised him to make his pictures elsewhere and to sign a "personal services" contract, which authorized Kennedy to organize and run a new corporate entity, Fred Thomson Productions.

Having let Thomson go, Kennedy offered a contract to a photogenic Detroit weight lifter named Vincent Markowski, whom he renamed Tom Tyler and to whom he paid a portion of what Thomson had been getting. He offered movie contracts as well to three other photogenic athletes: football great Red Grange and tennis champions Suzanne Lenglen and Mary Browne.[31]

Kennedy had never visited Hollywood, held any studio position, or produced any pictures, but he did not apologize for his lack of experience. On the contrary, he trumpeted his outsider status as a Harvard-educated banker born of American-born parents, a Bostonian whose only language was English, a baseball-playing, suburban-house-owning father of seven, and he made the case persistently and passionately that the picture industry—plagued by charges of immorality, sullied by sex scandals and divorce suits, and struggling to protect its products and profits from increasingly aggressive state censorship boards—needed someone like him. He would be Hollywood's white, non-Jewish knight and rescue it from the suspicion that its pictures were not to be trusted because they were produced by men who through breeding and background were morally untrustworthy. "While anti-Semitic sentiments were never openly voiced," writes film historian Garth Jowett, "it seemed as if there was a basic resentment that this 'art of the people' should be in the hands of 'Jewish ex–clothing merchants' who sold their product like so many cheap garments."[32]

He introduced himself to the larger public and industry insiders in a July 9, 1926, advertisement, published in the *New York Times* and elsewhere, for *The Two-Gun Man,* starring Fred Thomson, world's greatest western star, and his miracle horse, Silver King. Referencing Florenz Ziegfeld, who the week before had jumped on the censorship bandwagon and proposed that the secretary of the New York Society for the Suppression of Vice chair a six-person committee to clean up the stage,

Kennedy's ad had his western hero address the Broadway impresario directly.

"You Tell 'Em ZIEGGY. Clean up the stage. Make it clean as the screen. I produce CLEAN photoplays with my pal, SILVER KING—But I make 'em hum with action—flame with romance—boom with comedy—whizz with thrills—and Silver performs some of the greatest tricks you ever saw! You please the whole family. SO DO I!"

The very next day, Kennedy made his point again, this time in a huge ad for another of his superclean, homegrown American pictures, *Bigger than Barnum's*: "BRING THE CHILDREN! Re-live the Golden Hours of Youth! The Ecstasy of Circus Days when Main Street reared and rocked with the Smashing Pageantry of the Greatest Show on Earth."

As he told a gathering of newspaper reporters he had invited to Adams House in Boston, highlighting once more the fact that he was not an immigrant, but American-born and -bred, he intended to make "American films for Americans."

"Wholesomeness, Mr. Kennedy pointed out to his guests," according to the *Boston Daily Globe*, "is intended to form the keynote of the pictures which the new concern will present, and there is to be a very general elimination of the sex problem movies and of those which depend upon sex appeal." There were no foreign names in FBO productions, no dark, swarthy heroes or exotic-looking heroines, and little intimation of sex, divorce, or debauchery. As part of his branding strategy, Kennedy placed his own, distinctly non-Jewish face with his name in large capital letters in each display ad. Smiling, wearing his spectacles, dressed in a conservative suit jacket and tie, he was the best advertisement he could find for FBO's clean entertainment.[33]

As a full-time "picture man" with offices in New York City and a studio in Los Angeles, Kennedy spent most of the week away from home. Every Friday night, he and Eddie Moore took the train to Boston, returning to New York on Sunday night. "Occasionally," Rose remembered, "I went to New York with him for the weekend, saw some plays and did some shopping, but life at home with seven children [Robert Francis, or Bobby, had been born in November 1925] was a busy one. The New England winters were bitter, cold, and snowy, and the spring weather was changeable which gave everyone constant colds." "I didn't want to move. I didn't want to interrupt the children's schools. They were having their teeth straightened—orthodontia work—and I didn't want to interrupt that, until he was certain that this was going to be a success."[34]

That summer, his first at FBO, Kennedy again rented the house at Hyannis Port for Rose, the children, and his father, who after the death of Mary Augusta was spending more time with his son's family. When Joe Jr., now a big boy of eleven, went away to camp, Kennedy took it upon himself to keep him informed of what the rest of the family was doing at the Hyannis Port house. So began the series of letters that would continue for the next thirty-five years, with father, then mother, filling in the children on the comings, goings, and misdeeds of their siblings. Kennedy wrote to Joe Jr. in July 1926 and told him that his younger brother Jack, left to fend for himself for the first time in his life, was "really very lonesome for you and wants me to be sure and promise him that he will go to camp next summer. He is taking swimming lessons to see if he can improve his stroke."[35]

A few weeks later, after visiting Joe Jr. at camp, Kennedy wrote to say that he and Rose had been "all tickled to death with the way you seem to be getting along." He reassured his son that the bit of schoolwork he was doing at camp in preparation for his next term would in the end be well worth it. "You will be much better prepared in the Fall and then you will be thankful that you did a little work. Remember that Jack is practicing at the piano each day an hour and studying from one-half to three-quarters of an hour on his books so that he is really spending more time than you are."[36]

In August, Kennedy sailed to Europe again, this time with Rose. Two of their six weeks were spent at the Hotel du Palais in Biarritz, the other four in Paris and London, where Rose shopped and her husband held business meetings with film executives, including one at the Pathé offices, set up by Lord Beaverbrook, with whom Kennedy had been in correspondence since his last visit abroad. "With the calculating eye of the banker," the *Boston Daily Globe* reported on his return, Kennedy had "observed industrial conditions in the Old World from an unbiased viewpoint" and found England, especially, recovering well from the war and ready and willing to import more American films.[37]

On his return, he hosted a luncheon for theater owners at the Hotel

Astor in New York, to which he invited Will Hays, Fred Thomson, and Gene Tunney, the new heavyweight champion, thereby assuring that the event would be covered by the Hollywood trade press. Serving as master of ceremonies, Kennedy introduced Hays, who, he announced based on what film executives in England had told him, was largely responsible for the boom in American film exports. Hays responded with fulsome praise for Kennedy, who had "honored the motion picture industry by coming into it, and it is better for your presence. You are a distinct asset. . . . For a long time I have wanted to state publicly my opinion of Joseph P. Kennedy and the significance of his entrance into the motion picture industry. . . . I see three champions here. Champion Gene Tunney, Champion Fred Thomson and Champion Joe Kennedy: all champions in their lines!"[38]

Everywhere he went—to New York and Hollywood dinner parties, business meetings, and film openings—Joseph P. Kennedy flashed his toothy Boston smile and put on the charm. "A new figure has appeared among the big men of the motion picture industry," *Moving Picture World* exulted in a multipage December 11, 1926, profile. "A new personality—in his manner of thought, in his cultural backgrounds . . . a new, big figure on the motion picture horizon, a natural leader and organizer, Joseph P. Kennedy's shadow looms larger every minute."[39]

Over the Christmas holidays and January, part of which he spent with the family in Brookline, Kennedy visited Harvard Business School and opened negotiations to organize and present a lecture series on the picture industry, with a star-studded roster of top executives from every branch of the industry. To sweeten the deal, he promised to fund a research project on the industry with the princely sum of $10,000 a year for three years.[40]

The lecture series was well worth $30,000 to Kennedy. If he could bring it off, he would manage to shine yet another spotlight on his Harvard diploma and business connections and burnish his reputation as a go-to, get-it-done magic man who possessed not only the genius to come up with a brilliant idea, but the organizational talents to produce the season-long Harvard show, starring Adolph Zukor, Marcus Loew, Cecil B. DeMille, and Jesse Lasky. Was there any better way to demonstrate to the public and politicians alike that the pictures had outgrown their origins in vaudeville and penny arcades and were entirely legitimate—as art and business—than by parading before a Harvard audience the biggest names in the industry?

Kennedy consulted with Will Hays on the speaker list for his lecture series. He also volunteered to coordinate an industry-wide effort to lend films that represented "the best artistic achievements in the industry" to a Fogg Museum film library and archive. When the chair of the Harvard Department of Fine Arts signed off on the proposal, Kennedy wrote Hays that "it would be of great interest to Harvard if *New York Times* commented on their progressive steps editorially. I merely make this suggestion for your consideration. Believe Times would do it." Two days later, the *New York Times* ran the requested story.[41]

After clearing the names with Hays, Kennedy got in touch with Adolph Zukor, Jesse Lasky, Marcus Loew, William Fox, Harry Warner, and Cecil B. DeMille, not as a supplicant who needed a favor, but as a potential collaborator in an industry-enhancing project. To Adolph Zukor, arguably the most powerful individual in moving pictures, he explained that the alliance with Harvard Business School, the Fogg Museum, and the Harvard Department of Fine Arts was "a step of world-wide importance" for the film industry. "It means a recognition of the artistic work by the oldest university in the United States and by a department that is second to none in the world." In a separate letter, written the same day to one of Zukor's top executives, Kennedy suggested that Zukor might want to delay his promised gift to Yale and consider Harvard instead.[42]

In March, he wrote Cecil B. DeMille, who had asked if he could change the date of his lecture. "If you had any idea how anxious the Harvard authorities are to see you, you would forgive my keeping after Hays to have you come here. I spent most of my first lecture at Harvard telling them about the marvelous work you have done in 'The King of Kings.' . . . President Lowell," Kennedy added, was "very anxious to meet you personally." DeMille, who apparently took well to flattery, agreed to give his lecture in April.[43]

Kennedy acted as host and master of ceremonies for the lecture series that spring and editor of the collected lectures, which he published in book form. He introduced the speakers, took them on tours of the campus, hosted special luncheons where they met "Harvard people," and had his picture taken with each of them. He also offered his services to students who wanted to work in the industry, helped to set up the film library at Fogg, and got from Hays "passes" at Boston's leading moving theaters for the "members of the Fine Arts Department who are to select the films for the archives at Harvard."

His stature—at Harvard and in Hollywood—was, as he had hoped and expected, boosted by his service as liaison between the two. Later that spring, he was asked by the dean's office to secure newsreel coverage for the dedication of the Harvard Business School's new building. "They are very anxious to have the news reels take shots of the buildings," he telegraphed Hays in Hollywood, "so that the whole world will have an opportunity to see what Harvard is doing. Incidentally, it will be good advertising for us. Would you care to call up the various companies that have news reels and make this suggestion?"[44]

In the late spring of 1927, Kennedy, for the first and only time, took Rose with him to the West Coast. Frances Marion hosted a dinner for the Kennedys, followed by a ladies' luncheon for "the boss's wife" at "The Enchanted Hill," the name bestowed on her and Fred Thomson's twenty-room, two-story "Andalusian farmhouse" in Beverly Hills, complete with an indoor movie theater and outdoor pool, aviary, tennis court, riding ring, and stables for several horses, including Silver King and his double. Rose, who had come to Los Angeles to scout out the possibility of moving the family there, found the estate "magnificent" but confided to Marion that "she would never want to surround her children with such an overabundance of luxuries."[45]

Like other movie moguls in Hollywood and New York, Kennedy that spring offered a picture contract to America's newest and cleanest-cut homegrown hero, Charles A. Lindbergh. Joseph W. Powell, Kennedy's former boss at Fore River, who had a small financial interest in FBO, was enlisted to tender the offer. As Powell explained to a Captain Alan Buchanan after Lindbergh had rejected their overture, while recognizing "that the chances were 100 to 1 against us," FBO had felt obligated as "the only Christians in the moving picture business . . . to offer to do a good job for this very fine young gentleman."[46]

In the fall of 1927, a year and a half after he had bought FBO, an old family friend from Boston, James Quirk, now the editor of *Photoplay*, commissioned a multipage profile by Terry Ramsaye, the industry's unofficial spokesperson, complete with photos of the newest movie mogul, his wife, and his seven children. Ramsaye's article, like all the other publicity on Kennedy, made the none-too-subtle point that the Boston banker had nothing in common with other "famous film magnates" who had entered the industry by accident. Kennedy, by contrast, after a "career of business success behind him in . . . banking and shipbuilding, came in the amusement world and the motion pictures deliberately, consciously and with his eyes open." To drive home his point that Kennedy was a new breed of studio head, Ramsaye offered what he claimed was Marcus Loew's reaction on being introduced to Joseph Kennedy. " 'A banker! . . . A banker?—why I thought this business was just for furriers.' " According to Ramsaye, Kennedy had arrived at just the right moment to "endow the febrile motion picture industry with an atmosphere of Americanism and substantiality. Kennedy is a valuable personality from this point of view. He is exceedingly American, with a background of lofty and conservative financial connections, an atmosphere of much home and family life and all those fireside virtues of which the public never hears in the current news from Hollywood." Ramsaye's piece was so much to Kennedy's liking that he would soon afterward hire him as a publicist.[47]

Rose Kennedy, always a shrewd observer, concurred entirely with Ramsaye's observations about her husband's Hollywood career. "One reason he was so much in demand was because he was a banker and no banker was directly in the business in those days. . . . They were also all of Jewish extraction and Kennedy was the only one of Irish extraction in the movie business company and there were a lot of jokes around how the Jews were going to take the Irishman. However, he did very well."[48]

According to Rose, Kennedy was astonished not only at the number of Jews in positions of power and influence in Hollywood, but at the way in which they clung together and protected one another. As she later told her collaborator Robert Coughlin, her husband brought home from Hollywood an important lesson for his children: that they too "should stick together."[49]

Rose and her husband could not help but look at Hollywood, as they did every other community, through ethnic-tinged glasses. They had grown up rich, powerful, and privileged, but in a city sharply and irremediably divided between "us" and "them," Irish Catholics and Yankee Protestants. Kennedy discovered an entirely different social environment in Hollywood, one in which the major division was not between Irish Catholics and Anglo-Protestants, but between Christians and Jews. As an Irish Catholic studio executive in Hollywood, Kennedy was the odd man out, part of a minority so small, it was of little consequence. There were Catholics in the media, such as Quirk at *Photoplay* and Martin Quigley, the publisher of the *Exhibitors Herald,* but during Kennedy's time in Hollywood, they did not exercise the powerful influence they would with the organization of the Catholic Legion of Decency in 1933. Kennedy strategically cast his lot in Hollywood with Presbyterian Will Hays and the Protestant establishment that had so effectively excluded him from positions of power and influence in Boston.

Seven

HOLLYWOOD

In the spring of 1927, "we decided," Rose recalled, "that Joe was definitely in a successful movie business" and that the time had come to move the family from Boston to New York. Years later, answering a question asked her by Robert Coughlin, her ghostwriter, she denied emphatically that Kennedy had moved the family "to New York because he felt he had been socially snubbed in Boston and it was difficult for the children." They had moved for one reason only, "because his business was exclusively in New York at that time." What she neglected to add was that Kennedy had never had any great love for the city he left behind.[1]

He would later advise his friend John Burns, the brilliant Boston-born Irish Catholic lawyer, Harvard Law School professor, and former superior court judge, to move his family from Boston to New York: "Boston is a bigoted place." The Burns boys would never succeed there as they might in New York City. Wall Street, he told Burns, was a meritocracy in ways that Boston, with its anti-Irish sentiments, would never be.[2]

Eddie Moore, dispatched to find a home for the Kennedys in New York, located one large enough for a family of nine—plus servants—and grand enough for a picture studio head, at 5040 Independence

Avenue, on the corner of 252nd Street in Riverdale. White stucco, with several floors of bedrooms, the top ones overlooking the Hudson River, the house was enormous, by far the largest in the neighborhood, with a multiple-car garage and a spacious backyard. Kennedy rented the house and held on to the one in Brookline as insurance should all fall apart. Rose, who was pregnant with their eighth child, wanted to return there to give birth.

On September 24, 1927, the Kennedy children, Rose, and the servants boarded the private railroad car her husband had leased for the trip from Boston to New York. "Rose and children arrive New York Saturday," Kennedy wired Fred Thomson, whose first big feature for Paramount was opening in October. "Because of the newness of the place and number of things to be done to get them settled in house I feel I really should bring them over or at least take care of them when they arrive."[3]

The five older children were enrolled in the private school nearest their home, Riverdale Country School. With its well-groomed playing fields, emphasis on athletics, solid academics, and supervised after-school play program, it was perfect for Joe Jr. and Jack. Rosemary, Kick, and Eunice, who attended the lower school, took the school bus with their big brothers. Joe Jr., never a particularly good student, plodded through with grades in the lower eighties, solidly in the middle rank. Jack started off well, then tailed off. Their school photos reveal two very different-looking boys: the athletically built Joe Jr., proud and composed, with a smirk on his face; and Jack, thin, frail, looking a bit frightened.[4]

K ennedy's daily life was not appreciably impacted by his family's move to Riverdale. He saw little of them that fall, worked late hours, and spent many nights at the Harvard Club or at a hotel near the FBO offices at 1560 Broadway.

He had made great strides in his year and a half as FBO chief executive. By adhering closely to his business model, he had not only cut losses but had begun to make a profit feeding the small-theater audiences' endless appetite for "B" features. FBO brought out fifty-one forgettable films in 1927, including *South Sea Love, Aflame in the Sky,*

Jake the Plumber, Toupay or Not Toupay, A Racing Romeo, Skinny, and *Bee Cause.* Kennedy profited as well from his "personal services" contract with Fred Thomson. He had negotiated a contract for Thomson with Jesse Lasky at Paramount, which provided him with a sizable fee for each picture Thompson made. For his first big-budget feature, Thomson had decided to play Jesse James—but as a Confederate war hero, not a villain. Regrettably, there was no way in the world that a film portraying Jesse James as a hero was going to pass censorship. When Thomson stuck to his guns and refused to play Jesse as a villain, Kennedy was forced to use his considerable charm and negotiating skills to work out an acceptable compromise with Paramount and the censors. The film was re-edited so that James died in the end, which angered Thomson's fans but satisfied the censors. To make sure audiences got the right moral, the closing title was changed from "He was shot in the back by Bob Ford" to "After all, Jesse was wrong—it had to end this way."[5]

The film opened in October on Broadway at the Rialto. The reviews were mixed, the box office poor. Fred and Silver King followed with three additional westerns for Paramount. They too did poorly. Kennedy saw the handwriting on the wall. The public had grown weary of westerns, even Paramount-produced, big-budget ones. There were too many of them, with the same plots, stunts, characters, costumes, and interchangeable athletes on horseback. Kennedy did everything he could to keep Fred's career alive, but ultimately he failed. Thomson's stardom had crested at FBO. There was nowhere left to go but down.[6]

Fortunately for Kennedy, another star whose light burned much brighter than Fred Thomson's was gravitating in his direction. On November 7, 1927, he got a cable from a Hollywood acquaintance, Robert Kane, asking if he would meet with Gloria Swanson, who was on her way to New York City. "Gloria needs handling," Kane wrote, "needs being properly financed and having her organization placed in proper hands and I have taken the liberty of asking her to see you."[7]

They met at Barclay's, the hotel where Swanson was staying. "The maître d' led me to the table," Gloria recounted in her memoirs, "and Mr. Kennedy rose and energetically introduced himself. I was amused by his heavy Boston accent, and I could tell he was surprised that I was so tiny. He didn't resemble any banker I knew. His suit was too bulky, and the knot of his tie was not pushed up tight. With his spectacles and prominent chin, he looked like any average working-class person's uncle. A man of about forty, he still retained a certain boyishness. Apart from his accent, his hands were the most noticeable thing about him. They looked unused to work, and there were wide spaces between his fingers. He gestured often and animatedly with them when he talked." The meeting went well, for the most part. Swanson showed Kennedy "a memorandum from her accountant outlining the two propositions I had received for financing my third picture for United Artists." Kennedy seized the opportunity to show off his banker's vocabulary and declaim on the studio's failures to properly finance and account for production and distribution costs. "Nobody in Hollywood, he declared, knew how to make a balance sheet that gave a banker what he needed. . . . Certainly nobody knew how to depreciate, to amortize, to capitalize—those very things, he said, that spelled success or failure in any other business."

Despite herself, Swanson was enchanted by the boyish banker who was trying so hard to impress her with his knowledge of finance. When he wasn't expatiating on the failures of Hollywood to follow reasonable accounting procedures, he was bellowing with laughter "and whacking his thighs" at her little jokes. She was a bit surprised and disappointed when instead of offering a proposal of his own for financing her next film, he suggested that she stay with United Artists. Kennedy was playing hard to get; he had no intention of letting the opportunity to work with one of Hollywood's greatest stars slip away. When Swanson returned to her hotel room that evening, the hotel telephone operator informed her that she had had several calls from a Mr. Kennedy, who was now downstairs and had asked to see her. "I was bemused and told her to send him up," she recounted in her memoirs. Kennedy asked her to dinner. "He added in a different tone altogether that he had a proposition to discuss with me."[8]

They drove for three quarters of an hour over the Queensboro Bridge into Long Island, Kennedy talking all the time about banking and moving pictures. When they sat down for dinner, Swanson recalled in handwritten notes for her autobiography, Kennedy looked a bit uncomfortable. "It was obvious he was ill at ease not knowing what to do next—I'm sure he was not accustomed to dining alone with a lady." Swanson was only half right. Kennedy had been out with ladies before, but not with glamorous movie stars. He had lured her to dinner to discuss a business proposition, but both of them knew that if that was all he intended, he would not have felt obliged to have a chauffeur drive them to Long Island.[9]

He presented her with a copy of his Harvard lectures, now in book form. They laughed together at the idea of Zukor lecturing at Harvard, and Swanson "imitated Mr. Zukor's heavy Hungarian accent." Kennedy was in his element here, the Harvard-educated banker alternately railing against and mocking the immigrant Jewish amateurs in Hollywood who didn't understand business, banking, or accounting—and never would. "There is no question that one of the bonds between them that Joe exploited was that she had been taken advantage of by Jews," William Dufty, Swanson's sixth and final husband, told author Cari Beauchamp.[10]

As the night wore on, Kennedy laid out his proposition. He offered to take her on as his personal client, to put her finances in order, reduce her debts, finance her next picture, and manage the business aspects of her career.

After nearly two years of making cheap, grade-B pictures, he was ready to move up a notch in the Hollywood pecking order and join the rest of the studio heads in throwing money at overpriced, self-indulgent stars. In his Harvard lecture he had joked that when told by a magazine writer that he "had some good pictures this year," he'd asked, "What were they?" His most successful film to date had been *The Gorilla Hunt*, which, he told the Harvard students, he had watched for five minutes before leaving the room "in disgust." There was money to be made in cheap westerns, melodramas, and adventure stories starring dogs, but little prestige accrued to studio heads who turned them out like cookies from a cooker cutter. Having hobnobbed with the industry's elites at Harvard, Kennedy did not relish returning to his lowly perch at FBO.[11]

Gloria Swanson offered him the vehicle he needed to climb to the top of his profession. At the time, she was arguably one of Hollywood's two or three greatest stars. In the 1924 *Photoplay* fan poll, she had come in third, behind Mary Pickford and Douglas Fairbanks. In the *Film Daily*'s rating of box office attractions, she had ranked second behind Harold Lloyd. The year before, Jesse Lasky had offered her $1 million to re-sign with Paramount, but she had turned him down to join her fellow megastars Pickford, Fairbanks, Charlie Chaplin, Rudolph Valentino, and Buster Keaton at United Artists.[12]

There was no one quite like her. Physically, she was eerily like Rose. Both were tiny, with sparkling eyes, the whitest of teeth, and curly dark hair. But Gloria was tinier, her eyes (always well mascaraed) shone brighter, her hair was darker and curlier, her features were sharper and more defined. And unlike Rose Kennedy—or for that matter Mary Pickford, her only real rival at the box office—Swanson would never be mistaken for the girl next door. She exuded a devil-may-care sensuality that, under Cecil B. DeMille's direction, had been transposed early in her career into box office magic. She avoided being stereotyped, took different roles, and enjoyed breaking the rules for public appearances. She was among the first female stars to be photographed with her children and the first to marry and divorce one husband after another. She stopped at six. When she met Kennedy she was on her third, the dashing Frenchman Henri, Marquis de la Falaise de la Coudraye, who with his perfect physique and posture, greased-back dark hair parted on the left, elegant suits, and well-manicured mustache looked as much the movie star as she did.

That Kennedy and Swanson met in the fall of 1927 was fortuitous for both. He needed her to escape being typecast as the chief executive of a minor studio. She needed him to put her financial house in order so that she could secure funding for her next film. That they were sexually attracted to each other was icing on the cake.

Swanson returned west soon after their dinner on Long Island. Kennedy stayed in touch with her and her longtime attorney and adviser, Milton Cohen, by telephone, telegram, and letter. "From the very sketchy outline I am able to obtain from Miss Swanson," he wrote Cohen on December 20, "it rather appears to me as if she has so heavily mortgaged her future that very drastic steps must be taken if she hopes to straighten herself out." Kennedy informed Cohen that he would be "very glad, after receiving word from you, to put myself and some people in my organization at her disposal to work out her problems as best we could without any cost to her."[13]

Kennedy did not follow Swanson to Los Angeles but remained in New York, where there was much to do. It was becoming clearer by the minute, especially after the opening of Al Jolson's *The Jazz Singer* in October, that picture audiences wanted and were willing to pay a bit extra to hear their stars talk and sing. Converting the studios and theaters to sound would require huge amounts of capital. Fortunately, Wall Street was in the midst of what appeared to be an unstoppable upward trend in stock prices and profits. With but a few minor dips along the way, the Dow Jones Industrial Average had doubled from 92 in May 1924 to over 200 in December 1927. In 1927 alone, $7.8 billion in stocks and bonds had been floated, a postwar record; corporate-bonded debt had reached an all-time high of $35.2 billion.

By late 1927, the remaining question for most of the major studios was not when or whether to convert to sound, but which system to install. Western Electric had taken an early lead in the multimillion-dollar sweepstakes by signing Vitaphone contracts with most of the leading studios. David Sarnoff was desperate to demonstrate the superiority of the RCA Photophone, but he hadn't yet found a studio willing to install and produce pictures with it.

Sarnoff, born in Russia, raised on the Lower East Side, apprenticed as a newsboy and telegraph operator, had developed an early expertise and interest in wireless radio communications. In 1921, he had been named general manager of General Electric's subsidiary, the Radio Corporation of America (RCA). It was Louis Kirstein, the department store owner, Sarnoff's friend from Boston, and an investor in FBO, who suggested that he talk to Kennedy about installing his RCA Photophone equipment in the FBO studios. Sarnoff met with Kennedy and came away enormously impressed with his "clear grasp of the opportunities in sound recording and talking pictures."[14]

The two young chief executives, one tall and Irish, the other a small, broad-faced Eastern European Jew, quickly struck a deal. FBO agreed to install RCA Photophone equipment in its studios and produce sound pictures with it. In turn, RCA would purchase $500,000 of FBO stock, enough to pay for the installation and provide Kennedy and Guy Currier, the chief stockholders, with a sizable profit. To maximize those profits, Currier and Kennedy cornered as much FBO stock as they could, then pooled their holdings in a newly organized corporate entity, the Gower Street Company.

As Kennedy had predicted long before, the men in New York who had invested in and now controlled the picture business had begun to merge, consolidate, and combine their studios into larger and, they hoped, more productive and profitable enterprises. To manage these new companies—and watch over the millions of dollars invested in them—they needed managers with the skill set Kennedy had brought with him to the picture business, businessmen who cared only for the bottom line and were not afraid to slash production costs to increase profits and boost stock and bond prices. The latest megadeals organized by Wall Street investment banker Elisha Walker, president of Blair & Co., and Jeremiah Milbank, a conservative Republican who had been attracted to the picture business after seeing DeMille's *The King of Kings,* had brought together Pathé, which made newsreels and short films, and DeMille's company, Producers Distributing Corporation, which made features. A year later, in a complicated cross-ownership and affiliation agreement, Walker undertook the near impossible task of consolidating into one enterprise the merged Pathé/DeMille studio in Hollywood and the Keith-Albee-Orpheum (K-A-O) chain of vaudeville theaters.

J. J. Murdock, the sixty-eight-year-old Scotsman who had managed the Keith-Albee-Orpheum theaters, was put in charge of the new company. A vaudeville theater man who knew nothing about producing pictures, Murdock, with Walker's encouragement, approached Kennedy about running the Hollywood side of the operation. Kennedy had been selling Pathé stock short since the previous August through an account registered in Eddie Moore's name at E. F. Hutton. He now demanded and was given access to the company's financial records, which confirmed what he had guessed when he started selling the stock short. Pathé was badly in debt and desperately needed to cut operating costs at the studio.

Joseph Kennedy had learned through experience that the best way to get a job was to act as if one didn't need or want it. This was what he had done with Swanson and what he did again with Murdock. In late January 1928, insisting that he could not possibly postpone his winter vacation, he cut off negotiations with Murdock and boarded a train at Grand Central for Palm Beach, via Jacksonville. If Murdock wanted to make a deal, he'd have to wait until Kennedy returned to New York.

As we shall see, it was not the best time to go on vacation, but Kennedy was a creature of habit and refused to let anyone or anything interfere with his schedule. Days before he boarded the train to Palm Beach, Rose had left Riverdale for Brookline to await the arrival of her eighth child under the care of Dr. Good, who had delivered her previous seven.

The Kennedy children who had arrived in Riverdale only months earlier would spend their first winter in a new home, new schools, and a new neighborhood, with mother, father, aunts, uncles, and grandparents hundreds of miles away. The older boys, Joe Jr., twelve, and Jack, ten, stepped into the breach and watched out for the younger Kennedys, as they had been raised to do. Kick kept an eye on her little sister Eunice. Mary Moore, Eddie's wife, who lived nearby, and the nannies and nurses looked after three-and-a-half-year-old Patricia and two-year-old Bobby.

Though the family had relocated to Riverdale to be closer to Kennedy's workplace, neither wife nor children would see very much of him for the next three years. His trips to the West Coast grew more frequent and of longer duration. He might have compensated by cutting back on his winter vacations. But this he would not do, and no one who knew how hard he worked, not wife or children or business associates, dared suggest that he give up or curtail his rest-and-recuperation pilgrimage to Palm Beach.

In Palm Beach, Kennedy stayed at the Royal Poinciana, one of the world's great resort hotels, on thirty acres, with one thousand rooms, a twelve-hundred-seat dining room, gardens, tennis courts, golf courses, and the Coconut Grove with dancing every evening. The center of social life remained the hotels—and, a short walk from them, Colonel Edward Riley Bradley's Beach Club, a members-only, evening-dress-required gambling resort with the best food in town. As Palm Beach grew in size and population through the 1920s, the richest of the rich moved out of the hotels and into wildly eclectic Spanish-Mediterranean "cottages" with terra-cotta tiles, stucco façades, and tastefully oversize turrets, columns, arcades, cloisters, and high wood-beamed ceilings. High-toned restaurants, nightclubs, and shops spread along Worth Avenue, anchored by the exclusive Everglades Club, designed as a convalescent hospital for Great War veterans but converted to the island's most luxurious and exclusive private club.

Kennedy and his friends were not members of the Everglades or part of Palm Beach haute society. They came south to play golf, eat fresh seafood, soak in the sun and the air, swim in the pools and in the ocean, and do a bit of gambling at Bradley's. Or such had been the program in past years. January 1928 would be different.

Joe and Gloria had spoken regularly on the phone since her return to Los Angeles. Simultaneously, Kennedy's associates E. B. Derr and C. J. Scollard were doing their best to sort out Swanson's business affairs, reincorporate her production company, renegotiate her film contracts and debt to United Artists, and reduce her financial obligations by firing several of her personal attendants, closing down her New York office, selling her furniture, and eliminating redundant and oversize insurance policies. On January 25, Derr wired Kennedy in Palm Beach that he had discovered Swanson employed a full-time production manager, accountant, publicist, stenographer, dressmaker, seamstress, secretary, chauffeur, butler, and three servants. "New bills [were] turning up every day," he telegrammed Eddie Moore three days later. "Funds are getting short. Was not startled when partial payment bill came in on foreign car but new bill just arrived demanding immediately payment $700 to Professor Faust Squadrilli for three paintings Marquis supposed to have bought recently. Can I pay the bill by returning the paintings? Could he [the marquis] possibly make the supreme sacrifice by giving up the paintings until we get some money together?"[15]

In late December, the Marquis de la Falaise de la Coudraye returned to Los Angeles to celebrate Christmas with Gloria and her children. "There were," Swanson recalled in the unpublished notes she wrote for her autobiography, "wild telephone calls for us to come to Palm Beach—

there was of course lots to talk about and I supposed lots of business things to settle." Swanson was due in New York City in early February for the premiere of her latest picture, *Sadie Thompson,* but she agreed to stop off in Palm Beach. Kennedy and Eddie Moore met her, Henri, and her full entourage on January 28 and escorted them to the Whitehall Hotel, which was as luxurious as (but a bit more exclusive than) the Royal Poinciana.

Kennedy and Swanson would see a great deal of each other during their week together. In handwritten notes for her autobiography, Swanson would later claim that while members of Kennedy's entourage took Henri fishing, she and Kennedy had sex for the first time. "After every unruly storm you look for the damage. Was Henry [her husband] hurt or even aware?" she asked. "Apparently everything had happened so fast and the confusion so great that the obvious was buried for the moment at least. . . . Henry was being introduced to fishing in a very big way by the four shadows who were now shadowing him and I was being untrue to my husband—what a hell emotionally I was going through. It was against every fibre and my conscience gnawing at me—I loved Henry, he mustn't be hurt—and at the same time I was completely caught up in this wild man's passion and the world he represented rather than Henry's."[16]

While Swanson was vacationing with Kennedy and her husband in Palm Beach, Derr was in Los Angeles trying to renegotiate her contract with United Artists. Joe Schenck agreed to release her from her commitments, he told Derr, because "he liked Kennedy" and wanted to help him out. The truth was that Schenck knew he had no chance of holding on to Swanson and wasn't sure she was worth the trouble.[17]

Swanson was free now to sign the papers Kennedy had prepared, giving him full power of attorney and placing her assets past, present, and future in Gloria Productions, a new company he had incorporated. After her week in the sun, Swanson and Henri, who was still not indicating that he had any knowledge of what had gone on between his wife and her new business manager, left Palm Beach for New York. Kennedy took a separate train north with Eddie Moore.

On his return, he sat down with Murdock and Elisha Walker and concluded the negotiations over Pathé that he had suspended when he'd left for his winter vacation. Anticipating that the Pathé stock price would rise once the news of his hiring was officially confirmed, Kennedy bought eight hundred shares of preferred, in Eddie Moore's name, on February 14. The following day, after the official announcement, he sold all his Pathé stock for a profit of $16,318 on an investment of $21,772.50.[18]

On February 20, his fifth daughter and eighth child, Jean Ann, was born at St. Elizabeth's Hospital in Brookline. This time, the Boston newspapers put the father's name first and left out his father-in-law's. Befitting Kennedy's new status in the moving picture industry, even *Variety* reported on Jean's birth. Fred Thomson telegrammed his "congratulations and very best wishes to Rose and the daughter. My road to fame is now clear. In future years I will be able to say I knew Joe and Rose Kennedy when they had only seven children." Bill LeBaron, FBO's production chief, joked in his telegram to Rose that he had just telephoned Joe, who was so excited and so busy "that he doesn't know whether this is his eighth or ninth child. Think you should wire him correct information as I hate to see an otherwise good father so demoralized by the movies." Gloria Swanson de la Falaise sent flowers.[19]

Though he had told the *Los Angeles Times* that he was working for Pathé "without compensation," he had negotiated a healthy salary, $2,000 a week, equivalent to more than $3.4 million in purchasing power today, "plus out of pocket expenses and disbursements." The real reward for his new part-time job was "100,000 fully paid shares" of Pathé stock, which was to be delivered to him in four installments: 25,000 shares on May 15, 1928; another 25,000 on August 15; the third installment on November 15; and the final one on February 15, 1929. The net profits from the sale of these shares, which Kennedy disposed of at or just before delivery, totaled a little over $579,000, worth more than $7 million in purchasing power today.[20]

On February 15, Kennedy announced that he would be traveling to the West Coast to reorganize the Pathé studio and meet with Cecil B. DeMille, the putative studio head and major culprit in the cost overruns. A week later, *Variety* reported that weekly overhead at the Pathé studios had been reduced from $110,000 to $80,000 and fifty salesmen and two division managers in the distribution department had been let go. What was not reported then or subsequently was that simultaneously with slashing costs in Hollywood, Kennedy had created a position in Paris for Henri as Pathé sales representative, thereby removing him from Gloria's payroll and from the United States for longer periods of time.[21]

Kennedy's major achievement that spring was working out a mutually acceptable exit strategy with Cecil B. DeMille. With his $7,500-a-week salary, his $100,000 bonus for each finished feature, and the outrageous luxuries he lavished on subordinates, retainers, and his mistress/screenwriter, DeMille had to be taken off the payroll. DeMille was furious that Pathé executives—including, he suspected, Joe Kennedy—had leaked stories about his profligacy as a producer and studio head, and he demanded that all derogatory comments cease at once and that from this point on, Pathé executives praise his production unit as the only efficient and profit-making one in the conglomerate.[22]

Kennedy agreed and wrote Elisha Walker, demanding that chatter out of New York stop at once. If he was to run the company, as he had been hired to do, he had to have complete control of everything, including publicity. "I do not wish to appear arbitrary in the matter of this DeMille settlement but the conduct of this business must either be left in our hands here or else we cannot make any promises as to its success. We are more vitally interested in any publicity which vitally affects future success of the Company than anybody can possibly be in New York. We realize if the wrong statements get out the future success of the Company is seriously in danger and therefore I think it necessary that the question of publicity be left to [the Pathé publicist] and me. We of course will try to get it to you if possible." Walker made sure the DeMille chatter ceased in New York. The deal was signed and DeMille exited, leaving the studio in better, but far from perfect, financial circumstances.[23]

On previous trips to the West Coast, Kennedy and Eddie Moore had stayed at the Ambassador Hotel. This time, in spring 1928— perhaps because Kennedy needed a more private place to rendezvous with Gloria and/or because as a studio head, he believed he had to have a mansion of his own—Moore rented a large house on Rodeo Drive, with gardens, a tennis court, a large formal dining room, and a full

complement of servants. E. B. Derr and two other business associates moved in with him and Moore. Gloria had her own house and
children nearby—and a husband in Paris—but she spent most of her
evenings and ate her dinners at Rodeo Drive with Kennedy and his entourage (whom she referred to alternately as his "four horsemen" or his
"shadows").

"It was the strangest house," she wrote in her memoirs. "An Irish
maid took my coat when I arrived, and another Irish maid served the
elaborate meal. In addition I saw a butler, and there was mention of the
gardener and the cook. Yet the mood of the place, despite its domestic
furnishings, was strictly that of a clubhouse or an office building."[24]

Their relationship—business and personal—deepened that spring in
Los Angeles as they began to plan their first joint venture together, a
Gloria Swanson feature produced by Joseph P. Kennedy. "It was certainly obvious to me," she would later recall in handwritten notes for
her memoir, "and I suppose anyone else in the same room that this
overpowering personality had a schoolboy crush on me." She was as
taken with him as he was with her. "I must confess I was impressed
with his sense of power— His sense of laughter or anger was always on
the edge of every situation. He went chalk white when angry and into
healthy peals of laughter when there was the slightest opening for it.
This man wanted me to lean on him—something I had never done in
my life. . . . It was good to have someone say I'll take care of whatever
worriment I had. Darling Henry wanted so much to be helpful but he
was bewildered and why not, having been transplanted from a sane
normal life to one of complete unreality and madness. I was caught up
in both these worlds because I loved both for different reasons."[25]

Kennedy had promised Swanson—and himself—that they would
make an "important" picture together. The prime ingredient in an
"important" picture was an "important" director, and one of the most
"important" was free to work with them. Swanson later claimed that
she was both delighted and a bit frightened when Eddie Moore called
to tell her that the "boss had got von Stroheim" to direct her next
picture.[26]

Erich von Stroheim was available because no one in Hollywood besides Kennedy was willing to put up with him. He was, it was true,
possessed of demonic genius—and with his bulldog head and pugilist

physique he looked the part—but he had also proven himself to be a self-destructive madman incapable of following orders or staying within the grandiose budgets allotted him. He had gone overbudget in his last five films, each of which had been taken away from him when he failed to edit it down to a workable length. His last film, *The Wedding March*, which he had made at Paramount after being fired by MGM and Universal, had come in too far overbudget, too long (between six and nine hours), and too misshapen to be saved. Paramount would neither allow him to finish the film nor give him a new project. By the time Joe Kennedy magically appeared to invite him to write and direct an original screenplay for Swanson, he was considered unemployable.

A meeting was arranged between producer, director, and star at Swanson's Hollywood residence. Von Stroheim appeared with the sketch of an idea, flattered Swanson with his attention, and virtually ignored Kennedy. After he left, Swanson reminded Kennedy of the director's reputation as being impossibly "difficult to handle." Kennedy was unfazed. He had decided to hire at least "two watchdogs" to make sure von Stroheim behaved in a businesslike and efficient manner. "I was not to worry about anything—just come on the set looking pretty."[27]

A t this point, Swanson and von Stroheim were the least of Kennedy's concerns. He was running two studios and being paid a huge amount to do so: $2,000 a week from FBO and $2,000 a week from Pathé for a combined annual salary of $208,000, three times what Babe Ruth made in 1928, the year after he hit his sixty home runs. Simultaneously with running these studios and preparing to produce Swanson's new film, he was completing negotiations to take over yet another entertainment conglomerate, the Keith-Albee-Orpheum chain of theaters. Elisha Walker and Jeremiah Milbank had tried earlier to merge K-A-O with the Pathé/DeMille studios but had been stymied by the aging but still tyrannical Edward Albee, who refused to allow his vaudeville theaters and performers to be engulfed by the moving picture behemoth. To protect their investments, the bankers were determined to buy out Albee, integrate the companies into one corporate entity, and provide Pathé with a nationwide theater chain in which to exhibit its pictures.

Kennedy returned to New York in early May to finalize a deal with Albee on behalf of Walker and his fellow investors. On May 15, 1928, Edward Albee agreed to turn over control of his company to the Kennedy and Walker consortium for $4.2 million. His only condition was that he retain his position as president. The deal consummated, Kennedy was rewarded for past and future services with a two-year option to buy seventy-five thousand shares of K-A-O stock for $21, another unlimited expense account, a five-year contract as chairman of the board, control of the executive committee, an exemption from the provision that directors should have no other "financial interest, etc. in any other theatrical or motion picture company," and an explicit agreement that he would "not be required to devote your entire time and attention to [the company's] affairs."[28]

Kennedy reached out at once to Johnnie Ford, with whom he had worked at Fore River and then hired to run the Maine and New Hampshire Theatre Company, which he had taken control of the year before. A skilled accountant and businessman, Ford would remain one of Kennedy's most trusted associates for the next twenty years. His long-term assignment was to reorganize the K-A-O management and retrofit its vaudeville theaters for sound. His short-term task was to deal with Albee. "Find out just how far we are obligated to pay him his salary: then go in and have a talk with him, explaining conditions and discuss with him the cuts. . . . I think he should be cut to $25,000" from his current salary of $100,000.[29]

Though the seventy-one-year-old Albee retained his title as president of his theater chain, "Mr. Kennedy," the *Los Angeles Times* reported on May 23, was "expected to assume the active management" of the company. While Kennedy would later pay homage to Albee and vaudeville, he had been brought in to push both the man and the live entertainment genre he had pioneered off the stage. House managers across the K-A-O circuit were instructed to make room for Pathé pictures on their bills and devote at least 50 percent of their advertising budget to them.[30]

Kennedy was now running three large entertainment companies at the same time, two picture studios and a chain of several hundred vaudeville theaters that were in the process of being converted to pictures. Even those who had worked with him in the past marveled at the energy he expended, the impossibly long hours he kept, his ability to concentrate on several matters at once, and his capacity for juggling numbers, accounts, personalities, staffs, employees, and contracts as he flitted back and forth from office to office, city to city, coast to coast.

That spring, while negotiating the takeover of the Albee company, he presided over the annual sales conventions for his movie studios. It appeared that 1928 was going to be FBO's biggest year ever—and he intended to take full credit for it. The multipage, full-color announcements of the upcoming season that appeared that spring in the trade journals prominently displayed a smiling photo of Joseph P. Kennedy, under the headline THE MAN . . . THE PRODUCT AND THE MASTER SHOWMAN OF THE WORLD. From that moment on, in posters, in press advertisements, or on the screen, every FBO film would be preceded in large letters by "Joseph P. Kennedy Presents."[31]

The first public announcement of the Swanson/von Stroheim deal appeared at the end of April 1928, though with no mention of Kennedy's involvement. "Here's one to make your eyes bulge," wrote one columnist, speculating on the likelihood that von Stroheim could complete the film within the rumored ten-week shooting schedule. "He's spent longer than that on a couple of scenes." In mid-May, Kennedy and his lieutenants in Hollywood, still below the radar, secured permission from Paramount to "borrow" von Stroheim for the project. The next step was getting a cameraman, which would not be easy, as the best ones were tied to major studio contracts. Kennedy wrote to Louis B. Mayer on May 25 to ask as a "personal favor" if he could "borrow Ollie Marsh," a cameraman agreeable to both Swanson and von Stroheim. "As you may or may not know, I have taken unto myself the responsibility of financing and producing the next Swanson picture. I have arranged to get von Stroheim to direct, and I can already hear you saying: 'You have had no troubles in the picture business yet—they have just started.' However we shall try to do the best we can under the circumstances." Kennedy closed his chatty, one-mogul-to-another letter with a joke about his latest coup, the takeover of K-A-O: "As you probably know, not feeling that there was enough excitement in the picture business, I have gone into the vaudeville game—God knows what will happen there."[32]

Though there was as yet no public connection with Swanson, Joseph Kennedy's fame was spreading beyond the confines of the Boston papers and the Hollywood trades. On May 23, 1928, following the K-A-O takeover, the *Los Angeles Times* ran its first feature on the "Banker Now Theater Man." That same week, *Time* magazine profiled him. Then, on June 3, the *New York Times* published a feature-length Sunday story titled "Movie Chief's Rapid Rise."

Two weeks later, Kennedy's name appeared in the headlines again, in even more spectacular fashion, with the announcement that he had been appointed "adviser" to a third film studio, First National, in anticipation of his taking over the company. First National was one of the five "majors," with a rich history, a stable of box office stars, a huge studio in Burbank, a chain of regional theaters, and many of the grandest big-city, first-run movie palaces. News of the deal reverberated through Hollywood and New York. How could any one man, even a Joe Kennedy, run four companies at the same time? Was a merger in the offing? Or some sort of market-sharing "specialization" plan under which, as *Variety* reported, FBO would stick to making "B" films for smaller theaters, First National would produce "A" features for first-run theaters, and "Pathé would distribute short subjects exclusively"? Or, as most industry insiders believed, had Kennedy been brought in to slash costs so that the company could be sold or merged with another?[33]

"If you hear a movie Paul Revere tearing down a studio street," Harry Carr of the *Los Angeles Times* reported in his weekly column on July 22, "you can be sure this is what he is yelling: 'Look out: Kennedy is coming!' The word 'Kennedy' whispered in any studio will send all the executives shrieking for the fire escapes. . . . Up to date, Mr. Kennedy has accumulated F.B.O. Studio, the Pathé interests, has done something or other to First National that no one can find out. And is said to be negotiating for the purchase of Universal. As I haven't inquired during the last few minutes, I don't know whether Kennedy by now owns Paramount, M.G.M. and Fox, or not. At any rate, every time the footfalls of Kennedy are heard approaching, they thrust all the little movie companies under the bed and block the doors." Carr did not regard Kennedy's appointment—as adviser/chief of First National—as necessarily bad for the industry. On the contrary, he welcomed the Boston banker and wished him well: "The point is . . . that Mr. Kennedy is turning things upside down in the studios where he holds sway. He is bringing business methods to Hollywood. . . . The picture business, in general, isn't feeling so healthy. A shakeup has long been necessary, and the resultant tremor is considerable." The industry was in the process of converting its studios and theaters from silence to sound. "Is it significant or providential," Carr asked rhetorically in his final paragraph, headed "The Kennedy Era," "that a great new financial force has come into pictures at the moment of this sweeping change in technical method?"[34]

While Hollywood was rife with rumors about who was going to be fired, hired, promoted, or demoted and how and when Kennedy was going to start merging his three studios and theater company, Hollywood's "big mystery man," as the *Film Daily* now referred to him, kept his counsel. He cooperated with the large-circulation dailies and magazines for their puff pieces but refused to talk to the trade journals about his plans for his studios, especially the latest one, First National. "Western Union niceties about California weather but nary a word about First National," the *Film Daily* reported. "If it means anything to you, dear reader, Joe is running true to form. He never discusses his business with outsiders. His business, so he reflects when you ask him, is nobody's business."[35]

Part of the reason he may have kept quiet was that he had nothing to say. Although he was the one getting the publicity, he was still working for Elisha Walker and the major stockholders in the companies he was running. The short-term agenda they had given him was to cut costs by reducing the payroll and, in so doing, raise the stock price. What happened next depended entirely on his partners on Wall Street and whether they were willing to spend more money buying or merging or consolidating more companies.

Though he was not charged with formulating long-term plans, he had taken on more than was humanly or organizationally possible for one man, even one as talented as Joseph P. Kennedy. He had built a personal organization of tough-minded, number-crunching, relentless negotiators, accountants, and managers, but the final decisions remained his to make. And there were now too many of them, too many moving parts, too many investors and bankers to satisfy in New York, too many budgets to cut, too many managements to revitalize and reconfigure. He was stretching himself too thin, entwining himself in increasingly tangled business relationships and, as he added new responsibilities and new companies, neglecting older ones.

David Sarnoff, to cite but one example, was near furious at the delay in converting FBO pictures to RCA Photophone sound and more furious still when it became apparent that First National, Kennedy's latest Hollywood conquest, was going to install his competitor's equipment. The *Film Daily* found the whole situation rather amusing: "You can never tell. Here Kennedy has RCA and General Electric as partners in FBO and yet, First National, one of Joe's 'specially advised' companies, signs with Western Electric for sound. Nobody would have believed it."[36]

Sarnoff, fearing now that Kennedy might double-cross him entirely and install Western Electric equipment in the FBO and Pathé studios, demanded that he sign an exclusive agreement with RCA for both studios and start spending studio money to make sound films. Elisha Walker met with Sarnoff in New York City to try to hammer out a settlement. Kennedy called in from Los Angeles and agreed, as the conference memorandum recorded in language much tamer than he must have used, "that there seemed to be some misunderstanding between the parties as to whom was to pay for the [sound] work already completed or in process."[37]

It had become clear to everyone in the room—and to Kennedy on the West Coast—that the partnership between Sarnoff and the Kennedy-run studios was not going to work. Sarnoff was interested in promoting his RCA Photophone equipment; Kennedy, in wringing maximum profits and personal publicity, with or without RCA Photophone sound, from the companies he now controlled. The *Film Daily,* which took great pleasure in Kennedy's misadventures—perhaps in retribution for his refusal to talk to it—gleefully reported the dispute in mid-August. "Kennedy may have one toy less to play with now. When he was in California, several telephone wires fairly burned up between the place where they make 'em [Hollywood] and the place where they finance 'em [New York]. The scene was something like this: Sarnoff at RCA headquarters in New York; Kennedy in the glorious West. A telephone call. 'Mr. Kennedy talking at length about RCA and sound. Mr. Sarnoff very much inclined not to listen.' That's one incident. There have been others. Result: Kennedy and Sarnoff decide to call it a day."[38]

Kennedy refused to acknowledge to himself or his associates that he might have been at blame for failing to follow through on the deal he had made with Sarnoff or that he had acted too precipitously in cutting costs at First National. Instead, he responded to his critics by lashing out at the industry that had welcomed him as its savior. In August 1928, he broke his silence in an angry interview with the *Los Angeles Times* that was picked up by the trades. "Dissatisfaction," he claimed, "permeates this business and it is the most harmful thing in its effect. . . . Legislators are introducing [censorship] bills that are aimed at pictures, and foreign countries are throwing up barriers to American film importations." These issues were "serious enough without any additional complications but they are complicated a hundred fold by the advent of the sound films. These throw the whole thing into a new form of chaos." The problems facing the industry were enormous, but they were all solvable, he insisted, given the right leadership. First Hollywood had to cure itself of the "psychological condition" that plagued it: "too many grumblers, too many growlers, too many people listening to every idle bit of comment, too many making mountains out of molehills."[39]

Having said his piece—and intimated, not very subtly, that there was no basis for the criticism he was getting and that the industry needed him more than he needed it—Joseph P. Kennedy returned from Los Angeles to New York to meet with the First National executives on August 10. The next day, a Saturday, First National president Irving Rossheim announced that Kennedy had signed "a contract which places him in charge of First National Pictures for five years. . . . He will have charge of all producing and distributing for First National." What was not made public was that the agreement guaranteed him $3,000 a week from First National (in addition to his $2,000 from FBO and $2,000 from Pathé), to be increased to 10 percent of profits after three years. This, Kennedy had argued, was more than reasonable, as he intended to eliminate three top First National executives who together were receiving $7,000 a week plus 10 percent of the profits.[40]

According to the *Film Daily,* which provided industry readers with a day-by-day account of the negotiations, directly after the Saturday meeting "Joe left for Cape Cod to see Mrs. Joe and his flock of children. It's been six weeks since last he made whoopee with them and he was right anxious to go home." E. B. Derr stayed behind in New York to sort out the details.[41]

For the fourth summer in a row, Kennedy had rented the sprawling cottage in Hyannis Port at the end of the block, with the large lawn leading down to the water. Joe Jr. had turned thirteen in July (his father had missed his birthday that year, as he had that of his other children), Jack was eleven, Rosemary was ten, Kick and Eunice were eight and seven, and the babies, Pat, Robert, and Jean, were four, three, and six months. That summer, Joe Jr. and Jack got their first boat, which they named the *Rose Elizabeth* for their mother; they also got their names in the papers for rescuing a young boy whose boat had been swamped a short distance from their front porch. Their father, who had been in New York and Los Angeles through most of the summer, spent a week in Hyannis Port before sailing to Europe with Rose in mid-August.

On Wednesday, August 15, two days before they were to sail, Irving Rossheim, the First National president, wired Kennedy at Hyannis Port with disturbing news. First National directors from all over the country had been calling him long-distance to express their "dissatisfaction with terms of your control outlined at meeting." Rossheim suggested that Kennedy meet with two of the most powerful dissidents, Barney Balaban of the one-hundred-theater Balaban & Katz chain in the Midwest and Spyros Skouras, who with his brothers owned another forty theaters.[42]

Kennedy took the train to New York to meet with Balaban and Skouras, who (with other company directors) wanted to change the terms of his contract and require him to consult with an executive committee before making any major decisions. Kennedy emphasized that he could not work effectively under such circumstances. The next day, after the *Île de France* had sailed with Kennedy on board, Rossheim telegraphed Al Rockett, the head of production in Burbank, that "by mutual consent the Board of Directors of First National Pictures and Joseph P. Kennedy had terminated an agreement under which Mr. Kennedy had been acting in an advisory capacity for First National Pictures and was to continue to do so for the next five years."[43]

"Some of the panting has ceased," the *Film Daily* reported. "Many of the folks at First National—East and West—are breathing lots easier. For Kennedy, that quiet and provocatively silent man, is no longer gunning on the organization's preserves, and, it seems, some of the game frequenting those woods will roam freely as of yore. The cheers that greeted news of the break might not have been stentorian in volume, but never doubt the degree of their sincerity."[44]

Kennedy, it appeared, didn't care in the slightest. He was by now, or so he thought, bigger than any individual studio. Whatever happened at First National, he sat astride the industry as its savior. There would be other studios bidding for his services and he would oblige them, but only on his terms. Or he would cash in his options and walk away to start over elsewhere, this time with millions of dollars in his bank accounts.

Eight

GLORIA AND ROSE

Dear Mr. Joe Kennedy: Aw, come back from Europe!
Life is tame when you are gone. You haven't bought
a motion-picture company for days and days.
—HARRY CARR, AUGUST 26, 1928, *LOS ANGELES TIMES*

The smiling, effervescent, freckle-faced boy wonder had been transformed into a silent man of mystery, but the magnetic field around him had not diminished in the slightest. There was no one like Joe Kennedy in Hollywood; the reporters and columnists knew it and tracked his every move. As the industry appeared at times to speed out of control into the new sound era, as rumors swirled about takeovers, mergers, consolidations, and buyouts, there remained one constant: Joseph P. Kennedy.

"The most intriguing personality in the motion picture world this autumn," according to the *New York Herald Tribune*'s Sunday magazine, "is not some newly discovered beauty from the corn belt, a new Valentino rescued from the obscurity of a tent show in Czechoslovakia or some hatchet-faced actor with the voice of a Barrymore to whom the 'talkies' have opened the door. . . . The person who now monopolizes conversation in the studios and on locations is not an actor, but one of the executives of this highly important new industry. His name is Joseph P. Kennedy."[1]

Kennedy's departure from First National had ended the speculation that the company would be merged with Pathé, FBO, and/or K-A-O, but it had set in motion a new set of negotiations—and rumors. In September, Warner Brothers bought First National and acquired hundreds of theaters in which to exhibit its Vitaphone talkies. David Sarnoff, worried that without a Hollywood studio in which to film RCA Photophone talkies or theaters to exhibit them, RCA would be shut out of the picture business forever, opened negotiations with Elisha Walker to buy and merge the FBO studio and the K-A-O theaters into a new corporate entity, known as Radio-Keith-Orpheum, or RKO. Though Kennedy was president of FBO and chairman of the board of K-A-O, the negotiations were initiated while he was abroad.

"Friday. The Aquitania nosed into its berth today and off the gangplank stepped Joe Kennedy," the *Film Daily* reported in its September 30 roundup. "Joe is peeved that anyone should start a deal to nab control of K-A-O without his knowledge and furthermore, while he was visiting such inexpensive pleasure haunts like Deauville and Le Touquet. Now he's back and almost anything you like may happen."

Kennedy wasted no time getting his name in the headlines. On Sunday, September 30, he was a guest on the weekly *Collier's Radio Hour,* broadcast live from WJZ in New York City at 8:15 P.M. He opened his talk with a strangely complicated introduction that managed to be both self-deprecating and boastful. "To tell you what little I have learned of the enormous activity we call show business," he declared, "would take so long that I tremble to think how much of your time, and my own, I could consume if I knew all there was to be known about the art of providing profitable and entertaining amusement to the masses." He proceeded to give his own capsule history of the medium before concluding that the days of "poor plots and pretty faces" were at an end because the "intelligent public . . . want substance to stories and real acting." With remarkable foresight, he predicted that television, the new entertainment medium that Sarnoff and RCA were experimenting with, might one day vanquish moving pictures, as the pictures had vaudeville. "Perhaps the time will come when television will carry the best of entertainment into the home. I don't know. The entire amusement industry is in a state of flux and experimentation. Novelties of today become obsolete tomorrow. But one thing I do know, and everybody who has any business in the amusement business should know—

that sophistication is on the increase, and that prizes in the form of profits only go the way of producers who bet their brains and money in the long run on popular intelligence."[2]

He said nothing about his future in the industry or about the negotiations going on to sell his companies out from under him.

On October 4, six days after his return from Europe, Sarnoff and Walker finalized RCA's purchase of K-A-O and FBO. Three days later, the *Los Angeles Times,* the *New York Times,* the *Film Daily,* and others reported the sale. The $300 million "Giant Born to Amuse" was destined to become "the General Motors of the entertainment field," predicted the *Los Angeles Times.* The *Film Daily* highlighted its story with a front-page banner: KENNEDY QUITTING AS RCA ACQUIRES K-A-O, FBO.

Sarnoff did not ask Kennedy to stay with the company; had he, Kennedy would not have accepted. He had nothing but respect for Sarnoff as a businessman, and the two would remain friendly, though never intimate, for the rest of their lives. But Sarnoff had his priorities and Kennedy had his. Sarnoff was committed to the future of RCA, Kennedy to the future of Joseph P. Kennedy and his family. In response to Sarnoff's perfunctory request "for your suggestions on anything you feel requires immediate action," Kennedy suggested with all the authority of his two years in Hollywood that before proceeding, Sarnoff should decide on "the type of production you want to make and the field of competition you want to enter." He added that he would be "glad to advise you on anything I think would be of any value whatsoever to you." His choice of personal pronouns was notable. He would advise Sarnoff on what he, Kennedy, considered of "value."[3]

When a reporter from the *Boston Daily Globe* asked about his future plans, he responded almost perfunctorily—but honestly—that he had never had any intention of remaining forever in the picture business. "I entered the amusement business with the viewpoint of a banker. If, after the organization of the new corporation it is running smoothly, I look around and get a good offer for my holdings, I will make a trade. I have wanted to get out of this business for some time." In the end, the sale of his companies to Sarnoff was a business deal, not a repudiation of his leadership. This was how he presented it to the press, and this was how he perceived it.[4]

On October 16, he sold the 5,500 shares of K-A-O he owned outright for a profit of $63,820. Two days later, he exchanged his option for 75,000 shares of K-A-O common stock for an option to purchase 75,000 shares of RKO. In December, he exercised the new RKO option and purchased 50,000 shares, which he then sold in several accounts, including one in the name of C. J. Scollard, his accountant, another in Rose's name, and a third in the name of his old friend and business partner Steve Fitzgibbon. His profit was $786,988.69. He would exercise his option on the remaining 25,000 RKO shares over the next two years for an additional profit of $489,494.10. In the end, he would emerge with a total profit of $1,276,482.79 on his K-A-O options, equivalent in today's currency to more than $15 million—for three months' part-time labor as chairman of the board.

And this was only the beginning of his profit taking.

On October 26, 1928, he agreed to swap his 37,500 shares of FBO for 37,500 shares of RKO, which he then sold for $35 a share on November 26, 1928. His minimum profit on this transaction alone (assuming he had actually paid $6 per share for his FBO stock) was $905,772.97, worth more than $11 million today. Additional shares of FBO and K-A-O stock registered in Kennedy's name or Honey Fitz's or in the name of the Gower Street Company, which Kennedy co-owned with Guy Currier, were also exchanged, one for one, for RKO shares and then sold for substantial profits.[5]

Although he remained employed by Pathé and would be for some time afterward, Kennedy sold short the options for the 50,000 shares he was to receive later that year, for a profit of another $310,000, worth almost $4 million in today's currency. That he was selling stock in a company in which he was an executive and doing it because of "insider" information may have been unethical, but it was not illegal and would not be until the SEC ruled it so under its first chairman, Joseph P. Kennedy.[6]

He had entered the industry a rich man, but he departed a multimillionaire with more than enough money in his and Rose's accounts and in the children's trust funds to support them all comfortably for the rest of their lives. He had been a good baseball player and a better than average shipping company executive, broker, banker, and studio executive, but when it came to making money, in up markets and down markets, good times and bad, Joseph P. Kennedy was in a league by himself.

For more than a decade, wherever he might happen to be, he had traded stocks, bonds, and options over the telephone with Mike Meehan, E. F. Hutton, Gurnett & Co., Palmer & Co., Hallgarten & Co., W. K. Johnson & Co., Halle & Stieglitz, Blair & Co., Lehman Brothers, Hayden, Stone, and others. He made his money as a trader, not an investor; he bought on bad news, sold on good news. During his years in the picture business, he stepped up his trading activity, taking full advantage of the insider knowledge he was privy to. He generated rumors, planted stories, spread gossip to drive prices up or down, depending on whether he was selling or buying. Rarely, if ever, did he hold on to a stock or bond for very long. He preferred getting out with generous profits to waiting for windfalls.

On November 30, 1926, after ten months in the film business, his "capital account" held $373,394 and his real estate holdings were limited to his modest house in Brookline. Less than three years later, on October 31, 1929, after the stock market crash, his capital account held $1,740,494 (more than $22 million today) and he had bought two new houses for the family. His net worth was five times what it had been three years earlier. And that didn't take into account his real estate holdings.[7]

A fabulously wealthy man now, he shifted his investment strategies, focusing more attention on preserving his fortune than on adding to it. He knew, from the inside, how easy it was to manipulate stock prices, that there was no necessary connection between share prices and the value or viability of companies. He had never trusted the market, and now, having put enough away in trust funds to support his family, he began to diversify and invest in real estate.

On November 6, 1928, he purchased in his and Rose's names the Hyannis Port house they had rented for the past several summers. According to Ted Kennedy, his father had had his eye on the larger, grander house on the edge of the water, but Rose preferred the smaller one they eventually purchased because it had room for a large lawn where the children could play in full sight of whoever was delegated to watch them from the front porch. The house was uncannily sited at the same distance from the sea as Kennedy's childhood home in East Boston had been. Because it was barely large enough for the family and Kennedy was not lacking in money to spend, he hired the Boston architect who had built it in 1903 to enlarge it to fourteen rooms and add a home theater in the basement.[8]

From this point on, the Hyannis Port house would be the Kennedy family's primary residence, though they seldom spent more than a few months together there every summer. Kennedy could well have afforded a larger, more luxurious house, even a mansion, in a more exclusive, high-end resort community. But he chose to stay in Hyannis Port. For the children, it was perfect. "Our whole lives were centered in this one place," Ted Kennedy recalled in his memoirs. "We didn't really go out to other places to play. We didn't go off to other kinds of events. It was all here, all here: all the playing, all the enjoyment, all the fun." They played games and cards and read and gossiped in the living room and on the porch and spent a good part of every day on the big lawn in front of the house: calisthenics in the morning, ball games in the afternoon, and after dark, the Kennedy family variation of "flashlight" tag, which they called "murder." At night, they watched first-run films in the basement, with fixed chairs for the children, a more comfortable easy chair in front for Kennedy. The bedrooms were on the second floor. Downstairs, in the kitchen, dining room, large living room, and porch, the children ruled, and the scene was one of barely controlled chaos, with young bodies flying madly back and forth, Rose trying to maintain order, and Kennedy, when he was there, taking it all in from his perch on his balcony outside his upstairs bedroom or his favorite chair in the corner of the living room.[9]

The family home in Riverdale was large and comfortable, but not for eight children, and it was rented, not owned. In May 1929, six months after he bought and remodeled the Hyannis Port house, Kennedy closed on the purchase of a "large brick Georgian residence" described by the *New York Times* as "one of the most imposing" in Bronxville. He paid $250,000 for the property, equivalent in today's currency to over $3 million. For it, he got a three-story colonnaded mansion on a crest of land, "its red-tiled roof," according to Ted, "catching the sun above a thick scattering of tall old trees." There were twenty rooms on six acres of landscaped gardens and playing spaces, a gardener's and a chauffeur's cottage, a basement billiards room, "such modern wonders as shower baths, an oil-burning hot water heater, and a number of enclosed porches," and a five-car garage. The younger children occupied the second floor. The older children had rooms on the third floor, which also contained a large playroom, the governess's bedroom, and a train room, where Joe Jr., Jack, and later Bobby ran the Lionel cars round and round. Ted, when he came along, was permitted to watch as long as he positioned himself away from the switches.[10]

Kennedy had a room of his own, on the ground floor, with a large sofa bed. When he was home, which was seldom, his door was always open to his children, who would spend time with him, sprawled on his sofa bed. Upon his return to Bronxville from wherever he might have been—New York City or Boston or Hollywood on business or Palm Beach for his winter vacation—he would pepper each of them with questions about friends, teachers, sports, their siblings. And they would talk, uninterrupted, about this and that and the other, while their father heard them out, his blue eyes focused directly and solely on the child in the room with him. He dispensed advice occasionally but listened more than he spoke, accepted what he was told as gospel, and was unfailingly supportive and sympathetic, especially when it came to problems with teachers.[11]

In mid-September 1928, Kennedy received an odd letter from Franklin Delano Roosevelt, who was managing the presidential campaign of New York's Irish Catholic governor, Al Smith: "Information comes to me, that, having weighed the attitude of the two candidates you have decided to support Governor Smith. I sincerely hope this is correct and if so, won't you write me confidentially, as there are some matters upon which I would appreciate your suggestions and counsel. . . . This is a personal letter. I am not writing you as a member of the Democratic National Executive Committee, nor am I leading up to the matter of a campaign contribution."[12]

There is no evidence that Kennedy ever answered Roosevelt's letter—and for good reason. Though Smith was from Kennedy's new home state, New York, an Irish American, and greeted in near messianic fashion by Honey Fitz and Mayor James Curley on his campaign visits to Boston, Joseph P. Kennedy, a lifelong Democrat, neither contributed to nor endorsed his candidacy. He had grown up revering gentlemen Irish Catholic businessmen/politicians such as the sainted Patrick Collins and wincing at loudmouthed, backslapping, plainspoken, stump-singing, and often corrupt Irish pols such as Honey Fitz and James Curley. Kennedy was proud of his heritage, proud of his parents, and a more devout Catholic than Al Smith would ever be. But he may have been slightly embarrassed by the informality of Smith's campaigning in his shirtsleeves and suspenders, singing "The Sidewalks of New York," and throwing kisses to his admirers as if he were a movie star, not a candidate for the highest office in the land.

Over the past few years, Kennedy had spent more time in Holly-wood and Los Angeles than in New York City or Boston, and with Republicans such as Louis B. Mayer, who revered Herbert Hoover as Irish Americans did Al Smith. Kennedy was not a political chameleon who changed parties when he changed environments. Still, in 1928 his interests as banker, businessman, and millionaire were more in line with those represented by the Republicans than the Democrats. He had profited enormously from the "Coolidge boom" and was convinced that Hoover was better positioned than Al Smith to keep it on track. So he resisted the pull of habit and tradition and the importuning of his father-in-law, who, Rose Fitzgerald Kennedy remembered, "was a big backer of Al Smith" and put "a lot of pressure . . . on Joe to back him." Although he would not publicly back Hoover, neither would he contribute any money to the Smith campaign. Instead, he sat out the election. He would later intimate to Charles Francis Adams III, whom Hoover had appointed secretary of the navy, that he had voted Republican. "I told Mr. Milbank at lunch the other day," he would confide to Adams, "that I considered your appointment was reason enough for President Hoover's election and sufficient justification for a good Democrat like myself to vote for him again."[13]

Though he had cashed out of K-A-O and FBO and no longer had any relationship with First National, Joseph P. Kennedy was still in charge of Pathé. He had been brought in to stabilize the Pathé stock and bond prices until such time as the company was swept up into a vertically integrated conglomerate with theaters to provide exhibition venues for its newsreels and features. While he awaited that outcome, his responsibility was to keep the films coming, the profits at a reasonable level, and stock and bond prices stable, which he accomplished without a great deal of effort. In truth, he paid little attention to the studio that fall. His major concern was *Queen Kelly,* as Swanson's picture with von Stroheim, formerly *The Swamp,* had been retitled.

The film had been scheduled to begin shooting in early fall, but as late as mid-October there was no sign of Swanson or von Stroheim on the lot. "Just why the dark and shivering mystery about the delay in starting the picture?" Harry Carr asked in his October 21, 1928, *Los Angeles Times* column. "Out at F.B.O. they seem to shudder at the mention. The picture was to have started on September 3; it was now to start about the first of November—maybe."[14]

Shooting did indeed begin on November 1, 1928. To make up for lost time and to satisfy his own obsessive work habits, von Stroheim pushed his crews night and day, then spent the evening viewing the rushes. Kennedy arrived in Los Angeles during the first week of shooting and sat in on some of these sessions, but more as a tourist than a producer. Swanson appeared delighted with the early scenes and the care von Stroheim was lavishing on her. Still, as E. B. Derr (who had been delegated to watch over von Stroheim) reported by "Confidential" telegram to Kennedy on December 6, von Stroheim had not yet scripted an "ending" and the film was already monstrously long. "Everything suggested [for possible cutting] he calls milestones. I wish he had one around his neck. . . . I will be with Glazer [another of Kennedy's advisers] to determine what items can definitely be cut and unless you object only way to cut out four excessive reels is to order von to abandon those episodes or sequences to get it down to ten reels."[15]

No one was pushing the panic button yet. Kennedy still trusted in the men Swanson had earlier referred to as his "watchdogs," Derr in particular, and had every reason to believe they would be as ruthlessly effective with von Stroheim as they had been at FBO and with C. B. DeMille at Pathé. None of them, unfortunately, had ever come up against anyone with the talent for self-deception, bravado, and abusive behavior that von Stroheim displayed every day. Vehemently and with unremitting concentration, he blamed everyone else for the delays and cost overruns and insisted that if left alone, he would turn out the masterpiece expected of him.

There is no telling whether Kennedy would have fared any better than Derr and his other advisers had he stayed in Hollywood, taken personal charge of scripting, shooting, and editing, and confronted von Stroheim directly. But as much as he wanted his first film with Gloria to be a glorious one, he was not going to let it interfere with his winter vacation in Palm Beach. Eddie Moore and Ted O'Leary, who worked for him in New York City, had taken the train south with him. They were joined by J. J. Murdock and Pat Casey, the former K-A-O executives with whom Kennedy had traveled to Europe that summer. After two weeks alone with the boys in Palm Beach, Rose arrived, then the Marquis de la Falaise de la Coudraye, Gloria's husband, who had decided to take a detour through Florida on his way back to Paris. The shifting constellation of bodies swirling around Kennedy kept the man who feared being alone fully occupied.

Never far from a telephone—except when he was on the golf course or at the beach—Kennedy fielded a constant stream of calls from the Pathé studio and the *Queen Kelly* set in Hollywood, none of them with particularly good news, but none foretelling the disaster unfolding. Edmund ("Eddie") Goulding, a British director who had established a reputation as a talking picture wizard, had been brought in to add sound sequences to accompany the silent footage. A voice coach had been hired on an eight-month contract to give Swanson daily lessons. The picture still appeared salvageable, though advance sales through United Artists, which was handling distribution, were tepid. Filming had been shifted from the FBO studios, which were now part of Sarnoff's RKO empire, to the Pathé studio in Culver City. To ease the transition—and demonstrate his affection for Gloria at a time when he was three thousand miles away—Kennedy built her a "bungalow" on the Pathé lot that was even more "elaborate" than the one William Randolph Hearst had built for his mistress, Marion Davies, in 1925. "Mine had a living room with a grand piano, a full kitchen, a wardrobe, a fitting room, and a big bedroom," Swanson wrote in her memoirs. "It also had a private entrance from the road and a private garage. I could only surmise that Joe Kennedy was starting to do very well for himself in the movie business. And that he loved me." What she didn't yet understand was that Kennedy's gift had cost him nothing; he had charged the bungalow costs to her production company.[16]

Von Stroheim, as was his wont, shot take after take—hours of film and crew time expended on scenes that would never make it into the final picture or, if they did, would consume only a few minutes. Eight weeks after shooting had commenced, he had finished only the first part of the film, set in the mythical kingdom in which the prince meets and falls in love with Patricia Kelly, played by Gloria Swanson. On January 2 he began shooting part two, which took place in Africa, where Patricia had been summoned by her dying aunt, who ran a dance hall there. Quite a few kinky scenes had already been shot, some involving nudity, but compared with what would come next, they were remarkably tame. As part two of the film opens, young Patricia, upon arriving in Africa, discovers that her aunt not only runs a bordello but has decided to marry off her convent-schooled niece to the wealthy brothel manager, Jan Vryheid—a drunkard and a degenerate, crippled, leering, and lascivious—played by character actor Tully Marshall.

Swanson had persevered through the filming of the European scenes and the first few days on the African ones, trusting that in the end E. B. Derr would succeed in reining in von Stroheim. As late as the morning of January 21, she had cabled Kennedy in Palm Beach with delight: "EB successful. Von toeing the mark. . . . Watch my smoke. Kindest regards."[17]

And then, that same day, it all fell apart. Von Stroheim had instructed Tully Marshall to drool tobacco juice on Swanson's hand as he put on her wedding ring. Swanson, disgusted and near nauseated, ran out of the studio and placed a call to Kennedy. "My first words were: 'You had better get out here fast,'" she recalled in her unpublished notes. "Then I went into everything that I had been concerned about—secretly."[18]

Kennedy was not prepared to cut short his vacation, even for Swanson. Instead, he picked up the phone, called von Stroheim in Hollywood, and fired him. Derr brought in playwright Eugene Walter to read von Stroheim's script, view the thirty reels (about five and a half hours) of film already shot, and offer suggestions on how the film might be completed. On January 25, Derr summarized Walter's findings in a long telegram to Eddie Moore in Palm Beach.

The sins of von Stroheim were legion, and Derr, citing Walter's report, expatiated on each and every one of them. The film as scripted and shot was "slovenly, gross, often revolting . . . in execrable taste . . .

not coherent nor believable nor in good taste nor human." Above all else, von Stroheim had failed to create a worthy "vehicle" for a star of Gloria Swanson's magnitude. "Her characterization as depicted is negative and retreating and passive and at no time does one single solitary thing which would show any evidence of strength or individuality or of charm or of any of her attributes. Her characterization as written could be played by any third-class leading woman. Up to end of first half she is depicted as either the most exasperating sap or a potential prostitute. . . . All she does is yield and weep which becomes deadly monotonous in spite of client's skill." The entire film, Derr concluded, had to be re-scripted with sound sequences added and additional scenes written to bring the story to an end and fill in the gaps von Stroheim had left behind him. No one wanted to abandon the project. A way had to be found to save it without damaging Swanson's "star value" or Kennedy's reputation as a take-charge studio executive.[19]

Money was also an issue. Though Kennedy had refrained from putting his own capital into the production, he had lent a considerable sum to Swanson's production company, money that would be lost should the project founder. "The boss suggests that I write you," E. B. Derr telegrammed Scollard in New York in mid-February, "so that you and Tom can discuss the effect on the boss's income tax in the event it is decided to abandon 'Queen Kelly.' . . . Generally, the total cost will be about $600,000."[20]

Kennedy arrived in Los Angeles in early February and was driven to the studio, where he met with his advisers and looked at some of the footage. "After more than an hour of waiting," Swanson recalled in the notes for her memoir, "a very anxious—a very white man charged into the bungalow living room alone. He slumped into a deep chair—put his head in his hands and grumbled and groaned like a hurt animal— His first words were in a quiet voice. 'I've never had a failure in my life.' . . . He put his arms around me and presently I felt his face was wet— Why, this big strong man had shed a few sultry emotions. Bravo—it can happen to the strongest of us."[21]

Swanson blamed Kennedy for the debacle. He had promised that his "watchdogs" would protect her from von Stroheim, then disappeared entirely. She refused even to contemplate returning to the set—or the project—and without Kennedy's knowledge had gone to see Jesse Lasky about doing her next picture for Paramount. Kennedy wrote his employee and mistress's husband, the Marquis de la Falaise, hoping that he would be able to exert whatever influence he had to get his wife back to work on *Queen Kelly*: "I went out there and found Gloria in very bad shape and in the hospital, as the result of practically a nervous collapse. She was down to 108 in weight and her attitude towards the picture, and everybody connected with it, was quite hostile. I looked at the picture and agreed that it certainly could not be released in its present form. . . . There is no need to go into the personal reaction of Gloria toward owing me considerable money on the picture, but it was far from a pleasant one. . . . I think her whole attitude was due to her overwrought condition and the discouragement over the whole situation. We had a very drastic showdown after the Lasky incident, and I insisted that some sort of a finish must be made because there was too much money at stake and too much loss of prestige if the picture was not finished. . . . Whether it will ever get started, whether it will ever see a finish, whether (when it is finished) it will be any good, I can give you no information whatsoever. If there is a reasonable chance of finishing the picture and my presence in California will help, Rose and I will go out there again. It is the chief concern now, as there is already over a million dollars invested with nothing to show. I am not giving you this story to annoy you but just to keep you posted on what is going on."[22]

In the midst of this Sturm und Drang, Kennedy was called back to the East Coast. His father had been taken ill with degenerative liver disease and been admitted to Deaconess Hospital in Boston. The train trip across the continent was never an easy one, though it had become faster and more luxurious since the Atchison, Topeka and Santa Fe Railway rolled out the *Chief* in November 1926. Those willing to pay the extra fare were whisked east—from Los Angeles to Chicago, with a brief layover in Albuquerque—in just under fifty-seven hours, three nights and two days, or so the timetable promised. Along the way, passengers were invited to make full use of the specially designed "two-car set" in the front of the train, which "included a dining car [with room for forty-two passengers] and club lounge, with bath, barbershop, and soda fountain." From Chicago, passengers such as Kennedy who could afford it boarded the *20th Century Limited* for the day-long trip to Grand Central Station in New York.[23]

Kennedy arrived in New York in mid-March and would remain there, commuting back and forth to see his father in Boston until early May, when the doctors told him (wrongly, it would turn out) that P.J. was out of immediate danger. Rescue work on *Queen Kelly* continued in his absence. He and Swanson talked regularly on the telephone, though that was not easy. It took several telegrams back and forth to set up each phone appointment. "Shopping today for house furnishings for Mrs. Kennedy," Kennedy wired Swanson on April 23. "Will call tomorrow. Nothing new."[24]

In early April, Swanson and the cast of *Queen Kelly* returned to the Pathé studio to shoot a new beginning and ending for the film. Gloria approved the script, then, after screening the footage from the ten days of filming, rejected it. As she had previously rejected every other suggestion for re-scripting and reshooting, the project was put on hiatus. None of this made Kennedy happy. Swanson was now interfering with his plans to get *Queen Kelly* finished and recoup at least some of his money—and reputation. On April 15, he called the marquis in Paris with the latest bad news: "Picture likely be shelved. Approximate loss between eight hundred and million. . . . Have been unable to get to California to find out how things are because my father's illness which is dragging on. Nothing can be done. Just keeping you advised."[25]

British director/writer Eddie Goulding, who in Kennedy's absence had grown closer than ever to Swanson, suggested that she draw attention away from the *Queen Kelly* fiasco by quickly making a lighthearted talkie, her first, which he offered to write and direct. Kennedy, perhaps worried that if he did not agree, Swanson would follow through on her threat to return to Paramount, gave the go-ahead and arranged for the film, which would be distributed by United Artists, to be shot at the Pathé studio.

With a new picture to work on, a director/writer she trusted, and a temporary surcease to her *Queen Kelly* travails, Swanson was satisfied for the time being. In New York, Kennedy was busy as usual, juggling multiple, and at times conflicting, business interests. In April, he solidified his control of Pathé, his only institutional connection to the film industry, by having himself elected chairman of the board.[26]

In May, after two full months in the East and persuaded by the doctors that his father was well past any danger, Kennedy boarded a train from Grand Central that would connect in Chicago with the westbound *Chief*. He arrived in Los Angeles on May 17. The next morning, a Saturday, he was at the Pathé studio when the news he had dreaded caught up with him. His father had died.

The funeral was scheduled for Monday, May 20, at the Church of St. John the Evangelist in Winthrop, not East Boston. Kennedy might have requested that the funeral be put off a few days so that he could attend. But what purpose would that have served? There was no widow to comfort. He had no desire to listen to hours of funeral tribute or attend wakes. His father's friends were not and had never been his. He would grieve by himself, three thousand miles away.

The Kennedy family, now of Bronxville, was represented at the funeral by Rose and Joe Jr. "I was terribly disappointed not to be there myself," Kennedy wrote Joe Jr., "but I was more than proud to have you there as my own representative and delighted everybody liked you so much. . . . I do not know how long I will have to stay here to finish the job I came out to do, but in the meanwhile, help mother and everybody out as much as you can and I will be with you as soon as possible."[27]

He also wrote Jack, whose birthday he was going to miss again, to say that he had tried but failed to finish up his work on the coast "so I could get home and have a little fun with you all at the beach. . . . You may be sure I will get home as quickly as possible and when I do I will get busy on that horse arrangement so that you can do some regular horseback riding. I hope everything finished up well at school and that you are helping mother out as much as possible."[28]

Queen Kelly had been quietly shelved, while Kennedy and Swanson figured out if and how it might be salvaged. Eddie Goulding was already at work on Swanson's next film and first talkie, *The Trespasser*, a "weepie" about a poor Chicago secretary who marries a rich young man. When the man's father has the marriage annulled, the secretary is left alone to raise the baby. Kennedy had read the script on the train returning to Los Angeles in mid-May. "Just finished reading story out loud to Ted [O'Leary] and we both cried," he cabled Swanson from the train. "If that isn't the greatest motion picture that anyone ever shot I want to go back to stock manipulation. I could see you in every scene. You certainly did a marvelous job. I am so happy for you."[29]

On arriving in Hollywood, he invited Swanson, Goulding, and a few others to lunch and a script reading at Rodeo Drive. During lunch, Goulding, having decided that the film needed music, asked Swanson if she could sing. "'She sings beautifully!'" Swanson recalled Joe calling "out like a proud parent. . . . 'Why, Gloria wanted to be an opera singer when she was young. She's told me so many times.' Before I could be embarrassed that he had, as it were, compromised me in front of strangers, I read easily in the eyes of [those present] that our secret was no secret to begin with. I realized that Hollywood saw us as a modified version of William Randolph Hearst and Marion Davies, only unimpeachable because we were both solidly married with children; beyond whispers, therefore, and entirely free of the possibility of louder accusations. So be it, I thought; at least I don't have to spend the next two months or two years or two decades playing games."[30]

The Trespasser was scripted, shot, and edited in just three months and previewed at the Rialto Theatre in New York in mid-July. Because United Artists, the distributors, had no first-run New York house available that summer, it was decided to open *The Trespasser* in London in August, then perhaps move it to Paris and Berlin to gather maximum publicity before an American opening later in the fall. Kennedy, who finally had a hit on his hands, though one he had had nothing to do with, was going to enjoy every minute of it. He was smart enough to realize he and Swanson could not attend the European premieres as a couple, so he invited Rose and his youngest sister, Margaret, to sail with him to London on the *Île de France*. Swanson would sail to Paris on the *Olympic* with her own traveling companion, her friend Virginia Bowker. In Paris, she would collect her husband, Henri, and then cross the English Channel with him for the London opening.

According to *Variety, The Trespasser* premiere was nothing less than "a sensational smash"—and both producer and star reveled in it.

Kennedy especially, Swanson recalled, was almost giddy with the adulation. His "constant fervent attention" embarrassed her and distressed Henri. Rose appeared oblivious to it all.

The two couples celebrated their London triumph in Deauville, then returned to Paris. While Kennedy attended a series of business meetings, Gloria and Rose went shopping at Lucien Lelong, at the time Paris's leading couturier, "and ordered our clothes there. It may sound easy, but it was hard work," Rose remembered. "Gloria had to order something spectacular . . . and, as she was quite short, it was always more difficult. It is always more difficult to dress a short woman than a tall woman. I am not very tall and she only came up to my shoulder."

While in Paris, Swanson discovered that her husband was having an affair with the American actress Constance Bennett, whom she suspected Kennedy had slept with as well. According to Rose, Swanson threatened to "get a divorce at once" and told Kennedy she would never again appear in public with Henri. "Joe was dumbfounded and flabbergasted." The last thing he needed was a divorce court scandal interfering with the publicity for his and Swanson's hit film. "Joe said he had put a lot of money into the picture, also time and effort and he was not going to lose it all for a personal disagreement on the part of the star and her husband." Swanson agreed and, accomplished actress that she was, made believe that she and Henri were still a loving married couple. "Henri moved to separate quarters in the hotel," but in public, Rose remembered, "Gloria and he were hand in hand, all smiles and to all appearances very happy." On September 18, as Rose, Kennedy, sister Margaret, Gloria, and Virginia Bowker boarded their ship bound for New York Harbor, the marquis was there to wave good-bye for the photographers.[31]

Swanson recalled in the notes for her memoir the near lunacy of sailing home with her lover and her lover's wife and sister. It was a particularly "crazy experience because by this time J. P. was brazen about his feeling for me, example: After dinner one night, he with his four ladies wife-sister-Virginia and me were sitting in the salon. At the next table was a man who obviously wanted to get a good look at me and was staring— It was embarrassing but was made worse by Mr. K's telling him to stop, turn around, in no uncertain terms—what his wife and sister thought Virginia and I could never figure out—the whole trip was nerve racking for me—because while someone may be difficult to find on a ship he never left me out of his sight—and if his wife wanted to find him all she had to do was find me. . . . The curious part of the whole situation was that I felt no guilt feeling about Rose. She was an enigma to me. She didn't show any sign of caring if Joe was possessive of me— She treated me as if I were one of the family—I wanted to say little do you know but I couldn't because there were times when I was sure she didn't know and times when I was sure she didn't care."[32]

To her dying day, Rose would deny that there was anything other than a business relationship between her husband and Gloria Swanson. The ridiculous rumors of her husband's relationship to Gloria, she told her ghostwriter, had begun only because when their boat docked in New York Harbor, she stayed behind in her cabin to avoid being photographed. The reporters greeting the boat, seeing Gloria and Joe on deck without her, assumed that they had vacationed together in Europe. Rose's story seemed so preposterous that her ghostwriter didn't include it in her published memoir.[33]

Swanson did not return immediately to the West Coast but stayed behind in New York to do some publicity work on her new film. Her children, her nanny, and a few friends were imported east to be with her. She no doubt spent some of her nights in New York City with Kennedy, but in hotels or borrowed apartments well out of public view. There was nothing out of the ordinary in Kennedy's staying overnight instead of returning to Bronxville. In February 1932, while Rose was in Boston giving birth to her ninth child, Kick would innocently include in her twelve-year-old stream-of-consciousness letter to her mother the fact that "Daddy did not come home last night. We do not know when he is coming."[34]

Swanson and her daughter visited Bronxville for a Halloween party in 1929, and "little Gloria" went to school with Kick, who was profoundly disappointed when her schoolmates refused to believe that her friend was actually Gloria Swanson's daughter. (In her memoir, Rose identifies Pat as the child who took little Gloria to school, but Pat was only five at the time, four years younger than little Gloria and not yet in school.) That Christmas, Rose made sure to send presents to Los Angeles for the Swanson children, and Swanson reciprocated by directing her New York assistant to buy the Kennedy children presents. Because her first choice, a "puff billiards game," was all sold out, the assistant bought a "large horse game . . . quite expensive but [it] was suitable for all six children. Sent army ambulance auto for Bobbie and unbreakable doll for Jean."[35]

Swanson and Kennedy's "secret" would remain Hollywood's secret, which meant it was never much of a secret within the industry but was guarded from those outside it. The trade press, anxious to protect Hollywood's image, was not going to turn on its own. Big-city publishers and editors, Hearst among them, had long ago reached gentlemen's agreements to stay away from gossip about adultery and infidelity. Such subjects were not to be mentioned, even hinted at, unless and until exposed publicly in divorce court proceedings.

There would later be hints, originating with Swanson, that Kennedy intended to leave Rose and his family for her. In the notes for her autobiography, she referred to a church official in a red robe with "a handsome face and beautiful hands" who summoned her to a clandestine meeting in New York and asked her to give up Kennedy. In her memoirs, her ghostwriters elaborated on the story and identified Cardinal William O'Connell of Boston as the red-robed churchman who informed Swanson "that Joe had spoken about our relationship with some of the higher representatives of the Catholic Church [and] sought permission to live apart from his wife and maintain a second household with me." The story, published in 1980 when there was no one left alive to refute it, does not ring true. Neither does the casual aside, also in the memoir, that Joe wanted Swanson to bear his child. Joseph P. Kennedy was every inch the realist. He did not engage in quixotic quests for the impossible. He had been in and of the church all his life and certainly knew enough about church doctrine and practice to realize that he would never be granted "permission" to live with Swanson. There was no way he would have prostrated himself before "some of the higher representatives of the Catholic Church" to make a request he knew would be denied.[36]

Kennedy had no intention of leaving Rose and his children to live with Swanson in Los Angeles—or anywhere else. Other men might have had to make a choice between wife and mistress, but not Joseph P. Kennedy. Having a wife at home and girlfriends away from home was neither an ethical nor a logistical problem for him. He had always been a ladies' man. Among men of his social set, this was far from unusual. Though we know nothing about P. J. Kennedy's marriage, there is abundant evidence that Honey Fitz, Rose's father, had been serially unfaithful to her mother. Kennedy followed in this family tradition, while Rose, like her mother before her, did her best to look the other way. Before Swanson, there had been flings with dozens of women, in Boston, New York, Chicago, Palm Beach, and Hollywood. But the liaison with Gloria was different—and he and his friends knew it. Swanson was a catch, the most famous, the most alluring film star in the world and a woman who, while married, had no compunction about having relations with other married men. Kennedy had to have been delighted with his conquest. It gave him a cachet in Hollywood and a badge of honor he wore proudly in the company of his male friends.

And yet, their affair was not as important to him as Swanson wanted it to be. Years later, she would be so appalled by Rose's rather dismissive account in her memoir, *Times to Remember,* of her relationship with Joe that she wrote her own memoir, *Swanson on Swanson,* to correct the story. Still, as much as she tried to impress on the reader how infatuated Kennedy was with her, it does not appear that they spent much time together. During their romance, they were never in the same place at the same time for more than six weeks or so. Had he wanted to, Kennedy could have spent up to ten months a year with Gloria in Los Angeles (while Henri was in Paris) and pleaded business necessity for doing so. But he did not.

The inescapable truth was that for Joseph P. Kennedy, Swanson was another sexual conquest, one of many he would fit into his busy life. That he wandered from the marriage bed was inconsequential to him. Adultery was a sin, but one easily forgiven.

In notes headed "Joe Rosebud," Swanson tried to make sense of the fact that Kennedy, a devout, churchgoing Catholic and married man, was able to carry on his affair with her, a married woman, without shame or guilt. "Joe believed in hell and he believed in Purgatory. It didn't worry him too much because he also believed in confession and the forgiveness of sins. He believed you could wipe the slate clean just by going to confession. It worked for him like sleeping pills for other people." Swanson teased him often about his confessors, who she claimed were "all after his money. That's why they let him off with a penance of a few Hail Marys. . . . Joe always had a confessor handy. Someone at the Church of the Good Shepherd in Beverly Hills. New York and Hyannisport. There was always one on the boat to Europe too. . . . Joe usually knew in advance what the penance would be. He never wanted to take a chance on running into some smarty pants priest there in a dark confessional from some poor diocese where he didn't have any real estate holdings."[37]

Nine

LAST EXIT FROM
HOLLYWOOD

In September 1929, the eight Kennedy children moved into their new Bronxville home and prepared to return to school. Their parents were thousands of miles away in Europe and not expected back until the end of the month.

First days are never easy, not even for Kennedys, but this one may have been particularly tough. They had changed schools before, three times in the past four years, but they had always moved as a pack. Now, in September 1929, with their parents overseas, their oldest brother and sister were sent away: Joe Jr. to Choate in Wallingford, Connecticut; Rosemary to the Devereux School in Berwyn, Pennsylvania.

"Joe and I had agreed," Rose wrote in her memoirs, "that the responsibility for education for the boys was primarily his, and that of the girls, primarily mine." Joe Jr. was now ready for high school and had done moderately well at Riverdale, though schoolwork did not come easily to him. His father, who had never been a particularly good student, never ceased to remind him (though usually gently) that he could do better if he worked harder. The last year at Riverdale had been a tough one, as Joe Jr. had had to compile a good enough record—and complete enough courses—to move on to a good high school. When he succeeded in doing so, his father made sure to congratulate him. "Your making up those subjects," Kennedy wrote his son from Los Angeles in June 1929, "was a real worthwhile achievement, and while we may have had a little disagreement once in a while about some particular thing, I am very proud of your effort and results."[1]

Kennedy had no real problem with Riverdale for his girls, but he wanted something better for his boys, a school like Boston Latin with rigorous academics and competitive sporting teams. "Joe did a lot of investigating, thinking, and discussing," Rose wrote in her memoirs. "For a time his chief adviser was Mr. Pennypacker, who had been headmaster of Boston Latin, and who became dean of admissions at Harvard." Kennedy also contacted his Harvard classmate Russell Ayres, who was coaching baseball and teaching history at Choate, to inquire about the possibility of Joe Jr., and maybe Jack, transferring there in September.[2]

Choate was seventy miles away, closer to Bronxville than the older, more prestigious New England prep schools, and though Protestant, it was neither rigidly Episcopal like Groton or St. Paul's nor overly celebratory of its WASPish ancestors and alumni like Andover and Exeter. The Kennedy boys would be welcomed at Choate, while they might not have been at the New England boarding schools that the "proper Bostonians" attended.

"My only hesitancy about doing it," he wrote C. Wardell St. John, the Choate assistant headmaster (and headmaster's son), "is I realize that when the boys go away now to school, they are practically gone forever, because it is three years there and then four years at college, and you realize how little you see of them after that. I may be selfish in wanting to hold on for another year at least. . . . However I am talking the matter over with his mother and will try to come to a decision and make out the applications as you suggest."[3]

Kennedy filled out the application for Joe Jr. to enter in September 1929, Jack two years later. St. John wrote to thank him and "confess that we 'fell' immediately for those attractive snap shots that were clipped to the applications. Both boys look like mighty good Harvard material." Still not sure whether Kennedy would actually send the boys, he invited him, Rose, Joe Jr., and Jack to visit "before the end of the school year." Kennedy did not visit the school, but he did enroll his oldest son.[4]

Joe Jr. did not take immediately to the rigidly ruled prep school environment. As the privileged older son, he had ruled the roost at home, lording it over Jack and his sisters. Rose had tried to keep an orderly home, but as the family grew in size, she had concentrated her attention on the babies and on Rosemary, who needed more guidance than her brothers and sisters. She made sure Joe Jr. and Jack remained in good health, did their homework, got to school and church on time, learned proper table manners, watched their language, and took care of their younger siblings. She had long ago given up trying to make them clean up after themselves. Joe Jr.'s room was always a mess, his clothes a bit disheveled; he never made his bed or put away his clothes; and he spent far too much time roughhousing with his scrawny little brother Jack, who never gave up and never won.

Choate did not countenance such behavior. Roughhousing and teasing were frowned on, rooms had to be clean and neat, beds made, ties and jackets worn to class. Joe Jr. struggled, then adjusted and thrived. His father watched over his progress, offering advice and encouragement and interceding with the school officials when necessary. When, days after arriving at Wallingford (probably escorted there by Eddie Moore), Joe Jr. wrote to ask his father to arrange for him to go horseback riding on a regular basis, Kennedy suggested he concentrate on football instead. "Perhaps both of these things can be done but I would not give up the chance of participating in school athletics for the sake of riding horseback. I also have written the school for permission for you to attend First Friday [Mass], and I know you will fix this up so that you can go."[5]

Rosemary would also be sent away to boarding school that fall. Her parents had put off this day as long as they could. It was no secret to any of the Kennedys that Rosemary, now eleven, was "different from them and from children of her age group," as Rose would put it in her memoirs. She was attractive, as pretty as her sisters, if a bit taller and plumper, round-faced, with a lovely smile. But she had none of their athletic grace; she lacked their sense of humor and whimsy, their gift of gab. She was shy, withdrawn, a bit distant. Nothing came easily to her.[6]

The Kennedys had been given the same advice that was offered other parents of "mentally retarded" children. Rosemary should be sent away to a training school or institution for "slow" children. Rose was a loving, devoted mother, but that, the experts believed, was part of the problem, not its solution. The love of mothers for their "retarded" offspring blinded them to the reality of their children's deficiencies, the impossibility of a cure, and the dangers and disappointments "slow" children faced in the world outside the institution. It also led to the mother's focusing exclusive attention on the "retarded" child and neglecting the needs of their other children and their husbands.[7]

Rose worried about these issues, but she never wavered in the belief that her daughter should not be sent away. "Much as I had begun to realize how very difficult it might be to keep her at home, everything about me—and my feelings for her—rebelled against that idea, and I rejected it except as a last resort." Kennedy was as adamant that his eldest daughter remain at home. "When psychologists recommended that Rosemary be placed in an institution," Eunice later recalled, "he said, 'What can they do in an institution that we can't do better for her at home—here with her family?' So my sister stayed at home." Rose encouraged the other children to include Rosemary in their activities. "They were merely told that Rosemary was 'a little slow' and that they should help her and encourage her. When she did something well, tell her so. If she made a joke, laugh with her, don't give her a quick retort," she remembered telling them all. "If there is some activity going on, let her participate, invite her to be involved."[8]

Rose had sent Rosemary to school with Kick in Brookline and with Kick and Eunice in Riverdale, but at age eleven she had fallen so far behind them—and her classmates—that it no longer made sense for her to continue in a regular public or private school. The same September that Joe Jr. was sent away to Choate, Rosemary was enrolled in the Devereux School in Berwyn, Pennsylvania, a private boarding school founded in 1920 by Helena Devereux of Philadelphia, who had studied with psychologist Henry Goddard, author of the *The Kallikak Family: A Study in the Heredity of Feeble-Mindedness*. At Devereux, Rosemary would be taught (or, more properly, drilled in) silent and oral reading, arithmetic and making change, spelling, social studies, and the womanly arts of handwork (making doilies), music, art, dramatics, and sewing.[9]

With her parents in Europe, Rosemary was probably taken to Berwyn by Mary Moore. She would not see her mother, her father, or her siblings until Thanksgiving; visiting at Devereux was strongly discouraged. In mid-November, Kennedy received his first letter and responded immediately. "I cannot tell you how excited and pleased I was to get your letter. . . . I think you were a darling to write me so soon." He filled her in with news of the family: "Mother went over to Boston to see Grandma Fitzgerald." He bragged a bit about his Hollywood connections: "Miss Swanson is sending you a picture and writing you a letter." And he congratulated her on her accomplishments, while exhorting her to do better: "I was very glad to see a lot of improvement in the report card, and I am sure that within the next couple of months it will be even better." He closed by asking her to write again: "Thanks again, my sweetheart, and if you have some time write me another letter. Lots of love."[10]

Rosemary had a difficult time at first, but as her teachers reported to her parents after her first year there, she had made the necessary "social adjustments" to life away from home. She also learned to sew, sing, and dance, exhibited "excellent social poise and is quite charming at times," had done reasonably well in her arithmetic and in social studies and had "written several very good stories about the robin and her trip to Washington." Her major problem was that she had little or no self-confidence, needed constant praise and encouragement, was too hard on herself, and was given to outbursts of impatience.[11]

Rosemary would return to Devereux in the fall of 1930 for a second year, but, as her teachers reported in November, she appeared to have given up on academics. She was "impatient" in silent reading and, instead of attempting to comprehend the story, "skips a good deal and fills in from her imagination." She was not progressing in arithmetic because she "dislikes making the effort necessary to attain good results. . . . She is very impatient and does not persevere." Her progress in English class was stalled because she "dislikes exerting the effort necessary to accomplish acceptable results." Her teachers were especially troubled by her almost total lack of self-confidence and difficulty in concentrating on any but the simplest tasks. "Rose's achievements in class work are seldom commensurate with her ability, and an effort is being made to bring her work up to the standard she is really capable of. This is a difficult task, as she has so definitely acquired the idea that her abilities are negligible and that her work cannot reach [any higher] standard."[12]

Rosemary's second year would be her last at Devereux. She would return to Bronxville, but not to school. "As we had a large family," Rose remembered, "life probably was easier for her with us, because she liked to play with the younger children who were less advanced than the older ones and she could sort of keep up with them." Because her father was absent so much of the time, he had less to do with his oldest daughter than anyone else in the household. Neither a patient man nor one who easily accepted defeat, he had a great deal of difficulty coming to terms with Rosemary's condition. Like her teachers at Devereux, he clung to the hope that she could do better if only she tried harder and were more patient. "My father supported her," Eunice Kennedy Shriver would later recall, "but he was much more emotional, and was easily upset by Rosemary's lack of progress, her inabilities to use opportunities for self-development."[13]

T he "GALA PREMIERE of GLORIA SWANSON in her ALL-TALKING Sensation 'The Trespasser'. . . A Joseph P. Kennedy presentation" was scheduled for Friday, November 1, 1929. Kennedy was proud enough of the film—and his role in it (minimal though it was)—to invite dozens of friends and former business associates to join him at the Rialto in Times Square for the opening.

Gloria Swanson was his mistress, but she was also his business property. The discovery that she had a decent speaking voice and could sing made her potentially more valuable than ever. No opportunity was overlooked in publicizing the arrival in New York of the "Voice that has Thrilled Two Continents!" Swanson sang on a nationwide radio hookup; her recording of "Love, Your Spell Is Everywhere" was widely distributed; sheet music covers, banners, posters, and newspaper ads ballyhooed her newfound talent, while reminding audiences of her past achievements: "Her talking and singing voice will amaze you! Her supreme dramatic acting will hold you spellbound—her clothes will delight you! Secure Your Tickets Now!"[14]

The Trespasser turned out to be an enormous box office attraction, and given its minimal cost, a huge moneymaker.

On Thursday, October 24, eight days before *The Trespasser*'s American premiere, the stock market crashed. Prices steadied on Friday and Saturday, then plunged again on Monday and Tuesday. By the second week in November, the Dow Jones Industrial Average had fallen 40 percent from its high in September. Only a few escaped unscathed. Joseph P. Kennedy was one of them. "The crash in the market left me untouched," he wrote the Boston attorney who was working on his father's estate. "I was more fortunate this time than usual."[15]

Having learned from the inside how markets worked, he knew enough to resist the trading euphoria of the late 1920s. At base, a conservative man who disliked gambling, he had shifted gears, taken his profits, and months before the crash, refocused his attention on protecting rather than increasing his already considerable fortune. On leaving Hollywood, he had cashed in his options, pocketing millions of dollars. A portion of his Hollywood windfall was used to buy real estate in Bronxville and Hyannis Port; the rest was put into family trust funds and invested in blue chips and secure bonds.

Though Kennedy had scored a big hit with *The Trespasser,* he had no desire to go back to Hollywood and reestablish himself as a studio head. His tenure as a "picture man," more than three and a half years, had outlasted his previous stints as bank examiner, bank president, assistant general manager at Fore River, broker at Hayden, Stone, and private investor. It was time to move on to something new.

There was, however, one piece of unfinished business: *Queen Kelly.* On returning to Hollywood in November 1929, he gathered his troops to try once again to rescue the project and recoup at least some of the money he had lent Gloria Productions, the company he had organized for Swanson when they went into business together.

He and his advisers entertained dozens of ideas for reshooting or re-editing the picture. They considered hiring new directors and screenwriters, adding slapstick comedy, or, to take advantage of Swanson's newly discovered singing voice, converting von Stroheim's dark melodrama into a breezy operetta. They brought in Franz Lehár, the composer of *The Merry Widow,* to write a "*Queen Kelly* waltz." But with each attempt at rescue they were struck anew by the unwelcome reality that what *Queen Kelly* needed was an entirely new script and new director, and that was going to take hundreds of thousands of dollars.

After spending the Christmas holidays in New York with his family, Kennedy returned to Hollywood in February. It would be his last trip for a long time. Rather than continue to pour good money after bad or take on more debt, Kennedy concluded that the project had to be scrapped. In mid-March 1930, it was announced that work on *Queen Kelly* would "not be resumed."[16]

Two months later, Kennedy announced that he had retired "from active management" of Gloria Productions. His affair with Gloria had also run its course.[17]

In her memoir, published a half century later, Swanson would complain that he had run out on her and ended their relationship when she confronted him, sometime in the spring of 1930, about financial matters and insisted rather bitterly that his creative bookkeeping arrangements at Pathé and Gloria Productions had left him rich and her poor. Despite her charges—and the fact that there was probably some truth to them—Swanson stayed in touch with Kennedy and sought his advice in late 1930 about signing a picture deal with Joe Schenck at United Artists. When that deal went bad, she sought him out again, in October 1932. He made several suggestions to her, including that she hire someone outside United Artists to look over her contracts and verify her earnings: "It might help . . . if they thought someone connected with me was checking. . . . Maybe not. . . . Hope you won't mind my suggestions. You probably have them all in mind, but I believed they might be helpful." When in 1935 she (or Bette Davis) became interested in remaking *The Trespasser,* she telegrammed Kennedy to ask that the rights to the film be reverted to her. They exchanged several phone calls, though Kennedy complained that it was "harder to get [her private phone numbers] than the White House" number. She solicited his advice and help in getting an American visa for her ex-husband Henri and his new wife in 1940 and in securing a transfer for her son from one army company to another during World War II. Swanson would, in the years to come, send Kennedy photos of her grandchildren and condolence letters after the deaths of Joe Jr. and Kick. In 1950, after her career was rekindled with the success of *Sunset Boulevard,* she and her advisers consulted Kennedy and his staff in New York on a variety of items, including a proposal for a Gloria Swanson fashion line, a *Sunset Boulevard* sequel, and help on her tax returns.[18]

Only in the late 1950s, pursued by tax bills, did she turn on her former lover and business partner. Struggling to find new sources of revenue to pay her debts, her lawyer came up with the idea of releasing her old pictures—perhaps for television—and completing and reissuing *Queen Kelly*. In an attempt to figure out the "cost basis" of the picture for tax purposes, Swanson's lawyer contacted Kennedy's office to find out if he had taken a "tax loss" on *Queen Kelly*. If he had not, Swanson might still be able to do so.[19]

After some delay, Kennedy responded by writing Swanson and belittling the attempt to rescue *Queen Kelly*. "Now, I am not the one to say that anything isn't possible, but I wouldn't bet 10 cents in this new proposition." Still, he made a few suggestions as to how to raise money to complete the film—and even offered "to get some bank to loan the money." As far as the tax losses, he reported that his accountant didn't know if any had been taken, but even if they had not, the statute of limitations forbade Swanson from taking them now.[20]

Swanson, distressed by Kennedy's lack of enthusiasm and inflamed by her lawyer's charge that Kennedy had cheated her by taking her tax credit for *Queen Kelly,* drafted a letter, which she may or may not have sent: "It's about time (the last lap of our lives) that the truth concerning the most important matters in my life had God's spotlight turned on them, for it is possible that they have contributed to the fact that I have had to continue to work instead of relaxing as you have so many times advised me to do. . . . You know as well as you know your right name that every penny spent on 'Kelly' was returned to you <u>out of the profits</u> of 'the Trespasser.' . . . Moreover, you alone benefited taxwise for I certainly did not." She blamed Kennedy entirely for her current financial state. He had stolen from her during the brief time they were in partnership together by billing her wrongfully for expenses he had incurred—for travel, entertainment, her bungalow, and, most outrageously, the car he had given actor Sidney Howard as a reward for suggesting the title *What a Widow!* for one of her films. In the early 1930s, after promising to lend her money if she needed it, he had "proceeded to evaporate into thin air . . . leaving me with no alternative" but to give up her only asset, her United Artists stock.[21]

Swanson claimed in her 1980 memoir that she had trusted Kennedy with her career and her finances and asked no questions. If that was true, she had been a royal fool. Kennedy was in the picture business to enrich himself—and his family. He looked after his interests and expected those he worked with to look after theirs. He could not be faulted if he was better with figures and corporate structures than those he did business with. He had structured his deal with Swanson and Gloria Productions so that he and Pathé, the studio he controlled and in which he had a major investment, would come out ahead, no matter what happened.

What galled Swanson most was Kennedy's blithe dismissal of any responsibility for the sorry financial state he had left her in. After having refused for decades to admit to herself that she had been bested in their business—and personal—relationship, Swanson lashed out at her former partner and lover, attributing his reprehensible behavior to his Catholicism. He had cheated her without remorse because he knew his God would absolve him. "Speaking of being absolved," she wrote in the letter she may or may not have sent him, "does one really set oneself free from one's conscience (on the assumption that everybody possess one) by confession? There is only one God—and Joseph—he is mine as well as yours, though I have not contributed money to his glorification, I have paid for my mistakes (by the sweat of my brow rather than another's) and my sins, I hope, by my own suffering rather than Christ's."[22]

Swanson was wrong. If Kennedy had taken advantage of her financially and felt no guilt about it, it was not because he was a Catholic, but because he was a businessman.

With *Queen Kelly* scrapped, his business and personal ties with Swanson at an end, and FBO sold out from under him, Kennedy's only institutional connection to the picture business was his position at Pathé. The studio was still turning out pictures, but for how long nobody dared guess. The insoluble problem Pathé faced was that it owned no theaters in which to exhibit its films, and after the October 1929 crash, there was not much chance that it would find the wherewithal to purchase any. Kennedy, though nominally in charge of the studio, had paid it less and less attention in recent months. In his absence, the studio's chances of survival had gone from bad to much worse.

In early December 1929, a fire destroyed the Pathé sound studios in

New York. Ten people lost their lives, the newspapers cried scandal (there were no sprinklers installed), and production on new films was halted. That same month, Kennedy discovered that his plan to make Pathé talking films in French, German, Italian, and Spanish to avoid the heavy tariffs placed on American-made products was also going nowhere, in large part because in the aftermath of the stock market crash, it was impossible to raise capital to invest in the project.

On May 7, 1930, Kennedy announced that he was retiring as the active manager of Pathé but would retain his position as chairman of the board of directors. The reason he gave for his retirement was that he had decided to return to banking with Elisha Walker, who had been named chairman of Transamerica, the investment banking conglomerate organized the year before by the merger of the Bank of America and Blair & Co.

In early summer, Kennedy and Walker opened negotiations with Hiram Brown, the president of RKO, which was the only company large enough and rich enough to buy Pathé and the only one that required additional studio space. Kennedy valued Pathé's assets at $12.7 million, which included $6 million for its stake in the DuPont-Pathé Film Manufacturing Corporation, which produced raw film stock. Hiram Brown recommended to David Sarnoff that instead of buying the entire company for $12 million, as Kennedy proposed, RKO should purchase its studio, stars' contracts, and newsreel operation for $5 million.[23]

A deal was struck in early December. The purchase price was large enough to cover the redemption of the company's 7 percent bonds, but not to buy back its common or preferred stock. The stock prices fell immediately and dramatically: the common, which had been priced at 1⅑ at the end of the year (12 percent of its pre-crash price of 9), to 25 cents; the preferred from 2⅞ to 1⅛. Kennedy had disposed of his stock before the October 1929 crash and his bonds in August and September 1930, so he was not affected. Elisha Walker, whose investments were in bonds, not stock, would be fully compensated. "Deal signed six forty-five tonight," Kennedy wrote Walker on December 4, 1930. "Think it magnificent one for us. I am happiest because I know you will like it."[24]

"I can't tell you what a relief it is to me to get this cleaned up," he wrote his friend and former business associate J. J. Murdock five days later. "It was so loaded with dynamite over the last three or four years that anything could have happened at any time. I think we have worked out a deal for the Pathé security stockholders which can't help but make them all more than satisfied. I believe this has probably taken another five years off my life. I am going to stay around until the Stockholders' Meeting in January and if there is anything left of me then, I am going away for three or four months."[25]

Kennedy and his associates might have been delighted with the RKO deal, which protected their investments in bonds. Not so the thousands of stockholders who were left holding near worthless Pathé common and preferred shares. As chairman of the board and Pathé's most visible executive officer, Kennedy was bombarded with angry letters, many of them handwritten and addressed to him personally, such as the ones from Margaret Walsh of Brighton and Anna Lawler of Jamaica Plain, each of whom claimed that she had bought Pathé stock because Kennedy was involved with the company. "Knowing your father, the late P. J. Kennedy [and Honey Fitz]," Anna Lawler wrote, "I put my money into your enterprise, only to see where you are willing or trying to pass it over to another concern for about nothing. This seems hardly Christian-like, fair or just of a man of your character. I wish you would think of the poor working women who had so much faith in you as to give their money to your Pathé."[26]

Kennedy thanked Margaret Walsh—and the others—for their letters but emphasized that as an inviolable practice, he "never urged any of my friends to buy securities of any company in which I may be interested. . . . I honestly believe that this proposed trade will be of great benefit to the corporation and I urge you to send along your own proxies with those of your friends."[27]

Other communications were not nearly as polite as Walsh's and Lawler's. Some stockholders threatened to sue unless the company bought their stock from them, which it did in some cases, on the advice of its attorneys, Cravath, de Gersdorff, Swaine & Wood. A few threatened violence. "We are not going to plug you or we are not going to stick you in the back, but we are going to cut your throat from ear to ear as a warning to others what pulls the same deal. Now you may go to Florida or Europe or any other place but we will get you anyway when you least expect it."[28]

On January 5, 1931, "at a boisterous meeting, at which," according to the *New York Times,* "heavily armed private detectives were unable to preserve order, although they did succeed in preventing physical violence," the Pathé stockholders gathered to consider the RKO deal. The deal's opponents were livid beyond words at the way Pathé officials had "'rushed stockholders off their feet' to induce them to sign proxies." When Joseph P. Kennedy, considered by most to be the evil mastermind of the deal, "entered the room, he was greeted with epithets from minority stockholders, who questioned and heckled him when he tried to reply to them. The shouts of the irate minority carried through the partitions into the elevator corridor." Kennedy was asked directly "if it were not true that directors of Pathé were also directors of R.K.O., implying that the sale had been engineered by an interlocking directorate. Mr. Kennedy said that some directors, but not all, were on the boards of both companies." He answered as many questions as he thought he had to, then made his exit before the balloting began.[29]

Though the opponents of the sale may have been in the majority at the meeting—and certainly made the most noise—they did not control anywhere near the one third plus one shares required to block the sale. They could shout and heckle all they wanted and organize lawsuits to overturn the sale, but the deal went through.

The price of the Pathé preferred and common stock, already at its low, continued to fall to the point where the stock was delisted from the New York Stock Exchange. The price of the 7 percent bonds also fell as uncertainty gripped the market. Kennedy, with insider knowledge that the bonds would be protected and that RKO had sufficient funds to redeem them at par when they came due, took advantage of the falling prices and bought bonds, which he held on to until mid-September 1931, when he sold them for a considerable profit. To guarantee that the sale remained secret, he executed it through J. H. Holmes, a broker he had never used before and never would again.[30]

Immediately after the Pathé stockholders' meeting and the approval of the RKO deal in late January 1931, Kennedy boarded the train for Palm Beach, where he would spend the rest of the winter and a sizable portion of the spring. He kept in touch with his children—and with

Rose—by telephone, telegram, and letter. To show his love, he sent them all crates of oranges. Joe Jr. got one at Choate, as did Rosemary at Devereux and Jack, who, having completed the seventh grade at Riverdale with decent grades, no apparent illnesses, and a sturdier frame, had been sent off not to Choate, which might have appeared a bit too formidable for him as yet, but to Canterbury, a smaller school closer to home—and Catholic.

Away from home for the first time since he'd contracted scarlet fever as an infant, Jack was miserable. He was also losing weight, which had become a matter of concern not only to his parents, but to the headmaster and his wife, who had taken it upon themselves to put more flesh on his slender frame. While the other boys were allowed to switch tables in the dining hall each week, Jack was stuck with Dr. and Mrs. Hume for five straight weeks.

At age thirteen, he was already making light of the physical ailments that defined his daily existence. In a letter to his father, he described how at Mass that morning, he "began to get sick dizzy and weak. I just about fainted and everything began to get black so I went out and then I fell and Mr. Hume caught me. I am O.K. now. Joe fainted twice in church so I guess I will live. . . . We are reading Ivanhoe in English and though I may not be able to remember material things such as tickets, gloves and so on I can remember things like Ivanhoe and the last time we had an exam on it I got a ninety eight."[31]

Kennedy was worried enough about Jack's health to bring him to Palm Beach for Easter to rest and relax in the sun. On returning to Canterbury, Jack came down with a serious case of appendicitis. His appendix was removed, but too frail to return to school, he stayed in Bronxville for the remainder of the term. Kennedy, who had never been entirely happy with Canterbury (it had been Rose's choice), decided that come September, Jack would join his brother at Choate.

In May 1931, after a four-month vacation in Palm Beach, Kennedy returned north, stopping over at the Homestead in Hot Springs, Virginia, one of the nation's most prestigious and expensive resorts. Accompanying him was Arthur Houghton, with whom he no longer had any business dealings, only a commitment to golf and good times. During his three weeks at Hot Springs, his every step was chronicled in the New York society columns as he lunched, dined, rode, golfed, entertained, and was entertained by the Hot Springs royalty, including Ben Smith, one of Wall Street's most notorious—and successful—traders. Two weeks into his stay, Rose joined him at the Homestead. Husband and wife spent only a few days together before Kennedy took the train north to New York, leaving Rose behind for another week of vacation. "They went their separate ways," Jean Kennedy Smith recalled, and no one in the family thought it odd. When together, they appeared, at least to their children, to be quite content with each other. "Strange as it might seem," Ted Kennedy recalled in his memoirs, "Dad and Mother never fought." When, much later, Caroline Kennedy asked Rose how she had handled her "differences" with her husband, Rose replied, "I would always just say, 'Yes dear,' and then I'd go to Paris."[32]

Nine months after her rendezvous with her husband at the Homestead in Hot Springs, Rose Kennedy, back in Brookline again with Dr. Good, gave birth to her ninth child, Edward Moore ("Ted") Kennedy. Her husband had left months before for Palm Beach. "There was no need keeping Joe around in the winter," Rose remembered, "not in the middle of February for a baby so he went to Palm Beach." Still, she insisted to her ghostwriter, he was a devoted husband. While she was in the hospital giving birth to Ted, he had her meals sent "from the Ritz in a taxi. He felt so sorry for me being in a hospital."[33]

PART III

Washington

Ten

ON THE
ROOSEVELT TRAIN

WORST OF DEPRESSION OVER, SAYS HOOVER . . . RECOVERY NEAR, HE STATES, read the May 2, 1930, headline in the *New York Times*. In a speech the night before to the Chamber of Commerce, the president had declared unequivocally that the nation had "passed the worst of the great economic storm. . . . There is one certainty in the future of a people of the resources, intelligence and character of the people of the United States—that is prosperity."

The stock market, reassured perhaps by the optimistic predictions that followed President Hoover's cheerleading conferences with business leaders, had risen steadily through the first three months of 1930, closing at 294 on April 17, almost one hundred points above the low reached five months earlier. And then it resumed its steady slide downward. It would fall another 52.7 percent in 1931 and continue downward until it reached 41 on July 8, 1932. The economy collapsed with the market. Between 1929 and 1932, thousands of banks and tens of thousands of businesses failed; national income fell from $87.4 billion to $41.7 billion; annual net farm income decreased from $6.1 billion to $2 billion; residential construction declined 82 percent; sales in automobile and electrical manufacturing shrank by over two thirds; iron and steel production fell by 59 percent; unemployment rose from under 5 percent to nearly 25 percent.[1]

And Joseph P. Kennedy made money, lots of it. Having left the film industry with no intention of returning, he could concentrate his attention on trading securities from wherever he happened to be: Bronxville, Palm Beach, Hyannis Port, or somewhere in between. All that he required was a telephone connection to 35 West Forty-fifth Street, his New York City office, where loyal and discreet accountants and associates kept track of his financial records, recorded his stock transactions, monitored the trusts he had set up in 1926 before going to Hollywood, compiled monthly reports and profit and loss statements on all his accounts, paid his bills, and filed his tax returns.

After 1930, he increased his short selling in the nation's largest companies, anticipating that stock prices would continue to fall, which they did. He made money as American Tobacco, DuPont, Standard Oil, Pennsylvania Railroad, Liggett & Myers, Reynolds Tobacco, Westinghouse, and other blue-chip companies lost it. His short positions in the blue chips were balanced by long positions in the stocks of companies he had some connection to, such as Transamerica, Todd Shipbuilding, and the Atchison, Topeka and Santa Fe Railway.

He had an almost uncanny knack for being in the right stock, short or long, at precisely the right time. His December 1931 balance sheets show him with large short positions in American Can, which fell from 113¾ on January 2, 1931, to 57¾ a year later, and U.S. Steel, which over the same period declined from 142 to 37⅛. The other blue-chip stocks that he shorted behaved in much the same way. In many regards, he was his own hedge fund. In his largest non-trust accounts, the ones in his and Rose's names, he balanced his short positions with investments in stocks he expected to rise over time and/or pay healthy dividends. If the market went up, he would lose on the short sales but gain on the longs, and vice versa. In good times and bad, he found a way to make money. His end-of-the-year balance sheet for 1931 listed assets of $2.1 million; for 1932, his assets were listed as $4.2 million. And this in a year when the Dow Jones Industrial Average fell by more than 20 percent.[2]

Unlike the vast majority of American families, the Kennedys were not obliged to do any belt-tightening during the Depression years. Kennedy felt no need to go back to work or earn a regular salary. Rose was not put on a tightened expense account or asked to reduce the increasing costs of household servants and expenditures or the amounts she spent on her wardrobe and travel. The children experienced no difference in their daily lives. Joe Jr.'s and Jack's allowances at Choate were not as capacious as those of some of their classmates, but large enough. When Jack needed a new pair of skates, he bought them and informed his parents afterward. For him, the Depression was almost something to joke about. He was, he wrote his father in December 1931, doing his "Christmas shopping Saturday with another boy. Due to financial difficulties at Wall Street we will not be encumbered by any weight in that direction. Woolworths five and ten store will probably be our object Saturday."[3]

Kennedy was proud of his wealth, but he worried that the children might become spoiled by it. Jack especially was becoming too undisciplined, too careless, and too devil-may-care about everything he came in contact with: his health, grades, clothes, and money. It was not Kennedy's nature to scold or tease or punish his children, but it was also not in his nature to look away when he believed they needed a bit of firm guidance. "In looking over the monthly statement from Choate," he wrote Jack in April 1932, "I notice there is a charge of $10.80 [$170 today] for suit pressing for the month of March. It strikes me that this is very high and while I want you to keep looking well, I think that if you spent a little more time picking up your clothes instead of leaving them on the floor, it wouldn't be necessary to have them pressed so often. Also, there are certain things during these times which it might not be a hardship to go without, such as the University hat. I think it would be well to watch all these expenditures in times like these, in order that the bills will not run too high."[4]

The news that the industry's wonder boy was leaving the picture business had surprised many of those who had charted his rapid rise. The *Boston Daily Globe* reported on May 19, 1930, days after the announcement of his retirement from Pathé and Gloria Productions, that "those few in Hollywood who know the 'Blonde Banker' from Boston have a 'hunch' that he is about to break out in a bigger and stronger way! They say Lon Chaney, 'the man of many faces,' is a piker compared with Joseph Kennedy, the man of many plans, who operates so quietly and mysteriously in perfecting them that his close associates never know what he's going to do until he's already done it."

Over the next few years, Kennedy would be contacted on several occasions by those who hoped he would reinvolve himself with the industry. His answer was always no. In November 1931, he declined B. P. Schulberg's invitation to become a member of the Academy of Motion Picture Arts and Sciences, "inasmuch as I am now definitely out of the motion picture industry." "When I retired from Pathé and the Swanson thing," he explained to a friend trying to interest him in a film start-up company, "I really washed up my entire interest in the picture business." Other offers came his way as well, but he deflected them all, including one to meet with Bob Quinn, the owner of the Boston Red Sox, during spring training in Florida to discuss the possible purchase of the team.[5]

With millions of dollars in safe investments and real estate, much of it in trusts, he had retired secure in the belief that neither he nor his children nor his grandchildren would ever have to worry about money. But as the market continued to fall and the economic picture darkened through a second and into a third year of depression, he began to worry that the large fortune he had accumulated might not be safe and secure. He accelerated short selling in his own accounts through 1931 and in 1932 shifted more than $200,000 of the $780,000 in the children's trust funds out of equities and into cash. These were short-term expediencies. If the market continued to deepen, there would be no safe haven for the riches he had accumulated.[6]

In 1936, he would recall that during the darkest days of the Depression, in the winter and early spring of 1932, he had "felt and said I would be willing to part with half of what I had if I could be sure of keeping, under law and order, the other half. Then it seemed that I should be able to hold nothing for the protection of my family." Note the emphasis on "law and order." What Kennedy was beginning to fear was not simply the diminution of his fortune, but the destruction of the capitalist system that had made that fortune possible.[7]

As the Depression deepened, so too did the anger at the bankers, the brokers, the financiers, the men who had led the nation into this disaster. Some could simply be accounted fools or dreamers. But many more were indicted by the public as confidence men, criminals, thieves, and parasites who had stolen the people's wealth and the American future.[8]

The Depression, as Arthur M. Schlesinger, Jr., noted in the first volume of his *The Age of Roosevelt,* offered "radicalism its long awaited chance." The unemployed, underemployed, dispossessed, and hungry were not sitting idly by waiting for prosperity to return. Many were too numbed, too crushed, to protest, but a small and vocal minority were not. The Socialist and Communist parties more than doubled their tiny memberships and exploded in visibility. Communist Party organizers were actively operating in city neighborhoods from Harlem to Detroit, in the coal fields of Pennsylvania and Kentucky, at the River Rouge plant in Dearborn, among tenants and sharecroppers in the South and migrant workers in California, and outside and inside closed and closing mills and factories in the Northeast. Their argument was simple: capitalism had failed and needed to be replaced.[9]

Did the Communist Party or the Socialists, union organizers, radical agrarians, and Bonus Marchers pose a genuine threat to American capitalism and democracy? In retrospect the answer is probably no, but at the time this was not self-evident, certainly not to those who, like Joseph P. Kennedy, having amassed a fortune for themselves, had a great deal to lose.

Kennedy had tacitly supported Hoover for the presidency in 1928, but by the spring of 1932 he was convinced—and he was certainly not the only one—that four more years of Hoover in the White House would only deepen the economic crisis and provoke more strikes, protests, and marches on the Capitol building. "I was really worried," Kennedy would later tell Boston reporter Joe McCarthy. "I knew that big, drastic changes had to be made in our system and I felt that Roosevelt was the one who could make those changes. I wanted him in the White House for my own security, and for the security of our kids, and I was ready to do anything to help elect him."[10]

He had backed Hoover in 1928 because he thought he would keep the economy moving forward and stock prices climbing. He would support Roosevelt in 1932 because he hoped he would reverse the economic decline and falling stock prices. In his actions as New York governor and his speeches as a candidate, Franklin Roosevelt had persuaded Kennedy that he too feared for the future. Taking direct issue with Hoover, Roosevelt had declared unequivocally in his major addresses in 1932 that the Depression posed a greater threat to the nation than had the Great War. Any solution to the crisis involved some combination of increasing farmer purchasing power, assisting homeowners in preventing mortgage foreclosures, stimulating the sale of goods overseas, and expanding government planning and regulation. Only government action from the top down was going to get the economy moving again and preserve and protect capitalism. And only a man as self-confident and as practiced in the game of politics as Franklin Delano Roosevelt could get Washington moving again. Or so the Roosevelt campaign preached—and Joseph P. Kennedy came to believe.[11]

By early 1932, Kennedy had been at leisure for more than a year. He had neither the inclination nor the need to go back to work, but was intrigued by the idea of attaching himself to a national campaign for a candidate he believed in. He had been turned away from electoral politics by his father's defeat in East Boston and the clownish antics of Democrats such as his father-in-law, James Michael Curley, and Al Smith. Roosevelt, now governor of New York, brought Kennedy back into politics because he was a different sort of Democrat. He was an American aristocrat, a gentleman farmer, a Protestant, a patrician, a product of Groton and Harvard, and the only man running for president who was capable of stemming the economic crisis before it turned into a political one.

In the months and years that followed the 1932 presidential campaign, Joseph P. Kennedy would come to alternately revere and revile Franklin Delano Roosevelt. The two could not have been more different—in temperament, religion, family background, and just about everything else—but they had one critical trait in common. Each was a consummate charmer and regularly deployed his charm as a tool or a weapon to get what he wanted. It was difficult, if not impossible, to resist their importuning when they smiled their toothsome smiles, their blue eyes blazing with warmth. For the professional charmer there is a fine line between

charming and dissembling. Kennedy and Roosevelt crossed it occasionally, certainly in their dealings with each other. What is remarkable
about their relationship is how adept Roosevelt was at getting from Kennedy what he needed and how regularly he would resist giving much
back.

Having joined the campaign, Kennedy fought to find a place for
himself on the inside. Aside from an open checkbook, it appeared he
had little to offer. He had no experience in a national campaign, few
political connections outside of Irish American Boston, which was
fiercely committed to Al Smith for the nomination in 1932, and almost
no rich friends or business associates who were not Republicans. What
he did have were some connections in Los Angeles and access to the
most powerful man in California, William Randolph Hearst.

Kennedy had become friendly with Hearst and Marion Davies during his time in Los Angeles. He had visited them, often with Swanson, at San Simeon and at Marion's "beach house" mansion in Santa
Monica. Both Hearst and Marion were taken with Kennedy's charm,
humor, smarts, and lack of pretense. They weren't so sure about Gloria.
Marion found her a lot of fun, but so ridiculously pretentious that she
felt compelled to impersonate her in her 1928 film *Show People* as the
unsophisticated, buck-toothed Peggy Pepper, who changes her name
to Patricia Pepoire and starts making "art" films after she meets her
phony European count.

On January 2, 1932, Hearst had announced in a nationwide radio
broadcast and on the front pages of his daily newspapers that he was
supporting John Nance Garner of Texas, the Speaker of the House, for
the Democratic nomination because he was the only candidate who was
not an internationalist. The Hearst papers had been relentlessly pushing
the Garner candidacy since then. On April 19, 1932, either on his own
or at the suggestion of the Roosevelt campaign, Kennedy returned to
Los Angeles after a two-year absence, checked into the Beverly Wilshire
Hotel, and wired Hearst at San Simeon to ask if he could "fly up tomorrow morning, arriving about 1 o'clock." They spent the next day talking politics, movies, business, and the campaign. Hearst listened politely

to everything Kennedy had to say but showed no signs of changing his mind about Roosevelt. His candidate remained John Nance Garner of Texas.[12]

Two weeks later, on May 3, Garner soundly defeated Roosevelt in the California primary. Garner had no chance of winning the nomination, but he—and Hearst, his sponsor—now controlled two of the largest delegations to the convention, Texas and California. Roosevelt invited Kennedy to spend the weekend at Warm Springs, no doubt to discuss Hearst. Anxious to establish himself as a campaign "insider," Kennedy intimated to the press that he was an old friend of the candidate, which he was not. "I have known Governor Roosevelt for fifteen years and I remember what a fighter he was in the Navy Department. He cut more red tape and accomplished more than anybody thought could be accomplished. Certainly his record then and since ought to persuade every one that he is a real doer."[13]

The day after his visit with Governor Roosevelt, Kennedy wired Hearst at San Simeon: "If you care to hear my observations will call you on phone between four thirty and seven your time Wednesday night."[14]

On June 1, Kennedy, identified in the press now as a "New York banker and long-time associate of the executive," was invited to lunch with the governor in Albany. It was a heady time for Kennedy, whose association with Roosevelt had opened the door to wealthy, well-placed New Yorkers he had never before had occasion to come into contact with. Among his newfound acquaintances was the influential and omnipresent Herbert Bayard Swope, the gregarious, well-connected man-about-town, Democratic insider, former editor of the *New York World,* and at age forty-seven so striking (redheaded and jut-jawed, according to *Time* magazine) that Lucky Strike cigarettes hired him to pose with a "Lucky" in his mouth in its full-page magazine advertisements. Swope, who had a talent for making, maintaining, and amusing friends, had taken to Kennedy on meeting him. Kennedy, who gravitated to those whose connections, wealth, and wit were equal to his own, took to Swope as well. "He used to be with him a lot," Rose remembered, "because [Swope] had a sharp mind and [was] interested in politics. . . . We used to go to the theater and to his house and eat. . . . It was gay and . . . Irving Berlin used to come there too." Through

Swope, Kennedy met Bernard Baruch, whom he had always admired from a distance. Baruch was a South Carolina Democrat and Jew, in his early sixties now, tall, stately, white-haired, fiercely handsome, always nattily dressed in the most expensive suits and ties. As Rose recalled, he was "quite a name in those days. And we had come from Boston where you'd heard about those people but didn't associate with them."[15]

Swope and Baruch became not only friends, but business partners when they joined Kennedy and Elisha Walker in a scheme to gain control of the Brooklyn-Manhattan Transit Corporation (BMT), in anticipation of the huge price rise that was expected when state officials concluded the "cooperative," cost-cutting, revenue-enhancing consolidation agreement among the city's three subway lines that had been in the works for some time. Kennedy invested nearly half a million dollars in BMT stock, ten to twenty times more than his other "long" investments. Though the consolidation agreement would not be consummated for several years, the stock price jumped as soon as the negotiations began. Within three years, Kennedy's $489,000 investment would be worth more than $1 million. By the time he sold his stock, it would be worth even more.[16]

In late June, Kennedy flew to Albany for lunch and a meeting with the governor and his campaign staff. Raymond Moley, the Columbia University professor who had become Roosevelt's chief adviser on policy issues, recalled Kennedy as "a ruddy-faced, vigorous, and highly colorful talker. I arrived just as Kennedy was leaving and I well remember that when he paused at the door he turned to Roosevelt and said, 'I will keep my contact with W.R. [Hearst] on a day-and-night basis.'"[17]

Together with a small team of Roosevelt advisers and accompanied, as always, by the amiable, effective, and ever-present Eddie Moore, Kennedy boarded the *20th Century Limited* in Albany, bound for Chicago and the nominating convention. They checked into the Blackstone Hotel, where Kennedy began at once to lobby arriving delegates, explaining why he, a banker and businessman, was for Roosevelt.

It was imperative, the Roosevelt team believed, that their candidate win on an early ballot. No one dared predict what would happen if he did not. Because Roosevelt already had a majority of the delegates, but not the two thirds necessary for nomination, several of his supporters wanted to petition the rules committee to change the two-thirds requirement to a simple majority. Senator Burton Wheeler, who was in Chicago at the time and supported the change, recalled that Kennedy opposed it because he thought, rightly, that it might needlessly alienate southern delegates. At some point during the internal debate on whether to petition for the change, Kennedy, according to Wheeler, called FDR in Albany and urged him to abandon the effort. We don't know if Kennedy's call had any effect, but on Monday morning, as the convention was officially gathered to order, Roosevelt "issued a statement from Albany abandoning the fight" for a rules change.[18]

The convention opened on Monday, but it was not until 4:28 A.M. on Friday, July 1, that the roll call of the states was called. Roosevelt polled 666¼ votes, 89 more than a majority but 104 short of the necessary two thirds. He picked up 11½ votes on the second ballot, then another 5 on the third, but when the convention adjourned at 9:15 that morning, he was still 87 votes short of nomination. The scenario that he and his advisers had so feared was unrolling before their eyes. The convention hall and hotels were filled with rumors that the anti-Roosevelt forces and those who feared a deadlocked convention were prepared to rally behind Newton Baker, a successful corporate attorney who as a former reform mayor of Cleveland, secretary of war, and advocate for the League of Nations appeared to be the perfect compromise candidate. Since Al Smith had no intention of releasing his delegates, Roosevelt was going to have to get the votes he needed from Garner and his sponsor, William Randolph Hearst.

All evening long, members of the Roosevelt team tried to reach Hearst at San Simeon by telephone. Kennedy got through early in the morning and was able to persuade Hearst that Garner was not a viable candidate and that if the convention remained deadlocked, the delegates were likely to turn to Newton Baker, who was even more of an internationalist that Roosevelt. "I felt there was nothing to do," Hearst later wrote his wife, Millicent, in New York, "but communicate with Speaker Garner and tell him the truth about the whole situation." Garner agreed to withdraw, the California and Texas delegations switched their votes to Roosevelt, and he was nominated. No one in the convention hall was terribly surprised when Roosevelt named Garner as his running mate.[19]

Hearst would take full credit for Roosevelt's nomination and Kennedy full credit for bringing Hearst into the fold. Both men exaggerated their roles. It is likely that even without Hearst's intervention enough delegates would have shifted to FDR on the fourth or fifth ballot to guarantee him the nomination. Still, whatever his role, Kennedy emerged from the Chicago convention an important member of the Roosevelt campaign team.

When, on July 11, nine days after he accepted the party's nomination, Franklin Roosevelt set sail from Port Jefferson, Long Island, on what was ostensibly a fishing trip with his sons, he invited key campaign advisers, financial backers, and Kennedy along. Kennedy rented a seaplane for the occasion and, with Edward Flynn, the Bronx political boss, made a spectacular entrance, flying out onto Long Island Sound to join the party. After two nights on Roosevelt's yacht, Kennedy flew off, returned that afternoon for another meeting, then took off again for New York City, this time with Jesse Straus, the president of Macy's, as his passenger.[20]

The summer of 1932 was a glorious one for all the Kennedys, save perhaps Jack, who had been in and out of the infirmary and done poorly in his first year at Choate, failing both French and Latin. George St. John, the headmaster, fearing that Rose was too soft on the boy, had written directly to Kennedy, imploring him to send Jack to summer school. "We have kept constantly in mind Mrs. Kennedy's desire that Jack should not have Summer work to do," but there was, the headmaster warned, no other alternative. "It hurts me to have to admit partial defeat with a boy to whose development we have given everything we had, but in Jack's case I have to admit it. If Jack were my own boy, I should send him to Summer School for the full six weeks." Kennedy ordered Jack to summer school.[21]

Kennedy, who had been absent—in Hollywood or in Europe—for the past several summers, planned to spend as much of this one as he could with his children at Hyannis Port. He enjoyed nothing so much as being with his children, who adored him as he did them. He was a near-perfect father as far as they were concerned. He never scolded or spanked, seldom raised his voice, was patient and generous. His only requirements were that they be courteous, watch out for one another, and always be on time.

Those who wanted to go riding with him had to get up at six A.M. when he did. They were given a five-minute warning—the amount of time it took to get the car out of the garage. If they weren't downstairs and ready to go when the car arrived, their father left without them. They rode on big, friendly Irish horses, side by side when possible, the children chattering away. Jean was a bit afraid of her horse but never let that get in the way of spending time with her father. When the farmer who owned the farm where they rode and stabled their horses raised the rent to what Kennedy thought was an exorbitant rate, he bought the property for $18,000, which, he claimed, was the best deal he ever made on any property.[22]

He played golf almost every day at the nearby Hyannisport Club, not the fanciest course in the land, but just right for him. As the children got older, they joined him. When the club, which had always teetered on the edge of solvency, came close to bankruptcy, he lent the board of directors 60 percent of what they required and helped raise the rest, his only condition being that should the club be sold or go bankrupt, he would get back his money.[23]

Though he never learned to sail, he made sure his children did, and cheered them on when they began to race. He had, he often told them, bought a house on the water (two, in fact—one in Hyannis Port, the other in Palm Beach) so that they would want to spend time there. Joe Jr., now seventeen, square-jawed and ruggedly handsome, was the family's master sailor. He collected brochures from the brokers, and advised his father on what boats to buy, from whom, and for how much. Jack crewed for him. Kick and Eunice learned by following the lead of their big brother.[24]

Franklin Roosevelt spent much of his summer in Albany, consulting with the professors who would come to be known as his brain trust and doing his damnedest to rid himself of his personal incubus, New

York City mayor James Walker. A state legislative committee, led by chief counsel Judge Samuel Seabury, had that past year investigated and uncovered widespread, blatant corruption in the Walker administration. Roosevelt, knowing that the Republicans would do everything possible to tie him to Tammany corruption, held his own hearings that summer and personally cross-examined Walker. "As long as the Walker hearings go on, I am engaged at the Capitol until about 5 P.M. but after that I am usually reasonably free," he wrote Kennedy, who had inquired if he might visit him. Mayor Walker resigned on September 1, sparing Roosevelt further political embarrassment.[25]

In early September, against the advice of several of his advisers who didn't think him strong enough, Roosevelt embarked on a whistle-stop, cross-country train tour that would eventually bring him from Albany to Los Angeles. Kennedy was invited along. On September 8, he telegraphed A. P. Giannini, president of the Bank of America, and asked him to meet with Roosevelt in San Francisco: "I know he would be anxious to have a chat with you." He contacted Hearst as well: "If you have a few minutes this afternoon or this evening, would like to discuss this political situation as I personally see it. I will telephone you whatever number or time at your convenience."[26]

The reporters who covered the campaign were intrigued by the fact that Kennedy had been invited on the Roosevelt train. "Is he the Barney Baruch of the Roosevelt campaign?" asked one westerner who was trying to puzzle out Mr. Kennedy's place in the picture. The *Boston Sunday Globe* insisted that while Kennedy was "officially listed. . . . as a 'member of the Democratic finance committee,'" he was now a member of the candidate's "inner circle," was consulting with Professor Moley on policy, and "discussing political tactics" and "business matters" with Governor Roosevelt himself.[27]

Whatever his role, Kennedy was given an honored place in one of the two front cars reserved for permanent members of the campaign entourage. Kennedy was unaccustomed to working as part of any group that he did not direct, but he seemed to get along well with everyone on board, especially Moley, who thought him smart and shrewd in the ways of the world and the perfect counterweight to old-school politicos like Louis Howe. The Roosevelt children, especially James and Anna, found him to be an "unusually warm human being." "Joseph P. Kennedy," James Roosevelt later recalled, "was a rather fabulous figure to a very young fellow on his father's first campaign train." Kennedy was blunt, terse, his language now earthy and laced with expletives, but when he spoke, Jimmy Roosevelt remembered, everyone, including his father, listened.[28]

Immaculately groomed in dark banker's suits, his brownish red hair perfectly in place, his freckles and toothsome smile seemingly at odds with his austere banker's uniform, Kennedy carried with him an aura of mystery and of gravitas. He alone among the candidate's advisers, he proudly proclaimed to a Boston reporter, had no ulterior motives. "There is nothing I want. . . . There is no public office that would interest me. Governor Roosevelt asked me to go with him on this trip and I agreed to accompany him." His major responsibility, he insisted, was to act as the candidate's eyes and ears. "I never go to the official functions. When the dinners and speeches are on, I go out on my own to talk to the barber or the druggist. I try to find out what the people are thinking and talking about."[29]

In what Raymond Moley referred to as "the friendly intimacy of the campaign train," Kennedy quickly "became one of the inner circle. I permitted him to read the speeches before their delivery and welcomed his shrewd suggestions. His political inheritance from his father and his understanding of very practical economic affairs were valuable." Kennedy's standing as a member of the campaign team was enhanced by the presence of Eddie Moore, his sidekick, secretary, and companion. "His infinite capacity to make friends made up for much of Kennedy's shortcomings in this respect." It quickly became clear that Moore was not there to act as Kennedy's toady or gofer or jester or yes-man. He was, recalled Eddie Dowling, former song-and-dance man, theatrical producer, and now campaign aide, a man possessed of "a tremendous amount of know how" and solid political instincts. Kennedy loved him like a brother, and he in turn revered Kennedy. "He never stopped telling me, and anybody else that would listen, about the greatness of Joseph P. Kennedy."[30]

Kennedy and Moore established themselves as the go-to problem solvers on the train. When James Farley and finance chairman Frank Walker decided to join the campaign in Salt Lake City, they wired Kennedy for assistance. "Have you sufficient influence to obtain suite of rooms and bath for us. Colonel House [Woodrow Wilson's former adviser and still a power in the party] joins party at Butte. Keep cool, calm, and collect," a not so subtle reference to Kennedy's role as campaign fund-raiser.[31]

The first stop on the campaign train was Jefferson City, Missouri, on September 13 at ten A.M.; then St. Louis, Kansas City, and Topeka for a major address on farm policy to be broadcast nationwide. Between Kansas City and Topeka, Kennedy attempted to inject "some typical New York expressions" into the farm speech, but according to the *Boston Daily Globe* reporter covering the campaign, he was overruled by Moley.[32]

With each stop on the way west, the crowds grew larger and more enthusiastic. In "Los Angeles, stronghold of Republicanism," two hundred thousand onlookers engulfed the motorcade as it made its way to the Hollywood Bowl, where Roosevelt addressed a crowd of twenty-five thousand. That evening, the candidate appeared at a star-studded salute at the Olympic Stadium, organized by Jack and Harry Warner. Kennedy had suggested to Jack Warner at an earlier meeting in New York that he try to get Hearst's support for the rally, which Warner did, he recalled, by fashioning it as a charity event and donating half the proceeds to the Marion Davies Foundation for Crippled Children and half to the Motion Picture Relief Fund. The evening was a smashing success, with nearly ninety thousand in the audience and dozens of Hollywood stars onstage. Warner remembered standing with "Joe looking over the enormous crowd. . . . He watched me for a moment then asked, 'What are you doing, Jack—counting the house?' 'No,' I replied. 'I was just wondering who's in the theatres tonight.'"[33]

Joseph P. Kennedy was having the time of his life. Roosevelt enjoyed campaigning, and his delight and enthusiasm rubbed off on the others. The hours were grueling, the pace relentless, the discussions over policy and what to include in the candidate's speeches endless and sometimes acrimonious, but the electricity surging through the train was palpable. The campaign entourage—often with the press in tow—ate in the best restaurants, stayed in the swankiest hotels, and rode only in limousines. Despite Depression conditions, no one seemed to mind.

After Los Angeles, Roosevelt stopped over in Arizona for a two-day vacation before returning east. Kennedy, with Farley and Flynn, flew back to New York City. For the remainder of September and most of October, he would be strangely absent from the campaign. He spent most of his days—and many nights—at his office at 35 West Forty-fifth Street and the nearby Ambassador Hotel, where he had rented an apartment for himself. He went home to Bronxville some nights—and always on weekends—to see the younger children and Rosemary. Though Choate was only a few hours' car ride from either Bronxville or New York City, Kennedy did not visit his boys that fall. Joe Jr. was particularly upset when his father missed the Choate football game with Hartford High on October 8. "I was not in the first team line-up but after about the first three minutes of the first quarter the coach sent me in for right-end, and I played there until the last two minutes of the game," he wrote his mother. "I wish Dad had come up yesterday, because I might not play so long next week. . . . P.S. Please be sure to show this letter to Dad."[34]

I n mid-October, Roosevelt (again against the advice of his chief strategists) set off on a second train tour, this one through the Midwest, then south to Atlanta, Warm Springs, Raleigh, and Baltimore. As the *New York Times* reported on October 18, he intended to take with him the same cast of characters who had accompanied him west in September. "Only Joseph P. Kennedy, banker and chief campaign fund raiser, and Edward Moore, his associate, are thus far not included."

There is no indication as to why Kennedy was not invited on the October tour. It might have been because he had outlived his usefulness to the campaign—and both he and Roosevelt knew it. His chief role, and the one for which he had been invited along on the western trip, was as a fund-raiser, but he had, in the end, turned out to be something of a failure in this regard. He had also been less than generous with his own contributions. His only gift had been $10,000, made on September 9, at the start of the western trip. He had, in addition, lent the campaign $50,000, which he expected to be repaid (and it was, much later). These were large contributions, but significantly less than those made by at least a dozen other Democratic contributors, including John Jakob Raskob, William Woodin, Bernard Baruch, and Hearst.

It is also possible that his continued presence in the campaign might have been vetoed by Louis Howe, the chain-smoking, wheezing, gruff gnome of a man who had been Roosevelt's most trusted adviser for more than twenty years. Howe not only distrusted and disliked Kennedy, but he worried that Roosevelt would be tarred by association with a Wall Street operator.[35]

On October 18, after the Roosevelt campaign train had left Albany without him, Kennedy received a letter from Joe Willicombe, William Randolph Hearst's secretary, with a check for $25,000 "for radio campaigning." Kennedy wrote to thank Hearst for funneling his campaign contribution through him. Well aware that while Hearst thought Roosevelt would make a better president than Herbert Hoover, he feared him as too much of a progressive and an internationalist. Kennedy inserted himself between the two, claiming that whatever happened in the future, he would remain Hearst's ally, defender, advocate, and liaison to Roosevelt. "As far as I am concerned. . . . I appreciate personally, more than I can ever express to you, your kindness in mailing [the check] to me because I realize that this check coming to the Committee through me helps a great deal in having consideration paid to any suggestions that I might want to make. You may rest assured, and this I want to say in order to go on record, that whenever your interests in this administration are not served well, my interest has ceased."[36]

Kennedy telephoned Jimmy Roosevelt as soon as he got Hearst's check and asked him to relay the news to his father. A few days later, Roosevelt telegraphed Kennedy from the campaign train: "Been having a great trip. Why don't you join up with us at Richmond, Washington, or Baltimore?" Kennedy caught up with the group on its final swing through the South and donated an additional $5,000 of his own money. He remained with the campaign after the tour and traveled north to Boston with Roosevelt for his last major speech, on October 31.[37]

On November 8, 1932, Franklin Delano Roosevelt carried forty-two of the forty-eight states in the Union, won the electoral college by 472 to 59, and received 57.4 percent of the popular vote. The following evening, Kennedy celebrated with a theater party for Roosevelt's two oldest children, Anna, twenty-six, and Jimmy, twenty-five, and their friends. (He tried to invite Elliott Roosevelt as well but could not reach him.) Whatever the future brought, Joseph P. Kennedy intended to stay close to the nation's new first family.[38]

Eleven

WAITING FOR THE CALL

On the Sunday after the election, President Herbert Hoover telegrammed the president-elect to ask that he join him in fashioning a response to the British request for a suspension of war debt payments, including $95 million due on December 15. Roosevelt was put in an awkward—and historically unprecedented—situation. If he refused to cooperate with Hoover, he could be blamed for contributing to the economic collapse; if he did, he risked being co-opted into support for Hoover's failed policies.

Assuming that Joseph P. Kennedy was in direct contact with Roosevelt, Hearst wired to warn him not to "let the incumbent unload on our friend any part of his unpopularity or any part of the responsibility for those things which cause his unpopularity. I think it far better for our friend to go into office with a clean state." Before Kennedy had a chance to forward the message, the president-elect declined Hoover's request. Hearst was delighted, as he indicated in a second telegram to Kennedy, sent the next day: "Our friend's letter pretty darn good. Incumbent has bad case unpopularity measles and wants to give them to our friend."[1]

Hearst was not the only one who assumed that Kennedy was part of Roosevelt's inner circle and would follow him to Washington. The *New*

York Times identifying him as the "fiery Boston and New York financier, who fights so hard in conferences for his proposals and his convictions that he sometimes arouses temporary enmity within the group," listed him among the fifteen or so members of "The 'Cabinet' Mr. Roosevelt Already Has: The Group of Advisers Who Assist Him in Plotting His Course on Political Seas." Will Hays only half jokingly addressed his election day telegram to Kennedy to "Dear Mr. Secretary."[2]

Kennedy responded to the congratulatory calls, letters, and telegrams on Roosevelt's victory and his imminent move to Washington by insisting that "accepting any position" in the new administration remained "the farthest thing from my mind." He had gone "into the fight," he wrote Hiram Brown at RKO, "for the fun it gave me, and there is no hope of an ultimate reward."[3]

That was not entirely true. As Raymond Moley recalled, Kennedy, having "ostentatiously" come out in support of Roosevelt, believed "quite realistically, and I believe properly . . . that he would be rewarded with a high place in the new Administration." Years later, Rose would recall that "what Joe really wanted from Roosevelt was to be Secretary of the Treasury and he felt he could and would do a good job in that capacity and restore confidence in the dollar." But if this was what he wanted, he had to know that it was not going to happen. Roosevelt had, in his longhand notes on cabinet appointees, identified Kennedy as one of the donors whom he hoped or thought he should reward, but he had penciled him in as a possible "Treasurer" of the United States, a largely honorary position, not as secretary of the treasury.[4]

All through November, Kennedy waited in New York for his invitation to confer with the president. Hearst had counted on him to forward his recommendations for the cabinet to the president-elect, but he had been unable to do even this. He had heard nothing from Roosevelt, who was in Warm Springs, but planned, he wrote Joe Willicombe, Hearst's secretary, to "go to the Gridiron dinner [in Washington] a week from Saturday night and meet there some of the folks coming up from Warm Springs. Have all W.R.'s suggestions and will try to get further reactions on this at this dinner." After the dinner, he would fly to Los Angeles "to visit W.R. for a few days" and fill him in on what he had learned.[5]

Kennedy attended the Gridiron Club dinner as planned, but he did not get to confer with the president-elect or any of his advisers. The following Monday, as promised, he flew to California to spend the weekend with Hearst and Marion Davies at San Simeon. The more strained his relationship with Roosevelt, the closer he was drawn into Hearst's orbit. In some ways, Hearst was what he aspired to be: the consummate insider, a shrewd and highly successful businessman with political connections, and a man who did exactly as he pleased in his personal life. On Christmas Eve 1932, he wrote to offer Hearst "my sincere appreciation of your kindnesses to me personally and your cooperation this year. Over a period of twenty years in business I have had to do with a great many people big and little. In all my experience I have never once met up with anyone who so nearly fitted my idea of a business associate. My sincerest wishes for a merry Christmas and a happy New Year with the hope that this year I may have the opportunity of being of some service to you."[6]

Hearst, not yet unwilling to give up on the president-elect, but sorely miffed that he had not been consulted on cabinet selections, asked Edmond Coblentz, the editor of the *New York American,* to hand deliver to Kennedy another memorandum for Roosevelt. Kennedy forwarded the "papers" to the president-elect. "I think that you will like to see them. If you want me to come to Albany right away, I will be very happy to do so, or call me on the telephone, or suit your convenience."[7]

Again, there was no response from the president-elect.

Snubbed by Roosevelt, Kennedy reached out to his family, friends, and advisers. He invited Jimmy Roosevelt and his wife, Betsey—and her sister—to stay with him and Rose in Palm Beach. Jimmy was unable to make it, but his wife and sister-in-law were. Eddie Flynn and Raymond Moley, both close advisers to the president-elect, were also invited to visit Palm Beach. Moley, who had been in touch with Kennedy since the election, recalled later how Kennedy's concern at being neglected by the president "turned very soon to deep indignation. . . . I heard plenty of Kennedy's excoriation of Roosevelt, of his criticisms of the President-elect, who, according to Kennedy, had no program—and what ideas he had were unworthy of note. There must have been hundreds of dollars in telephone calls to provide an exchange of abuse of Roosevelt between Kennedy and W. R. Hearst. . . . There was little I could do in 1933 either to pacify Kennedy or to move Roosevelt to offer some substantial recognition of his obligation. But while I never developed a real affection for Kennedy, I sympathized with his disappointment."[8]

Kennedy would have been better served by swallowing his disappointment and staying mute. Instead, he let everyone he came into contact with know what he felt, and in the bluest language. On the telephone, in letters, telegrams, and face-to-face conversations, Kennedy expressed his irritation, nearly exhausting his friends with his ceaseless criticism of the president-elect. Herbert Bayard Swope, with whom, according to Swope's biographer, Kennedy had a standing telephone appointment at eleven A.M. each morning, wrote him in Palm Beach to report on a conversation he had had with Raymond Moley, Frank Walker, and Forbes Morgan, a Roosevelt campaign donor. "All agreed, and thought" that Roosevelt's failure to do anything for Kennedy "was a damned outrage. They are going to send for you and have the Great White Father hold your hand. I am told that everybody agrees that not alone should you have what you want, but that you have the right to speak for any job you want for anybody else." Swope had heard that there was a movement to install Kennedy as under secretary of war. Louis Howe, he had been told, was "quite friendly, except he wants to keep you away from finance. That's his method, I suppose, of separating the Administration from Wall Street."[9]

There was a great deal of truth in Swope's observations. Whatever he might have done in Hollywood or on the campaign trail, Kennedy remained tied by reputation to the worst of the Wall Street stock manipulators. In January, the Senate Committee on Banking and Currency had again taken up its investigation of fraud and illegality in banking and the stock market. "As newspapermen watched with astonishment," Arthur Schlesinger has written, "leading figures of the banking world shuffled to the stand, where, under the patient and ruthless questioning of Ferdinand Pecora, the new Committee counsel, they squirmed, fidgeted and sweated, while reluctantly confessing to one breach after another both of normal ethics and of normal intelligence." Political prudence dictated that Roosevelt not tie himself or his administration to men like Kennedy.[10]

While Kennedy relentlessly and viciously criticized Roosevelt to his friends, in his few private communications with the president after the inauguration, to which he was not invited, he nearly prostrated himself in praise. On March 14, he telegraphed Roosevelt to report that the "Mother Superior" at the Sacred Heart Convent in Providence, "a real saintly woman," had told him that "the nuns were praying for you and then made a remarkable statement for a religious woman to make 'since your inauguration peace seemed to come on the earth; in fact it seemed like another resurrection.' Mortal men can pay you no higher compliment."[11]

Two weeks later, Roosevelt wrote Kennedy, ignoring, as Kennedy had, the fact that they had not communicated since the election, apologizing instead for the two-week delay in responding to Kennedy's fawning telegram: "I am sorry not to have written before to thank you for your awfully nice telegram. It was good of you to take the trouble to tell me of what you had heard. We are all keeping our fingers crossed and hoping to get in some real work while the temper of the country and the congress is so pleasant. Do be sure to let us know when you are going through Washington and stop off and see us."[12]

Kennedy spent the winter in Palm Beach, paying attention to his golf—and to his children. Joe Jr. was working hard and doing well in his last semester at Choate. Jack was doing neither. "It looks to me very much as if you were starting on the toboggan again," Kennedy wrote his second son, on receipt of his grades, "and the only possible result is grief and a bad summer. I am . . . sure . . . that you are trying lots harder now than you ever did before, but for some reason or other you evidently are missing again, and as it is now only February, you have plenty of time either to slide down or pull yourself up. I am much more hopeful that you can pull yourself up than I have ever been any other year, because I think your attitude is much better and I think that not only do you want to do well, but that you are really trying to; so, for goodness sake, don't spoil your spring and summer by not doing the job as well as you might."[13]

The four older children spent Easter in Palm Beach as they had the year before and, Kennedy hoped, would in the years to come. As he expected to be there for succeeding winters—with the children joining him for their vacations—he decided to buy a house that could accommodate all of them. He chose a faux Mediterranean Palm Beach–

style mansion that had been designed by architect Addison Mizner for Rodman Wanamaker of the Philadelphia department store family. Kennedy paid $105,000 for it and another $15,000 for the lot next door (a total equivalent to over $2 million today).[14]

By Palm Beach standards, the white Spanish-revival "hacienda" with its red-tile roof was modest, a minor Mizner, but it was perfect for the Kennedys with its several bedrooms, big garage, and room to install a pool and tennis courts. Located at 1095 North Ocean Boulevard, it was situated exactly like the Hyannis Port house—and the house Kennedy had grown up in in East Boston—on a slight incline and near the water. Ted would recall later that the house appeared to have been designed—and functioned—as a self-enclosed Kennedy town square, with an extended patio taking the place of the plaza. Kennedy would later build an enclosed "bullpen" where he could sunbathe nude and conduct business on the telephone.

In mid-May, Roosevelt wrote Kennedy again but made no offer of any sort: "I have been meaning for some time to write to you and tell you of my real appreciation of all that you did during the campaign. I need not tell you how helpful you were, to say nothing of the joy you added when things were most difficult. I gathered from someone that you were here for the Gridiron Dinner but failed to see you there. Do be sure to let me know when you expect to be here and come in to see me. Try to come on a weekend so that you can have a sail on the Sequoia. I know you would love it."[15]

Kennedy responded with an embarrassingly sycophantic note of his own: "You have made your place high—in the respect, admiration, faith and gratitude of the people you saved from despair, or worse, and high in history, for, I feel sure, your work will go on, widening in scope and results. . . . I owe you a debt for the privilege I feel it was to have come into contact with you, and to have been of such slight aid in your battle as was in my power. I shall always look upon that period as one of the most satisfactory in my life." Only in the final paragraph did Kennedy restore to himself a semblance of dignity by declining the president's invitation for a cruise: "I appreciate your consideration, but I am rarely in Washington. If I am, however, I shall certainly join you."[16]

He kept his lines open to the White House through the Roosevelt children, the president's secretary, Missy LeHand, whom he had befriended, and Raymond Moley, whom the president had appointed assistant secretary of state. Fearful that Moley would resign, which he eventually did, rather than work for Secretary of State Cordell Hull, Kennedy did all he could to keep him in Washington. "Our friendship," Moley recalled later, "reached a point when during the Hundred Days Kennedy invited me for lunch in New York. . . . After a few preliminaries, Kennedy came down to the business he had in mind. He said that my status in Washington required a certain standard of living that my limited private means could not sustain. Therefore, how would it be if he solicited some of his friends to contribute to a fund to provide me with the means to live as I should? I was sure then, as I am now, that there was nothing in this to suggest a bribe. I was already willing to do what I could to get him recognition but had failed."[17]

Moley did not accept Kennedy's offer, but he stayed in Washington long enough to recommend that Kennedy join him as a member of the delegation to the London Monetary and Economic Conference, scheduled to open on June 12. James Warburg, the young New York banker from the famous banking family whom Roosevelt had appointed to oversee conference planning, vetoed Moley's suggestion outright. He wanted no donors, no Wall Street speculators, and certainly no one like Kennedy, who, he had learned from businessman Harrison Williams, had been "spreading malicious stories about the President." When Moley raised Kennedy's name a second time, Warburg declared firmly that he would refuse to go to London if Kennedy was part of the delegation.[18]

Shut out of Washington, Kennedy returned to doing what he did best: making money on Wall Street. The Twenty-first Amendment (repealing Prohibition) had been approved by Congress during its lame-duck session but would not take effect until it had been ratified by specially called conventions in three quarters of the states. No one had any idea how long this was going to take. In the meantime, there was money to be made by those prepared to act quickly.

In June 1933, Kennedy joined a syndicate organized by Elisha Walker with Kuhn, Loeb; Lehman Brothers; and Walter Chrysler of the Chrysler Corporation to purchase sixty-five thousand shares in the Libbey-Owens-Ford Company, with options for tens of thousands more. With the repeal of Prohibition now set in motion, investors were lining up to purchase "repeal" stocks. One of the most popular was Owens-Illinois, which made glass bottles. Libbey-Owens-Ford was an entirely separate company, which manufactured plate glass for automobiles, not bottles, but its name was close enough to the bottle glass company to fool unwary investors.

The syndicate, of which Kennedy was the largest individual investor, placed its Libbey-Owens-Ford stock orders in the hands of two pool managers, who divided them into several parcels and began trading them wildly on the New York Stock Exchange. As one of the pool managers later admitted under questioning by Ferdinand Pecora before the Senate Committee on Banking and Currency, the enterprise was constructed on the correct assumption that if the pool managers pumped up volume by buying and selling shares to one another, investors would take notice and start buying shares of Libbey-Owens-Ford on the mistaken belief that they were buying shares of Owens-Illinois, the bottle manufacturer.[19]

Kennedy profited enormously from the stock pool and invested some of his profits in Owens-Illinois. He also bought sixty-three hundred shares of National Distillers at an average price of $8.64. By year's end, after the repeal of Prohibition, National Distillers was selling at $26 a share.[20] National Distillers specialized in blended ryes and bourbons, which could be produced domestically, as could gin and, of course, beer. Scotch whiskey would have to be imported.

There was no shortage of Americans poised to compete for the right to import Scotch whiskey as soon as it was legal to do so. But none had the advantages Kennedy enjoyed. He was known in London banking circles as the American who had purchased and revitalized the British film company FBO. He was fabulously wealthy, with abundant cash to spend. He was a brilliant businessman and a consummate salesman and promoter who could be counted on to get the whiskey into the right hands—for the right price. And perhaps most important of all, he had connections to the Roosevelt administration, which would determine import duties and issue licenses.

In the fall of 1933, Kennedy sailed to London to negotiate an agreement with the Distillers Company, which had a near monopoly on aged Scotch. To demonstrate the strength of his Washington connections, he brought with him the president's oldest son, Jimmy. "I did help him get the business going," Roosevelt recalled in his memoirs. "But I did not expect to become part of the business. . . . Joe and I never had an agreement to that effect." What Jimmy, who was starting out in the insurance business, got in return for his help were the contracts to insure the Distillers Company imports from fire (always a great risk in shipping huge quantities of alcohol).[21]

In early December, Kennedy was awarded contracts by the Distillers Company to import Haig & Haig and Dewar's Scotch whiskey and to distribute Gordon's gin and some secondary liquor brands that were imported in bulk, then bottled in Linden, New Jersey. Kennedy called his new company Somerset Importers, borrowing the name from the Somerset Club, the "proper Bostonian" establishment in the city he had left five years earlier.[22]

On December 5, the Prohibition amendment was fully ratified, and the Federal Alcohol Control Administration began issuing new licenses for the import of wines and spirits. One of them went to Kennedy's company. Days later, Somerset Importers was granted one of the first state "wholesaler's license" to sell in New York.

The liquor would soon come flowing in and with it the profits. In 1934 alone, Somerset would import some 130,000 cases of Scotch, with gross sales of $3 million and gross profits of $536,000 (equivalent to $8.73 million in purchasing power today). By 1936, profits had doubled to more than $1 million. For the fiscal year ending December 31, 1940, Paul Murphy, who oversaw Kennedy's operations in his New York City office, conservatively estimated Somerset net (not gross) profits at "approximately $560,000 to $600,000," somewhere around $9 million today. Until 1946, when Kennedy sold the company, Somerset would function as the family cash cow.

To protect his Somerset income from taxation, Kennedy established nine new "irrevocable trusts" on November 28, 1936, and transferred into them ownership of most of his Somerset stock. Because Rose and his children were already comfortably provided for by the 1926 trusts, the new ones were designed with the grandchildren in mind. The boys could begin to withdraw annual income from the trusts when they reached the age of thirty-one (Joe Jr., the eldest, would not reach thirty-one until 1946); the girls would have to wait until the age of forty-one. The corpus of the trusts would be distributed to the grandchildren on the death of their parents.[23]

With Rose vacationing in Europe for much of the fall of 1933, Kennedy stepped in to watch over the older girls, Kick and Eunice. Kick, small, brown-haired, with a gorgeous dimpled smile, full of energy, and always the most popular girl in her class, had been transferred from the Riverdale Country School to the Sacred Heart Convent at Noroton that fall. "She was quite pretty," Rose remembered, "and was getting altogether too popular with boys, which she enjoyed. She was on the telephone with them for hours at a time and was being distracted from her schoolwork and other duties. . . . My answer to the situation was to send her away to school."[24]

Kick, with Joe Jr., Jack, Rosemary, and Eunice, spent her Christmas holidays with her father in Palm Beach. She had no trouble adjusting to the delightfully schizophrenic life she now lived, shuttling back and forth between the highly disciplined, tightly scheduled, cloistered life of the convent and the almost no-holds-barred sociability of the clubs and house parties in Palm Beach. "Now I suppose you are glad you have me stuck back behind convent walls," she wrote her father after returning to the convent in January. "I am all safe and sound now and can't go skipping around to 'El Studio' or the 'Everglades,' etc. . . . I am already counting the days until our week-end Feb. 16. In fact the whole school is. And then spring vacation and Palm Beach again. Thanks loads for the wonderful vacation Daddy. It was the best one I have ever had. Each one gets better. I hope we go to Palm Beach next Xmas again in fact anytime is alright with me. Jack confided to me that he would rather go to Palm Beach than stay in Bronxville. So I guess you will have no peace in Florida any more. I feel very rested and everyone thinks I look very well so a few parties never did anyone any harm."[25]

Kick wouldn't have long to wait. In January, she had her appendix removed, and Rose took her to Palm Beach to recuperate along with Eunice, who had been ill most of the fall and suffered from chronic stomach problems (she would later be diagnosed with Addison's disease).

Kennedy's major concern was Jack, who was now at Choate. The problem with the boy, his father was convinced, was that he was too lighthearted, too whimsical, and too smart for his own good. Kennedy had tried everything—as had Jack's headmasters, masters, tutors, teachers, and housemasters—but failed to turn him around. In November 1933, he wrote Joe Jr. and asked him to intervene. Kennedy had just returned from Choate, where he had watched "Jack play football with the Juniors. . . . Jack plays tackle and played very well, but still with that careless indifference of his. . . . I wish you would write Jack and really set forth some ideas that will give him a sense of responsibility. . . . It will be too bad if with the brains that he has he really doesn't go as far up the ladder as he should. If you can think of anything that you think will help him, by all means do it."[26]

Kennedy also wrote George St. John, the Choate headmaster, who he feared wasn't pushing Jack hard enough. Jack was doing well in those subjects he cared about, particularly history, but "the happy-go-lucky manner with a degree of indifference that he shows towards the things that he has no interest in does not portend well for his future developing. I realize that you have many problems and that each parent's problems seems to him to be the most important one of the day. Nevertheless, I do wish you would give this some extra consideration to see if we can't devise some method of developing Jack's sense of responsibility."[27]

St. John replied with an overlong but artfully crafted letter. The gist of it was that he was not "seriously uneasy or worried about Jack. The longer I live and work with him, and the more I talk with him, the more confidence I have in him. . . . Jack has a clever, individualist mind. It is a harder mind to put in harness than Joe's—harder for Jack himself to put in harness. . . . A more conventional mind, and a more plodding and mature point of view, would help him a lot more right now; but we have to allow, my dear Mr. Kennedy, with boys like Jack, for a period of adjustment." The headmaster intimated that Kennedy might be expecting too much of his second son. For the moment, at least, Jack was working hard in plane geometry and in French, but with little effect. It was possible, the headmaster suggested, that Jack might not be "as able academically as his high I.Q. might lead us to think. . . . I think we over estimate Jack's present academic ability."

St. John suggested that the father might be contributing to the boy's problems. "I asked Jack if he had a good chance to talk with you when you were here, and he said that there really wasn't very much time. He said you had more time to talk with some of his Masters than with him, and that when you talked with him you were of course 'rather peeved.' Jack said there wasn't very much time to talk things over. That may or may not be so, my dear Mr. Kennedy. It may be a young boy's point of view; and he may be attributing his embarrassment and inability to express himself to some other cause—especially to a lack of time." But whatever the case, Kennedy had to pay more attention to Jack. "(1) Follow him up and check him up all the time for the best work he can do; (2) Treat him as man to man, and show him that we have confidence in him. I believe Jack will respond. . . . In all our work with Jack, we ought to show absolute confidence, and absolute vigilance; and if we are as good parents and teachers as we ought to be, I'll bet Jack will prove to us that he is the right kind of person, and that we don't need to worry about him."[28]

As had happened before—and would happen again—Jack Kennedy was rescued from the plight of overexpectations when, in early February 1934, he collapsed and was rushed to the New Haven Hospital with a nasty case of hives, a frighteningly low blood count, and a very high temperature. Kennedy took the train north from Palm Beach to be with his boy, leaving Rose behind. On arriving, he "called in a conference of Boston doctors and doctors from Mayo Clinic" to examine the boy, but they could reach no consensus on what ailed him: he was variously diagnosed as suffering from leukemia, hepatitis, and "agranulocytosis, a rare disease that impairs the production of granulated white blood cells by bone marrow." Fortunately, his condition improved as magically as it had developed, but it left him jaundiced and seriously underweight. It was agreed that he should spend the rest of his fall semester in Palm Beach, regaining his health and, with the help of private tutors, keeping up with his schoolwork. All past grievances were forgotten—by headmasters and parents. "He has been having a very miserable time," Kennedy wrote Joe Jr., "and has handled himself very well. . . . The doctors have very definitely told me that he has got to go very light on all athletics for at least six months, in order to get his strength back, but he is a good sport about it and seems pretty well reconciled."[29]

In his First Hundred Days, Franklin Delano Roosevelt, with a large Democratic majority in Congress, passed a great many bills with relatively little criticism.

By November 1933, a year after his election, the honeymoon was over. Critics from the press, the Republican Party, the banks, and the business community accused him of being too far to the left of the rest of the country and under the control of the radical left elements in his administration. His opponents, according to *New York Times* columnist Arthur Krock, believed that he had "definitely decided that State collectivism is the only solution of the nation's problems; that he will attempt to end the profit system, as we have known it; that the government, so long as controls it, will take control of all capital investment. . . . These same people insist that the President intends to introduce even more radical ideas and, by 1936, as the head of an extreme Left, set up the equivalent of a Labor Government in the United States." Krock did not discount such scenarios as being either far-fetched or conspiratorial. On the contrary, he buttressed them by pointing out that since his inauguration, Roosevelt had distanced himself from the conservative thinkers, bankers, and businessmen he had been "in close intimacy with" as a candidate. Joseph P. Kennedy was identified as among those former advisers who "rarely enter his office doors."[30]

While still furious at Roosevelt for ignoring him, Kennedy discounted the charge that the president had moved too far to the left. His problems with the White House were, for now, more personal than ideological.

"Roosevelt seems to be taking all the criticism smiling and I doubt if he has lost any of his popularity with the people," Kennedy wrote Harvard Law School professor Felix Frankfurter, who was spending the year at Oxford, on December 5, 1933. "What the future holds in store for us, God only knows. I am keeping shut and sitting on the rails, not even pretending to know anything."[31]

We don't know precisely when or how Kennedy met Frankfurter, but by the summer of 1933, the tall Irish Catholic from East Boston and the small, dapper Austrian Jew from the Lower East Side had become friendly enough for Kennedy to ask advice on Joe Jr.'s education. Kennedy had decided that instead of enrolling at Harvard immediately upon graduating from Choate, Joe Jr. should spend a year abroad. Frankfurter, who never turned down an occasion to offer advice on any subject, recommended that the boy study with Harold Laski at the London School of Economics and Political Science. Kennedy took his suggestion. There was, he believed, no better way to prepare his boy for a world turned upside down by the Depression, then right side up by New Dealers and Frankfurter liberals, than to send him abroad to study with a Socialist who had been a visiting professor at Harvard, was conversant with America and its politics, in regular correspondence with Oliver Wendell Holmes, Walter Lippmann, and Franklin Roosevelt, and entirely supportive of Roosevelt's "revolution by consent," which, Laski claimed, was laying "the foundations of a new social order" in the United States.[32]

Joe Jr. enrolled in the General Course at the London School of Economics, where he took classes in French and German as well as history and economics with Laski. Kennedy wrote his eldest son every ten days or so with detailed reports on Choate and Harvard football, news of the family, observations on the Roosevelt administration's efforts to right the economy, and suggestions as to whom Joe Jr. might look up in London. He never ordered or directed his son to do anything; he simply offered advice, expecting that his son would follow it. When he learned from Jack that Joe Jr., who had been sharing quarters with a Canadian, was now "rooming with an American," he recommended that he "keep your contacts with the foreigners as much as possible. You have Americans to live with the rest of your life." When Joe Jr. expressed an interest in racing yachts, Kennedy cabled that he "would much prefer you to

study and travel until time to return home. Racing boats in the middle
of the year does not appeal to me at all." Joe Jr. responded that "intention misunderstood. Racing intended for ten days during vacation. . . .
Still interested in school work."[33]

Kennedy had not only decided where and what and with whom his
boy would study on graduating from Choate. He also planned his summer vacation. Joe Jr. wanted to crew with writer and radio personality
Phil Lord, who was planning a round-the-world cruise on a ship
equipped not only with shortwave broadcast equipment, but with a specially designed diving chamber for underwater photography. Kennedy
investigated Lord, concluded that his round-the-world trip was badly
conceived and ill-funded, and urged his son to make other plans. He
suggested that he come back to "the States somewhere around the latter
part of July or the first of August to sort of get lined up on your courses
next year in Harvard and the Freshman Football Training Camp this
year begins rather early in September. Walter Cleary, the Head Coach,
called me up the other day to ask if you were coming back. Also, I think
it would be nice to spend a month at home at least with the family." If
Joe Jr. wanted to travel, he could do so over his spring break. "The
French and Italian situations seem to me to be most interesting and I
can arrange for you to meet Mussolini through Breckinridge Long, the
American Ambassador to Italy and also arrange an audience with the
Pope. I think also that it would be highly educational and instructive to
go into Germany and see something of Russia."[34]

That spring, in the used Chrysler convertible his father had bought
for him, Joe Jr., with his roommate, visited Rome as his father had suggested, had an audience with the pope, met with Ambassador Long, but
not Mussolini, then drove north to Munich, where he would spend the
rest of his vacation. A year had passed since Adolf Hitler had been
named chancellor, crushed his political opposition, assumed dictatorial
powers, outlawed unions and political parties, withdrawn Germany
from the League of Nations, and fomented what H. R. Knickerbocker
of the *New York Evening Post* described as a "violent campaign of murderous agitation. . . . An indeterminate number of Jews . . . have been
killed. Hundreds of Jews have been beaten or tortured. Thousands of
Jews have fled. Thousands of Jews have been, or will be, deprived of
their livelihood. All of Germany's 600,000 Jews are in terror." The vio-

lence of March 1933 had been followed by the passage of a series of laws that excluded Jews from working for municipal, state, or national government and limited the number of Jewish students who could attend German universities.[35]

No one who read the daily papers and weekly journals, especially the *Manchester Guardian* and the *Nation,* which Joe Jr. subscribed to, could have avoided reading about Nazi persecution of the Jews. Joseph Kennedy, Jr., was, if anything, better informed than most young Americans on what was going on in Germany.

"Before starting on my trip, I had heard the greatest condemnation of Hitler and his party. I had been to Laski's many times to tea, and heard him and many German Socialists tell of the frequent brutalities in Germany." Having visited Germany, he was now prepared to discount much that he had heard about Hitler and nazism. Driving north from Italy into Germany, he wrote his father, "I had the opportunity of talking with two different men, one in Pisa. . . . He was quite a learned man, did a lot of business in the States, and was pretty well informed all around. I discussed the usual points with him, and I was very much impressed by the enthusiasm and confidence which he had in the policies of Hitler. He of course agreed that it was regrettable that the Jews had to be driven out, but he said that the methods they employed in business were appalling."

Arriving in Munich, he was, he wrote his father, immediately "impressed by the quietness of the city. . . . The only signs of a Nazi Germany were the brown shirts, who were very numerous, parading the streets. . . . They are very nice and polite, however, at least to foreigners, and one sees no sign of brutality." While he had witnessed no overt anti-Semitism, he did not underestimate its presence in Germany but claimed now to understand its genesis and purpose. "The German people were scattered, despondent, and were divorced from hope. Hitler came in. He saw the need of a common enemy. Someone of whom to make the goat. Someone, by whose riddance the Germans would feel they had cast out the cause of their predicament. It was excellent psychology, and it was too bad that it had to be done to the Jews. This dislike of the Jews, however, was well founded. They were at the heads of all big business, in law etc. It is all to their credit for them to get so far, but their methods had been quite unscrupulous. A noted man told

Sir James [Calder, the head of the Distillers Company and a family friend] the other day that the [German] lawyers and prominent judges were Jews, and if you had a case against a Jew, you were nearly always sure to lose it. It's a sad state of affairs when things like that can take place. It is extremely sad, that noted professors, scientists, artists etc. so should have to suffer, but as you can see, it would be practically impossible to throw out only a part of them, from both the practical and psychological point of view. As far as the brutality is concerned, it must have been necessary to use some, to secure the whole hearted support of the people, which was necessary to put through this present program. . . . It was a horrible thing, but in every revolution you have to expect some bloodshed."

Almost as if following a script prepared for him by Nazi propagandists, Joe Jr. explained to his father that "a great deal of brutality was on private lines," perpetrated by Hitler's more rabid followers but never approved by him. Hitler now had "things well under control. The only danger would be if something happened to Hitler, and one of his crazy ministers came into power, which at this time does not seem likely."

Joe Jr., bizarrely for a practicing Catholic with a retarded sister, hailed as one of Hitler's great achievements "the sterilization law which I think is a great thing. I don't know how the Church feels about it, but it will do away with many of the disgusting specimens of men which inhabit this earth." "The Law for the Prevention of Hereditarily Diseased Offspring," which Joe Jr. so enthusiastically endorsed, mandated sterilization "by a surgical operation" for those afflicted with hereditary diseases, such as feeblemindedness, schizophrenia, manic-depression insanity, epilepsy, blindness, deafness, serious bodily deformities, and alcoholism.[36]

At this point, the most important thing in Joe Jr.'s life—at times, it appeared, the only important thing—was to make his father proud of him. He had written his lengthy essay on Nazi Germany for an audience of one. In it, he had presented his father with observations and analyses that he knew in advance he would agree with.

Kennedy, on receiving his son's long letter, wrote back at once, on May 4, 1934, that he was "very pleased and gratified at your observations of the German situation. I think they show a very keen sense of perception, and I think your conclusions are very sound. Of course, it is still possible that Hitler went far beyond his necessary requirements in his attitude towards the Jews, the evidence of which may be very well covered up from the observer who goes in there at this time."

Kennedy was correct, of course, to suggest that Hitler had gone further than was "required" in his "attitude towards the Jews" and that evidence of Nazi persecution might very well have been "covered up" and hidden from foreign visitors. Still, his dispassionate, distanced response to Joe Jr.'s extended apologia for Hitler and his regime suggests that he did not take great issue with his observations, that Nazi persecution of the Jews was not an issue that resonated with him. It was as if his son had written a theme paper on the races at Ascot and his father were grading it: "I think you show a great development in your mind in the last six or seven months. It is most gratifying to both Mother and me." The only hesitancy Kennedy had in offering more fulsome praise was that his son had not asked what for Kennedy was the most critical question. "What reason [do] you give for his present attitudes towards the Catholics? If he wanted to re-unite Germany, and picked the Jew as the focal point of his attack, and conditions in Germany are now so completely those of his own making, why then is it necessary to turn the front of his attack on the Catholics? When you go in there next time, I think it would be interesting to make some observations on this point."

On his return to London in late April, Joe Jr. was invited to travel to the Soviet Union with Harold Laski, who was lecturing in Moscow, and Felix Frankfurter, who planned to accompany him. In the end, Frankfurter would decline to go along, in large part because he had been advised not to by Ray Moley, Swope, and others who feared that a trip to the Soviet Union would embolden those who were already charging him with being a Communist. Roosevelt's move to the left on economic policy had been met by a red-baiting, anti-Semitic whispering campaign that the president had become a captive of left-wing Jews such as Frankfurter. "There is a terrific agitation and feeling against the so-called Frankfurter group in Washington," Kennedy wrote his son in early May, "and, even the topside Jews of the country are very much worried about the situation in Washington." Kennedy was outraged by the accusations but nonetheless hoped that Frankfurter would take them seriously and do nothing to aggravate the situation. "I can see his indignation on being advised against [traveling with Laski to the Soviet Union], but he is smart enough to know that we here in America are seeing and hearing a lot of things that he cannot possibly get abroad. So much for politics."

Since there was no way anyone would ever accuse a Kennedy of being a Communist, no impediment stood in the way of Joe Jr.'s accompanying Laski to Moscow. "It would be wise for you to go with Laski, particularly because it would give you a very favorable view point in consideration of things here, and with rounding out your year there, it strikes me that you would have a great start on any of your contemporaries, and you should be able to keep up very important contacts, so I am very hopeful that you will be able to make the trip."[37]

Kennedy was convinced now that Roosevelt's move to the left was not going to be reversed, and that being the case, the more his boys knew about state planning, the better off they would be. "The Frankfurter Liberals are still in the saddle," he had half jokingly written Frankfurter in mid-February, and they were going to remain there. "I hope when the revolution comes, my knowing you will at least get me a sergeantcy, if they have any sergeants now in your prospective Armies."[38]

Twelve

TO WASHINGTON

In late February 1934, Richard Whitney, a graduate of Groton and Harvard, former Kidder, Peabody broker, and now president of the New York Stock Exchange, summoned the senior partners of the nation's largest exchanges to meet with him. He simultaneously contacted "each and every one of the 800 corporation heads whose stock" was listed on the New York Stock Exchange. The securities exchange legislation making its way through Congress, he warned them all, was "a matter of grave concern to every owner of real estate or securities, to all officials of corporations or banks." No business, banking, or brokerage firm or executive could "afford to disregard this new menace to national recovery."[1]

The battle of the bankers and Wall Street against the New Deal was now fully engaged. A year earlier, in March 1933, the economic crisis had been so dire, the people so frightened, the Republicans so thoroughly defeated, and business and banking leaders so disgraced that there had been little opposition to the first wave of regulatory legislation. The banking bill had passed in March with almost no debate or opposition, the securities bill in May. Together they provided for a degree of regulation of the banks and of Wall Street that was unprecedented in the nation's history. Congress had more to do. The Securities

Act of 1933 regulated only the marketing of securities. A companion bill that provided for the regulation of the exchanges that traded those securities had been introduced in Congress in early 1934. It was this legislation that had enraged Whitney and led to an outpouring of criticism of a different order from anything that had come before.

Joseph P. Kennedy was nearly alone among those who had prospered on Wall Street *and* supported legislation to regulate it. In February, on his return from Palm Beach to New York, he had written Frankfurter that he had "found that another bombshell had been dropped, in the form of the new stock exchange bill and while I agree with 85% of it (which, by the way, is quite an acknowledgment from an old conservative like myself) I still think that it is unnecessarily severe in the other 15%." Frankfurter, whose students and protégés had drafted the bill, was delighted with what he took to be Kennedy's endorsement of the legislation. "When a guy like you agrees with 85% of the Stock Exchange Bill, that's good enough for me and makes me only wish that fellows with your sense were running the motor and the steel industry, or for that matter, running a lot of other things."[2]

Roosevelt recognized full well that getting the legislation passed would be difficult, but not nearly as difficult as getting it administered. Given the already intense opposition from Wall Street and the business community, he was wary of appointing commissioners with reputations for being anti–Wall Street, antibanking, or antibusiness. The economy was not going to get moving again until big business, the banks, and Wall Street began to invest their capital in job-creating enterprises. They would not do that unless they were assured that the new legislation would not be used as an anti–Wall Street bludgeon. What Roosevelt needed was a strong administrator who was also a conciliator and who could convince Wall Street that the legislation regulating the exchanges was not antibusiness and was not going to impede honest businessmen, brokers, and bankers from making honest profits. Kennedy was the perfect candidate because he was the only one who was both acceptable to Wall Street and trusted by Moley and the Frankfurter liberals who had drafted the legislation.

In late March and early April, while the bill was being pounded by conservative and business opponents in congressional committee hearings, the president went fishing off the Bahamas with his friend Vincent

Astor. Returning to Washington by train, Roosevelt, through his son Jimmy, asked if Kennedy would meet with him during a stopover in Palm Beach. The two chatted briefly in the president's private railcar. Roosevelt invited Kennedy to the White House for the weekend.

The very next day, Kennedy and Rose took the train north to Washington. They spent the afternoon at the racetrack with Jimmy and Betsey and the evening, as part of the president's party, at the Gridiron dinner at the Willard Hotel. Upon his return to the White House at midnight, Kennedy was summoned by the president to meet with him, Jimmy, and Louis Howe in his private study, where for more than three hours they talked politics, pending legislation, and tax policy.

At 11:15 the following morning, the two men met again, this time by themselves in the president's bedroom, where the president, suffering from a bad cold, was resting. "He told me," Kennedy noted in the notes he made afterward, "he thought the time had come when I should come to Washington. I told him I was perfectly happy and willing to come to Washington to be of service to him, but reiterated . . . that my only interest was my personal affection for him, and that I was not interested in taking a position for any other reason. I said I had been rather annoyed at the coolness that had sprung up between us, and for which I blamed Louis Howe. He passingly referred to my connection with Wall Street." Knowing that his reputation as a Wall Street manipulator was the major obstacle standing in the way of a possible appointment, Kennedy had come prepared with a detailed statement that he now presented to the president, "showing that the bulk of all my money had been made by business acumen rather than Wall Street operation." Roosevelt didn't want to look at it. He was not, he made clear, interested in rehashing the past. "He wanted me to forget all that and urged me to come to Washington. He suggested that it might be a very great idea to have me come down as charge of the Securities Commission, which bill was before Congress at that time. He made me no direct offer, and I made him no promise of acceptance."[3]

The president asked Kennedy and Rose to have lunch at the White House before they took the train to New York. To demonstrate the high esteem in which he held the man he had ignored since the election, the only other guests Roosevelt invited to that lunch were Secretary of State Cordell Hull and his wife.

Kennedy felt as if he had been run over by a bulldozer, which he had. In his letter to Joe Jr. in London, he reported that during the course of their conversations, Roosevelt had mentioned several possible government positions in addition to the Securities Commission, including "going to South America as the head of the Commission to regulate tariffs for South America, where he feels the great bulk of the prospects for foreign trade lies. I told him that I did not think [that was] the kind of work I was particularly interested in; in fact, I told him that I did not desire a position with the Government unless it really meant some prestige to my family. I felt my responsibilities with my large family were so great that I would be obliged to remain out of the Government's activities." The president was unwilling to take no for an answer. "He said that he thought I had an obligation to do something, and then suggested that I go to Ireland as Minister. He thought it would be a very nice thing for me to go back as Minister to a country from which my grandfather had come as an immigrant. But Mother and I talked it over, and we decided that this wasn't of any particular interest, and I told him so. Now he has in mind another position in Washington which he hasn't made clear to me as yet."[4]

From Washington, Kennedy traveled north to Bronxville, where he waited for Roosevelt to call and recuperated from a broken leg and smashed right ankle he had suffered while horseback riding. "By a strange coincidence," he wrote Louis Ruppel, one of the journalists he had befriended on the Roosevelt campaign train, "the horse's name was 'Louis,' named after you I hope, not after the President's secretary, Mr. Howe. But then, after all, I have been thrown pretty consistently by Louises this year. I will recover, however, and press on to greater efforts. [Eddie] Moore suggests that I ride one of those horses that they put in swimming pools, and when I fall off, I can only get wet."[5]

He was able to joke about Howe—who he believed had kept him out of the administration—only because he was convinced that a call to Washington was imminent. Roosevelt recognized the political pitfalls of inviting a former Wall Street plunger to regulate the other plungers, but he was ready to move forward with the appointment. As Harold Ickes, who opposed the nomination, confided to his diary, "The President has great confidence in him because he has made his pile . . . and knows all the tricks of the trade. Apparently he is going on the assumption that Kennedy would now like to make a name for himself for the sake of his family, but I have never known many of these cases to work out as expected."[6]

On May 11, 1934, while the securities exchange bill was still being debated in Congress, Tommy Corcoran—the charming, slick, accordion-playing, brilliant, and solitary Irish member of the Frankfurter team who, with stolid, hardworking, and frighteningly intelligent Ben Cohen, had drafted the bill—wrote Felix Frankfurter in London that the "ticket for the Stock Exchange Commission on which the Skipper had secretly smiled [includes] your friend, Joe K. in Boston—Democrat. The last is particularly 'deep well,' comes straight from the Skipper through Ray [Moley]."[7]

If Roosevelt had had any doubts about Kennedy's competence, they had been dispelled by Raymond Moley, whom he had brought back to Washington to lead the drive for the new legislation. Moley had submitted to the president eight names for the five slots on the commission. First on his list was Kennedy: "the best bet for Chairman because of executive ability, knowledge of habits and customs of business to be regulated and ability to moderate different points of view on Commission."[8]

In late June, Jimmy Roosevelt telephoned Kennedy in Hyannis Port to say that the president wanted to meet with him at the White House on Thursday, June 28. Kennedy had by now made up his mind that he would accept the appointment as chair, but would not serve as one of the four other commissioners. Ferdinand Pecora, counsel to the Senate Committee on Banking and Currency, had indicated that he too wanted to chair the SEC, and there had been a groundswell of left New Deal support for him. "I can well remember Joe saying goodbye in the morning on his way to Washington," Rose recalled later, "and his last words were, 'I shall probably be back tonight, for I shall not stay unless I get the chairmanship.'"[9]

As word leaked out that Kennedy was the leading candidate for chairman, public and private opposition mounted, led by Roy Howard of the Scripps Howard newspapers, who visited the president in the White House and then followed up with an editorial in the *Washington News* declaring that Roosevelt's appointment of Kennedy to the SEC chairmanship would register as "a slap in the face to his most loyal effective supporters." In the face of such opposition, Kennedy was advised by friends and supporters, including Swope and Moley, to accept an appointment as commissioner if, as now appeared likely, Roosevelt decided he could not name him chairman. Only William Randolph Hearst, to whom Kennedy placed a long-distance call to his castle in Wales, agreed that he deserved the chairmanship and should accept nothing less.[10]

On June 28, Kennedy was driven to the White House for his five o'clock meeting. Roosevelt was at his sadistically charming best. He had decided to offer Kennedy the chairmanship and knew how eager Kennedy was to accept, but instead of getting down to business, he delayed endlessly in speaking his mind. First he invited Kennedy to sit silently in the Oval Office while he made small talk, signed bills, and conferred with various staff members. "At six o'clock, having said nothing to me about the matter he had called me down for, he invited me to have a swim with him in the pool and stay for dinner." At dinner with Moley, Bernard Baruch, who was staying at the White House, Mrs. Roosevelt, and several others, the president continued to toy with Kennedy. There was more small talk and political gossip, but no mention of the SEC. "At the close of the dinner, Mrs. Roosevelt upon rising, said to the President, 'Franklin, when are you going to talk to Joe?' And he said, 'About two o'clock tomorrow morning.'" The president then rose, leaving Kennedy to chat with Baruch and Moley. Moley was summoned first, and then, about fifteen minutes later, Kennedy and Baruch were asked to join him and Roosevelt upstairs.

Roosevelt played with Kennedy, telling him that he had put him first on the SEC list he had made up two weeks earlier, but not saying whether he had changed his mind since then. "He talked on for about fifteen or twenty minutes without indicating [whether] he intended to make me the Chairman," Kennedy wrote in his notes of the meeting. "He finally said in a jocular manner, 'I think you can be a great liberal on that, and I think you would do a great job running it.'" Kennedy asked if the president might want to reconsider, given the opposition to his appointment. "I told him that I had been involved in Wall Street, and, over a business career of twenty-five years, had done plenty of things that people could find fault with."

"At this point," Moley would recall in his memoirs, "knowing what was in F.D.R.'s mind as well as if he had put it in writing for me, I said 'Joe, I know darned well you want this job. But if anything in your career in business could injure the President, this is the time to spill it. Let's forget the general criticism that you've made money on Wall Street.' Kennedy reacted precisely as I thought he would. With a burst of profanity he defied anyone to question his devotion to the public interest or to point to a single shady act in his whole life. The President did not need to worry about that, he said. What was more, he would give his critics—and here again the profanity flowed freely—an administration of the SEC that would be a credit to the country, the President, himself and his family—clear down to the ninth child."[11]

The initial reaction to Kennedy's appointment was hostile, as predicted, then grew worse after July 15, when the first chapters of the report of the Senate Committee on Banking and Currency investigations of Wall Street fraud were published and named Kennedy as a participant in the highly questionable, if not fraudulent, Libbey-Owens-Ford stock pool. New Dealers were outraged that their president had chosen a Wall Street denizen to regulate Wall Street. "Had Franklin D. Roosevelt's dearest enemy accused him of an intention of making so grotesque an appointment as Joseph P. Kennedy," the *New Republic* editorialized on July 11, 1934, "the charge might have been laid to malice. Yet the President has exceeded the expectations of his most ardent ill wishers."[12]

While New Dealers were distressed by the appointment, conservatives within and outside the Roosevelt camp were delighted. "He is all right," journalist Mark Sullivan, one of the most influential and outspoken of the New Deal opponents, wrote Swope on August 1, 1934, after an interview with Kennedy. "He is an unusual combination of Irish temperament to an extreme degree, with an exactness of mind and a head of figures which the Irish don't always have. . . . He can tell a long story carrying dramatic development hand in hand with logical development. I think he could have been a showman had he started out that way, but I suspect all that characteristic of him has been rather submerged by the traits of mind he developed in business. When he is tired he has a priest-like look that often comes to Irishmen of the intellectual type. That he will make friends goes without saying." What was most encouraging to Sullivan, who had publicly excoriated members of Roosevelt's brain trust for trying to turn America into Russia, was that Kennedy was a true conservative. "In the past the radicals have had it almost all their own way due largely to their greater energy and earnestness. . . . From now on, I imagine, Kennedy can be depended on as the conservative influence that will press on Roosevelt all the time. If Kennedy presses harder than the radicals, then Roosevelt will take the country reasonably to the right. . . . Kennedy is at once fighter enough and Irish enough and flexible and resourceful enough, to lick the radicals although the radicals may outclass him a little in steady persistence."[13]

Kennedy's meeting with Sullivan had been part of the carefully orchestrated media campaign conducted by his friends Bernard Baruch and Herbert Swope, who also arranged a long, one-on-one interview for him with Arthur Krock, the Washington bureau chief and columnist for the *New York Times*. This was the start of the Krock-Kennedy alliance, one of the stranger partnerships in the history of American politics and journalism. Arthur Krock, a stately, somewhat pompous man of medium height and nondescript, certainly not handsome, features, had been born in Kentucky of a not particularly prosperous Jewish father and half-Jewish mother. He had spent a year at Princeton, then dropped out and gone to work for the *Louisville Herald*. He eventually moved to the *New York World*, where he wrote editorials until Walter Lippmann, the editorial page editor, already upset with him for blatantly boosting Bernard Baruch, accused him of disclosing information about a future editorial to brokers from Dillon, Read, where he moonlighted.[14]

Krock left the *World* for the *New York Times* in 1927. In January 1932, he was named Washington bureau chief and the following year was given an opinion column. The Washington bureau was his fiefdom; the reporters who worked there did as he told them. In his column as well, he had complete autonomy. By 1934, Arthur Krock was one of the most powerful men in Washington. A born and bred southern conservative, he opposed big government, big spending, northern liberals, Franklin Roosevelt, and many, if not most, of the New Deal programs that he slyly but not subtly critiqued in his columns.

He had met Kennedy on the campaign trail in 1932 and been readily "impressed with the fact that for vigor, intelligence, forcefulness, political sagacity, and charm, this tall, red-haired, red-faced, boy-eyed man was outstanding in the circle dedicated" to electing Roosevelt president. Still, he did not, in his words, "become really acquainted with him" until 1934, when Kennedy accepted the appointment as chair of the SEC. Within a year, Krock was "an intimate of the family." For the next quarter century, while working as Washington bureau chief and as columnist, would serve as Kennedy's unofficial, clandestine press agent, speechwriter, political adviser, informant, and all-purpose consultant. Whenever Kennedy had something to say, Krock helped him say it and gave him space in his column or in those of the reporters in his bureau.

In his memoirs, Krock insisted that Kennedy "was as scrupulous as I in excluding material considerations from this relationship," but as we shall see, this may not have always been the case. In Kennedy's letters, there are offers to pay Krock generous weekly salaries for his editorial assistance, but no letters from Krock refusing such salaries. On the whole, the correspondence reveals something quite disturbing, if not corrupt, about Krock's willingness to do Kennedy's bidding, to advise him or write a speech for him, then praise it in his column, to take money for ghostwriting Kennedy's *I'm for Roosevelt* campaign book in 1936, to assist Jack in turning his college thesis into a book, *Why England Slept,* to allow Kennedy to pay for vacations in Palm Beach and travel to London, all without any acknowledgment to his superiors at the *Times* or his readers.[15]

The first fruits of the Krock-Kennedy relationship or partnership were a pair of *New York Times* articles, by Krock and by S. J. Woolf, who published an extended profile on August 12, 1934.

"His manner is buoyant, his spirit exuberant and his clear blue eyes are merry," Woolf reported. "As he discussed the future of the country's financial activities he interrupted his remarks with tales of his nine children. It is evident that he regards them as the best dividends he had ever received. One senses that he is solicitous of the future for their sakes; that the improvements for which he is striving are improvements which they will enjoy."

Kennedy pleasantly surprised Woolf, as he did Washington's other reporters, by answering "good-naturedly questions about his former activities—questions which might never have been asked had he been less free and candid in his manner." He claimed that he had "operated in stocks, but . . . with his own money." This was not quite true. Much of the money he invested was borrowed, in the early days largely from his own East Boston bank. Kennedy insisted as well that he had never been in a "bear pool." This too was untrue. He had taken part in almost every kind of investment scheme on Wall Street over the past two decades. As Kennedy proudly admitted at the end of his SEC tenure, "The President had appointed me as chairman of the SEC because he knew that I knew all the angles of trading, that I had studied pools and participated in them and was aware of all the intricacies and trickeries of market manipulation. . . . I had engaged in many a furious financial fight and knew the formulas—when to duck and when to hit."[16]

After being sworn in, Kennedy took a week off to get his affairs in order. He flew to Hyannis Port to kiss the children and Rose goodbye, then, in late July, returned to Washington with Eddie Moore, who would function as his personal secretary and chief of staff and whose salary he paid out of his own pocket.

Every step he took was now covered by reporters, columnists, and magazine writers who took great delight in reporting the comings and goings of the newest sensation on the Washington scene, a man who was not only highly accessible and quotable, but photogenic and the father of nine gorgeous children. He leased Marwood, the faux French Renaissance "near-palace," as the papers described it, which had been built by Chicago millionaire Samuel Klump Martin III for his wife, Mary Jane, who among other achievements had danced in Eddie Cantor's *Whoopee!* When Martin died, his widow sold Marwood to the Pulitzer family, who rented it to Kennedy. Everything about the mansion overlooking the Potomac was extraordinary. The "near-palace" was approached through "an arched gatehouse, which guards a mile-long roadway lined with trees." There was a pool, where Kennedy would swim naked every morning, and several bathhouses. Inside the mansion was an "enormous hotel-like living room. . . . The dining room is the kind in which sat King James I of England. A large library, dressing rooms, lavatories, and a sound-proof office completes the ground-floor symphony." Upstairs were fourteen master bedrooms and fourteen baths, each with gold fixtures, which delighted Rose. In the cellar was the game room. Below it, in the subcellar, was a "motion-picture theatre with lounges for 100 guests."[17]

The reporters explained that Kennedy needed so vast a mansion to house his nine children, but that was not quite true. None of the children were going to relocate to Washington. Neither was Rose, who that October accepted her husband's twentieth anniversary gift of a European vacation—without him. Kennedy had rented a Washington mansion not for the family, but because, as Rose would put it, he would be more comfortable there than in "a suite in a hotel [because] in a house he could rest better, away from the noise; he could eat better and at his own convenience . . . and he would be happier." He could also entertain whomever he wanted, whenever he chose.

Joseph Kennedy was not a particularly sociable man. His idea of the perfect evening was a dinner cooked by his chef for him, Eddie Moore, and a few of the guys, followed by an hour or so listening to classical music, reading a mystery novel, and going to bed on the early side. Unfortunately, men who went to bed early and did not socialize with their peers and betters did not succeed in business or politics.

To make a name for himself as a Washington insider, he had to entertain, and lavishly. Marwood was the perfect place to do so. "He got into the habit of ordering delicious live lobsters sent down from Maine or from Boston," Rose recalled. "Then he would invite different Senators out for a stag dinner. In those days, fresh lobsters were a great delicacy in Washington. In fact, many of the Westerners did not know exactly how to eat a lobster until initiated into the delicious salty briny flavor by omniscient Eddie Moore. When oysters and clams were at their best at Cape Cod, they too were shipped down. There was always plenty of the best Scotch around—[Haig & Haig] Pinch Bottle, which was prize Scotch. There different Senators were entertained weekly and often the President would drive out for an hour's relaxation and a heaping platter of seafood washed down with a choice beverage. Everyone was in a gay mood, a relaxed mood, and everybody enjoyed this form of Kennedy hospitality."[18]

The president enjoyed nothing more than a night with friends away from the White House, and he became a frequent visitor at Marwood, often with members of his inner circle and his son James. Arthur Krock reported on one such evening when Roosevelt and his party stayed late into the night, drinking mint juleps, enjoying a lavishly prepared and served dinner, watching a feature film in Kennedy's screening room, then retiring upstairs to sing along with Corcoran's accordion and tell jokes and stories, the president offering his own about college life and sailing adventures. "The party soon became very merry. The President's laughter rang out over all, and was most frequent."[19]

Kennedy began life in Washington in the height of summer, when the un-air-conditioned city was virtually uninhabitable. With the federal government expanding almost exponentially week by week with new agencies and commissions squeezed into old, already overcrowded buildings, there was no space available for the SEC. The commission was slated to move into two floors of the old Interstate Commerce Commission building but could not do so until the ICC had moved out. For the time being, it was housed in a wooden building that had been hastily constructed during the Great War and was famous (according to the July 6 *New York Times*) for being "one of the hottest spots in the capital."

As always, Kennedy rose early, exercised, breakfasted, and was at his desk by eight thirty A.M., where he would remain until after dark. As the chair of an entirely new commission with an extended mandate, he was in the enviable position—or so it appeared at first—of being able to hire dozens of lawyers, accountants, professors, and hungry young men eager to spend a tour in Washington.

Over the next few months everyone he had ever known, and several he did not, would petition him for jobs for themselves, their children, their friends, and their friends' friends and children. He received personalized letters and tried to act positively on recommendations from, among others, Eleanor Roosevelt, Secretary of the Treasury Henry Morgenthau, Jr., Mayor James Michael Curley of Boston, Senator David I. Walsh of Massachusetts, and dozens of other elected and appointed officials. Mrs. Roosevelt was particularly indefatigable in sending Kennedy and Eddie Moore the names of friends or the children of friends who needed work either in Washington or in Hollywood, where she knew Kennedy still had contacts.[20]

Loyalty was not just important to Kennedy, it was critical. As a

Washington outsider, he felt the need to construct a comfort zone of men he had worked with and trusted. He brought Eddie Moore with him to the SEC and then hired two other Irish Catholics from Boston, Joe Sheehan, a Boston Latin classmate, and James Fayne, a Harvard classmate, both of them efficient, hardworking businessmen whose primary loyalty would be to him. "After Frank Shea [another Harvard Law School graduate], no more Irish," Milton Freeman, one of the lawyers on the staff, remembered Kennedy joking. "This place is beginning to look like the Irish Free State Embassy."[21]

Kennedy's most important appointment was of a general counsel. Ben Cohen, the brilliant, quietly confident Frankfurter protégé who had been brought to Washington to draft the 1933 and 1934 securities and securities exchange bills, was on the top of every list. But Cohen, as everyone in Washington knew, was fiercely loyal to Frankfurter. Kennedy wanted his own man as his general counsel, preferably someone new to Washington, ideally an Irish Catholic. He chose Judge John Burns, a tough, smart Boston Irish Catholic who had worked his way through college and then Harvard Law School, had been named a full professor at age thirty, and a month later appointed to the Massachusetts Superior Court.

Kennedy wanted only the best and brightest working for him, and he was able to get just about anyone he wanted. His closest adviser was James Landis, the smallish, slim, humorless, intensely serious son of a missionary who, at Frankfurter's urging, had come to Washington from Harvard Law School, where he had been a professor of legislation. Landis had been one of the principal drafters of the Securities Act of 1933 and was appointed to the Federal Trade Commission (FTC), which administered the law until the SEC was created. His background and familiarity with the establishing legislation made him a logical candidate for the position of SEC chairman, but when he was passed over, he agreed to serve under Kennedy.

To head up the division that oversaw bankruptcies and receiverships, Kennedy hired another brilliant law professor in his middle thirties, William O. Douglas of Yale, who brought Abe Fortas with him as his chief assistant. Douglas accepted the position without ever having met Kennedy because he knew and admired James Landis and, like so many of his generation, was eager to spend time in Washington. He found Kennedy "friendly but brusque."[22]

Though Kennedy was nearly alone among his senior staff in not having a law degree, there was never any doubt as to who was in charge—or why. He was stern, tough, "funny and quick," and the most able administrator they had ever met. "Kennedy was very businesslike and polished," Milton Freeman recalled years later, "the rest of us New Dealers were pretty sloppy in our ways. I remember Kennedy sending out a memorandum saying, 'The Securities and Exchange Commission is a government organization. Businessmen and the public have to deal with it, and they have a right to have everybody here during office hours, which are 9:00 to 5:30.' He added that at 9:00 he had called up a number of people who had not answered. He went on, 'From now on everybody must be at his desk at 9:00 unless he received my personal permission to the contrary.'"[23]

Kennedy need not have worried about his staff not working sufficiently long hours. "The energies of the men seemed endless," Douglas noted in his memoirs. "We would all work until six, take two hours out for dinner, be back at eight, and work until midnight or later, reporting by nine o'clock the next morning for another day." Milton Freeman remembered his years at the SEC in precisely the same way: "Everybody was working very hard. We were remaking the world."[24]

The pressure on Kennedy and the SEC commissioners and staff was immense. What was referred to as the Roosevelt bounce, the stock market rise in the six months following the president's inauguration in March 1933, had restored a bit of confidence in the workings of the economy. But the momentum had stalled. Unemployment was still much too high. What was needed now was private investment to get the economy moving again. Unfortunately, it appeared that the nation's investment bankers and corporate leaders had gone on strike, unnerved by their own failures, frightened by Roosevelt's attacks on the "money changers," nearly unhinged by the Richard Whitney–led assault on the Securities Exchange Act of 1934, and leery of the heavy liabilities placed by that act on corporate directors, lawyers, and accountants who made errors in their registration statements. By the time Kennedy arrived at the SEC in the summer of 1934, the capital markets had nearly ceased to function, with virtually no new offerings of stocks and bonds. Trading had slowed on the major exchanges to the point that, as the *New York Times* reported on August 5, 1934, Wall Street firms had been forced "to cut expenses drastically by reductions in personnel, salary cuts and 'Scotch weeks' [a week per month without pay] for employees." Kennedy's mandate was to find a way to restore confidence in investors, large and small, who were unwilling to put more capital into the market after having lost much of it in the crash.

Roosevelt had already demonstrated that one way to soothe a frightened nation was to speak to it on the radio. Kennedy followed his lead, secured an invitation to address a luncheon of the National Press Club and fifteen minutes of airtime on the ABC radio network. "The brokerage community," the *New York Times* reported on July 25, the day of his talk, "is waiting eagerly if not anxiously for the radio address of Chairman Kennedy this afternoon . . . because there is a lot of talk in Wall Street to the effect that the talk may be reassuring if not actually encouraging to better markets. . . . It was facetiously suggested yesterday that the Exchange should either suspend operations for fifteen minutes between 2:30 and 2:45 this afternoon, or provide a loud-speaker to broadcast the talk to members on the floor."

With so much at stake, Kennedy, a witty correspondent, conversationalist, and storyteller, but not much of a writer, enlisted Swope and Moley to help draft his address. "Here is the smear," Swope wrote him the day before, "done in rough outline so that you may put in and take out, as you please, and also so that you may word it, wherever you wish, in Kennedyesque fashion. . . . What I want you to do is to strike a note that is definitely your own—one that is marked by courage, by independence and by understanding of the joy you have before you; also by a deep sense of fairness. And now my blessing—and to hell with you."[25]

Kennedy's radio address did precisely what he had hoped it would. Much like Roosevelt, he was able to project an aura of optimism grounded in his own confidence that he could get his job done and regulate the exchanges without doing them—or investors—any harm. "We of the SEC do not regard ourselves as coroners sitting on the corpse of financial enterprise. On the contrary, we think of ourselves as the means of bringing new life into the body of the security business." The market—and the businessmen who had made their fortunes issuing and trading securities—had prospered in the 1920s because during the Great War, the public at large had gotten into the habit of investing in war bonds and then "in the period succeeding the war . . . turned to the leading exchanges and to the investment bankers and brokers for further investment." Having encouraged ordinary Americans to invest in equities, "can there be any doubt the government owes them the responsibility to check improper financial practices—that it owes this vast army responsibility to supervise the industry?"

These were the ethical and historical arguments for government regulation. But there was a compelling practical necessity as well. The securities industry would not prosper again until investor confidence was restored and capital lying idle put to good use. As chairman of the SEC, Kennedy pledged to use the powers placed at his disposal—powers of registration, investigation, subpoena, public hearings, the bully pulpit, and criminal proceedings—to restore confidence and protect investors by weeding out the crooks, the sharks, the swindlers. "The Commission will make war without quarter on any who sell securities by fraud or misrepresentation." And it would do so without interfering with the work of honest brokers, businessmen, and investment bankers. The rules and regulations it would write and enforce would be "simple and honest. Only those who see things crookedly will find them harsh."[26]

Kennedy's speech delighted the investment community. As the *New York Times* reported the next morning, for the fifteen minutes Kennedy was on the air, Wall Street's brokers had "dropped their other duties and clustered around the portable radios in their offices" to hear his address. "Most of them left the loud-speaker with a smile of relief, and some enthusiastically commented that 'that is all the market needs.'" The speech had gone over brilliantly, Swope telegraphed Kennedy. "Whadya mean I done noble," Kennedy responded. "You done noble. Everybody seems to have liked it." Adolf Berle, who had returned to New York after his stint on Roosevelt's brain trust, congratulated Kennedy on striking "a note which was very much needed for the time being."[27]

Congress had given the SEC until October 1 to register every stock exchange in the nation and every security listed on them. Registering the exchanges was a relatively simple matter, as there were only a few dozen of them. Registering the thousands of securities listed on them and the tens of thousands of unlisted securities sold over-the-counter was going to be more difficult. The SEC solved what could have been an impossible problem by granting temporary registration for companies that applied for it and provisional registration for those that did not. It then set out to write permanent registration requirements and design application forms for every firm whose stock was listed on the twenty-one registered exchanges.

It is impossible to overstate the enormity of the task that lay ahead. Between October 1934 and June 1935, the commission, with Kennedy overseeing every action it took, formulated permanent rules governing trading on the exchanges and outlawing "manipulative and deceptive practices"; cooperated with the Federal Reserve System in setting margin rates; began an "intensive study" of the operation of over-the-counter markets with the goal of establishing registration procedures by January 1, 1936; and wrote and put into operation guidelines for the permanent registration of securities already traded and for new issues.[28]

K ennedy managed to get away for a few weekends at Hyannis Port that summer of 1934, his first in Washington, but not many. As his father recommended, Joe Jr. had spent the summer in Hyannis Port preparing for Harvard in the fall. Rose later recalled that he had returned from his trip to the Soviet Union "full of these ideas about the superiority of the communist system . . . over the capitalist system." After one such dinner table argument, at which Joe Jr. tried to enlighten his father on Soviet communism, "Dad set his knife and fork down," Ted later remembered. "'When you sell your Car, and sell your boat, and sell your horse, you can talk to me about that,' he exploded at Joe, 'but otherwise *I don't want to hear any more about it in this house!*' And boom! up he got, and out the door he went." Jack had been listening intently on the sidelines and later confided to his mother that "Joe seems to understand the situation better than Dad." Rose reported Jack's comments to her husband, who responded that he didn't "care what the hell they think about me. I will get along alright, if they stick together."[29]

Rose had arranged for Joe Jr. and Jack to go on retreat with the Passionist priests at their monastery in Brighton, Massachusetts, at the end of the summer. When after the retreat, Father Nilus McAllister wrote

Rose that he was concerned for her sons' piety, she forwarded the letter to her husband in Washington. Kennedy wrote Father McAllister directly to say that he agreed with his concerns about "both" of his boys. "I think they have great potentialities, but I think they are also very critical and rather of an inquisitive frame of mind." As for their relationship to the church, he was not worried that Joe would "become careless now" because at Harvard he would be in "direct contact with the St. Paul Catholic Club." It was Jack he was "very worried about." His year at Catholic school had been a failure, and he was now at Choate "with no help or cooperation whatsoever [from the local parish priests]—a fact I believe, to be a disgraceful proceeding on the part of the clergy." He asked Father McAllister to look after both boys and sent along a check to "defer some of the expenses of this retreat."[30]

If his boys were getting spoiled, it was because he was doing the spoiling, and he knew it. He had sent Joe Jr. to college with a healthy annual allowance to cover his expenses but suggested that he limit himself to an "allotment . . . of $125 a month merely for the moral effect of trying to live as reasonable as possible. If you try this for a couple of months and it doesn't work, let us look into the subject again." Joe Jr. got everything he asked for. When he needed a new shaving brush, Kennedy had Eddie Moore send him one. When he needed train reservations from Boston to Miami for spring break, Kennedy put him in touch with Paul Murphy, who worked at his New York office. When Joe Jr. was chosen chairman of the Freshman Smoker Committee, he got Rudy Vallee and his Connecticut Yankees to perform.[31]

Kennedy kept close tabs on his son and offered constant, often unsolicited advice. Joe Jr. was encouraged to play football at Harvard, because it would give him "a great chance to meet a lot of fellows, and after all, that is the first requisite of a successful college education—learning how to meet people, and getting along with them." He was reminded to stay in close touch with Sir James Calder and other aristocrats in the liquor business in England: "I think it would be a very good idea for you to drop them a line when you can. . . . You know, all that group may be your partners some day and it is well to build up a background for business reasons." When Joe Jr. informed him that he intended to study philosophy, Kennedy laid out the case against philosophy, then recommended that he get in touch with Felix Frankfurter, whose "judgment on the whole lay out would be invaluable." To make sure that Frankfurter said the right thing, Kennedy phoned him and, when he was not in, explained to Mrs. Frankfurter "what I hoped you would be able to do as far as Joe goes." Recognizing that Frankfurter might think he was being too intrusive and overbearing a father, Kennedy preemptively defended himself: "I really want to do the best thing for Joe. By that I mean that I don't wish to force on him anything he can't see himself. I still hope to be able to make suggestions and possibly help direct him. That's as far as I ever want to go."[32]

Five months later, in March 1935, Joe Jr. wrote to say that he had decided to major in government, which from his father's perspective was a great improvement on philosophy. "I think it is frightfully interesting and the type of work you may decide to take up. I wouldn't lose sight of the fact, however, that economics might be a very good sideline, on the basis that it would have many practical advantages."[33]

In Rose's absence—she was taking her "20th anniversary" vacation tour of Europe without her husband—and no doubt because he realized the burden was too great to be left to her alone, Kennedy looked after sixteen-year-old Rosemary that fall. For the past several years, he and Rose had struggled to find the right learning environment for their daughter. They had tried public school, a private boarding school for "slow" children, homeschooling, a Scared Heart convent, but nothing had quite worked out. In September 1934, in large part because her big brother Joe Jr. would be nearby in Cambridge, they sent her to study and live with a private tutor, Helen Newton, in Brookline.[34]

Kennedy, who was concerned that Rosemary would misinterpret the reasons for her relocation from the convent school in Providence to a private home in Brookline, asked Joe Jr. in Cambridge to "keep suggesting to her that she should work very hard in order to get all she can. In other words—she must not feel she is there for social purposes and nothing else." He asked Jack to write Rosemary regularly. "You know it is very important that we have a good job done up there [at Miss Newton's in Brookline] this year."[35]

In mid-October, Kennedy visited Rosemary. He was torn now between pushing her to work harder, as he did his other children, and letting her alone. When Miss Newton complained about his daughter's "bad disposition," Kennedy gently corrected her: "It is something else besides herself that must be blamed for her attitude. By that I mean, it is her inherent backwardness, rather than a bad disposition." He assured Miss Newton that he had "a very firm talk with Rosemary and told her that something must be done, and I am sure she really wants to do it. . . . She was pleased because you felt she had improved with her studying, and I think the other things will show an improvement too." With help from Miss Newton, Rosemary wrote to thank her father for visiting: "I would do anything to make you so happy. I hate to disappoint you in any way. Come to see me very soon. I get very lonesome every day."[36]

Miss Newton had suggested that Kennedy get in touch with Dr. Charles Lawrence, the chief endocrinologist at the New England Medical Center, who "had done wonders for a couple of her pupils." Years earlier, Dr. Frederick Good, who had delivered Rosemary and the other eight children, had discussed "the gland theory as affecting Rosemary." Kennedy now asked Good to look into the matter for him. Up until now, Rosemary's care and schooling, like that of his other daughters, had been Rose's province. But he was intervening now, substituting his judgment for hers while she was away in Europe. He asked Good to proceed with some haste, as he hoped to have the "gland" question fully "investigated before Rose got back on the twenty-eighth. We do not want to leave a stone unturned if there is anything possible to be done." Good visited Rosemary and Miss Newton in Brookline, checked up on Dr. Lawrence, found his "standing . . . one hundred percent," and made an appointment for Rosemary to see him.[37]

Nine days later, after taking Rosemary to see Lawrence, Good reported back to Kennedy the news he had been wishing for: "I am quite hopeful that a systematic treatment with Endocrines will do considerable good—in fact, I will make it even stronger and say that I am very, very hopeful that within a few years, as a result of these Endocrine treatments, Rosemary will be 100% all right."[38]

Kennedy was too much of a realist to believe in miracles, but, as he wrote Dr. Lawrence a month later after visiting Rosemary, while he had "told Dr. Good it was probably imagination, I am noticing considerable improvement. It will certainly be a blessing if possible to help her. I will be interested from time to time to hear any observations you may make in connection with the case, and I hope and pray that something can be done."[39]

That winter, with Joe Jr. during well at Harvard, Rosemary apparently benefiting from regular "gland" injections, Kick settled in at the Sacred Heart Convent, and Eunice putting on weight and getting over her asthma, Jack resumed his role as the Kennedy family problem child. It was his final year at Choate, and if he did reasonably well, his father had promised to send him to study with Laski in London, as his brother had the year before. Jack, as always, refused to fulfill anyone's expectations of him. He read what he wanted to when he wanted to and proudly sported the irreverent attitude that the Passionist priests had complained about.

Early in December, Jack wrote his father in Washington to confess that both he and his best friend were ashamed at "how poorly" they had done in the first "quarter, and we have definitely decided to stop fooling around. I really do realize how important it is that I get a good job done this year if I want to go to England."

His best friend at Choate and, arguably, for the rest of his life was Kirk LeMoyne Billings, or "Lem." Lem was from Pittsburgh, his father a noted but not terribly wealthy physician who had died while his son was at Choate and left almost nothing behind for him. Lem was a bespectacled teddy bear of a boy with curly blondish hair, glasses, and a perpetual grin. Jack was devoted to him. After his father died, he was virtually adopted and certainly assisted financially by Kennedy. Much later, he would look after Bobby's children when they were orphaned.

Kennedy, on receiving Jack's confession that he and Lem were doing less than they could at school, wrote back to say that he had taken "a great satisfaction out" of his son's uncharacteristically contrite letter. Then, having been given the opening, he launched into an almost standard-issue patriarchal exhortation: "Now Jack, I don't want to give the impression that I am a nagger, for goodness knows I think that is the worst thing any parent can be. . . . After long experience in sizing up people I definitely know you have the goods and you can go a long way. Now aren't you foolish not to get all there is out of what God has given you and what you can do with it yourself. After all, I would be lacking even as a friend if I did not urge you to take advantage of the qualities you have. . . . I am not expecting too much and I will not be disappointed if you don't turn out to be a real genius, but I think you can be a really worthwhile citizen with good judgment and good understanding. I like LeMoyne and think he is a very fine boy, with great possibilities, and I know that if both of you really made up your minds to do what you honestly could do with your talents, you would both be surprised and pleased."[40]

Despite his father's pep talk, Jack quickly got into trouble again. When headmaster St. John referred in chapel to the boys who failed to live up to the school's behavioral standards as "muckers," Jack and Lem promptly formed a "Muckers Club" and invited their classmates to join. St. John responded by threatening the "muckers" with expulsion. Kick made matters worse by telegraphing her support to her brother and Lem: "Dear Public Enemies one and two, All our prayers are united with you and the other eleven mucks. When the old men arrive sorry we won't be there for the burial." The telegram was intercepted and shown to St. John.[41]

On February 11, St. John wired Kennedy at his office in New York and at the SEC, "Will you please make every possible effort to come to Choate Saturday or Sunday for a conference with Jack and us which we think a necessity." Kennedy cabled back that he could not get away on Saturday but would arrive in Wallingford at 12:15 on Sunday.[42]

Kennedy's appearance on being summoned by St. John and Jack's contrition saved him from expulsion. Kick was admonished separately and warned not to send any more incriminating telegrams. "I know you want to do all you can for Jack, but I think I should tell you that one of the serious difficulties he found himself in was his characterization of 'public enemy' and that group of his with the frightful name 'muckers.' I really don't think there is anything smart about it and I hope it won't be the cause of having him expelled. . . . It has all been smoothed out temporarily, but have this in mind."[43]

As the school year came to a close, Kennedy was worried that Jack would not make it out of Choate if he didn't do better. Now thoroughly exasperated at the ups and downs in his son's scholastic career, he wrote him once again—this time in the harshest terms he could employ: "Don't let me lose confidence in you again, because it will be pretty nearly an impossible task to restore it—I am sure it will be a loss to you and a distinct loss to me. The mere trying to do a good job is not enough—real honest-to-goodness effort is what I expect. . . . You have the goods; why not try to show it?"[44]

In the pre-SEC days, there had, as historian Thomas McCraw has written, been "no requirement that corporate reporting be certified by independent public accountants. Some companies issued no reports or information of any kind." This dearth of reliable information on corporate assets, income, expenses, and liabilities had provided insiders such as Kennedy with an unfair advantage that they exploited to the full. Such practices had to cease now, Kennedy argued, and the playing field leveled, if investors were to be induced to get back into the market. The task set before the SEC was to determine precisely what kind of information companies should be compelled to divulge and how to make sure that this information was truthful, complete, and verifiable. "In case after case," recalled future Supreme Court justice William O. Douglas, "we had to determine whether registration statements filed contained false statements of material facts. Some representations were transparent." Stock or stock options issued to promoters were disguised; companies falsely advertised ownership of nonexistent timber, gold mines, or oil wells; the accountants who verified the financial statements were company officers. "These and thousands of other artifices and devices had been historically used to mulct the public, and in the early years . . . the mettle of the new agency was tested over and over again."[45]

The "blue sky" laws that the SEC wrote and enforced would, Kennedy believed, constitute the single most important tool in restoring confidence in the market by weeding out the crooks and charlatans. He took enormous pleasure in recounting in the articles and speeches he delivered in 1935 the success his lawyers, accountants, and field men had had in uncovering "gyps" perpetuated by the tipsters, swindlers, bucket-shop grafters, and confidence men who preyed on the public by spreading rumors. "Some folks believed they could win quick riches through buying Florida frogs to breed frogs legs and saddles on an enormous scale. . . . There were gold mines galore, because the public became gold-conscious when we slipped off the standard. One mine I recall sold plenty of stock based on an engineer's belief that a stone picked up by a schoolgirl at play showed rich gold deposits near her home." There were oil royalty rings and potash syndicates that made outrageously false claims in their prospectuses. These abuses the SEC intended to end—and, in fact, came very close to doing so.[46]

While bucket-shop gypsters and charlatans fleeced the public by making false claims about their stocks, seemingly reputable corporate directors and officers, exchange officials, investment bankers, and Wall Street's own brokers, dealers, and specialists had done more damage still by withholding information about their trading practices, manipulating stock prices, and clandestinely buying and selling large blocks of their own stock. Kennedy hoped to curb such "insider trading" abuses by requiring companies to promptly report when trades were executed by directors or officers or individuals who owned 10 percent or more of a stock. Directors and officers were furthermore prohibited from colluding with brokers and specialists to pump up prices or volumes by trading in multiple or falsely registered accounts. Also outlawed were pools, corners, wash sales and match orders (in which excessive volume is generated by the simultaneous sale and purchase of the same stock), dummy sales (pumping up prices on smaller exchanges before listing them on major ones), and all sorts of insider and specialist trading abuses.

Joseph P. Kennedy believed in capitalism, the market, the good sense of investors, and the honesty of most of those in the securities business. His primary task, as he never ceased to repeat, was a conservative one: to get the markets and the economy going again by pumping in new investment capital. He directed that the registration rules for new issues be rewritten to make the process less expensive and less cumbersome. He then took to the road with John Burns, the SEC counsel, to reassure corporations and underwriters that it was safe to return to the market and offering them assistance in writing up their registration statements. "You have been told when you sought to raise money or readjust corporation finances by refunding," he lectured Chicago business executives on February 8, 1935, "that the labor expense, and legal liabilities involved, imposed upon the issuer of new securities unbearable hardships. Gentlemen, I ask you now to disregard those warnings and to forget that bogie. Do your business as usual. Come down to Washington in person and present your problems to us, and I am confident that we can show you how to do new financing legally, pleasantly, and inexpensively."[47]

He saw his task as that of cheerleader, Wall Street enthusiast, civic booster. "In all frankness, I must say that this ace of American cities," he declared at a speech in New York City, "is not giving a good account of its stewardship as the pace-setter of business enterprise. . . . Gentlemen, I am deeply concerned about the low state to which courage and confidence among business men have fallen. . . . I urge you to seize the torch of leadership in this necessary crusade. . . . New York, which has been holding back largely because of misapprehension and unwarranted fears, we hope will provide that timely leadership."[48]

His tough talk in New York earned him front-page coverage and support in the editorial pages the next morning. "Most men of sober judgment will consider that [his] rebuke was merited," the *New York Times* declared.[49]

On February 19, after the Supreme Court had decided, in a 5–4 decision, that Congress had acted constitutionally in removing the nation from the gold standard, a decision that, had it gone the other way, would have caused chaos in the stock markets, Roosevelt playfully agreed to Kennedy's request that he take a week off. "In view of the sleepless nights and hectic days of the Chairman of the S.E.C., in view of his shrunken frame, sunken eyes, falling hair, and fallen arches, he is hereby directed to proceed to Palm Beach and return to Washington six hours after he gets there AND AFTER TEN INTERVENING DAYS HAVE PASSED BY (FOOLED AGAIN!)"[50]

Kennedy flew to Palm Beach but was back in Washington within the week. The workload was grinding him down, but he reveled in his new insider status. "Have important meeting White House tonight," he wrote Bernard Baruch, who had invited him to his South Carolina estate for the weekend. "Correspondents' dinner tomorrow night. Going to New York on midnight, coming down in time to join the Boss on *Sequoia* [FDR's yacht] Sunday afternoon. . . . I hope I live long enough to see you back here. At the clip I am going it won't be long now."[51]

Roosevelt had begun to call on Kennedy more and more now. He enjoyed socializing with him at the White House and Marwood, admired his blunt talk and lack of pretense, and recognized that there were political benefits in the reports of Kennedy's being one of his close advisers. Simply by consulting with his SEC chairman—and letting the press know that he was—Roosevelt disarmed opponents who portrayed him as having cut himself off from any but the most radical New Dealers. "The President," Arthur Krock reported on April 28, 1935, "is especially fond of him because of his agreeable personality, his ready laugh, his loyalty, his high ability and his Celtic pugnacity. The two argue constantly over acts and policies, and the President hears more objections than assents from the chairman of the SEC. But he consults Mr. Kennedy on everything, and, when the argument is over, President and adviser relax like two school boys." Charles Hurd, also of the *New York Times,* identified Kennedy in his May 26, 1935, column as the president's current "confidante, the individual outside the Cabinet circle" with whom he discussed his "pressing problems . . . the worries of the day." Exaggerating even more than Krock the position Kennedy occupied in the administration, Hurd reported that the SEC chairman dined "at the White House three or four evenings weekly and he is the last man before whom proposals are laid by Mr. Roosevelt after the President has discussed them with the specialists."

Had the business recovery been more rapid or more sustained, the president would not have needed Kennedy by his side. But although it was true, as Kennedy had reported in speeches in Chicago and New York earlier in the year, that business activity was on the rise, it was also the case that unemployment remained scandalously high, still over 20 percent, and the "forgotten men" whom Roosevelt had preached to and who had supported him for the presidency in 1932 and in the 1934 midterm elections were losing patience.

The president had several choices: (1) he could stay the course and hope to weather the attacks from left and right until the economy righted itself—if it did; (2) he could move closer to the business community by reducing government spending, easing up on reform, and letting business regulate itself; or (3) he could move to the left, raise taxes on the rich, support labor's attempts at unionization, and spend more money to put the unemployed back to work.

His decision to take the third option and embark on a new and massive jobs or "work relief" program was intended, in part, to shift attention—and support—away from the grandiose schemes for sharing the wealth and ending unemployment tossed onto the public agenda. Father Charles Coughlin, the Detroit radio priest, had by early 1935 attracted a loyal following of nearly forty million radio listeners and enrolled eight and a half million "persons qualified to vote" for his National Union for Social Justice, which advocated higher taxes on the wealthy, a guaranteed annual wage, the nationalization of public utilities, protection for organized labor, and much more. Dr. Francis Townsend of Long Beach, California, nearly seventy now, was listened to by millions more who believed that his plan to give pensions to every American sixty and over who promised to retire would solve poverty and unemployment. Roosevelt's most dangerous rival in 1934 was neither Coughlin nor Townsend, popular as they were, but Senator Huey Long of Louisiana, who had his own "Share the Wealth" program, clubs across the country, a mailing list of seven and a half million Americans, and a profound understanding of how elections were fought and won.

Early in 1935, Roosevelt convened a meeting to discuss a new work relief effort and public jobs program. In attendance were Harold Ickes, his secretary of the interior; Harry Hopkins, who ran the Federal Emergency Relief Administration; and Henry Morgenthau, secretary of the treasury. Though Kennedy was not a member of the cabinet or director of any of the New Deal relief agencies, he was invited to the first planning sessions. According to Harold Ickes, Kennedy was initially "quite cold on the matter of a public works program," but during the course of discussion he was "swung over and favored such a program."[52]

In January 1935, Roosevelt asked Congress for several billion dollars to put Americans back to work. In April, Congress gave him what he had asked for. Kennedy was called to the White House to advise the president on how to spend the money. "The President has just appointed me to the small Executive Committee for the spending of the $5,000,000 relief fund," he wrote Jack on April 26, 1935. "I don't know how in heaven's name I am going to find any time, but I will stick it out as long as I can. It looks very doubtful, however, if I will be able to finish this job by the first of July," the goal he had set himself.[53]

Having secured the funds he needed for his new work relief pro-

gram, Roosevelt required both a plan and an administrator to implement it. Harry Hopkins and Harold Ickes were the principal candidates
and rivals for the job. Morgenthau suggested that to avoid internal bick-
ering between the two, Roosevelt appoint Kennedy. Kennedy turned
down the proposal because he did not want to be put in a position
where he would have to work with "Honest Harold" Ickes. At age sixty,
the crusading midwestern Republican whom Roosevelt had made his
secretary of the interior and then entrusted with the Public Works
Administration was an indefatigable infighter, smart, ambitious, vain,
and incorruptible. Though Kennedy and Ickes would feign friendship at
times, neither had any use for the other. Kennedy thought Ickes a du-
plicitous, gossiping, fuzzy-minded, antibusiness radical. Ickes despised
and distrusted Kennedy as a confidence man and stock swindler. He
was also a bit jealous of Roosevelt's affection for and seeming trust in a
man he, Ickes, detested.[54]

A new relief program was a necessity, but it was not in itself going to
steal the thunder from the president's critics. The president had to also
demonstrate that he believed in sharing or redistributing the nation's
wealth. The only way to do this was by increasing taxes on inheritances
and the income of the wealthiest Americans. Knowing the opposition
such a measure was bound to elicit and hoping to defuse it, Roosevelt
invited Edmond Coblentz, William Randolph Hearst's senior editor, to
the White House. Over the course of a four-hour cocktails/dinner discussion, Roosevelt explained patiently but passionately to Coblentz that he
was fighting not just "Communism [but] Huey Longism, Coughlinism,
Townsendism. I want to save our system, the capitalistic system; to save
it is to give some heed to world thought of today. To combat . . . crackpot
ideas, it may be necessary to throw the forty-six men who are reported
to have incomes in excess of $1,000,000 a year to the wolves. In other
words, limit incomes through taxation to $1,000,000." Hearst was one
of those forty-six men whose income was about to be "limited."[55]

To emphasize that the tax message he was sending to Congress was
not a radical but a conservative measure intended to save the capitalist
system from its enemies, Roosevelt sent Kennedy to meet with Hearst.
Kennedy spent a week at San Simeon in early May, the longest time he
had been out of Washington since his Christmas vacation with his family in Palm Beach. Whatever he said did the trick. Hearst cabled his

editors across the country asking them to "please hold up articles critical of administration for a while. . . . I think we would be fairer to administration and also more effective in our criticism if we discriminated
more and also if we had commendation for some measures." One of the
administration measures Hearst identified as "beneficial to the country" and deserving commendation was the "securities act" that Kennedy administered.[56]

Franklin Roosevelt was so delighted with Kennedy's success at San
Simeon that he offered to bring him back to Washington "on Battleship
through Panama Canal. Happy Landings."[57]

There was, unfortunately for the president, a limit to the magic Kennedy could work. The Hearst papers held their fire for a month. Then
on June 19, 1935, after Roosevelt had formally requested that Congress
raise tax rates on incomes over $1 million, inherited fortunes, and large
corporations, Hearst went back on the attack. "President's taxation
program is essentially Communism," he telegraphed his editorial writers across the country. "It is to be sure, a bastard product of Communism and demagogic democracy, a mongrel creation which might
accurately be called demo-communism, evolved by a composite personality which might be labeled Stalin Delano Roosevelt."[58]

The Roosevelt administration, with Kennedy in the thick of it,
spent the spring and summer of 1935 designing and implementing its
$4 billion work relief program, preparing new tax legislation, watch-
ing anxiously as the Wagner Act (which provided workers with the
government-sanctioned-and-protected right to organize unions) wound
its way through Congress, waiting for the Supreme Court to issue its
decision on the legality of the National Recovery Act (which it did on
May 27, declaring it unconstitutional), and lobbying for a public utility
holding company bill.

Kennedy was involved in all these projects, but the one that took the
most time and caused the most trouble was the public utilities bill, an
essential part of the administration's rather dramatic turn to the left.
The aim of the legislation was to break up the large holding companies
that together controlled three quarters of the nation's privately owned
electricity-generating industry. The moment the bill was introduced in
Congress in February, Wall Street and the utility companies had

launched a mammoth lobbying and misinformation campaign against it, claiming that the legislation, if approved, would halt investment, curtail future innovations, raise consumer costs, and lead to government ownership of the utilities and the ruin of the millions of Americans who had invested their life savings in utility holding company stocks.

Louis Howe, whose job it was to protect the president politically, asked Kennedy if it was true, as the lobbyists claimed, that five million Americans owned utility company stock. Kennedy thought the number too high but agreed that Americans who had invested in utility stocks were right to worry about the legislation. That, however, was not sufficient reason not to go ahead. "After all, the total number of investors is so much smaller than the total number of the public affected by unjust public utility rates that the interest of the latter must prevail. It goes without saying that greater violence would be done the public as a whole if utility holding companies were allowed to continue as at present than that being done to investors by the proposed legislation."[59]

Washington was inundated by more utilities lobbyists than there were senators and congressmen combined. The public utility holding company bill was furiously lobbied, amended, and reamended all that spring and into the early summer of 1935. The bill that was passed by the Senate in June called on the holding companies to voluntarily restructure themselves into regional operating entities. To provide an incentive for such restructuring, the bill contained a "death sentence" provision mandating that companies that had not been so restructured by January 1, 1940, would be dissolved. Though Kennedy privately thought the "death sentence" a bit harsh and confrontational, what concerned him more was that the SEC was to be assigned responsibility for implementing it—this at a time when it was already overburdened with administering the Securities Act of 1933 and the Securities Exchange Act of 1934. "The four of us [Pecora had resigned at the end of his term and no replacement had been named]," he wrote Sam Rayburn, who was steering the legislation through the House, "have been carrying the load here for the last six months and we frankly are all shot to pieces, and need to get some rest before we take on this terrific new job." He asked Rayburn to amend the bill so that it would become effective on December 1, giving the SEC thirty extra days to prepare. "I just do not see how we can start off by the first of November."[60]

Worse was yet to come. Under pressure from the utility company lobbyists and business interests, Rayburn was forced to amend the bill in the House, replacing the mandatory "death sentence" with a watered-down provision that gave the SEC sole responsibility for determining whether the "public interest" was served by permitting a holding company to control two or more "integrated" systems in noncontiguous geographic areas. Kennedy was outraged. As he wrote the president and Burton Wheeler, the sponsor of the bill in the Senate, there were two essential problems with the amended House bill. The "administrative burden" imposed on the SEC in determining whether to dissolve a holding company was "overwhelming." Even more critical, however, he thought it exceedingly "poor policy to vest in any one group of men [the SEC commissioners] the tremendous responsibility involved in this grant of power. . . . In a matter of this kind where there are at stake the interests of millions of people, investors, and the consuming public alike, I do not believe that any Commission should be given unfettered discretion to decide matters of such transcendent importance."[61]

The debate over the public utility holding company legislation and the "death sentence" continued through the summer, to Kennedy's dismay. He had hoped to get away to Hyannis Port after July 4 but found himself interminably tied up in Washington. "I am spending the weekend here working on the Utility Bill," he wrote Swope on July 13, 1935. "Anybody could have made a lot of money betting me at odds of 100 to 1 that I would spend a summer weekend in Washington."[62]

On July 11, while he was in Washington working on the utility bill, Roosevelt cabled him from Hyde Park with yet another task: "A lot of business men feel that not the least important block to recovery lies in excessive steel prices. Do you want to do a little quiet looking into this for me?"[63]

Having now spent the largest part of two successive summers in Washington, knowing that come fall he would have to put into operation the public utility legislation, bone weary from having worked twelve-hour days and six-day weeks for the past year, Kennedy decided to resign. After visiting Hyde Park to tell the president of his plans, he delivered his formal letter of resignation on September 6, 1935. He was, he wrote the president, leaving government service for "personal reasons." He had agreed to serve for only a year but had remained in place for fifteen months. He was resigning now so that his successor would have ample time to prepare for the implementation of the new Public Utility Holding Company Act.[64]

Franklin Roosevelt had one more favor to ask. Concerned that Father Coughlin, whose radio audience was growing larger by the day, was moving closer to an alliance with Huey Long in preparation for the 1936 elections, the president asked Kennedy to phone Coughlin and tell him the "boss" wanted to see him. Kennedy placed the call while he was with Roosevelt at Hyde Park. Coughlin agreed to come at once, boarded the overnight train from Detroit, and arrived in Albany about four the next morning. According to Coughlin, Kennedy picked him up at the station in his Rolls-Royce and drove him to Hyde Park. When the president awoke later that morning, he greeted both men warmly, then, with a smile, "told Joe to 'go look at the pigs'—he didn't have any pigs of course," Coughlin later told a reporter. "It was just a little joke he used to make. Joe laughed and went out." Coughlin then presented the president with evidence he said he had received from his bishop that officials in the Roosevelt administration were "helping the Communist cause overseas."

Roosevelt listened intently but did not take the matter nearly as seriously as Coughlin had hoped. He didn't have to. That morning, he had learned that Huey Long had died in a Louisiana hospital after being shot in the abdomen in the corridor of the Louisiana Capitol. As a Canadian and a priest, Coughlin could not run for president and was thus rendered infinitely less of a threat to the president with Long out of the picture.

At the end of their conversation, Roosevelt asked Father Coughlin and Kennedy "to stay for dinner," but Coughlin replied that the two men had "already made plans to drive up to the home of a friend of ours in Great Barrington. On the way up I told Joe most of the story, and when we got there Kennedy asked the butler to bring him some writing paper . . . and wrote out his resignation as chairman of the SEC."[65]

Most of the story rings true, though the letter of resignation Cough-

lin claims Kennedy wrote in Great Barrington had been delivered earlier. Coughlin may have misremembered the details. More probably,
Kennedy had implied that he was so concerned with Roosevelt's move
to the left that he was resigning because of it.

Whatever he may have intimated to Coughlin or, later, to other Roosevelt critics, Kennedy was not resigning because of any policy differences, but because the thought of continuing in place, and gearing up to
administer yet another congressional mandate, the Public Utility Holding Company Act, was more than he could stomach. Drew Pearson and
Robert Allen, in their "Washington Merry-Go-Round" column, insisted that in the end it was boredom as well as overwork that had
forced his hand. He was resigning because the SEC was "functioning
smoothly. 'And,' says Joe, 'it is darn boring to sit around deciding
whether a clerk receiving $3,200 should now get $3,600.'"[66]

The news of his resignation prompted an outpouring of praise for the
man, his family, and the swell job he had done. In its July 22, 1935,
cover story on Kennedy, *Time* magazine had already crowned the SEC
with "the distinction of being the most ably administered New Deal
agency in Washington." Reporters and editorial writers from around the
country agreed. "The financial community's high esteem for Mr. Kennedy," the *Literary Digest* opined on August 24, 1935, "is remarkable,
perhaps unique. It involves a considerable measure of gratitude, since it
is felt that his understanding attitude has made the rigors of SEC control
not only bearable but, in many respects, acceptable."[67]

"He was," syndicated conservative columnist Frank Kent reported
on September 25 in the *Wall Street Journal* and elsewhere, "more consistently and unanimously praised by the press than any public official
of his time. . . . Mr. Kennedy happened to be in a class entirely alone"
among Roosevelt appointees and supporters. "He stood out among
these giddy New Dealers and carefree money-scatterers like a light-
house in a fog. . . . Instinctively, Mr. Kennedy, fond as he was of Mr.
Roosevelt personally, did not belong to the New Deal crowd, did not
pretend to be one of them, did not believe in the New Deal hokum."[68]

His greatest success, as the Kent article demonstrated, had been in
maintaining and promoting, with the help of influential friends like Arthur Krock, his unique political persona as the plainspoken, always
honest, nonideological, nonpartisan businessman who had come to

Washington to do a job for the president and, having completed it, was leaving. Unlike other members of the administration team, he had refrained from commenting publicly for or against the programs and proposals that characterized Roosevelt's turn to the left: the Wagner Act, the income tax proposals that had so angered Hearst, the massive deficit-spending work relief programs, or the "death sentence" provision of the public utility holding company legislation that he was rumored to oppose. If his conservative friends took his silence as disagreement with the administration, that was all to the good. It maintained his standing as their liaison to the White House, while keeping open the door to his return to Washington in some other role.

Thirteen

REELECTING ROOSEVELT

Kennedy sailed for Europe on the *Normandie* on September 25, 1935, taking Jack, Kick, and Rose with him. Jack would remain in London to study with Harold Laski, as his brother had. Kick was on her way to a convent school at Neuilly, outside Paris. Rose had shopping to do.

Unwilling to abandon his role as an administration insider, Kennedy, on resigning his post at the SEC, had lobbied for a new and special assignment from the president. He intended to spend that fall negotiating with officials in the European capitals for the registration of foreign stocks and bonds on the New York Stock Exchange. Befitting his position as presidential emissary, he was preceded by letters to the American ambassadors in Great Britain, the Netherlands, Germany, Italy, and France, asking them to arrange meetings with "one or two of the important people" in government and "also those in opposition." Arthur Krock wrote the *New York Times* bureaus and reporters, asking them to assist Kennedy as well.[1]

Meetings were arranged with officials in charge of finance and banking in the Western European capitals, including, in London, Chancellor of the Exchequer Neville Chamberlain and former chancellor Winston

Churchill. Bernard Baruch had cabled Churchill in advance, suggesting that he be sure to make an "appointment to see [Kennedy] as he is important and good relationship between you two might have far reaching results."[2]

After a visit to Chartwell, Churchill's estate in Kent, and a week spent mostly in London, Kennedy crossed the English Channel for meetings in Switzerland, Holland, France, and Italy. His tour was cut short when Jack, whom he had left behind to register for classes at the London School of Economics, took ill and had to be hospitalized. Kennedy returned to London, cabled Jack's doctors in the States, and was informed that Jack was probably suffering from a relapse of the "agranulocytosis" that had led to an earlier hospitalization. This time, as twice before, Jack miraculously recovered as quickly as he had taken ill. "I am once more baffling the doctors," he wrote Lem Billings from London. "I am a 'most amazing case.'"[3]

While Jack put on the bravest of fronts, his father was frightened. He had witnessed too many unexplained illnesses, too many relapses, too many emergency hospitalizations. There was no telling when the illness would fell him again. If and when it happened, Kennedy wanted his son nearby, not in London, an ocean away. With a bit of help from Swope, the master fixer, strings were pulled and Jack was admitted, after the semester had begun, to Princeton, where Billings and his friends were in residence and where he could go to school without being compared with his older brother, Joe Jr., who was still at Harvard.

His improvement, so rapid at first, stalled when he got home. "Jack is far from being a well boy," Kennedy wrote Ambassador Robert Bingham in London soon after his return, "and as a result I am afraid my time for the next six months will be devoted to trying to help him regain his health." After consulting with Jack's doctor at Princeton and the specialist who had been treating him at the Peter Bent Brigham Hospital in Boston, Kennedy decided to let him stay at school through Thanksgiving. "Then, if no real improvement has been made," he wrote Jack, "you and I will discuss whether or not it is best for you to lay off for a year and try and put yourself in condition. After all, the only consideration I have in the whole matter is your happiness, and I don't want you to lose a year of your college life (which ordinarily brings great pleasure to [a] boy) by wrestling with a bad physical condition and a jam in your studies. A year is important, but it isn't so important if it's going to leave a mark for the rest of your life."[4]

A month later, Jack was back at Peter Bent Brigham Hospital. In mid-December, he was officially withdrawn from Princeton. He spent the Christmas holidays in Palm Beach with friends from Princeton and would have preferred to recuperate there for the rest of the winter, but his father was determined to find out what ailed him and how to treat it. He sent Jack back to the hospital in Boston for two months of tests (with weekends off). In late February, the doctors released him to his father's care in Palm Beach. They had failed to come up with any diagnosis or treatment plan. It was too late to return to Princeton—and Kennedy was not convinced his son was up to it. What the boy needed, he decided, was to build his strength to the point where he could fight off future infections.

Arthur Krock, who was visiting in Palm Beach, recommended a cattle ranch in Arizona. Jack reluctantly agreed, and after a bit more time in the sun in Palm Beach and a trip to New York, he went west to work on the ranch. He came home that spring, hale, hearty, and relatively healthy, to inform his delighted father that he had decided not to return to Princeton, but to join his brother at Harvard.[5]

Kennedy wrote the Harvard dean of freshmen, with whom he had already been in correspondence, to push the boy's application forward. He was so anxious to have Jack admitted that he preemptively identified, then apologized for, his son's shortcomings: "Jack has a brilliant mind for the things in which he is interested, but is careless and lacks application in those in which he is not interested. This is, of course, a bad fault." Still, he wanted the dean to know that Jack was so committed to returning to school and catching up on his year away that he intended to complete the work for his degree in three years, not four (thereby accomplishing something his older brother had never imagined attempting). Kennedy applauded his son's ambition but requested that the dean's assistant "confer with Jack on whether or not this three-year idea is to be encouraged." He himself was on his way to Europe on business but would return in time for the opening of the school year. "I shall make it my business to go to Boston and talk with the teachers from whom Jack will receive instruction in his freshman year."[6]

In November 1935, after delivering his report to the president, Kennedy held an informal press conference to remind reporters of his existence, then in early December flew to Palm Beach for the rest of the winter. "Without me," Rose recalled, "he was an unattached male," that most coveted of dinner guests in Palm Beach. Still, he declined almost every invitation. Having his dinner anywhere but home, he risked getting "into an argument of some sort," Rose told an interviewer in 1972. "He often sat next to some prying female who asked stupid inarticulate questions and why should he be thus bothered." On those few occasions when he did go out, he was inevitably sorry the next morning, because he had gotten into "a fight about Roosevelt or he was asked advice about the Stock Market and was quoted or misquoted later."[7]

Rose visited Palm Beach occasionally, but she never stayed for long—and was seldom there alone with her husband. "I hope this letter reaches you in Florida," Kick wrote her mother on February 8, "as you seem to jump around like a frog between N.Y. and Florida—One minute in New York the next in Florida."[8]

Rose did not particularly enjoy sharing the Palm Beach house with her husband's golfing buddies, especially Arthur Houghton. When they were around—and they always were—she stuck out like a sore thumb. And then too there were the other women in Kennedy's life. Though she would never articulate it as such, Rose had to have known in some way that her husband did not remain celibate during the three hundred or so days a year they remained apart.

As Joe Jr. and Jack grew older, and sexually active, they began to take notice of the beautiful young women their father kept company with. During his brief stay in London in the fall of 1935, Jack wrote Lem of his own interest in the "very good looking blonde whom Dad seems to know, about 24, who is a divorcee." Joe Jr. wrote his father in Palm Beach the following February to say that the beautiful "Barbara Cushing [Barbara "Babe" Cushing, later Paley, was James Roosevelt's sister-in-law at the time] & a friend who was out with you in N.Y. hearing Toscanini, Persian Room etc. till 3 o'clock were up here and gave me the low down on you. They said they nearly went South [to Palm Beach].

I think Mother ought to keep a better eye on you." Kennedy responded lightheartedly that his son should not "worry too much about Barbara Cushing and her pal . . . 21 or 22 is still a little too young for me."[9]

From Palm Beach, Kennedy kept in touch with his children by letter. To Joe Jr., who was still more than a year away from graduation but had no real career plans, he suggested he consider the family business, politics. "Get yourself signed up and possibly make some speeches in the fall in the campaign throughout Massachusetts. It would be a very interesting experience and you could work up two or three subjects you wanted to discuss and go out through the State. Of course, the trouble is football may be on." He suggested that Joe Jr. might also want to "drop in at the bank [Columbia Trust Company in East Boston] and see Mr. Porter [the president] and look around. There may be some points of interest there you would like to follow up."[10]

Rosemary was still living in Brookline with Miss Newton and appeared to be doing well. Looking at her, one would not guess that she was "slow." Joe Jr. invited her to school dances and functions at Harvard, which she mightily enjoyed. She was also spending time with Rose's sister Agnes and other members and friends of the Fitzgerald family. Her letters home were chatty but rambling and disorganized— in the manner of a five- or six-year-old. "I take my red pills, injections in my arm 3 times a week. My new white shoes are ready. I have a new necktie red and white the color. I am going to study Napoleon."[11]

Kick had been homesick at first but had adjusted, as she always did, to her new circumstances at her convent school in France. Her father worried that she was a bit too eager to get away with her American friends for weekends and holidays in Paris, London, and Italy. Kennedy had no objection to her sightseeing, but he wanted her to make the most of her trips away from the convent. "Try to get all you can out of this trip, because it will be of great help to you in everything you do hereafter."[12]

Eunice, who never had to be prodded to focus on her schoolwork, had finished her "orals" and, her father supposed, was now "taking it nice and easy." He suggested that she work on her penmanship, which was still pretty bad. "By this time I suppose Bobby has that bugle and the house is pretty nearly a mad house. However, maybe you could arrange to send him down near the railroad station and let him play when the trains come in."[13]

He asked Bobby, though only ten, to step up and begin taking a bit of responsibility at home in Bronxville. "Joe, Jack and I talked it over the other night and decided we really depended on you to do a good job in the house now that you are . . . the only man left in it."[14]

In late February, in his letter thanking Eunice, Patricia, and Jean for their valentines, Kennedy announced that the "golf professor" their mother and brother Jack had taken lessons from would be staying with them at Cape Cod for the summer. You all can take lessons every day and become good golfers—and that means Jeannie, too." He wrote a separate thank-you note to Bobby and Ted. "I do not think you two boys would like to get a letter with the girls so am writing you one separately. . . . The girls will tell you about the golf lessons . . . I think Teddy would be a little too small, don't you?"[15]

As the world's leading authority on procedures and requirements for registering new issues with the SEC, Joseph P. Kennedy, private citizen, was in great demand. In early 1936, David Sarnoff asked for his help in putting together a recapitalization plan for RCA, which would include the issuance of new SEC-registered securities. Kennedy, who had remained on good terms with Sarnoff since they had parted company seven years earlier, flew north to discuss his new assignment with him and the RCA board. On the way back to Palm Beach, he stopped off in Washington to meet separately with the president and with his former associates at the SEC. The announcement of his contract with RCA, followed two days later by his visit to the White House and the SEC offices, the *New York Times* reported, had "set brokers to speculating whether he is in business or in politics, or in both." Colonel Robert McCormick, the publisher of the *Chicago Tribune* and at the time perhaps the New Deal's most acerbic critic, published an editorial on January 18, 1936, attacking the president for having appointed Kennedy to the SEC and Kennedy for parlaying that appointment into a lucrative consulting contract with RCA.

Kennedy asked John Boettiger, Anna Roosevelt's husband, who had worked for the *Chicago Tribune,* to help him draft a response. Though he did not say so to McCormick, he expected to return soon to Washington, and once he did so he would have to give up all moneymaking activities. Why not, then, while he was still a private citizen, make as much as he could?[16]

He began work on the RCA project by assembling a team of accountants, several of whom had worked for him at the SEC. In April 1936, he flew to New York City to deliver his recommendations at a stockholders meeting. Following his presentation, he took questions. The first one was about his fee. Betraying not the slightest sign of embarrassment at the question—or the answer he was about to give—Kennedy began by explaining that "at the SEC we always demanded the truth and I guess some of you will get a shock. . . . My fee was $150,000 [equivalent to about $2.25 million today], from which I paid $30,000 to accountants."

"The stockholders," *Time* magazine reported on April 20, "were indeed shocked [by Kennedy's disclosure], for a profound silence descended upon the rest of the meeting." Moments later, however, they voted to approve his plan and his fee. The next day, the RCA stock price began an upward climb.

Almost immediately on turning in his RCA report and pocketing his fee, Kennedy was hired as a special adviser to Paramount. His mandate was to offer recommendations on how the studio could cut costs, increase profits, and cover dividend payments on its preferred stock issues. Six weeks after taking the assignment, Kennedy submitted his report to the board of directors and asked that it be made public. He bit down hard on the hands that had fed him, recommending a shakeup in the board of directors, "drastic and courageous revision of management," and substantial cuts in executive salaries. He was paid a $50,000 fee, making his total consulting salary for three months' work $200,000. President Roosevelt's annual salary in 1936 was $75,000; Vice President Garner's was $20,000; the dean of Harvard Law School earned $14,000.

To make sure no one in the White House would forget him while he was on what he hoped would be a temporary hiatus from Washington, Kennedy sent bottles of Haig & Haig's best Scotch to the president for Christmas and stayed in close contact with the Roosevelt children and with Missy LeHand, the president's secretary since 1920, who now lived in the White House and, when Eleanor was absent, acted as presidential hostess. He called Missy regularly, got her brother Bernard a job with Somerset, and invited her to make use of the Palm Beach house, which she did on several occasions.[17]

In Washington, he had regularly invited the president, Anna and Jimmy Roosevelt, and Missy to Marwood for fresh seafood dinners and first-run films in his private theater. He tried to keep up with at least part of that tradition by airmailing stone crabs to the White House from Palm Beach. "If after what I called the air plane company yesterday morning [a reference to his foul mouth] they don't throw the stone crabs off the plane for spite, you will have them in Washington tomorrow afternoon," he wrote Missy LeHand on February 17, 1937. "They are being cooked and packed in dry ice and leaving here at nine-thirty Thursday morning. In fact the head of the air plane company said he would much rather carry stone crabs than carry one Kennedy, the worst crab he ever knew. . . . Anyhow the crab will be there tomorrow and they better be good." The following month, he sent lobsters to the president and his entourage in Warm Springs. "This is the first time live lobsters ever flew to Pine Mountain," FDR wrote back. "We are informing Smithsonian."[18]

Though he was not above criticizing the president behind his back to his conservative friends in the press, including William Randolph Hearst and Frank Kent, Kennedy considered himself a member of the Roosevelt team and intended to work for his reelection. In January 1936, the president sent him a list prepared by his secretary of commerce of fifty prominent businessmen who might be considered "friendly" to the administration. He followed up with a call to Palm Beach to ask Kennedy to solicit the businessmen on the list for endorsements and/or campaign contributions. Their conversation was cut short so that Kennedy could attend Mass. The next day, Kennedy followed up on the president's proposal with one of his own: "About the list you sent me, I feel it is not at all strong enough to do what we thought of, but I will go ahead and try to think out some plan and if any of your people have a suggestion as to how it can be well used, I wish they would let me know. It isn't that I am stubborn or stupid, but I am anxious to get a result that will merely not be just a superficial gesture. I still think I can do it."[19]

He had been both astounded and appalled by the depth of anti-Roosevelt sentiment he had encountered in Palm Beach among the wealthy. The very men and women who should have been among the president's strongest supporters because he had saved capitalism and their fortunes were his most venomous opponents. "We are witnessing," he would later write in his Roosevelt campaign book, *I'm for Roosevelt,* "the strangest hatred of history."[20]

Some among his conservative friends, especially those to whom he had voiced his doubts about New Deal programs and the antibusiness radicals who were running them, had hoped that when he left Washington he would join them in opposition. They were quite disappointed when he did not. "When you resigned as Chairman of the Securities Commission, the whole country rose up as one to acclaim you," Paul Block the conservative publisher of several newspapers, including the *Pittsburgh Post-Gazette,* wrote him on April 10, 1936. "And when you told me the various reasons for your resignation, I thought even more of you, but now I read in the paper that you are going back to Washington to start fighting for the re-election of the radical New Dealers. If this is true, then all I can say is, 'Poor Joe,' and I think I should also say 'Poor America.' We thought Joe would help the sane people, but he is going back to the asylum."[21]

Kennedy didn't see it that way, of course. He was supporting Roosevelt for a second term because in his first he had gotten the economy going again. On April 28, when Secretary of the Treasury Morgenthau phoned to ask for his assessment of market conditions and the recent drop in stock prices, Kennedy reassured him that there was nothing to worry about. Stock prices might drift a bit lower, but not by much; the bond markets were safe; the worst was over. He told Morgenthau he was drafting an answer to New Deal critics like Al Smith, Herbert Hoover, banker and former Roosevelt appointee James Warburg, and others who insisted, despite evidence to the contrary, that the Roosevelt administration had been bad for business.[22]

He had decided that the best help he could offer the president's re-election campaign was to concentrate his attention on businessmen and explain to them, as one businessman to another, why he was supporting Roosevelt—and why they should as well. He would put these thoughts into a booklet, *I'm for Roosevelt*, which would be subtitled *A Businessman's Estimate of the New Deal.* To help him with the writing, he recruited James Landis, his successor at the SEC, and John Burns, still general counsel there. On May 4, he asked Missy LeHand "to tell the president that the booklet is finished, but I am having it re-read and re-edited, and will send it down for comments a little later." In mid-June, he forwarded a draft to the president, who thought it "splendid and . . . of real service, not only from a campaign point of view but also as a distinct step in sane education of the country."[23]

Encouraged by the president's comments and thinking his "businessman's manifesto," properly edited, might reach a broader general audience, he contacted Arthur Krock with a proposal and forwarded a copy of the letter he had received from the president. "I gather from it that he is anxious to have it done," Kennedy wrote Krock, "and if it is done, I should like to have it done in bang-up shape. I imagine that you are going on your vacation after this convention, and I wonder if you could give some of your time each week, for, say the next five weeks, to help put it in shape. I shall avail myself of your services, however, if you will permit me to pay you for the work you do on it. I should like to make a deal with you for $1000 a week for five weeks, if that is worth your while." Krock, who had no business writing campaign literature while covering the White House for the *New York Times,* agreed to edit the book for him.[24]

In July, having now been away from Washington and without any official position for nearly a year, Kennedy invited reporters to Hyannis Port, where he entertained and lectured them for hours on why Roosevelt should be reelected.

JOE KENNEDY STICKS HIS NECK OUT: SAYS HIS BUSINESS FRIENDS WILL JUMP ON HIM, BUT TELLS WHY HE THINKS ROOSEVELT REELECTION WILL BE BEST THING FOR BUSINESS AND FUTURE OF COUNTRY, read the headline over the half-page spread that appeared in the *Boston Sunday Globe* on July 26, 1936. Kennedy was supporting Roosevelt for a second term, he explained, because in his four years in office, he had rescued capitalism from the worst depression in American history. "I was in Chicago in 1933 and I saw the mounted police charge in to drive the people out of the banks and I got a glimpse of the kind of powder barrel our system was sitting on without plan or leadership. That wasn't very long ago. Some people have forgotten very quickly." Every business index now pointed upward. The stock market was rising, production was up, the automobile and steel industries were "going ahead beyond anybody's expectation," railway car loadings were up. Even the bankers railing against the administration were stuffing their portfolios with government securities, proof positive that they were worth something. He urged his fellow businessmen to stop trying to turn the clock back to the Hoover years, but instead to follow his example, acknowledge the breadth of the recovery, and cooperate with the administration. There was nothing more dangerous to the future of the economy— and the nation—than misguided conservatism. "I remember my father was in the Massachusetts Legislature when the 54-hour law was being changed," he told the reporters gathered for his informal press briefing. "He has told me how the mill owners talked against the 48-hour law. Now nobody would go back. I remember the howl against the Federal Reserve act when it was new. Everybody is for it now." His endorsement of administration policies was indeed so powerful that he felt obligated to insist that there was no quid pro quo involved. He was "sticking his neck out" only because "he was interested in establishing a system that will make my family secure. Nothing that an administration can give me is as important as that. I'm all through in politics. I haven't any Government job. I won't take any."[25]

This was the only press interview Kennedy would give that summer. He remained at Hyannis Port the entire season, except for a few brief excursions elsewhere. One was a trip to Skowhegan, Maine, the home of Lakewood, among the country's premier summer theater colonies. During his stay there, Kennedy rented a cottage with Day Eliot, one of the actresses who was appearing in *Star Light, Star Bright,* a comedy by Owen Davis. Muriel Palmer, whose father rented the cottage to Kennedy, remembered her mother being upset that her family was a party to such goings-on.[26]

Having forfeited his last two summers to the SEC, Kennedy was set on enjoying this one. "You know when I go on vacation," he wrote Robert Allen, Drew Pearson's partner in Washington, "I don't ever write letters. I answer an occasional telephone call, and become a first-class bum. . . . Give my best to Drew and tell him that I am an economic royalist of the loafing type."[27]

I'm for Roosevelt was scheduled for publication in early fall. Kennedy's friend from the 1932 campaign train, Louis Ruppel, now at the *Chicago Daily Times,* wired him in Hyannis Port on August 4 to ask for prepublication rights: "Understand your book will be a sensation. . . . What do you say to making it available in whole or in part for the readers of Chicago's outstanding liberal newspaper, the *Times?* It's a cinch your old pal Bill Hearst won't print it and after you dispose of five hundred copies in Wall Street what will you do with the rest?" Three weeks later, after having read the manuscript, Ruppel told Kennedy that he was enormously impressed by the power of his manifesto. "Never let the Fascists prevail," he wrote Kennedy, "or it will be a toss up whether you or Tugwell [Rexford Tugwell, one of the original brain trusters and a strong advocate for economic planning] face the firing squad first. Really it is the clearest presentation of the facts which require Roosevelt's reelection that has yet been made. . . . Hurry, Hurry, Joe and give me a release remembering that whatever price you set you'll have to sue to collect."[28]

His campaign book was published, with excerpts splashed across the Scripps Howard papers and elsewhere, in September 1936. Kennedy paid the full costs of production, publication, and distribution, made hundreds of copies available to old friends from Boston and Hollywood, new friends from New York such as Ellin Mackay and her husband, Irving Berlin, and dozens of members of the Roosevelt administration. He was immensely proud of the book. "I have lots of letters about it—practically all of them favorable," he wrote Patrick Campbell, his old headmaster from Boston Latin, and dozens of others who wrote to congratulate him on his effort.[29]

I'm for Roosevelt presented Kennedy's profit and loss statement on the New Deal, which he claimed had succeeded in rescuing the economy from the depths of depression. Roosevelt deserved reelection because he had proven himself, time and again, "the real defender of American freedom" and American capitalism. "The New Deal is founded upon a basic belief in the efficacy of the capitalistic system. Every effort had been strained to preserve the system." The book, as published, made for rather dry reading, sold few copies, and probably won over few voters, but it received enough attention in the press to make the project a success for its author.[30]

In late September, after his summer in Hyannis Port and a brief trip to Europe on Somerset business, Kennedy joined the campaign on a full-time basis. "I'm so glad you're back," Tommy Corcoran wrote on September 21. "The Boss sorely needs paladins whose maces swing heavy and whose lances don't splinter." Kennedy helped arrange Jimmy Roosevelt's campaign tour of Massachusetts and paid for it out of his own pocket. When Stephen Early, the president's press secretary, permitted newsreel companies to film the president and his family at Hyde Park, Kennedy was asked to supervise the shooting and review the edited film and the narration. He also made several speeches, gave interviews, and buttonholed influential businessmen across the country, repeating, reemphasizing, and hammering home his one essential truth, that the Roosevelt presidency had been good for business. "It is the business man, large and small, who has chiefly prospered through the policies of the President," he wrote in an extended Sunday magazine article for the September 6 *New York Times*. "The wealthy have been the chief beneficiaries of the New Deal policies, as witness the financial pages of any paper. . . . He [Roosevelt] has never condemned wealth as such, but only the ignoble, the selfish, the irresponsible wealthy. Is it reasonable to suppose that he would sponsor an indiscriminate hatred against the whole class to which he and his kin have always belonged?"[31]

On October 1, the campaign suffered a major setback when Al Smith, in a nationally broadcast radio address from Carnegie Hall, endorsed Republican candidate Alf Landon, charging, as Hearst and Coughlin had, that the New Deal was rife with Communists. The next morning, Louis Ruppel asked Kennedy to answer Smith's charges at a meeting of the Chicago Bar Association. Kennedy spoke with campaign officials in Washington, then replied to Ruppel that he could not spare the time to come to Chicago. "Appointments have been made for practically every day and night from now until twenty-ninth of October. I never knew I was so good. Think our interest will be served best by my staying here."[32]

Four days later, he gave the first of several nationally broadcast radio speeches. He did not refer directly to Smith's accusations or the Communist issue. Instead, he repeated his "Roosevelt is good for business" mantra. "Incidentally," Drew Pearson joked with him a few days after the first talk, "did you know that your radio voice is a double for Groucho Marx? Any time Groucho is late at the broadcasting studio, all they will have to do is to get you to read his lines; no one would know the difference."[33]

By early October, the Democrats seemed headed for victory. "The campaign looks to me distinctly Roosevelt, but it will be by no means an easy fight," Kennedy wrote Ambassador Robert Bingham on October 6, 1936. "Father Coughlin has definitely made bother in the states that we need to carry, and the Communist cry has been raised rather successfully among the Catholics, I believe, to the damage of Roosevelt."[34]

As election day approached, Kennedy was everywhere at once, defending the president's record in newspapers and magazines, on the stump, over the radio. On October 23, from the Waldorf-Astoria in New York City, he introduced the president, who spoke from Washington via nationwide radio hookup to "businessmen's dinners" across the country.

The following evening, he delivered his own nationally broadcast address from the Copley Plaza in Boston, in which as a homegrown Irish Catholic he answered the charges hurled by Coughlin and Smith that Roosevelt was under the sway of Communist advisers. He reminded his audience that "nearly every piece of social legislation passed by the state to protect the laborer from oppression," like those passed by the Roosevelt administration, had "been denounced in their day as entering wedges of socialism and communism [by] Back-Bay Brahmins [and] Bourbons in all countries. It was against such attacks that the encyclicals of Poe Leo XIII and Poe Pius XI were aimed." Roosevelt was not a Communist for advocating social and economic reforms. "Tugwell, Hopkins and Frankfurter aren't Communists. . . . I know all three of these men very well and I can tell you unhesitatingly . . . they are no more communists than you and I." Communists, Kennedy declared, were opposed to private property, individual liberties, and religion. But the president and his advisers had time and time again demonstrated an "abiding belief in private property." As for a commitment to individual liberties, the president, Kennedy joked, had sent "no editors . . . to concentration camps, and my friends in the Harvard Club can call the

President anything they care to without fear of reprisal." Kennedy closed his speech by responding, as only he could, to the charge that Roosevelt was "an enemy of organized religion" by invoking the exalted names of Notre Dame, which had granted Roosevelt an honorary degree, and His Eminence George Cardinal Mundelein of Chicago, who had publicly commended the president. "In the face of this compelling evidence," he concluded, "certainly no American should be disturbed in the slightest by those who either in the name of politics or through ignorance or fear cry out 'Roosevelt is a Communist.'"[35]

In the next week, he gave speeches in Hartford, New York, and then Boston again and spoke on national radio at least twice more. On October 27, he forwarded to Harpo Marx a photograph of the president that he had asked for. "We always deliver, kid. Come on East after Tuesday and help us celebrate." "Win, lose, or draw," he wrote James Byrnes, senator from South Carolina and a big Roosevelt supporter, "after Tuesday—Joseph Patrick Kennedy retires from the political ring for ever and a day."[36]

The election of Roosevelt to a second term was a foregone conclusion by the time the polls opened on Tuesday, November 3, 1936. But no one had predicted the size of his victory. Roosevelt won forty-six of the forty-eight states, 523 of 531 electoral votes, and 61 percent of the votes. No candidate had ever done better.

There was little time for a victory lap—for the president or for Kennedy. In October, Eugenio Cardinal Pacelli, the Vatican secretary of state, had arrived in the Port of New York. While he insisted otherwise, the reason for the visit was to discuss with the president the possibility of the United States renewing diplomatic relations with the Vatican. Pacelli was accompanied by Enrico Galeazzi, the Rome liaison to the Knights of Columbus and a close friend to Francis Spellman, the highly influential auxiliary bishop of Boston. On Spellman's suggestion, Galeazzi visited Kennedy at his office at 30 Rockefeller Plaza to work out arrangements for a meeting with the president, which it was agreed would have to wait until after the election.

"The floor of all rooms of his office," Galeazzi remembered, "was covered with a thick light blue moquette, of the same color as the eyes of this man." He was impressed by Kennedy's take-charge attitude, his devotion to the church, and his charm. "Tall, elegant, gentlemanly," Galeazzi recalled, Kennedy "could be as gentle and kind as a gallant knight or as violent and cross as a general at war." The two men would become and remain the closest of friends and allies for the rest of their lives.

To be called upon to do a favor for the Vatican was the highest honor Joseph P. Kennedy could receive. He arranged for a private railroad car to transport Pacelli and his entourage between New York and Hyde Park and scheduled a lunch with the president for November 5, two days after the election. There would be no discussion in the press as to what the president and the Vatican secretary of state spoke about. Galeazzi would later recall only that Cardinal Pacelli had visited Hyde Park "in cordial intimacy and stayed for lunch. The aged mother of the President and his son James were present. Joe Kennedy was, with Bishop Spellman, the life of the party." On his return trip to New York City, Cardinal Pacelli stopped over in Bronxville to visit the Kennedy family. Teddy, who was four at the time, recalled being "fascinated by his long robe and scarlet skullcap, and his long aristocratic nose." Uninvited, he crawled up on the cardinal's lap while he was seated on the family's favorite sofa.[37]

Two and a half years later, Cardinal Pacelli would be crowned Pope Pius XII in St. Peter's Square before a gathering of church officials, worshippers, and foreign dignitaries, including Ambassador Joseph P. Kennedy, his wife, and eight of their children. When, in 1946, the Bronxville house was sold, Rose made sure that the sofa the cardinal, now pope, had sat on was moved to Hyannis Port with a plaque made and attached to it to commemorate the 1936 visit.

Fourteen

MARITIME COMMISSIONER

W illiam Randolph Hearst and his media empire were early
casualties of the Roosevelt victory.

By relentlessly referring to the president as "Moscow's
candidate" and Stalin's "comrade," Hearst had forced his largely urban,
working-class, Democratic readers to choose between him and the president. They had chosen the president and stopped buying Hearst papers. Hearst might have survived had he not already been deeply in debt
to newsprint suppliers and to the banks. As long as circulation remained
stable, his creditors had permitted him to roll over his debt, but with
circulation and advertising revenues falling, they refused to do so any
longer. Faced with a debt of $2.1 million to the International Paper
Company, $300,000 of which was due in early January, Thomas J.
White, Hearst's top lieutenant, contacted Kennedy in New York.

As with RCA and Paramount, Kennedy knew he had been called on
not simply because he was an astute businessman and banker, but because he had written the SEC rules that governed the issuance of the
new stocks and bonds the Hearst corporations would have to sell to
pay off their debts. To protect himself from conflict of interest charges,
Kennedy kept his work with Hearst quiet. There were no announcements,
no press conferences. He did not request a fee for his services, but asked

only that Hearst pay the men who worked with him on the project. He agreed to prepare a restructuring plan, write the registration statements required for the issuance of new stocks or bonds, and then, if warranted, assume some leadership role in the restructured corporation.

On January 20, Kennedy flew north from Palm Beach to Washington, D.C., for Franklin Delano Roosevelt's second inauguration. This time around, in acknowledgment of all he had done during the campaign, Roosevelt had not only invited him to the inauguration, but encouraged him to bring as many family members as he could gather. Jack and Joe Jr. were occupied with midterm examinations and could not make it, but the other seven children, escorted by a governess and Eddie and Mary Moore, took the train to Washington, were put up at the Brighton Hotel, had dinner at the Mayflower, and were asked to luncheon the next day in the White House ballroom and introduced to the president.

The following month, he heard from the president, who asked if he would accept appointment as the first chairman of the United States Maritime Commission. This was not the type of position Kennedy had hoped for, but he accepted it four days after it had been offered. While no promise was made, the presumption was that if he took on one more impossible task for the president, the next appointment would be more to his liking.

"I am planning to take the same house I had before if possible," he wrote James Byrnes, with whom he had become quite friendly during his days in Washington. "If by any chance the boys hold you in Session for the summer we'll at least have some nice cool mint juleps and Boston lobster. If I am confirmed I expect to be in Washington from next Friday on and then I'd like to see you as often as you can find time to see me."[1]

Anxious as he was to return to the capital, he did not want to appear too needy a suitor. He made clear to Byrnes and others that he had turned down some "very profitable" assignments to return to government service, because he could not say no to the president. "I should love to tell you the story how I got into this mess, and you and Anna [Roosevelt] would have plenty of laughs," he wrote John Boettiger, FDR's son-in-law, who with Kennedy's help had been appointed publisher of Hearst's *Seattle Post-Intelligencer*. "I give up my business, give up my leisure to take up the most unworkable bill I ever read in my life, but you know that man's winning ways. It is pretty good when you can give up a perfectly good reputation and throw it in the ash can when you can be of service, but you know, if you are going through with a guy you must go all the way through. Arthur Krock just telephoned me and he does not think my luck will hold and I probably will be confirmed, although there is still a great doubt."[2]

His friends in the press treated his return as if he were Agricola leaving his farm for battle. Krock, who may or may not have remained on the payroll after completing work on *I'm for Roosevelt,* led the cheerleading. In his columns of March 10 and 17, he identified Kennedy "as one of the outstanding figures in American life" and one of the president's "few 'miracle-men.'" *Time* magazine went even further by noting in its March 22 issue that after asking others to chair the commission, "the President turned to his most effective and trusted extra-Cabinet friend, red-headed Joe Kennedy. Every night for two weeks a White House limousine met Joe Kennedy as he landed from Manhattan at the Washington Airport, whisked him off to be cajoled by that persuasive pleader, Franklin Roosevelt."

While the press response to the nomination was near unanimous in its praise, there remained one serious obstacle to confirmation. The legislation that had established the Maritime Commission, though muddled on several particulars, was preemptively clear that only individuals who in the past three years had had no connection to or financial interest in any shipping company could serve as members. Kennedy had held on to the large position in Todd Shipbuilding, Inc., that he had purchased while at Hayden, Stone; he promised that if he was confirmed, he would sell it within sixty days. The solicitor general declared that possession of the stock did not render Kennedy ineligible for appointment. Several congressmen disagreed. To remove any doubts about Kennedy's eligibility, Senate Majority Leader Joe Robinson of Arkansas introduced a joint resolution certifying that Joseph P. Kennedy "shall not be deemed to be in violation" of the Merchant Marine Act (of 1936). The resolution was passed and signed into law on March 30. Kennedy was confirmed and took office two weeks later.

During the month he awaited confirmation, Kennedy redoubled his efforts to reorganize the Hearst empire. With John Burns, former counsel at the SEC, and accountant Arthur B. Poole, who had worked with him at Pathé, he oversaw the preparation of the registration statements the SEC required for the approval of new bond issues. On March 29, Kennedy sent Hearst a four-page, single-spaced letter outlining his work to date. He recommended that Hearst formulate a long-range plan for the "future management of the financial affairs of your properties" and hire Arthur Poole as a vice president at $20,000 a year to execute it. Much hinged on the development of this plan—including, Kennedy added bluntly, "my own whole-hearted efforts to make important contribution to the financial management of your properties."[3]

All through the spring of 1937 and into the summer, before and after he took office as chair of the Maritime Commission, Kennedy worked on the Hearst reorganization. Having submitted and gained approval for the registration statements, he and Poole tried to find an underwriter for the Hearst bond issue. While the bankers they talked to, including Elisha Walker, Harry Stuart of Halsey, Stuart, and top executives at Lehman Brothers and Lazard Freres, indicated interest in joining a consortium, not one of them was ready to take the lead. Ironically, as the *Nation* magazine pointed out on June 19, 1937, in an article titled "Will the SEC Wreck Hearst?" the rules that Kennedy had instituted had compelled the Hearst corporations to disclose information that frightened off potential investors. In the pre-SEC days, Hearst would have been able to float his issue without having to reveal the declining value of his assets, his indebtedness, or the fact that a considerable proportion of the money raised would be going to pay off debts he had personally guaranteed. But those days were gone now, a victim of the "blue sky" regulations that Kennedy had promulgated.

In late June, with the bond issue still without underwriters or subscribers and Hearst in desperate need of cash to stave off bankruptcy, Kennedy, as an act of friendship and because it was a solid investment, offered to buy one or both of Hearst's Boston newspapers for cash. He also renewed his offer to take over the financial management of the organization. Hearst thanked Kennedy "for the excellent and valuable advice you have given me so freely and so helpfully" and promised that he would give his proposals "the most thoughtful consideration."[4]

Kennedy never heard back from him.

In late July, Kennedy came up with another plan to rescue Hearst from his financial difficulties and provide the Kennedy family with a new income stream. He arranged a tentative deal with a Chicago bank, which agreed to lend the Hearst Corporation $2.2 million for ninety days, predicated on Kennedy "taking over the financial management of all the Hearst properties." The loan would be used to pay off the creditors, after which Kennedy would reorganize the Hearst empire and spin off the magazines into a new company that he would control.[5]

Hearst's advisers barely considered the plan before turning it down. Kennedy was disappointed. He had made a good-faith offer, one that would have benefited him and saved Hearst from bankruptcy. "Boy, that offer . . . still looks pretty good doesn't it," he wrote Tom White, the only one of Hearst's lieutenants he trusted, seven months later. "All those secret conversations that our friends had to the effect that this was stealing the magazines from Mr. Hearst sound like a joke. As I look at the picture, I still believe that every bit of advice I gave you and him is the best advice he will ever get. . . . I could cry when I think of his having turned the proposition down."[6]

As involved as he was with the Hearst reorganization, it was little more than a sideline. He was fully occupied that spring and summer in his new position, as the first chairman of the Maritime Commission. By 1937, it was impossible, even for an isolationist Congress and nation, to ignore the war clouds gathering over Europe. Hitler had quit the League of Nations in 1933, renounced the Treaty of Versailles, rearmed, and in 1936 seized the Rhineland; Italy had invaded Ethiopia; Japan was threatening China; there was civil war in Spain. Should a larger European or world war develop, American trade would be severely impacted, perhaps even cut off as the European-flagged ships that transported the bulk of goods across the Atlantic would be called into service.

To prepare for the worst-case scenarios, it was imperative that the American maritime industry be reorganized and revitalized. American shipbuilding had been in a sorry state for decades now. Most of the merchant vessels engaged in international trade had been built during or immediately after the Great War. It was estimated that within five years, 85 percent of them would be ready for retirement.

For the past eight years, federal aid to the moribund maritime industry had come in the form of lucrative contracts to deliver the mail from Europe. These subsidies had resulted in healthy profits for a few shipowners, but no new ships. In 1936, in an attempt to stimulate domestic shipbuilding, Congress had passed legislation establishing the Maritime Commission and directing it to replace the mail contracts with direct subsidies for new ships. Unfortunately, as Kennedy announced to reporters on arriving in Washington, the new maritime law was "lousy." The subsidies intended to stimulate shipbuilding had been saddled with onerous conditions, including restrictions on the salaries the shipbuilders could pay their executives (no more than $25,000) and the profit margins they could retain (no more than 10 percent). On taking the job, Kennedy declared that he would undertake his own survey of the industry and offer Congress recommendations on how it might amend and improve the 1936 law.

Though he would complain often—and in doing so call attention to his perseverance and dedication to his job—he was pleased to be back in harness and perversely delighted that he had been handed what everyone considered to be another impossible task. Even Harvard took notice of the distance he had traveled from East Boston and the reputation he had acquired as a Washington problem solver, a man who got things done. Barely a month after his return to Washington and his second "chairmanship," he received the highest honor his classmates could offer, an invitation to speak at his twenty-fifth reunion. His career at Harvard had been less than stellar—as a student or an athlete—but none of that mattered any longer. "I won't be like a coy debutante," he answered Bob Fisher, who had issued the invitation on behalf of the reunion committee, "but will say I'll be there. It is certain however, I'll not talk more than fifteen minutes and for the honor and glory of Kennedy . . . Fisher and Company, I'll do the best I can. Rose is in Boston this week and I told her to contact somebody to talk to seriously as to the arrangements to be made for the children there."[7]

Fisher asked Kennedy to get in touch with Robert Benchley, who, with Kennedy, had been a member of Delta Upsilon, and, like him, had become notorious as a Harvard graduate for doing something decidedly un-Harvard-like, writing humor pieces and screenplays for MGM in Hollywood. "There are forty-six mail contracts which have to be settled for the United States government in the amount of $400 million before June 30th," Kennedy bragged to Benchley, "but they are selling me the idea of coming to the reunion if only for a couple of days. . . . If I have to be there, there is no one I'll miss more if he isn't there than you. I could talk with all your bosses and get you a leave of absence if you wanted it. It is a long tough hot trip here . . . but after all you are the great boy of the class and my particular pet. So leave all the beautiful women or bring two on if you want to and try to come, if only for Saturday night dinner. I have to make the address and I want you to introduce me. My past is safe in your hands."[8]

Kennedy gave his speech at the reunion weekend's closing dinner. Instead of rehearsing (as was customary) the ways in which his success in life could be attributed to his four years on campus or telling silly stories and flattened-out jokes about his classmates, he delivered an uncalled-for, unexpected, and unpardonably political speech. Before an audience that was largely anti-Roosevelt and anti–New Deal, he defended not only big government, but Social Security and organized labor. And then, to add provocation to provocation, he praised John L. Lewis, the principal organizer of the Congress of Industrial Organizations (CIO) and perhaps the single most hated man in banks, boardrooms, and Harvard clubs. He had, he told his classmates, recently had lunch with Lewis and come away from the table with "a distinctly favorable impression of the man's character. . . . On the fundamental issues, that is—his faith in the democratic form of Government and his personal integrity—I entertain not the slightest doubt. We are reaping the whirlwind of a quarter century of mishandling of labor relations. We complain about the lack of responsibility of labor and for years we did our best to render labor organizations impotent." He closed by emphasizing to his classmates, "particularly to those . . . who have children that the scene is not as bad as it looks. Without wishing to appear in a 'Pollyanna' role, I frankly see nothing which justifies the hate and the despair which are all around us."[9]

It was a brave speech and a foolish one. Given the opportunity to demonstrate to his classmates that he was not an outsider, but one of them, he could not quite do it. Instead, he felt called upon to tell them—to their aristocratic, "proper Bostonian" Republican faces— that they had got it all wrong about Roosevelt and the New Deal, that he was their savior, not their executioner. Whether intended or not, and whether he knew it or not, he had insulted them all by bringing politics—and decidedly the wrong kind of politics—into the sanctified space of a Harvard class reunion.

His new position was not nearly as high-profile as his former one. He would have to make his own headlines, which, with the help of Arthur Krock, he did. He delivered his first official speech to the Propeller Club at the Hotel Astor on May 21, 1937. As the *New York Times* reported on its front page the next morning, he pledged a MER-CHANT MARINE TO EQUAL ANY RIVAL. MARITIME BOARD HEAD PLANS TO BUILD NEW AND FASTER SHIPS IN IMMEDIATE FUTURE. AID OF CAP-ITAL ASKED. GOVERNMENT IS READY TO TAKE INITIATIVE . . . "SQUARE DEAL" FOR LABOR. MEN AFLOAT TO BE TREATED AS THOSE ASHORE, BUT LOYALTY WILL BE DEMANDED OF THEM. There was nothing espe-cially controversial or even interesting in what Kennedy proposed, ex-cept, as the *Times* reported, for his "enunciation of the commission's labor policy."

The industry had been convulsed by two major strikes in three years, the first of which had escalated into the general strike that had virtually shut down San Francisco in the summer of 1934 and lasted a full eighty-three days; the second, less than two and a half years later, had para-lyzed West Coast shipping for ninety-nine days and cost the industry some $700 million. Had the labor problems that roiled the industry been confined to labor/management disputes, they might have been settled more easily and quickly. But through the 1930s, maritime labor had been engaged in an internal civil war between newly established and usually more militant locals with allegiance to the CIO and older ones affiliated with the American Federation of Labor.

There were, as Kennedy acknowledged in his inaugural speech, rea-sons for labor strife in the maritime industry, primary among them the low and irregular wages crewmen were paid and the impossibly poor working conditions they were forced to endure. The Maritime Commis-sion had been empowered to rectify these conditions—and would—by setting minimum hours and wage rates for seamen who worked for companies that received government subsidies. Kennedy promised to give the seamen "a square deal" and asked them, in turn, to "give the Commission and the tax-paying public a square deal. . . . Labor, the commission believes, must demonstrate that it is worthy of the special treatment which the American public is willing to give it. . . . There can be no excuse for costly and bitter factionalism which is harmful to everyone in the long run. . . . In particular, labor ought to be willing to forego resort to extreme measures when there exists peaceful machinery for adjusting its grievances."[10]

It was not difficult to read between the lines here. In asking the seamen to "forego resort to extreme measures," Kennedy was requesting that they give up their right to strike and accept arbitration in its place. In involving himself directly in the industry's labor problems, Kennedy believed he was doing what Roosevelt expected of him. In June, the president had forwarded to Kennedy a four-page letter he had received, detailing the deplorable conditions the letter writer, a distinguished author, had found on an American ship bound for China. The crew had been surly, incompetent, and undisciplined. Roosevelt noted that such conditions were "all too common on American ships." The implication was that Kennedy should do something about it.[11]

In May, Kennedy, who until now had received only praise for his work in Washington, was given a draft of a cover story that Earle Looker, a well-respected journalist, had written for *Fortune* magazine's forthcoming survey of the shipping industry. He immediately wrote Russell Davenport, the managing editor of *Fortune*, that the article was "permeated with distrust of my character, dislike of my occupations and social prejudice against my origin. . . . I have marked fifty-four inaccuracies in as many places." Davenport invited him to elaborate, which he did in a long letter, written with Arthur Krock's help, listing the false "statements" with his "observations" and corrections. He was particularly incensed at the characterization of his father as a saloon keeper who had entered government service to increase his "opportunities for the acquisition of wealth." "The inference here [that P.J. had been a corrupt politician] is mean and contemptible. My father's reputation could never be touched by any such aspersion." He was also disturbed by Looker's charge that he had been an operator of the Libbey-Owens-

Ford pool and a "cold blooded Bear of exceptional shrewdness." The fact that Looker had gotten this part of the portrait right was beside the point.

Davenport sent an associate to placate Kennedy, then wrote him personally to assure him that the article would be redrafted to incorporate his corrections. That wasn't enough. Kennedy demanded that the article be taken away from Earle Looker, "whose presentation of me is so cheap and tawdry that a rereading of the script sickened me. There are so many deliberate misrepresentations that I believe that either Looker has an ingrained hatred of the Irish, or a resentment against me personally. The only basis for personal antagonism I could think of might be Looker's anger at my failure to arrange for him a sale of his book to a moving picture company. The request was made to me in writing while he was engaged in working on the present draft. If such is the explanation for the article, the word 'blackmail' despite all its ugly imputations is not too extreme a characterization. After consulting with some friends in Washington, I am convinced that it would be useless to attempt to revise a draft so permeated with bias and incompetence."[12]

The implications were clear. Kennedy did not identify his "friends in Washington," but he didn't have to. They included the most powerful men in the Roosevelt administration and columnists like Arthur Krock and Drew Pearson. Davenport backed down, withdrew Looker's draft, and assigned the article to another author. In early August, he sent Kennedy the new draft and a copy of the photograph that was to run with it. Kennedy's threats had gotten him precisely what he wanted, a puff piece in a major financial magazine. He segued now from bullying Davenport to flattering him. "My dear Mr. Davenport," he wrote on August 6. "I want to tell you how very much I appreciate the picture. It will remind me of a great many things, not least of which is your masterful handling of a very difficult situation with a very irritable young man named Kennedy. . . . My warmest personal regards and assuring you it has been a great pleasure working with you."[13]

Occupied with both the Maritime Commission and, to a lesser extent, Hearst business, Kennedy commuted back and forth to Hyannis Port that summer of 1937. Jack, healthy now for almost a year, had left for Europe with Lem Billings in early July. Rose departed at the end of the month with Joe Jr. and Kick. Bobby and Pat went off to one camp, Rosemary to another. Eunice was left behind in Hyannis Port with her baby brother and youngest sister, but that was fine with her; she had learned to sail by crewing with Joe Jr. and had her best year yet, winning several races. Jean won some races herself that summer.

While Jack's trip to Europe was done on the cheap to accommodate Billings's relatively modest budget, there were, as befitted the son of a Washington insider, appointments at the American embassies in Paris and Rome, a private meeting with Vatican secretary of state Cardinal Pacelli, and an audience with Pope Pius XI. In late August, Kennedy wrote to thank Count Enrico Galeazzi for entertaining his son, joking that "the only trouble with all of this is that I have such a large family that those who have enjoyed your hospitality insist upon their return that the others must go to Rome to meet Mr. Galeazzi. So, if your patience will hold out, I will send the little Kennedys along as they gradually get old enough to travel."[14]

In summers past, Rosemary had joined the family at Hyannis Port, but this year, with her older brothers and sisters and mother going abroad and Bobby and Pat at camp, it was thought best to send her to camp, with an adult companion to look after her. In the fall, she would return for a second year to the Residence School at 37 East Eighty-third Street in Manhattan, which was run by Miss Mollie Hourigan. Her parents had sent her to New York so that she might, after being tutored one-on-one in Brookline for two years, be able to live with other girls, take a group class in choral singing, and go on group trips to the opera, concerts, lectures, and horse shows on Friday evenings. Her schoolwork was overseen by Miss Amanda Rohde at her studio on West Eightieth Street; Miss Rohde also took her to her dancing lessons once a week and to the doctor's offices on East Ninetieth Street for her "gland" injections.[15]

On paper, the arrangement appeared to be the best possible for Rosemary, who got the personal attention she required from a private tutor and, at Miss Hourigan's Residence School, the group activities that she had missed at Miss Newton's. Much like Miss Newton in Brookline, Miss Rohde found Rosemary difficult to teach and her "attitude towards her work, and consequently towards me" particularly troubling. "Rosemary," Rohde wrote Rose in mid-October, "has been allowed to escape too much for her own welfare. She has found it more pleasant to day-dream. Now she makes herself unpleasant when she finds herself in a situation in which she has to think. If she is allowed to continue in this, she will become more and more difficult to live with. Little by little she must be brought to face reality. It will be a long siege, but it can be done."[16]

That past spring, the Kennedys, still in search of the expert who could diagnose Rosemary's problems and prescribe a cure, had taken her to Dr. Walter Dearborn, a Harvard research scientist and clinician with degrees in experimental psychology and medicine and expertise in intelligence testing, growth studies, and the development of reading comprehension. Rosemary met with Dr. Dearborn at the Psycho-Educational Clinic at the Harvard Graduate School of Education. Like the other experts who had examined Rosemary, Dearborn assured her parents that he could help and designed a personalized curriculum that leaned heavily on the work of John Dewey and the first generation of progressive educators. To teach her "practical arithmetic," he proposed giving her an account in the "department store" with regular bills she would have to pay. "She should be trained to shop within a given budget and to go through step by step all of the processes of shopping accounts, records, and so forth."[17]

Dearborn had several recommendations for next year's course of study. Amanda Rohde could continue as Rosemary's tutor. What remained for Rose to decide was whether it would be best for her daughter to stay on for another year at the Residence School or move to the Sacred Heart Convent in Manhattanville, where she would be watched over by the nuns and live with girls her own age instead of the much younger Residence School students.

In July 1937, after much procrastination, Rose notified Miss Hourigan that she wanted Rosemary to return to the Residence School. She was caught entirely off guard when Miss Hourigan replied that it would be best if Rosemary boarded elsewhere. Although she was "drawn to Rosemary and I feel that I shall always be interested in her," she could not allow her to return for a second year. "Quite frankly, the responsibility was much greater for me, last year, than I had anticipated. Having accepted the child, and agreed upon the arrangements with you, it was only a short time before I realized that Rosemary needed continual protection or supervision. This entailed a constant checking, which was a responsibility that could never be let down. I do not think we have ever had a more lovable girl, dear Mrs. Kennedy but frankly, I have never before carried as great a responsibility, both for your child, and for my school." Miss Hourigan recommended that Rose try to arrange some sort of living arrangement for Rosemary at the Manhattanville Sacred Heart convent, which would be much more suitable for her, "because, in that large group there would be contacts of every kind, without ever leaving the convent grounds." With more to do at the convent, Rosemary, a rather pretty, though slightly overweight, nineteen-year-old, might have less incentive to wander away, unnoticed and unchaperoned, which either had already happened or, Miss Hourigan feared, would happen if she remained at the Residence School building on East Eighty-third Street.[18]

As Rosemary got older, the distance between what she was permitted to do and what she wanted to do had grown enormously. She had always been the only Kennedy child who was not allowed to go sailing or play in the yard or go for a walk or swim without her brothers, sisters, companions, or mother tagging along. "As she grew older and was a teenager," Rose remembered some three decades later, "I was always worried that she would run away from home someday and get lost, or that she would meet with an accident, or that [in the wake of the 1932 Lindbergh kidnapping] she would go off with someone who would flatter her or kidnap her as the kidnapping craze was on then."[19]

Her parents—and siblings—wanted more than anything else for Rosemary to feel comfortable in the world, to fit in, to belong, to be accepted, but that was becoming more difficult for her anywhere outside the Kennedy home. She was uneasy in public and often froze when confronted by a simple task, such as paying for something. Dr. Dearborn suggested that she was beset at such moments by a kind of "intellectual blocking as a result of failure in . . . tense social settings—'the concerned looks of all concerned.'"[20]

Kennedy spent more time at Hyannis Port that summer than he had planned. What had begun as a peaceful vacation had turned hectic when Pat was stricken at camp with an acute case of appendicitis and had to be transported to Boston for an emergency operation. Soon afterward, Bobby came down with pneumonia and was taken to the same hospital. Kennedy arranged for round-the-clock nursing for both children. When they were well enough to come home, Luella Hennessey, one of the six nurses who had cared for them, was asked and agreed to accompany them to Hyannis Port and remain there until they were well again. Luella would remain part of the Kennedy family for the rest of her life, caring for children, grandchildren, and after his stroke, Joe Kennedy himself.

It was not until after Labor Day that Kennedy was able to return to Washington. "I just got back to Washington this week," he wrote a business associate on September 9, "after having stayed up at the Cape with two very sick children. . . . I gave up all business and confined myself exclusively to them."[21]

Almost immediately upon his return, Kennedy got a phone call from the American vice consul in Montevideo, Uruguay. A group of American seamen on the S.S. *Algic* had defied the orders of their captain, refused to unload cargo, and gone on a sympathy strike with the local longshoremen. Because the ship was owned by the government, though leased to a private concern, the ship's captain wanted Kennedy to order the sailors back to work and punish them as mutineers if they refused. Kennedy could have ignored the request or deflected it elsewhere. But he did not. He had made it clear in May that he was going to involve himself in maritime labor disputes. The strike or mutiny of a few seamen, though thousands of miles away, presented him with the opportunity he had been looking for to dramatize—to the seamen, their unions, Congress, the president, the press, and the public—the need to reform labor practices in the maritime industry.

Kennedy notified the president that he needed to speak to him "about the terrible conditions on our American ships with regard to discipline." He had, he wrote Roosevelt, consulted with the assistant attorney general in charge of the criminal division, who had indicated that he was prepared to use the "Mutiny Statute" against any sailors who were guilty of refusing to "obey the lawful order of the Master." Kennedy was "firmly convinced that such action if promptly taken would go a long way toward clearing up insubordination and generally deplorable conditions in the American Merchant Marine." To make sure his letter was brought to the president's attention, Kennedy sent a separate note to James Roosevelt, who now worked as his father's secretary: "This thing is getting terribly serious. If you think it worthwhile to give it a little pressure, all right, but if you don't we will take it out of our files. Really though, something should be done."[22]

Arthur Krock claimed to be in Kennedy's office when Roosevelt called to urge restraint but was, according to Krock, talked out of it by his maritime commissioner. " 'No, sir, I don't go with that idea of compromise. . . . Listen, boy. If we do that we'll land in the ———.' (At which mention of the ignoble but functional edifice to which Kennedy was wont to refer, came a delighted roar . . . from the other end of the wire)."[23]

Kennedy cabled the ship's captain to "instruct crew to proceed with your lawful orders. If they still refuse warn crew that all still refusing . . . will be placed in irons and prosecuted to full extent of law on return to United States. If they still refuse, place ringleaders in irons. If other crew members still refuse duty, have them removed from ship and replace them with American, if available, and if not, foreign seamen." The cable was signed, "United States Maritime Commission," though as *Time* magazine reported, its "terse message . . . looked as if it had had the personal attention of Chairman Kennedy."[24]

The National Maritime Union (NMU), to which the sailors belonged, protested immediately that Kennedy and the commission had no right to intervene in a labor dispute in Uruguay. Nonetheless, the seamen returned to duty.

When the *Algic* landed in Baltimore a few weeks later, fourteen crew members were arrested by federal agents and indicted for "revolt and mutiny." Joseph Curran, the president of the NMU, publicly blamed Kennedy for the arrests, declared the union was "going to get Kennedy's scalp," and cabled Roosevelt at Hyde Park, "asking that justice be procured" for the jailed sailors and that Mr. Kennedy be fired. Secretary of Labor Frances Perkins, who was on good terms with Curran and the CIO officials who backed him defused the crisis by suggesting that Roosevelt ignore the telegram. She then persuaded Curran to apologize to Kennedy for making the *Algic* affair into a personal dispute. Kennedy accepted the apology but refused to back down. He was not, as he had made clear in his Harvard speech that spring, antiunion, but neither was he going to sit idly by and let unionized seamen disrupt commerce by going on sympathy strikes in Montevideo.[25]

The fourteen seamen were found guilty of violating a 1790 mutiny law. Nine were given two-month prison sentences, the remaining five $50 fines. The CIO unions would never forgive Kennedy. The business community, on the other hand, had nothing but praise for his tough talk and actions.

Kennedy sailed on from triumph to triumph. On July 1, 1937, he had announced at a press conference that the Maritime Commission had reached agreement with twenty-three of the shipping companies that for the past nine years had received bloated "disguised" subsidies for carrying the mail. That Kennedy had secured these agreements by July 1, less than three months into his tenure as chairman, and saved the government millions of dollars was, Arthur Krock reported, nothing less than miraculous. Even the president sent Kennedy a letter of congratulation or, rather, had his son James do so over his signature: "It was a grand job to get those contracts out of the way on time."[26]

In November, with consummate showmanship, Kennedy made even larger headlines with the release of a compendious report to Congress on the state of the merchant shipping industry. "Joe Kennedy was a genius at public relations," recalled Harvey Klemmer, who worked at the Maritime Commission in Washington and then with Kennedy in London. "He had the whole country waiting for the economic survey. He built up suspense until you thought it was the second coming of Christ." To gather maximum publicity for the commission's report— and its chairman—Kennedy sat for interviews with newspaper and magazine reporters and appeared in a *March of Time* and a Hearst newsreel. The *New York Times* declared in an extended editorial that Kennedy's report was "a model of what such a report should be. . . . It is informative, concise, lucid, and above all readable" and urged that Congress follow its recommendations.[27]

In early December, Kennedy appeared before the House Committee on Merchant Marine and Fisheries to present his report and answer questions about his progress—or lack of it—in getting new ships into the water.

"'You have been chairman of the Maritime Commission for eight months?'

"Kennedy nodded in agreement.

"'How many ships have you laid down in that time?'

"'One.'

"'Are any others to be built soon?'

"'I have no assurance under the act as it stands that any ships will be built.'

"'Do you think this act is workable as it now stands?'

"'No . . . I think it is about the worst I have ever seen.'"[28]

Kennedy insisted that until Congress passed the amendments to the 1936 maritime legislation the commission had recommended—and mandated compulsory arbitration of labor disputes—it would be impossible to get more American ships into the water.

The next week, he took his seat for a repeat performance, this time before a joint meeting of the Senate Committee on Commerce and the Committee on Education and Labor.

The president's second term had begun rather disastrously when, in February 1937, he proposed legislation to radically change the composition of a hostile Supreme Court by adding an additional justice for each sitting justice seventy years or older. The response of the public, the press, and members of both parties to what became known as his "court-packing" plan was decidedly negative. As a loyal member of the Roosevelt team, Kennedy agreed to line up support for the president. "Before I ask you in the name of the Holy Father to help on a plan," he wrote Bernard Baruch on March 3, 1937, "are you for or against the Holy Father's suggestion on the Supreme Court and if you are for his plan would you care to go along and help. Wire me care of the White House." In the end, there was nothing Baruch or Kennedy or anyone else friendly to Roosevelt could do to save him from the grievous political miscalculation that he would be able to bully the Congress into approving his plan.[29]

In late July, the doomed bill was "recommitted" to committee, where it would die of inaction. Weeks later, the bottom fell out of the economy.

The administration had decided earlier in the year that the recovery was proceeding so impressively, it was time to steer back to normalcy, reduce federal expenditures, and cut the budget. The result was economic disaster. Stock market prices began falling in August, the sell-off accelerated in October, and by December the Dow Jones Industrial Average was a third of what it had been at the start of the summer. The economy appeared to be going through the same kind of meltdown as at the start of the Great Depression eight years earlier. Corporate profits fell, national income declined, and unemployment increased dramatically.

Kennedy could have kept quiet and ridden out the storm, but he preferred not to. As an insider now, he defended the administration and, as he had in his 1936 campaign book, insisted that he was doing so not as a professional politician, but as a businessman who understood the workings of the economy.

On December 7, 1937, he took the pro-Roosevelt side in a debate organized before fifteen hundred members of the Economic Club of New York at its annual black-tie dinner at the Hotel Astor. The anti-Roosevelt position was presented by former budget director Lewis Douglas and Democratic senator Carter Glass of Virginia. Douglas attacked the administration for being antibusiness. He was followed to the podium by Senator Glass, who declared that he was "totally in disagreement with nearly everything that had been done in Washington" since Roosevelt took office. After Glass had received round after round of applause and shouts of "More!" from the crowd, Kennedy was called to the podium. He began by pledging to follow the instructions he had been given and not to make a speech. "I have only one thing to say. About three years ago I went to Washington as a real enthusiast of the New Deal, and in spite of everything that has been said, and in spite of everything that has happened, I still am an enthusiast for the New Deal." He urged the members of the Economic Club to stop "bellyaching" and if they had ideas about recovery, to do as he had, go to Washington and offer "to help and assist, not for Roosevelt, not for the New Deal, for yourselves, because by doing something now, you can help the whole cause." His speech, the *New York Times* reported the next morning, "was greeted with applause and an undercurrent of booing."[30]

As James Roosevelt recalled in his memoir, Kennedy had "made it clear" after the 1936 election "that he felt he deserved a reward—which he did—and he hinted broadly that the reward he had in mind was the post of secretary of the treasury—which was out of the question. Father was not going to remove Henry Morgenthau from office. Father did not tell Joe in so many words, but in time it became clear to him." A year later, after Kennedy had successfully organized the Maritime Commission as its first chairman, Roosevelt mentioned to his son that "we've got to do something for old Joe, but I don't know what. He wants what he can't have, but there must be something we can give him he'll be happy with." James was informally delegated to raise the subject of a future appointment with Kennedy, which he did "several times." "One evening Joe said that if he couldn't be secretary of the treasury, there was one other job he'd consider: 'I'd like to be ambassador to England.' I was surprised. I really liked Joe, but he was a crusty old cuss and I couldn't picture him as an ambassador, especially to England." James reported Kennedy's request to his father, who on first hearing it "laughed so hard he almost toppled from his wheelchair." Kennedy had never demonstrated any interest in or knowledge of foreign affairs, and he was among the least diplomatic men in Washington. He spoke his mind, got into fights with cabinet members such as Ickes and Frances Perkins, whom he considered softheaded, had no patience for ceremonial events or occasions, was possessed of a fierce temper and a foul mouth, and he was third-generation Irish and a practicing Catholic.[31]

Still, there was a logic to it all. The president was well aware, in late 1937, that whatever the future brought, he was going to have to find a way to confront the looming presence and increasingly aggressive behavior of Hitler and Mussolini on the continent and the Japanese in China. To do so effectively, he needed intelligence not only about internal political currents, but about the European economies, public opinion, what the bankers, industrialists, and political leaders were contemplating. This Kennedy might be able to provide. Say what you might about the man, he was a superb analyst and reporter, a clear-headed, tough-minded, independent thinker who appeared not to be swayed by ideology, belonged to no political faction, was beholden to no industrial sector, and was loyal to the president.

In early December 1937, James Roosevelt reported to Kennedy that his father was prepared to appoint him to the London post. A few days later James visited Kennedy at Marwood. Arthur Krock, who was dining alone with Kennedy that evening, as he did quite often now, recalled watching "as the pair retired to another room for a half hour or so, after which James Roosevelt departed and Kennedy returned to the table. He was fuming. 'You know what Jimmy proposed? That instead of going to London, I become Secretary of Commerce! Well, I'm not going to. FDR promised me London, and I told Jimmy to tell his father that's the job, and the only one, I'll accept.'"[32]

Roosevelt's trial balloon having been punctured, he notified Kennedy that he would be named ambassador to Great Britain. To make sure that the president could not change his mind a second time, Kennedy leaked the story to Arthur Krock, who went public with it on December 9, embarrassing the president, who still had an ambassador in place. Roosevelt was furious and confronted Krock, who intimated that the information had come from the State Department. The president wrote Sumner Welles, his newly appointed under secretary of state, to warn that such leaks had "become a 'positive scandal. . . . If there is a leak in future, everyone down the line will be sent to Siam!'"[33]

Roosevelt knew that the appointment of Kennedy to such an important and prestigious post as ambassador to the Court of St. James's was not going to sit well with his advisers. In his brief tenure in Washington, Kennedy had made a lot of enemies for himself: by speaking out when he shouldn't have, by criticizing the president behind his back to his conservative friends, by offering unsolicited advice on matters that were beyond his purview, and by, time and again, making it clear that he thought he was infinitely smarter, certainly about business and the economy, than anyone else who worked for the president. The general consensus was that he was not to be relied on, that his professed loyalty to the president and the New Deal was skin-deep, that he cared only about himself and his future.

In what may have been a preemptive attempt to push back against the inevitable criticism, Roosevelt "got started on Joe Kennedy" in a December 8 meeting with Secretary of the Treasury, Morgenthau. The president had learned that Floyd Odlum, the wealthy lawyer and industrialist who had extensive holdings in utilities, had "offered Kennedy one million dollars to represent the utilities in Washington." There was nothing illegal about making such an offer, if indeed one had been made. Still, the fact that the utilities industry, which had so bitterly opposed New Deal regulatory legislation, might think that Kennedy would work for them reflected badly on him and his loyalty to the White House. Roosevelt told Morgenthau that he had "faced Kennedy with this story and that he absolutely denied it." Still, Morgenthau noted in his diary, the president had agreed with him that Kennedy was "a very dangerous man." He was sending him to London, he told Morgenthau, "with the distinct understanding that the appointment was only good for six months and that furthermore by giving him this appointment any obligation that he had to Kennedy was paid out." Morgenthau was not convinced that even with such safeguards, the appointment should be made. "Don't you think," he asked Roosevelt, "you are taking considerable risks by sending Kennedy who has talked so freely and so critically against your Administration?" The president assured Morgenthau that he had "made arrangements to have Joe Kennedy watched hourly and the first time he opens his mouth and criticizes me, I will fire him." He closed the discussion by repeating "two or three times, 'Kennedy is too dangerous to have around here.'"[34]

Harold Ickes, Roosevelt's secretary of the interior, disliked and distrusted Kennedy even more than Morgenthau did. He was intensely jealous of Kennedy's relationship with Roosevelt, his fortune, his large family, his overwhelming self-confidence, and his rapport with the Washington press corps. "Kennedy has probably a better press right now than any member of the Administration," Ickes wrote in his diary for December 18, 1937. "He is a very rich man who is always doing favors for newspapermen. For instance, when he is to be away from his large and luxurious Washington house he will turn it over to some newspaper man who can entertain lavishly, leaving all the bills to Kennedy to pay when he returns." Ickes's major fear at the moment, which he noted in his diary was shared by Tom Corcoran, was that Kennedy would use his friendship with Jimmy Roosevelt to exert more and more influence over the president and his policies. "Kennedy . . . is pouring his conservative ideas into the sympathetic ears of Jimmy who relays them to the President. . . . Jimmy is riding with a high hand and, naturally, he is closer to the President than anyone else. Not only this, but he spends more time with him than anyone else." Ickes's fears were misplaced. It was true that on Louis Howe's death, Jimmy Roosevelt had taken over many of his responsibilities and been officially named his father's secretary in July, but it was sheer folly to believe that the president relied on him for advice or that Kennedy was suborning the New Deal or pushing it in a more conservative direction by feeding Jimmy ideas.[35]

While his enemies seethed, most of his friends were delighted for Kennedy, though a few begged him to consider carefully whether he was truly suited for a diplomatic position. When Boake Carter, the most popular radio commentator in the nation and a fiercely unrestrained New Deal critic, asked Kennedy if he could ever be happy in a position in which his main responsibilities would be conveying information back and forth from the State Department to the British Foreign Office, Kennedy responded that he had reached "an 'understanding' or an 'agreement'" with Roosevelt that he was not to be "simply an errand boy in London," but the president's eyes and ears abroad, whose advice and counsel would be sought and respected. Carter warned him not to trust such "agreements."

"My dear lad, agreements mean nothing in his [Roosevelt's] life," Carter wrote. "They never have and they never will. . . . If he thinks certain things should be done as far as Great Britain is concerned, which you may think are cockeyed, you'll either have to carry them out, a la order boy, or explode and resign. That is not a pleasant prospect. . . . Remember also no matter who is sent to London, he will remain there only so long as he does what he is told from Washington. The minute he shows independence, he's through." Carter strongly, "desperately" counseled Kennedy to remain in the country, where he could do much good, add to his reputation as an independent-thinking problem solver, and position himself for higher office, if he so chose. "The minute you accept a reward for your services in some key position or official job, you immediately become answerable to Roosevelt and in so doing, you have to sell out your ideals and thoughts, and work only for the things he directs. . . . You become his servant. You cease to become his consultant. . . . You are an honest man. But the job of Ambassador to London needs not only honesty, sincerity, faith and an abounding courage—it needs skill brought by years of training. And that, Joe, you simply don't possess. . . . Joe, in so complicated a job, there is no place for amateurs."[36]

Senator James Byrnes, among the most influential men on the Hill, also recommended that Kennedy remain at the Maritime Commission until a cabinet position, perhaps at the Treasury Department, opened up. Kennedy responded that had he thought it possible for him to exercise real influence over domestic policy, he might have considered staying behind, but "to continue where I am is certainly a waste of whatever talents I possess. . . . I have never had political ambitions and have none now. I am only vitally concerned with where we are headed. If fellows like yourself think I can help, I will stay and help in whatever job I can do the most good. If I can't help, I can always go back to my own private affairs and be quite happy."[37]

T he news that Roosevelt was going to appoint Kennedy to be the ambassador to Great Britain set the rumor mills in motion. The *Boston Sunday Post* declared on January 2 in a lengthy story, fronted by very large headlines that the WORLD'S FINANCIAL AND POLITICAL NERVE CENTRES RIFE WITH RUMORS KENNEDY TO BE 1940 PRESIDENTIAL CANDIDATE.

Three weeks later, the *St. Louis Star-Times* reported that a close business associate of Kennedy's was spreading the story that a deal had been finalized in Washington to send Morgenthau to London and replace him at the Treasury Department with Kennedy. Morgenthau, convinced that Kennedy had planted the story, called him in Palm Beach. According to the transcript of the conversation recorded by Morgenthau, Kennedy insisted that the story, wherever it came from, was "'god-damned' embarrassing and, of course, as you realize it's 'god-damned' embarrassing to me. . . . I'm 'God-damned' happy! I mean, I've got a 'God-damned' good job." Kennedy offered to find out who had written the story and demand a retraction. The two men hung up, Morgenthau convinced that Kennedy was a liar, Kennedy convinced that Morgenthau was a fool.[38]

Kennedy had told the truth to Morgenthau. He was indeed "'God-damned' happy" because he had a "'God-damned' good job." If he could not be secretary of the treasury, there was no better place for him than as the first Irish Catholic ambassador to Great Britain. The list of past ambassadors read like a *Who's Who* of America's most distinguished publishers, poets, historians, and statesmen. No fewer than five future presidents had held the post. Every one of the Kennedy children—and their children to come—would benefit from having a father and grandfather who had served his country as ambassador to the Court of St. James's.

"I know how you feel," Boake Carter had conceded after what appears to have been hours of conversation on the topic with Kennedy. "I know just how damn fine it would be to give a present like this to your family. I know how it touches your own pride, and what satisfaction one gets out of a thing like this. I know the attraction to you and the type of mind you have. But—I also know the underneath spirit—or at least I think I do—which runs through you. It's a spirit that likes to go out and do big things, fight big battles, win against huge odds."[39]

With an eerily accurate degree of prescience both men would have found frightening, Carter predicted that if Kennedy accepted the appointment, he would return from London defeated, his reputation destroyed, his progress toward higher office blocked. And he was right.

Kennedy was entirely unprepared to serve as ambassador. His businessman's skills, his head for numbers, his negotiating talents, his knowledge of domestic finance and markets, and his flair for publicity had served him well at the SEC and Maritime Commission, but they would not help him in London. Nor would his supreme self-confidence, his sense that he knew best, prepare him for a job in which he would have to answer to the secretary of state for everything he said or did.

He had planned to sail with Rose on February 9 (the children would join them at the end of the school term), but when she was stricken with appendicitis, he delayed his departure for two weeks and flew without her to Palm Beach to join James Roosevelt and Harry Hopkins, to whom he had lent his house, for a few days in the sun. Rose arrived in Palm Beach in the middle of February, and Kennedy flew that same day to Washington.

Two weeks earlier, Secretary of Labor Frances Perkins had made an appearance before the Senate Committee on Commerce to oppose the "compulsory arbitration" amendment to the Merchant Marine Act that Kennedy had proposed. Kennedy, invited to respond to her, indicated that he would be delighted to do so. The day before he appeared, committee chairman Royal Copeland predicted a "field day" in the hearing room. And that was what he got.

As a witness, future ambassador Joseph P. Kennedy was anything but diplomatic. In a letter read aloud to the committee and in comments afterward, he lashed out with undisguised contempt at Secretary Perkins and those who had sided with the CIO and opposed his call for mandatory arbitration. "His opinions of the Secretary of Labor are hardly printable," *Time* magazine would later report. "Mr. Kennedy was so steamed up that Senator Copeland cautioned: 'As chairman of this committee I welcome your fury, Joe, but as a doctor I must tell you it isn't doing your stomach ulcer any good.'" While we don't know what the president thought of Kennedy's attack on his secretary of labor, the newspapers by and large applauded it, as did several congressmen, including Senator Copeland, who, when Kennedy had concluded his remarks, "turned to him and said, 'The members of this committee are very sorry that you are leaving your present post to go to England. We wish you would stay here.'"[40]

He had resigned as chairman of the Maritime Commission after only eight months in office, but with a near universal roar of approval, his reputation among the press and the public enhanced by his tough-talking attack on the maritime unions and Frances Perkins. *Time* magazine marked his departure with an article titled "Kennedy Candor." "In a mood of mingled relief and regret, Chairman Joseph Patrick Kennedy of the U.S. Maritime Commission wrote President Roosevelt last week: 'I should like to report in relinquishing my post that the ills of American Shipping had been cured. . . . Candor compels me to say, however, that the shipping problem is far from solved.' . . . The President replied: 'My dear Joe. . . . You have maintained your justly earned reputation of being a two-fisted, hard-hitting executive."[41]

PART IV

London

Fifteen

A Plainspoken
Ambassador

The day before he was to sail to London, Kennedy was invited to Hyde Park to meet one last time with the president. They spent the morning discussing the faltering American economy, "the foreign situation in general," Kennedy wrote in his diary, British politics, and Anglo-American relations. The question of what the new ambassador would wear at court was brought up. The president had, from the moment he made the appointment, never stopped joking about how bad Kennedy would look in knee breeches, the traditional dress at court. "He told me of his mother's worry that I shall not wear knee breeches and suggested that, if she brought up the matter at luncheon, I might say I am waiting until I get to London to decide. If I didn't do something of the kind, the President warned me, no lunch might be eaten."[1]

Confronted by reporters after lunch, the president, with Kennedy beside him, good-naturedly turned aside any serious questions about their discussions. "When the interviewers finally turned to Mr. Kennedy and jokingly suggested that he come outside so they might 'work' on him, the President said that suggestion also had to be ruled out because Mr. Kennedy had to get his stomach ready for his ocean voyage."[2]

The press was out in force the next day to cover Kennedy's departure in the misconceived hope of a public confrontation between the seamen who manned the S.S. *Manhattan* and Kennedy, who had once claimed that maritime labor conditions were so bad that he would never allow a member of his family to take sail on an American-flagged ship. Regrettably for the reporters, there was no confrontation or ugliness of any sort, though for Kennedy the departure was "a nightmare. All of the children, except Jack, were there to see me off, but I couldn't get to them. Newspaper men, casual well-wishers, old friends and strangers by the thousand, it seemed to me, pressed into my cabin until we all nearly suffocated. . . . Jimmy Roosevelt managed to get to my cabin and I took him into the bedroom for a brief chat. Even there, the photographers had to snap us as we sat on the bed trying to make sense. Finally, I got up to the deck and the children."[3]

The Kennedy send-off was front-page news, in large part because the new ambassador was so unlike his predecessors. As Ferdinand Kuhn, Jr., of the *New York Times* reported from London, until Kennedy, American ambassadors had "sprung from . . . the 'chosen race' of Anglo-Scottish Protestants. . . . Almost invariably they have been chosen for the Englishness of their background and their manner, among their other qualities."[4]

This was one of the reasons Roosevelt had selected Kennedy for the London post. He was not an admirer of all things British, nor was it anticipated that he would become one. As Senator James Byrnes, citing Woodrow Wilson, wrote Kennedy just before his departure, "You can send an American to London, but it is difficult to keep an American there. . . . Notwithstanding President Wilson's statement, I venture to predict that in you we have one American who will remain an American."[5]

The month before, at the annual Mayflower Hotel dinner of the recently fabricated J. Russell Young School of Expression, named for the White House correspondent of the *Washington Star,* the president had awarded Kennedy and Eddie Moore mock "Doctor of Oratory" degrees. His delight at awarding the degrees was, he confessed, "conditioned by certain grave fears, nay, apprehensions—a veritable dread that our Joe's accent may suffer a change with the change of air just ahead of him. Not a few travelers to the bourne whither he is bound have returned with an intonation wholly unintelligible to American ears." Kennedy's degree was being offered provisionally and would be formally ratified only if "Joe, at some future time, shall demonstrate that he still speaks our mother tongue in its full American purity, free from all foreign entanglements."[6]

Kennedy did not disappoint Roosevelt. Aside from adding "bloody" to his already robust lexicon, he never abandoned his American accent. Nor did he appear anywhere in knee breeches. He broke with British tradition—and affirmed the American tradition that grown men do not appear in public in short pants—by wearing a formal evening suit to court. Having violated one sacred Anglo-American tradition, he modified another by declaring, after consultations abroad and at home, that in future he would limit the number of American debutantes presented at court to those whose fathers were working and residing in Great Britain.

He arrived in England already a celebrity. Newsreel cameras recorded his landing in Plymouth and were there when, later in the day, he inspected his new residence in London. Before and after he delivered his brief remarks, he bantered lightheartedly with the reporters. Once the cameras were turned on, he was all business, staging the scene as he wanted it shot, with just the right camera angles, yelling, "Cut!" when he stumbled or got his emphases misplaced.

He had only a few complaints, he wrote Jimmy Roosevelt. The new American embassy at 1 Grosvenor Square might look impressive from the exterior, but it was woefully designed. "If there was ever a badly laid out building for which the United States Government has to pay regular money this tops it all." His private office, decorated in the American style of the 1820s, was a joke. "I have a beautiful blue silk room and all I need to make it perfect is a Mother Hubbard dress and a wreath to make me Queen of the May. If a fairy didn't design this room, I never saw one in my life."[7]

He was more pleased with the ambassador's residence, a six-story, fifty-two-room mansion at 14 Prince's Gate, which J. Pierpont Morgan had donated to the government in 1920. The residence was well situated within walking distance of the embassy and just off Hyde Park and its Rotten Row bridle path, where Kennedy rode almost every morning before work. Though a large amount of money had already been spent to refurbish the interior of the mansion, it was not suitable for a family of eleven. It would take a fortune to renovate the space and another one to keep it up. Serving his country in London, Kennedy quickly realized, was going to cost him a great deal of money.

Because the family could not be expected to survive on English goods alone, Kennedy imported American products for them, including plenty of Maxwell House coffee, tons of candy, dozens of cans of clam chowder, and household supplies unavailable in London like Nivea skin oil, Jergens lotion, and bottles of Cherrico cough medicine. When he discovered that English freezers did not handle ice cream well, he had an American freezer shipped from New York. Through Carmel Offie, Ambassador William Bullitt's assistant at the U.S. embassy in Paris, he purchased cigars, fine wines, and fresh vegetables at wholesale prices. In May 1938, he ordered two thousand bottles of Pommery & Greno champagne, five hundred to be shipped to London at once, the remainder to be stored "in the Pommery cellars at Rheims." He himself seldom drank, and when he did, he preferred Haig & Haig with water before dinner, but a large part of his job as ambassador would be holding formal dinners—for visiting Americans, English gentlemen, and government officials—and he intended to be prepared.[8]

He spent his first Saturday in England playing a round of golf and shooting a hole in one off the second tee. The press roared with delight on both sides of the Atlantic, though his sons questioned whether some chicanery had been involved. After Mass on Sunday, he visited the Convent of the Sacred Heart at Roehampton to register his daughters for school.[9]

The first American to pay a formal visit to the embassy was Rabbi Stephen Wise, who was so impressed by the new ambassador that he wrote a "Private and Confidential" letter to the president, congratulating him on his appointment. "I know you will be glad to hear, through probably you will have heard it before this, that J.K. has already made a very good impression. These Britishers will hear, of course in private, language from him to which their dainty ears are not accustomed."[10]

Rabbi Wise had come to London to confer with Chaim Weizmann, David Ben-Gurion, and other leading Zionists on what appeared to be a shift in British policy on Palestine. He had cabled Felix Frankfurter the day before Kennedy's arrival to "ask him to send word to J.K. to the end that I may have the earliest and most favourable opportunity of meeting with him. He ought to be warned about the present situation." The Zionists feared, rightly, that the British government was intent on reneging on the Balfour Declaration pledge to establish a Jewish homeland, at precisely the moment when such a homeland was needed more than ever. Two and a half years earlier, in the fall of 1935, the Nazi government had instituted the Nuremberg Laws, which formally revoked all citizenship rights from Jews. German Jewish emigration did not increase immediately, but, as Saul Friedländer has written, "the very idea of leaving the country, previously unthinkable for many, was now accepted by all German-Jewish organizations."[11]

On meeting with Kennedy, Wise was delighted, as he wrote his colleagues in New York, to find that the new ambassador agreed with him entirely on the need to pressure the British on Palestine. "J.K. is going to be very helpful, as he is keenly understanding, and there is just enough Irish in him to make him sympathetic to those of us who resent the British promise [to permit Jewish immigration to Palestine] that is in danger of being broken." In the months to come, Wise predicted, the Zionist leadership would be able to count on Kennedy, as it did on Roosevelt, to support their position on Palestine.[12]

W ell, old boy," Kennedy wrote Jimmy Roosevelt the day after he arrived, "I may not last long over here, but it is going to be fast and furious while it's on." As Kennedy's friend Boake Carter had warned him, this was not the best of times for an amateur to enter the diplomatic ranks. In Asia, the Japanese armies that occupied Manchuria had begun their march southward in the summer of 1937, capturing Beijing, Shanghai, and other coastal cities. In Europe, Franco's attempted coup against the Republican government in Spain had turned into a full-scale proxy war, with the Soviets aiding the loyalists and Italian troops and German armaments sustaining Franco's rebels. Mussolini, having brutally conquered Ethiopia in 1936, was now pressuring the British for diplomatic recognition of his newly annexed prize. Hitler was making threatening noises about the future incorporation of Austria and portions of Czechoslovakia into the Third Reich.[13]

President Roosevelt's hands were tied by the Neutrality Acts of 1935 and 1936 that embargoed American trade in arms with belligerents and prohibited loans and credits to nations threatened or victimized by aggression, but he sought other ways to support resistance against what he characterized as "the present reign of terror and international lawlessness." In October 1937, in a major speech in Chicago, he had warned the American people, more bluntly and directly than they were used to, that if the contagion of international lawlessness, aggression, and treaty violations was not halted, the western hemisphere and America would be threatened. Drawing a bit awkwardly on the metaphor that war was a "contagion" spreading uncontrolled across the globe, he proposed that the peace-loving nations actively but nonviolently punish aggressor nations that violated treaties, engaged in violence, and threatened international anarchy by quarantining them. What he meant by this was not entirely clear, though the implication was that he favored some sort of collective economic sanctions. Vague as his proposal was, it was criticized for violating the spirit, if not the letter, of the Neutrality Acts.[14]

Under an attack broader and louder than he had anticipated, Roosevelt had to back away from his quarantine policy—and rhetoric. Unwilling to withdraw entirely from the international arena, however, he supported a proposal by Under Secretary of State Sumner Welles to convene an international conference on November 11, 1938, Armistice Day, and invite nations from every region of the world to the White House to draw "up programs for international conduct, arms reduction, methods of war, and equal access to raw materials." On February 2, 1938, as Kennedy prepared to leave for London, the president informed the British government that he would disclose his plans for the conference within a few days. But events, as they would too often in the months to come, got in the way of grand schemes for peacemaking.

On February 4, 1938, Hitler dismissed his war minister and his commander of the army, took personal control of the German armed forces, and elevated Hermann Goering to field marshal and Joachim von Ribbentrop to foreign minister. Taken together, these changes pointed in the direction of future military adventurism. On February 9, Sumner Welles informed the British ambassador in Washington that the president had decided not to push forward with the conference plans until he had better intelligence on the German situation.

All signs indicated an imminent invasion of Austria, which would be put off only if the Austrian government peacefully agreed to *Anschluss,* or annexation, by Germany. The Americans, Kennedy made clear on arriving in London, were going to stay out of the matter entirely. In his introductory meeting with Lord Halifax, who had been named foreign secretary two weeks earlier, Kennedy noted in his diary that he had "talked pretty frankly to him about the isolationist tendencies at home and found him prepared for that point of view." Two days later, Kennedy said much the same to Prime Minister Neville Chamberlain, who "was apparently prepared as Lord Halifax had been, for my assurances that the United States must not be counted upon to back Great Britain in any scrape, right or wrong. He said he was making his plans for pacification or fighting, as things might develop without counting on us, one way or the other. I talked to him quite plainly and he seemed to take it well."[15]

After returning to the embassy from his meeting with the prime minister, Kennedy called in the press and, feet planted firmly on his desk, volunteered that the average American was much "more interested in how he's going to eat and whether his insurance is good, than in foreign politics. Some, maybe, even, are more interested in how Casey Stengel's Boston Bees are going to do next season." Given the fact that at that moment Hitler was laying the groundwork for the invasion of Austria, Kennedy's remarks were meant to be provocative—and to demonstrate graphically that Americans were not and would never be as concerned with conflicts on the continent as the British were.[16]

For his part, Kennedy was fairly sanguine that the crisis would be settled peacefully. "Nothing is likely to happen except to have [Austrian chancellor Kurt von] Schuschnigg eventually give in unless there is some indication that France and England are prepared to back him up. . . . My own impression," he wrote Roosevelt on March 11, "is that Hitler and Mussolini, having done so very well for themselves by bluffing, are not going to stop bluffing until somebody very sharply calls their bluff." Since nobody, certainly not Great Britain, was going to call that bluff, war was not in the offing. "I am thoroughly convinced and the heads of the various departments in the Government and outside of the Government all feel that the United States would be very foolish to try to mix in. All they are interested in is to have the United States stay prosperous and build a strong navy. . . . This feeling is almost unanimous among the topside people. . . . I am more convinced than ever that the economic situation in Europe is becoming more and more acute and if our American business does not pick up so that trade is generated for these countries, we will have a situation that will far overshadow any political maneuverings."[17]

Kennedy's letter to Roosevelt was written at noon on March 11. His prediction that Hitler was bluffing would be proved wrong within hours. Chancellor Kurt von Schuschnigg had announced on March 9 that he would hold a plebiscite on Austrian independence. To prevent the plebiscite from being held, Hitler ordered an immediate invasion of Austria. Schuschnigg canceled the plebiscite and resigned on March 11. At two A.M. the next day, fourteen hours after Kennedy had declared Hitler was bluffing, German troops marched into Austria, followed soon afterward by Hitler. On March 13, 1938, the German government declared that Austria was henceforth a province of the Reich.

The annexation of Austria was accomplished quickly, efficiently, bloodlessly. The paramount question that remained was what *Anschluss* would mean for Czechoslovakia, which was now bordered by the Reich on the west, north, and south. Would Hitler attempt to annex the Sudetenland, which was populated by more than three million ethnic Germans? And if he did, would France and Britain fulfill their treaty obligations to protect Czechoslovakia from aggression? "We are helpless as regards Austria—that is finished," Sir Alexander Cadogan, the permanent under-secretary of state for foreign affairs, recorded ominously in his diary on March 13. "We *may* be helpless as regards Czechoslovakia, etc. *That* is what I want to get considered. Must we have a death-struggle with Germany again? Or can we stand aside? Former does no one any good. Will latter be fatal?"[18]

Neville Chamberlain downplayed the significance of the German invasion, called for calm, and argued against any saber-rattling gestures. His Conservative Party nemesis, Winston Churchill, on the other hand, declared in the House of Commons that the only way to prevent Hitler from engaging in further aggression was to proclaim Britain's "renewed, revivified, unflinching adherence to the Covenant of the League of Nations" and assemble a "Grand Alliance in a solemn treaty for mutual defense against aggression." To Kennedy, the choice between the two men and the two positions was simple. Chamberlain would appease Hitler and preserve the peace; Churchill would enrage him and provoke war. As Kennedy's first and only priority was preventing war in Europe—and Chamberlain was more committed to preserving the peace at any price than Churchill—the new ambassador was drawn at once into the Chamberlain camp.[19]

He had been impressed with Chamberlain from the moment he met him. Neville Chamberlain was tall, thin, and handsome, with a full mustache, upright posture, and a craggy, slightly rumpled look to him. As Kennedy noted in his diary on March 4 after their first meeting, he "found him a strong decisive man, evidently in full charge of the situation here." Chamberlain had been a businessman and, Kennedy believed, still behaved like one, which was all to the good. The prime minister understood the value of negotiation, the need to compromise with one's opponents, the dangers of rhetorical overkill. His preference was always to make the deal rather than walk away from the table empty-handed. Kennedy was impressed as well by Lord Halifax, the tall, one-armed, balding Uriah Heep–looking foreign secretary, and his dapper and meticulous second, Sir Alexander Cadogan, the permanent under-secretary of state.[20]

Chamberlain, Halifax, and Cadogan were equally taken with the new American ambassador. They appreciated his frankness and intelligence and, from the moment he arrived in London, treated him not as the oddity he was—the first Irish Catholic ambassador ever and a blunt, plain-speaking businessman to boot—but as a trusted colleague with whom they could speak freely and candidly and occasionally share information gathered by British intelligence.

It was customary for the newly arrived American ambassador to introduce himself to his British hosts with a speech at the Pilgrims Society. A month before sailing for London, Kennedy had hired Harold Hinton, a former *New York Times* reporter on foreign affairs, as his speechwriter and asked him, with Krock and a few others, to begin assembling ideas for his address. He continued to work on the speech after arriving in London and forwarded a copy to the State Department for review on March 11.[21]

As ambassador, Kennedy reported directly to Cordell Hull, the tall, lean, white-haired, former Tennessee congressman whom Roosevelt had asked to be his secretary of state. When Kennedy's speech arrived by cable in Washington, Hull delegated career diplomat Jay Pierrepont Moffat, chief of the Western European division, to look at it. Moffat suggested minor changes and passed the speech along the chain of command. The following day, Saturday, March 12, the speech was edited a second time and significant excisions made by Secretary Hull and other "internationalists" in the State Department who, Moffat reported in his diary, feared that Kennedy had "swung far too much towards the isolationist school." It was one thing to avoid comment on the *Anschluss,* quite another to emphasize that Americans believed they had no stake in European affairs, which was what Kennedy appeared to be implying.[22]

Moffat cabled Kennedy to explain that further cuts had been made in his speech, not because anyone in the department disagreed with what he had to say, but because the American press was hammering the State Department to respond "to the German rape of Austria" and any utterance by an American official would "be read as having been written with the Austrian situation in view." Hull emphasized the same point in a cable sent the same day. Although neither he nor the president found fault with Kennedy's address, they were "inclined to think that the tone of the speech is a little more rigid, and hence subject to possible misinterpretation, than would appear advisable at this precise moment." To make sure the international community understood that the American government was going to pursue a policy that avoided "the extremes of isolationism and internationalism," Hull told Kennedy that he had decided to give his own speech the day before Kennedy's was scheduled.[23]

What Hull was saying—and Kennedy understood it at once—was that he didn't trust his new ambassador to speak for the administration, and to prevent him from doing so, he had decided not only to censor his inaugural address, but to preempt it with one of his own. Kennedy should have backed off at this point, but he did not. The stakes were too high.

On Tuesday, March 15, Kennedy was visited at the embassy by Lord Astor, who told him "that some of the leading men here believe that immediate war is a greater danger than they like to let the public know." The antiappeasement faction in Parliament, led by Winston Churchill, was calling for a tougher stance against Germany, and if Churchill's group carried the debate, it would embarrass Chamberlain, anger Hitler, and push Europe closer to war.[24]

Kennedy placed a transatlantic call to the State Department to report what Astor had told him. It was nine thirty in the morning Washington time. He was in a panic now that Hull, in his forthcoming speech, would say something that would give the Churchill faction an edge in the parliamentary debate on the British response to Hitler's seizure of Austria.

> **Mr. Moffat:** The Secretary is here and you are talking to him on the receiver but he has a bad throat and I am his voice answering back to you. . . .
>
> **Ambassador:** Will you connect me up with the President after I finish talking with you? . . . I am very much concerned about the idea of the Secretary's making the speech outlined in the wire last night. The situation is very, very acute here. . . . They don't know what they are going to do and anything we say now would only complicate the situation. . . .
>
> **Moffat:** The Secretary has asked whether you have seen his speech.
>
> **Ambassador:** No, I have not. . . .

At this point, Secretary Hull, bad throat and all, felt compelled to get on the phone and explain that his speech contained nothing new but simply summed up the general principles under which the United States believed world order could be maintained.

> **Ambassador:** A speech of the Secretary's is not going to help at all. Why say anything when there is nothing you can say or do which will help the situation? Why not keep quiet?

Kennedy refused to let up. He continued to argue against Hull's giving his speech. Moffat mercifully brought the conversation to an end by expressing the secretary's appreciation for Kennedy's call and "point of view" and announcing that he had just received a note that the president was "with his dentist" and unable to talk to the ambassador.[25]

After hanging up, Hull and Moffat met with the department's senior advisers, including Sumner Welles. "A few of them," Moffat noted in his diary, "were quite brutal in their comment that Kennedy wanted the Secretary's speech canceled in order that his own which was more isolationist in trend would receive a better play. Had he offered to cancel the Pilgrims Society speech the situation might be different but in the circumstances the consensus of opinion was against any change of plans."[26]

Kennedy had indeed feared Hull's speech would undercut his own, but that was not his only concern. He feared that the secretary of state was going to offer some moralistic/legalistic condemnation of Hitler's move into Austria, that this would be interpreted as a sign that the United States would stand behind a tough British response to the *Anschluss,* and that such a "sign" would provide the Churchill saber rattlers with a boost in the House of Commons. Two weeks into his tenure, Ambassador Kennedy was already trying to usurp the authority of the secretary of state and interfere in British politics. And two weeks into his tenure, he had already been slapped down by Cordell Hull for doing so.

On March 18, 1938, Kennedy was formally welcomed by the Pilgrims Society at a dinner at Claridge's. The evening opened with a message from King George VI read by his youngest brother, the Duke of Kent, followed by introductions from the Earl of Derby, the society's president, and Lord Halifax. The new ambassador then took the podium, his posture perfect, his smile dazzling, his formal dinner dress perfectly tailored. He was going to be "frank" with his hosts, he warned them. Instead of soothing them with the "usual diplomatic niceties," he would "speak plainly" about "certain factors in American life which have a greater influence than some of you may realize on my countrymen's attitudes toward the outside world." Americans were "appalled by the prospect of war" and desired peace for themselves and for the peoples of the world, but "the great majority" were opposed to entering into any sort of "entangling alliances." Kennedy did not rule out the possibility that "circumstances, short of actual invasion," might arise in the future and compel Americans to "fight." But he wanted it fully understood that the assumption, widely held in both nations, "that the United States could never remain neutral in the event a general war should break out" was both dangerous and wrong.

The speech was carefully balanced between what were at the time the two shaky pillars of American foreign policy: diplomatic unilateralism and economic cooperation. After asserting that the United States was not interested in entering into diplomatic alliances, Kennedy insisted that it "would be glad to join and encourage any nation or group of nations in a peace program based on economic recovery, limitation of armaments and a revival of the sanctity of international commitments. . . . We regard the economic rapprochement of the nations as imperative. Economic appeasement . . . means a higher standard of living for the workers of the world and a consequent reduction in those internal pressures which all too frequently lead to war."[27]

There was nothing particularly inflammatory about Kennedy's speech—anything that might have been had been carefully deleted by the State Department editors. In fact, as the German ambassador to the United States reported in his dispatch to the German Foreign Ministry, Kennedy's address differed from Hull's, given the day before, "only in form. While Secretary Hull treats the problem with his usual academic and monotonous phraseology, Ambassador Kennedy does not shrink from employing an unmistakable and resolute tone. Mr. Kennedy really says nothing new. He merely says what he has to say more clearly than it has hitherto been expressed by the President or Mr. Hull."[28]

Strangely enough for one who identified himself and would be identified as an isolationist, Kennedy the businessman could not help but think globally. The continuing and, after mid-1937, deepening depression in the United States was going to have a disastrous effect on stability in Europe. "Our continual tail-spin," he wrote Tommy Corcoran from London, "is making this problem here and all through Europe more difficult, because the basis of the correction of conditions here is not political but economic." There could be no peace or political stability in the world without economic security. The most effective role the

United States could play in reducing tensions and preventing wars was to promote economic recovery at home, which would have positive domino-like effects abroad.[29]

The farther he got from Washington, the more disturbed he was that the president did not understand how critical it was—for European peace—to get the American economy going again. To stimulate recovery, the president had to convince American businessmen that the administration was on their side, as Kennedy had at the SEC and the Maritime Commission. Unfortunately, instead of cozying up to the nation's businessmen and assuring them it was safe to invest again, the president was continuing, Kennedy feared, to alienate them with pseudopopulist rhetoric. In a transatlantic phone call to Cordell Hull, Kennedy reported that at a recent dinner he had hosted, every one of the "eighteen . . . big bankers here in London" had expressed discomfort with the president's antibusiness outbursts at a speech in Gainesville, Georgia. A former chancellor of the Exchequer had gone so far as to tell Kennedy that he blamed Roosevelt's failure to promote capital investment in American industry for the "dismal economic condition of England." "Who was responsible for that Gainesville speech? Whoever was ought to be horsewhipped," Kennedy volunteered to Hull.[30]

His fear that economic distress could not help but foment political unrest in Europe was not an abstract possibility, but a recurring nightmare. Dutifully responding to a letter from Honey Fitz about Boston politics in early April, Kennedy remarked on the sorry state of the American economy. "Sometimes I wonder if I will have money enough to last out a decent term in London. I hate to think how much money I would give up rather than sacrifice Joe and Jack in a war, and there is no danger of that in America, whereas there is a real danger of it for boys of their age over here."[31]

In mid-March, Rose arrived in London with Kick and the four youngest children. The new Kennedy residence, Rose complained gently to the press, was large for any ordinary family, but a bit small for hers. "The house will be large enough for these five . . . but no place will be large enough in the summer when all the rest come with their friends from Harvard and Princeton." She brought with her the younger children's governess, Elizabeth Dunn; Luella Hennessey, the nurse who had cared for Patricia and Bobby when they got sick at camp; and the family cook. There were already at the residence handfuls of English butlers, chauffeurs, maids, and secretaries.[32]

On April 27, Rosemary and Eunice, accompanied by Eddie and Mary Moore, landed at Plymouth. Eunice, Patricia, and Jean were enrolled at the Sacred Heart Convent in Roehampton; Rosemary in a Montessori-oriented school; Bobby and Teddy at the nearby Gibbs Preparatory School. The boys had the hardest time adjusting. David Ormsby-Gore, later Lord Harlech, spent a good deal of time as a teenager with the Kennedys in London. Bobby, he recalled, "rather disliked the school he was sent to. . . . He thought it was rather ridiculous . . . that the uniform they had to wear was ridiculous. . . . He was always very sensitive about his appearance. . . . They were made to wear these red magenta hats which were made like a sort of tweed cap which was unique for any school, even in England. I think this acutely embarrassed him and I don't think he ever settled down."[33]

Teddy had his own difficulties. He was younger and smaller than his schoolmates and didn't make friends easily. "Bobby tried to keep me company," he recalled, "but he'd joined a circle of friends his age." For the first time in years, Kennedy was living in the same house as his children, and when he noticed his youngest son's discomfort, he tried to ease it. "Dad spent as much time with me as he could. . . . He came to my cricket games at school. He invited me with him on morning horseback rides. . . . In the evenings, before leaving the house with Mother for a dinner or the theater, he would come into my bedroom and read to me, sometimes for forty-five minutes or an hour."[34]

On May 11, Rosemary and Kick were presented at court. The preparations—the selection of the dresses, the fittings, the search for the perfect tiara for Rose, the practice walks and curtsies—had taken days. The ceremony itself took but a few minutes and went off without a hitch. Rose had worried that Rosemary, now twenty years of age, might not be up to the event, which was choreographed as carefully as a ballet, but she did beautifully.

There had been some talk—but not much—of Kick's attending college in England, but she decided not to. It was her first London "season" and she expected to take it all in, unencumbered by schoolwork. Almost on arrival she had become the darling of the London social set, her every evening and weekend taken up with dinner dances, excursions to grand country estates, racing and regattas and Scottish hunting parties.

The three Kennedys, sometimes separately but often together—the ambassador reluctantly, Rose and Kick more enthusiastically—spent much of that spring of 1938 attending garden parties, rowing regattas, formal balls, afternoon teas, dinner dances, racing at Epsom Downs and the Royal Ascot, tennis matches at Wimbledon. They were invited to a weekend with the Duchess of Marlborough at Blenheim Palace, an evening court at Buckingham Palace, and a ball given by Lady Astor for the king and queen.

Rose had been waiting all her life for this. To the press and her dinner companions, she appeared totally at ease and fully in control. In private, however, she worried a great deal about fitting in. She was horrified, as she confided to her diary, to discover that on Sunday lunch at Windsor Castle, she was the only one dressed in tweeds; the others wore afternoon dresses. She was so confused about when and where she should wear a tiara that she contacted officials at Buckingham Palace, who told her that it should be worn at any dinner at which a member of the royal family was present. She also asked in writing if she should provide "finger bowls at dinners at which Royalty are present" and was informed that there was no formal rule against them.[35]

With the arrival in London of all the Kennedys save the two older boys, who were still in school, the press on both sides of the Atlantic stepped up its parade of news items, photographs, and adoring profiles. Not a day, it seemed, had passed that spring of 1938 without a story or two about a Kennedy or two: about Joe Kennedy, Jr.'s decision not to dress in drag in a Harvard satirical review; Jack's recovery from illness so that he could swim for the Harvard varsity; Kick's possible engagements; Rosemary's hospitalization for an unnamed ailment; Eunice's graduation from the Sacred Heart Convent in Noroton; Patricia's and Jean's enrollment at the Sacred Heart Convent at Roehampton; Bobby's interview, on departing New York, with Mary Pickford, who was preparing for her next role as a reporter; Teddy's having "gone missing" for a moment upon the family's arrival at Plymouth; Rose's being selected with Ginger Rogers, Dolores del Rio, and Kitty Carlisle as one of the eleven "best dressed" women in the United States; and Elsa Maxwell's inclusion of Ambassador Kennedy as one of the six most "chic" males on the planet, with Crown Prince Umberto and Count Ciano of Italy, Fred Astaire, Joe DiMaggio, and William Rhinelander Stewart, the debonair New York socialite.[36]

It got to the point where even Honey Fitz began to joke about the coverage. Kennedy, who had little sense of humor when it came to his father-in-law, responded that he had had nothing to do with the avalanche of publicity. "We are not sending any pictures to any paper. . . . If you have an attractive daughter and attractive grandchildren, you can't get mad if their pictures appear in the papers."[37]

Kennedy did not shy away from the attention. On the contrary, he did everything he could to remind the folks back home that he was still serving his country. He employed one of the largest and most accomplished press, public relations, and speechwriting offices in the government, headed by Eddie Moore and James Seymour, whom Kennedy had lured away from Harvard a decade before to join his staff in Hollywood. Kennedy had also taken with him to London Harvey Klemmer, a speechwriter who had worked with him at the Maritime Commission and remained on its payroll; Arthur Houghton, whom he had borrowed from Will Hays's office in Hollywood; and an RKO publicist in London named Jack Kennedy, who was referred to as "London Jack" Kennedy.

Kennedy adjusted easily to the social demands of his new life. He was the perfect dinner companion, the consummate weekend guest, a magnificent host at the dinners he gave at the residence. Nobody in London had as star-studded an invitation list, with lords and ladies, American corporate and government leaders, and Hollywood royalty seated next to one another. Formal dinners, with guests in tuxedos and gowns greeted and served by liveried servants, were held for magazine publisher Henry Luce and his wife, Clare Boothe Luce, a former actress and now a celebrated writer; for Hollywood producer Darryl Zanuck and his wife, Virginia Fox Zanuck; for actress Rosalind Russell; and for Secretary of the Interior Harold Ickes when he toured Europe with his new wife, Jane. Although Ickes had nothing good to say of Kennedy in Washington, he was happy to be entertained by him in London. After dinner, the Kennedys veered sharply from London social customs and invited their guests, men and women alike, to watch the latest Hollywood films in the drawing room. At the May 17 dinner for Foreign Secretary Halifax and Lady Halifax, which Charles and Anne Morrow Lindbergh attended, Kennedy screened *Test Pilot* with Myrna Loy and Clark Gable. On May 30, he screened *The Adventures of Robin Hood* but arranged for the prime minister, one of the guests for the evening, to "stay out of the drawing room in order to talk with Arthur Sulzberger [of the *New York Times*], Harry Luce and one or two others." Luce, who did not much enjoy socializing, noted appreciatively that compared with other formal dinners, there was "not much conversation" at a Kennedy-hosted affair. "Old Joe wasn't much for that sort. We had a movie after dinner. That eliminated the necessity for postprandial conversation."[38]

Kennedy disliked the constant socializing he had to endure as American ambassador—he had never much enjoyed having to make idle chitchat with people he did not know or care about—but there were distinct advantages to being in London for the season. Kennedy had always been a Toscanini fan and was now able not only to attend each of the maestro's spring concerts with the BBC Symphony Orchestra, but also to sit in on the ten A.M. rehearsals as well. Joseph P. Kennedy was not a man given to hero worship, except perhaps for Arturo Toscanini. Among the most cherished possessions at Hyannis Port was a framed Toscanini baton.[39]

In London, as elsewhere, Kennedy awoke before seven A.M. After breakfast, he went for a horseback ride, then showered, dressed in his ambassadorial uniform—striped pants, short black jacket, white shirt, stiff collar, and dark necktie—and walked or was driven to the embassy, arriving by 8:45 at the latest. Every day brought another contingent of American journalists and publishers, Broadway and Hollywood big shots, businessmen and bankers, each of whom expected a private interview. The phone began ringing the moment he arrived at his office—and kept ringing all day long—interrupting the carefully laid-out schedules that Eddie Moore had prepared. "It is almost impossible to do any desk work when he is here," Moore confessed to Paul Murphy in New York, "for the telephone is popping from morning until night, and what with it and the newspaper men and visitors in addition, it leaves very little time for anything else."[40]

His hard work won the admiration of embassy personnel, who had not expected their new ambassador to be this dedicated to his new job. "Kennedy has started off very well, I think he will do a first class job," Alan Steyne, a minor official at the embassy, wrote his uncle, Boston department store owner Louis Kirstein, on April 16, 1938. "He arrived with quite a few preconceived notions and prejudices but he is very keen and is slowly dropping those which do not jibe with the facts here. . . . The pressure on his time is very great and the number of people who want to meet him makes Bingham [his predecessor] look as if he had the Measles. Kennedy's seen about more in one month than Bingham was in a year. . . . He's far more outspoken than the run of the mill Ambassador. . . . He is not easy to work for in that he is very nervous and suffers from stomach ulcers which doesn't improve his disposition the days when they bother him. However, he has a very keen, quick intellect and is open to conviction if you can marshal a good argument. His informality is delightful and his language longshoremanesque."[41]

The week after the dueling speeches brouhaha with Cordell Hull, Kennedy, recognizing that he would have to work with the man for the rest of his tenure in London, wrote to flatter him by reporting how much the queen had enjoyed his speech, which "came through nicely [over the radio] and, of course, made a terrific impression here." The war scare that had so unsettled him had passed. "Popular opinion has changed from being all upset regarding war as a real possibility to a much more complacent attitude and more inclined to follow Chamberlain's original thesis—to try every possible means of averting a war. . . . I imagine the England-Italy situations will be worked out within the next few weeks . . . and then Chamberlain is going definitely to work to try to fix up something with Hitler." The preliminaries cleared away, he got to the point of his dispatch: "From what I have seen of the job here and assuming nothing happens of world import, I can deliver your messages, but I probably can do nothing very constructive. I can talk Chamberlain's language and Halifax's language and if there were anything vital to do would have a reasonable chance of getting it done, but, as matters stand today, the only possible help I can give you is to express my opinion as to events in Europe. The annoying part of this is that, while I am busy from 9:30 in the morning until 11:00 at night, I don't feel I am doing you very much good and if anything occurs to you, outside of the ordinary instructions, where I can be of any real assistance, please let me know. . . . I hope you get some good out of my services; I am sure I will have a fine time."[42]

On March 24, Joseph Kennedy joined several other ambassadors in the Peers' Gallery of the House of Commons to listen to a major address by Prime Minister Chamberlain, who declared that Great Britain would not offer Czechoslovakia any "prior pledge" of assistance in case of a German invasion, nor would it agree in advance to join France should it decide to come to Czechoslovakia's rescue. Having made these statements, Chamberlain came close to emptying them of meaning by declaring that "if war broke out . . . the inexorable pressure of facts might well prove more powerful than formal pronouncements" and that there was every probability that countries such as Great Britain and France, not party to the "original dispute would almost immediately become involved." As the *New York Times* summarized the speech the morning after, "Prime Minister Neville Chamberlain today kept Germany and the rest of the world guessing as to whether Britain would fight in case of a German onslaught upon Czechoslovakia."[43]

Kennedy thought the speech nothing less than "a masterpiece. I sat spellbound and heard it all. It impressed me as a combination of high morals and politics such as I had never witnessed. . . . As I size it up, there will be no war if Chamberlain stays in power with strong public backing, which he seems to be acquiring day by day. A deal will be made with Italy (it may be practically complete by now), . . . Germany will get whatever it wants in Czechoslovakia without sending a single soldier across the border. The Czechs will go, hat in hand, to Berlin and ask the Fuhrer what he wants done, and it will be done. . . . The Germano-Czech situation will solve itself without interference."[44]

Kennedy's observations were made in one of the long "political letters" he had begun writing to influential friends in the press and in government. Though the letters were marked "Private and Confidential," Kennedy sent them to every major conservative columnist, senator, and Washington insider, clearly not shy about advertising his admiration and support for Chamberlain, Halifax, and their appeasement policy. Bob Allen, Drew Pearson's "Washington Merry-Go-Round" writing partner, warned Kennedy to tread lightly. "I wouldn't think of advising you," he wrote him from Washington, "but just as a friend, Joe, I'd keep my fingers crossed on Chamberlain and his Tory crew. You are going to see important changes in the British government in the not very distant future. . . . From the inside information we get here, the Chamberlain government is about as competent as Hoover's and is rapidly becoming as unpopular." Allen was wrong about Chamberlain, who would continue in office for another two years, but he was correct about the dangers of Kennedy remaining so close to him.[45]

On April 6, at the start of his second month in London, Kennedy met with Lord Halifax to discuss, among other things, the British negotiations with the Italian government, "with a view to the settlement of all matters outstanding between them." The most controversial part of the agreement under discussion was that in return for concessions from the Italians in a number of areas and professions of future friendship, the British were prepared to end any and all opposition to the Italian annexation of Ethiopia. Before proceeding, Halifax wanted Roosevelt to publicly signal that he approved or would not actively oppose British recognition of the Italian conquest. Kennedy told Halifax "that he would willingly mention the point to the President and thought it was the kind of thing he might well do."[46]

He cabled Hull that evening with details of his conversation with the foreign secretary on the "Italian situation." He then ventured his "own opinion . . . that ninety per cent of the people in Great Britain will hail [the Italian accord] with great acclaim and there is no question about its being the beginning of a step in the right direction." There was no direct response from the secretary of state.[47]

A week later, the negotiations with the Italians that much closer to conclusion, Halifax forwarded through Kennedy a "Personal and Confidential" letter for Hull and Under Secretary Welles, outlining the proposed terms of the Italian agreement and asking again that Roosevelt "give some public indication of his approval." Sumner Welles was delegated to draft Roosevelt's answer and did so in diplomatic doublespeak that withheld comment on the substance of the agreement but praised the fact that it had resulted from "peaceful negotiations."[48]

Because the statement failed to condemn or criticize Mussolini, it was greeted enthusiastically by Americans who favored further negotiation with the dictators and condemned by those who considered accommodation with aggression a sign of moral and diplomatic weakness. Welles took the brunt of the criticism, but Kennedy was singled out as having been an important influence on the president. The cruelest rebuke came from Kennedy's friends Drew Pearson and Bob Allen, who intimated that Kennedy had supported the British cave-in on Ethiopia because he had been brainwashed by Lord and Lady Astor and the Tory appeasers who were headquartered at Cliveden, the Astors' country estate. "Latest American to be wooed by the Cliveden group is genial Joe Kennedy," Pearson and Allen reported in their April 22, 1938, column. "Reports are that Joe has been taken in just a bit by the Cliveden charm, not on the Nazi-Fascist theories, but on the idea of cooperating with the Tories of Great Britain. Joe, who has a lot of Irish-American commonsense, will probably snap out of it. But the tragedy of the American diplomatic service for years has been its unabashed obeisance before the throne of British foreign policy."[49]

Kennedy was furious with the column, if only because it portrayed him as the dupe of Tory aristocrats. "I know you and Bob don't want to hurt me unless you have definite reasons," he wrote Drew Pearson. "Your story on the Cliveden set is complete bunk. There is not one single word of truth to it and it has done me great harm. You know I would not make this firm denial unless it was so. It is unfortunate when I am working as hard as I can to keep this situation straight that this kind of story should be published. The repercussions over here have been extremely bad. I don't know what you can do about it, but thought I should tell you."[50]

Pearson wrote back at once to say that he doubted his column would "have any serious effect. Let me add, however, that the information in the story came to us from very good friends in the State Department— friends both of yours and of ours." This news could not have come as any comfort to Kennedy. The gossip that he was a confirmed member of the Cliveden set was bad enough; that it had come from the State Department was worse.[51]

Kennedy was not a member of the Cliveden set, nor had he been unduly influenced by their views. He had come to believe that appeasement was the best, perhaps the only route to preserving the peace long before he had visited Cliveden. Still, he might have done well, as the representative of his nation, to follow the advice of Pearson and Allen and keep a bit of distance from Lady Astor and her circle.

The former Nancy Witcher Langhorne of Danville, Virginia, now Lady Astor and a Conservative member of the House of Commons since 1919, though magnetically charming at age sixty, had become more vituperative than ever in her condemnation of those who criticized the Germans, especially those who were Jewish. Ten months earlier, on boarding a ship to return to England after a brief stay in America, she had denounced to a *New York Times* reporter the "anti-German propaganda in the United States. . . . 'If the Jews are behind it they are going too far, and they need to take heed. . . . Anyone who reads the papers can see what is coming; it will react against them. And I tell all my Jewish friends the same thing.'" She was not, she insisted, "pro-German," but she felt obliged to point out that the "agitators against Germany . . . were forgetting completely the atrocities going on in other nations, in Russia, in Spain and Ethiopia."[52]

None of this prompted Kennedy to steer clear of her. He had no problem with Lady Astor's pronouncements about the Jews, in large part because she was simply saying in public what others, Kennedy included, were saying in private: that the Jews were too powerful in the media and too outspokenly anti-German. No matter how outrageous her comments and no matter what the press might make of his visits to the Astors and Cliveden, Kennedy had no intention of staying away or encouraging any member of his family to do so. The Astors would become fast family friends of the Kennedys, not just because of their political affinities, as the ambassador's critics back home would argue, but because they were British royalty, gloriously wealthy, glamorous, sociable, lots of fun, and loyal.

Asked by Lady Astor to speak at an event at Plymouth in December 1938, Kennedy readily agreed. "If you asked me to go to Plymouth or anywhere else you were interested in, I would get on a bicycle and go there. When I was very young, my father impressed upon me that I would notice as I went through life that gratitude was mostly found in the dictionary, and he always urged me never to be unappreciative of the kind things done for me and I have tried to keep that in mind all my life. I would seem very unappreciative indeed if I didn't express to you my thanks for your many kindnesses to Rose, Kathleen and the children. If my going to Plymouth gave you half as much pleasure as I had in going and making that speech and getting such a wonderful reception, then I am very happy."[53]

He continued to see a great deal of the Astors, almost in defiance of those who criticized him for doing so. He invited them to dinner at the residence and accepted their invitation for luncheon with George Bernard Shaw and Charles Lindbergh on May 5. When Drew Pearson and Robert Allen attacked him, he sent her a copy of the column, making light of what was the most offensive aspect: the insinuation that he was not his own man. "Well, you see what a terrible woman you are, and how a poor fellow like me is being politically seduced. O weh ist mir!"[54]

In any other context, Kennedy's use of a Yiddish expression might be interpreted as a weak attempt at humor. But at this time, in this place, after the promulgation of the Nuremberg Laws, the removal of citizenship rights from German Jews, their expulsion from the universities, the hospitals, the law courts, the military, and the civil service, the expropriation of their shops and small businesses, and the recent unprovoked and brutal acts of violence against Austrian Jews, and given Lady Astor's own penchant for anti-Semitic comments, his lighthearted remarks were particularly distasteful.

The *Anschluss* of March 1938 had had a devastating and immediate impact on the 190,000 Jewish citizens who were swept up into the new German empire. "The persecution in Austria, particularly in Vienna," Saul Friedländer has written, "outpaced that in the Reich. Public humiliation was more blatant and sadistic; expropriation better organized; forced emigration more rapid." The president, though outraged, refrained from saying or doing much, fearful that the simplest humanitarian efforts might be perceived and trumpeted by his opponents as proof of the pernicious influence of his Jewish advisers on what was too often referred to now as the "Jew Deal." Still, Roosevelt was disturbed enough by Nazi violence against Jews to instruct Secretary of State Hull on March 23, twelve days after the Germans entered Austria, to call on the governments of Europe and Latin America and ascertain "if they would be willing to co-operate with the Government of the United States in setting up a special committee . . . for the purpose of facilitating the emigration from Austria and presumably from Germany of political refugees." That the vast majority of these refugees were Jews was not mentioned. On the contrary, in a March 25 press conference, Roosevelt insisted that the new initiative "embraced Jews, Protestants and Catholics, as well as the persecuted minorities of Russia, Italy and Spain." When asked point-blank "if it were not true that the main purpose of the Government's cooperative gesture was the relief of Jews in Germany and Austria," he "answered in the affirmative," then emphasized again that a "very large number of Christians would be benefited by the plan."[55]

Kennedy conveyed Hull's request to Lord Halifax, who on April 6, 1938, officially accepted the invitation to send a British representative to the international conference scheduled to take place at Évian-les-Bains, France, in June. He handed Kennedy a memorandum with the "points" the British government expected to be "particularly borne in mind in handling the matter" of the Austrian refugees. The British had no intention of opening Palestine for Jewish settlement or of increasing immigration quotas for Jews to Great Britain or its overseas colonies and dominions. On the contrary, the Home Office had taken steps after the *Anschluss* to restrict the number of refugees. Austrian Jews were admitted on three-month visas, requiring them to register immediately with the police on entering the country, and prohibited from seeking or taking employment.[56]

The State Department neither questioned these actions nor protested the conditions the British government placed on the discussions that would take place at the Évian Conference. Kennedy adhered scrupulously to the letter and intent of the State Department instructions. When Joseph Karmel, a "reporter and literary critic" for two Polish newspapers, asked for a chance to interview him "on behalf, if I may say so, of thousands of Jewish readers," the ambassador agreed, on the understanding that their conversation was not "for publication. . . . You will appreciate, I am sure," Kennedy wrote Karmel, "that any official discussion of any government attitude must come from the proper authorities in Washington."[57]

While Kennedy made no public pronouncements on the British refusal to do anything for the Jewish refugees, it clearly did not sit well with him. This was a humanitarian crisis of the first order, and the British, like the Americans, had the responsibility to do what they could. Harold Ickes recalled in his diary that during his honeymoon in London in May 1938, Kennedy took him to "call on Lord Halifax at the Foreign Office. Halifax brought up the question of the Jews and the rough treatment they are receiving in the Fascist countries. Their position is rapidly being made untenable in Germany and Austria. . . . The question is where to find a place for them on the surface of the earth where they can be left alone in comparative peace and security." For the British, Palestine was a closed issue. Lord Halifax asked "whether it might be possible to locate these Jews in the United States, in South America, and in some of the British colonies." Ickes responded that though "the Jewish question with us was not as acute as elsewhere, there was a great deal of anti-Jewish sentiment which would undoubtedly increase if an attempt were made to bring in a large number of Jews." He and Kennedy turned the tables and suggested "that there ought to be plenty of room in some of the British Colonies to take care of all the Jews who need a new home, and it would also seem that there must be plenty of room in South America."[58]

In June, Kennedy met personally with Viscount Bearsted, one of the leaders of the British Jewish community, who impressed on the ambassador, as he had earlier on Lord Halifax, his sense that the Jewish refugee problem, now exacerbated by the inclusion of 190,000 Austrian Jews in the Third Reich, "could no longer be handled by private individuals. It has become an international question." Bearsted had hoped to get from Kennedy reassurance that progress toward a solution to the refugee problem might be made at Évian. Instead, he found Kennedy's "ideas somewhat hazy." The ambassador confided to Bearsted "his low opinion of Mr. Myron Taylor," the former head of U.S. Steel, whom Roosevelt had asked to represent the United States at Évian. Taylor, Kennedy insisted, had "not only no knowledge of the problem, but was making no attempt to get it up." Kennedy told Bearsted that he intended to "see the President on his return to America and endeavour to ensure that instructions, or fresh instructions, were sent to Mr. Taylor."[59]

Although Kennedy believed that the British could and should do more for the Jews of Austria and Germany, it was not his first priority. He felt quite differently about a group of Catholic refugees trapped in Spain.

The Sunday after he arrived in London, while visiting the Sacred Heart Convent at Roehampton to enroll his girls, he had been approached by the reverend mother, who told him about her efforts to rescue thirty-six Sacred Heart nuns in Barcelona who had been placed in mortal danger (as was every other civilian in the city) by German and Italian bombardment. On returning to the embassy, and without seeking permission of the State Department, Kennedy contacted the American consul in Spain to ask for assistance in getting the nuns evacuated. On April 6, he requested, again without informing the State Department, that the British use their influence to secure the release of the nuns. "Halifax," he reported in his diary, "asked if I was prepared to take the responsibility of saying that the American Government wanted those nuns to be permitted to leave, and I said I was. . . . I told him that I was willing to be hanged any time for trying to save those 28 innocent and devoted women (eight of them had already been killed in the bombings of Barcelona) and I assumed that responsibility for the expense it would entail to bring them to England." Three days later, on hearing from Halifax that progress had been made, Kennedy informed Secretary of State Hull of the "incident," which, he believed, now successfully concluded, would "bring joy to your heart." The British government's rescue of the Barcelona nuns was, he continued in a "Private and Confidential" cable to Hull, "a noble piece of work. . . . There are no official records on this anywhere, but I thought you would like to know it." Seven hours later, realizing that he had spoken prematurely and that the British had not secured the nuns' release, Kennedy asked Sumner Welles to step up American pressure. "It seems to me a strategic stroke for the State Department to get this class of person out of Spain." By "this class of person," Kennedy was referring to the fact that the nuns, though political refugees, were neither Austrian nor Jewish. Kennedy was suggesting that by demonstrating its commitment to securing the rescue of the nuns, the State Department would be rebutting accusations that the Roosevelt administration cared only about Jewish refugees.

It would take another three months of pressure and politicking until the nuns were finally afforded safe passage out of Spain.[60]

I n late April, Kennedy, in a confidential note to Jimmy Roosevelt, asked him to arrange a home leave so that he could attend Joe Jr.'s graduation from Harvard and confer, face-to-face, with the president and secretary of state. His request, though unusual for one who had been in office only since early March, was approved.[61]

Five days before he was scheduled to sail back to the United States, on June 10, 1938, Kennedy met with Ambassador Joachim von Ribbentrop, who was about to return to Berlin to serve as Hitler's foreign minister. There was nothing out of the ordinary here. The only thing that was peculiar about Kennedy's conversations with German diplomats in London in 1938 was that they would later be published. In 1946, American armed forces seized documents from the German Foreign Office archives and, with the British, edited and published excerpts from them. Included were transcripts of conversations held in London with Kennedy.

After his June 10, 1938, meeting with Kennedy, Ribbentrop reported to Berlin that the two had discussed "the subject of the agitation against us in the American press. The American Ambassador replied that he intended to do everything in his power to stem this press agitation. . . . His main objective was to keep America out of any conflict in Europe, and he would do everything in his power to accomplish this."[62]

Three days later, Kennedy met with the new German ambassador, Herbert von Dirksen. As Dirksen reported in his dispatch to Berlin, Kennedy indicated that the purpose of his upcoming trip to the United States was "to give President Roosevelt detailed information about European conditions. . . . The President desired friendly relations with Germany. However there was no one who had come from Europe and had spoken a friendly word to him regarding present-day Germany and her Government. When I [Dirksen] remarked that I feared he was right in this, Kennedy added that he *knew* he was right. Most of them were afraid of the Jews and did not dare to say anything good about Germany; others did not know any better, because they were not informed about Germany. . . . The Ambassador then touched upon the Jewish question and stated that it was naturally of great importance to German-American relations. In this connection it was not so much the fact that we wanted to get rid of the Jews that was so harmful to us, but rather the loud clamor with which we accompanied this purpose. He himself understood our Jewish policy completely; he was from Boston and there, in one golf club, and in other clubs, no Jews had been admitted for the past fifty years. His father had not been elected mayor because he was a Catholic [what Kennedy neglected to say was that his Irish Catholic father-in-law had]; in the United States, therefore, such pronounced attitudes were quite common, but people avoided making so much outward fuss about it." When Dirksen, taking up the same topic as Ribbentrop three days earlier, "mentioned the poisonous role of the American press in the relations between the two countries . . . [Kennedy] merely mentioned that the press on the east coast was unfortunately predominant in the formation of public opinion in America and that it was strongly influenced by Jews."[63]

When these transcripts were made public, Kennedy and his defenders would insist that Dirksen, new to the post and anxious to please his superiors in the Foreign Office, had grossly distorted his remarks. It is clear from the transcripts that Kennedy was doing his best to ingratiate himself with the German diplomats, as he did with all those he anticipated doing business with in the future. Still, while telling them what they wanted to hear about American anti-Semitism and Jewish media dominance, he was not saying anything he did not believe to be true.

Sixteen

A RATHER DREADFUL
HOMECOMING

Kennedy was preceded home by various rumors as to the reasons why he was returning after less than four months abroad. No one quite believed that the primary purpose was to see his son graduate from Harvard.

In a front-page story on May 17, the *Boston Post* declared that he was returning to accept an honorary doctorate from Harvard. Although he had hoped that would be the case, Kennedy had learned earlier that he had been passed over by the seven-member Harvard Corporation, which served as the university's principal governing body. "The sooner that Boston crowd [six of the seven corporation members were "proper Bostonians"; the seventh, a New Yorker, had attended Harvard Law School] is turned out of the management of Harvard University, the better it will be," he angrily wrote his friend and classmate Bob Fisher, "and it should be done before it is too late, so that Harvard won't suffer the way the banking business has in Boston."[1]

Kennedy would never forgive Harvard for its snub, never attend another reunion, and never donate another dollar to the university. He would make up for Harvard's rejection by collecting honorary degrees from other universities, the first, on July 7, from Trinity College, Dublin. So many followed within the next year that when he was awarded one from Cambridge University in June 1939, the British Pathé newsreel voice-over joked that "if Mr. Kennedy goes on collecting university degrees at this rate, he'll soon have one for each of" his children.[2]

Washington insiders, including members of the cabinet and the president, wondered if the real reason for Kennedy's early return was to assess his chances as a candidate for the Democratic presidential nomination should Roosevelt decide not to seek a third term. Almost from the moment he had left the country for London, rumors had begun to circulate that he was considering a run for the highest office in the land. He had, quite wisely, done nothing either to encourage or discourage such talk.

In mid-April 1938, Senator Byrnes jocularly raised the subject at the end of one of the newsy "Washington insider" letters he exchanged with Kennedy: "Speaking of gossip, when do you expect to announce your candidacy for the presidential nomination? Whatever doubts we may have had about your intentions in the past have been removed by this political stunt of turning down requests for an opportunity to bow for the King. I don't know what effect it will have in the B'nai B'rith, but it will be enthusiastically applauded by the Ancient Order of Hibernians."[3]

"I suppose you know that you are being mentioned very frequently as a candidate to succeed Mr. Roosevelt," William Randolph Hearst wrote a month later. "In fact, you are the most mentioned candidate, and the one most likely to unite the factions in which the Democracy is apparently divided. . . . Work seems to run off your shoulders like water off a duck's back. So you are generally looked on, I feel, as the one to straighten out the many kinks in the New Deal system, and to restore the government to soundness and sanity. If you think it is nice for your family's sake to be Ambassador, think how much nicer it would be for them for you to be President. So you would better be thinking seriously about that."[4]

The press had also begun talking about a possible candidacy. "There are only five Dionne Quints," *Life* magazine had joked in its April 11 photo essay on the family, "and the Kennedy Kids are nine. If Father Joseph Patrick Kennedy ever gets to be President, he will owe almost as much to that fact as to his abilities which earned him $9,000,000." A month later, in the May 21, 1938, issue of *Liberty* magazine, a national publication with a circulation of over one million, Ernest Lindley asked, "Will Kennedy Run for President?" and answered in the affirmative. Though the odds were heavily against him "at this stage," Lindley declared, "a few connoisseurs of Presidential material are willing to make long-shot bets that the next Democratic nominee for President will be Joseph Patrick Kennedy." The *Boston Sunday Advertiser* phrased the question a bit differently on June 5: CAN KENNEDY BE PRES-IDENT? DESTINY BECKONS BOSTON MAN: WILL HE REACH THE WHITE HOUSE? "College graduating classes throughout the country," including at "Tufts, with its Protestant background," were, the paper reported, "voting him their overwhelming choice for President in 1940" in straw polls.

Joseph P. Kennedy knew that his candidacy was a long shot and that it would make sense only if Roosevelt decided not to run for a third term. He was not going to let that deter him from putting the best possible gloss on his credentials. Though he had been in London for only a few months, he positioned himself now as an expert on European affairs. "I think it would be a very helpful thing if agitation could be started to have me address the Senate and House Foreign Relations Committee in Executive Session," he wrote Arthur Krock on May 24. "If you think this is worthwhile, you might start it in the works." Krock responded that he thought Kennedy's idea a "splendid" one "and I shall put it in the works. By the time you arrive, I think you will find everything ready unless the members have all got out of town by then."[5]

On landing at New York Harbor, Kennedy was given the type of greeting usually reserved for movie stars or presidential candidates. To the surprise and consternation of British heavyweight champion Tommy Farr, who thought he was the most famous man on board the *Queen Mary,* it was the ambassador who was thronged by reporters and photographers. The first question asked was whether he was going to be a candidate for president in 1940. He answered "emphatically that he would not consider being boomed for President in 1940. He added that any such move would be a breach of faith with the President."[6]

From New York Harbor, he was taken to the Waldorf-Astoria, where he visited with members of the Maritime Commission. The following morning, he was driven to Hyde Park to see the president. They met in Roosevelt's private office.

Roosevelt was, as Harold Ickes would write in his diary after having lunch with the president a few days later, furious at Kennedy for his presidential ambitions and for being so taken with his newfound expertise that he lectured the president on foreign policy. Kennedy, Roosevelt told Ickes, had "remonstrated with him for criticizing Fascism in his speeches. He wants him to attack Nazism but not Fascism. The President asked him why and he said very frankly that he thought that we would have to come to some form of Fascism here. The President thinks that Joe Kennedy, if he were in power, would give us a Fascist form of government. He would organize a small powerful committee under himself as chairman and this committee would run the country without much reference to Congress."

Kennedy had always been much more conservative, much more pro-business, than the president's other advisers, but during his months in England he had become so obsessed with the lack of progress toward economic recovery, the deleterious effects that prolonged depression in America was having on European prosperity and stability, and the threat of war that he appeared ready now, or so he had hinted, to sacrifice democratic principles and practices. Kennedy did not welcome the coming of a Fascist-like economic order—he much preferred the free-wheeling capitalist system through which he had made his fortune—but he believed that the unregulated, uncontrolled, private investment regime that had fueled economic expansion in the nineteenth and early twentieth centuries might not be a viable option in a global economy dominated by national actors who had centralized control of capital investment and foreign trade. It was time now for the United States government to extend its control over the economy, as the Italians had, and provide a few wise businessmen such as Joseph P. Kennedy with more authority.

There was nothing new in Kennedy's ambitions to play a larger role in economic matters. Everybody knew he had always wanted to be secretary of the treasury. What angered Roosevelt was that Kennedy now thought he should be president as well. "The President," Ickes wrote in his July 3 diary entry, "knows that he is a candidate but does not think that a Catholic could be elected."

Ickes tried to impress on Roosevelt the danger Kennedy posed as a potential candidate. "It is reported that Kennedy has come to an understanding with Arthur Krock of the *New York Times*. It is expected that there will soon be a vacancy in the editorship. . . . Krock is doing all that he can to boost Kennedy and Kennedy is ready to support Krock financially if necessary for this *New York Times* job. I have been told that Krock is going to take some time off to devote himself to spreading the Kennedy-for-President gospel. There is probably no doubt that Kennedy is spending a great deal of money to further his Presidential ambitions. He has plenty of it and he is willing to spend it freely. Neither is there any doubt that he is making a good deal of headway in conservative quarters."[7]

Ickes's reports on the Kennedy-Krock alliance were true, though much exaggerated. Krock had indeed hoped that with the retirement of Dr. John Huston Finley, who was quite ill, he would be named the new editor in chief of the *New York Times*. We don't know if Kennedy interceded on his behalf. What we do know is that after Krock had been passed over for the post in November 1938, Kennedy complained about it to Arthur Sulzberger, who was visiting London. "I remember saying to him that I was terribly disappointed that Arthur did not receive the post," he wrote Krock in October 1941. "Sulzberger seemed quite moved by my statement and hastened to explain that of course I understood that there was no reflection at all on your ability because he regarded you as a most able newspaper man, but he was of the opinion that he would be criticized if he appointed a Jew as Editor, since the ownership was in the hands of Jews. Of course to this I could make no answer except to again express my regret that any reason could be found not to give you the job." Kennedy did not protest or try to argue with Sulzberger, no doubt because he agreed with him that it would open Sulzberger to criticism if he, a Jew, appointed another Jew as editor.[8]

The president did not confront Kennedy directly on his ties to Krock. Nor did he say anything to him about his unseemly enthusiasm to be considered a candidate for the Democratic nomination in 1940. Instead, he cut short their meeting at Hyde Park, summoned Eleanor and asked her to "feed him lunch at her cottage and then see him to the train."[9]

On June 23, the day after Kennedy's visit with the president, Arthur Krock wrote to tell him that "there were reports of Presidential coolness toward you at Hyde Park Tuesday." Krock had inquired as to the source of these "reports" and been informed by one of his contacts in Washington that Steve Early, Roosevelt's press secretary, "had told one or two correspondents . . . that Roosevelt was annoyed with Kennedy partly because of the Presidential boomlet and partly on the ground that Kennedy had given what he (Roosevelt) considered outside (*foreign affairs*) information to correspondents before Roosevelt himself got it." The reference was to Kennedy's political letters, in which, sounding very much like a future candidate for office, he weekly forwarded his observations on foreign, domestic, and economic developments to the most influential men in Washington, including Arthur Krock, Walter Lippmann, Boake Carter, Roy Howard, Frank Kent, Drew Pearson and Robert Allen, Russell Davenport of *Fortune,* William Randolph Hearst and his chief lieutenant, Tom White, former New Dealer Hugh Johnson, Bernard Baruch, and senators James Byrnes, Key Pittman, and Burton Wheeler.[10]

Kennedy got Krock's letter in Hyannis Port. After attending the pre-commencement "Class Day" events, which his son, as chairman of the 1938 Class Day committee, had helped organize, he had left Cambridge, avoiding the next day's commencement exercises and the award of honorary degrees to Walt Disney and thirteen others but not to him. When asked by Boston reporters why he had not attended his son's graduation and whether he was disappointed not to have received an honorary degree, he claimed that he had left Cambridge because his younger son Jack had stomach problems and needed him in Hyannis Port. Jack, it was true, had a few days earlier checked into the New England Baptist Hospital, where doctors tried unsuccessfully to figure out why he was losing weight again. Whatever his condition—and the doctors remained baffled by it—he recovered quickly enough to join his brother and other members of the Harvard team in the intercollegiate sailing championship held that year at Wianno. As their father watched with pride, the Kennedy boys sailed well enough (though they took no firsts) to help the Harvard team take home the championship.

That same day, on June 23, the two reporters to whom Early had spoken, Walter Trohan of the *Chicago Tribune* and William Murphy, Jr., of the *Philadelphia Inquirer,* published nearly identical stories about the rift between the president and his ambassador to Great Britain. "One of the most notable friendships of the New Deal," Murphy wrote, "appeared tonight to be headed for possible wreckage on the jagged rocks of Presidential ambitions. The reason for this situation is that the Roosevelt inner circle has become convinced that Kennedy seriously cherishes the idea that he might be selected as the Democratic standard-bearer in 1940. The idea does not appear to be pleasing to the White House." Both reporters offered as evidence of the ambassador's nascent candidacy the "secret circular which Kennedy has been forwarding to selected Washington correspondents [his political letters]" and an offer to a "prominent Washington correspondent [Arthur Krock] to direct his presidential boom from London."

Usually so quick to respond to any perceived slight, Kennedy decided to let this one go. He could not confront Early directly without telling him that his information had come from Krock, which Krock had asked him not to do. Instead, he waited until he was back in London and then let his anger out in a letter to the editors who had published the articles. Colonel McCormick, the publisher of the *Chicago Tribune* and a Palm Beach neighbor of Kennedy's, wrote him at once to say that his anger was misdirected. Walter Trohan, who had broken the story, had had no malicious intent. He was simply repeating what he had been told by high administration officials. "He had complete authority for everything he said. . . . You are the victim not of the reporter, but of your political associates."[11]

Though the signs were there for the reading, Kennedy had refused to recognize that Roosevelt was the source of the story. Roosevelt had known for a long time that Kennedy was criticizing him behind his back, but he had let it go as long as Kennedy had been of use to him, as a campaigner, SEC and Maritime Commission chairman, and liaison with the business community. Roosevelt could tolerate a great deal, but not Kennedy's presumption in believing himself a viable candidate for president. He had no intention of breaking formally with his ambassador, but neither was he going to allow him to position himself as the president's dear friend, confidant, trusted adviser, and possible successor.

Kennedy either did not understand what was happening or, if he did, thought the break in his relationship with Roosevelt was easily repaired. Part of his confusion may have been caused by the president's demeanor. When they met for dinner at the White House only a few days after the published reports of Roosevelt's "coolness" toward him, the president not only evidenced no sign of displeasure or lack of confidence, but gave him a new and critically important assignment.

Roosevelt asked him to meet, on his behalf, with Thomas Lamont, who represented J. P. Morgan on the U.S. Steel board of directors. Under intense pressure from the White House, U.S. Steel had agreed to cut prices to stimulate the economy. The understanding was that it would do so without cutting wages. Only after the agreement had been reached did the company inform the White House that it was going to cut wages. The president was furious. Across-the-board wage reductions in a major industrial sector would inevitably lead to decreased purchasing power, declining consumption, and sustained unemployment.

Unbeknownst to the press, Kennedy met with Lamont at the Waldorf-Astoria the morning after his dinner at the White House. He brought along Arthur Krock, whom he was taking to Europe with him the next day. Krock did not write about the meeting in his newspaper, but he took notes that he published years later in his memoirs. According to Krock, Lamont insisted to Kennedy that U.S. Steel had no choice but to cut wages now that the government had pressured it to cut prices and that "John L. Lewis [then head of the CIO] understood its position."

Kennedy suggested that the company hold off wage reductions for at least ninety days to ascertain what, if any, effect the price cuts were going to have on revenues. If, after ninety days, there was proof that the price cuts were destroying the steel business, the company might then with impunity declare that it had no choice but to cut wages. Kennedy shared with Lamont a memorandum, written by Tommy Corcoran and Secretary Ickes and approved by Roosevelt, that recommended that if U.S. Steel agreed to cooperate with the White House and keep wages stable, the government would provide it and its subsidiaries with additional contracts while simultaneously depriving Bethlehem Steel of whatever competitive advantages it enjoyed from importing Canadian raw materials.

"Lamont," Krock observed, "turned pale. He said he would not ask the Steel Corporation to be a party to a deal of that sort. He said it was unfair and wrong. He asked what business was going to do in contention with a government holding such ideas.

"Kennedy answered, 'Tom, you are a respectable man. You can't understand these people. But you've got to. There they are. You don't have to be a party to any deal. I'm just telling you what you can expect if you hold off these wage cuts and follow my suggestion. But, forgetting the deal, my suggestion has greater value and some moral quality.'"

If U.S. Steel waited ninety days before cutting wages and then did so only after significant revenue loses, it would seize the upper hand. Under these circumstances, Roosevelt could not accuse the company "of failure to cooperate."

As he had at the SEC, Kennedy positioned himself as the corporate sector's best friend and protector and a man whose business sense and moral standing were superior to those of the New Deal politicians on whose behalf he was negotiating. Lamont did not formally sign off on any deal with the government, but U.S. Steel did not cut wages. Once again, Kennedy had done the president's bidding—and done it well.[12]

W hatever satisfaction Kennedy might have enjoyed was quickly washed away. On Tuesday, the day before he was to sail back to Europe, the latest issue of the *Saturday Evening Post* went on sale with an article by Alva Johnston titled "Jimmy's Got It" about James Roosevelt's insurance business, which, it claimed, earned between $250,000 and $2 million annually. Joseph P. Kennedy was identified as one of his boosters.[13]

Johnston was not the first to suggest that there was something slightly sinister about Kennedy's friendship with the much younger Jimmy Roosevelt, but he was the first to put the thought into print. His accusations reverberated through the daily press. Jimmy checked himself into the Mayo Clinic to avoid having to comment.

Kennedy dismissed Johnston's charges as malicious nonsense. Questioned by reporters as he prepared to depart for Europe on the *Normandie,* Kennedy declared that he was "not at all perturbed by" the article, which among other things had asserted "that he was the premier Scotch-whisky salesman in the United States." He joked with the reporters that while he tried to be the best in everything, he was not the nation's number one whiskey salesman. "This magazine article," he continued, "tries to make me out a phony, but if all of it is as true as the part I have read about myself, it is a complete, unadulterated lie."[14]

The next day Kennedy boarded the *Normandie* with his two oldest boys and Arthur Krock. Joe Jr., having graduated from Harvard only days before, was off to London to serve as his father's secretary, as Felix Frankfurter had recommended he do. Jack was going to take a long summer's vacation before returning to Harvard for his junior year—or at least that was what his father had planned for him. "You really should give yourself plenty of rest. You are almost 21 now and really should take very good care of your health and you can only do that by getting lots of rest. I don't like to close a letter with an admonition, but it is for your own good, and I am sure you realize it."[15]

There remained at the end of Kennedy's whirlwind nine-day trip the same confusion about its purpose that there had been at the beginning. Kennedy had told reporters that he had come home for his son's graduation, which he had missed, and for frank talks about the European situation with the president. He had told the German diplomats in London that the objective of his trip home was to brief the president on Germany. Only after he sailed did Drew Pearson and Robert Allen report in their "Washington Merry-Go-Round" column that despite "those sensational dope stories giving the real lowdown for Ambassador Joe Kennedy's hurried visit . . . the real purpose . . . was to confer with Roosevelt about the tragic German and Austrian refugee problem. . . . In his private talks with the President, Kennedy reported that the situation of German and Austrian Jews is extremely hazardous and that unless a plan for their migration is worked out at the Evian conference thousands of them are doomed. On top of all the other refugee complications, Kennedy reported that the secret policy of the Nazis is to demand ransoms for the release of these people whom they claim they are anxious to get rid of."[16]

Pearson and Allen had most likely gotten their story from Kennedy. In June, just before leaving London, Kennedy had warned Viscount Bearsted not to expect much from the Évian Conference or from Myron Taylor, the president's representative. He had no faith in Taylor's competence and inferred, in his talks with Bearsted, that he would tell the president as much when he saw him. And that was precisely what he did.

Few if any commentators were using language as stark as Kennedy was employing in the early summer of 1938; few understood, as he appeared to, the catastrophic consequences that would follow the failure to negotiate a viable plan for rescuing German and Austrian Jews. Still, he was optimistic.

Hitler, he believed—and this was still, in mid-1938, the dominant view in Washington and London—was not a madman but a calculating, rational actor. He would be willing to let the Jews emigrate with some portion of their assets, but only if Germany was given something in return. The proceedings at Évian were mere window dressing. Even if the nations assembled there agreed to offer safe havens for every one of the German Jewish refugees, which was not going to happen, no Jews would be rescued until Hitler gave them permission to emigrate.

Kennedy's position was clear: the only way to save the refugees was to negotiate a comprehensive settlement of Germany's grievances, one arrived at without sound and fury and certainly without the chorus of condemnation that Kennedy believed organized Jewry was mounting.

Seventeen

MUNICH

I n public, Ambassador Kennedy remained unfailingly optimistic. Times were tough, dangers lurked around every corner, but there was no need for concern, he insisted, certainly no reason to panic. Privately, he was more frightened of the future than he had ever been. Hitler, he expected, would sooner or later make a move to annex the Sudetenland, that part of Czechoslovakia in which three million ethnic Germans lived; the Czech government would resist; Hitler would invade; France, under treaty with the Czechs, would declare war on Germany; the British would fight to defend the French; the Americans would be drawn in to assist the British. And then the worst would come. World war, in the midst of depression, would lead to economic collapse and economic collapse to political upheaval and the end of democracy in Great Britain and the United States.

"Kennedy was much more worried and pessimistic than he was during my last conversation with him," the German ambassador reported to Berlin on July 20, 1938. "The idea that Germany might go to war against Czechoslovakia, which would then result in the intervention of England and France and, first indirectly and then directly, of the United States appeared to have a pretty firm hold on him."[1]

The only positive news was from Barcelona. The Sacred Heart nuns whose release he had sought were on a British warship bound for London. "I decided to let the newspapers know of the rescue of the nuns," Kennedy wrote in his diary, "for a variety of reasons. I wanted to emphasize that the Jews from Germany and Austria are not the only refugees in the world, and I wanted to depict Chamberlain and Halifax as human, good-hearted men, capable of taking an active interest in such a bona fide venture. I also wanted to give them credit for sending the warship after the poor women."[2]

The fact that the British government had intervened to assist a handful of refugee nuns did not, as the *New York Times* cautioned its readers on July 31, signify that it was willing to help Jewish refugees. On the contrary, the Chamberlain government had made it clear, most recently at the Évian Conference, that it had no intention of opening any territory in Great Britain or Palestine to Jewish refugees, though it claimed to have under consideration "the possibility [of] the small-scale settlement of Jewish refugees" in the colony of Kenya or another of the East African territories.[3]

In late July, Rose and the children left for Cap d'Antibes on the French Riviera. Kennedy remained behind in London until the end of July, when Parliament adjourned. Kick, now eighteen, stayed behind as well. She had accepted an invitation to weekend at Cliveden, where she hoped to spend some time with William Cavendish, the Marquess of Hartington, one of Britain's wealthiest and most eligible young bachelors. Billy Hartington, as he was known, was not just another British aristocrat, but a member of the Cavendish family, which since the 1530s had made its fortune and fame dispossessing Catholics of their assets and, more recently, opposing home rule for Ireland. Although Billy had not an ounce of anti-Irish or anti-Catholic prejudice in him, the same could not be said for his father, Edward William Spencer Cavendish, the 10th Duke of Devonshire, whom he would succeed.[4]

On August 3, twelve days after the rest of the family had departed, Kennedy flew with Kick to Paris, changed planes for Marseilles, and continued by limousine to Cap d'Antibes, between Nice and Cannes. The Domaine de Beaumont, which he had rented for the month, was perfect except for the pool, which was filled with water pumped from across the hills and (to Rose's disgust) changed only every few weeks. "It looks and feels so stagnant, so cloudy, so uninviting. Of course, I do not like the children to dive or put it in their mouths." Fortunately, the luxurious and exclusive Hôtel du Cap was nearby, with its rocky cliffs, saltwater pool, outdoor pavilion, and celebrated restaurant. Kennedy rented a cottage-sized cabana for the family. Among the guests and visitors at the hotel that season were Secretary of the Treasury Morgenthau and his family; Elsa Maxwell; tennis star Bill Tilden; the Duke and Duchess of Windsor; socialite decorator Elsie de Wolfe; and Marlene Dietrich, who was vacationing with her entourage, which this year included her husband, her latest lover, Erich Maria Remarque, her husband's lover, and her thirteen-year-old daughter, Maria, who would try to spend as much time with the Kennedys as she could.[5]

While awaiting her husband's arrival, Rose tried to find household help, reliable secretaries, and milk for the smaller children and Jack. A whirlwind of self-improvement schemes for herself and the children, Rose took the children on a "cook's tour" of the area, tried to interest Pat and Eunice in collecting autographs, and prodded them all to keep diaries. Now that her children were under one roof, she was able to focus her attention on fattening up Jack and slimming down the others. In her weight loss campaigns, Rose had her husband's full approval and gratitude. Kennedy, the son of an obese mother, could not countenance extra weight on himself or his children. He watched his diet, exercised, and kept slim. He expected his children to do the same.

For the next few weeks, the Kennedy world would revolve around the patriarch. His word was law, as it had always been. He didn't yell or scold or argue with his children. They knew he had a temper, but they seldom saw it. He said what he thought, with the understanding that his thoughts were deeper and more often correct than anyone else's. When Jack refused to drink the milk his mother gave him because it tasted sour, his father explained that it tasted that way because it was unpasteurized. He had had some like it in Wales and had gotten used to it, which he suggested Jack could do as well. Jack drank his milk. When Rose outlined her plans for returning to the United States so that Kick could make her formal debut at Thanksgiving, Kennedy quickly but gently vetoed the idea.

The older children were free during the day to do as they pleased.

Rose and the governesses took the little ones to the hotel for swimming and lunch. The family reconvened for dinner at the villa at a long table, the youngest at one end, their table manners monitored by their mother, the older children, at the other end, discussing "topics and issues proposed by their father. He ran the discussions like a master conductor," recalled Dietrich's daughter, Maria, "posing questions about world affairs, politics, the economy. Most of the questions were directed at the bigger boys, but the younger children, boys and girls, were expected to listen and contribute if and when they had something to add. He drew them out, prodded them to back up their arguments, filled in the blanks."[6]

A strange twist of fate had that summer of 1938 placed the ambassador together in the South of France with the man he had hoped to replace in the cabinet, Secretary of the Treasury Henry Morgenthau, Jr. Kennedy, supremely confident in his own charm—and his ability to disarm potential or past opponents—attempted to draw Morgenthau closer to him by running down his colleagues in the cabinet. His particular bête noire at the moment was Secretary of State Cordell Hull, whom he referred to only as "the old man." That spring and summer, Hull had pushed Kennedy hard for assistance in negotiating a bilateral trade treaty with Great Britain. Kennedy had been less than helpful because he thought Hull's demands ridiculous. "The old man" simply didn't understand business or international trade and was making requests that no British official was going to take seriously. Morgenthau listened carefully, and no doubt gleefully, as Kennedy explained why he was doing less than he might have to follow the instructions that came out of the State Department. He made mental notes of every disparaging word out of Kennedy's mouth, and as soon as he returned to Washington, he reported it all to the president.[7]

The Kennedys were not the most famous vacationers in Cannes that season, but they dominated the scene by sheer force of numbers and personality. Henry Morgenthau III, who was Jack's age, remembered him and Joe Jr. "chasing a shapely brunette in and out of the swimming pool." Joe Jr. led the way, with near godlike self-confidence, charm, good looks, and a well-chiseled athletic body; Jack, Morgenthau recalled, held back a bit. The rumors circulating among the other hotel guests were that he was suffering from some incurable ailment and had only two years to live.[8]

While Henry Morgenthau III was a bit cool toward the Kennedys, thirteen-year-old Maria, Dietrich's daughter, was smitten at first sight by the "wonderful" Kennedy children. "I would have gladly given up my right arm, the left, and any remaining limb, to be one of them. They looked, and were, so American. All had smiles that never ended, with such perfect teeth each of them could have advertised toothpaste." She found their father "kind of rakish. For a man with such a patient little wife, who had borne him so many children, I thought he flirted a bit too much, but outside of that, Mr. Kennedy was a very nice man." She saw a lot of the ambassador that August. He was, Maria recalled, "a regular visitor to our beach cabana" and made sure that everyone knew it.[9]

D espite the president's growing coolness toward the ambassador, John Burns, who was now in private practice but remained a friend and associate of Kennedy's, and Arthur Krock were confident that he still had a chance of winning the Democratic nomination in 1940—if Roosevelt decided not to put his own name forward. Kennedy's strength was with the party's conservative wing.

Burns cautioned him to reach out to the liberals. "I think it is important that you have the good will of the liberals, the kind of good will which I believe Tommy [Corcoran] is attempting to build up through Rabbi Wise, [labor leader] Sidney Hillman and the 100% New Dealers." He suggested that Kennedy, while pursuing "a policy of friendliness to the leftish group, but no identification . . . accentuate your New England [roots] rather than your New York association. . . . There is a surprisingly strong sentiment throughout the country, and particularly in New England, in favor of your designation." Burns recommended that Kennedy seek out at once "an expert politician" to begin lining up convention support for him.[10]

Krock's political advice was different, though not contradictory. "Your publicity continues good," he wrote Kennedy, "and on every hand one hears golden opinions of what you are doing." The problem was that much of that publicity was of the wrong kind. Kennedy's strength as a candidate—his down-home, plain-folk, blunt-spoken appeal—was being lost in the sea of photographs of him in top hat and tails, entertaining and being entertained by English aristocrats. "I don't want the impression to get round that you are anything of a prima donna. . . . I urge you to keep away for a goodish while from the Royal Family. Today again you were boating (in the paper) with the Windsors. My instinct tells me there has been enough of that, and I can see how it could be misused and distorted by unfriendly persons. Get some very different kind of social publicity for a while, and soon, is my unsought counsel."[11]

Krock may have been getting his information about Kennedy's growing reputation as a prima donna from his contacts at the State Department. Less than six months into his tenure, Kennedy was already making a nuisance of himself with continual complaints about procedures and pay rates. "I really believe you must be the most patient man in the world," he wrote George Messersmith, assistant secretary of state for administration, "to have to sit there and take all these letters from fussy Ambassadors and not lose your sense of humor or temper. It is an art I wish I had cultivated in my youth. However, maybe you will get your reward in Heaven." He then asked Messersmith to see that Joe Jr. was "added to my staff as my private secretary at a dollar a year. He is a graduate of Harvard and I want to keep him with me this year, because of the tremendous amount of personal work I find myself called upon to perform here. . . . The reason I am asking for diplomatic status for him is that I can use him on a lot of small events where they want members of the family, and to build up good-will."[12]

When he didn't get an immediate answer, Kennedy followed with an angry telegram. Messersmith replied a few days later that he could not grant Joe Jr. diplomatic status, as department rules precluded ambassadors from appointing family members to their staffs. Kennedy accepted Messersmith's explanation and apologized again for his impatience. "I was mad as hell when I didn't get an answer for a month [really two weeks] to what I considered a very simple request regarding young Joe."[13]

Instead of working for his father at the embassy, Joe Jr. would spend his year abroad between college and law school traveling from capital to capital, embassy to embassy, from Paris to Prague, Warsaw, and

Moscow, then the Scandinavian capitals, Berlin, The Hague, then Paris again, and if it could be arranged, Madrid. Wherever he went, he was treated like royalty. In Warsaw, Ambassador Anthony Joseph Drexel Biddle, Jr., allowed him to read "all his dispatches." When it came time to visit Spain, he asked his father to "write some letters to famous pals, possibly the Duke of Alba might do it, so they could show me the works. Also some letters from newspaper men to correspondents down there."[14]

On August 28, Kennedy ended his vacation and flew to Paris to attend a meeting on the Jewish refugee problem with Ambassador Bullitt, Myron Taylor, and George Rublee, who on Roosevelt's recommendation had been appointed director of the Intergovernmental Committee on Refugees, the organization set up at the Évian Conference. Rublee wanted to visit Germany as soon as possible to negotiate terms for the emigration of German and Austrian Jews, but he could not do so until he had some idea as to the number of refugees that Great Britain, France, and the United States would accept. Bullitt and Kennedy agreed to inquire of the French and British governments what they were prepared to do for the refugees.[15]

Kennedy arrived in London late on August 29 in the midst of several crises, the least important of which, certainly for Halifax, was the Jewish refugee one. The foreign secretary and the prime minister were too preoccupied with German threats to Czechoslovakia to pay much attention to the Jewish question. When asked by Kennedy "about the Jewish situation," Halifax responded that "he was not very well up on it." There had been some discussion, he told Kennedy, "about placing Jews in Rhodesia and Kenya, but just how many they cannot tell yet." He added that he was not sure the attempt to resettle the German and Austrian Jews was a good idea as "other countries who want to get rid of their Jews will be encouraged to throw them out, hoping that America, England and France will find some way of taking care of them."[16]

On August 30, Prime Minister Chamberlain convened an emergency cabinet meeting to consider whether the British government should issue a formal warning to Germany that it would defend the territorial integrity of Czechoslovakia by force, if necessary. It was decided to make no such commitment for now, but to keep Hitler guessing as to what the British might do should he invade Czechoslovakia. At the conclusion of the cabinet meeting, Chamberlain met with Kennedy at 10 Downing. Kennedy, who had not seen the prime minister in more than a month, was shocked at his appearance.

"He does not look well at all," he cabled Hull at five P.M. that afternoon. "The gist of the conversation was that he is very much disturbed about the Czechoslovakia situation. All the information that he gets . . . is that Hitler has made up his mind to take Czechoslovakia peacefully if possible but with arms if necessary." The nightmare scenarios that had haunted Kennedy since the *Anschluss* were one step closer to denouement. Only Chamberlain, Kennedy believed, stood between war and peace. "He still is the best bet in Europe today against war, but he is a very sick looking individual. He is worried but not jittery."[17]

The day after Kennedy's interview with the prime minister, he met with Halifax, who wanted to know "what would be the reaction in America if the Germans went into Czechoslovakia, with the Czechs fighting them, and England did not go along." Kennedy forwarded Halifax's request to Hull. He then, bizarrely, before he had received any reply, "called in a mixed audience of newspaper men" and told them about Halifax's request. Reporters on both sides of the Atlantic were aghast at his lack of discretion. As the *Chicago Tribune* asked rhetorically, "Why he touched on a subject considered a dark secret is best known to himself."[18]

Kennedy violated State Department protocol a second time that same day by giving an exclusive telephone interview to Hearst's *Boston Evening American,* without clearing it with the State Department.

Roosevelt directed Hull to inform Kennedy that the American government had no intention of specifying, in advance, how it would respond to the hypothetical scenario Halifax had described and to chastise him for granting interviews to selected newspaper chains. Morgenthau, who met with the president that same day, "got the impression that the President felt that not only was Kennedy talking to the press, but he was definitely trying to force the President's hand in this manner in his process of playing the Chamberlain game." By leaking the news of the British request, Kennedy had placed his government in an impossible situation. "We are in the position now," Morgenthau wrote in his diary, "that anything we do now makes us a party either way, a party to their fighting or not fighting. They have us, for the moment, stymied. Kennedy is playing with the British Foreign Office and the Prime Minister. He has spilled the beans, and the President knows this."[19]

Morgenthau reported to Roosevelt what Kennedy had said at Cannes about "the old man" (Secretary of State Hull) and his mishandling of the Anglo-American trade bill. When he had finished his Kennedy story, Roosevelt told one of his own. He had recently sent a commission to Britain "to study labor conditions abroad." Though the commission members were in London for a full three weeks, Kennedy had not entertained a single member "with the exception of Gerard Swope," chairman of General Electric and brother of Kennedy's friend Herbert Bayard Swope. At a dinner given by the British in honor of the commissioners, Kennedy "got up and gave a talk. He said that in America legislation was prepared on a ten minute study by the brain trust; it was then passed by Congress and subsequently found to be imperfect or unconstitutional and that's the way we did things in America, while in England everything was carefully prepared by Commissions so that it could be readily passed by Parliament and that it worked well. The President," Morgenthau noted in his diary, "was perfectly furious when he heard this and . . . tempted to recall Kennedy."

Morgenthau, stoking the president's anger, suggested that Kennedy's "popularity with the English" was due to such critical remarks about the United States. The president agreed. "I don't think there is much question but what Kennedy is disloyal to his country." He asked Morgenthau if, when they were together in the South of France, Kennedy had mentioned resigning. "If Kennedy wants to resign when he comes back [for his next leave, probably at the end of the year], I will accept it on the spot and . . . if Kennedy returns to private life he is through."[20]

On September 2, Kennedy and Jack took the train to Aberdeen, Scotland, to lay the cornerstone of a memorial chapel dedicated to an American bishop from Connecticut. Anxious not to get himself into any more trouble, the ambassador had forwarded a draft of his remarks to the State Department for review and marked those paragraphs that might cause "some concern on broad political grounds." One of them contained as clear an articulation of his views on war and peace as he would ever make: "I should like to ask you all if you know of any dispute or controversy existing in the world which is worth the life of your son, or of anyone else's son? Perhaps I am not well informed of the terrifically vital forces underlying all this unrest in the world, but for the life of me I cannot see anything involved which could be remotely considered worth shedding blood for."[21]

When Moffat received the draft and read the highlighted paragraph, he immediately went looking for Hull, who he hoped would show the draft to the president. "Joe Kennedy's star is not shining brightly these days," Moffat noted in his diary on September 1. "He cannot move without a blare of publicity and in tense moments like these publicity is the thing most to be avoided. . . . All of us thought that the Secretary should have Presidential authority to reject the paragraphs."[22]

Roosevelt, on reading the draft, was confirmed in his opinion that Kennedy had gone over to the other side. His position—that Czechoslovakia was not even "remotely" a cause "worth shedding blood for"—was but a paraphrase of Chamberlain's position—that Britain had no vital interest in going to war to preserve the territorial integrity of Czechoslovakia. "Who would have thought," he told Morgenthau on September 1, 1938, "that the English could take into camp a red-headed Irishman? . . . The young man needs his wrists slapped rather hard."[23]

It was apparent now, six months into his tenure, that Joseph P. Kennedy was unfit to serve as ambassador. Unfortunately, there was no way Roosevelt could recall him. On the contrary, he needed him in London more than ever. The nominating conventions were less than two years away and there was already, as Harold Ickes had written in his diary that summer, a strong feeling "in some quarters that there may be an understanding between [Vice President] Garner and [Postmaster General] Farley looking to a ticket consisting of these twain in 1940 [and this] has led to the suggestion that in such an event the President might have to turn to Joe Kennedy as a candidate for Vice President. This would match a Roman Catholic against a Roman Catholic."[24]

While Roosevelt, contrary to Ickes's speculations, was not considering Kennedy for the vice-presidential nomination, he knew that whether he ran for a third term or chose a liberal New Dealer like Hopkins to succeed him, he was going to need Kennedy's endorsement. The ambassador was too rich, too outspoken, too charming, and too well connected to the national media to have as an enemy. The solution would have been to bring Kennedy back to Washington and give him another position. However, the ambassador had made it clear that the only position he would accept, in lieu of his ambassadorship, was secretary of the treasury, and Roosevelt was not about to replace Morgenthau, whom he trusted, with a known renegade.

Roosevelt was trapped. In the months to come, the president would speak ill of his ambassador, trust him less and less, and detour around him to communicate with London, but he would never, as he had suggested to Morgenthau he should, slap his wrists, criticize him publicly, or let him know of his dissatisfaction. Kennedy, with no direct knowledge of the president's displeasure, would continue to follow his own agenda.

On September 6, Joseph P. Kennedy celebrated his fiftieth birthday by himself. Rose and Kick, who were shopping in Paris, called to wish him a happy birthday at 8:45 in the morning but missed him. Joe Jr., also in Paris, telegrammed his birthday wishes: "The first fifty they say are the toughest but it's going to be much tougher for your all too promising son to come anywhere near duplicating your great achievements. Love and Congratulations on your half century of phenomenal success." There were letters as well from Eunice and Rosemary, who reported that they were having a grand time on their tour of Scotland and Ireland. "We have been getting plenty of attention," Eunice, now seventeen, informed her father from County Cork. "We had the special De Luxe room on the boat. A couple of people wanted to interview us and two people have asked us for our autograph. . . . Well Daddy I hope you had a very happy birthday and a very 'quiet one.' I only wish you were with us."[25]

By early September, Lord Halifax had come up with a new strategy for keeping the peace, the very opposite of the one he and Chamberlain had pursued to this point. Hitler, Halifax now believed, might be persuaded to back away from his threat to seize the Sudetenland if he could be convinced that the British and the French, with American support, would go to war to protect Czechoslovakian territorial integrity. The problem with such a scenario was that the Americans had never evidenced any intention of joining a campaign, military or otherwise, against Germany.

Kennedy, informed by Halifax of his new strategy, thought it worth pursuing and offered his support. According to Halifax's summary of their meeting on September 10, Kennedy had declared that "American opinion was more excited against Germany now than he had ever known it. . . . If war should come, he anticipated that the immediate reaction would be a desire to keep out of it, but that, if we [Great Britain] were drawn into it and, for example, London was bombed, he thought there would be a strong revulsion of feeling and that the history of the last war would be repeated, leading a great deal more rapidly than in the last war, to American intervention."[26]

The next morning, on September 11, the foreign secretary and the ambassador met again. Knowing full well that neither Roosevelt nor Hull intended to make any public commitment to backing the British should they call Hitler's bluff, Kennedy set out to find a way to create the illusion of one. He "suggested," according to Halifax's notes, "that it might be useful were he to call on the Prime Minister this evening in order to encourage German speculation regarding the fact that our two countries were apparently keeping in such close touch. I welcomed the ambassador's suggestion and told him that I had no doubt that the Prime Minister would be glad to see him, quite apart from the political value which his visit might have in the eyes of the outside world." In his diplomatic dispatch, Kennedy reported to Hull that he was "seeing the Prime Minister at 7:30" but didn't tell him that the meeting had been his idea and was intended to create the illusion that the British and Americans were pursuing or formulating some joint declaration or action.[27]

Kennedy took a second and much more dangerous step toward constructing the appearance of an Anglo-American alliance by leaking news of one to officials in the German embassy. On September 12, the German chargé d'affaires in London cabled Ribbentrop that he had learned "from a reliable source [that] President Roosevelt has made it known through the Ambassador that Great Britain could count on the support of the United States if she should become involved in a war." The "reliable source" was Kennedy, who was cited in another dispatch to Berlin as having declared that while "he himself had two sons and would work" to keep America out of the war, he was "convinced that America would nevertheless intervene in the end." With the English, French, and ultimately the Americans poised to come to Czechoslovakia's rescue, Kennedy had told the German envoy that it now "depended on Hitler whether there was to be chaos, from which no country in the world could remain immune." Should Hitler back away from a military invasion and takeover of the Sudetenland, Kennedy assured the German envoy, "there would be a big change in public opinion through the world . . . and above all in the United States." Hitler would be hailed by the world as a "benefactor of mankind. . . . His ideas in the social and economic field which were responsible for such extraordinary achievements in Germany would be a determining influence on the economic development of the United States and economic cooperation between all nations." Desperately seeking to avert the catastrophe he saw just over the horizon, Kennedy was alternately threatening and flattering the Germans in the mistaken expectations that Hitler did not want war and that he cared about European and American public opinion.[28]

On the evening of September 12, Hitler delivered the long-awaited speech at Nuremberg, during which it was expected he would declare his intentions regarding Czechoslovakia. Transmission was erratic, crackling, but listeners across the English Channel and across the Atlantic had no difficulty making out the high-pitched, sometimes frantic screeching of the fuehrer, accompanied by hundreds of thousands of thunderous voices chanting, *"Sieg Heil!"* Hitler raged against the Czech government, insisted that its oppression of the Sudeten Germans cease at once, and, borrowing a phrase from the American political lexicon and Woodrow Wilson, demanded that they be given the right of self-determination. He did not, however, declare war on Czechoslovakia, as had been feared.[29]

Immediately after the speech, Kennedy made his rounds of British cabinet members to ascertain their reactions. He was unable to see either the prime minister or the foreign secretary, but at eleven P.M. he was invited to the office of the home secretary, Sir Samuel Hoare, who told him that the Foreign Office believed "the speech meant absolutely nothing except that the trouble was still present. He said Chamberlain, Halifax, Simon [Sir John Simon, chancellor of the Exchequer], and he felt there was more hope in the situation."[30]

Whatever hopes might have been raised by Hitler's speech were dashed almost instantly by news that the Sudeten Germans, incited by Hitler's provocations, had begun to riot, attack Czech soldiers and policemen in the streets, and plunder Jewish shops. When the Czech government declared martial law, Konrad Henlein, the leader of the Sudeten Germans, demanded that the government cease all police actions in the Sudetenland. British ambassador Sir Nevile Henderson reported from Berlin that the Germans were poised to invade and would be prevented from doing so only if the Czechoslovak government immediately granted full autonomy to the Sudeten Germans.

With war on the horizon, Kennedy called Rose, who was in Cannes, and suggested she return home the next morning. Rose tried to take the first plane out but was unable to get a seat. She waited until that evening and boarded a sleeper for Paris. "I think I should be in London," she wrote in her diary, "as Joe has Teddy [who was suffering from tonsillitis] on his mind and also, these crises in world politics."[31]

"Oh, to be back in America," Kennedy wrote his friend Arthur Goldsmith the next day, "hanging around with loafers like yourself. I am still trying to think of the fellow who suggested my name as Ambassador to Great Britain. Shooting would be too good for him. I want to tell you, boy, when you hit 50, you slow up. If these people would just stop fighting and let me get a rest, I promise I would never do an honest day's work again. Just be a bum like you."[32]

On September 14, the American ambassador was summoned to 10 Downing, where Chamberlain, exiting from his eleven A.M. cabinet meeting, informed him that he had the evening before telegrammed the fuehrer and asked for a meeting, to which Hitler had agreed. The next morning, the sixty-nine-year-old prime minister, who had never before been on an airplane, flew to Munich, where he was met at the airport by an open car sent by Hitler, driven to the train station, and transported in the fuehrer's special train to Berchtesgaden in the Bavarian Alps. The fuehrer and the prime minister met for three hours that day with only a translator in the room with them. Chamberlain returned to London on Friday, September 16, to meet with his "inner cabinet" of chief advisers, then with the full cabinet.

Kennedy, like the rest of the world, did everything in his power to find out what had occurred in Berchtesgaden and whether the prime minister's mission had met with success. He called several times at 10 Downing and the Foreign Office at Whitehall, buttonholing undersecretaries and private secretaries, hoping to get news on the negotiations. His every step was chronicled by the daily press and in newsreels in America. "You and Hitler are running neck and neck to see who has his picture more often in the New York papers," Arthur Goldsmith wrote from New York on September 16, "and if you think either of you is pretty, you're crazy! It is 'Kennedy goes to Downing Street,' 'Kennedy sees Halifax,' 'Kennedy has his shoes shined,' 'Kennedy thinks . . .'— that would be news. The implications in the New York newspapers are that Chamberlain does not dare go to the lavatory without consulting you."[33]

That evening, Kennedy was briefed by Chamberlain. Hitler, Kennedy cabled the State Department, had demanded full "self-determination" for the Sudeten Germans, by which he meant separation of the Sudetenland from Czechoslovakia and its annexation by Germany. "Chamberlain asked him then if that meant that he would attempt to get the results he wanted by using force and Hitler said, 'Absolutely, and I will chance a world war if necessary.'" The only concession he offered Chamberlain was that he would agree to refrain from giving "any military orders" until he had heard from the prime minister as to whether the British government would accept the principle of self-determination for the Sudeten Germans. Chamberlain, Kennedy added, had come away from meeting with Hitler "with an intense dislike for him. He said he is cruel, overbearing, has a hard look and would be completely ruthless in any of his aims and methods."[34]

Chamberlain, recognizing that Hitler was not going to be deterred from the Sudetenland by threat of war, was prepared to give him what he wanted. What he did not know was whether the Czech government would agree to peacefully hand over the Sudetenland to the Germans. Roosevelt, an ocean away, was "of the opinion," as he told Morgenthau, "that the Czechs will fight." He wanted to get word to the French that instead of sending soldiers across the border into Germany in support of the Czechs, thereby setting in motion a process that could only lead to another world war, French forces should "stay behind the Maginot line" and, with the other "countries surrounding Germany," make the war "a defensive one and then both on land and sea . . . shut off Germany's supplies." The president was, Morgenthau believed, "ready to go pretty far in demonstrating United States sympathy in such a move." Morgenthau asked Roosevelt how he intended to get his message delivered to the French and the British.

" 'What about Kennedy' the president asked.

"I said, 'You know, Mr. President, you can't trust Kennedy' and he said, 'That is right.' "

Roosevelt sent for British ambassador Ronald Lindsay and laid out his proposal for a blockade of Germany. Kennedy was never told of the president's plan. He was already, barely six months after his arrival, outside the diplomatic loop, though he didn't yet know it.[35]

Chamberlain did not want to go to war with Germany over the Sudetenland. Kennedy was determined to do whatever he could to support him on this. Brave talk about British military will notwithstanding, Kennedy had no doubt (nor, it appeared, did Chamberlain) that the British were woefully unprepared to take on the Germans. Should the British even attempt to send troops into battle, Hitler could be expected to retaliate with air raids. London would be the first casualty. Kennedy was convinced that if he could get this point across to British politicians and the public, they would fall into line behind Chamberlain and appeasement.[36]

On September 19, Kennedy cabled Charles Lindbergh in Paris and asked him and his wife, Anne Morrow Lindbergh, "to come to London as soon as possible." On Wednesday, September 21, the Lindberghs and Kennedys had lunch together at Prince's Gate. "After lunch,"

Anne Morrow Lindbergh recorded in her diary, "C. [Charles] and Ambassador Kennedy talk, Mrs. Kennedy and I listen. It is profoundly depressing."[37]

According to Charles Lindbergh's diary entry, Kennedy, referring to information he had secured from the British Foreign Office, reported that while Chamberlain realized "the disastrous effects of war with Germany at this time and is making every effort to avoid one, English opinion is pushing him toward war." Lindbergh was horrified. "The English," he wrote in his diary, "are in no shape for war. They do not realize what they are confronted with. They have always before had a fleet between themselves and their enemy, and they can't realize the change aviation has made. I am afraid this is the beginning of the end of England as a great power."[38]

Kennedy asked Lindbergh to prepare a report that he could circulate among British officials, outlining what would occur should Great Britain go to war. Lindbergh did as he was asked, wrote the report, and presented in it the most frightening scenario imaginable: "For the first time in history a nation has the power either to save or to ruin the great cities of Europe. Germany has such a preponderance of war planes that she can bomb any city in Europe with comparatively little resistance. England and France are far too weak in the air to protect themselves."[39]

Kennedy sent the report to Hull, without telling him that he had invited Lindbergh to London and asked him to write it. He suggested that Hull forward the report to "the president and to the War and Navy departments." He also had his secretary place a call to the office of the British chief of staff for the air force "to say that Colonel Charles Lindbergh was in London for a day or two . . . and would be willing to meet someone from the Air Staff and discuss the situation with him." In the next day or so, Lindbergh made the rounds of the Air Ministry, repeating his dire warnings. John Slessor, the deputy director of plans, invited Lindbergh to dine with him and the secretary to the air chief marshal. "His attitude," Slessor recorded at the time, "struck us as being entirely sympathetic to the British," though he exhibited "an enormous admiration for the Germans and likes them personally." Lindbergh made it as clear as he could "that our only sound policy is to avoid war now at almost any cost."[40]

The immediate threat of war receded on September 21 when the Czech government agreed to "make territorial concessions in return for an international guarantee against unprovoked aggression."

Chamberlain flew to Germany the next day to hammer out what he hoped would be the final details of a peace agreement. At a meeting at the Hotel Dreesen in Godesberg, overlooking the Rhine, Chamberlain presented Hitler with his proposal for an international commission to draw new Czech boundaries and organize the orderly exchange of populations. He was shocked when the fuehrer insisted on the immediate cession of the entire Sudetenland and the withdrawal of the Czech army. If the Czechs did not agree to these demands by October 1, he would take the Sudetenland by force. Chamberlain protested, then agreed to present Hitler's demands to the Czech government. The next morning, he flew back to London to report to his cabinet.[41]

Kennedy, who had been left in the dark again (with the rest of the diplomatic corps, the press, and the cabinet) while Hitler and Chamberlain conducted their negotiations, haunted 10 Downing and Whitehall in search of news. Under-Secretary Cadogan did his best to "hold . . . Joe Kennedy at arm's length," he wrote in his diary. The American ambassador, furious at being shut out, made "little secret of what he thinks of us." Finally, at one P.M. on Saturday, September 24, Kennedy was briefed on Hitler's "preposterous" demands. "Hitler not only wants what everybody was willing to give him but it looks as if he wants a great deal more," he cabled Hull at the State Department.[42]

Chamberlain, exhausted and disheartened, presented his "inner cabinet" with the "memorandum" the fuehrer had given him and recommended that Hitler's demands be met. That evening, Secretary of State Hull called Kennedy at the embassy. The cabinet was still meeting and he had no definitive word to offer Hull on what its decision would be. "I may see Halifax within the next hour. I am still up and will stay close to the telephone until late. . . . Everyone is frightfully nervous. We have been working until three or four o'clock in the morning. . . . I believe it is the Prime Minister's policy to have peace at any price. The other group [the Churchill faction in the House of Commons] says that they are not going to stand it any longer and they are going to fight anyhow."[43]

The Chamberlain cabinet met again the next morning to try to reach a decision on how to respond to Hitler—and how to hold on to a majority in the House of Commons. "There may be some crack-up this afternoon," Kennedy cabled Washington. "Mr. Chamberlain and Halifax are not seeing me because they have no policy outlined yet that they can get the Cabinet to agree to, and I have been frankly advised that they want to have their house in order before saying what they propose doing. . . . The question is peace or war."[44]

On Sunday evening, September 25, the order was sent out by the British government to mobilize the ARP (Air Raid Precautions). "War," Kennedy wrote in his unpublished *Diplomatic Memoir,* "seemed to have come appreciably nearer. All over London people were being fitted for gas-masks. In the churches, in the theatres, at the sports matches, announcements were made of the depots to which they should go. A motor van slowly cruised through Grosvenor Square with a loud speaker attachment urging people not to delay in getting their masks. It carried posters pleading for more recruits for the air protections services." Kennedy cabled the State Department twice on September 26, asking for an additional one thousand gas masks and for the authority to spend several thousand dollars without getting preliminary estimates to purchase "materials for safeguarding against infiltration of gas, for first aid and similar supplies." When he was told he could have the gas masks, but he could not get additional materials without first submitting an estimate, he "purchased the necessary materials with my own funds, to be reimbursed at a later date."[45]

On September 26, President Roosevelt issued a direct appeal to all parties involved—Czech, British, French, and German: "So long as negotiations continue, differences may be reconciled. Once they are broken off reason is banished and force asserts itself. And force produces no solution for the future good of humanity." Kennedy was neither consulted nor warned in advance of the telegram, which was sent out at 1:13 A.M. Washington time.[46]

The prime minister, in a last-ditch effort to preserve the peace, dispatched Sir Horace Wilson to Berlin to appeal to Hitler "for negotiation as against violence." He also arranged a radio address for the following day, September 27, to personally plead with Hitler for time to complete a peaceful transfer of the Sudetenland.

Kennedy suggested to Hull that Chamberlain's radio address be broadcast directly to the American public. Sumner Welles called London to tell Kennedy that the president did not want Chamberlain's speech "broadcast to the United States. . . . Any reference in that address to the similarity of ideals, to the similarity of love of peace of the two peoples would be all to the good but a direct message to the American public might be misconstrued."

Kennedy pressed his case. "Supposing it isn't just a broadcast to America but that American companies pick up this broadcast to England?" Welles tried again to impress his point on Kennedy. The American government was not about to prevent radio companies from broadcasting whatever they wished, but neither he nor Hull nor the president thought it a good idea for Chamberlain to speak live on the radio to the American people. "A direct broadcast would be interpreted as an appeal to the United States and would be undesirable at this moment."[47]

On Monday, September 26, the day he received Roosevelt's plea for renewed negotiations, Hitler addressed Germany and the world from the Sportpalast in Berlin. "Shouting and shrieking in the worst state of excitement I've ever seen him in," the CBS radio commentator in Germany, William Shirer, wrote in his diary, "he stated . . . that he would have his Sudetenland by October 1—next Saturday. . . . If [Czech president Eduard] Beneš doesn't hand it over to him, he will go to war. . . . For the first time in all the years I've observed him he seemed tonight to have completely lost control of himself."[48]

Chamberlain, who had been praised in Hitler's speech as a peacemaker, prostrated himself yet again by declaring in a public statement that if Germany refrained from using force, the British government would guarantee the cession of Czech territory without delay. Hitler remained intransigent.

Answering Roosevelt's telegram, he bluntly declared that the question of whether there would be peace or war in Europe rested not with him, but with the Czechoslovak government. Kennedy, frightened that war—and the German bombardment of London—was now imminent, cabled Washington to find out from the Maritime Commission "what ships could be made available for the hordes of American citizens clamoring to get home."[49]

That Tuesday, September 27, while "lunching at home with Teddy," who was still suffering from tonsillitis, Kennedy was interrupted by a phone call from 10 Downing. Sir Horace Wilson, Chamberlain's personal envoy, was flying back to London. "He had seen Hitler this morning and Hitler had remained 'obdurate.' They regard the situation as almost hopeless." Hitler had shouted at Wilson in their face-to-face meeting that as far as he was concerned, the British cabinet and the Czechoslovak government had only two choices: to accept his terms or to reject them. If they chose the latter, Hitler thundered, then repeated several times, "I will smash the Czechs." He gave the governments until two P.M. the following day to accept his terms.[50]

Kennedy cabled Hull the news and asked him to please make preparations for ships "to get the Americans out, because the panic would be great." Preparations for the coming bombardment were now in full swing. Even in Roehampton, which was outside the central city, the three Kennedy girls were fitted for gas masks in the basement bunker. In London, work had reached an almost fever pitch. "All during the night of September 26–7," Kennedy wrote in his *Diplomatic Memoir,* "workmen were busily digging trenches in the parks under the glare of flashlights. But there were not enough men for this work on the unemployment rolls. An SOS call had been issued for every able-bodied man to report to the nearest labor exchange to help to dig trenches. The distribution of gas masks also continued. In many of the city boroughs the schools had been closed in order to facilitate their distribution to the lengthening queues of applicants." Expecting the German invasion of Czechoslovakia the following afternoon, the Admiralty announced on the evening of September 27 that it was mobilizing the British fleet.[51]

That afternoon, Kennedy visited the king to deliver a "sealed" letter from Roosevelt. Since Kennedy knew that it contained an invitation to the royal family to visit the United States, which he had suggested, he was "annoyed" at having to deliver it "sealed." He was delighted when the king opened the letter and read its contents aloud. "The King then asked me to sit down and we discussed the foreign situation. He was noticeably disturbed. . . . The talk turned to the Duke of Windsor, whom I had seen at Cannes. . . . 'One of the minor calamities of a war,' the King said, 'will be his return.'" He was no doubt referring to the likelihood that should Hitler win the coming war, he would recall the pro-Nazi Duke of Windsor to London and restore him to the throne.[52]

Kennedy returned home to listen to Chamberlain address the nation over the radio on Hitler's latest demands. Across the Atlantic, a radio was set up in the cabinet room, where Ickes and his colleagues listened. "His words were carefully measured and several times his voice was at the breaking point. He spoke slowly and feelingly. He gave the impression that the tears were just beneath the surface."[53]

When the speech was over, Roosevelt called a cabinet meeting to explore the possibility of sending a second message to Hitler, asking him, as Chamberlain had, to delay any action that might lead to war. At three P.M. Washington time (eight P.M. in London), Sumner Welles phoned Kennedy in London with "a message from the President. He asks if you will see Mr. Chamberlain as quickly as possible and tell him that the President is considering making a reply to the message which he received from Berlin last night. In his reply he is considering doing two things. The first of them is to supplement the existing negotiations, should it be thought desirable, by the holding of a conference of the nations directly interested, immediately, in some neutral European capital. . . . The second point he has in mind is to make a direct appeal to the man [Hitler] who sent him the message last night and to limit the message to that man and no one else."[54]

Kennedy didn't call back until 1:45 A.M. London time. He had been delayed meeting with Chamberlain, who, he believed, had abandoned all hope for peace. The prime minister was terrified that Hitler was going to march on the following day, Wednesday, instead of waiting until Saturday, October 1. Ninety minutes later, 3:15 A.M. London time, 10:15 P.M. Washington time, Roosevelt sent his second telegram to Hitler, proposing an international peace conference.

On Wednesday, September 28, the day Hitler had demanded that the Czechoslovak government sign off by two P.M. on his demands, Kennedy phoned Rose at the nearly deserted Gleneagles Hotel in Perthshire, Scotland, where she had gone to vacation after returning from Cannes. "Said I should come back tonight, as we must make some sort of plans for the children because war is imminent," she recalled later. "Everyone depressed and sober. Waiters chattering in groups. Some of the reserves called out. Took golf lesson." What she didn't do was make plans to return to London. Her husband had the week before called her back from Cannes and it had been a false alarm.[55]

In Rose's absence, Kennedy began packing the household and making arrangements to get the girls back from Roehampton as soon as passage to America had been secured for them.

At eight A.M. on the morning of September 28, after being up all night cabling and talking by telephone to Washington, he placed a call to the Swedish American Line to ask that the *Kungsholm,* en route from Gothenburg, Sweden, to New York, stop "at a British port" to take on American passengers. When the company agreed to permit the ship to stop at Leith in Scotland at midnight, Kennedy organized a special train to transport Americans there from London. Later that afternoon, he received a call from the company "to say that they heard the Firth of Forth had been mined and they could not accept the responsibility of permitting the ship to go into Leith." Kennedy arranged for the ship and the trainload of passengers from London to be directed to Newcastle instead. "All this was done under the pressure of British mobilization . . . with telephone lines jammed and only priority messages permitted to get through."[56]

That afternoon, the president cabled Kennedy with a personal message: "In these difficult days I am proud of you." Kennedy, delighted with the cable but unaware that the same note had been sent to the American ambassadors in Paris, Prague, and Berlin, stuffed it into his pocket and left for the House of Commons to attend what everyone believed would be Chamberlain's final speech before war was declared.[57]

Kennedy was seated in the Peers' Gallery, listening to Chamberlain, when a messenger arrived with a note for Lord Halifax, who passed it on to former prime minister Stanley Baldwin, who then, as Kennedy watched, left his seat and went downstairs. The note was passed along the treasury bench to Sir John Simon, chancellor of the Exchequer, who handed it to Home Secretary Hoare. Chamberlain, approaching the end of his eighty-minute speech, was thanking Mussolini for requesting that Hitler postpone mobilization for twenty-four hours when Home Secretary Hoare handed him the note.

"It was twelve minutes after four," Harold Nicolson, a member of Parliament at the time, wrote in his diary. The prime minister "adjusted his pince-nez and read the document that had been handed to him. His whole face, his whole body, seemed to change. He raised his face so that the light from the ceiling fell full upon it. All the lines of anxiety and weariness seemed suddenly to have been smoothed out; he appeared ten years younger and triumphant. 'Herr Hitler,' he said, 'has just agreed to postpone his mobilization for twenty-four hours and to meet me in conference with Signor Mussolini and Signor Daladier at Munich.' . . . For a second, the House was hushed in absolute silence. And then the whole House burst into a roar of cheering, since they knew that this might mean peace"[58]

"The cheers in the House from both sides were terrific," Kennedy cabled Hull. "Everybody feels tremendously relieved tonight." While Chamberlain had pointedly thanked Mussolini, not Roosevelt, for his last-minute intervention with Hitler, Kennedy seized the occasion to flatter the president and claim, rather preposterously, that his cable to Hitler had changed the tide of history. He closed his note with the sort of light touch that had been absent for months. "Well, as they say on the radio, 'signing off' and will try to get 6 hours sleep which I have not had for 7 days."[59]

"As we left the House of Commons," Kennedy recalled in his *Diplomatic Memoir,* "the tone of the crowds had changed. They were cheering and laughing and waving at every passerby, crowding about the cars and even running beside them in their exuberance. I was happy, too. It was a smiling, grinning individual, I was told, who stepped into the Embassy that afternoon and said: 'Well, boys, the war is off.'"[60]

Chamberlain flew to Germany, this time to Munich, where he, Prime Minister Édouard Daladier of France, Benito Mussolini of Italy, and Hitler agreed in writing to the cession of the Sudetenland to Germany, the evacuation to commence on October 1 and be completed by October 10. In the years to come, those who were present in the House of Commons that afternoon or heard the news on their radios or read it in their newspapers or welcomed Chamberlain back from Munich, Germany, would take little pleasure in remembering the delight with which they had greeted the prime minister's declaration that after months of preparation for war, "peace was at hand." Even President Roosevelt, certainly no fan of Chamberlain's, was so pleased with news of the agreement signed in Munich that he asked Hull to cable Kennedy with his congratulations. "Personal for the Ambassador. Transmit urgently following message to Prime Minister Chamberlain: 'Good man. Signed Franklin D. Roosevelt.' "[61]

"Tonight," Kennedy wrote in his diary, "a feeling is spreading all over London that . . . war will be averted. . . . It may be the beginning of a new world policy which may mean peace and prosperity once again." Rose, who had waited out the crisis at Gleneagles, decided that she could now "stay on at least over the weekend."[62]

Eighteen

THE KENNEDY PLAN

The euphoria that greeted Neville Chamberlain's return from Munich was shared by most of those who would later turn against the agreement he carried with him. As the choice between no agreement and the one signed at Munich was a choice between war and peace, to argue against it was, in effect, to welcome war. Few were willing to do so. There were exceptions, of course. Duff Cooper, first lord of the Admiralty, resigned from the cabinet in opposition; Winston Churchill spoke eloquently against the notion that the Munich Agreement preserved the peace. "We have sustained a total and unmitigated defeat. . . . We are in the presence of a disaster of the first magnitude. . . . Do not let us blind ourselves to that. . . . Do not suppose that this is the end. This is only the beginning of the reckoning. This is only the first sip, the first foretaste of a bitter cup which will be proffered to us year by year unless by a supreme recovery of moral health and martial vigour, we arise again and take our stand for freedom." Despite such warnings, when the time came to stand for or against the government that had negotiated the agreement with Hitler, Churchill remained seated. So too did a dozen or so other Conservative Party critics of Munich and Chamberlain. In the end, the vote to approve the agreement was almost three to one in favor; no Conservative Party member voted in the negative; twenty abstained.[1]

President Roosevelt, apparently as swept up in this moment of hopeful expectation as his ambassador to Great Britain, cabled London on October 4 with a "personal message" he wanted Kennedy to convey "orally" to Chamberlain. Now that Chamberlain had succeeded in establishing "personal contact with Chancellor Hitler," Roosevelt suggested that he attempt to open discussions with the chancellor on the Jewish refugee problem. There were well over half a million Jews in the Reich, and their circumstances were growing more horrific by the day. The number who sought to leave was growing exponentially, but the German government would not allow Jews to take their assets with them; worse yet, no country was willing to accept them. Roosevelt knew better than to suggest that Chamberlain criticize or call into question "the present German policy of racial persecution." All he asked was that he try to negotiate an agreement that would permit Jewish refugees who wanted to leave Germany "to take with them a reasonable percentage of their property. . . . As time may be of the essence, I am sending you this message without further delay in the hope that you will be able to find an appropriate opportunity to lay these considerations before the Reich Chancellor."[2]

Kennedy did not, as he had been instructed to do, deliver the note "orally" to Chamberlain, who was occupied in the House of Commons by the debate over the Munich Agreement. Instead, he read it to Lord Halifax, then forwarded it in written form to the prime minister. When he visited 10 Downing the next day to say good-bye to Chamberlain, who was going off on a long overdue fishing holiday, he read aloud the president's request that the prime minister appeal directly to Hitler on behalf of the Jewish refugees. Chamberlain responded "that he had already given the Jewish problem much thought and that it was part of the series of problems that in due course could now be taken up with Hitler and Mussolini." The critical phrase was "in due course." The following day, October 7, Chamberlain cabled Roosevelt that he agreed that "the first suitable opportunity should be taken of urging . . . the German Government to make a practical contribution to the solution of the [refugee] problem."[3]

Roosevelt didn't press the issue. Neither did his ambassador. Kennedy had complete faith that Chamberlain would raise the issue of the Jewish refugees with Hitler when that "first suitable opportunity" arrived. The prime minister was, he wrote David Sarnoff on October 7, "the best bet in the world today on this question, so, if some of your high class Jewish friends will stop selling the American public that I am pro-British, I may be able to help the cause. Anyway, I will do the best I can."[4]

George Rublee, the director of the Intergovernmental Committee on Refugees, was not nearly as sanguine about the Chamberlain government's commitment to solving the refugee problem. The British government, he urged Sumner Welles in an October 10 phone call, had to "be persuaded to take the matter more seriously. This can only be done through Ambassador Kennedy," who, while "personally sympathetic" to the plight of the refugees, "feels that our undertaking is hopeless. He does not want to go out on it because he has other matters he considers more important." Welles promised to speak directly to the British ambassador in Washington.[5]

Rublee's fears were well-founded. A lawyer by training and a skilled negotiator, he had taken on the task Roosevelt had given him and was trying to do the best he could, but he was hitting obstacle after obstacle. Three days after his call to Welles, at a "buffet dinner given by Ambassador Kennedy," Rublee wrote an associate in Washington, "I remarked that he had told me that if I got into a 'jam' he would help me. 'Well,' I said, 'I am in a "jam" and I wish you would help me.' He assured me that he would talk to Lord Halifax when Halifax came back on Monday and that he would also talk to the Prime Minister. He said that he had had a talk with the German Ambassador earlier in the day and that the German Ambassador had said that Hitler was not quite 'right' for this matter yet. The Ambassador said that he had read all my cables to the Department and that he understood my situation. I was encouraged by his manner and tone which were much more reassuring than I expected."[6]

Rublee had every right to be alternately frustrated and encouraged by Kennedy. The ambassador was not insensitive to the plight of the German Jews, as Rublee had told Welles in their phone conversation, but he prided himself on being a realist and as such agreed with the

British that the priority in these halcyon, post-Munich days should be placed not on getting Jews out of Germany and Austria, but on securing a viable, long-term peace agreement with the dictators, one that would include but not be centered on the rescue of the Jews. There was, as Kennedy well knew, another reason, almost as important, for the British reluctance to engage with the Jewish refugee problem. The last thing Chamberlain and Halifax wanted at this moment was further discussion of the issue, if only because they feared that it would lead inevitably to the demand that Palestine be opened to Jewish emigration. A demand they had no intention of meeting.

In the ever more likely event of future hostilities with the Germans and/or the Italians, the strategic importance of the Middle East and the support of Arab regional leaders was paramount. The British had no intention of taking any step in Palestine that might endanger that support. Legal Jewish immigration, which had been hearty in the middle 1930s, had been drastically reduced from 61,800 in 1935 to 10,500 in 1937 to placate Arab leaders and stem cascading violence between Arabs and Jews.

The royal commission charged with finding a solution to the Palestine problem had, in the spring of 1937, suggested partition into two states, but the proposal—and the map the commission drew of the proposed states—had been withdrawn because of opposition from both Arabs and Jews. A second High Commission on Palestine had been appointed in February 1938 to try again to come up with a workable plan. Rumors abounded on both sides of the Atlantic in the fall of 1938 that within days the commission would recommend further restriction, perhaps curtailment of Jewish immigration to the Middle East, this at a moment in time when the numbers of Jews seeking to emigrate had increased exponentially.[7]

On October 6, Chaim Weizmann in London cabled Supreme Court justice Louis Brandeis, Felix Frankfurter, and other Zionist leaders in New York and Washington that he feared the British were about to restrict immigration to Palestine and that only pressure from the Americans was going to stop them. It was imperative that Roosevelt be asked at once to instruct his ambassador in London to express the American government's steadfast objection to any proposal by the British to reduce Jewish immigration to Palestine.[8]

Hull and Welles, on Roosevelt's instructions, cabled Kennedy in London to ask him to find out precisely what was in the British plan and to let the Chamberlain government know how significant the question of Palestine was to the American Jewish community. "Unless you perceive serious objection," Hull cabled Kennedy on October 12, "I should like to have you see Lord Halifax at your early convenience and, entirely personally and unofficially, inform him that during the past few days the White House and the Department have received thousands of telegrams and letters from all over the United States protesting against the alleged intention of the British Government to alter the terms of the Palestine Mandate in such a way as to curtail or eliminate Jewish immigration."[9]

Kennedy did as he was asked, exasperated at what he perceived to be the posturing going on in Washington. Hull, Welles, and Roosevelt had to know that the Chamberlain government was likely to restrict Jewish immigration to Palestine and that no matter what Roosevelt might say to Zionist leaders and sympathizers in Washington, the U.S. government was not going to involve itself in what it regarded as a British matter.

Joseph P. Kennedy had arrived in London believing that one of his major tasks would be negotiating the Anglo-American trade and tariff agreement that was at the top of Secretary of State Hull's agenda. On October 14, he called Hull in Washington to offer his assistance in the final round of negotiations. "I don't know anything about the terms of the agreement, but I know something about trading. I have been doing that for twenty-five years and I know how you have put your heart on this thing and I don't want to see it fall down. I am on the ground here and I think I know exactly what's going on here." Hull let Kennedy ramble on, to the point where the ambassador became concerned that no one was paying attention at the other end of the line and asked pointedly if someone was "taking this down." He then offered his recommendations on the terms that should be offered the British on lard, tobacco, lumber, plywood, corn, wheat flour, electric motors, typewriters, wool, and motorcars. Hull promised that he would stay in touch.[10]

Kennedy was angry about being shut out of the trade negotiations, but angrier still when the news of his exclusion was leaked to the press. As Drew Pearson and Robert Allen reported on October 31, "One sidelight on British treaty negotiations has been the attitude of Ambassador Joe Kennedy. . . . Much interested in the treaty negotiations, Joe frequently wired the State Department . . . for details. But the State Department never obliged. Joe's requests for information were not answered. Department officials feared Joe might use the information to chisel the treaty's progress."[11]

Such snubs from Washington were, he feared, having an adverse influence on his ability to conduct business in London. He had also been excluded from discussions about the royal family's visit to the United States. "While I do not like to bother you with this," he cabled the State Department in a "For the Secretary Personally" dispatch, "I am somewhat embarrassed by being questioned every day in connection with the King's trip by the King's Secretaries and by the Foreign Office. . . . Because I imagine my contacts and prestige here would be seriously jeopardized I hate to admit knowing nothing about it. Possibly nothing can be done about this and although it is difficult I can continue to look like a dummy and carry on the best I can."[12]

Five days later, Kennedy received a "Dear Joe" note from the president, asking "if he would be good enough" to deliver another letter to the king. "I feel sure," Roosevelt explained, offhandedly responding to the ambassador's complaints, "you will understand that the preliminary discussions about the proposed visit of Their Majesties next year is only in the preliminary stage and that, therefore, I am conducting it personally." Roosevelt's explanation was ridiculous (he could at one and the same time have conducted the discussions "personally" and consulted with his ambassador) and served only to reinforce Kennedy's sense of isolation now verging on paranoia.[13]

On October 19, Kennedy addressed the annual Trafalgar Day dinner of the Navy League, the first American ambassador ever invited to do so. The speech was, for the most part, a lighthearted, thoroughly conventional paean to the informal but grand alliance between the English and American navies. The ambassador began by jokingly listing the topics he had decided not to talk about, including "a theory of mine that it is unproductive for both democratic and dictator countries to widen the division now existing between them by empha- sizing their differences, which are self-apparent. Instead of hammering away at what are regarded as irreconcilables, they can advantageously bend their energies toward solving their remaining common problems and attempt to re-establish good relations on a world basis. . . . After all, we have to live together in the same world, whether we like it or not." The reporters covering the speech, not a few of them lurking in wait for him to say something off-color or blatantly undiplomatic, seized immediately on these sentences. The *New York Times,* reporting on the speech the next morning in an article titled KENNEDY FOR AMITY WITH FASCIST BLOC: URGES THAT DEMOCRACIES AND DICTATORSHIPS FORGET THEIR DIFFERENCES IN OUTLOOK. CALLS FOR DISARMAMENT, printed verbatim the two paragraphs in which Kennedy had called "for amity with Fascist bloc," labeling it "an excellent summary of the atti- tude repeatedly stated here by Prime Minister Neville Chamberlain" and asking whether Kennedy's pronouncements, vague as they were, indicated a shift in American policy from "quarantining" the dictators to making friends with them.[14]

The president and Hull were furious—not so much at Kennedy, whom they expected to say such things, but at the State Department, which had failed to censor him. "The Secretary," Moffat wrote in his diary on October 21, "is very upset over the effect of Kennedy's recent speech. . . . He thinks we should have definitely called Kennedy off in advance, despite his claim that he was advancing a 'pet theory of his own.' The Secretary asked Sumner why he did not see the danger of the speech. Sumner replied that he had been thinking of Mexico and had assumed that the Secretary himself had given attention to the matter and had initialed blind." Hull then turned to Moffat and blamed him for the fiasco. "A 'goat' is needed and I shall be the goat," Moffat con- cluded. "In the long run, however, no one is going to be hurt unless it be Mr. Kennedy himself."[15]

Hull held a press conference the morning after the speech to insist that Kennedy had been speaking for himself, not the government. This did nothing to quiet the storm. On October 26, just a week after the Trafalgar Day speech, the White House called Adolf Berle, one of the original members of Roosevelt's brain trust who now served as an assistant secretary of state, to ask him to "prepare a fifteen minute speech" for the president that "would undo the damage done by Kennedy's recent speech [and] make it clear that our foreign policy was unchanged." Without mentioning Kennedy by name, the president repudiated everything the ambassador had said in a speech broadcast from the White House. There could, he declared, be no peace with nations that threatened war as an instrument of national policy and persecuted and denied freedom of speech and religion to their own citizens.[16]

The president's clarification did not quiet the controversy over Kennedy's remarks but intensified it. Frank Kent reported in his October 28 column that Kennedy had that past week received a "journalistic lambasting so completely in contrast to his accustomed laudation that it could hardly help but be a shock to him." In a telephone conversation with Moffat the following week, Kennedy noted that he had "just received a week's batch of newspaper clippings and I should judge by them that I had never been right in anything since the war broke out in 1914." Without apologizing, and in fact confirming the major charge leveled against him, that he was too close to Chamberlain, Kennedy warned Moffat that "you fellows in Washington should know one thing, that if I am to get results here I can only do it by staying on the right side of the men in power."[17]

Arthur Krock and John Burns, who both thought that Kennedy's comments on the need to open negotiations with the dictators were so out of line that they might get him recalled from London, warned him to watch his temper and his mouth. "You ought not to talk with Tommy [Corcoran] or anyone else in a complaining or querulous tone about what has happened," Burns wrote on November 4. "It's much better to keep up, as I know you can very well, the appearance of being entirely confident of the goodness, sweetness and charity of the 'Great White Father' [Franklin Delano Roosevelt]."[18]

Publicly, Kennedy tried to disguise his anger. Privately, he let it all out. He could not, for the life of him, understand what he had said that should so offend anyone back home. The English, French, and Americans had two choices: either fight a war with the dictators or make peace with them. Since it made no sense to fight with an enemy that was so much stronger, the only available path was to seek a mutually acceptable accommodation.

It was ludicrous to believe that anything positive could come from verbally abusing Hitler and Mussolini. Nasty words, no matter how eloquently delivered, and moral posturing, no matter how sincere, were not going to get them to change their ways. Only war or economic boycott might, but these were alternatives no one was seriously advocating at the moment.

"I believe that unless England and France are prepared to fight and endanger civilization," Kennedy wrote Tom White in mid-November, "then there is no point in staying on the side lines and sticking your tongue out at somebody who is a good deal bigger than you are. As far as the United States goes, we ought to mind our own business, but that means minding our own business and not one minute kicking the dictators' head off and the next suggesting that they cooperate along certain lines. It is my theory in doing business with individuals or with nations that you must either keep away from them altogether or, if you are going to stick your tongue out at them or slap them on the wrist, you have better be prepared to punch them in the jaw."[19]

In his unpublished *Diplomatic Memoir,* Kennedy was still trying a decade later to understand the furor over his speech. Much of it, he claimed, came from those, including "a number of Jewish publishers and writers," who wanted to precipitate a war with Germany. In separate letters written to New York *Daily News* columnist Dorothy Fleeson and to Tom White, Kennedy insisted that "75% of the attacks made on me by mail were by Jews." In his memoir, he claimed that he understood why the Jews wanted Great Britain and America to go to war against Hitler and why they had attacked those who advocated appeasement. "After all, the lives and futures of their compatriots were being destroyed by Hitler. Compromise could hardly cure that situation; only the destruction of Nazism could do so." Still, even after excusing his Jewish critics for what he believed was their warmongering, he was not ready to forgive them for their unfair attacks on him: "Some of them in their zeal did not hesitate to resort to slander and falsehood to achieve their aims. I was naturally not the sole butt of their attack but I received my share of it." The only Jewish names he mentioned were journalists. Max Lerner, who he claimed had unfairly attacked him in a speech to a Boston audience, and Walter Lippmann, who had declared in his column that ambassadors had no business airing their personal views in public. Lippmann's was not a particularly nasty column, certainly not as damning as columns written at the same time by Heywood Broun, Dorothy Thompson, and Hugh Johnson, none of them Jewish.[20]

Joe Jr. defended his father by drafting a letter that was apparently never sent. "Mr. Lippmann['s] article shows the natural Jewish reaction to the speech of ambassadors calling for some kind of cooperation between the democratic and fascists nations." Almost parroting his father, young Joe lectured Lippmann: "Either you have to be prepared to destroy the fascist nations . . . or you might as well try to get along with them. I know this is extremely hard for the Jewish community in the US to stomach, but they should see by now that the course which they have followed the last few years has brought them nothing but additional hardship."[21]

Jack reported from Cambridge that while the Navy Day speech "seemed to be unpopular with the Jews, etc. [it] was considered to be very good by everyone who wasn't bitterly anti-Fascist."[22]

There was more than a hint of paranoiac rage here directed at Jewish letter writers, columnists, and newspaper reporters. The Kennedys had to blame someone for the criticism—and who better than Europe's most venerable scapegoats. One of the staples of twentieth-century anti-Semitism, on the continent, in Great Britain, and in America, was the notion that the Jews had unfairly, perhaps criminally, seized control of the news media and were using it for their own ends. Kennedy grabbed hold of this myth even though it was clear that in numbers and ferocity, his gentile critics far outnumbered the Jewish.

His prejudices were reinforced by his friends the Lindberghs, the Astors, and Lord Beaverbrook. In a particularly vicious letter to Anne Morrow Lindbergh written on November 2, 1938, Lady Astor had mentioned that "only yesterday I was talking to someone who traces the origin of the 'yellow press' to an American Jew, named Pulitzer. . . . It is horrible how much one can trace back to them. I don't believe in persecution, but there is something evidently wrong with their whole make-up." Lord Beaverbrook, who as a newspaper mogul should have known better, agreed entirely that the Jews had far too much influence on both sides of the Atlantic. "The Jews are after Mr. Chamberlain," he wrote American publisher Frank Gannett in December 1938.

"He is being terribly harassed by them. . . . All the Jews are against him. . . . They have got a big position in the press here. . . . I am shaken. The Jews may drive us into war . . . their political influence is moving us in that direction."[23]

Kennedy's anger at the Jewish community was stoked by his sense that they did not appreciate his efforts on their behalf. While the Roosevelt administration had given no indication that it intended to press the British government to permit increased Jewish immigration to Palestine, Kennedy had on his own been meeting with and trying to counsel the American Zionist leaders who had come to London to lobby the British. When Ben Cohen visited in October 1938, supposedly on vacation but in truth as an unofficial emissary of Justice Brandeis and Felix Frankfurter, Kennedy arranged an introduction and meeting for him with Colonial Secretary Malcolm MacDonald.[24]

Two weeks later, Kennedy met with Chaim Weizmann, the president of the World Zionist Organization. In a document marked "Secret" in the Weizmann archives in Jerusalem, Weizmann, referring to himself as "X," reported his "general impression . . . that Mr. K. was both friendly and optimistic. . . . He himself was keeping in close touch with the Palestine problem. As a Catholic in Boston he had reason to know what discrimination meant; his own father had been unable to find any entrée in Boston, and had eventually been forced to look elsewhere for a livelihood. But for the Jews the position was a hundred times worse. He knew that Bullitt was a friend of ours, but neither Bullitt nor the President, as Protestants, could feel about the Jewish question in the same way as he, K., felt about it." Kennedy assured Weizmann "that if any time the red light were to show [if the British decided to cut off all immigration to Palestine], we should not hesitate to give him the signal, and he would do whatever he could to help." Kennedy's meeting with Weizmann ended rather spectacularly when the ambassador inquired what Weizmann "would think if he, K., were to go and visit Hitler to discuss the Jewish question. 'X' replied that from all he had heard, this subject was an obsession with Hitler, so that he became virtually insane when it was raised. Mr. K. said that he had nevertheless more than half a mind to pay him such a visit. It might light a few bonfires in the United States, but all the same he was tempted to intervene."[25]

Kennedy also met with Rose Gell Jacobs, an American representative on the executive committee of the Jewish Agency for Palestine. As he had in his discussions with Weizmann, though this time more directly, Kennedy offered his opinion that the only way to solve the refugee problem was to negotiate a deal with Hitler. "He mentioned the attacks that are being made on him by the newspapers and Jewish columnists in America, because of his suggestion that efforts be made to come to terms with Hitler on the Jewish problem. He says he is ready to listen to any scheme that will work, as he has not yet come across any. To his mind, winning Hitler over to a plan is essential." Although Jacobs, like Weizmann, considered Kennedy an ally, she reported back to New York that he was not fully in tune with Zionist aspirations. He had intimated to her, without saying so directly, that the answer to the refugee problem was not going to be found in Palestine because the British were not going to permit increased immigration. Jacobs did not argue with Kennedy but reminded him only that more Jews were attempting to immigrate to Palestine, because at present there were no safe havens for them in central or Eastern Europe.[26]

Benjamin Cohen, Chaim Weizmann, and Rose Jacobs all came away impressed by what Jacobs referred to as the ambassador's "sincerity and genuine desire to be helpful." And they were right to be won over. Kennedy had nothing to gain by dissembling. He met with them—and other Zionist representatives in London, including Ze'ev Jabotinsky, the founder of the Zionist Revisionist movement—because he hoped to convince them that his was the only way to rescue the German Jews, that angry words and anti-German boycotts made things worse, that unless Hitler approved, no German Jews were going to be let out of Germany.

The outpouring of unrestrained anti-Semitic brutality and sadism that the world would come to know as *Kristallnacht* shattered overnight the hopes of those such as Joseph P. Kennedy who, in the weeks following Munich, had believed that the time was propitious for negotiating a comprehensive settlement with Hitler that included provision for the emigration of Germany's Jews. "The Munich pact . . . now seemed to be a mockery of the notion 'peace in our time,'" historian Deborah Lipstadt has written. "For the first time since the Nazi accession to power a nationwide anti-Semitic action had taken place in full public view."[27]

The events of *Kristallnacht* on November 9 and 10 were not the first acts of unprovoked violence against Jews in Germany or Austria, but never had that violence been so widespread, so obviously coordinated and state-sanctioned, so violent, so effective. German and Austrian Jews, men, women, children, and the elderly, were beaten, their homes vandalized, their shops broken into, their synagogues destroyed, many burned to the ground. "The only immediate aim," Saul Friedländer has concluded, "was to hurt the Jews as badly as the circumstances allowed, by all possible means: to hurt them and to humiliate them." It was hoped and expected that, terrified by the violence, their possessions and economic resources plundered, Germany's Jews would not only acquiesce but actively participate in their own removal.[28]

The policy of appeasement that Chamberlain had, to Kennedy's mind, pursued successfully to this point had been based on the expectation that the Germans would fulfill their side of the bargain. In return for being permitted to annex Austria and the Sudetenland without a shot fired, they would eschew aggression, abide by their treaty obligations, and, in short, behave like a "civilized" nation. All that had been called into question by the brutal excesses of *Kristallnacht*. "I am hopeful that something can be worked out, but this last drive on the Jews," Kennedy wrote Charles Lindbergh just days after *Kristallnacht*, "has really made the most ardent hopers for peace very sick at heart. . . . It is more and more difficult for those seeking peaceful solutions to advocate any plan when the papers are filled with such horror. So much is lost when so much could be gained."[29]

During his first six months in London, the American ambassador had been an enthusiastic, perhaps too enthusiastic, supporter of Chamberlain and Halifax, because he was convinced they knew what they were doing. After *Kristallnacht*, he was no longer sure this was the case. Besieged internally and internationally for what was now perceived as a sell-out at Munich, the Chamberlain government was floundering. Instead of answering its critics by offering up new policy initiatives, the prime minister remained largely silent, reinforcing the notion that he was spineless, ineffective, incapable of standing up to Hitler.

Kennedy was disturbed both by Chamberlain's seeming passivity and by the virulence of the attacks on him. The ambassador recommended that the Chamberlain government demonstrate that it was still a major actor in European affairs by reopening the question of Jewish rescue. He understood and sympathized with British reluctance to permit unrestricted or expanded immigration to Palestine. But the British Empire was vast with underpopulated dominions, colonies, and League of Nations mandates. Surely there was someplace, somewhere, for the German and Austrian Jews.

Like a terrier with a small animal in its mouth, the ambassador held on tight to his new project, wrestling it back and forth, up and down, refusing to let go. Here was the magic panacea for Europe's ills. If the British opened up territory for Jewish settlement, everything else would fall into place: Jewish hostility and agitation against Germany would abate, the reputation of the Chamberlain government would be improved, negotiations between the British and the Germans for a comprehensive peace settlement could proceed to a successful conclusion.

He first discussed his plans with Chamberlain at 10 Downing on November 12, just days after news of *Kristallnacht* had reached London. The next day, invited with Rose and Joe Jr. to a luncheon at Colonial Secretary Malcolm MacDonald's house in Essex, Kennedy dominated the discussion by putting forward his solution to the Jewish question. If Great Britain would take the lead in opening territory for Jewish resettlement, other nations would fall into line and the onus would be taken off the Chamberlain government for not opening up Palestine to Jewish refugees. Kennedy proposed that the British "call the bluff of all the countries immediately" by asking them "how much money they were willing to put up for the Jews, and how many they were prepared to take." MacDonald responded that he preferred to proceed slowly "for fear of the reaction."[30]

In retrospect, the Kennedy plan was not nearly as fanciful—or indeed as original—as it might have appeared. Since that spring, Roosevelt and the State Department had been involved in their own lobbying efforts to find territories outside Palestine in which to settle Jewish refugees. The United States had no intention of opening its own lands to Jewish resettlement; its contribution to the problem would be to pressure the Latin American republics to do so. Administration officials and friends floated plans to resettle European Jews in the Orinoco River valley in Venezuela, in Costa Rica near the Panama border, in Mexico, Haiti, and Brazil. As these plans fell flat, one after another, the administration latched on to what Roosevelt called "the big idea," promoted by Herbert Hoover and Bernard Baruch in the United States, and by Anthony Gustav de Rothschild in Great Britain, to raise $300 million of private moneys to establish a "United States of Africa" somewhere in Africa, perhaps in Portuguese Angola.[31]

Kennedy should, by rights, have coordinated his campaign to open up British territory for resettlement with the White House and the State Department. Instead, he leaked news of his "Kennedy plan" to *New York Times* London bureau chief Ferdinand Kuhn, Jr., who reported on it in a front-page story on November 15: KENNEDY IS ACTIVE. LARGE-SCALE MOVE BY 2 NATIONS TO RESETTLE JEWS HELD URGENT.

That afternoon at four P.M. in Washington, President Roosevelt was asked at a press conference about the "reports from London that Mr. Kennedy has made a suggestion to the British Government concerning a place wherein the Jewish refugees would be taken care of." Roosevelt responded tartly that he could not "comment on the report, because I know nothing of what has been happening in London." It was becoming increasingly evident, as Moffat noted in his diary, that the American ambassador was "negotiating on his own with the British Government." "We are still," Moffat added the following day, "in the dark as to what Kennedy is doing in London on refugees."[32]

At almost the same moment that Roosevelt was dismissing any knowledge of the Kennedy plan, the ambassador was promoting it at a dinner given by the king and queen for King Carol of Romania. He cornered the prime minister and urged him again "to do something for Jews." Chamberlain replied that he was familiar with Kennedy's plan, having heard about it from Halifax and MacDonald, and that he intended on doing something. What, he did not say.[33]

The next day, Kennedy met with Lord Halifax at Whitehall to push again for British assistance, if only for the sake of public opinion in the

United States, which, he warned, was becoming "generally less sympathetic to His Majesty's Government. The Ambassador stressed the need of finding some means of counteracting this development." To facilitate the resettlement process once the British had designated territory for Jewish refugees, Kennedy volunteered to Halifax that he "thought that private sources in America might well contribute $100 or $200 million if any large scheme of land settlement could be proposed."

Halifax could scarcely disguise his anger. According to the record of the conversation he cabled to Ambassador Lindsay in Washington, the foreign secretary told Kennedy that he was "at a loss to understand why American opinion should blame His Majesty's Government because German Government persecuted the Jews, especially as the United States did not show much desire to do anything substantial." Lord Halifax reminded the American ambassador that the United States had as yet refused to open up any of its own territory to Jewish resettlement. Kennedy responded that, if only for the "psychological effect," it was imperative that Britain take the "lead" by opening up some part of the empire to Jewish immigrants, then, after making "an offer of land and financial assistance," ask the United States government "to what extent they were prepared to support the effort."[34]

That day, at cabinet, Halifax declared that he had "reached the conclusion that perhaps the best course was to do nothing as any positive action on our part would only make the position of the German Jews still worse." The cabinet agreed with him that it was a mistake to muddy the diplomatic waters "with this Jewish question." When one of the ministers asked about the use of "economic sanctions" against Germany over its treatment of the Jews, Halifax responded that "his anxiety was that Germany should not go to war with us as a consequence of any action we might take to help the German Jews." Incensed that the Americans, Kennedy chief among them, were putting pressure on the British to solve the refugee problem while they refused to take in any more Jews, the cabinet instructed the foreign secretary to inquire of the U.S. government if it would allow German Jewish refugees to enter America under the unfilled sixty-thousand-person British quota. There was also some vague discussion of resettling German Jews in British Guiana.[35]

Despite the fact that Kennedy's proposal had been mentioned and then dismissed as impracticable by Chamberlain, Halifax, and the British cabinet, the American papers carried page-one stories about what was now referred to as "the Kennedy plan" to rescue the German Jews and resettle large numbers of them in British colonies or League of Nation mandates in Africa. The *New York Times, Washington Post, Chicago Daily Tribune, Los Angeles Times,* and dozens of other American papers reported on November 18 that Great Britain had called on its colonial and mandate administrators to report immediately on how many refugees they could accommodate.

On the morning of November 17, British ambassador Ronald Lindsay, as instructed by the cabinet, called on Sumner Welles and formally requested that the American government apply the unused portion of the sixty-thousand quota for British immigrants to German Jewish refugees. Welles dismissed the idea out of hand. The British quota, he informed Lindsay, was for British citizens and no one else. Lindsay then proceeded to tell Welles that "he had been very much disturbed by newspaper reports during the past two days of plans which it was alleged Ambassador Kennedy had presented to the British Government for the solution of the refugee question." Kennedy, the British ambassador claimed, had gone so far as to virtually blackmail the British government by insinuating that American revulsion against the "treatment accorded Jews and Catholics in Germany" was provoking "vehement and widespread criticism in America against the policy of appeasement pursued by Mr. Chamberlain." Welles responded by disowning Kennedy, much as Roosevelt had two days earlier. "I told the Ambassador that if Mr. Kennedy had any plan he had not reported it to us. . . . This Government had not sent any instructions to Mr. Kennedy in the matter, nor had it instructed him to present any plan."[36]

Washington may well have been playing a double game here. The president and secretary of state had to have known what Kennedy was doing, if only by reading the press reports. They had allowed him to proceed instead of instructing him to desist, hoping he would gain some traction with the British. Now that Ambassador Lindsay had lodged a complaint, however, Hull had no choice but to call his ambassador on the carpet and inquire of him, for the first time, precisely what he had been doing. Kennedy responded without apology that he had, that past

Sunday, at luncheon with Colonial Secretary Malcolm MacDonald discussed "among other subjects . . . Palestine and the atrocities in Germany. I asked him why in heaven's name England did not show more interest as she had all the land and if she offered some of it," it would be easier to negotiate an agreement with the Germans and raise private moneys for resettlement. "I told him it looked to me that everyone was feeling sorry for the Jews but that nobody was offering any solution." Kennedy insisted that he had not informed the State Department about the discussions because nothing concrete had come of them. "If I had any news of any description concerning this matter which I thought would be of interest to you, you would have had it as you always do from me. If I have made any contribution it is that I have urged the British to do something quickly . . . but then I have been doing that for four months."[37]

Kennedy's explanation satisfied no one in Washington. "Tension between Kennedy and the Administration is so acute," Moffat noted in his diary on November 22, "that he must be handled with kid gloves; in fact many people feel that he is merely looking for an opportunity to get out with a resounding attack on the Administration." Moffat admired Kennedy's work ethic and enthusiasm and his detailed diplomatic dispatches from London, but he too was growing weary with Kennedy's penchant for shooting himself in the foot. "He is in many ways a curious personality and one whom in many ways I like and admire. His record of accomplishment in England is good but it is spoiled by an inordinate pushing of personal publicity. . . . I doubt if he has been anything but helpful in pushing the British on the refugee matter, yet the whole tenor of the articles from London, which are apparently inspired, gives him the entire credit of accomplishment and has infuriated the friends of George Rublee, Myron Taylor, and others to a point where they can scarcely be civil."[38]

The ambassador was furious at the reprimands and frightened at the consequences that might follow from the White House disowning "the Kennedy plan." Unless something was done to rescue European Jews from Nazi terror, American and British Jews would become implacable opponents of further negotiations, and they would apply their media influence and political power to force America into war against Germany. The fact that there was no organized or unorganized effort by American Jews to push America or Britain into a war with Germany had no effect on his increasingly hysterical thinking.

In many ways, Joseph Kennedy had become a victim of his own prejudices. The more he exaggerated the extent of the Jews' political and media power, the more he worried about the future. "I get very disturbed reading about what's taking place in America on the Jewish question," he wrote Robert Fisher on November 25. "When I hear that America wants to be an isolationist country and then people get themselves into such a dither over this question, I wonder how safe your sons and mine are from war. Of course frightful things are happening in the world and we all feel terribly sorry about it, but we have a country of our own with problems that require all of our ingenuity and sympathy." He made the same point in a letter to Russell Davenport and in conversations with his son Joe. Jr. "He is alarmed," Joe Jr. wrote in his diary on December 10, "that the country should get so worried up by the treatment of the Jews, for if they can be roused to fever heat on this question, there doesn't seem to be much possibility of keeping them out of war."[39]

Kennedy had convinced himself that his was the only voice of sanity in a world veering closer and closer to another European war. And that voice was in danger of being silenced. He had been abandoned not only by the once friendly American press, but by his friends in the White House. His father-in-law had written that even Missy LeHand, for whom he had done so many favors in the past, was saying "very unkind things about me." "All I have been having poured into me for the last three months," he wrote the president's son-in-law, John Boettiger, "is how Roosevelt is off me, how the gang is batting my head off, and that I am persona non grata to the entire Roosevelt family. Well, of course I know a lot of this is hooey, but it is damned annoying three thousand miles away. When I add up my contributions to this cause over the past five years—and I do not mean monetary ones—I get damned sick that anybody close to the Boss finds it necessary to do anything but say a good word." He had, Joe Jr. wrote in his diary, begun to speak "about quitting. He is afraid that they are trying to knock him off at home, and may make a monkey out of him in some diplomatic undertaking."[40]

His reputation in the United States was dealt another, near fatal blow when, on November 23, under questioning in the House of Commons, Sir John Simon, the chancellor of the Exchequer, acknowledged that the American ambassador had been quite helpful in the government's recent attempts to get Paramount to censor newsreels that contained interviews with two furiously anti-Chamberlain, anti-appeasement journalists. The American newspapers, alerted to the two-minute debate in the House of Commons, seized on it as an occasion to attack Kennedy once again for, as the *Chicago Daily Tribune* put it, "playing the role of office boy of empire." "There was a bad break in the news for Joe Kennedy the other day," Harold Ickes noted with delight in his diary on November 25. "I suspect that this collaboration between Kennedy and the British Foreign Office looking to a censorship of a perfectly legitimate section of film will not go well either in this country or in England."[41]

In a phone conversation with Morgenthau, Jim Farley, Roosevelt's postmaster general and political adviser, mentioned that Roosevelt had been "quite annoyed" with the publicity over Kennedy's latest gaffe. "I think when Joe comes back [for his next home visit] that that will probably be the beginning of the end."[42]

Kennedy too was beginning to contemplate "the end" of his tenure in London. "After ten months of carrying out his ambassadorial duties, Dad is rather tired of his work," Joe Jr. wrote in his diary. "He claims that he would give it up in a minute if it wasn't for the benefits that Jack and I are getting out of it and the things Eunice will get when she comes out next Spring. He doesn't like the idea of taking orders and working for hours trying to keep things out of his speeches which an Ambassador shouldn't say. He also doesn't like the idea of sitting back and letting the Jewish columnists in American kick his head off. The papers have made up a pile of lies about him, and he can't do anything about it." Joe Jr. again paid no attention to the fact that the only "Jewish" columnist who had attacked his father was Walter Lippmann and that his chief supporter, Arthur Krock, was Jewish.[43]

On November 29, Sumner Welles announced that Kennedy was returning "on leave for the Christmas holidays, but his visit will have no official significance." "The trip is entirely his own idea," Drew

Pearson and Robert Allen confirmed in their column. "Two motives are behind it—politics and the press. Personable, ingratiating, and with the flair of the Irish for politics, Joe is very ambitious in this direction. He is a brilliant business man and stock market operator, but he has made his pile and now wants to carve a name for himself in public affairs. What he is secretly after is the 1940 nomination for Vice President. . . . He is using the disturbed European situation as an excuse to dash across the Atlantic for a few weeks to look over the lay of the land and do some quiet fence building."[44]

Kennedy's first stop on his fence-mending tour was Washington. He brought with him the long memorandum he and his staff had been working on in London, which laid out in harrowing detail "the effect on the United States of the decline or collapse of the British Empire" through defeat in war or appeasement to prevent war. Germany, Italy, and Japan were on the rise and on the move, determined to take—by military action if necessary, by negotiations if possible—what they believed rightfully belonged to them as world powers. Great Britain and France had only a few choices, none of them palatable. They could enter into and be defeated in war with the dictators; they could surrender territory piecemeal through appeasement; or they could join the ascendant powers, and the United States, in restructuring a new, post-Versailles world order. There was, Kennedy insisted, no other way forward.[45]

Kennedy met only briefly with the president in Washington. They did not share cocktails or a meal or much small talk, as they had in the past. Instead of apologizing or attempting to explain why he had acted without or contrary to instructions from Washington, Kennedy seized the offensive, blaming the president and Secretary of State Hull for ignoring his advice, bypassing him on decisions he should have been consulted on, failing to defend him in the press. Roosevelt, who didn't enjoy such confrontations and had no intention of letting Kennedy return home before the 1940 elections, quickly put out the fire. He assured him that he was doing a fine job in London. There was no talk of recall or resignation.

After his meetings in Washington and a short stay in New York, which included a night at the opera with Arthur Goldsmith, Kennedy flew to Palm Beach for a six-week vacation with Jack, who had decided to take the next semester off and serve as his father's secretary in London. As always, Kennedy imported his buddies to spend the vacation with him. At one time or another, he was joined in Palm Beach by Arthur Houghton, "London Jack" Kennedy, Jack's friends Lem Billings and Rip Horton, Hearst columnist Walter Winchell, radio commentator Boake Carter, and David Sarnoff. Except for a brief New Year's Day excursion to Miami for the Orange Bowl, Kennedy and his guests remained within the protective cocoon of the island, playing golf at the Palm Beach Country Club, eating fresh fish prepared at his home by his chef, and spending an evening or two at Colonel Bradley's casino, where Kennedy enjoyed the food, but never bet more than a dollar or two.

The rest of the Kennedy family spent their Christmas vacation at St. Moritz, skiing, sledding, and being photographed by the press. "The photographers were out en masse this morning," Rose wrote her husband at Palm Beach. "You probably will have seen the results by now." Sensitive as only a politician's daughter could be to the essential weirdness of her husband's spending his vacation in Palm Beach while his wife and eight children were in Switzerland, Rose suggested a preemptive remedy to whatever rumors might be set in motion. "Do you suppose you and Jack should have some pictures taken there as I do not think much publicity was given to the fact that you went home to be with Jack."[46]

Kennedy's vacation was interrupted when he was called back to Washington to testify, alongside Ambassador Bullitt, before a closed-door joint session of the House and Senate Committees on Military Affairs. The hearing was carefully staged and the secret testimony skillfully leaked to support the president's call for an unprecedented peacetime allocation of $2 billion for national defense. Both ambassadors, but Kennedy especially, relied on Charles Lindbergh's report to frighten Congress into allocating every dollar the president had requested. The *Los Angeles Times* headlined its page-one story EUROPE WAR NEAR, ENVOYS TELL CONGRESS.[47]

Kennedy had intended to spend a full six weeks in Palm Beach, then head north for two speaking engagements before sailing back to England on February 23. When Neville Chamberlain suggested that it might be better if he returned a bit sooner, the president, on Hull's request, called him in Palm Beach to ask that he cut short his vacation.[48]

He stopped over in Washington for a final meeting with Roosevelt before departing. "He had a bad cold that day and received me in his upstairs study," Kennedy would later write in his *Diplomatic Memoir*. "He had no particular instructions to give me, but once more I told him I did not want to go to London unless I had his confidence." Again, the two men sang their signature duet, with Kennedy complaining and Roosevelt patting him on the back and assuring him that he had had nothing to do with the criticism emanating from the White House. To cement their renewed relationship, they gossiped together about Bernard Baruch, whom neither professed to like or trust.[49]

Following his session with Roosevelt, Kennedy "turned up" at Moffat's office at the State Department for a brief chat. "Personally I think highly of Kennedy's work," Moffat commented in his diary on February 9, "but there is no doubt that the Secretary [Hull] has his fingers crossed. He is willing to admit that Kennedy reflects faithfully what Chamberlain is thinking and doing, but he does not think that Kennedy adequately presents the American point of view to Chamberlain."[50]

Nineteen

SIDELINED AND CENSORED

Kennedy had delayed his return to London as long as he could, not simply because of the strain of the job, but because he was haunted by the sense that something had gone wrong, very wrong. He had been pushed to the sidelines, a place he had never before occupied, not in Boston or Hollywood or New York or Washington. As he resumed his post in London after less than eleven months in service (four of which had been spent on two home leaves and a vacation at Cannes), he did so determined, it appeared, to make a new start, repair the damage done to his reputation, and work his way back into the inner circle of Roosevelt advisers.

Within hours of his arrival, he was on his rounds again, meeting with Prime Minister Chamberlain at 10 Downing, Lord Halifax and Permanent Under-Secretary Cadogan at Whitehall, Home Secretary Samuel Hoare, Chancellor of the Exchequer Sir John Simon, Colonial Secretary MacDonald, other cabinet members at their offices, and fellow ambassadors at their embassies. Every morsel of information he gathered from this moment on—on proposed British loans to the Chinese, trade negotiations with German industrialists, discussions of whether and when to recognize the Franco government, rumors that the Germans were about to invade Albania or the Netherlands, British initiatives to establish closer ties to the Soviet Union and Turkey—was that same day synthesized, digested, coded, and cabled to the State Department.

Try as he might, he could not quite do what was expected of him. He was simply unfitted by temperament for the position of impartial, impassive listener and reporter, especially at moments of crisis. Scarcely a day passed now when there was not some development, some incident or rumor of an incident, that raised or lowered tensions. He was buffeted back and forth, alternately elated and depressed by the news from Germany or Italy or Turkey, Albania, Romania, and Poland, as relayed to him by his British informants. World war was approaching—of that he was sure—and neither he nor his government could do anything to stop it. The Spanish Civil War dragged on; Hungary had fallen under German influence; Germany, having absorbed the Sudetenland, was preparing to annex the rest of Czechoslovakia, Poland, and the Ukraine; Mussolini threatened Tunisia. As if this were not enough to signal the coming apocalypse, in late January the British Foreign Office informed the U.S. State Department of its belief that Hitler was preparing to invade Holland.

On taking up his post again, Kennedy discovered to his dismay that the prime minister was out of touch with developments on the continent. He informed Kennedy at their first meeting, then at dinner three days later, that there was no indication of German "moves toward Holland, Switzerland, or elsewhere to the west or to the Ukraine." The German economy, Chamberlain told Kennedy, was in a shambles, leaving the fuehrer with two choices, war or trade, and he had chosen the latter.[1]

Chamberlain's assessment of Hitler's intentions was so out of line with other intelligence that Sumner Welles felt obligated to diplomatically question the British ambassador about the prime minister's competency. Ambassador Lindsay's reply was that Chamberlain, though a "very logical, and very clear thinker," did not always take "into account the human elements involved and the mercurial factors with which he was dealing." The British ambassador doubted that Chamberlain's optimism about the future was shared by his colleagues in the cabinet. "The Foreign Office," Ambassador Lindsay told Welles, "was exceedingly apprehensive."[2]

In early March 1939, Kennedy sent the president a second doomsday scenario memorandum, more powerful and pessimistic than the one he had delivered in December. His premise, which he believed unassailable, was that Great Britain, whose military power was based on its navy and its economic power on its colonial trade, could not possibly prevail in a war with Germany and Italy in Europe, or with Japan in the East. "Great Britain and France are no longer able to maintain the old world order. They are on the defensive; the totalitarian states are on the offensive with the rise of air power. The preeminence of Great Britain has disappeared, for obviously a country so vulnerable to air attack cannot be the center of a really stable world system." The British were going to lose their empire, he concluded, which would result in a reduction in American exports of "at least 50 percent in volume." To survive in a hostile world with few trading partners, the United States would have no choice but to replace free market capitalism with "a regimented industrial order under Government control. Such centralization would tend to reproduce, possibly under other names, the basic features of the Fascist state: to fight totalitarianism, we would have to adopt totalitarian methods. . . . In short, America, alone in a jealous and hostile world, would find that the effort and cost of maintaining 'splendid isolation' would be such as to bring about the destruction of all those values which the isolation policy has been designed to preserve."[3]

What did Kennedy propose to save the nation from the coming apocalypse? He didn't quite say, though the implication was clear. The only solution was to find some sort of modus vivendi with the dictators before it was too late.

Roosevelt did not respond to Kennedy's memorandum. He had heard it all before, especially the part about the inevitability of the United States having to adopt Fascist methods of centralized economic control. Recognizing nonetheless that Kennedy's estimates of German military strength, though perhaps overstated, might be useful in frightening the public and Congress into supporting rearmament, which he thought of paramount importance, he forwarded the memo to "the chief of Naval Operations," with the warning that it "be kept confidential but may be made available to Operations and the General Board."[4]

On February 10, while Kennedy was still in the United States, Pope Pius XI died in Rome. In a letter to Enrico Galeazzi, sent two weeks afterward from London, Kennedy held out hope that "our friend" Cardinal Eugenio Pacelli, whom Galeazzi worked for and whom Kennedy and his family had entertained during his 1936 visit to America, would be named his successor. When he was, Kennedy lobbied Sumner Welles for permission to represent the president at the coronation. On March 7, he was notified that his request had been granted.[5]

No president had ever before sent an official representative to Rome for a papal coronation. That Roosevelt had been persuaded to do so and had decided to send Kennedy instead of Ambassador William Phillips, who was already in Rome, was a considerable honor. It erased (if only momentarily) earlier presidential snubs and went a long way toward convincing Kennedy that it might still be possible for him to work his way back into the Roosevelt inner circle. Kennedy had earlier that spring forwarded to the president a long memorandum from Cardinal Pacelli, then Vatican secretary of state, explaining the church's attitude toward the *Anschluss*. With Pacelli now pope and Galeazzi one of his chief advisers, Kennedy would become the de facto liaison between the pope and the president, a not insignificant honor for an Irish Catholic kid from East Boston.

Without asking anyone's permission, Kennedy notified the American embassy in Rome that he intended to bring his family with him to the coronation. The Kennedy children had attended Roosevelt's second inaugural, but as grand as that had been, it would pale beside the experience of witnessing a papal coronation. Only Joe Jr., who was in Spain, and feared that he would have trouble getting back into the country if he left it, could not attend.

On Sunday, March 12, the eight Kennedy children were awakened at dawn, scrubbed, brushed, dressed, and packed into limousines for the ride to the Vatican. Kennedy and Rose drove with Count Galeazzi, who would serve as their escort; the children, with the Moores and two governesses, arrived in separate limousines. They were dropped off outside St. Peter's Square and ushered through the crowds to their seats in the outside portico of the Basilica, near the statue of Charlemagne. The original seating plan had made allowance for two Kennedys, the ambassador and his wife, but it had to be altered on the run to make room for twelve more. When Count Ciano, the Italian minister of foreign affairs who was married to Mussolini's daughter, found that his assigned seat in the portico was occupied by a Kennedy child, he protested loudly and, according to the future pope Paul VI, threatened "to leave the Basilica and to desert the ceremony. The situation was immediately resolved," Pope Paul VI later recalled, "but there remained in our memory the procession of the children of Ambassador Kennedy." Kennedy, who "heard that Ciano was mad," concluded that he "was a swell-headed Muggo," which indeed he was.[6]

The next morning, at around eleven A.M., the Kennedy entourage of Moores, governesses, and eight children, supplemented by Arthur Houghton, Franklin Gowen, second secretary at the U.S. embassy in London, and Rose's French maid, arrived for their audience with the pope in his anteroom. Two days later they would return, this time to the pope's private chapel, for Teddy's First Communion.

The ambassador's official business was concluded on Monday evening, March 13, at a dinner given by American ambassador William Phillips. Kennedy, always alert to opportunities to secure information that might be of use to the State Department, tried to engage Count Ciano in conversation but found it impossible as the count had eyes only for the "young attractive Italian girls" whom Phillips had invited to the dinner, "for otherwise he just would not come." With the count occupied, Kennedy chatted with Ciano's wife, Mussolini's daughter. She complained to him that Americans understood neither Italy nor fascism. Kennedy left the dinner disappointed and not a little disgruntled at having wasted his time. "As a result of my observations of Ciano," he wrote Hull, "and the gossip that Mussolini now has a German sweetheart, I came away believing that we would accomplish much more by sending a dozen beautiful chorus girls to Rome than a fleet of airplanes and a flock of diplomats."[7]

At six A.M. on March 15, as Teddy Kennedy was putting on his white suit in preparation for his First Communion, the German army crossed the Czechoslovak border. By nine A.M., German troops occupied Prague. That afternoon, Hitler and his entourage entered the former Czechoslovak capital in a fleet of Mercedes limousines.

Kennedy arrived in Paris two days later, at eight A.M. on March 17. Rose, who had left earlier, was not at the Hôtel Ritz where he had expected her to be, but at Madeleine Church, "praying with her eyes closed." Kennedy took her back to the hotel, then set off for breakfast with Ambassador Bullitt. That afternoon he flew back to London, where after a brief stop at the embassy, he visited with Lord Halifax at Whitehall, saw the Romanian minister, met with Clarence Dillon of Dillon, Read, the New York investment bank, and Roy Howard of the Scripps Howard newspaper chain, and had dinner at the embassy with Frederick Lonsdale, the British playwright. After his three months in the United States and his week in Rome, it was as if he were making up for lost time, devoting his every waking moment to gathering information on the deteriorating situation in Europe. On Tuesday, March 21, at a dinner the king held for the president of France at Buckingham Palace, Kennedy was so frantic for news that he monopolized conversation with Lord Halifax until "Lady Halifax came up to pull [her husband] away saying we had talked together all night." The ambassador sent her flowers the next day to "square" himself.[8]

The jubilation he had experienced in Rome forty-eight hours earlier had given way to despair. Hitler had demonstrated that he was not only untrustworthy, but on the march and unstoppable, his next step most likely Danzig, the "free city" on the Baltic, and the Polish Corridor, the strip of land running through that part of the German empire that had been ceded to Poland by the Treaty of Versailles.

On March 31, Prime Minister Chamberlain, as Kennedy had expected and feared, declared unequivocally in a speech to the House of Commons that "in the event of any action which clearly threatened Polish independence, and which the Polish Government accordingly considered it vital to resist with their national forces, His Majesty's Government would feel themselves bound to lend the Polish Government all support in their power." The French, he added, would respond in the same way.[9]

Kennedy, given advance notice of what Chamberlain was going to announce, called the president the night before the speech. He was told that Roosevelt, who was at Warm Springs, was sleeping. "About one-half hour later the President called me and was very friendly. Said he thought Chamberlain's plan was a good one but thought it probably would mean war. Then he asked me whether I thought now was the time to call a world conference for peace. I said that I did not think so until we had a better idea of how the People of Germany and Italy, in spite of their leaders, took this pronouncement. . . . I told him I would watch public opinion reports from both these countries and keep in touch with him."[10]

Despite the gloom, the disappointments, and the recurrent night-mares of the war that was surely coming, there were moments of joy that spring as Kennedy watched his older children grow into adulthood. When asked why he had accepted the appointment to London, he had never hesitated to answer that he had done it for his children. He wanted his boys in particular to get the kind of hands-on experience that, combined with their Harvard educations, would set them up for careers in politics or government or international business. He had encouraged first Joe Jr., then Jack, to tour the European capitals and had done the advance work necessary to guarantee that they got to meet the "topside" people wherever they traveled. That spring of 1939, Joe Jr. was traveling through war-torn Spain and writing his father long letters about conditions there.

Invited for a weekend at Cliveden in late February, Kennedy read aloud his son's latest letter first at teatime on Lady Astor's bidding, and then again, after supper, to a larger gathering that included the prime minister. "Everyone sits around quietly," Anne Morrow Lindbergh recalled in her diary. When Kennedy had finished reading, he took "off his glasses . . . and suddenly looks like a small boy, pleased and shy. He looks like an Irish terrier wagging his tail (a *very* nice Irish terrier)." Later that spring, Kennedy sent copies of his son's letters "and a clipping from the London *Evening Standard*" about Joe Jr. to Paul Murphy in New York and asked him to forward the material to journalist John Bright Kennedy to deliver to the *Saturday Evening Post* and Hearst's *Cosmopolitan* magazine. Any money earned from publication would, Kennedy instructed Murphy, be given to charity, "as I do not want [Joe Jr.] competing with newspaper men on the strength of being the

Ambassador's son. . . . My interest in the matter is to see young Joe get out on his own with what I consider a very worthwhile contribution in the form of these letters and some other articles [which] will give him international publicity."[11]

Jack, too, was traveling through Europe that spring. On returning from the pope's coronation in March, he had taken up residence in Paris as a sort of high-level embassy intern. From Paris, he moved on to German-occupied Prague, Poland, and the Soviet Union, then back west to Danzig and south to Romania, Turkey, and Palestine. Everywhere he went, he was, as his brother had been, preceded by introductions to the American embassy. George Kennan, who was serving in Prague in 1939, recalled receiving the "telegram from the embassy in London, the sense of which was that our ambassador there, Mr. Joseph Kennedy, had chosen this time to send one of his young sons on a fact-finding tour around Europe. . . . We were furious. . . . His son had no official status and was, in our eyes, obviously an upstart and an ignoramus. . . . That busy people should have their time taken up arranging his tour struck us as outrageous."[12]

Jack Kennedy, Kennan notwithstanding, was no "ignoramus." His letters to his father from Eastern Europe, Turkey, and the Middle East were wise and incisive and capitalized on the history he had read during his many lengthy periods of bed rest and convalescence. Jack had hoped to extend his tour through the summer and would have, had his father not cabled that the "girls would be disappointed" if he was not back in London for Eunice's "coming out" and the debutante parties that would precede it.[13]

The partying was more intense than ever that spring and summer of 1939, perhaps because of relief that war had not come or because of the fear that it was in the offing. Whatever the reason, Joe Jr., Jack, and Kick Kennedy, with no lack of resources, charm, or good looks, made their mark in London society. At the July Fourth party that the Kennedys gave at their residence, Rose sat next to the king's brother the Duke of Kent, who, she reported in her diary, "told me accidently he had seen Kennedys at every table at the 400 Club which is supposed to be rather gay and not a place for Kathleen. Joe reprimanded Kick for being there and a few moments later, the Duke apologized [to Kick] for telling on her."[14]

That August, with the social season at an end, Jack prepared to travel again, this time to Germany with Torbert Macdonald, his friend from Harvard. Just before their departure, the boys were called in to see the ambassador. "I recall very well indeed the Ambassador saying," Macdonald later remembered in an oral history, that "no matter what happened, [they were] not to cause any trouble and to bend over backwards to stay out of trouble. . . . He indicated that the Germans were very tough and paid no attention to laws and rules, and, if anything happened, just to back away."[15]

Kennedy visited often with his eldest daughter, Rosemary, who attended the Convent of the Assumption school in Kensington Square, a training center for Montessori teachers. She had been told that if she did well there, she would graduate in June with a diploma and be prepared to teach young children.

In late February, Rosemary wrote to thank her father "very much for taking me to the concert. It was very nice of you. I have been very busy making an Album for Dr. Montessori when she comes in March. It takes an awful lot of work. And your time. I have been taking elocution lessons up to the 14th of March. Then I will be too busy. So Mother Estelle wants me to stop then. Do they know what exactly what I am going to take? But it is wonderful to get a diploma. Then I will be a school teacher. I got a diploma for being a child of Mary." She wanted her father to be proud of her—and he was, especially as she was losing some weight, which she knew was important to him and to her mother. "This diet of Elizabeth Arden is very good. I have gone down between 5 and 7 pounds already living on salads, egg at night, meat once a day, fish if I want, spinach, soup. Wait to you see me. I will be thin when Jack sees me." The letter was written in the block letters of a six- or seven-year-old, sprawled all over the page, slanting awkwardly, with no margins, no paragraphs, few complete sentences, and lots of misspellings.[16]

The fact that Kennedy was now living in the same city and in the same residence with several of his children and with his wife (when she was not traveling) did not prevent him from entertaining his women friends, among whom he now counted Clare Boothe Luce. She and her husband, Henry, whom both the Kennedys considered family friends, had visited in the spring of 1938. Clare had returned, somewhat mysteriously, in the fall. The only sign of the latter trip was the inclusion of her name in the *Normandie* list of arriving New York passengers on October 10, 1938. That same day, she had cabled a four-word message to Kennedy in London: "Golly that was nice."[17]

She planned to visit again by herself in June, for the London opening of her hit play *The Women*. "You're angel," she cabled Kennedy from New York in April. "Make life so exciting for me. Sailing June first for Paris, then London until June thirtieth. Will you be there. Cable. Yes, do." She signed the cable with "love to Rose." Four days before she sailed, she cabled again, this time without mention of Rose: "Sailing *Normandie* Tuesday. Save me lunch and/or dinner. Chat. Alone. Love, Clare."[18]

Like the Kennedys, the Luces, within a few years of their wedding, had begun to spend more time apart than together. "Their sexual relationship," wrote Henry Luce's biographer Alan Brinkley, "troubled from the beginning, had come to a virtual end in 1939." This made Clare an ideal lover for Kennedy. Because she was a family friend, the two could appear together in public. Because she was virtually separated from her husband, they could also spend time alone as a couple. And perhaps because beginning in late 1942 Henry Luce would embark on his own affairs, he bore Kennedy no ill will for having had one with Clare.[19]

We have no idea whether Rose knew of her husband's affair with Clare. Still, either through coincidence or design, she and Clare traded places that spring. On May 24, Rose sailed west to New York on the *Normandie*. On its return journey, the *Normandie* brought Clare east to Southampton and Le Havre. Her biographer Sylvia Jukes Morris, noted that "Kennedy's name appears more frequently than any other" in Clare's diary during her stay in London. "As well as entertaining her à deux, 'Joe' squired her to the Ascot races and an evening performance of *The Women*."[20]

In April, Kennedy was given a new assignment, though not necessarily one he thought worthy of his talents. Should war break out, it would lead to shortages of the essential raw materials that American manufacturers imported from the British Empire. Hull asked Kennedy to "discuss with the British Government the possibility of arranging at once for an exchange of cotton and wheat for strategic materials, particularly rubber and tin." Kennedy took on the assignment and eventually secured terms even better than those Hull had envisioned possible.[21]

He was pleased with the assignment but wanted to be trusted with something more.

On April 5, he sent off a "Personal and Confidential" letter to Welles, bypassing State Department channels, offering his services as liaison to the pope. Like a chastened, unwanted employee, he reached out to a trusted colleague in the hope that he would vouch for him with the boss. He was languishing on the sidelines at a time in history when his energy and intelligence were becoming more and more valuable—or so he believed. "I had a couple of talks with the Holy Father—one at rather great length, both as to conditions in the United States and conditions in Europe," he informed Welles. "Besides having great prestige in countries like Great Britain and the United States, his influence in Italy is probably stronger than that of any Pope for the last 100 years." The pope was never going to intervene to "stop Mussolini from fighting a war," but his influence, Kennedy believed, "could be utilized for the cause of peace in ways under the surface rather than in a big gesture." Kennedy promised to "keep my contacts close to the Vatican. All with the view of watching the moves very carefully and with the hope that there might possibly be a spot for the President to do the big job—peace for the world."[22]

On April 1, Franco declared victory in the Spanish Civil War. On April 7, the Italians invaded and occupied Albania. On April 14, President Roosevelt wrote open letters to Hitler and Mussolini, asking for assurance that their armed forces would not attack or invade the territory or possessions of thirty-three European and Middle Eastern nations, which he identified by name. The president pledged, in return, to seek similar assurances from these nations and to call an international conference on limiting armaments and increasing world trade.[23]

Mussolini and Hitler dismissed the president and his message with contempt.

Kennedy, who had been invited to give a major address in Edinburgh the week after Roosevelt's telegram was released, planned to focus attention on the president's initiative and its significance. He was told instead to excise all reference to foreign affairs, which he did. "On my way to Edinburgh," he cabled Roosevelt and Hull the night before, "with speech all international affairs omitted, talking about flowers, birds and trees. The only thing I am afraid of is that instead of giving me the freedom of the city [a special municipal honor] they will make me queen of the May."[24]

On returning from Edinburgh, Kennedy placed a call to Washington to thank Secretary of State Hull for defending him against former Wisconsin governor Philip La Follette, who had called for his removal. After they had exchanged remarks about La Follette's bad behavior, Hull asked Kennedy in a rather perfunctory way, "How are things looking to you?" Kennedy responded with a lecture on the present economic situation. Hitler had run out of gold and foreign currency and would soon find it impossible to purchase the raw materials he needed to keep the German economy afloat. The only way to remedy this was to resume his path of territorial aggrandizement. It would be difficult, if not impossible, to appease him. "The price that you better get ready to pay him," he warned the secretary of state, "is something beyond anybody's imagination. . . . It isn't merely a question of giving him colonies and it isn't a question of sending over the leaders of British industry to effect trade. . . . What has to be done for him is beyond anyone's conception yet. He has no money and he can't change all those people who are engaged in war-time activities into peace-time activities without having a terrific problem."[25]

Kennedy was in effect laying the groundwork for a new appeasement strategy, one that would buy Hitler off by providing him with the means to convert his war economy to a peace economy. He was proceeding entirely on his own on this. His former allies in appeasement, Neville Chamberlain and Lord Halifax, had long since come to the conclusion that appeasement could not work because Hitler could not be trusted to fulfill any agreement he signed. Kennedy disagreed. He could not imagine that Hitler was so out of touch with reality that he would turn down a deal that would rescue his nation from its economic problems.

Kennedy's plan was to offer Hitler a comprehensive economic package that would enable Germany to trade on favorable terms for the raw materials it required, thereby removing the need for future aggression. Though there was abundant evidence now that Hitler was not a rational actor, that he was motivated by concerns other than the purely economic, that he had decided that the best way to solve Germany's trade problems was by territorial aggrandizement, Kennedy continued to regard him as if he were a rival business leader with whom it was possible to negotiate one's differences. He continued to hold tight to the idea that Hitler's absorption of first Austria, then the Sudetenland, and now what remained of Czechoslovakia had been prompted by economic problems and that Hitler would cease and desist from future aggression if and when the German economy was sound, foreign currency and gold reserves sufficient, and trade robust.

Kennedy was not alone in believing it might still be possible to make a deal with the fuehrer. On April 25, James Mooney, the president of General Motors Overseas and a businessman so well respected that Roosevelt would later employ him as an unofficial envoy to Germany, paid Kennedy a "courtesy call." He had met in Berlin on General Motors business with Dr. Emil Puhl, a Reichsbank director, and Dr. Helmuth Wohlthat, Hermann Goering's chief economic adviser. Mooney told Kennedy that he had inquired of Puhl and Wohlthat if, in return for "some sort of gold loan," the Reich would reverse the discriminatory practices that had led Great Britain and the United States to cease trading with it. "To my shock and surprise," Mooney reported to Kennedy, "they both answered immediately, 'Hell, yes, we'd give it all up if we thought there was the slightest chance of our negotiating a gold loan and come back into normal trading arrangements.'" On hearing this, Kennedy "suggested that he might be able to go over to Paris, ostensibly for a week-end visit," and meet secretly with the Germans to "discuss the subject."[26]

Here was Kennedy's chance to get back into the diplomatic game, doing what he did best, negotiating businessman to businessman with an

English-speaking German banker. Territorial appeasement had failed, but economic appeasement might yield results. American and British politicians and government officials might be unwilling even to contemplate entering such negotiations, but Kennedy was willing to give it a try. Still, he recognized from the onset that there would be serious risks involved in his initiating talks with German officials. The backlash—against him, the State Department, and the president—would be devastating should his private meeting become public knowledge.

Alert by now to the dangers of getting caught again violating State Department regulations, Kennedy cabled a "Strictly Confidential" dispatch to Sumner Welles: "I had a call this morning from Berlin from Mooney who is in charge of General Motors Export business and head of the German plant. He invited me to dine with him in Paris Saturday night. Another party at the dinner will be a personal friend of Hitler and high in influence in the Reichsbank. . . . This man is in the inner circle, from what Mooney said. . . . Is there any particular information regarding financial and political matters which you would like me to try to obtain?"[27]

Welles's reply was immediate and to the point: "I have talked over your message with the Secretary and we both feel very strongly that at this particular time it would be almost impossible to prevent your trip to Paris and the names of the persons you will see in Paris from being given a great deal of publicity. If an erroneous impression in the press here were given [regarding] your conference with this individual from Germany it would inevitably create speculation and unfortunate comment. . . . I hope very much for the reasons above expressed that you will not undertake this trip at this moment."[28]

When Mooney insisted it would be "unpardonable" to cancel the meeting he had set up with the German officials, Kennedy promised to contact the president and ask him for permission.

The next morning, Mooney phoned Kennedy from Paris and "found a gloomy Ambassador awaiting me. He had been up half the night, he said, getting the telephone call through to the White House, only to be refused permission for a second time." Disappointed, but undaunted and incapable of letting go of his grand opportunity, Kennedy suggested that the meeting with Dr. Wohlthat be moved from Paris to London. Welles and Hull had asked him not to fly to Paris to have dinner with an unnamed German, but they had said nothing about a meeting in London. Wohlthat agreed to move the meeting and arrived in London on Monday, May 8. The following morning, he and Kennedy met at eleven A.M. at Wohlthat's rooms at the Berkeley Hotel. Two days later, the *Daily Mail* reported on the front page: GOERING'S MYSTERY MAN IS HERE. Fortunately for Kennedy, the State Department, and the president, there was no mention of the reason for his visit.[29]

Nothing came of Kennedy's discussions with Wohlthat except an acquaintance that would be renewed after the war. Had Mooney not written about their meeting in his unpublished memoir, it would have remained a secret forever. What it reveals, in retrospect, is the degree of desperation that Kennedy felt that spring of 1939. Roosevelt's open letter to the dictators had been greeted with scorn and ridicule. Chamberlain had turned overnight from a potential peacemaker into a wreck of a man who was fighting for his political life. Kennedy had no sympathy for Hitler or the Nazis, nor was he inclined in any way to aid and abet their ambitions for territorial acquisition, but despite his instructions from Washington, he refused to sit on his hands as war approached. He set up the meeting with Wohlthat for one reason only, to try to find a way to restart negotiations with the Germans and succeed where others had failed, in turning Hitler away from future aggression.

In early 1939, the Chamberlain government convened an international conference in London on the future of Palestine. Representatives of the Palestinian Arabs, neighboring Arab countries, the Jewish Agency for Palestine, and leading Zionist organizations were invited to participate in formulating a plan for partition, which when arrived at would be presented to the British Parliament. There was not the slightest hope that anything would emerge from the deliberations. As the *New York Times* correspondent in London explained to his readers in the United States, with the Zionist and Arab positions "diametrically opposed . . . most observers seem to agree that the result will probably be a stalemate, after which the British Government will announce its own policy for Palestine."[30]

On February 27, while the conference was still in session, Kennedy cabled Hull that he had met with Lord Halifax at Whitehall "about the

Jewish question." Halifax had informed Kennedy that the British cabinet "had not arrived yet at a definite plan but it looked as though" it was going to give up its "present mandate" in Palestine and replace it with "a Palestinian state with the Jews a minority, with immigration allocated for the next 5 years to between 100,000 and 150,000 with 10,000 children additional every two years. He was a little hazy on the figures, but said this approximated it. . . . He just wanted to give me a bare outline and you can see this is because they are still talking it over. They are really sparring for time, and, I should judge, giving the Arabs the better of it." The ambassador closed his cable by reporting that he had asked Dr. Stephen Wise to "come in tomorrow to see if I can get any definite reactions or thoughts and will send them to you. Is there any angle on this that you want covered or have any suggestions for me to make to Halifax?"[31]

Hull's response was cold and blunt. He did not have "any suggestions which you might make to Halifax on the Palestine question." His concern was not with the substance of the British plan, but on insulating himself and the president from the protests that were sure to follow. "I may say in strict confidence that I feel we should be cautious about being drawn by the British into any of their preliminary proposals in advance of any final plan which they may decide upon for a solution of the Palestine problem. If any suggestions in that sense are made to you I am confident you will bear the above observation in mind and keep us promptly advised."[32]

Kennedy heeded Hull's warning and kept quiet. He broke ranks only once, when, having heard that the American Zionists were considering withdrawing from the conference, he "vigorously advised them not to . . . and thus avoid being blamed for the failure."[33]

The conference broke up on March 17 with the rejection by both the Arab and the Zionist delegations of the proposals the British had put forward. The Chamberlain cabinet, having made its show of involving Palestinians, Arabs, and Zionists in their deliberations, was now free to submit to Parliament the plan for restricting Jewish immigration that Halifax had earlier outlined to Kennedy. The same day the conference broke up, the British counselor in Washington delivered to the State Department a copy of the plan Chamberlain was going to lay before Parliament. Roosevelt and Hull received the plan without comment, lest they be drawn into negotiations and the United States become a partner to British policy. They asked only that Kennedy petition the British to delay any announcement. Kennedy requested such a postponement, which was agreed to with the proviso that it would be a temporary one.[34]

The British had decided to close down immigration to Palestine at a moment in time when the need for safe havens was greater than ever. More and more Jews were ready now to flee Germany, but there was no place for them to go and no guarantee that they would be able to take with them even a portion of their assets.

"The letters of inquiry that we are getting about the refugees would break your heart," Eddie Moore wrote John Burns in mid-February, "and the sad part of it is that little can be done on any of the cases." For Kennedy and Moore, who prided themselves on their ability to cut through red tape and get things done, the situation was intolerable. As the requests mounted in number, Moore lashed out at his and Kennedy's friend Arthur Goldsmith for offering refugees false hope that letters of introduction to the embassy would get them visas. "I am not going to let you or anybody else put me in a box. Neither am I going to allow anybody in distress to leave my office feeling that I haven't been of every assistance to them, so please don't tell any more people what you told Mrs. Egger [an American woman who had come to London to get visas for her parents] or write letters for them to me such as the one that you gave her."[35]

Goldsmith wrote back to explain, not to apologize. He did not know Mrs. Egger. It was her husband who had come "to see me, and as a matter of pure humanitarianism, the same emotion which always animates you, I took the one desperate chance that you might be able to be of some help to her as she was already set on going to Europe. . . . If Mrs. Egger appeared over-distressed or irritating, I can only say that in this horrible situation in which everybody in the world—particularly Jews—finds himself, this is understandable and I know you understand it. . . . At this particular writing, in this country, we are so low in spirit that we would have to mount a stepladder to kick a snake in the belly. How are you and your dear, sweet wife?"[36]

There were very few secrets in London that spring, least of all that the White Paper on Palestine, soon to be released, would recommend the restriction of Jewish immigration to Palestine. The only remaining hope for the Zionist leaders was that American government officials might intervene with British officials before the new policy was set in stone. On April 30, Moshe Sharett, in effect the Zionist movement's and Jewish Agency's ambassador to Great Britain, was delegated by the leadership to "go to Kennedy." In his diary entry, he "questioned whether it was worthwhile—I have no faith in Kennedy's good will. Besides, he won't do anything without instructions from Washington. My seeing him won't give him those instructions. Besides, today is Sunday and Kennedy is an observant Catholic. The embassy's office is closed. It is unlikely Kennedy is home on Sunday and it would be unpleasant to disturb him at his private apartment."[37]

Sharett waited until Monday morning, then "asked for a meeting with Kennedy and was invited for 4:30 P.M. . . . The doorman knew of my coming and took me upstairs. Since the ambassador hadn't come as yet, he took me into the waiting room. After a few minutes a butler came and took me to a waiting room closer to the ambassador's office. He asked me to be seated. Kennedy came in, greeted me but instead of ushering me into his office led me back to the outside waiting room, gave me a seat, sat down himself and asked me to begin. I was surprised at this procedure, but at the conclusion of our conversation I understood the secret." Sharett told the ambassador that he knew about his earlier talks with "our American friends" and with Weizmann, and that the Zionist leadership valued "his interest" in their cause. Sharett understood that the "ambassador of a government [Kennedy] receives his instructions from it" and was not a free agent. Still, he had "to inform him that we have come to the final hour. . . . If there is the inner strength to act, this is the moment. It will be tragic, a thousand times over if this moment is passed over." Kennedy, Sharett wrote, heard him out "without moving a muscle in his face. When I finished he said: 'You undoubtedly know . . . that we are doing all we can.'" Sharett emphasized again "the urgency" of acting now to prevent the British from closing off Palestine. Kennedy repeated, "We are doing all we can." He then rose, shook Sharett's hand, and "turned to return to his office. I could not but think: had he received me in his office he would not have been able to end the conversation so abruptly when it was convenient for him."[38]

Kennedy, for his part, had cut short his meeting with Sharett because he had nothing to say that Sharett wanted to hear and saw no reason to prolong the discomfort. The British had made their decisions on Palestine and were not going to budge. And Roosevelt, Kennedy knew, had no intention of interfering.

Eight days later, on May 9, Kennedy informed the State Department that the White Paper on Palestine was going to be presented to Parliament the following Monday. "The Jews will not be pleased with it, but the Government feels that it cannot delay the matter any longer and that it has made the only fair decision." Roosevelt asked Kennedy to seek another postponement. "Any announcement about Palestine at this time by the British Government," the president wrote Welles, "is a mistake, and I think we should tell them that. What can I say to Justice Brandeis?" The British agreed to delay the release of the White Paper, but only from Monday to Wednesday.[39]

In Washington, Justice Louis Brandeis, Felix Frankfurter, Ben Cohen, Rabbi Stephen Wise, Senator Robert Wagner, and William Green of the AFL-CIO converged on the White House to plead with Roosevelt to intervene with the British. The president assured them that he had instructed Kennedy to keep in touch with Chamberlain. The impression conveyed to the Zionist leaders in Washington, a Mapai (the most powerful political party in pre-state Israel) report concluded in June, was that "FDR cables the U.S. ambassador in England every day and demands that he be especially attentive to the Zionist stance." That was not the case, however. The president did not ask Kennedy to do anything other than ask for a delay in the release of the White Paper. By intimating to the Zionist leaders that he had instructed Kennedy to do otherwise, Roosevelt made it appear as if Kennedy were at fault for not doing more to stop the British from restricting immigration to Palestine.[40]

Kennedy, of course, had laid himself open to scapegoating by making it brutally clear to Zionist emissaries such as Sharett that there was nothing he could do to alter British policy on Palestine. Because he had, the previous November, confided to Weizmann that the "Jewish question" was one of his top priorities, the Zionists in London and Washington now regarded him as "two-faced." What they did not understand, the Mapai report later concluded, was that what Kennedy meant by the "Jewish question" was entirely different from what the Zionists meant. "When a Zionist official meets a government figure and hears 'the Jewish question' he assumes Eretz Israel [Palestine]. But this doesn't have to be the case. His interlocutor may have in mind solving the Jewish question in Guiana." This was certainly Kennedy's position. Knowing that the British would never open Palestine to substantial immigration, he had sought other outlets for the resettlement of German Jewish refugees. For him, and for Roosevelt, the questions of Jewish rescue and Palestine immigration were separate ones.[41]

Kennedy was caught unawares by what he perceived as the turn against him. He had been a friend of the Jews in London, had done what he could to find safe havens for them somewhere in the British Empire, had, in fact, been so outspoken on the issue that the State Department had warned him to cease and desist. And now, suddenly, he was accounted as the enemy, though the decision not to pressure the British to open immigration to Palestine had been made by Roosevelt and Hull, not by him. His problem was that, instead of dissimulating, as Roosevelt had, he had made it clear that, as far as the American government was concerned, Palestine was a British issue. Unlike Roosevelt, he had not expressed his sympathy with or commitment to the Zionist project of resettling German Jews in Palestine. On the contrary, he considered the issue closed and settled. His remarks on the hopelessness of the Zionist cause, had, in fact, so distressed Harold Laski that he got in touch with Louis Brandeis, who directed him to "convey some of the information about Kennedy to the 'skipper' [Roosevelt]."[42]

Kennedy continued to speak his mind, seemingly unaware of the consequences. In conversation with Colonial Secretary Malcolm Mac-Donald, he had remarked that while American Jews would be outraged at the new plan for Palestine, their protest would never be loud enough to get Roosevelt to intercede. And this was true. When word of what he had said was cabled to the Zionist leaders in the United States, as he had to have known it would, all hell broke lose. Ben Cohen, fearing that Kennedy was being set up as a scapegoat, cabled to warn him. Kennedy replied that he was shocked that "American Zionists are repeating these unfair stories. It is rather a peculiar slant for the Zionists to take at this late day after my work for their cause. However I am getting used to this type of experience."[43]

Solomon Goldman, the president of the Zionist Organization of America, cabled his apology from Washington the next day: "Feel it duty say American Zionists have always regarded you devoted friend. Recall with appreciation warm reception accorded me during visit London. Rumors between continents unavoidable but be assured we feel indebted for earnestness with which you have furthered interests American Jews and cause of people whose fate must be of deepest concern to you."[44]

Thanking Goldman for his note, Kennedy could still not resist complaining about his unjust treatment. "I can't tell you how pleased I was to receive your cable. I was really frightfully upset by the one I got from Ben, because, while realizing he sent it in the most friendly spirit, it seemed to me that it was another of those unfortunate things that happened to me no matter how much work I did on the Jewish problem. . . . Therefore your wire was a very pleasant relief. If you see Ben tell him I quite understand the reason for his sending it and that I am appreciative of his interest, but that I was very much upset to think that was the result of all my efforts."[45]

The British White Paper on Palestine was published on May 17 and was even worse than the pessimists among the Zionist leadership had anticipated. The British announced that they intended to establish an independent Palestine within ten years with a majority of Arabs. To safeguard against further violence and to preserve the present Arab majority, they were restricting Jewish immigration for the next five years to ten thousand a year, plus, "as a contribution towards the solution of the Jewish refugee problem," an additional twenty-five thousand, "special consideration being given to refugee children and dependents."[46]

WASHINGTON SILENT ON THE WHITE PAPER, read the *New York Times* front-page story on May 18. Roosevelt had nothing to say, and neither did the State Department, which claimed it had not received the full White Paper text. Over the next few days, when that excuse was no longer possible, Hull declined to comment on the White Paper, claiming that decisions on Palestine were Britain's to make. Roosevelt held his silence.

From Paris, Chaim Weizmann wrote Solomon Goldman on May 30 to find out what precisely was going on in Washington. He had learned from the head of the League of Nations Mandates Commission that the Americans, instead of protesting the British action on Palestine, were " 'behaving very nicely to them.' The British have been saying that all along and were somewhat amused at our reliance on America. . . . Again I feel a great deal will turn on the attitude of the President. But what the real attitude of your Government is—that is a point which needs elucidation. I shall try to see Bullitt here and perhaps he would explain something; I have not much faith in Kennedy."[47]

Goldman responded to Weizmann that he and his Zionist colleagues in the United States had "every reason to believe that the President has the finest understanding of, and the deepest sympathy with, our movement." Roosevelt had, in fact, been in conversations with Louis Brandeis on a new plan for Palestine. "He stated in so many words . . . that two to three hundred thousand Arabs can and must be moved from Palestine to Iraq. He estimated that we should need a sum of $300,000,000 to achieve such a wholesale transfer of Arabs. He thought that the Jews might be in a position to raise $100,000,000, that the British and French might extend a loan of $100,000,000, and that the United States an equal sum. He seemed to indicate that as soon as he was somewhat relieved from the pressure of other affairs, he might try to tackle the job. . . . I understand that on two occasions he used the trans-Atlantic telephone and spoke directly to Chamberlain."

Though Goldman reported enthusiastically on this "Iraq plan," he and Brandeis had to have recognized how difficult, if not impossible, it would be to implement. Given the economic and political realities of 1939, it was the height of folly to believe that the British, the French, or the Americans would extend $100 million loans with no possible hope of repayment to resettle Arabs in Iraq. And even should the money be raised, how was Roosevelt or anyone else going to determine which Arabs had "entered Palestine since 1917" and should be resettled? And

Left: Mrs. Patrick J. Kennedy in a formal posed studio photograph, probably just after her marriage to Patrick Joseph Kennedy in November 1887. The former Mary Augusta Hickey was the daughter of a well-to-do Irish-born contractor from a quite distinguished old East Boston family.

Right: Patrick Joseph Kennedy from the 1890s during his heyday as ward leader and East Boston businessman. P.J. was a rarity among Boston's Democratic leaders, a quiet man who did not enjoy making speeches, a politician known and respected not only for his ability to manage his ward and get out the vote but also for his integrity.

Spring, 1908: A photograph from the *Boston Daily Globe* of the starting first baseman on the Boston Interscholastic Nine. Joe Kennedy made his mark at Boston Latin, one of the finest public high schools in the nation as an athlete, not a scholar. He managed the football team in the fall, played basketball in the winter, and was captain of the tennis team and an all-star first baseman.

Kennedy had hoped to get a job with a major Boston bank on graduation from Harvard but had to settle instead for a civil service position as an assistant bank examiner. In January 1914, he resigned his position, and after helping to rescue the East Boston bank his father had founded from a hostile takeover, he was named its president. According to the Boston newspapers, he was at age twenty-five the youngest bank president in the nation.

1918: Fore River shipyard, Kennedy with J. W. Powell (far left), general manager of the shipyard, and Charles M. Schwab (center), chairman of the board of Bethlehem Steel. Though Kennedy knew nothing about shipbuilding, he accepted the position as assistant general manager at Fore River because he had gone as far as he could as president of a tiny East Boston bank and needed a job that would carry with it a draft exemption.

October 1914: The wedding photo of Joseph P. Kennedy and Rose Elizabeth Fitzgerald, the mayor's daughter, as published in the *Boston Daily Globe*. The marriage of the children of two of Boston's leading Irish Catholic politicians was performed by Cardinal William O'Connell in his private chapel.

Beside his 1919 Ford Model T, of which he was quite proud, with two-year-old Jack and four-year-old Joe Jr. In June 1919, Kennedy resigned his position at Fore River to take a job as manager of the brokerage business at the Hayden, Stone office in Boston. His next car would be a Rolls-Royce.

In 1920, the Kennedy family moved into a larger house in a wealthier section of Brookline. He is pictured here, in 1924, with his three girls, from left to right, Eunice, three, Rosemary, six, and Kick, four, probably on their way to church.

Another photograph from 1924 taken on the front steps of the Kennedy home in Brookline. Grandfather P. J. Kennedy is pictured here with Joe Jr., looking quite unhappy, and his three sisters, Rosemary, on the step below her brother, Eunice, on the top step, and Kick, only partially visible to the far left. Jack was not in the photograph, probably because he was ill in bed, as he was so much during his childhood.

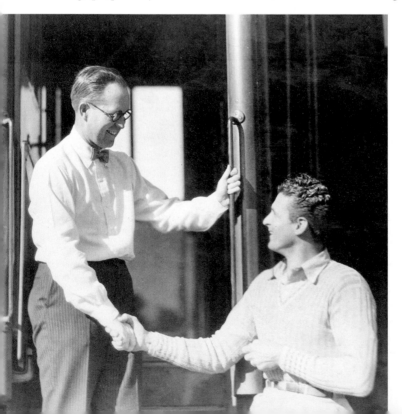

Beginning in the spring of 1926, Kennedy, now in the moving picture business, made frequent train trips back and forth to Hollywood. The first leg of the journey from Los Angeles took about sixty hours, three nights and two days. Passengers changed trains in Chicago, then spent another day on the train bound for New York City. In this photo, Kennedy is shaking hands with Fred Thomson, the cowboy movie star, whom he had signed to a personal services contract.

When Kennedy met Gloria Swanson, whose career he managed and with whom he would have an affair, she was married to her third husband, Henri, Marquis de la Falaise de la Coudraye. Swanson and the marquis are photographed here, looking rather somber, on the deck of one of the luxury liners on which they sailed back and forth to Europe.

Gloria Swanson, with Edmund Goulding, who wrote and directed her first talking picture, *The Trespasser*. Though Kennedy had had little to do with the writing or filming of the picture, he produced it and proudly introduced Gloria at the premieres in London and New York in the late summer and fall of 1929.

September 23, 1932: Kennedy is standing a bit right of center in the first row as the Roosevelt campaign train stops somewhere near the Oregon-California border. On the train platform is Franklin Delano Roosevelt. His son James is to his far right. Kennedy was delighted to be one of the few campaign officials invited to ride on the train with the candidate. And Roosevelt was delighted to have onboard the wealthy Irish Catholic businessman with connections to Hollywood, to Wall Street, and to William Randolph Hearst, the nation's most influential publisher.

July 19, 1934: Kennedy expected to be rewarded for his service during the campaign with a cabinet position and was infuriated when he was not invited to join the new administration. More than a year and a half after the election, Roosevelt, to the surprise and dismay of almost every member of his inner circle, appointed the ex–Wall Street operator as first chairman of the Securities and Exchange Commission. Here Kennedy poses for a press photograph with his fellow commissioners, Ferdinand Pecora and George Mathews on the left and James Landis and Robert Healy on the right. Pecora had served as chief counsel to the Senate Committee on Banking and Currency during its investigation of Wall Street in 1933 and 1934. Landis, a former Harvard Law School professor, had helped draft the 1933 securities legislation. He would serve as Kennedy's chief adviser on the commission and remain a family friend and adviser for the rest of his life.

February 18, 1938: Having done yeoman work for the president at the SEC, contributed to his 1936 reelection effort, then served as first chairman of the Maritime Commission, Kennedy was rewarded with appointment as the first Irish Catholic ambassador to the Court of St. James's. Here he is being sworn in by Supreme Court justice Stanley Reed, while the president looks on rather amused.

On arriving in Washington, Kennedy made a name for himself as an administration insider. He is seen here talking to Postmaster James Farley with Secretary of Treasury Henry Morgenthau listening in.

June 2, 1938: Kennedy and his oldest daughter, Rosemary, on one of their outings in London. Kennedy, who had, for the most part, lived apart from his children during his years in the picture business and then in Washington, very much enjoyed being in the same city and under the same roof with them in London. Rosemary, who had always had trouble in school, did so well in London that when the rest of the family left for America after Britain declared war on Germany, she remained behind with her father.

Kennedy, Joe Jr., and Teddy, just visible at the far left of the table, dining at the American ambassador's residence in London, probably in early September 1938, while the rest of the family was still on vacation at their villa in the south of France. Teddy had been sent back to London with his father because he was suffering from tonsillitis.

Kennedy was a forceful, persistent, and loyal advocate of Prime Minister Neville Chamberlain and his policy of appeasing the dictators rather than pushing them into a war Chamberlain and Kennedy were convinced Great Britain was not prepared to fight and could not win. Here we see Chamberlain returning, triumphant, from Munich after negotiating an agreement with Hitler, which gave Germany a large portion of Czechoslovakia, but, according to Chamberlain, preserved "peace in our time."

March 1939: Kennedy, Rose, and eight of their children (Joe Jr. was traveling in Spain) on their way to a private audience with Pope Pius XII. President Roosevelt had honored Kennedy by asking him to be his representative at the papal coronation.

The family on vacation in the south of France in the summer of 1939. They lived in a nearby villa but rented a beach cabana at the Hôtel Cap d'Antibes, where this photo was taken. Bobby and Jean are in the front row; Jack, Eunice, Kennedy, and Pat in the middle; Kick, Joe Jr., Rosemary, Rose, and Teddy in the rear.

May 4, 1939: Rose and Kennedy with Queen Elizabeth and King George VI at a dinner at the American embassy, held two days before the king and queen sailed to Canada and the United States on state visits. The official photos, released to the press, show all four staring straight ahead. This is a rare picture of a smiling king and queen.

On learning in late August 1939 that Germany and the Soviet Union had signed a nonaggression pact, Kennedy flew back from the south of France to London for consultations with British government leaders. He is pictured here with Lord Halifax, the foreign secretary, after a meeting at Whitehall. Within the week, Germany would invade Poland, and Great Britain and France would declare war on Germany.

December 11, 1939: Kennedy, on home leave from London, visited Boston for a checkup at the Lahey clinic and an informal reception at his old East Boston church. He also visited with his three oldest boys, Joe Jr. at Harvard Law, Jack at Harvard College, and Bobby, who was at Portsmouth Priory in Rhode Island. Note how immaculately dressed Joe Jr., the future politician, is compared to his younger, more carefree brother Jack, in his ill-fitting sports jacket and dark shoes with white socks.

Kennedy remained in London as ambassador through the early stages of the blitz, thoroughly discredited as an appeaser and an opponent of American aid to the British war effort. Roosevelt should have recalled him, but was afraid of angering a still influential Irish Catholic whose support he needed in his campaign for a third term. In October 1940, Kennedy returned to Washington, where to the surprise of many, he endorsed Roosevelt for reelection. He is pictured here two months after the election delivering a radio address on lend-lease, the administration's plan to assist the British war effort, in which he confused and angered both sides of the debate by refusing to take an unequivocal stand for or against the legislation.

April 1946: One of the rare photos of Kennedy with his son Jack during Jack's first campaign for Congress. Once his son decided to run for office, Kennedy retreated from public view, fearful that his decidedly unpopular views might damage Jack's chances for election. This photo was originally taken for a *Look* magazine feature. Kennedy might have felt obliged to be in it rather than leave the spotlight to his father-in-law, Honey Fitz (at left), the former mayor. As was so often the case, Honey Fitz, is saying something that Jack finds amusing but his father does not.

1948: On the porch of the Hyannis Port house with Eunice and Bobby in either the late summer or early fall of 1948. Bobby, age twenty-three, would that September begin law school at the University of Virginia; Eunice, twenty-seven, was working for the government in Washington

Christmas, 1947: The family gathers for Christmas in Palm Beach. There are two Kennedy children missing: Rosemary, who never returned home after her unsuccessful lobotomy in 1941, and Joe Jr., who, less than three years later, in 1944, was killed when his navy bomber crashed and burned. Kick, to the far left, is leaning into the frame of the photo over Jack. This would be her last Christmas. She would die in a plane crash the following spring.

September 12, 1953: Kissing the bride, with a smiling groom looking on. Kennedy was fond of all his children's spouses, but if he had a favorite, it might very well have been Jacqueline Bouvier Kennedy, who adored him as well.

With granddaughter Caroline on November 18, 1960, ten days after her father had been elected president. Kennedy enjoyed nothing more than riding early in the morning with his children when they were young, then with his grandchildren.

When the children were young, Jean overheard a conversation in which her father was referred to as a "bear" because he believed stock prices would fall. From that moment on, "beware of bear" became a family joke among the Kennedys. This photo is probably from 1958, around the time of Kennedy's seventieth birthday.

January 21, 1961: The president and his father on the reviewing stand during the inaugural parade.

Kennedy suffered a debilitating, near fatal stroke in December 1961. For the first time in more than four decades, he and Rose would spend more time together than apart.

September 7, 1963: An early celebration of Kennedy's seventy-fifth birthday in Hyannis Port. Jacqueline Kennedy sits next to Kennedy. Standing, from left to right, are Sargent Shriver, Stephen Smith, Ethel Kennedy, John Kennedy, Jean Kennedy Smith, Rose Kennedy, Robert Kennedy, Eunice Kennedy Shriver, Pat Kennedy, Ted Kennedy, and Joan Kennedy.

August 1963: The president and his father at Hyannis Port. No matter how busy the president and the attorney general might be, they found time to fly from Washington to Hyannis Port or Palm Beach to spend time with their father. President Kennedy would be assassinated in November.

what were the chances that the British or the local Arab leaders would allow such a transfer to proceed?

Still, the mere mention of an unworkable plan with no timetable for execution and only the vaguest commitment from the president that he "might tackle the job" when he was "relieved from the pressure of other affairs" was, for Goldman, "evidence of his interest in Zionism." Even Hull, who had done everything he could to absent himself and his government from intervening on Palestine, was still regarded by Goldman as "unquestionably a friend of ours." Goldman admitted that there were working for Hull in the State Department a number of "secretaries and under-secretaries and under-under-secretaries [who] have not escaped the virus anti-Semiticus." He did not place the American ambassador in this category, though he reported to Weizmann that "Kennedy has given us much concern."[48]

On May 8, the London newspapers reported that Kennedy "had fallen out of favor with President Roosevelt" and was going to be replaced by Myron Taylor, former president of U.S. Steel and currently the American representative to the Intergovernmental Committee on Refugees. On July 12, Drew Pearson and Robert Allen stated that Kennedy's replacement would be either Joe Davies, the current ambassador to Belgium, or Harry Woodring, the secretary of war.[49]

British journalist Claud Cockburn, in his antiappeasement newsletter, *The Week,* claimed, on the contrary, that though Kennedy should have been fired for being a Cliveden set sycophant, Roosevelt had decided for mysterious reasons to keep him on. Roosevelt, Cockburn wrote, had given his ambassador "a very severe dressing down" in December. Since then, Kennedy's "activities [had] become more remarkable than ever. He has for instance gone to the length of informing members of the British Government that they 'need not worry' about anything that Mr. Roosevelt may say, for the reason that (1) 'It will be my friends that are in the White House in 1940.' (2) 'Roosevelt is run by the Jews and all the anti-fascist sentiment in the United States is really created by the Jews, who control the press.'"[50]

Harold Ickes gave Cockburn's article to the president. The *New Republic,* in an editorial titled "Whose Ambassador Is Mr. Kennedy?," repeated his accusations verbatim, then concluded that although "we do not know whether these charges are true," if they were "even 10 percent true, Mr. Kennedy should come home."[51]

There was nothing Kennedy could do to rebut the rumors. Issuing formal denials would only have kept them current. When Boake Carter asked if he knew the basis for the reports that he was going to be recalled, he replied that he did not. Still, he could not deny that resignation had not crossed his mind. "Confidentially, I had hoped to get back after the end of July and possibly spend some part of a vacation at Cape Cod. Look over the situation and find out whether, from the point of view of the United States, I could safely discuss with the President my resignation. This, of course, pre-supposes a quiet condition here and a belief that Hitler would consider attending a round table conference. If this is not possible, of course, I see no prospect of returning to private life, because I would never forgive myself if I got out and something happened that would seemingly require my presence in London. While the situation does not seem acute, there is enough unrest and uncertainty at the moment to indicate that my job is still here."[52]

The Germans were poised to move on Danzig; the Japanese had blockaded Tientsin, a British protectorate in China. The Chamberlain government was checkmated on two continents. As Kennedy told Walter Lippmann, who met with him during his trip to London in June, Hitler had "every reason to go to war and is able to win. The British fleet is valueless. The German submarines can cut off shipping in the Atlantic. Franco is surrounded . . . Poland has no munitions. Russia is useless. Rumania can't fight. And the Japanese will attack in the East. . . . All Englishmen . . . in their hearts *know* this to be true, but a small group of brilliant people has created a public feeling which makes it impossible for the government to take a sensible course."[53]

In late July, before leaving London for his summer holiday, the ambassador called on Chamberlain and Halifax. The prime minister, Kennedy cabled Hull, was "fairly optimistic about the outlook for the next 30 days." Halifax was not. "He said he had no definite information, but in the next breath asked me how long it would take me to get back. I told him about 5 hours and he said he would keep my office informed and would call on me to come back if he saw the situation tightening."[54]

Since he had arrived in London, Kennedy's fears had multiplied one on another. "I am leaving tomorrow for a holiday," he wrote Roosevelt on July 20, "and before I go, I would like to write you about what I regard as the makings of the worst economic conditions the world has ever seen. As you know, I have been constantly bearish for the last two or three years and I see nothing tonight that makes me change my opinion, but, on the contrary, I feel more pessimistic than ever." Even should war be averted, the economic crisis in Europe would continue to worsen, prolonging the depression in America. Agricultural prices were falling, the precursor to general depression, the European nations remained deeply in debt, their economies steadily weakening, "the Japanese financial picture is a frightfully bad one . . . the Chinese financial picture is only kept alive with the help of the United States and Great Britain." All that Kennedy could recommend was that the United States do what it could to conserve its "financial position at least for one more year." There should be no new social expenditures and no legislation that would frighten the business community. He ended his letter by apologizing for "writing about something that is none of my business," implying, of course, that it should be. By harping on Washington's failure to push itself and the world out of depression, he was not very subtly auditioning to replace Morgenthau at the Treasury Department or, as an alternative, asking to be given more responsibilities in Europe.[55]

Kennedy's original plan had been to vacation in the United States that summer. But with the situation in Europe so unsettled, he had decided to return to the South of France. Arthur Krock, always on the alert to do his friend and patron a favor, dedicated his July 18, 1939, column to the topic "Why Ambassador Kennedy Is Not Coming Home." Kennedy, Krock declared, wanted "to come home." He was overworked, weary of being the object of a "propaganda campaign directed against him by the 'young New Dealers,'" concerned that his five youngest children had been "too long separated from the way of life in their native country," and burdened by the tremendous "expenses of his post" and the obligation "to disconnect himself from important sources of income." He had, in fact, according to Krock, decided that at the conclusion of the king and queen's triumphant visit to America, "which he had suggested and in great part planned," he would resign his post. He had changed his mind only because Roosevelt, increasingly reliant on his reports from London, had urged him to stay in place. Kennedy had reluctantly "agreed to await the events of the Summer and early Fall before returning to his private affairs in the United States which, he feels, acutely call for personal attention."[56]

Kennedy was pleased with Krock's column, and pleased even more when the president, who disliked and intensely distrusted Krock, sent him a personal note. "I suppose you know of the latest 'Krock' in the *Times* about you, and I think you begin to agree with me that that particular gentleman, with his distorted ideas of how to be helpful, has done you more harm in the past few years than all of your enemies put together." While Krock had insisted in his column that the rumors about "White House disfavor" and Kennedy "being dragged toward the doghouse" were false, by raising them again, he had, Roosevelt declared, done the ambassador a disservice. Roosevelt claimed he had "tried to correct the impression by telling several people the other day that I have complete confidence in you, that you have never mentioned leaving London, that you are doing a good job there, and that in these critical days I count on your carrying on." He concluded by asking Kennedy to "drop me a line to tell me your inside thoughts about the present situation." This, of course, was precisely what Kennedy wanted to hear.[57]

His response to the president was heartfelt but somewhat treacly. "Your letter made me happy—not only what you said but the whole tone of it." As far as his "inside thoughts" were concerned, most of them had been included in his dispatches and his recent letters. "But, in the mood of your letter, I should like to add some personal observations and comments. The chief thing I have noticed in the South of France, on the part of caddies, waiters and residents, is a very strong anti-Semitic feeling. Beyond that, and a general sense of wary waiting for almost anything to happen, I can contribute nothing to an understanding of the international state of affairs." Still, because the president had asked for his "inside thoughts about the present situation," Kennedy seized upon the occasion to return, like a homing pigeon, to his favorite theme.

"About my position in England my only thought was to wonder whether my experience and knowledge were not being completely wasted. After all, I recognize that in this day and age an Ambassador may be hardly more than a glorified errand boy. I do get a bit discouraged for, although I have worked harder and longer hours in this job than on any job I ever held, it seems that three quarters of my efforts are wasted because of the terrific number of things to be done which seem to have no close connection with the real job at hand." He did not want the president to think he was ungrateful for the honor granted him or that he was ready to abandon ship. "Of this one thing, though, you may be sure. Regardless of any personal inconvenience, as long as I am of any assistance to you, I shall remain for whatever time you like. . . . When I was a youngster, my father taught me two principles: gratitude and loyalty. . . . I have tried to live up to those two principles and, to you personally, I owe a debt on both counts." Even his complaints were softened, so grateful was he that the president had taken the time to write him.[58]

Kennedy leased the Domaine de Ranguin in 1939 with what was reported to be perhaps the "finest rose garden on the Riviera." It was here that the family would spend its last summer together. Kennedy played with his younger children, had long talks with the older ones, sunbathed, rented a yacht, played golf, and as he had the year before, took in the "leg shows" on the beaches, which he admitted to Rose were so numerous "that the old variety shows have lost their novelty and their allure." Rose, having seen those "leg shows" the summer before, had gone shopping for bathing suits for her girls in New York that June. It had been "impossible," she noted in her diary, "to find anything at Cannes last year. Everyone wore a little brassiere, a bare tummy and an abbreviated pair of shorts. Such a costume is O.K. for the gals there but not for the Kennedys."[59]

Marlene Dietrich was back at the Hôtel du Cap, with a slightly different and enlarged entourage. "Papa Joe," as Dietrich referred to Kennedy to distinguish him from the other Joes in her life, offered her career advice, persuading her to accept Joe Pasternak's offer to star in a western, *Destry Rides Again,* alongside Jimmy Stewart. To make sure she got the best deal possible, Kennedy called Arthur Houghton in Hollywood and found a new agent for her. Kennedy was happy to be of help, though by the end of the summer, Dietrich was beginning to get on his nerves. "Every time the telephone rings," Kennedy wrote Houghton in late August, "and Dietrich wants to speak to me, I know she wants some favor." Kennedy's pique might have been aroused because that summer, Dietrich—whose entourage now included her husband, Erich Maria Remarque, and a new addition, her "summer of '39 interlude," a woman named "Jo"—had less time for him. Fortunately, Kennedy had Amy, a beautiful young French girl who, he wrote Houghton, "caddied for me every day and she was good in every respect."

War was coming, and there was no way to escape it or ignore it. Before leaving the hotel that August, Dietrich, her daughter remembered, asked, "'Papa Joe—what will happen if there is a war? Do I have to take everyone with me to America, or can I leave them here?' . . . Kennedy [who had earlier helped secure her daughter's American citizenship papers] assured her that if and when he felt the danger of war was imminent, he would evacuate his family back to England and safety and that her family would be given the same protection as his."[60]

Twenty

"THIS COUNTRY IS AT WAR WITH GERMANY"

T he German official telegraphic agency and the German radio system has just announced that, 'The German and Soviet Governments have agreed to conclude a non-aggression pact,'" the American chargé d'affaires in Germany reported on August 21.[1]

Kennedy flew back to London from his villa in the South of France. With the threat that the Soviet Union would intervene to defend Poland now removed, there was no impediment to a German invasion. Prime Minister Chamberlain dispatched Ambassador Nevile Henderson to Salzburg with a letter requesting that Hitler peacefully resolve through negotiations any disputes he might have with the Polish government. He also reaffirmed Britain's determination to come to the assistance of Poland if Germany invaded. That same day, Wednesday, August 23, President Roosevelt cabled a message to the king of Italy asking that he and his government do all they could to bring Germany and Poland to the bargaining table.

The diplomatic efforts were cosmetic. It was generally agreed that there was only one way out of the crisis. Poland would have to agree at once to turn over Danzig and at least some segment of the Polish Corridor. By sending Henderson to Hitler and then agreeing to partake in a second, secret round of negotiations with Swedish industrialist

Birger Dahlerus, Goering's personal emissary, the Chamberlain government had set in motion the same process that had led to the Munich Agreement. Hitler played his part in the charade by agreeing to talk peace while preparing for war.

In the early evening of August 23, Kennedy visited Lord Halifax, who, he cabled to Washington, believed that the Polish government was not inclined to enter negotiations with Hitler. An hour later, Kennedy met with Chamberlain. "He said the spectre of the impending catastrophe was over him all the time. He looks very bad and is terribly depressed. I said to him, 'How does it look?' and he said, 'Very bad but I have done everything that I can think of and it seems as if all my work has come to naught.' . . . I asked him if he thought the Pope could do any good and he said no. . . . Although I talked with him for almost an hour the sum and substance of it all was sheer discouragement with the picture as it stands. . . . If the President is contemplating any action for peace, it seems to me the place to work is on Beck [Józef Beck, the Polish colonel and minister for foreign affairs who had negotiated with and remained on good terms with Hitler] and to make this effective it must happen quickly. I see no other possibility."[2]

In suggesting that Roosevelt "work on Beck," Kennedy was advising him to pressure the Polish government to peaceably cede territory to Germany, as the Czechs had. The alternative was war, which Kennedy believed had to be avoided at all costs.

At ten o'clock the following morning, Kennedy received a call from Sir Horace Wilson, one of Chamberlain's chief advisers, who wanted to know—as did the prime minister—what the president was going to do. Kennedy promised Wilson he would be back in touch with him as soon as he heard from the White House. After lunch, Wilson called again to find out if Kennedy had reached the president. He had not, but he reported that he had an appointment to speak to the White House at eleven P.M.

At midnight, the ambassador's call to the president was put through and answered by Under Secretary of State Sumner Welles, who was sitting with the president. Kennedy "asked Welles if he understood the import of my request for President to get in touch with Poland. [Welles] said, yes, but it could not be done the way I suggested. I said I didn't care how it was done so long as something was done and quickly.

"All right, came the President's voice. Something will be done to-night."[3]

The next morning, August 25, upon arriving at the embassy, Kennedy discovered that instead of following his advice and pressuring the Poles to negotiate with the Germans, the president had urged both Hitler and Ignacy Mościcki, the president of Poland, to refrain from hostilities and choose one of several methods to peaceably settle their differences. "Neither the president nor I," Hull would later write in his memoirs, "felt any disposition to bring any pressure to bear on Poland."[4]

On August 25, Hitler made what he deemed to be his final offer to Nevile Henderson. Kennedy spent all day trying, without much luck, to find out what Hitler had proposed and how the British intended to respond. He was invited to Downing Street at ten o'clock that evening, read the dispatches from Germany, and cabled Washington at midnight. The fuehrer had insisted that the Polish question be settled at once. As soon as the provocations against Germans in Poland ceased and the problems of Danzig and the Polish Corridor were resolved, Hitler declared that he would make Great Britain a comprehensive peace offer and "limit armaments, go back to peaceful pursuits, and become an artist, which is what he wanted to be. (Aside by Kennedy, he is now, but I would not care to say what kind.)" If his terms were not accepted, Hitler had declared, "it was going to be a war worse than '14–18."[5]

When he had finished reading the dispatches, Kennedy was invited to join the prime minister, the foreign secretary, Lord Cadogan, and their chief aides in the cabinet room. The prime minister asked Kennedy what he made of Hitler's proposals and what his recommendations were for a British response. "I said I felt strongly he could not quit on Poland no matter what else happened. He would jeopardize not only the honor of Britain, but would completely break his political party. . . . I then suggested that the answer could contain a suggestion that if [Hitler] accepted a reasonable Polish settlement perhaps he could get U.S. and other countries to get together on an economic plan that certainly would be more important to Germany than what he could possibly get out of getting anything in Poland.[6]

"'You must pass the hat before the corpse gets cold,' I said.

"'What do you mean by that?' asked Chamberlain.

"'You have to make your solution more attractive to Germany than what she is trying now to get out of Poland. Do it this way . . . Propose a general settlement that will bring Germany economic benefits more important than the territorial annexation of Danzig. Get the United States now to say what they would be willing to do in the cause of international peace and prosperity. After all, the United States will be the largest beneficiary of such a move. To put in a billion or two now will be worth it, for if it works we will get it back and more.'"[7]

Kennedy remained in the cabinet room "for another half hour and then I rose and as I went by the P.M.'s chair, I put my hand on the back of his shoulder and said, 'Don't worry, Neville, I still believe God is working with you.' . . . When I left No. 10, I thought to myself that incident has probably been the most important thing that has ever happened to me. Here I was an American Ambassador, called into discussion with the P.M. and Foreign Secretary over probably the most important event in the history of the British Empire. I had been called in before the Cabinet and had been trusted not only for my discretion but for my intelligence. It was a moving experience."[8]

Kennedy's recommendations were dismissed as soon as they were offered. He was proposing nothing less than rewarding Hitler for past aggressions and preventing future ones by settling on him an appeasement package so magnificent, it would divert him from occupying Danzig and the Polish Corridor. It defied the logic of events to believe that Hitler could be bought off with cash or credits or promises of more favorable trade agreements. It was even more preposterous to believe that the Chamberlain government, having failed in its attempt at appeasement at Munich, would try again less than a year later.

The next morning, a Saturday, Kennedy was up early as always. After his horseback ride and breakfast, he went to the embassy, where he spent the remainder of the day attempting to cajole, threaten, and beg American and European shipowners to stop at British ports and evacuate Americans. The liners that regularly serviced the British ports were already filled to capacity, having been booked weeks before to bring vacationing Americans home. Several companies, fearful that war was about to be declared, had canceled their sailings, leaving thousands stranded with no way to cross the Atlantic.

On August 28, Sir Nevile Henderson delivered to Hitler the British cabinet's reply to his "peace offer." The British proposed that Germany and Poland engage in direct negotiations to settle their differences, that the settlement be guaranteed by the European powers, and that once that settlement was achieved, the British would proceed with further discussions toward a comprehensive Anglo-German agreement.

"I am sitting at my desk," Kennedy wrote Arthur Houghton on August 29, "waiting to hear what Mr. Hitler says to Sir Nevile and wondering whether it is to be peace or war. The children are all back in London, but I don't feel I should send them home until I have the rest of the Americans out of London. Another one of those great moral gestures that the American people expect you to make; that is, get your own family killed, but be sure and get Miss Smith of Peoria on the boat."[9]

Both Lord Derby and J. P. "Jack" Morgan (who had decided that "whatever the result of the immediate reply from Hitler may be," he was sailing home) had offered Kennedy use of their country estates. Kennedy chose Morgan's Wall Hall, with its hundreds of acres of gorgeously landscaped grounds and gigantic faux Gothic castle, in large part because it was fully equipped and staffed by an army of servants, cooks, gardeners, and chauffeurs who, unlike Morgan, could not escape to America. Unable to get his children out of England yet, he moved them away from London and harm's way.[10]

At midnight on Tuesday, August 29, Kennedy cabled Hull in Washington that Hitler had agreed to "direct negotiations with Poland solely out of a desire to insure friendship with Great Britain," but insisted that a Polish plenipotentiary with full decision-making powers appear in Berlin within twenty-four hours to receive and agree to his demands. "Ambassador Henderson remarked that this last stipulation sounded like an ultimatum. After a heated exchange of remarks Hitler and Ribbentrop assured him it was intended only to stress the urgency of the matter, at a moment when two fully mobilized armies were facing each other."[11]

The next morning, the full text of Henderson's communication arrived in London and Kennedy hurried off to Whitehall to read it. He

met briefly with Halifax, who told him that he thought Hitler's demands that the Polish representative arrive in Berlin and sign an agreement within twenty-four hours were both "impudent and impertinent."
Still, the fact that Hitler had kept open the door to negotiations made
the foreign secretary a "little more optimistic" than he had been the day
before.

Halifax departed for 10 Downing and Kennedy was ushered into the
office of Under-Secretary Rab Butler, where he was given "the text of
Hitler's reply to Britain" and a draft of the cabinet's reply. Butler asked
him "what he thought" of the British reply. Kennedy, according to his
diary entry for that day, answered that he thought it was so "tough"
that Hitler might well respond, "Well, if this is the attitude the British
are going to take the minute I make the slightest concession, what possibility have I got to ever work out any big political or economic scheme
with them."

Kennedy suggested that the British offer Hitler a counterproposal
with "something to hang his hat on." Butler, according to Kennedy's
diary and memoirs, was in full agreement with him and suggested that
Kennedy "should see the P.M. and give him my reactions." Both men
believed that Hitler, though erratic and probably a bit of a madman, did
not want to go to war with the British. Kennedy reported to Butler that
when Joe Jr. had lunched last week in Berlin with Unity Mitford (who,
according to Joe Jr., was "the most fervent Nazi imaginable, and is
probably in love with Hitler"), Mitford said that "Hitler had really
great admiration for the British—they really knew how to rule, but that
he was heartbroken when Chamberlain had gone home after Munich"
instead of staying behind to negotiate a comprehensive peace treaty between their two nations.[12]

Rab Butler, hoping that Kennedy would push Chamberlain back
onto the appeasement track, arranged a meeting for the ambassador
and the prime minister early that evening. "At 6:30, I went to 10 Downing Street and on arriving Sir Horace [Wilson] met me with 'How is the
Stormy Petrel today?' I said, 'Fine' and asked him how he felt." (Kennedy apparently had no problem with being referred to as a "stormy
petrel," the bird sailors regarded as a harbinger of trouble.) On being
ushered in to see the prime minister, Kennedy repeated what he had told
Butler and then suggested that Chamberlain "put in some war regula-

tion that will affect the whole people and give them a little taste of what is to come. They then might not be so anxious for Poland to refuse to negotiate and start a war when they saw what they would suffer themselves." According to Kennedy, even at this very late date, Chamberlain had still not given up hope that war could be prevented. "If he only could get the Poles and Germans really negotiating something could be done. . . . The big thing was a European settlement. . . . 'It could be done,' said Chamberlain, 'if I could only get the chance.'"[13]

As Kennedy sat in his office that night, distracting himself by writing to his friends in the United States, he still held on to the belief that war might be averted. The Poles, he cabled Hull at seven P.M., had agreed to negotiate, but no one knew what the Germans were going to demand of them. Still, "the mere fact that the Germans have actually formulated proposals is regarded as a slightly favorable sign. The impression given by the Foreign Office is that they are a little more hopeful than they were yesterday, but the general public seems more depressed."[14]

At midnight, the ambassador spoke with the president over a secure phone line. Roosevelt had learned that Germany had made sixteen separate demands of the Poles. Kennedy knew nothing about them.

The next morning, September 1, Kennedy called Bill Bullitt in Paris, who agreed that "things were much better." Hitler, Bullitt told him, "didn't have the guts to fight."

"I had hardly hung up the telephone when the news came. It came with a rush, like a torrent spewing from the wires—German troops had crossed the border; German planes were bombing Polish cities and killing civilians; the Germans were using poison gas." Kennedy called Lord Halifax at the Foreign Office to report that he had heard, but could not confirm, that Warsaw had been bombed. Hull telephoned him at noon to ask for more information. Kennedy cabled him at four P.M., five P.M., eight P.M., eleven P.M., and twelve midnight, each time to confirm that he knew nothing more than that German troops had crossed into Poland.[15]

The French and British governments tried one more time to defuse the situation. Before declaring war on Germany, which they were obligated by treaty to do once German soldiers crossed into Poland, they delivered formal diplomatic notes demanding that Germany cease its aggression and withdraw its troops from Polish soil.

Kennedy commuted back and forth that weekend from the Morgan estate in Hertfordshire, where he had gathered his family until passage to America could be arranged. He and Rose preferred to travel separately—and usually did, lest an accident deprive the children of both their parents. Kennedy now made plans for his children also to travel in installments.

Luella Hennessey, the younger children's nurse, wanted to remain in London to get married to the man she had been seeing. Kennedy tried to talk her out of it. "He said it was going to be a long, hard war, and eggs were going to be rationed to one a month. And he gave me quite a bleak picture of the future there, but I still thought that love would take care of everything. So then he said, 'Well, I'll tell you, you come back with us, and when you land in New York, you can do whatever you want. You can wait for the boat to turn around, and come right back again, or you can stay in America. But Mrs. Kennedy and I feel that we brought you over single, and we'll return you to America single.'" Hennessey obeyed Kennedy's wishes, "the same as all his children do. I wouldn't dare argue with him."[16]

On Sunday, September 3, Kennedy and Rose drove back from Hertfordshire to their church in London for ten-thirty Mass, only to discover that it had been canceled. Kennedy dropped Rose off at the Brompton Oratory in South Kensington so she could attend Mass there, then proceeded to the embassy.

The prime minister was scheduled to address the nation at 11:15 that morning. "I cleaned up my desk, sent for a small radio from the house in a hurry and had it set up. I listened to the speech in my office with several of the staff. It was terribly moving. And when he got to the part of his 'efforts have failed,' I almost cried. I had participated very closely in this struggle and I saw my hope crash too."[17]

"This country is at war with Germany," Chamberlain announced that morning. "This is a sad day for all of us, and to none is it sadder than to me. Everything that I have worked for, everything that I have hoped for, everything that I believed in during my public life, has crashed into ruins. There is only one thing left for me to do; that is, to devote what strength and powers I have to forwarding the victory of the cause for which we have to sacrifice so much. I cannot tell what part I may be allowed to play myself; I trust I may live to see the day when Hitlerism has been destroyed and a liberated Europe has been reestablished."[18]

When the speech was over, Kennedy called 10 Downing. To his surprise, Chamberlain came to the phone. "Neville, I have just listened to the broadcast. It was terrifically moving. . . . I feel deeply our failure to save a world war." Chamberlain thanked Kennedy for the call and his steadfast support. "We did the best we could have done but it looks as though we have failed. . . . Thanks, Joe, my best to you always and my deep gratitude for your constant help—Goodbye—Goodbye."

At 11:27, the air raid sirens started screaming. For a brief moment, tragedy gave way to farce. As there was no shelter at the embassy, Kennedy directed the staff to "Molyneaux [*sic*], the dressmaker," whose establishment was just around the corner on Grosvenor Street and "had a reasonably good basement." When Joe Jr., Jack, and Rose appeared in front of the embassy to drive with their father to the House of Commons, Kennedy directed the boys to take their mother "at once to Molyneaux. . . . I went over to Molyneaux's to cheer people up and found most of them in pretty good shape." It was not the worst place to spend the first few minutes of the Second World War.[19]

Twenty-one

THE LIVES OF AMERICANS
ARE AT STAKE

Asense of panic was in the air." Kennedy rearranged schedules to provide twenty-four-hour staffing at the embassy and begged the State Department for funding for air raid protection. When he was informed that Americans in England might have to wait until early October for ships to bring them home, he lashed out in rage. "After all there is a war on, and it is quite conceivable that England will be bombed. If so, it is probable that Americans will be killed, because there is no place in England where we can store these people and promise them immunity."[1]

At two thirty A.M. on September 4, he was awakened at home by a phone call routed through the embassy. "The Foreign Office was on the line. The clipped accents of an unknown clerk spelled out a message that he said had just been received—'S.S. *Athenia,* Donaldson Line, torpedoed 200 Miles off Malin Head [Ireland's most northern point], 1400 passengers aboard, S.O.S. received, ship sinking fast.'" The survivors were being evacuated by a British destroyer and taken to Glasgow. Kennedy directed embassy officials to compile a list of deceased and surviving Americans. He then called Eddie Moore to ask him to leave at once for Glasgow and take Jack Kennedy along as the ambassador's personal representative.

The sinking of the *Athenia* reinforced Kennedy's fears that Americans were unsafe on any but United States–flagged vessels. As sternly as he could, he issued a warning to them not to sail in British ships. And again he implored the State Department to redirect all American-owned ships, including those bound elsewhere, to British ports. When State Department officials did not respond immediately, he blew past them and placed a call to his friend Max Truitt at the Maritime Commission to request that the commission pressure shipowners to dispatch ships to Britain. Secretary of State Hull was furious when, the next morning, the *Herald Tribune* reported on the contents of Kennedy's call to Truitt—which included a bitter, foulmouthed denunciation of the State Department. Instead of apologizing, Kennedy pushed back harder.

"Of course," he cabled Hull, "I know you realize the situation is bad here but I am sure you do not realize how bad it is. There are a great many newspapermen trying to get their wives and children and friends on boats and it is very difficult and people are constantly complaining that no ships are being sent from America. We are doing our best to keep them quiet but when you are bombarded by the Press every minute of the day and night as to what you are going to do about it, the press is going to publish something. . . . With the danger of submarine warfare . . . a critical situation might well arise with Americans sailing on British boats. All I am working for is to get them out as quickly and safely as we can."[2]

Day after day now, there were articles, columns, and editorials about the sinking of the *Athenia,* German perfidy and denials of perfidy (the Germans claimed the British had sunk the ship to outrage American opinion), fleeing refugees, torpedoes, fire on the deck, and the rescue at sea of more than a thousand survivors. Kennedy's office, staffed by the most savvy publicists in the diplomatic corps, tried and largely succeeded in positioning the ambassador as the hero of the story.

Time magazine put his face on the cover of its September 18 issue under a "The U.S. and The War" banner. "Last week Joe Kennedy had already shuttered and barred the palatial Embassy house at No. 14 Prince's Gate . . . and moved to a country house away from the terror of bombs. Thence each morning he drove into London in a Chrysler, waved swiftly through traffic by bobbies. . . . With 9,000 Americans to shepherd in England, with tangible U.S. business interests under his eye, with 150 Americans cabling from the U.S. daily for information on *Athenia* survivors, with British bigwigs to see, Franklin Roosevelt to keep informed, Joe Kennedy had a bigger job."

Within the confines of the State Department, Joseph P. Kennedy was not a hero, but a troublesome publicity hound who made impossible demands, then blamed Washington when they could not be met. "Kennedy has been terribly explosive," Breckinridge Long, former ambassador to Italy and now special assistant secretary of state in charge of repatriation efforts, wrote in his September 7 diary entry. "Kennedy seems to think that the only people needing repatriation are in the lobby of the American Embassy in London. As a matter of fact, there are 2800 in Ireland; there are many thousand in France, and there are scattered and spread hundreds of them in [countries across Europe]. . . . Kennedy had been condemning everybody and criticizing everything and has antagonized most of the people in the Administration. . . . I talked to Truitt this afternoon and told him I thought Kennedy was hurting himself and that the impression that was created in this country and that the news stories and publicity items which went out of London with his permission if not with his origination indicated that he did not view the situation normally."[3]

Eleven days after the declaration of war, Kennedy began sending his family home. Kick, Eunice, and Bobby sailed with their mother on the *Washington* on September 14. On September 18, Joe Jr. left on the *Mauretania;* Jack, who had been granted permission from Harvard to arrive a few days late, flew to New York on the Pan Am Clipper on September 19; on September 20, the final contingent of Kennedys, Patricia, Teddy, and Jean, sailed on the *Manhattan* with Miss Hennessey, who, Jean reported to her father, "was very sad to be leaving Roy [her English boyfriend] and was morning [*sic*] all the way over."[4]

Only Rosemary stayed behind in England with her father. She was doing so well—and seemed so content—at the Montessori-method convent school, it would have been foolish to uproot her. Instead, she was evacuated with the other students and nuns and Miss Gibbs, her companion, to Boxmoor, a village in Hertfordshire, where the convent school was reestablished on the grounds of the local Catholic church.

Boxmoor was conveniently close to Wall Hall, the Morgan estate where Kennedy now spent his weekends.

On Saturday morning, two days after Rose had sailed home, Kennedy visited Mother Isabel, the mother superior at the convent, "and had a nice talk about Rose[mary]." That same night, he called Rosemary to tell her that "she was going to be the one to keep me company, and as this house [Wall Hall] was very handy to her new school I would invite some of her girl friends and herself down to spend every other weekend with me and I would have a picture show at the house. That tickled her no end. So we will see how that works out. I think I will have the Moores stay over . . . until I see how serious this bombing turns out and then if it gets real bad they can take her home. And in the meantime the Moores can take Rose[mary] out every once in a while and between us all she will be really happy and enjoy herself." He was going to have a telephone installed at the school so he could talk regularly to his daughter. He had also, he wanted Rose to know, arranged for "an extra girl" to spell Miss Gibbs. "So," he reassured his wife, "that's that. Don't give it a moment's thought at least for the present. . . . Now darling, as to me. With all of the family safe in America I have no worries. I will miss you terribly but that can't be helped. . . . This position at the minute is probably the most interesting and exciting in the world, and in addition I may be of some help in helping to end this catastrophic chaos."[5]

The war was but two weeks old and Kennedy was already attempting to put himself in a position where he could be of "some help" in ending it. Secretary of State Hull detoured around Kennedy, fully aware that in wartime, as in peacetime, Kennedy would try to set his own agenda. When he had information or questions for the British, Hull conveyed them through Lord Lothian, the newly installed British ambassador in Washington.

Within days of the declaration of war, Secretary of the Treasury Morgenthau had proposed that the U.S. government, in partial payment for British war debts, take possession of the *Normandie* and *Queen Mary*, which were in American ports. Charged with negotiating the transfer, the State Department opened talks with Lord Lothian in Washington. Kennedy found out about the proposal two days later when British Treasury officials, assuming he was involved, asked for clarification. Embarrassed and furious, Kennedy accused Morgenthau of excluding him from the talks. Morgenthau, who had never suggested that Kennedy be shut out, asked Welles to please make that clear. "I'm willing to take the blame," the treasury secretary told Welles over the telephone, "when the blame is mine, but I don't think it is this time."[6]

Morgenthau called Kennedy in London to explain that it had been the State Department's decision, not his, to negotiate through Lothian in Washington. Kennedy made it clear he didn't hold Morgenthau responsible. "It's dead as far as I'm concerned, Henry, and I'm glad you called me up. And you know how I feel about it. . . . I know very well that I can save you a lot of bumps as far as this place goes . . . if I know what's going on, but this one struck me so between the eyes that I didn't know whether I was afoot or horseback."[7]

Still unaware or unwilling to recognize that his policy recommendations were dismissed the moment they arrived, not only by Hull but by Roosevelt, Kennedy wrote the president a long letter the week after war was declared, marked it "Personal and Confidential," and offered "a few of my impressions as to what is taking place here." The British government, he warned the president, was going to do everything it possibly could to influence American public opinion, "figuring that sooner or later they can obtain real help from America." For the moment, they were preparing for war—and the economic emergency it would entail.

"The place where the real works are going on is in the economic and financial departments. There the best brains in England have been concentrated. . . . England is as much a totalitarian country tonight from an economic and trade point of view as any other country in Europe—all that is needed is time to perfect the organization. All trade will be directly or indirectly controlled by the Government." It was imperative, given this developing reality, that the Americans make changes accordingly so as not to be bested in the rounds of trade negotiations over raw materials, finished products, and currency regulations. "This all adds up into one suggestion: That we should be on our guard to protect our own interests. In the economic and financial field the best possible brains should be concentrated on the problems which the European war is bound to raise."[8]

A day later, Kennedy sent off a "Triple Priority" telegram labeled "Strictly Confidential and Most Personal for the Secretary and the President." He had visited for an hour with the king and queen and then spent forty minutes with Home Secretary Sir Samuel Hoare. The king had told him that he was convinced Poland would be defeated within three or four weeks, after which Hitler would forward a proposal "to France and England to put a stop to this war and to arrive at some understanding." When that happened, the Chamberlain government would, Kennedy "inferred" from what Hoare had told him, be faced with either entering into negotiations and being voted out of office for doing so; or refusing to enter into negotiations and preparing for endless, probably unwinnable war on the continent and bombardment from the air at home. Each path led to disaster. "They know that if the war continues or if a Government is maintained on a war basis, it signifies entire social, financial and economic breakdown and that after the war is over nothing will be saved. If the war were stopped, on the other hand, it would provide Herr Hitler with so much more prestige that it is a question of how far he would be carried by it." There was only one way out. Roosevelt, Kennedy suggested, should step in where the British could not and forge a deal with Hitler. "It appears to me that this situation may resolve itself to a point where the President may play the role of savior of the world. As such the English Government definitely cannot accept any understanding with the present German Chancellor but there may be a situation when President Roosevelt himself may evolve world peace plans. . . . Having been a practical person all my life, I am of the opinion that it is quite conceivable that President Roosevelt can manoeuver himself into a position where he can save the world."[9]

Kennedy's recommendation was recklessly bizarre. Roosevelt could not make peace in Europe because he had nothing of substance to offer Hitler, other than perhaps Poland, which was already within his grasp. To even get Hitler to the bargaining table, Roosevelt would have had to recognize his seizure of Austria and Czechoslovakia, which he could not possibly do without making a mockery of American pronouncements and principles. The attempt to appease Hitler would surely fail, and failure this time would be catastrophic. It would weaken Roosevelt internationally, cripple him politically a year before a presidential election, embolden Hitler to continue his aggression, offer Italy and Japan tacit assurance that the "democracies" would eventually recognize their conquests, and represent one of the grandest double crosses in world history. Had the ambassador taken an hour or two to think through his proposal before sending it off, he might have realized this. But he had not. His cable was dispatched at two o'clock, only hours after he had met with Hoare. Given the time it took to dictate, type, review, and "Triple Priority" encode a message this long, it was clear that Kennedy had not had the opportunity to reflect on what he was recommending.

Kennedy got his answer two hours after he sent his cable. It was brutally terse. Hull informed him, on a strictly confidential basis, that the president would never, "so long as present European conditions continue," initiate any peace move. "The people of the United States would not support any move for peace initiated by this Government that would consolidate or make possible a survival of a regime of force and of aggression."[10]

Roosevelt and Hull were astounded by Kennedy's suggestions that the president initiate negotiations with Hitler while Great Britain and France were at war with him. The president, according to James Farley, thought that Kennedy's cable was "the silliest message to me I have ever received. It urged me to do this, that, and the other thing in a frantic sort of way."[11]

It may not have been coincidental that the day he received Kennedy's dispatch, the president initiated direct contact with Winston Churchill, now first lord of the Admiralty and Chamberlain's expected successor at 10 Downing. "It is because you and I occupied similar positions in the World War that I want you to know how glad I am that you are back again in the Admiralty," Roosevelt explained in his first letter to Churchill, sent by diplomatic pouch to the embassy but sealed so that no one would open or read it at Grosvenor Square. "Your problems are, I realize, complicated by new factors, but the essential is not very different. What I want you and the Prime Minister to know is that I shall at all times welcome it, if you will keep me in touch personally with anything you want me to know about. You can always send sealed letters through your pouch or my pouch."[12]

There was something daring and wholly irregular in the American president bypassing his ambassador and opening a secret channel of communication with a British cabinet member at a moment when the nation was bound by strict neutrality laws and its people overwhelmingly opposed to engagement in another European war. Churchill covered himself by clearing every message he sent with Prime Minister Chamberlain. Roosevelt had no superior to provide him cover.

Three weeks after the correspondence had been initiated, Kennedy found out about it from Churchill. Embarrassed and infuriated, he referred in that evening's diary entry to the president's clandestine correspondence with Churchill as yet "another instance of Roosevelt's conniving mind which never indicates he knows how to handle any organization. It's a rotten way to treat his Ambassador and I think shows him up to the other people. I am disgusted." What made the matter worse to Kennedy's mind was that Roosevelt's overtures to Churchill indicated that he trusted him. Kennedy most certainly did not. "I can't help feeling he's not on the level. He is just an actor and a politician. He always impressed me that he'd blow up the American Embassy and say it was the Germans if it would get the U.S. in. Maybe I do him an injustice but I just don't trust him."[13]

On October 6, the evening after Churchill confided in him that he was receiving secret communications from the president, Kennedy was awakened after midnight by the first lord of the Admiralty, who apparently not only never slept but didn't want anyone else to. Churchill had had a call from the president and wanted Kennedy to cable his reply from the American embassy. Kennedy had the cable coded and sent that same evening. "Again I am amazed at Roosevelt's complete lack of understanding of organization. He calls Churchill up and never contacts me. A rotten way to win men's loyalty . . . I'll have my say some day!"[14]

On Sunday morning, September 17, two weeks after the declaration of war, Lord Beaverbrook called Kennedy with the news that "the Russians had crossed the borders into Poland. He was frightfully disturbed. He said, 'This puts a terrible new aspect on the war.'" Beaverbrook wanted Kennedy to "get your President to see what plans can be worked out to save this catastrophe." The news was indeed terrible and terrifying. If the Soviet invasion of Poland was the first move in a Soviet-German military alliance to divide up Europe (with Italy as junior partner), there was no conceivable way to save the democracies.[15]

Chamberlain, whom Kennedy visited the next day, downplayed the significance of "the Russian situation." The prime minister did not believe that the move into Poland signaled the beginning of "a straight military alliance with Germany." In that evening's dispatch to the State Department, Kennedy recounted and then dismissed Chamberlain's relative equanimity. "I think he is probably doing some wishful thinking."[16]

The American ambassador showered Washington regularly now with Cassandra-like predictions of the end of civilization, capitalism, and representative government in Europe. On September 30 alone, he wrote three separate letters to the president, each arguing that there was no way to save the British from defeat—and it might not be worth even trying to do so. The British claimed for themselves the highest moral ground, but the government had gone to war not to save Poland or Western civilization, but to protect and preserve its colonial "possessions and place in the sun, just as she has in the past." This was not a war to protect "democracy—the only form of government I want to live under." It was another war to preserve the British Empire.[17]

He was disgusted by the drumbeating for war, by the moral certainty of the British and their American supporters that war had to be waged. "Of course, I am not carried away by this war for idealism," he wrote Missy LeHand on October 3. "I can't see any use in everybody in Europe going busted and having communism run riot. My own belief is that the economics of Germany would have taken care of Hitler long before this if he didn't have a chance to wave that flag every once in a while. But, of course, one isn't supposed to say this out loud. The British are going into this war hating it, but with determination to fight it out. I still don't know what they are fighting for that is possible of accomplishment."[18]

As long as Chamberlain and Halifax had pursued a peace agreement with Hitler, the ambassador had been their uncompromising supporter—so uncompromising, in fact, that he had been accused of going over to the other side. Now that the Chamberlain government had declared war and the prime minister and foreign secretary ruled out the possibility of further negotiations, Kennedy distanced himself from them both. As he told Lord Halifax, who reported their conversation to Lord Lothian in Washington, it was "his opinion [that] the consequences of indefinite continuance of the war were so serious that every effort should be made by diplomatic resources to find the way of peace." Halifax answered that while "everyone would agree that peace was desirable if it could be achieved [insofar as] the present German Government were quite untrustworthy nothing was to be gained by deluding ourselves into supposing that any paper peace terms proposed by them could . . . offer the way of peace. The Ambassador did not seem to disagree with this, but recurred to the tragic results that prolongation of the war must involve."[19]

The British Foreign Office now began to monitor the ambassador's activities as if he were an enemy agent. A secret "Kennedyiana" file was opened, and under the heading "U.S. Ambassador's Views as to the Outcome of the War," Foreign Office officials filed their reports, all secondhand, of the "defeatist" remarks the ambassador had supposedly made to foreign journalists, colleagues in the diplomatic corps, and whoever happened to be at the dinner table with him. They were so concerned by the ambassador's endless badmouthing of British war efforts that they debated whether to notify Lord Lothian in Washington and, if "necessary . . . ask him to speak to Mr. Roosevelt." Another option was for the Foreign Office to voice the government's concerns to career diplomat Herschel Johnson so that he might "take the hint" and report his chief's indiscretions to Washington. A third was to confront the ambassador directly and ask him to desist.

In late September, the Foreign Office sent Lord Lothian "a specimen of the reports" gathered in the "Kennedyiana" file. "While it is very regrettable that Kennedy should be adopting this attitude, we do not propose, for the time being at any rate, to pursue the matter further. We had thought it well, however, to let you know about his indiscreet utterances in case it should later become necessary for us to ask you to drop a hint in the proper quarters." The consensus was that any attempt at "'splitting' Mr. Kennedy at the state department or elsewhere" might only backfire. "A complaint might, of course, make him shut up, but in that case we shall neither know what he is thinking nor what he is telling the U.S. Government." As one officer suggested, Kennedy's "defeat-ism" might also, in a perverse sort of way, "have its good side in jogging the Americans out of their eighty-two percent [according to a recent Gallup poll] wishful thinking that the French and we are going to win!" The more frightened the American public and politicians were that the British were going to lose, the more likely Congress might be to amend the Neutrality Acts to permit direct assistance of the British war effort.

Various explanations were offered for the ambassador's defeatism: that as an Irish American, he was "naturally predisposed to twist the lion's tale"; that he had been convinced, wrongly, of German air supe-riority, first by Lindbergh and then by his son Joe Jr., recently returned from a visit to the continent; that as a politically ambitious American, he had "to make sure that he is not tarred with the pro-British brush." The shrewdest observation was made by an officer (whose handwritten signature is indecipherable) who noted that because Kennedy was "pri-marily interested in the financial side of things, he cannot, poor man, see the imponderables which, in a war like this, will be decisive."[20]

In mid-October, Charles Peake on the American desk at the For-eign Office sought out William Hillman, the former Hearst foreign cor-respondent in London, hoping that Hillman, who knew Kennedy well, might offer some insight into his character. Hillman told Peake that the key to understanding Kennedy was to recognize that he was not only "a professing Catholic who loathed Hitler and Hitlerism, almost, though perhaps not quite, as much as he loathed Bolshevism, but he was also a self-made man" who feared for his and his family's economic future. He had made a pile of money—and was fearful now that it would be lost in the economic catastrophe that would accompany the fighting of another European war. "Mr. Kennedy was convinced that this war un-less it was soon stopped would bankrupt the British Empire and also bankrupt the United States, who would be bound to come in before it was over. . . . Bankruptcy and defeat, said Mr. Hillman, were obses-sions now in the American Ambassador's mind and though he had tried to reason with him, he was not amenable to reason, his argument being that Hitler and the Nazis could not last forever and that there was bound to be a change in regime in Germany one day if we had only let it alone."[21]

The Foreign Office fully accepted Hillman's assessment. As Sir Oliver Harvey, Halifax's private secretary, noted in his diary on November 1, 1939, Kennedy was "engaged in defeatist propaganda" because "he only thinks of his wealth and how capitalism will suffer if the war should last long."[22]

The excitement of the first weeks of war quickly dissipated. All of the Americans who had wanted to go home had done so; trenches and shelters had been dug; the barrage balloons launched; London's children (and their dogs with them) evacuated to the countryside, their older brothers sent away to military training camps. Even the blackouts and sirens, at first so distressing, had become second nature. And while the theaters and movie houses were empty, the nightclubs had opened again.

Kennedy spent more time now at Wall Hall, where he was well cared for by Jack Morgan's staff. On weekends, Rosemary, her companion, the Moores, and two golf-playing colleagues from the embassy, Jim Seymour and "London Jack" Kennedy, stayed with him. He was alone most of the time. "I'm running true to form," he wrote his wife, the one person who could always be counted on to sympathize with him. "I'm sick of everybody and so I'm alone tonight by choice. It's funny that nobody in the world can be with me very long without boring me to death. I just can't help it. You are the only individual in the world that I love more every day. . . . This job without you is comparable with a street cleaner's at home."[23]

He had never expected he would miss the children so much, because he never had before. "Having to live this life with the family in America," he wrote Boake Carter, "is nothing short of hell, and it adds greatly to my boredom and depression over the present situation." "I notice it much more, I suppose," he confided to Johnnie Ford, "because they were with me so much the last year and a half and because I had such a great time with them."[24]

While he complained of the boredom, he also took great pleasure in being in the middle of the action. "I have to admit," he wrote Phil Reisman on October 3, 1939, "that I wouldn't have missed the opportunity of having a front row seat for the show that's going on here. It may become a hot seat later on, but at any rate, exciting adventures make life interesting, and to be in business with this going on would irk me no end."[25]

His guess was that it was going to be a short war. The German army had marched into Poland almost unimpeded. On September 27, Warsaw had surrendered. There had been no bombardment of Great Britain—and no counterattack by the Royal Air Force (RAF). There were battles at sea as German U-boats went after British merchant ships, but the naval war, though intense at first, had subsided by late September. A month after the declaration of war, hostilities on land, air, and sea had ceased.

The peace offer that Kennedy and everyone else had expected Hitler to make after the Polish surrender arrived in mid-October. It was a nonstarter. Hitler refused to even discuss the restoration of Polish sovereignty. When Chamberlain rejected his peace offer, Hitler declared that the war would continue. He didn't say where or when.

"Everyone here is amazed that the war is going as it is," Kennedy wrote Johnnie Ford on October 26. "They can't understand it and don't know just where it will finally lead to. I can't believe that, even if it starts in real earnest, it can go on for a long time. It is too potentially catastrophic in character, but if anybody thinks he can tell in advance what's going to happen in Europe, he is crazy."[26]

Kennedy's hours at the embassy were consumed now by what he considered to be necessary work, but not the kind that required his elevated skill set or brought much satisfaction. He found transportation home for those Americans still in England; he opened negotiations to guarantee that U.S. manufacturers would not suffer from price gouging or shortages of necessary raw materials, particularly rubber and tin; he made the rounds of the embassies and met with British cabinet officials and reported his findings in dispatches to the State Department; and he and his embassy served as liaison in repatriating the thousands of Germans still in the British Empire and the far fewer number of British nationals marooned in Germany.

His main task was protecting American business from British import restrictions. The British, desperate to retain as many dollars as possible, cut back severely on American imports. Kennedy did his best on behalf of the tobacco, cotton, and fruit exporters, but he worked over-time for the Hollywood film industry. He negotiated so ferociously on behalf of the picture industry and secured such a favorable agreement that, as he wrote Johnnie Ford, had he been employed by the film companies as a lawyer, they "would probably have to pay me a million dollars." Phil Reisman, who worked in Hollywood, agreed that "every one of the boys in the picture business should get down on their knees and thank God that you were over there watching out for their interests."[27]

He still considered himself a film man and industry watchdog, though he had not been in Hollywood in more than a decade. In mid-November, after watching Jimmy Stewart, the star of Frank Capra's *Mr. Smith Goes to Washington*, confront widespread and blatant corruption, dishonesty, and criminality in Congress, he notified Will Hays by cable that he considered the film to be "one of the most disgraceful things I have ever seen done to our country. To permit this film to be shown in foreign countries," he wrote Hays, "and to give people the impression that anything like this could happen in the United State Senate is to me nothing short of criminal. I am sending a copy of this wire to the President of the United States." "I do not question that in 'Mr. Smith,' you have made a sincere attempt to attack crooked politics," he wrote Harry Cohn, the head of Columbia Pictures, which released the film, "but I am also convinced that the picture will definitely discredit American Government and American civilization in the eyes of the English public. . . . In foreign countries this film must inevitably strengthen the mistaken impression that the United States is full of graft, corruption and lawlessness."[28]

He was once again, unbidden, taking on the role of moral guardian for the picture industry.

Although he was not a man prone to self-pity, Kennedy couldn't help feeling sorry for himself, marooned in London with nothing of importance to do at the embassy and with friends and family an ocean away. "When I read about those Philadelphia Symphony concerts, those dinners with those beautiful women, those dances . . . and various and sundry night clubs," he wrote Arthur Goldsmith, his friend since Harvard, "and I think of myself in the blackouts, carrying a gas mask, spending all day long—and most of the night—working on rubber and tin and films and shipping and securities, why it just isn't right. . . . It looks to me as if I were back running a business now, with nothing to get you in the headlines except perhaps a scandal. Of course that is liable to happen anywhere and any time about my past life, but I assure you it couldn't happen about my present! Not because I haven't those inclinations; but age has done its bit."[29]

"It isn't that the work is so terribly hard now," he repeated in a letter to another classmate, Bob Fisher, "it's really the atmosphere one works in. I mean—seeing youngsters, whom you had to the house for dinner with your own daughters, going off to war and some of them already killed in airplanes; seeing business shot to pieces; seeing, with the vision or imagination I think I have, what's going to happen to America, even though they never get into the war, and, of course, they shouldn't. It all makes you sick at heart."[30]

The stress was getting to him, though he preferred to blame his weak stomach on a rich diet. "My stomach has been terrible," he wrote Rose, "due the doctor says to too much rich milk, cream, eggs and butter & bacon. So I go to bed early read and get up to a most uninteresting life. . . . I've got to cut out rich food for a while. So between, no liquor [not even his one Haig & Haig with water before dinner], no tobacco, no sweets, no women, and now no food, well I might just as well get hit by a bomb." His boredom and loneliness and stress were exacerbated by the horrific state of transatlantic communications. Letters arrived weeks after they were sent and were read by censors before they were delivered. To spare Rosemary—and the rest of the family—any embarrassment over the infantile state of her penmanship, Kennedy had decided to evade the censors by forwarding her notes by diplomatic pouch. "I don't see any point in having any of her letters go to America and be talked about. Over here it doesn't make any difference."[31]

Worse than the delay in the mail was the prohibition against transatlantic phone calls that the British had instituted when they declared war. Kennedy, outraged that he could not call home, wrote Rose that he had complained in person to Lord Halifax: "I've got to be permitted to talk to the U.S.A. I've got more sense than to discuss the war, in a way to help the Germans, but must keep track of my family. . . . I said I didn't much care what action had to be taken. I wasn't going to be of much help to anyone if I didn't get that privilege. Well anyhow I have it with a warning not to let the Germans know anything. . . . So that's that!! You'll be hearing from me."[32]

For the rest of the war, Kennedy would place a call to Bronxville or Hyannis Port or Palm Beach every Sunday. The children would line up at the phone, awaiting their turn to talk to their father. The children and Rose also wrote regularly, though they never knew when Kennedy would receive their letters.

Everyone seemed to be thriving in America, as they had in London. Joe Jr. was working hard at Harvard Law School. Kick wrote to say that she had not gotten into Sarah Lawrence but was thinking about applying to "Finch in New York. It is a Junior College and one can get a diploma which is something." Eunice, in a series of newsy letters, reported that she was doing well at Manhattanville, where she was on the tennis and swimming teams. She had begun the term as a boarding student but had been removed when "mother heard a rumor there were a few mice running around there and she took me out so fast that I couldn't even explain although she said there were no explanations needed." Eunice told her father about Jack's girlfriends, Kick's new beaus, Pat's suitor, whom "everyone in the family thought . . . was wonderful" but she thought "a dope," and Teddy's weight, which, though only fifteen pounds more than it should be, left him looking "like two boys instead of one." Jean, almost twelve now, wanted her father to know that Pat's new boyfriend was "six feet seven [and Pat] can wear her high heel shoes without looking tall" and that Eunice had gotten a "lovely painting from an elderly gentleman who came down one day with Conde Nast and he went crazy over Eunice."[33]

Kennedy tried to answer every letter. "Well, old lady," he replied to Pat's latest in a handwritten note, "you are doing yourself proud on the letters. I certainly think that you are having a much gayer time there than you possibly could have had over here. . . . I still go out to the country every night, and between you and me, it is pretty lonesome. . . . Tell someone to send me Bobbie's address and I will write him. Explain that is the reason he hasn't heard from me. Work hard dear, have fun and think of me."[34]

From London, he helped the children with their hobbies and their schoolwork. He had letters sent to the American consuls general in

Montreal, Bangkok, Tunis, Algiers, Calcutta, Moscow, Istanbul, and every European and South American embassy, asking them to purchase "small dolls, about 8 to 10 inches high, dressed in the native costume of the country" for his daughter Jean's collection; he directed embassy staff to save special stamps for Bobby; and when Jack decided to write his senior thesis on British foreign policy and preparedness after the Great War, he mobilized his public affairs office to collect research materials for him.

Back in Cambridge, Massachusetts, John Burns was keeping a close watch on Jack's progress at Harvard and Joe Jr.'s in law school, as Kennedy had asked him to. That fall, when Jack published an "isolationist" editorial in the *Crimson,* Burns suggested that he might be better served by not making his opinions known in public. Burns helped Joe Jr. choose his courses and professors at law school and tutored him for his examinations. In November, Kennedy wrote Burns that he had "been thinking, if there is a soft place, it might not be a bad idea to have young Joe a delegate to the [1940 Democratic] National Convention—primarily for the experience, but, everything considered, it might be good for him. I wish you would give this some thought, and then, in that event, I would probably have Jack appointed an officer of the Convention by the National Committee and they could both be there."[35]

While Jack and Joe Jr. were firmly settled at Harvard and Teddy appeared to be doing fine in Bronxville, Bobby was floundering a bit. Kennedy had arranged to get him admitted to St. Paul's, arguably the most prestigious prep school in New England. Rose had never been happy about sending her boy to an Episcopalian school, and two weeks after the term began, she suggested to her husband that Bobby transfer to Priory, a Catholic preparatory school in Rhode Island. She had raised her concerns about St. Paul's with Johnnie Burns, who "thinks that you as the leading Catholic should not have a son in a definitely Episcopal School." If Priory didn't work out, Bobby could transfer to Andover for his final two years. Kennedy assured his wife that "whatever you do will turn out OK."[36]

Kennedy focused his attention on Rosemary that fall. He was, Rose recalled in her diary, "especially attentive to her during that time, supervising everything from her studies to her pocket money and dental care, and writing to her often, and visiting the school." "She is wonderful," Kennedy wrote his wife in mid-October, "and Mary Moore who was here [at Wall Hall] said she had never seen such a change in her life. She is completely happy in her work [with the younger children at the school], enjoys being the boss here and is no bother or strain at all. . . . It becomes definitely apparent now that this is the ideal life for Rose[mary]. . . . She is happy, looks better than she ever did in her life, not the slightest bit lonesome, and loves to get letters from the children telling her how lucky she is to be over here. (Tell them to keep writing that way.) She is much happier when she sees the children just casually. For everyone peace of mind, particularly hers, she shouldn't go on vacation or anything else with them. It certainly isn't a hardship when everyone especially Rose[mary] is 1,000 times better off. I'm not sure she isn't better staying over here indefinitely with all of us making our regular trips, as we will be doing, and seeing her then. I have given her a lot of time and thought and I'm convinced that's the answer."[37]

He had come to the conclusion that despite the kindnesses shown her by her brothers and sisters, Rosemary did better on her own. The rest of the family might also do better knowing that she was well cared for by others, that they did not have to worry about her, or feel guilty, or be afraid that she might embarrass herself—or them. For twenty years, Rosemary had tried to keep up, to join in the fun, to dance and swim, joke and flirt, play tennis and golf, go sledding, boating, and skiing, to smile a hearty smile for the cameras, exude glamour and gaiety and self-confidence in being one of the worshipped, privileged Kennedys. Joe Jr. and Jack had escorted "her to dances at the Yacht Club at the Cape, or to the Stork Club in New York." Kick and Eunice had gone swimming and sailed and traveled with her. Jean Kennedy had spent hours hitting tennis balls with her on vacation in the South of France. Teddy "looked out for her too, when I could, though I was fourteen years younger," he recalled in his memoirs. As her brothers and sisters grew up and progressed intellectually, Rosemary, who did not, fell further behind. She was "slow" but not stupid and had to have been cognizant of the growing separation from her brothers and sisters. Her attempts to keep pace, coupled with the realization that, try as she might, she could not, had been too much for her.[38]

In Rose's absence and without consulting her, Kennedy decided that he was going to separate Rosemary from the family. She would stay at the convent school in England as a full-time resident and part-time teacher after he returned to the United States. Rosemary would no longer travel or go on vacation or live with the rest of the family. "She must never be at home for her sake as well as everybody else's."[39]

In mid-November, Kennedy put his new proposal into operation. He was not, he wrote Rose, bringing Rosemary with him when he returned for home leave in December 1939. "Now as to Rosie for Christmas, I think she should stay here, by all means. First of all she would not be able to come back once she got over there. No passports being granted. Second she is so much happier here than she could possibly be in the United States that it would be doing her a disservice rather than helping her. She had another nice girl with her yesterday for the weekend. The girls are very nice and fit in with her limitations without anyone being the wiser. In the meantime she is 'cock of the walk' by being by herself so that builds up her self-confidence. She is no bother when she is away from the other children. She gets along very well with Mary Moore and they have lots of fun together. . . . So I think everything is getting along OK. . . . Pray that everything stays quiet for me to get home."[40]

Twenty-two

DEFEATIST

On November 22, Kennedy was granted permission to return to the United States on home leave. In his final meetings with the king and queen, prime minister, foreign secretary, first lord of the Admiralty, and other members of the war cabinet, he repeated the message he had been delivering since the war began. It was better to attempt to appease Hitler while the war was still a "phony" one than to wait for him to turn his troops and planes west and, after defeating the British and French, dictate terms for surrender.

Having swallowed whole Lindbergh's analysis of Germany's overwhelming military advantages, Kennedy had no doubt that the German army, aided by the air force, would sweep through Western Europe and then invade and conquer Britain. Sir Henry "Chips" Channon, the American-born Conservative member of Parliament, wrote in his diary that Kennedy had prophesied to him "the end of everything and goes about saying that England is committing suicide." Even the ambassador's devoted friend and admirer Lady Astor was worried about his pessimism. At their final meeting before his return to the States, she gave Kennedy a sealed letter for her dear friend Philip Kerr, Lord Lothian, now the ambassador to Washington. In it she remarked that Kennedy had "said to someone the other day, that if the war did not stop soon, there would be no markets!!! It looks as though he may be a bit of a defeatist, so you had better watch out for this. (I trust he does not open this letter!) He has been a splendid Ambassador, but people are just a little frightened of that."[1]

On November 29, Kennedy left London for Paris to meet with the American ambassadors to France, Russia, and the Netherlands, after which he proceeded to Lisbon. After a three-day weather delay, he boarded the *Dixie Clipper,* a twenty-seat seaplane, bound for Port Washington. He carried with him an important and very secret message for the president from the first lord of the Admiralty. Churchill was preparing to mine the waters off the western coast of neutral Norway, as the British Navy had in 1918, to prevent the Germans from shipping Swedish iron ore south during the winter months when ice blocked the Baltic Sea. Before he moved ahead with this plan, he wanted to know what the president thought of it. "The code arranged between the First Lord and Mr. Kennedy for communication on this matter was that if Mr. Kennedy replied 'My wife cannot express an opinion,' this would mean that while the President was not prepared to commit himself, he did not receive the notion too badly. If he reacted very unfavourably the message was to be something like the following: 'My daughter [or Eunice] is unable to accept the invitation.'"[2]

On landing in Port Washington, Kennedy was met by Rose and dozens of reporters with whom he chatted about London in the blackout, the mood of the British people, their acceptance of the fact that the Americans were not going to join them in war, and the importance of his home visit. He was, he announced, on his way to Washington at once to confer with the president and secretary of state. "I want to tell them some things that it might not be wise to put on the cables." Roosevelt tried to slow him down and called him in Bronxville to suggest that he delay his trip to Washington until he had spent time with his family. "In postponing the conference with Kennedy for a day," the *Chicago Tribune* opined, "the President was seen as minimizing the importance of the conference and the secret nature of the report the ambassador will offer."[3]

Kennedy, undeterred, arrived in Washington at seven thirty the next morning, declared his support for a Roosevelt third term to the reporters who met him at Union Station, and was driven to the "Carlton

Hotel, shaved, changed my clothes, had breakfast, arrived White House at 9 A.M." Roosevelt was "in bed; looked terribly tired; was most cordial in his reception." Kennedy delivered Churchill's letter with his plan to mine Norway's waters and, when the president raised no objections, cabled as much to London. The president and his ambassador then discussed economic affairs, with Kennedy trespassing into matters that were not within his mandate. The ambassador recommended that the United States provide the British with American-flagged ships to transport American goods and warned that the sale of British securities to raise dollars would have a "disastrous" effect on American markets.

On the whole, he was delighted by his reception in Washington. Roosevelt had charmed him out of any complaints he might have had, greeting him as if he were a long-lost friend. He offered Kennedy the treasured first and last appointments of the day, had breakfast in his presence, and then, during their afternoon meeting, shared the latest political gossip and prognostications. When Kennedy asked about a third term, imploring Roosevelt to seek one, the president responded that he wouldn't run again " 'unless we are in war.' He added, almost as an aside, 'Even if we are in war, I'll never send an army over there. We'll help them with supplies.' "[4]

Encouraged to speak his mind—as if he needed any such encouragement—Kennedy warned again of the coming apocalypse. "Joe Kennedy was utterly pessimistic," the president later reported to Harold Ickes. "He believes that Germany and Russia will win the war and that the end of the world is just down the road."[5]

Jay Pierrepont Moffat, who was one of the few men in the State Department with whom Kennedy enjoyed a reasonably good relationship, was delighted when the ambassador dropped by and "spent about forty minutes between appointments in my office, summarizing in staccato fashion his views." The Chamberlain government, Kennedy told Moffat, understood that the United States had no intention of entering the war in Europe. "Churchill, however, wants us there as soon as he can get us there. He is ruthless and scheming. He is also in touch with groups in America which have the same idea, notably, certain strong Jewish leaders. All told," Moffat concluded, "K. is very bearish. He sees little hope for a prosperous England after the war, and little hope for the Continent to preserve its social structure. He says the British are a combination of cleverness and stupidity; but where they are really clever, and can walk circles around us, is in matters financial. . . . He says there is no question but that they have all our codes [the secret codes the embassy used to cable dispatches to Washington]. Three or four times Ministers have by references and allusions given the show away. . . . He said that his main work was now done, and that pretty soon the British would start trying to undermine him, as he was too much of a fighter. If so, they would do it via Washington and not in London. I gathered that he would prefer a key job here in Washington, but, lacking that, will go back in mid-January with pleasure."[6]

The ambassador was correct that the British had broken the American codes and with such remarkable ease that the Foreign Office was worried that others, including the Germans, had done or would do the same. On March 18, 1940, the Foreign Office would recommend that the minister of economic warfare "warn members of your Department that what they may say in confidence to members of the United States Embassy may easily get round rather quickly . . . to our enemies, and that they should therefore frame their remarks with this consideration in mind."[7]

Kennedy was also on the mark when he told Moffat that British officials would endeavor to "undermine" him because he was too much of "a fighter." The Foreign Office had indeed been debating since autumn if, when, and how to get him recalled. These discussions would continue—and, in fact, intensify—during Kennedy's home visit. T. North Whitehead, the son of philosopher Alfred North Whitehead and himself a Harvard professor who consulted from Cambridge with the American desk at Whitehall, had informed London in January that he believed that as necessary as it might be to get Kennedy removed from office, it would be best to delay any action until after the 1940 elections. "Mr. Roosevelt has had some difficulties in handling the unconventional political habits of the Irish in the United States without thereby antagonising them. I think it possible that Mr. Kennedy is a valuable asset to the Administration in view of the forthcoming election. I question the wisdom of letting the Administration know of our objections to Mr. Kennedy, however informally." Whitehead's comments set off a new round of sniping, snarling, and rumormongering in the Foreign Office and cabinet about Kennedy, his "défaitiste activities," the "perpetual 'spilling'" of his views, and his "gastric troubles." "Mr. Kennedy is a very foul specimen of double-crosser and defeatist," scrawled Sir Robert Vansittart, a close ally of Churchill's and now chief diplomatic adviser to the cabinet. "He thinks of nothing but his own pocket. I hope that this war will at least see the elimination of his type."[8]

From Washington, Kennedy traveled to East Boston for a reunion of parishioners at Our Lady of the Assumption Church, where he had once been an altar boy. He hadn't prepared a speech for the occasion—none had been requested—but spoke extemporaneously to his fellow parishioners. "There's no place in this fight for us. It is going to be bad enough as it is. . . . There is no reason—economic, financial or social—to justify the United States entering the war." The following day, his remarks were picked up by the British press. The Foreign Office was aghast that the ambassador was now saying in public what he had been saying privately: that the British were finished and that the United States should not come to their assistance.[9]

Kennedy stayed overnight in Boston and the next day checked into the Lahey Clinic. His doctors could find nothing organically the matter with his stomach but wanted him to have another set of tests before he returned to London in February. Because he feared, and rightly, that no one in Washington would understand how serious his stomach condition was, he asked Dr. Sara Jordan, his gastroenterologist, to write Roosevelt, which she did, declaring that Kennedy's "chronic gastritis" had reached "an acute phase." Under ordinary circumstances, Dr. Jordan told the president, Kennedy's condition would require "hospitalization, with rest and medication; but in view of the fact that Mr. Kennedy has such excellent facilities for rest in Florida, we feel he should go there and follow a very careful routine, which to be effective should be of at least two months duration."[10]

Back in Washington, Kennedy continued to pour out his cataclysmic predictions. "To anyone who comes within hailing distance," Joe Alsop and Bob Kintner reported in their nationally syndicated December 19 column, "our ambassador to England freely predicts the collapse of capitalism, the destruction of democracy and the onset of the dark ages. He says that only an early peace, at almost any price, can save the world." A prolonged war would inevitably, no matter which side won, lead to "general ruin. This must not be taken to mean that either Kennedy or his English friends do not believe that Hitler must be stopped. While they thought capitalism might survive in a Europe only partly Nazi-dominated, they know general Nazi rule would sweep away the landmarks as efficiently as a bloody world conflict. Naturally, however, Kennedy is desperately anxious to see the war stopped as soon as possible." Alsop and Kintner hoped he would remain in place in London. "A pessimist is always more useful than an optimist in international affairs."[11]

Kennedy did not spend any time in Westchester. Instead, he flew from D.C. to Palm Beach, where he would spend the Christmas holidays with the family and January and most of February recuperating from his stomach problems.

On February 24, he returned to New York City to board the *Manhattan*, bound for Naples in neutral Italy. It was not safe to land in Great Britain or France, as it had once been. He wrote Rose, as if it were entirely coincidental, that "Clare Luce and Miss [Margaret] Case of Vogue" happened to be on the same ship. "The trip across the Atlantic," he would recall in his unpublished memoir, "was uneventful, marked by inclement weather and poor food. Happily, Clare Luce was on hand. . . . Her gay conversation was a contrast to the greyness of sea and sky." Kennedy and Luce, who was on assignment to report for *Life* magazine on the effect of the war in Europe, disembarked in Naples at noon on March 4, visited Pompeii, then returned to Rome together. "Jo and I walk in moonlight, coliseum," Clare noted in her diary. The next evening, they dined together and attended the opera.[12]

One might have thought that the ambassador, after more than three months away from his post, would hurry back to London. But Kennedy was in no great rush. After two days in Rome with Clare Boothe Luce, he boarded a train with his valet and "London Jack" Kennedy, whom he had arranged to meet him in Naples. On their way north, they stopped off in Milan, where he was able to secure a private viewing of Leonardo da Vinci's *Last Supper* and visit the fourteenth-century Duomo.[13]

Kennedy returned to his post in March, having been away since late November. Rather than taking up residence at Prince's Gate, he moved into St. Leonard's, a sixty-room castlelike mansion in Windsor (since 1996 home of the Legoland Windsor Theme Park), which automobile mogul Horace Dodge had invited him to use rent-free.

His extended absence had not been taken well by the British, who considered it something of an insult for the American ambassador to remove himself from London in this, their time of troubles. The once popular American ambassador had become very much persona non grata. Clare Boothe Luce was so concerned that she asked the *Time* magazine offices in London to prepare a "research memorandum" explaining the causes of "this present wave of unpopularity." She received back a lengthy report listing several reasons for Kennedy's unpopularity: "(1) His [antiwar] speech on arrival [in America] before Christmas in which he advised Americans 'to keep out of it.' . . . (2) His long absence from England, following the speech. . . . (3) The fact that he has not brought his family back. (4) That he has given up his London house and lives in the country."[14]

Had the British government, press, and public known how far out of the policy-making loop Kennedy was, they would have rested easier. But it was assumed in London that the ambassador remained a valuable adviser to Roosevelt. When in early March Washington announced that the president was sending Sumner Welles to consult with German, Italian, French, and British officials, the Chamberlain government worried that he was going to launch peace negotiations with the Germans and Italians, as Kennedy had advocated.[15] Welles had been sent instead to find out if there was any chance to end the war before it started up again. Roosevelt did not believe there was but wanted to make sure.

The under secretary of state arrived in London on March 10. Kennedy met him at the airport and, as he wrote Rose, the two men "have been spinning ever since. . . . We have had two or three conferences with the Prime Minister and Halifax and saw Churchill, Lloyd George, Eden, Atlee, Sinclair [future secretary of state for air], and all the rest. They treated Welles exceptionally well here. . . . Welles is very intelligent and is hoping that out of all the mess some plan may be devised that can save the world from this devastating war. There is always a hope, but the chances look like about one in a thousand." Kennedy did not tell his wife that he had been left off the invitation list for Welles's visit "to the palace to have tea with the King and Queen," which vexed him no end. Welles offered several explanations for the snub—none of which was ever confirmed—then intervened to have Kennedy added to the list. The ambassador interpreted his exclusion as further sign of the disfavor with which he was now held in British government circles.[16]

Welles returned to Washington at the end of March. The exercise had been a total failure. "The leaders he talked to," Hull recalled in his memoirs, had "offered no real hope for peace."[17]

You would never believe the way public opinion in this country has turned anti-American and incidentally anti-US Ambassador Kennedy," he wrote Rose on March 20. "The things they say about me from the fact I've sent my family home because they were afraid, to the fact that I live in the country because I am afraid of being bombed etc. etc. All rotten stuff but all the favorite dinner parties at Mayfair go right to work hauling the U.S. Ambassador down. It's for that reason it would be silly for you or the children to come over. It might spoil your pleasant impressions." As in the past, Kennedy blamed much of his unpopularity on the Jews, believing they were against him because he was not sufficiently bellicose. "Walter Lippmann is around saying he hasn't liked the US Ambassador for the last 6 months. Of course the fact he is a Jew has something to do with that. It is all a little annoying, but not very serious."[18]

Rose gently suggested that Kennedy might want to do something to rescue his reputation. "Joe, dear, I have a definite idea that it would be a wonderful feat if you could put over the idea that although you are against America's entering the war—still you are encouraging help to England in some way. It seems to me most people in America would be sympathetic to that idea, & it would endear you to the hearts of the British. It may be impractical, but I have felt it strongly the last two weeks."[19]

Kennedy, unwilling or unable to apologize for saying what was on his mind, did nothing of the sort.

He spent Easter 1940 with Clare Boothe Luce at St. Leonard's in Windsor. Rosemary remained with Miss Gibbs and Mother Isabel in Hertfordshire. Her eight brothers and sisters spent the holiday with their mother at Palm Beach. "It is lovely weather down here," Jean wrote her father. "We all flew down and the trip was very smooth. No one was sick except Miss Dunn. Everyone is down except Joe. He is coming down later. Teddy is learning how to play tennis and is using everybody's tennis racket. It's a wonder he hasn't broken any by now. I am working very hard trying to make a sweater and I am nearly finished."[20]

Jack arrived in Palm Beach in a triumphant mood, having finished the senior thesis he had been working on all winter: "Appeasement at Munich: The Inevitable Result of the Slowness of Conversion of the British Democracy to Change from a Disarmament Policy to a Rearmament Policy." "Jack rushed madly around the last week with his thesis," Joe Jr. wrote his father on March 17, "and finally with the aid of five stenographers the last day got it in under the wire. I read it before he had finished it up and it seemed to represent a lot of work but did not prove anything. However, he said he shaped it up the last few days and he seemed to have some good ideas so it ought to be very good."[21]

As proud as Jack was of his thesis, what he wanted more than anything else was his father's approval. "Arthur Krock read it and feels that I should get it published," he wrote his father. "Please let me know what you think about the thesis as soon as you can— Am sending it to an agent Krock gave me—and see what he thinks—the chief questions are 1. Whether it is worth publishing if polished up. 2. If it can be published while you're still in office."[22]

Kennedy read the thesis and showed it "to various people around here. Everyone agrees that it is a swell job, and that you must have put in some long hard hours assembling, digesting and documenting all of this material." The thesis was, as it now stood, a well-documented, though not entirely convincing, defense of Neville Chamberlain's actions at Munich. The prime minister, Jack concluded, had had no choice but to appease Hitler because an antiwar, antimilitary British public had refused to spend money in the 1930s on maintaining and modernizing the British army, navy, and air force. "I believe that the basis of your case—that the blame must be placed on the people as a whole—is sound," Kennedy wrote Jack. The danger was that because Jack blamed the "people," not the politicians, his thesis was susceptible to being read as a "complete whitewash" of Chamberlain and Stanley Baldwin, his predecessor. This had to be corrected. "You might also be trying to improve the writing," Kennedy concluded his long letter to his son. "After you are satisfied with it, ask Arthur Krock to go over it again. If Krock is willing, let his agent handle the publication. I suggest that, when you are going over the material again, you check your references. We have found several misspellings of names and a couple of wrong dates."[23]

It had not been a particularly good spring for Kennedy. On March 26, he learned of the death of Joe Sheehan, his oldest friend from East Boston, Boston Latin, and Harvard. Days later, he received word that Eddie Moore had been taken ill in Paris with a bad case of the "flu." Kennedy flew to Paris at once, visited Moore, spent two nights with Clare Boothe Luce, then brought Eddie and his wife, Mary, back to London and moved them both into his estate in Windsor. "He doesn't want to go home, of course," he wrote Rose after getting the Moores safely back to England, "because he figures we will all be going home pretty soon and he would rather stay so that we can all go back together."[24]

He still had no idea how long he was going to be in place as ambassador, or indeed how long he wanted to remain in place. "The news all seems to be Roosevelt won't run so automatically I'm out," he wrote Rose on April 5. "The only thing is how soon? . . . Well darling I guess it's right nothing is perfect in this life and I just don't like being so completely away from you. Yet knowing myself as I do when I've been home 6 months I'll want to get going again. Maybe old age and a bad stomach will change me. I don't know. I guess I'm a restless soul: Some people call it ambition. I guess I'm just <u>nuts</u>. Nevertheless, I love you so much."[25]

Kennedy's brief period of ennui came to an abrupt end four days later when, at three in the morning on April 9, German ships entered Oslo, Bergen, and Norway's southern port cities; at five A.M., more ships landed in Copenhagen and German soldiers crossed the Danish frontier. Denmark, under threat of aerial bombardment, surrendered without a fight. The Norwegians chose to resist.

While the rest of the world reeled at the ease, the speed, the secrecy, and the success with which the Germans occupied Copenhagen and every major Norwegian port, Lord Halifax, whom Kennedy visited at three thirty in the afternoon of April 9, "seemed more cheerful than usual. Kept repeating 'a very interesting situation.' Felt the Germans had made a false move." Churchill, Halifax told Kennedy, had been "almost thrilled with the news and he had convinced the Cabinet that Hitler had made a major strategic error." The British military was prepared for the landing, Churchill declared in the House of Commons on April 11, and would quickly repel it.[26]

Exhibiting an exquisitely poor sense of timing, Kennedy wrote Roosevelt two days after the phony war turned real to complain about British finances: "It may seem strange that I should be writing to you at this moment about such matters as gold and British holdings of American securities, but although the necessity to face up to this situation is not yet as urgent as events which are now taking place in Scandinavia, it is nevertheless real and soon may be the none-the-less urgent." The British were buying the dollars they needed to pay for American imports and military supplies by selling gold in the United States at $35 an ounce instead of liquidating their investments in American securities, as they had pledged to do. Kennedy recommended that Roosevelt step in immediately and curtail British gold sales by legislation, if necessary, before the treasury was overrun with gold it did not need and could not exchange.[27]

On April 29, Secretary of the Treasury Morgenthau, whom Roosevelt had asked to answer Kennedy's four-page letter, assembled his chief advisers for a 10:15 meeting. "Now, the reason I have got you fellows in here, this is extra confidential. I got one of these typical Joe Kennedy letters to the President on gold. . . . It is one of these typical asinine Joe Kennedy letters." Morgenthau was opposed to Kennedy's recommendation that the British be pressured to sell their securities to fund the war effort, because he feared that dumping those securities on the market would result in a dramatic fall of American stock prices. Only months earlier, Kennedy had warned of this eventuality. When a colleague asked Morgenthau why the ambassador might now be pushing the president in the opposite direction, Morgenthau, furious that Kennedy had dared interfere with treasury policy from the other side of the ocean, exploded with rage and insisted that Kennedy wanted to depress stock prices so he could make money selling short. "The only thing that has explained Joe Kennedy to me for the last couple of years is that he has been consistently short in the market. . . . Every single move he has made is to depress [the prices of] our securities and our commodities."[28]

Morgenthau had no evidence for this charge, other than the fact that Ben Smith, a notorious short seller with whom Kennedy had traded a decade earlier, had recently been in London. But lack of evidence did not stop him from adding his voice to the whispering campaign against the ambassador. The reality that no one in London or Washington would have believed was that Kennedy had virtually stopped trading stocks when he'd entered government service, first, because the rules he had written at the SEC made selling short much more difficult, and second, because he knew that there were spies everywhere looking to brand him as an unscrupulous, unpatriotic stock swindler. He wasn't going to give them the chance to do so.

The situation tonight," Kennedy wrote Rose a week after the German landing in Norway and Denmark, "is more bewildering than ever. The Norwegian situation is far from being a simple one. . . . It is going to take a lot of work to drive the Germans out. . . . But the difficulty is that nobody really knows what [Hitler] is liable to do or what's going to come out of this whole Scandinavian episode. . . . I am more convinced than ever that the children should not come over here. I quite understand Kathleen's interest [she was desperate to see Billy Hartington again], but she can take my word for it that she would have the dullest time she ever had in her life. All the young fellows are being shuttled off to war."[29]

As it quickly became apparent that the British attempt to dislodge the Germans in Norway was turning out disastrously, the public and press, having been fed only good news by Prime Minister Chamberlain and First Lord of the Admiralty Churchill, began to turn against the government. "Had a long call from Joe Kennedy," Lord Halifax wrote in his diary for April 25, "who came to talk about the inefficiency of what he called our showmanship. I thought there was a good deal in what he said. . . . I become more and more convinced that the Minister of Information ought to sit in at the Cabinet, but the P.M. is very sticky about this."[30]

While the Norwegian operation had been planned and executed by Churchill as first lord of the Admiralty, it was Chamberlain who, as head of the government, was going to take the fall for its failure. On the evening of May 8, after a two-day debate on the prosecution of the war capped by Churchill's eloquent defense of the Norwegian exercise, a "division" was called, ostensibly on an adjournment motion but, in fact, on whether or not to censure the present government. Chamberlain's majority, recently over two hundred, was cut to eighty-one. Thirty-three Tories, including Anthony Eden, defected; another sixty, including Lady Astor, abstained.[31]

Kennedy, as had become his habit, "went to Beaverbrook's house to get his slant on the situation." Beaverbrook "felt that Chamberlain would have to go—if not right away, very shortly." Concerned that the Chamberlain government was about to fall, Kennedy placed a call to the White House at midnight. The president came to the phone and Kennedy reported what he had heard. The president replied that "he had just heard that Germany had delivered an ultimatum to Holland." What it all meant, Roosevelt did not yet know. "There is," Kennedy concluded in his diary entry that evening, "a very definite undercurrent of despair because of the hopelessness of the whole task for England."

The following morning, May 10, at six A.M., the "telephone rang and they said it was Secretary Hull. I held on five minutes and the Secretary came on and asked me if I knew of anything that was going on. I said, 'Nothing.'" Hull reported that he had heard from Ambassador John Cudahy in Belgium that "the Germans had attacked Holland and Belgium, and that there was great concentration of airplanes over Luxembourg."

On ringing off, Kennedy "called the Admiralty and got the map room and they indicated that the only news they had was that Holland had been invaded. . . . Again it struck me that they didn't have the slightest idea of what was going on." Kennedy got dressed and was driven to his office, where he placed calls to the American embassies in Holland, Belgium, and Italy. The Germans, he learned, had mined the Dutch harbors, bombed The Hague, were attacking Brussels from the air, and were concentrating airplanes over Luxembourg. There was no news from Rome. He called Lord Halifax at Whitehall and "asked him what the British were doing and he said, 'We are moving all ways—air, navy, and army." He then called Sumner Welles at the State Department, "gave him all this information" he had gathered, and promised to remain in touch as long as the telephone lines remained open. Welles thanked him. "He said they hadn't been able to get through to anybody, not even Paris, and he was very anxious to keep in touch with the countries and to know what was going on."[32]

The first British casualty of the German assault was the prime minister, who resigned his position on May 10. He had preferred that his successor be Lord Halifax, but when the foreign secretary declined the offer, he turned to Churchill. Kennedy was distraught by the fall from power of the man he admired most in Great Britain, and devastated by the news that the gentlemanly Chamberlain would be succeeded by the warmongering, near alcoholic Winston Churchill.

As Prime Minister Churchill assembled his war cabinet, naming himself minister of defense, the German Panzer divisions pushed through Holland, Belgium, and into France. Barely ninety hours after the initial attacks, Paul Reynaud, the French premier, reported to Churchill by telephone that the French lines had been broken and the army cut in two. He called again the next morning at seven A.M. "The battle is lost," he told Churchill in English.[33]

Kennedy was fully occupied at the embassy with evacuating those Americans still in England. The State Department had suggested ferrying them across the English Channel to the southern coast of France, where they could be picked up by American ships. For Kennedy, the notion of ferrying anyone across the English Channel, "the most dangerous stretch of water now being used by any passenger service in the world," was further proof that Washington had no idea what was happening on the continent. Kennedy suggested that Irish ports were far more accessible from England and far safer. After much back and forth, his recommendation was accepted.[34]

The evening of May 14, Kennedy went to the theater with Franklin Gowen from his embassy and Bill Hillman, the former Hearst correspondent. On the way back to Windsor, he stopped off to see Lord Beaverbrook, who told him that he had just accepted an appointment as minister of aircraft production in the Churchill government and was on his way to a midnight appointment with the prime minister. Minutes later, the telephone rang at Beaverbrook's residence, and Kennedy, who hadn't left yet, was asked to "come right away to the Admiralty; that Churchill would like to see me."

Kennedy had never liked or trusted Churchill. Now, confronted with the rotund red-faced little man, surrounded by his aides, he was truly frightened. "I couldn't help but think as I sat there talking to Churchill how ill-conditioned he looked and the fact that there was a tray with plenty of liquor on it alongside him and he was drinking a scotch highball, which I felt was indeed not the first one he had drunk that night, that, after all, the affairs of Great Britain might be in the hands of the most dynamic individual in Great Britain but certainly not in the hands of the best judgment in Great Britain."[35]

"I just left Churchill at one o'clock," Kennedy cabled Roosevelt and Hull an hour later. "He is sending you a message tomorrow morning. . . . The reason for the message to you is that he needs help badly. I asked him what the United States could do to help that would not leave the United States holding the bag for a war in which the Allies expected to be beaten. It seems to me that if we had to fight to protect our lives we would do better fighting in our own backyard. I said you know our strength. What could we do if we wanted to help you all we can? You do not need money or credit now. The bulk of our Navy is in the Pacific and we have not enough airplanes for our own use and our Army is not up to requirements. So if this is going to be a quick war all over in a few months what could we do. He said it was his intention to ask now for a loan of 30 or 40 of our old destroyers and also whatever airplanes we could spare right now. He said that regardless of what Germany does to England and France, England will never give up as long as he remains a power in public life even if England is burnt to the ground. Why, said he, the government will move to Canada and take the fleet and fight on."[36]

This was precisely what Kennedy expected and feared Churchill was going to say. The newly installed prime minister intended to push the British to fight on until the Americans had no choice but to enter the war or watch from the sidelines as Great Britain was conquered.

On May 16, Roosevelt called on Congress to appropriate $896 million to upgrade American air, ground, and naval defenses. "New powers of destruction, incredibly swift and ready, have been developed; and those who wield them are ruthless and daring. . . . No old defense is so strong that it requires no further strengthening, and no attack is so unlikely or impossible that it may be ignored." He made no mention of supplying any military assistance to the British or the French.[37]

After delivering his message to Congress, the president returned to the White House and wrote to inform Churchill that the United States could not loan the British any destroyers, no matter how old, without congressional approval, which he declined to seek. On the matter of airplanes, he promised nothing, insisting only that the United States would do "everything within our power to make it possible for the Allied Governments to obtain the latest types of aircraft in the United States." As to the American fleet, which Churchill hoped would be repositioned to the Atlantic, it was "now concentrated in Hawaii where it will remain at least for the time being." Roosevelt was, however, prepared to permit the British to purchase steel in the United States, and he pledged to give "the most favorable consideration . . . to the request" for antiaircraft equipment and ammunition, though he added that the request would have to be considered "in the light of our own defense needs and requirements."[38]

Churchill responded by pressing his case and posing a frightening scenario. Although he had no intention of negotiating with the Germans, he could not vouch for his successors, who might, as part of a peace settlement, hand over the British fleet. For the moment, the United States was seemingly impregnable, but should the Germans gain control of the British fleet, they would rule the seas as well as the European continent and be free to do as they pleased in the western hemisphere. "Excuse me, Mr. President, putting this nightmare bluntly. . . . However, there is happily no need at present to dwell upon such ideas."[39]

Roosevelt was persuaded by Churchill's argument that the defeat of the British would pose a direct threat to American security, especially if the fleet fell into Germany's hands. In his May 15 dispatch, Kennedy had argued that "if we had to fight to protect our lives we would do better fighting in our own backyard." Roosevelt disagreed.

"The President and I," Cordell Hull recalled decades later in his *Memoirs*, "reached a different conclusion from Kennedy's. It seemed to us we should do better to keep fighting away from our own back yard. This we could do by helping Britain and France remain on their feet." Although it was unclear as yet what could be done to assist the British given the neutrality laws and public opinion, "of one point, the President and I had not the slightest doubt; namely, that an Allied victory was essential to the security of the United States."[40]

Twenty-three

THE FALL OF FRANCE

It was Saturday, May 18, 1940. The ambassador was spending his weekend at St. Leonard's. Late in the evening, Herschel Johnson, his number two man at the embassy, called to say that he had been visited that afternoon by Maxwell Knight of MI5, British Military Intelligence. "Johnson's language," Kennedy recalled in his unpublished *Diplomatic Memoir,* "was guarded but I gathered enough from what he said to learn that one of our clerks was suspected of having given out confidential information to sources allied to the Nazis."

Johnson met with Kennedy at St. Leonard's the next morning and told Kennedy a most "extraordinary story" of espionage at the American embassy. Tyler Kent, a twenty-nine-year-old code specialist from an old Virginia family who had joined the U.S. Foreign Service after college, served in Moscow, and been transferred to London in October 1939, had been consorting with Anna Wolkoff, the daughter of a former admiral in the czar's navy. Wolkoff was connected to the Right Club, a secret society of English Fascists led by Captain Archibald Maule Ramsay, a Conservative member of Parliament. Through the use of undercover agents, MI5 had learned that Wolkoff had bragged about receiving information from Kent that could only have come from the embassy. Scotland Yard was preparing to arrest Wolkoff the next morning, Monday, "and would search Kent's rooms at the same time provided that we would waive any diplomatic immunity that might prevent such a search." Kennedy agreed to waive immunity.[1]

The ambassador arrived at the embassy early on Monday morning, May 20. That same morning, Maxwell Knight of MI5, Franklin Gowen of the embassy, and three men from Scotland Yard made their way to Tyler Kent's flat. They arrived at 11:15. On being refused entrance, they broke down the door, took Kent into custody, let the woman he was with go home, and searched his rooms, where according to Knight they discovered "a most amazing collection of documents [including] copies of secret and confidential code telegrams between various United States Embassies and Washington." An hour or so later, they returned to the embassy, where Kennedy and Johnson took a quick look at the stolen materials: almost two thousand documents, two sets of duplicate keys to the code and file rooms, a tin box, and a locked, leather-bound book. Kent was brought into the office, where he insisted that he was not a spy but had taken the documents "only for my own information."[2]

Tyler Kent had not been the highest-ranking or most efficient of the decoders, but it had fallen to him to code and decode the clandestine Churchill-Roosevelt cables. Had it become public knowledge in the spring of 1940 that the president of the United States, whose actions in the international arena were bound by strict neutrality laws, had been in secret communication with the bellicose first lord of the British Admiralty, Roosevelt and the Democrats would have been severely embarrassed six months before the presidential elections.[3]

The ambassador in London was frightened to the core at the possible repercussions. There were too many unanswered questions. For how long had MI5 suspected that Tyler Kent was a spy? Did the British have potentially embarrassing information about other embassy employees? Was Kent part of a larger spy ring? Were officials at other American embassies involved? To whom had Kent and his British Fascist accomplices given the materials they had stolen from the code and file rooms?

At seven o'clock that evening, Kennedy cabled Washington with the news he knew would set off alarms. He did his best to pretend that he had the situation fully in control, though it was obvious that he did not. "Following the receipt on Saturday of information that Tyler Kent associated with a gang of spies working in the interests of Germany and Russia, I today caused his private quarters to be searched, finding there substantial amounts of confidential embassy material, including true readings of messages in most confidential codes; also evidence of his personal connections with the spy group." He had waived Kent's immunity, participated fully with MI5 and Scotland Yard, and permitted Kent to be placed in custody. Kennedy "urgently requested . . . the department's approval and instructions."[4]

Within hours, he received a cable from Washington with orders that all further communications be decoded by Herschel Johnson and no one else. Hull needed to know at once if the strip cipher system, the most secret of the codes used by the State Department, had been compromised. A second cable informed the ambassador that Tyler Kent had been dismissed. A third directed him to keep a careful watch of all code clerks, their associates, and their outside activities.

The State Department was near frantic. To determine whether Kent had associates in other American embassies in Europe, Breckinridge Long, with J. Edgar Hoover's assistance, recruited and dispatched teams of undercover agents, disguised as special couriers, to several European embassies.[5]

Embassy staff in London were instructed to put together a catalog of the stolen documents. "They are a complete history of our diplomatic correspondence since 1938," Long wrote in his diary on receiving the documents. "It is appalling. Hundreds of copies—true readings—of dispatches, cables, messages. Some months every single message going into and out from the London Embassy were copied and the copies found in his room. It means not only that our codes are cracked a dozen ways but that our every diplomatic maneuver was exposed to Germany and Russia. . . . It is a terrible blow—almost a major catastrophe."[6]

Long was overreacting. Kennedy proved remarkably adept at damage control. He met with the under-secretary at the Home Office, who spoke with the chief censor on his behalf. "They assure me," he cabled Hull on May 24, that "nothing will be permitted to be printed here or abroad." To avoid the spectacle of a public espionage trial, Kent was not deported but tried in London under the British Official Secrets Act, with no reporters, visitors, or spectators allowed into the courtroom and no documents from the Churchill-Roosevelt correspondence, or indeed any other sensitive dispatches or cables, put into evidence. The jury returned a verdict of guilty on all counts after deliberating for twenty-four minutes and sentenced Kent to seven years penal servitude, of which he would serve a little more than five.[7]

Breckinridge Long's investigation revealed that Tyler Kent had acted alone. There had been no leak of the secret Churchill-Roosevelt communiqués. The "catastrophe" that the State Department had anticipated had not come to pass. In the end, the Tyler Kent affair was a sideshow, though a thoroughly frightening one.

Meanwhile, on the continent all that Kennedy had feared and expected had come to pass. The Germans pushed on, almost unimpeded, pounding the French army and the British Expeditionary Force from the air and on the ground.

"The situation is terrible," Kennedy wrote Rose on May 20 in his own hand, as he did not want to share what he had to say with his typists. "I think the jig is up. The situation is more than critical. It means a terrible finish for the Allies. I'm planning to get Rose[mary] and the Moores out either to Ireland or Lisbon. We will be in for a terrific bombing pretty soon and I'll do better if I just have myself to look after. The English will fight to the end but I just don't think they can stand up to the bombing indefinitely. What will happen then is probably a dictated peace with Hitler probably getting the British Navy, and we will find ourselves in a terrible mess. My God how right I've been in my predictions. I wish I'd been wrong. Well darling it's certainly been a great adventure. It's getting near the finish."[8]

During the last week in May, after the failure of a French counteroffensive, General John Gort, the commander of the British Expeditionary Force in Europe, established a safe haven at the port of Dunkirk, just northeast of the advancing German troops, and began to evacuate his army across the English Channel. Churchill, who had urged his generals to fight on, reluctantly agreed that the army would be destroyed or captured by the Germans if it did not leave the continent at once. "My impression of the situation here," Kennedy cabled Washington on the evening of May 27, "is that it could not be worse. Only a miracle can save the British expeditionary force from being wiped out or as I said yesterday, surrender." Kennedy insisted that the Allies had no choice now but to sue for peace. "I suspect that the Germans would be willing to make peace with both the French and British now—of course on their own terms, but on terms that would be a great deal better than they would be if the war continues. . . . I realize this is a terrific telegram, but there is no question that it's in the air here. . . . Churchill, Atlee and others will want to fight to the death, but there will be other numbers who realize that physical destruction of men and property in England will not be a proper offset to a loss of pride. In addition to that, the English people, while they suspect a terrible situation, really do not realize how bad it is. When they do, I don't know which group they will follow—the do or die, or the group that want a settlement. It is critical no matter which way you look at it."[9]

Kennedy's suggestion that the British and French attempt "to make peace" before it was too late was not an outlandish one. Lord Halifax, still foreign secretary, had already proposed to the cabinet that the British consider joining with the French and inquiring of Mussolini, perhaps through President Roosevelt, what his terms were for staying out of the war and whether he would be willing to attend a four-power conference, with Germany, France, and Great Britain, to negotiate an end to the crisis. After three days of strenuous internal debate, Churchill convinced his colleagues not to approach Mussolini.[10]

"With France apparently falling," Hull called together senior State Department officials "to consider the possible eventualities of the war situation in Europe. . . . We came to the general conclusion that the position of the Allied armies was desperate, and our attention centered on the necessity" of keeping the French and British navies out of German hands. Roosevelt cabled both governments asking for assurances, which were given, that they would not surrender their fleets to the Germans.[11]

The possibility that Britain's gold supplies might be seized or surrendered to the Germans was no less frightening. Kennedy, on instructions from Hull, suggested to Kingsley Wood, the British chancellor of the Exchequer, and Montague Norman, the governor of the Bank of England, that it might be prudent for the government to consider shipping its gold and securities to Canada. "Kingsley Wood said he would consult the Prime Minister. . . . The next day he told me that Churchill would not agree to ship valuables to Canada because it might make the country think that the government was in panic. . . . I was learning rapidly," Kennedy recalled in his *Diplomatic Memoir,* "that one can become unpopular by offering advice that people don't want to hear. My contacts with the Churchill cabinet were certainly far less friendly than with the old government."[12]

All of these scenarios, one more nightmarish than the next, were founded on the anticipated loss of most, if not all, of the quarter-million-man British Expeditionary Force. What neither Washington nor London knew was that Hitler, for reasons that remain open to debate to this day, instead of pressing forward to capture the British Army, had on May 24 halted the forward movement of his Panzer divisions fifteen miles south of Dunkirk. By the time he revoked that order two days later, the British evacuation was under way. On May 26 and 27, some 8,000 troops crossed the English Channel; on May 28, another 19,000; on May 29, some 47,000 more. By June 4, when the last boats departed from the beaches and harbor of Dunkirk, the impossible had happened: the bulk of the British Army and more than 100,000 French and Belgium troops had been saved.[13]

"We must be very careful not to assign to this deliverance," Churchill told the House of Commons on June 4, "the attributes of a victory. Wars are not won by evacuations." Still, the army had been saved to fight again. "I have, myself, full confidence that if all do their duty, if nothing is neglected, and if the best arrangements are made, as they are being made, we shall prove ourselves once again able to defend our island home, to ride out the storm of war, and to outlive the menace of tyranny, if necessary for years, if necessary alone. . . . We shall go on to the end. We shall fight in France, we shall fight on the seas and oceans, we shall fight with growing confidence and growing strength in the air, we shall defend our island, whatever the cost may be. We shall fight on the beaches, we shall fight on the landing grounds, we shall fight in the fields and in the streets, we shall fight in the hills; we shall never surrender, and even if, which I do not for a moment believe, this island or a large part of it were subjugated and starving, then our Empire beyond the seas, armed and guarded by the British Fleet, would carry on the struggle, until, in God's good time, the new world, with all its power and might, steps forth to the rescue and the liberation of the old."[14]

Kennedy was stirred by Churchill's eloquence. Still, for him, the most significant passages of the speech, as he recalled them years later in his *Diplomatic Memoir,* were not those devoted to the call to arms, struggle, sacrifice, and endless battle, but the prime minister's admission and warning that "our thankfulness at the escape of our army . . . must not blind us to the fact that what has happened in France and Belgium is a colossal military disaster."[15]

"If the French break—and the consensus here is that they will—," Kennedy wrote Joe Jr. on June 6, two days after Churchill's address, "then I should think the finish may come quite quickly. The British, of course, will fight, but only through pride and courage. With the French out of the way and the Germans in control of all the ports I can see nothing but slaughter ahead. I am arranging to send everybody away with the exception of about ten of us . . . who will stay and sleep at the Chancery [the embassy]. I am going to try to keep this place operating as long as they leave the building standing up."[16]

"The strain is terrible," he wrote that same day to Bob Fisher. "I hate to think what is going to happen to England, but since I am sure that I was born not to be bombed to death, I am very optimistic. I have got all the family and Eddie and Mary home. I propose to stick in London as long as there are any buildings left. I am moving my bed into the office this week, and here I stick."[17]

His letter to Rose was almost wistful. "Didn't someone say in the Bible once that you 'have to pay for all your pleasures sooner or later.' Well if they didn't they should have because I'm satisfied everyone thinks it's time and it would be nice to have the Bible as an authority." He expected that France would fall soon now and "the Germans will invade England. . . . I of course will have to stay here through Bombing and Invasion but once this has happened I will expect F.D.R. to send for me. . . . Americans will have gone home and since there won't be much to do, my place is home, I've done my duty. . . . We've been lucky so far that none of our friends have been killed but lots of boys have been. The atmosphere is very depressing. . . . On the whole I'm fine, lonesome and anxious to see if I can take it." With Rosemary back in the United States, the burden of caring for her had returned to Rose, but that he assured his wife was only temporary. "When things settle down here under any regime, they [the nuns at her convent school] will be delighted to have her back and I'm sure she'll come back hopping. This state of the world can't keep on long at this tension."[18]

On June 10, Mussolini appeared on the balcony of the Palazzo Venezia to declare Italy's entrance into the war. On June 11, Churchill and key cabinet members and military advisers flew to the relocated French headquarters seventy miles from Paris to confer with Premier Reynaud and French army leaders.

The end was in sight. The only questions now were how long the French would be able to hold out, what would be the terms of surrender, and what would become of the fleet.

Returning from his meeting with the French, the prime minister summoned Kennedy. On greeting him, he offered the American ambassador a Scotch, as he always did; Kennedy refused, as he always did. Churchill had nothing much to report on France. "He still was not quite frank with me about the situation and hastens to remark on all occasions that England is going to fight to a finish" and that even if the French lost their fleet, which he did not think likely, "the British would still fight on." Again, he asked for American destroyers, which, he insisted, were more important now than planes "because of the terrific problem of protecting the Island from invasion and at the same time keeping trade routes open." Kennedy promised to forward his request to the president.[19]

The next evening, Kennedy received a cable from Roosevelt, which he was asked to hand-deliver to Churchill. It was a copy of his reply to Premier Reynaud, who had three days earlier on evacuating his government from Paris requested that the president "declare publicly that the United States will give the Allies aid and material support by all means 'short of an expeditionary force.' I beseech you to do this before it is too late." Roosevelt had delayed replying, but having learned from Churchill that the French were about to capitulate, he delivered an answer of stunning ambiguity: "As I have already stated to you and to Mr. Churchill, this Government is doing everything in its power to make available to the Allied Governments the material they so urgently require, and our efforts to do still more are being redoubled."[20]

Kennedy found Churchill at dinner with his wife and two daughters and was asked to read aloud the president's note to Reynaud. "Churchill then read it himself three or four times during dinner and was visibly moved by, I think, excitement, but possibly by champagne, which he was drinking, and told me he would immediately convey to Reynaud that his understanding of this message was that America assumed a responsibility if the French continued to fight." He then rushed away to read the note to his cabinet, which did not interpret it as he had. "It was pointed out," in the minutes taken of that evening session, that the president "had not stated in terms that the United States would declare war." Churchill was not to be deterred. He insisted again and again that the message "could only mean that the United States intended to enter the war on our side" and told the cabinet that he intended to say so to Premier Reynaud.[21]

Kennedy, meanwhile, had returned to the ambassador's residence at Prince's Gate, "drank my bottle of milk and had a sponge cake . . . and tried to lie down for a few minutes." At eleven P.M., the phone rang. It was the prime minister requesting that Kennedy return to Downing Street. Churchill wanted him to call Washington immediately and get permission from the president to publish the cable to Reynaud. A call was put through to the White House. Roosevelt came to the phone and "indicated that he didn't think the message should be printed, but it was not with great firmness that he said that. He said Hull objected to printing it because he thought it was too much of a commitment." Kennedy urged the president to make no final decision until he was fully aware of conditions in France. He promised to cable him "an outline" of what had occurred, after which he could decide whether or not to publish the note to Reynaud.[22]

Kennedy hurried back to the embassy, where he cabled Roosevelt and Hull what he had learned from the "minutes" of the British-French summit. The French, he informed Washington, were ready to surrender. Churchill had urged them not to. The prime minister was insistent that Roosevelt's message be published because he thought it was the only way to revive French morale and "keep them in the fight. . . . I realize the tragedy of the present moment and how important it is for the success of these poor people that their morale should be bucked up; nevertheless I see a great danger in the message as a commitment at a later date."[23]

No sooner had he cabled his dispatch than the phone at the embassy rang. It was Churchill, who had drafted another message to Roosevelt that he hoped could be coded and cabled at once. Kennedy "dashed down" to 10 Downing, retrieved Churchill's message, and suggested that if the prime minister wanted to speak directly to the president, he should call him at two thirty A.M. London time. Churchill replied that "he would be sound asleep long before that time." Kennedy returned to the embassy, roused Herschel Johnson, who was now in charge of coding all critical messages, sent off Churchill's cable, then stumbled back to his residence and to bed, hoping to get a few hours' sleep.

"About 4:30, the telephone rang and the President was on the phone." He was adamant now, no longer tentative as he had been a few hours earlier, that he did not want his note to Reynaud published. He asked Kennedy to convey this information to Churchill. To make sure Kennedy understood, the president cabled him the next morning: "My message to Reynaud not to be published in any circumstances. It was in no sense intended to commit and does not commit this Government to the slightest military activities in support of the Allies. . . . If there is any possibility of misunderstanding please insist that Churchill at once convey this statement to the appropriate French officials."[24]

At 9:20 that morning, Churchill called Kennedy at home and was informed that Roosevelt was not going to permit publication of the message to Reynaud. "Churchill, in a very subdued voice, said if that were the case all would be lost in France. My impression," Kennedy wrote in his diary, "is that all will be lost in France anyway, and I am sure the publication of the President's reply would have only delayed the demise very slightly and merely temporarily."[25]

Kennedy spent his weekend at St. Leonard's, working himself into a rage at the president for delaying his response to Reynaud's message for almost three days and then writing a note that could be and was interpreted as a "commitment" to come to France's assistance. Roosevelt had, Kennedy wrote in his diary after midnight on Saturday, June 15, unconscionably played "ducks and drakes with the destinies of millions." Instead of making it clear that the Americans were not going to enter this war, no matter how bad things got for the Allies, he had stalled and then spoken out of both sides of his mouth.

By refusing to follow Kennedy's advice and explain clearly but definitively why American assistance—in airplanes, destroyers, armaments, and ammunition—would not be forthcoming, Roosevelt had endangered the future friendship of the British, who would now blame the United States government for promising to come to the aid of the Allies and then abandoning them. Should the British find themselves in the position where they had to sue for peace after a German bombardment, would they send their fleet to Canada to protect it from falling into German hands? Or would they say to hell with the Americans and use it as a bargaining chip to get better terms?

All Friday night into Saturday, Kennedy ruminated on the possible consequences of the president's actions. None were reassuring. Unlike other parts of his diary, which were dictated, transcribed, and corrected, then put away to be resurrected and rewritten into his *Diplomatic Memoir* years later, the stream-of-consciousness notes he jotted down that night were unmediated, uncensored, and not for publication in any form.

"We've fought with everybody."
"Here we are tonight flat on our fannies—without a friend in the world."
"What is the aftermath to be?"
"Even if we keep out of war."
"What kind of country are we going to have? . . . How're we going to live in it?"

He was exhausted, lonely, frightened, bitter, and self-pitying:

"Great place for a guy who came for a rest and who has a bad stomach!"

He was angry at Roosevelt:

"Don't see how FDR could go off on cruise today!" [The president had left Washington for a cruise on the Potomac.]

He was worried that no one in Washington was taking seriously or preparing militarily for the possibility that, having seized control of the French fleet, with the British fleet next in line, the Germans would move aggressively toward the western hemisphere:

"JPK Program: Take over N[orth] A[merica] to Panama Canal; 1st guy who opens mouth, shoot the sucker. Right of free speech doesn't mean talking against duly delegated authority and gov't. Put in universal military service right now."

He was frustrated beyond words that he had been kept on a tight leash instead of being allowed to play a larger part in securing the peace:

"Navy Day Speech re 'getting along with neighbors.'"
"Twice A[dolf] H[itler] invited JPK to come to Berlin and see him."
"If Roosevelt had followed my advice, we'd have stopped the war."[26]

On Sunday morning, June 16, Churchill phoned Kennedy at St. Leonard's to report that Premier Reynaud had resigned and been replaced by Marshal Philippe Pétain, who, "with a heavy heart," announced the next day that he had "applied to our adversary to ask if he is prepared to seek with me, soldier to soldier, after the battle, honourably the means whereby hostilities may cease."[27]

The armistice was signed on June 22. The French army was to assemble in specified ports to be demobilized and disarmed. Pétain's government would remain in place, but a huge swath of the nation, including Paris, northern France, the borders with Belgium and Switzerland, and the entire coastline from Dover in the north to the border with Spain in the south, was placed under German occupation.

Fortunately, the worst-case scenario did not unfold. The French fleet was permitted to sail to ports in North Africa, where it remained under the nominal control of the Pétain government, until on July 3, the British, rather than risk having it fall into German hands, opened fire upon it. The bulk of the French fleet was destroyed, and some 1,250 French seamen lost their lives.

Twenty-four

THE WORST OF TIMES

Kennedy tried to keep his spirits up, tried to control his rage, tried to look on the positive side. His family and fortune were intact, if an ocean away. The news from home was good. Joe Jr. was doing okay in law school and had made a name for himself by holding tight at the Democratic National Convention in Chicago and voting for James Farley, to whom he had been committed, rather than giving in to formidable pressure to switch to Roosevelt. Jack had graduated from Harvard with honors and was about to publish his first book. Rosemary had been able to spend part of the summer as a junior camp counselor before withdrawing because the responsibility was too much. Kick was at Hyannis Port, surrounded, as always, by admiring boys. Eunice was winning prizes sailing. Pat had lost ten pounds and had decided to go to college in the fall. Bobby was not taking much interest in sailing or his stamps but was avidly following the war news. Jean was making bandages twice a week for the Red Cross and sailing. Teddy had become "completely self-sufficient." And Rose, exhausted by a month with the children and not looking forward to August, which would be even more hectic, was at "Elizabeth Arden's Camp in Maine . . . a quiet place where they have exercises, swimming, golf and massage."[1]

Kennedy had moved back to 14 Prince's Gate but opened up only his own bedroom and study "so the house," as he wrote his daughter Jean, "looks pretty lonesome." He spent his weekends at St. Leonard's in Windsor. After a nasty fall in the spring, he had temporaily given up horseback riding, but he played golf when he could. His stomach was better, but he worried about it and ate lightly. He drank not at all.[2]

The government was Churchill's now, and he had his own set of advisers and confidants, none of whom, with the possible exception of Lord Beaverbrook, minister of aircraft production, had much time to spare the American ambassador. Kennedy spent long days at the embassy, but there was precious little of importance for him to do. As honorary chairman of the American Red Cross war relief fund, he made speeches and thanked donors for their generosity. As chief negotiator for a ludicrously ill-conceived and underthought scheme to save the lives of British children by sending them to the United States, he wasted days on a rescue plan that was destined to fail because British citizens didn't want to part with their children, and even if they had, there were not enough ships—or military convoys—to get them across the Atlantic.

Like everyone else, he waited for the German invasion. Since late May and with renewed urgency after the fall of France, the question voiced in the newspapers, in war cabinet meetings, and in the streets was not if but when the Germans would attempt to cross the English Channel. When July 1, the supposed "zero hour for Hitler's invasion of England," passed without incident, Lord Cadogan marked in his diary that the date now favored by the tipsters was "about July 8." Lord Halifax thought it would be July 9. Kennedy thought July 9 or July 15.[3]

Churchill had been preparing for the invasion since he'd assumed the position of prime minister, perhaps even earlier. "We expect to be attacked here ourselves . . . in the near future, and are getting ready for them," he had written Roosevelt in his May 15 request for "the loan of forty or fifty of your older destroyers to bridge the gap between what we have now and the large new construction we put in hand at the beginning of the war." Kennedy had advised Roosevelt and Hull to turn down this and other requests for military assistance, but the president and his secretary of state had made up their minds to not only not listen to Kennedy, but to do precisely what he advised against. In a major speech at the University of Virginia at Charlottesville on June 10, 1940, Roosevelt had signaled a shift in American policy by declaring that the United States while rearming would "extend to the opponents of force the material resources of this nation."[4]

Though the president, the secretary of state, and the newly appointed secretaries of war and the navy, Republicans Henry Stimson and Frank Knox, were prepared to provide the British with all available military assistance consistent with the Neutrality Acts, they could not entirely dismiss Kennedy's warnings from London. If the British were as woefully unprepared as the ambassador said they were, then any American military supplies shipped to the British would, when the war was lost, end up in German hands. That, obviously, was unacceptable.

Because Kennedy was thoroughly convinced that the German military machine was invincible, neither Roosevelt nor Hull nor, for that matter, anyone in the cabinet and few in the State Department believed him capable of providing any sort of objective evaluation of the state of British military preparedness and civilian morale. He should rightly have been removed from office and replaced by someone the president and Hull could trust. But given the political realities and the fact that the November elections were only a few months away, this was out of the question. It was decided instead to let him remain in place, safely isolated in London, but detour all fact-finding initiatives around him.

In July, Secretary of the Navy Knox, with Stimson's support and Roosevelt's approval, enlisted "Wild Bill" Donovan, a Republican lawyer, law school classmate of Roosevelt's, and Medal of Honor hero, to travel to London to evaluate Britain's military capacities and will to fight. Knox, the former editor of the *Chicago Daily News,* asked Edgar Mowrer, a foreign correspondent for that newspaper, to assist Donovan in gathering information. To provide both men with cover, he suggested that they announce they were going overseas to investigate—and prepare a series of articles on—Nazi/fifth column activities.

Kennedy, who had been told nothing about the Donovan mission, was furious when he heard about it secondhand from Edgar Mowrer in London. His own staff, he cabled Hull, was already engaged "in getting all the information that possibly can be gathered and to send a new man in here at this time, with all due respect to Colonel Knox, is to me the height of nonsense and a definite blow to good organization." Four hours later, he cabled Hull again, at nine P.M. London time, that "if Colonel Knox doesn't stop sending Mowrers and Colonel Donovans over here this organization is not going to function efficiently." Still not convinced he was being heard, he cabled his complaints to Roosevelt, sent a copy to Welles, called Welles in Washington to ask him to intervene with the president to get the mission canceled, and the next day had Jim Seymour, his chief assistant now that Moore had gone home, phone the State Department and follow up with a "Triple Priority" telegram.[5]

Roosevelt, who had enthusiastically supported the Donovan mission, was more amused than distressed by Kennedy's communications avalanche. He asked Knox to take up the ambassador's complaint "with Secretary Hull and try to straighten it out. Somebody's nose seems to be out of joint!"[6]

On July 14, Colonel Donovan flew from Port Washington to Lisbon, en route to England. Though he carried no official credentials, he was greeted by the British government as a conquering hero, granted an audience with the king, ushered into the new subterranean war bunker underneath Whitehall to talk with Churchill, shown all sorts of secret documents, including intercepted German dispatches, invited to sit down, man to man, with the leaders of the government and the military, and taken on tours of key military installations, arms and aircraft plants, and RAF airfields and command centers. While gathering his information and formulating his conclusions, Donovan kept Kennedy's military attachés close and the ambassador at a distance.

On August 2, the day before he was to return to the United States with his recommendations, the colonel breakfasted at Claridge's with General Raymond E. Lee, Kennedy's army attaché. Lee was delighted, as he wrote in his diary, to find that Donovan, unlike Ambassador Kennedy, was "not at all defeatist" and put the odds of the British repelling a German attack at 60/40. General Lee thought the odds "a little better, say 2 to 1, barring some magical secret weapon."[7]

On returning to Washington, Colonel Donovan reported to the president and Secretary of State Hull that the British were willing to fight, were prepared to fight, and should be given American assistance to do so. Almost everything he had to say contradicted the recommendations of the American ambassador, who had warned time and again that the British were going to be beaten and that it made no sense to waste planes or destroyers, already in short supply in America, on a losing cause.

The German Luftwaffe launched its first waves of air attacks on Great Britain on July 10. The objective was to inflict damage on the RAF, the Royal Navy, and the south coast towns and defense installations in preparation for an invasion later in the summer or early fall. As the bombing continued through July and into early August, Kennedy's letters and cables home grew more pessimistic, not because the Germans were achieving their goal, but because it was apparent that the Luftwaffe was not nearly as invincible as he had believed. The more effective the RAF was in battling the Luftwaffe, the longer the war would go on and the greater the likelihood that the Americans would be drawn in. "If the British air force cannot be knocked out," he cabled Hull on August 2, "then the war will drag out with the whole world continuously upset, with the final result the starvation of England and God knows what happening to the rest of Europe." He was, it appeared, furious at the RAF for refusing to "be knocked out," for making it impossible for the Germans to invade, and for thereby prolonging the war. He scoffed at Churchill's high oratory, his self-congratulatory paeans to British morale, the government's relentless exaggeration of RAF triumphs and German losses. He looked past the rhetoric and saw trouble brewing everywhere. The soldiers who had been evacuated from Dunkirk and were now stationed in England were angry at being denied "free smokes" and being paid far less than the munitions workers; the poor worried about their lives deteriorating further; the "intelligent people" were concerned about the effects of the war on colonial holdings. And as the bombardment continued, British military capacity, already weak, was further degraded. The British might succeed in delaying but they could not prevent a victory by the German military.[8]

The phone rang first a bit after midnight on July 31. "They told me the President was calling." The connection was so poor that the call was rescheduled for the next afternoon.

Two weeks earlier, Franklin Delano Roosevelt had been nominated for a third term. His opponent was lawyer-businessman Wendell Willkie, whom Roosevelt considered his strongest opponent yet. The first step in launching his reelection campaign was to pull back into camp those who had wandered off or whose enthusiasm might have dwindled. And so the call to London.

Roosevelt did not want an angry, volatile Kennedy, conspicuously sitting out the election or, worse yet, preaching to fellow Irish Americans on his favorite subject: British unpreparedness and perfidy. Whatever happened, Roosevelt had to mollify Kennedy and keep him in London, out of harm's way, muzzled but content, until the election was over and won.

> FDR: Hello, Joe. . . . I wanted to ring you up about the situation that has arisen here so that you would get the dope straight from me and not from somebody else. The sub-committee of the Democratic Committee desire you to come home and run the Democratic campaign this year, but the State Department is very much against your leaving England.
>
> JPK: That's very nice of the State Department and I am also very flattered by the sub-committee.
>
> FDR: Yes, they were very anxious to have you and you know how happy I would be to have you in charge, but the general impression is that it would do the cause of England a great deal of harm if you left there at this time and I didn't want you to hear that you had been named and that your name had been turned down by me.

Kennedy replied that he "wouldn't take the job even if it were offered to me." He felt an obligation to remain at the embassy "as long as there was any prospect of the British going through a bad bombing."

However, if at the end of the month the Germans had not intensified or extended their bombing to civilian populations, he would consider resigning his post. "As far as I can see, I am not doing a damn thing here that amounts to anything and my services, if they are needed, could be used to much better advantage if I were home."

Roosevelt disagreed. Lying through his teeth, the president declared that he was getting "constant reports of how valuable you are to them over there and that it helps the morale of the British to have you there and they would feel let down if you were to leave. In addition to that, the people in our country who are already complaining that we are not doing enough in Great Britain feel well satisfied with you being in England." This, of course, was contrary to everything Kennedy knew was being said and written about his unrelenting "defeatism." Anxious for reassurance, for praise, for the hearty confirmation that he remained an important member of the team, a vital insider, the ambassador simply thanked the president for his vote of confidence. "Then with the usual 'Take care of yourselves' and 'Goodlucks' we rang off." Nothing was mentioned by the president or the ambassador about Colonel Donovan's recent mission.[9]

Kennedy had sent home with Colonel Donovan letters to each of his children, to Rose, Clare Boothe Luce, Eddie Moore, John Burns, and others. He reported to Rosemary about his latest talk with Mother Isabel; he brought Kick up-to-date on the doings of the Astors and her friends in London; he encouraged Pat to keep up with her tennis and play some golf; he told Eunice about his difficulties getting eggs and "handling my food supplies"; he explained to Jean that her friend Stella Jean's parents were wavering on their earlier decision to send her to live with the Kennedys; he gave Jack a full report on "the situation here" vis-à-vis the air war and possible invasion. His feat of letter writing impressed even Eunice, who had always been convinced her father was a superman. "How you could write to 8 Kennedys [he hadn't written Joe Jr., who was out west and couldn't be reached] and make them all so interesting and amusing is way above me. But then there are a heck of a lot of things above me!"[10]

In every letter he wrote, he mentioned the fact that the president had called him the day before. Only in his letter to Rose did he explain why: "My own feeling is that the reason Roosevelt rang me up . . . was that he is afraid I will walk out because of my dissatisfaction with things and he wanted to 'soft-soap' me." He understood fully, as he wrote both Clare Boothe Luce and Joseph Davies at the State Department, that Roosevelt's remarks "that he had heard from various sources that I was doing a fine job" were nothing more than "apple sauce," his favorite nonexpletive term for bullshit.[11]

He was staying at his post, he made clear to Rose, Eddie Moore, and the others, not out of loyalty to the president, but to protect and preserve his and his family's reputation. He had been dogged for some time by whispered accusations that his antiwar stance and long absences from London were due, as John Balfour at the American desk in the Foreign Office had put it, not to his being "anti-British," but to his being "a coward." Should he leave London now, such slanders would become commonplace. "After having worked as hard as I have the last six years and a half," he wrote Rose, "I don't want to do anything that would reflect on the family. After all that's why we went into this and I don't want to spoil it for the sake of a month or two. The boys are doing so well."[12]

He had, he reported to Rose and to Dr. Jordan, gained some weight and was "feeling surprisingly well, considering everything"—so well, in fact, that he had stopped taking belladonna for his stomach troubles. When the French ambassador closed up "his house" in London, Kennedy had inherited the wines in the cellar and "his French chef," who was "terrific" and could puree vegetables, which the English chefs could not master. "I think he could puree a bale of hay and make it taste like chocolate ice cream. He is having quite a time making those egg muffins and broiling bacon so that I can eat it."[13]

Less than a week after his phone call from the president—and Donovan's departure—it happened all over again. Washington, he learned, again secondhand, had gone behind his back and informed the British War Office that it was sending a military fact-finding delegation to London, this one led by an admiral and two generals. "Now there is probably a good reason why it is necessary to go around the Ambassador in London and take up the matter with the British before he knows about it," he cabled Hull. "However, I do not like it and I either want to run this job or get out. At this time, this job is a delicate one and to do the job well, requires that I know what is going on. Not to know what is going on causes embarrassment and confusion. I want to know, in other words, what is going to happen before the British are notified. Not to tell me, is very poor treatment of me, and is bad organization."[14]

When told that he had not been informed about the delegation because "secretary Stimson desires 'to avoid any publicity whatever,'" Kennedy exploded in righteous anger. "I just do not figure what you people are getting at in Washington," he cabled Welles on August 8. "All I can say is that you are laying the groundwork . . . for a real bombshell for your foreign policy." There was no way to keep the arrival in London of an admiral, a brigadier general, and a major general a secret from the British and American press. "You had better tell the Army and whoever else has anything to do with them to get their story fixed up and get it fixed up quickly because pretty soon everybody in the world is going to know all about them and there is nothing that can be done about it by this Embassy."[15]

On July 31, after a six-week pause, Churchill renewed his secret correspondence with Roosevelt. "It has now become most urgent for you to let us have the destroyers, motor boats, and flying boats for which we have asked." He requested "50 or 60 of your oldest destroyers. . . . Mr. President, with great respect I must tell you that in the long history of the world this is a thing to do *now*. . . . I am beginning to feel very hopeful about this war if we can get 'round the next 3 or 4 months. The air is holding well. We are hitting that man hard, both in repelling attacks and in bombing Germany. But the loss of destroyers by air attacks may well be so serious as to break down our defense of the food and trade routes across the Atlantic. . . . I am sure that with your comprehension of the sea affair, you will not let this crux of the battle go wrong for the want of these destroyers. I cabled to Lothian some days ago, and now send this through Kennedy, who is a grand help to us and the common cause." (The reference to Kennedy would be excised from the "copy" of the telegram that Churchill included in his multivolume history of the war. Churchill had put it in only because he knew Kennedy was going to read the message before having it coded and cabled and saw no reason not to flatter the man.) While Churchill did not offer Roosevelt any quid pro quo in exchange for the destroyers, he was willing, he cabled Lord Lothian, should it be necessary, to lease the Americans military bases in the West Indies and Bermuda.[16]

On August 2, Roosevelt met with his cabinet to consider Churchill's request. He was convinced now, his conviction bolstered by Colonel Donovan's report, that while the odds were against a British victory, they had at least a fighting chance of surviving German air attacks and preventing a full-scale invasion. That being the case, he saw no reason not to give them the fifty aged destroyers. Although Churchill had made no mention of the British fleet, its future disposition, should the British be defeated, remained of paramount importance to the president. "It was agreed," he wrote in his summary of the cabinet meeting held to consider Churchill's destroyer request, "that the British be approached through Lord Lothian to find out if they would agree to give positive assurance that the British Navy, in the event of German success in Great Britain, would not under any conceivable circumstances fall into the hands of the Germans."[17]

Churchill desperately needed the destroyers and was willing to gift or lease the bases in return, but, as he cabled Lord Lothian in Washington, he refused to make any declarations about what might happen to the fleet should Great Britain be defeated. "We have no intention of relieving United States from any well-grounded anxieties on this point. . . . There is no warrant for discussing any question of the transference of the Fleet to American or Canadian shores. I should refuse to allow the subject even to be mentioned in any Staff conversations, still less that any technical preparations should be made or even planned. . . . Pray make it clear at once that we could never agree to the slightest compromising of our full liberty of action, nor tolerate any such defeatist announcement, the effect of which would be disastrous."[18]

On August 14, Kennedy inquired if he might visit the prime minister at three thirty to hand-deliver a message from the president. Churchill put off the meeting "because he said he has a sleep then. . . . He said after his sleep he was good until two o'clock in the morning." At their meeting held later that afternoon, after the ritual offer of a Scotch highball, Churchill read the president's terms for delivering the destroyers, reiterated that he had no problems with providing leases on the bases, then repeated that he could make no public pronouncements about the fleet. Kennedy emphasized how important the issue was for the president. Churchill promised to do what he could. "I am seeing the Admiralty tonight and I will have a statement for you tonight. We will get around it somehow."[19]

The very next day, Kennedy greeted the military delegation whose visit he had so strenuously opposed and invited them and his military attaché, General Lee, to his estate in Windsor to brief them before the British War Office had a chance to.

He spent the afternoon berating Churchill for military blunders in Norway, Belgium, and France and declaring the British were on "the brink of disaster." He told his visitors that he "saw dynamite in their visit because if they were here for staff talks that meant we were getting ready to go in." Rear Admiral Robert Lee Ghormley, who had met with Roosevelt before leaving Washington, reported that he had asked the president directly if their mission—and the speed with which they were being rushed to London—meant that the United States was about to enter the war. "Positively not" had been Roosevelt's answer. Kennedy came away from the meeting wholly befuddled by what was on the president's mind. "I don't understand Roosevelt," he wrote in his diary. "I feel all the time he wants to get us into war and yet take what he says to Ghormley. I just can't follow him."[20]

The British, when they finally got the chance to brief the American military men, tried desperately to undo the damage they were sure Kennedy had caused. "It is only to be hoped," an American desk official at the Foreign Office wrote his colleagues after the visit was concluded, "that what these . . . officers have seen will have demolished any wrong impressions that may have been created upon their minds by their having been sequestrated by Mr. Kennedy for five whole days after their arrival in England."[21]

At 7:20 the first air raid warning in London since the day of the declaration of war," Kennedy wrote in his diary late in the evening on August 15. He had been dining at 14 Prince's Gate when the alert was sounded, but having heard no bombs detonate, he'd decided against the advice of his butler not to retreat to the cellar. Instead, he continued with his dinner, after which he and his guest, a Mrs. James King, proceeded to Queen's Hall to hear Sir Henry Wood conduct the London Symphony. (Eight months later, Queen's Hall would be demolished by German bombs.) "It was remarkable to see how well behaved and quiet the whole audience was. A young man came on the platform to apologize saying, since some of the orchestra were missing due to air raid warning did we mind waiting 4 or [5] minutes. (I tell you they are a strange people, I can't make out whether they're stupid, courageous, or complacent.)"[22]

Kennedy did not get to hear the entire concert at Queen's Hall that evening. At 10:20, he was approached by an usher who "told me American Embassy wanted me on phone. . . . PM wanted to see me at 11." The ambassador left at once for 10 Downing, where he met Churchill. "We went into Cabinet room and he told the guard to mix me a scotch & soda. (He never seems to remember I don't drink.) I turned it over to him. He then offered me a cigar; again I said I'm not smoking or drinking for the duration of the war. 'My God' he said 'you make me feel as if I should go round in sackcloth & ashes.'"

Churchill then went into his monologue. He was one of the few individuals alive whom Kennedy did not even attempt to interrupt once he got going. He wanted Kennedy to know that as a favor to Roosevelt, he was arranging for the Tyler Kent trial to be postponed until after the November elections, which would prevent the release of any "telegrams [that] showed too close a connection between the Prime Minister and the President." He remained certain that England would win the war and that it was in a better situation now that it was fighting alone. He didn't want or need the American military to fight the war, but he could use some "volunteer aviators," as the RAF was short of pilots. He closed their meeting—it was by now well after midnight—by inviting Kennedy to "come in and see me any time . . . I'm always glad to see you."[23]

The German bombing campaign, with pauses for bad weather, continued through the third week of August. On August 25, Windsor was hit with a bomb falling within three hundred yards of Kennedy's house. It being a Sunday, Kennedy was in residence and, according to the American papers, personally inspected the crater. For those— and there were many in government, the diplomatic corps, the press, and the public—who thought it disgraceful and cowardly for the American ambassador to spend even the weekends outside of London, the bombing of Windsor came as a sort of divine intervention. When, a few days later, now back in London, Kennedy told Lord Halifax about "the bombs that had fallen near his house," the foreign minister half joked in his diary that the fact that they had fallen "pretty close" to his house "everybody is no doubt inclined to think a judgment on Joe for feeling he was likely to be safer there than in London."[24]

The truth was that Kennedy feared neither German bombs nor an invasion. What bothered him no end—and precipitated his decision to leave London—was his accelerating boredom and growing unease at being ignored in Washington. His worry now was that Roosevelt, afraid of what he might say should he return, had decided to keep him at his post until after the election. Clare Boothe Luce had the opposite worry, that he would return before the election and succumb to the pressure to support Roosevelt again. "I'd rather see you, my sweet stay right in dangerous old London than to come home and identify yourself with the Third Term campaign. . . . If the British do hold on to September, you can—I'm sure, come home quite gracefully. And this would be a fine occasion for you to make a public speech in England before you leave—handing lots of bouquets to the British for their stamina and guts, and saying frankly, 'Boys, I didn't think you could do it—you did. Thank God, I was wrong—!' And then say, 'I'll be seeing you later in the winter' (I hope), . . . and you'll leave a popular man with a free conscience, and their blessings, I know. Quite simple. So shall we have luncheon at the end of September, here?"[25]

All through August, while Kennedy watched angrily from the sidelines, the negotiations for the destroyers proceeded. His only information on the status of the talks came, ironically, from Churchill, who shared with him the contents of the cables he sent Roosevelt. The British had now decided that the destroyers-for-bases deal was too one-sided—with the Americans getting long-term leases on valuable military bases in return for sixty overage, worthless destroyer. Fearful of the political fallout in Britain, Churchill suggested that instead of swapping bases for destroyers, he would offer the bases as a gift, made out of friendship; he hoped that the United States would do the same with its destroyers.

At a dinner for the visiting American military delegation, which Kennedy attended, the prime minister declared that he sought only material assistance, not soldiers. "This is not going to be a battle of men, it is going to be a battle of industry and what we want from America is that it shall be a manufacturing depot. Of course, we will pay as long as we can and after that you will have to give us the money." The British, Kennedy concluded, with more than a bit of fear and trembling, had "made up their minds that America will have no alternative except to give them whatever money they need to finish this campaign, on the ground that they will be fighting it to our advantage and, having that in mind, they have no scruples about ordering or buying anything from us. It is a problem we will have to face soon."[26]

On August 27, Kennedy, unable to contain himself any longer, confronted Roosevelt head-on in a "Triple Priority" cable marked "For the President, Personal and Confidential." For weeks now, he had known about but been excluded from any participation in the destroyers-for-bases negotiations. "I am sure you must be aware of the very embarrassing situation I feel myself in this connection. . . . I would have no knowledge whatsoever of the situation had it not been for the fact that the Prime Minister had seen fit to send some cables back through me and also has furnished me with supplementary data. You may properly say there is no reason for my knowing anything about it but if I am not acquainted with facts of vital importance to both countries I fail to see how I can function with any degree of efficiency. . . . Rarely, as a matter of fact, am I ever advised when important conversations are held in Washington with the British Ambassador. . . . I have been fairly active in any enterprise which I have taken up for the last twenty-five years. Frankly and honestly I do not enjoy being a dummy. I am very unhappy about the whole position and of course there is always the alternative of resigning, which I would not hesitate to do if conditions were not as they are."[27]

Roosevelt could not ignore Kennedy's complaints this time or delegate someone else to answer them. Not daring to risk a congressional vote on the destroyers-for-bases deal, which he had been assured he would lose, he had decided to detour around Congress and assert his constitutional authority as commander in chief to sign an agreement that strengthened American defenses, as this one would. He expected, and rightly, that the Republicans would attack him as soon as the deal was announced and that there might even be calls for his impeachment. The last thing he needed, in such circumstances, was to have Kennedy join the opposition.

Roosevelt wrote Kennedy back the day after he received his letter. He did not apologize for excluding Kennedy from the negotiations but reassured him that he was still a vital member of his team. "The destroyer and base matter was handled in part through you and in part through Lothian but the situation developed into a mapping proposition where the Army and Navy are in constant consultation with me here and the daily developments have had to be explained verbally to Lothian. There is no thought of embarrassing you and only a practical necessity for personal conversations makes it easier to handle details here. . . . Don't forget that you are not only not a dummy but are essential to all of us both in the Government and in the Nation." Roosevelt asked Kennedy to "explain" to Churchill why he could not give the destroyers as a gift. Only if he offered them in return for military bases could he argue that he had made the swap to strengthen America's defenses.[28]

Kennedy was gratified by the president's letter, especially by what he thought was the request that he assume a role in the negotiations by consulting with Churchill. He did as he was asked and explained to the prime minister why the bases could not be gifted but had to be offered as a quid pro quo for the destroyers. Churchill, he notified Washington, understood and was agreeable.

There was no response from the president or the State Department. Days later, Kennedy was shocked and embarrassed to learn from

Admiral Ghormley that "the agreement was to be signed at six o'clock the following day." Even after the Sturm und Drang of the previous week, his angry cable to the president, and the president's conciliatory letter, Kennedy discovered that he had not only been excluded from the final negotiations, but was, in fact, considered so incidental to the process that he was not even informed when an agreement was reached.[29]

Twenty-five

THERE'S HELL
TO PAY TONIGHT

On his fifty-second birthday, the ambassador went riding at St. Leonard's. "The air-raid warning was on and it was interesting to be riding through the fields and looking up in the sky looking for air raiders and bombs. One interesting sight was the movement of a lot of training planes from the airport to an ordinary field near where we rode."[1]

The next afternoon, the sirens sounded in London, which had not yet been attacked from the air. It was Saturday, 4:25 P.M. General Raymond Lee, who was at the embassy catching up on his correspondence, "heard some antiaircraft guns cracking away in the distance and then a series of heavy explosions to the northeast and not as far away. They kept on, and at the same time the droning of planes overhead increased and I went out on the square where I could see little flecks like bits of tinfoil darting about overhead, so high that they were almost out of sight. Only an occasional burst of machine-gun fire showed that fierce combat was going on in the heavens." One of his colleagues went up on the roof to see what was going on, then "came down and reported that great fires were raging as a result of the bombardment."[2]

Some 100 German airplanes were approaching London in formation, the large bombers in the middle, the fighters outside. Less than an hour later, at 5:18, the second wave of 250 airplanes attacked. Dusk turned to dark, and the raids continued. The first targets were the docks, warehouses, and small factories on the East End, which, hit spot-on, burst into flames. The London fire brigades did their best but, lacking resources and experience, were overwhelmed by the number and magnitude of the conflagrations. When the all-clear sounded at five that morning, after twelve hours of nearly continuous attack, much of East London lay in ruins; some 430 people were dead.[3]

The bombers came again the following evening and 400 more lives were lost. The next day, a Monday, they took 370 lives. Discovering that the shelters provided little or no protection from the bombs that fell and the fires they set off, the people of London took to the tube stations, which offered better protection and, more critically, an escape from the aboveground cacophony that made sleep impossible: the drone of the aircraft, the clatter of the machine guns, the whistling, screaming bombs, the alerts and all-clears and alerts again, the nonstop wailing of the sirens.[4]

For Kennedy it was the beginning of the end. "The first night of the blitz," Harvey Klemmer recalled, "we walked down Piccadilly and he said I'll bet you five to one any sum that Hitler will be in Buckingham Palace in two weeks."[5]

"The last three nights in London have been simply hell," Kennedy wrote Rose on September 10. "Last night I put on my steel helmet and went up on the roof of the Chancery and stayed up there until two o'clock in the morning watching the Germans come over in relays every ten minutes and drop bombs, setting terrific fires. You could see the dome of St. Paul's silhouetted against a blazing inferno that the Germans kept adding to from time to time by flying over and dropping more bombs. 14 Prince's Gate has just missed being hit. One of the bombs hit the barracks, you know, facing Rotten Row; one last night dropped in the bridle path opposite the house; and Herschel Johnson was almost killed the other night when the house next door to his was completely demolished. . . . Last night, after I had looked the situation over, I slept in the air raid shelter at the Chancery and did very nicely for myself. When I have to stay in town I am planning to sleep there and the rest of the time go out to Windsor. . . . I am completely a fatalist about bombing accidents. I don't think anything is going to happen to me, and for that reason it doesn't worry me the slightest bit."[6]

He wrote the children separate letters and asked them to hand them around. "For a man with a weak stomach," he wrote Jack, "these last three days have proven very conclusively that you can worry about much more important things than whether you are going to have an ulcer or not. . . . The only thing I am afraid of is that I won't be able to live long enough to tell all that I see and feel about this crisis. When I hear these mental midgets talking about my desire for appeasement and being critical of it, my blood fairly boils. What is this war going to prove? And what is it going to do to civilization? The answer to the first question is nothing; and to the second I shudder even to think about it."[7]

Bobby, who had been following the war with unusual intensity and focus for a fourteen-year-old, received the most detailed descriptions and nightmarish analysis. If the Germans joined forces with the Italians, his father predicted, there would be no stopping them from marching through Turkey into the Middle East and gaining control of the Suez Canal and the oil wells that supplied British needs. "Should Italy and Germany get control of these oil fields the prospect for England becomes darker by the minute. The whole problem will finally be dropped in the lap of the United States, because as the manufacturing facilities here are destroyed or disorganized, we in the United States will have to furnish more supplies, and that means that England will have to have more money, and they can't get more money unless we give it to them." He concluded by saying how sorry he was not to have "had a chance to see you this summer Bob, but I do hope you will put in a good effort this year. It is boys of your age who are going to find themselves in a very changed world and the only way you can hold up your end is to prepare your mind so that you will be able to accept each situation as it comes along, so don't, I beg of you, waste any time."[8]

To Ted, he wrote of the fires in East London "and all those poor women and children and homeless people . . . all seeing their places destroyed," and then, rather poignantly and presciently, he added that he hoped "when you grow up you will dedicate your life to trying to work out plans to make people happy instead of making them miserable as war does today." In happier days, Ted had been invited into his father's bedroom to chat while the ambassador dressed for his evening engagement. Now, to illustrate how much had changed in so little time, he wrote Ted about an incident the night before when he had dashed home to "put on my dinner jacket" before a concert at Queen's Hall and dinner with Duff Cooper, Churchill's minister of information. "When I got to Queens Hall I found the concert was cancelled, and then I went back to my office, and after sitting there three-quarters of an hour I noticed by the merest chance that I had forgotten to shave for a couple of days, and I was going out to a dinner party without being shaved. So you can see how busy I am. I am sure everybody will laugh at this. Well, old boy, write me some letters and I want you to know that I miss seeing you a lot, for after all, you are my pal, aren't you."[9]

He wanted to remain in London now to see "how this thing is going to work out," he wrote John Burns, "but I also want to have something to do or say about my family in the few years I have got left to enjoy them." Joe Jr. was doing okay at Harvard Law, but Jack had been sidelined again by health problems and, on Dr. Jordan's recommendation, was taking a year off before beginning law school. "I received a cable from him today about possibly going to Stanford," Kennedy wrote Burns in mid-September. "It is almost impossible to make up your mind over here what is the best thing for him to do over there, and I am sure you will give him the best advice."[10]

His major concern was not what the boys were going to do that September, but what would come next. The conscription bill that President Roosevelt had endorsed in July had been signed into law. Jack and Joe Jr., along with other American males twenty-one to thirty-five years of age, would register for the draft on October 16 and receive their "numbers" on October 29.

If war came, Kennedy would not be able to keep his boys out of uniform—and he knew it. All he could do was make sure they got the most out of their military service. The war was going to be a proving ground for the next generation of American leaders. Those who advanced quickly through the ranks and covered themselves in glory would have a step up on those who had merely served their time.

"I have had with me rather intimately," he wrote Joe Jr. on September 11, "Major General Emmons, in charge of the Air Force of the U.S.A., General Strong, second in command of the Army, and Admiral

Ghormley, second in command of the Navy, and I have been having discussions about you and Jack. Strong, who is really the topside man in the Army feels that the chance for promotion and for position is much better in the Air Force than in anything else, principally because it is going to be expanded quickly and because it isn't as hidebound as the regular army. . . . As far as Jack goes, I don't know what to say. If he isn't well enough to continue his law school course, I don't see how he is going to be well enough to go in the army, but I am going to talk to Emmons and Ghormley about him, so that when you fellows talk your own situations over we will have somebody you can talk with to get good advice."[11]

As the bombs fell on London, Kennedy, perpetually out of step with everyone around him, constructed and forwarded alternative narratives to the heroic ones proffered by Churchill and the British press. "After four days of bombing, the people in the East End . . . have taken on the aspect of refugees. The rest of the people living in London are also affected by having to spend most of their nights in air raid shelters and by the noise of the constant attacks," he wrote in a dispatch to the State Department on September 11. No one was getting any sleep, and without sleep, vital work was not being performed in government offices or defense plants. "Leaving aside all the direct damage to military objectives done by explosions and fires, the war effort is being very definitely hampered by the lack of efficiency of the people who are tired and also by the lack of efficiency of the transportation units. . . . In spite of all, I don't mean that the people are going to quit." On the contrary, they appeared ready to follow Churchill's lead and fight on until they had nothing left with which to fight. This, Kennedy believed, was the tragic underside of their heroism. The best outcome—the one that would spare the most lives and halt the slaughter and sacrifice—would have been for the British to accept defeat. The worst outcome—and the most likely one—would be that they kept fighting in the expectation that the Americans would, responding to their misery, "come into this war and sign a blank check." What nobody on the other side of the ocean wanted to accept was the harsh reality that American intervention would only prolong the war and the agony of civilians caught in it.

Americans who were in favor of intervention did not want to look the tragedy in the face. "Their desire to help this country fight this war, I can quite appreciate, but I do think they should very clearly understand what the responsibility will entail."[12]

He wanted the American public to know the truth: that tales of heroism and sacrifice were not the whole story; that the British could not survive without massive infusions of American assistance; that the dollars loaned would never be repaid; that a prolonged war would mean prolonged slaughter and suffering; and that in the final analysis, American boys in uniform might be compelled to follow American dollars across the Atlantic and into battle.

And the bombs continued to fall. The cacophony in the air was now accentuated by the rounds fired from antiaircraft guns mounted on trucks or on ships in the Thames. In the days and weeks that followed the first raids on East London, bombs would hit Buckingham Palace, St. Paul's, the Tower of London, the Natural History Museum, the BBC, Queen's Hall, the Zoo, and London's residential areas. They fell in the parks and in the squares and on churches, tube stations, and theaters, on small row houses that burned to cinders and great brick town houses that collapsed into ruins. London's East End, West End, and the City were pockmarked by craters and smoldering ruins, streets and parks cordoned off by unexploded and delayed-action bombs. Nothing and no one was spared, from the humblest East Enders to the king and queen to the ambassador and those who worked with him at Grosvenor Square.

On Saturday, September 14, during the second week of bombing, Kennedy called Sumner Welles "to report to him that everybody was getting along well here. Of course," he added in his diary entry, "my telephone conversation was sarcastic, because I was amazed that the Department showed so little interest in the welfare of the people." As Kennedy had anticipated, the president, no doubt alerted by Welles, phoned at three o'clock on Sunday afternoon to cheer him up. "Taking into account that everybody might be listening," Kennedy recorded in his diary, "he made a rather perfunctory inquiry as to how we were all getting along and said he hoped we were all right. I wasn't particularly impressed with it."[13]

The next day, a Monday, Kennedy cabled Welles. "For ten days now there has been continual day and night bombing. It has been aggravated by an anti-aircraft barrage that has lasted all during the night. The members of my staff who are living in London have not had much sleep under these conditions. . . . The Embassy has been able to function in the last several days for only three hours daily; the rest of the time has been spent in the air raid shelter. I have taken the risk of keeping the staff at their desks until the spotter on the roof telephoned me that planes are nearby; I should not be called upon to take that risk indefinitely." He had "been living at St. Leonard's with about ten officers during weekends" and would be sleeping there, whenever possible, "since 14 Prince's Gate is now considered in a danger zone." He intended to relocate several embassy functions and officers to St. Leonard's, Coworth Park, which Lord Derby had made available to him, and Headley Park, a facility near Epsom that had been placed at the disposal of the American embassy by its owner, an American banker. He would continue to work out of "London as long as there is an Embassy there."[14]

On September 17, after ten days and nights of bombing, with Luftwaffe losses exceeding those of the RAF, the Germans no closer to clearing the airspace over the English Channel, and the British more unwilling than ever to entertain peace talks, Hitler canceled plans for the invasion. Kennedy's pessimism remained untouched and unbounded.

In his dispatches to Washington, he did everything he could to counter the propaganda efforts of the British and downplay their preparedness to fight an extended war. In his September 27 cable, written after the announcement that Japan had joined Germany and Italy in a "tripartite pact," he derided British claims of stepped-up war production. "Production is definitely falling, regardless of what reports you may be getting. . . . I cannot impress upon you strongly enough my complete lack of confidence in the entire conduct of this war. . . . If by any chance we should ever come to the point of getting into the war we can make up our minds that it will be the United States against Germany, Italy and Japan, aided by a badly shot to pieces country which in the last analysis can give little if any assistance to the cause. It breaks my heart to draw these conclusions about a people that I sincerely hoped might be victorious, but I cannot get myself to the point where I believe they can be of any assistance to the cause in which they are involved."[15]

K ennedy had made it clear to the president during their August 2 phone call that he was anxious to return home but would remain in place for at least a month and then evaluate the situation in London. Two months had passed since then with not a word from Washington about his coming home. His strongest argument for leaving his post, which he had repeated time and again, was that he was no longer serving any purpose in London. "The only thing I am unhappy about," he wrote Missy LeHand, "is that I have nothing important to do. If it hadn't been for the fact that I didn't want it to look as if I was leaving here before the bombing began, I would have left long ago. I have never been very happy sitting around and not making a real contribution to the job I was supposed to do." On the final day of September, he declared to his wife that he could take no more. "For all the good I am doing the United States or England now, I might as well be in Palm Beach. . . . I have . . . made up my mind that I shall come home, either for consultation or to resign—that is entirely dependent on Mr. Roosevelt. Frankly, I don't care which."[16]

On October 5, the *Chicago Daily News,* in an article picked up by papers across the country, reported in language that suggested the story came from Kennedy or someone close to him that the ambassador planned to leave his post "within the next 10 days or 2 weeks. . . . It has been an open secret for many weeks that Kennedy considered his continued stay in London as superfluous [but] didn't wish to leave Great Britain while the course of the war was completely in the air and that, under no circumstances, did he wish anyone to be able to say that he was running away from the blitzkrieg. Now that he has gone through one solid month of the Battle of Britain and on several occasions has been within sound of falling bombs, he feels that nobody will accuse him of running out on the show."[17]

Joe Alsop and Robert Kintner commented on the story in their October 8 column. Under the title, "Kennedy, Unwilling Sojourner," they reported on the "mercurial" ambassador's preemptive move "in an obscure but exciting little game. The players are Kennedy and the President. For Kennedy, the goal has been to come home as soon as he decently could; for the President, to keep Kennedy in London as long as possible." It was clear why Kennedy wanted to come home. The question was why Roosevelt wouldn't let him. Alsop and Kintner believed that the president wanted him to remain in London because he could "do less harm there. . . . An emotional fellow, he has strong convictions and less than no remaining fondness for his chief. He will certainly express his opinions to every available American listener the instant he gets through the customs. He will be in a position to speak impressively and persuasively. The President is represented as fearing he will reduce large numbers of leaders of opinion to such a state of hopeless blue funk that our foreign policy will be half-immobilized by fear." Alsop and Kintner, with the help of cables and other materials leaked to them by the State Department, went on to ridicule Kennedy for his "gloom," which was "now so intense that while the American military mission headed by General George Strong was in London, Kennedy constantly tried to persuade them they had not seen the worst" and insisted that munitions plants that had been bombed "were wholly out of commission," when, in fact, they were up and running in weeks. "If Kennedy does come home," they warned their readers, "it will be well to listen to him carefully, but to take his jeremiads with a grain of salt."[18]

Kennedy was infuriated by the article, but more so by the realization that someone in the White House or the State Department was leaking his confidential dispatches to Alsop and Kintner. When, two days after the article had appeared, Summer Welles called him in London, Kennedy declared unequivocally that he was coming home, preferably "for consultation," but if the State Department "did not want to call me home, then I would extend my resignation, to take effect here and at once; that I was damned sick and disgusted with sitting here and doing nothing, and having that little pimp Alsop write nasty columns." He told both Arthur Krock and Frank Murphy that he had warned Welles that "he had written a full account of the facts to Edward Moore, his secretary in New York, with instructions to release the story to the press if the Ambassador were not back in New York by a certain date." He threatened Welles that if he was not officially recalled, he would come home on his own and tell the American public that the destroyer-for-bases deal was "the worst ever," that no written contract had ever been signed for the bases, and that when "'all the facts are known' they will 'shock the American people.'"[19]

The day after their telephone conversation, Welles reported what Kennedy had told him in a meeting with Roosevelt. Breckinridge Long, who sat in, recalled in his diary that Welles was in favor of permitting Kennedy to return to the United States, but "the President did not want him to come. He looks upon him as a trouble-maker and a person entirely out of hand and out of sympathy. Welles insisted upon [his] recommendation and [Roosevelt] finally compromised by saying he could come home the latter part of this month and that he would himself send him a personal letter, which Welles was to draft, giving him instructions about his conversation and conduct when he got here." Welles raised his concern that Kennedy "might come out for Willkie. He realizes Kennedy is in a terrible blue funk about England, would give that impression here, and would advise the public probably that England was about to collapse. The president thought that it would be very unfortunate. He also thought Kennedy's resentment would carry him so far as to urge the election of Willkie."[20]

Welles cabled Kennedy that he was going to be recalled for consultations. Six days later, the president sent the letter he had asked Welles to draft for him:

"Dear Joe: I know what an increasingly severe strain you have been under during the past weeks and I think it is altogether owing to you that you get a chance to get away and get some relief. The State Department has consequently telegraphed you by my desire to come back for consultation during the week commencing October 21." The rest of the telegram contained the toughest possible warning to Kennedy to keep his mouth shut. "I need not tell you that a great deal of unnecessary confusion and undesirable complications have been caused in the last few months by statements which have been made to the press by some of our chiefs of mission who have been coming back to this country. In your particular case the press will be very anxious to get some statements from you and no matter how proper and appropriate your statements might be, every effort will be made to misinterpret and to distort what you say. I am, consequently, asking you specifically not to make any statement to the press on your way over nor when you arrive in New York until you and I have had a chance to agree upon what should be said. Please come straight through to Washington on your arrival since I will want to talk with you as soon as you get here."[21]

The request was clear and Kennedy honored it—in his way, by not talking to the press. Only in his final interviews with British government officials, including Lord Halifax, did he make clear his dissatisfaction with his shabby treatment by Washington and his intention to protect his reputation. As Halifax reported to Lord Lothian in Washington, Kennedy had told him that he had forwarded an article "to the United States to appear on November 1, if by any accident he was not able to get there, which would be of considerable importance appearing five days before the Presidential election. When I asked him what would be the main burden of his song, he gave me to understand that it would be an indictment of President Roosevelt's administration for having talked a lot and done very little. He is plainly a very disappointed man. I did what I could to soothe his feelings."[22]

Halifax's memo set off a flurry of activity in the Foreign Office, which like the rest of the British government had a good deal invested in Roosevelt's reelection. Halifax kept calm. He didn't much like Kennedy, but he trusted that he would do no harm in Washington. The American ambassador, he knew from experience, took great pleasure in foulmouthed histrionics, but more often than not, his bark was much worse than his bite. "He was breathing threats of brutal speech to Roosevelt when he gets back but he does not intend to make things any more difficult for him in the election and will indeed, I have no doubt, when he gets there, help him."[23]

The ambassador spent his last days in London, as he had his first, calling upon his colleagues in the diplomatic corps. Rather like a lawyer constructing a brief, he was gathering evidence to support the position he had arrived at, that the British could not possibly defeat the Germans. Not surprisingly, nearly everyone he spoke to agreed with him.

The Brazilian ambassador "was very pessimistic." The Portuguese ambassador "was very bearish on the outlook for England, and saw very little if any hope." The Turkish ambassador was "particularly pessimistic on the whole picture, unless the United States comes in and quickly." The only diplomat who held any hope for the future was Ivan Maisky of the Soviet Union, whom Kennedy liked but had never much trusted.[24]

He spent time as well with the leaders of the Labour Party. What he wanted from them—and they gladly supplied it—was confirmation that the end result of war, no matter who might win, would be some sort of socialism in Great Britain. He asked his "friend" Herbert Morrison, the Labour Party stalwart who had recently become home secretary, "point-blank just what type of government he visualized in England at the close of the war; at what point did he think he could stop short of National Socialism? He said he quite agreed that the old form of Government was gone. He thought Democracy could function, however, and get the advantages of National Socialism without the Gestapo and other disagreeable features. However, when I asked him to tell me how that was going to happen, he was at a loss—as are all the other leaders of the Socialist party. They see their opportunity to come to the leadership of the country and they believe they can fix their brand of Socialism so that it will be palatable to the country." Kennedy posed the same question to Clement Attlee, the head of the Labour Party, who admitted that he was "spending a great deal of time trying to work out just what form of government England is going to have." Kennedy concluded, "All those in authority believe they will have to have something pretty soon to sell to the people of England which will give them an idea of what they are fighting for." John Reith, a Chamberlain Conservative, now minister of works and buildings, told Kennedy the government had decided that when it rebuilt East London, it wouldn't put "workers' houses up against the docks any more; we'll have green lawns." Kennedy's response, as recorded in his diary: "Oh boy! I'm beginning to see National Socialism budding up so fast that these fellows don't recognize it."[25]

The more he probed and learned, the more he was convinced that the free market capitalism he had known and profited from in the 1920s was doomed. He had recognized this years before—and that recognition had prompted his decision to support the New Deal and to send his older boys to study with the Socialist Harold Laski. The unfettered, unregulated markets on which he had built his fortune were artifacts of the past. Should the Americans enter the war, they would, he feared, have no option but to follow the British and control imports, exports, currency exchange, investment opportunities; dictate what should be produced and how and when; and set profits and wage rates. American capitalism would not survive the coming of war, as the British had not. Here, in a nutshell, was the most basic reason he was committed to doing everything he could, inside or outside the government, to keep his country out of war.

His final London farewell was the most difficult. Neville Chamberlain, the man who had welcomed him to Great Britain and had treated him as an insider, a partner, a collaborator for peace, was dying a dreadful death from cancer. Kennedy visited to say good-bye in person, then, the night before he left, wrote a final note: "Here I am tonight getting ready to fly at daybreak tomorrow. Before I go, I must tell you what I feel in my heart about you. . . . Your conception of what the world must do in order to be a fit place to live in, is the last sensible thing we shall see before the pall of anarchy falls on us all. For me to have been any service to you in your struggle is the real worthwhile epoch in my career. You have retired but mark my words the world will yet see that your struggle was never in vain. My job from now on is to tell the world of your hopes." He signed his letter, "Now and forever, Your devoted friend, Joe Kennedy."[26]

He would be good to his word. Whenever the occasion arose—and sometimes when it didn't—he would defend Chamberlain. If the British were now, in 1940, able to hold their own and forestall invasion and defeat, Kennedy was convinced it was because Chamberlain at Munich had bought them two years to rearm. His actions in 1938, more than Churchill's in 1940, had made possible whatever military success the British would achieve.

Joseph P. Kennedy left London on Tuesday, October 22, two and a half years after his arrival. He had been warned before he ever set foot in London that he had neither the training nor the temperament for a diplomatic position, but his self-confidence, buoyed by successes in Boston, New York, Hollywood, Washington, and on Wall Street, was such that he could not imagine he would not do himself and his family proud. And he did—for the first few weeks—before that same self-confidence led him to speak his mind rather than follow State Department orders.

He had sought to be an insider but refused to be a team player because he was convinced that he knew better than his superiors and that it was his responsibility to speak the truth, not tie it up in diplomatic obfuscations. He prided himself on being a realist, unlike Cordell Hull, who he feared was too moralistic, too sentimental, and Roosevelt, who did not always think rationally and relied too much on academics and politicians who knew little of the real world.

As ambassador, he had had his priorities and he'd pursued them relentlessly, breaking rules and protocol whenever he thought it necessary. It was essential that the economy be righted, that prosperity return, and that the free enterprise system be preserved. None of this would be possible without peace in Europe. In the final analysis, he believed anything, even giving Hitler more than he justly deserved, was better than fighting a war against him. He had sympathy with the victims of Nazi aggression but would not allow that sympathy to interfere with his better judgment, that war with Germany had to be avoided no matter what the cost. If the well-being of Austrians and Czechs and Poles and Europe's Jews had to be sacrificed, so be it. That millions of those Jews would later be murdered was not a consideration—as neither he nor anyone else in Washington or London considered it a possible outcome.

Wiser heads had failed to prevent war from engulfing Europe in 1940, but that war could and had to be contained and brought to a negotiated end. Whatever happened to Great Britain, it was imperative that America not go to war.

PART V

Washington,
but Briefly

Twenty-six

HOME AGAIN

Upon arriving in Lisbon, the only safe place from which to fly across the Atlantic, Kennedy was "handed a note from Roosevelt specifically requesting me to come to the White House and make no statements to the newspaper men. I was, of course indignant," Kennedy wrote in his diary, "but could understand Roosevelt's position particularly when I came home and saw what the status was." There was a second telegram waiting in Lisbon, this one from Clare Boothe Luce, who with her husband was backing Wendell Willkie and expected Kennedy to do so as well. Clare urged Kennedy to "tell the press and the people the truth as you have always told it to me. . . . If you say what you have never said to me or never believed that the boy on the burning deck [FDR] is the master of foreign policy of all time, then you will have to pay my funeral expenses and after that nothing in this land will be safe or sure. Them's me parting words, my hero."[1]

Bad weather forced a day's delay in Lisbon. The White House and the State Department, increasingly anxious lest Kennedy talk to the press before he spoke with the president, monitored his every move. When the Pan Am Clipper on which Kennedy was flying was held over a second day in the Azores, Sumner Welles called the White House and spoke with Edwin "Pa" Watson, the president's secretary and adviser, who relayed the message to Roosevelt. Kennedy was not expected to arrive "until sometime Sunday. He [Welles] is going ahead with arrangements to get Joe Kennedy down here Sunday afternoon, as that would be the only place he could see you before (as Sumner Welles expresses it) any one else got at him to talk." Lauchlin Currie, chief economic adviser in the White House, wrote Missy LeHand that "Arthur Goldsmith, a very close personal friend of Joe Kennedy's, called Jerome Frank today and suggested that it would be most helpful if the President were to send Kennedy a little note on his arrival tomorrow and arrange to have him met by somebody important from the State Department."[2]

In Bermuda, the next leg of his journey, Kennedy was handed another telegram from the president, this one inviting him and Rose to "come to Washington immediately after your arrival in New York to spend Saturday night at the White House." From Bermuda he called the White House to explain that he would be late arriving in New York, and got Missy LeHand on the phone. She "turned me over to the President whom they evidently had to awaken. The President was very pleasant. . . . He urged Rose and me to come down immediately on arrival."[3]

The ambassador arrived in New York at two thirty on Sunday afternoon, two days late. The White House sent Max Truitt, his closest friend still in government service, to hand-deliver yet another note from Roosevelt. Truitt was accompanied by Robert Stewart, who headed up the British Empire desk at the State Department and had been ordered to stay at Kennedy's side until he arrived in Washington.

On exiting the plane, Kennedy was besieged by reporters and photographers. "Do I have to go through this before I even see my family?" he asked, laughing. At almost the same moment, he caught sight of Rose, Jean (nearly thirteen), Patricia (sixteen), Eunice (nineteen), and Kick (almost twenty-one)—mother and three older daughters in fur coats, Jean in cloth. Teddy, not yet nine, was missing, his car having been delayed in traffic. After embraces, tears, and smiles all around, the girls and Rose left the room momentarily so that Kennedy could greet the reporters. Looking "for all the world like a man bursting with things to say," the *New York Times* reported the next morning, the ambassador "limited himself to these words: 'I have nothing to say until I have seen the President.' . . . He promised to 'talk a lot' when he had had his discussion with the President."⁴

He left the reporters and the newsreel cameras to see his daughters, then for a meeting with Rose, John Burns, Eddie Moore, Ted O'Leary, and a trusted and political-savvy Boston friend, Cornelius Fitzgerald. They "talked the situation over as to whether or not I would be for or against the President. I told them that I had many personal grievances, but questioned as to whether or not they were sufficient grounds on which to take a definite stand." Rose argued rather strenuously that for the good of the family, Kennedy had to back Roosevelt. The president had appointed him as the first Roman Catholic ambassador to London, something no other president had or would have done. He had sent him as his representative to the pope's coronation. To abandon him now would forever mark Kennedy as an "ingrate." Burns agreed and warned Kennedy that if he backed away from Roosevelt, it would "turn him into a pariah. . . . None of his boys will able to hold their heads up at a Democratic convention ever again. It will be destructive for all his dreams and hopes for his children."⁵

In the end, there was no real question as to what Kennedy would do. He had no faith that Willkie was qualified to serve as president, and despite his dissatisfactions with Roosevelt, he thought him infinitely more competent. He believed as well that Roosevelt would be true to his word and keep America out of the war in Europe.

A little after five P.M., only a few hours after his plane from Bermuda had landed, the ambassador was in the air again, this time with Rose and the State Department official as their chaperon. They arrived in Washington at six thirty and, after posing for photographers and waving to reporters, were whisked away to the White House in a presidential limousine.

Roosevelt brilliantly orchestrated Kennedy's reception, as he had every step of his journey from London to Lisbon to the Azores to Bermuda to New York to Washington. With James Farley having abandoned the administration and Al Smith campaigning for Willkie, the president needed a high-profile Irish American to come to his defense and declare unequivocally that he was not plotting to send American boys to die in trenches to save the British Empire. The week before Kennedy's arrival, Felix Frankfurter, now a Supreme Court justice but still among Roosevelt's most trusted advisers, had approached Frank Murphy, the former governor of Michigan, recent attorney general, and now Supreme Court justice, while they were both "sitting on the bench" and asked his advice on saving "the Catholic vote, which was rapidly leaving Roosevelt." Murphy, Kennedy wrote later in his diary, had suggested to Frankfurter that the ambassador be asked to make a speech on the president's behalf. A few days later, Justice Murphy was called to the White House for a meeting with Harry Hopkins and his two colleagues on the Supreme Court, Felix Frankfurter and William O. Douglas. The subject, Murphy told Kennedy, was "how they could get me [Kennedy] to come out for them. Douglas and Murphy agreed that I was absolutely important to get. Frankfurter appreciated that I was, but hated to ask me. . . . There was a lot of conversation and it was left to the President to get in touch before (as they said) Krock could get me."[6]

Roosevelt, knowing Kennedy's desire to be treated as an insider, invited him and Rose to spend the night at the White House and arranged for an informal scrambled eggs and sausages dinner to be served not in the dining room, but "on the Upper Floor right off his Study," with Missy sitting in for Eleanor, and James Byrnes and his wife the only other guests. "When we were about half through the dinner," Kennedy noted in his diary, "Jim Byrnes, acting as though a wonderful idea had just struck him, said he thought it would be a great idea if I would go on the radio Tuesday night on my own. He thought it absolutely essential that I go and most necessary for the success of the Roosevelt campaign. . . . I didn't say, Yes, Aye, or No. The President worked very hard on Rose, who I suspect he had come down because of her great influence on me. He talked to her about her father. All through dinner, Byrnes kept selling me the idea, but I made no comment, because I wanted to talk alone with the President before making any decision."

When, after dinner, the group reassembled in the president's study, Kennedy announced that "since it doesn't seem possible for me to see the President alone, I guess I'll just have to say what I am going to say in front of everybody." He was, he told the president, "damn sore at the way I have been treated. I feel that it is entirely unreasonable and I don't think I rated it." He reminded Roosevelt how, at a rather low point in his presidency, he had "come out for you for a Third Term." Still, in spite of all that he had done, "you have given me a bad deal." He cataloged his complaints, from Donovan to the generals to the destroyer deal, as if he were talking to a business associate, not the president of the United States. As he had anticipated, Roosevelt "promptly denied everything," blaming Knox and Welles and the "career men" in the State Department. After Kennedy confronted him about the leak of one of his cables to Alsop, Roosevelt "disclaimed any responsibility, and protested his friendship for me. Rose chimed in at this point and said it was difficult to get the right perspective on a situation that was 3,000 miles away." "Somebody is lying very seriously," Kennedy noted in his diary, "and I suspect the President."

The discussion "went on and on." There was, tellingly, no mention of foreign policy initiatives, no questions from Kennedy as to what the president planned to do next, no talk of anything other than the ambassador's grievances. Rose, in her diary entry, recalled that "Joe did most of the talking. The President looks pale." After what seemed like hours of Kennedy complaints and Roosevelt explanations, the ambassador brought the long evening to an end, as he recalled in his diary, by telling the president that he would "make the God damned speech for you and I will pay for it myself. It will cost twenty-two or twenty-three thousand dollars but that is alright. . . . I will write the speech myself. I don't want anyone else to do it for me. . . . I am not going to show it to anyone. You will all trust me or you won't get it. . . . I have my own ideas about this and I want to get it out my own way."

Everyone thought that a fine idea; Missy LeHand called the Democratic National Committee and arranged for radio time for the following Tuesday. "I made up my own mind," Kennedy later told Frank Murphy, "that I was going to acquit myself of all my indebtedness to the President, that I would stand by him, that I would go down the line for him, that I would pay for it myself."[7]

Roosevelt had suggested that Kennedy and Rose spend the night at the White House, then return to New York with him on his campaign train. Kennedy declined. If he took the train with Roosevelt, everyone would know he was going to endorse him. It would be better to maintain the suspense and build as large an audience as possible for the Tuesday radio broadcast. Though he hadn't seen his wife, much less spent the night with her, in more than eight months, he took the late flight back to New York. Rose slept over at the White House in the bedroom where, according to a plaque under the mantelpiece, the Queen of England had slept on her recent visit. "There was no mention made of the King." Rose could not help but wonder where he had slept.[8]

The ambassador had promised the reporters who met him at the airport that he would talk to them at eleven A.M. the following morning at the Waldorf. But instead of doing so, he had his secretary issue a press release declaring that he would "speak over the nation-wide Columbia network on Tuesday at 9 P.M." The Democratic National Committee announced only that it had released one half of the one-hour block it had previously booked and that Kennedy's radio time would be paid for by his wife and nine children. Kennedy sequestered himself in his hotel suite with John Burns and a few others to draft his speech. He saw no visitors, took no calls, and leaked nothing of what he might say.

"I've tried all day long to get you," Clare Boothe Luce telegraphed on Monday. "The fact that I can't is I'm afraid answer to a number of questions. <u>First</u> and foremost I'm so happy you are home and <u>safe</u> and you are to me, like millions of others, as well as Ambassador, a grand guy—even a bit of a hero. I want only for you to know, when you make that radio address tomorrow night . . . you'll probably help to turn the trick for him. And I want you also to know that I believe with all my heart and soul you will be doing America a terrible disservice. I know too well your private opinions not also to know that half of what you say (<u>if</u> you say it) you <u>really</u> won't believe in your heart. . . . I know you will, in the end, do what you think is the right thing. But please remember that the rift that the election of FDR will drive through the National heart is the same rift your speech in support of a third term is going to drive through mine tomorrow."[9]

Kennedy's radio endorsement of Franklin Roosevelt on October 29 was not nearly as full-throated or enthusiastic as four and eight years before. Instead, he delivered an extended, almost pedantic policy statement on the need for the United States to rearm. He had taken to heart the lessons of Jack's senior thesis, that only rearmament on a grand scale would protect the United States from being bullied by Hitler and the dictators. To preserve the peace, the United States was going to have to quickly rebuild its military strength until it rivaled that of the dictators. "What counts in this hour of crisis is what we in the United States of America are prepared to do in order to make ourselves strong. . . . We are re-arming because it is the only way in which America can stay out of war. . . . It is today our guarantee of peace." To those who might charge that his was "an unduly pessimistic view of the world situation," that he was "steeped in gloom," he asked where in the "world picture" was there "any excuse for gaiety. A large part of the productive capacity of the world is devoted to the cause of killing; millions are facing starvation; millions are facing disease. Great peoples are being sacrificed. . . . Gloom, under such circumstances, is nothing more than 'facing the facts.'" He closed his talk by focusing attention back to himself, his experience, and his family. "As a servant of the American people I feel that they are entitled to my honest conclusions. In my years of service for the Government, both at home and abroad, I have sought to have honest judgment as my goal. . . . After all, I have a great stake in this country. My wife and I have given nine hostages to fortune. Our children and your children are more important than anything else in the world. The kind of America that they and their children will inherit is of grave concern to us all. In the light of these considerations, I believe that Franklin D. Roosevelt should be re-elected President of the United States."[10]

His address was over by 9:30. At 10:18, the president sent a telegram to his suite at the Waldorf. "We have all just listened to a grand speech. Many thanks. Looking forward to seeing you all tomorrow evening." Jack cabled from California, "Proud to have sponsored you."[11]

The following day, at a rally and speech at the Boston Garden, Franklin Delano Roosevelt told his audience how pleased he had been to "welcome back to the shores of America that Boston boy, beloved by all of Boston and a lot of other places, my Ambassador in the Court of St. James's, Joe Kennedy." Kennedy, who had decided not to accompany the president to Boston, got a telegram that night from Kick, who reported from Eddie Moore that "the Pres really went to town for you tonight in Boston amidst terrific cheers from the crowd. . . . It's great to be famous. Goodnight from your 4th hostage."[12]

The Republicans picked up on the president's reference in his Boston speech to "my" rather than "our" ambassador as further evidence of the president's dictatorial pretensions. The White House issued a legal opinion that the ambassador, having been appointed by the president, was indeed "his" ambassador, but the critiques continued. Roosevelt could have cared less. Kennedy's address had done what he had wanted it to do and more. It had rallied reluctant Irish Catholic voters to his side, buttressed his claims that he was not going to take the nation into war, and emphasized that he alone had the experience to lead the nation in these difficult times.

On the Saturday before election day, Kennedy joined seventy-six thousand fans at Yankee Stadium to watch Notre Dame defeat Army, 7–0. After the game, he visited with Frank Murphy, who recorded their conversation in his diary notes. "'For heaven sakes, get me some tea and cinnamon toast at once—I am starved,' he [Kennedy] remarked as he sprawled out on the davenport to rest." For the next hour or so, he recounted in a stream of unbroken bitterness all the affronts he had suffered in London. "He was violent and profane in explaining it all. He practically left no one uncursed but that is the style of this able and dynamic man and so it ought not to be given too much emphasis. That he was filled with wrath and possessed contempt for those who have tried to undo him was plain."[13]

Three days later, on November 5, 1940, the American people went to the polls and elected Franklin Delano Roosevelt, with 55 percent of the popular vote and 449 of 531 of the electoral college votes.

The Wednesday after the election, Kennedy returned to Washington and visited the White House, congratulated the president, and told him he wanted to resign his position. Roosevelt asked him to wait until he had found and named a replacement.

The ambassador's next stop was the State Department, where he met with Cordell Hull, Sumner Welles, and Assistant Secretary of State Breckinridge Long, now head of a special division handling problems related to the European war, including the refugees. Nothing could shake or temper Kennedy's pessimism, which was so stark and out of line with recent events that Long attributed it to a kind of battle fatigue. The ambassador refused to see what everyone else in Washington saw: that the RAF had turned back the Luftwaffe campaign to free the airspace over the English Channel; that the Germans had called off their invasion plans; that Spain had not entered the war on the side of Germany and Italy; that there had been no coordinated German-Italian thrust toward the Suez Canal; that Italy, in fact, had turned away from the Middle East and invaded Greece instead; that the British were already and the Americans would soon begin turning out more fighters and bombers than the Germans.

None of this had had any effect on Kennedy. The cataclysm he had feared had come to pass. Even Breckinridge Long, no cheery-eyed optimist, was frightened and disturbed by Kennedy's relentless negativity. "He sees a new philosophy, both political and economic, with the United States excluded from European markets and from Far Eastern markets and from South American markets. . . . Consequently he thinks that we ought to take some steps to implement a realistic policy and make some approach to Germany and to Japan which would result in an economic collaboration. He does not see how or what. He has no suggestion to make. He only feels that what we are doing is wrong but does not know how to do it right. . . . He does not believe in our present policy. He does not believe in the continuing of democracy. He thinks that we will have to assume a Fascist form of government here or something similar to it if we are to survive in a world of concentrated and centralized power." At the conclusion of their meeting, Kennedy told Long that "he was going to the west coast and would see Hearst and try and set him right and see other publishers like McCormick and I [Long] told him that he ought not to talk to the press or to talk in a way that would scare the American people . . . that the American people needed education in foreign affairs and that to thrust it upon them too suddenly would be disastrous. He agreed and said that he would not do that."[14]

Kennedy would have been wise to heed Long's counsel.

On November 7, the day after Long had warned him not to talk to the press, the ambassador flew to Boston to visit with Joe Jr. in Cambridge and Bob at Priory, catch up with friends and family, and check into the Lahey Clinic for a full physical examination. When he arrived at the Ritz-Carlton, he found a note from *Boston Daily Globe* reporter Louis Lyons, who had interviewed him four years earlier for a favorable story that received wide national coverage: "The *Globe* hopes I can persuade you to talk to me a little for our people—just as a traveler home from the wars, not political talk. . . . Anytime, anywhere that you can spare me a snatch of time, I'd like to make the most of it."[15]

Kennedy could not say no.

On Saturday afternoon, Lyons arrived at the Ritz-Carlton for the interview. With him were Charles Edmonson of the *St. Louis Post-Dispatch,* a Nieman Fellow at Harvard, and his editor, Ralph Coghlan, to whom Kennedy had promised a "background" briefing on the war. The three journalists found Kennedy in his shirtsleeves, eating apple pie, perhaps celebrating the clean bill of health he had gotten the day before at the Lahey Clinic. Thinking that he was among friends—after all, Lyons was a Boston reporter—and assuming that he was speaking off the record and would not be quoted directly, Kennedy held court for the next ninety minutes. He was at his best that afternoon: jovial, warm, opinionated, a reporter's dream. He never stopped talking and did not censor what he had to say. He repeated in clear, plain, tough talk what he had been putting into his diplomatic dispatches for more than a year. Lyons took it all down.

"People call me a pessimist. I say, 'What is there to be gay about? Democracy is all done.'"

"You mean in England or this country, too?" he was asked.

"Well, I don't know. If we get into war it will be in this country, too. A bureaucracy would take over right off. Everything we hold dear would be gone. They tell me that after 1918 we got it all back again. But this is different. There's a different pattern in the world."

Asked about British democracy and what it meant "to have labor men now at the center of government," he answered bluntly, "It means national socialism is coming out of it. . . . Democracy is finished in England. It may be here. Because it comes to a question of feeding people. It's all an economic question. . . . We haven't felt the pinch of it yet. It's ahead of us."

He insisted it was important to provide Great Britain with military aid "to give us time" to rearm. He would not even try to guess how the war would end but was insistent that America stay out.

"'I'm willing to spend all I've got to keep us out of the war,' Kennedy flashed towards the end of his talk. 'There's no sense in our getting in. We'd just be holding the bag.'" He claimed that he was starting up his own "determined and fighting crusade, to 'keep us out. . . . I know more about the European situation than anybody else, and it's up to me to see that the country gets it,' he says in explanation of the role of carrying the torch that he has cut out for himself."

The reporters left the hotel that afternoon with more than they had bargained for. Coghlan, assuming the interview remained off the record and "for background," did not publish anything. But Lyons, knowing a big story when he saw one, wrote up what Kennedy had told him.

To make it clear to his readers—many of whom were Kennedy fans—that he had not intended to hang Kennedy and that any damage done was self-inflicted, he embedded a paragraph, subheaded "Reporter's Dilemma," in the middle of his article, explaining that he had planned to do a "soft" Sunday piece but had been given much more, which he now felt obligated to share with his readers.[16]

The next morning, back in Bronxville, Kennedy was called to the phone by Joe Dinneen, another *Boston Daily Globe* reporter. Neville Chamberlain had died and Dinneen wanted a quote from Kennedy.

"'That's quite an interview you gave Louis Lyons for this morning's paper,' the reporter [Dinneen] said.

"'Why? What did he say?' Joe asked.

"'What did he say?' [Dinneen] repeated. 'He wrote everything you told him.'

"Dinneen proceeded to read some of Kennedy's quotes from the story.

"There was a dead silence on the other end. [Dinneen] thought they had been cut off. . . .

"'He wrote all that?' Kennedy asked incredulously.

"'All that and a lot more,' he was told. 'Anything wrong with it? You said it, didn't you?'

"There was another pause. 'I said it,' he agreed."[17]

The interview appeared in Boston in full, with an edited and more volatile version syndicated by the Associated Press on front pages across the country. Kennedy claimed the next day that the interview had been "off the record" and not for publication and that Lyons, who took no notes, had gotten several quotes wrong and manipulated others to "create a different impression entirely than I would want to set forth." The problem with his explanation, as Arthur Krock wrote him, was that "the general impression here seems to be—and this goes for the State Department also—that whatever the facts about the off-the-record restrictions the sentiments sound very much like yours, with one or two exceptions."[18]

The *New York Herald Tribune* called on Kennedy to explain himself or resign. Alsop and Kintner had a field day. "The history of American diplomacy is replete with fantastic incidents," they wrote forty-eight hours after the article appeared, "but a good many State Department officials agree that the recent interview given by Joseph P. Kennedy . . . comes near to winning the prize." The two reporters concluded, without any evidence, that the ambassador's "crusade for 'peace' . . . is obviously a potential front, behind which Kennedy and the men who go along with him may be able to start the first articulate, unblushing movement for appeasement the country has yet seen." That Kennedy had mentioned nothing about "appeasing" Hitler did not register with Alsop and Kintner, who had gone looking for and found numerous "indications of appeasement-mindedness" in the interview.[19]

To protect himself from the onslaught in London, Kennedy cabled a warning to Lord Beaverbrook. "The bombers may be tough in London but the ill-disposed newspapers are tougher in America. . . . Tell my friends not to pay any attention to anything they read that I say unless I sign or deliver it myself. There is as much conniving . . . in this country as there is in Russia."[20]

On November 19, Republican congressman George Tinkham inserted into the *Congressional Record* a verbatim copy of the article and follow-up stories in the *New York Times* and the *Boston Evening Transcript.*

Kennedy reluctantly and belatedly recognized that he had to now issue a "restatement of his position." Bluntly, unapologetically, and quite untruthfully, he denied having made "anti-British statements in this country [or] saying that I do not expect the British to win the war." His chief concern, he emphasized, remained "keeping America out of the war—but there has never been any secret about that. Everyone has known from the beginning that I have been against American entry into the war."[21]

General Raymond E. Lee, Kennedy's military attaché in London, had noted earlier the ambassador's penchant for "going off into a tirade or oration" at the drop of a hat. He "used almost to get drunk on his own verbosity, and I am inclined to think that is what betrayed him on many occasions." This was precisely what had happened at the Ritz-Carlton in Boston. It would happen again a week later, on the other end of the continent.

Kennedy had flown west to visit with Jack, who was taking courses at Stanford, and drive with him to see Hearst and Marion at Wyntoon, their estate in northern California. On his way back to New York, he accepted an invitation from the Warner brothers to speak at a luncheon at their studio. His topic was supposed to have been the difficulties of importing films to Europe in wartime, but he instead delivered a thundering three-hour monologue, in which he declared with an almost manic urgency that the British were doomed, that Britain's Jews were being blamed for the war in Europe, and that Hollywood and America's Jews would be similarly blamed for whatever hardships might occur should the United States enter the war. According to one Hollywood insider who provided columnists Joseph Alsop and Robert Kintner with an account of the talk, Kennedy's discussion of anti-Semitism was not only "strangely irrelevant," but in the view of most of those assembled had been "introduced into the discussion for scare-head purposes."[22]

"He apparently threw the fear of God into many of our producers and executives," Douglas Fairbanks, Jr., wrote President Roosevelt the day after the speech, "by telling them that the Jews were on the spot, and that they should stop making anti-Nazi pictures or using the film medium to promote or show sympathy to the cause of the 'democracies' versus the 'dictators.' . . . He continued to underline the fact that the film business was using its power to influence the public dangerously and that we all, and the Jews in particular, would be in jeopardy, if they continued to abuse that power."[23]

Three weeks earlier, Charlie Chaplin's *The Great Dictator* had opened in New York City. It was drawing good crowds at premium ticket prices across the country. Knowing Hollywood's herd mentality and understanding the endemic yet often unexpressed rage in Holly-wood against Hitler, nazism, and Germany, Kennedy feared that Chap-lin's picture and the earlier release of *The Mortal Storm,* another successful anti-Nazi film starring Jimmy Stewart, would set the stage for similar films. His message to the studio executives was to stay away from the subject entirely, that demonizing Germans, though emotion-ally satisfying, was going to prolong the war and the suffering by mak-ing it more difficult for both sides to approach the bargaining table. The longer war raged in Europe, the greater the likelihood that Americans would be drawn in. And if that happened, Kennedy warned, the cry would go out across the nation that American boys and resources were being sacrificed because the Hollywood Jews had hoodwinked the na-tion into fighting a war it had no business getting into.[24]

Kennedy's attack on Jewish producers was so intemperate, so un-called for, and ultimately so provocative that it left observers struggling to figure out if some ulterior motive was in play. "His campaign of ter-rorism," British Foreign Service officer Eric Cleugh reported, might have been "prompted by a hope that it will cause some of the Jews to get out of the business, so leaving a gap for Mr. Kennedy." Several of those who had heard him speak at Warner Brothers "and who 'sit in high places' in this industry," Fairbanks Jr. noted in his letter to Roos-evelt, "feel that . . . he is personally ambitious to take over powers in the film business. He has suggested 'clean-ups' and 'clean-outs.'" Darryl Zanuck, who was not Jewish, was asked the day after the luncheon what he thought Kennedy's motives had been in bringing up the subject of anti-Semitism. He replied, "He wants to scare the Jews out of the film business so that he can get back into it again."[25]

Kennedy's remarks at the Warner Brothers luncheon were not re-corded or reported in the newspapers. But news of what he had said was quickly relayed to Washington and to New York, where the Cen-tury Group, a loosely organized committee of journalists, lawyers, re-tired military men, and politicians who advocated expanded assistance to the British, if not an American declaration of war on Germany, drafted a letter demanding that Roosevelt repudiate Kennedy "as an official spokesman for the United States in any capacity" and remove him from his ambassadorial position, "not on the soft cushion with a 'well-done' accolade, but with a summary and indignant discharge."[26]

Roosevelt, who already knew Kennedy was going to resign, saw no need to do anything.

From Hollywood, Kennedy flew back to New York to continue his one-man antiwar crusade, not in public but in a series of meetings at the Waldorf Towers with the country's most influential opponents of intervention. On Friday, November 22, the day after Thanksgiving, he visited with ex-president Herbert Hoover. The ex-president, delighted but perhaps a bit puzzled by the visit of a Roosevelt appointee who had worked so hard to defeat him in 1932, agreed entirely with Kennedy on the futility of war and the need for a negotiated end to the hostilities, before Europe's great cities were reduced "to rubble heaps." Hoover kept a detailed record of the meeting and recalled Kennedy telling him that "if we went into the war, we would have a National Socialist state—he said he could see no return to democratic forms. He said that as between a bet on the British going down and our becoming a totalitarian government, we have to take the risk of British defeat . . . to avoid totalitarianism by keeping out of the war." On leaving the ex-president, the ambassador announced, unbidden, "that he would keep in communication with me, that we have a joint mission to keep America out of the war, and that he wanted to devote his every energy to it."[27]

Following his session with Hoover, Kennedy met with Joseph Patterson of the New York *Daily News,* Roy Howard, Charles Lindbergh, and others. To all of them, he insisted that the British position was "hopeless" and the best possible outcome to the war was a "negotiated peace."[28]

On December 1, Kennedy stopped off in Washington on his way to Palm Beach to meet with Roosevelt and formally submit his resignation. Though the president had not yet chosen a replacement, he accepted Kennedy's resignation with the caveat that he remain in office until a new ambassador could be named and confirmed. He did not rebuke him for telling Lyons that "democracy was finished" in Britain or for mouthing off about Jewish influence in Hollywood. Well aware that he might have need of Kennedy's support in the recurring battles he anticipated over rearmament and assistance to Great Britain, Roosevelt had no intention of alienating him further. Instead, he discussed

with him, as he would with a senior adviser or a man he was considering for a new appointment, "several problems bothering him," including economic relations with Canada and South America, potential labor
problems at defense plants, and the hard road ahead "fitting Naval
plans in with naval production contractors, etc." Kennedy, for his part,
greeted the president as he would an old and trusted friend. "When he
complained that people don't understand all the problems and mentioned his own physical indisposition [he was suffering from a bad
cold], I said: 'For God sake don't let anything happen to you and then
have to take Wallace [Henry Wallace, his vice president]—you're responsible for him and he has no experience.' He replied, 'That's right,
I'll be careful.'"[29]

In a statement released to the press on exiting the White House,
Kennedy announced that he was resigning.

"Today the President was good enough to express regret over my
decision, but to say that, not yet being prepared to appoint my successor, he wishes me to retain my designation as ambassador until he is
prepared. But I shall not return to London in that capacity. My plan is,
after a short holiday, to devote my efforts to what seems to me the great
cause in the world today—and means, if successful, the preservation of
the American form of democracy. That cause is to help the President
keep the United States out of war."[30]

Twenty-seven

THE MAN WHO
OUT-HAMLETED HAMLET

Apparently Joe Kennedy is out to do whatever damage he can," Harold Ickes wrote in his diary on December 1, 1940, the same day Kennedy had his cordial reunion with the president at the White House. "He has had an interview with Hearst with a view to starting a campaign for appeasement in this country. He has seen, or is about to see, Roy Howard and Joe Patterson, of the *New York News,* who for some reason has been talking appeasement. . . . This would make a powerful combination. Kennedy has lots of money and can probably raise all that he needs."[1]

Four days later, Alsop and Kintner sounded the same warning, but in public: "Let there be no mistake about it. When Joseph P. Kennedy grandiloquently announced he was laying down his office to fight for the cause of peace, he really meant he was going to peddle appeasement all across the United States. . . . Indeed, he seems to have been at it already. For it must be more than a coincidence that wherever Kennedy has gone in the country since his return from London, there have been sudden crops of defeatist rumors and appeasement talk. By following his announced plan of seeking out leading men and telling them his story, Kennedy may have a great effect on public opinion."[2]

On December 11, 1940, General Robert E. Wood of Sears, Roebuck, the chairman of the anti-interventionist America First Committee, approached Kennedy with a proposal. Believing (as did most foes and friends of the president) that Kennedy was ready to campaign full-time now against the administration, he suggested that he succeed him as chairman of the committee. Kennedy's reply was courteous, if noncommittal: "My own hunch is, at least for the time being while I am still Ambassador in name, I won't join any Committees, and after I get out I think I will have to decide just how I think I can work best." He agreed, nonetheless, to meet in Palm Beach with Robert Stuart, Jr., who had founded the America First Committee while a law student at Yale and now served as its national director. After the meeting, Kennedy wrote Wood again to confirm that he was not going to join the committee just yet, but that he was prepared to "do everything I possibly can to help you."[3]

Less than two weeks after leaving Washington for Palm Beach, Kennedy was called back for the funeral of Lord Lothian, the British ambassador to the United States and dear friend of Lady Astor's. Met at Washington Airport by reporters, "he seemed determined as he strode along the concrete runway to avoid political matters," until he was asked a question about preparedness. He answered "dryly" that what the nation needed was "less talk about going to war and more action about building up our defenses." This was taken by some as an indication that Kennedy was ready to return to Washington to help build those defenses. "Guessing what Joseph P. Kennedy will do next," the Los Angeles Times reported on December 16, 1940, "is one of Washington's most popular sports."[4]

Arthur Krock, who defended Kennedy in his December 8 column against "the close-knit and sincere, but intolerant group" that attacked him as an "appeaser," was working on his own plan to bring Kennedy back into the government. He proposed to Roosevelt and to Hull that Kennedy be appointed as a special presidential envoy and sent to Ireland, ostensibly to discuss food supplies but secretly to negotiate with President Éamon de Valera on behalf of the British, who wanted to be able to make use of Irish military bases. The proposal was outlandish, noted Neville Butler, currently in charge of the British embassy in Washington. Still, Butler warned, the suggestion had to be taken seriously, as it came from Krock and Kennedy, "people of importance in this world here with correspondent capacity for mischief." Butler was instructed by Halifax, with Churchill's full agreement, to meet with Hull and tell him that the British government "do not consider that good is likely to come of [the initiative]. For your own information, we regard Mr. Kennedy as a highly unsuitable emissary though we appreciate that we must not antagonize him or such Irish-American opinion as is under his influence."[5]

On the Sunday of the Lothian funeral, Kennedy noted in his diary that before attending Mass at St. Matthew's, he had "read in *Washington Post,* owned by Eugene Meyer, a Jew, that five prominent men had written short eulogies on Lothian." Four of the five were active in the campaign for American assistance to the British war effort: Felix Frankfurter, "who is supposed directly and indirectly to influence Roosevelt on Foreign Policy over Hull's and Welles's heads [and] whose cohort of young lawyers are in practically every government department, all aiding the cause of Jewish refugees getting into America"; "John W. Davis attorney for J. P. Morgan . . . Tom Lamont, head of Morgans, who would certainly like to get U.S. in"; and William Allen White, the publisher/editor of the Kansas *Emporia Gazette* and chairman of the Committee to Defend America by Aiding the Allies. "It looks to me," Kennedy noted in his diary, "as if the English sympathizers were tying their cause in with the Jews because they figure they've got all the influence in U.S."[6]

He was not alone in his fear that the Jews had too much influence in Washington. Kennedy reported in his diary that Justice Frank Murphy had told him the month before, when they met in New York City, that "it was Frankfurter and Ben Cohen who wrote the Attorney General's opinion on destroyers and bases. Murphy regards the Jewish influence as most dangerous. He said that after all, Hopkins' wife was a Jew; Hull's wife is a Jew; and Frankfurter and Cohen and that group are all

Jews." Sumner Welles had also told Kennedy that he thought Frankfurter "dangerous." Frankfurter, he told Kennedy, "read all the papers
[diplomatic dispatches?] and made suggestions to Roosevelt— *He's* a
Jew chiseler."[7]

Assistant Secretary of State Breckinridge Long reported to Kennedy
that he too was having difficulties with the Jewish organizations that
were lobbying for an immediate and significant increase in "emergency
visas" for refugees from Nazi-occupied territories. With the support of
Martin Dies, chairman of the House Committee on Un-American Activities, and in partnership with J. Edgar Hoover, Long had demanded
that visa requirements for Jewish refugees be tightened, not loosened,
to prevent the Nazis from flooding the nation with spies. "Saw Long,"
Kennedy noted in his diary. "Getting madder and madder at tactics of
Frankfurter, Meyer [Eugene, publisher of the *Washington Post*], and
other Jews to get Jew political refugees in U.S.— They were constantly
harassing him. . . . The Department of Justice was split up—[Solicitor
General Francis] Biddle headed up the Jews and their connection. They
wouldn't let the FBI investigate the names of the refugees. Just an un-
holy show. (Looks like it needs an investigation.) [Long] told me again
[about] the copy of the letter from big Jew who offered German cause
$300,000 to get some Jews out. This refugee situation stinks to Heaven
but no paper will print the story."[8]

Long, in slightly more decorous and disguised language, confirmed
in his diary that same day that he was under siege by organized Jewry.
"The attacks on the Department and the unpleasant situation in the
press over the refugee matter seems to continue. It is more widespread
than it was and seems to be joined up with the small element in this
country which wants to push us into this war. Those persons are largely
concentrated along the Atlantic seaboard, and principally around New
York. There are elements of them in the Government here. They are all
woven together in the barrage of opposition against the State Department which makes me the bull's eye."[9]

Upon his return to Palm Beach, Kennedy wrote John Burns, recounting what he had learned from Long. The British government and the
American Jews were "getting together in this whole campaign to get
America into this war" and no one dared speak out against it. Worse
yet, the Jews had become so powerful that they were steamrolling their

proposals for refugee resettlement through Washington. "A greater fraud and well-engineered scheme was never perpetrated on the American public than that a thousand refugees have been taken into the United States; not one of them, I know, had ever been investigated by the F.B.I., and yet I don't suppose any newspaper in the United States would print the truth for fear of losing advertisers—and then we boast of the freedom of the press. Nuts, I say." He still trusted Roosevelt to "make the right decision, if left alone," he claimed in a letter to Frank Murphy in late December. "It is the influence around him, I fear."[10]

Since returning to the United States, Kennedy's paranoia about Jewish influence had gotten the better of him. The more he found himself on the outside, scorned and criticized as an appeaser, a man out of touch with reality, a traitor to the Roosevelt cause, the more he blamed the Jews. Incapable of understanding why his warnings that the British were doomed and were doing all they could to bring down America with them was nowhere heeded, he looked for conspiracy—and found it. The Jews opposed him and orchestrated the attacks on him, he convinced himself, because he was committed to finding a way to live at peace with Hitler, while they were committed to going to war. That there was no basis for such conclusions did not deter him from voicing them in gratuitous and increasingly grotesque anti-Semitic language.

His fears that the Jews had become too powerful in Washington were, of course, entirely misplaced. Jewish influence on foreign policy was negligible, its influence on the State Department nonexistent. In the months and years to come, Breckinridge Long would, virtually unopposed, institute visa requirements that succeeded in cutting back the number of Jewish refugees admitted to the United States. By mid-1941, new regulations, supposedly written to keep out Nazi spies masquerading as German Jews, had reduced the number of visas offered to about 25 percent of the available quota. After Pearl Harbor, visa procedures would be tightened again, preventing even more Jewish refugees from entering the country.[11]

As Kennedy had feared, and warned, and as Lord Lothian had undiplomatically announced in November two weeks before his death, the British were "broke"—or if not yet "broke," very close to running out of the dollars they needed to pay for the military hardware they were requesting. Giving them any armaments on credit was illegal according to the current Neutrality Acts; giving them away as a gift was politically impossible. Roosevelt found a third option, which he explained at a December 17 press conference. "Suppose my neighbor's home catches fire, and I have a length of garden hose four or five hundred feet away. If he can take my garden hose and connect it up with his hydrant, I may help him put out his fire. Now, what do I do? I don't say to him before that operation, 'Neighbor, my garden hose cost me fifteen dollars; you have to pay me fifteen dollars for it.' What is the transaction that goes on? I don't want fifteen dollars—I want my garden hose back after the fire is over."[12]

In a fireside chat on December 29, Roosevelt further elaborated on what has become known as "lend-lease"—a program, he declared at the onset, that was about national security, not war. He began by ruling out any possibility that the United States would ever attempt to broker or "encourage talk of peace" with the "aggressor nations." "The experience of the past two years has proven beyond doubt that no nation can appease the Nazis. No man can tame a tiger into a kitten by stroking it." There were those, he admitted, who believed "that wars in Europe and in Asia are of no concern to us," but they were dangerously wrong. National security depended on the survival of Britain. "If Great Britain goes down, the Axis powers will control the continents of Europe, Asia, Africa, Australia, and the high seas—and they will be in a position to bring enormous military and naval resources against this hemisphere." The British had not asked for American troops, and even if they had, the president had no intention of sending them. "The people of Europe who are defending themselves do not ask us to do their fighting. They ask us for the implements of war, the planes, the tanks, the guns, the freighters which will enable them to fight for their liberty and for our security." To protect the nation from future attacks and assist the British in repelling the current one, America had to become "the great arsenal of democracy."[13]

While Roosevelt put his cabinet to work on writing legislation to implement the lend-lease program, the America First Committee, disturbed by both his declaration that he would not seek a negotiated peace and his intention to supply the British with increased military assistance, marshaled its arguments and its forces. On January 4, Robert Stuart, Jr., the national America First Committee director who had earlier met with Kennedy in Palm Beach, wrote Page Hufty, the coordinator of the Florida branch, to ask him to get back in touch with the ambassador. "With relation to Ambassador Kennedy, I feel more than ever that he is one of our most important cards. He has got to be played right. . . . More than any other man in the country today, he can cut through the confusion that exists in so many people's thinking. I do hope that if you have any influence with him, or know anyone who has, you will prevail upon him to come out and take a stand at the earliest possible moment."[14]

Hufty tried but got nowhere. Kennedy did not, he wrote Stuart, "feel it was wise for him to make a move until the Administration's program had been presented in tangible form which would give him something more specific to attack. He felt that the American people would not be interested in what he had to say much more than once and that therefore he should be very careful to pick his spot for that time." Though Kennedy had left the door open to joining the anti-intervention campaign, Hufty held out little hope that he ever would. "Ambassador Kennedy still clings to his conviction that President Roosevelt is sincerely anxious to keep us out of war."[15]

Hufty was correct. In a letter to Cornelius Fitzgerald in Boston, Kennedy directly contradicted the America Firsters' assumption that Roosevelt wanted to get Americans into the European war. "Until Hitler decides that it is to his best interest to have the United States in, we won't go in. Maybe I am one of those who has too much confidence in what Roosevelt says, but . . . I just don't believe that we are going in."[16]

On January 10, Roosevelt's lend-lease bill was introduced in both houses of Congress, with hearings scheduled to begin before the House Committee on Foreign Affairs the following Wednesday. The Democratic majority called as its first witnesses the secretaries of state, treasury, war, and the navy, and William Knudsen, director of the president's Office of Production Management. After a recess for the inauguration, to which Kennedy was invited but did not attend, Hamilton Fish, the senior Republican on the committee, called his witnesses. First on the list was Joseph P. Kennedy, whom Fish and nearly everyone else in Washington believed would forcefully and persuasively oppose the legislation.

Kennedy, aware that the spotlight was going to be turned on him and there was no way to avoid it, booked a half hour of radio time two days before he was scheduled to testify. He was not going to allow his first public appearance since his resignation to be choreographed by congressional committee protocols. Because he was still nominally ambassador to Great Britain (his successor had not yet been named), he called Sumner Welles to inquire whether there were any procedures he should be aware of, and to tell him that he had booked time for himself "to go on the radio and broadcast Saturday night—I am sick and tired of being attacked by both sides and think I am at least entitled to state my position clearly." He was, he added, particularly "sore" at the president for not "calling off his 'Henchmen'" who were preemptively attacking him for his opposition to the lend-lease bill.

Welles called back the next day to report that Hull wanted to go over his testimony with him. This Kennedy would not do. He did, however, agree to meet with the president on Thursday morning, two days before his radio address and four days before his House testimony. Because the weather was bad and he was afraid his plane might be grounded, Kennedy took the 12:50 A.M. train to Washington. He arrived at the White House on schedule that morning. After a fifteen-minute wait, he was "ushered into [Roosevelt's] bedroom and found he was in his bathroom in his wheel chair. He was attired in sort of grey pajamas and was starting to shave himself. I sat on the toilet-seat and talked with him." As he had every time he had encountered the president over the past few years, Kennedy began by complaining about "the treatment I had received." Roosevelt listened, then commented almost casually that no one had "received worse treatment than he had in the last eight years." The preliminaries out of the way, they proceeded to the business at hand: the lend-lease legislation. Kennedy told the president that he believed the bill might be passed without amendments, but it would be difficult, because as now written, it expanded presidential powers in a way the American people would oppose "unless they understood it better." Kennedy suggested that Roosevelt allow the Democrats to amend the bill to give Congress more oversight, rather than risk having the Republicans push through their own amendments. The president replied that he would not oppose an amendment that would establish a joint committee that he would "keep posted on what was going on," but he was not going to delegate to Congress powers that the Constitution had given the executive branch.

Kennedy asked Roosevelt if he had decided on his successor as ambassador to Great Britain. They discussed a number of possibilities, then talked a bit about Jimmy Roosevelt's decision to try his hand in Hollywood, the administration's difficulty in getting reliable information about the extent of British dollar holdings, and a few other matters. "His whole attitude was very friendly," Kennedy recalled in his diary. "I said numerous times that I couldn't understand why so many people were so anxious about our not being friends. He said he paid no attention to this, but he wouldn't have been human if he hadn't." Roosevelt kept the meeting going to the point where "he was about an hour late on his appointments." Nothing, of course, could have pleased Kennedy more. He was back on the inside again, an intimate, a trusted presidential confidant and adviser. Roosevelt was also pleased with the meeting. Later that afternoon, he told his cabinet that he now "thought that Kennedy would not go too far overboard, although he realized that he was always unpredictable and might say anything."[17]

That was not the impression Kennedy gave the newspaper reporters he spoke to on leaving the White House. The last thing he wanted was to appear as the president's stooge. And he did not. The *New York Times,* in a front-page story, headlined KENNEDY TO URGE OUR "STAYING OUT," quoted the ambassador as declaring emphatically that "for once, I am going to say for myself what I have in my mind." The New York *Daily News* reported on Kennedy's meeting with Roosevelt in a syndicated front-page story that the *Los Angeles Times* carried under the headline PRESIDENT GIVEN REBUFF BY KENNEDY: ENVOY SECRETLY CALLED TO WHITE HOUSE OPPOSES AID-TO-BRITAIN BILL. As evidence that Kennedy was going to oppose the president, the *Daily News* reported that on leaving the White House, he had returned to his suite at the Carlton to meet Burton Wheeler, the leader of the opposition. When reporters finally caught up with the ambassador, he was uncharacteristically "tight lipped and terse. All he would say for publication was: 'In order that there be no misunderstanding about this at this time, I am going to tell my story in full on Saturday. The accent will be on keeping this country out of war.' "[18]

Joseph Kennedy had been preparing to deliver this, his first major foreign policy speech as a private citizen, for months now. His primary consultant was his twenty-four-year-old son, Jack, who had proven his worth as a foreign policy analyst in his senior thesis. Father and son had spent hours together during the ambassador's November trip to California, discussing how Kennedy might best respond to the accelerating attacks that had followed the Lyons article in the *Boston Sunday Globe*. He trusted Jack's judgment because he knew his son had listened carefully and absorbed into his thinking much of what he had told him. Kennedy expected Jack to put his thoughts into words that were less provocative than he was likely to come up with himself.

Jack advised his father to take the high road and avoid personal attacks on the columnists who had been savaging him, as journalists "have 365 days a year to strike back." "I think it is important that you write in a very calm and a judicious manner, not as though you were on the defensive." Jack also urged his father to correct the impression that he was still an "appeaser." "It seems to me that if this label is tied to you it may nullify your immediate effectiveness. . . . Lindbergh may prove a good example of this. I don't mean that you should change your ideas or be all things to all men, but I do mean that you should express your views in such a way that it will be difficult to indict you as an appeaser." "Where I think Lindbergh has run afoul is in his declarations that we do not care what happens over there—that we can live at peace with a world controlled by the dictators. . . . I would think that your best angle would be that of course you do not believe this, you with your background cannot stand the idea personally of dictatorships—you hate them—you have achieved the abundant life under a democratic capitalistic system—you wish to preserve it. . . . The point that I am trying to get at is that it is <u>important that you stress how much you dislike the idea of dealing with dictatorships,</u> how you wouldn't trust their word a minute—how you have no confidence in them."[19]

A little less than six weeks after Jack had laid out his guidelines for his father, on Saturday evening, January 18, 1941, Kennedy spoke into the microphones at the WEAF station in New York, first in several takes for the newsreel cameras, then at seven P.M. live over the NBC Red Network. He opened with a call for "tolerance." Too many well-meaning public servants, himself included, were being smeared by "a few ruthless and irresponsible Washington columnists [who] have claimed for themselves the right to speak for the nation." He intended to set the record straight and correct the "many false statements regarding my views on foreign policy." He rejected the label of "defeatist." As ambassador, he had reported accurately and faithfully on the problems facing Great Britain, but he had never predicted defeat.

Jack had asked him to tone down his rhetoric and avoid the term *appeaser,* but his father was too stubborn, too proud, and too loyal to the master appeaser, Neville Chamberlain, to do this. Instead, he tried to deflect criticism by redefining the term. "Another label used as a smear against certain citizens who favor keeping America out of war is the word 'appeaser.' I have been called one. Here is my answer. If by that word, now possessed of hateful implications, it is charged that I advocate a deal with the dictators contrary to the British desires, or that I advocate placing any trust or confidence in their promises, the charge is false and malicious. . . . But, if I am called an appeaser because I oppose the entrance of this country into the present war, I cheerfully plead guilty. So must every one of you who want to keep America out of war." What precisely he meant by this was far from clear. How could one be an appeaser and yet agree with Roosevelt that it was futile to attempt to negotiate with, to "appease," Hitler?

Since his primary objective was to support Roosevelt without appearing to be his toady, Kennedy had to refocus the discussion. Instead of entering the debate over the lend-lease bill, he spoke on a topic of his own choosing and presented a series of disjointed arguments against the United States entering the war in Europe. He claimed that the

United States was not "prepared to fight a war"; that there had been no national debate over "war aims"; that defeating Germany and rescuing Great Britain was insufficient cause to sacrifice American lives and fortune; that there was no danger of a German invasion of the western hemisphere, even after the defeat of Great Britain.

"It is said that we cannot exist in a world where totalitarianism rules. I grant you—it is a terrible future to contemplate. But why should anyone think that our getting into a war would preserve our ideals, a war which would then practically leave Russia alone outside the war area getting stronger while the rest of the world approached exhaustion? . . . Well, at the end of the war we win—so what? What is the status of the world? Who is going to reorganize Europe? . . . To keep defeated Germany and the other counties from going completely Communistic we will have to reorganize them as well as ourselves, probably standing guard while this reorganization is taking place. I shudder to contemplate it. Are our children's and our grandchildren's lives to be spent standing guard in Europe while Heaven knows what happens in America?"

Only at the end of his address did he refer to the lend-lease legislation, but in such a desultory, confused, conflicted manner that it was near impossible to know whether he opposed or supported it. He declared, to the delight of the president, that he was a firm believer "in centralized responsibility and . . . in conferring all powers necessary to carry out that responsibility. Moreover, I appreciate full well that time is of the essence." And then, out of nowhere, he voiced his objection to the bill in two sentences: "I am unable to agree with the proponents of this bill that it has yet been shown that we face such immediate danger as to justify this surrender of the authority and responsibility of the Congress. I believe that after the hearings have been completed there will be revealed less drastic ways of meeting the problem of adequate authority for the President."[20]

No one knew quite what to make of his performance. Harold Ickes, who listened on the tiny radio he had placed on the dinner table, wrote in his diary that "Kennedy gave all of us the impression last night that he was doing some tightrope walking. He would seem to take one position and then to reverse himself. The speech was not impressive." Democratic senator James Byrnes, who was in favor of the president's bill, praised Kennedy in public for his "very strong statement of the reasons why this country should render all aid to Britain—promptly—short of war." Burton Wheeler, who opposed the legislation, declared, also publicly, that he was "in entire accord with Kennedy's remarks concerning the vital necessity of keeping out of war."[21]

Fifteen-year-old Robert Kennedy was relieved, as he wrote his mother, that his father had "really cleared himself from what people have been calling him." And his father had indeed succeeded in making it clear that he was not an "isolationist" or a "defeatist" or in favor of opening negotiations with the Germans. But he had given Roosevelt's opponents an opening large enough to drive a truck through by almost casually suggesting that the lend-lease bill might be amended to give Congress some oversight. The *Chicago Tribune,* published by Colonel Robert McCormick, who would later testify against what he and his paper referred to as the "dictator bill," reported on the speech in a front-page story headlined in large type, boldface, **DON'T ENTER WAR**—Kennedy, with the subhead "Opposes F.D.R. Bill."[22]

Kennedy had not intended to position himself as an opponent of the president or an advocate of the America First position. He supported the bill in principle and in substance; his objections were minor. There were myriad reasons for him to back the president, as he thought he had. He accepted Roosevelt's argument that it made sense to aid the British in their fight against the Germans if only to buy time until the United States was fully rearmed; he trusted that Roosevelt was telling the truth when he declared that he had no intention of going to war with Germany; and he supported the president's full-throttle rearmament campaign, which he expected would produce more than enough military goods to share some with the British. More practically, even had he disagreed with the legislation, it is likely he would have kept his complaints to himself or muttered them in private rather than go on the radio and testify to Congress about them. If he or, more probably, his boys, were to have any future in politics, it would be as Democrats. Irish Catholic politicians did not go very far in the Republican Party.

Why, then, did he not come right out and endorse the legislation? Because he was too proud to permit himself to be viewed, again, as the president's yes-man; too independent-minded to unequivocally support legislation he had not been consulted on; too obsessed by his own fears to focus on anyone else's agenda, even that of the president of the United States; too caught up with his own importance to speak to the issue that mattered.

In the end, he failed to understand what was required of him in a wartime emergency. Joseph P. Kennedy had battled all his life to become an insider, to get inside the Boston banking establishment, inside Hollywood, inside the Roosevelt circle of trusted advisers. But he had never been able to accept the reality that being an "insider" meant sacrificing something to the team. His sense of his own wisdom and unique talents was so overblown that he truly believed he could stake out an independent position for himself and still remain a trusted and vital part of the Roosevelt team.

His abbreviated, curiously ambiguous, almost obscurantist remarks in his radio address on Saturday night focused added attention on his Tuesday morning testimony before the House Committee on Foreign Affairs. Again, the consensus opinion was that he would speak in opposition to the bill as written. Walter Trohan of the anti-Roosevelt *Chicago Tribune* recalled in a letter written years later that he had been with Kennedy "the night before he testified. . . . He screamed, bellowed, and beat his breast that lend-lease meant war and shouted that war must be stopped because it would wreck our way of life."[23]

He was called to testify at ten A.M. as the lead-off Republican witness. He would hold the floor for the next five hours. "Mr. Kennedy's testimony," the *New York Times* reported the next morning in a front-page story, "drew the largest gallery of any witness so far heard on the lease-lend bill. A throng of several hundred, predominantly women, including many inaugural visitors, jammed all available space in the Ways and Means Committee auditorium. On many occasions the audience broke into applause as Mr. Kennedy, with Irish wit and Boston straight-talk, shot his answer back to a searching question." No one could nail him down; he treated congressmen from both sides of the debate and both sides of the aisle with studied contempt as they tried to get him to say something he did not intend to say. He did not think the president had made any secret deals with the British or that the bill, if passed in its present form, would bring the nation closer to war. He was in favor of giving the president the powers needed to provide the British with immediate assistance, but he was opposed to the bill as written because it did not provide for a "coordinating function" for Congress. When asked what he meant by "coordinating function" or if he might suggest how the bill should be amended to provide it, he declined to elaborate, insisting only that he was sure that after the debate in Congress, the matter would be resolved.[24]

He left the hearing room satisfied with his performance, unprepared for the reaction that would follow. Taken together, his radio address and congressional testimony would prove an unmitigated disaster. His final descent into the political purgatory in which he would spend the remainder of his years can be dated from the moment he left the hearing room on Tuesday afternoon.

The press coverage was devastating. He had "out-Hamleted Hamlet," wrote columnist Dorothy Thompson, who supported the lend-lease bill. "Instead of posing the question 'To be or not to be' he managed to make it, 'To be and not to be.'" Even *Time* and *Life,* Henry Luce's large-circulation weeklies that were usually so friendly, mocked him heartlessly, perhaps in retaliation for his decision to endorse Roosevelt for a third term. "Joseph Patrick Kennedy, who smilingly took the stand," *Time* reported in its summary of the first week's hearings, filled "the room with obfuscation [and] could not even make up his mind whether he should be called 'Mister' or 'ambassador.' Said Mr. Kennedy cheerfully: 'Whichever way you want me is all right with me.' It was the nearest he got to defining his position." *Life* reported that "Joe Kennedy had entangled himself in ambiguities from which even his best friends seemed unable to extract him." The Republicans and America Firsters were astounded by his refusal to come out against the bill or attack the president as a warmonger; the administration accounted him nothing less than a traitor for his reluctance to stand behind the president and his bill.[25]

"I tried to be as fair as I could at the testimony before the House Committee," he wrote John Boettiger from Palm Beach on February 10, "and if you read it sometime you will be convinced that under the circumstances I got out quite well. Now, if my statements and my position means that, outside of the ever loyal Boettigers, I am to be a social outcast by the administration, well so be it. I will be sorry but if that's the way it is, it's just too bad. I will, at least, have the satisfaction of having fulfilled all my obligations."[26]

Boettiger sent a copy of Kennedy's note to the White House, hoping that the president might reassure and welcome the ambassador back into the fold. Roosevelt was reluctant to do either. He was furious that Kennedy, while agreeing in principle with the lend-lease legislation, had refused to give it his unqualified support. "It is, I think, a little pathetic that he worries about being, with his family, social outcasts," Roosevelt replied to his son-in-law. "As a matter of fact, he ought to realize of course that he has only himself to blame for the country's opinion as to his testimony before the Committees. Most people and most papers got the feeling that he was blowing hot and blowing cold at the same time—trying to carry water on both shoulders."

Displaying an anger that he seldom allowed to be glimpsed outside family confines—and a touch of WASPish condescension that he also hid well—Roosevelt explained to his son-in-law that Joe Kennedy was an unreliable ally, and would always be—not because he was ambitious, which he was, not because he enjoyed wielding power, which he did, but because all he cared about was preserving the fortune he had accumulated and handing it on to his children. "The truth of the matter," Roosevelt continued, "is that Joe is and always has been a temperamental Irish boy, terrifically spoiled at an early age by huge financial success; thoroughly patriotic, thoroughly selfish, and thoroughly obsessed with the idea that he must leave each of his nine children with a million dollars apiece, when he dies (he has told me that often). He had a positive horror of any change in the present methods of life in America. To him, the future of a small capitalistic class is safer under a Hitler than under a Churchill. This is sub-conscious on his part and he does not admit it. Personally, I am very fond of Joe and he is wrong in referring to being hurt by my 'hatchet men.' I have none of course, though there are lots of people who speak out on both sides of the fence! After the lend-lease Bill goes through, I will write Joe to ask him to stop off on his way North. Sometimes I think I am 200 years older than he is."[27]

It is difficult to argue with any of this, save Roosevelt's unnecessary reference to Kennedy as being Irish or his thoughtless remark that Kennedy believed the "small capitalistic class . . . safer under a Hitler." He most definitely did not. Had he, he would have been much less frightened by the likelihood of a German victory in Europe.

PART VI

Palm Beach and Hyannis Port

Twenty-eight

A FORCED RETIREMENT

Press attention over Kennedy's lend-lease testimony subsided soon enough and, with it, any interest in what he had to say or was doing. Except for an item or two in the Palm Beach society pages, his name all but disappeared from the daily newspapers and weekly magazines. Only Arthur Krock made mention of him in columns published in April, May, July, and September 1941, each of which suggested that Kennedy was one of several "brilliant 'unemployed'" business executives who belonged in Washington.

There were no more invitations from the America Firsters to write or broadcast or speak out on their behalf. The whirlwind antiwar crusade that he had promised—and that some in the Roosevelt camp had so feared—never materialized. If he had wanted, he could have found venues for his views, or bought them, but he had said his piece, and until the situation changed, he had nothing more to say. "As I promised at the time of my appearance before the Foreign Relations Committee," he wrote Franklin Gowen, still at the U.S. embassy in London, "if the Lease-Lend Bill were passed after proper debate, I would go along with it, so I have kept religiously quiet. I have disappeared from the stage and will let new faces take on."[1]

Early in the following year, Jack Kennedy would tell his girlfriend

Inga Arvad, whose conversations the FBI monitored because they feared she might be a German spy, that "his father's greatest mistake was not talking enough; that he stopped too quickly and was accused of being an appeaser" because he feared that his comments "might hurt his two sons later in politics."[2]

On resigning as ambassador, Kennedy had, indeed, stopped talking to the press. He retreated into a closed Palm Beach universe, surrounded by adoring children and golfing buddies. He was not a recluse or a shut-away, but preferred to spend time at home—and at the Palm Beach Country Club, the "Jewish club," which was only a few minutes distant. (He was, he boasted, one of the club's two non-Jewish members. The other was the Duke of Windsor.) He had given up playing tennis with his boys when Joe Jr. got good enough to beat him. But he still enjoyed a round of golf with them, probably because he still played better than they did. He played fast, never wasted time, never lost a ball (to his children's and his caddy's amazement), though he spent a good deal of time looking for the ones that went astray, and seldom lost any money on his bets. His favorite ploy with his boys was to remind them, on those few occasions when they were leading, that they had only "two up with three to go," ratcheting up the pressure on them not to mess up, which, Ted remembers, they inevitably did.[3]

He saw his children over their Christmas and Easter vacations but was alone with his buddies most of the winter. Rose visited occasionally but didn't stay for long. Joe Jr. was still at Harvard Law School, Kick at Finch College on Manhattan's East Side, Bob at Priory in Rhode Island, Pat and Jean at the Sacred Heart Convent school in the Bronx, and Rosemary in Washington, D.C., at St. Gertrude's School of Arts and Crafts, a residential school for "retarded" girls staffed by Benedictine sisters from St. Scholastica Priory in Duluth, Minnesota.

St. Gertrude's was a temporary solution for Rosemary until the situation improved in England and she could return to live with Mother Isabel. At twenty-two years of age, Rosemary was much older than the other students at St. Gertrude's, but there were few other institutions in the country that could accommodate the special needs of a woman her age. She was still quite pretty, with short, curly brown hair, a tooth-some Kennedy smile, rounder than her waiflike sisters, Patricia and Eunice, but not terribly overweight. Kennedy monitored his daughter's care, as he had in England, visited her, and kept in touch with Dr. Thomas Moore, the priest who oversaw St. Gertrude's.[4]

Jack and Eunice, both plagued by undiagnosed medical problems (later identified as Addison's disease), did not go to school that spring. After a short stay in the hospital, Eunice traveled to Latin America with her mother. Jack, after yet another inconclusive battery of tests in Boston, returned south to help his father with his memoirs, then joined his mother and sister on their Latin American tour.

Ted, the youngest, was the only Kennedy afforded the dubious honor of being allowed to remain in Florida after the Christmas holidays. He was enrolled in a local Palm Beach elementary school for three months until Easter. Then, with the "season" at an end and his parents heading north, his mother arranged for him to attend Priory with his brother Bob. "I entered the seventh grade at Portsmouth Priory in the spring of 1941," Ted wrote later in his memoirs, "when I was barely nine years old, boarding and competing with boys who were four years older than me. It was a recipe for disaster. My time at Portsmouth Priory was not an education; it was a battle." His only friend was his pet turtle, who died a few weeks after he arrived.[5]

Though it was Rose who made the decisions as to where the younger children went to school, Kennedy was becoming more active as a parent now that he was home from London and unemployed. When Rose left for her extended tour of Latin America, Kennedy became not only "housekeeper," as he wrote Hearst, but was put in charge of finding a companion to accompany Rosemary to Wyonegonic Camps in Denmark, Maine, that summer. He monitored Teddy's schooling, arranged for Pat to "take the [Wellesley] entrance examinations" now that she was about to graduate from the Sacred Heart Convent in the Bronx, and worked with his contacts in the military to secure the right placements for his boys, who had decided to enlist instead of waiting to be drafted.[6]

Joe Jr., athletic, healthy, and now in his second year at Harvard Law School, was going to have no trouble getting a plum assignment in whatever branch or unit he chose, but Jack, almost grotesquely underweight and with a slew of unresolved health problems, needed all the help his father could give him. That spring of 1941, Kennedy wrote George McDonald at the "Office of the Chief of the Air Corps" on

Jack's behalf. An army air corps unit was being organized at Harvard, and Kennedy wondered whether Jack should apply in Boston, from Palm Beach (where he was now residing), or from California, where he had registered for the draft. "To be perfectly honest with you I am more confused as to what my two sons are going to do than I have ever been on any job I have ever tackled in my life. Joe is planning on entering the Air Corps, but if Jack goes into the Army Air Corps, I understand that Joe is entering the Naval branch of the service. I hope they know what they're doing because I am frank to say that I don't. I get dizzier and dizzier."[7]

In June 1941, after his second year at law school, Joe Jr. enlisted in a special unit of the U.S. Naval Air Corps that was being organized at Harvard. He would spend his summer training at Squantum, a stone's throw from the Fore River shipbuilding plant where his father had done his service in the Great War.

Jack, on returning from Latin America, went to work as an intern in the East Boston bank his grandfather had founded and in which his father had served as president. Kennedy, knowing how anxious his second son was to follow his brother into the military and how impossible it would be for him to pass his physical, got in touch with Captain Alan Kirk, whom he had met in London. Kirk pulled whatever strings he had to and arranged for Jack to take and pass his physical in Boston in early August. Jack then filled in some questionnaires, sat for an interview, received his security clearance, and was commissioned an officer in the navy and ordered to report in the fall to Captain Kirk at the Office of Naval Intelligence in Washington. For the time being, both Kennedy boys were where they wanted to be: in uniform in Uncle Sam's peacetime military.

With the children scattered across the country, Rose traveling, and Kennedy in Palm Beach, there was no need to hold on to the Bronxville mansion. Kennedy had put it on the market while he was in London and kept it there awaiting a reasonable offer. He certainly didn't need the money from the sale. Whatever happened, he was confident that the family trust funds would keep growing and the cash flow from Somerset Importers remain large enough to fund the family's living expenses. The British needed dollars and would continue to export Scotch to ever-thirsty Americans. To protect himself against the unlikely possibility that the Germans might close down transatlantic trade, Kennedy had, while still in London, pulled all the strings he could to secure precious cargo space for his Scotch. He now had enough of it stockpiled in American warehouses to last the war.[8]

He had feared that war in Europe would further depress the American economy, but the opposite seemed to have been the case. As government funds for military spending poured into the industrial sector, the domestic economy showed signs of heating up. The most likely short-term effect would be inflation, but a shrewd investor such as Kennedy could adjust for that.

He was going to play it safe from now on. The world economy remained too shaky, the equity markets too volatile, and the rules he had written and enforced at the SEC too restrictive for him to return to the trading patterns that had served him so well in the 1920s. Whatever spare capital he had would go into real estate and oil, the soundest of investments in an inflationary economy. When Honey Fitz asked him to take a position in Eastern Massachusetts Street Railway, a fairly safe stock, Kennedy turned him down. "It probably is all that you say that it is, but I have made up my mind that my day of buying securities is over and it looks like I will have to live on my capital until I pass out of the picture." "I don't feel much like putting any capital into anything at this time," he wrote a Boston associate who had inquired about his interest in buying the *Boston Post*. "I think if I do any work at all, I will furnish my brain as my capital from now on."[9]

He was, he wrote his friends, tongue only partly in cheek, "developing my career as a first-class bum" in Palm Beach, watching "the idle rich enjoy their last fling" in Hot Springs, and making "arrangements to join the 'Fishermen's Union'" in Hyannis Port.[10]

The spring of 1941 had been a dreadful one for the British. They had done well against the Italians in Greece but were no match for the Germans, who had invaded Yugoslavia and then cut through Greece and Crete. The same scenario played out in North Africa, where the British had held their own against Italian troops but were pushed onto the defensive with the arrival of General Field Marshal Erwin Rommel and the Afrika Korps. In the Atlantic, they were losing more shipping to German U-boats and battle cruisers than they could replace. The question asked on both sides of the Atlantic was where would Hitler strike next. Would he move his troops from Greece and the Balkans into Turkey, solidify his control of the Mediterranean, and move on to conquer the Middle East and take over the Suez Canal? Or would he prepare for a 1941 invasion of Great Britain?

In late spring, Kennedy accepted invitations to give commencement addresses and receive honorary degrees at Oglethorpe University and Notre Dame. While he reemphasized his hatred for the Nazis, "their philosophy, their silly racism and their nightmare of world domination," he repeated in his Oglethorpe speech what he had said in his January radio address, that it was "nonsense to say that an Axis victory spells ruin for us." Ignoring the consequences for European Jews or, in fact, for any of the peoples or nations that were or might be brought under Nazi rule should the British lose the war, he argued that whatever happened across the ocean, the United States would survive and endure. "From 90 to 95% of our trade is internal. We depend less on foreign markets than any great nation. If worse came to worst, we could gear ourselves to an intelligent self-contained national economy and still enjoy a fair degree of prosperity." That such a reconfiguration in the direction of a "self-contained national economy" would entail increased centralization of decision making in Washington and an end to free market capitalism, as he had earlier predicted, no longer appeared to bother him.[11]

On May 27, three days after Kennedy's Oglethorpe speech, the president delivered his first radio address since the "Arsenal of Democracy" talk five months earlier. Directly contradicting everything Kennedy had said about the United States surviving a totalitarian victory in Europe, Roosevelt described in detail the catastrophic consequences that would follow. Quislings would arise to destroy American democracy and freedom from the inside. "The American laborer would have to compete with slave labor in the rest of the world." Tariff walls would descend against American goods. "The whole fabric of working life as we know it . . . could be mangled and crippled. . . . Yes, even our right of worship would be threatened." After cataloging the dangers facing America should Great Britain be conquered, Roosevelt "issued a proclamation that an unlimited national emergency exists and requires the strengthening of our defense to the extreme limit of our national power and authority." What he didn't do was even hint that the United States might consider going to war to save the British from defeat.[12]

On the Sunday following the president's speech, Kennedy delivered his commencement address at Notre Dame. He began by acknowledging the president's proclamation of an unlimited emergency, one that, he told his audience, demanded "unlimited loyalty" from all Americans. The rest of the speech was stuffed with emptied-out, high-toned platitudes that sounded as if they had been lifted directly from papal encyclicals. The president having declared that America was not going to war, there was no necessity for Kennedy to say anything more, especially at Notre Dame, where political speeches were frowned upon.[13]

Three weeks later, the Germans invaded the Soviet Union. The danger of British defeat had been deterred, at least until the Germans could turn west again.

Ten days after the invasion, Herbert Hoover invited Kennedy to join former governor Alf Landon of Kansas, President Maynard Hutchins of the University of Chicago, and "some ten or fifteen men . . . outside of the Congress and outside of the America First group" in putting his name to an anti-intervention statement. Kennedy declined. When he was asked a second time, he declined again. "As I have said to you before I much prefer to go my way alone. I can then take my position on any subject and at any time as the occasion demands without consultation with anyone. I am well aware of the magnificent work you have done to keep us out of war. . . . Nevertheless I feel so strongly about pursuing my course alone that I feel that I would like to stick to this decision."[14]

He visited Washington that fall to see Jack, who was working for naval intelligence, and Kick, whom he had gotten a job at the *Washington Times-Herald* as secretary to associate editor Frank Waldrop. Kick enjoyed the work, the social life in the nation's capital, and the opportunity to spend time with her brother, but what she wanted more than anything else was to return to London and her friends there, especially Billy Hartington. In October 1941, she wrote her father with a plan she had worked out with Carmel Offie, Bullitt's former assistant in France and Kennedy's friend. Offie would ask Tony Biddle, whom Roosevelt had dispatched to London as ambassador to the European governments in exile, "to give me a passport. . . . Tony will do anything for him. The only thing that remains is your consent. . . . I have a lot of great friends that I should really like to see and even if the British feel a little embittered about your opinion in the present struggle I don't think any real friends such as I have would let that bother them. And even if it does as Offie says 'the hell with them.'" She knew bombs were still falling in London but figured her chance of being hit by one was about the same as her getting hit by a car in Washington. Two weeks later, not having been given the go-ahead, she wrote her father again. "I am so anxious to go back that I can hardly sit still. I received a letter from Andrew and Debo [Billy's brother and his wife, Deborah, the future Duchess of Devonshire] pleading with me to come back and save Billy from Sally Norton who apparently has got him in the bag. No one wants him to marry her and all told [me] to come back and save him. Apparently they are going to announce it in Jan. I haven't heard from him for simply ages and that no doubt is the reason."[15]

Kick never did get to London that fall. It would be another year and a half before she was able to return to London and to Billy Hartington.

The continuing war in Europe made it impossible for Rosemary as well to return to England and Mother Isabel's Convent of the Assumption. She was marooned at St. Gertrude's and terribly discontent there. "In the year or so following her return from England," Rose wrote in her memoirs, "disquieting symptoms began to develop. Not only was there noticeable retrogression in the mental skills she had worked so hard to attain, but her customary good nature gave way increasingly to tension and irritability. She was upset easily and unpredictable. Some of these upsets became tantrums, or rages, during which she broke things or hit out at people. Since she was quite strong, her blows were hard. Also there were convulsive episodes."[16]

In July 1941, Kennedy contacted Monsignor Casey at St. Patrick's in New York with a list of convents, hoping that the monsignor would "institute inquiries through the channels we talked about." The monsignor failed to find an alternative institution, and Rosemary was enrolled at St. Gertrude's for a second year. Kennedy kept in touch with her by telephone and mail.

"Well, how is my old darling today?" he wrote on October 10, 1941. "I just got an idea I thought you might think about. Do you think Dr. Moore and the Nuns would like to have a picture show sometime this fall and also do you think the children would like it? If they would, what kind of a picture do you think they'd like. . . . Incidentally, Mother and I will be down there in a couple of weeks or so and Eddie and Mary [Moore] are coming down and they were thinking perhaps that they might take you for a trip up to Philadelphia to look the situation [and a possible place for her to live] over up there." In late October, Kennedy asked Father John Cavanaugh, his friend and now a vice president at Notre Dame, for tickets to the November 8 Notre Dame–Navy game at Municipal Park in Baltimore for himself and his "three children in Washington," Jack, Kick, and Rosemary.[17]

The change in Rosemary's behavior, which Rose had noticed on her daughter's return from Europe, got worse that fall, not better. At twenty-three, Rosemary was frustrated, angry, and disturbed at being confined at St. Gertrude's. Father Moore, worried about her welfare and the effect of her behavior on others at St. Gertrude's, brought in a Miss Slavin to assist. "I trust," he reported to Kennedy, "that she will be able to help a great deal." He then asked Kennedy for a loan or gift of $25,000 for a new building.[18]

The problem at St. Gertrude's was much the same, if more aggravated than it had been at the Residence School in Manhattan. These schools were not shuttered cloisters with closed gates. St. Gertrude's was located in the heart of Washington. There was no way short of locking her in at night to keep Rosemary from wandering the streets. "She was a beautiful girl," remembered her cousin Ann Gargan, who had spent most summers and vacations with the Kennedys since 1936. The thought that she was incapable of making the proper judgments or protecting herself from strangers was simply "horrifying." "Many nights," Ann Gargan told Doris Kearns Goodwin, "the school would call to say she was missing, only to find her out walking around the streets at 2 A.M. Can you imagine what it must have been like to know your daughter was walking the streets in the darkness of the night, the perfect prey for an unsuspecting male?"[19]

Her father, Jean Kennedy Smith recalled, believed that Rosemary's irritability, which her teachers and tutors had been commenting on for years now, might have had something to do with her "mind." Her mother also was beginning to believe, as she put it in her memoirs, that "there were other factors at work besides retardation. A neurological disturbance or disease of some sort seemingly had overtaken her, and it was becoming progressively worse."[20]

As he did whenever there was a medical problem to be diagnosed and solved, Kennedy consulted the leading practitioners. He probably did so alone, though Rose, in her memoirs, claimed that she took part. The children's medical problems had always been his responsibility, not his wife's. In the case of their daughter Rosemary, there was an additional reason he may have proceeded to seek a medical solution without involving his wife. As historian Janice Brockley has written, mental health professionals in midcentury "urged parents to be 'realistic' about their disabled children" and believed that in the final analysis, only fathers had the capacity to do so. "The job of maintaining objectivity was often given to fathers, who supposedly had the skills, emotional detachment, and rational judgment that mothers lacked. Mothers were the caregivers, however flawed; fathers were the ultimate decision makers about major issues such as institutionalization. . . . Fathers were often expected to take the burden of decision making from their wives."[21]

This was precisely what Kennedy did. At some point in the late fall of 1941, he met with Dr. Walter Freeman, the chair of the Department of Neurology at George Washington University Medical School, and perhaps with his colleague James Watts, a Yale-trained neurosurgeon. Freeman and Watts had five years earlier performed their first psychosurgery at George Washington University, borrowing from the techniques of and with instruments invented by a Portuguese doctor, Egas Moniz, who in 1949 would be awarded the Nobel Prize in Physiology or Medicine for "his invention of a surgical treatment for mental illness."[22]

By 1941, Freeman and Watts had performed hundreds of lobotomies. The operation was relatively simple. A tubelike surgical instrument with a sharp blade was inserted into the frontal lobe of the brain through two entry holes at the top of the skull and then used to cut away brain tissue. The intent was to sever the connections between the frontal lobes, the cognitive regions of the brain, and the thalamus, the emotional center, the hypothesis being that after the operation, lobotomized patients would no longer experience emotional distress, depression, anxiety, or tension. The operation was controversial and not indicated for patients with mental retardation. Freeman, a master salesman who had written and lectured widely on the procedure, had by 1941 succeeded in convincing large numbers of well-placed medical experts that it was relatively harmless, with few side effects, and of great benefit to depressed and agitated patients, especially women. "Between 1937 and the end of World War II," medical historian Jack D. Pressman had written, "a consensus emerged among many American physicians that psychosurgery was a treatment that indeed offered certain benefit."[23]

Because Joseph P. Kennedy never wrote or talked about his communications with Dr. Freeman, we can only speculate what he asked or what the doctor told him. It is likely that Freeman repeated what he had said to others in consultations, that the operation, if successful—and there was no reason to believe it would not be—would treat Rosemary's agitated depression and reduce, if not eliminate, the tantrums, irritation, and violence. In the book on psychosurgery he published in 1941, Freeman claimed that follow-up data on the operations he had performed with Watts demonstrated that "63% of their patients had improved, 23 percent had not changed, and 14 percent were in poorer condition." He no doubt shared these results with Kennedy.[24]

If there was a 63 percent chance that Dr. Freeman could solve Rosemary's emotional problems without causing any additional deterioration of her already diminished mental capacities, that was a chance Kennedy thought worth taking. The operation was performed between November 12, when Father Moore last wrote to Kennedy, and November 28, 1941, when Kennedy, in a letter to a friend, mentioned that he was coming to Washington to see an eye doctor and "visit with my two [not three] youngsters who are there."[25]

Like many (but not all) lobotomy patients, Rosemary came out of the operation inert, unable to speak or walk. She was moved to Craig House, a private psychiatric hospital in Beacon, New York, to recuperate. With its 380 acres, an indoor swimming pool, golf course, stables and horseback riding trails, arts and crafts center, and trained medical personnel, Craig House offered its patients the best possible custodial care as well as discretion and secrecy. Zelda Fitzgerald had been a patient, as had Alfred Stieglitz's daughter, Kitty. Henry Fonda's wife, Frances Ford Seymour, would arrive in early 1950 and commit suicide that same spring. There was as yet no indication of when or to what extent Rosemary would regain her mobility and speech.

In a January 1942 round-robin letter to the children, Rose did not refer to Rosemary, which was highly unusual. She would not mention her again in a letter for the next twenty years.

Kennedy kept the rest of the family informed about Rosemary's recovery. A year after the operation, Kennedy wrote Rose, who was vacationing in California, that he had "stopped off to see Rosemary and she was getting along very nicely. She looks very well." The following July, in a letter to Jack, he reported that "Rosemary is feeling much better and is swimming in the pool every day." In February 1944, he wrote Joe Jr. that Rosemary was "feeling quite well, so everybody is getting along quite happily," and in March, he wrote Kick that her older sister was "about the same, but seems quite cheerful."[26]

Rosemary regained some of her motor skills at Craig House, but she did not recover her memory or her speech. She had been mildly retarded, but after her failed lobotomy she was severely so. There was nothing the staff at Craig House could do for her save make her comfortable. The 1948 bills "for care and treatment of Miss Rosemary Kennedy" included not just the usual fees for room, board, and custodial care, but additional amounts for three extra private-duty nurses, laundry, hairdresser, druggist, stationer, tailor, and cash, for a monthly total of $2,385.85, which in purchasing power today would be equivalent to more than a quarter of a million dollars annually.[27]

Kennedy was the only one in the family who visited Rosemary or consulted with her doctors at Craig House. We don't know what he told Rose or the children about Rosemary after February 1944, the last letter in which he referred to her. Nor do we know what they inquired of him. In her memoirs, Rose did not raise the possibility that Kennedy might have made an error in allowing Dr. Freeman to operate on Rosemary. She simply recorded the outcome: "The operation eliminated the violence and the convulsive seizures, but it also had the effect of leaving

Rosemary permanently incapacitated. She lost everything that had been gained during the years by her own gallant efforts and our loving efforts for her. She had no possibility of ever again being able to function in a viable way in the world at large."[28]

What Kennedy himself thought about his decision to have his daughter lobotomized we do not know. There is in his correspondence only one reference to her, from May 29, 1958, when, in answering a letter from Sister Anastasia at the St. Coletta school in Jefferson, Wisconsin, where Rosemary had been moved years before, he expressed his gratitude for the sister's "persevering kindness" in making a home for Rosemary. He added that "the solution of Rosemary's problem has been a major factor in the ability of all the Kennedys to go about their life's work and to try and do it as well as they can."[29]

"Rosemary's," her mother recalled in her memoirs, "was the first of the tragedies that were to befall us."[30]

Twenty-nine

WAR

On July 24, Japan sent forty thousand soldiers into French Indo-China. Roosevelt demanded that the troops be withdrawn, and when they were not, he seized Japanese assets in the United States and instituted a new "licensing" system that drastically reduced trade with Japan and cut oil exports by some two thirds. Negotiations between Japan's ambassador in Washington and the State Department were held to defuse the crisis, but it was clear now, with Japan running short of oil and having insufficient reserves of rubber, rice, and iron ore, that the two powers were on a collision course.

The attack came on December 7, at Pearl Harbor. The following day, President Roosevelt asked Congress for and received a declaration of war. On December 11, for reasons historians are still debating, Hitler declared war on the United States. Kennedy's nightmare had become reality.

At 6:20 on the evening of December 7, less than five hours after word of the attack reached the White House, he wired Roosevelt: "Dear Mr. President: In this great crisis all Americans are with you. Name the battle post. I'm yours to command." Two days later, Steve Early,

Roosevelt's press secretary, replied for the president: "For the splendid assurance conveyed in your message he is more appreciative than he can say."[1]

Kennedy expected to be called to Washington at once. When he heard nothing from the White House, he asked House Majority Leader John McCormack of Boston to intervene on his behalf. The president told McCormack he had never gotten Kennedy's telegram. But even though he now knew—through McCormack—that Kennedy was prepared to return to Washington, he did not get in touch with him.[2]

Surprised and angered, Kennedy leaped to the conclusion, which he recorded in his diary, that the president's reluctance to recall him was due to "a decidedly anti-Catholic feeling. . . . He has not appointed a prominent Catholic to any important post since a year ago last November." Kennedy was not the only one who harbored suspicions that Roosevelt and his closest advisers were prejudiced against Irish Catholics. When Felix Frankfurter complained to Supreme Court justice Frank Murphy that "'Roosevelt haters and self-promoters' were attempting to 'poison American opinion' by claiming that Catholics like Joseph Kennedy were being denied a role in the war effort by 'British bootlickers and Bolshevik Jews' . . . Murphy retorted that it was a 'fact' that Catholics had been excluded from the war effort, 'except to fight,' because the 'party clique mistrusted them.'"[3]

The truth, of course, was that Roosevelt had not called Kennedy to Washington not because he was Irish and Catholic, but because he didn't trust him in any position of importance and knew he would accept nothing less.

As the weeks passed with no summons to Washington, even Rose, who was not always attentive to his moods, noticed Kennedy's growing discontent. "Dad seems quite well," she wrote the children on January 26, 1943, "although he gets very depressed at times about the whole war situation. I suppose he knows too much about the people who are running things. I really wish he were running something himself." Kennedy was indeed so desperate to get back into the mix that on February 5, 1942, he telegrammed Lord Beaverbrook, now Churchill's minister of supply, and offered "my services in any capacity here that would be of any value to England and to you."[4]

On December 7, 1941, Joe Jr. was training at an air base in Jacksonville and Jack was working at naval intelligence headquarters in Washington. Six weeks later, without warning of any sort, Jack was transferred to the Charleston Navy Yard in South Carolina. He had, he told his mother, been "completely mystified as to why he was changed and he was quite stunned by the suddenness of the news. His only explanation was that I guess they just take those things out of a hat and his happened to be the name that was uppermost."[5]

There was a better explanation. On Monday, January 12, Walter Winchell had announced in his syndicated column that "one of Ex-Ambassador Kennedy's eligible sons is the target of a Washington gal columnist's affections. So much so she has consulted her barrister about divorcing her exploring groom." Winchell had gotten his information from Drew Pearson, who had written him on January 6 that Inga Arvad was "casting eyes in the direction of ex-ambassador Joseph P. Kennedy's offspring [and that] Old Joe is reported to be very hot and bothered about it."[6]

Why Pearson gave the story to Winchell we do not know, but Winchell ran with it. Although he did not use either Inga's or Jack's name in his column, everyone in Washington knew whom he was referring to. Naval intelligence, which had been investigating Inga as a possible German agent and/or knew that the FBI was, removed Jack Kennedy from harm's way by transferring him to Charleston.

Jack had been introduced to Inga Arvad by Kick Kennedy, her colleague at the *Washington Times-Herald*. A Danish native who had worked in Germany and gone to the Columbia Graduate School of Journalism, Arvad was four years older than Jack, blond, blue-eyed, gorgeous, and one of the few women he had been with who was as witty, bright, well traveled, well connected, and glamorous as he was. In November 1940, a classmate at Columbia had sent the FBI a letter detailing his suspicions about the Danish student who complained bitterly about the large number of Jews in their class and who "speaks very convincingly of her intimacy with Goering, Goebbels, Himmler and Hess, and of the delightful impression she made on Hitler in her two interviews with him." A little more than a year later, while Inga was working at the *Times-Herald,* a colleague reported that she might be a spy, and publisher Cissy Patterson directed editor Frank Waldrop to take the matter to the FBI. The FBI interviewed Inga, then assigned agents to monitor her activities, wiretap her phone calls, and when she left Washington for Charleston to visit Jack Kennedy, bug her hotel room. The decision was also made, probably by Hoover himself, that as a courtesy, whatever information the FBI gathered on young Jack Kennedy would be shared with his father, the ambassador.[7]

Kennedy kept close watch on his children, wherever they happened to be. He knew that Joe Jr. and Jack had lots of lovers. As a rule he left them alone, but not this time. Inga was older than Jack and Danish and Protestant. She was divorced from her first husband and still married to her second, a mysterious Hungarian film director who was currently employed by a Swedish millionaire suspected of being a Nazi sympathizer or operative. This much, at least, Kennedy had probably learned from Arthur Krock, who was jokingly referred to by Kick, Jack, and Inga as the ambassador's spy in Washington.[8]

When Kennedy found out—from Kick or Krock—that Jack might be serious about Inga, he got in touch with his son. We don't know precisely what he said, but whatever it was, his son listened, took it to heart, and pulled back. "I know who prompted you to believe or rather disbelieve in me, but still I dislike it," Inga wrote him in late January. "I am not going to try and make you change—it would be without result anyway—because big Joe has a stronger hand than I." She had no illusions about where Jack's loyalties lay. "You belong so wholeheartedly to the Kennedy-clan," she wrote him in mid-March, "and I don't want you ever to get into an argument with your father on account of me. As I have told you a dozen times, if I were but 18 summers, I would fight like a tigress for her young, in order to get you and keep you."[9]

By the end of February, Jack and Inga had agreed that they would stop seeing each other. Jack apparently was having trouble making a final break, because days later, on March 6, he called Inga at a little after ten P.M. to invite her to Charleston. Inga turned him down. In the course of their conversation, which was monitored by the FBI, Jack mentioned that he had talked to his father the Sunday before. "He said he got the report. He said he had just talked to Max Truitt and he said things aren't quite right up there [in Washington]. I said I didn't believe that. He said he was just telling me what he heard. . . . You are mixed up in something. . . . You're not holding out on me, are you?"[10]

Though still infatuated with Inga, Jack was ready to move on, with or without his father's prodding. Bored by his current situation, tired of being chained to a desk in Charleston, jealous of his brother and his friends who were preparing for active duty, he was desperate for a new assignment, preferably overseas on a battleship.

Inga understood that her twenty-four-year-old lover had no intention of staying stateside to be with her. She had dreamed of moving out west with him but understood now that there was no way that was going to happen. "Put a match to the smoldering ambition," she wrote him, "and you will go like wild fire. (It is all against the ranch out West, but it is the unequalled highway to the White House.)" Arvad had grasped the truth that Jack usually kept hidden, that beneath the carefree, jocular appearance was a serious young man with "smoldering ambition."[11]

Kennedy knew this and had already begun to prepare for the possibility that both of his older boys were going to enter politics in some capacity. In early 1942, after having shifted the entire family's legal residence to Florida, he arranged for the two to become Massachusetts residents and began lining up the local media outlets that would be required should they ever run for public office. "Since my two boys are eventually going to make their homes in Massachusetts, if they get through this war successfully," he wrote David Sarnoff on February 2, 1942, "I would be interested in purchasing any radio station that you might have for sale in Boston or Massachusetts. . . . My energy from now on will be tied up in their careers rather than my own."[12]

On March 4, 1942, three months after he had first volunteered his services, Kennedy wrote Roosevelt a second time, enclosed a copy of his December 7 telegram, and sent the package to Grace Tully, who had taken over as Roosevelt's personal secretary when Missy LeHand suffered a stroke in 1941. "I don't want to appear in the role of a man looking for a job for the sake of getting an appointment," he wrote Roosevelt, "but Joe and Jack are in the service and I feel that my experience in these critical times might be worth something in some position. I just want to say that if you want me, I am yours to command." His letter, preceded and followed by calls and letters to friends in Washington, set in motion a scenario that would be repeated at regular intervals over the next few years.[13]

This time Roosevelt responded with a warm letter and a vague job offer. Kennedy had burned most of his bridges, but he still had friends in Congress, was an able administrator, and had experience in the shipping industry.

"I was," Roosevelt wrote, "of course, sure that you wanted to do everything possible to help and I have had the suggestion from the Maritime Commission that you, knowing its earlier work and having had former experience with Fore River people, could be of real service in stepping up the great increase in our shipbuilding—especially in getting some of the new production under way. I know, for example, that you do not want to be merely a member of one of the many Commissions— that you do want actual, practical and effective responsibility in turning out ships. [Maritime Commission chairman Vice Admiral Emory Scott] Land and [Vice Chairman Howard] Vickery are keen to have you do this. Will you? I do hope to see you soon."[14]

Kennedy called Land at once to find out exactly what he had in mind and what kind of authority he was willing to delegate. Land offered a few options, but none of them with the decision-making authority Kennedy wanted. He was well aware of his limitations. He could run an agency but not work for one run by anyone else. "He is in quite a quandary," Kick wrote Jack in Charleston. "I am not sure what he is going to do." After conferring with James Byrnes, now on the Supreme Court, and Jim Landis, Kennedy turned down the positions Land had outlined for him. "I think you know," he wrote Roosevelt, "that if I am given a job cleanly and concisely I will work hard to get you the results you want, but running around without a definite assignment and authority, I'd just be a hindrance to the program."[15]

Roosevelt was not pleased. "What do I do about this?" he wrote Land and Vickery. "My own personal slant is that you should offer him a specific, definite job: (a) To run a shipyard; (b) To head a small hurry-up inspecting organization under Vickery, to iron out kinks and speed up production in all yards doing Maritime Commission Work."

Knowing full well what a nuisance Kennedy could be carping on the sidelines and how effective he might be in the right position, Roosevelt had decided to bring him back to Washington, though he realized it was not going to be easy to find a position for him. Kennedy was demanding the kind of authority Roosevelt was reluctant to yield to anybody. In war as in peace, the president excelled at designing confused, often contradictory organizational charts, with competing responsibilities and overlapping authority. There was an added and not insignificant complication. In his tenure at the Maritime Commission and his two years in London, Kennedy had acquired a great many enemies. Every time the press even hinted that he was being considered for a job, the White House was flooded by letters, calls, and telegrams denouncing him and anyone who dared suggest that he be brought back into government. Whatever position he was offered would have to be one that required no congressional hearings, oversight, or approval.[16]

Tentative job offers began to flow into Palm Beach: positions at the Maritime Commission, at the newly created Office of Defense Transportation, in the office of the alien property custodian. In mid-April, Kennedy stopped over in Washington and explained to the president why he was not going to accept any of the jobs that had been offered him. He was convinced that the president intended to "put me to work not particularly to help the war effort, but to help his politics."[17]

His pessimism was unshakable—though it is not clear he ever tried to shake it. He worried that the president and his cabinet were not up to mobilizing to fight effectively on two fronts, that the war would go on forever, that the economy would be devastated, that prosperity would never return. Clare Boothe Luce cautioned him not to infect his children, Jack especially, with his overpowering sense that their future was doomed. "It alarms him . . . and dispirits him, and I do think that you . . . and I have no right to add the burden of doubt to the other burdens that he, and a million like him, must carry from here out." Kennedy trusted Clare's judgment and was disturbed enough by her warning to forward her letter to Jack. "This is Clare's letter. After you've read it, send it back because I'd like to keep it for my files. Heaven knows, I don't want any pessimism of mine to have any effect on you, but I don't know how to tell you what I think unless I tell you what I think."[18]

To keep himself occupied for at least part of the spring and summer of 1942 and to reestablish credibility as a political force in Massachusetts, he got behind a quixotic effort to send his father-in-law to Washington. "We are considering Grandpa going into the fight for the Senate," he wrote Joe Jr. on July 6, 1942. "Whether he'll go or not we don't know, but at least we'll have some fun." A victory for Honey Fitz in the primary, whether or not he beat Henry Cabot Lodge, Jr., in the general election, would weaken the hold of the Roosevelt camp in the state, strengthen the Fitzgerald-Kennedy power base, and pave the way for a Kennedy to run for the Senate when the seventy-nine-year-old Honey Fitz stepped aside.[19]

From Hyannis Port and Boston, Kennedy lined up support for "Grandpa," solicited the endorsement of the local Hearst papers, reviewed campaign literature, and contributed money. It was not easy to run a seventy-nine-year-old who had been out of office for more than two decades against a Democratic Party primary opponent who had been endorsed by every elected official in the state, and every newspaper save those owned by Hearst. Fortunately, there were scandals brewing that Kennedy hoped might boost his father-in-law's candidacy. The Republicans, Kennedy wrote Joe Jr. in mid-July, had begun a whispering campaign against Joseph Casey, Honey Fitz's primary opponent, "on the ground that he married a Protestant and had a baby five months after his marriage. Politics is a great game! You better be sure to marry yourself a nice Irish Catholic girl," Kennedy warned his son, knowing full well that he was dating a Protestant girl in Florida, where he was stationed. To hammer the lesson home, Kennedy wrote Joe Jr. again three weeks later. "One thing that impresses me very much that I pass on to you is that there is a great deal of criticism by the Catholic women that Casey married a Protestant. You wouldn't think this was important but it definitely is, and I am thoroughly convinced that an Irish Catholic with a name like yours and with your record, married to an Irish Catholic girl, would be a pushover in this State for a political office. They just wouldn't have anything to fight about. It seems like a silly thing, but I can't impress it on you too strongly."[20]

To no great surprise, Honey Fitz was defeated in the primary. Joe Jr. sent his condolences from Florida, adding that "maybe I'll get a shot at Casey, when this thing is over." In one of her round-robin letters to the children, Rose wrote that Jack, acknowledging his brother's ambition, had joked that he thought "it would be good for Joe's political career if he died for the grand old flag, although I don't believe he feels that is absolutely necessary."[21]

Joe Jr. was in the last phase of what he hoped would be his final training before combat. His father had advised him that spring to make out his will. "You still have quite a substantial amount of cash due you out of the Trust, so your will has to be carefully drawn. If I can help you with any suggestions, let me know."[22]

Jack had graduated from naval training school in Chicago and, with his father's help, had been accepted into the newly organized and elite PT (patrol torpedo) boat school at Melville, Rhode Island. Though Kennedy had helped his son get the assignment at Melville, he was aghast at the thought of Jack spending the war on tiny boats at sea.

Jack's health problems had grown steadily worse since 1940. Now, in addition to a chronically bad stomach, he was afflicted with a chronically bad back. As with his other ailments, his back problems resisted diagnosis. The doctors he had visited in the spring of 1940 suggested back surgery, but he had resisted. By the fall of 1942, the pain had become so debilitating that he could no longer endure it. "What he wants to do," Kennedy wrote Joe Jr. on October 1, 1942, "is to be operated on and then have me fix it so he can go back in that service when he gets better. This will require considerable manipulation and I have given up the idea of going to California with mother to see if I can be of any help to him."[23]

Rose was on her way to Palo Alto and Stanford to live, eat, and go to class with Eunice, who she feared was too unhealthy and far too skinny to be on her own. Not for the first time, Kennedy assured his wife that he had everything under control and she could stay away as long as she pleased. "Don't go bothering your head about anything around here," he wrote her in California. "Everything is moving along and it is certainly no bother for me. I'm not giving it your thorough handling, but we'll be all right."[24]

Jean and Pat were in Philadelphia, Jean at Eden Hall, a Sacred Heart Convent school, Pat at Rosemont College just eleven miles from the city center. Teddy and Bobby were outside Boston starting over at new schools, Ted in West Newton at Fessenden, Bobby at Milton Academy, where he had been moved because his father worried that without better grades from an established prep school he would never get into Harvard.

In mid-October, Kennedy left Hyannis Port and moved into his hotel suite at the Waldorf Towers. Almost every weekend he entertained another contingent of children. "I have had a talk with Pat about Stanford," he wrote his wife, "and she really doesn't want to go. I have had her up here practically every weekend since I have been here and I have had lots of talks with her. I still find a great deal of difficulty in getting close to her, and yet she seems to be perfectly sweet and nice about everything. . . . Of course, I thoroughly understand our talks that children of eighteen don't know what is good for themselves, but I don't think you could force her to go out there and get any results at all."[25]

He traveled to Beacon, New York, just after election day to visit Rosemary at Craig House. She was, he wrote Rose, "getting along very nicely" and looked well. He continued on to Washington, where he saw Kick and "all the important people" in town, including Lord Halifax, now British ambassador to Washington. After he reported to Halifax that he was thinking "of making a speech which . . . might be expected to have considerable influence with such sections as Roman Catholics, Irish, and some others," Halifax confided in his diary that he didn't "fancy Joe Kennedy has as much influence as he thinks." Kennedy, perhaps recognizing as much, never drafted or gave the speech.[26]

From Washington, it was off to Boston "to see Teddy play football. He was a riot, as usual," he wrote Rose in California. "Mr. Fessenden [the founder and headmaster of Teddy's new school] arranged a meeting in a room with all of his teachers . . . and I should think that the consensus of opinion was that he had a fine head, is getting along much better with boys than he did when he first started, that he goes off half-cocked when anybody asks any questions and he gives them an answer even though most times it is wrong. . . . I am convinced, however, that the school is good for him."[27]

He also visited Bobby at Milton Academy. Understandably worried about starting over at a new school and making new friends, Bobby had been advised by Jack "to sort of sit back and let the boys come to you rather than for you to go to the boys." Kennedy wrote Bobby that he thought Jack's advice "a big mistake. . . . I think as a matter of general policy, it is much better to be sociable with everyone and make your intimate friends after you have appraised their various values, but for goodness sake don't stand off. Try to cultivate as many people as you can and know as many people as you can. That's all life is—whether it's in business or a profession or anything. . . . You have a lot on the ball and you have a personality that will make friends, so by all means hop in there and meet everybody, be pleasant to everyone, and don't stand off. That's much more likely to make a bad impression. Go to games with your friends in the school, arrange to take some to luncheon when you go out to lunch, etc., etc. But for the next two years that's probably going to be your life and you might as well have as many friends as you can."[28]

His major concern was that Bobby, perhaps the most independent-minded of his sons, was hell-bent on getting out of school as soon as he possibly could and following his brothers into the military. Kennedy thought this a dreadful idea, but because he knew his son was set on it, he made inquiries in Washington about getting Bobby into officer candidate school when he graduated from Milton Academy in the spring.

While at Milton, he met with the headmaster and told him of Bobby's plans. It was decided to change "Bobby over from chemistry to physics because that will help him in the Army." After meeting with the headmaster, Kennedy "went to Harvard and had a talk with the Dean of Admissions about Bobby's position. . . . He'll be eighteen next November and will not have finished Milton, and if he has to go in the Army then he will be between the devil and the deep blue sea—he will not have graduated from his secondary school and he will not be entered at college. However," he wrote Rose, "I think I got an agreement with the Dean out there that if Bobby does good work this year they will give him an Aptitude Test and if he is well recommended by Milton, I think I may be able to get him admitted to Harvard. At any rate, I think I made real developments in this matter."[29]

The ironies were overwhelming. Kennedy had done everything he possibly could to prevent this war. Now he was doing everything he possibly could to assist and prepare his three sons to fight in it. "Young Jack has gone to the Motor Torpedo Division and that is causing his mother and me plenty of anxiety," he wrote Father Maurice Sheehy, Joe Jr.'s chaplain in Florida. "And now with Bobby going next, he is begging and pleading to be permitted to enlist so that he can get into the Navy Aviation. I suppose that I should be proud that my sons should pick the most hazardous branches of the service in this war and, of course, there is pride in my heart but quite a measure of grief in my mind."[30]

On December 7, 1942, Bobby Kennedy, who had already developed a wit as mordant as that of any of his brothers or sisters, casually informed his mother that "Dad just phoned from N.Y. and said he was going down to Washington with Jack to see the president tomorrow which sounds pretty exciting for the president, but I suppose there are other almost as exciting things happening in his life now." Aside from idle chatter and a few encouraging words, Roosevelt had nothing to offer Kennedy. Kennedy reminded the president that he "hadn't appointed a Catholic to any important post since election 1940. He seemed stunned at this, actually, and said 'I must have,'" but the only name he could come up with was historian Carlton Hayes, whom he had made his ambassador to Spain. "He then paused and said nobody had brought that to his attention ever before and he would look into it."[31]

In mid-January 1943, James Byrnes, who had left the Supreme Court in October to accept the directorship of the newly created Office of Economic Stabilization, called Palm Beach with yet another job offer for Kennedy, "to take charge of the small business situation." Kennedy pointed out that the job made no sense, as every small business in the country had a different set of problems and there was no way of designing one policy to assist them all. As he later wrote his friend and lawyer in Boston, Bart Brickley, "Jimmie acted rather shamefaced about offering me this job, and although he argued with me for forty-five minutes . . . he said he understood my position and would tell the President that I didn't think I could get him the results he wanted. . . . I told Jimmie that he had a hell of a gall to offer me this stinking job. . . . Also, that there were countless other positions, and although they were very difficult, they offered one an opportunity for getting results. I told him I wanted a job to do, not to just have a number put on my back. I have stayed out this long, so I might just as hold out now for something better or get nothing at all." Byrnes, who had been one of Kennedy's few remaining friends and supporters in Washington, protested but got nowhere.[32]

Two months later, after yet another call and another job offer, this one from Sidney Weinberg, the assistant to Donald Nelson, director of the War Production Board, Kennedy informed the president that he was not only turning down the job, but was "withdrawing myself from consideration of any position from now on. . . . I've made up my mind that as long as I stay here I become more critical of the Administration and I don't know what percentage of it is instinctive and what part of it is just criticism and so for that reason I think I'll go to South America . . . stay there for a couple of months and see what that will do to my viewpoint." The president thought that was a good idea, then chattered on until it was time for his next appointment.[33]

Later that spring, at a meeting in New York City with his friend Lord Beaverbrook, Kennedy insisted that he was not only out of government for good, but had no intention of playing any role in the 1944 elections. When Beaverbrook suggested that he might consider running "for an elective office," Kennedy responded directly and emphatically that he had "no desire to return to public life. The political career of my two sons, if that is what they want to follow, is the only concern of mine now. . . . I could get all the thrills and excitement watching the careers of my children. I do not have to have it centered on me anymore, I have had mine."[34]

Jack was the first to leave the country. On completing PT boat school, he was assigned to a noncombat training squadron in Jacksonville, Florida. He and his friends considered himself so "shafted" by the stateside noncombat assignment that from this point on, he would be known among his PT boat buddies as "Shafty," to the horror of his mother, who asked pointedly not to be told what it stood for. Devastated at the thought he might never get to see combat, Jack got in touch with his grandfather Honey Fitz, who was on good terms with Massachusetts senator David Walsh, chairman of the Naval Affairs Committee. Walsh arranged for Jack's transfer. In February 1943, he left Florida for San Francisco. In early March, he boarded a troopship for the New Hebrides, en route to Tulagi, a small island in the Solomons. His father sent his "Amphogel [antacid] Tablets" to San Francisco, hoping they'd be forwarded across the Pacific.[35]

The next to depart was Kick, twenty-three, who intended to follow her big brothers into public service. She enlisted in the Red Cross and requested assignment to one of the many canteens for American servicemen in Great Britain, Australia, and North Africa. Given her and her father's connections, she hoped to be assigned to London to be with Billy Hartington, who had long since broken off his engagement. Lord Halifax, on hearing from Kennedy that Kick was "going over to England with the Red Cross," noted in his diary that he imagined "this will not give any particular pleasure to Eddy Devonshire," Billy's father.[36]

Kennedy would have preferred to have his daughter remain in Washington, but as with the boys, once she had made up her mind to leave, he supported her decision, though not without warning her of what she might encounter.

"Don't get too upset if you hear the British talking about your Dad," he wrote her as soon as he received the telegram that she had landed safely in London. "After all, the only crime I can be accused of is that I was pro-American instead of pro-English. I don't blame them for being mad at me for not wanting America to go into the war to help them out, but that wasn't my job, any more than I could be critical of Churchill for having such a terrific influence in our affairs. I resent him as an

American, but I don't blame him as an Englishman. But oftentimes the British aren't that tolerant. I don't care what they say, so don't you let it bother you. You have your own life to live and you needn't answer any of my problems, responsibilities or difficulties—so just smile and say 'Fight with him; he can take care of himself.' After all, no one has been more sympathetic to the British cause than you, so you shouldn't have to take any of the criticism, but I'm just saying this to you so that you'll be prepared for it. I don't mind it; don't you."[37]

When Kick had last been in London, the Kennedys had been treated as a mixture of American royalty and Hollywood celebrity, loved, admired, obsessed over. A great deal had happened since then. "Everyone is very surprised & I do mean surprised to see me," she wrote Jack on arriving in London. There was "much more anti-Kennedy feeling than I imagined and I am determined to get my stories straight as I think I'll get it on all sides." Fortunately, the British she met were too polite to say anything about her father. "No one with the exception of Mr. [Aneurin] Bevan, [Independent Labour] MP from Wales has mentioned a thing about Pop's views which fact has quite amazed me. In Washington hardly a night would pass that someone didn't ask about them, make remarks etc. and they were Americans. Now here are the British who are directly concerned and not a peep out of them."[38]

Kick worked days and occasionally nights at the Red Cross greeting center and canteen but managed to lead a full social life. She dined with Americans stationed in London, including the Biddles and the Harrimans, visited family friends like the Beaverbrooks and the Astors, and saw as much as she could of Billy Hartington. "Billy and I went out together for the first time in London last Saturday," she wrote the family on July 14. "It really is funny to see people put their heads together the minute we arrive any place. There's heavy betting on when we are going to announce it. Some people have gotten the idea that I'm going to give in. Little do they know."[39]

In late July, she wrote Jack after "a day and a half spent in the country with Billy. . . . For 24 hours I forgot all about the war. Billy is just the same, a bit older, a bit more ducal, but we get on as well as ever. It is queer as he is so unlike anyone I have ever known at home or any place really. Of course I know he would never give in about the religion and he knows I never would. . . . It's really too bad because I'm sure I would be a most efficient Duchess of Devonshire in the postwar world and as I'd have a castle in Ireland, one in Scotland, one in Yorkshire and one in Sussex I could keep my old nautical brothers in their old age. But that's the way it goes. Everyone in London is buzzing with rumors and no matter what happens we've given them something to talk about."[40]

Without saying anything about her intentions—in large part because she had no idea where her romance with Billy was going to take her—Kick wrote regularly about Billy. "Billy came down from Yorkshire and had to sleep on the floor," she informed her parents after a "bank holiday" weekend in August at Cliveden. "I wish his father could have seen him. It really is funny how much worried and how much talking is being done, by all those old Cecil and Devonshire spooks. Of course on Sunday morning there was the great problem of my going to church. They all told me that the church was miles away and I couldn't possibly go. I think they would have considered it a moral triumph if I hadn't so I was determined to get there no matter how far away it was. Had a chat with the priest who said it was about four miles each way and it was just according to my conscience whether I should attend mass. Finally hopped on a bike and was there in twenty-five minutes."[41]

Wherever she went now, the press remained hard on her heels. "Someone rings up every morning and wants to know who I am announcing my engagement to. Each time it's a different person."[42]

Kennedy responded to her letters and cables with long newsy letters about her siblings, her friends, her co-workers at the Washington paper, and the political situation back home. He offered no advice, other than to repeat that he trusted her and would support her in whatever she decided to do. He said nothing about Rose, who was adamantly opposed to any of her children marrying outside the church. "As far as I'm concerned, I'll gamble with your judgment. The best is none too good for you, baby, but if you decide it's a Chinaman, it's okay with me. That's how much I think of you." The church was important to him, but not more so than his daughter's happiness.[43]

L ike every parent of draft-age children, Kennedy was suspended in time, holding his breath until the war was over and his children out of harm's way. The summer before, he had busied himself by running his father-in-law's primary campaign. In 1943, he sought refuge from his worries in two very different ventures: farming and show business.

He had earlier bought the Osterville farm, where he kept his horses and where he and the children had ridden for years along the bridle paths through "wet, peaty terrain" that was perfect for cranberry growing. Now, with the war on and rationing in place, he converted it into a working farm to supply the family with fresh vegetables, dairy products, and beef.

"Your father is nuts about the farm," Rose wrote the children in late August 1943, "and is reading farm reports assiduously and discussing the merits of having registered cattle. He is also busy preserving everything from string beans to steers." No one was as shocked as he was by his newfound vocation. The farm had become so much a part of his life that he included regular progress reports on it in his letters to his children overseas. "Our little farm down here is still doing very well," he wrote Jack in the South Pacific in November 1943. "We've got four cows and three steers. We're killing four pigs on Saturday and three lambs in a couple of weeks. I hope to keep it going until two or three years after the war, at least, and possibly as long as we stay at the Cape."[44]

His adventures in show business did not go nearly as well. An acquaintance of sorts, the English playwright Frederick Lonsdale (who, Kennedy wrote Arthur Houghton, had "had a very hard time with the Jewish boys and has had plenty of guts to stand up and fight for no war"), had written a play, *Another Love Story*, which Kennedy had volunteered to produce. "After all, I need something to keep my mind active." The problem was that it wasn't a very good play. Kennedy tried but failed to get Lonsdale to consult first with Eddie Goulding, then with Clare Boothe Luce. When Lonsdale refused, Kennedy, more bemused than angry, walked away. The play opened on Broadway on October 12, 1943, and ran for 104 performances. Kennedy got back most of his investment, but not enough to inspire him to produce or invest in any more Broadway shows.[45]

The farming and the Broadway play provided some distraction that summer and fall. But they were no substitute for news from the war zones where his children were stationed. He heard regularly from Kick, but not nearly enough from either Joe Jr., who was on his way to fly "Liberator bombers—B-24's" from an air base in England, or Jack, who was in the Pacific.

"We haven't heard from Jack since the battle started in the Pacific, around the 27th of June," he wrote Tim McInerny, a former Boston editor and friend, in August. "I wish to God he was back here with me—and that goes for every man or woman who is in the war. . . . Bobby has joined the Navy, but will finish out the next four or five months of his last year at Milton Academy. I've threatened Teddy—age 11—to punch him in the nose if I find him around any recruiting station, even though it is against the law to threaten anybody against any enlistment."[46]

He followed events in the newspapers as assiduously as every other parent with a son in the military, but with the knowledge that the news that got into the papers was already heavily censored. "Well, we spent the last five days reading about the battle [for two of the Trobriand Islands, which was widely reported in the press that summer]," he wrote Jack in the Pacific, "and they don't tell us very much. . . . We hope and pray that this wasn't the time for the back and stomach to go bad on you so that at least you had a chance to do your stuff."[47]

There was no answer from Jack and would be none through July and August. Kennedy, growing increasingly frantic about his son, called Clare Boothe Luce, who had won election to Congress in 1942 and sat on the Military Affairs Committee. "Clare Luce," Kennedy wrote Kick on August 7, "checked with the Navy Department and apparently everything was all right." Jack's unit had been engaged in battle on Munda, the island just north of Rendova, where he was stationed. "After [M]unda," Kennedy continued in his letter to Kick, "the battle in his section will probably quiet down again and maybe he'll be content—with his bad back and his bad stomach—to come back home and lead a normal life, but I don't know my children very well I guess."[48]

That same day, Kennedy wrote Jack again. "We haven't heard from you since the 24th of June and naturally we've been concerned with all the battles going on there as to just how you are making out. . . . I talked with Angela Green [an actress whom Jack had been dating in New York before his departure]. . . . I told her we hadn't heard anything from you and she seemed quite concerned. She says you are still her favorite boy friend."[49]

Kennedy's letter, and a second one written four days later, were acts of faith—and desperation. Though he had written to reassure Kick that "everything" was "all right," it was far from that. Kennedy, who would later boast that he had his "sleuths . . . on the job in Guadalcanal as well as at the Stork Club," had learned from his contacts in the South Pacific that Jack had gone "missing." More than that he did not know.

In the early morning of August 2, 1943, PT 109, which Jack commanded, had been rammed by a Japanese destroyer while on patrol in the Blackett Strait in the mid-Solomons. The boat's plywood hull had been ripped in two. Its gasoline tanks exploded in flames. Two members of the thirteen-member crew were killed instantly, several others badly injured. The commanders of the nearby PT boats, witnessing the collision and explosion, concluded that all hands on PT 109 had been lost and after a cursory search for survivors returned to base with the news that Lieutenant Kennedy and his crew had been killed. "They believed us lost for a week," Jack later wrote a friend, "but luckily thank God—they did not send the telegrams." The decision not to send the "telegrams" had kept the news from Rose and the rest of the family, but not, as we have seen, from Kennedy.[50]

Jack and his crew stayed afloat in the water until the fire was out, then swam back to the remaining piece of the hull, which they held on to as long as they could before swimming another four hours to the nearest island, Lieutenant Kennedy towing one of the injured men behind him. After several days on the tiny island, they were discovered by two natives, whom Jack asked to take a message, carved inside a coconut (there was no paper on the island), to the naval station at Rendova. The next morning, he awoke to the sight of a canoe with eight locals landing on the island, with a stove, food, and a message from a British officer that he was sending a rescue party.[51]

From the "tent" hospital where he and his crewmates were put in sick bay after their rescue, Jack wrote his family "a short note to tell you that I am alive—and <u>not</u> kicking—in spite of any reports that you may happen to hear. It was believed otherwise for a few days—so reports or rumors may have gotten back to you. Fortunately they misjudged the durability of a Kennedy—and am back at the base now and am O.K. As soon as possible I shall try to give you the whole story." The note was postmarked August 13, San Francisco. We have no idea when it reached Hyannis Port.[52]

In a letter to the children, Rose claimed that she first heard about the rescue on August 19. "The *Globe* called me up about 8:20 in the morning . . . when I was in your father's room waiting to hear the morning radio news. Of course, I was very much surprised and excited and I told them I would contact your father, who had gone over to the farm for his early morning ride. . . . Dad knew he was missing for two weeks, although he gave no sign—for which I am very thankful—as I know we should all have been terribly worried. He just complained about his arthritis and I said it was funny he was nervous now, little knowing what he had to be nervous about."[53]

Kennedy later told his son Ted and nephew Joey Gargan that he had heard about Jack's rescue on the radio when he was driving back from his early morning horseback ride at the Osterville farm. "He said that he was so excited that he drove the car off the road and into a field."[54]

The news of Lieutenant Kennedy's heroism burst onto the front pages on August 20. KENNEDY'S SON IS HERO IN PACIFIC AS DESTROYER SPLITS HIS PT BOAT, the *New York Times* reported on page one, in a story datelined "Aug. 8 (delayed)." The family was besieged by congratulatory telegrams from all over the country. "Several people," Rose wrote the children in her round-robin letter of August 25, "have said they always knew Jack would do it and they always felt that Joe had the same sort of stuff, which is all very wonderful for a mother to hear. I believe I would be just as happy though if Joe did not have to risk his life in such a fashion."[55]

Kennedy tried to answer every telegram and letter the family received. "I've been a little lax in writing you recently," he wrote Tim McInerny in London, "but Jack's exploits in the South Pacific have kept me pretty well tied up. It is the consensus of the newspaper men here that there hasn't been a better story since the war started than the one of young Jack. He really came through with flying colors." Convinced that his son's heroism should not go unrewarded, he began a quiet lobbying campaign with his friends in Washington and in the press to get him a "decoration" of some sort.[56]

As exhilarated as he was by the good news from the South Pacific, Kennedy's relief from his fears was only partial—and temporary. He was sick with worry about Jack's health (how could a dangerously underweight man with a bad stomach have survived on coconuts for a week?), furious with the navy for not sending the boy home, and angry with Jack (though he would never tell him) for not demanding to be repatriated. To a friend whose son was also in the military, he confided, only partly in jest, that he thought "the ones that really suffer in this war are the parents. The boys love it and they have a great time, particularly those that are flying or on PT boats."[57]

He was desperate to see Jack in the flesh. In the fall, he left Hyannis Port for New York City, still with no word as to when Jack would return home. "We have not heard from Jack for a couple of weeks," Rose wrote the children on October 27 from Hyannis Port, "and I think Dad worries a bit as he telephones from New York every day. We rather think he is in the midst of the fighting again as we got one report that he volunteered for all the hazardous assignments. I am hoping he will surprise us by suddenly telling us he is on his way home, as he really hoped and believed he would be here by Christmas."[58]

When Kennedy did hear again from his son, the news was not good. "They will not send anyone back while there is fighting in this area—when its over—I'll get back," Jack wrote from his island base in the South Pacific. "As a matter of fact—I am in a bad spot for getting out as am now Capt. of a gunboat— It's the first one they've ever had of its type—it's a former P.T. and is very interesting. . . . It was a sort of a dubious honor to be given the first—so I will have to stick around & try to make a go of it. . . . Don't worry at all about me— I've learned to duck—and have learned the wisdom of the old naval doctrine of keeping your bowels—your mouth shut—and never volunteering."[59]

"If you are going to be out there until we clean up that area,"

Kennedy wrote back on November 4, "I should think it would be Teddy who would relieve you instead of Bobby. I'm told by some of the group here that roughly a year is the limit so that at least puts an outside time of around February for you. Of course I know you'd hate to have anybody mix into your schedule so I'm leaving it at that until I hear from you further."[60]

Sometime that summer or fall of 1943, while awaiting word from his boys in the war zones, Kennedy contacted the local FBI office and volunteered "to assist the Bureau in any way possible should his services be needed." Why he did so at this time, we don't know. It might have been to belatedly thank J. Edgar Hoover for alerting him about Jack's involvement with Inga Arvad.

After a cursory investigation in Washington, Kennedy was enlisted as a "special service contact." In discussions that fall with Special Agent William H. Carpenter, his FBI liaison in Hyannis Port, Kennedy offered to use his connections in the liquor business in New York and the moving picture industry in California and in South America to "benefit the Bureau." According to Special Agent Carpenter, he volunteered that he had "many Jewish friends in the moving picture industry who would furnish him, upon request, with any information in their possession pertaining to Communist infiltration. . . . He feels also that he is in a position to secure any information the Bureau may desire from his contacts in the industry with reference to any individuals who have Communistic sympathies."[61]

Though Kennedy would remain a fawning, outspoken admirer of J. Edgar Hoover and his bureau in the years to come, there is no evidence that he ever offered the FBI tips on Communist infiltrators or individuals who might have "Communistic sympathies." His communications consisted almost entirely of flattering letters to the director, complaints about articles and columnists critical of the FBI, and invitations to Hoover and his companion, Clyde Tolson, to join him in Palm Beach or at Hialeah. His ceaseless flattery of and attention to Hoover was multipurposed. It gave him access, as we shall see, to the FBI and to J. Edgar Hoover's assistance whenever he or anyone else in the family needed it.

Another presidential election was approaching and Kennedy was going to sit it out. He had little faith in Roosevelt, but less in the opponents the Republicans might put up against him. "I am beginning to be courted very strongly by both sides now," he wrote Sir James Calder on December 20, 1943, "because they are starting to think of the election next year, but I am minding my own business and praying that the war will be over and I'll get my children back. That's the thing that concerns me at the minute—not who's going to be the candidate."[62]

With the "courting" came a new set of rumors that he was going to be named secretary of commerce. "So that you'll be all straightened out on the common gossip regarding your Dad's future," he wrote Pat on March 8, 1944, "I am not considering an offer to be Secretary of Commerce and wouldn't if it were offered to me. They've got to do better than that 'to get papa back into this awful mess.'"[63]

In January 1944, Jack finally returned to the United States, five months after his PT boat had been sunk. His medical condition, as his father had feared, was so poor that even before seeing his family, he flew to the Mayo Clinic, where he was told that he would have to have an operation on his back. He suffered as well from an early duodenal ulcer and a still undiagnosed case of malaria. The photographs of the lieutenant in his disheveled navy uniform reveal a tanned, smiling, but unhealthy-looking, frightfully thin young man. "He got back," Kennedy wrote Joe Jr. in late February, "having lost about twenty odd pounds, with his stomach in pretty poor shape. . . . His back, however, was in very bad shape and finally, after spending three weeks here getting in reasonable condition, he is now in the New England Baptist Hospital in Boston where he's having pictures taken of his back and at the same time having his stomach treated. He expects to get an assignment to Miami for about six weeks, and then if his back isn't right he's going to have it operated on. How serious that is they are not really able to tell me until they start to do the job. His future depends on how his back turns out. If it isn't going to be all right, I imagine he'll be through with the Navy; if he gets fixed up, I imagine he'll be on his way again, without too much enthusiasm."[64]

While stateside, Jack met with journalist John Hersey, whom he had known earlier and remained friendly with even after Hersey had wed a woman, Frances Ann Cannon, he had himself considered marrying. Hersey was so taken with the PT boat story that he proposed to write an article about it. The article was rejected by *Life* magazine, then accepted by the *New Yorker*. Kennedy and the navy, hoping for a larger readership, tried to get it published in *Reader's Digest* instead. "I'm hopeful I can work it out. It would be a great boost for the Kennedy clan," Kennedy wrote Joe Jr. in late May. In the end, the article was published first in the *New Yorker* and then in condensed form in *Reader's Digest*.[65]

Kennedy's pessimism, his sense that the world was spinning out of control, was intertwined with and augmented by his loss of control over his own life and those of his children.

Though Kick had said nothing about marrying Billy Hartington, she was acting more and more as if she intended to. In January 1944, when Billy decided to run for the seat in Parliament that had belonged to his family for almost two centuries, Kick joined him on the campaign trail. She wrote to tell her parents that she had "paid a visit to Bishop Matthew," the auxiliary bishop of Westminster, to find out what her options might be should she marry a Protestant. "He had nothing to offer me as a possible solution and went so far as to say that in a case like this the Church would have to be very careful so as to avoid all criticism. In fact bend the other way about making any concessions. When I returned home I picked up the paper and found that the Archbishop of York had just made a statement saying that any Anglican who gave in to the Roman Catholic Church at marriage was guilty of a great weakness. He must have gotten wind of something I should think. Well, in any case there is no immediate rush for a solution but I must say it would be a great load off my mind."[66]

Had the circumstances been otherwise, Kennedy would have flown to London to be with his daughter. But it was wartime, flights were restricted, and the press would be all over him once he arrived, with the publicity making matters worse for everyone involved. Fortunately, Joe Jr. was now stationed in England. "I do hope you'll give her the benefit of your counsel and sympathy," Kennedy wrote him in late February, "because after all she has done a swell job and she's entitled to the best and with us over here it's awfully difficult to be as helpful as we'd like to be. As far as I personally am concerned, Kick can do no wrong and whatever she did would be great with me." It is noteworthy that Kennedy switched from the "we" to "I personally" in declaring his belief that Kick could "do no wrong." Rose Kennedy was not so sure.[67]

On February 22, Kick wrote her family about the results of the by-election, which Billy had lost. In the middle of her letter, she drew back from politics to talk about Billy and the Cavendish family, with whom she had celebrated her twenty-fourth birthday on February 20. "Received a lovely old leather book from the Duke for my birthday. The Duchess said she had nothing to do with it, and when I opened it I knew why. It was the Book of Common Prayer of the Church of England. I laughed and thanked him very much." The duke, by now as taken with Kick as everyone else in the family, was reconciled to his son marrying her, but only because he expected that she would convert to the Church of England. Kick reported that Billy's mother, the duchess, with whom she had had a "long chat . . . longs to make things easy. Please try and discover loopholes although I keep feeling that the particular parties involved would make any compromise impossible. The Catholics would say it would give scandal. This situation, Daddy, is a stickler."[68]

Kennedy cabled Count Enrico Galeazzi to inquire as to whether there was any way for Kick to get a "dispensation" to marry an Anglican. The news was not encouraging. "Frankly I do not seem to think Dad can do anything," Rose wrote her daughter on February 24. "He feels terribly sympathetic and so do I and I only wish we could offer some suggestions. When both people have been handed something all their lives, how ironic it is that they cannot have what they want most. I wonder if the next generation will feel that it is worth sacrificing a life's happiness for all the old family tradition." It was not difficult to read between Rose's lines. She did not tell Kick, as Kennedy had on several occasions, that she would support her whatever she decided. Instead, she sounded very much as if she took it for granted that her daughter would make the "sacrifice" necessary to maintain "the old family tradition."[69]

In early March, Kennedy wrote to thank Kick on her wise and witty letter on Billy's electoral campaign. Midway through his four-and-a-half-page letter, fearing (rightly) that it would be read by the censors, he referred "to the other problem," on which he was "working in every way I know. The prominence of the situation makes it most difficult, neither side wishing to look as though it were making concessions. I am afraid the individuals themselves will have to work it out with some give and take on their part and let all the rest of us go jump in the lake." In true Kennedy fashion, he closed with a bit of dark gallows Irish humor, the joke that arouses the "mirthless laugh," as Samuel Beckett has written, the laugh "at that which is unhappy." He had heard from London that Kick had been making "converts" among the American soldiers at her canteen. "Maybe if you made enough of them a couple of them could take your place." Knowing that Rose would not have appreciated his joking about the church and converts, he added that if she "ever saw that sentence I'd be thrown right out in the street."[70]

Kick's troubles were enough to try any parent's heart. She had, she told her parents in a March 22 letter, just returned from a visit to Churchdale, the Cavendish estate in Derbyshire, where the duchess had arranged, with Kick's full approval, for her to meet with the duchess's "very great friend . . . Father Ted Talbot" of the Church of England, so that he might "explain what the Cavendish family stood for in the English Church, the impossibilities of Billy permitting his son to be brought up a Roman Catholic." Father Talbot and the duchess asked Kick to at least explore the possibility of converting. Kick was adamant. Almost paraphrasing her mother's sentiments in her recent letter, she explained that because she had "been blessed with so many of this world's goods . . . it seemed rather cheap and weak to give in at the first real crisis in my life." She left Churchdale feeling "most discouraged and rather sad. I want to do the right thing so badly and yet I hope I'm not giving up the most important thing in my life." She understood now that Billy could neither convert nor allow his children to be raised as Catholics. "Poor Billy is very, very sad but he sees his duty must come first. He is a fanatic on this subject." If she and Billy were to be married, she would have to be the one to "give in."[71]

In the best of circumstances, the choices that Kick faced would have been near debilitating. But this was wartime and every decision was more difficult. It was common knowledge that the second front in Europe would soon be opened and Billy, with tens of thousands of other British soldiers and officers, would be swept across the English Channel and into combat. Kick could not afford the luxury of putting off her choice.

On April 4, she wrote to say that she, Joe Jr., and Billy had visited Bishop Matthew again and learned from him that there would no "dispensations," no "concessions," from the church. "The Bishop told me that it would put the Church in a very difficult position for us to get a dispensation and it would be better if we went ahead and got married and then something might possibly be done afterwards. Of course he wouldn't guarantee that anything could be done." As a married woman, she could still "go to Church but not Communion. . . . If I do marry Billy within the next two months, please be quite sure that I am going it with the full knowledge of what I am doing and that I'm quite happy about it and feel quite sure that I am doing the right thing." She added as a postscript that Billy had "called last night and said that there wasn't much hope of getting any more leave. That's our latest difficulty. Goodness, when will they ever stop."[72]

Kennedy held out hope that some sort of compromise could be reached. "Jack," he wrote on April 27, "much to my amazement because I am not particularly impressed with the depth of his Catholic faith, feels that some kind of concession should be made on the part of Billy. . . . In the meantime, I want you to know that I feel for you very deeply. . . . When I think of you alone over there, even though I am sure you are with people you like to be with, I am also conceited enough to know that you would value the counsel of Mother and I. . . . Now none of this means that I am attempting to tell you how you should handle your life. You are the one that has to live it and it is a long one and also quite a difficult one, but as I have said to you before you are 'tops' with me and you always will be."[73]

R ose and Kennedy did not learn of Kick's decision until April 29, when she cabled that she and Billy were going to be married in a registry office, not a church, but she did not know precisely when.

"Naturally," Rose wrote in her diary, "I was disturbed horrified—heartbroken." Kick was setting a bad example for every Catholic girl who was attracted to a Protestant boy. "Every little young girl would say if K. Kennedy can—why can't I? . . . What a blow to our family prestige." She recognized that she was overreacting, but that didn't stop her. "No one seemed to be as excited about that as I & I was sick & supposed to keep from any emotional upset so I prayed with all my heart. . . . Joe told me I had done all that could be done. . . . I would like Joe to fly to her but he seemed to think that was impossible altho' now I know he should have gone over a month or 2 ago."[74]

Frantic and unwilling to trust her husband because he was not frantic, Rose sent another cable to her daughter, then returned to Boston and checked into the New England Baptist Hospital, where, according to the newspapers, she remained for the next "two weeks for a routine physical checkup." Kennedy, worried that his youngest daughter, Jean, might be distressed by the news from London, visited her at the Sacred Heart Convent. The two went for a long walk and Kennedy told Jean that Kick was going to marry outside the church, but to a good man whom she loved. He was happy for her and Jean should be also. She assured her father that she was not upset and promised to write her sister, as Kennedy had suggested.[75]

Meanwhile, on Kennedy's behalf, Archbishop Spellman contacted Archbishop Godfrey in London, who visited Kick and asked her to reconsider, because her mother was "greatly distressed." "Effort in vain," Archbishop Godfrey cabled Spellman on May 4. That same day, the engagement of Kathleen Kennedy and Lord Hartington, heir of the Duke of Devonshire, was announced in *The Times* of London.[76]

Having heard nothing from her father, Kick cabled him the day before the wedding. "Religion everything to us both. Will always live according to Catholic teaching. Praying that time will heal all wounds. Your support in this as in everything else means so much. Please beseech mother not to worry. Am very happy and quite convinced have taken right step. Love to all."[77]

Rose's distress was predictable, but not Kennedy's silence. He had supported his daughter from the very beginning, urged her to forget the rest of the world, and told her that "whatever she did would be great" with him. Still, he had never quite believed that she would marry a

Protestant. Now that she had, he was momentarily stunned—and speechless. There was no congratulatory cable from him when the engagement was announced or immediately before, or after, the wedding at the Chelsea registry office in London on May 6.

Joe Jr., who was not in the habit of reprimanding or correcting his father, felt obliged to do so. From London, he sent a six-word cable the day after the wedding: "The power of silence is great." The next morning, Kennedy sent his congratulations to his daughter. There was no message from Rose Kennedy. "Most distressed about mother," Kick cabled Palm Beach. "Please tell her not to worry. Your cable made my happiest day. . . . Have American papers been bad? All love."[78]

When Kennedy responded that Rose was well, Kathleen wrote her directly. "Goodness mother—I owe so much to you and Daddy that nothing in the world could have made me go against your will. However, I felt that you expected the action I took and would judge that it was the course to make under the circumstances. . . . Please don't take responsibility for an action, which you think bad (and I do not). You did everything in your power to stop it. You did your duty as a Roman Catholic mother. You have not failed. There was nothing lacking in my religious education. Not by any means am I giving up my faith—it is most precious to me. . . . Of course it was too bad that the papers made such an issue of the religious question. However, I must admit that I expected it. I hope they weren't too bad in Boston." Kick was filled with gratitude that her big brother, Joe Jr., had not only attended the wedding but had been on her side from day one. In her letter to her mother, she joked that giving his sister away in marriage to a Protestant aristocrat might not have been a terribly wise move politically. Joe Jr. agreed that with "his face plastered all over the papers . . . he was 'finished in Boston.'"[79]

Kick and Joe Jr. need not have worried. Kennedy had used all the influence he could muster to make sure that the local papers either ignored or downplayed the wedding of his daughter to an English Protestant aristocrat. "In fact," Kennedy reassured his son, "Arthur Krock said that in twenty-five years of newspaper work he had never seen such a difficult situation handled so tactfully." Only "gabby grandfather" had had anything to say to the press. "Naturally, when you get leading questions, such as . . . 'How do you feel about your daughter renouncing the Catholic Religion?' . . . and . . . 'Do you favor the marriage of your daughter outside of the Church?' it was a very difficult situation. I couldn't say that I didn't like it because after all, I think the world of Kick and as I've often said, whatever she did would be all right with me, because I feel she's a girl of great character, great instincts, and great experience, and when she makes up her mind to do anything—then boy, I know she's got some reason for it and that's enough for me. But of course with Mother, it's different."[80]

In the end, what troubled Kennedy the most, perhaps, was not that his daughter had married a Protestant, but that, having wed an Englishman, she would not be coming home. "I have lost one of my daughters to England," he wrote Lord Beaverbrook on May 24. "She was the apple of my eye and I feel the loss because I won't have her near me all the time, but I'm sure she's going to be wonderfully happy and I can assure you that England is getting a great girl."[81]

On June 6, 1944, one month after the marriage of William Hartington and Kathleen Kennedy, the Allied invasion of Europe was launched. Two weeks later, Billy Hartington crossed the English Channel. Joe Jr., who could have come home on leave in mid-May, stayed behind to fly support missions for the invading troops.

Kennedy, waiting for the return from the battlefields of his son-in-law and his son, busied himself by giving a few speeches. He spoke in Boston on National Maritime Day, then in May flew to Chicago to address the American Gastroenterological Association at the invitation of its president, his friend and doctor, Sara Jordan, of the Lahey Clinic. Before Pearl Harbor, he had insisted that Americans stay out of European battles and refrain from trying to save the world from tyrannical dictators, even those as evil as Adolf Hitler. Now he repeated his message again and urged his fellow Americans "with all the strength I command" to resist the call "to bear an onerous share of the expenses of world-wide social service, foreign trade and world currencies." He had no patience with those who claimed that because American cities had not been "devastated and gutted" as London had, Americans "have not suffered from this war." In a sentence large with foreboding, he declared, "You can't tell that to the family whose boy is not coming home at the end of the war."[82]

On June 11, Lieutenant John F. Kennedy was admitted to the Chelsea Naval Hospital, then transferred to New England Baptist for back surgery. "Isn't it lovely," Clare Boothe Luce wrote his father on June 12, "to have him tucked away safely in a plaster Paris cast for a few months, anyway?" The plan had been to repair a disk, but when the doctors found abnormally soft tissue they removed it. Jack "has had a very hard time," Kennedy wrote Joe Jr. on August 9. "He has not recovered nearly as fast as he should have and is now having a great deal of trouble with his leg. Of course, he can't correct the stomach difficulties until his back gets right. He is back in the Chelsea Naval Hospital, and we are hoping that he may get a little time off to recuperate if another operation is not necessary."[83]

Jack at least was safe. Nothing had been heard from Billy since he'd crossed the Channel in late June. "We hear from Kathleen and she is very, very happy," Kennedy wrote Houghton on July 7, "but a little bit worried about her husband as she hasn't heard from him for quite a while. You know they stick those Grenadier and Coldstream guards with the Irish guards right out in front."[84]

Joe Jr. had still not come home. "Although he's had a large number of casualties in his squadron," Kennedy wrote Lord Beaverbrook, "I'm still hoping and praying we'll see him around the first of July."[85]

The first of July came and went, and no Joe Jr. "No doubt you are surprised that I haven't arrived home," he wrote his parents on July 26. "I am going to do something different for the next three weeks. It is secret, and I am not allowed to say what it is, but it isn't dangerous so don't worry. So probably I won't be home till sometime in September."

He had never told a bigger lie. He had volunteered for a dangerous, near suicidal mission. German V-1 flying bombs had been pummeling London since D-Day, causing death, destruction, and constant fear. Even brave Kick, who had been through so much, was, according to her brother, "terrified of the Doodles [the name given the aerial bombs] as is everyone else, and I think she is smart not to work in London." Joe Jr.'s assignment was to take out a major V-1 launching site in Belgium. The navy had stripped down one of the Liberator bombers that he had been flying so that it could be fully loaded with explosives. His instructions were to fly the overloaded B-24 across the English Channel, turn over control of his plane to the two B-17s flying with him when he reached his target, and parachute to safety.[86]

Kennedy hid his disappointment and fears as best he could. "The reason I haven't been writing you is that I have been expecting to hear the telephone ring any time and to hear that you were in Norfolk and were on your way home. Not until we got your letter night before last did we know that you were not likely to make it until September. I can quite understand how you feel about staying there because the worst of it is certainly better than anything in the Pacific, but don't force your luck too much."[87]

Thirty

"A MELANCHOLY
BUSINESS"

It was a warm, pleasant Sunday in Hyannis Port; the date was August 13, 1944, the time about two o'clock in the afternoon. Jack was home from the hospital, still in pain, neither his back nor his stomach problems resolved. He and his sisters Jean and Eunice and his little brother Teddy were sitting on the porch after a long, leisurely picnic-style lunch. Bing Crosby's "I'll Be Seeing You" was playing on the phonograph. Rose was reading the Sunday paper. Kennedy had gone upstairs for an afternoon nap.

A dark car drove down the street and into the driveway in front of the house. "Two naval chaplains got out, walked up the steps to the porch, and knocked on the screen door," Ted recalled a half century later. They told Rose that they had come to speak to her husband. There was nothing unusual here, no reason to be frightened. "Priests and nuns fairly often came to call, wanting to talk with Joe about some charity or other matter," Rose would later write in her memoirs. "So I invited them to come into the living room and join us comfortably until Joe finished his nap. One of the priests said no, that the reason for calling was urgent. That there was a message both Joe and I must hear. Our son was missing in action and presumed lost."

Ted and the other children heard only "a few words: 'missing—lost.' All of us froze."

Rose raced upstairs to wake her husband. "Moments later, the two of them came back down. They took the clergymen into another room and talked briefly. When they emerged, Dad's face was twisted. He got the words out that confirmed what we already suspected. Joe Jr. was dead. . . . Suddenly the sunroom was awash in tears. Mother, my sisters, our guest, myself—everybody was crying; some wailed. Dad turned himself around and stumbled back up the stairs; he did not want us to witness his own dissolution into sobs." Sixteen-year-old Jean got on her bicycle and rode off by herself to church. Jack turned to his little brother. " 'Joe wouldn't want us sitting here crying,' my brother said. 'He would want us to go sailing. Let's go sailing.' . . . And that was what we did. We went sailing."[1]

Kick was called in London. On Wednesday, August 16, she flew home on an army transport plane. Billy did not accompany her; he was somewhere in France with his regiment, she didn't know where, not having heard from him in weeks.

The Kennedys remained at Hyannis Port through Labor Day, trying to live their lives. The children sailed, played tennis, entertained their friends, ate dinner around the big table on the porch; Jack rested and recuperated; Eunice and Ted raced competitively. Each Kennedy grieved in his or her own way. Jean, who had had a very special relationship with Joe Jr., who was her godfather, who taught her how to dance, who listened to her jokes and reassured her that she would pass her exams, suffered quietly and worried about her father.[2]

Joseph P. Kennedy would never recover from the death of his oldest son and namesake, the handsome, charming, charismatic young man who believed—with his father—that he could do anything he set his mind to. Kennedy mourned privately, out of public view. For the first time in his life, he feared he had lost his faith. Years later, in a letter to his friend Walter Howey, whose wife had died after a debilitating illness, Kennedy would marvel at the different ways he and Rose had responded to their son's death. "When young Joe was killed, my faith, even though I am a Catholic did not seem strong enough to make me understand that . . . he had won his eternal reward. . . . My faith should have made me realize this and I should not have indulged in the great self-pity the way I did. . . . Rose, on the other hand, with her supreme faith has just gone on and prayed for him and has not let it affect her life. I am sure that you are more in my class than either of us are in hers; so we are going to be unhappy at the loss of those we love until we die."[3]

The horror he had most dreaded had come to pass. The war in Europe he had done so much to oppose had taken his son. "Joe's death has shocked me beyond belief," he wrote James Forrestal, now secretary of the navy, on September 5. The letter was handwritten because he did not want to share its contents with a secretary or typist. "All of my children are equally dear to me, but there is something about the first born that sets him a little apart—he is for always a bit of a miracle. . . . He represents our youth, its joys & problems."[4]

He busied himself by responding to the hundreds of condolence notes the family had received, from the president, the prime minister, government officials and private citizens, family friends, Joe Jr.'s classmates and service mates. For the first time in his life, he was stuck in time, unable to see past the present moment. Joe Jr. had been his future, and now he was gone. To his cousin Joe Kane, the family's political representative in Boston, he apologized that he just couldn't "get in the mood to write letters about young Joe. You more than anyone else know how much I had tied my whole life up to his from here on. You know what great things I saw in the future for him, and now it's all over." To Arthur Houghton, he confided that he was "considering a proposition with [producer] Mike Todd but not too seriously. I think I probably have to interest myself in something because all my plans for my future were all tied up with young Joe, and that has gone smash."[5]

After Labor Day, still adhering to his regular routines, he left Hyannis Port for his suite at the Waldorf Towers. Rose, as was her custom, moved into the Plaza, where she was joined by her daughters. On September 16, a month and four days after Joe Jr.'s death, a telegram arrived for Joseph P. Kennedy at the Waldorf. Kick's husband, Billy Hartington, had been killed in action in France. Eunice was with her father when the telegram arrived. Kennedy sent her to find Kick, who was shopping at Bonwit Teller. She did not tell her sister what had happened, only that "Dad" wanted to see her at once. The two returned to the Waldorf, where Kennedy told Kick that her husband of four months—only one of which she had spent with him—was dead.

That night, the family went to dinner at Le Pavillon. Jean Kennedy remembers that she, Pat, and Eunice tried their best to cheer up their sister. There was little or no talk of Billy. The Kennedy family did not mourn the dead by speaking of or telling stories about them.[6]

The next day or the day after, Kick called Lord Halifax at the British embassy in London. "I told her that the War Office had confirmed her bad news. She seemed very good and brave on the telephone. . . . She is going up to Quebec tomorrow to fly home. . . . It is a melancholy business."[7]

Kennedy retreated further into himself. He had not really known Billy Hartington, but he grieved for him and his parents and for his daughter Kick, who returned to England to be with Billy's family and friends. He saw no one, gave no speeches, wrote fewer letters.

In late October, Kennedy was visited at the Waldorf Towers by Morton Downey, one of his Palm Beach friends, who brought with him Bob Hannegan, chairman of the Democratic National Committee. Kennedy, who had always enjoyed being courted by men in high places, was not surprised that the Democrats had come calling as election day drew near.

"Hannegan admitted, starting off, that he had heard a great deal about my difficulties with the group behind Roosevelt and made no bones about the matter that he despised the group also. . . . He insinuated that Roosevelt was not as well as they thought and that it was extremely likely that Truman [Roosevelt's running mate] would be President, would throw that gang out bodily, and would want fellows like myself to come back into the Government and make it work. He asked me if I would be willing to see Roosevelt, and I said, 'Of course, if Roosevelt asked me to go there, I would go.'" The fact that he was willing to visit the White House did not, he made clear to Hannegan, mean that he was going to endorse the president. On the contrary, he was "seriously contemplating making a speech for Dewey [Thomas

E. Dewey, the Republican candidate]. . . . With one son in the hospital, one son dead, and my son-in-law killed," Kennedy told Hannegan, he didn't think any speech he might make "would be very helpful to Roosevelt."

On October 26, Kennedy visited Washington for the first time in more than a year and the White House for the first time since the spring of 1943. He found Roosevelt looking "very badly," sicker than he had ever seen him. "His face was as gray as his hair," he wrote later. "He is thin, he has an unhealthy color. His hands shake violently when he tries to take a drink of water." They made small talk, as they always did, Roosevelt "speaking of Kathleen's husband" but getting his name wrong. Roosevelt then launched into a discussion of current politics, the upcoming election, and the forecasts for Massachusetts and New Jersey. Kennedy recalled in his notes of the meeting that he told the president that the 5 percentage undecided vote in those states was "not the independent vote, but . . . the old line Democrats—the Irish, and the Italians—all of whom should be in the Democratic columns but this year were off for two or three good reasons. First, they felt that Roosevelt was Jew controlled. Second, they felt that the Communists were coming into control. . . . Third, that this group, along with many others, felt that there were more incompetents in Roosevelt's cabinet than you could possibly stand in this country." Kennedy paused to add that he agreed "with the group who felt that the Hopkins, Rosenmans [Samuel Rosenman was one of Roosevelt's chief advisers], and Frankfurters, and the rest of the incompetents would rob Roosevelt of the place in history that he hoped, I am sure, to have. . . . Roosevelt went on to say 'Why, I don't see Frankfurter twice a year.' And I said to him, 'You see him twenty times a day but you don't know it because he works through all these other groups of people without your knowing it.'"

Kennedy kept on, his rage and bitterness tumbling out, his complaints mounting one on top of the other, most of them old ones, some new. "I am sore and indignant because of the way I have been treated," he told the president. "The last blow was when Jack was recommended for a medal by all his officers in direct command which was two degrees higher than what he finally received. He was reduced . . . for reasons unknown to me, but which I suspect were because I was persona non grata to the powers that be in Washington."

The president tried to change the subject to conditions in Italy, which were deplorable, then to de Gaulle, whom he thought a buffoon. Kennedy would not be deterred. Though the war was coming to an end—and that was good—he was consumed with fear about the postwar world. "I told Roosevelt that I didn't take much stock in any plans I had seen for post-war peace because I thought that Stalin was, after all, the dominating influence in the world." Roosevelt could only reply, "Well, he doesn't always get what he wants."

Whatever topic Roosevelt brought up, whatever he said, Kennedy argued with him. When Roosevelt mentioned that he thought he had made the right decision in responding to recent Republican attacks on him and his family "in a very light manner," Kennedy "disagreed completely by saying that so many families had lost boys in the war that they didn't want such light treatment."[8]

Roosevelt was not the only one Kennedy spoke with that day in Washington. Just before his appointment at the White House, he had called up Lord Halifax, now the British ambassador, to see if he could come by "to shake us by the hand." In his diary entry, Halifax recalled that Kennedy "was in his usual unsatisfactory mood and I really did not begin to know what he thinks or wants." As with the president, then afterward with James Byrnes and Archbishop Spellman, Kennedy complained nonstop about Roosevelt and the outlook for a postwar world dominated in Europe, at least, by Stalin. "His attitude," Halifax recalled, "seemed to be a compound of a surviving and quite futile feeling that America ought never to have gotten into the war . . . and unhappiness at the consequences of the war on people like himself who used to have a lot of money." Halifax had little sympathy with Kennedy, having lost one son in Europe and a second return from combat in Africa with both legs amputated. On the contrary, he was rather disgusted. "I am afraid," he concluded his diary entry, "I think he is a rotten fellow."[9]

On October 28, Kennedy flew to Boston to meet with Democratic National Committee chairman Hannegan and vice-presidential candidate Harry Truman. According to Kennedy's notes of the meeting, Truman "begged me to make a speech" for the Democratic ticket. He and Hannegan reiterated that Roosevelt was not well and would most likely not live out his term. And in that event, Truman declared, confirming what Hannegan had earlier told Kennedy, he would "kick all these incompetents and Jews out of Washington and ask fellows like myself and others to come back and run the government." Though this was precisely what Kennedy wanted to hear, it was not enough to win him back. He could not, he repeated to Truman, endorse Roosevelt. "Knowing my experience," Truman and Hannegan told Kennedy, "they didn't blame me a bit, but they still hoped I would come out for him."[10]

Twenty-five years later, in a conversation with writer Merle Miller, Truman offered a different version of the meeting: "Old man Kennedy started throwing rocks at Roosevelt, saying he'd caused the war and so on. And then he said, 'Harry, what the hell are you doing campaigning for that crippled son of a bitch that killed my son, Joe?' I'd stood it just as long as I could, and I said, 'If you say another word about Roosevelt, I'm going to throw you out that window. . . . I haven't seen [Kennedy] since." Some (but not all) of this account rings true. Truman might, in retrospect, have wished that he had defended Roosevelt, as he claimed he had, instead of nodding silently as Kennedy excoriated him. Ten days before the election, he was not about to antagonize the country's most prominent Irish Catholic on his home turf. Hannegan and Truman bit their tongues, heard Kennedy out, and accepted the campaign donation he offered them.[11]

By courting Kennedy directly, asking for his support, making him feel wanted again, and inferring that he would have a place of importance in the upcoming Truman administration, Hannegan and Truman—with an assist from the president, who had invited Kennedy to the White House—had accomplished what they'd set out to do. Kennedy did not make any speeches for the Democratic ticket as he had four, eight, and twelve years earlier, but neither did he endorse Dewey nor say a word in his favor. Irish Catholics voted for the president in the same proportions they had in earlier elections. Franklin Delano Roosevelt was elected president for a fourth term on November 7, 1944.

In Europe and the Pacific, the killing of young men continued without pause. The war was not yet over, nor did its end appear imminent. Through the autumn and early winter of 1944, more and more soldiers—and millions of civilians—died as the Russians drove west, reoccupying the Ukraine, moving into Poland and toward East Prussia, while the British and Americans pushed east, their momentum stalled as the Germans, instead of surrendering as they had in World War I, pushed back relentlessly and with some success. In the Pacific, the Japanese fleet had been defeated at the Battle of Leyte Gulf in the Philippines, but the war continued.

The passage of time healed no wounds. On the contrary, the hurt became worse as the months passed, and for Kennedy, at least, the problems that would have to be faced after the war became larger and more unmanageable. "For a fellow who didn't want this war to touch your country or mine," Kennedy wrote Lord Beaverbrook in late October 1944, "I have had rather a bad dose—Joe dead, Billy Hartington dead, my son in the Naval Hospital. . . . As I sit here and write you this letter with the natural cynicism that I know you and I share about a great many things, I wonder if this war will do anything for the world. No matter what peace outline I read, looking behind it, I see the problems of living standards, economics, stability, and national pride are all still standing on shaky ground. . . . To have boys like ours killed for a futile effort would be the greatest reflection on us all. Yet, if you would ask me what I am doing to help, I would tell you nothing. However, I assure you it is not by choice rather by circumstances."[12]

Six weeks later, Kennedy wrote Sir James Calder, another old friend, to thank him for his condolence letter. Only to a friend on the other side of the Atlantic whom he did not expect to encounter in person could Kennedy reveal the depth of his pain. "I am trying to reconcile myself to your magnificent spiritual outlook but I, very frankly, haven't arrived at it yet. I think Jack's illness and the death of the two boys along with the horrible conditions in the world have left me rather a long road to travel back to arrive at the spiritual point of view. It will come, I know, but it just hasn't come yet."[13]

In May 1945, Kennedy heard from Arthur Houghton that his son, Andy, had been killed in the Pacific. Kennedy tried to find words that might console Houghton but could not. "I don't think you ever get over the shock. . . . I won't offer you that hocus-pocus that some people offer—that he died for a great cause—I don't believe he did. I believe he died like young Joe as a result of the stupidity of our generation.

The one thing he did die a martyr to was his own conscience. He wanted to do the right thing because it was his idea of the thing to do, and for that—and that alone—he died. This is the satisfaction which you and I will always have."

To heal his own wounds, Jack Kennedy had solicited essays from Joe Jr.'s school and navy buddies, some family friends, and Honey Fitz, Kathleen, and Ted for a privately published tribute to his brother, *As We Remember Joe*. Kennedy was able to read only one "article at a time," and that with much difficulty. He sent Houghton a copy of the book, and Houghton responded by forwarding "the little tribute" he had written about Andy. Again Kennedy tried to find words that might help his friend come to grips with his loss. "You'll never get it out of your mind no matter what you think or what you do. Everyday interests naturally relieve the strain, but the thought will always be there. . . . It is things like this that darken the few years that we have left, and for that reason I am now telling you that we must get what happiness we can out of the time that we have left to enjoy it."[14]

Franklin Delano Roosevelt would not survive to greet the peace in Europe or in Asia. He died on April 12, 1945, exactly eight months after Joe Kennedy, Jr.'s bomber had gone down in flames. "The news hit America like nothing since Pearl Harbor," wrote Roosevelt biographer H. W. Brands. Restaurants, bars, theaters, concert halls, and nightclubs closed for the night. The first baseball games of the year were canceled. The radio networks suspended commercial programming. The New York Stock Exchange announced that it would be closed on the following day. The nation grieved. Joseph P. Kennedy did not.[15]

"Evidently he'd been slipping very badly," he wrote Kick in London, "and it becomes more and more apparent to all of us that Hopkins and the rest of them were really running this country for the last year and a half, and, if I do say so, damn near ran it into the ground." He admitted that there had been "real sorrow on the announcement of his death and for two or three days after." But now, two weeks later, "you rarely, if ever hear his name mentioned, and there is also no doubt that it was a great thing for the country. He had stirred up a hatred in the minds of at least half the country, and no matter whether he proposed anything good or bad, half the country would be against it and half for it." Roosevelt had lost control of Congress to the point where the federal government was nearly paralyzed. And he had not laid the foundation for a peaceful postwar. "It's a horrible thing to contemplate, with the death of all these boys and with the world economically and socially in chaos, that we haven't anything to look forward to in the line of peace for the world as the pay-off for everyone's sacrifices."[16]

His anger was unbounded at those he held accountable for bringing on the war that had led to Joe Jr.'s death and Jack's near fatal illnesses. On April 19, a week after the president's death, he told former president Herbert Hoover, according to Hoover's notes, that he had dozens of diplomatic dispatches in his possession that fully documented Roosevelt's role in pushing the British toward war. On May 15, at a second meeting with Hoover, he elaborated on his theory, insisting that in the spring of 1939, Roosevelt had encouraged Chamberlain to guarantee Polish sovereignty and provide British military support in the event of German aggression. "Kennedy said that if it had not been for Roosevelt the British would not have made this, the most gigantic blunder in history."[17]

Kennedy's conspiracy theory of the origins of the war was clearly incendiary, but that did not stop him from repeating it, always in private, usually to those he believed might agree with him. In his diary, James Forrestal recounted a discussion he had on December 27, 1945, while golfing with Kennedy in Palm Beach; almost to the word, it mirrored the one Kennedy had had with Hoover seven months earlier. Kennedy declared unequivocally that there would have been no war in Western Europe had Roosevelt not forced Chamberlain to face down the Germans over Poland. Left to his own devices, Kennedy insisted, Hitler would have turned east toward Russia. There were two separate claims here: one was defensible, that Hitler preferred to move east rather than west; the other, that Roosevelt was somehow responsible for the war, was preposterous.[18]

On May 7, 1945, a little more than three weeks after Roosevelt's death and almost a year after the landings on Normandy, the German military, with Hitler dead by suicide, agreed to the only terms the

British and Americans would accept, unconditional surrender. The American people celebrated briefly before turning their attention to the war in the Pacific. Three months later, that war, too, came to an end. On the morning of August 6, 1945, the first atomic bomb was dropped on Hiroshima. President Harry Truman demanded Japan's unconditional surrender and threatened a further "rain of ruin from the sky." On August 8, the Soviet Union, as promised at Yalta, entered the war, its armies marching south the next day into Manchuria.

Kennedy, who had opposed unconditional surrender in Europe, was appalled at the American attempt to secure it in Japan by dropping atomic bombs on civilian populations. On August 8, he and Harry Luce visited Archbishop Spellman and implored him to request of the president a few days' truce to give Japan's leaders the opportunity to formally surrender. We do not know whether Spellman ever contacted Truman. On August 9, a second atomic bomb was dropped on Nagasaki. On August 14, Emperor Hirohito agreed to American terms.[19]

While others basked in the glory of unconditional victory, Kennedy's anger at the results of the war washed away any sense of relief that the bloodshed might now be at an end. "It does seem ironical that somebody who opposed the war as bitterly as I did should lose his oldest son, his son-in-law, and have his second son badly banged up," he wrote Cissy Patterson on November 26, 1945. "At the minute it does seem that it is rather too much to hope for that the world will be any better as a result of the sacrifices of all these fine young men—but then again, I never thought it would be."[20]

He tried to control his rage and succeeded for the most part, certainly with his children. But the anger within him was such that it sprang out, unbidden, at rather inappropriate moments: at lunch with President Hoover, golf with Secretary Forrestal, on the telephone and in letters to friends. In January 1946, he was invited to have "a chat" with Winston Churchill at Hialeah during the ex–prime minister's post-election, post-defeat tour of the United States. Churchill offered his condolences for Kennedy's losses. Kennedy thanked him. Churchill, making small talk with a man he knew despised him and might hold him accountable in some way for his son's death, remarked almost casually that "the world seems to be in a frightful condition." Kennedy agreed, then added, "After all, what did we accomplish by this war?"

Churchill had to have been momentarily stunned. The war had accomplished a great deal from his perspective: the destruction of Nazi Germany, Fascist Italy, and Japan, the restoration of the Western European republics, the rescue of Great Britain. Instead of confronting Kennedy and launching into a debate at the Hialeah racetrack, Churchill tried to defuse the situation. "He turned sharply, saying, 'Well, at least, we have our lives [to which Kennedy] replied, 'Not all of us.' With that," Kennedy recalled, Churchill "dropped the subject at once."[21]

He did not dispute the reality that the world war had saved Europe from Nazi domination and much of Asia from Japanese domination. But had it made the world a safer or more tolerant place? Had it brought the American people any added measure of security? In Europe, one enemy, Germany, had been replaced by another, the Soviet Union; one alien, un-Christian, freedom-denying, authoritarian ideology, nazism, by another, communism. To those who argued that the war had eliminated a great evil from the world, Kennedy countered in a June 1946 commencement address at Colby Junior College for Women in New Hampshire that "evil forces there will always be . . . if not Hitler and his gang, then their prototype." War, he insisted, was not the answer to evil in the world; it solved nothing, protected no one.[22]

Knowing as we do today the full extent of Hitler's murderous intent, it is difficult for us, as it was difficult for those who greeted victory in 1945, not to celebrate World War II as a triumph of good over evil. From Kennedy's perspective, the victory over Hitler had cost much and accomplished little. It would not bring back his son or the millions of young men murdered on the battlefields of Europe. And it would most certainly not bring back to life the six million Jews who had perished. Their fate, he believed, had been determined long before American troops set off across the ocean. As he had argued in 1938 and 1939, there was only one way the Jews of Europe might have been protected: through a comprehensive agreement with Hitler that provided for their rescue and resettlement. Once that effort failed and was abandoned, the future of European Jewry was left in the hands of one man, Adolf Hitler.

Unlike his friend Frank Murphy, who in early January 1944 announced that he would serve as chairman of the National Committee Against Nazi Persecution and Extermination of the Jews, Kennedy said nothing, wrote nothing, voiced no concern over the fate of European

Jews, no outrage at anti-Semitism abroad or at home. As he told Boston reporter Joseph Dinneen in an unpublished interview in May 1944, "Anti-Semitism is their fight—just as anti-Irishism was my fight and the fight of my fathers in this country. . . . I have never discussed anti-Semitism in public, because I could never see how it would be helpful. Whenever I have been asked for a statement condemning anti-Semitism, I have answered: 'What good would it do?' If the Jews themselves would pay less attention to advertising their racial problem, and more attention to solving it, the whole thing would recede into its proper perspective. It's entirely out of focus now, and that is chiefly their fault. . . . Publicizing unjust attacks upon the Jews may help to cure the injustice, but continually publicizing the whole problem only serves to keep it alive in the public mind."[23]

As far as he had journeyed from East Boston "outsider" to "insider," Kennedy still divided the worlds he inhabited between "us" and "them," Irish Catholics and everyone else. Though Protestants constituted the bulk of the "them" category, the Jews remained the quintessential "other" for him, as they did for most Catholics and Protestants alike. He had several close Jewish friends, Arthur Goldsmith and later in life Carroll Rosenbloom, the Baltimore businessman and future National Football League owner who lived in Palm Beach. As much as he enjoyed their company, he could never look past the fact that they were Jews. His letters to them were filled with joking references to their Jewishness. He meant no harm in this—and none was taken, but it was symptomatic of his worldview. The Jews were a different people with different values, talents, and objectives. Like Irish Catholics, they looked after their own, but with unparalleled intensity, dedication, and success. And that was what made them dangerous. He understood and sympathized with Jewish attempts to protect Jews in Nazi-occupied Europe, but he remained convinced that such loyalties had biased their judgment and made them unfit for government service.

All through the war, he had privately criticized Roosevelt for his reliance on Jewish advisers like Felix Frankfurter. Now, in 1945, after the world had learned of the death camps, he complained once again at what he still believed was the overrepresentation of Jews in high positions. As always, he disguised his criticism as concern.

In March 1945, he told his cousin Joe Kane that he had warned Arthur Krock, who happened to be Jewish, that he "couldn't think of anything worse for the Jewish people" than that so many of them had been appointed by Roosevelt to postwar planning positions. A month later, in April, he complained about Bernard Baruch, whose trip to Europe as the president's "special economic adviser," he claimed, "makes a perfect answer for the German charge that the Jews control the situation."[24]

His relief was almost palpable when Truman took office in mid-April 1945 and, as he had promised, dismissed Henry Morgenthau as treasury secretary, removed Samuel Rosenman from the White House, and sidelined Felix Frankfurter as presidential adviser. "The Jews are crying that they've lost their greatest friend and benefactor," Kennedy wrote Kick soon after Roosevelt's death. "It's again a clear indication of the serious mistake that the Jews had in spite of their marvelous organizing capacity. They made all their bets on one man rather than on some real social improvement. Then the man dies, and their hope for social improvement dies with him. . . . Fundamentally, what has happened in this country is that the people believe that the day of free spending and the power of certain groups to control the future life of this country are finished."[25]

Kennedy was temporarily invigorated by the accession of the new president and would not have been surprised, he told Kick, if Truman offered him a position. "If it's anything I can do, I'll probably take it on the basis that everybody should help if they can."

Still, he preferred sticking to his plan of retiring from public life in favor of his children. If Truman did get around to offering him a job, he was "seriously considering . . . whether I might not say to him that I'd like to help any way I can; but if he's going to give me a job, I'd rather have him give it to Jack and maybe make him the minister to some country or Assistant Secretary of State or Assistant Secretary of the Navy, or something of that sort. I haven't mentioned it to Jack yet, but I'm thinking it over."[26]

For a brief moment that spring, it was almost as if the old days had returned and his advice, friendship, and support were again valued in Washington. On May 15, he met with Herbert Hoover, who had heard that Truman wanted to see him but didn't think it appropriate for a Republican ex-president to request an appointment with the Democratic president. Kennedy agreed that the invitation should come from Truman and called a contact at the White House to suggest as much. When Truman subsequently invited Hoover to the White House, Kennedy took it as a sign that he was a Washington insider again. "My observation to Rose . . . was that it is a strange thing that a little fellow from East Boston, who had been out with the Administration for four or five years because of his war position, should be called upon to bring an Ex-President of the United States and the new President of the United States together for the first time."[27]

J oe Jr. was gone, Jack was an invalid, and Rosemary was still at Craig House, able to walk but unable to speak, write, or perform the simplest tasks, and in need of twenty-four-hour custodial care. Kick had decided that she was going to remain in England and was attempting now to build a life for herself. Her father wrote her long letters every week. There was little more he could do for his oldest children. But he had five others who were approaching adulthood and needed his guidance.

Bobby had enlisted in the navy and was in training in Lewiston, Maine. In January 1945, put off because he was nineteen and his father still wrote to him as if he were a child, he asked him to "write me a letter as you used to Joe & Jack about what you think about the different political events and the war as I'd like to understand what's going on better than I now do." Kennedy was only too happy to oblige. The main point of tension between father and son remained Bobby's burning desire to get into the war. Kennedy was able to delay that moment by convincing Bobby to go to officer candidate school, as his brothers had. "I should like to have him get as far along in his school as possible and then get him out as reasonably soon after the war as I can," Kennedy wrote Joe Kane on March 19, 1945. "I want Bobby to have a college education and then really get busy. With Joe gone and Jack still a long way from being well, there is plenty of slack for Bobby to take up."[28]

Ted, at thirteen years of age, was too young to even contemplate military service, but not too young, his father believed, to think seriously about his future. "When I was thirteen or fourteen years old, Dad called me into his room for a chat. I must have done something that prompted the conversation, but I don't remember what it was." He had expected some sort of reprimand. Instead, he got a gentle lecture on what it meant to be a Kennedy. "There are a lot of children in this family and they are all trying to do useful things. If you don't want to do important and useful things, that's your choice, but I don't have time to waste. If you want to do something important and useful, then I'll help you out." Ted left the room, ecstatic that instead of scolding him, his father had offered his assistance.[29]

He held his daughters to the same standard. At a time when most American parents, particularly those who were rich and Irish Catholic, pushed their daughters to find husbands, Kennedy encouraged and assisted his in finding work. Although the median age at which women married in the 1940s and 1950s was twenty, the three youngest Kennedy daughters would go into the workplace first, then marry later: Eunice at thirty-two, Pat at thirty, and Jean at twenty-eight.[30]

Eunice's first job, secured for her by her father, was at the State Department working with returning POWs in the Special War Problems Division. Her next job, which her father also got for her, was with the Justice Department. If she wasn't happy with it, he advised her, she should "have no hesitancy in dropping it. Don't stick it out just because you think you should. The important thing is to be happy with your job." When Eunice, as Bobby had, asked her father to send his thoughts on politics and the economic situation, he happily complied, answered her questions, and sent her a copy of a recent speech he had given in Boston.[31]

Because Patricia was particularly good with numbers, when she graduated, Kennedy found a place for her at the Bache firm on Wall Street. When she decided not to take it, he found her work with Father Patrick Peyton, "the Rosary Priest," who staged radio, television, and live theater performances to promote the praying of the family rosary.[32]

After Jean, the youngest of his daughters, confided to her father that she had no idea what she wanted to do when she graduated, he suggested that she start out in public relations and see if that kind of work suited her. She agreed and he found jobs at the Merchandise Mart, which he now owned, and a place for her and a friend to live in Chicago. After two years in public relations, Jean took a position with Father James Keller on his weekly television show, *The Christophers.*[33]

T hough Kennedy would continue his Cassandra-like pronouncements about postwar economic collapse, he and his family had little to fear. The bulk of their fortune was safely invested in trusts for Rose, the children, and the children's children. Rosemary's trust was handled separately from the others, and on his death, Joe Jr.'s had been divided among the other children. To provide for maximum growth, the children were not permitted to withdraw anything from the 1936 trusts until the boys reached thirty-one and the girls forty-one, at which time they would be permitted to spend the annual earned income only, the corpus being reserved for their children. The 1926 trusts allowed earlier withdrawals, at age twenty-five. What this meant was that by 1946, very little had been taken out of the accounts, allowing the principal to grow unimpeded. By the end of 1946, the sum total in the trusts was about $8 million, equivalent to almost $90 million today.[34]

Kennedy left nothing to chance. Because he had little or no expectation of strong economic growth in the immediate future, he reinvested his profits in what he believed to be the safest haven for his capital, commercial real estate, and chose as his primary broker John J. Reynolds, who bought and sold properties for Archbishop Spellman and the New York Archdiocese. With the city's premier broker working for him, connections to the Catholic Church (one of the city's largest real estate owners), cash reserves for down payments, easy access to large mortgages at low rates, and an almost uncanny ability to do the numbers and spot undervalued properties, Kennedy ended up defying his own expectations and making at least as much money from real estate as he had from trading stocks.

It was a very good time to buy prime urban real estate. For fifteen years, since the stock market crash of 1929, there had been little new construction. With increased war spending and inadequate and aging residential and commercial space, rental prices had soared.

Kennedy real estate deals were all big ones. From 1943 on, he purchased dozens of high-priced, prime real estate parcels in midtown Manhattan, several on Lexington Avenue between Forty-sixth Street and Fifty-ninth Street, the entire block front between Eighty-second and Eighty-third on the west side of Broadway, the Siegel-Cooper building between Eighteenth and Nineteenth on Sixth Avenue, and the old Fahnestock mansion at Madison Avenue and Fifty-first. He bought these properties not as income-producing investments, but with the intent to turn them over quickly. He sold the Siegel-Cooper building after a year to J. C. Penney for a healthy profit. He sold the Fahnestock mansion to Random House less than ten months after he had purchased it, again at a sizable profit. Had he held on to these properties longer, he would have made even more money. But that was not his style. Better to get out with a healthy profit than to hold on and risk a loss.[35]

The real estate market had become so lucrative—with rents rising so high and so fast during the war years—that both the federal Office of Price Administration and the New York State Legislature debated instituting rent controls. On September 28, 1944, at a hearing on rent controls held by the general welfare committee of the city council, Kennedy was "cited as a rent gouger" for raising rents in the Siegel-Cooper building when he purchased it. A week later, at a second public hearing, this one held by a joint state legislative committee investigating commercial rent increases, John J. Reynolds, representing Kennedy, struck back. "After Mr. Kennedy's name had been mentioned several times," the *New York Times* reported on October 4, "Mr. Reynolds retorted: 'Why spread the name of Mr. Kennedy all over the case? Mr. Kennedy didn't buy the property, and he never saw it. It was bought by John J. Ford of Boston, in trust for the children of Joseph P. Kennedy, and I operate it for him.'" Reynolds's defense of Kennedy was ludicrous. No matter whose name the trusts were in, he retained full control over them—and the properties they owned.[36]

The outcry against rent gouging was such that the New York State government passed commercial rent control laws for New York City that were signed into law and approved by the courts in early 1945. By the time they went into effect, Kennedy had diversified his real estate portfolio beyond the reach of the new legislation. By mid-1945, he had purchased a thirteen-story office building in Albany, a large commercial plot on Boston Post Road in Pelham Manor, and the crown jewel in the Kennedy real estate empire, the Merchandise Mart in Chicago.

The Mart, a gigantic building with ninety-three acres of rentable space, had been built fifteen years earlier by Marshall Field. In 1945, Field, with excess profits tax liabilities he could not afford to pay, decided to sell the building at a loss, therefore reducing his excess profits and his taxes. Kennedy negotiated a price of $13.2 million on the property, which had cost $30 million to build and been valued on Field's recent financial statement at $31 million. There was one catch. Before Field finalized the deal, Kennedy had to assure him that rumors that Congress might repeal the excess profits tax were false and that it indeed made sense for him to take a tax loss on the Merchandise Mart sale. Kennedy got such assurances—which he immediately relayed to Field—from John W. McCormack, the House majority leader, who had checked with his colleagues on the Ways and Means Committee and received confirmation that the excess profits tax would remain in effect for 1945.[37]

Kennedy secured a mortgage of $12.5 million on the property, which meant the Merchandise Mart cost him a little less than $1 million in cash. To protect himself from huge tax bills, he then asked for and received IRS approval to vest ownership of the Mart in the family trusts.

On a Saturday in mid-November 1945, Kennedy flew to Chicago to sign the final sales documents and take control of his new building, the largest in the country, save the Pentagon. At nine the next morning, a Sunday, he met with his new CEO, Wally Ollman, and looked over his purchase in person for the first time. "In pungent phraseology," Ollman recalled, Kennedy "recounted that he had never been identified with a loser and did not intend to blemish that record in the operation of The Mart. Those desiring to work with him . . . were welcome to stay and those finding the task too difficult or demanding were invited to leave as all employees were informed on the following day in his first organization meeting."[38]

This would be the first of many meetings between the two. They would begin with each man standing, then, according to Merchandise Mart insiders, go into their dance. Kennedy would sit down on the couch; Ollman, a large, imposing man, would perch on a chair and look down at his boss. Kennedy would then move to higher ground, on the arm of the couch, from where he would be the one looking down. Eventually, neither man willing to concede anything, they would rise to their feet and continue their meeting.[39]

At the time Kennedy purchased the Mart, 40 percent of the space was rented by government agencies that paid submarket prices for their leases. Ollman wanted to replace these tenants with corporations that would pay full market price, but he knew he would be taking a considerable risk, politically and fiscally, if he did so. Kennedy listened carefully to his presentation, then told him to go ahead. To make the property more attractive, Ollman suggested putting in air-conditioning, still comparatively rare in office buildings, at a cost of over $5 million. Kennedy agreed that air-conditioning was needed, then came up with a plan for raising the capital required by levying additional charges on Mart leases. The tenants agreed—and the Merchandise Mart became "the first and . . . still [as late as 1965] the largest property to supply this much-needed facility."[40]

From the outside, Kennedy appeared to be the same man. He did not talk about his losses: one son dead, another nearly an invalid; one daughter nearly destroyed by a botched lobotomy, the other a childless widow at twenty-five. He could still light up any room he entered, dominate the conversation no matter who was in that room. Though now retired from private business and public service, he dressed immaculately in bespoke dark suits up north, white ones in Palm Beach, but never brown (which he abhorred). His white tailored shirts from Sulka were always crisply laundered; his ties were still those of the conservative Boston banker; his black shoes were always polished to a perfect shine. His cook, Mathilda Heddal, on seeing him for the first time in 1940 when he was fifty-two, had remarked that "he was handsomest man I had ever seen." And he was still, at fifty-seven, a strikingly handsome man. His sandy brown hair was graying and thinning, brushed back now, not a strand out of place. His posture was military perfect. He wore spectacles, but only occasionally. With or without them, his eyes still shone the same piercing blue; his smile, when he chose to flash it, was as broad as ever.[41]

But inside, he had been changed forever by the death of his firstborn son.

Thirty-one

THE CANDIDATE'S
FATHER

Every man in this room, because of the position he occupies, owes something to our state." It was April 17, 1945, a week after Roosevelt's death. Joseph P. Kennedy, on the invitation of Massachusetts governor Maurice Tobin, was lecturing Boston's business and political leaders on what they had to do to rebuild their city and state economy.

He had come home because there was nowhere else that he felt as comfortable, as beloved and respected. He had come home because nowhere else did he enjoy the same degree of political power. And he had come home to establish a power base for his son Jack, should he decide to enter politics. Two days earlier, he had marked his return with an almost ritual offering of $10,000 to the Guild of Saint Apollonia, the organization of Catholic dentists he had given money to when Jack recovered from scarlet fever twenty-five years earlier.

"Your future is in your hands," he exhorted the businessmen in the main ballroom of the Copley Plaza. History, he warned them, was "not made by inaction, indifference and timidity." Thousands of young men and women were about to return to New England, and they required jobs, good jobs consonant with their training and ambition. "If they do not find an opportunity to apply their skills here at home they will go elsewhere. . . . It is not a pleasant thing for a young man born and reared and educated in Boston to have to pull up his stakes and seek opportunities elsewhere. I know, for I had to do it."[1]

Less than two weeks after his homecoming speech, Kennedy was invited by Governor Tobin to become chairman of a special commission to determine whether the state should establish a department of commerce.

As he toured the state that summer, giving speeches, granting interviews, and meeting with local bankers and businessmen, he attacked the "proper Bostonian" bankers and businessmen who refused to invest in the state's future. His blunt talk disturbed some but charmed the newspapermen who followed him from town to town. He made for good copy wherever he was.

"I'm willing to come back to live because this is where my heart is. But I don't expect to come back to stay until I think there has been a change for the better. For the past 25 years Massachusetts has consistently been losing business—in that time 2,300 industries have left the state. . . . We haven't done a blessed thing to find out why they are leaving or to keep them here. During the next five years Massachusetts will have its last chance to keep itself out of the grave." When he was asked why, if he was so concerned about his home city and state, he had spent millions of dollars buying the Chicago Merchandise Mart, he "shot back, 'Because the condition of real estate is scandalous [in Massachusetts] and that of politics is worse.'"[2]

"Joseph Patrick Kennedy, now 57 and with red hair graying, came out of self-imposed political exile last week and went back to work for his native state of Massachusetts," reported *Time* magazine on September 24, 1945. "Last week Joe Kennedy seemed to have his old zest again. In a midnight blue Chrysler, he rode like a Paul Revere through the textile, shoe and machinery-producing towns in Middlesex, Essex, and Berkshire counties. All the way from Greenfield to Salem, in some 30 speeches within ten days, he spread the alarm."

Giving speeches, granting interviews, and grabbing headlines distracted him from his grief and relieved him of his boredom. It also gave him the opportunity to raise high again the Kennedy banner and extend it across the state, preparing the way for his son Jack, should he ever fully recover his health, to run for elective office.

In a game of political musical chairs that would have been inconceivable anywhere else, Boston's politicians were changing places. James Michael Curley, after losing elections for mayor to Maurice Tobin in 1937 and 1941, had in 1942 run for and been elected to Congress. In November 1944, when Tobin ran for and was elected governor, replacing Leverett Saltonstall, who had run for and been elected to the Senate, Congressman Curley announced that he would be returning to Boston to run for Tobin's seat the following year. (John Kerrigan, Boston City Council president, would preside as acting mayor in the interim.)

In declaring his candidacy, Curley made no mention of either his federal indictment for fraud or the six-year-old court order to pay back $37,000 plus interest he had "improperly received" from a city contractor. Six weeks later, on December 26, 1944, he announced that he had paid off all his debts. The funds, it has been whispered from that day to this had to have come from Joseph P. Kennedy, who had a very good reason to smooth Curley's return to Boston. Should Curley be elected mayor in 1945, he would have to vacate the congressional seat in the eleventh district, once held by Honey Fitz.

If ever a district was made for a Kennedy candidacy, it was this one: the eleventh district included Cambridge, where Jack had gone to school; East Boston, the Kennedys' ancestral home; the North End, the Fitzgerald bailiwick; and predominantly Irish wards in Brighton, Somerville, and Charlestown.

Before Jack could even consider running for office, however, he had to get his health back. "Jack told me . . . something about his plans" to spend the winter recuperating at a resort in Arizona, John Burns wrote Kennedy in Palm Beach on December 29, 1944. "I think he is very wise in taking a Boston residence now and when he returns from the West he ought to be off to a flying start for whatever objective he should determine upon. . . . He certainly has real stuff."[3]

By that spring, after several months in Arizona, Jack was feeling well enough to relocate to San Francisco, where with the help of his father he was hired by Hearst's *Chicago Herald-American* to cover the founding conference of the United Nations. That June, he relocated across the Atlantic to report on postwar British elections and Ireland, again for the Hearst papers.

Though Jack was good at his job—his articles were informative, nicely crafted, and rather persuasive—no one believed that he had any real desire to become a full-time journalist. Reporting for the Hearst papers was a temporary diversion, one that allowed him to improve his writing skills, add to his already extensive knowledge of European affairs, and visit his sister Kick in England. His father, hoping to find a temporary resting place for his decorated war hero son in the Department of the Navy, arranged for James Forrestal (whom Truman had retained as secretary of the navy) to meet with Jack in Paris during the secretary's post-surrender tour of the continent. Jack traveled with Forrestal to Berlin for the Potsdam Conference, continued on to Bremen, and then flew back on the secretary's plane to Washington following an emergency stopover in London, where he was hospitalized with severe abdominal pains, nausea, and fever—debilitating and frightening symptoms that, as in past episodes, vanished undiagnosed.[4]

Secretary Forrestal was sufficiently impressed with young Kennedy to invite him to visit Washington in mid-September to "see what there is in hand." Jack did not follow up on the offer. Other options, more attractive than sitting at a desk at the Navy Department, had presented themselves.[5]

"Jack arrived home," Kennedy wrote Sir James Calder on August 22, 1945, "and is very thin but he is becoming quite active in the political life in Massachusetts. It wouldn't surprise me to see him go into public life to take Joe's place."[6]

In 1945, when he made the decision to run for Curley's seat in Congress should Curley be elected mayor, John Fitzgerald Kennedy was twenty-eight and old enough to represent the eleventh district in Congress, though he looked five to ten years younger. He was frighteningly frail-looking and skeletally thin. No matter how well tailored his suit jacket and shirt collar, he looked like a child in his father's clothes. He had never lived in the eleventh district—or, for that matter, anywhere else in Boston. (Brookline was outside the city lines.) And he had no political experience of any sort; he had never been to a precinct meeting or a ward hall, never stumped for a candidate or rung a doorbell, never shaken a stranger's hand and asked for a vote.

That fall, Jack Kennedy moved into a two-room suite at Boston's Bellevue Hotel, where his grandfather lived. Honey Fitz, though white-haired and stouter, was the same garrulous firebrand at eighty that he had been at twenty-eight when he was elected to the Boston Common Council. He intended to act as his grandson's chief adviser and counselor, to give speeches for him. His excitement was such that he had to be restrained from taking over the campaign.

Election day was more than a year away, but there was an enormous amount of work to be done for a candidate who was unknown in the district and unschooled in politics. Father and son put together a campaign team, with advice from Honey Fitz; cousin Joe Kane, a skilled local political operative who had always thought Jack Kennedy a golden boy and candidate; "the Commish," Joe Timilty, former police commissioner and now Kennedy retainer, errand boy, and golf partner; and Eddie Moore, who had retired briefly after London but was now called back into Kennedy service. John Dowd, who ran the agency that handled the Somerset advertising, was brought in to do the initial public relations and advertising work. Billy Sutton and Patsy Mulkern, whom Honey Fitz knew and trusted, and a few other young streetwise politicos such as Dave Powers were put on the payroll. Jack, who understood the need to surround himself with men whose first loyalty was to him, not his father or grandfather, recruited his old friends Lem Billings, Torb Macdonald from Harvard, and Paul ("Red") Fay, whom he had met in the South Pacific.

John Fitzgerald Kennedy had many assets as a candidate, but none more valuable than his record as a war hero. No one knew if, how, or for whom the returning veterans were going to vote in 1946, but it was expected that they would go to the polls in large numbers.

In New York, where the Democrats hoped to defeat Thomas Dewey for governor, they had organized a special "Democratic Veterans Association" to get as large a share as possible of the one-million veteran vote. In California, in the twelfth congressional district, Republican Party leaders recruited navy veteran Richard M. Nixon to run against incumbent Jerry Voorhis. In Wisconsin, ex-marine Joseph McCarthy challenged Bob La Follette, Jr., for the Republican senatorial primary. In Florida, another ex-marine, George Smathers, ran for a House seat against another long-term, fully entrenched incumbent. Nixon, McCarthy, and Smathers would all win their elections. Overall, some forty veterans would be elected to the House and eight more to the Senate in November 1946.[7]

Jack Kennedy introduced himself to the district as a veteran returning to help guide the nation he had fought for. He did not run from his family history but refocused it to concentrate on his and his brother's service and heroism. In December 1945, he organized a new Veterans of Foreign Wars post named for his brother. He loaded his staff with veterans, referred to his mother as a "Gold Star Mother" (one who had lost a son in the war), and sought invitations to speak at every American Legion hall and VFW post in the district.[8]

His first major speech was to an American Legion post in Boston on September 10. His father arranged to have it broadcast on the radio. He would spend the next year on the campaign trail. He shook thousands of hands and spoke to hundreds of gatherings, formal and informal, of veterans associations, church groups, charitable organizations, fraternal orders, and social clubs, at firehouses, in front of post offices, at factories and shops, and at teas, receptions, and house parties in every part of his district.

Most every evening, after the day's events were finished, he called his father or visited him at the Ritz-Carlton when he was in town. "Many a night when he'd come over to see Daddy after a speech," Eunice Kennedy Shriver recounted to Doris Kearns Goodwin, "he'd be feeling rather down, admitting that the speech hadn't really gone very well or believing that his delivery had put people in the front row fast asleep. 'What do you mean?' Father would immediately ask. 'Why, I talked to Mr. X and Mrs. Y on the phone right after they got home and they told me they were sitting right in the front row and that it was a fine speech.' . . . Father would go on to elicit from Jack what he thought he could change to make it better the next time. I can still see the two of them sitting together, analyzing the entire speech and talking about the pace of delivery to see where it had worked and where it had gone wrong."[9]

His father's enthusiasm was contagious, as was that of grandfather Honey Fitz, cousin Joe Kane, and the young men who accompanied Jack on his speaking engagements and campaign stops. It didn't take long for them to recognize, and for Jack to realize, that strange as it might have seemed, he had a talent for campaigning—and the stamina to keep at it all day and night long. He learned to control his voice, which was a bit high-pitched, and to slow down his rapid-fire, staccato diction; to make eye contact with his audiences; to blend enthusiasm with earnestness; to be (or at least appear to be) at ease with strangers; and to harness his irrepressible charm to win friends and disarm potential enemies.

Boston's voters were worried, as were voters across the country in 1945 and 1946, about shortages of housing and jobs and the specter of a returning depression. Jack's message was much like his father's. He was in favor of government funding for economic development, jobs creation, and a strong military. Where he differed from his father was in his emphasis on the bread-and-butter concerns of his mostly working-class constituency: affordable housing (which his father ignored), the continuation of price controls (his father wasn't sure), and a national health care system (about which his father had nothing to say).

In November 1945, James Michael Curley was elected mayor. Jack Kennedy accelerated his campaigning, though he held off formally declaring for Curley's seat.

In early December, Kennedy flew south to Palm Beach for the winter. Jack had decided it was time to promote his own people to positions of authority in the campaign, but only those his father approved of. He asked navy veteran Mark Dalton, who had gone to Boston College and then Harvard Law School, to serve as campaign manager. All that winter, Joseph Kennedy and Dalton would confer by telephone. "He would talk at great length and wanted to know about every facet of the campaign," Dalton recalled in an oral history. "As a matter of fact that was one of my problems. He'd keep you on the phone for an hour and a half, two hours." Kennedy kept in touch as well with the old pols he had attached to his son's campaign. In early February, he dropped a quick line to Joe Kane to report that although he knew Jack was "working like a beaver," he had heard "from some other people up there that they think he should visit more Jewish organizations. Perhaps you should speak to him about that."[10]

By now, there were half a dozen declared and almost declared contenders for Curley's seat, including the mayor of Cambridge, candidates with roots and organizations in Somerville, Charlestown, Brighton, and the North End, and a man named Joe Russo, whose major appeal was the fact that he was the only Italian in the campaign—or at least he was until another Joe Russo declared his candidacy. Mark Dalton, who was mystified by the appearance of the second Joe Russo, was convinced that Joe Kennedy and his money had persuaded him to run for office.[11]

Jack Kennedy didn't expect to sweep any of the wards in his district, but he hoped to come in at least second in each of them, perhaps first in East Boston. He established campaign offices in central Boston at the Bellevue Hotel, where he lived, and in Cambridge, Charlestown, East Boston, Somerville, and Brighton. This cost money. So did plastering the district with billboards and campaign literature, organizing bell-ringing, door-to-door operations, buying radio advertising, mailing copies of John Hersey's PT 109 article to voters, and organizing the dozens of volunteers who had flocked to the campaign. Fortunately, money was never a problem in any Kennedy campaign. From Palm Beach, Kennedy made sure the funds flowed freely through trusted lieutenants such as Eddie Moore, who served as unofficial campaign cashier.

Through February and March, while Jack built his organization with an eye on Curley's congressional seat, another possibility surfaced. Governor Maurice Tobin was up for reelection in 1946 and required a fresh face with lots of money, preferably a veteran, to run on his ticket as lieutenant governor. Kennedy, worried now that his son might be too young and inexperienced to prevail in a wide-open primary, was attracted to the idea of his running with Tobin and gaining the seasoning he needed for a later run for senator or governor. Honey Fitz was bitterly opposed to the idea, as was Jack. Kennedy was eventually won over to their side after commissioning a poll that showed that Jack had a much greater chance of being elected congressman in a safe district than lieutenant governor in a state that was leaning Republican.

Almost fifteen hundred miles from Boston, Kennedy tried to stay quiet that winter and spring so as not to steal any thunder from or embarrass his candidate son up north. But, having made the round-trip from outsider to Washington insider and back to outsider, he craved the attention he had once enjoyed.

Congress was in the midst of debating whether to approve the $3.75 billion 2 percent loan to Great Britain that Truman had proposed in December. Kennedy, as former ambassador, had expected to be called upon to give his opinion on the loan, but had received no invitation to do so. Intent on inserting himself into the debate, nonetheless, he drafted a statement that he sent to Krock at the *New York Times* Washington bureau. "This is approximately what I think about the loan. It needs punch and polish. Will you look it over, shape it up, and then send me what you think will do the most good for us?"

Krock edited the statement and gave it to John H. Crider, one of the reporters who worked under him in Washington. A few days later, on March 4, Crider published a front-page story headlined KENNEDY BACKS AID TO BRITAIN AS GIFT: FORMER AMBASSADOR CALLS IT IN OUR SELF-INTEREST AND A BAR TO COMMUNISM. Kennedy's statement on the loan, edited by Krock, was inserted in the article. "The United Kingdom fought from 1939 to 1942 to save its own skin," not to protect Western civilization or the United States. "So we owe the British nothing on that basis. . . . However, the British are in a bad economic situation, and they are a fine people. Also, it is to our interest to help them now to maintain the balance of world trade and world salvation lest otherwise they be driven into the arms of communism. But in so doing let us not practice deceit on the American people." Kennedy favored giving the British the funds they required to stabilize their economy, but as a gift rather than a loan. Great Britain and the European nation had not paid back their old World War I debts and were certainly not going to pay back any new ones.[12]

Although it was doubtful that his position in favor of a multibillion-dollar gift to the British was going to help Jack with Irish voters in the eleventh district, he was sure, he wrote Joe Kane in Boston, that "with the exception of a few Coughlinites . . . the statement won't hurt Jack in that district, and it certainly will help him with the Canadians and English in the state at some later time." He then added, preparing Kane for another potential problem, that "this next issue of LIFE will have my big article on foreign policy. It can't possibly hurt him, and I think you will like it very much."[13]

There was too much going on in the world for Kennedy to remain in political exile forever. "Over the space of about five weeks in February and early March," historians Craig Campbell and Fredrik Logevall would later write, "the political climate in Washington shifted dramatically toward the view . . . that the United States must confront the Soviet Union decisively as a serious enemy." On his nationally broadcast radio program, Drew Pearson frightened listeners with the tale of an extensive Soviet atomic espionage network working out of Canada. Days later, Stalin gave a speech, more bellicose in tone than in substance, that affirmed the essential differences between communism and capitalism and predicted that only one would survive.[14]

"Well, last night on the radio," Kennedy wrote Ralph Cropley at the Maritime Commission, on February 25, "I heard Pearson and Winchell both talk about incidents which mean World War No. III—and at once! Pearson prophesies that the Russians and the Turks will be fighting within three months. Winchell just sees a third World War right handy. As I look back to my speeches of five years ago, I can't help but feel that I predicted chaos for the world, and if this isn't it, I never saw chaos. . . . The Washington situation leaves me completely cold. All in all things don't look very good."[15]

For a second time in less than a decade, the United States, Kennedy worried, instead of retreating to its fortress America, building up its domestic economy, and constructing an impregnable military defense, was on the brink of launching a wasteful, quixotic, and potentially deadly quest "to establish liberal democracy throughout the world." Determined to push back against the developing consensus that the Soviet Union was the enemy of the United States, and so fixated on world conquest that negotiations with it were not possible, Kennedy decided to offer his own policy recommendations in *Life* magazine.

The magazine accepted his article, cut it down in size, and published it on March 18. It also took the precaution, lest readers find Kennedy's dismissive views on the Soviet threat too persuasive, of prefacing his article with a caustically dismissive front-of-the-book editorial. Kennedy, the *Life* editors declared, just didn't understand the Communist threat. "In Mr. Kennedy's political geography, the U.S. and Russia appear to be just a couple of nation-states trying to come to terms." But

Russia was not "just a nation-state," it was the epicenter of an international Communist conspiracy that intended to spread its poison across the globe.[16]

Kennedy's piece was fiercely out of touch with the saber-rattling, anti-Soviet speeches that had followed Pearson's spy story and Stalin's speech. On February 27, Republican senator Arthur Vandenberg, the former isolationist and now fierce anti-Soviet ideologue, had risen in the Senate to ask rhetorically, "What is Russia up to now?" The implied answer was world conquest. Secretary of State James Byrnes, pushed by Truman, declared only days later that the United States would not "stand aloof if force or the threat of force is used contrary to the purposes of the" United Nations Charter. On March 5, Winston Churchill, speaking with the president at his side, raised the rhetoric by declaring that an "iron curtain" had already descended across Europe.

Kennedy did not mention any of these speakers directly, but he countered them all by arguing that "the nationalistic policy of Russia . . . is much the same as that of any other nation: to maintain its territorial integrity and security and to advance its political, economic and social well-being." Instead of attempting to reach a sustainable modus vivendi with the Soviets and withdrawing forces and funds from Europe, the administration appeared committed to meddling in the affairs of other nations and trying to force the rest of the world to "establish liberal democracy." This was the path to a third world war. To safeguard peace abroad and reestablish prosperity at home, it was imperative, Kennedy argued, that the United States stop "minding other people's business": in Greece, Palestine, the Balkans, India, Spain, Asia, everywhere outside the western hemisphere.

Kennedy's article, poorly written and organized, numbingly dull, and buried in the back of a magazine known more for its photos than its text, received little attention. Arthur Krock tried to remedy this by sending the unedited version to publisher Alfred Knopf with the suggestion that it be expanded into a full-length book. Knopf's reader, Columbia professor Louis Hacker, a former student of Charles Beard's who had traveled from Marxism in the 1930s to conservatism in the 1950s, recommended it be rejected. He suggested instead that Kennedy write a two-part book on domestic and foreign policy. Kennedy toyed with the idea, then dismissed it. He realized, as Hacker had, that he'd said all he had to say in the *Life* article.[17]

In early April, Kennedy moved back to Boston, where he would remain through primary day, commuting back and forth on the weekends to Hyannis Port. Jack had officially declared his candidacy for the Curley seat in late April and was campaigning sixteen or more hours a day. He was joined in Boston by his mother, his sisters Eunice, Patricia, and Jean, Bobby in his sailor's uniform, and Ted, who though just fourteen was big enough to run errands for the campaign.

Kennedy remained offstage. Except for a brief visit to introduce himself to the campaign workers and volunteers, he stayed away from headquarters and neighborhood storefronts, didn't attend any "teas" or house parties or receptions, granted no interviews, gave no speeches, never even appeared in the same room or at the same rally or political forum with his son. When asked in May if he would address the Lincoln Public School in Lincoln, Massachusetts, he replied that he could not. "Unfortunately, my son is running for Congress in Boston, and because of that I am not making any speeches in Massachusetts, at least not for the summer. I think one Kennedy in the public eye is enough."[18]

Kennedy kept his distance not simply because he was afraid he had too many enemies, but because Jack's greatest handicaps were his age, his inexperience, and his tourist status in the district. Should he ever be seen as a daddy's boy, a puppet whose strings were pulled by his father, his credibility as a new voice for a new generation would be destroyed. "Your father," Rose wrote Kick in London on June 6, "has kept out of it and is only doing a little work behind the scenes so whatever success there is will be due entirely to Jack and the younger group."[19]

Still, as John Droney, a navy veteran and attorney who ran the Cambridge office, recalled, "Even though he stayed out of it, he wasn't out of it. He was very much in it. Anytime I ever had a problem, I'd call him and he'd help us." Mark Dalton remained the "official" campaign manager, but as he too would later admit, "The campaigns were run by

Joseph P. Kennedy. . . . There never indeed was any campaign manager except Joseph P. Kennedy."[20]

From his suite at the Ritz-Carlton or from Hyannis Port, Kennedy watched over everything, consulted with the young men Jack had hired and the old pols he himself had enlisted, made suggestions on the content of billboards, advertisements, radio spots, and the candidate's speeches, and set strategy with Jack and his senior advisers. He had learned how to spend money and sell a "star" in Hollywood and applied that knowledge in the Roosevelt campaigns in 1932 and 1936 and to promoting himself at the SEC and the Maritime Commission and in London. Now he focused those skills on branding his son as the fresh-faced, charming young war hero, with a bit of glamour and a whole-some down-to-earth quality; a Harvard man and a man of the people; a book-writing intellectual who was everyone's friend.

Primary day was held early that year, in June rather than September, so there would be ample time to get the general election ballots printed and distributed to servicemen overseas. On Tuesday, June 18, 1946, Jack voted with his grandfather and grandmother, then toured the wards to thank his workers. That night, he escaped to see the Marx Brothers in *A Night in Casablanca*. He returned to his headquarters at the Bellevue, where he was joined by his father, Eunice, Bobby, and Jean to listen to the returns. He won five of the eleven wards in the district, polled 42 percent of the vote, and beat his nearest challenger, the mayor of Cambridge, by almost two to one. His opponents had tried hard to label him as an interloper, a rich idler, the spoiled son of a Palm Beach millionaire, but what voters saw instead was a thin, well-mannered, charming, humble, and very handsome young man who had risked his life to serve his country. It didn't hurt that he was able to outspend his opponents by a large margin or that he had started earlier and campaigned harder than any of them.

"How terrifically pleased I am for you. Everyone says you were so good in the Election and that the outcome must have been a great source of satisfaction," Kick wrote from England. "It's nice to know you are as appreciated in the 11th district as you are among your brothers & sisters. Gee, aren't you lucky."[21]

Jack took a few days off in Hyannis Port, then flew to Hollywood to enjoy a last fling. "I saw in Jack Lait's column," Kennedy wrote Houghton on July 30, 1946, "that my congressman son was paying attention to Peggy Cummins [the glamorous British actress] and another columnist had him seeing Inga Arvard, Hitler's Nordic. Well, I suppose youth must be served! We haven't heard anything from him. Do you know when he is coming back?"[22]

Jack returned to Boston to give a few speeches before the general election. In mid-August, he presented Archbishop of Boston Richard Cushing, a family friend, with a $600,000 check to build a convalescent home and hospital for poor children in Brighton, which just happened to be in the eleventh district in which he was running for Congress. The funds came from the newly organized Joseph P. Kennedy, Jr. Foundation, of which John F. Kennedy was the first president. The day after the ceremonies, photographs of the candidate handing the check to Bishop Cushing, with his mother, the daughter of a former mayor, at his side, appeared in all the Boston papers.

The publicity given the grant led to several requests for funding addressed to John F. Kennedy in Boston. His form letter responses thanked the writers for their letters and explained that there were no funds available as "the work that the foundation is planning to do has already been mapped out for the next three years." A "Kennedy for Congress" flyer was stuffed into every envelope.[23]

In November, to no one's surprise, John Fitzgerald Kennedy was elected to Congress. What was startling was the size of his victory. He polled 69,093 votes to his Republican opponent's 26,007. Statewide, the Democrats took a beating. Senator Walsh was defeated in a landslide victory by Henry Cabot Lodge, Jr. Governor Maurice Tobin and his running mate for lieutenant governor, Paul Dever, were beaten almost as badly.

With John Fitzgerald Kennedy now elected to a seat it would be nearly impossible for him to lose, his father could speak out with impunity. And he did.

I n the year that had passed since Kennedy's *Life* magazine article, the national debate over what would soon be known as the Cold War had intensified. Isolationist Republicans on the right, led by Senators Robert

A. Taft and John Bricker of Ohio, and internationalists on the left, led by Secretary of Commerce Henry Wallace, argued, as Kennedy had, against government spending abroad to counter the so-called Communist threat. Within the White House, the debate was nearly over. A near consensus had been built around the "Long Telegram" written by George F. Kennan, counselor at the American embassy in Moscow. Kennan, asked to make sense of Stalin's rhetoric and actions, had argued persuasively that Russia's historic suspicion of the West and the Soviet Union's ideological commitment to expansion and conquest posed a threat, though a containable one, to American interests in Europe. It was incumbent on the American government to "contain" that threat by the careful but persistent application of counterforce.

On March 12, 1947, President Truman went before a joint session of Congress to declare that, the British government having concluded it could no longer provide Greece and Turkey with political, economic, or military assistance to contain Soviet aggression, the American government had to step into the breach. "The very existence of the Greek state," the president announced in his request for $400 million in aid, "is today threatened by the terrorist activities of several thousand armed men, led by Communists. . . . It must be the policy of the United States to support free peoples who are resisting attempted subjugation by armed minorities or by outside pressures. . . . The free peoples of the world look to us for support in maintaining their freedoms."[24]

Kennedy was unalterably opposed to supplying military or financial assistance to Greece or Turkey. Instead of ratcheting up anti-Communist rhetoric and actions, he believed it advisable to try to negotiate with the Soviets. Anything was better than heightening tensions and pushing the world a step closer to another war.

In the late 1930s, the United States had, he had argued, no business going to war with Germany or assisting the British and the French in doing so, for the simple reason that Hitler posed no threat to American interests. The same was now true, a decade later, of the Soviet Union. Kennedy's "consuming public concern" in the postwar period was, as Arthur Schlesinger, Jr., would later write in his biography of Robert Kennedy, "as it had been before the war: that the United States might be deluded into mounting a world crusade for democracy. He was perfectly consistent. He saw communism in the forties as he had seen Nazism in the thirties—as a detestable system but not as a mortal threat to American security."[25]

Kennedy's chief concern in the spring of 1947 was that he had no way of making his voice heard, no means of countering what was becoming a groundswell of bipartisan support for Truman's foreign policy initiatives. Arthur Krock, who visited him in Palm Beach that spring, came to his rescue. Either because Krock was on retainer or believed Kennedy's views still newsworthy or because, as a Jew who had been passed over for promotion, he sympathized with Kennedy's struggle to cross over from outsider to insider, he made sure that his patron's ideas got maximum coverage.

At Kennedy's "instance," Krock recalled in his *Memoirs,* the two "designed [an interview] for publication." On March 12, 1947, the day of Truman's speech to Congress calling for assistance to Greece and Turkey, Krock published his "interview" with Kennedy. He disguised the genesis of the column by claiming that while in Palm Beach on vacation, he had happened upon "an informal round table the other evening, the subject being our future economic foreign policy," at which "the most emphatic view offered was that of Joseph P. Kennedy." Ambassador Kennedy, he reported, was opposed to spending large sums of money overseas when the American economy was still in the doldrums. Given the task of reconverting the economy from wartime to peacetime and the need to keep taxes low to encourage investment, the United States could not "possibly finance resistance to other systems of government, to the extent and for the period proposed or required, without impoverishing this nation. . . . The wise policy is to keep the American way of life as strong as our resources can make it, and permit communism to have its trial outside the Soviet Union if that shall be the fate or will of certain peoples. In most of these countries a few years will demonstrate the inability of communism to achieve its promises." The United States should, in other words, back off and "permit communism to have its trial."[26]

Krock's column thrust Kennedy into the center of the national debate. His recommendations were immediately and universally condemned in editorial pages across the country as "the new appeasement." Ten days later, James Reston of the *New York Times* declared that while a small coalition of the Far Right and the Far Left was assembling to oppose financial assistance to Turkey and/or Greece, no one was "prepared to take the responsibility involved in adopting publicly the Joseph P. Kennedy thesis that we should take our chances with the spread of communism." The only positive responses to Kennedy's remarks were editorials in the Hearst papers and a letter to the editor of the *New York Times* from pacifist A. J. Muste of the Fellowship of Reconciliation.[27]

On April 22, the Senate took up and approved Truman's proposal for assistance to Greece and Turkey by a vote of almost three to one, with Republican senators Arthur Vandenberg and Henry Cabot Lodge, Jr., of Massachusetts not only enthusiastically supporting the measure, but gathering a large number of their party's votes in support of it. On May 8, the House followed with an overwhelming bipartisan endorsement of the president, approving his bill by a vote of 287 in favor, only 107 opposed. Recorded in favor of the bill was the young congressman from the eleventh district of Massachusetts, John F. Kennedy.

Joseph P. Kennedy had raised his boys to argue with him—and this was the result. It didn't make him particularly happy, but he accepted that there was nothing he could do about it. Supreme Court justice William O. Douglas, whom Kennedy had hired at the SEC, stayed close with, and promoted several times for national office, remembered a visit to Palm Beach in 1949. "I must be nuts," Kennedy said to him. "The two men in public life that I love the most are Jack and you. And I disagree with you guys more than anyone else. What's wrong with me?"[28]

Years before, his son Jack had warned Kennedy to temper his language, to stay away from labels like "isolationist" and "appeaser." And he had done so, for a time. Now, in 1947, with all hope gone of his returning to Washington—and with his son elected to a safe seat in Congress—there was no longer any incentive to hold his tongue or mind his manners. In late April, he spoke at length to Hearst *New York Journal American* columnist Frank Conniff on "the heavier problems which harass the world today" and declared he was ready "to admit from now on that the term 'isolationist' described my sentiments perfectly. We never gave 'isolationism' a chance. The 'interventionists' had their way and look what happened. I'm proud I warned against participation in a war which could only leave the world in a worse condition than before." Communism would, he predicted, fall by itself. The people of Eastern Europe were fiercely patriotic. "You can't tell me indifferent administrators like the Russians are going to have everything their way in such strongly nationalistic countries. It's against the probabilities to expect it."[29]

On May 18, the *New York Times* provided Kennedy with space, on the front page of the business section, in which he declared forcefully that Truman's plan to spend millions on Greece and Turkey should be opposed on economic grounds alone. To pay for foreign assistance projects, the government was going to have to level exorbitant taxes at home, which would rob business of the capital it needed to expand, deprive Americans of well-paying jobs, and decrease the resources required to defend the homeland. "Personally, as I have said before, I believe our efforts to stem communism in Europe with dollars will eventually prove an overwhelming tax on our resources that will seriously affect the economic well-being of our country."

He repeated himself the following week in an interview that was splashed across the front pages of the Hearst papers on May 25. "Approximately $10 billion is the staggering price we have already paid for the dubious privilege of taking up the 'white man's burden' now that England has slipped from its prewar world stature." And what would come of it? Neither peace nor prosperity nor any possibility that these dollars would buy reliable anti-Communist allies overseas. "I suggest that our statesmen read something of modern history before going all out for saving the world. . . . With nations as with individuals, the ALLY YOU HAVE TO BUY WILL NOT STAY BOUGHT."

Again, the response to his broadsides was overwhelmingly negative. Again, Kennedy didn't much care.

The depression that he feared would result from escalating military spending overseas did not come to pass in his lifetime. The American economy would be transformed, as he predicted, but money spent abroad, much of it on military projects, would not destroy "economic well-being," but rather stimulate growth and increase per capita income at home. Only over the long term would it become apparent that this Cold War spending spree might have had other, perhaps less positive impacts on American "economic well-being" by diverting capital from infrastructure, nonmilitary industrial modernization, and social welfare projects.

Thirty-two

FAMILY MATTERS

I have given up all my favorite sports—golf and kissing girls—and expect to devote my life to serious business," he wrote Lucius Ordway, his millionaire friend from Palm Beach, in November 1950. He was joking, of course—about the golf and the girls and the serious business.

He played golf every day he could, which was every day of the week now that he'd retired from business. He had no trouble finding partners. His children all played golf, except for Rosemary, and visited Palm Beach during the holidays. When they weren't around, he played with "the Commish," Joe Timilty, who had virtually moved in after being denied reappointment as police commissioner; or with Arthur Houghton, who after his resignation from his position in Hollywood and the death of his wife was free to spend long periods with Kennedy in Palm Beach.

Nothing pleased Kennedy more than a day with his buddies golfing or at the baseball park or the racetrack (Hialeah in the winter and Saratoga in August). "That's one thing about Houghton and me," he joked with Lucius Ordway, "women have never had any effect on our lives—we're men's men!" And he meant it. As important as female companionship was to him, he had never let the women in his life, not Rose or

Gloria Swanson or any of the others, take him away from his male friends.[1]

At age sixty, as at every stage of his life, his eye still wandered, though perhaps not the way it once had. Kick, in England, found it hysterically funny that her father had been identified in a *Sunday Pictorial* article about the Florida Gold Coast as "the playboy of Palm Beach. . . . I think it shows a lot of life left in that old man of ours if he can start being a playboy at his ripe old age!!! I wouldn't have been a bit surprised if they had named Grandpa, but I didn't expect Daddy to have the title." Even Rose, on occasion, made light of her husband's flirtatious ways. From Hyannis Port on June 25, 1949, she wrote her daughters that Teddy had brought home with him "a girl called Nancy who was here last year, and she stayed here last night. She is really very pretty but looks about fifteen. Your Father made the startling announcement to her that when she was about eighteen he would be waiting for her. As she is already eighteen, she was really dumbfounded."[2]

In late 1946, Kennedy sold Somerset Importers. The liquor importing business had served the family well, but it was no longer the cash cow it had once been, and with Jack launched on a political career it had become a source of potential embarrassment. "In Jack's campaign for Congress," Kennedy wrote Sir James Calder after the primary victory in 1946, "they made the real issue my support of the British Loan and said the only reason for it was that I had a franchise from Haig & Haig. It occurs to me that from here in it is going to be necessary for me to take a great many positions for England as against Russia, and it is silly to have wrong interpretations put on my actions." In the final analysis, it made no sense to remain in the liquor business now that Kennedy owned the Merchandise Mart, which generated more money than Somerset ever had, much of it tax-free.[3]

Kennedy had minimized tax liabilities by placing ownership of the Merchandise Mart—and its annual income—in a partnership: 12.5 percent for him, another 12.5 percent for Rose, 50 percent for the family trusts, and the remaining 25 percent for the newly incorporated Joseph P. Kennedy, Jr. Foundation. Because the property was owned by a "partnership" rather than a corporation or an individual, he and Rose paid lower rates on their shares; the family trusts paid lower rates still; and the foundation paid nearly nothing. The Mart would continue to generate income for the Kennedy family until 1998, when it was sold for $625 million, fifty times what Kennedy had paid for it.[4]

On the second anniversary of Joe Jr.'s death, Kennedy established a foundation in his name and in his honor. Having put away more than enough money to provide for three generations of Kennedys and earning sufficient income to cover current expenses for all of them, he was prepared now to increase his charitable giving. He would have been a fool to do so without taking advantage of the tax benefits offered family foundations.

"Although the philanthropic impulse, like human nature, is immutable," *Fortune* magazine declared in August 1947 in an article titled "How to Have Your Own Foundation," that impulse reacted "to external influences. These influences today happen to be progressive surtaxes and fixed exemptions for charitable contributions." With the top bracket in 1946–1947 fixed at 86.45 percent for taxable income over $200,000, estate taxes at 77 percent, and gift taxes at 58 percent, wealthy individuals had every incentive to make use of the charitable deductions afforded them by the tax code. The taxpayer who established a family foundation did not have to spend any of the money put into it to get a deduction. One hundred percent of the funds could sit, accumulating untaxed interest and dividends, until the directors chosen by the donor decided to spend it. Better yet, for individuals such as Kennedy with assets that appreciated over time—stocks, real estate, and, later, stakes in oil wells—the amount of the tax deduction was based not on the original cost of the asset, but on its present value. What this meant was that Kennedy could donate to the foundation a building he had bought for $100,000 that was now worth $1 million, deduct $1 million from his income taxes, and avoid whatever capital gains he would have had to pay if he cashed out.[5]

The mission statement of the Joseph P. Kennedy, Jr. Foundation read much like those of Progressive-era settlement houses: its "purposes . . . are for the relief, shelter, support, education, protection and maintenance of the indigent, sick or infirm; to prevent pauperism and to promote by all lawful means social and sanitary reforms, habits of thrift, as well as savings and self-dependence among the poorer classes, without discrimination owing to race, color, or creed." The fact was that none of the Kennedys truly knew how best to commemorate Joe Jr.'s life. He had been a good Catholic, a good student, a good athlete, a man-about-town, and a very good brother. But he had not lived long enough to demonstrate any commitments to philanthropic purposes.[6]

Kennedy had given money earlier to Catholic charities and institutions and expected to do the same with the foundation's funds. He had asked nothing in return for his earlier gifts, but he wanted those given by the foundation to be named for and to serve as memorials to his son. Buildings were a poor substitute for a living body, but they would, he hoped, sustain the memory of his firstborn. There was less vanity here than a genuine and desperate desire of a father to keep his son's name alive.

The foundation would serve other purposes as well, at least in its early years. It would solidify the family's political base in Boston and Massachusetts and, by calling attention to Kennedy beneficence, subtly shift the conversation away from the source and size of his fortune to the uses he intended to make of it on behalf of the community. The first foundation gift had been the $600,000 check that Jack had presented to Archbishop Cushing just before election day in 1946. In his second year of giving and thereafter, Kennedy maximized the political impact of the donations by giving money not only to Irish Catholic institutions, but to Italian Catholic and Polish Catholic and a few Jewish and non-sectarian ones as well.[7]

Kennedy appointed as foundation directors four of the men closest to him: Eddie Moore, Johnnie Ford, Paul Murphy, and James Fayne, whom Kennedy had worked with at Hayden, Stone, brought to the SEC, and would hire full-time to work in the New York office in 1949. Jack was the fifth director and the first president. (In 1947, Ford would be replaced on the board by Eunice; in 1953, after Jack's election to the Senate, he would be replaced as president by Bobby.)

So as not to waste money on unnecessary infrastructure, the Joseph P. Kennedy, Jr. Foundation had no program officers, accountants, evaluators, or staff of any sort. It was run out of Kennedy's New York office. As foundation president, Jack did little more than sign letters and appear at ceremonies.

Kennedy had surrounded himself with an extraordinary group of business executives, accountants, researchers, tax men, and real estate experts who he had no doubt could run a foundation in addition to overseeing his investments. A large number of them had worked with him in Boston, New York, Washington, and London. Several, after leaving his employment, had returned. Paul Murphy was in operational control of the office; Johnnie Ford oversaw the New England concerns, including Kennedy's theater business; John Reynolds ran the real estate operation; John Burns, the former Harvard Law School professor and superior court justice whom Kennedy had brought to the SEC as general counsel and who had remained a close friend and business associate ever since, was now in private practice. He continued to work on retainer for Kennedy, who insisted that his business concerns be given precedence over those of Burns's other clients.

Sometime after the war, Burns, who had taken on several important clients, including Hearst and the New York Archdiocese, informed Kennedy that he needed more time for them. He was weary of being on constant call and of having to work on whatever Kennedy threw him, no matter how trivial it might be ("I didn't go to Harvard Law School to spend my life disputing Rose's bills at Bergdorf's"). Kennedy threatened that if Burns left, he would tell everyone who mattered that he had been fired. Burns responded that he knew enough to sink Kennedy and that if Kennedy dared do anything to threaten his livelihood and interfere with his capacity to provide for his family, he would open doors that Kennedy needed closed and locked. Burns left Kennedy's employment, but neither man ever said anything about the circumstances under which he departed. Remarkably, while their fathers remained estranged, the Burns and Kennedy children would remain closely connected for the rest of their lives.[8]

James Landis, former Harvard Law School dean, chair of the SEC and the Civil Aeronautics Board, and as distinguished a jurist as Burns, stepped into the role that he had occupied. In December 1947, Tommy

Corcoran called Kennedy in Palm Beach to say that he had learned that President Truman was not going to reappoint Landis as chairman of the Civil Aeronautics Board. Kennedy contacted Landis to offer him a job. "Come on down to Palm Beach and just announce that 'I'm associated with the Kennedy enterprises.' . . . I'll get hold of Arthur Krock and see to it that the *Times* carries that story, that you are leaving in order to take a job with the Kennedy enterprises." When Landis asked what he would be doing in this job, Kennedy responded, "We'll figure that out after you're down here. You'll need a rest for a while." Kennedy's intervention saved Landis "from a great deal of embarrassment," financial and personal, at having been ousted from his Washington position.[9]

Kennedy quickly found work for Landis, most of it far beneath his capacities. Landis drafted letters, wrote speeches, reviewed legal contracts, and when Clare Boothe Luce decided to run for Congress, undertook a "racial and religious makeup of Fairfield County" for her. He also served as Kennedy's research assistant and coauthor for an article in *Life* magazine and a pamphlet, *The Surrender of King Leopold*, which refuted Churchill's claim that because the Belgian king had not notified the Allies in advance, his surrender to the Germans in May 1940 had had dire effects on the course of the fighting in Europe and the evacuation of the British troops at Dunkirk.

Landis's primary task, however, was trying to put Kennedy's diplomatic memoirs into publishable order. Since returning from London ten years earlier, Kennedy had been working on the project with help from a variety of editors, researchers, and several of his children. With Elizabeth Walsh, who also worked full-time for Kennedy, and for a time Jean Kennedy, Landis did the historical research that was required to fill in the narrative, fact-checked the manuscript, contacted men cited in the document (such as Sumner Welles and Arthur Krock) to check their recollections, organized and redrafted and rewrote. Several drafts and many years later, a readable, rather accurate, but insensately ponderous history of the prewar years, with Kennedy at its center, was completed. The book was never published—not, as would later be charged, because Kennedy's analysis of American diplomacy from 1938 to 1940 might cause difficulties for his boys' political careers, but because it was too boring for a general audience and too light for a specialized academic readership. "As I look at the book," Kennedy reluctantly concluded in a letter to publisher Paul Palmer in March 1955, "I am not dead sure that there are very many things that are of any great import."[10]

Six and a half years after his resignation as ambassador, in July 1947, Kennedy accepted another government appointment, this one unpaid and part-time, on the Commission on Organization of the Executive Branch of the Government, which, chaired by former president Herbert Hoover, would become known as the Hoover Commission. The legislation establishing the commission provided for a membership of twelve, half government officials, half private citizens, appointed in equal portions by the president; Joe Martin, the Republican Speaker of the House; and the Republican president pro tempore of the Senate, Arthur Vandenberg. Kennedy accepted appointment out of respect for Hoover and only after being assured that he would not have to attend any meetings. Instead, he met occasionally with Hoover at his Waldorf Towers suite. Though Dean Acheson and James Forrestal, representing the Truman administration, did their best to influence the course of the deliberations, Hoover controlled the proceedings, the staffing of task forces, and the flow of information to commission members. Kennedy had no difficulties with any of this, as he trusted and respected former president Hoover much more than he did President Truman or any of his advisers.

As Kennedy had predicted, President Truman's proposal to spend hundreds of millions of dollars to save Greece and Turkey from communism was followed by even larger requests.

In June 1947, Secretary of State George Marshall, speaking at the Harvard commencement, invited the nations of Europe to design a comprehensive economic recovery plan that the United States would fund. The proposal, which would be known as the Marshall Plan, had several objectives: to provide dollars to European nations to pay for American imports, to stabilize the European economies, and, most important, to forestall the economic crises that, it was widely feared, local Communist parties would capitalize on to win elections and seize power. When Kennedy wrote Kick that spring that he was sure "Italy and France will be definitely in the Communist orbit before the end of this year," he was voicing what had become the accepted wisdom among Washington's wise men.[11]

While Kennedy did not relish the idea of Communist-dominated governments and economies in Europe, he doubted that spending millions of American dollars was going to succeed in preserving democracy and capitalism abroad. On the contrary, he feared, it would exacerbate tensions with the Soviets and bring the world a step closer to war. He, of course, had the luxury of carefully balancing the pros and cons of Marshall's plan before coming out for or against it. His son, the congressman from Massachusetts, did not. The voters in the eleventh district were staunchly anti-Communist and more than willing to spend American dollars to defeat or push back the Red menace.

Jack not only enthusiastically backed the Marshall Plan, but in the fall of 1947, undertook a fact-finding trip to Europe with two other congressman, one of them Richard Nixon, to investigate Communist influence on French and Italian labor. His first stop was Ireland, where he visited Kick at a castle owned by her in-laws. He was ill most of the time, though he did manage a visit to Dunganstown to meet his Irish cousins, the first of his family to do so.

On September 21, he returned to London en route to the continent and his fact-finding investigation. Arriving in London, he became so ill that he placed an emergency call to Kick's friend Pamela Churchill. A doctor was located, examined Jack, and put him into the hospital, where he was diagnosed with Addison's disease. He was flown home at once and admitted to a Boston hospital. The public was told that he suffered from a recurrence of his wartime malaria. For the rest of his life, Jack Kennedy would suffer and be treated for Addison's disease while publicly declaring that he did not have it.

Jack had earlier agreed to be the keynote speaker at the fiftieth anniversary of the Cambridge Knights of Columbus on October 23. He was too ill to do so now and asked his father to pinch-hit. Though Kennedy's views on the British loan, the Truman Doctrine, and the Marshall Plan were out of line with his son's, he remained enough of a political asset to serve as the congressman's stand-in.

"I suppose a father is primarily interested more in his family than in any honor that can possibly come to him no matter how great it may be," Kennedy began that evening in Cambridge. "My oldest boy ran for office here for the first time and became a delegate to the Democratic National Convention." The next line was going to be about Jack, but, Mark Dalton recalled, "the tears welled up in his eyes as he spoke of Joe and it took him about two minutes to get the grip."[12]

Kennedy gathered himself and continued. He had, he reminded his audience, "opposed very bitterly the Truman Plan," which, he did not add, his son had voted for. "I thought it was pouring money down the rathole." He thought much the same about the Marshall Plan. Still, because the European nations were in dire economic distress, he was willing to "loan them five or six billion dollars or give it to them," but only for a year. If, after that year, productivity was still low and organized labor uncooperative, or if any of the nations receiving American aid voted Socialists or Communists into their governments, the loans or gifts would not be renewed. He was not an anti-Communist hard-liner—and he made this clear. "I do not think it is the spread of Communism that is dangerous. . . . People are not embracing Communism as Communism, but they are discontented, insecure and unsettled and they embrace anything that looks like it might be better than what they have to endure. . . . It is very easy for anybody who has a job and is getting along all right to cry for democracy . . . but if you cannot feed your children and you do not know where the next meal is coming from, nobody knows what kind of freak you will follow."[13]

In the spring of 1948, Kennedy returned to Europe for his first extended visit since he had left seven and a half years before. He was on a personal fact-finding mission of sorts, looking for material to use as ammunition in his fight against the Marshall Plan. He sailed on the *America* on April 14 and took "the Commish," Joe Timilty, with him. Although he commanded far less press and attention than he once had, the Boston papers kept track of his trip and his pronouncements. While he was in Paris, on April 18, the Christian Democrats in Italy, with the assistance of millions of dollars provided clandestinely by the CIA, defeated the Popular Front coalition of Socialists and Communists by nearly two to one. When the *Boston Post* contacted Kennedy for his reaction, he responded, consistent with his undying pessimism, that the results of the election, with 35 percent of the electorate voting Communist [in reality, the vote was 31 percent for the coalition of Socialists and Communists], were "more alarming than reassuring."[14]

Interviewed in Paris by Bill Cunningham of the *Boston Herald* about his aspirations for his children, he declared: "In two words, it's Public Service." Bobby had graduated from Harvard and was "traveling through Europe, and even down into Greece, Turkey and such troublous districts." Travel abroad, Kennedy told Cunningham, had been instrumental in interesting and equipping Jack "for a career of public service." He hoped and expected "the same for Robert, in fact, for all his children. Cunningham asked about the girls, and Kennedy cited the instance of "daughter Eunice, who's in Washington as a special assistant to Atty.-Gen. Tom Clark, working particularly upon the problem of juvenile delinquency." "What we need now is selfless, informed, sincere representation and service at home and abroad. . . . Please don't misunderstand me as trying to imply that my children are any smarter, or any better qualified than anybody else's children. But we chance to be in a position in which they can be spared the necessity of supporting themselves. Spared that, why shouldn't they better try to qualify to serve their country in some needed capacity, great or small, as they can prove themselves worthy?" He had, he insisted, "no copyright on the idea," but he hoped nonetheless that it "spread widely. There are many other young men and women in the United States whose families could easily afford to make the same decision, and who are possibly better qualified than my own children for great service to America and to the world. . . . That has been our family plan for our children from the first. If it doesn't work out with them, it could work out with some others."[15]

In May, Kennedy took the train to Rome for an audience with the pope, then returned to Paris to meet up with Kick, who was flying in with her fiancé, Peter Fitzwilliam. Only a few weeks earlier, Kick, at the tail end of her winter vacation in the United States, had informed the family that she intended to marry Fitzwilliam, an immensely wealthy, titled British Protestant, like Billy Hartington, but married, considerably older than Kick, and widely known as something of a bounder.

Kathleen Kennedy Hartington was, at age twenty-eight, three and a half years a widow and ready to move on. The year before, she had contemplated marriage to another "notorious ladies' man," also a Protestant, but her father had talked her out of it and she had been grateful to him for doing so. "Any ideas about that particular southern gentleman were passing fancies!" she had written him on her return to Great Britain. "You told me what you thought. I listened. The rest was up to me and in the cold light of morning after having the life I have had one doesn't waste it going from El Morocco to the Stork Club. Not if one has any sense, one doesn't."[16]

She wasn't going to be talked out of this marriage. Fitzwilliam was simply too charming, too rich, too gallant, too much fun. He had promised to divorce his wife to marry Kick. Jack had been the first to learn about Fitzwilliam during his trip to Ireland in August 1947, but he'd said nothing to his parents. When Rose heard about him that winter, she was so distraught at the prospect of her daughter besmirching her family's good name by marrying a Protestant divorcé that she threatened to sever all ties with her and cut off her allowance. Kennedy was crushed into silence by the news, though he agreed, to his daughter's surprise and joy, to meet with her and Fitzwilliam in Paris, perhaps to try one final time to convince them to back away from their marriage plans.

Fitzwilliam had planned to spend a few days with Kick in Cannes before they met Kennedy in Paris. He chartered a private two-engine, eight-seat plane for the trip. When they stopped over to refuel in Paris, he decided to have lunch with a few of his friends rather than fly at once to Cannes. By the time he and Kick were ready to proceed, a thunderstorm was developing over the Rhone Valley and all commercial flights had been grounded. Fitzwilliam argued with the pilot until he agreed to fly. Their plane took off at 3:20 P.M. It never arrived.

Eunice Kennedy, who was working in Washington and shared a town house with Jack, was called to the phone at midnight by a *Washington Post* reporter who asked if the Lady Hartington reported killed in an airplane crash in France was her sister. She replied that there were two Lady Hartingtons. The reporter said that a passport had been found with the name Kathleen on it. Jack was reclining on a sofa listening to a recording of *Finian's Rainbow* when Eunice told him what the reporter had said. He got in touch with Ted Reardon, his congressional assistant, and asked him to check on the story. Reardon phoned an hour later to confirm that it was indeed Kathleen who had died in the crash, along with Peter Fitzwilliam, and the plane's pilot and co-pilot.

Kennedy was awakened in Paris at six thirty A.M. by Joe Timilty, who had gotten a call from Joe Dinneen of the *Boston Globe*. A half hour after he learned of his daughter's death, he sat down to write her epitaph. "No one who ever knew her didn't feel that life was much better that minute. And we know so little about the next world that we must think that they wanted just such a wonderful girl for themselves. We must not feel sorry for her but for ourselves." He then arranged to be taken to the crash site, just outside the town of Privas, and from there to the Town Hall, where four lead-lined coffins, covered by flowers, were awaiting identification. An official opened the lid on the coffin with the woman. It was Kick.[17]

Kick's body was removed to a church in Paris until a decision could be made about where she should be buried. Kennedy had hoped that Jack would make arrangements to fly her body back to the United States for burial at Cape Cod, but Jack was too debilitated by grief to do anything. When Billy's parents volunteered to bury her in the family plot at Chatsworth, Kennedy agreed.

We can only speculate as to why no member of the family save Kennedy attended Kick's funeral. Had Jack been ready to fly to England, his sisters and perhaps his mother might have followed. But he was too broken to attempt the journey. Rose might have flown by herself or with her daughters. But she too was devastated. Rather than permit themselves to be swallowed up in the sea of mourners at Chatsworth—and grieve their daughter's death with a Protestant family that held tight to Kathleen as one of their own—the Kennedys mourned Kick in their own way, in their own home.

On May 20, a High Mass was held for Kathleen Kennedy at the Farm Street Church near Berkeley Square in London. Joseph P. Kennedy was the only family member in attendance. After the Mass, he boarded a specially chartered train, with two hundred of Kick's friends and her coffin, for the final journey to Derbyshire. "He wore a crumpled blue suit," recalled Debo Devonshire, Kick's sister-in-law, to author Barbara Leaming, "and he was crumpled just like the suit. I never saw anything like it."[18]

The next day, Kennedy sailed for home. "He asked," the *Boston Herald* announced on May 30, "that he be excused from being interviewed and photographed." His wishes were respected.

He had lost the second of his four oldest children, a third was institutionalized, and he worried incessantly about the life expectancy of the fourth.

There would be no memorials to Kathleen Kennedy, no foundations or charities, no book of remembrances like the one Jack had put together for Joe Jr. The sad truth was that the family did not know how to tell her story. There were rumors at the time of her death that she had left the church, rumors put to rest by an article planted in the *Boston Post*. Rather than attempting to defend Kick's decision to marry a Protestant or covering up the circumstances of her death, the Kennedys laid her public memory to rest with her. They would never cease to love her or to miss her or to speak lovingly of her among themselves, but they would not mention her life or the circumstances of her death in public.

Her death, just four years after Joe Jr.'s, was almost too much for her father to bear. The fact that his son had died in battle for a cause he thought just and died alongside so many other brave young men imbued his death with some meaning. Kathleen's death had no meaning, had not been foretold or foreseen, as was the death of a soldier, and was, in that regard, more debilitating.

On July 27, he wrote Lord Beaverbrook, apologizing for his uncharacteristic two-month delay in responding to his condolence message. "Reluctance to address my mind to a distressing subject is the excuse I offer for my tardiness in acknowledging your comforting expression of sympathy. . . . The sudden death of young Joe and Kathleen, within a period of three years, has left a mark with me that I find very difficult to erase."[19]

Only in September, three and a half months after his daughter's death, was he finally able to write and thank the Duchess of Devonshire for her kindness. "I thought about you a great deal since I came back to America. I think that the only thing that helped me retain my sanity was your understanding manner in the whole sad affair. I would like to be able to tell you that I am very much better, but I just can't. I can't seem to get out of my mind that there is no possibility of seeing Kick next winter and that there are no more weeks and months to be made gay by her presence. I realize that people say, 'You have so many other children, you can't be too depressed by Kick's death,' and I think that, to all intents and purposes, no one knows that I am depressed. In fact, I have never acknowledged it even to Rose who, by the way, is ten thousand per-cent better than I am. Her terrifically strong faith has been a great help to her, along with her very strong will and determination not to give way.

Jack, Bobby, the girls, and Rose would all visit and correspond with Billy's family in the months and years to come. Kennedy could not. Everything and everyone associated with his daughter brought him too much pain, pain that would not lessen as the years passed.

"Even in his prime," his friend Father John Cavanaugh would later write, "he could not speak of [Joe and Kathleen] without great emotional disturbance." Cavanaugh recalled driving with Kennedy "along a highway in Southern France. He wanted me to know that off to the left towards the lower Alps was the spot where Kathleen had dropped. He simply gripped my arm and made me realize with a quick look in his eyes what he could not speak in words. For several minutes we rode along without saying anything."[21]

A year after Kick's death, in the summer of 1949, the family marked the fifth anniversary of Joe Jr.'s death by giving Archbishop Richard Cushing $125,000 more for the Brighton hospital for poor children and $100,000 for the St. Coletta school in Hanover, a residential facility for what were known at the time as "feeble-minded children," which had been built in the summer of 1947 on 175 acres of waterfront land in Hanover, Massachusetts, about twenty-five miles from Boston. The Sisters of St. Francis of Assisi, the order that had established a similar school in Jefferson, Wisconsin, in 1904, had agreed to staff the new school, which was to be called St. Coletta's by the Sea.[22]

The Brighton hospital, officially known as the Joseph P. Kennedy, Jr.

Memorial, opened in September 1949. Kennedy was so delighted with it that he asked Eunice to keep her eyes open for "a very good project that will measure up to the Memorial Hospital, not necessarily in bricks and mortar, but in ideals." All the children had been invited to take part in the foundation work, but from the onset it had been Eunice who demonstrated the most interest. In the years to come, she would play a larger and larger role in the management of the foundation.[23]

Though the hospital had been named after his son, Kennedy was dismayed to discover that the publicity materials the nuns had prepared for the dedication referred to "a convalescent Home and Hospital for Underprivileged Children." "I just don't understand, and haven't from the beginning, why there is any hesitancy or disinclination to have everything identified with this new home described as being the Joseph P. Kennedy, Jr. Memorial Home," he wrote Mother Marie Emile Ange on January 31, 1950. He was angry as well with the "description of the hospital" that Archbishop Cushing's office had given to the press, which had identified the total cost of the building at $2 million and Kennedy's contribution as $700,000. "I did not like that kind of publicity at all." He had agreed to build the hospital, been told the cost, and written a check. If in the end the final costs of the project came to $2 million, that was because Cushing had added a "chapel and the convent, for which at no time had I assumed any responsibility." He did not know who was at fault for making him look cheap, but it didn't matter. "I am not at all happy," he wrote Mother Ange, "and I want the Archbishop to know it, and I want him to have this letter after you have finished with it. As far as I am concerned, I do not propose to discuss it ever again, except to say that I am not at all pleased."[24]

Joseph P. Kennedy was discovering, as Andrew Carnegie had a half century earlier, that it was not easy to give away one's money. To leverage his gifts—as Carnegie had—Kennedy provided seed money for construction costs, not funds or an endowment for operational costs. Where Carnegie had held local governments accountable for maintaining, staffing, and buying books for the libraries he built, Kennedy expected the Catholic Church and its charities to provide the funds necessary to operate the institutions his foundation built. He was more than a little taken aback when in August 1951, less than two years after the hospital in Brighton had opened, Mother Ange wrote to say that she was having "difficulty making ends meet." He replied that before giving his donation for the building, he had "asked you just how you proposed to operate this new home. I did so because my business experience over the past 40 years has proved to me conclusively that it is not the initial cost that is the substantial one but it is the continuing deficit in operating expenses. You assured me that was no problem." He insisted he had made no commitment to cover the hospital's operating expenses.[25]

He did not want to appear stingy or unfeeling, but neither was he going to make promises he was not certain he could keep. "The Foundation's chief source of income at the present is from the Merchandise Mart," he wrote Father John Wright, Archbishop Cushing's secretary. "A fire, a bomb, an accident of serious nature, a move of the home furnishings business away from Chicago to New York would leave the Mart a liability instead of an asset." The suggestion Cushing had made, that the Kennedys "make a commitment based on" their own funds, he regarded as "hazardous." With tax rates rising to pay for the Cold War, he feared that personal incomes over $25,000 would soon be taxed out of existence. Kennedy was temperamentally a bear. No matter how well he was doing in the present, he could not help fearing for the future.[26]

Relations between Kennedy and Archbishop Cushing were further strained by the appearance of an article in the *Boston Post* that quoted the archbishop as saying that since their original contribution, the Kennedys had given nothing to the Brighton hospital and that if funds were not forthcoming, new arrangements, including putting the children in the hospital up for adoption, might have to be made. Cushing wrote Kennedy immediately to disown the words attributed to him. "Having read the article, I was shocked to put it mildly." The hospital was "not in need of funds. Everything is going along very well." Cushing assured Kennedy "that never again, either directly or indirectly, will publicity ever appear unless it is personally written by me." And he kept that promise.[27]

Part of the underlying tension between the two men was that Cushing was not a businessman and had little interest in behaving like one. Deficits did not trouble him. When they got too big to handle, he relied on God's beneficence or, more concretely, on his and the church's fund-raising prowess to raise the money he needed. Kennedy, who had no such faith, preferred that the institutions he funded be operated in the black.

In the summer of 1952, he sent two of his ablest associates to Brighton to review the Joseph P. Kennedy, Jr. Memorial hospital's financial statements. He followed up with personal visits and extended interviews with the sisters. "The original plan of the institution has been entirely set aside," he wrote Cushing in early August. "The idea of the care of convalescent children and the care of children from broken homes . . . has given way to the care of mentally deficient children." Though the sisters were doing a remarkable job, they had no training in this area. "They must start hiring professional help, which will be expensive."[28]

Cushing insisted that things were not nearly as bad as "Joe" imagined them. "The Kennedy Memorial is one of the greatest institutions, of its kind, in this country. It is now what it was always intended to be—a haven for physically and mentally handicapped children." There was no financial emergency. "The Finger of God is on this place." And so was Cushing's. "I had as much to do with the planning of this project as anyone and I can tell you there isn't any institution, under Catholic auspices, in this country, that has attracted more favorable comments. I also planned St. Coletta's in Hanover. . . . This is an entirely different institution. Saint Coletta's is a school for exceptional children of a certain grade of intelligence. It could never accept the poor tots who go to the Kennedy Memorial. In fact, the latter has taken a few of the hopeless cases from the former. Honestly, Joe, I cannot understand what the 'shouting' is all about. There are no immediate problems at Kennedy."[29]

The ambassador, Cushing later recalled, was "very demanding of his friends. But we all like it. He wants things done well and you fulfill his requests or 'you get off the team.'" Because he got things done— and done well—Archbishop (later Cardinal) Richard Cushing would become a lifelong member of the team, friend of the Kennedy family, and recipient of large foundation grants for the projects he sponsored.[30]

Kennedy would enter into a working relationship with Archbishop Francis Spellman in New York similar to the one he had forged with Cushing in Boston for the same reason. Spellman could be counted on to get things done. The two men who would become rivals for Kennedy foundation funding could not have been more different. Cushing was fun-loving, informal, and outgoing. He looked rather like a tough, handsome, Irish cop and behaved more like a ward politician than a high church cleric. Spellman, on the other hand, was small, round, bespectacled, humorless, distant. Unlike Cushing, he spoke Italian and had powerful friends not only in the Vatican, but in the upper reaches of national politics, business, and banking.

Kennedy and Spellman shared the same real estate adviser, John Reynolds, who may have been instrumental in arranging the family's first gift to the New York Archdiocese: a valuable piece of land on Pelham Parkway. In August 1951, Spellman wrote Kennedy with a request: "I realize that for many reasons your charitable interests should be in Massachusetts but nevertheless I think that New York can offer you bigger and better bargains." The particular "bargain" Spellman was writing about was a boys' home and school at 1770 Stillwell Avenue in the Bronx, "available for immediate dedication and occupancy. There are no maintenance charges. Better terms may be had if desired." Spellman's unchurchmanly reference to "bargains" and "terms" was offered tongue-in-cheek, but the archbishop was deadly serious. He understood Kennedy's reluctance to commit funds for operational costs and was more than willing to accommodate him. The boys' home in the Bronx had formerly been run by the Edwin Gould Foundation (founded by railroad tycoon Jay Gould's son Edwin), which had had to abandon it "because of the high cost of operation." Spellman anticipated no such difficulties. "Since the Sisters work for nothing but their food and clothing, we shall be able to conduct this institution for two hundred and eighty children at an anticipated annual operating deficit of less than $50,000 which deficit can be met by annual appropriations from Catholic Charities."[31]

Kennedy agreed to provide Spellman with the funds he needed—with the proviso that whatever donation he made be spread over several years. On September 8, 1950, the archbishop invited reporters to the site of the new Bronx children's home, which he announced "would be named the Lieut. Joseph P. Kennedy Jr. Home," its name to be "placed in bronze letters over the entrance." Six weeks later, the press was welcomed back for the official dedication of the facility. Spellman and no fewer than four auxiliary bishops blessed the buildings, following which Joe, Rose, Jack, Eunice, Patricia, and Bobby posed solemnly for a photograph in front of an oil painting of Lieutenant Joseph P. Kennedy, Jr.[32]

In the fall of 1948, a year and a half after Kathleen's death, Kennedy took up what he wrote Johnnie Ford was "the most important unfinished business I have." He had come to the conclusion that he could no longer keep Rosemary at Craig House (perhaps after speaking with Mary Moore, Eddie's wife, who had made several visits there, the last in October). The year before, in October 1947, St. Coletta's by the Sea, the school for the "feeble-minded" founded by Archbishop Cushing, had opened its doors in Hanover. Sometime during the fall of 1948, Kennedy visited the school or sent Johnnie Ford to talk to the sisters about moving Rosemary there. "The Sisters confided in me the nature of their recent contacts with you and yours," Archbishop Cushing wrote Kennedy on December 4. "From the beginning, I told them I was not enthusiastic because I was fearful of publicity." While he regarded the Sisters of St. Francis of Assisi as "the finest group of religious that I have ever met," he recommended against placing Rosemary with them in Hanover. "Humanly speaking, it would be impossible to avoid public attention to any plans you had." He suggested instead that Rosemary be sent a thousand miles away to the St. Coletta school in Jefferson, Wisconsin. "There, and not Hanover, will solve your personal problems. That's the recommendation that I wish to make. . . . Once again, I hesitate to make this recommendation for I have no reason for entering the picture save my devotion to you and the family."[33]

Kennedy did as Cushing recommended. It was imperative, for his and his family's peace of mind, that Rosemary not become an object of public pity or an embarrassment for the family. It was better for all of them that she live her life in privacy in a protected, secluded, sequestered environment a thousand miles away. Three weeks after Cushing wrote Kennedy, Johnnie Ford, who was his intermediary in this matter, heard from Sister Maureen of the St. Coletta school in Hanover that "word has come from Mother Mary Bartholomew that the school at Jefferson, Wisconsin will cooperate in every way concerning the placement of Rosemary." Sister Maureen was, she told Ford, "sure that everything can be arranged to Mr. Kennedy's satisfaction. Both you and Mr. Kennedy have been especially kind to us and we are deeply grateful. May the Christ Child reward you with abundant blessings on Christmas Day and throughout the New Year."[34]

On New Year's Eve, Kennedy wrote to ask if Ford, when he was next in Chicago, could "run up to the school at Jefferson, Wisconsin, and have a talk with Mary Bartholomew. . . . You know just what I have in mind and, after an examination of the place and a talk with the Nuns, I am sure you will be in a position to tell me what to think. I thought I would follow up with a visit myself, possibly in March or April."[35]

Sometime that spring, Rosemary was moved from Craig House in Beacon, New York, to the St. Coletta school in Jefferson, Wisconsin. She would remain there for the rest of her life.

The school, as Cushing had said, was the "finest of its kind in the nation." It was situated on a large, rural campus with rolling fields, parkland, gardens, and a farm that provided residents with fresh vegetables and meat. The buildings were old-fashioned multistory brick ones like the large parochial schools then found in every city in the nation. There was a beautiful church and chapel on the grounds, an auditorium with a stage for live shows and a Hollywood-style projector that Kennedy might very well have contributed, indoor and outdoor swimming pools, playgrounds and recreation facilities, boys' and girls' dormitories, and a graveyard for sisters and former residents.

Rosemary lived in her own ranch-style cottage about a mile from the school with two nun caretakers. She visited the main campus often to watch movies on Saturday nights, to go to church, and to take part in special events. According to her sister Jean, Rosemary was content and loved by the nuns and the other residents. "She has remained physically healthy and generally happy," Rose would write several decades after Rosemary moved to St. Coletta. "She functions on a childlike level but is able to have excursions . . . and to do a little personal shopping for her needs—always with an attendant—and to enjoy life to the limit of her capacities. She is perfectly happy in her own environment and would be confused and disturbed at being anywhere else."[36]

Johnnie Ford was charged with communicating with Sister M. Anastasia at St. Coletta. There is no evidence that anyone in the family

either visited or was in contact with Rosemary or the nuns for the first
ten or so years. Sometime in the late 1950s, after she had married and
moved to Chicago, Eunice may have either visited St. Coletta or corre-
sponded with Sister Anastasia.[37]

The nuns never ceased working with Rosemary to improve her mental and motor skills. In the spring of 1958, Sister Anastasia asked Johnnie Ford to "kindly assure Mr. Kennedy that Rosemary's doctor will be
here soon and we will discuss the possibility of speech improvement.
Also, the summer school speech therapist will be here in June and we
shall have her work with Rosemary along these lines." There had, she
reported, been a man who had asked to see Rosemary. He had said he
was "in the army with Joe," but "we told him that Rosemary does not
wish to see anyone without the parents' consent." There had also been,
that week alone, "three to four different parties and also children's
folks inquiring about Rosemary." Rosemary's presence, Sister Anastasia confided reluctantly, was posing quite a problem for fund-raising.
"When we come with our sponsor drive, some folks flatly refuse, telling
us we are endowed. One party went as far as to say that the entire estate
of Rosemary's was ours; also that 'Kennedy' supports the school."[38]

Kennedy answered Sister Anastasia directly. He was "glad to see
that you are considering the possibility of a speech therapist. Of course,
you have always been authorized to do anything that you think would
be of any help to Rosemary. All you have to do is to do it and send me
the bill." He was not surprised "that people are still inquiring about
Rosemary. We still have hundreds of people riding down a private road
here in Hyannis Port to take a look at our house. Natural curiosity does
that." He had no idea who the visitor had been, "and I do not care who
the rest of them were or what their arguments were—your rules still
stand." As for fund-raising efforts, "we certainly do not want to hurt
any of your drives, but anyone who knows of the great work which you
are doing and looks for the excuses which you cite in your letter, I am
afraid would never be of much help to you anyway." He was, however,
going to increase his financial support for the school. He expressed his
gratitude for Sister Anastasia's "persevering kindness" in making a
home for Rosemary.[39]

Given the fact that the results of the lobotomy were irreversible, he
was convinced, and probably rightly, that there was no better place for

Rosemary than at St. Coletta. The fact that she was well taken care of and content was a godsend for the family, who would no longer have to worry about her and whether they were doing enough to watch out for and care for her.

The question that confounds us in the end is not why Rosemary was sent to live at St. Coletta, but why, once she was there, Kennedy did not attempt to visit her or to encourage his wife and children to do so. The most likely answer is that he thought it best for all of them to effect a permanent separation. It was certainly best for him, especially after the pain inflicted by the death of Kick, not to have to confront, face-to-face, what had become of his Rosie.

Only after Kennedy suffered his debilitating stroke and, like his daughter, lost his ability to speak, write, or communicate in words did his wife and children begin to visit Rosemary in Wisconsin and invite her to their homes. They did so still respecting his wishes and neither reporting back to him about his daughter nor suggesting that he see her again.

Joseph P. Kennedy would die in 1969 not having seen his eldest daughter for a quarter of a century.

Thirty-three

"THE GREAT DEBATE"

M y dear Mr. President," Kennedy wrote Harry Truman on January 31, 1950. "It is with great reluctance that I write you as I know how busy you are in these momentous days. I am writing you not as a Catholic but as the man more responsible than anyone for the suggestion of establishing the so-called Taylor mission at the Vatican." He was concerned, as were Catholics everywhere, with Truman's failure to appoint a successor to Myron Taylor, who had resigned in mid-January as the president's representative to the Vatican. "At the present," Kennedy informed Truman, "I am living in Palm Beach, Florida, but I could leave on Monday and would be available any day thereafter."[1]

Six months later, no plan having been made to replace Taylor, Kennedy set up an appointment to meet with Truman in person. By the time he arrived at the White House at noon on June 30, there were other items of greater importance to discuss.

Five days earlier, the North Korean military had crossed the thirty-eighth parallel into South Korea. The American response had been immediate and dramatic. The United States delegate called for an immediate session of the UN Security Council and introduced a resolution condemning North Korea for its actions and demanding it withdraw all troops. In the absence of the Soviet delegates, who were boycotting the council, the resolution passed. On June 27, the United States introduced a second resolution, which also passed, calling on member nations to provide military assistance to South Korea to repel the attack from the North, That same day, Truman announced that American military forces would come to the defense of South Korea.

Kennedy was ushered in to see Truman at twelve thirty on June 30, just as an emergency cabinet meeting ended. "He told me he had been up since 4:30 that morning and that he was not going to let those sons of bitches push him around. His own impression was that he did not think the Russians would fight on this particular occasion. . . . He realizes that these are horrible times and that the decisions he is making are going to affect all civilization, but he considers it his responsibility and he is taking it on. . . . I said that I felt mentally very much as I did when Chamberlain guaranteed Poland because I felt that was the step that really made it impossible to leave anything further to negotiations." The implication was that Truman, by coming to the military defense of South Korea, might be precipitating another world war. "If the French and British had stood up to Hitler," Truman responded, as he was to the Communists in Korea, "the Germans would have retreated. Then he said Chamberlain quit at Munich and he was not going to appease." Only half in jest, Kennedy asked if Truman "didn't feel as if he was handling this like a poker game. He looked up very much surprised, but I added there had to be a great deal of bluff in this sort of thing." Truman, convinced the Russians were behind the North Korean incursion, responded that he had no choice now but "to make a firm gesture and didn't think the Russians would accept the challenge."

Kennedy let the issue die for the moment. "We then took up the question of the Vatican, which was my prime reason" for asking for the meeting. Again the president and his visitor disagreed on virtually everything.

On Myron Taylor: "I said I thought Taylor was a horse's ass. He said he liked him. . . . He said he had received some fine information from Taylor and I said if he did he got it very incidentally."

On eighty-four-year-old Cardinal Dennis Dougherty of Philadelphia: "He said that Cardinal Dougherty had been down to see him and that he was a great man. I said that I thought he was in his dotage."

On the closing of Taylor's office in Rome: "I understood that the American office at the Vatican had been closed without consultation with the Pope, and he said that was not so."

On the clandestine aid that the United States had funneled through the Vatican to the Christian Democrats to support their election contest with the Communists: "I also told him that the Vatican had not been very well treated on the question of money in the last Italian election. He told me that the United States spent one billion dollars. . . . I said if they did the Vatican did not even get the six million dollars which I understood they had been promised."

The president was as blunt and plainspoken with Kennedy as Kennedy was with him. "As far as the Vatican is concerned, he is not going to take all the abuse that the Protestants and Oxnam [Garfield Bromley Oxnam, the Methodist bishop of New York who was leading the opposition to American diplomatic relations with the Vatican] have been heaping on him all the time for keeping Taylor there. He is going to let Congress take it from here in." He would make no recommendations about renewing or discontinuing American representation to the Vatican until after the midterm elections.

After thirty-five minutes, Kennedy withdrew. The president, he recorded in his diary, had been "most agreeable and pleasant and was not the slightest bit rushed in getting me out of the office."[2]

In his report to Count Galeazzi on his meeting, Kennedy did not blame Truman for playing politics with the question of American diplomatic relations with the Vatican. The bitter truth was that there were more Protestant voters in America than Catholic ones. If the Catholic minority was to get the respect—and diplomatic representation—it deserved and required, it would have to follow the example of American Jews and organize itself better. "I still believe, as I told the Pope, and as I told you, that until the day comes when the hierarchy of the United States make up their minds that they should have political influence, we are not going to fare well in this country, and unless we do it right away, the opportunity will be lost. A Jewish minority group, well-organized, gets whatever it wants and we get nothing."[3]

On September 27, 1950, in the third month of the war, President Truman authorized Douglas MacArthur to cross the thirty-eighth parallel into North Korea. The invasion was launched on October 9. American troops pushed north along two flanks, one on the eastern coast and the other on the western coast of the peninsula. By late October, the invasion was proceeding so smoothly that the *New York Times* declared editorially that "we can now be easy in our minds as to the military outcome." On November 24, the day after Thanksgiving, when his troops were within shouting distance of China, General Mac-Arthur announced his final "home by Christmas" offensive.

The following evening, three hundred thousand Chinese troops crossed the border into North Korea and mounted a full-scale attack on the UN/American troops. "We face an entirely new war," MacArthur cabled the Joint Chiefs of Staff on November 28.

Truman chose to fight on and so informed the American people at a November 30 press conference. When asked if "use of the atomic bomb [was] under active consideration," he answered, "Always has been. It is one of our weapons."[4]

On October 2, 1950, Honey Fitz died. Beloved by his grandchildren, tolerated by his son-in-law, he had been a force in all of their lives, but, perhaps, most particularly in Jack's. No one had been more delighted than Honey Fitz when Jack decided to run for the seat he had held; no one worked harder on his behalf; and no one enjoyed the campaign and the victory more than he had.

A month after his grandfather's death, John Fitzgerald Kennedy was elected to his third term in Congress.

In mid-December, Joseph P. Kennedy spoke at the University of Virginia Law School Student Legal Forum at the invitation of its president, Robert F. Kennedy. James Landis had drafted a serviceable, entirely uncontroversial address on lawyers and public service, but

Kennedy put it aside in favor of his first major foreign policy speech since leaving government service.

He seized the occasion—and the press coverage he was able to garner for it—to restate and reemphasize his opposition to Truman Doctrine aid to Turkey and Greece, Marshall Plan assistance to Europe, the organization of NATO, and recent congressional appropriations for military assistance overseas. What, he asked, had these billions of dollars accomplished? Nothing. The Truman policy was "suicidal" and "politically and morally" bankrupt. Kennedy called for a complete about-face. He challenged every central tenet of the Cold War consensus: that the Soviets were ideologically and politically committed to expanding their empire; that Moscow controlled Communist parties and regimes everywhere and always would; that the United States was rich enough to police the world against Communist aggression without damaging the domestic economy; that any attempt at negotiation with Communists would embolden them to further aggression as "appeasement" in the 1930s had emboldened the Japanese, Italians, and Germans.

The policy recommendations that followed from these premises were startling in their radicalism, their coherence, and their distance from Truman's policies. "A first step . . . is to get out of Korea—indeed, to get out of every point in Asia we do not plan realistically to hold in our own defense. . . . The next step . . . is to apply the same principle in Europe." Communism was neither monolithic nor eternal; Soviet influence might spread into Europe, but only for the short term. Communist parties outside the Soviet Union "will soon develop splinter organizations that will destroy the singleness that today characterizes Russian Communism. Tito in Yugoslavia is already demonstrating this fact. Mao in China is not likely to take his orders too long from Stalin."

Kennedy recognized that his recommendations would "be criticized as 'appeasement.'" But he did not run away from the term. "If it is wise in our interest not to make commitments that endanger our security, and this is appeasement, then I am for 'appeasement.'" His was a realistic foreign policy, one that, unlike Truman's, was "in accord with our historic traditions. We have never wanted a part of other peoples' scrapes. . . . What business is it of ours to support French colonial policy in Indo-China or to achieve Mr. Syngman Rhee's concepts of democracy in Korea. . . . We can do well to mind our business and interfere only where somebody threatens our business and our homes. . . . The suggestions I make . . . would—and I count this most—conserve American lives for American ends, not waste them in the freezing hills of Korea or on the battle-scarred plains of Western Europe."[5]

Kennedy made sure that his speech got attention in the papers the next morning by sending out advanced copies. The Hearst papers responded, as he knew they would, with glowing editorials and long excerpts. "We think it offers a clear and hard-headed basis of hope in these times when people's faces are clouded with fear and sickly anxiety for the future." Arthur Krock claimed that "a bipartisan group [was already] veering towards the position stated this week by Joseph P. Kennedy . . . that the United States should build the greatest military power in history, concentrate it in the Western Hemisphere and on our Pacific security line, and let Europe and Asia go Communist in the meantime if that shall be the result." Even Walter Lippmann found Kennedy's arguments oddly compelling. The American public, Lippmann wrote in his December 19, 1950, column, had become so out of sympathy with Truman's thunderous globalism and bombastic rhetoric that it was willing now to give isolationists like Kennedy a hearing. What Lippmann feared was that Kennedy's brand of extremist isolationism, which would take the nation back "to the positions we occupied in 1939," would overwhelm more moderate approaches. "A new doctrine which is far short of the globalism of the Truman Doctrine on the one hand and of the isolationism of Mr. Kennedy on the other will have to be formulated if the isolationist sentiment is not to become irresistible and overwhelming."[6]

Kennedy would later claim, and with some justification, that his speech launched what *Life* magazine would on January 8, 1951, refer to as "the great debate." While Henry Luce—and his magazines— disagreed with almost everything Kennedy espoused, particularly his recommendation that the United States withdraw from Korea (Luce wanted instead to extend the war and liberate China), the editors admitted that the speech had "created a minor stir." Printing three columns of letters endorsing Kennedy's speech, the *Wall Street Journal* explained the omission of critical letters by saying it just hadn't received any yet.

A week after Kennedy spoke, Herbert Hoover delivered his own heavily promoted and nationally broadcast address. Whether Hoover's speech was occasioned by Kennedy's, we do not know, but the similarities in their isolationist sentiments and recommendations were such that they were soon conflated into what James Reston and others began to refer to as the Hoover-Kennedy side of the debate. Kennedy could be dismissed as a quirky, bitter voice of negativity. But when Hoover took up many of the same themes, the Cold Warriors felt obliged to hit back hard. The ex-president and the ex-ambassador were derided as reactionaries, defeatists, isolationists, appeasers, and Communist sympathizers or dupes. A *New York Times* editorial noted almost gleefully that *Pravda* had published the full texts of both their speeches.

Kennedy took the brunt of the criticism, as his proposals for total withdrawal from Europe and Asia were far more extreme. Joe Alsop, now writing with his brother Stewart led the charge. "Under normal circumstances," they wrote, "there would be no great interest in the political views of a successful stock market speculator who makes it a habit to propose surrender whenever surrender is feasible. At present, however, when the threat of Soviet triumph is actually greater than the threat of Nazi triumph ten years ago, the Kennedy program deserves analysis." Kennedy's recommendations, if followed, the Alsops declared, would ensure "total triumph for Stalin. . . . Perhaps, of course, during the early stages of our digestion as a Soviet satellite, men like Kennedy, the advocates of isolation, the gravediggers of the republic, might be permitted to keep their villas at Palm Beach. The best Christmas thought that can be offered this year is that most Americans would rather be dead."[7]

On January 5, 1951, three weeks after Kennedy's speech in Virginia, Senator Robert Taft of Ohio, "Mr. Republican," joined the "great debate" with a ten-thousand-word address on the Senate floor that sounded very much like an affirmation of Kennedy's views. Why, he wanted to know, was President Truman preparing to send General Dwight David Eisenhower to Europe as supreme commander of NATO forces? Why was he planning to send hundreds of thousands of American troops to Europe? What did he hope to accomplish by provoking the Soviets? Truman, Secretary of State Dean Acheson, and a variety of

Democratic senators attacked Taft viciously, as Kennedy and Hoover had been attacked, for being a muddle-headed appeaser and Communist dupe. Among his harshest critics was his fellow Republican, Senator Henry Cabot Lodge, Jr., of Massachusetts.

What had begun as a policy argument quickly turned into a larger debate about congressional authority. Could the president send American troops overseas on his own, or did he require explicit congressional approval to do so? Two days before Taft's speech, Republican congressman Frederic Coudert, Jr., from New York introduced a resolution in the House that would have required such approval. On January 8, Republican senator Kenneth Wherry of Nebraska introduced a parallel resolution in the Senate.

Congressman John Kennedy, knowing he would eventually have to take a position siding either with his party, his president, and Henry Cabot Lodge, Jr., whom he was considering running against in 1952, or with his father and Republicans Taft and Coudert, announced the day after Taft's speech that he was going to "spend the next four weeks in Europe," determining for himself whether the nations of Western Europe were committed to "rearming themselves." If not, it made no sense sending American troops to defend them against communism.[8]

It was a brilliant maneuver—and it worked well. Congressman Kennedy would be absent from the country for at least a month, during the height of what was going to be a highly contentious debate. When he returned, it would be as an expert who had made an independent, on-the-ground study and was guided by that, not party orthodoxy or his father's opinions. Kennedy thought the trip a grand idea and recommended that Jack issue regular press releases from Europe, detailing his meetings with American and European diplomats, military experts, Pope Pius XII, and Marshal Tito. When he returned, his father purchased radio time for him to report his findings to the country over the Mutual-Yankee Networks.

In early February, Kennedy flew north to welcome Jack home, help him prepare for his radio speech, and give his own talk at a luncheon at the Harmonie Club, where he declared without equivocation that he opposed sending any financial assistance to Europe or Asia. "Asia for the Asiatics is an intelligible theme, as plain to Pakistan as to Peiping. . . . The overthrow of Communism in China is rightly a crusade for the

Chinese, but not the responsibility of an alien race." He called for the withdrawal of American troops from Korea, the end of support for Chiang Kai-shek in Formosa, and the cessation of financial assistance to the French in Indo-China.[9]

Every time he opened his mouth now, Kennedy made it easier and more necessary for Jack to separate himself from his rabble-rouser, extremist, provocateur father. Three days after his father had spoken at the Harmonie Club, Congressman Kennedy presented his findings calmly, almost dispassionately, in a nationwide radio broadcast. He reported on European military readiness and civilian morale, but it was near impossible to tell where he stood on the major issue: whether American troops should be sent to Europe. That, of course, was his intention. The *Boston Herald* chose to emphasize his dismay "that Europe is not making the sacrifices necessary for survival and by no means is making an effort to match America's contribution. . . . It is important that Western Europe be saved, but we cannot do so ourselves or pay a price that will endanger our own survival." The *Boston Traveler* declared, on the contrary, that the congressman had repudiated "the gloomy defeatism of his father's December speech," that he did not, "like the ex-Ambassador, declare that Europe is physically and morally bankrupt and that Americans had better huddle within their borders until the Communist storm blows itself out."[10]

Two weeks later, on February 22, Congressman Kennedy presented his findings before the Senate Committees on Foreign Relations and Armed Services, which were meeting jointly to consider Senator Wherry's resolution prohibiting the president from dispatching troops to Europe without congressional approval. Of the thirty-seven witnesses called in eleven days, he was the youngest, least experienced, least known, and only junior congressman called to testify. He read his report on rearmament programs in Great Britain, France, and Italy and, based on it, offered a compromise proposal, that the United States supply military assistance to its European allies but limit it to the four divisions Truman had already asked for. In the future, American troop deployments to Europe would be determined by a ratio system policed by Congress: no more than one American division for every six supplied by the Europeans. Congressman Kennedy's compromise solution was similar to that already put forward by several Republican senators, but it was in direct opposition to his party's refusal to approve any restrictions on the president's right to send troops to Europe.

After he had read his report, the congressman was questioned by committee members, including Henry Cabot Lodge, Jr., whom Jack Kennedy would soon challenge for his seat in the Senate. Senator Walter George of Georgia prefaced his remarks by assuring Congressman Kennedy "in advance that the question I am going to ask is an impersonal one. . . . You come from a very distinguished American family that exercises a great influence on American public opinion. I want to ask you impersonally whether you remember the able speech of your father in December 1950? I think you know me well enough to know that I do not share his point of view, but I respect his sincerity." The senator then cited Joseph P. Kennedy's statement that the United States should get out of Europe because if the Soviets chose to move west or should any European nation "turn communistic," there was little the United States could do about it. "Now, my question is this," Senator George continued. "Am I right in my interpretation of your testimony here today that although you think there is a danger or a possibility that Europe might go communistic, nevertheless you think we should take such steps as we can in cooperation with our allies in Europe, to prevent her from going communistic, and not get out of Europe now, as was indicated, if I read his language right, by your father in his December speech?"

Having been fed a friendly softball from the distinguished senator, Jack Kennedy proceeded to knock it out of the park. "I do not like to speak for my father, because I think he could do that better than I could." He then declared that the effect of "losing Europe and losing its productive facilities, and so forth, would be such that while I think we could survive, it would be difficult and I think we should do our utmost within reason to save it. Therefore, I am in favor of sending these four divisions. . . . I still feel that we should take the risk to save Western Europe. . . . This is my position. I think you should ask my father directly as to his position."

Congressman Kennedy had demonstrated precisely what he had hoped to: that he was not a marionette controlled by his father or his party. In opposition to Joseph P. Kennedy, Congressman Kennedy favored sending four divisions of American troops to Europe. In opposition to the Democratic majority, he was not, however, in favor of giving Truman carte blanche. When Senator Tom Connally of Texas, chairman of the Foreign Relations Committee, asked if he was in favor of the Wherry resolution, which the Republicans supported but the Democrats opposed, he answered with a definitive yes and no. He was not in favor of the resolution if it was going to mandate that Truman withdraw the four divisions that he had already requested. But he did favor one that regulated the dispatch of additional divisions.[11]

In the end, the nonbinding and therefore meaningless resolution that was passed by the Senate was close to the compromise Congressman Kennedy—and the majority of Republican senators—had pushed for. After three long months of debate, acrimony, and much name-calling, the Senate approved the sending of four divisions to Europe but admonished Truman to send no more without congressional approval. Each side claimed victory and blamed the other for attempting to desecrate the Constitution and bring havoc to the world. Congressman Kennedy was one of the few winners, having established a name for himself as a reasoned and independent voice in foreign policy.

While the son was enjoying a fleeting moment in the spotlight, one he cherished to the point of having ten thousand copies of his Senate testimony printed up and distributed, the father was on his way to Europe for his spring vacation. Rose was already in Europe and met up with him in Paris. "Dad is in very good form," she wrote the children back in the States, "and takes me out every night so I have never been so gay. The last time he was here with me was just after Bobby was born, so there are quite a few new sights since then."[12]

From Paris, Kennedy took the train to Rome, where Count Galeazzi had arranged an audience with the pope and discussions with Vatican officials, including the secretary of state. Upon his return to Paris, he met with Anthony Biddle, who, after a distinguished career as a diplomat and in the military, was serving as the army's foreign liaison officer. Biddle invited Kennedy to visit U.S. Army headquarters "and see some of the topside men." The next day, he called to say that General Eisenhower wanted to see Kennedy on Friday morning at the Astoria Hotel, where he had set up his offices. After being held up by security officers who didn't know who he was, Kennedy was escorted upstairs, where Eisenhower saw him without delay.

"I had never met him before," Kennedy recalled in his diary, "and he unquestionably is a very attractive man to meet. He was sitting behind his desk, got up and shook hands, and said let's sit over here where it is more comfortable and so we sat in lounge chairs facing one another. He started off by asking me what I had noticed." Kennedy told him that most of the Frenchmen he had talked with claimed to prefer occupation by the Soviets to "all-out war." Eisenhower did not disagree. He had come to Europe, in part, to "make the people realize that they must improve their spiritual attitudes towards this whole problem of Russia." Eisenhower then launched into a general discussion of American foreign policy by "saying he was against my general plan to withdraw to the North American continent." Kennedy corrected him by saying that he would "be willing to give some help provided Europe showed the real attitude of a desire to fight; but, in the absence of that, I thought we would be just pouring our resources down a rat-hole." They moved on to other subjects "because I was convinced neither could persuade the other." Kennedy questioned Eisenhower about his views, then tore them apart one after another. He was aggressive, relentless, without a hint of deference to the general, who was arguably the most popular and respected American on two continents. As Kennedy continued to pummel him, Eisenhower got more defensive. He wasn't part of the Truman-Acheson team, he insisted; he didn't want to get the country involved in any more wars; he understood the great difficulties and potential consequences of standing up to the Soviets.[13]

Kennedy came away from their meeting, as he wrote Galeazzi, assured that though Eisenhower agreed with the Democrats on foreign policy issues, he "would much prefer, I would think, to be the candidate of the Republican party. . . . I am sure he is going to get in there somewhere along the line. Personally I don't like to see any military man president of the United States but I think I would take anybody in preference to Truman."[14]

Joseph P. Kennedy had always prided himself on being an independent thinker who said what he thought regardless of the consequences. In great part, that had been part of his downfall and exile from Washington.

What he feared now was that he was the last of his breed. Regardless of his disputes with individual journalists and columnists, Kennedy had always believed in the power of an independent press, and he wanted to now. But as he looked around him, he found that everyone he could once have counted on to make noise was gone—the naysayers, the provocateurs, the newspaper editors and publishers—all gone. William Randolph Hearst had died that August. Colonel Robert McCormick of the *Chicago Tribune* was still alive, but ailing. They had been replaced by a generation of sycophants, men who catered to the powerful instead of holding them to account for their mistakes. In the fall of 1951, Kennedy accused James Reston, chief diplomatic correspondent for the *New York Times* and, within government circles, as powerful as any journalist in the country, of being less than "independent" in his judgments, of being too close to the government, too uncritical of the administration. The world was falling apart, the future was dire. Why couldn't Reston see this—and write about it? (Kennedy was not the only one who thought Reston was too close to his sources. It was widely known that Dean Acheson, a good friend of Reston's, regularly leaked information to him.)

Reston defended himself by insisting that Kennedy was the one who was unable to see clearly what was going on in the world. "Your view of our time is one of unrelieved anxiety. You see the policy of the present as a catastrophe for your country. . . . I do not, however, share your melancholy view of our time." Although Kennedy refused to concede to Reston that his judgment might be biased by his "unrelieved anxiety," he came close to admitting as much in a condolence letter to the Duchess of Devonshire on the death of her husband: "I suppose the fact that nothing in the world seems to be right these days may be the result, for some of us, of having lost those who were near and dear to us. When that kind of love goes out of one's life it is very difficult to replace it with anything else, and it is almost impossible to see with any degree of reasonableness all the good things that are left."[15]

Approaching his middle sixties, Joseph P. Kennedy lived a strangely bifurcated life, swinging back and forth between what Reston had referred to as his "melancholy" and a kind of manic exhilaration. When he was with his friends and family, he was a very different man from the one who delivered angry speeches and lectured President Truman in the White House and General Eisenhower in Paris.

Now that he was retired and had more free time, his need to surround himself with family and friends was stronger than ever. His buddies—old friends such as Arthur Houghton, Phil Reisman, Morton Downey, and Joe Timilty and new ones such as Lucius Ordway, the St. Paul businessman and founder of 3M who had retired to Palm Beach, Carroll Rosenbloom, Baltimore businessman and NFL team owner, and Father Cavanaugh of Notre Dame—took his mind off his cares, made him laugh, and gave him an outlet for the caustic, mocking, but usually good-natured teasing at which he excelled. His letters to Houghton and Ordway and Rosenbloom, written in his sixties, were (absent the anatomical references) very much like those his son Jack had written in his teens and early twenties to his college friends: sophomorically funny, cuttingly sarcastic, irreverent.

"You were very smart to go to Mayo," he wrote Ordway from Hyannis Port in June 1951. "Of course I go to the Lahey Clinic twice a year; but then, I always do things twice as well as you. . . . Houghton and I are thoroughly convinced that there is something more than just slightly wrong with that. You crab in a golf game; you abuse the nice woman who is now your wife; you're anti-social; you don't spend any of that thirty million dollars you have; in fact, we think you're pretty nearly hopeless regardless of your condition from your neck down. I can imagine we could get testimony that that isn't so good either! However, we like you for some strange reason and we like your wife even better."[16]

For those he counted as his friends, he would do anything. There were times when he almost begged them to let him help them, to accept his business advice, to visit his doctors at his expense, to accept his offers of loans or investment capital. When William O. Douglas suffered a dreadful mountain-climbing accident in 1949, Kennedy paid his hospital bills and invited him to recuperate in Palm Beach. He worried especially about friends such as Count Enrico Galeazzi, whose employment as a lay adviser to an aging, infirm pope did not afford him much financial security. In the summer of 1950, he offered to secure for Galeazzi and his son-in-law a Coca-Cola distributorship, but Galeazzi was not interested. Kennedy promised to keep looking. "I spend most of my life writing how grateful I am to you for all the favors you do for me and my family, and I just feel that I never have a chance to do anything for you."[17]

Carroll Rosenbloom believed that Kennedy kept secret many of these acts of kindness because "he rather enjoyed being thought of as 'tough' rather than 'soft.' . . . In his personal relationships, he has always been the 'softest touch' I have ever known." Friendship was, for him, a priceless commodity. "I remember his telling me once that a man was fortunate if he could count his real friends on the fingers of one hand. . . . Friendship has always meant a great deal to him—it is a deep, abiding thing. To him friendship could never be casual."[18]

He had a gift for friendship, though he knew it did not always come easily, that one had to work at it, stay in touch, celebrate the good times, offer condolences in the bad. When Walter Howey lost his wife in the spring of 1954, Kennedy wrote him from Palm Beach, even though they had not spent time together in years. "I am not sure I will do well with this letter even though I want to write it," he began, aware that Howey had suffered severe professional and financial setbacks. "I have known that you have been hurt and that you are having a terrible time. I also know that your dear wife died. I just couldn't write you a letter because what could I say? . . . All I can say is what I feel deeply— that my best and dearest friend has suffered a great loss and that his sorrow is shared by me. I can't do anything for you except pray for you and that I will do. If you want me for anything, just let me know."[19]

The only thing that mattered more to him than his friends was his children. The Kennedy boys and girls, he was convinced, could do whatever they wanted once they made up their minds to do it. Each had his or her minor flaws—Jack was rarely punctual, was very messy, and had still not, his father complained, "learned the art of taking care of himself"; Bobby never quite knew what he wanted to do next; Teddy was too much of a playboy; Eunice didn't take care of her health; Patricia couldn't make up her mind; Jean never seemed to take anything seriously. Each of these shortcomings could and, he was sure, would be corrected as they grew up.[20]

The Kennedys were beginning to expand in size now. The first newcomer was Ethel Skakel, whom Bobby married in June 1950, at the end of his second year of law school in Virginia. Ethel Skakel was the daughter of a self-made Protestant millionaire father and an Irish Catholic mother. She had grown up in a mansion outside Greenwich and gone to Manhattanville with Jean, who had introduced her to Bobby. Wealthy, Catholic, athletic, pretty, with a grand sense of humor and six siblings of her own, she had no trouble fitting into the Kennedy clan and ended up adoring her father-in-law as much as he adored her. The same would happen with Robert Sargent Shriver, the next to join the family.

Eunice had met Sarge in Washington in 1946 when she was working at the State Department and sharing a town house with Jack. Shriver, whose father, once wealthy, had lost the family fortune during the Depression, had gone to Yale College and Yale Law School, seen action as a battleship gunner during the war, then returned to work at *Newsweek*. Soon after they met, Eunice introduced Shriver to Kennedy, who was looking for someone to edit Joe Jr.'s letters from Spain for publication. When Shriver reported that the letters were unpublishable, Kennedy, admiring his honesty and intelligence, recruited him to work in Chicago at the Merchandise Mart. After eight months there, his employer—and future father-in-law—called Shriver back to Washington to help Eunice in her new job, organizing a committee on juvenile delinquency in the office of the attorney general. In the summer of 1948, Shriver was sent back to Chicago as assistant general manager of the Merchandise Mart and chief representative of the Kennedy family's political interests. Three years later, Eunice moved to Chicago to work with the House of the Good Shepherd and the Chicago Juvenile Court. They would marry two years after this, in May 1953.

In 1950, Ted Kennedy followed his three brothers and father to Harvard. He played freshman ball in the fall and did quite well. "Dad made all my home games, where he helped out the coach by pacing the sidelines wearing a beret and shouting instructions." When spring came, Ted threw himself into practice "to the extent that my grades suffered, my Spanish grade especially. I worried that if I flunked or made a D on the final exam, I wouldn't be eligible to play football in the fall." He might have studied harder or gotten tutoring, but he took what he thought was the simple way out and had a friend take his exam for him. The boys were caught, given a year's suspension, and "told we could come back if we'd done something useful with that time."

Ted's first call on being suspended was to his brother Jack, who agreed to prepare their father for the news. He then left Cambridge for Hyannis Port. "My father met me in the sunroom," Ted recalled in his memoirs. "He alternated between disappointment and anger for quite a while. . . . The more we talked, the quieter his voice would get. But then the phone would ring; one of my brothers expressing concern, offering advice. And when I came back into the room, he'd tee off on me again. 'There are people who can mess up in life and not get caught,' he advised me at one point, 'but you're not one of them, Teddy.'" The day after their first go-round, as his father began to understand the possible fallout from his son's suspension for cheating, "he was absolutely wild and went up through the roof. For about five hours. From then on he was calm. It was just 'How do we help you?' And he never brought the thing up again." Ted might have transferred and continued his schooling, but he didn't want to. He and his father decided that he would enlist in the army and return to Harvard after two years of service.[21]

On June 25, Ted took his physical and was assigned to basic training at Fort Dix. He wanted to volunteer for duty in Korea but was talked out of it by his brothers during a lunch in New York. "Both were appalled, and strenuously argued against my volunteering. 'Mother and Dad have suffered enough. . . . We can't afford to have you go over and risk getting killed. You just can't do this kind of thing. Go where the army assigns you.'"[22]

Kennedy, who knew nothing of Ted's dreams of becoming a war hero like his two oldest brothers, arranged to get him an assignment with the CIC, the Counter Intelligence Corps. Ted trained with the CIC for two months, after which he was transferred to Camp Gordon in Georgia, ostensibly because he was too young for the CIC and never should have been there in the first place.

On learning that his son was now going to be a MP, Kennedy contacted Anthony Biddle with "a tremendous personal favor to ask you." He wanted Biddle, who had joined the army from the diplomatic corps during the war and still had contacts there, to arrange to get Ted "an interesting assignment, Paris, for instance, where he could learn the language and learn something about the place. . . . Now you know I wouldn't bother you with this if it did not mean a great deal to me. I hate to ask favors from my personal friends but since he is only a private and we are not asking for transfer from one sphere of his duty to another but rather an assignment in his own present branch of activity, I would appreciate it if you could arrange this for me." Biddle did Kennedy the favor he asked and Ted was assigned to Paris, where he served out his time.[23]

Fortunately for everyone, the cheating incident was kept quiet. Ted had left Harvard, his father told his friend Sir James Calder, "because he got restless and enlisted in the regular army." That he had been suspended for cheating would not become public knowledge until the spring of 1962, when Ted was running in a primary election for the U.S. Senate and got a call from brother Jack in the White House, warning him to "get that Harvard story out." Whether the president had learned that the press already had the story, we do not know. Ted took his brother's advice and had the story released to the *Boston Globe,* which ran it on the front page. He was castigated for his cheating, then praised for his candor in admitting to it.[24]

Although Ted's dismissal from Harvard was kept secret, the ninety West Point cadets who were expelled for cheating that same spring had no such luck. Their story was front-page news for weeks.

Editorials demanded that Army football coach Earl Blaik, whose team had been decimated by the scandal, resign or be fired; President Truman expressed his concern; the Senate launched an investigation; Senator William Fulbright of Arkansas demanded that the football programs at West Point and Annapolis be suspended, if not permanently ended. Cardinal Spellman, on the other hand, declared that "to err is human, to forgive is divine" and asked the presidents of three Catholic colleges in New York, Fordham, Iona, and Manhattan, to admit West Point students who applied for transfer.

Father Cavanaugh of Notre Dame recalled years later that he, Arthur Houghton, and Kennedy had discussed the scandal during an August cruise on the *Marlin,* Kennedy's fifty-one-foot yacht. They had just finished their fish chowder luncheon and were looking at yet another story about the expelled cadets in the *New York Times* when, Cavanaugh recalled in his oral history, "Kennedy shot a question at me. 'What would it cost to send all of these young fellows through Notre Dame?'" Cavanaugh, without knowing how many of the students were in their first, second, third, or fourth year, quickly calculated that it would "run almost to a half million dollars" (about $12.4 million in purchasing power today). Kennedy's response was immediate: "I want every one of them to have an opportunity to go through Notre Dame, all expenses paid. Let us agree upon two conditions. My name will not be made known, and none of these young men should participate in intercollegiate athletics. . . . Otherwise, people will think that Notre Dame's benefactor is trying to buy athletes for the university."[25]

The offer was announced on August 21, 1951. Each of the ninety expelled West Point students was sent a Notre Dame application and an offer letter that explained that while the unnamed benefactor did "not condone the act of the cadets," he realized "the limitations of means for the purpose of getting an education by which some of the cadets and their families are restricted. . . . The offer is made to athletes and non-athletes, to Catholics and non-Catholics." The only requirement was that the students "meet the standards and academic requirements of Notre Dame."[26]

Thirteen West Point students registered at Notre Dame that September, twelve received funds from Kennedy, and every one of them graduated. Upon graduation they were given the name of their benefactor. The story made it to the back pages of a few newspapers, but nobody took notice, as by then the scandal was very old news. Kennedy wanted it that way, not because he shied away from positive publicity, but because there were too many loose ends he didn't want to unravel. Jack was getting ready to run for higher office and wouldn't be helped by stories of how his father had rescued West Point cheaters. Worse yet, Kennedy feared the story might lead reporters from West Point to Harvard and Ted Kennedy. It was better to keep the matter quiet.

It would not be entirely accurate to say that Joseph P. Kennedy was mellowing with age. But it would be foolish to believe that he had not been affected by the passage of time and the tragedies that had befallen three of his four eldest children. He was as opinionated, volatile, argumentative, driven, fearful of boredom, and anxious to be doing something significant and remain in the public eye as he had ever been. But now well into his second decade of retirement and knowing that he would never again return to Washington or take on a full-time position in private business, he was in the process of creating a new life for himself. Rather than push back against his status—as senior citizen, retired businessman and public servant, philanthropist, and grandfather-to-be—he took hold of it, spent more time with his friends, welcomed daughters- and sons-in-law, presided over the family foundation, and concentrated his considerable attention and talents on pushing his children wherever they wanted to go.

Thirty-four

THE NEXT SENATOR
FROM MASSACHUSETTS

Jack had been reelected without opposition in 1948. He had a Republican opponent in 1950 but crushed him with 82 percent of the vote. That same year, two of the young veterans he had entered Congress with, Richard Nixon of California and his good friend George Smathers of Florida, ran for and were elected to the Senate.

Jack had never much liked the House of Representatives and never been much of a congressman. He had sided with labor and voted for health care reform, housing relief, and every New Deal or Fair Deal welfare issue that came before him. But these were not "his" issues, not his specialty. His forte was foreign policy, which to a great extent was the purview of the Senate.

His seat from the eleventh district was as safe as any in Washington. He could have remained in the House, his mother remembered, "for the next thirty or forty years, rising by seniority . . . to become an extremely influential old man, perhaps Speaker of the House. The prospect of spending his life that way bored Jack intensely."[1]

The only way up and out was to run for higher office. In 1952, he was faced with two possibilities. He could run against incumbent senator Henry Cabot Lodge, Jr., or, if Democratic governor Paul Dever chose to campaign for the Senate, Jack could run for governor. In either case, he had to make himself better known to the voters of the state, as he had earlier to the men and women of the eleventh district.

He began his campaign for statewide office—he didn't yet know which it would be—in the spring of 1949. For the next three years, he spent almost every weekend traveling the state, "driving to various civic, fraternal, political or veteran group meetings on Friday night and Saturday, appearing at Catholic communion breakfasts or Protestant church socials on Sunday and then hurrying back to Boston to catch the Federal at Back Bay station on Sunday night and crawling into a sleeping-car berth for the trip to Washington." "No town was too small or too Republican for him," recalled Dave Powers, his "booking agent" for these weekend campaign trips. "He was willing to go anywhere, and every group was glad to have him, not only because he was an interesting political figure and a well-known war hero, but because he never charged a dime for expenses."[2]

The congressman pushed himself and his aides relentlessly. They marveled at his stamina, his unflappable affability, his ability to connect with audiences, his willingness to shake as many hands as were extended to him. His back still bothered him—and would for the rest of his life—but it didn't stop him or slow him down. Wherever he went that spring, he told his listeners that although he had no set plans for the future, if they would be so kind as to give him their names and addresses, he would contact them later if he needed them. Large numbers obliged. His list of contacts, some of them Democrats, some independents or Republicans, grew until it included hundreds of names from every part of the state.

His father supported him through it all, offering advice, solicited and unsolicited, and making sure he had all the money he needed. In August 1951, with statewide elections still fifteen months away, Kennedy wrote Tim McInerny, a former *Boston Post* editor whom he had known and worked with for years, about joining his son's campaign as researcher and publicist. It would not, he cautioned McInerny, be a big job, at least for now. Much of the work would be done by Kennedy, James Landis, who had connections in Washington, and the staff at the New York office. "I know you will remember that we are not strangers in Washington, and I am not a stranger to the newspaper men or columnists, and when the campaign starts I, myself, will do all the things I think are necessary, and, therefore, it will not require very much of your time. . . . I wanted your services occasionally for digging up an item that might be of value in the state." When McInerny asked for more money than Kennedy was willing to give him, Kennedy cautioned him that there would be "no occasion for entertainment and travel. . . . We are not exploiting somebody whom nobody has ever heard of, and we are not going to ask any favors from people that I have not done some favors for before or that I can do at some future time."[3]

To burnish his foreign policy credentials, Congressman Kennedy set off that fall of 1951 on a twenty-five-thousand-mile, seven-week tour of the Middle East and Asia. Accompanying him were his sister Patricia and his brother Bob, who left behind him his wife of sixteen months, Ethel Skakel, and the first Kennedy granddaughter, Kathleen, born in July 1951. The three Kennedys met with Generals Dwight Eisenhower and Matthew Ridgway in Paris; Jean de Lattre de Tassigny, the French military commander, and Premier Bao Dai in Vietnam; Prime Minister David Ben-Gurion and Arab leaders in Israel; British officials and national leaders in Iran; Prime Minister Jawaharlal Nehru in India; and Liaquat Ali Khan, the prime minister of Pakistan, just hours before he was assassinated. Their final stop was Korea, where Jack was taken ill—a common occurrence on trips during which he pushed himself beyond his limits—and flown to Okinawa with a temperature of 106. After a course of penicillin and adrenal hormones for his Addison's disease, he was judged well enough to fly home.

His father cheered him on and offered public relations assistance from the United States. "If possible," he cabled him in New Delhi on October 13, 1951, at the start of his journey, "try and get some news service to report your activities each location. Good for build up here." On November 2, he informed Jack of the media campaign he had set up for him on his return: "Radio program National hookup night November 14. Boston Chamber of Commerce Lunch Nov. 19. What about Kate Smith's afternoon television hour? [At the time, Patricia was working for Kate Smith.] Have interview National Hookup probably night of

15th. Write me names important people you talked with for newspaper publicity and air talks. Telephone me upon arrival in Europe."[4]

Jack cabled that he would be returning to Boston "on the morning of the 12th or perhaps on the 11th for publicity—and then I could come to N.Y. on the same day to work on the speech." He asked his father to get hold of recent articles by Justice Douglas on Iran, William Bullitt on India, and Gardner Cowles, the founder and publisher of *Look* magazine. He also wanted to look at the articles and speeches Governor Dewey had delivered when he returned from abroad and the "last 8 weeks copies of the *Economist*."[5]

After his last "fact-finding" trip in February, Jack had taken a position in direct opposition to that of his father. Now, nine months later and after weeks of extended discussions with diplomats, military officials, anticolonial leaders, and journalists in the field, his thinking had begun to move closer to his father's on the need for the United States to reduce its presence overseas. With a specificity that was absent from his father's broad-stroked attacks, but in line with his overall policy recommendations, Congressman Kennedy, in his half-hour radio address, broadcast nationwide on November 14, 1951, from New York at ten thirty P.M., urged American withdrawal from the "desperate effort of a French regime to hang on to the remnants of empire. . . . These Indo-Chinese states are puppet states . . . as typical examples of empire and of colonialism as can be found anywhere." In the Arab world as well, the United States appeared "too frequently . . . too ready to buttress an inequitable status quo." He was opposed to the government's unthinking, unwavering support for European colonial interests, to American "intervention in behalf of England's oil investments in Iran . . . our avowed willingness to assume an almost imperial military responsibility for the safety of the Suez, our failure to deal effectively after these years with the terrible human tragedy of the more than 700,000 Arab refugees [from Palestine]."

The similarities between his father's speeches of the year before and his radio address were remarkable. Joseph P. Kennedy had declared on December 12, 1950, "We have far fewer friends than we had in 1945!" Jack, nine months later: "It is tragic to report that not only have we made no new friends, but we have lost old ones." Joseph Kennedy had, on February 3, 1951, asserted that the United States, because of its support of European imperialism, had come to "represent in Asia, as the French in Indo-China, the revival of the white man's burden." Jack now insisted that American support of British interests in Iran and French colonialism in Indo-China had "intensified the feeling of hostility towards us until today we are definitely classed with the imperialist powers of Western Europe."[6]

There were differences between the two men's positions, differences that would be emphasized in the years to come. Unlike the ex-ambassador, Congressman Kennedy thought it was in the best interests of the United States to fight communism abroad, but by force of example, not force of arms, by celebrating and exporting the "American spirit," supporting nationalist attempts to break free of colonial rule, combating poverty and want, and contributing to the building of "strong native non-Communist sentiment." His father, on the other hand, believed the United States had no business fighting communism in any manner, anywhere outside the western hemisphere.

The New York *Daily News,* in the past one of the few and most dynamic supporters of the senior Kennedy's views, saw at once the significance of the congressman's decision to come over to his father's side. John O'Donnell, the paper's Washington correspondent, declared on November 20, 1951, that in his radio address, John Fitzgerald Kennedy had dropped "a couple of political blockbusters." He was not only taking aim at the Truman administration's foreign policy but had signaled his intentions to challenge Truman's most loyal Republican champion, "Senator Henry Cabot Lodge, Jr., long a supporter of the Roosevelt-Truman foreign policy." If, as now seemed to be the case, Congressman Kennedy decided to run for Lodge's Senate seat, Massachusetts politics would be turned topsy-turvy with "a Democrat who challenges both Truman's foreign policy and its Republican backer. The future will be lively."

Though an unannounced candidate and unsure as to whether he would be running for senator or governor, the congressman was in full campaign mode now. "Jack," his father wrote Arthur Poole on November 20, "was in pretty bad shape when he arrived and, with the radio broadcast that he made followed by a . . . speech before the Chamber of Commerce yesterday, and another television appearance that evening, and a half dozen speeches in the eastern part of the state, and three days in the hospital here, we expect him home tonight. His mental courage is so much superior to his physical strength that I sometimes wonder what the final result will be."[7]

Jack was facing a much more difficult campaign than in 1946. Henry Cabot Lodge, Jr., was as handsome as Jack Kennedy and a better speaker, paraded a family name as distinguished as any in Massachusetts (or the nation), had his own Harvard degree, a distinguished war record, a stellar record as an anti-Communist, and lots of money. George Smathers, perhaps Jack's best friend in Congress, urged him not to oppose Lodge. So did almost everyone outside the family. There were whispers everywhere about whether Jack was making the right choice, Eunice Shriver recalled, but none "in our home about Lodge. Only a mighty roar every time Jack came home. . . . 'Jack run for the Senate. You'll knock Lodge's block off.' My father had analyzed the situation thoroughly, and decided that Jack could win. Jack made the decision on his own after campaigning in every town in Massachusetts and finding support. But the greatest influence on his decision was my father's encouragement, and his belief that Jack could win."[8]

Joseph Kennedy's reasoning, as he laid it out to Cornelius Fitzgerald in late October 1951, was simple. Massachusetts was a Democratic state; all Jack had to do was to hold the Democratic vote and add to it some Republicans and independents. "It's ridiculous in this Democratic state that has been able to elect Curleys and Hurleys and even Dever that we should have Republican senators for almost twenty years. Lodge is very weak with the Republicans, themselves, and he had always been elected because he was able to get the Democratic vote. Nobody has ever fought him . . . who was competent to take him on, but Jack can easily do that. If Jack holds the Democratic vote in this state, he will get a substantial Republican vote and a very substantial independent vote."[9]

There was something daring, almost reckless, about Kennedy's analysis. To everyone else, Henry Cabot Lodge, Jr., looked unbeatable in 1952. The last four statewide elections for senator had gone to Republicans. Lodge himself, first elected in 1936, had been reelected in 1942; after his stint in the military, he had run against and easily defeated Democrat incumbent David Walsh in 1946, with 60 percent of the vote. Leverett Saltonstall, another Republican, had been elected to Lodge's seat by a landslide in 1944, then reelected in 1948 by a comfortable margin.

No matter what his father might say, Jack faced a difficult battle. "I am interesting myself in Jack's candidacy which probably will be for the U.S. Senate," Kennedy wrote Sir James Calder on November 24, 1951. "I have turned the conduct of most of my business over to an organization that I have gotten together in my office in New York and I am not paying too much attention to anything except in a very supervisory capacity."[10]

Kennedy canvassed friends, acquaintances, business associates, and former colleagues for help in getting his son's name before the voting public. And he was successful.

The year before, in the wake of the uproar over his University of Virginia speech, Kennedy had been invited by Lawrence Spivak, the founder, permanent panelist, and producer, to appear on *Meet the Press*. Kennedy declined but remained in touch with Spivak, who, a year later, issued an invitation for December 2, 1951, to Jack Kennedy, one of the few congressmen ever granted a half-hour interview on what was the premier news program on radio or television.

Jack looked remarkably young and almost painfully thin, with his ears sticking out on either side of his freshly trimmed haircut (thick on top, short on the sides). He answered questions from Spivak, James Reston, May Craig of the *Portland Press Herald*, and Ernest Lindley of *Newsweek* about whether Eisenhower was a Democrat or a Republican, whether Truman was the strongest candidate, what effect ongoing bribery and influence-peddling scandals would have on Democratic chances in 1952, and what he had learned on his recent trip abroad. His responses were dutiful and rather dull. On Korea, he tiptoed around, saying he agreed with General MacArthur on some points, but not on bombing Manchuria, that he supported the ongoing truce talks, and that he did not regard it as a sell-out of American troops that Truman had agreed with the enemy to establish a "truce line." "We ought to take agreement where we can take it." On most issues, he sounded like any other Democrat. Only when it came to questions about American intervention in the Middle East and Asia did he sound like his father. On Indo-China, he criticized the U.S. government for giving the French everything they had asked for. On Iran, he criticized it for taking the

British side and turning its back on the nationalists. When asked what he would do differently, he responded that he would send more "technical assistance" to the Middle East and Asia, improve the Voice of America and other propaganda tools, and back off support for the French in Indo-China until they declared their intention to cede independence to the native peoples of the region.

It was a good—though not a great—entrance onto the national stage for the young congressman. He made no mistakes, appeared intelligent, answered all the questions, resisted the traps laid, and found several occasions to flash a bit of Kennedy charm. The fact that, while still a comparatively junior congressman with no real accomplishments to his name, Jack had appeared on *Meet the Press* was, in the final analysis, more important than anything he happened to say.

His father acknowledged as much in a letter to Spivak a month after the appearance. Spivak had sent Joseph Kennedy a pair of suspenders as a Christmas gift. "Is there any significance to the fact that you sent out suspenders?" Kennedy had responded. "Does that indicate that people could lose their pants on the program, or anything like that? From what I have seen of it, I can't imagine trying to keep up with the brains of your panel. Maybe I could have done it in my younger days but I am sure I couldn't today. On the other hand, *Meet the Press* established Jack once and for all as a major personality, so there you are! Anyway, my very deep appreciation for all your favors and kindnesses."[11]

Two weeks after Congressman Kennedy's appearance on national television, his father spoke on the Mutual Broadcasting System radio network from 10:35 to 11:00 P.M. via a live hookup from Chicago. Written with James Landis and James Fayne, and reviewed and edited by Arthur Krock, his address to the Economic Club, titled "Our Foreign Policy—Its Casualties and Prospects," was another direct assault on Cold War assumptions and policies. The amount the nation spent fighting so-called enemies abroad, Kennedy insisted, limited "how much we can and dare expend for social purposes." Without firing a single shot, the Russians had succeeded in impoverishing America by forcing "upon us peacetime expenditures beyond what could have been their wildest hopes." The Truman administration had been "wasting our resources in the pursuit of a dream [the defeat of communism everywhere] which, worthy though it might be, was impossible of accomplishment. . . . The Korean War becomes more ghastly, more utterly futile as each day follows the next. . . . In Indo-China, American arms, American military aid, and American dollars are going to support France's desperate effort to keep her old colonial empire. In the Suez and on the Persian Gulf, we may soon become embroiled by the actions of the British. The Arab world, whose friendship had been ours, has turned against us. . . . America is no longer seen as a champion of democratic self-determination but as a nation indistinguishable from her imperial allies."

His anti-imperialist, anticolonialist rhetoric sounded much like his son's, but as he was not running for office, he had no need to moderate his positions, disguise his anger, or conceal his fears for the future. While the congressman could not distance himself from the ultimate Cold War objective—the destruction of communism—and remain a viable candidate for any office, his father could and did. Looking into the future, Kennedy underscored what he believed would be the ultimate consequence of an extended Cold War arms race. "Since armaments quickly become obsolescent and need replacement, this will mean the continuation of vast expenditures for the North Atlantic world. . . . Taxes will remain extravagantly high and life regimented to the austere needs of a war economy. It is not too difficult to predict that our democratic institutions cannot long survive such a strain." He had made much the same case in arguing against American involvement in the war against Germany, Italy, and Japan. To fight a dictatorship, even in a "cold" war, democratic governments had to employ the tools of dictatorship. Political and economic freedoms would be curtailed, markets reined in, investments controlled, prices and profits regulated.

He had tried the year before to set in motion a "great debate" about the Cold War, and perhaps he had. But, aside from Senator Robert Taft, who would be seriously challenged that year for leadership of his party and the Republican nomination for president, there were fewer and fewer politicians who were actively dissenting from what appeared to be a growing bipartisan consensus. The Democrats supported Cold War spending because they believed that the country could afford both guns and butter and that enhanced military expenditures were not detracting from but driving economic recovery and growth. The Republicans did not publically disagree but argued only that they could fight communism more efficiently and effectively than Truman.[12]

As the year before, reaction to Joseph Kennedy's speech was largely negative. He was not one to make excuses, but he felt obliged to explain himself in a letter to Adlai Stevenson, the governor of Illinois and the front-runner for the Democratic presidential nomination in 1952. "I have no ax to grind in politics," he explained, "but I am tremendously disturbed by the results of our foreign policy." His "sincere doubt" that the nation could afford the current program of foreign aid and his "growing conviction" that overseas expenditures were not buying added security had led him "to what I set forth in my talk. I hope it will at least stimulate thought, for the burden of the solution must be borne by younger men like yourself."[13]

This was to be his "last hurrah." With his son now a candidate for the Senate and, he hoped, in the foreseeable future, for the presidency, Joseph Kennedy recognized he would have to take a backseat. "As you may know," he explained to Dave Powers, who had invited him to speak in Detroit, "I made a speech in Chicago on the 17th and that finishes my speech making for quite some time. I have a son who is a Congressman and who is active in public life. I have tried to retire more or less from making speeches and let him carry on, and I make only one speech about once a year."[14]

W̶ith my boy Jack a probable candidate for the Senate against Lodge in Massachusetts," he wrote Lord Beaverbrook on February 18, 1952, "I am finding myself with plenty to do." During the Hialeah meet that winter, Rose remembered her husband spending at least three days a week working "in a political way, because a lot of people would come to Miami for the winter who were influential politically and he'd give them a sales talk." In Palm Beach, he solicited support for Jack on the phone from his bullpen, where he sunbathed from about eleven thirty to lunchtime every day, naked, save for the hat on his head and the coconut butter he smeared all over his torso. "Joe used a telephone the way Heifetz played a fiddle," his friend Morton Downey remembered. "He could do business on a telephone in a few minutes that took his supposed peers a day or a week to accomplish across a desk in an office and conference room."[15]

To court the Italian American vote, he sought Galeazzi's assistance in arranging for Jack to be awarded "the Star of Solidarity" from the Italian government for his service to Americans of Italian descent. Lodge was so disturbed by the award that he petitioned for his own "Star of Solidarity," as did Senator John Pastore of Rhode Island. It didn't matter. As Kennedy gleefully wrote Galeazzi, the announcement that Jack was getting the award came out first. And, as his campaign literature noted, he was the only congressman to have ever been so honored.[16]

In early April, Governor Dever finally called Jack to say that he intended to stand for reelection, leaving the path to the Senate nomination wide open. Mark Dalton, whom Jack had asked to return as campaign manager, drafted the announcement that Congressman Kennedy would be a candidate for Lodge's seat and read it over the phone to Kennedy, Jim Landis, and Arthur Krock, who, though still Washington bureau chief for the *New York Times,* remained a Kennedy adviser. The statement was issued on Palm Sunday, which Archbishop Cushing thought augured well for the campaign.

The Palm Beach season at an end, Kennedy returned north to take residence at 84 Beacon Street in Boston, just around the corner from Jack's residence at 122 Bowdoin. The apartment had three bedrooms, one for Sargent Shriver, whom Kennedy imported from Chicago to work on the campaign, another for Rose, the third for Kennedy. The campaign team, built with Kennedy's money, included the motley crew of volunteers and "secretaries" whom Jack had recruited during his visits through the state; professionals from previous campaigns; new advisers and media consultants like Ralph Coghlan, formerly of the *St. Louis Post-Dispatch,* and Larry O'Brien, who had been brought in because of his contacts in Springfield and western Massachusetts; and family retainers like Landis, Fayne, Krock, and Johnnie Ford.

The ambassador (his preferred title of address) approved every piece of campaign literature no matter where it originated; designed and oversaw radio and TV advertising; served as personal liaison with newspapers across the state, especially the Republican ones; and personally recruited Taft Republicans and independents who distrusted Lodge's steadfast support for Truman's foreign policy initiatives. He had spent the winter working on a position book with Elizabeth Walsh, a member of his New York staff, that referenced Jack's record and public statements on every issue that might come up during the campaign, and on the "tabloid," a glossy photo-and-text magazine that could be distributed door-to-door or through the mails. "He picked out the pictures and what stories went into it. He knew how to do that." According to Sargent Shriver, Kennedy was also responsible for the campaign slogan "He will do <u>more</u> for Massachusetts," with the "more" underlined.[17]

Lodge was known as a foreign policy expert and the man who had engineered Eisenhower's nomination for the presidency. But had he done enough for Massachusetts? Kennedy commissioned James Landis and James Fayne to take the materials he had accumulated during his "economic development" commission work in 1945 and produce a series of position papers and speeches that emphasized Congressman Kennedy's commitment to bringing new capital, new industries, new jobs, and improved transportation links to the state's depressed cities. Positioning his son as someone who cared about the Massachusetts economy would strengthen his standing not only with working-class Democrats, but, as Landis put it, "with many of the basic financial interests in New England who would normally be Republican and . . . felt that here was a man that was going to do more for them than Lodge had been able to do or was inclined to do."[18]

Sargent Shriver, who was not yet married to Eunice, was astounded at the way Kennedy took charge. "He was the campaign manager, no doubt about it." "He was such a strong personality," Kenneth O'Donnell, Bobby's Harvard roommate who had been recruited to work on Jack's 1946 congressional campaign and was called back to work on the Senate campaign, recalled, "that nobody could—nobody *dared*—fight back." Campaign staff were frightened to death, never knowing when they visited headquarters or attended a meeting at Kennedy's apartment whether they would find a kindly grandfatherly figure waiting for them or a tyrannical screamer "in the throes of the 'itch,' as he called his fits of nervous irritation."[19]

Kennedy's constant and public carping at Mark Dalton, the nominal campaign manager, was such that it undermined his leadership. The campaign, which had begun with much enthusiasm, John Droney remembered, "bogged down early. . . . Nobody seemed to be the leader; we could get away with that in a congressional fight, but it was obvious to everyone that we couldn't go on like that if [Congressman Kennedy] were going to beat Lodge."[20]

"We were headed for disaster," Kenny O'Donnell recalled. "The only time the campaign got any direction was when John Kennedy . . . was able to get up to Massachusetts to overrule his father. . . . The Congressman and I had a big argument one day, and I told him that the campaign could only be handled by somebody who could talk up to his father; nobody had the courage to, and *I* certainly didn't have the qualifications, and it just wasn't going to work unless Bobby came up." Jack asked O'Donnell to get in touch with Bobby, which he did, but the younger brother, who had graduated from law school in 1951 and had just taken his first job at the Justice Department, was reluctant to drop everything, resign his post, leave his pregnant wife and first child behind, and move to a state he didn't know and had never lived in to take over a campaign that was in trouble. A week later, Bobby called O'Donnell back. "I'm coming up; I've thought it all over, and I suppose I'll have to do it."[21]

Working eighteen to twenty hours a day seven days a week, Bobby pulled the disparate pieces of the campaign staff together into a statewide organization whose allegiance was not to the Democratic Party, but to John Fitzgerald Kennedy. Along the way, he acquired the reputation as the "ruthless" Kennedy. Every adjective ever applied to his father was now visited upon the son: abrasive, driven, aggressive, and a screamer. But, like his father, he got things done—brilliantly.

With Bobby in control, someone in whom he had confidence, the ambassador could back away from day-to-day operations. It was Bobby and Jack's campaign now—and they would make the decisions. When Paul Dever tried to get the Kennedy camp to join forces with it in a Kennedy-Dever campaign, "Ambassador Kennedy called Bobby and told him to let the Dever organization work with us." Bobby and his senior aides disagreed. They feared that Dever would drag Jack down, and the greater the distance and distinction between the two campaigns, the better it would be. In this instance—as in several others—it was Bobby who prevailed and his father who conceded.[22]

Kennedy's major contribution to the campaign in its final months was to brilliantly use television in a way few others had ever done to market John Fitzgerald Kennedy as a senatorial candidate. For more than two decades now, Kennedy had been a student of the arts and crafts of the newsreel. When the Roosevelt campaign arranged to film the candidate at Hyde Park in 1932, Kennedy oversaw the placement of the cameras and the editing of the film. Later, in Washington and in London, he perfected his own performance in front of the newsreel camera. He taught himself how and when to look serious, how to stride masterfully to the microphone, flash a full-toothed, eyes-twinkling, but never goofy smile, and look straight into the camera with a fearless gaze that betokened intelligence and honesty.

He raised his children to be as comfortable on camera as he had become. He bought 8 mm home movie cameras for their nurses and nannies, who filmed the Kennedy boys and girls at home, at play, on vacation. As the children grew older, they were given their own cameras to film one another and their friends.

Kennedy adapted what he had learned about the newsreel camera to the new medium of television. "Mr. Kennedy was a genius about how Jack should be handled on television," Sargent Shriver recalled. "He was the guy who really understood the tube. How Jack should appear on it. . . . He figured that television was going to be the greatest thing in the history of politics and he set out studying it and how Jack could utilize it most effectively. . . . He knew how Jack should be dressed and how his hair should be." On television, the congressman's youthful glamour and experience as a man of the world could be combined into one persuasive image.

"I remember one night," Shriver recalled in an oral history, "eight of us were in Mr. Kennedy's apartment watching Jack make a TV speech. There was the guy that wrote the speech and the guy from the advertising agency and all the yes men sitting there with Mr. Kennedy smack in front of the tube. After it was all over, Kennedy asked what they thought of it. They gave these mealy-mouthed answers and all of a sudden Mr. Kennedy got ferocious, just *ferocious*. He told them it was the worst speech he'd ever heard and they were destroying Jack and he never wanted to see his son have to get up on TV and make such a fool of himself again. The guy who wrote the speech said he couldn't talk to him like that and Mr. Kennedy got red and furious and told him if he didn't like it to get out. He told them they would have a meeting in the morning and come up with a whole new concept because they were ruining this precious commodity they had. . . . Then Jack called and Mr. Kennedy said, 'Boy, Jack, you were great.' "[23]

Kennedy exploited his standing as an administration opponent to reach out to Taft Republicans who could not forgive Senator Lodge, first for backing Truman's foreign policy initiatives, then for throwing support behind President Eisenhower for the Republican presidential nomination. The leader of the Taft wing of the Republican Party in Massachusetts was Basil Brewer, the publisher of the New Bedford *Standard-Times*. "The 1952 campaign," Charles J. Lewin, Brewer's editor at the *Standard-Times* recalled, "began for us in 1951. Mr. Basil Brewer . . . and I worked closely with Mr. Kennedy. We had frequent communication with him." Kennedy actively exploited this Taft-Lodge split by pointing out as often as he could that on foreign policy, his son was closer to Taft than to Lodge.[24]

While Kennedy worked on the Republicans, he delegated James Landis, who was on good terms with Massachusetts liberals, to get in touch with Arthur Schlesinger, Jr., a founder of Americans for Democratic Action (ADA), and arrange for Jack to appear before the executive committee. Schlesinger, writing Landis in July after the candidate's appearance, reported that he had been "favorably impressed by Jack's presentation as I have in general been by his voting record and his performance in Congress. . . . My own view is that Jack is better than Cabot on most domestic issues, they are about the same on foreign policy, and where Jack is weak (from my viewpoint) Cabot is equally weak. So I am inclined at this point to favor endorsement." Still, Schlesinger wanted Landis to know that there was, among the ADA leadership in Massachusetts, "some disappointment expressed about an occasional tendency to vote to reduce foreign aid appropriations . . . and Jack's inclination to stay out of the civil liberties fight."[25]

The ADA would have found it easier to endorse Jack Kennedy had he ever criticized Wisconsin senator Joseph McCarthy, but the congressman, like every other elected Massachusetts Democrat, had kept quiet, fearful of McCarthy's popularity in the state, especially among Irish Catholic voters.

Though his silence was dictated in large part by political considerations, Jack also refrained from criticizing Joe McCarthy because he had become a friend of the family—and of his father. He himself had spent time with McCarthy during his first years in Washington. The senator from Wisconsin was fun to be around and had dated first Eunice, then Pat, and visited the Kennedy family at Hyannis Port, where he had gotten along rather famously with Joe Kennedy. "He was always pleasant; he was never a crab," Kennedy recalled in a 1960 interview, describing a Joe McCarthy very unlike the nasty, scowling politician the rest of the world had come to know. "He went out on my boat one day and he almost drowned swimming behind it, but he never complained. If somebody was against him, he never tried to cut his heart out. He never said that anybody was a stinker. He was a pleasant fellow."[26]

Joe Kennedy not only enjoyed McCarthy's company, he admired him for his big mouth, his outspoken confrontations with the government establishment (especially the State Department), his take-no-prisoners attacks on the Truman administration, and his contempt for diplomacy and decorum. When McCarthy ran for reelection to the Senate in 1952, Kennedy, to express his friendship, loyalty, and provide another reason for the Republican senator not to campaign against his son, contributed to his campaign.[27]

Kennedy the father was adamant, for political and personal reasons, that his son not be pushed into the position where he would have to say anything in public about the senator from Wisconsin. The CIO had, James MacGregor Burns wrote in his 1960 campaign biography, lent the Kennedy campaign the use of "Pat" Jackson, a staunch liberal who on his own prepared an anti-McCarthy statement for the candidate. When Jackson brought the statement to Jack's apartment, a meeting was in progress with senior staff and Joseph Kennedy. Jackson was asked to read the statement aloud. "He had got through three sentences," Burns wrote, "when Joseph Kennedy sprang to his feet with such force that he upset a small table in front of him. . . . 'You and your friends are trying to ruin my son's career!' . . . Again and again he returned to the charge that liberals and union people were hurting his son. The Jews were against him, too." When asked to explain his father's tirade, Jack attributed it to "pride of family."

No anti-McCarthy ad was ever run, not because the Kennedys felt any great need to protect McCarthy, but because they were convinced that any attack on a popular Irish Catholic was bad politics. When Adlai Stevenson, the Democratic candidate for president in 1952, called Sargent Shriver to ask how he could be of use to the Kennedy campaign during his swing through Massachusetts, Shriver requested only that he refrain from attacking McCarthy. Jack, he told Stevenson, was hoping to position himself as the candidate who was strongest "on communism and domestic subversives. . . . Up here," Shriver wrote Stevenson, "this anti-communist business is a good thing to emphasize."[28]

Up until the last minute, the campaign worried that McCarthy would succumb to party pressure, campaign for Lodge, and pull away a sizable number of Irish Catholic votes. We do not know whether, as has been claimed, Kennedy himself called McCarthy or had Westbrook Pegler call to ask him not to campaign for Lodge. In the end, Joseph McCarthy's biographer David Oshinsky concluded, "The man most responsible for keeping McCarthy out of Massachusetts was not Joe Kennedy; it was Henry Cabot Lodge." Lodge told Oshinsky that he had never asked McCarthy to campaign for him and only at the very last minute "asked him whether he would come into Massachusetts and campaign against Kennedy *without* mentioning me in any way. He told me that he couldn't do this. He would endorse me but he would say nothing against the son of Joe Kennedy. I told McCarthy 'thanks but no thanks.' So he never did come into Massachusetts."[29]

Every member of the Kennedy family except Rosemary, who was in Wisconsin, and Ted, who was stationed in Europe, campaigned in 1952. "Jean is, as you know, the Office Manager of Headquarters and is working from 9 in the morning until 10:30 at night," Kennedy wrote Ted in June. "Pat and Mary Jo [Gargan, Rose's niece] are on the Women's Committees throughout the state and were in Worcester this week and Springfield next. Eunice appeared at a luncheon that Mayor Hynes gave for Jack on Bunker Hill Day, June 17th, but Jack was unable to attend. After lunch she wandered through the streets of Charlestown looking at the parade and made her usual big hit. Bobby has taken over the management of the whole campaign and is doing a great job. He works fifteen hours a day and is showing remarkable good sense and judgment. . . . Houghton and I spend three days a week in Boston on the campaign and this week we are going to New York. We will probably see the [Sugar Ray] Robinson-[Joey] Maxim fight Monday night and then line up the television procedure for Jack's campaign. As busy as everybody is, Mother is the busiest. Her door is constantly open and whether I go out at 6:30 A.M. or get in at 12:30 at night she has three sheets of paper full of suggestions for me to get busy on. She is planning to fly on the 27th of July for Paris but I suggested to her she should leave tomorrow or I won't be alive by the end of July."[30]

As in 1946, Kennedy supplied the campaign with an almost unlimited budget for receptions and "ladies teas," telephones, posters, flyers, billboards, radio and TV, and almost one million copies of the "tabloid" campaign booklet that were distributed by mail and by hand throughout the state. That much was public. But there were other expenditures that also bought votes.

Days before the election, the *Boston Post*, which had supported the Republican candidates for governor and senator, abruptly switched sides and endorsed Democrats Paul Dever and John Kennedy. Almost six years after the election, John Fox, the rabidly anti-Communist publisher of the newspaper, appearing before a congressional committee, claimed that the day before the *Boston Post* endorsed Congressman Kennedy, he had "talked to Joseph Patrick Kennedy . . . who agreed to lend" him $500,000. When the story surfaced in 1958, Kennedy's New York office declared that the loan had not been discussed until after the election and was repaid in full within sixty days. Robert Kennedy, questioned years later, claimed that he had forgotten the details, but he did not deny that "there was a connection between the two events," the loan and the endorsement.[31]

Early on November 4, 1952, it became clear that it was going to be a Republican year in Massachusetts and almost everywhere else in the nation. Eisenhower carried Massachusetts by 208,800 votes, but John Kennedy defeated Henry Cabot Lodge, Jr., by more than 70,000. His victory was made all the more remarkable by the defeat of the incumbent Democratic governor, Paul Dever. "God!" Kennedy half joked to Lucius Ordway in Palm Beach. "I suppose I'll have you sucking around me all this winter trying to re-establish your social contacts by claiming that you know the former Ambassador and father of a United States Senator."[32]

As delighted as he was at Jack's victory, Kennedy was disturbed that his son was not getting the recognition he deserved for knocking off an "unbeatable," powerful, articulate, and wealthy Republican incumbent. "Sometimes in reading the papers," he wrote a friend in mid-November, "I wonder whether they are not all mad at Jack for having had the temerity to lick this fair-haired Goliath. It seems to me that if there was ever an attempt to play down a real worth-while victory this was it. In an effort to save Lodge, Eisenhower and Nixon came into the city the night before election and paraded through the city and pleaded over the radio and television for his re-election. In spite of the fact that Eisenhower won by 200,000 votes, Jack licked Lodge by 70,000. Don't make any mistake, this was a real desire on the people's part to lick the Democrats. Of course, we are all tickled to death and I am sure Jack will do a fine job in Washington."[33]

Thirty-five

RETIREMENT

J ack had been elected to the Senate, but there was work to be done. From Palm Beach, Kennedy contacted James Rowe, a Lyndon Johnson supporter and adviser, and had Jim Landis write him as well, to request "a good" committee assignment for the newly elected junior senator from Massachusetts. Kennedy also phoned Joseph Mc-Carthy, who, with the Republicans now in the majority, would take over as chair of the Permanent Subcommittee on Investigations, to rec-ommend that he appoint Bobby as his chief counsel. McCarthy agreed to take Bobby on, but not as chief counsel. That position was going to Roy Cohn, the lawyer from New York who had distinguished himself as an anti-Communist crusader by helping to convict Julius and Ethel Rosenberg of espionage.[1]

Kennedy did not expect Bobby to remain long as assistant counsel on a Senate subcommittee. In managing his brother's campaign, his third son had shown an aptitude for politics. Kennedy hoped he too would someday run for office. The question was where. "Confiden-tially, Bobby is considering taking up residence in Connecticut," Ken-nedy wrote family friend and lawyer Bart Brickley in March. "It's the same old story, he doesn't want to interfere with Jack's career by going into politics himself. We have looked into where the best place would be to establish residence in that state and have come to the conclusion that it probably is around Hartford. In that event, we will want to have him make a good legal connection and, if possible, buy some business that would keep him interested—a paper or television station, or something like that. Have you any ideas or connections in that part of the world?" A month later, the Connecticut idea having been discarded, Kennedy contacted Cornelius Fitzgerald in Boston for advice on Bobby's running for office in Massachusetts. "After all, that is going to be his ambition, but the problem is whether Jack's being in politics there would hurt him very much. He is giving very serious consideration to it and might move out of the state" if it wasn't feasible to run for office there.[2]

Bobby's first assignment for McCarthy's committee was to compile statistics on foreign commerce and prepare a report on the extent to which British and Greek shippers were trading with Communist China. Five months later, after completing the report, he resigned. His problem was not with McCarthy, whom he liked, or the anti-Communist crusade, which he supported, but with Roy Cohn, his nominal boss, who preferred grandstanding to research and, Bobby Kennedy was convinced, was going to get McCarthy and everyone who worked for him into trouble.

After leaving the committee, Bobby remained loyal to McCarthy, as did his father. McCarthy was vulgar, scanted on his research, relied on an unscrupulous twenty-five-year-old as his chief counsel, lied when he thought he needed to, employed demagogic language and tactics, and drank too much. But these were not sins unique to him. He was being singled out for criticism, Kennedy believed, because he was a Catholic who spoke his mind and angered leftists who were either Jews or allied with Jews.

In July 1953, the month Bobby resigned, J. B. Matthews, the anti-Communist crusader whom McCarthy had hired as research director, charged that "the largest single group supporting the Communist apparatus in the United States is composed of Protestant clergymen" and that "at least 7,000 Protestant clergymen had served 'the Kremlin's conspiracy.'" When three leaders of the National Conference of Christians and Jews, including Monsignor John A. O'Brien of Notre Dame, asked President Eisenhower to repudiate Matthews's allegations, he did so, calling them "deplorable" and "unjustified."

Furious that Notre Dame, a Catholic institution whose board of lay advisers he would soon join, had allowed one of its faculty members to publicly criticize McCarthy, Kennedy wrote Father Cavanaugh, the former president of Notre Dame, to complain. "I don't think it does Notre Dame any good to have Father O'Brien signing petitions for the Christians and Jews with Notre Dame behind his name; in fact, I think it does it immeasurable harm. I always thought that organization was completely dominated by the Jews and they just use Catholic names for the impression it makes throughout the country. I was disgusted to see him sign a petition to fire Matthews and I know nothing about Matthews. I am not suggesting eliminating freedom of speech but I certainly am against using the name of Notre Dame for the benefit of that type of organization."[3]

The senator from Wisconsin, spiraling out of control into depression, alcoholism, and a frighteningly self-destructive sense of his own importance, fired Matthews, but instead of retreating, launched a new investigation of subversives in the U.S. Army. Early in 1954, six months after he had resigned as assistant counsel to the subcommittee's Republican majority, Robert Kennedy was hired by the Democratic minority. On April 22, 1954, when the Army-McCarthy hearings were broadcast live on television to some twenty million Americans, Bobby Kennedy, twenty-nine years of age but looking much younger, could be glimpsed in the rear of the hearing room, behind Democratic senators John McClellan, Henry Jackson, and Stuart Symington.

The hearings ended in mid-June 1954, with McCarthy having lost the support of the millions who had watched as he growled, snarled, and bullied his way through the proceedings. His colleagues were now prepared to take action against him. On July 30, 1954, Republican senator Ralph Flanders of Vermont submitted a resolution of censure. Senator Kennedy, who had never had any use for McCarthy, asked his chief aide and speechwriter, Ted Sorensen, to prepare a speech explaining why, though he disagreed with Flanders's broad condemnation, he intended to vote for censure. That speech was never given, as the Senate leadership, instead of calling for a vote, referred the Flanders resolution to special committee.

In Europe that summer, Joseph P. Kennedy continued to defend McCarthy. "I had dinner with Lord Beaverbrook a couple of times," he wrote Bobby on August 15, 1954, "and the other night Lady Diana Cooper, the widow of Duff Cooper, asked me, 'How much longer will McCarthy amount to anything in the United States?' That, of course, rubbed me the wrong way because it was true pontification. I said he was the strongest man in the United States next to Eisenhower. Then I said to the small English group, 'What have you got against McCarthy?'" Lord Beaverbrook objected to McCarthy's "calling Marshall a traitor. He, Beaverbrook, had no objection to him saying he was a bad Secretary of State and that he had lost China for the world, but he said people just know he isn't a traitor. I said I had never heard that he said he was a traitor by condemning him for being an incompetent; but my own feeling is that Joe went further than that. I then asked Lady Diana what she had against him. She said she thought people she talked with felt he ruled by fear and added, 'You know we British don't like anybody to do things like that.' I said that was poppycock. . . . The only thing I regret is that they seem to be forgetting Cohn in the picture and concentrating on McCarthy."[4]

Four days later, still incensed at the beating McCarthy was taking, Kennedy wrote his son Jack on the same topic. "All this poppycock about McCarthy having any effect on America's standing in Europe is the biggest lot of dribble I ever read. Unless you're a newspaperman or a politician, the masses haven't the slightest idea what McCarthy stands for, what he does or what's wrong with him, and 99% never heard of him long enough to remember him."[5]

His defense of McCarthy that summer was all the more remarkable given the fact that only months before he had experienced first-hand the damage that reckless accusations posed to innocent young men. In May 1954, Kennedy learned that reporter Jack Anderson, who was then working for Drew Pearson, was pursuing a story that Ted Kennedy had been dismissed from the CIC (Counter Intelligence Corps) training school "because of an adverse report which linked him to a group of 'pinkos.'" Kennedy was livid and "sent word to Drew Pearson that if he so much as printed a word about this that he would sue him for libel in a manner such as Drew Pearson had never been sued before." He then placed a call to J. Edgar Hoover and, after being informed he was "in a travel status," was connected to Assistant Director Louis Nichols. Knowing that Nichols "had the Director's confidence," Kennedy told him that he was "sick of the Washington situation; that the Army-Stevens Hearings [usually referred to as the Army-McCarthy hearings] were a disgrace and that he simply was not going to tolerate his son being victimized in any way, shape or form." Nichols promised that the bureau "would check into this matter immediately." He later called Kennedy "back and told him that I could find no record and that we certainly had not investigated his son. . . . I told Mr. Kennedy that he was authorized to state, if need be, that he checked with the FBI and the FBI had not investigated his son."[6]

This was the second time that the bureau had done Kennedy a big favor—the first was during Jack's affair with Inga Arvad—and he was not about to forget it. In early July 1954, he invited Special Agent H. G. Foster to visit with him at Hyannis Port. As Foster wrote Hoover after the meeting, "He had met many many people who are great admirers of yours, but I believe that Mr. Kennedy is the most vocal and forceful admirer that I have met. I found him to be a forceful, outspoken gentleman who takes great pride in his friendship with you."[7]

Kennedy's flattery of Hoover was effusive to the point of near parody. "I think I have become too cynical in my old age," he wrote the director in October 1955, "but the only two men that I know in public life today for whose opinion I give one continental both happen to be named Hoover—one John Edgar and one Herbert—and I am proud to think that both of them hold me in some esteem. . . . I listened to Walter Winchell mention your name as a candidate for President. If that could come to pass, it would be the most wonderful thing for the United States, and whether you were on a Republican or Democratic ticket, I would guarantee you the largest contribution that you would ever get from anybody and the hardest work by either a Democrat or a Republican. I think the United States deserves you. I only hope it gets you."[8]

In December 1957, he reported to his local FBI contact in Hyannis Port that Teddy, who was at the University of Virginia Law School, had told him "that several people have talked to the students there and have more or less unfavorably slanted their talk against the FBI. . . . He stated," the Hyannis Port agent continued, that "he has taught his children to respect the FBI, that it is provoking to them, as well as to himself, to hear anyone speak ill of the work of the FBI." He suggested that the FBI send someone to the University of Virginia to "give our side of the picture as to loyalty and security investigations."[9]

I am promising myself every year that I will take it easy. I haven't done too well so far, but I am hoping I will make a real effort in '53." Or so he had promised himself. But when the Republicans, on taking over the reins of government in 1953, convened a second Commission on Organization of the Executive Branch of the Government, enlisted Herbert Hoover to chair it, and asked Kennedy to serve as a member, he agreed. The chance to return to Washington, if only on a part-time basis, was too good to pass up. He hired Bobby, who had resigned from the McCarthy committee, as his assistant and went to work.[10]

Herbert Hoover ruled the second commission, as he had the first, with an iron hand, which was fine with Kennedy, who supported him enthusiastically. He was "the least frequent dissenter" on the commission, "entering a public dissent on only one of the commissions' 314 recommendations." This time around, he attended commission meetings, ably chaired his subcommittees, participated in the writing of several of the reports, and introduced and pushed through proposals of his own. As he proudly wrote Rose in April 1955, he had gotten the commission "to recommend increased appropriations for basic medical research for cancer, mentally retarded patients and various others" and was "overwhelmed with thank-yous" from the directors of medical research clinics.[11]

He was delighted to be a Washington insider again, especially as it gave him the opportunity to leak classified information to J. Edgar Hoover as thanks for past favors and down payment for future ones. "President Eisenhower," he told Agent Foster, who forwarded the information directly to the director, "had requested Hoover Commission to investigate CIA . He [Kennedy] advised that General Mark Clark would probably head up their investigative efforts. He also indicated he was leaving for Europe in just a little over a week and left the inference he expects to do some inquiring concerning CIA while he is abroad. He also advised it was his personal thought that President Eisenhower had asked the Hoover Commission to make this inquiry to forestall an investigation into CIA by Senator McCarthy."[12]

Kennedy had no business divulging confidential information about possible investigations of the CIA to J. Edgar Hoover, who considered the agency the bureau's chief rival. But he owed Hoover something—and information such as this was worth its weight in gold to the director. A firm believer in the ethics of the quid pro quo, Kennedy would continue to leak "insider" information to the director, who in turn, he hoped, would protect his boys by guarding whatever "insider" information he had on them.

The Kennedy family had much to celebrate. In May 1953, Eunice married Sargent Shriver at St. Patrick's Cathedral, Cardinal Francis Spellman officiating. The reception dinner and dance was held at the Waldorf. The bride looked beautiful, the groom handsome, the bride's parents glowed with delight.

The following month, Jack announced his engagement to Miss Jacqueline Bouvier, whom the *New York Times* identified as a "Newport society girl." She was more than that, of course. She was the perfect Kennedy daughter-in-law: educated at Vassar, the Sorbonne, and George Washington University, from a good (if divorced) Catholic family, gorgeous, trim, with a quiet but rather wicked sense of humor, and unflappable. She was also genuinely interested in and admiring of her new father-in-law, and he of her.

The wedding was scheduled for September. Jack planned to spend his last summer as a bachelor traveling in Europe with his friend Torb Macdonald. His father did everything he could to stop him. He urged Macdonald not to accompany Jack, then relented but begged him to do what he could to protect Jack's health—and reputation.

"Jack needs a rest. Unquestionably he has the best time with you. I am a bit concerned that he may get restless about the prospect of getting married. Most people do and he is more likely to do so than others. As I told you, I am hoping that he will take a rest and not jump from place to place, and be especially mindful of whom he sees. Certainly one can't take anything for granted since he has become a United States Senator.

That is a price he should be willing to pay and gladly. I understand your love and devotion to Jack and I know you wish him nothing but the best and I hope you both will have a good vacation."[13]

Jack returned home, his reputation intact, to marry Jacqueline Bouvier on September 12, 1953, at Newport, Rhode Island, where her mother and stepfather lived, before hundreds of guests, hundreds more gawking onlookers, and dozens of newsreel cameramen and still photographers. Archbishop Cushing officiated. Kennedy, who had been uncharacteristically camera-shy through his son's 1952 campaign for the Senate, came out of hiding to smile broadly for the cameras as he arrived at the church, then danced with his daughter-in-law at the reception and presented her with a stack of congratulatory telegrams.

Patricia was the next to marry, to British actor Peter Lawford, who though not a Catholic promised to raise their children as Catholics. In April, Patricia and Peter were married at the Church of St. Thomas More in New York City by Father Cavanaugh. The newsreel cameras were out in force again, and Joseph P. Kennedy looked perfectly regal in his formal wear. There would be stories, the most persuasive ones from Patricia and Peter Lawford's son, Christopher, that Kennedy was disturbed at the prospect of his daughter marrying a Englishman, an actor, and a Protestant, but if he was, he never said so in public or in correspondence with family or friends.[14]

By the summer of 1954, the rapid expansion of the Kennedy family, with two sons-in-law, two daughters-in-law, and four grandchildren, had resulted in a "housing crisis" at Hyannis Port, as Rose would later put it. Bobby and Ethel would soon rent and then buy a house next door to the main house; Jack and Jackie would a few years later purchase their own just in back, followed by Sarge and Eunice, and Jean and Steve Smith, whom she would marry in 1956. But that was in the future.

Kennedy loved his children, warmly welcomed their husbands and wives into the family, and adored his grandchildren. But there were now a great many of them, and they all wanted to spend their summers at Hyannis Port. He enjoyed being a grandfather—but he also enjoyed a bit of solitude to read his mysteries and listen to his music in the evening. He had never been much of a disciplinarian and certainly didn't want to become one now. "He didn't want to have to tell them to be quiet—but couldn't take the bedlam on a steady basis." His solution was to hand over the big house to the children and spend the summer in a villa in the South of France.[15]

To his friend Morton Downey, he proudly explained that he had "no relatives anywhere in the world now except in my house this summer. Well. That's the way life is!" "Grandpa is staying in Europe," he cabled his oldest grandson, Bobby and Ethel's boy, Joseph II, on his second birthday, "so he will live long enough to celebrate your 21st with you."[16]

We arrive on the 13th of July," he wrote Albert Champion, whom he had asked to make the arrangements for the visit and hire a staff for the villa he had rented in Èze, six miles east of Nice. "Mr. Houghton and Mr. Reisman will be with me and my secretary, Miss Des Rosiers, and my masseur, Mr. Thomas Mushyn, who will need a room—not necessarily an important one—either in the same hotel or in the general neighborhood. I certainly would like to see your smiling face at Le Havre on our arrival and as we are bringing along a Cadillac car, maybe we should hire a chauffeur to pick it up and drive it to Paris, and then we could decide whether we wanted to hire him permanently or not."[17]

As had become his standard routine, his first stop after Paris was Rome to see Galeazzi and get the latest gossip about the new list of cardinals and Vatican intrigues. He was fascinated by the ins and outs of Italian politics, the machinations of the Communists, the maneuverings of the Christian Democrats, the back-channel influence of the Vatican. As a former diplomat, the father of a U.S. senator, and now a member of a federal commission, he was welcomed—or at least tolerated—wherever he went. On this trip, he spent a full day in Versailles at NATO military headquarters, where he was briefed by General Alfred Gruenther, the supreme Allied commander, Europe. He also made plans to meet with President Éamon de Valera in Ireland, Foreign Secretary Anthony Eden in England, Chancellor Konrad Adenauer in Bonn, and General Francisco Franco in Spain.

His fact-finding excursions were the bookends to his summer abroad, most of which was spent at his marvelous villa. Even Rose, who visited for a brief time, was impressed. "Here I am in the Cote d'Azur," she wrote her children in early August, "and it is beautiful, as you know, and as you have seen in all the travel catalogues. Your father and his confreres picked out a very beautiful house for us all. It is a villa on the water and is terraced in the front with 5 or 6 terraces of beautiful flowers, all very lovely and all very different. The same is true on the sides and all around are very lovely little garden paths where, if I was not a three-mile walker, I would be quite content to wander." Albert Champion had staffed the villa with butlers, cooks, gardeners, chauffeurs, and even a lady's maid who, when there were no ladies present, which was most of the time, did the "washing and sewing and what not." The chef, Kennedy bragged to son Ted and daughter Jean, was the best "in all of France" and had worked for the Duke and Duchess of Windsor for ten years. "He can even make American ice cream as good as Pavillon."[18]

To stave off boredom (and loneliness), Kennedy brought with him to the South of France a large staff, including his secretary, Janet des Rosiers, who would later claim to have been his mistress since around 1948. He surrounded himself as well with his buddies Houghton, Reisman, "the Commish," Morton Downey, Bart Brickley, and Fathers Theodore Hesburgh and John Cavanaugh, whom he imported in groups of two and three. "I get the boys all up in the morning at 6:45," he wrote Ted. "I have a swim and we all have breakfast at 7:40; leave for the golf course at 8 o'clock, and then after the golf game three days a week we swim at Eden Roc and come home for lunch, have a sleep, dictate my mail when I wake up, have a rub at 6:15, and then have a little cold soup, cheese and red wine for supper at 7:30; then we sit on the veranda and listen to the radio until 10:30. We go out Friday nights to the Monte Carlo Galas. This isn't the kind of existence that should appeal to anybody under 65, but . . . it seems to fill the bill. . . . I haven't seen all those beautiful girls that everybody talks about being here in the South of France, but maybe when Jack arrives here next week he'll find them."[19]

He and his buddies were older now, more conscious of their weight and their hairlines, but with their wives left behind in the States, they felt obligated to at least tease one another and self-mockingly refer to their sexual appetites and attractiveness. "Houghton has lost the sight of both eyes," he wrote Tim McInerny in August, "and twisted his neck out of position gaping at the young Marilyn Monroes, of which he tells me there are millions! As he repeatedly says—oh! If I were only 70 again I would spend the next 25 years on the Riviera!"[20]

For most of the summer, Èze was a bachelor's paradise. Rose never stayed for long even when Kennedy assured her, as he did in July 1955, that he was not expecting any more guests, "except Bart Brickley and possibly Morton Downey and his wife for ten days or so. . . . You won't have to see Houghton except for possibly one meal and they [the chauffeurs] can drive you over to play golf . . . whenever you want to. So, for heaven's sake please don't think that we can't have any fun if you're here because that is utter nonsense. It's merely a question whether you like the place well enough and whether you get bored with so few things to do. We never go out at night except on Friday night to the Gala but sit up above and listen to the radio. Up to date nobody has arrived here whom you would know." All in all, he was not making the best possible case for Rose to visit. In any event, she preferred to vacation on her own. Kennedy consulted with "the best hotel man in France," who recommended that "if you do not want to stay on the Riviera, Switzerland is by far the best place to go unless you want to go to the musical festival in Salzburg." Rose took the suggestion and spent her summer and fall vacations at a resort in Lausanne.[21]

There was nothing new or out of the ordinary here, as Jack, Eunice, and Jean acknowledged in their fortieth anniversary cable to their father:

> *Forty years you are wed to Rose*
> *Where she goes nobody knows*
> *But why she goes we are all aware*
> *Because you are a great big bear*
> *But this is all said in jest*
> *After Houghton she loves you the best.*[22]

As on previous trips to Europe, Kennedy intended to write about his findings when he returned to the States. "I expect when I get home," Kennedy wrote Morton Downey on August 23, 1954, "I will have enough material for one good speech or article." He had decided that as long as he didn't speak in Massachusetts, he wouldn't get in his son's way or cause him any particular political problems.[23]

By mid-August, he had come up with an outline for the article or speech he would complete when he returned to the United States. "From my preliminary talks and my observations, I have come to the conclusion that there are three basic courses for the United States to follow in its foreign policy. One, to accept any of the challenges of the Russians or Chinese and drop the bombs or the guided missiles. . . . The Second alternative is really a continuation of our present policy—talking about the Communists all the time . . . and continue our efforts to maintain a cold war. . . . The Third alternative is to find out on what basis we can live in peace with the Russians." Option three, he had concluded, was the only reasonable one. Fighting an endless cold war made no sense. The notion of deterrence was an absurdity. It was worse than futile to pile "up bombs we will never use except for defensive purposes, which unfortunately must come second after an attack." Now was the time to negotiate, when the United States enjoyed military superiority.[24]

He still worried a bit about drawing attention away from his son or, worse yet, forcing Jack to have to distance himself or apologize for his father's intemperance. Fortunately, the Senate would not convene in 1954 until after election day, in part to spare senators from having to publicly declare for or against a resolution to censure Senator McCarthy. "I have made quite a few observations on our foreign policy," he wrote Tim McInerny in late August, "and I think if I get these various interviews and some others I am planning, I will have a very interesting story when I get back and, since the Senate is not in session, I can say what I want without hurting Jack."[25]

John Fitzgerald Kennedy celebrated his thirty-seventh birthday in May 1954. For thirty-four of those thirty-seven years, his father had worried about his health—and longevity. The steady dose of cortisone he took for his Addison's disease had calmed his stomach, but his back was no better, perhaps worse, than it had ever been. By the spring of 1954, the pain had become so intense that he was using crutches everywhere, even in the Senate chambers, in the mistaken belief that taking pressure off his back would help it heal. In April, he visited the Lahey Clinic. In July, he checked into the Bethesda Naval Hospital, looking for relief but finding none. His father knew he was ailing but believed that with a bit of rest he would feel better. "I hope that you will take care of yourself for the next two or three months," he wrote him on August 19, the day before the Senate went into a recess that would last until November 8, "and see if you can get in good shape before you have to go back to Washington."[26]

In August, Jack was visited in Hyannis Port by the team from the Lahey Clinic that had examined him earlier in the spring. They recommended that he undergo surgery to fuse his spinal disks. If he did not do so, they warned, there was a good chance that he would be confined to a wheelchair for the rest of his life. If he went ahead, however, there was a high risk of infection because of his Addison's disease. Jackie visited Kennedy in the South of France at the end of the month and brought with her the news of Jack's decision to have the operation. Jack remained in Hyannis Port. He should have been resting his back but instead had accepted a number of speaking engagements.[27]

Kennedy returned from Europe that fall with every intention of making headlines again for himself and his ideas. On visiting Hyannis Port and finding Jack more seriously debilitated than he had imagined and about to submit to major and highly risky surgery, he put everything aside and, as he had thirty-five years ago when Jack's life was threatened with scarlet fever, focused his attention entirely on his son.

Having lost one child to an operation that went terribly wrong, and knowing the risks entailed in this one, Kennedy advised against surgery. "Joe first tried to convince Jack that even confined to a wheelchair he could lead a full and rich life," Rose recalled in a later interview with Doris Kearns Goodwin. "After all, he argued, one need only look at the incredible life FDR had managed to lead despite his physical incapacity. But even as Joe spoke, seeing that Jack was determined to go ahead, he finally told his son he'd do everything he could to help. 'Don't worry, dad,' Jack replied. 'I'll make it through.'" Her husband didn't sleep at all that first night at Hyannis Port. "His mind kept wandering back to the last letter he received from Joe Junior, the letter written right before his death, assuring his father that there was no danger involved and that he would be sure to return. The memory was so painful that Joe actually cried out in the darkness with a sound so loud that I was awakened from sleep."[28]

Jack checked into the Hospital for Special Surgery in New York City on October 10. After three postponements, the operation was performed on October 21. Three days later, Jack Kennedy developed the infection that almost killed him. His temperature rose precipitously and he sank into a coma. A priest was called to administer the last rites. And then, as he had so many times before, Jack Kennedy rose from the near dead. He remained desperately but no longer mortally ill, with a wound eight inches long that would not heal.

Kennedy stayed in New York while Jack was in the hospital, answering questions about his health, responding to well-wishers and the hundreds of notes of encouragement that had been sent from all over the world. "Your cards came at a time when a little gayety was a much sought after thing," Kennedy wrote to thank Carroll Rosenbloom in early November. "We have had quite a tough time with Jack and he has really suffered way beyond what anybody should be expected to endure and he has a long, long road still ahead."[29]

On November 8, Congress reconvened with Jack still in the hospital, looking very much as if he would be absent for the entire session. The Democrats' victory in the midterm elections in 1954 had won for the party a majority in the Senate and opened up new possibilities for committee assignments. Jack had served only one third of one term and would now be absent for much of the next year. He was in no position to ask any favors of the Democratic leadership, but his father, who had carefully spread his largesse among the party's leaders in the form of generous campaign donations, was.

On the very first day of the session, Kennedy phoned Senator George Smathers of Florida to ask him to lobby Lyndon Johnson to put Jack on the Foreign Relations Committee. "After your call yesterday," Smathers wrote Kennedy on November 9, "I went over and had another long talk with Lyndon about Jack. He is thoroughly sympathetic, but he certainly has his problems. . . . Lyndon has assured me he will do the best he can for Jack within the limitations imposed upon him by the seniority of these other fellows." In the end, Johnson bypassed Kennedy, which made sense, as he was neither a Johnson loyalist nor a powerful Democrat whom the majority leader needed in his camp.[30]

On December 2, while Jack was still in the hospital, "most of the time in severe pain," the Senate approved the McCarthy censure resolution by a vote of 67–22. Only one Democrat, John F. Kennedy of Massachusetts, did not vote for censure, though he did not vote against it; his vote was marked as "unrecorded." The senator might, had he chosen to, have instructed Ted Sorensen to pair him in favor of censure with an absent Republican who was opposed to it. He chose not to, either because he did not, at this moment in his life, want to go against his father's wishes or because he believed that his constituents, like his father, did not believe that McCarthy had done anything to merit public censure.[31]

The Kennedys, Bobby and his father in particular, would remain loyal to Joe McCarthy until the very end, which was not far off. Overcome by alcoholism, depression, and acute hepatitis, Senator McCarthy died in May 1957. Kennedy telegraphed his wife, Jean Kerr McCarthy, to say how "shocked and deeply grieved" he had been "to hear of Joe's passing. His indomitable courage in adhering to the cause in which he believed evoked my warm admiration. His friendship was deeply appreciated and reciprocated."[32]

While the Kennedys were all too ready to forgive the senator's trespasses, they would for the rest of their lives nurture an abiding hatred for Roy Cohn, who they believed had brought him down. When, in the summer of 1955, Morton Downey invited Cohn to his home in Hyannis Port for a weekend, Rose wrote Kennedy in France that "Bob was livid . . . Bob is sure he would not do it, if you were around." Kennedy, whose temper was no longer what it had once been—and certainly not as volatile as his second living son's—wrote him in Hyannis Port to say that while Downey shouldn't have invited Cohn, "in the last analysis, we can't tell people whom they should invite to their home; nevertheless, I am annoyed."[33]

On December 21, 1954, two months after his surgery, Jack was well enough to leave the hospital. He was transported by stretcher to a limousine that took him to the airport, then loaded him onto a private plane for the flight to Palm Beach. Covered from head to toe with a checked blanket, he managed a wan smile but looked more dead than alive. When his father saw the television footage, he worried that Jack might have reinjured his back on being carried into the airplane.[34]

Jack convalesced in Palm Beach in a makeshift hospital wing on the ground floor, cared for by a team of doctors and nurses and his wife and parents. The wound in his back opened up during the surgery did not heal; the pain did not subside. By February, Rose recalled to Doris Kearns Goodwin, "Joe came to the conclusion that something had to be done, so he flew to New York to see the doctors, and came back with a recommendation for a second operation. He recognized the high risk involved, but now he understood what Jack had meant in the beginning about not wanting to live unless he could really live."[35]

Jack's second operation, the chief purpose of which appeared to have been to remove the metal plate that had been inserted in his back during the first, was performed on February 15 and brought him a measure of relief. Early in March, he was able to walk without his crutches for the first time. "The Ambassador," Dave Powers recalled, "said to me later when we were eating lunch, 'God, Dave, he's getting stronger all the time. Did you see the legs on him? He's got the legs of a fighter or a swimming champion.' Then the Ambassador said, and I often thought of it later, 'I know nothing can happen to him now, because I've stood by his deathbed three times and each time I said good-bye to him, and each time he came back stronger.'"[36]

On May 27, 1955, seven months after his surgery and two days before his thirty-eighth birthday, Jack returned to the Senate, still in pain, but pain he could live with. "The results from the back operation," Kennedy had written Galeazzi the month before, were "not what we had hoped for, but maybe time will correct it. [Jack] has gone through such a terrible ordeal."[37]

Kennedy would continue to monitor Jack's recovery and meet with his doctors. As heartbroken as he was about his son's infirmities, he never let on—to Jack, especially—that he had any doubts that he would make a full recovery. "I am sorry you have been having trouble again with your physical condition," he wrote from France in late July, "but I keep meeting people who have suffered a couple of years after operations and felt they would never be well and who are now playing 18 holes of golf every day and doing all the things that you want to do; but, as you say, let's forget it as best as we can and see if being away from the scene of all your difficulties might not have a very good effect."[38]

During his long convalescence in Palm Beach, Jack had begun work on an article on political courage that was soon extended to a book-length manuscript. Like his father, who always sought research and editorial advice from his advisers, Jack asked Ted Sorensen, his chief aide in Washington, and to a lesser degree Arthur Krock, Jim Landis, and others, for assistance. By the summer of 1955, he and Sorensen had completed most of a first draft. Jack asked his mother, who was on her way to the South of France, to deliver the first and last chapters to his father. Jack showed up at the villa in early September with the rest of the book. "As usual," Kennedy wrote his son Ted, sharing an insider Kennedy joke, "he arrived without his studs, with two different stockings and no underpants; so he walked off with a pair of brand new Sulka stockings of mine, a new pair of Sulka underpants of mine, and the last pair of evening studs I possessed. . . . He is back on crutches after having tried to open a screen in his hotel room, but if he hasn't any more brains than to try that, maybe he should stay on crutches. His general attitude towards life seems to be quite gay. He is very intrigued with the constant rumors that he is being considered for the Vice Presidency, which idea I think is one of the silliest I have heard in a long time for Jack."[39]

Although Kennedy made light of Jack's possibilities as a vice-presidential candidate in 1956, he was in fact taking them seriously. His fear was that Adlai Stevenson, who looked to be the probable candidate at the top of the ticket, had little chance of winning and that Jack, if nominated, would go down to defeat with him. The only Democrat he thought strong enough to defeat Eisenhower in 1956 was Lyndon Baines Johnson. In October 1955, Kennedy called Johnson to tell him that he "and Jack wanted to support [him] for President in 1956" in return for Johnson's putting Jack on the ticket as vice president. Johnson told Kennedy that he "was not interested" in running.[40]

With the return of the Democrats to the Senate majority in the 1954 midterm elections, Senator John McClellan, one of the many recipients of Kennedy campaign contributions, had become chairman of the Permanent Subcommittee on Investigations and hired Bobby as chief counsel. Bobby was, Kennedy wrote Ethel in July 1955, "gradually earning a place in the sun that he so well deserves." He was delighted, he told Ethel, that Bobby no longer gave "a damn whether McClellan likes him or not." "He has arrived at a period in his education when he has awakened to the realization that if you have the real goods yourself, you don't care a continental what the other fellow thinks, and that's a very important milestone to pass. . . . Now if Mr. Eisenhower decides not to run [for reelection in 1956], I am sure the Democrats can win and he'll have the opportunity to get a very topside job out of that sort of a setup."[41]

To broaden Bobby's résumé, Kennedy had suggested that he travel that summer with Supreme Court justice William O. Douglas in Soviet Central Asia. "In 1955, when I finally got a visa," Douglas recalled in his memoirs, "Joe Kennedy telephoned me and asked if I would take Bobby to Russia with me. He said, 'I think Bobby ought to see how the other half lives.' I told Joe that I would be happy to take his son. Joe was a crusty reactionary and a difficult man, but he was very fond of me and he cared a great deal about his boys. He had big plans for Bobby and probably thought that the Russian trip would be important in his education."[42]

Kennedy stage-managed Bobby's trip as he had those of his brothers. Before his son had even arrived in Russia, his father had hired a publicity agent for him. "I am quite sure you agree with me that Bobby has been doing an outstanding job as Counsel for the Senate Subcommittee," he wrote Edward Dunn, who had worked for Jack's Senate campaign, "and I imagine you agree with me that because of Jack's position in Massachusetts politics it will be very difficult for Bobby to enter into politics. Nevertheless, I think that when he returns from this trip through Russia's provinces he will have a background that will need some building up, and if this kind of a job is the province of your present day work, I would like you to give some consideration to it and I am enclosing my check for $1000 as a retainer."[43]

"I think that the value of the trip," he wrote Bobby, "besides adding stature to your background, is the articles and lectures you might give on it. . . . By all means I would extend the trip into Poland and any other places under Russian influence. That would give a new slant on your interview when you get to the States. In addition to all of this, if you are going to do any articles for 'Life' or the 'Saturday Evening Post,' I would do them jointly [with Douglas], if possible; at least as far as the one big article is concerned; after that each one on his own. Up to date the publicity has been fine for both of you, but as I have said a thousand times, things don't happen, they are made to happen in the public relations field. As much as you and Ethel would love to be in Èze and take a seven-day trip home in a boat, I think it would be a mistake unless Douglas is going to stay somewhere out of America until you get back. From your point of view, the Americans must not think of this trip just in relationship to Justice Douglas. . . . These are just suggestions; there may be perfectly good reasons why they do not make sense. In any event, we would love to see you both if you can make it."[44]

Bobby tried to do as his father had suggested, but he took ill in Siberia with a high fever and was not able to extend his tour into Poland. Jean and Ethel met him in Moscow, then traveled with him to Leningrad and to the Kennedys' villa in the South of France. On his return to the United States, Bobby gave speeches and wrote articles about his observations for *U.S. News & World Report* and the *New York Times Magazine*. He had become a rather strident Cold Warrior, though with a particular Kennedy twist. He did not, according to his biographer Arthur Schlesinger, Jr., like "more obdurate Cold Warriors . . . see western empire as a bulwark against communism nor suppose that anti-colonialism in Asia and Africa was organized in Moscow." He remained as much an anticolonialist as an anti-Communist. "If we are going to win the present conflict with the Soviet Union," he declared in one of the speeches he gave on his return, sounding very much like his father, "we can no longer support the exploitation of native people by Western nations. We supported the French in Indochina far too long."[45]

Jack's book, now titled *Profiles in Courage*, appeared officially on New Year's Day 1956 to positive reviews and rather extraordinary sales. Kennedy had predicted as much in a letter to Sorensen he had written in August, after reading the draft and going over it with Jack. The following May, Kennedy was awarded the Pulitzer Prize in Biography. Arthur Krock would later claim credit for pushing the jurors in Kennedy's direction, but he was probably overstating his importance. The book was lucidly written, had received terrific reviews, and was selling well: all ingredients that were taken into account by the jurors who gave it the prize.

Ted returned to Harvard and football in the fall of 1955. For Kennedy, his success on the football field—he was the starting end—almost made up for his earlier academic lapses. For the final game of the 1955 season, Kennedy organized a trip of family and friends from Boston to New Haven. As John Droney, one of Jack's campaign aides who was invited along, recalled in his oral history, Kennedy arranged for three or four cars to meet the group at the train station and, with police escort, drive them to the stadium. "He had them play the sirens all the way from the train to the game—not because he wanted to get there quicker, but he said it would embarrass Jack. He said, 'Look behind and Jack will have his head down on the floor.' We did and saw that nobody could see him. The father said, 'I don't know what's wrong with him. Now, if I were a senator and I was going to a game, I'd have them using those sirens, and I'd let the people see me. Jack hates anything like that.' "[46]

Harvard lost the game, but, as Ted remembered, "Dad . . . charged into the locker room with Jack and Bobby to noisily congratulate me. I knew they should tone it down, but with Dad and my brothers smiling so broadly over the TD catch and the earning of my letter, I can't say that I was sorry for their enthusiasm."[47]

A unwanted by-product of the victory was a shoulder injury, the severity of which didn't become apparent until later in the winter. Kennedy, unwilling to leave anything to chance, called together every top orthopedist in the Boston area to consult on Ted's shoulder, put them in a room, and flew to Boston to listen to their recommendations. At the end of the session, he graciously thanked them all, then announced that he had to leave for the airport and that Ted would make the final decision on his treatment. He added that if it were his decision to make, which it was not, he would follow the advice of the one doctor in the room who had not advocated surgery.

Ted decided not to have surgery. Bobby, to whom Ted later described the meeting, agreed with him that their father had been so traumatized by Jack's botched operation (and probably, though he didn't say so, by Rosemary's as well) that he found it impossible to imagine another of his children going under the knife.[48]

That fear would never leave him. In June 1964, in a wheelchair and unable to speak after his stroke, Kennedy was brought into the hospital room where Ted was recovering from the plane crash that had left him with a broken back and a collapsed lung. Kennedy listened as the doctors debated whether to perform back surgery or to leave Ted immobilized for months on a Stryker frame in the hope that his spine would fuse on its own. When the doctors were finished, Kennedy, unable to speak, made his opinion known as forcefully as he was able. "Whipping his head from side to side, he shouted out, 'Naaa, naaa, naaa!' I understood that Dad was recalling the back operation on Jack that had left him in permanent pain." Ted followed his father's recommendation and decided against surgery. It was the right choice this time, as it had been eight years earlier.[49]

Thirty-six

MAKING MONEY AND
GIVING IT AWAY

I n the booming 1920s, Joseph P. Kennedy had made his money investing in stocks; in the 1930s, he made more by selling them short; in the 1940s and early 1950s, he invested in real estate and oil, and the money kept rolling in.

Like every good businessman, he looked at the tax implications before investing in anything. He never paid a penny more than he had to or a penny less than he was required to. Leo Racine, one of the accountants in his New York office, recalled that Kennedy had worked out an arrangement with the IRS for a sort of pre-audit. Every year, the IRS sent a man to the Park Avenue offices to review the family's tax returns. If he found a problem, it was discussed and remedied before the returns were filed.[1]

As marginal tax rates for the wealthiest went up to 91 percent in 1950, where they would remain until his son's administration lowered them, Kennedy adjusted his investments accordingly, moving large amounts of capital into oil and gas production to take advantage of generous depletion allowances and tax benefits. Tulsa businessman Raymond Kravis, the father of financier Henry Kravis, recalled getting a call from Kennedy in September 1945 while he was visiting New York. "He asked me to study oil investments he was considering and to make recommendations as to their desirability. . . . It wasn't until five years later that something came along I felt he would be interested in." Kravis called Kennedy's attention to an oil company that was for sale and recommended he buy it. Kennedy interrupted him in the middle of his pitch, claiming not to have understood "a damn thing you're talking about." Then he added, to Kravis's surprise, "You're the doctor in the oil business as far as I'm concerned. . . . You know more about it than I do. If you say this is a good deal for me, I'll take it."[2]

In November 1957, *Fortune* magazine published its list of the richest Americans. Number one was J. Paul Getty with an estimated fortune of between $700 million and $1 billion; next came seven individuals worth between $400 million and $700 million; Kennedy was in the third group of eight with $200 million to $400 million. The source of his income, the magazine reported, was altogether "difficult . . . to catalogue; he says he does his best work floating around in his Florida pool." Alone among *Fortune*'s sixteen wealthiest Americans, Kennedy owned no substantial portion of or stock in any one corporation, firm, or business enterprise, save the Merchandise Mart, which was held in partnership with Rose and the family trusts. He had owned a piece of Hialeah but had sold it in 1954 "because the political pulling and hauling in Florida" made the investment too risky for his tastes. He had been offered scores of investments in buildings, companies, businesses, and even baseball clubs and turned them all down. Most recently, in the spring of 1954, Jack had written his father from Washington to report that he had been approached by a congressman from Philadelphia who "at the suggestions of Roy Mack [the owner] talked to me about the sale of the Philadelphia Athletics. . . . I thought perhaps if you would send me a line on this I could then let them know how you felt about it." Kennedy was not interested. "I feel as I do when Rickey offered me the Brooklyn club that one of the prime necessities for success in any ball club is local ownership." He had no intention of spending any time in Philadelphia.[3]

Joseph P. Kennedy lived a very good life. He stayed in the best hotels, ate in the top restaurants, dressed in custom-made suits, shirts, and ties, was cared for by a small army of servants, traveled in style wherever he went. It was assumed that his children would live lives of wealth and luxury as he did. Occasionally, their father and their mother felt obliged to remind them to be more careful, to watch their spending. When, in late January 1952, Jean had $34,000 of jewelry stolen out of the car she had parked in front of Jack's home in Washington, the newspapers reported the story with apparent glee. Rose wrote Jean, Eunice, and Pat at once, pointing out that each of them had recently lost an earring and admonishing them for their carelessness. "I think the best thing to do is wear pearls at night. You probably can buy those pearl and fake diamond earrings, which look quite well now. I am very sorry as I like you to have jewelry like everybody else." Precisely whom she meant by "everybody else" we do not know.[4]

Kennedy also commented on the incident, which he declared had brought the family "a lot of very bad publicity, not as bad as if somebody got drunk in a night club, but it shows a disregard for money on the part of people who are supposed to have it which irritates the masses beyond belief and it creates a very bad impression." He suggested that Eunice, Pat, and Jean "put all the important jewelry you all have in a safety deposit box and let it stay there . . . and just wear ordinary stuff around to whatever parties you attend. It may be sad but it's essential." He wanted them as well to "stop traveling by air planes, and by trains, particularly air planes, unless the trip is essential. This commuting back and forth besides being expensive becomes a matter of danger. I think you all should just get used to settling down in one spot and not rush away weekends to a different place from where you are located. Let's forget that for a while." Having raised the subject of finances, which he so rarely did, he concluded by adding "that while all of you have incomes that sound substantially large, to all intents and purposes . . . all of you are spending more than your income, so you need to readjust your sights and cut down on the spending, because if anything happens to me this income is liable to be affected and you may have to live on lots less so you might just as well get used to it. Just a word of advice from Daddy on this Monday morning. Love and kisses."[5]

The Joseph P. Kennedy, Jr. Foundation, which was a 25 percent owner of the Merchandise Mart and whose income Kennedy may have supplemented with additional donations, continued through the middle 1950s to give away large sums of money, most of it to church-affiliated institutions in the Boston area and Massachusetts, with smaller grants to out-of-state Catholic organizations, including $250,000 to Notre Dame, where Kennedy was now a trustee; $400,000 to Manhattanville College in the Bronx, where the girls had gone to college; and $240,000 to St. Coletta in Jefferson, Wisconsin, where Rosemary lived.[6]

"It was our original intention," Kennedy explained to Father Denomy, who had asked for a donation for the Pontifical Institute of Mediaeval Studies, "to spread this money amongst all religions, Catholics, Protestants, and Jews; but in practice, well over 95 per cent has been given to Catholic institutions." When John Royal of NBC asked him to see Father Max Jordan, the radio broadcaster who had become a Benedictine monk, Kennedy replied that he would be "glad to meet the Father but you and I know that none of these fellows want to meet me unless it's a touch, and I am so committed now to Catholic priests, hierarchy, and nuns that I will be paying off for the next three years. In addition to that, I don't have much of a chance to do anything except for the Catholics, and I don't think that's right either. They all stand for very worthy causes but it's just impossible to keep up with them. Every day requests come in from Trappists, Carthusians, Franciscans, etc., and I have to duck them because it's time wasted for them."[7]

As the children relocated across the country—Bobby and Ethel to Washington, Eunice and Sarge to Chicago, Pat and Peter to Los Angeles—foundation gifts followed them. "We have felt that where the family or the Foundation received substantial parts of their income," Kennedy explained to one petitioner, "that community deserved first consideration, after our native city of Boston and state of Massachusetts received their share." The foundation in early 1952 gave a $1.25 million grant to the St. Coletta school for retarded boys in Palos Park, just outside Chicago; in 1958, it provided $500,000 to the Washington Archdiocese for a school for retarded children and a teachers center; in 1959, $800,000 was donated to the Los Angeles Archdiocese for a center for mentally retarded and emotionally disturbed children.

For the first five or so years, the foundation had concentrated its giving on Catholic institutions that cared for "underprivileged" children, because that cause, the family believed, was closest to Joseph P.

Kennedy, Jr. By the middle 1950s, the focus was narrowed to "the cause of retarded children." As Kennedy explained to one applicant in October 1957, he had "at times . . . thought that we should set aside some proportion of our funds for other causes but the need is so great in the case of retarded children that, for the present at least, I feel it important to confine my efforts to this cause." Although he would never say so or even hint at it, the motivating factor behind the focus on the retarded was the memory of how impossible it had been to find schools, treatment centers, counseling programs, recreation facilities, or clinics for Rosemary. There was also the influence of Archbishop Cushing, who had taken up the cause of the retarded as his special mission.[8]

As Kennedy quickly discovered, the need was much greater than his resources. "As you become acquainted with this subject," he wrote Cardinal Spellman on June 21, 1958, "you also become aware that the surface is just being scratched and nothing short of the United States Government can maintain the services the mentally retarded children will require. . . . No matter how many of these institutions are built or started, we will only be 'scratching the surface.' Custodial care for mentally retarded children is too costly for any foundation or the Church. Specialized schools for the mildly retarded, or the children who are educable, seems to me to be the responsibility of the Government on every level. The religious instructions of the children is the responsibility of the Church authorities."[9]

Eunice later recalled that "the problem with the schools" for the retarded that the foundation had funded "was that no sooner was one built than there was a waiting list of over 1,000 people waiting to get in. Also, we were not graduating many mentally retarded each year, so new mentally retarded children coming along wouldn't be able to get into our institutions. Dad wanted new programs for the foundation."[10]

Sometime in 1958, frustrated by his inability to make much of an impact, Kennedy decided to shift foundation support from medical care and education of the retarded to research into the causes of mental retardation and preventive measures. He contacted Howard Rusk, the director of the Institute of Physical Medicine and Rehabilitation in New York and the nation's primary authority on rehabilitative medicine. He also contacted Harvard dean McGeorge Bundy, who had been trying against very long odds to get Kennedy to contribute something to the university. "I am considering the idea of changing the policy of the Foundation and, possibly, of spending a million dollars a year on research in the field of mental health. Of course, I realize that it is a very broad field and that it will be difficult to set up a line of demarcation. . . . If you feel that Harvard might help me in the pursuit of this new idea of mine and, at the same time, help itself, we could get together again and talk. . . . I am interested in the problem of retarded children and I would like to do as much as I can for them."[11]

Kennedy arranged for a meeting in New York City of experts to solicit their proposals. The "experts" assembled, with no knowledge of or experience with retardation, came up with large, general programs on "mental health rather than ones targeted on retardation." "I felt," Eunice recalled, "that the Foundation should be staffed with people previously interested in mental retardation . . . and that we should support programs designed specifically to serve the mentally retarded themselves." She asked her father to "'give Sarge and me six weeks and we'll get back to you with a plan.' He said, 'OK—but if you haven't anything in the next six weeks I'm going ahead with the plan of today.'"[12]

As a Kennedy, Eunice held no one in awe, except perhaps her father and the pope. She was now in her middle thirties, as gaunt as her brother Jack, with as toothsome a smile, and every bit as driven. Unlike her brothers, she couldn't go into politics. With two small children at home, she felt that it would not be right for her to take on a full-time job or appointment. Yet she too had been brought up to do something worthwhile with her life, to be of public service in some way. Her solution was to take a more active role in the family foundation.

Though a grown woman, Eunice Kennedy Shriver still needed her father's approbation, sometimes, it appeared, more than anything else. As Sarge wrote Kennedy, Eunice was possessed of an "ever-present desire—deep and emotional—to be important in your mind & heart. As she often says, you are the greatest father in the world. You must know she has a 'father complex.'"[13]

She had to have been delighted when Kennedy agreed to her proposal. Though she had no expertise in mental retardation or scientific research, if her father thought her qualified to take on this project, then she must have been qualified to do so. She and Sarge dropped what they were doing and spent the next few months traveling the country, interviewing researchers, lining up consultants to serve on an informal advisory board, and drawing up the guidelines for the new grants. By the time they were done they had met with dozens of experts on and practitioners in the field of mental retardation.

Kennedy was so impressed by their work that he asked Sarge to become the foundation's first executive director and Eunice its first executive vice president, a position she would relinquish only on her death. (The post of foundation president would be reserved for her brothers.) "I am withdrawing, more or less, from the work of the Foundation," Kennedy wrote Brandeis president Abram L. Sachar, who had applied for funding in the spring of 1959. "I have explained to my son-in-law that we are anxious to explore the possibility of doing something with Brandeis, and I am sure you will be hearing from him. When he has the situation lined up, I can get into it myself."[14]

Although Eunice and Sargent Shriver were committed to the Catholic Church and its institutions, they recognized, as Kennedy did, that the church did not have the expertise or financial resources to focus on the research mission the foundation intended to pursue. Instead, they solicited proposals from the "topside" people in the nation's research universities and teaching hospitals. In early 1959, the foundation awarded a grant of $1 million, the largest for research in mental retardation ever given, to Massachusetts General to establish the Joseph P. Kennedy, Jr. Laboratories for Research on Mental Retardation. Negotiations for additional grants, Kennedy explained to a priest who had requested funding for a "Catholic Guidance Center in Trenton," were already under way "with Johns Hopkins, Stanford, Wisconsin and Yale whose faculties include many of the outstanding research men." A year later, in February 1960, the foundation awarded a grant of $1.26 million to Johns Hopkins.[15]

As large as these grants were, they were not enough. Only the federal government, Kennedy had noted in his letter to Cardinal Spellman, had the resources to attack the problems. Regrettably, in fiscal 1956, Congress had allocated only $750,000 to research on retardation, $500,000 for a survey of projects currently under way and $250,000 to the National Institute of Mental Health. "NIMH staff members privately doubted whether as much as $250,000 could be well spent on a subject as unglamorous as mental retardation." That would change, dramatically and suddenly, when a Kennedy entered the White House, unleashing a torrent of energy, expertise, and money focused on the problems that the Kennedy foundation had addressed itself to after 1958.[16]

The Second Hoover Commission completed its work in the spring of 1955, just as Kennedy prepared for his four months in the South of France. One of its recommendations had been the establishment of a permanent presidential civilian watchdog committee for the CIA and other government entities engaged in intelligence gathering and interpretation. President Eisenhower accepted the recommendation, and in January 1956 wrote to ask Kennedy to serve on the newly organized President's Board of Consultants on Foreign Intelligence Activities. Kennedy telegraphed Allen Dulles, the head of the CIA and brother of the secretary of state, that he was both "delighted and honored to serve on the consultants' committee. I will enjoy the prospect of working with you and assure you that I will give my best efforts to be of any help that I can in this."[17]

The board met infrequently and had only advisory authority, but because it was chaired by James R. Killian, Jr., president of MIT, appointment to it conferred no small measure of prestige. More important to Kennedy, it put him in closer contact with Allen Dulles. Kennedy already knew that part of Dulles's portfolio was to oversee what future CIA director William Colby, who took over the Italian station in 1953, later referred to as "by far the CIA's largest covert political action program untaken until then": spending American money and using American influence "to prevent Italy from being taken over by the Communists in the next—1958 elections." Some of the CIA money was funneled through the Vatican, which had become a critical agent in the anti-Communist crusade in Italy. Because the United States government had no embassy or official representative at the Vatican, Dulles sought to make use of Kennedy. Information leaked by Dulles to Kennedy was conveyed to Count Enrico Galeazzi, who could be trusted to deliver it to the appropriate authorities in the Vatican, including the secretary of state and the pope.[18]

"I have just returned from Washington," Kennedy wrote Galeazzi on January 30, "where I participated in a meeting of a new board which has been formed by the President to supervise all the foreign intelligence agencies, including our friends in the CIA. . . . Very confidentially, I understand that you are aware of [Christian Democrat leader Amintore] Fanfani's request for financial aid for the Christian Democratic Party. If you do not approve of what is being done, by all means contact me as soon as possible and tell me what should be done. . . . I saw the Cardinal [Spellman] in New York and told him that I had suggested to Dulles that he come to New York and see him and alerted him on the Fanfani request."[19]

In March 1956, Kennedy began planning another of his "fact-finding" trips to Europe. "My position on President Eisenhower's Board of Consultants," he wrote Galeazzi at the Vatican, grossly exaggerating the importance of the advisory board, "brings me in close touch now with all questions of foreign policy and will probably necessitate some official visits to Spain, Italy, France, England, Germany and Switzerland during the coming summer. . . . Let me know if there is anything that should be looked after in connection with the Italian elections."[20]

In May, he wrote Father Cavanaugh to ask for his help. "The situation in Italy needs the attention that you can give it. There are a great many things being contemplated that are most secret in nature and most important in their implications." He then proceeded to break confidence and describe those "most secret" things. In 1948, the U.S. government had promised to funnel money through the Vatican to support the Christian Democrats in their electoral campaign against the Communists. The Vatican, expecting to be reimbursed, had secretly spent large sums of money on the campaign but had never been repaid by the Americans, "which was a terrible blow to the Vatican finances." Kennedy wanted Father Cavanaugh's assistance in making sure the Vatican got what it had been promised. He also hoped that Cavanaugh would assist him in reaching out secretly to Vatican-funded and -sponsored "Catholic action groups" that were expected to play a future role in Italian politics. He closed his letter by asking Cavanaugh to "destroy it" as soon as he had read it.[21]

Kennedy, on arriving in Rome that summer, called on Colby, the CIA station chief. Colby briefed him fully on agency activities. According to Colby, Kennedy demanded to know the name of the "outside [Italian] officer" handling one of the agency's programs. When Colby said he couldn't disclose that information, "Kennedy bore in; clearly, he was out to prove that he was entitled to know all and every secret. . . . He sharply said that either he would be given the name of the outside officer or he would return to Washington and resign from the President's Foreign Intelligence Advisory Board." Kennedy was given the name he had asked for.[22]

We do not know what Kennedy did with this name or any other information he gathered that summer on his self-initiated fact-finding mission. He was a man who knew the value of secrets and, no doubt, intended to make the best use of them.

P OLS THINK KENNEDY WILL BE ADLAI'S RUNNING MATE, read the headline in the *Boston Globe* on March 4, 1956. "When supporters of Adlai Stevenson discuss a possible running-mate for their candidate, they seldom fail to mention young Jack Kennedy of Massachusetts. . . . Kennedy would seem to have the necessary Democratic assets. He is young (38). He is handsome. He is liberal, but not radical. He is a Navy veteran with a brilliant record. . . . He is a vote-getter of proven ability. . . . He is a strong Stevenson supporter." All of this was no doubt true, but there remained substantial obstacles in Jack's way, including his youth, health, failure to vote against McCarthy, and Catholicism. There was little to be done about the youth issue, other than point out that Teddy Roosevelt had also been a young vice president. The health issue would, the Kennedys believed, disappear as soon as voters saw how hard he campaigned. The McCarthy problem would never disappear but would haunt his candidacy in 1956 and again in 1960. Fortunately, only a minority of voters would continue to hold it against him that he had not risen from his hospital bed to vote for censure.

It was the Catholic question that overshadowed every other one, especially for Democrats with memories of the Al Smith debacle in 1928.

Kennedy was against his son campaigning for the vice-presidential nomination from the moment it was mentioned as a possibility. The objection he voiced most often and most loudly was that the Democratic ticket was going to lose, and when it did, fingers would be pointed at the Catholic on the ticket. He had other concerns as well, which he voiced to Charles Wyzanski, chairman of the Harvard Board of Overseers, who was attempting yet again to get Kennedy to contribute money to his alma mater. The two had lunch on April 11, 1956, at the Tavern Club in Boston. When Wyzanski mentioned that he had heard that Kennedy was against his son running as vice president, Kennedy responded "that he had nothing like so much influence with his son as people tended to suppose. Only the other day," he told Wyzanski, "Senator Kennedy had voted to extend federal regulation over natural gas companies despite the fact that this was against the financial interest of his father (who was one of the largest individual owners of stock in natural gas companies). More important, the Ambassador stated was the fact that if JFK were then to run for vice president it was not clear that he had the stamina to withstand the strain, and even if he did, people would contend that his health was not good enough to bear the rigors of the Presidency if the office devolved upon him. The Ambassador said that the saddest day of his life was the day 'Joe' died; he thought of it every morning; and he didn't want another son to die."[23]

Ted Sorensen had early in 1956 started assembling data and constructing the argument that a Catholic candidate on the national ticket would add more votes than he would take away. He claimed, based on his research and pushing the numbers a bit to support his thesis, that (1) the Catholic vote would be pivotal in key cities in fourteen states with 261 electoral votes, not one of which Stevenson had carried in 1952; (2) while most Catholics still voted Democratic, the "Catholic Democratic vote was noticeably off in 1948—and showed a critical decline in 1952"; (3) Catholic candidates for state office had, in 1952, run ahead of the national ticket; (4) the Al Smith myth was just that. Smith had been beaten in 1928 for a number of reasons, not simply because he was a Catholic. Although Sorensen would later acknowledge the report's "limitations as a scientific analysis," there was no discounting its potential political impact. To protect Kennedy from the charge that he was pushing himself too aggressively as a national candidate, which he, in fact, was, Sorensen arranged for John Bailey, the Connecticut state chairman of the Democratic Party and a Catholic, to claim authorship.

Under Bailey's name, Sorensen's report was distributed to Democratic operatives, Stevenson supporters, and the press. Material from it would later be published, in full or in part, in several magazines, including *U.S. News & World Report* and *Time* magazine.[24]

The more the press trumpeted the findings of the Sorensen-Bailey memorandum, the more Kennedy feared that a trap had been set for his son. Worse than denying Jack the nomination because he was a Catholic was giving it to him because he was a Catholic. Even Clare Boothe Luce, one of Jack's "greatest rooters," Kennedy wrote his son in late May, "hopes you will not accept the nomination for the Vice Presidency. She has many arguments, not the least of which is that if you are chosen, it will be because you are a Catholic and not because you are big enough to do a good job. She feels that a defeat would be a devastating blow to your prestige, which at the moment is great, and nonpartisan."[25]

Jack listened to his father's arguments but wasn't swayed by them. "Arthur Schlesinger wrote to me yesterday," he informed his father, "and stated that he thought it should be done and that he was going to do everything he possibly could. . . . Competition is mostly from Hubert Humphrey, who had his Governor make a statement that I would not be acceptable because of my vote on the farm bill. [Senator Kennedy had opposed the continuance of farm subsidies at present levels.] . . . I have done nothing about it and do not plan to although if it looks worthwhile I may have George Smathers talk to some of the southern Governors. While I think the prospects are rather limited, it does seem of some use to have all this churning up. If I don't get it I can always tell them in the State that it was because of my vote on the farm bill."[26]

Jack's primary concern that spring was taking control of the Massachusetts Democratic Party from William "Onions" Burke, who had embarrassed Adlai Stevenson, the presumptive candidate in 1956, by running John McCormack as a favorite-son candidate and defeating Stevenson in the Massachusetts primary. Kennedy warned his son as strongly as he could to "leave it alone and don't get into the gutter with those bums up there in Boston," but Jack was convinced that to be a player on the national stage he had to gain control of his own state party. He organized a slate of candidates for the eighty committee seats that were up for grabs, outworked, outspent, outcampaigned, and outsmarted the party stalwarts lined up behind Burke, and installed his own people in leadership positions. The Stevenson campaign could not help being impressed, as were Democrats everywhere, including Joseph P. Kennedy.[27]

For a brief moment that spring, Kennedy considered the possibility that it might be in Jack's interest to join the Stevenson ticket. "The political situation seems to be changing rapidly," Kennedy wrote Lord Beaverbrook in mid-June. It appeared that Eisenhower's health—he had suffered a massive heart attack in September 1955—might become a major issue. If Eisenhower decided not to run, the Democrats would have an excellent chance. If he did run "as a sick man—and he will have to," Kennedy wrote Morton Downey, he might be beatable. In any event, Kennedy was considering returning from the South of France to attend the convention in Chicago. "We'll watch it from the sidelines for another week or ten days and if you get any real news, let me know."[28]

By mid-July, Kennedy had decided that he had been right in the first place. Eisenhower was invincible. His recent illness, rather than a liability, had made him a stronger candidate, more sympathetic than before. "I think Eisenhower is the most popular man that we have seen in our time," Kennedy wrote Sargent Shriver on July 18, "and to make attacks on him in the coming campaign is to me a sure way to commit suicide." He advised Shriver, who during his years in Chicago had become close to Governor Stevenson and his advisers, that the Democrats should focus their attention not on Eisenhower's illness, but on the fact that the nation needed a full-time president and Eisenhower was no longer prepared to be one. A Stevenson-Kennedy ticket, which now seemed likely, would, he concluded, "certainly do better than the last time," but it would not win.[29]

"Talked to Jack twice," he wrote his son Ted on July 18. "After conversation with Bill Blair [one of Stevenson's top advisers] on Cape on Sunday, he is giving serious consideration to the job. Last night, however, he was worried because the *New York Evening Post* was coming out with an article that said he had Addison's disease. I told him he should co-operate with the reporter and admit that he had had it but that the disease was not a killer as it was eight years ago, and I feel that it should be brought out now and not after he gets the nomination, if he gets it. He thought he might come over [to France] for a week to talk things over, but I doubt it." Fortunately for Jack, the article did not appear, or if it did, no one took notice.[30]

As late as July 30, less than two weeks before the convention opened, Jack had still not decided whether to actively campaign for the vice-presidential nomination. "There are a great many pros and cons," Kennedy wrote Galeazzi, "and I have been talking with him on the telephone frequently of late and I expect that I'll hear from him a great deal in the next two weeks. . . . If the political situation gets very exciting, it will become necessary for me to resign my position on the President's Board, at least until after the elections. I have written to the President and I am waiting to hear from him. Having a member of your family in this fight makes it a bit embarrassing. If Jack runs, I shall have to attack the Eisenhower administration; if he does not run, they may say because of my relationship with Eisenhower, I did not want him to run—so there you are! I will keep you posted in any event."[31]

That July, as the convention grew closer, still with no word from the Stevenson campaign as to whom they were going to consider for vice president, Kennedy wrote Jack from France. "If you make up your mind that you either don't want it and that you are not going to get it . . . you should get out a statement to the effect that representing Mass. is one of the greatest jobs in the world and there is lots to be done for your state and her people, and while you are most grateful for the national support offered you for the Vice Presidency, your heart belongs to Massachusetts." If, on the other hand, Jack decided to keep his name in the running and "ride the thing through to see whether you can get it, why couldn't I give an interview here in France to either Joe Smith of the I.N.S. [the Hearst news service], or the New York TIMES reporter, arranged by Krock or Jimmy Reston . . . in which I might say something like this: 'I stand prepared to back my son's decision whatever it may be. My own impression, however, is that his choice is being swayed by his heart and his head. His devotion to Massachusetts and its people has made him most reluctant to accept any position until he has done everything he possibly can for that state. On the other hand, he has a loyalty to his friends in the leadership of the Democratic Party who feel that his record and his integrity and ability would be of great assistance to the Democratic ticket. . . . I stand ready to support him in whatever his decision may be, and if he is nominated by his party, I am dead sure he will give a fine account of himself.' I think this statement should be got out by either you or me in some way or another the minute you make up your mind that you are not going to try the V.P. so that the full good effect will accrue to you. You or I might both add that being a U.S. Senator from Massachusetts is the finest position any young man could aim for."[32]

Senator Kennedy wisely made no statement of any kind, nor did he enlist his father to make one for him. It would have been the height of folly for him to preemptively withdraw his name from consideration. To do so would have made him sound as if he expected or deserved the nomination. Kennedy should have known this, but he so desperately wanted to be of help to his son that his better judgment deserted him.

Jack Kennedy departed for the Chicago convention still having heard nothing from the Stevenson camp. He had, however, been selected by producer Dore Schary to narrate and introduce the opening-day film on the history of the party. When the lights came up after the film, he was escorted onto the platform and given a standing ovation. "Senator John F. Kennedy of Massachusetts, a prospect for the Democratic vice-presidential nomination," the *New York Times* reported on August 14, "came before the convention tonight as a movie star." The next day, he was asked to give one of the nominating speeches for Stevenson, which he did, but only after discarding the text handed him and, with Sorensen, writing his own. He assumed now that he was out of the running for the vice-presidential nomination. The tradition was that those called on to give nominating speeches were not being considered as possible running mates. Half a world away, in their villa in France, Kennedy and Rose listened to his speech on the "short-wave radio and thought it extremely good."[33]

After being nominated for the presidency, Stevenson returned to his hotel suite, where he announced that he had decided to leave the choice of his running mate to the convention delegates. At midnight, the Kennedy clan, missing only the parents and Rosemary, gathered in Jack's hotel room with his senior advisers. As Charles Bartlett, Washington insider, journalist, and Jack's friend, later recalled, a challenge like the one Stevenson had laid before them was irresistible for the Kennedys. "I remember the whole family was milling around ready to go. . . . As soon as the competition arose, why . . . he really went for it. . . . I was really amazed because I hadn't been that aware before that he really wanted it that much."[34]

Jack "turned to Bobby and said, 'call Dad and tell him I'm going for it.'" Bobby, according to Ken O'Donnell, placed the call, "by no means an enviable assignment. Jack disappeared from the room, leaving me alone with Bobby when the call came through. The Ambassador's blue language flashed all over the room. The connection was broken before he was finished denouncing Jack as an idiot who was ruining his political career. Bobby quickly hung up the telephone and made no effort to get his father back on the line. 'Whew!' Bobby said. 'Is he mad!'"[35]

For the senior Kennedy, the scenario that was developing was the worst one possible. Either Jack would lose the fight to Senator Estes Kefauver, his first political loss ever, or he would win the nomination and, when the ticket went down to defeat, be blamed for having put his own ambition ahead of the party and, as a Catholic, siphoning off enough votes to elect Eisenhower to a second term. He would be tagged as a loser either way.

On the first ballot, Kefauver of Tennessee, who had been campaigning all year for the presidential nomination, received 483½ votes for vice president to Jack Kennedy's 304. The thought of a Kefauver victory, which now seemed imminent, galvanized the anti-Kefauver faction, including southern conservatives, into coalescing around Kennedy. On the second ballot, Jack Kennedy rallied to within 39 votes of the needed majority; then, on the brink of a Kennedy victory, Senator Albert Gore of Tennessee rose to request that his name be withdrawn from nomination and all his votes be switched to Kefauver. In quick succession, the chairs of the Oklahoma, Minnesota, Tennessee, and Missouri delegations rose to announce that their delegations were shifting their votes to Kefauver. Senator Kennedy, recognizing that the fight was lost, left his room at the Stock Yard Inn and went directly to the convention hall, where he was recognized by convention chairman Sam Rayburn, mounted the rostrum, thanked the convention for its support, released his delegates, and moved that Kefauver be nominated by acclamation.

Although he would later thank his lucky stars that he had not been part of the losing ticket, Jack did not take defeat easily. He asked Bobby to call their father in France. "In bad times," Bobby would later recall, they had always turned to their father, who "more than anyone else . . . has seen the bright side. . . . The greater the disaster, the brighter he was, the more support he gave." And so it was on this occasion. Kennedy, who had been following the nomination fight on shortwave radio, congratulated his boys on their valiant efforts and assured them that when the Stevenson-Kefauver team went down in defeat, which Kennedy believed all but assured, Senator John Fitzgerald Kennedy would be left standing as the only viable candidate for the 1960 presidential nomination.[36]

Exhausted and depressed after the convention, Jack left his pregnant wife behind in Newport with her mother and stepfather and flew to France to see his father and take a brief sailing vacation in the Mediterranean with his brother Ted and his friend Torb Macdonald.

"Jack arrived here very tired," Kennedy wrote Morton Downey on August 24, "but I think very happy because he came out of the convention so much better than anyone could have hoped. As far as I am concerned, you know how I feel—if you're going to get licked, get licked trying for the best, not the second best. His time is surely coming!"[37]

Thirty-seven

THE CATHOLIC CANDIDATE

The short item in the *Boston Globe* for September 18, 1956, reported only that Joseph Kennedy had had a prostate gland operation, followed by some sort of abdominal surgery. That is all we know aside from the fact that his recovery took longer than expected. "The reason you haven't heard from me," he wrote Lord Beaverbrook at the end of October, "is because since the 6th of September, beginning in the hospital in Paris until last Saturday, I have been in the hospital under the care of the doctors, having had four operations. I am recovering now and feel reasonably well but not well enough to do or write very much."[1]

While their father recuperated in Boston that fall, Bobby and Jack campaigned for Stevenson. Jack, according to Ted Sorensen, covered "more than thirty thousand miles in twenty-four states [making] over 150 speeches and appearances in the course of six weeks." Bobby, who it was anticipated would be Jack's campaign manager when he ran for president, "was sent on the Stevenson train . . . to see what was being done and how. A boring experience for Bob," his mother recalled, but a necessary one. Both sons learned an enormous amount about how and how not to run a presidential campaign. Jack broadened his exposure to voters outside Massachusetts.[2]

In November, Eisenhower was elected—and by a larger margin than 1952. He carried forty-one states out of forty-eight and polled 57.4 percent of the vote, the largest margin since Roosevelt's reelection in 1936. Kennedy, still recovering from his surgeries, was not displeased by the Republican victory. In 1960, after eight years of a Republican presidency and with the unpopular Nixon the heir apparent, the Democrats would, he believed, be well positioned to take back the White House. "It is not too much to expect that the Democratic Party could be successful in 1960," Kennedy wrote Galeazzi on November 9, "and it may interest you to know that Jack is a most likely candidate."[3]

On Thanksgiving Day 1956, Kennedy and Rose hosted their children and grandchildren at Hyannis Port. Later that day, after long conversations with his father, Jack told Dave Powers that he had decided to run. "With only about four hours of work and a handful of supporters, I came within thirty-three and a half votes of winning the Vice-Presidential nomination. . . . If I work hard for four years, I ought to be able to pick up all the marbles." There would be no official announcement. Before he could declare for the presidency, the senator had to run for reelection in 1958 and, if he wished to be considered a viable candidate, win in a landslide.[4]

Bobby too made a decision about his future after election day. Still chief counsel to the Permanent Subcommittee on Investigations, he had flown to the West Coast in November 1956 to follow up on a tip he had received on labor racketeering. Finding much more than he had bargained for, he returned east with a new agenda for himself and the Senate subcommittee: they would take on labor racketeering and corruption, beginning with the Teamsters and their president, Dave Beck.

The Kennedy family spent its Christmas in Hyannis Port, because Kennedy was not well enough to fly to Palm Beach. It was there that Bobby told his father of his plans to ask the Senate subcommittee to undertake a thorough investigation of labor corruption and the Teamsters. Kennedy was aghast at his son's recklessness. If Bobby went ahead, he would succeed only in alienating organized labor and making it impossible for his brother to win the 1960 nomination—or election. When Bobby would not yield, Kennedy brought in family friend and Supreme Court justice William O. Douglas to argue with him. Bobby refused to back down. He returned to Washington and convinced the senators he worked with to open an investigation of labor racketeering. A new subcommittee, chaired by Senator John McClellan of Arkansas, was impaneled to investigate labor corruption. As the second ranking Democrat on labor, Senator John Kennedy was offered a position on the new subcommittee. Senator Kennedy knew his father would be opposed to his accepting the position, but Bobby had asked for his help, and he could not refuse him. Besides, as a student of history, he knew how the reputations of Harry Truman and Estes Kefauver had been burnished by Senate investigations into corruption.[5]

In January 1957, Lyndon Johnson agreed to give Senator Kennedy the committee assignment on foreign relations that he and his father had been lobbying for since he'd arrived in the Senate. Jack may have sealed the deal with a telegram to Johnson, sent on July 27, 1956, thanking the majority leader for the "first class job you did for us all this year" and declaring that it was a "pleasure to be a Johnson man." Jack's rival for the position was Estes Kefauver, who was certainly not a "Johnson man," especially on civil rights, which was expected to be a major item before Congress in the next session. Jack had never taken much of a position on civil rights, either in his speeches in his district, where there were few African Americans, or in his campaign for the Senate. His silence on the issue had stood him well in the vice-presidential race, where he received the bulk of the southern delegate votes.[6]

In July 1957, six months after being named to the Senate Committee on Foreign Relations, Jack publicly criticized the French for refusing to negotiate with Algerian nationalists and suggested that the United States use its best efforts to effect a settlement that guaranteed eventual Algerian independence. President Eisenhower, Secretary of State Dulles, and former Democratic secretary of state Acheson rebuked the junior senator from Massachusetts for interfering in French internal affairs. When Jack confided to his father that he feared he had made a mistake by speaking out so forcefully, Kennedy assured him he would be okay. "I have to smile. For years, the political sharpshooters have raised hell with me because I wanted to keep the United States out of all countries except South America. Now they are raising hell with you because you want the United States in. I don't think they hurt me, and I'm sure they won't hurt you."[7]

On August 2, Jack voted with Lyndon Johnson on the amendment to the 1957 civil rights bill, which required a jury trial before any official could be convicted of voting rights violations. Senate liberals had argued that requiring jury trials would render the bill meaningless, but Jack had voted for the amendment, insisting, alternately, that without it southern senators would filibuster the bill to death and that the jury trial provision was necessary to protect basic constitutional rights. He was widely criticized by liberals for giving Johnson and the South everything they had asked for. His father assured him again that he had nothing to worry about, that he would soon "be out of the woods" on Algeria and civil rights.[8]

On September 7, 1957, the *Saturday Evening Post* published an embarrassingly effusive puff piece titled "The Amazing Kennedys," focusing not just on Jack's campaign for the presidency, but on the public service achievements of the other Kennedy children, including Rosemary, who it claimed was caring for and teaching "exceptional" children in a Catholic school near Milwaukee. The author summed up his unrelentingly cheery family history by declaring that "fervent admirers of the Kennedys profess to see in their rise to national prominence the flowering of another great political family, such as the Adamses, the Lodges and the La Follettes. They confidently look forward to the day when Jack will be in the White House, Bobby will serve in the Cabinet as Attorney General, and Teddy will be the senator from Massachusetts." Although there is no evidence for it, this last prediction sounds very much as if it had come from Kennedy—or someone close to him.[9]

On October 28, 1957, the same day that the *New York Times* (on page twenty) declared his father one of the nation's fifteen wealthiest men, Jack Kennedy received his own headlines (on page nineteen) for a speech he had given at a Yeshiva University dinner at the Waldorf-Astoria. In it, he refuted by clever analogy the charges that as a Catholic he might have conflicting loyalties: to the Vatican as well as the United States. Referring to the "Zionist activities of the large Jewish organizations" (which his father had been so critical of) and to "Americans of Irish, Hungarian, Italian, Greek and Latin American extraction," Senator Kennedy insisted that the interest such Americans took in their "homelands" was not "incompatible with loyalty to America. . . . American freedom had its deepest traditions in the toleration of multiple group loyalties."[10]

On November 18, *Time* magazine referred to his presidential campaign as a "soaring satellite" but asked if "the Democratic whiz of 1957 [would] still be the whiz of 1960." Jack Kennedy's virtues were manifold, but so were the obstacles to his candidacy, the article declared. He was Catholic, young, and "in many aspects, a conservative" in a liberal party. "Nobody," Senator Kennedy told the *Time* writers, "is going to hand me the nomination. If I were governor of a large state, Protestant and 55, I could sit back and let it come to me. But if I am going to get it, I'll have to work for it—and damn hard."

Two weeks later, on December 2, 1957, Senator Kennedy appeared on the *Time* cover, with the story inside describing in great detail his nationwide campaign. The article was unstinting in its praise of Kennedy's parents and grandparents, highlighting the political careers of grandfathers Patrick Kennedy and Honey Fitz and father Joe's skills as a moneymaker. Jackie defended her father-in-law "against charges that he runs his children's careers. 'You'd think he was a mastermind playing chess,' says Jackie, 'when actually he's a nice old gentleman we see at Thanksgiving and Christmas.' "

"The nice old gentleman" was delighted by the coverage, though, he joked, not particularly by Jackie's quote. "TIME did a great job for Jack," Kennedy wrote Luce, "but that 'nice old gentleman' quote has resulted in Jackie's being cut out of my will and I am having a talk with my lawyers about suing you for libel. The build-up in the FORTUNE article [which had listed Kennedy as one of the nation's wealthiest men] was great but what good is all that money to a 'nice old man.' "[11]

Kennedy was lulled by the positive publicity into thinking that the path to his son's nomination might not be as difficult as he had believed. "Strangely enough," he wrote Count Galeazzi in September, "the religious issue isn't nearly as bothersome at the minute as his age." He and his son's advisers had "decided now that Jack has addressed himself enough to the Catholic issue and unless pressed by a difficult question, will assume that from now on a Catholic can be elected. We'll see how this works out." To make sure the campaign was fully prepared, Kennedy enlisted Bishop John Wright, Cushing's former secretary and now bishop of Worcester, Massachusetts, to help him get "a few articles written" for national magazines on the subject of how one could be a good Catholic and a good American at the same time.[12]

Everything seemed to be going well when, in December 1957, almost two years after *Profiles in Courage* was published, and seven months after it had been awarded a Pulitzer Prize, Drew Pearson, interviewed on television by Mike Wallace, declared that he knew "for a fact" that Jack Kennedy had not written the book. The Kennedys got in touch at once with Washington insider and former White House counsel Clark Clifford, then in private practice. Clifford suggested that Jack Kennedy demand a retraction from ABC, the television station that had broadcast the Pearson interview. While the senator was in his office, Clifford recalled in his memoirs, "the telephone rang. It was Ambassador Kennedy. . . . I could hear the old man screaming at Jack. Very calmly, [Senator] Kennedy said, 'I will let you talk to Clark, Father.' . . . Before I could even say hello, Joe Kennedy said: 'I want you to sue the bastards for fifty million dollars. Get it started right away. It's dishonest and they know it. My boy wrote the book. This is a plot against us.'" Clifford explained that he and Jack had decided to ask instead for a retraction and that he was flying to New York at once to "sit down with the people at ABC. '*Sit down with them, hell!*' he shouted into my ear. His son watched me with a faint air of amusement." Kennedy demanded again that suits be filed at once against "ABC, Pearson, Wallace, and anyone else in sight." This time, the decision on how to proceed was not his call, but his son's, and Jack preferred to request a retraction. Clifford was able to persuade ABC officials that there was no basis for Pearson's claim and a retraction was issued and read by a vice president at the beginning of the next Mike Wallace show. After the retraction, Kennedy indicated "that we had followed the right course—which was," Clifford recalled, "as close as the old man ever came to an admission of error."[13]

K ennedy had been much too optimistic in his belief that his son's Catholicism was not going to be as big an issue as he had feared. In early January 1958, an organization known as POAU, Protestants and Other Americans United for Separation of Church and State, demanded that Catholic candidates for national office "take a definite stand for or against" on several issues, including state aid for parochial schools and the appointment of an American ambassador to the Vatican. Kennedy contacted Father John Cavanaugh, who suggested that Jack get in touch with three liberal Catholic theologians who, he believed, could help him answer questions such as those raised by the POAU.[14]

Questions about Jack's faith continued to be raised, even more so now that he appeared to be the front-runner for the nomination. In May 1958, Kennedy wrote Father Theodore Hesburgh, the Notre Dame president, about problems that were beginning "to arise" and requested that Father Cavanaugh, who was still attached to the university, be released from his responsibilities for "possibly a week or ten days in July and during the month of August [to] offer advice and suggestions on Jack's campaign." A master of the quid pro quo, he assured Hesburgh that it was "always possible, of course, that in these discussions with Father Cavanaugh, I might come up with some ideas that might be beneficial to Notre Dame and that would help pay my debt to you for the loan of his services."[15]

Though the Catholic issue would be with him through nomination and election, Jack's whirlwind campaigning was muting most other objections to his candidacy. Questions were still being raised, however, about the extent of his father's influence over him, but these too appeared not to pose any major problem. In Boston, Palm Beach, New York, and Washington, he might be Joe Kennedy's son; everywhere else he was Jack Kennedy, the young, dynamic, affable, and very handsome candidate from Massachusetts. To mute the criticism that he was in control of his son's campaign, Kennedy stayed put that winter in Palm Beach and offered no interviews or comments on the activities of either of his sons. Still, he spent so much time on the phone with them that Rose felt obliged to warn Bobby "again to please not telephone to your father around 7:15 P.M., as we have dinner then and if he gets too excited before dinner, as he did the other night when he talked to you about the labor investigation, it is not very good for his little tummy. It is nothing to worry about, dearest Bobby. It is just a little help for the grandfather of eleven or maybe twelve."[16]

Despite the resurfacing questions about Jack's faith, Kennedy was more than content with his son's progress toward the nomination. "The lineup today," Kennedy wrote Galeazzi in early February 1958, "is still Jack in front, with the runner-up at this time the Democratic leader of the Senate, Lyndon Johnson. He is from Texas and has had one coronary attack. Either, or both of these will probably be more hurtful than Jack's being a Catholic."[17]

In February 1958, Kennedy began planning for Jack's reelection campaign and asked Francis X. ("Frank") Morrissey, his and Jack's Boston assistant, to lease the apartment "which we had during the campaign in '52. It was very handy and I would like to get into the same building again for two months, say for the day after Labor Day until the day after the election." In April, already looking beyond November 1958, he inquired about buying a Convair airplane for Jack's presidential campaign.[18]

The money that Kennedy was spending on Jack's campaigns—for reelection to the Senate in 1958 and the presidential nomination in 1960—did not go unnoticed. In March 1958, at the Gridiron dinner in Washington, an actor playing Jack Kennedy appeared onstage to sing "a tribute to his father":

> I'll have a ball and votes this fall
> Will crown this Bostonian lady
> Then I will run for the top-most gun—
> And I learned it all from Daddy
> Now some hob-nob with brother Bob
> The boy who drove old Dave Beck batty,
> But Bob will chime that it ain't no crime
> For us to take our cue from daddy.
> Yes, I'll do it just like daddy
> And I hope he will not be mad
> When I send the bill to daddy
> Da-da, da-da-da, da-da-da-dad!
> So don't try to get this lady,

Though your aim be perfectly swell
For the bill belongs to daddy
'Cause my daddy, he pays it so well.

Jack had learned early that the best way to parry such attacks was with humor, which was never in short supply among the Kennedys. When he took the stage to deliver his own remarks, he prefaced them by reading from a telegram he ostentatiously pulled from his pocket. It was, he said, from his father: "Dear Jack—Don't buy a single vote more than is necessary—I'll be damned if I'm going to pay for a landslide."[19]

The following year, after Jack's victory in Massachusetts and another year of campaigning had set him further out front in the race for the Democratic nomination, the Gridiron dinner honored him again with a skit. He was introduced this time "as the first candidate to run for President on the 'family plan.'" The plan was explained by a Joseph P. Kennedy impersonator to the tune of "All of Me."

All of us
Why not take all of us
Fabulous
You can't live without us
My son Jack
Heads the procession,
Then comes Bob
Groomed for succession. . . .
I've got the dough
You might as well know
With one—
You get all of us.[20]

Jack Kennedy took the gibes about his father and his family with good nature, but when Eleanor Roosevelt in a December 1958 television interview criticized Joseph Kennedy by name for "spending oodles of money all over the country" and buying "a representative in every state by now" to advance his son's presidential ambitions, Jack responded by letter, rebutting her charges and demanding that she provide evidence to back them up. Mrs. Roosevelt admitted that she had no such evidence but refused to issue any apology.[21]

Despite himself, Joseph P. Kennedy was, two and a half years before the election, already looking forward to the possibility that he might one day be the father of a United States president. As he wrote Galeazzi in April, he had met with Allen Dulles, who, he reported, "was very happy with [Christian Democrat leader Amintore] Fanfani and was doing something for him. . . . I think that if there is anything that you want me to do, you could let me know at once and I will contact him. He is very aware of the fact that Jack may be the next President and while he has always been very friendly to me, I think that he is more than ever anxious to please."[22]

Kennedy returned to Boston in the spring of 1958 to contribute what he could to Jack's reelection campaign. Ted Kennedy and Steve Smith, Jean's husband, were already in place. Steve, whom Jean had married two years earlier, was a Georgetown graduate and a talented businessman who had run his family's transportation business in New York. He would quickly develop into a gifted political organizer. In 1958, he coordinated Jack's schedule in Boston. Ted was nominally in charge of the office, but when problems or controversies arose that could not be settled within the campaign staff, he called "dad up from the Cape." As in 1952, Kennedy concentrated his attention on Jack's print, radio, and television ads. He relentlessly pushed John Dowd, the advertising man, to come up with a new campaign slogan. Dowd would "write out a slogan and hand it to Dad, and Dad would look at it and say, 'No, that doesn't work, Dowd. That's not good. You can do better than that. That's not good.' And Dad went across the street to Bailey's restaurant and had his lunch, a chocolate soda. That's all he'd eat. He loved ice cream, but he didn't want to gain weight, so he had just this one chocolate soda." He returned after lunch and kept pushing at Dowd, no doubt in stronger language than Ted reported, until he got it right.[23]

Kennedy's greatest concern in 1958 was that Jack was going to campaign himself into an early grave. Even Lyndon Johnson, in his condescending way, had written Kennedy in late March that Jack was "working too hard. Make him take it easier." When he was presented with the schedule that Larry O'Brien and Kenny O'Donnell had drawn up for Jack, Kennedy exploded. "It's crazy. . . . You're going to kill him. You don't have to run him all over the state, just put him on television. . . . O'Brien, you'll wind up with a dead candidate on your hands and you'll be responsible. This schedule is ridiculous and I'm completely opposed to it." Jack, with his father in the room, agreed that the schedule was "rugged" and asked that it be retooled to give him "some time off. Dad's got a valid point about my health." After his first full day of campaigning, as he, O'Donnell, and O'Brien prepared to meet with his father at his apartment in Boston, the senator cautioned them not to argue anymore about the schedule. "Just ride with it. Your point is valid, but just don't make it." A compromise was reached. Jack would tour the state, but time would be set aside "every day for a quiet and quite leisurely lunch, because Ambassador Kennedy insisted upon it. 'You've got to see to it that he eats,'" he had warned O'Donnell and O'Brien. To make sure that his rules were being followed, Kennedy had Frank Morrissey, who ostensibly worked for the senator, call him daily with news of his son's health.[24]

As Hyannis Port, filled again with children, spouses, and grandchildren, was more chaotic than ever that spring, Kennedy altered his usual routine and spent the last weeks of June and July on the north shore of Lake Tahoe at the Cal-Neva Lodge, so named because it sat on the border straddling the two states. The principal owner of the lodge, at the time Kennedy stayed there, was "Wingy" (or "Wingie"), the nickname cruelly given Bert Grober, the shriveled-arm gambler and owner of the Park Avenue Steak House in Miami. The Cal-Neva, or "Wingy's place," as Kennedy would refer to it, was a first-class resort that had everything Kennedy required. It was on the water, as was every house Kennedy had lived in since he was a child in East Boston; the rooms were large and the dining superb; there were trails for horseback riding, a bay and pools for swimming, a fine golf course, a casino, which Kennedy did not patronize, and attractive, available women in no short supply. As an added bonus, Lake Tahoe was a short flight from Los Angeles, where Pat and her family now lived and where Kennedy was in negotiations over a new foundation project.[25]

There was nothing very remarkable about Kennedy's summers at the

Cal-Neva—he would return the next year as well. Only in the middle 1970s, as journalists, historians, and conspiracy hunters looked high and low for clues to tie John F. Kennedy's assassination to organized crime, would attention be paid to his father's stays at Cal-Neva and the "gang" connections he supposedly made, renewed, and exploited there. Joe Kennedy did not go out of his way to avoid the presence of unsavory characters, nor did he stay away from the places they frequented: Cal-Neva, Hialeah, and nightclubs and restaurants in New York, Chicago, Miami, and Palm Beach. But neither did he seek their company.

He had disposed of his liquor import business and his stake in Hialeah because he did not want his children to be tarnished with the stereotypes he had so scrupulously avoided all his life. He had lived his life and made and kept his millions by carefully evaluating risk/reward ratios and avoiding any and all unnecessary dangers, in business and politics. It would have been extraordinarily reckless—and he was not a reckless man—for him to do business with or consort with known mobsters, especially as they had nothing to offer him he could not obtain elsewhere. He had more than enough money to finance his son's presidential campaign and ties with big-city Democratic bosses across the country, including Mayor Richard Daley in Chicago, whom Shriver had cultivated on behalf of the family.

Jack easily won reelection to the Senate in November 1958 with nearly three quarters of the votes cast in his favor. His oversize victory, on the heels of a successful two-year speaking campaign across the country, cemented his position as the front-runner for the presidential nomination. *Time* magazine devoted its November 24, 1958, cover story to the "Democratic hopefuls." The cover illustration had Jack Kennedy seated comfortably in the center of the group, with Governors Robert Meyner of New Jersey and Pat Brown of California seated on either side, and Hubert Humphrey, Stuart Symington, and Lyndon Johnson standing behind him. "Jack Kennedy is the early-season Democratic favorite by general agreement. Says an aide to Michigan's hopeful 'Soapy' Williams: 'If the convention were held today, Kennedy would win on the first ballot, period.'" The remaining dangers to the Kennedy candidacy, the article reminded its readers, were the perception that his father was trying to buy the election and, more critically, his "Catholicism [which] could still be held against him when kingmakers are looking for winners at convention time."

Five weeks later, on January 1, 1959, James Reston took up this issue in his *New York Times* column, declaring that "the political implications of nominating a Roman Catholic for the Presidency are now coming increasingly to the fore in the Capital." Reston predicted, rightly, that the "religious issue" would, as the campaign swung into higher gear, "be debated more and more. And in the process Kennedy is likely to become, not just another candidate, but a symbol and center of political and religious controversy."

The scenario that Joseph Kennedy had so feared was unfolding before him and there was no way to escape it. Here he was, in 1959, at seventy years of age, after a lifetime spent on the quintessential American journey from outsider to insiders, suddenly and unexpectedly thrust back in time. His son had gone to Choate and Harvard, nearly lost his life in military service, written two books, won a Pulitzer Prize, been elected to national office five times, served thirteen years in Washington, and emerged as the front-runner in the race for the Democratic nomination—yet he was now identified not as the best-qualified candidate, but as the "Catholic" candidate. And he would have to run his campaign as such.

Father and son and Jack's senior campaign advisers were agreed that they had no choice but to confront the "Catholic issue" and head it off eighteen months before the nominating convention convened. The senator sat for an interview with Fletcher Knebel for a *Look* magazine article, "Democratic Forecast: A Catholic in 1960," and defended himself from charges that he was under the control of his church by reminding Knebel that he "had opposed a number of positions taken by Catholic organizations and members of the hierarchy . . . attended non-Catholic schools, from the elementary grades to Harvard," and, contrary to the church leadership, "favored aid to Yugoslavia, aid to Communist satellite states and the naming of Dr. James B. Conant [an outspoken critic of parochial schools] as our first ambassador to West Germany." He then answered the questions that the POAU had asked fifteen months earlier. "In a capsule," Knebel concluded, "his theme is that religion is personal, politics are public, and the twain need never meet and conflict."[26]

Jack Kennedy's attempt at candor and at redefining his religion as a private matter backfired badly. His explanations not only did not mollify Protestants who feared that, as a Catholic, he was less of an American, but they incurred the almost universal wrath of Catholic columnists and editorial writers. "I don't think you can exaggerate the reaction to that *Look* article, in the Catholic press, particularly," recalled John Cogley, a former editor of the Catholic magazine *Commonweal,* who would later became a campaign adviser, "because it was the first public reaction to Kennedy and it was a very negative and a very naïve reaction and, I thought a very politically unsophisticated reaction."[27]

Why, Catholic critics asked, did Kennedy think it necessary or proper to speak about his faith? Baptists, Presbyterians, Episcopalians, Lutherans, and Mormons weren't required to answer questions about their religion and their allegiance to the Constitution. Why should Catholics?

CATHOLIC CENSURE OF KENNEDY RISES, the *New York Times* reported on March 1. *America,* a Jesuit journal, accused Senator Kennedy of pandering to bigots by discounting the influence of his religion on his beliefs and decisions and compartmentalizing his faith as a private matter. *Ave Maria,* the weekly published by the Holy Cross Fathers at Notre Dame, declared that despite what Kennedy claimed in the interview, a man's religious faith was never solely a private matter and always had a bearing on his actions in the public sphere. "No man may rightfully act against his conscience. To relegate your conscience to your 'private life' is not only unrealistic, but dangerous as well . . . because it leads to secularism in public life." Diocesan newspapers across the country assailed him for affirming the extremist Protestant position that the separation between church and state was "absolute."[28]

Jack was upset, but his father was outraged at Catholic criticism of a Catholic candidate and waited expectantly for his friends in the church hierarchy to defend Jack's statements. In the end, only Cardinal Cushing issued any such defense. Kennedy was now livid. He had poured millions of dollars into diocesan projects in New York, Washington, Los Angeles, and Chicago. Yet there was no word, public or private, in support of Jack's position as a Catholic candidate from Cardinal Spellman, or Archbishops O'Boyle, McIntyre, and Stritch, or Father Hesburgh, the president of Notre Dame. "I am more than ordinarily bitter about the whole subject," he wrote Galeazzi on March 30, 1959. "I doubt very much if my relations with the Church and the hierarchy, with the exception of Cardinal Cushing, will ever be the same. I do not care now whether Jack is elected President or not and I have told him so. I certainly will never ask the hierarchy for anything ever again—not that I have ever asked them for much. And I have always been anxious to do everything I could, but that also has ceased. I just believe that they do not deserve to improve their position one single bit."[29]

Galeazzi tried his best to calm his friend but could not. "I value your suggestions and advice," Kennedy wrote Galeazzi on April 17, "but I am really more than annoyed or upset—I am downright disgusted! And I do not imagine that anything is ever going to change that. I deplore the pettiness of the Catholic Press and I deplore the weakness of some of the hierarchy for not speaking out, at least in some measure, in Jack's defense. I have had time to think it over and quiet down—if I were ever going to quiet down—but I know now that I never will."

All his life, Kennedy had bemoaned the lack of political sophistication among Catholics, comparing it unfavorably with that of the Jews, who had achieved political influence beyond their numbers because they knew how to organize themselves into a powerful lobbying group. Kennedy had imagined—and hoped—that the Catholic community would come together, as the Jews surely would have, in support of Jack's candidacy because he was a Catholic, because he was the best candidate for the office, and because electing a Catholic as president might help alleviate prejudices that still existed. No matter what his son's qualifications, the bigoted and biased were going to vote against him because he was a Catholic. To offset those lost votes, Jack needed Catholics to vote for him in even larger numbers than they usually did for Democratic candidates. Kennedy feared that without the support of the church hierarchy, his son would not get those additional votes.

He was now convinced that the leaders of the American church did not want a Catholic president or, at least, they did not want Jack Kennedy to be president. The *Look* article had, he wrote Galeazzi, provided "an excuse for a lot of stupid bishops and editors to say out loud what they have been saying privately for the last year and a half," that it would be better if Jack Kennedy did not run for the presidency in 1960.[30]

Kennedy was not the only one who had come to this conclusion. "Some of the hierarchy of the church," Cardinal Cushing would concede in a 1966 oral history interview, "were not in favor of John F. Kennedy being elected President. They feared that the time had not arrived when a president who was a Catholic could be elected." The senator, according to John Cogley, "felt that some members of the hierarchy" were against his candidacy "mainly because they were Republicans or because they didn't like what they thought was the liberal tenor of his thinking. Also, there was, among not only bishops but among priests, as we could tell by the mail that came in, a kind of a resentment sometimes that here he was, a Harvard man, the boy who didn't go to Catholic schools, being the nation's number one representative of Catholicism—I think there was a little of that there, too—and also a fear that his style was altogether too secularized for their tastes." The American church had, until now, spoken unchallenged, with one voice: that of its priests, bishops, and cardinals. The idea that if Kennedy was elected, the most prominent, the most influential, Catholic in the nation would be a layman, not a churchman, was for them a situation to be avoided at all costs. There were political considerations as well. It was widely and accurately believed that a Catholic president would be less likely to openly support federal funding for parochial schools or the establishment of full diplomatic relations with the Vatican.[31]

Opposing or remaining neutral to Jack's candidacy, as the church leaders now appeared to be doing, was, Kennedy believed, a betrayal not only of him, his son, and his family, but of the millions of American Catholics who stood to benefit from the election of one of their own to the presidency of the United States. For perhaps the first time in his life, certainly for the first time since the death of Joe Jr., Joseph P. Kennedy was forced to reconsider, to reevaluate, the ties that bound him to his church. "My relationship with the Church will never be the same," he confessed to Galeazzi in an April 17 letter, "and certainly, never the same with the hierarchy. But that will not make any difference to them, I am sure, and I can assure you that it will not make any difference to me. For the last few years which I have left, I will indulge myself at least in continuing to believe that friends are friends when you need them. Please do not be upset yourself about my attitude. I would not want anything to annoy you."[32]

Thirty-eight

ELECTING A PRESIDENT

The first organizational summit meeting for the 1960 campaign was held in Palm Beach on April 1, 1959. Four of the nine men present, Kennedy, Jack, Bobby, and Steve Smith, were family members. They were joined by Ted Sorensen, Larry O'Brien, Kenny O'Donnell, pollster Lou Harris, whom Joe Kennedy had put on retainer, and Bob Wallace, who had worked for Senator Paul Douglas of Illinois. "When the matter of financial requirements was raised, Ambassador Kennedy," Ted Sorensen recalled, "said, 'We've come this far, we're not going to let money stand in our way, whatever it takes, even if it requires every dime I have.' RFK piped up: 'Wait a minute now—there are others in the family.'"[1]

By October 28, 1959, when a second summit was convened, this one at the Robert Kennedy residence in Hyannis Port, the group of nine had been expanded by a dozen more, none of them chosen by Joseph P. Kennedy or beholden to him in any way. Jack ran the first part of the meeting, then after lunch, which was held at his parents' house next door, the group reconvened and Bobby took over. Joe Kennedy did more listening than talking. He was not in charge now, nor did he want to be. He could not match anyone in the room for sheer hands-on, data-driven knowledge of the political situation in each of the states Jack would have to campaign in for primary votes.

The week before, Jack had been one of two speakers—Governor Nelson Rockefeller the other one—at the annual Alfred E. Smith Memorial Foundation dinner at the Waldorf-Astoria. While Rose and members of the family sat at one of the tables in the ballroom, Kennedy, too nervous to sit with them, "stayed in the back of the hall where he could sense the reactions from the speeches." Jack didn't get to speak until eleven o'clock, at the end of a very long evening in a hot, stuffy, crowded room. According to the *New York Times* the next morning, he easily "took the honors in audience reception." He opened by telling the story of a past candidate for president who had failed miserably, carrying "fewer states than any other of his party, losing even his own state. 'You all know his name and his religion.'" He paused with the timing of a seasoned comedian: "'Alfred M. Landon, Protestant. . . . The memory of that election still burns deeply in our minds,' Senator Kennedy continued, amid laughter. 'But I am not prepared to tell Governor Rockefeller that a Protestant should not be nominated in 1960.'"[2]

While his father was delighted at the applause that greeted his son's lighthearted approach to a decidedly serious subject, he remained furious at the leaders of the Catholic Church, including Cardinal Spellman, one of the dinner's hosts, for not doing more for his son. "Arthur Krock of the *New York Times*," Kennedy wrote Galeazzi on New Year's Day 1960, "called me up to tell me that he was about to write an article saying that not only did he believe the hierarchy were not helping Jack; but he thought that they were going out of their way to hurt him. I told this to Cardinal Spellman and he just asked if Krock had any proof and I said that he did. And the Cardinal just kept quiet. . . . In addition to that," Kennedy continued, "practically every statement out of Rome hurts. This is not just my opinion—it is the opinion of the topside newspaper men in the country. However, we are all reconciled to the fact that the most we can hope is that they do not do us too much harm, not that they will do us any good."[3]

Here was vintage Kennedy, wisely deploying his strengths to push

Spellman by threatening him with a Krock column in the *New York Times*. Whether Krock had any intention of writing such a column we do not know. What we do know was that he continued, in his columns, to repeat that Senator Kennedy was a man of courage and character, that Catholic voters made up a large percentage of the Democratic faithful, and that at no time in American history had either party denied the nomination to a candidate because of his religion.[4]

The only way to put to rest Democratic Party leaders' fears that Protestants would not vote for a Catholic was for Jack to prove the opposite by doing well in the primaries. The first major primary was in Wisconsin, where Catholics were in a sizable minority at about 30 percent. "That is going to be a real tough fight—but we should win," Kennedy wrote Galeazzi. "Then he goes from there to West Virginia where the Catholics total around three or four percent. They may use the religious issue there and it may be very, very tough."[5]

Kennedy had originally, he wrote Sir James Calder in mid-January, expected to travel the country with his son. He decided not to because he had concluded, reluctantly, that his presence on the campaign trail might do his son more harm than good, especially in Wisconsin, a liberal state and the home of Joe McCarthy. He would spend the primary season in Palm Beach. Turning down an invitation to a fund-raising dinner at which Jack was scheduled to speak, he explained that while he was "sure that all of my friends are going to be there . . . I have tried to make it a rule never to be anywhere my boys or girls speak. It is just an old-fashioned notion, but I have stuck to it pretty much now for eight years."[6]

His plan, for the moment, was to make a few trips north to talk to old friends and acquaintances, but for the most part to work the phones from Palm Beach. He had accumulated a lifetime of contacts and intended, it appeared, to approach every one of them. "This is a list of names that Duffy Lewis, a former Bostonian and now, Secretary of the Braves [the baseball team that had left Boston for Milwaukee after the 1952 season], had made up for me," he wrote Bobby on February 8, 1960. "The dots indicate people with a great many friends, but they all should be contacted."[7]

Preoccupied with the religious question, as he had been since the campaign began, he took it upon himself—with Steve Smith's assistance—

to get "some of our friends in different states to get up a Protestant clergymen's committee to see if we can use such committees to offset some of the bigoted spokesmen." Frank Morrissey would do the same for Massachusetts, John Bailey in Connecticut, "and I will try to do it in New York. I really think that it is worth looking into."[8]

He focused his primary attention on Catholic politicians such as Governor David Lawrence of Pennsylvania who were not supporting Jack because they did not believe he could win the nomination. Archbishop Cushing arranged the first meeting with Lawrence in the spring of 1959 at the Penn Harris Hotel in Harrisburg. "The papers never discovered it," Lawrence later recalled. "I went down there and had lunch with him instead of at the mansion because the mansion would have been covered by newspapermen if they'd ever found it. Of course he couldn't understand why I wasn't for his boy, Jack. . . . I said to him, 'Mr. Kennedy, I'd love to be for your boy. I'd love to see him president of the United States, but I don't think he can win. I don't think any Catholic can win.'" Kennedy responded by telling the story of the young New York bank president who had been "shooting his mouth off about, 'Who's this young Kennedy think he is? What right's he got to be president of the United States?'" When Kennedy, who did a lot of business at the bank, was asked by the vice president if he wanted to meet the new president, he said he would. They met at Kennedy's office. "I had nine million dollars in that bank and I felt like I'd pull out of that bank that day." Kennedy and Lawrence parted friends, with Lawrence reminded of how much money Kennedy had, how committed he was to his son's victory, and how dangerous it was to cross him.[9]

Kennedy also lobbied Charles Buckley of the Bronx, Eugene Keogh of Brooklyn, Daniel P. O'Connell of Albany, Mayor Richard Daley of Chicago, and John McCormack of Boston. "If Jack had known about some of the telephone calls his father made on his behalf to Tammany-type bosses during the 1960 campaign," Kenny O'Donnell recalled, "Jack's hair would have turned white."[10]

On March 8, the voters went to the polls in the nation's first primary, in New Hampshire, where Senator Kennedy, as expected, polled 85 percent of the Democratic votes. His father, who was in New

York City for a luncheon with Cardinal Spellman, was delighted. "I think a lot of those who have been on the side line are amazed by yesterday's performance and may now start to think that maybe he can be elected." He was engaging in a bit of wishful thinking here. The make-or-break primary contest was going to be the one in Wisconsin on April 5, as Kennedy admitted in a letter to Galeazzi on March 31. "If we do not do very well there, I would say that we should get out of the fight. . . . If we do very well in Wisconsin, and I mean very well, I would think we would go on to win the nomination."[11]

While the rest of the family campaigned with Jack in Wisconsin, Kennedy remained in touch by phone from Palm Beach. In earlier campaigns, Kennedy had relied on Frank Morrissey for information about Jack's health. In 1960, according to Doris Kearns Goodwin, he "worked out an arrangement with Dave Powers to report to him every evening between six-thirty and seven to tell him about Jack's health, checking to see whether he took his vitamins, ate his prescribed New York–cut sirloin and drank his orange juice. 'Dave, if you want him to win, keep him healthy,' the Ambassador implored night after night."[12]

It was a dirty campaign and promised to get dirtier. The Humphrey campaign made constant references to millionaires and "high level" fixers and operators to draw attention to Joseph P. Kennedy. "I am watching what they say and do to Jack ten thousand times more than what they say and do to me," he confided to Lord Beaverbrook. "Everything is very unimportant now except his nomination and election."[13]

The attacks, real and threatened, came from every direction. Through Peter Lawford, the family had been introduced to Frank Sinatra, who had become a vocal Jack Kennedy supporter. Sinatra visited the Palm Beach house in March during the Wisconsin campaign. When actor Leo Carrillo, whom Kennedy had not seen in years, wrote to warn that Sinatra had hired a blacklisted Communist writer, Albert Maltz, for his next film and this would reflect badly on Jack, Kennedy drafted a blistering letter. "As to the Sinatra hiring of this writer, you know as well as I that there is nothing in the world that I can do about it. . . . To try and ring Jack in on this because Sinatra sang a campaign song for him is about as unfair as anything I can think of."[14]

Kennedy never had to send the letter to Carrillo. On April 8, Sinatra dismissed Maltz. "It was considered possible," claimed the *New York Times*, which reported the dismissal on page one, "that Mr. Sinatra may have changed his position . . . for political reasons." Sinatra replied angrily that he had had no pressure from or discussions with Senator Kennedy about Maltz, and those who said he had were "hitting below the belt. 'I make movies. I do not ask the advice of Senator Kennedy on whom I should hire. Senator Kennedy does not ask me how he should vote in the Senate.'" That much, of course, was true. What Sinatra didn't say was whether Kennedy Sr. had called to ask him, for Jack's sake, to get rid of Maltz.[15]

Kennedy was far more concerned with attacks on him—and his son—from the Left. One of the stories circulating through Wisconsin was that Kennedy was not just a conservative, but a friend and supporter of Nixon's. While it was true that he had contributed $1,000 to Nixon's 1950 campaign against Democrat Helen Gahagan Douglas, whom he regarded as much too far to the left, Kennedy had had no other contact with the presumptive Republican nominee. When Cyril Clemens, the editor of the *Mark Twain Journal,* raised the Nixon charges and asked why, if they were untrue, Kennedy had not said so directly, Kennedy wrote rather testily that if he "were to start to answer all the charges that have been made or are going to be made, I would not be able to do anything else. If people do not like Jack for what he is and what he stands for, then they should not vote for him. But if they do, they should support him—and never mind what the 'old man' says or does."[16]

Though he had stayed fifteen hundred miles away and kept his mouth shut, Kennedy found it impossible to escape the publicity that trailed after him. On April 5, 1960, primary election day in Wisconsin, Drew Pearson devoted his column to a lengthy conversation he'd had earlier with the senator at his home in Washington. The first question he had raised was about the senator's Catholicism, the next about his father.

" 'I confess to being skeptical about your father's influence over you,' I said. This is a tough statement to throw at a man who has been close to his father, but young Kennedy took it with good humor.

" 'Well, father wants me to be President all right,' he said. 'He tells everyone that I'm going to be President. But as far as influencing me, I think my voting record in the Senate speaks for itself. He and I have disagreed on foreign policy and domestic issues for many years, but always very amicably.'"

When asked "about reports that your father poured money into the New Hampshire primary," the senator responded that his father hadn't spent "'a penny in New Hampshire. . . . I would have been foolish to spend a lot of money in New Hampshire, even if I'd wanted to. It's a small state and all my friends were out bursting with energy and working without any money.'" He confessed that he was spending money in Wisconsin, but not more than Humphrey.[17]

J ack won the Wisconsin primary, but not by the landslide he needed. Worse yet, he lost three predominantly Protestant districts in the west of the state.

"What does it all mean, Johnny?" Eunice asked her brother as the returns came in.

"It means that we've got to go on to West Virginia in the morning and do it all over again," Jack said. "And then we've got to go on to Maryland and Indiana and Oregon, and win all of them."[18]

There were several primaries to come, and Jack needed to win them all to demonstrate to the party bosses who controlled the bulk of the delegates—only a minority were selected on the basis of primary voting—that he was a viable candidate. In states with significant Catholic populations, such as Pennsylvania, Illinois, and Maryland, he was going to need the help of those who remained on the sidelines because they did not think he could win and feared the long-term repercussions of his losing. "I can understand why a great many people might not like Jack—some say that he's too young, some that he's a Catholic, etc., etc.," Kennedy wrote Michael Morrissey, the Catholic publisher of a string of Massachusetts newspapers, in early April. "But I really have no patience with the Catholics who want to duck a fight. . . . When you said to me that you hated to see these bigoted ideas arise, I asked you what we were supposed to do, just duck this question for the rest of our lives. If Jack's heart is broken because he may be beaten on the religious question, then so be it. He has demonstrated that he is the greatest vote getter in the Democratic Party and it is certainly up to him to carry on the battle. A little help from a lot of people might bring him victory."[19]

From Wisconsin, the Kennedy and Humphrey campaigns turned their attention to West Virginia. It was here that Jack would have to demonstrate that Protestants were willing to vote for him. "Only about 3 percent of the state is Catholic, probably the smallest percentage in the United States," Kennedy wrote Lord Beaverbrook on April 20. "And they are passing out religious leaflets up and down the line. The Baptists are the most bigoted group. The Gallup Poll came out today and showed that Jack is pulling farther and farther ahead of all the other candidates; so that he will have a very good call on the nomination. If he is thrown out because he is a Catholic, I doubt very much if a Democrat will win."[20]

According to Ben Bradlee of *Newsweek,* who was invited to sit in on one high-level strategy meeting at Palm Beach, Kennedy had "argued strenuously against JFK's entering [the West Virginia primary]. 'It's a nothing state and they'll kill him over the Catholic thing.' A few minutes later JFK spoke out: 'Well, we've heard from the ambassador, and we're all very grateful, Dad, but I've got to run in West Virginia.' "[21]

Once the decision was made, Kennedy backed his son completely. Winning in West Virginia would require bags of money for local candidates who agreed to put Senator Kennedy on the primary election slates they headed and for party professionals, officeholders, poll watchers, election officials, drivers, and, it appeared, everyone else who stuck out a hand. The Kennedy camp was not the only one to throw money around, but it had more of it and did it better. Leo Racine, who worked out of Kennedy's New York office, had been dispatched to Wisconsin and West Virginia for the campaign. He recalled that money arrived in satchels. "It just kept flowing in. . . . All anyone in the campaign had to say was 'we need money' and it was on the way."[22]

To help his son win the Protestant vote in West Virginia, Kennedy got in touch with Franklin Roosevelt, Jr., who, like his brother James, had done well neither in politics nor in business and was at the moment selling Fiats in New York and contemplating a return to politics. Kennedy asked Roosevelt Jr. to fly to Palm Beach to meet with Bobby and Jack. After speaking with them, he agreed to join the campaign. His presence—and physical likeness to his father—bolstered Jack's attempt to define himself as a New Deal liberal who, much like FDR, would employ the power and resources of the federal government to rescue West Virginia's impoverished miners. Roosevelt called attention as well to the fact that Kennedy had fought overseas in World War II while Humphrey had stayed at home. "'You know why I'm here in West Virginia today?' Frank would say. 'Because Jack Kennedy and I fought side by side in the Pacific. He was on the PT boats and I was on the destroyers.'"[23]

In the midst of campaigning in West Virginia, Senator Kennedy returned to Washington to deliver a major speech to the American Society of Newspaper Editors, in yet another attempt to counter the anti-Catholic literature, speeches, whispers, and rumors that he feared were pushing every other issue to the side. He was not, he declared as emphatically as he could, "the Catholic candidate for President. I do not speak for the Catholic church on issues of public policy, and no one in that Church speaks for me. My record . . . has displeased some prominent Catholic clergymen and organizations and it has been approved by others. The fact is that the Catholic church is not a monolith—it is committed in this country to the principles of individual liberty." He was even more emphatic back on the campaign trail in West Virginia. In his final television speech, he repeated again that as president he "would not take orders from any Pope, Cardinal, Bishop or priest, nor would they try to give me orders. . . . If any Pope attempted to influence me as President, I would have to tell him it was completely improper."[24]

On May 10, 1960, Jack Kennedy won the West Virginia primary with 61 percent of the vote, which should have, but did not, put to rest the question of whether Protestants would vote for a Catholic. A week later, he won the Maryland primary with 70 percent, his ninth consecutive primary victory. The *New York Times* reported the Maryland primary victory on the front page. Just below, it ran a second front-page story with a Rome dateline: VATICAN PAPER PROCLAIMS RIGHT OF CHURCH TO ROLE IN POLITICS. The official Vatican newspaper had declared in an editorial that "the Roman Catholic hierarchy had 'the right and the duty to intervene' in the political field to guide its flock. It rejected what it termed 'the absurd split of conscience between the believer and the citizen.' . . . The Roman Catholic religion, the editorial asserted, is a force that 'commits and guides the entire existence of man.' The Catholic, it went on, 'may never disregard the teaching and directions of the church but must inspire his private and public conduct in every sphere of his activity by the laws, instructions and teachings of the hierarchy.'"[25]

The timing, placement, language, and emphasis of the Vatican paper editorial called into question everything Jack Kennedy had been saying about his religion. Pierre Salinger, his press spokesman, responded at once that Senator Kennedy supported "the principle of separation of church and state as provided in the United States Constitution [and] that this support is not subject to change under any condition." His statement was buried on page thirty-one.

The following day, May 19, lest there be any confusion, the *New York Times* confirmed that the editorial in the Vatican paper had "been given to the newspaper for publication by the Vatican Secretariat of State, the Department of the Church's Central Government that assists the Pope in political business," and that earlier reports that the "editorialist . . . did not have in mind the United States Presidential campaign" were inaccurate.

Joseph Kennedy was both distressed and baffled. His fears that the church was out to defeat his son were now fully confirmed. "You must have been aware," he wrote Galeazzi, "of how terribly shocked we were by that editorial in *L'Osservatore Romano* on the separation of church and state. . . . It was a bad shaking up and it did not do us a bit of good. I cannot understand why my two friends, Tardini [the Vatican secretary of state] and the other man [another papal adviser on foreign affairs] could ever have let anything like that come to America when it could create so much difficulty over something that has already been established as a fact here in the country, namely, the separation of church and state."[26]

The Vatican pronouncement, fortunately, did not do the immediate harm that Kennedy had feared it might. Though featured in the *New York Times,* the story was buried elsewhere by the news that Senator Kennedy had won the Maryland primary. For his father, it was an omen of things to come.

The final primary for Kennedy was held in Oregon on May 20. With every possible candidate listed on the ballot, Kennedy took 51 percent of the vote; favorite son Wayne Morse got 31.9 percent; Humphrey, 5.7 percent.

To celebrate the victorious conclusion of the primary season—and Jack's birthday—the family gathered for a long weekend at Hyannis Port. Frank Falacci of the *Boston Post* was among the throng of reporters who awaited the senator's arrival at the Barnstable Airport terminal on Cape Cod. "For a long time," he reported, "no one noticed the man in the blue suit with the yachtsman-type buttons, who carefully checked his watch against the wall clocks. When recognition did come, the reporters made a rush towards him, and Joseph P. Kennedy, tycoon, former ambassador, and father of the presidential candidate, greeted them with a grin.

"His first concern, he said, was for 'the boys.'

"'They all look tired in their pictures,' he said. 'Bob especially seems to have lost weight.'

"His eyes glowed when he spoke of the work his three sons had done in the primaries across the country. . . . He had special praise for his youngest son, Ted. 'When Jack's voice was gone in West Virginia, Ted really took over and kept the ball rolling.'"[27]

Kennedy was more and more convinced that his son was going to win the nomination, though there remained obstacles in his path—primarily Adlai Stevenson and Lyndon Johnson, each of whom wanted the nomination; and Harry Truman, who had declared that Jack Kennedy was too young and inexperienced to be president. On July 4, a week before the convention was to open, Senator Kennedy held a televised press conference to answer President Truman. If "fourteen years in major elective office is insufficient experience," he said, "that rules out . . . all but a handful of American Presidents, and every President of the twentieth century—including Wilson, Roosevelt and Truman." His father, listening on the radio from his cottage at Cal-Neva, told Joe Timilty, who was with him, that he thought it was the best speech his son had ever given. "That evening," Timilty later recalled, "we went over to the Tahoe Lodge for dinner and were joined by one Wingie Grober, who had the reputation of being quite a character. Mr. Kennedy said to Wingie, 'Wingie, you go out and beg and borrow as much money as you possibly can and place it on Jack to win on the 1st ballot.'"[28]

Kennedy, who had absented himself from every stop on the campaign trail, accepted Marion Davies's invitation to stay at her beach house in Santa Monica during the convention. The house was fully staffed, had a pool, rooms for children and grandchildren, a large television set, and it was outside the reach of the press. SEN. KENNEDY'S FATHER WATCHES IN HIDEAWAY, reported the *Los Angeles Times* on July 14. "Joe Kennedy, 71, has refused to grant any interviews. His wife explains that he has always been a rather controversial figure and thinks it is easier for his sons if he does not appear on the scene."

On July 5, Lyndon Johnson—the man whom Joe Kennedy had always considered the strongest threat to his son's candidacy—after staying out of the primaries, declared himself a candidate for the nomination. Johnson and his supporters, who had never had much of anything positive to say about Jack Kennedy, now began raising questions about his health and his father. Johnson's spokesmen told the press that Jack Kennedy had Addison's disease. Lyndon Johnson attacked the candidate's father directly. "I wasn't any Chamberlain umbrella man. I never thought Hitler was right." With the nomination almost within their grasp, the Kennedys ignored the charges about Joe Kennedy, claimed that Jack didn't have "classically described Addison's disease," and concentrated their attention on securing the last few delegate votes they needed for a first-ballot nomination.[29]

Joseph Kennedy stayed out of sight, declining every interview request except one from John Seigenthaler of the Nashville *Tennessean,* who had worked with Bobby and whom Bobby suggested his father talk to. "He was wearing swimming trunks and a . . . matching sports shirt, and he had on a straw hat with the brim turned down—a very narrow brim which he had turned down all the way round," Seigenthaler later recalled. The two men talked outside on Marion Davies's patio in the blazing Los Angeles sunshine for about two hours. Most of the interview was off the record, as Kennedy insisted that he didn't want to draw attention from his son's campaign. "This is Jack's fight, and this is his effort. He doesn't need me making wise cracks or making speeches for him. . . . I don't want my enemies to be my son's enemies or my wars to be my son's wars. I lived my life, fought my fights, and I'm not apologizing for them. . . . It's now time for a younger generation. . . . I don't want to hang on. . . . They'll make it on their own. They don't need me to fight my fight again." While they talked, the radio was playing in the background. When it was announced that Johnson had invited Jack to debate before the Texas delegation, Kennedy insisted that if he "were Jack, I wouldn't get within a hundred yards of him. We got this won. Jack's got the votes. Johnson can't change them, and he's desperate. . . . Hell, I wouldn't touch him. I wouldn't go near him." Then, a bit later, came the report that Jack had accepted Johnson's challenge, and without a moment's hesitation Kennedy declared that Jack would easily win the debate.

Seigenthaler was astounded at how forthcoming Kennedy was on every issue that he raised. When he asked about Rosemary (whom *Time* magazine had that week reported suffered from "spinal meningitis," a known cause of mental retardation, and was in a "nursing home in Wisconsin"), Kennedy responded that he didn't "know what it is that makes eight children shine like a dollar and another one dull. I guess it's the hand of God. But we just do the best we can and try to help wherever we can. . . . Eunie knows more about helping the mentally retarded than any individual in America." He had never before spoken publicly about Rosemary.[30]

On the evening of July 13, 1960, John Fitzgerald Kennedy, as his father had predicted, was nominated on the first ballot. Bobby, Ted, Jack's sisters and their husbands, Rose, and the grandchildren watched the proceedings or worked the floor. We don't know where Joe was. Rose said he stayed at home; Ted recalled that he watched the vote, then "slipped out of the convention hall with no fanfare."[31]

That evening, the candidate, his brother, and his senior advisers gathered to discuss the vice-presidential nomination. Kennedy had already made clear that his preference was Lyndon Johnson. When Jack offered the nomination to Johnson and Johnson accepted, the fallout from the liberal wing of the party was considerable. Kennedy remained upbeat. Charles Bartlett, visiting at Marion Davies's mansion, recalled "Mr. Kennedy . . . standing in the doorway . . . with his smoking jacket on and slippers. And the whole scene was rather downcast, considering this was the day after a great Kennedy triumph. And I remember old

Mr. Kennedy saying, 'Don't worry, Jack, in two weeks, they'll be saying it's the smartest thing you ever did.' "[32]

On Friday, the day that his son was to accept the nomination for president of the United States, Kennedy was nowhere to be found. Chuck Spalding, Jack's friend, later remembered having found Kennedy packing the night before. "I said, 'Where are you going?' He said, 'I have to get on a plane tonight and get back to New York and get working on this thing. We've got to keep moving.' "[33]

Kennedy had telephoned Henry Luce in New York and, Luce later recalled, "asked whether he could come to see me, I think he mentioned around five o'clock in my apartment at the Waldorf." In the long run up to the convention, the Luce magazines not only had provided Jack with plenty of coverage, but had been exceedingly fair on the religious issue. Kennedy expected that Luce, a lifelong Republican, would endorse Nixon, but he was not going to leave the country for France (which he planned to do on Monday, July 18) without trying to change his mind.

When Kennedy's morning flight was delayed, he called to ask if he could see Luce for dinner instead. Luce asked what he wanted to eat. "Well, he wanted lobster, so by the time he got there we had the dinner about ready and, as I remember, two lobsters. He ate a very hearty meal and he was in great form. . . . [Dinner] was over about nine o'clock and, as I remember it, the television [and Jack's acceptance speech] wasn't going on till ten. I thought that Joe hadn't come to see me just for chit-chat about the convention, so I thought I better get down to cases. I said to him when we were in the living room: 'Well, now, Joe, I suppose you are interested in the attitudes *Time* and *Life,* and I, might take about Jack's candidacy. And I think I can put it quite simply.' I divided the matter into domestic and foreign affairs, and I said, 'As to domestic affairs, of course Jack will have to be left of center.' Whereupon Joe burst out with, 'How can you say that? How can you think that any son of mine would ever be a so-and-so liberal?' . . . It's well known that Joe Kennedy's colorful manner of speech is not always suitable for the tape recording. . . . I think the conversation may have gone on about that for a while, but not very much. Then pretty soon the moment came, the television was on and the nominee, Jack Kennedy, got up to make his speech while the three of us [Luce's son was with them] were watching the television screen." Luce thought the speech was acceptable, but not great, and he objected to something in the opening, to which Joe had replied, "Oh, well, now, don't mind that." When the speech was finished, "Joe left and at the door he said, 'I want to thank you for all that you've done for Jack.' I think this was said with great sincerity and, if I recall, he repeated it."[34]

Kennedy's preemptive strike was not enough. The Luce publications would endorse Nixon, but tepidly.

On Monday morning, July 18, three days after his son accepted the Democratic nomination for the presidency of the United States, Kennedy flew to France. In early August, *Newsweek* dispatched a reporter to Cap d'Antibes to interview him. The reporter, having discovered that Kennedy swam in the hotel pool every day "'regular as a clock' from noon to 1 and 5 to 6 . . . followed him into the water." While the two treaded water, he asked why Kennedy "hadn't appeared with his son at the Democratic convention.

"'I wasn't on the stand with Jack because I wasn't in Los Angeles at the time,' he answered. 'I cannot think of a better reason than that. I was in New York on business and had left Los Angeles Friday morning.'

"'Can you explain why you've been staying in the background?' I asked.

"'I've been in this for 25 years now and never denied newsmen's questions,' Kennedy said, 'but I'm keeping out of it now because it's better that way. There'll be no questions about whether Jack is doing things himself if nobody else is around. Jack has already proved he is doing a fantastically good job.'

"'Isn't it a fact that you're something of a controversial figure?' I asked.

"Kennedy started a slow breast stroke toward shore while he thought about the question.

"'They've been saying those things about me for years,' he finally said. 'I'm used to it. . . . There is such a thing as staying in politics too long. . . . It's time for young men to step in. It's going to be their world.'

"Then, turning to climb up the concrete path to his cabin, Kennedy grinned. 'But Jack, Bobby, Ted, they're the ones to interview. They're the ones making the copy.'"[35]

The *Newsweek* reporter was followed by one from *U.S. News & World Report*. "I stood up and took them and batted them out for 25 years," Kennedy told him. "Now it's somebody else's turn. I called them as I saw them at the time, even when it got me in trouble, which is more than some people did." The only person who would talk to the reporter was Kennedy's caddy, "an attractive French girl named Françoise, about 21 years old. . . . The blonde Françoise says [Kennedy's] fairway shots are 'short' but very straight. . . . Mr. Kennedy speaks no French, but has been teaching Françoise English during the golf rounds."[36]

Kennedy hid out, an ocean away from the campaign, because he feared becoming a campaign issue. It was too late. He already was.

On July 11, the day the Democratic convention had been gaveled to order, Drew Pearson reported that "Republican researchers have been doing a job on the prospective Democratic candidates, especially on Jack Kennedy [and] have dug up some ammunition which they think will make the young Massachusetts Senator a sitting duck next November." The first two pieces of "ammunition"—namely, that the Kennedys had bought votes in West Virginia and were pals and admirers of Joe McCarthy—were old and stale. But the third, "Joe Kennedy on Hitlerism," was not. According to Pearson, Republican researchers had "dug up . . . the correspondence between the Nazi ambassador in London and the German foreign office shortly before Pearl Harbor [which] show Jack's father, then ambassador to London, having intimate talks with the German ambassador in order to keep the United States out of war. Young Kennedy, who had a great war record, is in no way involved. Nevertheless, because of the closeness between father and son, Republican strategists believe the Nazi letters will be effective."[37]

The letters Pearson was referring to were the memorandums Ambassador Herbert von Dirksen had sent to the German Foreign Office after his conversations with Kennedy in 1938. They had been among the thousands of documents discovered by units of the United States First Army in the Harz mountain range and Thuringia in April 1945 and published in the summer of 1949. Kennedy had dismissed the reports as "poppycock" when they were released, and the public at large appeared to have agreed with him. When Jack ran against Lodge for the Senate in 1952, he polled remarkably well in the Jewish districts of Boston. Now, twenty-two years after the conversations took place and eleven years after they had been placed into the public record, Republican operatives planned to use them again.

On September 1, as the campaign heated up after the summer recess, the *New York Times,* in a front-page story, PARTIES WORRIED BY "JEWISH VOTE," reported on what it characterized as Jewish voters' "active dislike of . . . Joseph P. Kennedy. . . . A Democratic worker in a heavily Jewish Brooklyn district called the elder Kennedy 'the number one bogy' of the campaign. . . . Asked why they felt so strongly about Mr. Kennedy's father, some Jewish voters said they had heard of the existence of a letter in which Joseph P. Kennedy had indicated approval of the Hitler regime." Democratic leaders in the state were agreed that "something had to be done to neutralize the whispering campaign."[38]

Kennedy asked James Landis to review the documents. Landis did so, then declared to the press that they proved nothing other than that Dirksen was trying to make a good impression on officials in Berlin by reporting what they wanted to hear.

As the campaign wound into higher gear after Labor Day, the Republicans doubled their efforts to smear the father to get at the son. "The Dirksen dispatches," *Newsweek* reported on September 12, "have been circulated among Jewish voters and they have been given wide credence." Flyers distributed by the New York Young Republicans for Nixon and Lodge and by ad hoc groups like the Committee for Human Dignity, with a Fort Washington Avenue address, flooded the city.[39]

There would be no public defense of Kennedy by his son or his family or anyone on the campaign team. Well aware that the easiest way to keep allegations alive in an endless news loop was to defend against them, the campaign and the Kennedys held their silence. "As I told you over the phone," Justin Feldman, Landis's law partner, wrote him on October 11, "we all agree it would be a mistake to try to counter it publicly." Instead, Feldman prepared a memorandum, with instructions that it should be "put in the hands of the five county leaders of New York City and . . . given to about a dozen of their district leaders with strict instructions not to distribute it or to reproduce it but to use it for their own information and to furnish answers to their workers."[40]

I came home," Kennedy wrote Lord Beaverbrook on September 9, "to find the campaign not between a Democrat and a Republican, but between a Catholic and a Protestant. How effectively we can work against it, I do not know. Jack gave it a bad licking in West Virginia and we are confident that we can lick it now. But with the Baptist ministers working in the pulpit every Sunday, it is going to be tough. All I can say is that they have a hell of a nerve to be talking about freedom for the world when we have this kind of a condition right here in our own country. It seems to me that it is more important than ever to fight this thing with everything we have. And that is what we are going to do."[41]

On September 7, Norman Vincent Peale, whom the *New York Times* identified as "an avowed supporter of Vice President Nixon," announced the organization of the National Conference of Citizens for Religious Freedom, comprising 150 leading clergymen "more or less representative of the evangelical, conservative Protestants," including the Reverend Dr. Billy Graham. They were united in their belief that Protestants had "legitimate grounds for concern about having a Catholic in the White House."[42]

Senator Kennedy was forced to confront head-on the subject he had hoped, after his win in the Democratic primaries, might be laid to rest. He did so by accepting an invitation to speak to the Greater Houston Ministerial Association, a gathering of Protestant leaders, many of them evangelicals. He began his address by declaring that while he was going to speak on the "so-called religious issue," he believed that there were "far more critical issues in the 1960 election." Still, "because I am a Catholic, and no Catholic has ever been elected President, the real issues . . . have been obscured—perhaps deliberately." He proceeded to say what he had been saying for almost two years: "I believe in an America where the separation of church and state is absolute. . . . I believe in an America that is officially neither Catholic, Protestant, nor Jewish . . . and where religious liberty is so indivisible that an act against one church is treated as an act against all." He reminded his audience that no one had asked him or his brother whether they "might have a 'divided loyalty'" when they fought—and his brother died—in the Second World War and that at the Battle of the Alamo, "side by side with Bowie and

Crockett died Fuentes and McCafferty and Bailey and Bedillio and Carey—but no one knows whether they were Catholic or not. For there was no religious test there." Knowing that this might be his best and perhaps last chance to put to rest the religious issue, he arranged to have the speech—and question period—broadcast nationwide.[43]

Though Jack did brilliantly in Houston, it was almost taken for granted now that he was going to lose Protestant votes that usually went Democratic and would have to compensate by polling a larger than usual big-city Catholic vote. Unfortunately, it appeared as late as six weeks before the election that Catholic voters might not be solidly behind the Democratic candidate. CITY'S CATHOLICS SPLIT ON ELEC-TION, the *New York Times* reported in a page-one headline on September 20, confirming Joseph Kennedy's worst nightmares. "If Jack Kennedy thinks he has the Catholic vote in his back pocket, he's wrong," an Irish Catholic party official was quoted as telling the *Times* reporter. Neither of the two major Catholic papers—the *Catholic News*, the New York diocesan newspaper, and *The Tablet*, the Brooklyn diocesan paper—"has ever been suspected of favoring either the Democrats or Senator Kennedy." The *Catholic News* had put a photograph of Nixon visiting with a group of nuns on its cover but had never so honored Senator Kennedy. *The Tablet* had denounced the Democratic Party platform in an editorial in July and had had nothing positive of any sort to say about Jack Kennedy. When both candidates appeared at the Al Smith dinner at the Waldorf on October 19, 1960, an event organized and presided over by Cardinal Spellman, Nixon received far greater applause. It was becoming abundantly clear that he was the cardinal's favored candidate.

On September 26, two weeks after the Houston speech, Senator Kennedy met Vice President Nixon in Chicago for their (and the nation's) first live televised debate. Since 1952, Joe Kennedy had preached the importance of television as a campaign vehicle and prepared his son well for this moment before the cameras. In this and the succeeding four televised debates, John Fitzgerald Kennedy did his father proud. He spoke directly to the camera and looked relaxed, comfortable, "calm and nerveless," as author Theodore White later described him.[44]

On his way out of the television studio, Senator Kennedy, seeing a pay phone on the wall, asked Ted Sorensen for change (he never carried any money with him) to call his father.

" 'Dad, what did you think?' were his first words," Sorensen recalled in his memoirs. "A long period of listening ensued, while I stepped a few feet away. 'Thanks, Dad, I've got to go to Ohio,' he concluded, and hung up the phone. 'I still don't know how I did,' he said, turning to me. 'If just now I had slipped and fallen flat on the floor, my dad would have said: "The way you picked yourself up was terrific!" ' "[45]

The second debate was held on October 8 and focused on foreign policy. From this point on, questions about missile gaps, the defense of Quemoy and Matsu, two islands off the shore of China, and the loss of Cuba would occupy the candidates. Although Senator Kennedy had always insisted that his ideas on foreign policy were very different from his father's, a reading of his statements counterpoised with those of his father's reveals remarkable similarities. It would be wrong to say that Jack simply parroted his father's positions. On the contrary, Jack's analyses in his Harvard thesis of the conditions that led Great Britain to Munich and on to World War II had had a significant effect in sharpening his father's thinking on these issues. The "Kennedy" position on foreign policy was as much a joint effort as one imposed on father by son.

In his warnings about missile gaps and the Eisenhower administration's failure to keep the military strong, as in his calls for increased military spending, John Kennedy had been updating the argument that his father had made in the 1930s and 1940s about the Nazis and, more recently, about the Soviets and that he had made in *Why England Slept*. The best defense against aggression was a mighty military. The stronger that military, the more likely one's enemy would be forced to negotiate— and on favorable terms. For father and son, negotiations with the enemy were always preferable to confrontations. Joseph Kennedy had been criticized for suggesting in 1950 that the United States open negotiations with the Soviets. Ten years later, when Soviet premier Nikita Khrushchev pulled out of the Paris four-power summit, angrily denouncing President Eisenhower for allowing a U-2 spy plane to penetrate Soviet territory, Senator Kennedy declared that Eisenhower should express his regrets over the incident, if this was what it took to get the talks restarted. He later issued his own call "for an early summit meeting between the next President and Premier Khrushchev" and declared that he would, as president, suspend all spy flights. His position on the paramount need to lay the groundwork for reopening negotiations had been promptly criticized by Lyndon Johnson, at the time his undeclared rival for the nomination, who made it clear to a cheering audience that he would neither apologize nor "send regrets to Mr. Khrushchev."[46]

Like his father, Jack Kennedy espoused an approach to foreign policy that he considered realistic, pragmatic, and nonideological. Just as his father had criticized President Truman for pouring "arms and men into the Quixotic military adventure" to defend Berlin and for entering into alliances that, under the guise of collective security, guaranteed nations across the globe that America would defend them, with arms if necessary, from potential Communist aggression, so did Senator Kennedy criticize Republican efforts to defend Quemoy and Matsu from Communist China.

In the second debate, Edward P. Morgan of ABC asked Senator Kennedy to elaborate on his statement "that Quemoy and Matsu were unwise places to draw our defense line in the Far East. . . . Couldn't a pull-back from those islands be interpreted as appeasement?" Senator Kennedy, ignoring the accusation of appeasement, echoed what his father had said ten years earlier. He declared that it was pure folly for the United States to allow itself to be drawn into a war over the defense of two indefensible islands four or five miles from Communist China's shores. Nixon disagreed. "These two islands are in the area of freedom. . . . We should not force our Nationalist allies to get off of them and give them to the Communists. If we do that we start a chain reaction."[47]

That Senator Kennedy should take a position on Cuba opposite that on Quemoy and Matsu was also consistent with the "realistic" approach to the Cold War his father had outlined in earlier articles and speeches. It might be impossible, Joseph P. Kennedy had argued in 1950, to contain the spread of communism in Asia and Europe, but it was possible—and necessary—to "keep Russia, if she chooses to march, on the other sides of the Atlantic and Pacific." The Republicans, Jack Kennedy argued in 1960, had done the opposite. They had poured resources into fighting communism abroad, while leaving the western hemisphere vulnerable to Communist influence. "Their short-sighted policies in recent years have helped make communism's first island base, the island of Cuba." Senator Kennedy insisted that the priority for American foreign policy should be the defense of the Americas and that unless something was done in that regard, "the same grievances, the same poverty, the same discontent, the same distrust of America, on which Castro rode to power," would spread through the rest of the western hemisphere.[48]

There is always a distance, of course, between what a candidate promises and the policies he pursues once elected. This would be the case with President John Fitzgerald Kennedy. Under the pressure of events, he would move in directions he had not envisioned during the campaign. It is important, nonetheless, to note that his starting point in foreign policy was much closer to his father's than we had previously recognized.

Joseph Kennedy spent the fall sequestered at Hyannis Port. He did not grant interviews or answer questions or allow himself to be photographed. He went out less than usual but kept working the telephones on behalf of his son. Frank Stanton, at the time the president of CBS, recalled in his oral history getting a call from Hyannis Port. "I had just come into the house around noon and the phone was ringing and I picked it up and it was Joe Kennedy: he was very abusive because we had the practice, which I didn't initiate but which I certainly supported, of switching our correspondents in the middle of a campaign. . . . That turnover took place when Jack Kennedy was campaigning in Minnesota. . . . He was demanding that we keep the correspondents that we had with Jack Kennedy with Jack Kennedy. And I explained the policy and the reason for it. It made no difference to him. He wanted what he wanted and that's all there was to it. And threatened me. Threatened my job."[49]

On October 22, two weeks before election day, the religious issue, which had been submerged during the debates, was brought to the surface again, this time not by the organized Protestant opposition, but by the Catholic bishops in Puerto Rico, who issued a pastoral leader forbidding Catholics to vote for Governor Luis Muñoz Marín's Popular Democratic Party and implying that they should vote for the newly formed Christian Action Party instead. Cardinal Cushing declared immediately that what had occurred in Puerto Rico was an anomaly, that "ecclesiastical authority here would not attempt to dictate the political voting of citizens." Cardinal Spellman did not criticize the bishops or their letter, but he remarked that Catholic voters who did not obey the bishops' directive would not be committing a sin.[50]

"Senator Kennedy," Sorensen recalled, "knew he had been hurt." His only hope, he told Sorensen, was that American voters would not "realize that Puerto Rico is American soil." If they did, he feared, "this election is lost."[51]

"The Ambassador," Ken O'Donnell and Dave Powers recalled in their memoir, "said that he was thinking of joining the Jewish religion. 'The Jews are giving us more help than we're getting from the Catholics.'"[52]

On November 3, two months and two days after its first article on the issue, the *New York Times* reported in a front-page article, SHIFT TO KENNEDY BY JEWS, that the attacks on the Catholic candidate by Protestant organizations, especially Norman Vincent Peale's, had produced "a backfire of sympathy for Mr. Kennedy." Republicans continued to circulate pamphlets "attacking former Ambassador Kennedy as a 'notorious appeaser of Hitler,'" but they were "not having much effect" on Jewish voters. "The fear that the elder Kennedy's views might have 'rubbed off' on Mr. Kennedy was 'slowly being whittled away.'"

Senator Kennedy had succeeded in convincing Jewish voters that he was the type of liberal they wanted in the White House. The shift toward Senator Kennedy did not mean that they had rejected the charges that Joseph P. Kennedy had been a Nazi sympathizer and anti-Semite, but that they refused to hold the sins of the father against the son.

Thirty-nine

"HE BELONGS TO
THE COUNTRY"

On election day 1960, the Kennedys gathered at Hyannis Port. "People filtered in throughout the afternoon and evening," Ted recalled in his memoirs, "the candidate and his wife, Bobby and Ethel, Sarge and Eunice, Pat and Peter, Jean and Steve, Joan and myself. The Gargans [Joey and Ann, Rose's nephew and niece, who had virtually grown up with the Kennedys] were there. Dad had invited some of his eclectic friends," Father Cavanaugh, Arthur Houghton, Carroll Rosenbloom, and Morton Downey. "We dined on Maryland crabs and then found comfortable places for viewing the returns, most of us at Bobby's house next door," which, Ken O'Donnell and Dave Powers later wrote, had been converted into "a communications and vote analysis center. Downstairs on the big enclosed porch there were telephones, staffed by fourteen girl operators, to be used for calling party leaders and poll watchers all over the country. In the dining room, there was a tabulating machine, more telephones connected to direct lines from various Democratic headquarters, and news service teletype machines." Lou Harris, the pollster, had taken over "the children's large bedroom, where the cribs and playpens had been cleared away to make room for tables full of data sheets and past election records."[1]

It was going to be a long night. The early returns—from the Northeast—were positive. But as the votes were recorded in the Midwest and border states, it became clear that Jack Kennedy was not going to do as well as he had thought he would. "For once," Rose remembered, "there wasn't much kidding or much gaiety. The race was extremely close, and there was tension in the air. Now and then people came over to our house for a sandwich or a drink or a change of scene. Jack would come in to tell his father about a new development. And Joe and I would be wandering in and out of Bobby's house. He and I had very little conversation that evening. He was trying to get the latest exact figures and to project from them how the counts in critical districts were likely to develop. I didn't want to interrupt his train of thought."[2]

They watched and listened and analyzed the votes as they came in. By eleven or twelve, "everyone knew that it would be an all-night thing." Jackie, who was eight months pregnant, was, she later remembered, "sent up to bed. . . . Jack came up and sort of kissed me goodnight—and then all the Kennedy girls came up, and one by one we just sort of hugged each other, and they were all going to wait up all night." At three A.M. a haggard-looking Richard Nixon appeared on television to say it appeared that Kennedy was going to win. Still he refused to concede. At about four, Jack went to bed. Bobby stayed up. We don't know when or if his father went to sleep that evening or if he was awake when, just after six A.M., a detail of sixteen Secret Service agents quietly formed a cordon around the three Kennedy houses.[3]

The president-elect was awakened at about nine thirty and told that he had carried Minnesota and won the election. There was no concession from Nixon. After breakfast with his wife and daughter, Jack Kennedy took Caroline to his parents' house. She spent part of the morning riding with her grandfather. At about one P.M., the Kennedys reassembled to watch Nixon's press secretary concede the election. Jack's photographer had tried desperately but failed to get the group to sit for a family portrait. He now appealed "to the Ambassador, the patriarch Joe Kennedy. . . . He agreed it would be the only chance and announced that a photograph was to be taken prior to the trip to the Armory," where the president-elect was to hold his first press conference. Everyone was herded into the library except for Jackie, who had gone for a long walk by herself. Jack went down to the beach to get her. "When

Jackie, having changed clothes, finally arrived at the door . . . the entire family rose and applauded."[4]

Kennedy helped position his family for the photograph. Jack was placed, standing, in the middle; his father sat next to him, on the arm of Rose's chair, dressed in a dark suit, his tie perfectly tied, his white handkerchief in his pocket. He smiled wanly, more exhausted than joyful. After the photographs were taken, they all moved outside, where the cars had assembled to take them to the armory. "We all got into the caravan of cars in the circle in front of the house," Pat recalled, "everybody but Dad, who was on the front porch, back a little in the shadows, looking very happy. . . . He had decided to stay at home out of the range of photographers and reporters. Jack suddenly realized what was happening. He got out of the car, went back up to the porch, and told Dad to come along and hear his speech. Jack insisted on it. And finally he talked Daddy into getting into our car."[5]

Arriving at the armory, Kennedy trailed behind his son, daughter-in-law, and wife, hanging back a step, just out of the cameramen's range. He looked near enervated, shrunken, frail. As the family took its place on the "bunting-draped stage," he positioned himself on the outside of the row of wooden folding chairs set up on either side of the podium. When the president-elect's brief speech was concluded and the family posed for photos, Kennedy hung back again.

The reporters who covered the president-elect's acceptance speech at the armory were struck by the fact that the "Kennedys showed no evidence of jubilation. All wore expressions of solemnity. Mr. Kennedy's margin of victory was too slender to stir much elation." The president-elect, when pressed to comment on the size of his victory, had nothing to say. Neither did his wife. When asked how she had felt watching the returns, she responded only that it had been "the longest night in history."[6]

Kennedy, who had expected his son to win easily, would never quite recover from the ordeal of waiting for the returns to come in, then waiting for Nixon to concede. When his son Ted joked that he had been so sure of his brother's victory that he had "placed a Las Vegas bet on it . . . [his father] hit the roof. 'This is just—this just makes no sense!' he fulminated," his anger out of all proportion to the crime. "'Foolish!

I'm appalled that you'd get into this kind of thing!' . . . He really went after me tooth and nail."[7]

A month after the election, he was still troubled by the results. "I didn't think it would be that close," he confessed to Hugh Sidey in an interview for *Life* magazine. "I was wrong on two things. First, I thought he would get a bigger Catholic vote than he did. Second, I did not think so many would vote against him because of his religion."[8]

"All of us," Ted Sorensen recalled, "predicted his proportion of the two-party popular vote would be in the 53–57 percent range." This was indeed what the University of Michigan political scientists tracking the campaign (with the most sophisticated techniques then available) had also predicted. That prediction was remarkably accurate with respect to the congressional vote, which broke 54.7 percent for Democratic candidates. John F. Kennedy's vote for the president was 49.8 percent, a full 5 percent below the vote for other Democratic candidates.[9]

The conclusion Joseph P. Kennedy reached, which was also that of the professionals and the academics, was that despite his son's performance in Protestant West Virginia, despite the speeches and the interviews and the press conferences and the reassurances he gave over and over that he was not the Catholic candidate and would not think or act as a Catholic president, huge numbers of Protestant voters refused to believe him. "There can be little doubt," the University of Michigan political scientists concluded, "that the religious issue was the strongest single factor overlaid on basic partisan loyalties in the 1960 election." They calculated that John Fitzgerald Kennedy had lost 6.5 percent of the national vote of Protestant Democrats and independents and 17.2 percent of the southern vote because he was a Catholic. He was the first president elected with a minority of Protestant votes. That their defection had not cost the election was due to the fact that Jewish and black voters supported him in larger than expected numbers.[10]

The vote was so close, especially in Illinois and Texas, that Nixon supporters across the country and Senator Thurston Morton of Kentucky, the Republican National Committee chairman, urged legal action. Nixon remained silent on the issue, but Kennedy, fearful that he might change his mind, called Herbert Hoover to ask him to arrange a meeting between his son and Nixon, which he hoped would put the matter of contesting the election to rest forever. Jack Kennedy flew to Key Biscayne, where Nixon was vacationing. "The meeting," Chris Matthews has written, "accomplished just what the Kennedys intended: providing a photo op to showcase the image of loser meeting winner. . . . The results had been validated by the face-to-face meeting on Nixon's own turf."[11]

The questions about Chicago would not go away as easily, even though Jack Kennedy would still have won the election even if he'd lost Illinois to Nixon. In the years to come, those who would try to tie Joe Kennedy to organized crime would cite the Chicago vote as an example of how Mob-controlled unions swung the election to his son. Statistical analysis of the actual vote demonstrates, on the contrary, that labor-union members in Chicago, suburban wards, and those districts and states that were supposedly Mob-influenced did not vote "unusually heavily Democratic in the 1960 presidential election."[12]

Joseph Kennedy was, at one and the same time, overjoyed that his son had won the election, bitterly disappointed that so many Democratic Protestants had voted against his son, and infuriated by the absence of the Catholic landslide he had hoped would compensate for it. His son had polled 80 percent of the Catholic vote, but that was only slightly more than Democratic congressional candidates, most of them non-Catholic, had polled in 1958 or than Lyndon Johnson would poll in 1964. Kennedy understood that Cardinal Francis Spellman, the most influential Catholic in the country, was much more conservative and anti-Communist than he or his son. Still, he had hoped that Spellman's ties to the Kennedy family and the millions of dollars the foundation had contributed to his favorite projects in New York City and in Italy would hold sway. As the campaign proceeded, there had been abundant opportunity for Spellman to do the right thing or at least to dispel the notion that he favored Nixon. But he had not.

On January 6, almost two months after election day, Kennedy wrote Enrico Galeazzi, the only person to whom he could express his anger with Spellman and the church. "I have a very strong feeling that the time for friends to be together is when you need them the most. I have never asked for many things, but I needed all the help I could get in this campaign. I don't think he [Spellman] gave the help he should have and I think we did as badly in New York amongst the Catholics as we did anywhere in the country. He was asked to do two or three things and he just didn't deliver. In my book we are all even for past services and I haven't any interest in the future. . . . As far as I am concerned, I am through working for them or with them, with the exception of Cushing in Boston. For him I will do anything and for anybody else, I am not interested. . . . Don't think that I am irrational or too mad about the situation. I am just fed up with the whole crowd."[13]

Galeazzi was close to Spellman and could not bear the thought of any permanent estrangement between Kennedy and the cardinal or Kennedy and the church. He tried to mend fences, but he failed, in large part because Spellman, having attempted (Kennedy believed) to sabotage Jack's candidacy, now set out to undermine his presidency. On January 17, three days before the inauguration, the cardinal "assailed" a proposal by President-Elect John F. Kennedy's "task force on education" to provide federal aid for public but not parochial schools. The cardinal, the *New York Times* reported in a front-page story on January 18, had "rarely . . . taken so strong a stand on a legislative proposal."

The president-elect had no comment to make, nor did his father dare say anything publicly. Only to Galeazzi did he let down his guard in what would be his last word on the subject. "And now I am going to write you once more about our friend, and I will not write you ever again about it. . . . I was shocked by his attitude in the Presidential campaign. I was shocked at the reception Jack got at the Al Smith dinner, and with many other incidents about which I have written you. That last fit of temper in which he came out publicly against the Task Force Report on Education, and on which report the President had not expressed any opinion whatsoever, and considering that Eisenhower has personally made this recommendation for the last five years, and our friend has never opened his mouth, I consider it another exhibition of the judgment of a man who should know better. As far as I am concerned, I am disgusted, and I prefer not to have any further contacts. . . . If we can continue our friendship without any further mention of your friend, there is nothing in God's world I would like better. But if my attitude makes you unhappy, I will quite understand it, and my friendship for you will never die."[14]

Galeazzi did not give up. He invited Kennedy to Rome and to meet the new pope, John XXIII, but to no avail. "I know that I shall not go back to Rome much any more. I will leave that to Rose and the children." As to further relations with Spellman or other members of the church hierarchy, in America or the Vatican, "I am sorry to say," he wrote Galeazzi in late October 1961, "I am less in the mood than ever to 'straighten the matter.' I am not like my older son who makes up to the people who attack him. When I have a bad experience, I remember it forever. It is very bad, I realize, and I know that I should be more charitable in my old age, but I seem to get worse instead of better."[15]

Joseph P. Kennedy had finally, through his son, accomplished all he had hoped for. The Kennedy family had completed its four-generation journey from outsiders to insiders, but at a cost greater than Kennedy had ever imagined. The Catholic Church, its American hierarchy, and the Vatican, instead of supporting the family's journey from East Boston to the White House, had stood in its way. And this the patriarch would not forget or forgive.

He did not broadcast his disaffection or speak openly of it to anyone, save Galeazzi and perhaps Cushing. Still, the signs that Spellman was out of favor with the Kennedys were not difficult to find. The cardinal was not invited to the inaugural: Cushing was asked to give a prayer instead. And the family foundation never followed up on the promise of $1 million for the Kennedy Child Study Center, sponsored and administered by the New York Archdiocese. Cardinal Spellman, in a draft of an April 1961 letter to Bobby that was never sent, expressed his sorrow "that your father cancelled the benefit for this providential enterprise which he encouraged me to start with a promise of one million dollars of which . . . we have received _____." He left the final figure blank and asked his staff to find out exactly how much had indeed been received. They calculated the total as $580,109.33, including a "personal contribution of Ambassador Kennedy made payable to St. Vincent's Hospital," a bit more than half what had been promised. Hoping that Eunice, who had recently visited the center, would extract more from her father and the foundation, Spellman decided not to send the note he had drafted. There is no evidence that the remainder of the money promised was ever delivered.[16]

During his son's campaign for the presidency, Kennedy had let go much of his bearish pessimism about the future, but now, with Jack about to move into the White House and take on the problems of the nation and the world, his father was visited again by his old fears.

Three weeks after the election, he invited Dorothy Schiff, publisher of the *New York Post,* to dinner to thank her for her support of Jack's candidacy. Schiff "found Joe quite changed. He looks his age," she noted after their dinner, "although he has retained his figure. He seemed depressed and nervous. . . . Joe asked me if I would like a drink and I ordered my usual. He ordered tomato juice and didn't drink a drop, which wasn't much fun for me. I don't know whether he never drinks or whether he was on guard. He ate sparingly and after dinner, instead of coffee, he had hot water with sliced lemon. . . . I realized that Joe is a worrier. I tried to get him to talk about his business interests. He said he didn't care any more about making money or making women." He had that afternoon, he told Schiff, been visited by the "top steel people [who] had expressed their concern [about] Jack's changing the oil depletion allowance. . . . He said he told them that if they tried to destroy Jack in the next four years they would have nothing—the country would also be destroyed. He repeated this several times. He said the economic situation was terrible and if Jack didn't receive cooperation, all would be lost. . . . He talked about the national debt and seemed very worried about it. . . . He talked about his concern about what would happen after January 20th—what if Mr. K. decided to recognize East Germany."[17]

If, in the past, the father's confidence had buoyed the children's, the converse was now the case. His children's full-throttled belief in their ability to control their futures restored his own faith. "Jack will be faced in the future with a horrible situation," he wrote his friend Galeazzi two weeks after his dinner with Schiff. "The Laos problem is in an awful state. The Cuban situation couldn't be any worse. There is an undercurrent of unrest among the Western Allies and Africa is in bad shape. In the United States business is bad and there are many, many problems to be faced. Jack himself recognizes all these problems and just seems to feel that something can be done about them all. . . . I am worried but hopeful."[18]

To Hugh Sidey, a faithful family supporter to whom he granted an interview in December, Kennedy confessed the strange mixed emotions that were running through his mind as he awaited his son's inauguration. "Just after his son was elected President," Sidey reported, "Joseph P. Kennedy got a call from a friend asking how it felt. 'Hell, I don't know how it feels,' he said. 'Of course I'm proud, but I don't feel any different. I don't know how I feel.' It was not until a few weeks later that the difference began to sink in. 'Jack doesn't belong anymore to just a family. . . . He belongs to the country. That's probably the saddest thing about all this. The family can be there, but there is not much they can do for the President of the United States.'"[19]

Joseph Kennedy could afford the luxury of nursing his grudges. His son could not. Kennedy urged him to reach out to his opponents and asked George Smathers to set up a meeting with Billy Graham in Palm Beach.

Graham, on arriving at the Palm Beach house in mid-January, was greeted by the president-elect. "My father's out by the pool. He wants to talk to you." At poolside, the two shook hands, then Kennedy, Graham recalled in his autobiography, "came straight to the point: 'Do you know why you're here?'" Kennedy told the evangelist (and Nixon supporter) that he and Father Cavanaugh had been in Stuttgart, Germany, when Graham lectured through an interpreter to an audience of sixty thousand. "'When we visited the pope three days later, we told him about it. He said he wished he had a dozen such evangelists in our church. When Jack was elected, I told him that one of the first things he should do was to get acquainted with you. I told you you could be a great asset to the country, helping heal the division over the religious problem in the campaign.'"

That afternoon, after a round of golf with the president-elect, Graham was reluctantly corralled into an impromptu press conference and did just as Kennedy had hoped: he told the press that he didn't "think that Mr. Kennedy's being a Catholic should be held against him by any Protestant. . . . They should judge him on his ability and his character. We should trust and support our new President."[20]

Kennedy left Hyannis Port for Palm Beach immediately after election day. His son, who had decided to make the Palm Beach house his headquarters, followed soon afterward.

Rose had spent a lifetime complaining with a smile on her face about her children's habit of bringing home flocks of friends who would track sand into the house. But never before had any of their many residences been as crowded and chaotic as the house on North Ocean Boulevard would be that holiday season. Jack brought with him his valet and secretary; Jackie, who arrived in early December after the birth of John Kennedy, Jr., brought a children's nurse, a maid, a private secretary, and a press secretary. The beach house was overflowing with "cooks, maids, gardeners, pool men, chauffeurs, hairdressers, and barbers commuting or living in the servants' wing," Thurston Clarke has written. "Add to this cast of characters politicians and dignitaries flowing through the house at all hours, Secret Service agents patrolling the grounds, and reporters camped outside the gate, and you have the ingredients of a Preston Sturges or Kaufman and Hart screwball comedy, in which several generations of an eccentric family trip over one another in a creaky mansion where the phones never stop ringing, doors never cease slamming, typewriters clack around the clock, doorbells sound perpetually, and guests never stop arriving and departing."[21]

Kennedy did not seem to mind at all. He had his own bedroom on the top floor, his own servants, chauffeurs, chefs, a gorgeous secretary, and an even more gorgeous masseuse. Despite the hubbub, he stuck to his regular routines: mornings in his bullpen, nude and smeared with coconut oil, swims in the ocean and the pool, a daily round of golf, sometimes with the president-elect. He did not sit in on any of the meetings his son held with staff, advisers, and potential cabinet appointees.

The only cabinet post he had any interest in was attorney general, which he insisted go to Bobby. The president-elect, Bobby later told Arthur Schlesinger, Jr., offered him the position "immediately after the election," but he turned it down. "I said I didn't want to be Attorney General," he later confided in an oral history. "In the first place, I thought nepotism was a problem. Secondly, I had been chasing bad men for three years and I didn't want to spend the rest of my life doing that." After Bobby said no, the position was offered to Connecticut governor Abe Ribicoff, one of Jack's earliest supporters, who also declined. On Thanksgiving, after Bobby returned to Palm Beach from a brief Acapulco vacation, Jack asked him again and he again said no.

Joseph Kennedy refused to budge. His sons listened as he explained why Jack needed someone in the cabinet in whom he had complete and absolute trust. The Kennedys would always be outsiders, unable to fully trust anyone but family members. Jack needed all the protection he could get; only Bobby was going to put his welfare first.

The president-elect was uneasy about pressuring Bobby anymore and concerned, as Bobby was, about the nepotism issue. He decided to offer Bobby the number two position at the Defense Department and asked Clark Clifford, who was running his transition team, to go to New York to explain to Kennedy, who had flown there after visiting Jackie and his new grandson in the hospital, why Bobby should not be named attorney general. Clifford agreed, though he thought it rather odd that the president-elect had asked "a third party to try to talk to his father about his brother." Clifford met Kennedy at Kennedy's apartment and presented his carefully rehearsed case against the appointment. "I was pleased with my presentation; it was, I thought, persuasive. When I had finished, Kennedy said, 'Thank you very much, Clark. I am so glad to have heard your views.' Then, pausing a moment, he said, 'I do want to leave you with one thought, however—one firm thought.' He paused again, and looked me straight in the eye. '*Bobby is going to be Attorney General.* All of us have worked our tails off for Jack, and now that we have succeeded I am going to see to it that Bobby gets the same chance that we gave to Jack.' I would always," Clifford recalled years later, "remember the intense but matter-of-fact tone with which he had spoken—there was no rancor, no anger, no challenge." The father had spoken, and his sons, on this issue at least, were expected to obey.[22]

Jack was the first to come around. He did not want to disappoint his father, and just as important, past experiences had proven to him that more often than not Joseph P. Kennedy knew what he was talking about. The initial criticism of his choice of his brother as attorney general would be brutal, he knew, but it would subside. He had, he told Bobby, assembled a sterling cabinet, but most of them, including Robert McNamara as secretary of defense and Dean Rusk as secretary of state, were strangers. He repeated now to his brother—as his father had to him—that he needed someone in the cabinet whom he could trust to tell him the truth at all times.

Bobby might have been able to withstand pressure from his father or from his brother, but the two together were too much for him. In mid-December, he accepted the position of attorney general.

Though Kennedy made only this one demand on his son, he encouraged his daughter Eunice to add one more. Eunice had spent much of November recuperating from an operation in a Boston hospital, for what, we do not know. While there, she read the annual report to Congress of the Mental Health Association and was dismayed to find no significant mention of "mental retardation." She called Dr. Robert Cooke of Johns Hopkins, one of the Kennedy foundation's key consultants, and suggested that the foundation take up the slack and sponsor its own national conference on mental retardation. Her next call was to her father, to whom she repeated her idea for a national conference, sponsored by the Joseph P. Kennedy, Jr. Foundation. " 'Just lie down and get well, for God's sake,' he replied, 'and when you come to Florida, we'll discuss it again and see what turns up.' " Eunice, persistent as ever, raised the subject again in Palm Beach. Her father listened carefully, then suggested that the two of them go upstairs and talk to Jack. "This movement needs the federal government behind it. The President can give it the prestige and momentum we can't give it if we work for 100 years and had 100 times as much money to put into the field."[23]

Kennedy suggested that his son follow the Hoover Commission model and establish a presidential commission on mental retardation. When the commission had delivered its recommendations, he could ask Congress for legislation and funding to implement them. Eunice and Dr. Cooke contacted ex-president Herbert Hoover to solicit his advice on "what sort of an organizational structure was needed to have a commission like this."[24]

The president-elect supported the plan, asked Myer Feldman, who would become special deputy counsel in the White House, to work with Eunice, and suggested that she ask Dr. Howard Rusk to recommend a panel chairman. Nine months later, on October 11, 1961, President John Fitzgerald Kennedy announced that he was creating a presidential panel on mental retardation in a statement so strong that it landed on the front page of the *New York Times*. There were, the president declared, approximately five million mentally retarded persons in the country. Mental retardation "disables ten times as many as diabetes, twenty times as many as tuberculosis, twenty-five times as many as muscular dystrophy and 600 times as many as infantile paralysis. . . . Our goal should be to prevent retardation. . . . Failing this, we must provide for the retarded the same opportunity for full social development that is the birthright of every American child."[25]

The inauguration of the thirty-fifth president—the youngest ever to be elected—was scheduled for January 20, 1961. Three days before, Joseph P. Kennedy took a commercial flight to Washington and moved into the house on P Street that he had rented for the week. On his arrival, he made it clear to his friends in the press and to Jack's staff that he didn't "want to have any calls from anybody." Instead, he spent the next "three days in the Senator's office in the Old Senate Office Building, doing the same kind of work I did when I was fifteen years old—sorting out letters and answering telephones." Invited by several of his friends in the press to a dinner for his son, he procrastinated, then declined. "While it seems silly for me not to have it over and say I would love to come, I just still haven't got used to going to dinners where my son is. Perhaps after another six months I will become calmer about it. But since I haven't attended one in my life while he has been in public office, I find it hard now to start."[26]

Until the Kennedys arrived in Washington, America had for the most part kept its entertainment, political, and intellectual elites carefully compartmentalized. This would all change, and rather dramatically, in January 1961. The mixing and matching of elites was noticed first at a dinner that Jean and Steve Smith gave at their Georgetown home on January 17 for family members, friends, and some of the entertainers Frank Sinatra had brought with him for the pre-inaugural gala at the National Armory.

It was the father who had introduced the Kennedys to Hollywood and vice versa, but it was his children—Pat, who married Peter Lawford; Jack, who had wined and dined and dated his way through Hollywood as a young man; and the rest of them—who built the bridges between the entertainment and political worlds that would stand for the next fifty years and more. And it was Jack who added to this mixture the intellectuals: Arthur Schlesinger, Jr., John Kenneth Galbraith, Robert Frost, and Norman Mailer.

The gala, the ostensible purpose of which was to raise enough money at $100 a ticket to retire the Democratic Party debt, was scheduled for nine P.M., the night before the inauguration. The snow had started falling at noon, become a near blizzard by four P.M., and paralyzed a city not known for its skill in handling poor weather. After a concert of classical music at Constitution Hall that started late, Kennedy and Rose, with Ted and Joan in their limousine, drove to the National Armory for the gala, which had been held up because neither entertainers nor audience could get there on time.

Never before (or since, perhaps) have the stars of Hollywood, Broadway, the London stage, television, and the recording industry come together for a night like this one. Joseph Kennedy, ever alert to the possibilities of combining entertainment and politics, had arranged for the gala to be filmed and for the rights to belong to him exclusively. Frank Sinatra was the star, but he had brought with him Harry Belafonte, Milton Berle, Leonard Bernstein, Nat King Cole, Tony Curtis, Bette Davis, Jimmy Durante, Ella Fitzgerald, Mahalia Jackson, Gene Kelly, Janet Leigh, Fredric March, Shirley MacLaine, Ethel Merman, Laurence Olivier, Sidney Poitier, Juliet Prowse, Anthony Quinn, and many others. The only one missing from the extended Sinatra entourage was Sammy Davis, Jr., who had been subject to the vilest whispers, jokes, and hate mail since he had announced his engagement to the beautiful blond Swedish actress May Britt. The decision to exclude him would wrongly be blamed on Joe Kennedy, but not by Davis Jr., who insisted in his autobiographies that it had been made by the president-elect.[27]

The gala began late and went on until after one thirty in the morning, when the president-elect concluded it with a short speech, thanking Sinatra and "the happy relationship between the arts and politics which has characterized our long history [and] reached culmination tonight." Rose and Jackie had gone home long before and missed the dinner and party at Paul Young's restaurant, planned and paid for by Joseph Kennedy and scheduled for midnight. The party did not begin until two A.M. or so when the guests arrived from the gala to dance to the music of Lester Lanin's band and eat "a buffet of high-WASP food such as Lobster Newburg and Strawberries Romanoff." Jack's friend "Red" Fay, who had somehow ended up escorting Angie Dickinson, recalled in his memoirs being "greeted by Mr. Kennedy, who barked with no intent to bite, 'Wait until I tell your wife how you are conducting yourself.' Then, without missing a comma, he turned to Angie, 'How are you, dear? You look lovely. Why are you wasting your time with a bum like this fellow?' With a friendly wave he sent us into the room so as to greet the next guests."

It had indeed been a glorious party. Even the president-elect was impressed. Early that morning, as the dinner was coming to an end, he motioned "Red" Fay to join him in the "pantry just off the kitchen. Out of earshot of the others, he said with emphasis, 'Have you ever seen so many attractive people in one room? I'll tell you Dad knows how to give a party.'" The *Washington Post* reported the next day that when the dinner finally broke up at about four A.M., Joe Kennedy told his departing guests, 'Just wait until you see the party we throw four years from now.'"[28]

The morning of the inauguration, it was so cold that the snow that had fallen the day before had hardened into ice. Rose woke early and went to Mass, where she saw her son but didn't join him in his pew. The dignitaries who had been assigned seats on the Capitol steps were supposed to be in them by eleven A.M. Kennedy, Rose, Ted, his wife, Joan, and cousin Ann Gargan were dressed and ready to go early enough, but the snow- and ice-covered streets and sidewalks made getting anywhere near impossible. "As our driver tried to pull out of his parking place," Ted recalled in his autobiography, "we heard nothing but the sound of the engine and the whirring of the tires as they spun around and around. . . . None of us was happy, but my father was furious. 'Hurry up. We're going to be late,' he shouted. But we were stuck. Finally, my father decided to take things into his own hands. I can still see him getting out of the car in his full dress clothes, shouting and gesturing at the driver and directing him on how to turn the wheel, how to back up, move forward, while Dad finally just pushed the car, providing the necessary muscle to power the vehicle out of the parking spot. It was classic Joe Kennedy: take charge and do it right, even if it means having to do it yourself. We made it to the inauguration."[29]

Joseph P. Kennedy and Rose Fitzgerald Kennedy were seated at the far end of the first row, which displeased Rose enormously, as they "were left out of everything except the panoramic pictures." Cardinal Cushing began the ceremonies with an endless invocation, enlivened only when smoke caused by an electrical fire rose from the lectern. After Cushing was finished—and the fire extinguished—Marian Anderson sang "The Star-Spangled Banner," Sam Rayburn administered the oath of office to Lyndon Johnson, Robert Frost stumbled through a poem, and Chief Justice Earl Warren administered the oath of office to John Fitzgerald Kennedy, who, after shaking hands with Richard Nixon, delivered his inaugural address.

Joseph Kennedy had tried on a few occasions to get a peek at the address but had been politely refused. His chief worry was that his son, having given a magnificent farewell address to the Massachusetts State Legislature, could not possibly do as well in Washington. He was wrong. The speech was electrifying. Jack had had many collaborators, advisers, and editors—and solicited and reviewed drafts from Adlai Stevenson, John Kenneth Galbraith, and Ted Sorensen, among others. Still, the words he delivered from the Capitol steps on January 20 were his, including the one sentence that was most remarked upon at the time—and continues to be fifty years later: "And so, my fellow Americans: ask not what your country can do for you—ask what you can do for your country." The thought was not a new one. It had been included in earlier speeches, including the acceptance speech in Los Angeles.

It would be fruitless indeed—though many have tried—to figure out exactly how this particular thought got put into these particular words. The resemblance is nonetheless striking between this idea as expressed in John Fitzgerald Kennedy's inaugural address and his father's lifelong insistence that his children enter public service and do something worthwhile, that they devote themselves not to making money—he had done that for them—but to the greater good of the larger community.

After the inauguration, while the new president and vice president and their wives were honored at a lunch given by the Joint Congressional Committee on Inaugural Ceremonies, Kennedy hosted a luncheon for about 150 family members and friends in a private room at the Mayflower Hotel. He and Rose were then driven to the White House, where they watched the inaugural parade from the front row of the reviewing stand.

As the lead-off car with the president approached the reviewing stand, Joseph P. Kennedy stood up and took off his hat in a gesture of deference to his son. "It was an extraordinary moment," Eunice would later remark. "Father had never stood up for any of us before. He was always proud of us, but he was always the authority we stood up for. Then, just as Jack passed by and saw Dad on his feet, Jack too stood up and tipped his hat to Dad, the only person he honored that day."[30]

That evening, his wife recalled, "Joe wore the white tie tails he had seldom worn since the ambassadorship, and had found to his satisfaction that they still fit quite well, nearly twenty years later." He and Rose attended the largest of the five inaugural balls, then returned to their rented house on P Street. "We didn't stop for a visit or farewells at the White House. . . . Joe was so determined to avoid any appearance of influencing Jack that he did not set foot in the White House except once during the rest of that year," when Jackie invited him to visit his grandchildren in their new home.[31]

With his two oldest boys settled in Washington—and his daughters, except for Rosemary, all married with children of their own—Kennedy's attention was now turned to the baby in the family, Edward Moore Kennedy. Sometime after the inauguration, Ted visited

Hyannis Port and went out on the *Marlin* with his father and Cardinal Cushing. After they had finished their fish stew lunch, Kennedy turned to his younger son, "Now that Jack and Bobby are where they should be, we have to find something for you." At twenty-eight, Ted was too young to run for the Senate, but in two years, when the term of Jack's Senate replacement, Benjamin A. Smith II, expired (an interim appointment in Massachusetts could be for only two years), he would be thirty, the minimum age to serve. Before even contemplating a run for elective office, Ted needed to get some seasoning in Washington or elsewhere. "When Jack became President and Bob Attorney General," Joseph Kennedy wrote Richard Steele of the *Worcester Telegram* on February 20, "I urged Ted not to move out West, as he thought of doing, but to dig our roots even deeper in Massachusetts. I am glad to see that he is doing just that." Ted took a house in Boston and a job as assistant district attorney for Suffolk County.[32]

Like Jack before him and with the family fortune at his disposal, Ted spent the two years running up to the election touring the state and lining up support. His father assigned Frank Morrissey to look after him and introduce him to everyone he should know. Kennedy went through his old lists of Massachusetts contacts compiled for Jack years ago and sent them on to his youngest son. "They are likely out-of-date now, but could be of some use." Eunice, watching from the sidelines, was impressed with the way her father turned aside the rather vocal objections to Ted's running for Jack's seat. "He predicted unparalleled success for Teddy in politics and argued that Teddy's success, and his differences in temperament and approach, would actually strengthen Jack and Bobby. . . . He was just as interested in Ted and his generation as he had been in the future of my older brother eighteen years before."[33]

His children were grown up and doing quite well for themselves, but Joseph P. Kennedy was still head of the family—and lord of Hyannis Port. Jean Kennedy Smith remembers the afternoon just after her brother's election when the president, the attorney general, and assorted family members and friends were playing touch football in the front yard. Lunch at Hyannis Port was served promptly at 1:15. At about 1:12, Joe Kennedy appeared on the porch and hollered at his children to come inside. "Come on, hurry up, food's getting cold." Jean and Jack were the farthest from the house and the last ones up the stairs. As they approached the house, Jack whispered to his sister, "Doesn't he know I'm the President of the United States?"[34]

Ted recalled a similar scene. Caroline was crying over something and the president had picked her up to comfort her when an aide appeared to say there was an urgent call. The president put his daughter down and went into the next room to take the call. When he returned, his father told him sternly that he didn't care what the emergency was, "never leave a crying child."[35]

The older I get the less inclined I seem to want to write an autobiography," Kennedy wrote Jess Stearn of *Newsweek* on February 6. "The real reason may be that after reporters have made an investigation of my past life and I read it, I can't imagine adding enough to the reports to make a dent anywhere. Of course, a lot of the 'facts' have been repeated so often that they are considered true by most people. That applies to the bad as well as the good. As I sit in my office and try to dig out from all the correspondence that I have received, I am realizing how insignificant it is compared to the fact that I am now the father of the President of the United States. I will probably just let the history of my life stand as it stands, and I am quite sure that nobody will care a damn. I have never written this long about the subject before because I never had a son President of the United States, and I felt I was entitled to a better break than I was getting. But I think I am over it now."[36]

He took up again—with new enjoyment—his old familiar role as family cheerleader. There was, in those first hundred days, much to cheer about. The president's approval ratings were extraordinary through March and into April. And then, in the middle of the month, came the Bay of Pigs fiasco: the bombing raids organized by the CIA, the invasion of the fourteen hundred Cuban exiles, the death of one hundred of them, the capture of the others, and the administration's embarrassment at getting caught in a series of lies and being so thoroughly and publicly humiliated by Fidel Castro. When Rose heard what had happened in Cuba, she put in a call to "Joe who said Jack had been on the phone with him much of the day, also Bobby. I asked him how he was feeling and he said 'dying'—result of trying to bring up Jack's morale after the Cuban debacle." Like his sons, Joseph Kennedy was furious with the CIA for misleading the president. "I know that outfit and I wouldn't pay them a hundred bucks a week. It's a lucky thing they were found out early."[37]

Later, after the president had issued a statement taking full responsibility for what had happened, Bobby suggested that they "call Dad, maybe he can cheer us up. And they did." Their father told them they had done the right thing. They were lucky that their most serious crisis had occurred early in the administration. He predicted Jack's approval ratings would start to climb again after he accepted responsibility for the fiasco. "Americans love those who admit their mistakes."[38]

He forwarded to his sons in Washington only a few names for appointment and did so gently for the most part. The exception was Francis Morrissey, who had been his eyes and ears in Boston since 1946 and was now Ted's chaperon and adviser in Boston. Morrissey had been lobbying for the appointment for almost two years now, well before Jack had been nominated or elected. Kennedy had insisted that he would "help" if he could but that Morrissey was "mistaken" if he thought the position had been "marked" for him. "You know that I would work very hard to get the job for you. But when you say that it has been 'marked' for you, you are way off base. . . . I cannot imagine I could ever have said that to you. Help you to get it, I would. But to promise it to you would be kidding you as well as myself."[39]

True to his word, Kennedy asked his son the president to forward Morrissey's name for the vacant federal judgeship in Boston. The president, knowing full well that Morrissey was not the first—and would certainly not be the last—unqualified nominee to be put forward, was noticeably peeved by the negative comments in the press.

"Look," Arthur Schlesinger recalled him complaining, "my father has come to me and said that he has never asked me for anything, that he wants to ask me only this one thing—to make Frank Morrissey a federal judge. What can I do?" McGeorge Bundy responded that his father shouldn't have asked, but having been asked, the president had no choice but to turn him down. And indeed that was precisely what he did—or almost. When the Justice Department, as was standard procedure in such nominations, requested a report on Morrissey's qualifications from the American Bar Association Standing Committee on the Federal Judiciary, the response was that he was unqualified for the post. President Kennedy let the nomination die, but to placate Morrissey and his father, he did not appoint anyone else to the vacancy, causing a serious backlog in the courts but leaving open the possibility that he would try again later.[40]

James Landis was one of the only Joseph Kennedy associates to accompany his son to the White House. At his first full news conference in Hyannis Port on November 11, the president-elect announced that he was reappointing Allen Dulles at the CIA and J. Edgar Hoover at the FBI, asking Clark Clifford to lead his transition team, and bringing Pierre Salinger, Ken O'Donnell, and Ted Sorensen with him to the White House. He then added that he had asked James Landis, "former dean of the Harvard Law School, member of the SEC, chairman of the CAB, to undertake a study" of the federal regulatory agencies. Landis would subsequently be appointed as a special adviser to the president and his responsibilities enhanced. Kennedy was delighted. Next to Bobby, he trusted no one to watch out for his son as he did Jim Landis.

As a special assistant, there was no need for Landis to undergo an FBI investigation, until President Kennedy, embarrassed in June 1961 when a White House aide was found to be in arrears on his taxes, "ordered routine post hoc FBI checks on all White House staffers, regardless of status or rank, including Special Assistant James Landis." The FBI asked the IRS for Landis's tax returns, but the IRS couldn't find them. Instead of going through channels, the district director in charge called Joseph Kennedy's New York office and reported the problem to Tom Walsh, his tax expert, who got in touch with Kennedy at once. Joe Kennedy put through a call to Landis, who couldn't be located; he then phoned Landis's law partner, Justin Feldman, to find out who at the firm did the partners' tax returns. A half hour later, he called Feldman again to say that he had located Landis, who admitted that he hadn't filed the missing tax returns. "I got him off a platform in Pittsburgh, told him to go see Bobby and then to get his ass back to New York. I told him I want those goddam tax returns filed and those taxes paid as soon as possible."

After learning first from his father and then from Landis that he had not filed any tax returns for at least five years, Bobby called the commissioner of internal revenue and asked him to see Landis. The commissioner advised Landis to get in his returns as quickly as possible. Kennedy lent him the money he required to pay the penalties he had incurred.

Landis resigned his position at the White House. No reason was given for the resignation, though the *New York Times* reported on September 8 that he had been accused of adultery in a divorce suit filed by his wife. The White House said only that Landis had made it clear on accepting the appointment that he didn't want to remain in place past June.

The intelligence division of the IRS opened an investigation as to whether Landis had voluntarily paid his back taxes, which would have protected him from criminal charges, or done so "involuntarily" after being discovered as delinquent. Landis, under questioning, admitted that he had filed the returns only after being warned to do so by Joseph P. Kennedy, who had heard about the problem from an IRS employee. The question of whether this constituted a "voluntary" filing was referred to the attorney general's office.

Bobby disqualified himself and handed the case off to Deputy Attorney General Nicholas Katzenbach, who decided he had no choice but to prosecute. Landis, by this time near suicidal, pleaded guilty and was sentenced to thirty days in jail, most of them spent at Columbia Presbyterian under guard. He was released in October 1963, disbarred in July 1964, and found dead in his pool, an apparent suicide, that same month. Bobby Kennedy, loyal to the end and devastated that he had been unable to protect his family's dearest friend, attended the funeral but did not speak.[41]

K ennedy spent the summer of 1961, as he had the previous ones, at his villa at Cap d'Antibes. He kept in touch with his children by telegram and telephone and made sure to send along his observations and advice to the president and the attorney general.

To Bobby's secretary, Angie Novello, he reported that he had been monitoring *Voice of America* broadcasts, which he found "much better this year than the last five years." He recommended that the attorney general "find out whether the USIA are finding out what countries are listening to these reports and what kind of circulation they have."

To Evelyn Lincoln, the president's secretary, he reported on his conversations with the "topside" people in Europe and recommended that "it would be a good idea to have somebody read the national press of each country every day. It would be of great help to the President." He also asked Lincoln, almost conspiratorially, to "please tell the President my friend [Galeazzi] came over from Rome on Sunday and talked with the important man [Pope John XXIII] on Friday and told him that he was seeing me, and the important man said that he [President Kennedy] was doing very good work and that all of his people should definitely let him alone. That order could go out if the President wants it." The implication was that the Vatican had finally come to terms with the fact that there was a Catholic president in the White House.[42]

To Lyndon Johnson, who remained on much better terms with him than with his sons, Kennedy jokingly suggested "a conference on the state of French political affairs that might be held here at Antibes. . . . Our agenda would be something as follows:[43]

9:00	Golf
12:00	Swimming at Eden Roc
1:00	Cocktails
1:30	No Metrecal, but plenty of lamb and chicken
2:30	Nap
3:30	Talk about Khrushchev and Berlin
3:35	" " de Gaulle and Bizerte
3:40	A little ride up the mountain
6:00	Day's agenda
6:30	A little swim
7:30	Cocktails
8:30	Dinner
10:00	Voice of America
10:15	Discussion on what everyone is doing in Washington
11:00	Sleep

"Hearing from you was a pleasure," Johnson wrote back, "and I must say that I have never met a man with a greater ability to lay out an agenda for a conference. I think that after a month of such activity, we would certainly have the problems of the world solved—or at least we would be better rested and better able to solve them."[44]

Kennedy flew home on September 4 to celebrate his seventy-third birthday with the grandchildren in Hyannis Port. "My own children," he wrote Walter Annenberg, who wanted to get a photograph for his *Philadelphia Inquirer,* "seem to feel a sense of obligation to their father for permitting their children to ruin the carpets, spoil the lawn, mess up the house in good style, and so forth and so forth. So the least they can do is to bring them all to the birthday party, and hope and pray that at least their children will look good in the picture."[45]

In October, he consulted with John Royal of NBC about the three-hour film of the pre-inaugural gala that he had commissioned and owned the rights to. If the network did not want to buy it, he was considering spending his own money to have it edited down to an hour or so and used "for Democratic meetings and possibly local stations." He was also thinking about producing a record of the concert but had made no firm plans as yet. Nothing would come of either idea for a half century until, in January 2011, on the fiftieth anniversary of the inauguration, the JFK Library released footage of the gala.[46]

In November, Kennedy checked himself into the Lahey Clinic for his annual checkup, which found him in good health. His blood and urine tests were normal. "The electrocardiogram showed no change from all the ones you have had in recent years. I thought your general physical condition was excellent," the examining doctor reported. "Hope you have a good Winter."[47]

He sought closure that month on what had been one of his—and the family's—more contentious and embarrassing real estate deals, the sale of a twelve-story apartment building on Columbus Avenue between Sixty-second and Sixty-third streets in New York City.

Time and age had not softened the old man's anger at those he thought had dealt unfairly with the Kennedys. John D. Rockefeller III had fallen into this category when, as president of Lincoln Center, he had agreed two years earlier to pay the grossly inflated price of $2.5 million for the Kennedy property that was located on the future site of Lincoln Center. Regrettably, as both men later learned, Rockefeller had no right to set the price, as the property was owned by the city, which had condemned it. The price was reset by the courts at $2,403,000, which though a bit lower than Rockefeller's first offer was a third higher than the assessed valuation. To square himself with Kennedy, Rockefeller sent the foundation a check for $100,000 to make up the difference. Joseph Kennedy returned it. He had been embarrassed by the wrangling over the final sales price and, unfairly, blamed Rockefeller for it. "My real annoyance was that I thought that when I made a deal with John D. Rockefeller, it was a deal, but instead of this I was put in the position of trying to get money from the city unreasonably, and my family was showered with abuse. . . . For me to accept $100,000 for the Foundation might make it appear that my 'annoyances and worries' are a matter of dollars and cents. They are not."[48]

Thanksgiving, with dinner for thirty-three, was celebrated at Hyannis Port that year. The night before, Kennedy served the oysters and lobster tails Carroll Rosenbloom had sent from Maryland. On Thanksgiving Day, there were oysters again in the sunroom, then a full-course meal with squash, which Kennedy insisted, though his wife frowned on it, be served with the sweet potatoes. (Rose objected to serving two vegetables of the same color.) On Friday night and Saturday night, the family gathered again for dinner, with lobsters the central part of the menu.

Ten days earlier, Joseph Kennedy had had what Rose referred to in her diary as an "attack," probably one of his periodic but prolonged stomach upsets. He "is not at all himself but quiet," Rose wrote in her diary, "complains about a lack of taste in his mouth & feels blah—he says— For first time—I have noticed he has grown old— Sargent noticed & said was plain he was not himself. Doctor [Janet] Travell here with Jack & says cold wind & air bad for Joe but he keeps going out." Kennedy tried to behave as if nothing were the matter. He presided over the festivities, carved the turkey, and, as always, dispensed advice to his children, suggesting to Bob that "he should move to Maryland & become governor—then President 1968." But something was wrong. Jack had noticed it, too, and "expressed his concern" to Ted Sorensen when he returned to Washington.[49]

Kennedy flew back to Florida in the second week of December, as was his habit. He was delighted to be in Palm Beach again and supervised the details incumbent on getting the residence in order, the phones hooked up, the newspapers ordered, the accounts with shopkeepers reinstated. On December 11, he turned down yet another request for an article, this one from a *Life* magazine Washington correspondent.

"As far as I am concerned, I have had it. The future reputation of the Kennedys will be made by the President, the Attorney General, and I am very hopeful, by Ted. They and their families will furnish all the interesting facts that the public should be asked to read."[50]

Forty

"NO!"

O n the morning of December 19, 1961, we were again on the move," recalled Ann Gargan, Rose's niece, in her contribution to Ted Kennedy's unpublished collection of reminiscences of his father. "We generally played golf about 8:30, but Jack was down in Palm Beach and leaving for Washington that morning. Your father rode to the airport with him. I followed in another car so that I could bring Caroline and 'Grandpa' back from the airport. We dropped Caroline off at home and went directly to the Palm Beach Country Club to play nine holes. Being later than usual the front nine was crowded so we played the back nine and not very well. We finished the sixteenth and as your Dad picked up his ball he said he felt rather faint, but for me to tee-off the seventeenth as there were people waiting behind us. I did. He was sitting on the bench, I asked if he wanted his ball tee'd up; he said no. He would just walk along. So we started out—his balance was all off so I asked his Caddy 'Red' to run and get a cart. Then though with some difficulty your father asked if we had gotten Caroline home alright. I assured him we had. This seemed to ease his mind. The golf cart arrived. I got the car and we drove home. Upon reaching the house he felt better and was delighted to find Jackie and Caroline waiting to have a swim with him. . . . He went upstairs under his own power and wanted to change right away for his swim. I persuaded him to rest and have something to eat as he didn't have any breakfast. He fell fast asleep, then awoke in about five minutes coughing and unable to speak or move on the right side."[1]

Ann Gargan called the doctor, who took one look at Kennedy and summoned an ambulance to take him to St. Mary's Hospital. Jackie and Ann went with him, Jackie shielding his contorted body—and face—from onlookers as he was wheeled into the hospital. Because Jack was still in the air, on his flight back to Washington, Bobby was called first. When Jack returned to the White House, his "hot line" was flashing amber.

The president and the attorney general flew in Air Force One to Palm Beach; Ted Kennedy took a military jet from Boston with a vascular specialist; Eunice flew in from Boston; Pat from California; Jean was already in Palm Beach. By the time his sons and daughters gathered at his bedside, pneumonia had set in and the last rites had been performed. There was nothing to do but wait and hope and, if you were so inclined, pray.

Joseph P. Kennedy had suffered an "intracranial thrombosis," a blood clot in the artery in the brain, which had triggered a massive stroke. The clot was inoperable. It left Kennedy paralyzed on his right side and unable to speak.

He woke from his coma the next day and appeared to recognize his children. By Christmas Eve, four days after the stroke, the doctors reported that he was out of any immediate danger, but the degree of recovery was unpredictable. By December 29, he was able to sit up. On January 8, three weeks after he had been felled, he was discharged from the hospital. The fact that he was alive—his vital signs good, with no fever, no pneumonia, his heart strong—was near miraculous. But there had been no improvement in his paralysis. He remained in a wheelchair. He had lost the use of language: he could not speak or write or communicate in words. And he never would be able to.

He returned to his Palm Beach home, which had been refitted, restaffed, reconfigured. A wheelchair ramp had been installed so that he could use the pool, with a plastic roof put over it to shield him from the sun. A nurse's station was set up outside his bedroom and an intercom installed inside. He was watched over twenty-four hours a day by teams of rotating nurses; by Luella Hennessey, who having cared for his children now cared for him; and by several men large enough to lift him into and out of bed. Ann Gargan, who had moved in with the Kennedys when she was taken ill with what was thought to be multiple sclerosis, took on the role of chief caregiver.

The family's first concern was to protect "Grandpa's" dignity, to encourage him and cheer him on, as he had them. For sixty years, Joseph P. Kennedy had imposed himself and his will on family members, friends, and acquaintances, on those he worked for or with, on political associates, business colleagues, and the hundreds of topside and not so topside men and women he came into contact with. Now, suddenly, on day 322 of his son's presidential term, three months into his seventy-fourth year, he was in an instant transformed from the most vital, the smartest, the dominant one in the room to a gnarled, crippled, drooling, speechless, wheelchair-bound, utterly dependent shell of a man. His right arm and leg were paralyzed, his right hand had frozen into a clawlike appendage curled up at the wrist; the right side of his face drooped; he could not dress himself, feed himself, shave or shower, or communicate his thoughts, desires, fears, or hopes in spoken or written language. Yet he appeared to understand everything that was said to him, everything he read or heard or saw.

He learned to feed himself, with some help, and to make his wishes known. He was not mute: he could growl, shout, scream, bellow—and he did. But the words did not come. Except, that is, for "No!" That, he could say easily and clearly. He would bellow, "No!" until the question came he could answer yes, and then he would change his tone of voice and signal with a smile, his blue eyes blazing, and say, "No," again but in such a way that everyone who heard him knew it meant yes. "He never could speak," Rose recalled in a difficult interview with Robert Coughlin. "I don't think he improved very much. . . . Something disturbed him . . . and then you'd give him a drink of water and he'd shake his head and then [you would] put on the radio and then he was happy so you'd conclude he wanted you to put on the radio. . . . Sometimes you couldn't understand and sometimes Ann couldn't understand and that of course irritated him, was very depressing for us."[2]

In April 1962, the Palm Beach season at an end, it was time to move north again, as he did every year. Dr. Howard Rusk, who had become a friend and adviser to the family and whose work the Kennedy foundation had generously supported, invited Kennedy to get further treatment at his Institute of Physical Medicine and Rehabilitation in New York and live in Horizon House, the bungalow, outfitted for disabled, wheelchair-confined patients that he had commissioned builder Sam LeFrak to construct on the hospital grounds. On April 30, with Dr. Rusk at his side, Joseph P. Kennedy was driven from North Ocean Avenue in Palm Beach to the airport, lifted and strapped into the *Caroline,* and flown to LaGuardia.

On landing, he looked out the window, and when he saw the parade of dignitaries waiting to greet him, refused to leave the plane. He had always had a temper but had learned to keep it under control, to turn it on and off as he chose. Now, without the ability to speak, he descended into rages when he feared he would be made to do something he did not want to do. He stormed, shouted, grunted, and lashed out with his strong arm at anyone who came to unstrap him. Only when Dr. Rusk told him he could wait no longer and had to get back to his patients did Kennedy allow himself to be removed from the plane. As he was carried down the ramp, he held his head high and greeted those who had come to meet him. "He did not try to speak but acknowledged each person with a nod of his head." He was put into a limousine and, accompanied by a full motorcade, driven to the institute.[3]

The scene at Horizon House was one of controlled chaos. With Kennedy were Dr. Rusk and his staff, Rose, Ann Gargan, Luella Hennessey, Rita Dallas, who had become his primary nurse in Palm Beach, his Hyannis Port cook and waitress, Jean, Eunice, Pat, Bobby, son-in-law Peter Lawford, and daughter-in-law Ethel. Bemused but delighted to see his family, Kennedy let them flutter about him, and then, when he was ready to settle in, he signaled by stamping his foot that it was time for them to go. Later that afternoon, Jackie arrived, and then the president.

Dr. Henry Betts, whom Dr. Rusk had assigned to the case, was impressed from the first by the way Kennedy's sons and daughters communicated with their father, the frequency of their visits, and their "constructiveness." They spoke rapidly. Their talk was "direct," "fresh." They smiled, laughed, and joked. There was no pity in their voices, no mourning—and that was precisely, Dr. Betts believed, what a patient in Kennedy's condition required. Rose stayed with him at the bungalow—

and, like an old married couple, they ate their dinner, then quietly watched television every evening. His daughters visited every day. Pat Kennedy, Dr. Betts recalled, was particularly good with her father, quieter than the others, gentle and sweet. Eunice never failed to get full progress reports from the doctors—and she pushed her father hard. Jean filled him in on her day's activities. Ted, who was busy running for the Senate, could not visit as often as he wanted. The attorney general and the president made time for weekly visits. Jackie came more often. Of all the family, she was the only one who dared to acknowledge in her eyes and gestures that something had happened. "While the others pretended not to notice the side of his body that was affected by the paralysis, she always held his deformed hand and kissed the affected side of his face."[4]

Joseph P. Kennedy had come to the institute to learn to walk again—and to speak. He was, Dr. Betts recalled, a "tragic figure—very disabled, very affected." He tried his best and made good progress at first, but it was difficult for him to find his way as one among many patients. It was even more difficult for the doctors, nurses, and staff; he was, after all, the father of the president of the United States and the only patient in the facility who was accompanied wherever he went by two Secret Service agents and whose meals arrived from La Caravelle with a waiter to serve them.

Every morning he was given his schedule of activities and told what would occur that day and why. As he had all his life, he made sure he was on time for every appointment, "following his schedule by his own Timex to the minute. . . . He also would refuse therapy or a visit from anyone except his own family who was even one minute late and, when any of his children did not arrive on schedule, he would be irritated and show obvious displeasure to them in the first stage of their visit." The most difficult part of the day was the trip from his bungalow to the main building, up and down the elevators, through the long corridors. Joseph P. Kennedy was used to having things his own way, to giving the commands, to setting the schedule. On several occasions early in his stay, he abruptly canceled therapy sessions or refused to follow directions or leave his bungalow. The effect of his outbursts, his mood changes, his tantrums, reverberated through the halls, upsetting staff and patients to the point where Dr. Betts confronted him in person and informed him that he had to follow orders. If he felt disinclined to do this, he should so indicate and leave the institute. Dr. Betts acknowledged that it might be difficult for Kennedy to follow the instructions of a doctor who was only thirty-one years of age, but he insisted there was no alternative. As he spoke, Kennedy's eyes gleamed "with a most ferocious hate I have ever seen and he wheeled out of the room." By the next morning, however, he was fully agreeable and prepared to follow instructions. Dr. Betts never again had any trouble with his patient, leading him to conclude that Kennedy understood everything he had said and had that night made up his mind to go forward. He worked hard over the next month or so and got to the point where he could stand and, with a heavy brace on his leg and a cumbersome surgical shoe, walk a bit. There was no improvement in his speech.[5]

Kennedy returned to Hyannis Port for the July 4 weekend. Contractors built a pool in the backyard (probably the most expensive of its kind ever built, Dr. Betts later joked) with a walkway from the house and a wheelchair ramp. Another wheelchair ramp was constructed off the pier where the *Marlin* was moored.

At Hyannis Port, Kennedy was surrounded not only by sons, daughters, and in-laws, but by his twenty grandchildren, each of whom, Ethel Kennedy recalled, he treated as an individual. Kathleen Kennedy and Joe Kennedy II, ten and nine years old, respectively, when their grandfather suffered his stroke, were struck by the hole in their lives. Grandpa could no longer take them riding three times a week at 7:15 in the morning or for picnics on the boat or read them stories, answer their questions, correct their grammar, and watch them when they went swimming. "It's a lot of fun to see him," Kathleen recalled four years after the stroke, "but not like before when we played with him all the time." He could no longer speak to them, but they were encouraged to speak to him. Every morning, they would troop into his bedroom to say good morning and then, when their day was done, return in their pajamas and one after another approach the old man in his bed, report on what they had done that day, and give him a kiss good night. Bobby Jr., who was seven when his grandfather had his stroke, remembered that his arm was "twisted grotesquely," but the kids got used to it. They knew that all he could say was "no," but they learned from his intonation when he meant yes. He could, Bobby Jr. recalled, express "happiness" or "anger" with his eyes. "The grown-ups were all scared of him and asked each other on entering the house, 'How's his mood.' Or told the kids and one another, 'Don't get him cross.'" But if he got cross, it was not with his grandchildren. When he saw them, his face lit up in a smile and he would reach out to hug or pat them.[6]

He had to have been lonely when, after September, the children and the grandchildren left Hyannis Port. He watched television, looked at the newspapers, watched baseball games with the Secret Service agents, and made ten-cent bets on the outcome. "He had more fun collecting a dime from me than anything else," Secret Service agent Hamilton Brown recalled later. "The funny part of it, he seldom lost. I only won a few bets in two years. The Chief [Kennedy] had a bank beside his bed that held my dimes and as soon as I won we made a big thing of it. He would take the dime out of the bank, look it over to see if anything was wrong with it (I accused him of slipping me counterfeits), and then with a great deal of reluctance, he would give me my dime back."[7]

He said nothing at all now, though Dr. Betts remembered him joining in an "automatic speech" happy birthday song to one of the grandchildren, and several family members recalled a curse or two coming from his lips. And yet, it was never difficult to discern his mood. When he was pleased, his eyes shone and his face opened in a twisted grin. He was happiest hearing from his children, in person or on the phone. "He looks for phone calls and feels rather hurt if no one calls him," Rose wrote her children from Hyannis Port in September 1962. "The best time to call is during the cocktail hour—between 5:15 and 6:45, as we have dinner now at 7:00. I might suggest that the boys telephone Monday, Tuesday, and Wednesday, and the girls Thursday, Friday, and Saturday, although this is optional."[8]

The progress he had made at Rusk was not maintained. He had begun to walk, but doing so required that he wear a heavy, uncomfortable brace. It was so much easier to get around by wheelchair. The decision to suspend his rehabilitation work was, in large part, his own—and his family accepted it. If he preferred not to suffer the indignities of trying to walk and the pain of wearing his brace, so be it. They were not going to argue with him, especially as they did not know how long he had left.

The prognosis was not good. The second summer of his illness, he had two separate incidents of cardiac arrests. Rose suffered most from the uncertainty, from never knowing when the alarms in his room would go off or if she would wake in the morning to find him gone. She had spent their married life traveling but now felt obligated to stay close by.

He had all his life prided himself on his appearance, on his perfectly tailored business suits and leisure suits, on his military posture, and on the smile he could turn on whenever it was needed. He had been a handsome young man, and he'd aged gracefully into the most handsome of older men. The stroke reversed all that. He was now—and he had to have known it—a twisted, gaunt old skeleton, bound to a wheelchair, unable to make himself understood. He was faced, as was his family, with the most distasteful choice between isolating himself in his room or going out and subjecting himself to the frightened or pitying stares of friends and onlookers.

The family tried not to interrupt the routines that had defined his life. He traveled back and forth, as he had when he was healthy, from Hyannis Port in late spring to Palm Beach in December. He made regular trips to Chicago, where he visited the Merchandise Mart and received maintenance therapy from Dr. Betts, who had moved there from the Rusk Institute. He continued to stop over for a few days in New York City on his trips to and from Palm Beach and made a point of visiting at his Park Avenue office for business updates and lunching at his favorite restaurant, La Caravelle. "He wanted his old table in the middle of the restaurant, so they'd wheel him in his wheelchair and move him onto the bench." When he was finished with his meal, his male attendant and nurse would return to his table, help him back into his wheelchair, and wheel him out of the restaurant. "He didn't seem to mind. . . . He could feed himself pretty well but his meat had to be cut."[9]

He had stayed away from the White House when healthy but accepted two dinner invitations after his stroke, on April 9 and May 9. On both occasions, Ben Bradlee, Jack's former neighbor and friend, and his wife were invited to dinner. "The old man," Bradlee recalled in *Conversations with Kennedy,* "is bent all out of shape, his right side paralyzed from head to toe, unable to say anything but meaningless sounds and 'no, no, no, no,' over and over again. But the evening was movingly gay, because the old man's gallantry shows in his eyes and his crooked smile and the steel in his left hand. And because his children involve him in their every thought and action. They talk to him all the time. They ask him 'Don't you think so, Dad?' or 'Isn't that right, Dad?' And before he has a chance to embarrass himself or his guests by not being able to answer, they are off on the next subject." When Teddy and Bobby sang a little song, in two-part harmony, frighteningly off-key for their father, "everyone applauded, especially old Joe. Only he applauds with his eyes." The only awkward moment occurred when dinner was announced and Kennedy insisted on walking into the dining room. "Jackie supported her father-in-law on one side, with Ann Gargan slightly to the rear of the other side. She has to stand slightly behind him so that she can kick his right leg forward between steps. He can't do it himself. When he eats, he drools out of the right side of his mouth, but Jackie was wiping it off quickly, and by the middle of dinner there really is no embarrassment left. Kennedy senior had brought along crabs from Florida for dinner. . . . 'I must say,' [President] Kennedy said as he ate his crabs, 'there is one thing about Dad: When you go with him you go first class.' There is a gaggle of agreement, and the ambassador, jabbing the air with his left hand, much as his son jabs the air with his right hand to make a point, says 'No, no, no, no,' and everyone knows what he means. In the old days it would have been some teasing wisecrack. Tonight it's a 'no' that means 'yes.'"[10]

He tried not to snub his oldest, dearest friends, but there were moments when he simply could not face them in his present condition. On May 16, 1963, during their spring visit to New York, he and Rose were invited to have lunch with President Hoover at his suite at the Waldorf. "The day of the luncheon," Rose recalled in an oral history, "Mr. Kennedy seemed rather upset and didn't just seem to be able to get ready and go down to the Waldorf. He wept a little and he was really quite upset emotionally, so we finally decided that I would go down and lunch with the former President, and hopefully Mr. Kennedy would follow. . . . Then, happily, my husband joined us [with Ann Gargan and a nurse] in about ten or fifteen minutes and it was wonderful to see the delight in both their faces when they met. . . . Of course, at that time their faculties were diminishing and it was very difficult for both of them, but you could see that they felt great emotion and great joy on that occasion from the fact that they had met once more."[11]

Two years shy of a month after his stroke, at approximately 1:40 in the afternoon on Friday, November 22, 1963, while Kennedy was napping after lunch in Hyannis Port, his youngest son, Edward Kennedy (who had been elected to the Senate the year before), presided over a routine debate on federal aid to public libraries. There was a noticeable shout from the lobby. The press liaison went out to investigate, then came back to the floor and motioned to Senator Kennedy to follow him out of the chamber.

The president had been shot in Dallas. The senator rushed home and phoned the attorney general, who confirmed that their brother was dead. Their mother, in Hyannis Port, had already heard the news; their father, still napping in his bedroom, had not. It was decided that no one would say anything to him until Ted and Eunice arrived.

When Kennedy awoke from his afternoon nap, he wanted to watch television but was told that it was broken. Ted and Eunice arrived and went upstairs to chat with him. They decided to wait until the next morning to tell him that his second son was dead. Kennedy ate an early supper in his bedroom, with his children beside him, then tried again to watch television but was told the set in his room was still broken, as was the one downstairs.

The next morning after breakfast, Ted—with Eunice, Ann Gargan, and the doctor, who had been summoned the night before from Boston—went upstairs to tell Kennedy that Jack was dead. Rose stayed outside. "I couldn't stand it."[12]

"To this day," Ted Kennedy recalled in his autobiography, "the memory of that conversation brings me to tears." Kennedy wept with his children. The television was turned on and he watched it intently. "He began to sob again, and for the next several hours—indeed, throughout most of the next two and a half days—he alternated between a yearning for information and a revulsion against it."[13]

That afternoon, Kennedy indicated that he wanted to go downstairs. His nurse wrapped a heavy blanket around him and helped him get into his wheelchair. Ted was sitting alone downstairs. Kennedy gestured toward the car outside, then, after he was bundled into the front seat and his wheelchair lifted into the trunk, he signaled—by grunts and saying "no" until he was asked the right question—that he wanted to be driven to the airport. His intention, clearly, was to fly to Washington for his son's funeral. When he saw that the *Caroline,* the only plane outfitted for him to fly in, was not there, he gestured to Ann Gargan and Ted that he wanted to leave. They drove on, through the back roads, with Joseph P. Kennedy pointing the way he wanted to go, until they reached the house.[14]

He did not attend the funeral with the rest of his family. Father Cavanaugh came to stay with him. His daughters except for Rosemary, Ted, and their spouses and children celebrated Thanksgiving at Hyannis Port that year, but this time without Jack and without Bobby, who was consumed by a grief that would not go away. When only a few weeks later Kennedy flew south to Palm Beach for the winter, he did so without the Secret Service agents who had played so large a part in his life. He was no longer the father of the president.

President Lyndon Baines Johnson made a point of visiting Kennedy at Palm Beach during a quick trip to Florida in late February. The following month, he called to congratulate Kennedy on Ted's appearance on *Meet the Press.* While Johnson chattered away at how well Ted had done, Kennedy could be heard in the background, mumbling incoherently, sounding more like a wounded animal than a seventy-five-year-old man. The call was painful for both parties, but Johnson soldiered on, talking nonstop until Ann Gargan came back on the phone to thank him.

In July, on Bobby's suggestion, Lyndon Johnson phoned again. When he asked Bobby whether his phone calls upset Kennedy, Bobby responded that they did, but that they also made "a big difference." Following Bobby's advice, Johnson talked to Kennedy about the economy and the stock market. There was no sound on the other end of the phone. Ann Gargan came on the line and apologized to Johnson. Uncle Joe "gets sort of emotional when you call."[15]

In the spring of 1964, there had been an attempt to start up his rehabilitation with a trip to a new facility in Philadelphia, but nothing had
come of it. "It was a little encouraging there for a while," son-in-law
Steve Smith told President Johnson, "and then he tired a little bit of it."[16]

Ann and Rose and the nurses and attendants and therapists did what
they could to make him comfortable. Ted tried to cheer him by taking
up the matter of the Frank Morrissey nomination with Lyndon Johnson. On September 24, the president, with Ted in his office, called Kennedy in Hyannis Port to tell him that he was "getting ready to recommend
your friend Judge Morrissey for the federal bench and we wanted to tell
you about it first." He then put Ted on the phone.

"Oh Dad. Well it looks you're the man with all the influence still. . . .
President says he's doing it for you and Jack and Bob and myself. And I
think he's giving it a little extra push because of your interest in it."[17]

This time, the nomination went as far as but no further than the
Judiciary Committee. After a series of damning revelations about Morrissey's out-of-state legal education, failed bar examinations, and claims
of residence in two states at the same time, Senator Kennedy had no
choice but to withdraw it from consideration.

Against all the odds and the medical prognostications, Joseph P.
Kennedy remained alive for nearly nine years after his stroke. With
every passing year, he withdrew further, seemed to shrink in presence,
to collapse into himself, to spend more time in his room, in his bed.
"He was engrossed in TV all the time," Rose later recalled. "He'd look
at television upstairs and downstairs." The visits to New York or Chicago came to a halt. He was still taken out on the boat—and for an
occasional drive—and still flown back and forth between Palm Beach
and Hyannis Port. His children still visited and filled him in on the details of their lives, except for their reunions with Rosemary. He received
visits from old friends: Morton Downey, Carroll Rosenbloom, Cardinal
Cushing, Father Cavanaugh. His grandchildren always brought a smile
back to his face.

And then, the unthinkable.

Rose did not learn of her third son's death until the morning after. She asked her chauffeur to drive her to Mass, then returned through the throng of reporters and photographers that had encircled the house. Quietly, she went upstairs and, after a few moments alone in her room, went in to tell her husband, by herself, that Bobby too was dead. This time, he watched it all on television, in his room, refusing to allow anyone to turn off the set. Hour after hour after hour, he stared at the screen without blinking, without moving, without a sound. And he wept.

"After Bobby's death," Rose recalled years later, "Joe's condition declined until by the fall of that year he was approaching helplessness, not even able to feed himself the greater part of the time, suffering all the annoyances and discomforts and indignities of hopeless infirmity." On November 18, 1969, nine years and one week after John Fitzgerald Kennedy's election as president and four days before the sixth anniversary of his assassination, the end came.[18]

Joseph P. Kennedy died peacefully in the place he loved more than any other, at Hyannis Port. He was eighty-one years of age and had outlived four of his nine children.

ACKNOWLEDGMENTS

No work of history is possible without archivists and librarians. Some of those who went out of their way to assist me on this project include Verity Andrews, Special Collections Service, University of Reading; Barbara Cline at the LBJ library in Austin; James Edward Cross, Special Collections, Clemson University Libraries; Cynthia Curtner, Boston Latin School archives; Al Davis, Riverdale Country School; Ana Guimaraes, Division of Rare and Manuscript Collections, Cornell University; Robert Johnson-Lally, Archdiocese of Boston; Donna Maxwell, Special Olympics; Malgosia Myc, Bentley Historical Library, University of Michigan; Matthew Schaefer, Herbert Hoover Presidential Library; Sister Marguerita Smith, Archdiocese of New York; Father Tom Sullivan, Archdiocese of Worcester; Marc Thomas, Maryland Historical Society; Florence Turcotte, Special and Area Studies Collections, University of Florida; and the staffs of the Cohasset, Quincy, and Palm Beach historical societies.

I did much of my research at the JFK library in Boston, one of the gems in our nation's superb Presidential Library system. I would like to thank Paul Kirk, Tom Putnam, Allan Goodrich, Jennifer Quan, Maryrose Grossman, Laurie Austin, and, in particular, Stephen Plotkin, who always found time to answer my calls and locate whatever I was looking for.

One of the drawbacks of taking several years to write a book is that you are unable to thank in person all those who contributed to it. Senator Edward Kennedy was from day one unfailingly generous with his time. Arthur Schlesinger, Jr., got me started by sharing his memories and thoughts about Joseph P. Kennedy. My mother, Beatrice Nasaw, as always, served as my chief research assistant as long as she was able.

I am enormously grateful to Jean Kennedy Smith for her encouragement and for answering every question I put to her. Vicki Reggie Kennedy was helpful throughout. Amanda Smith, the author of a superbly assembled and annotated collection of her grandfather's letters, shared her research with me. I was able to speak with Eunice Kennedy Shriver before her death. I profited as well from conversations with Ethel Skakel Kennedy, Robert Kennedy, Jr., Christopher Kennedy, Rory Kennedy, Timothy Shriver, and Ann Gargan. I thank the Shriver family for permitting me to look at and cite letters from Eunice Kennedy Shriver's personal papers.

Will Swift provided me with much of the research he had done on Kennedy's years in London. Cari Beauchamp talked to me about Kennedy's career in Hollywood. FBI historian John Fox helped me secure FBI records. Lucy White showed me letters to Joseph P. Kennedy written by her grandfather, Thomas White. Arthur J. Goldsmith, Jr., sent me letters written by his father, Arthur Goldsmith. William Gowen spoke about his father, Franklin Gowen, and his association with Kennedy at the London embassy and elsewhere. Brian Burns not only took time to talk with me about his father, Judge John Burns, and the role he played in Kennedy's life, but offered me copies of his father's letters. Muriel Palmer told me of an incident involving Kennedy from her childhood.

Robert Caro, E. L. Doctorow, Henry Feingold, Arthur Goren, Nigel Hamilton, Susan Hertog, Michael Janeway, Laurence Leamer, Jeff Madrick, Nancy Milford, Anne Navaksy, Victor Navasky, Dan Okrent, Ron Powers, David Rosner, and Richard Whalen were of enormous help.

Steve Brier, Alan Brinkley, Steve Fraser, Joshua Freeman, Robert

(K.C.) Johnson, and Thomas Kessner read portions of the manuscript and offered suggestions that guided my final rewrites.

There is no better place to teach, research, and write history than the Graduate Center of the City University of New York. I thank the Graduate Center president and my friend, William Kelly, for his support; and my colleagues in the history department, Martin Burke, Blanche Wiesen Cook, James Oakes, Judith Stein, and the late John Diggins for their assistance. I am greatly in the debt of the graduate students who assisted me with my research: Andrew Battle, Benjamin Becker, Rachel Burstein, Brendan Cooper, Mariel Isaacson, Fabio Mattioli, Brendan O'Malley, and Brian Sholis. Noah Simmons put my endnotes into order; Tracy Robey Masterovaya did yeoman service in fact-checking and securing permissions.

I received research assistance from Lauren Dinger in Boston, Tami Katz in Jerusalem, Ben Kopit in Los Angeles, Sarah Meier in Wyoming, Kelly Kelleher Richter in San Francisco, Alessandro Visani in Rome, and Corey Elliott Walker in Washington, D.C. Marilyn Farnell did photo research for me at the JFK library.

I learned much from conversations with Kennedy family friends and acquaintances, particularly Dr. Henry Betts, John Seigenthaler, Leo Racine, Theodore Sorensen, William vanden Heuvel, and Gore Vidal.

Lindsay Whalen at Penguin Press has, with good cheer and enormous competence, aided me in the final stages of getting the manuscript into publishable form; Sona Vogel did a masterful job of copyediting.

Ann Godoff remains, from my perspective, the best editor there is; Andrew Wylie, the best agent an author could wish for.

There are no words grand enough to express my love and gratitude to Dinitia Smith, my superb in-house editor, who read every word in every draft, and by her presence, persistence, and patience made this a much better book than it would have been without her.

NOTES

LIBRARIES AND ARCHIVAL DEPOSITORIES

Baker Library   Baker Library, Harvard Business School, Boston, Massachusetts

Bancroft   Bancroft Library, University of California, Berkeley, California

BPL-EB   Boston Public Library, East Boston Branch, East Boston, Massachusetts

Cohasset   Cohasset Historical Society, Cohasset, Massachusetts

CUOH   Columbia Center for Oral History, New York, New York

CZA   Central Zionist Archives, Jerusalem, Israel

FDRL   Franklin D. Roosevelt Presidential Library, Hyde Park, New York

HI   Hoover Institution Archives, Stanford University, Stanford, California

HHPL   Herbert Hoover Presidential Library, West Branch, Iowa

JFKL   John F. Kennedy Presidential Library, Boston, Massachusetts

JFKNHS   John Fitzgerald Kennedy National Historic Site, Brookline, Massachusetts

LBJL   Lyndon Baines Johnson Library, Austin, Texas

LC   Library of Congress, Manuscript Division, Washington, D.C.

Longfellow   Longfellow House–Washington Headquarters National Historic Site, Cambridge, Massachusetts

Mudd   Seeley G. Mudd Manuscript Library, Princeton University, Princeton, New Jersey

NAUK   National Archives of the United Kingdom, Kew, Richmond, Surrey, U.K.

NAUS   National Archives of the United States, Washington, D.C.

NYPL   The New York Public Library, Manuscripts and Archives Division, Astor, Lenox, and Tilden Foundations, New York City

Ransom   Harry Ransom Center, The University of Texas at Austin, Austin, Texas

SEC   Securities and Exchange Commission Historical Society

ARCHIVAL COLLECTIONS

AANY   Spellman Papers, Archives of the Roman Catholic Archdiocese of New York, Saint Joseph's Seminary, Dunwoodie, Yonkers, New York

Alsop   Joseph Alsop and Stewart Alsop Papers, LC

America First   America First Committee Papers, HI

Astor   Papers of Nancy Astor, Special
    Collections, University of Reading,
    Reading, U.K.
Baker   Newton Diehl Baker Papers, LC
Baruch   Bernard Baruch Papers, Mudd
Beaverbrook   Lord Beaverbrook Papers,
    House of Lords, Parliamentary Archives,
    London, U.K.
Berle   Adolf A. Berle Papers, FDRL
Blair   Clay Blair Papers, American Heritage
    Center, University of Wyoming, Laramie,
    Wyoming
BLS   Boston Latin School, Boston,
    Massachusetts
Boettiger   John Boettiger Papers, FDRL
Byrnes   James F. Byrnes Papers, Special
    Collections, Clemson University
    Libraries, Clemson, South Carolina
Cavanaugh   John J. Cavanaugh Papers
    (JJC), The Archives of the University of
    Notre Dame, Notre Dame, Indiana.
CBLP   Clare Boothe Luce Papers, LC
CHAR   Chartwell Papers, Churchill Papers,
    Churchill Archives Centre, Churchill
    College, Cambridge, U.K.
Clifford   Clark M. Clifford Papers, LC
Coblentz   Edmond Coblentz Papers,
    Bancroft
Corcoran   Thomas G. Corcoran Papers, LC
Cushing   Cushing Papers, Archives of the
    Roman Catholic Archdiocese of Boston,
    Braintree, Massachusetts
DeMille   Cecil B. DeMille Productions
    Records; Arts and Communications
    Archives; L. Tom Perry Special
    Collections, Harold B. Lee Library,
    Brigham Young University, Provo, Utah
Democrat   Democratic National Committee
    Papers, FDRL
Douglas   William O. Douglas Papers, LC
EKSP   Eunice Kennedy Shriver Papers,
    Special Olympics, Washington, D.C.
EMKP   Edward M. Kennedy Personal
    Papers, JFKL
FBI   Federal Bureau of Investigation,
    Washington, D.C.
FDRSF   President's Secretary Files, FDRL
FFF   Fight for Freedom, Inc., Records,
    Mudd
Forrestal   James V. Forrestal Papers, 20th
    Century Public Policy Papers, Mudd
Frankfurter   Felix Frankfurter Papers, LC
Gannett   Frank Ernest Gannett Papers,
    1900 Division of Rare and Manuscript

Collections, Cornell University Library,
    Ithaca, New York
Gressman   Eugene Gressman Papers, Bentley
    Historical Library, The University of
    Michigan, Ann Arbor, Michigan
Halifax   Papers of the 1st Earl of Halifax
    (Edward Frederick Lindley Wood),
    Borthwick Institute for Archives,
    University of York, York, U.K.
Hearst   William Randolph Hearst Papers,
    Bancroft
HHOHP   Herbert Hoover Oral History
    Project, HHPL
HHPLPPI   Post-Presidential
    Correspondence, HHPL
Hopkins   Harry Hopkins Papers, Special
    Collections Research Center,
    Georgetown University Library,
    Washington, D.C.
Hornbeck   Stanley Hornbeck Papers, HI
HUA   Harvard University Archives, Pusey
    Library, Harvard University, Cambridge,
    Massachusetts
Hull   Cordell Hull Papers, LC
Ickes   Harold L. Ickes Papers, LC
Krock   Arthur Krock Papers, 20th Century
    Public Policy Papers, Mudd
Jacobs   Rose Jacobs Papers, CZA
JFKOF   President's Office Files, JFKL
JFKOHP   John F. Kennedy Oral History
    Project, JFKL
JFKPP   John F. Kennedy Personal Papers,
    JFKL
JPKP   Joseph P. Kennedy Personal Papers,
    JFKL
JR   James Roosevelt Papers, FDRL
KBMPP   Kirk LeMoyne "Lem" Billings
    Personal Papers, JFKL
Kent   Frank Kent Scrapbooks, Maryland
    Historical Society, Baltimore, Maryland
Kirstein   Louis E. Kirstein Collection, Baker
    Library
Knopf   Alfred A. Knopf, Inc., Papers,
    Ransom
Knopf Records   Alfred A. Knopf, Inc.,
    Records, NYPL
LandisLC   James McCauley Landis Papers,
    LC
LandisHU   James McCauley Landis Papers,
    Harvard Law School, Cambridge,
    Massachusetts
LBJP   Papers of Lyndon B. Johnson, LBJL
LeHand   Marguerite A. ("Missy") LeHand
    Papers, Grace Tully Collections, FDRL

Lehman   Lehman Brothers Collection,
Baker Library

Lindbergh   Charles Augustus Lindbergh
Gift Collection, Manuscripts and
Archives, Yale University Library, New
Haven, Connecticut.

Long   Breckinridge Long Papers, LC

McCormick   Robert R. McCormick:
Business Correspondence, Colonel
Robert McCormick Research Center,
First Division Museum at Cantigny,
Wheaton, Illinois

Moffat   Jay Pierrepont Moffat Diplomatic
Papers, Houghton Library, Harvard
University, Cambridge, Massachusetts

Mooney   James D. Mooney Papers, Special
Collections Research Center, Georgetown
University Library, Georgetown
University, Washington, D.C.

Morgenthau   Morgenthau Diaries, LC

NHP   Nigel Hamilton Papers,
Massachusetts Historical Society,
Boston, Massachusetts

OF   President's Official Files, FDRL

Pathé   Pathé Exchange Records, Margaret
Herrick Library, Academy of Motion
Picture Arts and Sciences, Beverly Hills,
California

Pearson   Drew Pearson Personal Papers,
LBJL

Pegler   Westbrook Pegler Papers, HHPL

PPF   President's Personal Files, FDRL

Quigley   Martin J. Quigley Papers, Special
Collections, Georgetown University
Library, Washington, D.C.

REFKP   Rose [Elizabeth] Fitzgerald
Kennedy Personal Papers, JFKL

Riverdale   Riverdale Country Day School,
Riverdale, New York

Ross   Harold Ross Papers, *New Yorker*
Records, NYPL

Schiff   Dorothy Schiff Papers, NYPL

Schlesinger   Arthur M. Schlesinger, Jr.,
Papers, NYPL

Sulzberger   New York Times Company
Records, Arthur Hays Sulzberger
Papers, NYPL

Swanson   Gloria Swanson Papers, Ransom

Szold   Robert Szold Papers, CZA

Toscanini   Cia Fornaroli and Walter
Toscanini Papers, NYPL

Trohan   Walter Trohan Papers, HHPL

Weizmann   The Chaim Weizmann Archives,
Rehoboth, Israel

Wilson   Hugh Wilson Papers, HHPL

Wood   R. E. Wood Papers, HHPL

Wright   Papers of John J. Wright, Archives
of the Roman Catholic Diocese of
Worcester, Worcester, Massachusetts

NEWSPAPERS

AC   Atlanta Constitution

BDG   Boston Daily Globe

BH   Boston Herald

BRA   Boston Record-American

BSG   Boston Sunday Globe

BP   Boston Post

BSP   Boston Sunday Post

BT   Boston Traveler

CDT   Chicago Daily Tribune

CSM   Christian Science Monitor

*EHMPW   Exhibitor Herald Motion Picture
World*

FD   Film Daily

HC   Hartford Courant

LAE   Los Angeles Examiner

LAT   Los Angeles Times

MPN   Motion Picture News

MPW   Moving Picture World

NYDM   New York Daily Mirror

NYJA   New York Journal American

NYHT   New York Herald Tribune

NYT   New York Times

V   Variety

WP   Washington Post

WSJ   Wall Street Journal

INDIVIDUALS

BB   Bernard Baruch

CBL   Clare Boothe Luce

CK   Christopher Kennedy

EKS   Eunice Kennedy Shriver

EMK   Edward M. Kennedy

ER   Eleanor Roosevelt

ESK   Ethel Skakel Kennedy

FDR   Franklin Delano Roosevelt

FF   Felix Frankfurter

GS   Gloria Swanson

HH   Herbert Hoover

JB   John Boettiger

JF   John F. "Honey" Fitzgerald

JFK   John Fitzgerald Kennedy

JKS   Jean Kennedy Smith

JPK   Joseph P. Kennedy

JR   James Roosevelt

KKH   Kathleen "Kick" Kennedy Hartington

LB   Kirk LeMoyne "Lem" Billings

NA   Lady Nancy Astor

PKL   Patricia Kennedy
RC   Robert Coughlin
REFK   Rose [Elizabeth] Fitzgerald Kennedy
RFK   Robert Fitzgerald Kennedy
RK   Rosemary Kennedy
SS   Secretary of State (Cordell Hull)
WRH   William Randolph Hearst

PUBLICATIONS

FB   *The Fruitful Bough*
FRUS   *Foreign Relations of the United States*
HTF   *Hostage to Fortune*
TTR   *Times to Remember*
TC   *True Compass*

ONE: DUNGANSTOWN TO EAST BOSTON

1. David Noel Doyle, "The Remaking of Irish America, 1845–1880," in *Making the Irish American: History and Heritage of the Irish in the United States,* ed. Joseph Lee and Marion R. Casey (New York: New York University Press, 2006), 222.
2. *East Boston: A Survey and a Comprehensive Plan* (City of Boston, 1916), 1.
3. William H. Sumner, *History of East Boston* (Boston: J. E. Tilton & Co., 1858), 529; Samuel Eliot Morrison, *The Maritime History of Massachusetts: 1783–1860* (1921; reprint, Boston: Houghton Mifflin, 1961), 367–68.
4. U.S. Department of Labor, Bureau of Labor Statistics, *History of Wages in the United States from Colonial Times to 1928* (Washington, DC: Government Printing Office, 1934), 178, 253, 448, 460.
5. "The Catholic Church of New England," box 8, Boston, Church History folder, BPL-EB.
6. U.S. Department of Labor, *History of Wages in the United States,* 460.
7. Thomas O'Connor, *The Boston Irish: A Political History* (Boston: Back Bay Books, 1995), 99.
8. Kennedy, Bridget (1860 U.S. Census) Massachusetts, Suffolk County, Ward Two, Boston, Mass.
9. Suffolk County Probate and Family Court Administration. Docket 81567. Bridget Kennedy, 1889, Massachusetts Archives, Boston, Mass.

10. Frederick Bushee, "The Growth of the Population of Boston," *Publications of the American Statistical Association* 6 (June 1899): 262, 264.
11. Frederick Bushee, *Ethnic Factors in the Population of Boston* (New York: Macmillan, 1903), 122–23.
12. *BDG,* Dec. 12, 1888, 1; Lois Bannister Merk, "Boston's Historic Public School Crisis," *New England Quarterly* 31 (June 1958): 189–92.
13. John Higham, *Strangers in the Land* (1955; repr., New York: Atheneum, 1971), 101–3.
14. *BDG,* Nov. 18, 1899, 6.
15. *BDG,* Oct. 17, 1893.
16. Duncliffe, "Irish Surge as Pat Pulls Strings," *BRA,* Jan. 7, 1964.
17. *The Fruitful Bough (FB),* collected by Edward M. Kennedy (privately printed, 1965), 8.
18. John F. Murphy, *Up-to-Date Guide Book of Greater Boston* (Boston: John Murray, 1904), 118–19.
19. Loretta Connelly, *FB* folders, EMKP; Max Grossman, "The Life Story of Joseph P. Kennedy," *BSP,* Dec. 12, 1937.
20. *BDG,* Nov. 18, 1899, 6.
21. *BDG,* Feb. 1, 1899; Dec. 13, 22, 1899; Apr. 29, 1902.

TWO: SCHOOL DAYS

1. E. Digby Baltzell, *Puritan Boston and Quaker Philadelphia* (New York: Free Press, 1979), 426.
2. Boston Latin School, *Catalogue,* 1903, 28, BLS.
3. Boston Latin School, *Catalogue,* Oct. 1907, 37–42, BLS.
4. Boston Latin School, *Tercentenary Catalogue,* 1904–1905, 76, BLS.
5. O'Connor, *The Boston Irish,* 266–67.
6. *BDG,* Sept. 21, 1906; Mar. 30, 1907; Pengra, *FB* folders, EMKP.
7. REFK, *Times to Remember (TTR)* (New York: Doubleday, 1974), 17–18; REFK and RC, Jan. 21, 1972, box 10, REFKP.
8. REFK, *TTR,* 49–50.
9. REFK, *TTR,* 50; REFK and RC, Jan. 21, 1972, box 10, REFKP; REFK, *TTR,* 50–51.
10. Charles F. Hennessey, "Prophecy for the Class of 1908," in R. J. Dobbyn to JPK, Jan. 24, 1934, box 34, JPKP.

11. *Boston Latin School Register,* Dec. 1907, 13; May 1908, 14, BLS; *BDG,* June 13, 1908; *BSP,* May 9, 1908.

12. Harvard University, student records, UAIII, 15.88.10, 1890–1968, box 2600, HUA.

13. V. W. Brooks, "Harvard and American Life," *Contemporary Review* 94 (1908): 613; Harvard University, student records, HUA.

14. Seymour Martin Lipset and David Ries- man, *Education and Politics at Harvard* (New York: McGraw-Hill, 1975), 106; *Report of the Committee Appointed to Consider the Advisability of Revising the Present System of Examinations for Admission to Harvard College,* Harvard College Class of 1912, class book, 1913; "List of Secondary Schools, Universities and Colleges . . . from Which Students Have Entered Harvard College During the Years 1901–1910," HUA.

15. Campbell, *FB* folders, EMKP.

16. "1912 Harvard Class Album," HUA.

17. *BDG,* Mar. 19, 1911; Apr. 18, 24, 1911; Campbell, *FB* folders, EMKP.

18. *The H Book of Harvard Athletics, 1852–1922,* ed. John A. Blanchard (Cambridge, MA: Harvard Varsity Club, 1923); Richard Whalen, *The Founding Father* (1964; repr., New York: Regnery, 1993), 4, 27; Kelly, Potter, *FB* folders, EMKP.

19. Kelly, Potter, *FB* folders, EMKP.

20. *BDG,* Nov. 19, 20, 23, 1908.

21. O'Connor, *The Boston Irish,* 178.

22. REFK, *TTR,* 46–47.

23. REFK and RC, Jan. 24, 1972, box 10, REFKP; *BDG,* Jan. 3, 1911.

24. REFK, *TTR,* 51–52.

25. REFK and RC, Feb. 23, 1972, box 10, REFKP; REFK, *TTR,* 51–52.

26. REFK and RC, Jan. 4, 1972, box 10, REFKP; REFK, *TTR,* 54.

27. John B. Kennedy, "Joe Kennedy Has Never Liked Any Job He's Tackled," *American Magazine,* May 1928, 145–46.

28. Cram to P. J. Kennedy, Sept. 30, 1911, Harvard University, student records, UAIII, 15.88.10, 1890–1968, box 2600, HUA.

29. Harvard University, Joseph P. Kennedy, grade card, UAIII 15.75.12 1910–1919, box 12, HUA.

THREE: STARTING OUT

1. REFK, *TTR,* 56.

2. John B. Kennedy, "Joe Kennedy Has . . . ," 146.

3. Naomi Lamoreaux, "Bank Mergers in Late Nineteenth-Century New England," *Journal of Economic History* (Sept. 1991): 547–48; John Gunther, *Inside U.S.A.* (1947; repr., New York: New Press, 1997), 512.

4. O'Meara to JPK, May 15, 1937, box 91, JPKP.

5. Richard Whalen interview with Goldsmith, cited in Laurence Leamer, *The Kennedy Men* (New York: HarperCollins, 2001), 23.

6. JPK to Goldsmith, Apr. 17, 1912, in author's possession.

7. JPK to Goldsmith, n.d., 1913, in author's possession.

8. *BDG,* Apr. 6, 1911.

9. Merrill, *FB* folders, 1964, EMKP.

10. Goldsmith to JPK, n.d., in author's possession.

11. *BDG,* Jan. 3, Mar. 25, Oct. 14, 1913.

12. *BDG,* Dec. 19, 1913.

13. Boston News Bureau, Jan. 21, 1914, 5.

14. JPK to Goldsmith, n.d. [Jan. 1914], in author's possession.

15. "Deny They Gave $1,000," *BDG,* Feb. 13, 1914.

16. Massachusetts Bank Commissioners, *Annual Report of the Bank Commissioners, 1912–1915* (Boston: Commonwealth of Massachusetts, 1912–1915).

17. REFK, *TTR,* 59; "Bars Improper Dancing," *BDG,* Oct. 11, 1913.

18. REFK, *TTR,* 59.

19. REFK interview, Nov. 20, 1967, John Fitzgerald Kennedy National Historic Site resources management records, box 10, Longfellow.

20. REFK, "The Wedding Log," box 1, REFKP.

21. Alexander von Hoffman, *John F. Kennedy's Birthplace: A Presidential Home in History and Memory* (National Park Service, U.S. Department of the Interior, Aug. 2004), 29, 33.

22. Von Hoffman, 109–16, 189–93; Anne Coxe Toogood, *John Fitzgerald Kennedy National Historic Site: Historic Furnishings Plan* (Department of the

Interior, National Park Service, July 31, 1971), 23.

23. REFK and RC, Jan. 7, 1972, box 10, REFKP.

24. On collateral loan scandal, *BDG,* Dec. 3, 4, 5, 11, 1914; "Rowley Collateral Loan Director," Feb. 5, 1914.

25. Massachusetts Bank Commissioners, *Annual Report.*

26. Campbell, *FB* folders, EMKP.

27. JPK notes payable and receivable, 1921–1936, assorted materials, box 42, JPKP.

28. REFK, *TTR,* 62–63.

FOUR: WAR

1. *BDG,* Apr. 8, 1915.

2. REFK, *TTR,* 63.

3. REFK, in Doris Kearns Goodwin, *The Fitzgeralds and the Kennedys* (New York: Simon & Schuster, 1987), 272.

4. John Whiteclay Chambers II, *To Raise an Army: The Draft Comes to Modern America* (New York: Free Press, 1987), 126.

5. JPK draft card, NAUS.

6. *BDG,* Aug. 9, 10, 14, 16, 1917.

7. *BDG,* Oct. 21, 1917; U.S. War Department, *Second Report of the Provost Marshal General to the Secretary of War on the Operations of the Selective Service System to December 20, 1918* (Washington, DC: U.S. War Department, 1919), 45, 62–66; Samuel W. McCall, "Massachusetts in Action," *American Review of Reviews* 57 (May 1918): 506.

8. Powell to JPK, Nov. 14, 1917, box 37, JPKP.

9. *Preliminary Report on Bethlehem Shipbuilding Corp.—Quincy Plant,* July 31 and Aug. 1, 1918, record group 3, Records of the United States Housing Corporation PI-140, entry 39, box 6, NAUS.

10. See correspondence and memorandums in NAUS, record group 3, "Records of the United States Housing Corporation," PI-140, entry 39, box 6; JPK to James Richards, Sept. 9, 1918, Amanda Smith, *Hostage to Fortune: The Letters of Joseph P. Kennedy,* HTF (New York: Viking, 2001), 18–19.

11. Fore River Log 4, no. 3 (Oct. 1918), 15.

12. JPK to District Board No. 5, Feb. 18,

1918; Powell to T. F. Harrington, Feb. 17, 1918; Powell to Meyer Bloomfield, Feb. 25, 1918, box 37, JPKP.

13. *BDG,* Apr. 6, July 27, 1918.

14. *BDG,* Apr. 18, 1918; "Praises Work at Fore River," *BDG,* Aug. 3, 1918.

15. "Fore River Makes a Good Home Start," *BDG,* May 19, 1918.

16. *Forging America: The History of Bethlehem Steel,* chap. 3, http://www.baltimoresun.com/topic/all-bethsteel-c3p13,0,4940413.story; *BDG,* May 14, July 5, 1918; JPK to Joseph Larkin, Sept. 16, 1918, Smith, *HTF,* 19–22.

17. *BDG,* Sept. 6, 17, 21, 1918; REFK, *TTR,* 131.

18. *BDG,* Nov. 8, 1918; John B. Kennedy, "Joe Kennedy Has . . . ," 148.

FIVE: MAKING A MILLION

1. REFK and RC, Jan. 21, 1972, box 10, REFKP.

2. Fenway Building Trust transactions, box 45; bank loans secured by notes, box 42; JPK loans, withdrawn box (hereafter w.b.) 10, JPKP.

3. REFK, *TTR,* 77.

4. Gloria Swanson, *Swanson on Swanson* (New York: Random House, 1980), 344.

5. Coolidge to JPK, Oct. 8, 1920; JPK to Coolidge, Oct. 16, Nov. 26, 1920, box 35, JPKP.

6. REFK and RC, Jan. 24, 1972, box 12, REFKP.

7. REFK, *TTR,* 70, 73–74; REFK and RC, Jan. 20, 21, 1972, box 10, REFKP.

8. Peters to JPK, Feb. 25, 1920, box 36, JPKP; JPK to Place, July 2, 1920, Smith, *HTF,* 24.

9. St. Apollonia Guild, *FB* folders, EMKP.

10. Edwin Place, "Scarlet Fever," *American Journal of Public Health* 4 (September 1914): 772.

11. REFK and RC, Jan. 17, 1972, box 10, REFKP.

12. Von Hoffman, 43–46.

13. Houghton, *FB* folders, EMKP.

14. Armond Fields, *Fred Stone* (Jefferson, NC: McFarland, 2002), 193–94, 202–3; agreement among Gurnett, Kennedy, and Stone, May 2, 1919, box 49; JPK to Wellington, June 29, 1921, box 37, JPKP.

15. "Babe Ruth Signs to Enter Movies," *BDG,* Sept. 6, 1919; JPK and Babe Ruth:

Agreement, n.d.; Robbins to JPK, Oct. 8, 1919; Ruth to JPK, Oct. 31, 1919, box 68, JPKP.

16. David Stoneman to JPK, Nov. 6, 1919; minutes of Columbia Films board, Jan. 7, 1921, and assorted documents, w.b. 31, JPKP.

17. JPK to Treman, Jan. 2, 1920; JPK to E. B. Dane, Jan. 21, 1920, box 68, JPKP.

18. JPK to Hayden, Dec. 4, 1919; memorandum on loan to Frank Hall, June 20, 1920, box 68, JPKP; *NYT*, July 2, 1921.

19. Peters to Houston, Apr. 21, 1920, box 47; Houston to Peters, Apr. 26, 1920; Peters to JPK, Apr. 29, 1920; JPK to Peters, May 7, 1920, box 36, JPKP.

20. Dunphy to JPK, Aug. 11, 1920, box 35, JPKP.

21. JPK to Dunphy, Aug. 12, 23, 1920, box 35, JPKP.

22. JPK to Cole, Aug. 30, 1920, box 48, JPKP.

23. Hunter, Dublin and Company prospectus, 1927, in Janet Wasko, *Movies and Money* (Norwood, NJ: Ablex, 1982), 22.

24. JPK to Cole, Sept. 30, 1920, box 48, JPKP.

25. JPK to Cole, Nov. 19, 30, 1920, box 48, JPKP.

26. JPK to Turner, Dec. 23, 1920, box 37, JPKP.

27. Information on these loans, box 42; Thayer to JPK, June 8, 1921, w.b. 10, JPKP.

28. JPK to Dunphy, Dec. 31, 1920, box 35, JPKP.

29. Grace to JPK, Dec. 30, 1920, Jan. 17, Feb. 2, 1921; JPK to Grace, Jan. 11, 1921, box 37, JPKP.

30. JPK to JF, Jan. 21, 1921, box 48, JPKP.

31. Crum to JPK, Mar. 27, 1921, box 48, JPKP.

32. JPK to Thayer, Mar. 28, 1921, box 45, JPKP.

33. Graham's of London to JPK, June 21, 1921, box 48, JPKP.

34. JPK to Granville MacFarland, June 18, 1921; JPK to Godsol, June 17, 27, 30, 1921; JPK to Hurd, July 26, 1921; JPK to Hodkinson, Dec. 31, 1921, Jan. 12, 1922, box 48, JPKP.

35. JPK to Schnitzer, July 13, 1922, box 48, JPKP.

36. JPK to S. R. Kent, May 3, 1922, w.b. 31, JPKP.

37. JPK to Hays, Sept. 28, 1922, box 48, JPKP.

38. JPK to Franklin, Sept. 28, 1922, box 48; JPK to Yamins, Dec. 1, 1922, box 43; memorandum, Jan. 11, 1923, box 42, JPKP.

39. REFK, "Married Life," box 12, REFKP.

40. JPK to Murray, Aug. 15, 1921, Smith, *HTF 29*.

41. JPK to Houghton, Sept. 19, 1921, Smith, *HTF, 30–31*.

42. JPK to Turner, Aug. 16, 1921, box 37, JPKP.

43. JPK to Brush, June 24, 1922, box 45, JPKP; JPK to Thayer, Feb. 14, 1921, Smith, *HTF, 27*.

44. REFK, "Married Life," box 12, REFKP.

45. Haussermann, *FB* folders, EMKP.

46. JPK to Brush, June 24, 26, 29, 1922, box 45, JPKP.

47. JPK to Potter, Aug. 17, 1920, w.b. 23; Albert Garceau to JPK, Nov. 2, 1920; JPK to Turner, Dec. 1, 1921, box 37; "duplicate inventory," w.b. 23, JPKP.

48. Canada Royal Commission on Customs and Excise, *Royal Commission on Customs and Excise Interim Reports*, Joseph Kennedy Ltd., dissolved company file BC7534, Oct. 18, 1931, GR-1526 (B05158), British Columbia Archives.

49. Daniel Okrent, *Last Call: The Rise and Fall of Prohibition* (New York: Scribner, 2010), 366–71.

50. Information on 25 Sheldon Road home, Cohasset Historical Society, Cohasset, Massachusetts; Dean to Fisher, May 7, 1922, box 35, JPKP.

51. REFK and RC, Jan. 7, 1972, box 10, REFKP.

SIX: "MY OWN MASTER IN MY OWN BUSINESS"

1. *BDG*, July 11, 1921.

2. Miss F. to Guy, Jan. 5, 1922, box 48, JPKP.

3. REFK and RC, Jan. 4, 1972, box 10, REFKP.

4. REFK, diary, 1923, box 1, REFKP

5. REFK to JPK, n.d., box 1, JPKP.

6. REFK to JPK, n.d., box 1, JPKP.

7. JPK to REFK, Apr. 8, 1923, box 1, JPKP.
8. JPK to REFK, Apr. 15, 1923, box 1, JPKP.
9. REFK, diary, 1923, box 1, REFKP.
10. John B. Kennedy, "Joe Kennedy Has . . . ," 148.
11. Minutes of Columbia Advertising, Feb. 1924, box 37, JPKP.
12. JPK to Fitzgibbon, Jan. 2, 1924, Mar. 24, 1925, box 37, JPKP.
13. JPK to Brush, Dec. 14, 1923, Smith, *HTF,* 40.
14. JPK to John Borden, June 19, 1924, Smith, *HTF,* 42.
15. Hank Searls, *The Lost Prince* (New York: Ballantine Books, 1969), 39–40.
16. REFK, *TTR,* 132–34; REFK, autobiography notes, box 10, REKFP.
17. REFK, *TTR,* 120–21.
18. Cari Beauchamp, *Joseph P. Kennedy Presents* (New York: Alfred A. Knopf, 2009), 66.
19. JPK to Turner, Apr. 6, 15, May 6, July 2, 1925, box 37, JPKP; REFK, "Married Life," box 12, REFKP.
20. JPK to REFK, Aug. 17, 18, 1925, box 1, JPKP.
21. JPK to REFK, family, Aug. 23, 1925; JPK to JFK, Sept. 1, 1925, Smith, *HTF,* 44–45.
22. JPK to REFK, Sept. 6, 1925, box 55, REFKP.
23. Terry Ramsaye, "Intimate Visits to the Homes of Famous Film Magnates," *Photoplay,* Sept. 1927, 50.
24. JPK to William Gray, Feb. 5, 1926, box 69; Byrnes to JPK, Feb. 8, 1926; JPK to Byrnes, Feb. 9, 1926, box 68, JPKP.
25. JPK to Schnitzer, Feb. 11, 1926, box 48, JPKP, Beauchamp, *Joseph P. Kennedy Presents,* 73–74.
26. John B. Kennedy, "Joe Kennedy Has . . . , 148.
27. Gray to JPK, Mar. 6, 1926, w.b. 31, JPKP.
28. JPK to Quigley, [Aug.] 20, 1926, Martin J. Quigley Papers, special collections, Georgetown University Library.
29. Scollard to Silverman, Feb. 6, 1930, w.b. 31, JPKP.
30. Frances Marion, *Off With their Heads!* (New York: Macmillan, 1972), 90–91.
31. Beauchamp, *Joseph P. Kennedy Presents,* 82–83.
32. Garth Jowett, *Film: The Democratic Art* (Boston: Little, Brown & Co., 1976), 87–88.
33. *BDG,* Aug. 4, 1926.
34. REFK, "Married Life," box 12; REFK and RC, Feb. 23, 1972, box 1, REFKP.
35. JPK to JPK, Jr., July 13, 1926, box 1, JPKP.
36. JPK to JPK, Jr., July 28, 1926, box 1, JPKP.
37. Beaverbrook to JPK, July 23, 1926, box 48, JPKP; *BDG,* Sept. 29, 1926.
38. *MPW,* Oct. 16, 1926.
39. *MPW,* Dec. 11, 1926.
40. JPK to W. B. Dunham, Apr. 27, 1927, box 49, JPKP.
41. JPK to Hays, Jan. 22, 1927, box 49, JPKP.
42. JPK to Zukor, Jan. 22, 1927; JPK to Kent, Jan. 22, 1927, box 49, JPKP.
43. DeMille to JPK, Feb. 25, 1927, JPK to DeMille, Mar. 18, 1927, box 285, folder 7, DeMille.
44. JPK to Hays, May 6, 1927, box 49, JPKP.
45. Cari Beauchamp, *Without Lying Down* (Berkeley: University of California Press, 1997), 162–64, 188; Marion, *Off With Their Heads!* 166.
46. J. W. Powell to Lackey, June 7, 1927; Powell to Buchanan, June 10, 1927, box 48, JPKP.
47. Ramsaye, "Intimate Visits to the Homes of Famous Film Magnates," 50.
48. REFK, "Married Life," box 12, REFKP.
49. RC and REFK, Jan. 4, 1972, box 10, REFKP.

SEVEN: HOLLYWOOD

1. REFK, autobiography notes, box 10, REFKP.
2. Brian Burns to author, Apr. 22, 2010.
3. REFK, "Married Life," box 12, REFKP; JPK to Thomson, Sept. 20, 1927, Smith, *HTF,* 54.
4. Student records, school photos, Riverdale.
5. JPK to Julian Johnson, Sept. 30, 1927; JPK to Motion Picture Commission, State of New York, Oct. 14, 1927, box 51, JPKP.
6. Beauchamp, *Joseph P. Kennedy Presents,* 166–67.
7. Kane to JPK, Nov. 7, box 55, JPKP.
8. Swanson, *Swanson on Swanson,* 327–33.

9. GS, notes, box 270, folder 7, Swanson.

10. Beauchamp, *Joseph P. Kennedy Presents,* 125.

11. Joseph P. Kennedy, ed., *The Story of the Films* (Chicago: A. W. Shaw Co., 1927), 16–17.

12. Richard Koszarski, *An Evening's Entertainment* (1990; repr., Berkeley: University of California Press, 1994), 262.

13. JPK to Milton Cohen, Dec. 20, 1927, box 55, JPKP.

14. Sarnoff, *FB* folders, EMKP.

15. Derr to JPK, Jan. 25, 1928, w.b. 29; Derr to Moore, Jan. 31, 1928, box 55, JPKP.

16. GS, notes, box 270, folder 7, Swanson.

17. Derr to JPK, Feb. 10, 1928, box 55, JPKP; FBO Studios, memorandum, n.d., box 114, folder 2, Swanson.

18. "Pathé A stock" memorandum, box 63, JPKP.

19. LeBaron to REFK, n.d., box 130, REFKP.

20. Memorandum headed Pathé Exchange Inc., n.d., w.b. 30, JPKP.

21. Murdock to JPK, Feb. 15, 1928, box 63, JPKP; *FD,* Feb. 15, 1928; *V,* Feb. 22, 1928.

22. DeMille to JPK, draft, n.d., CBDMA XII, Cecil B. DeMille Productions, correspondence, box 778, DeMille.

23. JPK to Walker, Mar. 23, 1928, box 63, JPKP.

24. Swanson, *Swanson on Swanson,* 342, 359.

25. GS, notes, box 7, folder 7, Swanson.

26. Swanson, *Swanson on Swanson,* 344.

27. GS, notes, box 270, folder 7, Swanson.

28. Walker to JPK, May 9, 1928; JPK to Albee, May 10, 1928, box 63, JPKP; "Deal Book," Radio-Keith-Orpheum Corporation, 1928, Lehman.

29. JPK to Ford, two letters, July 2, 1928, Smith, *HTF,* 76.

30. *LAT,* May 23, 1928; *EHMPW,* Aug. 4, 1928.

31. *EHMPW,* May 19, 1928.

32. Richard Koszarski, *Von* (1983; repr., New York: Limelight, 2002), 236; JPK to Mayer, May 25, 1928, Smith, *HTF,* 74–75.

33. *V,* June 16, 1928.

34. Carr, *LAT,* July 22, 1928.

35. *FD,* July 23, 24, 1928.

36. *FD,* July 22, 1928.

37. Memorandum of conference, July 24, 1928, box 63, JPKP.

38. *FD,* Aug. 19, 1928.

39. *FD,* Aug. 5, 1928.

40. *NYT,* Aug. 11, 1928; "Points for Consideration," Aug. 9, 1928, box 68, JPKP.

41. *FD,* Aug. 12, 1928.

42. Rossheim to JPK, Aug. 15, 1928, box 68, JPKP.

43. *LAT,* Aug. 19, 1928.

44. *FD,* Aug. 23, 1928.

EIGHT: GLORIA AND ROSE

1. Thomas Carens, "A New Mogul of the Movies," *NYHT,* Sunday Magazine, Sept. 16, 1928, 8.

2. "Address by Joseph P. Kennedy," Sept. 30, 1928, box 68, JPKP.

3. Sarnoff to JPK, Nov. 5, 1928; JPK to Sarnoff, Nov. 6, 1928, box 64, JPKP.

4. *BDG,* Oct. 25, 1928.

5. Film Booking Office and Keith-Albee-Orpheum memos, w.b. 30; statements, w.b. 12, JPKP.

6. Pathé Exchange, Inc., memorandums, n.d., w.b. 30, JPKP.

7. Trial balances, 1926, withdrawn oversize box 3.6.1; trial balances, 1929, w.b. 8, JPKP.

8. EMK to author, Aug. 21, 2007; Leo Damore, *The Cape Cod Years of John Fitzgerald Kennedy* (Englewood Cliffs, NJ: Prentice-Hall, 1967), 21.

9. Edward M. Kennedy, *True Compass* (*TC*) (New York: Twelve, 2009), 31.

10. REFK, *TTR,* 145; *NYT,* June 6, 1929; EMK, *TC,* 37, 39–40.

11. JKS to author, July 15, 2008.

12. FDR to JPK, Sept. 13, 1928, box 36, JPKP.

13. REFK and RC, Jan. 6, 1972, box 10, REFKP; JPK to Adams, Apr. 13, 1929, Smith, *HTF,* 83.

14. *LAT,* Oct. 21, 1928.

15. Derr to JPK, Dec. 6, 1928, box 57, JPKP.

16. Scollard to Mark Markoff, Jan. 8, 1929, box 56, JPKP; Swanson, *Swanson on Swanson,* 372.

17. GS to JPK, Jan. 21, 1929, box 56, JPKP.

18. GS, notes, box 270, folder 10, Swanson.

19. Derr to Moore, Jan. 25, 1929, Smith, *HTF,* 78–81.

20. Derr to Scollard, Feb. 15, 1929, w.b. 29, JPKP.

21. GS, notes, box 270, folder 7, Swanson.

22. JPK to Marquis de la Falaise, Mar. 13, 1929, Smith, *HTF,* 81–82.

23. Bill Yen, *Santa Fe Chiefs* (St. Paul, MN: MBI, 1905), 41, 46.

24. JPK to GS, Apr. 23, 1929, box 56, JPKP.

25. JPK to Marquis de la Falaise, Apr. 15, 1929, box 57, JPKP.

26. Assorted memorandums, w.b. 30; "Agreement Made as of the 1st Day of April, 1929 . . . Pathé," box 63, JPKP.

27. JPK to JPK, Jr., June 3, 1929, Smith, *HTF,* 84.

28. JPK to JFK, June 3, 1929, Smith, *HTF,* 85.

29. JPK to Watson [Swanson], n.d., box 100, folder 15, Swanson.

30. Swanson, *Swanson on Swanson,* 383.

31. Swanson, *Swanson on Swanson,* 388–89; REFK, "Married Life," box 12, REFKP.

32. GS, notes, box 270, folder 8, Swanson.

33. REFK to RC, Jan. 4, 1972, box 10, REFKP.

34. KKH to REFK, Feb. 12, 1932, box 1, JPKP.

35. REFK, *TTR,* 101–2; Crossman to GS, Dec. 26, 1929, box 33, folder 8, Swanson.

36. GS, notes, n.d., box 270, folder 8, Swanson; Swanson, *Swanson on Swanson,* 392–95.

37. GS, "Joe Rosebud," n.d., box 271, folder 6, Swanson.

NINE: LAST EXIT FROM HOLLYWOOD

1. REFK, *TTR,* 145; JPK to JPK, Jr., June 3, 1929, Smith, *HTF,* 84.

2. REFK, *TTR,* 147.

3. JPK to W. St. John, Apr. 20, 1929, in Nigel Hamilton, *JFK: Reckless Youth* (New York: Random House, 1992), 82.

4. St. John to JPK, May 20, 1929, box 20, JPKP.

5. JPK to JPK, Jr., Oct. 1, 1929, box 1, JPKP.

6. REFK, *TTR,* 134.

7. Janice Brockley, "Rearing the Child Who Never Grew," in *Mental Retardation in America: A Historical Reader,* ed. Steven Noll and James W. Trent, Jr. (New York: New York University Press, 2004), 139–40, 144–45.

8. JKS to author, Apr. 27, 2009; REFK, *TTR,* 132–35.

9. "Helen Devereux biography," http://www.devereux.org/site/DocServer/ HTDBio.pdf?docID=281.

10. JPK to RK, Nov. 13, 1929, box 1, JPKP.

11. Report on Rosemary Kennedy, June 23, 1930, w.b. 3, JPKP.

12. Report on Rosemary Kennedy, Nov. 21, 1930, w.b. 3, JPKP.

13. REFK, diary notes, box 10, REFKP; EKS, in REFK, *TTR,* 133.

14. Classified ad, *NYT,* Oct. 31, 1929.

15. Assorted statements, w.b. 30; JPK to Keating, Nov. 1, 1929, Smith, *HTF,* 87.

16. *V,* Mar. 12, 1930.

17. *V,* May 7, 1930.

18. GS to JPK, Oct. 21, 1930, box 56, JPKP; JPK to GS, Oct. 19, 1932, box 101, folder 10; JPK to GS, June 26, 1944; GS to JPK, JPK to GS, various telegrams, Sept. to Dec. 1935, box 33, folder 8; Phil [Reisman] to JPK, Feb. 9, 1951, box 32, folder 5, Swanson.

19. R. Lawrence Siegel to GS, Feb. 11, 1957; Siegel to JPK, Mar. 6, 1957, box 56, folder 1, Swanson.

20. JPK to GS, Mar. 15, 1957, box 202, folder 15, Swanson.

21. GS to JPK, n.d., box 33, folder 8, Swanson.

22. Siegel to GS, Mar. 26, 1957, box 56, folder 1; GS to JPK, n.d., box 33, folder 8, Swanson.

23. Brown to Sarnoff, Oct. 8, 24, 1930, box 64, JPKP.

24. JPK to Walker, Dec. 4, 1930, box 64, JPKP.

25. JPK to Murdock, Dec. 9, 1930, box 64, JPKP.

26. Lawler to JPK, Dec. 30, 1930, box 64, JPKP.

27. JPK to Walsh, Dec. 19, 1930, box 64, JPKP.

28. Assorted letters, anonymous to JPK, [Dec. 1930], box 63, JPKP.

29. *NYT,* Jan. 6, 1931.

30. Pathé Exchange, Inc., 7% bonds, box 63; Pathé stock memo, w.b. 30; 1931–1932 statements, J. H. Holmes, Sept. 14–18, 1931, w.b. oversize, series 3.6.2, JPKP.

31. JFK to JPK, n.d., Smith, *HTF,* 94–95.

32. JKS to author, July 16, 2008; EMK, *TC,* 68.

33. REFK and RC, Jan. 6, 21, 1972, box 10, REFKP.

TEN: ON THE ROOSEVELT TRAIN

1. Anthony J. Badger, *The New Deal: The Depression Years, 1933–1940* (New York: Hill & Wang, 1989), 14, 2–22; John Kenneth Galbraith, *The Great Crash* (1955; New York: Houghton Mifflin, 1997), 141, 151.
2. Information on JPK's accounts found in w.b. 8–10, JPKP.
3. JFK to REFK and JPK, Dec. 6, 1931; JFK to JPK, Dec. 9, 1931, box 1, JPKP.
4. JPK to JFK, Apr. 12, 1932, box 1, JPKP.
5. JPK to Schulberg, Nov. 29, 1931, box 68; JPK to Poppe, Dec. 30, 1931, box 68; Gurnett to JPK, Mar. 9, 1931, box 37, JPKP.
6. Assorted statements, w.b. 8, JPKP.
7. Joseph P. Kennedy, *I'm for Roosevelt* (New York: Reynal & Hitchcock, 1936), 3.
8. Steve Fraser, *Every Man a Speculator* (New York: HarperCollins, 2005), 413, 415.
9. Arthur Schlesinger, Jr., *The Crisis of the Old Order: 1919–1933* (Boston: Houghton Mifflin, 1957), 206.
10. Joe McCarthy, *The Remarkable Kennedys* (New York: Popular Library, 1960), 46.
11. William E. Leuchtenburg, *Franklin D. Roosevelt and the New Deal* (New York: Harper, 1963), 4.
12. JPK to WRH, Apr. 19, 1982; WRH to JPR Apr. 19, 30, 1932, box 7, Hearst.
13. *NYT,* May 9, 10, 1932.
14. JPK to WRH, May 10, 1932, box 7, Hearst.
15. REFK and RC, Jan. 4, 1972, box 10, REFKP.
16. *NYT,* July 14, 1932; statements, w.b. 8, JPKP.
17. Raymond Moley, *The First New Deal* (New York, Harcourt, Brace & World, 1966), 379.
18. Wheeler, *FB* folders, EMKP; Schlesinger, *Crisis of the Old Order,* 300.
19. Roy Howard to Newton Baker, July 12, 1932, box 122, Baker; WRH to Millicent Hearst, July 3, 1932, carton 12, Hearst.
20. *NYT,* July 11, 12, 13, 1932.

21. St. John to JPK, June 14, 1932, box 20, JPKP.
22. JKS to author, Oct. 19, 2009.
23. EMK to author, Aug. 21, 2007.
24. JPK, Jr., to JPK, Jan. 26, 1930, Smith, *HTF,* 89; JKS to author, Oct. 19, 2009.
25. FDR to JPK, Aug. 23, 1932, in *FDR: His Personal Letters,* ed. Elliott Roosevelt (New York: Duell, Sloan & Pearce, 1947–1950), 3:294.
26. JPK to Giannini, Sept. 8, 1932, Smith, *HTF,* 98–9; JPK to WRH, Sept. 6, 1932, box 7, Hearst.
27. *NYT,* Sept. 9, 1932; James L. Wright, "Joe Kennedy Sits in Inner Circle," *BSG,* Sept. 25, 1932.
28. James Roosevelt, *FB* folders, EMKP.
29. Wright, *BSG,* Sept. 25, 1932.
30. Moley, *First New Deal,* 380; Dowling, oral history, 311–12, CUOH.
31. Farley and Walker to JPK, Sept. 16, 1932, box 72, JPKP.
32. Wright, *BSG,* Sept. 25, 1932.
33. Jack Warner, with Dean Jennings, *My First Hundred Years in Hollywood* (New York: Random House, 1965), 215–16; Jack Warner, *FB* folders, EMKP.
34. JPK, Jr., to REFK, Oct. 9, 1932, Smith, *HTF,* 99.
35. On campaign contributions, w.b. 31, JPKP; Louise Overacker, "American Government and Politics: Campaign Funds in a Depression Year," *American Political Science Review* (October 1933), 778–79.
36. JPK to WRH, Oct. 19, 1932, box 7, Hearst.
37. FDR to JPK, Oct. 24, 1932, box 70, JPKP; Raymond Moley, *After Seven Years* (New York: Harper & Brothers, 1939), 63.
38. JPK to Elliott Roosevelt, [Nov. 10, 1932], Smith, *HTF,* 101–2.

ELEVEN: WAITING FOR THE CALL

1. WRH to JPK, Nov. 14, 15, Hearst.
2. *NYT,* Nov. 20, 1932; Hays to JPK, Nov. 9, 1932, box 70, JPKP.
3. JPK to Hiram Brown, box 70, JPKP.
4. Moley, *First New Deal,* 381; REFK, "Married Life," box 12, REFKP; Frank Friedel, *FDR: Launching the New Deal,* (Boston: Little, Brown & Co., 1973) 138; Democratic National Committee papers, box 460, FDRL.

5. JPK to Willicombe, Dec. 1, 1932, box 7, Hearst.

6. JPK to WRH, Dec. 14, 24, 1932, box 7, Hearst.

7. WRH to JPK, Dec. 28, 1932, box 7, Hearst; JPK to FDR, Dec. 29, 1932, box 70, JPKP.

8. Moley, *First New Deal,* 381.

9. E. J. Kahn, Jr., *The World of Swope* (New York: Simon & Schuster, 1965), 378–79.

10. Schlesinger, *Crisis of the Old Order,* 457.

11. JPK to FDR, Mar. 14, 1933, Smith, *HTF,* 116.

12. FDR to JFK, Mar. 29, 1933, PPF 227, FDRL.

13. JPK to JFK, Feb. 10, 1933, Smith, *HTF,* 116.

14. Details of sale, w.b. 23, JPKP.

15. FDR to JPK, May 11, 1933, PPF 207, FDRL.

16. JPK to FDR, May 19, 1933, Smith, *HTF,* 117.

17. Moley, *First New Deal,* 381–82.

18. Warburg, oral history, vol. 3, 233, 407, 410, CUOH.

19. U.S. Congress, U.S. Senate, "Hearings Before the Committee on Banking and Currency," 73rd Cong., 2nd sess., 1933, 6,218–46.

20. Consolidated balance statement, Dec. 31, 1933, w.b. 9, JPKP.

21. James Roosevelt, with Bill Libby, *My Parents: A Differing View* (New York: Playboy Press, 1976), 210; Ronald Weir, *The History of the Distillers Company, 1877–1939* (Oxford: Clarendon Press, 1995), 280; Alva Johnson, "'Jimmy's Got It,'" *Saturday Evening Post,* July 2, 1938.

22. JPK to JPK, Jr., Nov. 21, Dec. 4, 1933, box 1, JPKP; Weir, *History of the Distillers Company,* 280.

23. Murphy to JPK, Sept. 19, 1940, w.b. 32; abstract of trust agreements, w.b. 22, JPKP.

24. REFK, *TTR,* 145.

25. KKH to JPK, Jan. 8, 1934, Smith, *HTF,* 123.

26. JPK to JPK, Jr., Nov. 21, 1933, box 1, JPKP.

27. JPK to G. St. John, Nov. 21, 1933, Smith, *HTF,* 120.

28. G. St. John to JPK, Nov. 27, 1933, box 20, JPKP.

29. Michael O'Brien, *John F. Kennedy* (New York: Thomas Dunne Books, 2005), 70; JPK to JPK, Jr., Feb. 14, 1934, Smith, *HTF,* 126.

30. Krock, "Sweeping Changes," *NYT,* Nov. 12, 1933.

31. JPK to FF, Dec. 5, 1933, Smith, *HTF,* 121–220.

32. FF, oral history, JFKOHP; Isaac Kramnick and Barry Sheerman, *Harold Laski: A Life on the Left* (New York: Penguin Press, 1993), 187, 309.

33. JPK to JPK, Jr., Feb. 14, 1934, Smith, *HTF,* 126–27; JPK to JPK, Jr., Feb. 21, JPK, Jr., to JPK, Feb. 23, 1934, box 1, JPKP.

34. JPK to JPK, Jr., Feb. 14, 1934, Smith, *HTF,* 126–27.

35. Cited in Deborah E. Lipstadt, *Beyond Belief* (New York: Free Press, 1986), 14.

36. JPK, Jr., to JPK, Apr. 23, 1934, Smith, *HTF,* 130–31.

37. JPK to JPK, Jr., May 4, 1934, Smith, *HTF,* 133–35.

38. JPK to FF, Feb. 14, 1934, Smith, *HTF,* 124–25.

TWELVE: TO WASHINGTON

1. *Time,* Feb. 26, 1934.

2. JPK to FF, Feb. 14, 1934, Smith, *HTF,* 124; FF to JPK, Mar. 19, 1934, box 37, JPKP.

3. JPK, memorandum, n.d., Smith, *HTF,* 127–29.

4. JPK to JPK, Jr., May 4, 1934, Smith, *HTF,* 133–36.

5. JPK to Louis Ruppel, May 18, 1934, box 71, JPKP.

6. Harold Ickes, *The Secret Diary of Harold L. Ickes* (New York, Simon & Schuster, 1953), 1:172.

7. Corcoran to FF, May 11, 1934, http://www.sechistorical.org/museum/papers/1930.

8. Moley, *After Seven Years,* 286.

9. REFK, "Married Life," box 12, REFKP.

10. Arthur M. Schlesinger, Jr., *The Coming of the New Deal* (1958: Boston: Houghton Mifflin, 1988), 468; Dowling, oral history, 366–67, CUOH; JPK, memorandum, n.d., Smith, *HTF,* 137.

11. JPK, memorandum, n.d., Smith, *HTF,* 136–39; Moley, *After Seven Years,* 288.

12. *New Republic,* July 11, 18, 1934.
13. Sullivan to Swope, Aug. 1, 1934, w.b. 1, JPKP.
14. Ronald Steele, *Walter Lippmann and the American Century* (Boston: Little Brown & Co., 1980), 200–201.
15. Arthur Krock, *Memoirs* (New York: Funk & Wagnalls, 1968), 330–32.
16. S. J. Woolf, *NYT,* Aug. 12, 1934; JPK, as told to John B. Kennedy, "Shielding the Sheep," *Saturday Evening Post,* Jan. 18, 1936, 61, 64.
17. *News-Week,* Aug. 4, 1934, 28; *Time,* July 22, 1935, 43, Mark Walston, "Riverside Palace," *Bethesda Magazine,* March–April, 2009.
18. REFK, "Married Life," box 12, REFKP.
19. Krock, memorandum, July 1, 1936, box 1, vol. 1, 64–66, Krock.
20. Assorted letters, box 76; ER to Moore, Nov. 22, 1934, box 80, JPKP.
21. Milton Freeman, in *The Making of the New Deal*, ed. Katie Louchheim and Jonathan Dembo (Cambridge, MA: Harvard University Press, 1983), 142.
22. William O. Douglas, *Go East, Young Man: The Early Years* (New York: Random House, 1973), 258–59.
23. Freeman, in *The Making of the New Deal,* 141–42.
24. Douglas, *Go East, Young Man,* 269; Freeman, in *The Making of the New Deal,* 141.
25. Swope to JPK, July 24, 1934, http://www.sechistorical.org/museum/papers/1930.
26. JPK, "Address . . . at National Press Club," July 25, 1934, http://www.sechistorical.org/museum/papers/1930.
27. "Topics in Wall Street," *NYT,* July 26, 1934, *NYT;* Swope to JPK, July 25, 1934, http://www.sechistorical.org/museum/papers/1930; Berle to JPK, July 30, 1934, box 8, Berle.
28. "First Annual Report . . . June 30, 1935," http://www.sechistorical.org/museum/papers/1930.
29. EMK, *TC,* 34; REFK and RC, Jan. 4, 1972, box 10, REFKP.
30. JPK to Father Nilus McAllister, Oct. 2, 1934, Smith, *HTF,* 142.
31. JPK to JPK, Jr., Oct. 2, 1934, Mar. 14, May 2, 1935, box 1, JPKP; JPK to JPK, Jr., Dec. 7, 1934, Smith, *HTF,* 147.
32. JPK to JPK, Jr., Oct. 2, 1934, box 1, JPKP; JPK to FF Oct. 9, 1934, Smith, *HTF,* 143–34.
33. JPK to JPK, Jr., Mar. 14, 1935, box 1, JPKP.
34. Newton to REFK, n.d., w.b. 3, JPKP.
35. JPK to JPK, Jr., Oct. 2, 1934; JPK to JFK, Oct. 10, 1934, box 1, JPKP.
36. JPK to Newton, Oct. 14, 1934, Smith, *HTF,* 145–46; RK to JPK, Oct. 15, 1934, Smith, *HTF,* 146.
37. JPK to Newton, Oct. 15, 1934, Smith, *HTF,* 145; JPK to Good, Oct. 15, 1934; Good to JPK, Oct. 18, 1934, w.b. 3, JPKP.
38. Good to JPK, Oct. 24, 1934, w.b. 3, JPKP.
39. JPK to Lawrence, Nov. 21, 1934, w.b. 3, JPKP.
40. JFK to JPK, Dec. 2, 1934; JPK to JFK, Dec. 5, 1934, Smith, *HTF,* 146–47.
41. KKH to JFK, n.d., in Hamilton, *JFK,* 126.
42. G. St. John to JPK, Feb. 9, 1935; JPK to G. St. John, Feb. 16, 1935, in Hamilton, *JFK,* 126.
43. JPK to KKH, Feb. 20, 1935, Smith, *HTF,* 151.
44. JPK to JFK, Apr. 29, 1935, box 1, JPKP.
45. Thomas K. McCraw, *Prophets of Regulation* (Cambridge, MA: Harvard University Press, 1984), 165; Douglas, *Go East, Young Man,* 273–74.
46. JPK, "Shielding the Sheep," 68; JPK, "Address . . . at Union League Club of Chicago, Illinois," Feb. 8, 1935, http://www.sechistorical.org/museum/papers/1930.
47. "Address of Hon. Joseph P. Kennedy . . . at Union League Club of Chicago, Illinois," Feb. 5, 1935, http://www.sechistorical.org/museum/papers/1930.
48. "Address of Hon. Joseph P. Kennedy . . . Before American Arbitration Association, New York City," Mar. 19, 1935, http://www.sechistorical.org/museum/papers/1930.
49. *NYT,* Mar. 20, 1935.
50. JPK to FDR, FDR to JPK, Feb. 19, 1935, OF 229, FDRL.
51. JPK to BB, Apr. 26, 1935, box 79, JPKP.
52. Ickes, *Secret Diary,* 1:203, 206.

53. JPK to JFK, Apr. 26, 1935, box 1, JPKP.
54. Arthur Schlesinger, Jr., *The Politics of Upheaval* (Boston: Houghton Mifflin, 1960), 345.
55. Coblentz to WRH, May 9, 1935, outgoing box 1, Coblentz.
56. WRH to Coblentz, May 15, 1935, box 4, Coblentz.
57. FDR to JPK, May 15, 1935, PPF 207, FDRL.
58. Edmond D. Coblentz, ed., *William Randolph Hearst: A Portrait in His Own Words* (New York: Simon & Schuster, 1953), 179–80.
59. JPK to Howe, Feb. 14, 1935, http://www.sechistorical.org/museum/papers/1930.
60. JPK to Rayburn, June 28, 1935, Smith, *HTF,* 154.
61. JPK to FDR, July 2, 1935, JPK to Wheeler, July 8, 1935, JPK to Pettengill, July 12, 1935; Pettengill to JPK, July 10, 15, 1935, http://www.sechistorical.org/museum/papers/1930.
62. JPK to Swope, July 13, 1935, http://www.sechistorical.org/museum/papers/1930.
63. FDR to JPK, July 11, 1935, box 71, JPKP.
64. JPK to FDR, Sept. 6, 1935, OF 1060, FDRL.
65. Robert S. Gallagher, "The Radio Priest," *American Heritage,* Oct. 1972.
66. Pearson and Allen, Sept. 3, 1935, http://www.aladin.wrlc.org/gsdl/collect/pearson/pearson.shtml.
67. *Time,* July 22, 1935; *Literary Digest,* Aug. 24, 1935.
68. *WSJ,* Sept. 25, 1935.

THIRTEEN: REELECTING ROOSEVELT

1. FDR to Bingham, Emmet, Dodd, Long, Straus, Sept. 23, 1935, PPF 207, FDRL; Krock letters, box 70, JPKP.
2. BB to Churchill, Sept. 25, 1935, 2/237, CHAR.
3. Hamilton, *JFK,* 141.
4. JPK to Bingham, JPK to JFK, Nov. 11, 1935, Smith, *HTF,* 164.
5. JFK to JPK, May 9, 1936, w.b. 1, JPKP.
6. JPK to Delmar Leighton, Aug. 28, 1936, in Smith, *HTF,* 187–88.
7. RFK, "Married Life," box 12; "Joe Kennedy's Friends," box 7, REFKP.
8. KKH to RFK, Feb. 8, 1936, Smith, *HTF,* 172–73.
9. Hamilton, *JFK,* 142; JPK, Jr., to JPK, n.d.; JPK to JPK, Jr., Feb. 27, 1936, Smith, *HTF,* 176.
10. JPK to JPK, Jr., Feb. 27, 1936, Smith, *HTF,* 176.
11. RK to RFK and JPK, Jan. 12, 1936, Smith, *HTF,* 167–68.
12. JPK to KKH, Jan. 20, 1936, Smith, *HTF,* 170.
13. JPK to EKS, Feb. 11, 1936, Smith, *HTF,* 174.
14. JPK to RFK, Jan. 11, 1936, Smith, *HTF,* 167.
15. JPK to EKS, PKL, JKS, Feb. 27, 1936; JPK to RFK, EMK, Feb. 27, 1936, Smith, *HTF,* 177.
16. Correspondence between JPK and JB, box 70, JPKP; JPK to McCormick, Jan. 31, 1936, Smith, *HTF,* 171.
17. LeHand to JPK, Aug. 5, 1936, JPKP.
18. JPK to LeHand, Feb. 17, 1937; JR to JPK, Feb. 19, 1937, JR; FDR to JPK, Mar. 18, 1937, PPF 207, FDRL.
19. JPK to FDR, Jan. 20, 1936, Smith, *HTF,* 169–70.
20. JPK, *I'm for Roosevelt,* 7.
21. Block to JPK, Apr. 10, 1936, box 69, JPKP.
22. Morgenthau, diaries, transcript of telephone conversation, vol. 22, Apr. 28, 1936, Morgenthau.
23. JPK to LeHand, May 4, 1936; FDR to JPK, June 17, 1936, PPF 207, FDRL.
24. JPK to Krock, June 24, Aug. 19, 1936, box 70, JPKP; Krock, *Memoirs,* 331–32.
25. *BSG,* July 26, 1936.
26. Muriel Palmer to author, Apr. 12–13, 2010.
27. JPK to Allen, Aug. 8, 1936, Smith, *HTF,* 186–87.
28. Ruppel to JPK, Aug. 4, 25, 1936, box 71, JPKP.
29. JPK to Campbell, Oct. 1, 1936, letters of congratulation, box 70, JPKP.
30. JPK, *I'm for Roosevelt,* 106.
31. Corcoran to JPK, Sept. 21, 1936, box 70; JR to JPK, Sept. 18, 1936, box 71; Early to JPK, Oct. 7, 1936, box 71, JPKP.
32. Ruppel to JPK, Oct. 2, 1936; JPK to Ruppel, Oct. 9, 1936, box 71, JPKP.
33. Pearson to JPK, Oct. 7, 1936, box 71, JPKP.

34. JPK to Bingham, Oct. 6, 1936, box 69, JPKP.

35. JPK, Oct. 24, 1936, radio address, box 75, JPKP.

36. JPK to Marx, Oct. 27, 1936, box 70; JPK to Byrnes, Oct. 30, 1936, series 2 senatorial, box 47, Byrnes.

37. Galeazzi, *FB* folders, EMKP; EMK, *TC*, 42.

FOURTEEN: MARITIME COMMISSIONER

1. JPK to Byrnes, Mar. 15, 1937, box 47, Byrnes.

2. JPK to JB, Mar. 22, 1937, box 21, Boettiger.

3. JPK to WRH, Mar. 29, 1937, box 7, Hearst.

4. Poole to WRH, June 23, 1937; WRH to JPK, June 27, 1937, box 45, JPKP.

5. Walter Cummings to JPK, July 31, 1937; JPK to Cummings, Aug. 2, 1937, box 45, JPKP.

6. JPK to White, Mar. 28, 1938, box 117, JPKP.

7. JPK to Fisher, May 12, 1937, Smith, *HTF*, 199.

8. JPK to Benchley, May 24, 1937, Smith, *HTF*, 210.

9. JPK, commencement address, June 1937, box 92, JPKP.

10. JPK, "New Blood in American Shipping," *Vital Speeches of the Day,* vol. 3, issue 317, June 15, 1937, 532–35.

11. Oursler to FDR, June 7, 1937; FDR to JPK, June 18, 1937, OF 1705, FDRL.

12. JPK to Davenport, May 25, 1937, Smith, *HTF*, 211.

13. JPK to Davenport, Aug. 6, 1937, Smith, *HTF*, 212.

14. JPK to Galeazzi, Aug. 25, 1937, Smith, *HTF*, 213.

15. Herrick to REFK, June 16, 1937; Rohde to REFK, Oct. 18, 1936, w.b. 3, JPKP.

16. Rohde to REFK, Oct. 18, 1936, w.b. 3, JPKP.

17. Dearborn to REFK, June 28, 1937, w.b. 3, JPKP.

18. Hourigan to REFK, July 23, 1937, w.b. 3, JPKP.

19. REFK, diary notes, box 10, REFKP.

20. Dearborn to REFK, June 28, 1937, w.b. 3, JPKP.

21. Hennessey-Donovan, oral history,

Sept. 25, 1991, 1–2, JFKOHP; JPK to Cummings, Sept. 9, 1937, w.b. 32, JPKP.

22. JPK to FDR; JPK to JR, Sept. 8, 1937, OF 1705, FDRL.

23. Krock, *Memoirs,* 332.

24. *NYT,* Sept. 11, 1937; *Time,* Sept. 20, 1937.

25. Curran and Perkins correspondence, OF 1705, FDRL; JPK to Curran, Nov. 4, 1937, Smith, *HTF,* 215–16.

26. FDR [dictated by James Roosevelt] to JPK, July 10, 1937, OF 1705, FDRL.

27. Klemmer, Philip Whitehead et al., *The Kennedys,* DVD (Thames/PBS, 1992); JPK to Wesley Stout, Nov. 7, 1937, Smith, *HTF,* 216; *NYT,* Nov. 11, 1937.

28. *NYT,* Dec. 3, 1937.

29. JPK to BB, Mar. 3, 1937, PPF 207, FDRL.

30. *NYT,* Dec. 8, 1937, 1, 22.

31. James Roosevelt, *My Parents,* 208–9.

32. Krock, *Memoirs,* 333.

33. Byrnes to JPK, Dec. 13, 1937, Byrnes; Krock to JPK, Dec. 8, 1938, box 93, JPKP; FDR to Welles, Jan. 7, 1938, in Benjamin Welles, *Sumner Welles: FDR's Global Strategist* (New York: St. Martin's Press, 1997), 200.

34. Morgenthau, diaries, Dec. 8, 1937, vol. 101, Morgenthau.

35. Ickes, diary, Dec. 18, 1937, Ickes.

36. Carter to JPK, Dec. 28, 1937, box 90, JPKP.

37. JPK to Byrnes, Dec. 23, 1937, Smith, *HTF,* 219–20.

38. Morgenthau, diaries, transcript of telephone conversation, vol. 107, Jan. 28, 1938, Morgenthau.

39. Carter to JPK, Dec. 28, 1937, box 90, JPKP.

40. *NYT,* Feb. 17, 1938, 1, 15; *Time,* Feb. 28, 1938.

41. *Time,* Feb. 28, 1938.

FIFTEEN: A PLAINSPOKEN AMBASSADOR

1. JPK, diary, Feb. 22, 1938, Smith, *HTF,* 236–37.

2. *NYT,* Feb. 23, 1938.

3. JPK, diary, Feb. 23, 1938, Smith, *HTF,* 237.

4. *NYT,* Mar. 13, 1938.

5. Byrnes to JPK, Feb. 21, 1938, box 47, Byrnes.

6. *Time,* July 5, 1937; FDR to Young, Jan. 28, 1938, in author's possession.

7. JPK to JR, Mar. 3, 1938, Smith, *HTF,* 237–39.

8. Moore to Murphy, Mar. 6, 1940, box 134; JPK to Offie, May 13, 1938, w.b. 32, JPKP.

9. JPK, diary, Mar. 2–9, 11, 1938, box 100, JPKP.

10. Wise to FDR, Mar. 4, 1938, PSF 37, FDRL.

11. Saul Friedländer, *Nazi Germany and the Jews* (New York: HarperCollins, 1997), 1:168.

12. Wise to Szold, Mar. 1, 1938, Weizmann Archives; Wise to FDR, Mar. 4, 1938, PSF 37, FDRL.

13. JPK to JR, Mar. 3, 1938, Smith, *HTF,* 239.

14. FDR, Quarantine Speech, Oct. 5, 1937, http://millercenter.org/president/speeches/detail/3310.

15. JPK, diary, Mar. 2, 1938, box 100, JPKP.

16. *NYT,* Mar. 5, 1938.

17. JPK to FDR, Mar. 11, 1938, Smith, *HTF,* 240–43.

18. *Diaries of Sir Alexander Cadogan, 1838–1945,* ed. David Dilks (New York: G. P. Putnam's Sons, 1972), 62.

19. Winston S. Churchill, "The Annexation of Austria, March 14, 1938," in Churchill, *His Complete Speeches* (New York: Chelsea House Publishers, 1974), 6:5, 923–27.

20. JPK, diary, Mar. 4, 1938, Smith, *HTF,* 239.

21. Hinton to JPK, Feb. 3, 1938, box 93, JPKP.

22. Moffat, diary, Mar. 11, 12, 1938, Moffat; Hull to JPK, Mar. 11, 1938, box 265, Hornbeck.

23. Moffat to JPK, Mar. 14, 1938, Moffat; Hull to JPK, Mar. 14, 1938, box 265, Hornbeck.

24. JPK, diary, Mar. 15, 1938, box 100, JPKP.

25. Moffat, diary, Mar. 15, 1938, Moffat; transcript of telephone conversation between Hull and Kennedy, Mar. 15, 1938, box 66, Hull.

26. Moffat, diary, Mar. 15, 1938, Moffat.

27. JPK, Pilgrims Society speech, Mar. 18, 1938, box 155, JPKP.

28. Dieckhoff to German Foreign Ministry, Mar. 22, 1938, in *Documents on German Foreign Policy,* series D, vol. 1, *From Neurath to Ribbentrop* (Washington, DC: Government Printing Office, 1949), 694–95.

29. JPK to Corcoran, Apr. 2, 1938, box 104, JPKP.

30. Transcript of telephone conversation, JPK to Hull, Mar. 30, 1938, box 66, Hull.

31. JPK to JF, Apr. 7, 1938, box 107, JPKP.

32. *New York World Telegram,* Mar. 9, 1938.

33. Lord Harlech, Aug. 27, 1969, Robert F. Kennedy Oral History Program, JFKL.

34. EMK, *TC,* 54–55.

35. REFK, diary, Mar. 24, Apr. 10, 1938, box 1, 2, REFKP.

36. *Washington Herald,* Apr. 27, 1938.

37. JPK to JF, Apr. 7, 1938, box 107, JPKP.

38. JPK, diary, May 30, 1938, box 100, JPKP; REFK, diary, May 17, 1938, Smith, *HTF,* 238; CBL, appointment calendar, 1938, box 29, CBLP; Luce, oral history, Nov. 11, 1965, 8, JFKOHP.

39. JPK, appointment books, box 99, 100, JPKP; EMK to author, Aug. 21, 2007.

40. Moore to Murphy, May 19, 1939, box 135, JPKP.

41. Styne to Kirstein, Apr. 16, 1938, Kirstein.

42. JPK to Hull, Mar. 22, 1938, box 109, JPKP.

43. *NYT,* Mar. 25, 1938.

44. JPK to Krock et al., Mar. 28, 1938, Smith, *HTF,* 248.

45. Allen to JPK, Apr. 5, 1938, JPKP.

46. Halifax, Apr. 6, 1938, FO 371/214934, NAUK.

47. JPK to Hull, Apr. 6, 1938, Wilson.

48. JPK to Welles, Apr. 15, 1938; Welles to JPK, *FRUS,* 1938, 1:143–45, 127–28.

49. Pearson and Allen, Apr. 22, 1938, http://www.aladin.wrlc.org/gsdl/collect/pearson/pearson.shtml.

50. JPK to Pearson, May 3, 1938, Smith, *HTF,* 255.

51. Pearson to JPK, May 4, 1938, G210, 3 of 5, "Public Figures," Pearson.

52. *NYT,* July 1, 1937.

53. KKH to NA, n.d., MS 1416/1/2/478; JPK, Jr. to NA, Apr. 27, 1939, MS 1416/1/2/478, Astor; JPK to NA, Dec. 8, 1938, 1416/1/2/471, Astor.

54. JPK to NA, May 10, 1938, in Smith, *HTF,* 256.
55. Friedländer, *Nazi Germany and the Jews,* 1:241; SS to [American ambassadors], Mar. 23, *FRUS,* 1938, 1: 740–41; *NYT,* Mar. 26, 1938.
56. Halifax, Apr. 6, 1938, FO 371/21494, NAUK; Louise London, *Whitehall and the Jews: 1933–1948* (Cambridge, UK: Cambridge University Press, 2000), 60–61.
57. Karmel to JPK, Mar. 25, 1938; JPK to Karmel, Mar. 29, 1938, box 109, JPKP.
58. Ickes, diary, July 3, 1938, Ickes.
59. Foreign Office minutes, June 9, 1938, FO 371, NAUK.
60. JPK, diary, Apr. 6, 1938, JPK to Hull, Apr. 9, 1938, box 100; JPK to Welles, Apr. 19, 1938, box 117, JPKP.
61. JPK to JR, Apr. 26, 1938, box 71, JPKP.
62. Ribbentrop memorandum, June 10, 1938, in *Documents on German Foreign Policy,* series D, vol. 1, 713–18.
63. Dirksen to Weizsäcker, June 13, 1938, in *Documents on German Foreign Policy,* series D, vol. 1, 713–18.

SIXTEEN: A RATHER DREADFUL HOMECOMING

1. JPK to Fisher, May 20, 1938, box 106, JPKP.
2. British Pathé newsreel, June 8, 1939.
3. Byrnes to JPK, Apr. 12, 1938, box 47, Byrnes.
4. WRH to JPK, May 16, 1938, box 109, JPKP.
5. JPK to Krock, May 24, 1938; Krock to JPK, June 1, 1938, box 110, JPKP.
6. *NYT,* June 21, 1938.
7. Ickes, diary, July 3, 1938, Ickes.
8. JPK to Krock, Oct. 10, 1941, box 56, Krock.
9. Joseph P. Lash, *Eleanor: The Years Alone* (New York: Norton, 1972), 287; Gore Vidal to author, Oct. 21, 2009.
10. Krock to JPK, Clark to Krock, June 23, 1938, box 109, JPKP.
11. JPK to Bignay, July 22, 1938, Smith, *HTF,* 268–69; McCormick to JPK, n.d., Smith, *HTF,* 269, n. 109.
12. Krock, *Memoirs,* 187–89.
13. Alva Johnston, "'Jimmy's Got It.'"
14. *NYT,* June 30, 1938.
15. JPK to JFK, May 2, 1938, box 1, JPKP.
16. Pearson and Allen, July 1, 1938, http://www.aladin.wrlc.org/gsdl/collect/pearson/pearson.shtml.

SEVENTEEN: MUNICH

1. Dirksen to state secretary in the German Foreign Ministry, July 20, 1938, in *Documents on German Foreign Policy, 1918–1945,* series D, vol. 1, 721–23.
2. JPK, diary, July 20, 1938, box 100, JPKP.
3. S. Adler-Rudel, "The Evian Conference on the Refugee Question," in *Yearbook of the Leo Baeck Institute,* 1968, 13: 246–47.
4. Catherine Bailey, *Black Diamonds* (London: Viking, 2007), 349–51; Barbara Leaming, *Jack Kennedy: The Education of a Statesman* (New York: Norton, 2006), 86.
5. REFK, diary, July 24, 1938, box 2, REFK.
6. Maria Riva, *Marlene Dietrich* (New York: Ballantine Books, 1992), 469.
7. Morgenthau, diaries, Aug. 30, 1938, vol. 140, item 7, Morgenthau.
8. Henry Morgenthau III, *Mostly Morgenthaus: A Family History* (New York: Ticknor & Fields, 1991), 290–91.
9. Riva, *Marlene Dietrich,* 469.
10 Burns to JPK, Aug. 2, 1938, box 103, JPKP.
11 Krock to JPK, Aug. 11, 1938, box 109, JPKP.
12 JPK to Messersmith, Sept. 12, 1938, box 112, JPKP.
13 Messersmith to JPK, Oct. 1, 1938, w.b. 32; JPK to Messersmith, Oct. 13, 1938, box 112, JPKP.
14 REFK, diary, Aug. 17, 21, 1938, box 2, REFKP; JPK, Jr., to JPK, n.d., box 1, JPKP.
15 Bullitt to SS, Aug. 29, *FRUS,* 1938, 1:776–78.
16 JPK to SS, Aug. 31, *FRUS,* 1938, 1:566.
17 JPK to SS, Aug. 30, *FRUS,* 1938, 1:560–61.
18 JPK to SS, Sept. 1, *FRUS,* 1938, 1:565–66; *CDT,* Sept. 3, 1938.
19 FDR to Hull, Sept. 1, 1938, box 170, Hull; Morgenthau, diaries, Sept. 1, 1938, vol. 138, 33–35, Morgenthau.
20 Morgenthau, diaries, Aug. 30, 1938, vol. 140, item 7, Morgenthau.

21 JPK to SS, Aug 31, 1938, box 37, FDRRSF.
22 Moffat, diary, Aug. 31, 1938, Moffat.
23 Morgenthau, diaries, Sept. 1, 1938, vol. 138, Morgenthau.
24 Ickes, diary, July 16, 1938, Ickes.
25 JPK, Jr., to JPK, Sept. 6, 1938; EKS to JPK, Sept. 4, 1938, box 2, JPKP.
26 JPK to SS, Sept. 10, *FRUS,* 1938, 1:585–86; Halifax to Lindsay, Sept. 10, 1938, FO 371/21636, NAUK.
27 Halifax to Lindsay, Sept. 11, 1938, FO 371/21736, NAUK; JPK to Hull, Sept. 11, *FRUS,* 1938, 1:587–88.
28 Kordt to German Foreign Ministry, Sept. 12, 1938, *Documents on German Foreign Policy,* series D, vol. 2, 742–43; Selzam, memorandum, in Kordt to German Foreign Ministry, Sept. 12, 1938, in *Documents on German Foreign Policy,* series D, vol. 2, 743–44.
29 JPK to SS, Sept. 12, *FRUS,* 1938, 1:591.
30 JPK to SS, Sept. 13, *FRUS,* 1938, 1:592.
31 REFK, diary, Sept. 13, 14, 1938, box 2, REFKP.
32 JPK to Goldsmith, Sept. 14, 1938, box 108, JPKP.
33 Goldsmith to JPK, Sept. 16, 1938, box 108, JPKP.
34 JPK to SS, Sept. 17, [two cables], *FRUS,* 1938, 1:607–12.
35 Morgenthau, diaries, Sept. 19, 1938, vol. 141, 115, Morgenthau.
36 JPK to SS, Sept. 19, *FRUS,* 1938, 1: 622; JPK, "DM," 14:28, JPKP.
37 Anne Morrow Lindbergh: *The Flower and the Nettle: Diaries and Letters, 1936–1939* (New York: Harcourt Brace Jovanovich, 1976), 409.
38 Charles Lindbergh, *The Wartime Journals of Charles A. Lindbergh* (New York: Harcourt Brace Jovanovich, 1970), 72.
39 Lindbergh, in JPK to Hull, Sept. 22, 1938, box 450, Lindbergh.
40 John Slessor, *The Central Blue* (New York: Praeger, 1957), 218–19.
41 Ian Kershaw, *Hitler: 1936–1945, Nemesis* (New York: Norton, 2000), 112–15.
42 *Diaries of Sir Alexander Cadogan,* 102–3; JPK to SS, Sept. 24, *FRUS,* 1938, 1:642–43.
43 Transcript of telephone conversation,

Hull and JPK, Sept. 24, 1938, box 66, Hull.
44 JPK to SS, Sept. 25, *FRUS,* 1938, 1:652.
45 JPK, "DM," 15:11; JPK to SS, Sept. 26, 1938, box 170; JPK, "DM," 14:1, 2, JPKP.
46 FDR to Hitler, Sept. 26, *FRUS,* 1938, 1: 657–58.
47 Transcript of telephone conversation, Welles to JPK, Sept. 26, *FRUS,* 1938, 1:660–61.
48 William Shirer, *Berlin Diary* (New York: Alfred A. Knopf, 1941), 141–42.
49 Hitler to FDR, received Sept. 26, *FRUS,* 1938, 1:669–72; JPK, "DM," 16:4, JPKP.
50 JPK, diary, Sept. 27, 1938, box 100, JPKP; John Wheeler-Bennett, *Munich: Prologue to Tragedy* (New York: Duell, Sloan & Pearce, 1948), 151–52.
51 JPK, diary, Sept. 27, 1938, Smith, *HTF,* 286–87; JKS to author, Dec. 11, 2009; JPK, "DM," 16:7, JPKP.
52 JPK, diary, Sept. 27, 1938, box 100, JPKP.
53 Ickes, *Secret Diary,* 2:477.
54 Transcript of telephone conversation, Welles to JPK, Sept. 27, *FRUS,* 1938, 1: 678–79.
55 REFK, diary, Sept. 28, 1938, box 2, REFKP.
56 JPK, "DM," 16:12–13.
57 JPK, "DM," 16:13.
58 Harold George Nicolson, *Diaries and Letters,* ed. Nigel Nicolson (New York: Atheneum, 1966–1968), 1:370–71.
59 JPK to SS, Sept. 28, *FRUS,* 1938, 1:692–93.
60 JPK, "DM," 16:16, JPKP.
61 SS to JPK, Sept. 28, *FRUS,* 1938, 1:688.
62 JPK, diary, Sept. 28, 1938, box 100, JPKP; REFK, diary, Sept. 28, 1938, box 2, REFKP.

EIGHTEEN: THE KENNEDY PLAN
1. Churchill, speech, http://hansard .millbanksystems.com/commons/1938/ oct/05/policy-of-his-majestys -government.
2. Welles to JPK, Oct. 5, *FRUS,* 1938, 1:791–92.
3. JPK, "DM," 29:1–2, JPKP; Chamberlain to FDR, Oct. 7, *FRUS,* 1938, 1:794–95, sequence of clauses rearranged.
4. JPK to Sarnoff, Oct. 7, 1938, box 115, JPKP.

5. Rublee and Welles, "Memorandum of Trans-Atlantic Telephone Conversation," [Oct. 10], *FRUS,* 1938, 1:795–96.

6. Rublee to Warren, in Rublee to Taylor, Oct. 14, 1938, *The Holocaust,* vol. 6, *Jewish Emigration 1938–1940* (New York: Garland Publishing, 1982), 1–3.

7. Walter Laqueur, *A History of Zionism* (New York: MJF Books, 1972), 509; Martin Gilbert, *Israel: A History* (New York: Morrow, 1998), 80–95; *NYT,* Oct. 2, 4, 6, 1938.

8. Weizmann to Brandeis et al., Oct. 6, 1936, Szold Papers, CZA.

9. SS to JPK, Oct. 12, *FRUS,* 1938, 2:951–53.

10. Transcript of telephone conversation, Hull and JPK, Oct. 14, 1938, Hull.

11. Pearson and Allen, Oct. 31, 1938, http://www.aladin.wrlc.org/gsdl/collect/pearson/pearson.shtml.

12. JPK to Hull, Oct. 28, 1938, Smith, *HTF,* 297.

13. FDR to JPK, Nov. 2, 1938, PSF 38, FDRL.

14. Trafalgar Day address, Oct. 19, 1938, box 155, JPKP; *NYT,* Oct. 20, 1938.

15. Moffat, diary, Oct. 21, 1938, Moffat.

16. Moffat, diary, Oct. 26, 1938, Moffat; *NYT,* Oct. 27, 1938.

17. Frank Kent, "The Great Game of Politics," *WSJ,* Oct. 28, 1938; Moffat, diary, Nov. 4, 1938, Moffat.

18. Burns to JPK, Nov. 4, 1938, box 103, JPKP.

19. JPK to White, Nov. 12, 1938, Smith, *HTF,* 299–300.

20. JPK, "DM," 18:4–6; JPK to Fleeson, Nov. 9, 1938, Smith, *HTF,* 298–99; JPK to White, Nov. 12, 1938, Smith, *HTF,* 299–300.

21. JPK, Jr., draft, Nov. 14, 1938, Smith, *HTF,* 301–2.

22. JFK to parents, n.d., box 1, JFKP.

23. NA to Anne Lindbergh, Nov. 2, 1938, Lindbergh-Astor correspondence, MS 1416/1/2/471, Astor; Beaverbrook to Gannett, Dec. 9, 1938, Gannett.

24. Cohen to Szold, Oct. 12, 1938, Jacobs.

25. "X's" interview with Kennedy, Nov. 2, 1938, Weizmann.

26. Jacobs to Szold, Nov. 4, 1938, Jacobs.

27. Lipstadt, *Beyond Belief,* 98.

28. Friedländer, *Nazi Germany and the Jews,* 277.

29. JPK to Lindbergh, Nov. 12, 1938, Smith, *HTF,* 300–301.

30. REFK, diary, Nov. 13, 1938, box 2, REFKP; JPK, Jr., diary, Nov. 14, 1938, in author's possession.

31. Henry Feingold, *The Politics of Rescue* (New Brunswick, N.J.: Rutgers University Press, 1970, 31, 92, 102–5.

32. Press conference no. 500, Nov. 15, 1938, FDRL; Moffat, diary, Nov. 16, 17, 1938, Moffat.

33. REFK, diary, Nov. 15, 1938, box 2, REFKP; JPK, diary, Nov. 15, 1938, box 100, JPKP.

34. Halifax to Lindsay, Nov. 16, 1938, FO 371/21637, NAUK.

35. Minutes of cabinet meeting, Nov. 16, 1938, FO 371/21658, NAUK.

36. Welles, memorandum of conversation, Nov. 17, *FRUS,* 1938, 1:829–31.

37. JPK to SS, Nov. 18, 1938, PSF 31, FDRL.

38. Moffat, diary, Nov. 22, 1938, Moffat.

39. JPK to Fisher, Nov. 25, 1938, 106; JPK to Davenport, Nov. 25, 1938, box 105, JPKP; JPK, Jr., Dec. 10, 1938, Smith, *HTF,* 305–6.

40. JPK to Fleeson, Nov. 9, 1938, Smith, *HTF,* 298–9; JPK to Boettiger, Nov. 25, 1938, Smith, *HTF,* 304; JPK, Jr., "November 21," Smith, *HTF,* 303–4.

41. *CDT,* Dec. 5, 1938; Ickes, diary, Nov. 25, 1938, Ickes.

42. Morgenthau, diaries, Dec. 5, 1938, vol. 154, 367–68, Morgenthau.

43. JPK, Jr., mss., Dec. 10, 1938, Smith, *HTF,* 305–6.

44. Pearson and Allen, Dec. 8, 1938, http://www.aladin.wrlc.org/gsdl/collect/pearson/pearson.shtml.

45. JPK, memorandum, Dec. 19, 1938, PSF 37, FDRL.

46. REFK to JPK, n.d., box 2, JPKP.

47. *LAT,* Jan. 11, 1939, 1.

48. Halifax to Chamberlain, Chamberlain to Halifax, Feb. 3, 1939, FO 371/22827, NAUK.

49. JPK, "DM," 21:13, JPKP.

50. Moffat, diary, Feb. 9, 1939, Moffat.

NINETEEN: SIDELINED AND CENSORED

1. JPK to SS, Feb. 17, *FRUS,* 1939, 1:14–17.

2. Welles, memorandum, Feb. 20, *FRUS,* 1939, 1:18–20.

3. JPK to FDR, Mar. 3, 1939, PSF 37, FDRL.
4. FDR to Chief of Naval Operations, PSF Navy, Mar. 13, 1939, FDRL.
5. JPK to Galeazzi, Feb. 25, 1939, box 107; Hull to JPK, Mar. 7, 1939, box 172, JPKP.
6. Pope Paul VI, oral history, 1964, JPKOHP; JPK, diary, Mar. 12, 1938, box 100, JPKP.
7. JPK to Hull, Mar. 18, 1939, Smith, *HTF,* 321-22.
8. JPK, diary, Mar. 21, 1939, box 100, JPKP.
9. JPK to SS, Mar. 31, *FRUS,* 1939, 1:105-6.
10. JPK, diary, Mar. 30, 1939, box 100, JPKP.
11. Lindbergh, *The Flower and the Nettle,* 526-29; JPK to Murphy, Apr. 18, 1939, Smith, *HTF,* 330.
12. George F. Kennan, *Memoirs: 1925-1950* (Boston: Little, Brown & Co., 1967), 91-92.
13. JPK to JFK, June 7, 1939, box 2, JPKP.
14. REFK, diary, July 4, 1939, box 2, REFKP.
15. Torbert Macdonald, oral history, Aug. 11, 1968, JFKOHP.
16. RK to JPK, Feb. 27, 1939, box 2, JPKP.
17. CBL to JPK, Oct. 10, 1938, box 91, CBLP.
18. CBL to JPK, May 26, 1939, box 93, CBLP.
19. Alan Brinkley, *The Publisher* (New York: Alfred A. Knopf, 2010), 306.
20. Sylvia Jukes Morris, *Rage for Fame* (New York: Random House, 1997), 340-41.
21. SS to JPK, Apr. 18, *FRUS,* 1939, 2:234-35; June 20, 2:256-57.
22. JPK to Welles, Apr. 5, 1939, box 117, JPKP.
23. FDR to Hitler and Mussolini, Apr. 14, *FRUS,* 1939, 1:130-33.
24. JPK to Roosevelt, Hull, Apr. 20, 1939, Smith, *HTF,* 330.
25. Transcript of telephone conversation, Hull and JPK, Apr. 24, 1939, Hull.
26. James D. Mooney, notes on European travel, box 1, Mooney.
27. JPK to Welles, May 4, 1939, Smith, *HTF,* 331-32.
28. Welles to JPK, May 4, 1939, box 174, JPKP.
29. Mooney, notes on European travel, box 1, Mooney.
30. *NYT,* Feb. 12, 1939.
31. JPK to SS, Feb. 27, *FRUS,* 1939, 4:718.
32. SS to JPK, Mar. 2, *FRUS,* 1939, 4:722.
33. Moshe Sharett, "Political Journal of Moshe Sharett," Feb. 28, 1939, Lavon Institute, Tel Aviv; translation from Hebrew by A. Goren.
34. Murray, memorandum of conversation, Mar. 17, *FRUS,* 1939, 4:732; Welles to JPK, Mar. 19; JPK to SS, Mar. 20, *FRUS,* 1939, 4:737-38.
35. Moore to Burns, Feb. 13, 1939, box 133; Moore to Goldsmith, Feb. 15, Mar. 6, 27, 1939, box 134, JPKP.
36. Goldsmith to Moore, Apr. 10, 1939, box 134, JPKP.
37. Sharett, "Political Journal," Apr. 30, 1939.
38. Sharett, "Political Journal," May 1, 1939.
39. JPK to SS, May 9; FDR to Welles, May 10; JPK to SS, May 11, *FRUS,* 1939, 4:748-50.
40. Mapai report, in Sharett, "Political Journal," June 14, 1938; Sharett, "Political Journal," May 11, 1939.
41. Mapai report, in Sharett, "Political Journal," June 14, 1939.
42. Goldman to Weizmann, June 20, 1939, Weizmann.
43. Zioniburo [London] to AMZO [American Zionist Organization, Washington] A407/130, Szold; JPK to Cohen, May 16, 1939, Szold.
44. Goldman to JPK, May 17, 1939, Szold.
45. JPK to Goldman, June 2, 1939, Szold.
46. British White Paper of 1939, Avalon Project, http://avalon.law.yale.edu/20th _century?brwh1939.asp.
47. Weizmann to Goldman, May 30, 1939, Weizmann.
48. Goldman to Weizmann, June 20, 1939, Weizmann.
49. *LAT,* May 8, 1939, 1; Pearson and Allen, July 12, 1939, http://www.aladin.wrlc .org/gsdl/collect/pearson/pearson.shtml.
50. *The Week,* May 17, 1939.
51. Ickes, diary, July 2, 1939; *New Republic,* June 21, 1939, 1.
52. JPK to Carter, June 13, 1939, box 104, JPKP.

53. "Reminiscences of Walter Lippmann," 1950, 183, CUOH.

54. JPK to SS, July 19, 20, *FRUS, 1939,* 1:286–88.

55. JPK to FDR, July 20, 1939, PSF 37, FDRL.

56. Arthur Krock, "Why Ambassador Kennedy Is Not Coming Home," *NYT,* July 18, 1939.

57. FDR to JPK, July 22, 1939, Smith, *HTF,* 353–54.

58. JPK to FDR, Aug. 9, 1939, Smith, *HTF,* 354–55.

59. JPK to Houghton, Aug. 29, 1939, box 109; REFK, diary, June 13, 1939, box 2, REFKP.

60. JPK to Houghton, Aug. 31, 1939, box 109, JPKP; Riva, 486–87.

TWENTY: "THIS COUNTRY IS AT WAR WITH GERMANY"

1. Kirk to SS, Aug. 21, 1939, *FRUS, 1939,* 1:337.

2. JPK to SS, Aug. 23, *FRUS, 1939,* 1: 339–42, 355–56.

3. JPK, diary, Aug. 24, 1939, Smith, *HTF,* 356–60; "DM," 23:5–6, JPKP.

4. Cordell Hull, *The Memoirs of Cordell Hull,* 2 vols. (New York: Macmillan, 1948), 1:662.

5. JPK to SS, Aug. 25, *FRUS, 1939,* 1:369–70.

6. JPK, diary, Aug. 24, 1939, Smith, *HTF,* 356–60.

7. JPK, "DM," 23:7–8, JPKP.

8. JPK, diary, Aug. 24 [25], 1939, Smith, *HTF,* 356–60.

9. JPK to Houghton, Aug. 29, 1939, box 108, JPKP.

10. Derby to JPK, Aug. 26; JPK to Derby, Aug. 29, 1939, box 106; Morgan to JPK, Aug. 29, 1939, box 112, JPKP.

11. JPK to SS, Aug. 29, *FRUS, 1939,* 1:381–82.

12. JPK, diary, Aug. 31, 1939, box 100; JPK, "DM," 33:12–14, JPKP; JPK, Jr., diary Aug. 21, 1939, Smith, 355–56.

13. JPK, diary, Aug. 30, 1939, box 100; JPK, "DM," 33:14–15, JPKP.

14. JPK to SS, Aug. 31, *FRUS, 1939,* 1:397–98.

15. JPK, diary, Aug. 31, 1939, box 100; "DM," 33:16–17, JPKP; Sidney Aster, *1939: The Making of the Second World War* (New York: Simon & Schuster, 1974), 371.

16. Luella Hennessey-Donovan, oral history, Sept. 25, 1991, JFKOHP.

17. JPK, diary, Sept. 3, 1939, box 100, JPKP.

18. Chamberlain, Sept. 3, 1939, http:// avalon.law.yale.edu/wwii/gb2.asp.

19. JPK, diary, Sept. 3, 1939, box 100, JPKP.

TWENTY-ONE: THE LIVES OF AMERICANS ARE AT STAKE

1. JPK, "DM," 34:4, JPKP; JPK to SS, Sept. 3, *FRUS, 1939,* 1:595–96.

2. JPK to Hull, Sept. 8, 1939, Smith, *HTF,* 370–71.

3. Long, diaries, Sept. 7, 1939, box 5, Long.

4. JKS to JPK, Oct. 3, 1939, box 2, JPKP.

5. JPK to REFK, Sept. 18, 1939, Smith, *HTF,* 379–80.

6. Morgenthau, diaries, transcript of telephone conversation, Welles and Morgenthau, Sept. 7, 1939, vol. 209, 43, Morgenthau.

7. Morgenthau, diaries, transcript of telephone conversation, Morgenthau and JPK, Sept. 11, 1939, vol. 210, 228, Morgenthau.

8. JPK to FDR, Sept. 10, 1939, Smith, *HTF,* 372–74.

9. JPK to Hull and FDR, Sept. 11, 1939, in Smith, *HTF,* 374–76.

10. SS to JPK, Sept. 11, *FRUS, 1939,* 1:424.

11. James Farley, *Jim Farley's Story* (New York: McGraw-Hill, 1948), 198–99.

12. Winston Churchill, *The Gathering Storm* (Boston: Houghton Mifflin, 1948), 440–41.

13. JPK, diary, Oct. 5, 1939, box 100, JPKP.

14. JPK, diary, Oct. 6, 1939, box 100, JPKP.

15. JPK, diary, Sept. 17, 1939, box 100, JPKP.

16. JPK to SS, Sept. 18, *FRUS, 1939,* I:439–40.

17. JPK to FDR, three letters, Sept. 30, 1939, PSF 37, FDRL.

18. JPK to LeHand, Oct. 3, 1939, LeHand.

19. Halifax to Lothian, Oct. 31, 1939, FO 371/22830, NAUK.

20. All comments above, from FO 371/22827, NAUK.

21. Peake to Cadogan, Oct. 12, 1939, FO 371/22827, NAUK.

22. *The Diplomatic Diaries of Oliver Harvey, 1937–1940,* ed. John

Harvey (New York: St. Martin's Press, 1970), 326.

23. JPK to REFK, Oct. 2, 1939, Smith, *HTF,* 391–92.

24. JPK to Carter, Nov. 3, 1939, box 104; JPK to Ford, Oct. 26, 1939, box 107, JPKP.

25. JPK to Reisman, Oct. 3, 1939, box 115, JPKP.

26. JPK to Ford, Oct. 26, 1939, box 107, JPKP.

27. Reisman to JPK, Nov. 13, 1939, w.b. 30, JPKP.

28. JPK to Hays, Nov. 12, 1939, Smith, *HTF,* 400; JPK to Cohn, Nov. 17, 1939, Smith, *HTF,* 400–401.

29. JPK to Goldsmith, Nov. 3, 1939, box 108, JPKP.

30. JPK to Fisher, Oct. 23, 1939, Smith, *HTF,* 396–97.

31. JPK to REFK, Oct. 23, 1939, in author's possession.

32. JPK to REFK, Oct. 11, 1939, Smith, *HTF,* 393–94.

33. KKH to JPK, Sept. 26, 1939; EKS to JPK, Nov. 20, n.d; JKS to JPK, n.d., box 2, JPKP.

34. JPK to PKL, Nov. 3, 1939, box 55, REFKP.

35. JPK to Burns, Nov. 17, 1939, w.b. 32, JPKP.

36. REFK to JPK, Oct. 6, 10, 1939, box 2, JPKP; JPK to REFK, Oct. 11, 1939, Smith, *HTF,* 393–94.

37. REFK, *TTR,* 137; JPK to REFK, Oct. 11, 1939, Smith, *HTF,* 393–94.

38. EMK, *TC,* 26.

39. JPK to REFK, Oct. 11, 1939, Smith, *HTF,* 393–94.

40. JPK to REFK, Nov. 13, 1939, in author's possession.

TWENTY-TWO: DEFEATIST

1. *Chips: The Diaries of Sir Henry Channon,* ed. Robert Rhodes James (London: Weidenfeld & Nicolson, 1989), 225; NA to Lothian, Nov. 27, 1939, Astor.

2. Cabinet minutes, Dec. 11, 1939, CAB 65/50, NAUK.

3. *WP,* Dec. 7, 1939; *CDT,* Dec. 8, 1939.

4. JPK, diary, Dec. 10, 1939, Smith, *HTF,* 404–6.

5. Ickes, diary, Dec. 10, 1939, Ickes.

6. Moffat, Dec. 8, 1939, Moffat.

7. Minute, Mar. 18, 1940, FO 371/24251, NAUK.

8. Cabinet minutes, Jan 18–25, 1940, in FO 371/24251; cabinet minutes, Jan. 26, 1940, CAB 65/56, NAUK.

9. *London Times,* Dec. 12, 1939, in FO 371/22827, NAUK.

10. Jordan to FDR, Dec. 13, 1939, PPF 207, FDRL.

11. Alsop and Kintner, *AC,* Dec. 19, 1939.

12. JPK to REFK, Mar. 14, 1940, Smith, *HTF,* 406–8; JPKP, "DM," 30:1, JPK; CBL, Mar. 4, 5, "Diaries, 1939–40," box 56, CBLP.

13. JPK to REFK, Mar. 14, 1940, Smith, *HTF,* 406–8.

14. Von Hofmannsthal to CLB, Mar. 27, 1940, box 96, CBLP.

15. Minute, Mar. 3, 1940, FO 371/24251, NAUK.

16. JPK to REFK, Mar. 14, 1940, Smith, *HTF,* 408.

17. Hull, *Memoirs,* 1:740.

18. JPK to REFK, Mar. 20, 1938, Smith, *HTF,* 410–11.

19. REFK to JPK, Mar. 31, 1940, box 2, JPKP.

20. JKS to JPK, Mar. 25, 1940, box 2, JPKP.

21. JPK, Jr., to JPK, Mar. 17, 1940, Smith, *HTF,* 410.

22. JFK to JPK, n.d., Smith, *HTF,* 417–18.

23. JPK to JFK, May 20, 1940, Smith, *HTF,* 433–35.

24. JPK to McAdoo, Mar. 31, 1940, box 136, JPKP; CBL, Apr. 2, 3, 1940, "Diaries, 1939–1940," box 56, CBLP; JPK to REFK, Apr. 5, 1940, Smith, *HTF,* 413–15.

25. JPK to REFK, Apr. 5, 1940, two letters, Smith, *HTF,* 413–15.

26. JPK, diary, Apr. 9, 1940, box 100; "DM," 42:4, JPKP; Churchill, http://hansard.millbanksystems.com/commons/1940/apr/11/the-war-at-sea#S5CV0359P0_19400411_HOC_320.

27. JPK to FDR, Apr. 11, 1940, OF 229, FDRL.

28. Morgenthau, diaries, Apr. 29, 1940, vol. 258, Morgenthau.

29. JPK to REFK, Apr. 16, 1940, in author's possession.

30. Halifax, diary, Apr. 25, 1940, Halifax.

31. JPK to Welles, May 8, 1940, RG 59, NAUS.
32. JPK, diary, May 10, 1940, Smith, *HTF,* 423–24; transcript of telephone calls, May 10, 1940, Hull.
33. Max Hastings, *Winston's War* (New York: Alfred A. Knopf, 2010), 22.
34. Assorted cables between SS and JPK, May 15–June 26, *FRUS,* 1940, 2:91–133.
35. JPK, diary, May 15, 1940, Smith, *HTF,* 425–26.
36. JPK to SS, May 15, *FRUS,* 1940, 1: 29–30.
37. *NYT,* May 17, 1940.
38. SS to JPK, May 16, *FRUS,* 1940, 3:49–50.
39. Churchill to FDR, May 20, 1940, in *Roosevelt and Churchill,* ed. Francis L. Loewenheim et al. (New York: Dutton, 1975), 97.
40. Hull, *Memoirs,* 1:766.

TWENTY-THREE: THE FALL OF FRANCE
1. JPK, "DM," 34:14–15, JPKP.
2. "Case of Anna Wolkoff, Tyler Kent, and Others," May 21, 1940, KV2/840; "Transcript of Interrogation of Kent," May 20, 1940, KV2/543, NAUK.
3. Warren Kimball and Bruce Bartlett, "Roosevelt and Prewar Commitments to Churchill: The Tyler Kent Affair," *Diplomatic History* (October 1981): 300.
4. JPK to Hull, May 20, 1940, RG 84, NAUS, in Ray Bearse and Anthony Read, *Conspirator: The Untold Story of Tyler Kent* (New York: Doubleday, 1991), 160–61.
5. Long, diaries, May 22, June 6, 12, 1940, Long.
6. Long, diaries, June 24, 1940, Long.
7. JPK to Hull, May 24, 1940, RG 84, NAUS.
8. JPK to REFK, May 20, 1940, Smith, *HTF,* 432–33.
9. JPK to SS, May 27, *FRUS,* 1940, 1:233.
10. Ian Kershaw, *Fateful Choices* (New York: Penguin, 2008), 30–47.
11. Hull, *Memoirs,* 1:771–72.
12. JPK, "DM," 35:6–7, JPKP.
13. John Keegan, *The Second World War* (New York: Penguin, 1990), 80–81.
14. Churchill, June 4, 1940, http://hansard .millbanksystems.com/commons/1940/

jun/04/war-situation#S5CV0361P0_ 19400604_HOC_231.
15. JPK, "DM," 35:18, JPKP.
16. JPK to JPK, Jr., June 6, 1940, box 2, JPKP.
17. JPK to Fisher, June 6, 1940, box 106, JPKP.
18. JPK to REFK, June 7, 1940, box 2, JPKP.
19. JPK, diary, June 13, 1940, Smith, *HTF,* 439–40.
20. Bullitt to SS, June 10, *FRUS,* 1940, 1:245–46; SS to First Secretary of Embassy in France, June 13, *FRUS,* 1940, 1:247–48.
21. JPK, diary, June 14, 1940, Smith, *HTF,* 440–43; War Cabinet minutes, June 13, 1940, CAB/65/7/60, NAUK.
22. JPK, diary, June 14, 1940, Smith, *HTF,* 440–43.
23. JPK to SS, June 14, *FRUS,* 1940, 1:248–49.
24. JPK, diary, June 14, 1940, Smith, *HTF,* 443; SS to JPK, June 13, *FRUS,* 1940, 1:250.
25. JPK, diary, June 14, 1940, Smith, *HTF,* 443.
26. JPK, diary, June 15, 16, 1940, box 100, JPKP.
27. JPK, "DM," 36:40, JPKP.

TWENTY-FOUR: THE WORST OF TIMES
1. REFK to JPK, July 27, 1940, box 2; assorted letters from children to JPK, box 2, JPKP.
2. JPK to JKS, Aug. 2, 1940, box 2, JPKP.
3. *Diaries of Sir Alexander Cadogan,* 308; Halifax, diary, July 9, 1940, Halifax.
4. Winston Churchill, *Their Finest Hour* (New York: Houghton Mifflin, 1949), 24; FDR, Charlottesville speech, June 10, 1940, http://millercenter.org/president/ speeches/detail/3317.
5. JPK to Hull, July 12, 1940, two cables, box 176, JPKP; Welles to FDR, July 12, 1940, PSF 62 FDRL; JPK to Hull, July 13, 1940, box 176, JPKP.
6. FDR to Knox, July 13, 1940, PSF 62, FDRL.
7. *The London Journal of General Raymond E. Lee,* ed. James Leutze (Boston: Little, Brown & Co., 1971), 27–28.
8. JPK to Hull, Aug. 2, 1940, 700.0001, RG 59, NAUS.

9. JPK, diary, Aug. 1, 1940, Smith, *HTF,* 452–53.
10. JPK to children, Aug. 2, 1940; EKS to JPK, n.d., box 2, JPKP.
11. JPK to REFK, Aug. 2, 1940, Smith, *HTF,* 454–57; JPK to Davies, Aug. 2, 1940, box 105; JPK to CBL, Aug. 2, 1940, box 96, CBLP.
12. Balfour minutes, May 23, 1940, FO 371/24251, NAUK; JPK to REFK, Aug. 2, 1940, Smith, *HTF,* 454–57.
13. JPK to REFK, Aug. 2, 1940, Smith, *HTF,* 454–55.
14. JPK to Hull, Aug. 7, 1940, box 176, JPKP.
15. JPK to Hull, Aug. 8, 1940, box 176, JPKP.
16. JPK to SS, July 31, 1940, *FRUS,* 1940, 3:57–58; Churchill, *Their Finest Hour,* 401–3.
17. FDR, memorandum, Aug. 2, 1940, *FRUS,* 1940, 3:58.
18. Churchill to Lothian, Aug. 7, 1940, in Churchill, *Their Finest Hour,* 405–6.
19. JPK, diary, Aug. 14, 1940, Smith, *HTF,* 460–61.
20. Leutze, ed., *London Journal of General Raymond E. Lee,* 36; JPK, diary, Aug. 15, 16, 1940, box 100, JPKP.
21. Perrone, Sept. 3, 1940, FO 371/24251, NAUK.
22. JPK, diary, handwritten entry, Aug. 15, 1940, box 100, JPKP.
23. JPK, diary, handwritten and typed entries, Aug. 15, 1940, box 100, JPKP.
24. Halifax, diary, Aug. 29, 1940, Halifax.
25. CBL to JPK, Aug. 26, 1940, box 96, CBLP.
26. JPK, diary, Aug. 23, 1940, box 100, JPKP.
27. JPK to FDR, Aug. 27, 1940, Smith, *HTF,* 463.
28. FDR to JPK, Aug. 28, 1940, PSF 62, Navy (Destroyers-Bases), FDRL.
29. JPK, diary, Sept 2, 1940, box 100, JPKP.

TWENTY-FIVE: THERE'S HELL TO PAY TONIGHT
1. JPK, diary, Sept. 6, 1940, box 100, JPKP.
2. *London Journal of General Raymond E. Lee,* 47.
3. Royal Air Force, "Battle of Britain Campaign Diaries," Sept. 7, 1940, http://www.raf.mod.uk/history/campaign_diaries.cfm?diarymonth=9&diaryyear=1940&diaryday-7.

4. Philip Ziegler, *London at War* (New York: Alfred A. Knopf, 1995), 113–16.
5. Klemmer, in Whitehead et al., *The Kennedys.*
6. JPK to REFK, Sept. 10, 1940, Smith, *HTF,* 466–67.
7. JPK to JFK, Sept. 10, 1940, Smith, *HTF,* 468–69.
8. JPK to RFK, Sept. 11, 1940, Smith, *HTF,* 469–70.
9. JPK to EMK, Sept. 11, 1940, Smith, *HTF,* 470–71.
10. JPK to Burns, Sept. 11, 1940, Burns to JPK, Sept. 18, 1940, box 103, JPKP.
11. JPK to JPK, Jr., Sept. 10, 1940, box 2, JPKP.
12. JPK to Hull, Sept. 11, 1940, 740.0011, RG 59, NAUS.
13. JPK, diary, Sept. 15, 1940, box 100, JPKP.
14. JPK to Welles, Sept. 16, 1940, box 176, JPKP.
15. JPK to SS, Sept. 27, *FRUS,* 1940, 3:48–49.
16. JPK to LeHand, Sept. 30, 1940, box 111; JPK to REFK, Sept. 30, 1940, box 2, JPKP.
17. *LAT,* Oct. 5, 1940.
18. Alsop and Kintner, *AC,* Oct. 8, 1940.
19. JPK, diary, Oct. 11, 1940, box 100, JPKP; Krock, private memorandum, Dec. 1, 1940, box 37, folder 2, Sulzberger.
20. Long, diaries, Oct. 11, 1940, Long.
21. FDR to JPK, Oct. 17, 1940, Smith, *HTF,* 475.
22. JPK, diary, Oct. 11, 1940, box 100, JPKP. Minutes, Oct. 10, 1940, FO 371/24251, NAUK.
23. Halifax, diary, Oct. 17, 1940, Halifax.
24. JPK, diary, Oct. 15, 1940, box 100, JPKP.
25. JPK, diary, Oct. 16, 18, 1940, box 100, JPKP.
26. JPK, diary, Oct. 19, 1940, box 100; JPK to Chamberlain, Oct. 22, 1940, box 104, JPKP.

TWENTY-SIX: HOME AGAIN
1. CBL to JPK, Oct. 21, 1940, box 103, CBLP; JPK, diary, "Account of Ambassador's Trip," Smith, *HTF,* 478–79.
2. Edwin M. Watson, "Memorandum for the President," Oct. 25, 1940; Lauchlin

Currie, "Memorandum for Miss LeHand," Oct. 25, 1940, PSF 37, FDRL.

3. FDR to JPK, Oct. 25, 1940, Smith, *HTF,* 479; JPK, diary, "Account of Ambassador's trip," Smith, *HTF,* 478–79.

4. *NYT,* Oct. 28, 1940; British Pathé newsreel, Nov. 21, 1940.

5. JPK, diary, "Account of Ambassador's Trip," Smith, *HTF,* 478–79; Krock, *Memoirs,* 334–35; Brian Burns to author, Apr. 22, 2010.

6. JPK, diary, Nov. 4, 1940, Smith, *HTF,* 491.

7. JPK, diary, n.d., Smith, *HTF,* 480–82; REFK, diary, "Visit to Washington," Oct. 29, 1940, box 3, REFKP; Frank Murphy, diary notes, Nov. 2, 1941, Gressman.

8. JPK, diary, n.d., Smith, *HTF,* 480–82; REFK, diary, "Visit to Washington," Oct. 29, 1940, REFKP.

9. CBL to JPK, Oct. 28, 1940, in JPK, diary, box 100, JPKP.

10. JPK, radio address, Oct. 29, 1940, Smith, *HTF,* 482–89.

11. FDR to JPK, Oct. 29; JFK to JPK, Oct. 30, 1940, Smith, *HTF,* 489.

12. KKH to JPK, Oct. 31, 1940, box 2, JPKP.

13. Murphy, diary notes, Nov. 2, 1940, box 1, Gressman.

14. Long, diaries, Nov. 6, 1940, box 5, Long.

15. Lyons to JPK, Nov. 8, 1940, box 111, JPKP.

16. Lyons, *BSC,* Nov. 10, 1940.

17. Joseph F. Dinneen, *The Kennedy Family* (Boston: Little, Brown & Co., 1959), 84.

18. *NYT,* Nov. 12, 1940; Krock to JPK, Nov. 12, 1940, box 31, Krock.

19. Alsop and Kintner, *HC,* Nov. 12, 1940.

20. JPK to Beaverbrook, Nov. 13, 1940, d/400, Beaverbrook.

21. *LAT,* Nov. 30, 1940.

22. Unsigned memorandums to Alsop and Kintner, box 33, Alsop.

23. Fairbanks to FDR, Nov. 19, 1940, PSF 37, FDRL.

24. David Welky, *The Moguls and the Dictators* (Baltimore: Johns Hopkins University Press, 2008), 201–2.

25. Cleugh, memorandum, Nov. 22, 1940, FO 371/339, NAUK; Fairbanks, Jr., to FDR, Nov. 19, 1940, PSF 37, FDRL; unsigned memorandum to Alsop and Kintner, box 33, Alsop.

26. Balderston to Bell, telegram and letter, Nov. 18, 1940, box 30; "Dinner Meeting Agenda," Nov. 20, 1940, box 50, FFF.

27. Herbert Hoover, memorandum, Nov. 22, 1940, box 110, HHLPPI.

28. Lindbergh, *Wartime Journals of Charles A. Lindbergh,* 419–21.

29. JPK, "DM," 52:4–6, JPKP.

30. JPK, diary, Nov. 30, Dec. 1, 1940, Smith, *HTF,* 494–97; *CDT,* Dec. 2, 1940.

TWENTY-SEVEN: THE MAN WHO OUT-HAMLETED HAMLET

1. Ickes, diary, Dec. 1, 1940, Ickes.

2. Alsop and Kintner, *WP,* Dec. 5, 1940.

3. Wood to JPK, Dec. 11, 1940, Wood; JPK to Wood, Dec. 11, 14, 1940, box 237, JPKP.

4. *WP,* Dec. 15, 1940; *LAT,* Dec. 16, 1940.

5. Butler, Jan. 2, 1941, PRED 3/133/1, NAUK.

6. JPK, diary, Dec. 14–18, 1940, box 100, JPKP.

7. JPK, diary, Nov. 4, 1940, Smith, *HTF,* 491; Sidney Fine, *Frank Murphy: The Washington Years* (Ann Arbor: University of Michigan Press, 1984), 221–22, 229–31; JPK, diary, Nov. 30, 1940, Smith, *HTF,* 494–95; Murphy, diary notes, box 1, Gressman.

8. JPK, diary, Dec. 16, 1940, box 100, JPKP.

9. Long, diaries, Dec. 16, 1940, Long.

10. JPK to Burns, Dec. 19, 1940, box 141; JPK to Murphy, Dec. 27, 1940, box 144, JPKP.

11. David Wyman, *The Abandonment of the Jews* (New York: Pantheon Books, 1984), 124–25.

12. FDR, press conference, Dec. 17, 1940, vol. 16, 360–65, FDRL.

13. FDR, Dec. 29, 1940, http://docs.fdrlibrary.marist.edu/122940.html.

14. Stuart to Hufty, Jan. 4, 1941, box 64, America First.

15. Hufty to Stuart, Jan. 7, 1941, box 7, America First.

16. JPK to C. Fitzgerald, Jan. 2, 1941, box 220, JPKP.

17. JPK, diary, Jan. 21, 1941, Smith, *HTF,* 524–29; Ickes, diary, Jan. 19, 1941, Ickes.

18. *LAT,* Jan. 17, 1941.

19. JFK to JPK, Dec. 6, 1940, Smith, *HTF,* 498–506.

20. JPK, radio address, Jan. 18, 1941, box 253, JPKP.
21. Ickes, diary, Jan. 19, 1941, Ickes; *NYT,* Jan. 19, 1941.
22. RFK to REFK, [Jan. 19, 1940], box 2, JPKP.
23. Trohan to Maloney, Nov. 17, no year, box 45, I-60 Robert R. McCormick: Business Correspondence, 1927–1965, McCormick.
24. U.S. Congress, *Lend-Lease Bill: Hearings Before the Committee on Foreign Affairs,* Seventy-seventh Congress, First Session (Washington, DC: Government Printing Office, 1941), 231.
25. Thompson, *WP,* Jan. 22, 1941; *Time,* Feb. 3, 1941; *Life,* Feb. 3, 1941.
26. JPK to JB, Feb. 10, 1941, box 21, Boettiger.
27. FDR to JB, Mar. 3, 1941, box 21, Boettiger.

TWENTY-EIGHT: A FORCED RETIREMENT

1. JPK to Gowen, May 14, 1941, box 222, JPKP.
2. Memo to director, Feb. 23, 1942, Arvad file, J. Edgar Hoover official and confidential file, FBI.
3. EMK to author, Aug. 21, Oct. 8, 2007, May 15, 2008; JKS to author, Oct. 4, 2007, July 16, 17, 2008, Oct. 19, Dec. 11, 2009.
4. Benedict Neenan, *Thomas Verner Moore* (New York: Paulist Press, 2000), 183–90; REFK's secretary to mother superior, St. Gertrude's, Oct. 24, 1940, box 26, REFKP.
5. EMK, *TC,* 61–62.
6. JPK to WRH, June 25, 1941, box 7, WHRP; JPK to Wellington, May 28, 1941, box 215, JPKP.
7. JPK to MacDonald, Apr. 22, 1941, box 229, JPKP.
8. Klemmer, in Whitehead et al., *The Kennedys.*
9. JPK to JF, Dec. 18, 1940, box 220; JPK to Gurnett, Mar. 13, 1941, box 221, JPKP.
10. JPK to J. Russell Young, Apr. 24, 1941, box 245, JPKP.
11. JPK, Oglethorpe address, May 24, 1941, box 253, JPKP.
12. FDR, May 27, 1941, http://docs.fdrlibrary.marist.edu/052741.html.

13. JPK, Notre Dame commencement address, May 29, 1941, box 254, JPKP.
14. HH to JPK, July 1, 1941; JPK to HH, July 11, 31, 1941, box 110, HHPP.
15. KKH to JPK, Oct. 3, 1941, box 7, folder 59, EKSP; KKH to JPK, Oct. 20, 1941, box 2, JPKP.
16. REFK, *TTR,* 244–45.
17. JPK to Casey, July 26 [1941], box 215; JPK to RK, Oct. 10, 1941, in author's possession; JPK to Cavanaugh, Oct. 28, 1941, box 216, JPKP.
18. Thomas Moore to JPK, Nov. 12, 1941, w.b. 34, JPKP.
19. Ann Gargan to author, Sept. 30, 2008; Gargan, in Goodwin, *The Fitzgeralds and the Kennedys,* 640.
20. JKS to author, Apr. 27, 2009; REFK, *TTR,* 245.
21. Brockley, "Rearing the Child Who Never Grew," in *Mental Retardation in America,* 147.
22. Jack El-Hai, *The Lobotomist* (New York: Wiley, 2005), 226–27.
23. Jack D. Pressman, *Last Resort: Psychosurgery and the Limits of Medicine* (New York: Cambridge University Press, 1998), 102.
24. El-Hai, *The Lobotomist,* 167.
25. El-Hai, *The Lobotomist,* 167; JPK to Woodward, Nov. 28, 1941, JPKP.
26. JPK to REFK, Nov. 23, 1942, box 2; JPK to JFK, July 5, 1943; JPK to JPK, Jr., Feb. 21, 1944; JPK to KKH, Mar. 8, 1944, box 2, 3, JPKP.
27. Assorted bills, 1948, w.b. 3, JPKP.
28. REFK, *TTR,* 245.
29. JPK to Sister Anastasia, May 29, 1958, w.b. 3, JPKP.
30. REFK, *TTR,* 245.

TWENTY-NINE: WAR

1. JPK to FDR, Dec. 7, 1941; Early to JPK, Dec. 9. 1941, PPF 207, FDRL.
2. JPK to FDR, Mar. 4, 1942, Smith, *HTF,* 541.
3. JPK, diary, Jan. 17, 1942, box 100, JPKP; Fine, *Frank Murphy,* 221.
4. REFK to children, Jan. 26, 1943, box 2; JPK to Beaverbrook, Feb. 5, 1942, box 214, JPKP.
5. REFK to children, Jan. 20, 1942, box 2, JPKP.
6. Pearson to Winchell, Jan. 6, 1942,

G 210, 3 of 5, "Public Figures,"
Pearson.

7. See letter dated Nov. 16, 1940, from
Columbia University and other
documents in Inga Arvad file, J. Edgar
Hoover official and confidential file, FBI.

8. Arvad to JFK, "Tuesday," n.d., box 4,
JFKPP.

9. Arvad to JPK, Jan. 27, Mar. 11, 1942,
box 4, JFKPP.

10. JFK to Arvad, Mar. 7, 1942, ARV
summary, Inga Arvad file, J. Edgar
Hoover official and confidential file, FBI.

11. Arvad to JFK, "Wednesday," n.d.; Feb.
23, 1942, box 4, JFKPP.

12. JPK to Kane, Jan. 25, 1943, box 225;
JPK to Sarnoff, Feb. 2, 1942, box 234,
JPKP.

13. JPK to FDR, Mar. 4, 1942, Smith, *HTF,*
541–42.

14. FDR to JPK, Mar. 7, 1942, PPF 207,
FDRL.

15. KKH to JPK, n.d., box 4, JPKP; JPK to
FDR, Mar. 12, 1942, PPF 207, FDRL

16. FDR, "Presidential Memorandum for
Admiral Land, Commissioner Vickery,"
Mar. 16, 1942, PPF 207, FDRL.

17. JPK, diary, Apr. 10, 1942, Smith, *HTF,*
544–46.

18. CBL to JPK, Feb. 5, 1942, JPK to JFK,
Feb. 9, 1942, box 4, JPKP.

19. JPK to JPK, Jr., July 6, 1942, box 2,
JPKP.

20. JPK to JPK, Jr., July 18, Aug. 7, 1942,
box 2, JPKP.

21. JPK, Jr., to REFK and JPK, [Sept. 1942],
box 2; REFK to children, Oct. 9, 1942,
box 2, JPKP.

22. JPK to JPK, Jr., June 20, 1942, box 2,
JPKP.

23. Robert Dallek, *An Unfinished Life*
(Boston: Little, Brown & Co., 2003) 81,
85–87; JPK to JPK, Jr., Oct. 1, 1942,
box 2, JPKP.

24. JPK to REFK, Nov. 23, 1942, box 2,
JPKP.

25. JPK to REFK, Nov. 23, 1942, box 2,
JPKP.

26. JPK to REFK, Nov. 23, 1942, box 2,
JPKP; Halifax, diary, Nov. 10, 1942,
Halifax.

27. JPK to REFK, Nov. 23, 1942, box 2,
JPKP.

28. JPK to RFK, Oct. 14, 1942, box 2, JPKP.

29. JPK to REFK, Nov. 23, 1942, box 2,
JPKP.

30. JPK to Sheehy, Oct. 28, 1942, box 235,
JPKP.

31. RFK to REFK, Dec. 7, 1941, box 2; JPK,
diary, Dec. 5, 1942, box 101, JPKP.

32. JKP, diary, Jan. 14, 1943, box 101; JPK
to Brickley, Jan. 25, 1943, box 215,
JPKP.

33. REFK to children, Mar. 11, 1943, box 2;
JPK, diary, Mar. 12, 1943, box 101,
JPKP.

34. JPK, diary, June 17, 1943, box 101,
JPKP.

35. JPK to JFK, Apr. 22, 1943, box 2,
JPKP.

36. Halifax, diary, Mar. 11, 1943, Halifax.

37. JPK to KKH, July 3, 1943, box 2, JPKP.

38. KKH to JFK, July 29, 1943, box 2, JPKP.

39. KKH to family, July 14, 1943, box 2,
JPKP.

40. KKH to JFK, July 29, 1943, box 2, JPKP.

41. KKH to family, Aug. 10, 1943, box 128,
REFKP.

42. KKH to family, Aug. 31, 1943, box 128,
REFKP.

43. JPK to KKH, Sept. 8, 1943, box 2, JPKP.

44. REFK to children, Aug. 25, 1943, box 2;
JPK to JFK, Nov. 16, 1943, box 3, JPKP.

45. JPK to Houghton, June 3, July 13,
Aug. 16, Sept. 14, 1943, box 224, JPKP.

46. JPK to McInerny, Aug. 3, 1943, box 230,
JPKP.

47. JPK to JFK, July 6, 1943, box 2, JPKP.

48. JPK to KKH, Aug. 7, 1943, box 128,
REFKP.

49. JPK to JFK, Aug. 7, 1943, box 2, JPKP.

50. John Hersey, "A Reporter at Large:
Survival," *New Yorker,* June 17, 1944,
31; JPK to JFK, Oct. 15, 1943, box 2,
JPKP.

51. Joan and Clay Blair, Jr., *The Search for
JFK* (New York: Berkley, 1976),
267–306; on PT incident, see Hamilton,
JFK, 581–602.

52. JFK to family, Aug. 13, 1943, box 2,
JPKP.

53. REFK to children, Aug. 25, 1943, box 2,
JPKP.

54. Joey Gargan, *FB* folders, EMKP.

55. REFK to children, Aug. 25, 1943, box 2,
JPKP.

56. JPK to McInerny, Aug. 31, 1943,
box 230, JPKP.

57. JPK to Taylor, Jr., Aug. 24, 1943, box 237, JPKP.
58. REFK to children, Oct. 27, 1943, box 2, JPKP.
59. JFK to JPK, Oct. 30, 1943, box 2, JPKP.
60. JPK to JFK, Nov. 4, 1943, box 3, JPKP.
61. Soucy to director, Oct. 18, 1943, Dec. 27, 1943, Hoover file, A 0729, FBI.
62. JPK to Calder, Dec. 20, 1943, box 216, JPKP.
63. JPK to PKL, Mar. 8, 1944, box 3, JPKP.
64. JPK to JPK, Jr., Feb. 21, 1944, box 3, JPKP.
65. Ross to JPK, May 18, 1944, box 52, *New Yorker*; JPK to JPK, Jr., May 24, 1944, JPKP.
66. KKH to family, Jan. 29, 1944, box 3, JPKP.
67. JPK to JPK, Jr., Feb. 21, 1944, box 3, JPKP.
68. KKH to family, Feb. 22, 1944, Smith, *HTF,* 574–77.
69. REFK to KKH, Feb. 24, 1944, Smith, *HTF,* 577–78.
70. Vivian Mercier, *The Irish Comic Tradition* (London: Oxford University Press, 1962), 47; JPK to KK, Mar. 8, 1944, box 3, JPKP.
71. KKH to JPK, REFK, Mar. 22, 1944, Smith, *HTF,* 580.
72. KKH to family, Apr. 4, 1944, Smith, *HTF,* 581–82.
73. JPK to KKH, Apr. 27, 1944, box 498, folder 11, Schlesinger.
74. REFK, "Notes," n.d., Smith, *HTF,* 584.
75. JKS to author, Feb. 2, 2011.
76. Godfrey to Spellman, May 4, 1944, Smith, *HTF,* 586.
77. KKH to JPK, May 5, 1944, Smith, *HTF,* 586.
78. JPK, Jr., to JPK, May 7, 1944; KKH to JPK, May 8, 1944, Smith, *HTF,* 587.
79. KKH to REFK, May 9, 1944, Smith, *HTF,* 589–91.
80. JPK to JPK, Jr., May 24, 1944, box 3, JPKP.
81. JPK to Beaverbrook, May 24, 1944, d/400, Beaverbrook.
82. JPK, "Address . . . June 12, 1944," box 255, JPKP.
83. CBL to JPK, June 12, 1944, box 228; JPK to JPK, Jr., Aug. 9, 1944, box 3, JPKP.
84. JPK to Houghton, July 7, 1944, box 224, JPKP.
85. JPK to Beaverbrook, May 24, 1944, d/400, Beaverbrook.
86. JPK, Jr., to REFK and JPK, July 26, 1944, Smith, *HTF,* 598.
87. JPK to JPK, Jr., Aug. 9, 1944, box 3, JPKP.

THIRTY: "A MELANCHOLY BUSINESS"
1. EMK, *TC,* 85–86; REFK, *TTR,* 257; JKS to author, Feb. 2, 2011.
2. JKS to author, Feb. 2, 2011; JPK, Jr., to JKS, n.d. [1942–1943], in author's possession.
3. JPK to Howey, Mar. 4, 1954, box 223, JPKP.
4. JPK to Forrestal, Sept. 5, 1944, box 27, folder 86, Forrestal.
5. JPK to Kane, Sept. 8, 1944, box 225; JPK to Houghton, Sept. 11, 1944, box 224, JPKP.
6. JKS to author, Feb. 2, 2011.
7. Halifax, diaries, Sept. 19, 1944, Halifax.
8. JPK, "Diary Notes on the 1944 Political Campaign," Smith, *HTF,* 605–12.
9. Halifax, diaries, Oct. 26, 1944, Halifax.
10. JPK, "Diary Notes on the 1944 Political Campaign," Smith, *HTF,* 605–12.
11. Merle Miller, ed., *Plain Speaking* (New York: Berkley, 1974), 186.
12. JPK to Beaverbrook, Oct. 23, 1944, d/400, Beaverbrook.
13. JPK to Calder, Dec. 5, 1944, box 216, JPKP.
14. JPK to Houghton, May 28, June 21, 1945, box 224, JPKP.
15. H. W. Brands, *Traitor to His Class* (New York: Doubleday, 2008), 813.
16. JPK to KKH, May 1, 1945, Smith, *HTF,* 615–18.
17. HH, notes on meetings of Apr. 19, May 15, 1945, box 110, HHPLPPI.
18. Forrestal, diary, Dec. 27, 1945, Forrestal.
19. Robert I. Gannon, *The Cardinal Spellman Story* (Garden City, NY: Doubleday, 1962), 359.
20. JPK to C. Patterson, Nov. 26, 1945, Smith, *HTF,* 622.
21. JPK, memorandum of conversation, Jan. 31, 1946, box 101, JPKP.
22. JPK, Colby Junior College

commencement, June 17, 1946, box 255, JPKP.

23. Dinneen, cited in Whalen, *The Founding Father,* 388.

24. JPK to Kane, Mar. 19, Apr. 6, 1945, box 225, JPKP.

25. JPK to KKH, May 1, 1945, Smith, *HTF,* 615–18.

26. JPK to KKH, May 1, 1945, box 3, JPKP.

27. JPK, memorandum, June, 1945, box 101, JPKP.

28. Arthur M. Schlesinger, Jr., *Robert Kennedy and His Times* (1978; Boston: Houghton Mifflin, 2002), 59; JPK to Kane, Mar. 19, 1945, box 225, JPKP.

29. EMK, *TC,* 40; EMK to author, Aug. 21, 2007.

30. EKS, oral history, box 42, Blair; http://www.census.gov/population/socdemo/hh-fam/ms2.csv.

31. JPK to EKS, Feb. 12, Oct. 7, 1945, box 8, folder 60, EKSP.

32. Fayne to JPK, Mar. 25, 1945, box 219, JPKP.

33. JKS to author, Feb. 2, Oct. 5, 2011.

34. See statements from Arthur Andersen & Co., Mar. 1947, JPKP.

35. Real estate records, w.b. 34, JPKP.

36. *NYT,* Sept. 29, Oct. 4, 1944.

37. CK to author, Apr. 2, 2009; JPK to Office of Commissioner of Internal Revenue, "In re Merchandise Mart," n.d., w.b. 22; JPK to McCormack, Sept. 5, 1945, box 230, JPKP.

38. Ollman, *FB* folders, EMKP.

39. CK to author, Apr. 2, 2009.

40. Ollman, *FB* folders, EMKP.

41. Heddal, *FB* folders, EMKP.

THIRTY-ONE: THE CANDIDATE'S FATHER

1. JPK, address, Apr. 17, 1945, box 255, JPKP.

2. *CSM,* Aug. 18, 1945.

3. Burns to JPK, Dec. 29, 1944, in author's possession.

4. Forrestal to JPK, July 14, 1945, folder 86, box 27, Forrestal.

5. Forrestal to JPK, Sept. 8, 1945, in Blair and Blair, Jr., *The Search for JFK,* 440.

6. JPK to Calder, Aug. 22, 1945, box 216, JPKP.

7. Sam Stavisky, "Where Does the Veteran Stand Today?" *Annals of the American Academy of Political and Social Science* 259 (Sept. 1948): 134.

8. JFK to Donnelly, Dec. 17, 1945, box 11, JFKPP.

9. EKS in Goodwin, *The Fitzgeralds and the Kennedys,* 707.

10. Mark Dalton, oral history, Aug. 4, 1964, JPKOHP; JPK to Kane, Feb. 11, 1946, box 225, JPKP.

11. Dalton, in Whitehead et al., *The Kennedys.*

12. JPK to Krock, Feb. 28, 1946, Smith, *HTF,* 625.

13. JPK to Kane, Smith, *HTF,* 625–26.

14. Campbell Craig and Fredrik Logevall, *America's Cold War* (Cambridge, MA: Harvard University Press, 2009), 67.

15. JPK to Cropley, Feb. 25, 1946, box 217, JPKP.

16. *Life,* Mar. 18, 1946, 36.

17. Hacker report, Mar. 14, 1946, series III, box 51, folder 11, Knopf records; JPK to Emily Morison, Mar. 25, 1946, general correspondence, box 7, folder 7, Knopf.

18. Samuel Bornstein, oral history, Apr. 15, 1977, JFKOHP; Kenneth P. O'Donnell and David F. Powers, with Joe McCarthy, *"Johnny, We Hardly Knew Ye"* (Boston: Little, Brown & Co., 1970), 72; JPK to McKelvey, May 4, 1946, box 31, JPKP.

19. REFK to KK, June 6, 1946, box 3, JPKP.

20. John Droney, oral history, Nov. 30, 1964, JFKOHP; Dalton, in Whitehead et al., *The Kennedys.*

21. KKH to JFK, July 13, 1946, Smith, *HTF,* 627.

22. JPK to Houghton, July 30, 1946, box 224, JPKP.

23. See materials in Joseph P. Kennedy, Jr. Foundation, box 9, JFKPP.

24. Truman, "Address Before a Joint Session of Congress, Mar. 12, 1947, in http://avalon.law.yale.edu/20th_century/trudoc.asp.

25. Schlesinger, *Robert Kennedy and His Times,* 69.

26. Krock, *Memoirs,* 338; *NYT,* Mar. 12, 1947.

27. "The New Appeasement," Mar. 29, 1947; Reston, *NYT,* Mar. 23, 1947; A. J. Muste, *NYT,* Mar. 16, 1947.

28. Douglas, *Go East, Young Man*, 200.

29. Coniff, *NYJA*, Apr. 30, 1947.

THIRTY-TWO: FAMILY MATTERS

1. JPK to Ordway, Nov. 17, 1950, box 232, JPKP.

2. KKH to family, n.d., box 3; REFK to girls, July 25, 1949, box 3, JPKP.

3. JPK to Calder, July 31, 1946, box 216, JPKP.

4. Commissioner of Internal Revenue to JPK, [1947], w.b. 22, JPKP.

5. "How to Have Your Own Foundation," *Fortune*, Aug. 1947.

6. "Information guide," Aug. 8, 1946, box 9, JFKPP.

7. *BP*, Aug. 13, 1947; "Archbishop Cushing Announces," Feb. 16, 1956, box 221, JPKP.

8. Brian Burns to author, Apr. 22, 2010.

9. Landis, oral history, 552–53, CUOH.

10. Landis to JPK, July 20, 1951, box 51, LandisLC; JPK to Palmer, Mar. 22, 1955, box 233, JPKP.

11. JPK to KKH, June 10, 1947, box 3, JPKP.

12. JPK, Hotel Continental speech, Oct. 23, 1947, box 256, JPKP; Dalton, oral history, JPKOHP.

13. JPK, Hotel Continental speech, Oct. 23, 1947, box 256, JPKP.

14. *BP*, Apr. 18, 1948.

15. Cunningham, "Kennedy Plan Purposeful," *BH*, May 20, 1948.

16. KKH to JKP, July 2, 1947, box 3, JPKP.

17. JPK, May 14, 1948, Smith, *HTF*, 636.

18. Much of this account is taken from Lynn McTaggart, *Kathleen Kennedy: Her Life and Times* (New York: Holt, Rinehart, & Winston, 1983), 224–38; Leaming, *Jack Kennedy: The Education of a Statesman*, 194.

19. JPK to Beaverbrook, July 27, 1948, c/193, Beaverbrook.

20. JPK to Duchess of Devonshire, Sept. 1, 1948, Smith, *HTF*, 637.

21. Cavanaugh, *FB* folders, EMKP.

22. Landis, memorandum on Joseph P. Kennedy, Jr. Memorial, Sept. 26, 1951, box 217, JPKP.

23. JPK to EKS, Jan. 25, 1950, box 4, JPKP.

24. Ange to JPK, Jan. 25, 1950, box 266; JPK to Ange, Jan. 31, 1950, box 266, JPKP.

25. Landis, memorandum on Joseph P. Kennedy, Jr. Memorial," Sept. 26, 1951, box 217; JPK to Ange, Aug. 8, 1951, box 266, JPKP.

26. JPK to Wright, Sept. 18, 1951, box 266, JPKP.

27. Cushing to JPK, Sept. 27, 1951, box 217, JPKP.

28. JPK to Cushing, Aug. 6, 1952, box 217, JPKP.

29. Cushing to JPK, Aug. 10, 1952, box 217, JPKP.

30. Cushing, *FB* folders, EMKP.

31. Spellman to JPK, Aug. 21, 1950, with enclosure of Spellman to Hartford, July 31, 1950, S/C-78, folder 10, AANY.

32. *NYT*, Sept. 8, Oct. 30, 1950.

33. JPK to Ford, Dec. 3, 1948, box 220, JPKP; Cushing to JPK, Dec. 4, 1948, Cushing.

34. Sister Maureen to Ford, Dec. 21, 1948, box 220, JPKP.

35. JPK to Ford, Dec. 31, 1948, box 220, JPKP.

36. Daniel Bellei to author, June 2, 2010; JKS to author, Apr. 27, 2009; REFK, *TTR*, 245.

37. Ford to Sister Anastasia; Ford to Danforth, Jan. 16, 1950; JPK to Ford, Sept. 24, 1951, box 220, JPKP.

38. Sister Anastasia to Ford, May 21, 1958, w.b. 3, JPKP.

39. JPK to Sister Anastasia, May 29, 1958, w.b. 3, JPKP.

THIRTY-THREE: "THE GREAT DEBATE"

1. JPK to Truman, Jan. 31, 1950, box 237, JPKP.

2. JPK, "Summary of Talk," June 30, 1950, Smith, *HTF*, 638–41.

3. JPK to Galeazzi, July 3, 1950, box 221, JPKP.

4. Robert Donovan, *Tumultuous Years* (New York: Norton, 1982), 309, 275; Melvyn Leffler, *A Preponderance of Power* (Stanford, CA: Stanford University Press, 1992), 398; Arnold A. Offner, *Another Such Victory: President Truman and the Cold War, 1945–1953* (Stanford: Stanford University Press, 2002), 396.

5. JPK, Virginia Law School Forum speech, Dec. 12, 1950, 256, JPKP.

6. *NYDM*, Dec. 13, 1950; Krock, *NYT*,

Dec. 15, 1950; Lippmann, *NYHT,*
Dec. 19, 1950.

7. Joseph and Stewart Alsop, *NYHT,*
Dec. 24, 1950.

8. Press release, Jan. 6, 1951, box 8, JFKPP.

9. JPK, Harmonie Club remarks, Feb. 3,
1951, box 258, JPKP.

10. *BH,* Feb. 7, 1951; *BT,* Feb. 8, 1951.

11. JFK, statement before the Committee on
Foreign Relations, Feb. 22, 1951, box 6,
JFKPP.

12. JFK to JPK, Mar. 13, 1951, box 6,
JFKPP; REFK to children, May 7, 1951,
box 4, JPKP.

13. JPK, meeting with Eisenhower, Apr.
1951, Smith, *HTF,* 646–50.

14. JPK to Galeazzi, May 18, 1951, box 221,
JPKP.

15. Reston to JPK, Nov. 7, 1951, box 233,
JPKP; JPK to Duchess of Devonshire,
June 22, 1951, Smith, *HTF,* 650.

16. JPK to Ordway, June 11, 1951, box 232,
JPKP.

17. JPK to Galeazzi, July 3, 1950, May 18,
1951, box 221, JPKP.

18. Rosenbloom, *FB* folders, EMKP.

19. JPK to Howey, Mar. 4, 1954, box 223,
JPKP.

20. JPK to Poole, Nov. 20, 1951, box 233,
JPKP.

21. EMK, *TC,* 95–56; EMK, in REFK, *TTR,*
123.

22. EMK, *TC,* 99.

23. JPK to Biddle, Jan. 18, 1952, box 214,
JPKP.

24. JPK to Calder, Nov. 24, 1951, box 216,
JPKP; EMK, *TC,* 95–97.

25. Cavanaugh, *FB* folders, EMKP.

26. John Cavanaugh to JPK, with
attachments, Sept. 24, 1951, box 249,
JPKL.

**THIRTY-FOUR: THE NEXT SENATOR
FROM MASSACHUSETTS**

1. REFK, *TTR,* 274.

2. O'Donnell and Powers, *"Johnny, We
Hardly Knew Ye,"* 86–87.

3. JPK to McInerny, Aug. 10, 1951,
box 230, JPKP.

4. JPK to JFK, Oct. 13, Nov. 2, 1951,
box 4, JPKP.

5. JFK to JPK, Oct. 31, 1951, box 4, JPKP.

6. JFK, transcript of radio address, Nov. 14,
1951, box 135, JFKOF.

7. JPK to Poole, Nov. 20, 1951, box 233,
JPKP.

8. Eunice Shriver, *FB* folders, EMKP.

9. JPK to C. Fitzgerald, Oct. 22, 1951,
box 220, JPKP.

10. JPK to Calder, Nov. 24, 1951, box 216,
JPKP.

11. JPK to Spivak, Jan. 4, 1952, box 235,
JPKP.

12. JPK, Dec. 17, 1951 radio address,
box 259, JPKP.

13. JPK to Stevenson, Jan. 8, 1952, box 259,
JPKP.

14. JPK to Powers, Dec. 21, 1951, box 233,
JPKP.

15. JPK to Beaverbrook, Feb. 18, 1952,
c/193, Beaverbrook; REFK and RC,
Jan. 4, 1972, REFKP; EMK to author,
Oct. 8, 2007; Downey, *FB* folders,
EMKP.

16. JPK to Galeazzi, Jan. 15, Feb. 19, 1952,
box 221, JPKP.

17. Sargent Shriver, oral history, Blair.

18. Landis, oral history, 590, CUOH.

19. Sargent Shriver, oral history, Blair;
O'Donnell, in *American Journey: The
Times of Robert Kennedy,* interviews by
Jean Stein, ed. George Plimpton (New
York: Harcourt Brace Jovanovich, 1970),
40–41; O'Donnell and Powers, *"Johnny,
We Hardly Knew Ye,"* 159.

20. Droney, oral history, Nov. 30, 1964,
JFKOHP.

21. O'Donnell, in *American Journey,* 41.

22. O'Donnell and Powers, *"Johnny, We
Hardly Knew Ye,"* 98–99.

23. Sargent Shriver, oral history, Blair.

24. Robert David Johnson, *Congress and the
Cold War* (New York: Cambridge
University Press, 2006), 42–43; Lewin,
FB folders, EMKP.

25. Schlesinger to Landis, July 10, 1952,
box 288, JPKP.

26. Irwin Ross, "Joseph P. Kennedy: The
True Story," *New York Post,* Jan. 9,
1960.

27. Trohan, *LAT,* July 25, 1960.

28. James MacGregor Burns, *John Kennedy:
A Political Profile* (New York: Harcourt,
Brace & World, 1959), 113–14; Scott
Stossel, *Sarge: The Life and Times of
Sargent Shriver* (Washington, DC:
Smithsonian Books, 2004), 109.

29. David Oshinsky, *A Conspiracy So*

Immense (New York: Free Press, 1983), 239–42.

30. JPK to EMK, June 25, 1952, box 4, JPKP.

31. "Up from South Boston: The Rise & Fall of John Fox," *Time,* July 7, 1958; RFK, in O'Brien, *John F. Kennedy,* 257.

32. JPK to Ordway, Nov. 13, 1952, 232, JPKP.

33. JPK to Clark, Nov. 15, 1952, box 216, JPKP.

THIRTY-FIVE: RETIREMENT

1. Rowe to LBJ, Jan. 12, 1953, Rowe to JPK, James Landis, Jan. 12, 1953, LBJA Famous Names, James H., Jr., LBJL.

2. JPK to Brickley, Mar. 12, 1953, box 215; JPK to C. Fitzgerald, Apr. 6, 1953, box 220, JPKP.

3. *NYT,* July 10, 1953; Kevin Michael Schultz, *Tri-Faith America* (New York: Oxford University Press, 2011), 76–77; JPK to Cavanaugh, July 22, 1953, box 216, JPKP.

4. JPK to RFK, Aug. 15, 1954, box 4, JPKP.

5. JPK to JFK, Aug. 19, 1954, box 4, JPKP.

6. Nichols to Tolson, May 11, 1954, part ID, JPK file, FBI.

7. Foster to JEH, July 2, 1954, JPK file, in JEH O&C, FBI.

8. JPK to JEH, Oct. 11, 1955, box 224, JPKP.

9. Memo to Tolson, Dec. 18, 1957, part VII, JPK file, FBI.

10. JPK to Calder, Dec. 31, 1952, box 288, JPKP.

11. Timothy Walch, "Some of My Best Friends Are Democrats," in Walch, *Uncommon Americans: The Lives and Legacies of Herbert and Lou Henry Hoover* (Westport, CT: Greenwood Publishing Group, 2003), 225–35; JPK to REFK, Apr. 20, 1955, box 4, JPKP.

12. Foster to JEH, July 2, 1954, JPK file, in J. Edgar Hoover O&C, FBI.

13. Macdonald to JPK, n.d.; JPK to Macdonald, July 22, 1953, box 229, JPKP.

14. Christopher Lawford, *Symptoms of Withdrawal* (New York: HarperCollins, 2005), 6.

15. EMK to author, Aug. 21, 2007.

16. JPK to Downey, Aug. 23, 1954, box 218;

17. JPK to Champion, June 19, 1954, box 243, JPKP.

18. REFK to children, Aug. 4, 1954, box 4; JPK to REFK, July 12, 1955; JPK to JKS, July 20, 1955, box 4, JPKP.

19. JPK to EMK, Aug. 13, 1955, box 4, JPKP.

20. JPK to McInerny, Aug. 29, 1954, box 230, JPKP.

21. JPK to REFK, July 12, 1955, box 4, JPKP.

22. JFK, EKS, JKS to JPK, Oct., 1954, box 4, JPKP.

23. JPK to Downey, Aug. 23, 1954, box 218; JPK to Polly Fitzgerald, May 11, 1953, box 246, JPKP.

24. JPK, diary, Aug. 14, 1954, box 101, JPKP.

25. JPK to McInerny, Aug. 29, 1954, box 230, JPKP.

26. JPK to JFK, Aug. 19, 1954, box 4, JPKP.

27. JPK to McInerny, Aug. 29, 1954, box 230, JPKP.

28. Goodwin, *The Fitzgeralds and the Kennedys,* 774–75.

29. JPK to Rosenbloom, Nov. 9, 1954, box 234, JPKP.

30. Smathers to JPK, Nov. 9, 1954, box 235, JPKP.

31. JPK to Watson, Dec. 3, 1954, box 252, JPKP.

32. JPK to Jean Kerr McCarthy, n.d., box 230, JPKP.

33. REFK to JPK, July 10, 1955, box 4; JPK to RFK, July 16, 1955, box 4, JPKP.

34. JPK to Heffernan, Jan. 5, 1955, box 223, JPKP.

35. Goodwin, *The Fitzgeralds and the Kennedys,* 776.

36. O'Donnell and Powers, *"Johnny, We Hardly Knew Ye,"* 115.

37. JPK to Galeazzi, Apr. 28, 1955, box 221, JPKP.

38. JPK to JFK, July 30, 1955, box 4, JPKP.

39. JPK to EMK, Sept. 3, 1955, box 4, JPKP.

40. LBJ to JPK, Aug. 25, 1956, box 225, JPKP.

41. McClellan to JPK, Sept. 11, 1954, box 230; JPK to ESK, July 20, Aug. 8, 1955, box 4, JPKP.

42. William O. Douglas, *The Court Years,*

1939–1975 (New York: Random House, 1980), 306.

43. JPK to Dunn, July 30, 1955, box 218, JPKP.
44. JPK to REFK, Aug. 24, 1955, box 4, JPKP.
45. Schlesinger, *Robert Kennedy and His Times,* 137–38.
46. Droney, oral history, Nov. 30, 1964, JFKOHP.
47. EMK, *TC,* 108–9.
48. EMK to author, May 15, 2008.
49. EMK to author, May 15, 2008; EMK, *TC,* 222.

THIRTY-SIX: MAKING MONEY AND GIVING IT AWAY

1. Racine to author, Aug. 21, 2008.
2. Kravis, *FB* folders, EMKP.
3. Richard Austin Smith, "The Fifty-Million-Dollar Man," *Fortune,* Nov. 1957; JPK to Ford, Aug. 3, 1954, box 226; JFK to JPK, July 31, 1954, box 4; JPK to JFK, Aug. 19, 1954, box 4, JPKP.
4. REFK to girls, January 1952, box 4, JPKP.
5. JPK to daughters, Feb. 18, 1952, box 4, JPKP.
6. Wright to JPK, July 3, 1953, Wright; "Miscellaneous Donations," box 267; "Archbishop Cushing Announces," Feb. 16, 1956, box 221, JPKP.
7. JPK to Denomy, Jan. 7, 1957, box 266; JPK to Royal, Jan. 27, 1953, box 235, JPKP.
8. JPK to Edison, Oct. 31, 1957, box 267, JPKP.
9. JPK to Spellman, June 21, 1958, S/C-27, folder 2, AANY.
10. EKS, *FB* folders, EMKP.
11. JPK to Rusk, Feb. 7, 1958, June 4, 1958, box 233; JPK to Bundy, May 13, 1958, box 267, JPKP.
12. EKS, *FB* folders, EMKP.
13. Sargent Shriver to JPK, n.d., box 2, folder 4, EKSP.
14. JPK to Sachar, May 11, 1959, box 11, JFKOF.
15. JPK to Opdenaker, Oct. 29, 1959, box 267, JPKP.
16. Elizabeth Boggs, "Federal Legislation Affecting the Mentally Retarded, 1955–1967," *Mental Retardation* 3 (1971).
17. JPK to Eisenhower, Dulles, Jan. 14, 1956, box 263, JPKP.

18. William Colby and Peter Forbath, *Honorable Men: My Life in the CIA* (New York: Simon & Schuster, 1978), 109.
19. JPK to Galeazzi, Jan. 30, 1956, box 221, JPKP.
20. JPK to Galeazzi, Mar. 5, 1956, box 221, JPKP.
21. JPK to Cavanaugh, May 5, 1956, box 216, JPKP.
22. Colby and Forbath, *Honorable Men,* 129.
23. Wyzanski memo, Oct. 20, 1964, box 498, folder 11, Schlesinger.
24. "Bailey Report," Victor Lasky, *JFK: The Man and the Myth* (New York: Macmillan, 1963), appendix B, 587–98; Theodore C. Sorensen, *Counselor: A Life at the Edge of History* (New York: Harper Collins, 2008), 159.
25. JPK to JFK, May 25, 1956, box 4, JPKP.
26. JFK to JPK, June 29, 1956, box 4, JPKP.
27. O'Donnell and Powers, *"Johnny, We Hardly Knew Ye,"* 105.
28. JPK to Beaverbrook, June 15, 1956, c/194a, Beaverbrook; JPK to Downey, n.d., box 218, JPKP.
29. JPK to Sargent Shriver, July 18, 1956, box 236, JPKP.
30. JPK to EMK, July 18, 1956, box 4, JPKP; Dallek, *An Unfinished Life,* 262.
31. JPK to Galeazzi, July 30, 1956, box 222, JPKP.
32. JPK to JFK, July 23, 1956, box 4, JPKP.
33. REFK, *TTR,* 281.
34. Bartlett, oral history, Jan. 6, 1965, JFKOHP.
35. O'Donnell and Powers, *"Johnny, We Hardly Knew Ye,"* 138.
36. RFK, *FB* folders, EMKP; JKS to author, Oct. 5, 2011.
37. JPK to Downey, Aug. 24, 1956, box 218, JPKP.

THIRTY-SEVEN: THE CATHOLIC CANDIDATE

1. JPK to Beaverbrook, Oct. 27, 1956, c/194a, Beaverbrook.
2. Theodore Sorensen, *Kennedy* (New York: Harper & Row, 1965), 100; REFK, diary, June 23, 1960, box 4, REFKP.
3. JPK to Galeazzi, Nov. 9, 1956, box 222, JPKP.
4. O'Donnell and Powers, *"Johnny, We Hardly Knew Ye,"* 144.

5. Schlesinger, *Robert Kennedy and His Times*, 153–54.

6. JFK to LBJ, July 27, 1956, "Three Western Union Telegrams," JFKL.

7. Burns, *John Kennedy*, 187; JPK to JFK, July 18, 1957, box 4, JPKP.

8. JPK to JFK, Aug. 7, 1957, box 4, JPKP.

9. Harold Martin, "The Amazing Kennedys," *Saturday Evening Post*, Sept. 17, 1957, 48.

10. *NYT,* Oct. 28, 1957.

11. JPK to Henry Luce, Nov. 28, 1957, box 228, JPKP.

12. JPK to Galeazzi, Sept. 12, Dec. 9, 1957, box 222, JPKP.

13. Clark Clifford, with Richard Holbrooke, *Counsel to the President* (New York: Random House, 1991), 306–10.

14. *NYT,* Jan. 5, 1958; JPK to JFK, Jan. 14, 1958, box 4, JPKP.

15. JPK to Hesburgh, May 21, 1958, box 250, JPKP.

16. REFK to RFK, Feb. 19, 1958, box 4, JPKP.

17. JPK to Galeazzi, Feb. 7, 1958, box 222, JPKP.

18. JPK to Morrissey, Feb. 4, 1958, box 231; JPK to des Rosiers, Apr. 10, 1958, box 218, JPKP.

19. *WP,* Mar. 16, 1958.

20. *WP,* Mar. 15, 1959.

21. O'Brien, *John F. Kennedy,* 400–401.

22. JPK to Galeazzi, Apr. 15, 1958, box 222, JPKP.

23. EMK, *TC,* 124.

24. LBJ to JPK, Mar. 25, 1958, Senate, master file index KEM-KEQ, box 103, folder 143, LBJL; Lawrence O'Brien, *No Final Victories* (Garden City, NY: Doubleday, 1954), 54–55; O'Donnell and Powers, *"Johnny, We Hardly Knew Ye,"* 160.

25. JPK to McIntyre, June 6, 1958, box 230, JPKP.

26. Knebel, "Democratic Forecast: A Catholic in 1960," *Look,* Mar. 3, 1959.

27. Cogley, oral history, Feb. 20, 1966, JFKOHP.

28. *Commonweal,* Mar. 20, 1959.

29. JPK to Galeazzi, Mar. 30, 1959, box 222, JPKP.

30. JPK to Galeazzi, Apr. 17, 1959, box 222, JPKP.

31. Cushing, oral history, 1966; Cogley, oral history, 1968, JFKOHP.

32. JPK to Galeazzi, Apr. 17, 1959, box 222, JPKP.

THIRTY-EIGHT: ELECTING A PRESIDENT

1. Sorensen, *Kennedy,* 119–21; Sorensen, *Counselor,* 180.

2. REFK, diary, June 23, 1960, box 4, REFKP; *NYT,* Oct. 23, 1959.

3. JPK to Galeazzi, Jan. 1, 1960, box 222, JPKP.

4. Krock, *NYT,* Jan. 10, 1958.

5. JPK to Galeazzi, Mar. 9, 1960, box 222, JPKP.

6. JPK to Harry Brandt, Jan. 27, 1960, box 214, JPKP.

7. JPK to RFK, Feb. 8, 1960, box 248, JFKPP.

8. JPK to Steve Smith, Feb. 8, 1960, box 4, JPKP.

9. David Lawrence, oral history, Jan. 26, 1966, JFKOHP.

10. O'Donnell and Powers, *"Johnny, We Hardly Knew Ye,"* 92.

11. JPK to Galeazzi, Mar. 9, 31, 1960, box 222, JPKP.

12. Goodwin, *The Fitzgeralds and the Kennedys,* 797.

13. *NYT,* Feb. 21, 1960; JPK to Beaverbrook, Feb. 18, 1960, c/194b; Beaverbrook.

14. Carrillo to JPK, Mar. 25, 1960; JPK to Carrillo, Apr. 4, 1960, box 216, JPKP.

15. *NYT,* Apr. 9, 1960.

16. JPK to Clemens, Apr. 4, 1960, box 216, JPKP.

17. Drew Pearson, *WP,* Apr. 5, 1960.

18. O'Donnell and Powers, *"Johnny, We Hardly Knew Ye,"* 180.

19. JPK to M. Morrissey, Apr. 8, 1960, box 230, JPKP.

20. JPK to Beaverbrook, Apr. 20, 1960, c/194b, Beaverbrook.

21. Benjamin C. Bradlee, *Conversations with Kennedy* (New York: Norton, 1975), 16.

22. Racine to author, Mar. 19, 2009.

23. O'Donnell and Powers, *"Johnny, We Hardly Knew Ye,"* 186–88.

24. *NYT,* Apr. 22, 1960; O'Donnell and Powers, *"Johnny, We Hardly Knew Ye,"* 187–88; Sorensen, *Kennedy,* 145.

25. *NYT,* May 18, 1960.

26. JPK to Galeazzi, May 27, 1960, box 222, JPKP.

27. *BP,* May 22, 1960.

28. Sorensen, *Kennedy,* 152; Timilty, *FB* folders, EMKP.

29. Robert A. Caro, *The Passage of Power* (New York: Random House, 2012), 95–97.

30. Seigenthaler, oral history, July 22, 1964, JFKOHP; "Pride of the Clan," *Time,* July 11, 1960.

31. EMK, *TC,* 150.

32. Charles Bartlett, oral history, Jan 6, 1965, JFKOHP.

33. Charles Spalding, oral history, Blair.

34. Henry Luce, oral history, Nov. 11, 1965, JPKOHP.

35. *Newsweek,* Aug. 8, 1960.

36. "A Talk with the Silent Kennedy," *U.S. News & World Report,* Aug. 22, 1960.

37. Pearson, "The Daily Washington Merry-Go-Round," July 11, 1960, http://www.aladin.wrlc.org/gsdl/collect/pearson/pearson.shtml.

38. *NYT,* Sept. 1, 1960.

39. Anti-Kennedy pamphlet, box 31, Schiff.

40. Feldman to JPK, Oct. 11, 1960, box 219, JPKP.

41. JPK to Beaverbrook, Sept. 9, 1960, c/194b, Beaverbrook.

42. "Protestant Unit Wary on Kennedy," *NYT,* Sep. 8, 1960.

43. JFK, "Address to the Greater Houston Ministerial Association," Sept. 12, 1960, JFKL.

44. Theodore White, *The Making of the President* (New York: Atheneum, 1960), 346.

45. Sorensen, *Counselor,* 190.

46. *NYT,* May 25, 1960, 13; *NYT,* May 31, 1960, 23.

47. Debate transcript, *NYT,* Oct. 8, 1960.

48. JPK, "An American Foreign Policy for Americans," Dec. 12, 1950, box 256; "Excerpts from Kennedy Talk on Cuba," *NYT,* Oct. 7, 1960.

49. Frank Stanton, oral history, 331–32, CUOH.

50. "Spellman Sees," *NYT,* Oct. 24, 1960, 1.

51. Sorensen, *Kennedy,* 208–9; Lawrence Fuchs, *Kennedy and American Catholicism* (New York: Meredith Press, 1967), 184–85.

52. O'Donnell and Powers, *"Johnny, We Hardly Knew Ye,"* 245.

THIRTY-NINE: "HE BELONGS TO THE COUNTRY"

1. EMK, *TC,* 158; O'Donnell and Powers, *"Johnny, We Hardly Knew Ye,"* 250–51.

2. REFK, *TTR,* 322.

3. Jacqueline Kennedy, *Historic Conversations on Life with John F. Kennedy* (New York: Hyperion, 2011), 97.

4. Jacques Lowe, *JFK Remembered* (New York: Random House, 1993), 100.

5. REFK, *TTR,* 323.

6. "Winner's Pledge," *NYT,* Nov. 10, 1960, 1.

7. EMK, *TC,* 158.

8. Hugh Sidey, "Joe Kennedy's Feelings About His Son, *Life,* Dec. 19, 1960, 32.

9. Sorensen, *Kennedy,* 223; Philip E. Converse et al., "Stability and Change in 1960: A Reinstating Election," *American Political Science Review* 55, no. 2 (June 1961): 278.

10. Converse et al., "Stability and Change," 275; Dallek, *An Unfinished Life,* 296.

11. Chris Matthews, *Jack Kennedy: Elusive Hero* (New York: Simon & Schuster, 2011), 318–19.

12. John J. Binder, "Organized Crime and the 1960 Presidential Election," *Public Choice* 130 (2007): 241–66.

13. JPK to Galeazzi, Jan. 6, 1961, box 222, JPKP.

14. JPK to Galeazzi, Feb. 6, 1961, box 222, JPKP.

15. JPK to Galeazzi, Oct. 24, 1961, box 222, JPKP.

16. Spellman to RFK, Apr. 10, 1961; "Memorandum for His Eminence, Apr. 11, 1961," folder 10, S/C-78, AANY.

17. Schiff, memorandum, Dec. 1, 1960, box 31, Schiff.

18. JPK to Galeazzi, Jan. 6, 1961, box 222, JPKP.

19. Sidey, "Joe Kennedy's Feelings About His Son," 32.

20. Billy Graham, *Just As I Am* (San Francisco: HarperSanFrancisco, 1997), 394–96.

21. Thurston Clarke, *Ask Not: The Inauguration of John F. Kennedy and the Speech That Changed America* (New York: Henry Holt, 2004), 39–40.

22. Clifford, *Counsel to the President,* 336–37.

23. EKS, *FB* folders, EMKP; EKS, oral history, May 7, 1968, JFKOHP.
24. Robert E. Cooke, oral history, Mar. 29, 1968, JFKOHP.
25. *NYT,* Oct. 12, 1961, 1.
26. JPK to Rogers, Jan. 14, 1961, box 234; JPK to Regan, Feb. 2, 1961, box 234; JPK to Henry, Jan. 16, 1961, box 247, JPKP.
27. Sammy Davis, Jr., and Jane and Burt Boyar, *Sammy: An Autobiography* (New York: Farrar, Straus & Giroux, 2000), 388–89.
28. Clarke, *Ask Not,* 158–61; Paul B. Fay, *The Pleasure of His Company* (New York: Harper & Row, 1966), 90.
29. EMK, *TC,* 165.
30. Goodwin, *The Fitzgeralds and the Kennedys,* 815–16.
31. REFK, *TTR,* 335, 337.
32. EMK to author, Aug. 21, 2007; JPK to Steele, Feb. 20, 1961, box 226, JPKP.
33. EMK, *TC,* 170; EKS, *FB* folders, EMKP; JPK to EMK, Apr. 15, 1961, box 4, JPKP.
34. JKS to author, July 16, 2008.
35. EMK to author, Oct. 8, 2007.
36. JPK to Stearn, Feb. 6, 1961, box 251, JPKP.
37. REFK, diary, Apr. 19, 1961, in *TTR,* 342; William Manchester, *Portrait of a President* (Boston: Little, Brown & Co., 1962), 35.
38. EMK to author, Aug. 21, 2007, May 15, 2008.
39. JPK to Morrissey, June 3, 1960, box 231, JPKP.
40. Schlesinger, *Robert Kennedy and His Times,* 375–76; Victor Navasky, *Kennedy Justice* (1971; repr., New York: Authors Guild Backinprint.com, 2000), 410.
41. Navasky, *Kennedy Justice,* 429–40.
42. JPK to Novello, July 19, 1961, box 231; JPK to Lincoln, July 18, 1961, box 227, JPKP.
43. JPK to LBJ, Aug. 1, 1961, box 252, JPKP.
44. LBJ to JPK, Aug. 14, 1961, box 27, folder 143, LBJP.
45. JPK to Annenberg, Sept. 14, 1961, box 213, JPKP.
46. JPK to Royal, Oct. 6, 1961, box 245, JPKP.
47. Hurxthal to JPK, Nov. 3, 1961, w.b. 1, JPKP.
48. *NYT,* Nov. 12, 1959; *LAT,* Nov. 13,

1959; JPK to Rockefeller III, Nov. 8, 1961, w.b. 34, JPKP.
49. Sorensen, *Kennedy,* 367; REFK, diary, "Thanksgiving '61," box 4, REFKP.
50. JPK to Suydam, Dec. 11, 1961, box 251, JPKP.

FORTY: "NO!"

1. Ann Gargan, *FB* folders, EMKP.
2. REFK and Coughlin, Jan. 13, 1972, box 8, REFKP.
3. Rita Dallas and Jeanira Ratcliffe, *The Kennedy Case* (New York: G. P. Putnam's Sons, 1973), 80–81; *NYT,* Apr. 30, 1962, 9.
4. Dallas and Ratcliffe, *The Kennedy Case,* 87.
5. Betts to author, Apr. 2, 2009.
6. Kathleen Kennedy Townsend, Joseph P. Kennedy, Jr., *FB* folders, EMKP; Robert Kennedy, Jr., to author, Jan. 5, 2011.
7. Hamilton Brown, *FB* folders, EMKP.
8. REFK to children, Sept. 1962; EMK, ed., *Her Grace Above Gold: In Loving Remembrance of Rose Fitzgerald Kennedy* (Joseph P. Kennedy, Jr. Foundation, 1997), 54.
9. REFK to Coughlin, Jan. 13, 1972, box 8, REFKP.
10. Bradlee, *Conversations with Kennedy,* 167–69.
11. REFK, oral history, Feb. 1, 1968, box 12, HHOHP.
12. REFK, *TTR,* 381.
13. EMK, *TC,* 210; William Manchester, *The Death of a President* (1967; repr., New York: Penguin, 1977), 502.
14. Dallas and Ratcliffe, *The Kennedy Case,* 242–48; REFK, box 8, folder 8, REFKP; Manchester, *Death of a President,* 502.
15. Recorded telephone conversations, #2709, Mar. 30, 1964; #3386, May 11, 1964; #4139, July 3, 1964; #4180, July 8, 1964, http://millercenter.org/scripps/archive/presidentialrecordings/johnson.
16. Recorded telephone conversations, Steven Smith, #3381–3382, May 11, 1964, http://millercenter.org/scripps/archive/presidentialrecordings/johnson.
17. Recorded telephone conversations, #8902, Sept. 24, 1965, http://millercenter.org/scripps/archive/presidentialrecordings/johnson.
18. REFK, *TTR,* 410.

BIBLIOGRAPHY OF WORKS CITED

Adler-Rudel, S. "The Evian Conference on the Refugee Question." *Yearbook of the Leo Baeck Institute* 13 (1968).

Aster, Sidney. *1939: The Making of the Second World War.* New York: Simon & Schuster, 1974.

Badger, Anthony J. *The New Deal: The Depression Years, 1933–1940.* New York: Hill & Wang, 1989.

Bailey, Catherine. *Black Diamonds: The Rise and Fall of an English Dynasty.* London: Penguin, 2007.

Baltimore Sun. "Forging America: The History of Bethlehem Steel," 2003. http://www.balti moresun.com/topic/all-bethsteel-c3p13,0,4940413.story.

Baltzell, E. Digby. *Puritan Boston and Quaker Philadelphia.* New York: Free Press, 1979.

Bearse, Ray, and Anthony Read. *Conspirator: The Untold Story of Tyler Kent.* London: Macmillan London, 1991.

Beauchamp, Cari. *Joseph P. Kennedy Presents.* New York: Alfred A. Knopf, 2009.

———. *Without Lying Down.* Berkeley: University of California Press, 1997.

Berg, Scott. *Lindbergh.* New York: G. P. Putnam's Sons, 1998.

Beschloss, Michael. *Kennedy and Roosevelt.* New York: Norton, 1981.

Bilainkin, George. *Diary of a Diplomatic Correspondent.* London: Allen & Unwin, 1942.

Binder, John J. "Organized Crime and the 1960 Presidential Election." *Public Choice* 130, no. 3/4 (March 2007): 251–66.

Blair, Jr., Joan and Clay. *The Search for JFK.* New York: Berkley, 1976.

Blanchard, John A. *The H Book of Harvard Athletics, 1852–1922.* Cambridge, MA: Harvard Varsity Club, 1923.

Boggs, Elizabeth. "Federal Legislation Affecting the Mentally Retarded, 1955–1967." *Mental Retardation* 3 (1971).

Bradlee, Benjamin C. *Conversations with Kennedy.* New York: W. W. Norton & Co., 1975.

Brands, H. W. *Traitor to His Class.* New York: Doubleday, 2008.

Brind, David. *Reaching the Mind, Touching the Spirit: The Helena T. Devereux Biography,* n.d., http://www.devereux.org/site/DocServer/HTDBio.pdf?docID=281.

Brinkley, Alan. *The Publisher.* New York: Alfred A. Knopf, 2010.

Brockley, Janice. "Rearing the Child Who Never Grew." In *Mental Retardation in America: A Historical Reader.* Edited by Steven Noll and James W. Trent, Jr. New York: New York University Press, 2004, 130–64.

Brooks, V. W. "Harvard and American Life." *Contemporary Review,* no. 94 (n.d.): 1908.

Burns, James MacGregor. *John Kennedy: A Political Profile.* New York: Harcourt, Brace & World, 1959.

———. *Roosevelt: The Lion and the Fox.* New York: Harcourt, Brace & World, 1956.

———. *Roosevelt: The Soldier of Freedom.* New York: Harcourt Brace Jovanovich, 1970.

Bushee, Frederick. *Ethnic Factors in the Population of Boston.* New York: Macmillan, 1903.

———. "The Growth of the Population of Boston." *Publications of the American Statistical Association,* no. 6 (1899): 239–74.

Caro, Robert. *The Years of Lyndon Johnson: Master of the Senate,* New York: Alfred A Knopf, 2002.

———. *The Years of Lyndon Johnson: Passage of Power.* New York: Alfred A. Knopf, 2012.

Chambers II, John Whiteclay. *To Raise an Army: The Draft Comes to Modern America.* New York: Free Press, 1987.

Channon, Henry. *Chips: The Diaries of Sir Henry Channon.* Edited by Robert Rhodes James. 1967. Reprint, London: Weidenfeld & Nicolson, 1989.

Churchill, Winston S. *His Complete Speeches.* New York: Chelsea House, 1974.

———. *The Second World War.* Vol. 1, *The Gathering Storm.* Boston: Houghton Mifflin, 1948.

———.   *The Second World War.* Vol. 2, *Their Finest Hour.* Boston: Houghton Mifflin, 1949.

Clarke, Thurston. *Ask Not: The Inauguration of John F. Kennedy and the Speech That Changed America.* New York: Henry Holt, 2004.

Clifford, Clark, with Richard Holbrooke. *Counsel to the President: A Memoir.* New York: Random House, 1991.

Coblentz, Edmond D., ed. *William Randolph Hearst: A Portrait in His Own Words.* New York: Simon & Schuster, 1953.

Colby, William, and Peter Forbath. *Honorable Men: My Life in the CIA.* New York: Simon & Schuster, 1978.

Converse, Philip E., Angus Campbell, Warren E. Miller, and Donald E. Stokes. "Stability and Change in 1960: A Reinstating Election." *American Political Science Review* 55, no. 2 (June 1961): 269–80.

Craig, Campbell, and Fredrik Logevall. *America's Cold War: The Politics of Insecurity.* Cambridge, MA: Harvard University Press, 2009.

Dallas, Rita, and Jeanira Ratcliffe. *The Kennedy Case.* New York: G. P. Putnam's Sons, 1973.

Dallek, Robert. *An Unfinished Life: John F. Kennedy, 1917–1963.* Boston: Little, Brown & Co., 2003.

Damore, Leo. *The Cape Cod Years of John Fitzgerald Kennedy.* Englewood Cliffs, NJ: Prentice-Hall, 1967.

Davis, Kenneth. *FDR: The War President.* New York: Random House, 2001.

Davis, Jr., Sammy, Burt Boyar, and Jane Boyar. *Sammy: An Autobiography.* New York: Farrar, Straus & Giroux, 2000.

Dilks, David, ed. *Diaries of Sir Alexander Cadogan, 1838–1945.* New York: G. P. Putnam's Sons, 1972.

Dinneen, Joseph F. *The Kennedy Family.* Boston: Little, Brown & Co., 1949.

Documents on German Foreign Policy. Series D, vol. 1, *From Neurath to Ribbentrop.* Washington, DC: Government Printing Office, 1949.

Doenecke, Justus D. *Storm on the Horizon.* New York: Rowman & Littlefield, 2003.

Donovan, Robert. *Tumultuous Years: The Presidency of Harry S. Truman, 1949–1953.* New York: W. W. Norton & Co., 1982.

Douglas, William O. *Go East, Young Man: The Early Years.* New York: Random House, 1973.

———. *The Court Years, 1939–1975.* New York: Random House, 1980.

Doyle, David Noel. "The Remaking of Irish America, 1845–1880." In *Making the Irish Ameri-*

can: *History and Heritage of the Irish in the United States*. Edited by J. J. Lee and Marion Casey. New York: New York University Press, 2006.

East Boston: A Survey and a Comprehensive Plan. Boston: City of Boston, 1916.

El-Hai, Jack. *The Lobotomist: A Maverick Medical Genius and His Tragic Quest to Rid the World of Mental Illness*. New York: Wiley, 2005.

Farley, James. *Jim Farley's Story: The Roosevelt Years*. New York: McGraw-Hill, 1948.

Fay, Jr., Paul B. *The Pleasure of His Company*. New York: Harper & Row, 1966.

Feingold, Henry. *The Politics of Rescue*. New Brunswick, NJ: Rutgers University Press, 1970.

Fields, Armond. *Fred Stone: Circus Performer and Musical Comedy Star*. Jefferson, NC: McFarland, 2002.

Fine, Sidney. *Frank Murphy: The Washington Years*. Ann Arbor: University of Michigan Press, 1984.

Fraser, Steve. *Every Man a Speculator: A History of Wall Street in American Life*. New York: HarperCollins, 2005.

Freidel, Frank. *Franklin D. Roosevelt: Launching the New Deal*. Boston: Little, Brown & Co., 1973.

Friedlander, Saul. *Nazi Germany and the Jews*. Vol. 1, *The Years of Persecution 1933–1939*. New York: HarperCollins, 1997.

Fuchs, Lawrence H. *John F. Kennedy and American Catholicism*. New York: Meredith Press, 1967.

Gaddis, John Lewis. *George F. Kennan: An American Life*. New York: Penguin Press, 2011.

Galbraith, John Kenneth. *The Great Crash*. 1955. Reprint, New York: Houghton Mifflin, 1997.

Gannon, Robert Ignatius. *The Cardinal Spellman Story*. Garden City, NY: Doubleday, 1962.

Gilbert, Martin. *Israel: A History*. New York: William Morrow, 1998.

Goodwin, Doris Kearns. *The Fitzgeralds and the Kennedys*. New York: Simon & Schuster, 1987.

Gunther, John. *Inside U.S.A.* 1947. Reprint, New York: New Press, 1997.

Hamilton, Nigel. *JFK: Reckless Youth*. New York: Random House, 1992.

Harvey, John, ed. *The Diplomatic Diaries of Oliver Harvey, 1937–1940*. New York: St. Martin's Press, 1970.

Hastings, Max. *Winston's War: Churchill, 1940–1945*. New York: Alfred A. Knopf, 2010.

Hertog, Susan. *Anne Morrow Lindbergh*. New York: Anchor, 2000.

Higham, John. *Strangers in the Land*. 1955. Reprint, New York: Atheneum, 1971.

Hull, Cordell. *The Memoirs of Cordell Hull*. 2 vols. New York: Macmillan, 1948.

Ickes, Harold. *The Secret Diary of Harold L. Ickes*. New York: Simon & Schuster, 1953.

Johnson, Robert David. *Congress and the Cold War*. Cambridge, UK: Cambridge University Press, 2006.

Jowett, Garth. *Film: The Democratic Art*. Boston: Little, Brown & Co., 1976.

Kahn, Jr., E. J. *The World of Swope*. New York: Simon & Schuster, 1965.

Keegan, John. *The Second World War*. New York: Penguin, 1990.

Kennan, George F. *Memoirs: 1925–1950*. Boston: Little, Brown & Co., 1967.

Kennedy, Edward Moore, ed. *The Fruitful Bough*. Privately printed, 1965.

———. *Her Grace Above Gold: In Loving Remembrance of Rose Fitzgerald Kennedy*. Joseph P. Kennedy, Jr. Foundation, 1997.

Kennedy, Edward Moore, *True Compass*. New York: Twelve, 2009.

Kennedy, Jacqueline. *Jacqueline Kennedy: Historic Conversations on Life with John F. Kennedy*. New York: Hyperion, 2011.

Kennedy, Joseph P. *I'm for Roosevelt*. New York: Reynal & Hitchcock, 1936.

———. *The Story of the Films*. Chicago: A. W. Show Co., 1927.

Kennedy, Paul. "A Time to Appease." *National Interest* (July–August 2010).

Kennedy, Rose Elizabeth Fitzgerald. *Times to Remember*. Garden City, NY: Doubleday, 1974.

Kershaw, Ian. *Fateful Choices*. New York: Penguin, 2008.

———. *Hitler: 1936–1945: Nemesis*. New York: W. W. Norton & Co., 2000.

Kessner, Thomas. *Flight of the Century*. New York: Oxford University Press, 2010.

Kimball, Warren F., and Bruce Bartlett. "Roosevelt and Prewar Commitments to Churchill: The Tyler Kent Affair." *Diplomatic History 5*, no. 4 (October 1981): 291–312.

Kimball, Warren F. *The Most Unsordid Act: Lend-Lease, 1939–1941*. Baltimore: Johns Hopkins University Press, 1969.

Koskoff, David. *Joseph P. Kennedy: A Life and Times*. Englewood Cliffs, NJ: Prentice-Hall, 1974.

Koszarski, Richard. *An Evening's Entertainment: The Age of the Silent Feature Picture, 1915–1928*. 1990. Reprint, Berkeley: University of California Press, 1994.

———. *Von: The Life and Films of Erich Von Stroheim*. 1983. Reprint, New York: Limelight, 2002.

Kramnick, Isaac, and Sheerman, Barry. *Harold Laski: A Life on the Left*. New York: Penguin Press, 1993.

Krock, Arthur. *Memoirs*. New York: Funk & Wagnalls, 1968.

Lamoreaux, Naomi. "Bank Mergers in Late Nineteenth-Century New England." *Journal of Economic History 51*, no. 3 (September 1991): 537–57.

Laqueur, Walter. *A History of Zionism*. New York: MJF Books, 1972.

Lash, Joseph P. *Eleanor: The Years Alone*. New York: W. W. Norton & Co., 1972.

Lasky, Victor. *J.F.K.: The Man & the Myth*. New York: Macmillan, 1963.

Lawford, Christopher Kennedy. *Symptoms of Withdrawal: A Memoir of Snapshots and Redemption*. New York: HarperCollins, 2005.

Leamer, Lawrence. *The Kennedy Men*. New York: HarperCollins, 2001.

———. *The Kennedy Women*. New York: Villard, 1994.

Leaming, Barbara. *Jack Kennedy: The Education of a Statesman*. New York: W. W. Norton & Co., 2006.

Lee, General Raymond E. *The London Journal of General Raymond E. Lee, 1940–1941*. Edited by James Leutze. Boston: Little, Brown & Co., 1971.

Leffler, Melvyn. *A Preponderance of Power: National Security, the Truman Administration, and the Cold War*. Palo Alto, CA: Stanford University Press, 1992.

Leuchtenburg, William E. *Franklin D. Roosevelt and the New Deal*. New York: Harper & Row, 1963.

Lindbergh, Anne Morrow. *The Flower and the Nettle: Diaries and Letters of Anne Morrow Lindbergh, 1936–1939*. New York: Harcourt Brace Jovanovich, 1976.

Lindbergh, Charles A. "Aviation, Geography and Race." *Reader's Digest* (November 1939).

———. *The Wartime Journals of Charles A. Lindbergh*. New York: Harcourt Brace Jovanovich, 1970.

Lipset, Seymour Martin, and David Riesman. *Education and Politics at Harvard*. New York: McGraw-Hill, 1975.

Loewenheim, Francis L., Harold D. Langley, and Manfred Jonas, eds. *Roosevelt and Churchill: Their Secret Wartime Correspondence*. New York: Dutton, 1975.

London, Louise. *Whitehall and the Jews, 1933–1948: British Immigration Policy, Jewish Refugees and the Holocaust*. Cambridge, UK: Cambridge University Press, 2000.

Louchheim, Katie, and Jonathan Dembo, eds. *The Making of the New Deal: The Insiders Speak*. Cambridge, MA: Harvard University Press, 1983.

Lowe, Jacques. *JFK Remembered*. New York: Random House, 1993.

Luce, Clare Boothe. *Europe in the Spring*. New York: Alfred A. Knopf, 1940.

Maier, Thomas. *The Kennedys: America's Emerald Kings*. New York: Basic Books, 2004.

Manchester, William. *Death of a President*. New York: Harper & Row, 1967.

———. *Portrait of a President: John F. Kennedy in Profile*. Boston: Little, Brown & Co., 1962.

Marion, Frances. *Off with Their Heads!* New York: Macmillan, 1972.

Massachusetts Bank Commissioners. *Annual Report of the Bank Commissioners, 1912–1915*. Boston: Commonwealth of Massachusetts, 1912.

Matthews, Chris. *Jack Kennedy: Elusive Hero*. New York: Simon & Schuster, 2011.

McCall, Samuel W. "Massachusetts in Action." *American Review of Reviews*, no. 57 (May 1918).

McCarthy, Joe. *The Remarkable Kennedys*. New York: Popular Library, 1960.

McCraw, Thomas K. *Prophets of Regulation*. Cambridge, MA: Belknap Press of Harvard University Press, 1984.

McTaggart, Lynne. *Kathleen Kennedy: Her Life and Times*. Garden City, NY: Doubleday, 1983.

Mendelsohn, John, ed. *The Holocaust*, Vol. 6, *Jewish Emigration 1938–1940*. New York: Garland Publishing, 1982.

Mercier, Vivian. *The Irish Comic Tradition*. London: Oxford University Press, 1962.

Merk, Lois Bannister. "Boston's Historic Public School Crisis." *New England Quarterly*, no. 31 (June 1958): 172–99.

Miller, Merle. *Plain Speaking: An Oral Biography of Harry S. Truman*. New York: Berkley, 1974.

Moley, Raymond. *After Seven Years*. New York: Harper & Brothers, 1939.

———. *The First New Deal*. New York: Harcourt, Brace & World, 1966.

Morgenthau III, Henry. *Mostly Morgenthaus: A Family History*. New York: Ticknor & Fields, 1991.

Morris, Sylvia. *Rage for Fame: The Ascent of Clare Boothe Luce*. New York: Random House, 1997.

Morrison, Samuel Eliot. *The Maritime History of Massachusetts: 1783–1860*. 1923. Reprint, Boston: Houghton Mifflin, 1961.

Murphy, John F. *Up-to-Date Guide Book of Greater Boston*. Boston: John Murray, 1904.

Navasky, Victor S. *Kennedy Justice*. New York: Scribner, 1971. Reprint, New York: Author's Guild Backinprint.com, 2000.

Neenan, Benedict. *Thomas Verner Moore: Psychiatrist, Educator and Monk*. New York: Paulist Press, 2000.

Nicolson, Harold George. *Diaries and Letters*. Edited by Nigel Nicolson. New York: Atheneum, 1966.

O'Brien, Lawrence F. *No Final Victories: A Life in Politics—From John F. Kennedy to Watergate*. Garden City, NY: Doubleday, 1954.

O'Brien, Michael. *John F. Kennedy*. New York: Thomas Dunne Books, 2005.

O'Connor, Thomas H. *The Boston Irish: A Political History*. Boston: Back Bay Books, 1995.

O'Donnell, Kenneth P., David F. Powers, and Joe McCarthy. *"Johnny, We Hardly Knew Ye": Memories of John Fitzgerald Kennedy*. Boston: Little, Brown & Co., 1970.

Offner, Arnold. *Another Such Victory: President Truman and the Cold War, 1945–1953*. Palo Alto, CA: Stanford University Press, 2002.

Okrent, Daniel. *Last Call: The Rise and Fall of Prohibition*. New York: Scribner, 2010.

Oshinsky, David M. *A Conspiracy So Immense: The World of Joe McCarthy*. New York: Free Press, 1983.

Overacker, Louise. "American Government and Politics: Campaign Funds in a Depression Year." *American Political Science Review* 27, no. 5 (October 1933): 769–83.

Place, Edwin. "Scarlet Fever." *American Journal of Public Health*, no. 4 (September 1914).

Plimpton, George, ed. Interviews by Jean Stein. *American Journey: The Times of Robert Kennedy*. New York: Harcourt Brace Jovanovich, 1970.

Pressman, Jack D. *Last Resort: Psychosurgery and the Limits of Medicine*. Cambridge, UK: Cambridge University Press, 1998.

Renehan, Jr., Edward. *The Kennedys at War*. New York: Doubleday, 2002.

Ritchie, Donald. *James M. Landis*. Cambridge, MA: Harvard University Press, 1980.

Riva, Maria. *Marlene Dietrich*. New York: Ballantine Books, 1992.

Roosevelt, Elliott, ed. *FDR: His Personal Letters*. New York: Duell, Sloan & Pearce, 1947.

Roosevelt, James. *My Parents: A Differing View*. New York: Playboy Press, 1976.

Schlesinger, Jr., Arthur M. *The Coming of the New Deal*. 1958. Reprint, Boston: Houghton Mifflin, 1988.

———. *The Crisis of the Old Order: 1919–1933*. Boston: Houghton Mifflin, 1957.

————. *Journals.* New York: Penguin Press, 2007.

————. *The Politics of Upheaval: 1935–1936.* Boston: Houghton Mifflin, 1960.

————. *Robert Kennedy and His Times.* 1978. Reprint, Boston: Houghton Mifflin, 2002.

Searls, Hank. *The Lost Prince.* New York: Ballantine Books, 1969.

Shirer, William L. *Berlin Diary: The Journal of a Foreign Correspondent 1934–1941.* New York: Alfred A. Knopf, 1941.

Shorter, Edward. *The Kennedy Family and the Story of Mental Retardation.* Philadelphia: Temple University Press, 2000.

Slessor, John. *The Central Blue.* New York: Praeger, 1957.

Smith, Amanda. *Hostage to Fortune: The Letters of Joseph P. Kennedy.* New York: Viking, 2001.

Sorensen, Theodore C. *Counselor: A Life at the Edge of History.* New York: HarperCollins, 2008.

————. *Kennedy.* New York: Harper & Row, 1965.

Stavisky, Sam. "Where Does the Veteran Stand Today?" *Annals of the American Academy of Political and Social Science* 259 (1948): 128–35.

Steele, Ronald. *Walter Lippmann and the American Century.* 1980. Boston: Little, Brown & Co., 1980.

Stossel, Scott. *Sarge: The Life and Times of Sargent Shriver.* Washington, DC: Smithsonian Books, 2004.

Sumner, William H. *History of East Boston.* Boston: J. E. Tilton & Co., 1858.

Swanson, Gloria. *Swanson on Swanson.* New York: Random House, 1980.

Swift, Will. *The Kennedys Amidst the Gathering Storm.* New York: HarperCollins, 2008.

Toogood, Anne Coxe. *John Fitzgerald Kennedy National Historic Site: Historic Furnishings Plan.* Washington, DC: Department of the Interior, National Park Service, 1971.

U.S. Department of Labor, Bureau of Labor Statistics. *History of Wages in the United States from Colonial Times to 1928.* Washington, DC: Government Printing Office, 1934.

U.S. War Department. *Second Report of the Provost Marshal General to the Secretary of War on the Operations of the Selective Service System to December 20, 1918.* Washington, DC: U.S. War Department, 1919.

Von Hoffman, Alexander. *John F. Kennedy's Birthplace: A Presidential Home in History and Memory.* National Park Service, U.S. Department of the Interior, August 2004.

Walch, Timothy. "Some of My Best Friends Are Democrats." In *Uncommon Americans: The Lives and Legacies of Herbert and Lou Henry Hoover.* Edited by Timothy Walch. Westport, CT: Greenwood Publishing Group, 2003.

Warner, Jack. *My First Hundred Years in Hollywood.* New York: Random House, 1965.

Wasko, Janet. *Movies and Money.* Norwood, NJ: Albex, 1982.

Weir, Ronald. *The History of the Distillers Company, 1877–1939.* Oxford: Clarendon Press, 1995.

Welky, David. *The Moguls and the Dictators: Hollywood and the Coming of World War II.* Baltimore: Johns Hopkins University Press, 2008.

Welles, Benjamin. *Sumner Welles: FDR's Global Strategist.* New York: St. Martin's Press, 1997.

Whalen, Richard. *The Founding Father.* 1964. Reprint, New York: Regnery, 1993.

Wheeler-Bennett, J. W. *Munich: Prologue to Tragedy.* New York: Duell, Sloan & Pearce, 1948.

Wyatt, Edgar M. *More Than a Cowboy: The Life and Films of Fred Thomson and Silver King.* Raleigh, NC: Wyatt Classics, 1988.

Wyman, David. *The Abandonment of the Jews.* New York: Pantheon Books, 1984.

Yenne, Bill. *Santa Fe Chiefs.* St. Paul, MN: MBI, 2005.

Ziegler, Philip. *London at War.* New York: Alfred A. Knopf, 1995.

INDEX

Aberdeen, Scotland, 331
Academy of Motion Picture Arts and
    Sciences, 170
Acheson, Dean, 616, 638–39, 643, 644,
    711
Adams, Charles Francis, III, 135
Adenauer, Konrad, 679
Africa, 529–30, 756–57
    as possible destination for Jewish
        refugees, 324, 329, 362, 364
Age of Roosevelt, The (Schlesinger), 171
Albania, 381
Albee, Edward, 65, 119–20
Alfred E. Smith Memorial Foundation,
    727
Algeria, 711, 712
Algic, S.S., 267–69
Ali Khan, Liaquat, 654
Allen, Robert, 236, 248–49, 303,
    304–5, 306, 317, 321–22, 353,
    368, 393
Alsop, Joe, 431–32, 481, 493, 500,
    501, 505, 638
Alsop, Stewart, 638
America, 722
America First Committee, 506, 510–11,
    517, 519, 525, 531

American Federation of Labor (AFL),
    60, 261
Americans for Democratic Action
    (ADA), 666
American Society of Newspaper
    Editors, 734
Anderson, Jack, 674
Anderson, Marion, 764
Ange, Mother Marie Emile, 624, 625
Annenberg, Walter, 772
Another Love Story, 554–55
Anschluss (Germany's annexation of
    Austria), 287–90, 292, 293, 294,
    306–7, 308–9, 322, 329, 351, 360,
    361, 383, 413, 486
anti-Semitism, 396
    JPK and, 202, 311, 501–2, 509,
        581–82, 748
    Kristallnacht, 359–60, 361
    motion picture industry and, 75, 97
    Nazi persecution, 199–200, 287,
        307–9, 311, 322, 329, 349–52,
        359, 363, 364–65, 486, 508,
        581–82
    perceptions of media influence and
        political power of Jews, 357,
        365–66, 507–9

anti-Semitism (*cont.*)
  Roosevelt's economic policy and,
    202–3
appeasement, 639
  JFK and, 746
  JPK and, 636–38
  of Soviet Union, xxii, 605–7
appeasement of Nazi Germany, 293,
    295, 302–3, 304–5, 338, 356, 359,
    505, 510
  Chamberlain and, 290–91, 292–93,
    301, 302–3, 333, 338, 340, 360,
    382, 416, 435–36, 515, 633
  economic, 382–84, 402
  JPK and, 295, 302–3, 304–5, 338,
    359, 368, 382–84, 402, 413–14,
    427, 475, 500, 505, 506, 509, 514,
    515, 526, 748
  JPK's Navy League speech and,
    353–57
  Munich Agreement, 346–47,
    348–49, 359–60, 400, 402,
    435–36, 485, 633, 745
Arab world, 351, 385, 386, 391,
    392–93, 655, 660
Arbuckle, Fatty, 75
Army-McCarthy hearings, 673, 675
Arvad, Inga, 525–26, 540–42, 559,
    604, 675
Astaire, Fred, 299
Astor, Nancy, Lady Astor, 298, 304–6,
    357, 377, 427–28, 439, 463, 506
Astor, Vincent, 205–6
Astor, Waldorf, Lord Astor, 292–93,
    304–6, 357, 463
As We Remember Joe (JFK),
    578, 622
Atchison, Topeka and Santa Fe
    Railway, 168
Athenia, S.S., 408–10
Attlee, Clement, 433, 448, 484
atomic bombs, 580, 682
Austria, Germany's annexation of
    (*Anschluss*), 287–90, 292, 293,
    294, 306–7, 308–9, 322, 329, 351,
    360, 361, 383, 413, 486
Ave Maria, 722
Ayres, Russell, 150

Bailey, John, 702, 729
Baker, Newton, 49, 176

Balaban, Barney, 126
Baldwin, Stanley, 345, 436
Balfour, John, 464
Balfour Declaration, 287
Bancroft, Hugh, 81
Bao Dai, 654
Bartholomew, Mary, 628–29
Bartlett, Charles, 706
Baruch, Bernard, 175, 183, 209, 211,
    228, 239, 270, 317, 362, 370, 583
Bay of Pigs, 767–68
Beard, Charles, 601
Bearsted, Viscount, 308, 322
Beauchamp, Cari, 109
Beaverbrook, Max Aitken, Lord, 99,
    415, 439, 441, 458, 500, 539, 550,
    567, 568, 577, 622, 661, 673, 704,
    709, 730, 733, 743
Beck, Dave, 710
Beck, Józef, 400
Belgium, 439–40, 449, 450
Benchley, Robert, 26, 259–60
Ben-Gurion, David, 286, 654
Bennett, Constance, 144
Berle, Adolf, 219, 354–55
Berlin, Irving, 174, 249
Bethlehem Shipbuilding, 54, 55, 57
Bethlehem Steel, 51, 52, 55, 56, 57, 72,
    320
  baseball league organized by, 55–56
Betts, Dr. Henry, 778–79, 780,
    781, 782
Bevan, Aneurin, 552
Biddle, Anthony Joseph Drexel, 329,
    532, 642, 648–49
Biddle, Francis, 508
Billings, Kirk LeMoyne "Lem," 224,
    225, 239, 241, 264, 369
  JFK's congressional campaign
    and, 595
Bingham, Robert, 239, 251, 301
Blaik, Earl, 649
Blair, Bill, 704
Block, Paul, 246
Boettiger, John, 243–44, 255–56, 366,
    519–20
Bonanno, Joe, 80
bootlegging, 71, 79–81
Boston, Mass.:
  East Boston, 5–7, 13, 593
  financial institutions in, 32–33

influenza epidemic in, 56–57
Irish Catholics in, *see* Irish Catholics, in Boston
JPK's return to, 591–92
Kennedy family's move to New York from, 105–6, 113
P. J. Kennedy's political career in, 8–9, 10, 11–12, 14, 15, 18, 23, 26–27, 172, 262–63, 311
policemen's strike in, 60–61, 67
Protestants in, 10–11, 15, 22
Republicans in, 10–11, 15
Boston Daily Advertiser, 591
Boston Daily Globe, 11, 14, 18, 21, 24, 26, 36–37, 51, 55, 56, 69, 85, 98, 99, 130, 169–70, 181, 557, 591, 621, 649, 701, 709
Lyons' interview with JPK in, 497–500, 514
Boston Evening American, 330
Boston Evening Transcript, 500
Boston Herald, 619, 622, 640
Boston Latin School, 16–25, 90, 150
Boston Post, 312, 529, 618–19, 622, 625, 653, 736
JFK's Senate campaign and, 669
Boston Red Sox, 170
Boston Sunday Advertiser, 314
Boston Sunday Globe, 179, 247
Boston Sunday Post, 276
Boston Transcript, 47
Boston Traveler, 640
Bowker, Virginia, 143, 144, 145
Bradlee, Ben, 733, 782–83
Bradley, Colonel Edward Riley, 113, 114, 369
Brandeis, Louis, 351, 358, 389, 390, 392
Brands, H. W., 578
Brewer, Basil, 666
Bricker, John, 605
Brickley, Bart, 550, 671–72, 680, 681
Brinkley, Alan, 380
Britain, *see* Great Britain
British Foreign Office, 275, 331, 339, 367, 372, 419, 431, 464, 467, 483
"Kennedyiana" file of, 417
Britt, May, 762
Broadway, 554–55
Brockley, Janice, 534

Brookline Trust, 66, 71
Brooklyn-Manhattan Transit (BMT) Corporation, 175
Brooks, Van Wyck, 22
Broun, Heywood, 357
Brown, Hamilton, 781
Brown, Hiram, 159, 186
Brown, Pat, 720
Browne, Mary, 97
Brush, Matthew, 78, 79, 88
Buchanan, Alan, 102
Buckley, Charles, 729
Bullitt, William, 286, 329, 358, 369, 376, 392, 405, 532, 655
Bundy, McGeorge, 696–97, 768
Burke, William "Onions," 703
Burns, James MacGregor, 667
Burns, John, 105, 216, 227–28, 247, 256–57, 355, 387, 424, 463, 476, 491, 494, 508, 593
JPK's break with, 614
JPK's employment of, 614
Butler, Neville, 507
Butler, Rab, 404–5
Byrnes, George, 94
Byrnes, James, 252, 255, 276, 284, 313, 317, 492, 516–17, 543, 549–50, 575, 601

Cadogan, Alexander, 290, 291, 340, 371, 401, 458
Calder, James, 200–201, 221, 559–60, 577, 594, 611, 649, 658, 728
Cal-Neva Lodge, 719–20
Campbell, Craig, 600
Campbell, Patrick, 249
Campbell, Tom, 23, 25, 29, 44, 54
Canada, 449, 454, 504
Cannes, 324, 326, 336, 397
Cannon, Frances Ann, 561
capitalism, xxi, 220, 227, 514–15, 530, 600, 617
Depression as threat to, 170–71
Roosevelt's policies and, 231–32, 246, 247, 249
World War II as threat to, 431–32, 485
Capone, Al, 80
Capra, Frank, 421
Carlisle, Kitty, 299
Carnegie, Andrew, 624

Carpenter, William H., 559
Carr, Harry, 122–23, 128, 136
Carrillo, Leo, 730
Carter, Boake, 275–76, 277, 287, 317,
    369, 394, 419
Case, Margaret, 432
Casey, Joseph, 545–46
Casey, Pat, 137
Castle, Irene, 66
Castle, Vernon, 66
Castro, Fidel, 747, 767
Catholic Church, 251, 586,
    624–25, 672
  in Boston, *see* Irish Catholics, in
    Boston
  at Harvard, xx, 22
  JFK's presidential campaign and,
    701–3, 707, 712–16, 721–25,
    727–29, 731–35, 743–44, 747–48,
    752, 753–55, 757–58
  JPK's faith, 146, 147–48, 158, 491,
    571–72, 724–25
  Joseph P. Kennedy, Jr. Foundation
    and, 695, 698
  in media and Hollywood, 104
  prejudice against, 10, 539
  Roosevelt and, 539, 549
  Vatican, *see* Vatican
  see also Irish Catholics
Catholic News, 744
Cavanaugh, Father John, 533, 623,
    645, 649, 673, 680, 700, 715, 749,
    757, 785, 786
Century Group, 502
Chamberlain, Neville, 324, 354,
    360–61, 376–77, 385, 394, 400,
    401, 413, 414, 429, 433, 438
  appeasement policy of, 290–91, 292–
    93, 301, 302–3, 333, 338, 340,
    360, 382, 416, 435–36, 515, 633
  Churchill vs., 290–91, 293
  Czechoslovakia and, 329–30, 332,
    336, 337–39, 340, 342–43
  death of, 485, 499
  Hitler's meetings with, 336–38, 340
  Jewish refugees and, 349–52, 361,
    363–64
  JFK's Harvard thesis and, 435–36
  JPK and, xxii, 238, 289, 290–91,
    302–3, 330–31, 336–37, 344, 349,
    355, 360–61, 363–64, 369, 370,

371, 372, 401–2, 404–5, 416–17,
    485, 737
  JPK's defense of, 485
  Munich Agreement and, 346–47,
    348–49, 360, 400, 435–36, 485,
    633
  Palestine and, 386–87, 389
  Poland and, 376, 399, 401–2, 405,
    413, 416, 420, 633
  resignation of, 440
  Roosevelt and, 330–31, 343, 344,
    376–77, 579
  speech declaring war on Germany,
    406–7
  speeches of, 342, 344, 345–46, 376
Champion, Albert, 679, 680
Channon, Henry "Chips," 427
Chaplin, Charlie, 110, 501–2
Chase National Bank, 71
Chiang Kai-shek, 640
Chicago Daily News, 459, 480
Chicago Daily Times, 249
Chicago Herald-American, 593
Chicago Tribune, 243–44, 318, 330,
    364, 367, 428, 517, 518, 644
China, 258, 272, 394, 395, 636, 639,
    672, 674, 682
  Korea and, 635
  Manchuria, 287, 658
  Quemoy and Matsu and, 745, 746
Choate, 150
  JFK at, 150–51, 162, 163, 169, 177,
    182, 189, 195–97, 221, 224–26
  Joe Kennedy, Jr. at, 150–51, 152,
    162, 169, 182, 189, 198
Christophers, The, 586
Chrysler, Walter, 192
Churchill, Pamela, 617
Churchill, Winston, 19, 238–39,
    290–94, 340, 414, 429, 433, 437,
    439, 441, 447–53, 455, 458, 461,
    477, 507, 551, 601
  becomes Prime Minister, 440
  Chamberlain vs., 290–91, 293
  in destroyers-for-bases negotiations,
    466–67, 469–72, 493
  House of Commons address of,
    449–50
  JPK's meetings with, 441, 468,
    580–81
  JPK's view of, 440, 441

King Leopold and, 615
Munich Agreement and, 348
Roosevelt and, 414–15, 428–29, 441,
  442, 445, 447, 51–53, 465–70, 504
CIA (Central Intelligence Agency), 618,
  676–77, 699–701, 769
  Bay of Pigs and, 767, 768
Ciano, Count Galeazzo, 299, 375
CIC (Counter Intelligence Corps), 648,
  674–75
Cinema Credits Corporation, 95
CIO (Congress of Industrial
  Organizations), 260, 261, 268,
  278, 319, 667
Civil Rights Act of 1957, 711–12
Clark, Mark, 676
Clark, Tom, 619
Clarke, Thurston, 758
Cleary, Walter, 199
Clemens, Cyril, 731
Cleugh, Eric, 502
Cleveland, Grover, 14
Clifford, Clark, 714, 759, 769
Coblentz, Edmond, 187, 231
Cockburn, Claud, 393–94
Coghlan, Ralph, 498–99, 662
Cogley, John, 722, 724
Cohasset, Mass., 81, 82, 87, 92
  golf club of, 81–82
Cohen, Benjamin, 208, 216, 358, 359,
  389, 391, 507–8
Cohen, Milton, 110
Cohn, Harry, 421
Cohn, Roy, 671, 672, 674, 685
Colby, William, 699, 700
Colby Junior College for Women, 581
Cold War, xxii, 604–5, 609, 625, 636,
  659, 660–61, 682, 689, 746
Cole, Rufus, 68, 70–71, 73, 74
Collateral Loan Company, 39, 43–44
Collier's Radio Hour, 129–30
Collins, Patrick, 9, 14–15, 18, 134–35
Columbia Advertising, 87–88
Columbia Films, Inc., 66
Columbia Pictures, 421
Columbia Trust Company, 10, 33, 36,
  38, 65, 71, 72, 78, 91, 96, 242
  JFK as intern at, 528
  JPK as president of, 38, 39–40, 42,
    43, 44, 45, 47–49
  World War I and, 40–41, 48–49

Commission on Organization of the
  Executive Branch of the
  Government (Hoover
  Commission), 616
  second, 676–77, 679, 699
Committee of One Hundred,
  Boston, 10
Commonweal, 722
Communists, communism, 202, 574,
  581, 639, 640, 660–61
  Cohn and, 671, 672
  Cold War, xxii, 604–5, 609, 625,
    636, 659, 660–61, 682, 689, 746
  Depression and, 171
  isolationism and, 604–5, 607–8
  JFK's views on, 641, 656, 668,
    746–47
  Joe Kennedy, Jr.'s views on, 220,
    606–7
  JPK's offer of assistance to FBI on,
    559
  JPK's views on, 516, 600–601,
    616–17, 618, 636–39, 641, 656,
    659–60, 682, 746
  Marshall Plan and, 616–17, 618, 636
  McCarthy and, 672–73
  Robert Kennedy's views on, 689
  Roosevelt and, 231, 232, 235,
    250–52
  Truman Doctrine (aid to Greece and
    Turkey) and, 605, 607, 608, 616,
    617, 618, 636, 637
Conant, James B., 721–22
Congressional Record, 500
Connally, Tom, 642
Conniff, Frank, 607
Conversations with Kennedy
  (Bradlee), 782
Cooke, Robert, 760–61
Coolidge, Calvin, 61, 88
  policemen's strike and, 60–61, 67
Coolidge, Louis, 61
Cooper, Duff, 348, 476, 674
Cooper, Lady Diane, 674
Copeland, Charles, 23
Copeland, Royal, 278
Corcoran, Tommy, 208, 215, 250, 275,
  295, 319, 327, 355, 614–15
Cosmopolitan, 377
Costello, Frank, 80
Coudert, Frederic, Jr., 639

Coughlin, Father Charles, 230, 231, 235, 250, 251, 599
    JPK and, 235–36
Coughlin, Robert, 86, 103, 105, 777
Cowles, Gardner, 655
Craig, May, 658
Crete, 529
Crider, John H., 599
Cropley, Ralph, 600
Crum, Erskine, 73, 74
Cuba, 746–47, 756
    Bay of Pigs and, 767–68
Cudahy, John, 439
Cummins, Peggy, 604
Cunard, Samuel, 5
Cunningham, Bill, 619
Curley, James Michael, 37, 38, 39, 59, 134, 135, 172, 215, 593, 594, 597, 602
Curran, Joseph, 268
Currie, Lauchlin, 490
Currier, Guy, 52, 58, 61, 91, 111–12, 131
Cushing, Barbara "Babe," 241–42
Cushing, Richard Cardinal, 604, 623–27, 628, 662, 678, 696, 714, 722–24, 748, 754, 755, 764, 765–66, 786
Czechoslovakia, 372, 375–76, 383, 400, 413, 486
    Sudetenland, 287, 290, 302, 323, 329–30, 332, 334–47, 360, 383

Dahlerus, Birger, 400
Daily Mail, 385
Daladier, Édouard, 346
Daley, Richard, 720, 729
Dallas, Rita, 778
Dalton, Mark, 597, 598, 602–3, 662, 663
Dane, E. B., 66, 71
Danzig, 376, 394, 399, 402
Davenport, Russell, 262–63, 317, 366
Davies, Joseph, 464
Davies, Marion, 137, 143, 173, 187, 501, 737, 738
Davis, Bette, 156
Davis, John W., 507
Davis, Owen, 248
Davis, Sammy, Jr., 762–63

Dean, Dudley, 81
Dearborn, Walter, 265, 266
De Gaulle, Charles, 575
De Lattre de Tassigny, Jean, 654
del Rio, Dolores, 299
DeMille, Cecil B., 100, 101, 110, 112, 116, 117, 119, 136
democracy, 171, 323, 484, 504, 514–15, 601, 606, 617, 618
    JPK's pessimism about future of, xxi, 323, 431, 497, 498, 503
Democratic National Committee, 493, 494
Democratic Party:
    Boston Irish Catholics and, 9, 10–11, 14, 15
    JPK's allegiance to, 22–23, 27, 61, 134, 135, 517
Denmark, 437
Denomy, Father, 695
Depression, Great, xxi, 171–72, 181, 198, 271, 295, 315, 395
    Hoover and, 167, 171, 172
    Kennedy family during, 168–69, 170
    public anger about, 171
    Roosevelt and, 172, 247
Derby, Lord, 403, 479
Derr, E. B., 114, 115, 118, 126, 136, 137, 138–39
Des Rosiers, Janet, 679, 680
De Valera, Éamon, 507, 679
Dever, Paul, 604, 657, 662, 664, 669
Devereux, Helena, 152
Devereux School, 149, 152–54, 162
Devonshire, Andrew Cavendish, Duke of, 532, 644
Devonshire, Deborah Cavendish, Duchess of ("Debo"), 532, 622–23, 644
Devonshire, Edward Cavendish, Duke of, 324, 551
Devotion School, 85
Dewey, John, 265
Dewey, Thomas E., 573–74, 576, 595, 655
De Wolfe, Elsie, 325
Dexter School, 89–90
Dickinson, Angie, 763
Dies, Martin, 508
Dietrich, Marlene, 325, 397–98

Dillingham, Charles, 77
Dillon, Clarence, 376
DiMaggio, Joe, 299
Dinneen, Joe, 499, 582, 621
Diplomatic Memoir (JPK), 341, 343, 346, 356, 370, 444, 449, 450, 454–55, 615–16
Dirksen, Herbert von, 310–11, 741–42
Disney, Walt, 317
Dodge, Horace, 433
Domaine de Beaumont, 324–25
Domaine de Ranguin, 397
Donovan, Joe, 16, 30, 41
Donovan, Ned, 18–19
Donovan, William "Wild Bill," 459–61, 463, 464, 466, 493
Dougherty, Dennis Cardinal, 633–34
Douglas, Helen Gahagan, 731
Douglas, Lewis, 271
Douglas, Paul, 726
Douglas, William O., 216–17, 226, 492, 607, 645, 655
  Robert Kennedy and, 688, 689, 710
Dowd, John, 595, 718
Dowling, Eddie, 180
Downey, Morton, 573, 645, 661–62, 679, 680, 681–82, 685, 704, 708, 749, 786
Doyle, David, 4
Droney, John, 602, 663–64, 690
Dufty, William, 109
Dulles, Allen, 699–700, 711, 718, 769
Dunkirk, 447, 449, 461, 615
Dunn, Edward, 688–89
Dunn, Elizabeth, 296–97
Dunphy, Chris, 68, 72
DuPont-Pathé Film Manufacturing Corporation, 159

Early, Stephen, 250, 317, 318, 538–39
East Boston, Mass., 5–7, 13, 593
  Kennedy house in, 13
  see also Boston, Mass.
Eastern Steamship Lines, 67–68, 78, 92
Economic Club of New York, 271–72
Economist, 655
economy, U.S., 608–9, 756
  JPK's views on, 530, 544, 586, 601, 606

peacekeeping and, 295–96, 315
Roosevelt's policies and, 202–3, 229–30, 246–49, 271–72, 295–96, 315
World War II and, 529
Eden, Anthony, 433, 439, 679
Edmonson, Charles, 498
Edwin Gould Foundation, 627
Eisenhower, Dwight David, 638, 564, 658, 663, 666, 669, 670, 672, 677, 688, 711, 745, 754
  Board of Consultants on Foreign Intelligence Activities, 699–701, 705
  illness of, 704
  JPK's meeting with, 642–43, 644
  Khrushchev and, 745–46
  reelection of, 704, 707, 710
Eliot, Day, 248
Emmons, Major General, 476–77
Ethiopia, 258, 287, 303–4
Évian Conference, 307, 308, 321, 324, 329
Exhibitors Herald, 95, 104
Èze, 681

Fairbanks, Douglas, 110
Fairbanks, Douglas, Jr., 501, 502
Fairbanks Company, 59
Falacci, Frank, 736
Famous Players-Lasky Corporation, 75, 76, 94
Fanfani, Amintore, 700, 718
Farley, James, 180–81, 182, 332, 367, 414, 457, 491
Farr, Tommy, 314
fascism, 315, 373, 375, 497
Fay, Paul "Red," 595, 763
Fayne, James, 216, 613, 659, 662, 663
FBI (Federal Bureau of Investigation), 80, 508, 509, 675–76, 769
  Arvad and, 526, 540, 541, 559, 675
  JPK and, 559
FBO (Film Booking Offices of America), 74, 91–99, 102, 103, 106–7, 109, 119, 121, 122, 125, 128, 130, 131, 135–37, 158, 192
  RCA and, 111, 124
Feldman, Justin, 742, 769–70
Feldman, Myer, 761

Fenway Building Trust, 59
Field, Marshall, 588
Film Daily, 110, 123, 124, 125–26, 126, 129, 130
film industry, *see* motion picture industry
Finley, John Huston, 316
First National Pictures, 122–27, 128–29, 135, 158
Fish, Hamilton, 512
Fisher, Carl, 93
Fisher, Robert, 23, 25, 29, 78, 81, 259, 312, 366, 422, 450
Fitzgerald, Agnes, 28, 41, 242
Fitzgerald, Cornelius, 491, 657, 672
Fitzgerald, John F. "Honey Fitz," 11, 16, 20, 21, 71, 73, 91, 131, 134, 135, 160, 172, 296, 299, 529, 551, 578, 593, 594–95, 713
    death of, 635
    JFK's congressional campaign and, 594–95, 596, 598
    and JPK's marriage to Rose, 41–42
    and JPK's romance with Rose, 20, 29–30, 36, 40
    marital infidelities of, 48, 147
    mayoral campaigns of, 18–19, 26, 27–28, 36–38, 41, 311
    P. J. Kennedy and, 18–19, 20, 26–27, 29, 38
    retirement of, 37–38, 41
    Selective Service System and, 51
    Senate campaign of, 545–46
    Smith and, 135
Fitzgerald, Mary Josephine "Josie," 28, 91
Fitzgerald, Zelda, 536
Fitzgibbon, Steve, 88, 131
Fitzwilliam, Peter, 619–20
    death of, 621
Flanders, Ralph, 673
Fleeson, Dorothy, 356
Flynn, Edward, 177, 182, 187
Fogg Museum, 101, 102
Forbes, Allan, 39
Ford, Johnnie, 120, 419, 420, 421, 662
    JPK's employment of, 613, 614
    Rosemary Kennedy and, 628–30
Fore River Lunch Company, 53, 72, 88

Fore River Shipbuilding Company, 51–57, 58, 59, 64, 65, 67, 91, 120, 543
    baseball team of, 55–56
Forrestal, James, 572, 579, 580, 616
    JFK and, 594
Fortas, Abe, 216
Fortune, 262–63, 317, 366, 612, 693, 713
Foster, H. G., 675, 676
Fox, John, 669
Fox, William, 94, 101
Fox Film Corporation, 66, 94
France, 410, 617
    Algeria and, 711, 712
    Dunkirk, 447, 449, 461, 615
    Germany's conquest of, 440, 441, 447–56, 458
    Indo-China and, 636, 640, 655, 656, 658–59, 660, 689
    U.S. aid to, 451–54, 605
    in World War I, 40, 49
    in World War II, 289, 290, 302, 323, 329, 334, 338, 339, 341, 368, 373, 376, 405, 413, 414, 443, 447–56, 633
Franco, Francisco, 287, 381, 394, 679
Frank, Jerome, 490
Frankfurter, Felix, 198, 202–3, 205, 208, 216, 221, 251, 321, 351, 358, 389, 491–92, 507–8, 539, 574, 582, 583
Freeman, Milton, 216, 217
Freeman, Walter, 534, 535, 536
Friedländer, Saul, 287, 306, 360
Frost, Robert, 762, 764
Fulbright, William, 649

Galbraith, John Kenneth, 762, 764
Galeazzi, Enrico, 252–53, 264, 374, 562, 634, 642, 643, 645, 662, 679, 686, 699, 705, 710, 713, 716, 718, 723, 724–25, 727–28, 730, 753–55, 756, 771
Gannett, Frank, 357–58
Gargan, Ann, 533–34, 749, 763, 775–78, 783–86
Gargan, Joey, 557, 749
Gargan, Mary Jo, 668
Garner, John Nance, 174, 332
    as Roosevelt's running mate, 176–77
    salary of, 244

George, Prince, Duke of Kent, 294, 378
George, Walter, 641
George VI, King, 294, 343–44
Germany, 636, 756
  Lusitania and, 44–45
  in World War I, 40, 44
  see also Nazi Germany
Getty, J. Paul, 693
Ghormley, Robert Lee, 467, 471–72
Giannini, A. P., 70, 179
Gibbs, Miss (Rosemary's companion), 410, 411, 419, 426, 435
Glass, Carter, 271
Gloria Productions, 115, 155, 156, 158, 169–70
Goddard, Henry, 152
Godsol, Joe, 74
Goering, Hermann, 400
Goldman, Solomon, 391, 392–93
Goldsmith, Arthur, 25, 34–35, 38, 336, 337, 368, 387, 421–22, 490, 582
gold standard, 228
Goldwyn Pictures, 73, 74
Good, Frederick, 113, 163, 223
Goodwin, Doris Kearns, 50, 533, 596, 683, 686, 730
Gore, Albert, 707
Gort, John, 447
Gould, Edwin, 627
Gould, Jay, 627
Goulding, Eddie, 137, 141, 142–43, 554
Gowen, Franklin, 375, 441, 445, 525
Gower Street Company, 112, 131
Grace, Eugene, 52, 55, 56, 72
Graham, Billy, 743, 757–58
Graham, Cecil, 73
Graham's of London, 73, 74
Grange, Red, 97
Gray, William, 94, 95
Great Britain:
  bombing preparations in, 341, 343
  in buildup to World War II, 289, 290, 292–94, 301, 302–3, 323, 329–31, 332, 334–35, 338–47, 368, 373, 399–407
  declaration of war against Germany, 406–7, 408, 410, 411, 415, 416
  economic difficulties of, 509–10

German attacks on, 458, 461, 462–63, 466, 468, 469, 473–75, 477, 478, 479, 480–81, 496, 516, 529–31, 568
  gold sales and, 437–38
  gold supplies of, 448–49
  import restrictions of, 420–21
  Italy and, 303–4
  Jewish refugees and, 308–9, 324, 329, 349–52, 361–65
  JPK as ambassador to, xxi, 80, 272–78, 283–311, 323–47, 249–70, 371–97, 399–407, 408–22, 427–43, 444–56, 457–72, 473–86, 491, 496, 512
  JPK's resignation as ambassador to, 496, 502–4, 526
  Labour Party in, 484
  lend-lease program and, 510, 511–13, 515, 516–20, 525
  oil needs of, 475
  Palestine and, 286–87, 307, 351–52, 358, 359, 361–62, 385–93
  U.S. aid to, 441–43, 451–54, 458–59, 461, 466–72, 498, 503, 510, 517, 519, 605
  U.S. loan to, 599, 617
  U.S. trade agreements with, 352–53, 380–81
  war debt payments of, 185, 411
  in World War I, 40, 44, 49–50
  in World War II, 408–20, 427–31, 433–34, 438–43, 448–55, 458, 460–63, 466, 468, 469, 473–75, 477–81, 483, 486, 496, 516, 529–31, 579, 581, 633, 745
Great Depression, *see* Depression, Great
Great Dictator, The, 501–2
Greater Houston Ministerial Association, 743
Greece, 497, 529, 530, 605
  U.S. aid to, 605, 607, 608, 616, 617, 618, 636, 637
Green, Angela, 556
Green, William, 389
Gridiron Club dinner, 186–87, 190, 206, 716–17
Grober, Bert "Wingie," 719, 736
Gruenther, Alfred, 679
Guild of Saint Apollonia, 62–63, 591

Gunther, John, 33
Gurnett, Daniel, 65

Hacker, Louis, 601–2
Halifax, E. F. L. Wood, Lord, 289,
    291, 294, 300, 302, 303, 307, 336,
    340–41, 345, 360, 376, 394–95,
    416–17, 422, 433, 437, 439, 440,
    448, 483, 507, 547, 575
  appeasement policy of, 303, 382,
    416
  Catholic refugees and, 309
  Czechoslovakia and, 330, 333–34
  and German attacks on England,
    458, 469
  Jewish refugees and, 308, 329, 349,
    350, 351, 352, 362, 363–64
  Kathleen Kennedy and, 551, 573
  Palestine and, 352, 385–86
  Poland and, 400, 403–4, 405
Halifax, Lady, 300, 376
Hall, Frank, 66–67
Hallmark Pictures, 66–67
Hannegan, Bob, 573, 575–76
Harmonie Club, 639–40
Harris, Lou, 726, 749
Hartington, William Cavendish,
    Marquess of (Billy Hartington),
    324
  death of, 572–73, 577, 580, 589
  Kathleen Kennedy's marriage to,
    564–67
  Kathleen Kennedy's relationship
    with, 324, 438, 531–32, 551,
    552–53, 561–67, 620
  military service of, 567, 568, 571,
    572
Harvard Business School, JPK's lecture
    series at, 100–102, 109
Harvard College, 78, 89
  Boston Latin and, 17, 22
  Edward Kennedy at, 647–48, 649,
    650
  JFK at, 240, 298, 317, 321, 424,
    457
  Joe Kennedy, Jr. at, 221–22, 239,
    298, 310, 312, 317, 321
  JPK at, xx, 21–26, 30–31, 55, 64–
    65, 259
  JPK passed over for honorary
    doctorate from, 312

JPK's degree from, 32, 33, 34, 100
JPK's 1936 reunion speech at,
    259–61, 269
reunions of, 47, 78–79, 259–61,
    312
social life at, 25
Harvard Crimson, 424
Harvard Department of Fine Arts,
    101, 102
Harvard Law School, 216, 244
  Joe Kennedy, Jr. at, 423, 424, 457,
    476, 526, 527
Harvard University, 696–97, 702
Harvey, Oliver, 419
Haussermann, Oscar, 79
Hawaii, 442
  Pearl Harbor, xxii, 509, 538, 567
Hayden, Charles, 58, 64, 66
Hayden, Stone & Co., 58, 59, 60, 63,
    64, 66, 67, 69, 70, 77–78, 87, 88,
    91, 256, 613
Hayes, Carlton, 549
Hays, Will, 75–76, 100, 101, 104, 421
Headley Park, 479
Hearst, Millicent, 28, 176
Hearst, William Randolph, 28, 74, 96,
    137, 143, 146, 173–74, 175, 187,
    209, 245, 249, 250, 313, 317, 501,
    505, 545
  death of, 644
  Garner and, 173–74, 176–77
  JPK's work on restructuring business
    of, 254–55, 257–58, 264
  Roosevelt and, 176–77, 179, 181,
    182, 183, 185, 186, 187, 254
  tax measures and, 231–32, 237
Heddal, Mathilda, 589
Henlein, Konrad, 336
Henderson, Nevile, 336, 399–400, 401,
    403, 404
Hennessey, Luella, 267, 297, 406, 410,
    777, 778
Henri, Marquis de la Falaise de la
    Coudraye, 110, 114, 115, 116–17,
    118, 137, 140, 141, 143–44, 147,
    156
Hersey, John, 561, 598
Hertz, John, 88, 89
Hesburgh, Father Theodore, 680, 715,
    723
Hialeah, 559, 580, 581, 610, 693, 720

Hillman, Sidney, 327
Hillman, William, 418–19, 441
Hinton, Harold, 291
Hirohito, 580
Hitler, Adolf, 272, 287–90, 293,
    341–46, 356, 372, 376, 385, 394,
    399–407, 413, 416, 418, 432, 437,
    438, 447, 479, 486, 494, 511, 530,
    567, 579, 581, 605, 633
  appeasement of, *see* appeasement of
    Nazi Germany
  Arvad and, 540–41
  assumption of power and first actions
    of, 199–200, 258
  Chamberlain's meetings with,
    336–38, 340
  death of, 579
  declaration of war against U.S., 538
  Dirksen and, 741–42
  Dunkirk and, 449
  Hollywood and, 501–2
  Jewish emigration and, 322,
    358–59
  Jewish persecution initiated by,
    199–200
  Joe Kennedy, Jr. on, 200, 201–2
  JPK and, 741–42, 748; *see also*
    appeasement of Nazi Germany,
    JPK and
  Munich Agreement with, 346–47,
    348–49, 359–60, 400, 402,
    435–36, 485, 633, 745
  Roosevelt and, 341, 344, 346,
    381–82, 385, 413–14
  speeches of, 335–36, 342
  sterilization law and, 201
  see also Nazi Germany
Hoare, Samuel, 336, 346, 371, 413,
    414
Hodkinson, W. W., 74, 85
Holland, 439–40
Hollywood, *see* motion picture
    industry
Holmes, J. H., 161
Holmes, Oliver Wendell, 198
Hoover, Herbert, 135, 171, 183, 246,
    248, 362, 503, 531, 579, 580, 616,
    637–38, 675, 676, 752–53,
    760–61, 783
  British war debt payments and, 185
  Depression and, 167, 171, 172

JPK's leaking of information to,
    676–77
  Truman and, 584
Hoover, J. Edgar, 446, 508, 541, 559,
    675, 769
Hoover Commission, *see* Commission
    on Organization of the Executive
    Branch of the Government
Hopkins, Harry, 230, 231, 251, 278,
    332, 492
Horizon House, 778
Horton, Rip, 369
Hot Springs, Va., 162
Houghton, Arthur, 65, 77, 78, 162,
    241, 299, 369, 375, 398, 403, 554,
    572, 578, 604, 610, 645, 649,
    668–69, 679–81, 749
  death of son, 577–78
Hourigan, Mollie, 264, 265–66
House, Edward M., 181
House Committee on Foreign Affairs,
    511–12, 518–20, 525
House Committee on Un-American
    Activities, 508
Houston, David, 67
Howard, Roy, 208, 317, 376, 503, 505
Howard, Sidney, 157
Howe, Louis, 179, 182, 183, 188, 206,
    207, 233, 275
Howey, Walter, 88, 571, 646
Hufty, Page, 511
Hull, Cordell, 191, 206, 296, 301–3,
    326, 330–32, 334, 340, 342, 343,
    346, 347, 364, 368–70, 382, 384–
    85, 394, 403, 405, 411, 414, 434,
    439, 441, 443, 446, 448–49, 452,
    458–61, 465, 496, 507–8, 512
  Catholic refugees and, 309
  Jewish refugees and, 307
  and JPK as proposed envoy to
    Ireland, 506–7
  JPK's speeches and, 292–95, 354
  Lindbergh report and, 339
  Palestine and, 352, 385–86, 387,
    392, 393
  and safety of British ships, 409
  U.S.-British trade agreement and, 381
Humphrey, Hubert, 703, 720, 730,
    732, 733, 734, 735
Hurd, James, 74, 229
Hutchins, Maynard, 531

Hyannis Port, Mass., 92, 99, 126,
    132–33, 190, 220, 247, 248,
    263–64, 266, 678–79, 719,
    766–67, 782, 786
Hyannisport Club, 178

Ickes, Harold, 207, 230, 231, 272,
    299–300, 308, 315–16, 319, 332,
    344, 367, 393, 429, 505, 516
    JPK and, 231, 274–75, 299
I'm for Roosevelt (JPK), 212, 246, 247,
    249–50, 256, 271
Indo-China, 636, 640, 655, 656,
    658–59, 660, 689
influenza epidemic, 56–57
Inside U.S.A. (Gunther), 33
Intergovernmental Committee on
    Refugees, 329, 350, 393
Iran, 655, 656, 658–59
Iraq, 392
Ireland, 410
    emigration from, 4, 9
    Irish Poor Law Extension Act and,
        3–4
    JFK's visit to, 617
    JPK proposed as envoy to, 506–7
    Kennedy family in, 4
    potato blight in, 3, 4–5, 9
Irish Catholics, 582
    JPK's identity as one of, xix, xx,
        22–23, 33, 49, 58, 61, 80, 104,
        251, 272, 277, 291, 374
    Roosevelt and, 539, 549
Irish Catholics, in Boston, 9, 12
    Democratic Party and, 9, 10–11,
        14, 15
    political success of, 10
    prejudice against, 10–11, 105
isolationism:
    communism and, 604–5, 607–8
    JPK and, xxii, 289, 292, 295, 366,
        431, 433, 434, 486, 498–500, 503,
        504, 517, 607–8, 637–38, 639, 641
    World War II and, 289, 292, 295,
        431, 433, 434, 486, 498–500, 503,
        504, 517, 607–8
Italy, 301, 368, 373, 377, 381, 414,
    416, 433, 440, 475, 575, 617, 636,
    679, 753
    Christian Democrats vs. Communists
        in, 618–19, 634, 679, 699, 700

Ethiopia invaded by, 258, 287, 303–4
    Great Britain and, 303–4
    Star of Solidarity award of, 662
    in Tripartite Pact, 479–80
    Vatican, *see* Vatican
    in World War II, 451, 479–80, 497,
        529, 581

Jabotinsky, Ze'ev, 359
Jackson, Henry, 673
Jackson, "Pat," 667
Jackson, Shoeless Joe, 55–56
Jacobs, Rose Gell, 359
Japan, 258, 272, 287, 368, 373, 394,
    395, 414, 497, 636
    atomic bombs dropped on, 580
    Pearl Harbor attack, xxii, 509, 538,
        567
    in Tripartite Pact, 479–80
    U.S. trade with, 538
    in World War II, 479–80, 538, 577,
        580, 581
Jewish Agency for Palestine, 359, 385
Jews, 22, 202, 316, 356–58, 393, 540,
    576, 634, 672–73
    in Hollywood, 75, 97, 103, 104,
        501–2, 503, 559
    JFK and, 742, 743, 748
    JPK and, 356–57, 358, 359, 367, 434,
        501–2, 507–9, 539, 559, 582–83,
        667, 742
    Joseph P. Kennedy, Jr. Foundation
        and, 695
    Lady Astor's statements about,
        305, 357
    media influence of, 357, 365, 393
    Palestine and, *see* Palestine
    political influence of, 365–66, 507–9,
        574, 582–83, 723
    refugees, 306–9, 322, 324, 329,
        349–52, 361–65, 387, 390, 507,
        508–9
    Roosevelt and, 349–52, 362, 390,
        508, 509, 583
    Zionism and, 286–87, 351–52, 358,
        359, 385, 386, 388–93, 712
    see also anti-Semitism
John XXIII, Pope, 755, 771
Johns Hopkins University, 698, 760
Johnson, Herschel, 417, 444, 445, 446,
    453, 474

Johnson, Hugh, 317, 357
Johnson, Lyndon B., 684–85, 687,
  711–12, 716, 718, 720, 736, 754,
  786
  Committee on Foreign Relations and,
    684–85, 711
  JPK and, 771–72, 785
  as presidential candidate, 737,
    738, 746
  as vice-presidential candidate, 738–39
Johnston, Alva, 320
Jordan, Father Max, 695
Jordan, Sara, 431, 464, 476, 567
Joseph P. Kennedy, Jr. Foundation, 604,
  611, 612–14, 625, 694–96,
  755–56, 773, 778
  directors and infrastructure of,
    613–14
  Eunice Kennedy Shriver's work at,
    613, 624, 696, 697–98, 760
  first gift of, 613
  mission statement of, 612–13
Joseph P. Kennedy, Jr. Laboratories for
  Research on Mental Retardation,
  698
Joseph P. Kennedy, Jr. Memorial,
  623–26
Jowett, Garth, 97
J. Russell Young School of Expression,
  284–85

Kahn, Otto, 70
Kaiserin Auguste Victoria, 35
Kane, Joe, 572, 583, 584, 595, 596,
  599–600
Kane, Robert, 107
K-A-O (Keith-Albee-Orpheum), 112,
  119–20, 121, 122, 128–29,
  130–31, 135, 137
Karmel, Joseph, 307
Katzenbach, Nicholas, 770
Keaton, Buster, 110
Kefauver, Estes, 707–8, 711
Keith, Benjamin Franklin, 65
Keller, Father James, 586
Kelly, Arthur, 24, 25, 54
Kennan, George F., 378, 605
Kennedy, Bridget Murphy
  (grandmother), 6
Kennedy, Caroline (granddaughter),
  163, 750, 767, 775

Kennedy, Edward Moore "Ted" (son),
  xxiii, 132, 336, 343, 435, 457,
  475–76, 490, 526, 557, 559, 611,
  646, 668, 718, 749, 751–52,
  765–66, 767, 775, 785, 786
  birth of, 60, 145, 163–64
  childhood of, 133, 134, 243, 253,
    375, 423, 555
  in Counter Intelligence Corps, 648,
    674–75
  education of, 424, 527, 547–48
  in England during JPK's
    ambassadorship, 297, 298
  at Harvard, 647–48, 649, 650,
    690–91
  JFK's assassination and, 784–85
  JFK's congressional campaign and,
    602
  JFK's inauguration and, 762, 763–64
  JFK's presidential campaign and,
    736, 738, 740
  Joe Jr.'s death and, 570, 571, 578
  JPK's correspondence with, 12, 35–
    36, 680, 704
  JPK's lecture to, 585
  JPK's stroke and, 776, 779, 783
  Kathleen's death and, 621
  military service of, 648–49
  in plane crash, 691
  Rosemary and, 425
  Senate campaign of, 649, 766, 779
  as senator, 712, 784
  shoulder injury of, 690–91
  at University of Virginia, 675–76
  World War II and, 410
Kennedy, Ethel Skakel (daughter-in-
  law), 647, 654, 678, 688, 689, 695,
  778, 780
  Robert Kennedy's marriage to,
    646–47
Kennedy, Eunice Mary (daughter), *see*
  Shriver, Eunice Kennedy
Kennedy, Francis B. (brother), 10
Kennedy, Jacqueline Bouvier "Jackie"
  (daughter-in-law), 677, 678, 683,
  713, 750–51, 758, 763
  JPK's stroke and, 776, 779, 783
Kennedy, Jean Ann (daughter), *see*
  Smith, Jean Kennedy
Kennedy, Joan Bennett (daughter-in-
  law), 762, 763

Kennedy, John Bright (journalist), 377

Kennedy, John Fitzgerald, Jr.
(grandson), 758

Kennedy, John Fitzgerald "Jack" (son),
241, 243, 255, 284, 325, 326, 331,
408, 423, 463, 475, 525–26, 541,
543, 548, 552, 554, 574, 645, 646,
678, 681, 709, 767
Addison's disease of, 527, 617, 654,
682, 683, 704–5, 737
Algerian issue and, 711, 712
appeasement issue and, 357
appendicitis of, 163
Arvad and, 525–26, 540–42, 559,
604, 675
assassination of, xxiii, 80, 720,
784–85
back surgeries of, 568, 570, 682–84,
685, 686–87, 691
bank internship of, 528
Bay of Pigs and, 767–68
birth of, 49
cabinet of, 760
Catholicism of, 701–3, 707, 712–16,
721–25, 727–29, 731–35, 743–44,
747–48, 752, 753–55, 757–58
childhood of, 61–63, 85, 90, 99, 113,
126, 134, 142, 151, 169, 178
at Choate, 150–51, 162, 163, 169,
177, 182, 189, 195–97, 221,
224–26
civil rights and, 711–12
communism and, 641, 656, 668
congressional campaign of, 594–98,
599, 602–4, 611, 635
as congressman, 607, 617, 635,
639–42, 652–59, 663
during Depression years, 169
early schooling of, 85–86, 87, 89–90,
106, 149, 221
elected to Congress, 604
elected president, 749–57, 766
in England during JPK's
ambassadorship, 378
European travels of, 264, 377, 378,
379, 619, 639
Fitzwilliam and, 620
foreign policy of, 745–47
Foreign Relations Committee
assignment of, 640–42, 684–85,
711

Forrestal and, 594
Graham and, 743, 757–58
Gridiron dinner and, 716–17
at Harvard, 240, 298, 317, 321, 424,
457
health problems of, xxiii, 56, 61–63,
85, 90, 106, 162, 177, 196–97,
239–40, 263–64, 298, 317,
326–27, 476, 477, 527, 528, 546,
549, 555, 558, 560, 568, 570, 579,
584, 589, 592–93, 617, 654, 677,
682–87, 701, 702, 704–5, 715,
719, 730, 737
Honey Fitz and, 635
inaugural address of, 764–65
inaugural gala of, 761–63, 772
inauguration of, 761, 764–65
Johnson offered vice-presidential
nomination by, 738–39
JPK given advice by, 514–15, 607
Joe Jr.'s death and, 571, 578
as Joseph P. Kennedy, Jr. Foundation
president, 604, 613
JPK's bond with, 63, 85, 162
and JPK's fears of war, 296
JPK's financial contribution to
presidential campaign of, 716–18,
720, 721, 732
JPK's involvement in campaigns of,
27, 602–3, 653, 658, 661–66,
668–69, 726–33, 736–41
JPK's pessimism and, 544–45
JPK's political ambitions for, 542,
550, 591, 592–93
JPK's stroke and, 775, 776, 779
Kathleen's death and, 620–21
Kathleen's marriage and, 564
labor corruption investigation
and, 711
Landis and, 769–70
in London in 1935, 238, 239, 241
marriage of, 677, 678
Marshall Plan and, 617
McCarthy and, 666–67, 674, 685, 701
on *Meet the Press*, 658–59
mental retardation panel created by,
760–61
in Middle East and Asia, 654
military service of, 527–28, 531,
540, 542, 543, 549, 551, 555–59,
560, 734

on monastery retreat, 220
and Morrissey as candidate for
    judgeship, 768–69
Nixon's debates with, 744–45
and outbreak of World War II, 410
presidential campaign of, 709, 710,
    712–25, 726–48
presidential nomination of, 738–40
in presidential primaries, 729–30,
    732–36, 743
at Princeton, 239–40
Profiles in Courage, 687, 690, 714
PT boat training of, 546, 551
as PT 109 commander, 556–58, 560,
    561, 598
Pulitzer Prize awarded to, 690, 714
as reporter for Hearst papers, 593–94
Rosemary and, 222, 425
scarlet fever of, 61–63, 591, 683
Selective Service System and, 476–77
Senate campaign of, 652, 656, 657–
    58, 661, 662–70, 711, 741–42
Senate reelection of, 716, 718, 720
as senator, 671, 682–83, 684, 731–32
speeches of, 596, 639–40, 655–56,
    665–66, 706, 712, 727, 734, 736,
    739–40, 743–44, 764–65
at Stanford, 476, 501
Star of Solidarity awarded to, 662
television as utilized by, 664–65,
    744
Truman and, 583–84
as vice-presidential candidate, 687–
    88, 701–8, 710
as war hero, 556–58, 561, 595, 603,
    653
Why England Slept, 212, 424,
    435–36, 457, 494, 514, 745
World War II outbreak and, 407
Kennedy, Joseph P.:
as ambassador to Britain, xxi, 80,
    272–78, 283–311, 323–47,
    249–70, 371–97, 399–407,
    408–22, 427–43, 444–56, 457–72,
    473–86, 491, 496, 512
ambassador's residence of, 285–86,
    296
as athlete, 19, 21, 23, 24–25, 30, 55,
    131
automobiles of, 45–46, 89
banking and finance career of, xx,

32–36, 38–44, 47–49, 65, 72, 91,
    131, 518
birth of, 10
bootlegging stories about, 71, 79–81
British Foreign Office's monitoring
    of, 417
Broadway play produced by, 554–55
business trips of, 86, 90, 113
at Cal-Neva Lodge, 719–20
cameras and, 665, 744
cardiac arrests of, 781–82
Catholicism of, 146, 147–48, 158,
    491, 571–72, 724–25
charitable giving of, 62–63, 591,
    612, 613, 623–28, 694–95; *see
    also* Joseph P. Kennedy, Jr.
    Foundation
charm of, 23, 172–73
childhood of, xx, 12–14
children's medical problems and,
    534
commencement addresses given by,
    530, 531
criticisms of, xix, xxii, 430–31, 433,
    434, 464, 509, 544, 638
death of, 631, 787
as Democrat, 22–23, 27, 61, 134,
    135, 517
Diplomatic Memoir, 341, 343, 346,
    356, 370, 444, 449, 450, 454–55,
    615–16
early European trips of, 35, 92–93,
    99, 143–45
education of, xx, 15, 16–31, 149
farm of, 554, 555
as father, xxii–xxiii, 61, 90, 134,
    149–50, 161, 177–78, 221–22,
    325–26, 527, 534
fiftieth birthday of, 333–34
financial advice to children, 694
financing methods of, 71–72, 91,
    213, 720
fortieth anniversary of, 681
fortune made by, xxi, xxii, 14,
    44–45, 89, 131–32, 155, 169, 170,
    171, 613, 693–94, 712, 713, 765
foundation established by, *see* Joseph
    P. Kennedy, Jr. Foundation
French villa of, 679, 680–81, 689,
    770
friendships of, 610–11, 644–46

Kennedy, Joseph P. (*cont.*)
  golfing of, 82, 86, 163, 172, 178,
    189, 286, 458, 526, 610
  homes of, 42–43, 63–64, 81, 90, 92,
    105–6, 132–34, 190, 214, 528–29,
    679, 680–81
  honorary degrees of, 312–13, 530
  on Hoover Commission, 616
  I'm for Roosevelt, 212, 246, 247,
    249–50, 256, 271
  as insider in Washington, 180–81,
    183, 185–86, 215, 371, 374, 492,
    513, 518, 582, 584, 599, 606, 676
  Irish Catholic identity of, xix, xx,
    22–23, 33, 49, 58, 61, 80, 104,
    251, 272, 277, 291, 374
  lecture series presented by, 100–102,
    109
  liquor importing business of,
    192–94, 245, 528–29, 611, 720
  marital relationship and infidelities
    of, 47–48, 76–77, 86, 146–47,
    163–64, 241, 379–80, 610–11, 680
  as Maritime Commission chairman,
    xxi, 80, 255–56, 258–59, 261–62,
    264, 267–70, 272, 276, 277,
    278–79, 296, 544
  marriage and honeymoon of, 34, 36,
    40, 41–42, 48, 65
  at Marwood in Washington, D.C.,
    213–15, 228–29, 245, 273
  in motion picture industry, xx,
    65–71, 73–76, 91–104, 105–27,
    128–32, 135–46, 154–62, 168,
    169–70, 518; *see also* motion
    picture industry
  Navy League speech of, 353–57
  negative portrayals of, xix–xx
  oil investments of, 529, 612, 692–93
  optimism of, xxii, 756
  as outsider, xx, xxi, 75, 80, 97, 104,
    260–61, 509, 582, 598–99, 606
  pessimism of, xxii, 395, 495, 496–97,
    498, 501, 503, 544–45, 561,
    618–19, 644, 756–57
  physical appearance of, 22, 60, 172,
    589–90, 782
  political ambitions for sons, 542,
    545–46, 550, 731
  on political leaders in London,
    302–3, 317, 318
  as possible presidential candidate,
    313–19, 327–28
  on President's Board of Consultants
    on Foreign Intelligence Activities,
    699–701, 705
  as private broker/banker, 87–89,
    91, 131
  public service expected for children
    of, 619, 765
  radio addresses of, 218–19, 250–52,
    493–96, 512, 515–18, 519, 530,
    659
  real estate investments of, 44, 59,
    529, 586–89, 592, 612, 692, 772
  reduced political influence of,
    371–72, 381, 412, 459, 464–65,
    469, 470–72, 519, 525, 539, 574,
    600, 643
  resignation as ambassador, 496,
    502–4, 526
  resignation as SEC chairman,
    234–36, 246
  retirement of, 525–29, 550, 592,
    600, 644–45, 651, 661, 671–91
  return home after ambassadorship,
    489–504
  as SEC chairman, xxi, 67, 80, 131,
    206–11, 212–20, 226–29, 232–37,
    243, 244, 246, 248, 254, 277, 296,
    320, 438, 529; *see also* Securities
    and Exchange Commission
  Selective Service System and,
    50–51, 54
  shipyard management position of,
    51–57, 58, 59, 64, 65, 67, 91, 120,
    131, 543
  socializing of, 48, 76–77, 86,
    214–15, 299–300
  speeches of, 218–19, 250–52,
    493–96, 512, 515–18, 519, 530,
    567, 591–92, 617–18, 635–37,
    639–40, 641, 655–56, 658,
    659–61, 682
  as stock broker, 58, 60, 63, 64, 66,
    67, 68
  stock market trading of, xx–xxi,
    44–45, 58–59, 67, 77–78, 131–32,
    155, 161–62, 168, 170, 175, 188,
    191–92, 205, 206, 209–10,
    212–13, 226, 438, 529, 692,
    693

stomach problems of, 57, 278, 422, 431, 432, 458, 464, 475, 773
stroke of, 775–76, 784, 786
stroke incapacitation of, xxiii, 267, 631, 776–87
surgeries of, 709, 710
taxes and, 157, 194, 588, 611, 612, 625
theaters purchased by, 76
tour bus company of, 30, 34
trusts established by, 92, 131, 155, 170, 193–94, 528–29, 586, 587, 612
vacations of, 86, 113–14, 137, 138, 163–64, 248–49, 324–27, 329, 368–69, 642
Kennedy, Joseph P., II (grandson), 679, 780
Kennedy, Joseph Patrick, Jr. (son), 194, 224, 241, 243, 255, 264, 326, 333, 361, 366, 367, 404, 418, 435, 463, 497, 526, 560, 564, 568, 618, 647
appeasement issue and, 357
birth of, 48
book of remembrances of, 578, 622
childhood of, 56, 62, 90, 99, 113, 126, 134, 151
at Choate, 150–51, 152, 162, 169, 182, 189, 198
death of, xxiii, 156, 570–72, 577, 578, 579, 580, 584, 585, 586, 589, 590, 622, 623, 683–84, 702
early schooling of, 85–86, 87, 89–90, 106, 149–50
in England during JPK's ambassadorship, 321, 328, 378
European travels of, 199, 200–202, 374, 377
foundation established in name of, *see* Joseph P. Kennedy, Jr. Foundation
in Germany, 199, 200–202
at Harvard College, 221–22, 239, 298, 310, 312, 317, 321
at Harvard Law, 423, 424, 457, 476, 526, 527
Hitler as viewed by, 200, 201, 202
JPK's correspondence with, 195, 207, 221–22, 242, 450, 545–46
and JPK's fears of war, 296

JPK's political ambitions for, 542, 545–46, 550
as JPK's secretary, 321, 328
JPK's spoiling of, 221
Kathleen's marriage and, 566
at London School of Economics, 198–99
military service of, 527, 528, 540, 542, 543, 546, 549, 555, 562, 567, 568–69, 570–71
on monastery retreat, 220
P.J.'s funeral and, 142
post-college travels of, 328–29
publicity on, 377–78
Rosemary and, 222, 242, 425, 536
sailing of, 178
Selective Service System and, 476–77
Soviet Union trip of, 199, 202, 203, 220
tribute to, 578
World War II outbreak and, 407, 410
Kennedy, Kathleen (granddaughter), 654, 780
Kennedy, Kathleen Agnes "Kick" (daughter), 194–95, 224, 238, 241, 264, 325, 333, 457, 463, 490, 495, 541, 543, 547, 555, 556, 568, 578, 583, 584, 594, 611, 617
Arvad and, 540
birth of, 61, 62
childhood of, 90, 113, 126, 145, 178
death of, xxiii, 156, 620–23
education of, 106, 149, 152, 194, 238, 242, 423, 526
in England during JPK's ambassadorship, 296, 297–98, 378
Fitzwilliam and, 619–20
funeral of, 621–22
Hartington's death and, 572–73, 589
Hartington's marriage to, 564–67
Hartington's military service and, 568, 571, 572
Hartington's relationship with, 324, 438, 531–32, 551, 552–53, 561–67, 620
JFK's congressional campaign and, 602, 603
Joe Jr.'s death and, 571, 578
Red Cross service of, 551, 552, 555
Rosemary and, 425, 536
secretarial job of, 531, 540

Kennedy, Kathleen Agnes "Kick" (*cont.*)
　telegram to Jack at Choate, 225
　World War II and, 410
Kennedy, "London Jack" (RKO
　publicist), 299, 369, 419, 432
Kennedy, Margaret Louise (sister), 10,
　12, 14, 143, 144, 145
Kennedy, Mary Augusta Hickey
　(mother), 14, 29
　death of, 87, 99
　East Boston home of, 13
　family of, 9–10, 12
　marriage of, 9–10
　Winthrop home of, 27, 34
Kennedy, Mary Loretta (sister), 10, 14
Kennedy, Patricia Helen (daughter), *see*
　Lawford, Patricia Kennedy
Kennedy, Patrick (grandfather), 4, 713
　emigration and arrival in Boston, 3,
　4–5, 6, 12
　marriage of, 6
Kennedy, Patrick Joseph "P.J." (father),
　14, 29, 30, 91, 99, 160
　Columbia Trust Company and, 10,
　38
　death and funeral of, 142
　East Boston home of, 13
　Honey Fitz and, 18–19, 20, 26–27,
　29, 37–38
　illness of, 140–41, 142
　liquor stores of, 10, 79
　marriage of, 9–10
　political career of, 8–9, 10, 11–12,
　14, 15, 18, 23, 26–27, 172,
　262–63, 311
　wealth of, 10, 15, 27
　Winthrop home of, 27, 34
Kennedy, Robert Francis "Bobby"
　(son), 264, 267, 457, 497, 517, 559,
　619, 635, 646, 671–72, 674, 676,
　678, 688, 691, 695, 709, 715–16,
　736, 755, 767, 769
　at Army-McCarthy hearings, 673
　assassination of, xxiii, 786–87
　as Attorney General, 712, 758–60,
　766
　birth of, 98
　childhood of, 113, 126, 134, 146,
　242–43, 424
　education of, 424, 526, 527, 547,
　548–49, 584

　in England during JPK's
　ambassadorship, 297, 298
　JFK's assassination and, 785
　JFK's congressional campaign and,
　602, 603
　JFK's presidential campaign and,
　709, 726, 733, 738, 740
　JFK's Senate campaign and, 664,
　668, 669, 671
　JFK's vice-presidential bid and, 707,
　708
　as Joseph P. Kennedy, Jr. Foundation
　president, 613
　JPK's stroke and, 778, 779, 783
　at Justice Department, 664
　labor corruption investigated by,
　710–11
　Landis and, 770
　marriage of, 646
　McCarthy and, 671, 672, 685
　military aspirations of, 549
　military service of, 584–85
　Permanent Subcommittee on
　Investigations and, 671, 673, 688,
　710–11
　reputation of, 664
　Russian trip of, 688–89
　travels of, 619, 688–89
　World War II and, 410, 475
Kennedy, Robert Francis, Jr.
　(grandson), 780–81
Kennedy, Rose Fitzgerald (wife), 78, 89,
　131, 137, 142, 220, 238, 253, 264,
　278, 299, 333, 347, 376, 378, 397,
　406, 428, 457, 526, 539, 546–47,
　558, 572, 584, 602, 642, 661, 662,
　669, 678, 686, 715–16, 738, 750,
　758, 773
　on Baruch, 174–75
　Bay of Pigs and, 767–68
　births of children, 48, 49, 61, 85,
　116, 145, 163–64
　children's education and, 149–50,
　163, 177, 424, 527, 549
　Cohasset golf club and, 82
　debut of, 28
　during Depression years, 169
　Eddie and Mary Moore and, 59–60
　in England during JPK's
　ambassadorship, 296–98, 361
　father's retirement and, 37–38

fortieth anniversary of, 681
French villa and, 680, 681
homes of, 42–43, 63–64, 105–6,
    132–34
influenza epidemic and, 57
Jack's health problems and, 61–63,
    683
jewelry and, 694
JFK's assassination and, 784
at JFK's inaugural gala, 762, 763
at JFK's inauguration, 764, 765
JFK's military service and, 540, 556,
    557
Joe Jr.'s death and, 570–72
and JPK's affair with Swanson,
    143–47
and JPK's appointment as SEC
    chairman, 206, 207, 208, 213, 214
on JPK's aspirations for role in
    Roosevelt administration, 186
JPK's banking career and, 32
JPK's correspondence with, 92, 93,
    162, 221, 265, 411, 422–23, 426,
    432, 433–34, 436, 438, 447,
    450–51, 463–64, 474–75, 547–48,
    549, 676, 685
on JPK's farming, 554
JPK's Hollywood career and, 98–99,
    102, 103–4, 105
and JPK's return to Washington after
    ambassadorship, 490–94
JPK's romance with, 19–21, 29–30,
    34, 35, 36, 39, 40
JPK's stroke and, 777, 778, 779, 781,
    782, 783, 786
Kathleen's death and, 621, 623
Kathleen's marriage and, 553, 562,
    563, 564–65, 566
and Kathleen's relationship with
    Fitzwilliam, 620
marital relationship of, 47–48,
    76–77, 86, 146–47, 163–64, 241,
    379–80, 610–11
marriage and honeymoon of, 34, 36,
    40, 41–42, 48, 65
Merchandise Mart and, 611–12, 693
Model T and, 45–46
Robert's assassination and, 787
Rosemary's difficulties and, 90, 152,
    265–66, 451, 532, 533, 534,
    536–37

at school, 28, 106
Swanson compared with, 110
on Swope, 174
trusts and, 92, 194, 586
vacations of, 86–87, 194, 214,
    222, 325–26, 336, 344–45,
    369, 681
World War II outbreak and, 407
Kennedy, Rose Marie "Rosemary"
    (daughter), 56–57, 62, 126, 194,
    222–24, 264–67, 333, 419,
    424–26, 435, 447, 457, 463,
    526–27, 532–37, 547, 584, 586,
    610, 668, 712, 738, 765, 786
behavior change of, 532–33
birth of, 57
childhood of, 90, 151
at Craig House, 535–36, 547, 584,
    628–29
in England during JPK's
    ambassadorship, 297, 298
glandular treatments of, 223–24,
    242, 264
at Helen Newton's, 222–23, 242,
    264
lobotomy of, xxiii, 535–37, 589,
    630–31, 683, 691
mental and social difficulties of,
    xxiii, 90, 151–52, 153–54, 201,
    222–23, 242, 266, 379, 422, 425,
    534, 536, 696
Miss Gibbs as companion of, 410,
    411, 419, 426, 435
and outbreak of World War II, 410
at St. Coletta, 628–31, 695
schooling of, 106, 149, 152–54, 162,
    222, 264–66, 297, 379, 410–11,
    451, 526, 532–33
separation from family, 425–26, 631
worries about, 266, 425,
    533–34, 631
Kennedy Child Study Center, 755–56
Kennedy family:
cameras and, 665
during Depression years, 168–69, 170
French villa of, 679, 680–81, 689,
    770
Hyannis Port home of, 92, 99, 126,
    132–33, 190, 220, 247, 248,
    263–64, 266, 678–79, 719,
    766–67, 782, 786

Kennedy family (*cont.*)
  Irish roots of, 4
  last group photograph of, 750–51
  move from Boston to New York,
    105–6, 113
  Palm Beach home of, 189; *see also*
    Palm Beach, Fla.
  trusts for, 91–92, 131, 155, 170, 194,
    528–29, 586, 587, 612
  wealth of, 15
Kenny, Thomas, 38
Kent, Duke of, 294, 378
Kent, Frank, 236, 245, 317, 355
Kent, Sidney, 75
Kent, Tyler, 444–47, 468
Keogh, Eugene, 729
Kerrigan, John, 593
Khrushchev, Nikita, 745–46
Killian, James R., Jr., 699
Kintner, Robert, 431–32, 481, 500,
    501, 505
Kirk, Alan, 528
Kirstein, Louis, 111, 301
Klemmer, Harvey, 269, 299, 474
Knebel, Fletcher, 721–22
Knickerbocker, H. R., 199
Knight, Maxwell, 444, 445
Knox, Frank, 459–60, 493
Knudsen, William, 511
Korea, 654
Korean War, 632–33, 634–35, 637
  Edward Kennedy and, 648
  JFK's views on, 658
  JPK's views on, 636, 637, 660
Kravis, Henry, 692
Kravis, Raymond, 692–93
Kristallnacht, 359–60, 361
Krock, Arthur, 215, 238, 240, 256,
    261, 268, 269, 273, 291, 314, 317,
    319, 321, 355, 482, 492, 500, 525,
    541, 566, 583, 599, 601, 615, 637,
    659, 662, 687, 690, 705
  background of, 211
  Fortune article and, 262–63
  I'm for Roosevelt and, 247, 256
  JFK's Harvard thesis and, 212,
    435–36
  JFK's presidential campaign and,
    727–28
  JPK's alliance with, 211, 316, 367
  on JPK's ambassadorship, 395–96

JPK's interviews with, 211, 606
JPK's presidential ambitions and,
    316, 318, 327–28
JPK proposed as envoy to Ireland by,
    506–7
JPK's relationship with, 211–12, 236
New York Times editor-in-chief
    position and, 316
on Roosevelt, 197
on Roosevelt's relationship with JPK,
    229
Kuhn, Ferdinand, Jr., 284, 362

labor, 229, 232, 260, 504
  maritime, 261–62, 267–69, 278–79,
    284
  1960 presidential election and, 753
  racketeering and, 710–11
Labour Party, 484
Laemmle, Carl, 74, 94
La Follette, Philip, 382
Lait, Jack, 604
Lakewood, 248
Lamont, Thomas, 319–20, 507
Land, Emory Scott, 543–44
Landis, James, 216, 217, 247, 543,
    614–15, 635, 653, 659, 662, 663,
    666, 671, 687, 742, 769
  death of, 770
  tax problems of, 769–70
Landon, Alfred M., 250, 531
Lansky, Meyer, 80
Laos, 756
Laski, Harold, 198, 200, 202, 203,
    224, 128, 390, 484
Lasky, Jesse, 94, 100, 101, 107, 110,
    139–40
Lawford, Christopher, 678
Lawford, Patricia Kennedy (daughter),
    90, 113, 126, 243, 264, 266–67,
    325, 423, 457, 463, 490, 560, 602,
    646, 654, 667, 695, 719, 762
  birth of, 90
  education of, 526, 527, 547
  in England during JPK's
    ambassadorship, 286, 297, 298
  Hartington's death and, 573
  JPK's stroke and, 776, 778, 779
  Kathleen's death and, 621
  marriage of, 585, 678
  work life of, 585

World War II and, 410
Lawford, Peter, 695, 730, 762, 778
 Patricia Kennedy's marriage to, 585, 678
Lawler, Anna, 160–61
Lawrence, Charles, 223–24
Lawrence, David, 729
League of Nations, 176, 199, 258, 290, 361
Leaming, Barbara, 622
LeBaron, Bill, 116
Lee, Raymond E., 460, 467, 473, 501
Leffingwell, Russell, 67
LeFrak, Sam, 778
LeHand, Missy, 191, 244–45, 247, 366, 416, 480, 490, 492, 493, 542–43
Lehár, Franz, 155
lend-lease program, 510, 511–13, 515, 516–20, 525
Lenglen, Suzanne, 97
Leonard, Dutch, 56
Lerner, Max, 356
Lewin, Charles J., 666
Lewis, Duffy, 728
Lewis, John L., 260, 319
Libbey-Owens-Ford Company, 192, 210, 262–63
Liberty, 314
Liberty Loans, 54
Lieut. Joseph P. Kennedy Jr. Home, 627–28
Life, 313, 432, 519, 561, 615, 637, 739, 752, 774
 JPK's article in, 599–602, 604–5
Lincoln, Evelyn, 771
Lincoln Center, 773
Lindbergh, Anne Morrow, 300, 338–39, 377
Lindbergh, Charles A., 102, 266, 300, 306, 338–40, 357, 360, 369, 418, 427, 503, 514
Lindley, Ernest, 658
Lindsay, Ronald, 338, 363, 364, 372
Lippmann, Walter, 198, 211, 317, 356–57, 367, 394, 434, 637
Lipstadt, Deborah, 360
liquor:
 JPK bootlegging stories, 71, 79–81
 JPK's Somerset Importers business, 192–94, 245, 528–29, 611, 720
 Prohibition and, 79, 191, 192, 193

Literary Digest, 236
Lloyd, Harold, 110
Lloyd George, David, 433
lobotomy, 534–35
 of Rosemary Kennedy, xxiii, 535–37, 589, 630–31, 683, 691
Lodge, Henry Cabot, 11
Lodge, Henry Cabot, Jr., 545, 604, 607, 639, 641, 656
 JFK's Senate campaign against, 652, 656, 657–58, 661, 662–70, 741–42
Loew, Marcus, 94, 100, 101, 103
Logevall, Fredrik, 600
London *Evening Standard,* 377
London Monetary and Economic Conference, 191
London School of Economics, 198–99, 239
Long, Breckinridge, 199, 410, 446, 447, 482, 496, 497, 508, 509
Long, Huey, 230, 231, 235
Lonsdale, Frederick, 376, 554
Look, 655, 721–22, 724
Looker, Earle, 262–63
Los Angeles Examiner, 96
Los Angeles Times, 116, 120, 122–23, 125, 128, 130, 136, 364, 369, 506, 513, 737
Lothian, Philip Kerr, Lord, 411–12, 416–17, 427–28, 465, 466, 483, 506, 507, 509
Lowell, Abbott, 61
Lowell, Ralph, 24
Luce, Clare Boothe, 299, 379–80, 432, 433, 435, 436, 463, 464, 469, 489, 494, 544–45, 554, 555, 568, 615, 703
Luce, Henry, 299, 300, 379, 380, 519, 580, 637, 739–40
Lusitania, 44–45
Lyons, Louis, 497–500, 503, 514

MacArthur, Douglas, 635, 658
MacDonald, Malcolm, 358, 361, 362, 365, 371, 390
MacDonald, Torbert, 379, 595, 677–78, 708
Mack, Roy, 693
Mackay, Ellin, 249
Mailer, Norman, 762

Maine and New Hampshire Theatre
    Company, 91, 94, 120
Maisky, Ivan, 484
Maltz, Albert, 730–31
Manhattan, S.S., 284
Manhattanville College, 695
Mao Zedong, 636
Marion, Frances, 96, 102
Maritime Commission, 315, 343, 409,
    543–44
    congressional report of, 269–70
    establishment of, 259
    JPK as chairman of, xxi, 80, 255–56,
        258–59, 261–62, 264, 267–70,
        272, 276, 277, 278–79, 296, 544
maritime industry, 258–59
    labor practices and disputes in,
        261–62, 267–69, 278–79, 284
Mark Twain Journal, 731
Marsh, Ollie, 121
Marshall, George, 616, 674
Marshall, Tully, 138
Marshall Plan, 616–17, 618, 636
Martin, Joe, 616
Martin, Mary Jane, 213
Martin, Samuel Klump, III, 213
Marwood mansion, 213–15, 228–29,
    245, 273
Marx, Groucho, 251
Marx, Harpo, 252
Massachusetts Electric, 59
Matsu, 745, 746
Matthews, Chris, 753
Matthews, J. B., 672–73
Maverick Congregational Church, 7
Maxwell, Elsa, 299, 325
Mayer, Louis B., 121, 135
McAllister, Father Nilus, 220
McCarthy, Jean Kerr, 685
McCarthy, Joe (reporter), 171
McCarthy, Joseph (senator), 595–96,
    667–68, 671, 672–74, 677, 682,
    685, 728, 741
    Army hearings, 673, 675
    death of, 685
    JFK and, 666–67, 685, 701
    JPK and, 667, 672, 674, 685
    Robert Kennedy and, 671, 672, 685
McClellan, John, 673, 688, 711
McCormack, John W., 539, 588, 703,
    729

McCormick, Colonel Robert, 243–44,
    318, 497, 517, 644
McCraw, Thomas, 226
McDonald, George, 527–28
McInerny, Tim, 555, 557–58, 653–54,
    681, 682
McNamara, Robert, 760
Meet the Press, 658–59, 785
mental retardation, 698–99, 760
    Joseph P. Kennedy, Jr. Foundation
        and, 696–99
    presidential panel on, 760–61
Merchandise Mart, 588–89, 592,
    611–12, 625, 647, 693, 694, 782
Merchants Bank of Boston, 38, 39, 45,
    49, 59
Merrill, Joe, 35–36
Messersmith, George, 328
Meyer, Eugene, 507, 508
Meyner, Robert, 720
MGM, 94, 119, 259
Middle East, 351, 497, 530, 658–59
    JFK's tour of, 654
Middlesex Club, 61
Milbank, Jeremiah, 112, 119
Miller, Merle, 576
Mr. Smith Goes to Washington, 421
Mitford, Unity, 404
Mizner, Addison, 190
Moffat, Jay Pierrepont, 292, 293–94,
    332, 354, 355, 362, 365, 370,
    429–30
Moley, Raymond, 175, 179, 180, 181,
    186, 187, 191, 202, 205, 208,
    209–10, 218
Moniz, Egas, 534
Mooney, James, 383, 384, 385
Moore, Edward "Eddie," 63, 67, 77,
    87, 89, 93, 98, 105, 114, 117, 137,
    151, 175, 180, 207, 213, 214, 215,
    221, 255, 284, 375, 387, 408, 419,
    436, 447, 450, 463, 464, 491, 495
    in England during JPK's
        ambassadorship, 297, 299, 300
    JFK's congressional campaign and,
        595, 598
    JPK's first business transaction
        with, 59
    JPK's relationship with, 59–60, 180
    Joseph P. Kennedy, Jr. Foundation
        and, 613

motion picture industry and, 94, 95,
112, 115–16, 118, 138–39
Rosemary Kennedy and, 411, 533
Moore, Mary, 59–60, 63, 113, 255,
297, 375, 419, 436, 447, 450
Rosemary Kennedy and, 152, 411,
425, 426, 533, 628
Moore, Owen, 86
Moore, Father Thomas, 527, 535
Morgan, Edward P., 746
Morgan, Forbes, 188
Morgan, J. P. "Jack," 285, 403, 419
Morgenthau, Henry, Jr., 215, 230, 231,
246, 272, 274, 276–77, 325, 326,
330, 331, 333, 338, 367, 395, 412,
437–38, 583
Morgenthau, Henry, III, 326–27
Morris, Sylvia Jukes, 380
Morrissey, Francis X. "Frank," 716,
719, 729, 730, 766
judgeship and, 768–69, 786
Morrissey, Michael, 732
Morrison, Herbert, 484
Morse, Wayne, 735
Mortal Storm, The, 502
Morton, Thurston, 752
Moscicki, Ignacy, 401
motion picture industry, xx
British import restrictions and,
420–21
censorship and, xx, 75–76, 97, 107
FBO and, *see* FBO
First National and, 122–27, 128–29,
135, 158
Jews in, 75, 97, 103, 104, 501–2,
503, 559
JPK in, xx, 65–71, 73–76, 91–104,
105–27, 128–32, 135–46, 154–62,
168, 169–70, 518
JPK's Harvard lecture series on,
100–102, 109
K-A-O and, 112, 119–20, 121, 122,
128–29, 130–31, 135, 137
Pathé and, *see* Pathé
RKO and, *see* RKO
Robertson-Cole Distributing
Corporation and, 71, 73–75
sound systems and, 111, 124
Moving Picture World, 95, 100
Mowrer, Edgar, 459–60
Mulkern, Patsy, 595

Mundelein, George Cardinal, 252
Munich Agreement, 346–47, 348–49,
359–60, 400, 402, 435–36, 485,
633, 745
Muñoz Marin, Luis, 748
Murdock, J. J., 112–13, 115, 137, 159
Murphy, Frank, 482, 492, 493, 496,
507, 509, 539, 581
Murphy, Paul, 193, 221, 301, 377
JPK's employment of, 613, 614
Murphy, William, Jr., 318
Murray, Vera, 77
Mushyn, Thomas, 679
Mussolini, Benito, 199, 272, 287, 289,
304, 346, 356, 375, 381, 448, 451
Roosevelt's April, 1939 letter to,
381–82, 385
Muste, A. J., 607

Nantasket, Mass., 81
Nashville *Tennessean,* 737
Nation, 257
National Conference of Christians and
Jews, 672
National Conference of Citizens for
Religious Freedom, 743
National Distillers, 192
National Maritime Union (NMU), 268
National Recovery Act, 232
National Shawmut Bank, 33, 45, 59,
71, 88
National Socialism, 484, 498, 503
National Union for Social Justice, 230
NATO (North Atlantic Treaty
Organization), 636, 638, 679
Navy, U.S., 504
JFK's service in, 527–28, 531, 540,
542, 543, 549, 551, 555–59, 560
Joe Kennedy, Jr.'s service in, 527,
528, 540, 542, 543, 546, 549, 555,
561, 567, 568–69, 567, 568–69,
570–71
Robert Kennedy's service in, 584–85
Navy League, Trafalgar Day dinner of,
353–54
Nazi Germany, 199, 200, 287, 288,
302, 315, 334–47, 356, 372–73,
377–78, 385, 394, 399–407, 418,
427, 432, 433, 438, 459, 475, 483,
486, 496–97, 516, 531, 577, 581,
605, 606, 638, 745

Nazi Germany (*cont.*)
  anti-Nazi films and, 501–2
  appeasement of, *see* appeasement of
    Nazi Germany
  Athenia and, 409
  Austria annexed by (*Anschluss*),
    287–90, 292, 293, 294, 306–7,
    308–9, 322, 329, 351, 360, 361,
    383, 413, 486
  Belgium and, 439–40, 449, 450
  Britain attacked by, 458, 461,
    462–63, 466, 468, 469, 473–75,
    477, 478, 479, 480–81, 496, 516,
    529–31, 568
  Britain's declaration of war against,
    406–7, 408, 410, 411, 415, 416
  Czechoslovakia and, 287, 290, 302,
    323, 329–30, 332, 334–47, 360,
    375–76, 383, 400, 413, 486
  Denmark and, 437
  Dirksen and, 310–11, 741–42
  economy of, 372, 382–84, 416
  France invaded by, 440, 441,
    447–56, 458
  Holland and, 439–40
  Joe Kennedy, Jr. in, 199, 200–202
  JPK's conversations with diplomats
    in, 310–11, 321
  JPK's fears about, xxii, 323
  King Leopold and, 615
  Kristallnacht in, 359–60, 361
  Norway and, 428, 429, 437, 438,
    439
  Nuremberg Laws in, 287, 306
  persecution of Jews in, 199–200,
    287, 306–9, 310–11, 322, 329,
    349–52, 359, 363, 364–65, 508,
    581–82
  Poland and, 376, 399–405, 413, 420,
    486, 579, 633
  Roosevelt and, 307, 309, 310,
    321–22, 334, 338, 341, 344, 349
  Soviet alliance with, 399, 415–16
  Soviet Union invaded by, 531
  surrender of, 579–80
  in Tripartite Pact, 479–80
  see also Hitler, Adolf
Nehru, Jawaharlal, 654
Nelson, Donald, 550
neutrality:
  JPK and, 294–95

laws on, 288, 415, 418, 443, 459,
    510
  World War I and, 40, 44
  World War II and, 294–95
New Bedford *Standard-Times,* 666
New Deal, 198, 204, 210, 211, 212,
    229, 230, 236–37, 243, 246, 249,
    250, 260–61, 271, 274, 275, 313,
    484
  work relief program, 229–31, 232,
    237
New Republic, 210, 393–94
Newsweek, 733, 740–41, 742, 767
Newton, Helen, 222–23, 242, 264
New York *Daily News,* 356, 503,
    513–14, 656
New Yorker, 561
New York Evening Post, 199, 704–5
New York Herald Tribune, 128, 409,
    500
New York Journal American, 607
New York News, 505
New York Post, 756
New York Stock Exchange (NYSE),
    578
  registration of foreign stocks and
    bonds on, 238–39
  see also stock market
New York Times, 42, 97, 101, 122,
    130, 133, 161, 167, 182, 186, 197,
    212, 215, 218, 219, 228, 229, 238,
    243, 250, 261, 270, 272, 284, 302,
    305, 324, 354, 362, 364, 385, 391,
    490, 500, 513, 518, 557, 587,
    606–7, 608, 635, 638, 644, 650,
    677, 705, 706, 712, 754, 761, 770
  editor-in-chief position at, 316
  JFK's presidential campaign and,
    722, 727, 731, 734–35, 742, 743,
    744, 748
  Krock at, 211, 212, 247, 316, 395,
    396, 599, 615, 662, 727–28; *see
    also* Krock, Arthur
New York Times Magazine, 689
New York World, 174, 211
Nichols, Louis, 675
Nicolson, Harold, 346
Nixon, Richard M., 595–96, 617, 652,
    670, 746, 757, 764
  JFK's debates with, 744–45
  JPK and, 731

in 1960 presidential election, 710,
715, 739, 740, 743, 744–45,
750–53
Norman, Montague, 449
Normandie, 238, 321, 380, 411–12
Norton, Sally, 532
Notre Dame, 252, 530, 531, 672, 695,
715
West Point cheating scandal and,
649–50
Norway, 428, 429, 437, 438, 439
Novello, Angie, 771

O'Brien, Hugh, 9, 11
O'Brien, John A., 672
O'Brien, Larry, 662, 719, 726
O'Connell, Daniel P., 729
O'Connell, Joseph, 38
O'Connell, William Cardinal, 38,
41, 146
Offie, Carmel, 286, 532
Odlum, Floyd, 274
O'Donnell, John, 656
O'Donnell, Kenneth, 663, 664, 707,
719, 726, 729, 748, 749, 769
oil, 475, 538, 655, 756
JPK's investments in, 529, 612,
692–93
Oglethorpe University, 530
Okrent, Daniel, 81
Old Colony Realty, 34, 44, 59
O'Leary, Ted, 137, 143, 491
Ollman, Wally, 588–89
O'Meara, Harry, 34
Ordway, Lucius, 610, 645, 669
organized crime:
JFK assassination and, 80, 720
JPK and, 80, 720, 753
1960 presidential election and, 753
Ormsby-Gore, David, 297
Oshinsky, David, 668
Osservatore Romano, 734–35
Our Lady of the Assumption Church,
10, 12–13, 15
Owens-Illinois, 192
Oxnam, Garfield Bromely, 634

Pacelli, Eugenio Cardinal, *see* Pius XII,
Pope
Palestine, 286–87, 307, 351–52, 358,
359, 361–62, 385–93, 655

JPK and, 385–93
Roosevelt and, 387, 389, 390,
391–93
White Paper on, 388–92
Paley, Barbara "Babe," 241–42
Palm Beach, Fla., 113–15, 137, 161–64,
172, 178, 187, 189, 190, 194–95,
197, 241–42, 245, 246, 369, 432,
435, 525–29, 610–11, 715, 728,
729, 758, 774, 775–78, 782, 786
Kennedy house in, 189
Palm Beach Country Club, 526, 775
Palmer, Muriel, 248
Palmer, Paul, 616
Paramount Pictures, 74, 106, 107, 110,
119, 121, 140, 141, 254, 367
JPK as adviser to, 244
Pasternak, Joe, 398
Pastore, John, 662
Pathé, 112, 115–17, 122, 124, 125,
128, 131, 135, 137, 141, 156,
158–59, 169–70, 257
RKO's purchase of, 159–62
Patterson, Cissy, 541, 580
Patterson, Joseph, 503, 505
Paul VI, Pope, 375
Peake, Charles, 418
Peale, Norman Vincent, 743, 748
Pearl Harbor, xxii, 509, 538, 567
Pearson, Drew, 236, 248–49, 251, 263,
303, 304–5, 306, 317, 321–22,
353, 367–68, 393, 540, 600, 601,
674–75, 714
JFK's presidential campaign and,
731, 741
Pecora, Ferdinand, 188, 192, 208
Pegler, Westbrook, 668
Perkins, Frances, 268–69, 272, 278
Persian Gulf, 660
Pétain, Philippe, 455, 456
Peters, Andrew, 59, 61, 62, 67
Peyton, Father Patrick, 585
Philadelphia Inquirer, 318, 772
Phillips, William, 374, 375
Photoplay, 93, 103, 104, 109
Pickford, Mary, 110, 298
Pilgrims Society, 291–95
Pittman, Key, 317
Pittsburgh Post-Gazette, 246
Place, Edward, 62, 63
Pius XI, Pope, 264, 374

Pius XII, Pope (Eugenio Cardinal
    Pacelli), 252–53, 264, 374–75,
    381, 491, 639
POAU (Protestants and Other
    Americans United for Separation
    of Church and State), 715,
    721–22
Poland, 577
    Germany and, 376, 394, 399–405,
        413, 420, 486, 579, 633
    Soviet Union and, 416
Ponzi, Charles, 67
Poole, Arthur B., 257, 656
Potter, Bob, 25, 33, 45, 54, 59, 71, 88
Potter, Jack, 93
Powell, Joseph W., 52, 54, 102
Powers, Dave, 595, 653, 661, 686, 710,
    730, 748, 749
Powers, Pat, 74, 91
Pravda, 638
President's Board of Consultants on
    Foreign Intelligence Activities,
    699–701, 705
Pressman, Jack D., 535
Princeton University, 239–40
Producers Distributing Corporation,
    112
Profiles in Courage (JFK), 687,
    690, 714
Prohibition, 79, 191, 192, 193
Protestants, in Boston, 10–11,
    15, 22
PT 109, 556–58, 560, 561, 598
Puerto Rico, 748
Puhl, Emil, 383

Queen Kelly, 118–19, 121, 136–42,
    155–56, 157, 158, 159
Queen Mary, 314, 411–12
Quemoy, 745, 746
Quigley, Martin J., 95–96, 104
Quincy, Josiah, 14
Quinn, Bob, 170
Quirk, James, 103, 104

Racine, Leo, 692, 733
rail travel, transcontinental, 140
Ramsay, Archibald Maule, 444
Ramsaye, Terry, 93, 103
Raskob, John Jakob, 183
Rayburn, Sam, 233, 707, 764

RCA (Radio Corporation of America),
    111, 124, 129, 130, 254
    JPK's consulting contract with,
        243–44
Rea, Ruth, 35–36
Reader's Digest, 561
real estate:
    JPK's investments in, 44, 59, 529,
        586–89, 592, 612, 692, 772
    rent controls and, 587–88
Reardon, Ted, 621
Red Cross, 458, 551, 552, 555
Reisman, Phil, 419–20, 421, 645,
    679, 680
Reith, John, 484
Remarque, Erich Maria, 325, 398
Republican Party, 135, 181, 197, 204,
    517
    in Boston, 10–11, 15
Reston, James, 606–7, 638, 644, 658,
    705, 721
Reynaud, Paul, 440, 451–53, 455
Reynolds, John J., 586–87, 627
    JPK's employment of, 614
Rhee, Syngman, 636
Ribbentrop, Joachim von, 310, 311,
    334, 403
Ribicoff, Abe, 759
Richardson, Hill & Co., 59
Ridgway, Matthew, 654
Right Club, 444, 445
Riley, John, 35
Riva, Maria (daughter of Marlene
    Dietrich), 325, 326, 327, 398
Riverdale Country School, 106, 149,
    150, 152, 162
RKO (Radio-Keith-Orpheum), 129,
    131, 137
    Pathé purchased by, 159–62
Robertson-Cole, 68–69, 70–71
Robertson-Cole Distributing
    Corporation, 71, 73–75
Robinson, Joe, 256
Rockefeller, John D., III, 772
Rockefeller, Nelson, 727
Rockett, Al, 126
Rogers, Ginger, 299
Rohde, Amanda, 264–65
Rommel, Erwin, 530
Roosevelt, Anna, 179, 184, 243, 245,
    255

Roosevelt, Betsey, 187, 206
Roosevelt, Eleanor, 209, 215, 245,
    316–17, 492
  JPK criticized by, 717–18
Roosevelt, Elliott, 184
Roosevelt, Franklin D., xxii, 262,
    268, 303–4, 368–70, 433, 448,
    455, 460, 462–64, 469, 476,
    481, 482, 483, 665, 683, 733–34,
    736
  and aid to Allies, 441–43, 451–54,
    458–59, 466–72, 503
  as Assistant Secretary of the Navy,
    55, 174
  "brain trust" advisers to, 178–79,
    331, 354
  British war debt payments and, 185,
    411
  cabinet selections of, 186, 187
  campaign contributions to,
    182–83
  Catholics and, 539, 549
  Chamberlain and, 330–31, 343, 344,
    376–77, 579
  Churchill and, 414–15, 428–29, 441,
    442, 445, 447, 451–53, 465–70,
    504
  court-packing plan of, 270–71
  criticisms of, 197–98, 246, 248,
    251–52, 271
  death of, 578–79, 583
  on the Depression, 172
  in destroyers-for-bases negotiations,
    466–67, 469–72, 493
  economic policies of, 202–3,
    229–30, 246–49, 271–72, 295–96,
    315
  elected president, 183–84, 186
  First Hundred Days of, 197
  fourth term campaign and election,
    560, 573–74, 575–76
  Garner as running mate of, 176–77
  as governor, 172
  Hearst and, 176–77, 179, 181, 182,
    183, 185, 186, 187, 254
  Hitler and, 341, 344, 346, 381–82,
    385, 413–14
  ill health of, 574, 575–76
  inner circle of, 180–81, 183, 185–86,
    215, 371, 374, 518
  Japan and, 538

Jews and, 309–10, 349–52, 362,
    390, 508, 509, 583
  on JPK, 520–21
  JPK appointed ambassador by,
    272–78, 283, 284, 491, 496
  JPK appointed Maritime Commission
    chairman by, 255
  JPK appointed SEC chairman by,
    206–11
  JPK offered jobs by, 543–44,
    549–60
  JPK's correspondence with, 189,
    190–91, 412
  JPK's first meetings with, 174, 175
  JPK's meeting with, after
    ambassadorship, 489–93, 505
  JPK's offering of services to, after
    U.S. entry into World War II, 539,
    542–44
  JPK's presidential aspirations and,
    315–19, 327
  JPK's relationship with, 172–73,
    180–81, 183, 185–86, 215,
    228–29, 231, 244–45, 274,
    318–19, 327, 331, 332–33, 393–94,
    396–97, 429, 513
  and JPK's resignation as ambassador,
    502–4
  and JPK's resignation from SEC,
    234–36
  JPK's speech at 1936 Harvard
    Reunion and, 260–61
  JPK's support for presidential
    campaign of, xxi, 171–73, 175–77,
    179–83, 186, 188, 190
  JPK's support for reelection of,
    245–52, 255
  JPK's support for third term of, 428,
    429, 489–96, 519
  Krock and, 211
  lend-lease program of, 510, 511–13,
    515, 516–20, 525
  letter to JPK regarding Al Smith, 134
  at Marwood in Washington, D.C.,
    215, 228–29, 245
  Munich Agreement and, 347
  Mussolini and, 381–82, 385
  and Nazi Germany, in buildup to
    World War II, 307, 309, 310,
    321–22, 334, 338, 341, 344, 349,
    373, 376–77, 399–401, 405

Roosevelt, Franklin D. (*cont.*)
  negotiations appeal in buildup
    to World War II, 341, 342,
    343, 344
  neutrality laws and, 288, 415, 445
  New Deal of, 198, 204, 210, 211,
    212, 229, 230, 236–37, 243, 246,
    249, 250, 260–61, 272, 274, 275,
    313, 484
  1932 presidential campaign of,
    171–77, 179–83
  Palestine and, 387, 389, 390, 391–93
  public utilities bill and, 232–35, 236,
    237
  radio addresses of, 530–31
  Reynaud and, 451–53
  salary of, 244
  second term election of, 252, 254,
    710
  second term inauguration of, 255
  tax proposals of, 229, 231–32, 237
  third term, decision to seek, 313,
    333, 428, 429, 436, 492
  third term election of, 496
  third term nomination of, 462
  and U.S. entry into World War II,
    538
  and U.S. involvement in World War
    II, 443, 454, 467, 491, 504
  Walker and, 178–79
  Wall Street regulation and, 205
  whistle-stop tours of, 179–83
  work relief program of, 229–31,
    232, 237
Roosevelt, Franklin, Jr., 733–34
Roosevelt, James "Jimmy," 179–80,
    183, 184, 187, 193, 206, 208, 241,
    245, 250, 253, 268, 269, 275, 278,
    513, 733
  insurance business of, 320
  and JPK's ambassadorship, 272, 273,
    284, 285, 287, 310
  JPK's friendship with, 320
Roosevelt, Theodore, 701
Rosenberg, Julius and Ethel, 671
Rosenbloom, Carroll, 582, 645, 646,
    684, 749, 773, 786
Rosenman, Samuel, 583
Rossheim, Irving, 125, 126
Rothschild, Anthony Gustav de, 362
Rowe, James, 671

Royal, John, 695, 772
Rublee, George, 329, 350–51, 365
Ruppel, Louis, 207, 249, 250
Rusk, Dean, 760
Rusk, Howard, 696, 761, 777–78
Rusk Institute, 778, 781, 782
Russell, Rosalind, 299
Russia, *see* Soviet Union
Russo, Joe, 598
Ruth, Babe, 66, 119

Sachar, Abram L., 698
Sacred Heart Convent, 309, 323–24
St. Coletta School, Hanover, Mass.,
    623–24, 626, 628–29
St. Coletta School, Jefferson, Wisc.,
    537, 695
  Rosemary at, 628–31
St. Coletta school, Palos Park, Calif.,
    695
St. John, C. Wardell, 150
St. John, George, 177, 195–96, 225
St. Leonard's Mansion, 433, 435, 444,
    458, 473, 479
St. Louis Post-Dispatch, 80, 498
St. Louis Star-Times, 276–77
Salinger, Pierre, 735, 769
Saltonstall, Leverett, 593, 657–58
Sarnoff, David, 111, 124–25, 129, 130,
    137, 243, 350, 369, 542
Saturday Evening Post, 320, 377, 712
Schary, Dore, 706
Schenck, Joseph, 96, 115, 156
Schenck, Nick, 94
Schiff, Dorothy, 756
Schlesinger, Arthur M., Jr., 171, 188,
    605–6, 666, 689, 703, 758, 762,
    768
Schnitzer, Joseph, 74–75, 94
Schulberg, B. P., 170
Schuschnigg, Kurt von, 289, 290
Schwab, Charles M., 52, 55
Scollard, C. J., 114, 131, 139
Seabury, Samuel, 179
Seattle Post-Intelligencer, 255–56
Securities Act of 1933, 204–5,
    216, 233
Securities and Exchange Commission
    (SEC), 226–28, 247, 257, 296, 613,
    614
  blue sky laws of, 226

Hearst and, 254, 257
insider trading and, 67, 131, 226, 227
JPK as chairman of, xxi, 67, 80, 131, 206–11, 212–20, 226–29, 232–37, 243, 244, 248, 254, 277, 320, 438, 529
JPK's 1934 radio address and, 218–19
JPK's resignation from, 234–36, 246
JPK's staff appointments for, 216–17
public utilities bill and, 232–35, 236, 237
Securities Exchange Act of 1934, 205, 208, 217, 233
Seigenthaler, John, 737–38
Selective Service System:
JPK's registration with, 50–51, 54
in World War I, 50
in World War II, 476
Senate Committee on Banking and Currency, 188, 192, 208, 210
Senate Committee on Foreign Relations, 314, 640, 711
JFK and, 640–42, 684–85, 711
Senate Permanent Subcommittee on Investigations, 671, 673, 688, 710–11
Seymour, Frances Ford, 536
Seymour, James, 299, 419, 460
Sharett, Moshe, 388–89, 390
Shaw, George Bernard, 306
Shea, Frank, 216
Sheehan, Joe, 16, 54, 216, 436
Sheehy, Father Maurice, 549
Shirer, William, 342
Show People, 173
Shriver, Eunice Kennedy (daughter), 194, 242–43, 264, 325, 333, 423, 457, 463, 490, 526, 527, 646, 657, 667, 668, 678, 681, 695, 732, 738, 755, 760, 765, 766, 784
Addison's disease of, 527
birth of, 85
childhood of, 90, 113, 126, 178
education of, 106, 149, 152, 242, 297, 298
in England during JPK's ambassadorship, 297
Hartington's death and, 572–73

health problems of, 195, 224, 527, 546–47
JFK's congressional campaign and, 596, 602, 603
Joe Jr.'s death and, 570, 571
Joseph P. Kennedy, Jr. Foundation and, 613, 624, 696, 697–98, 760
JPK's stroke and, 776, 778, 779, 784
Kathleen's death and, 620–21
marriage of, 585, 647, 677
and outbreak of World War II, 410
Rosemary and, 152, 154, 425, 630
work life of, 585, 619, 647, 697
Shriver, Robert Sargent (son-in-law), 647, 662, 663, 665, 668, 678, 695, 697–98, 704, 720, 773
Eunice Kennedy's marriage to, 585, 647, 677
Sidey, Hugh, 752, 757
Silverman, Sime, 96
Simon, John, 336, 345, 367, 371
Sinatra, Frank, 730–31, 762, 763
Sisters of St. Francis of Assisi, 623, 628
Skinner, Otis, 73
Skouras, Spyros, 126
Slessor, John, 339
Smathers, George, 595–96, 652, 657, 684, 703, 757
Smith, Al, 134–35, 172, 173, 176, 246, 250–51, 491, 701, 744, 754
Smith, Ben (Wall Street trader), 163, 438
Smith, Benjamin A., II (senator), 766
Smith, Jean Kennedy (daughter), xxiii, 163, 243, 264, 423, 435, 457, 458, 463, 490, 534, 565, 615, 646, 668, 678, 681, 718, 762, 766–67
birth of, 116
childhood of, 126, 146, 178
doll collection of, 423–24
education of, 526, 547
in England during JPK's ambassadorship, 286, 297, 298
Hartington's death and, 573
jewelry theft and, 694
JFK's congressional campaign and, 602, 603
Joe Jr.'s death and, 570, 571
JPK's stroke and, 776, 778, 779
Kathleen's death and, 621
marriage of, 585, 678, 718
and outbreak of World War II, 410

Smith, Jean Kennedy (*cont.*)
Rosemary and, 425, 629
work life of, 585–86
Smith, Joe, 705
Smith, Kate, 654
Smith, Steve (son-in-law), 718, 726,
728, 762, 786
Jean Kennedy's marriage to, 585,
678, 718
socialism, 251, 484, 618
Depression and, 171
Social Security, 260
Somerset Importers, 192–94, 245,
528–29, 611, 720
Sorensen, Ted, 673, 685, 687, 690,
702–3, 709, 726, 745, 748, 752,
764, 769, 774
Southard, Louis K., 38
Soviet Union, 287, 394, 484, 577, 580,
581, 600–601, 604–5, 638, 643
appeasement of, xxii, 605–7
in Cold War, xxii, 604–5, 609, 625,
636, 659, 660–61, 682, 689
German alliance with, 399, 415–16
German invasion of, 531
Joe Kennedy, Jr.'s trip to, 199, 202,
203, 220
JPK's views on, xxii, 600–601,
605–6, 617, 659, 682, 745, 746
Korea and, 632, 633, 636, 641
Poland invaded by, 416
Robert Kennedy's views on, 689–90
U.S. negotiations with, 745–46
Spain, 374, 377, 496–97
Catholic refugees in, 309, 323–24
civil war in, 258, 287, 377, 381
Spalding, Chuck, 739
Spellman, Francis Cardinal, 252–53,
575, 580, 586, 626–28, 649,
677, 696, 698, 700, 730, 748,
755–56
JFK's presidential campaign and,
723, 727–28, 744, 753–55
Spivak, Lawrence, 658–59
Stalin, Joseph, 254, 575, 600, 601, 605,
636, 638
Stanford University, 476, 501
Stanton, Frank, 747
State Street Trust, 45
Stearn, Jess, 767
Steele, Richard, 766

Stevenson, Adlai, 661, 668, 687, 701–8,
709, 736, 764
Stewart, Jimmy, 398, 421, 502
Stewart, Robert, 490
Stewart, William Rhinelander, 299
Steyne, Alan, 301
Stieglitz, Katherine "Kitty," 536
Stimson, Henry, 459, 465
stock market:
and British sales of securities, 437–38
crash of 1929, xxi, 132, 154,
159–60, 218, 586–87
insider trading and, 67–68, 78, 131,
132, 161–62, 226, 227
investigation of fraud in, 188
JPK's trading in, xx–xxi, 44–45,
58–59, 67, 77–78, 131–32, 155,
161–62, 168, 170, 175, 188,
191–92, 205, 206, 209–10,
212–13, 226, 438, 529, 692, 693
JPK's work as broker, 58, 60, 63, 64,
66, 67, 68
Libbey-Owens-Ford stock pool and,
192, 210, 262–63
registration of foreign stocks and
bonds on NYSE, 238–39
regulation of, 204–5, 219; *see also*
Securities and Exchange
Commission
Roosevelt and, 217, 246, 248, 271
short selling and, 88, 168, 170, 438,
692
upward climb of, 77, 111, 167
Stone, Fred, 65, 76, 77
Stone, Galen, 58, 64, 67, 69, 74, 87
Straus, Jesse, 177
Strong, George, 481
Stuart, Harry, 257
Stuart, Robert, Jr., 506, 511
Sudetenland, Czechoslovakia, 287, 290,
302, 323, 329–30, 332, 334–47,
360, 383
Suez Canal, 475, 497, 530, 655, 660
Sullivan, Mark, 210–11
Sulzberger, Arthur, 300, 316
Sumner, William, 5, 6
Sunday Pictorial, 611
Sunset Boulevard, 156
Supreme Court, 228, 232
Roosevelt's plan to change
composition of, 270–71

Surrender of King Leopold,
    The (Kennedy and Landis),
    615
Sutton, Billy, 595
Swanson, Gloria, 86, 107–10, 113,
    114–15, 116–19, 121, 122, 153,
    155–59, 173, 611
  bungalow built for, 137, 157
  financial problems of, 157–58
  Gloria Productions, 115, 155, 156,
    158, 169–70
  JPK's affair with, xx, 115, 117, 118,
    137, 143–48, 154, 156, 158
  JPK's meeting of, 107–8, 110
  Moore and, 60
  Queen Kelly, 118–19, 121, 136–42,
    155–56, 157, 158, 159
  Rose Kennedy and, 143–47
  Rose Kennedy compared with, 110
  singing of, 143, 154–56
  Sunset Boulevard, 157
  The Trespasser, 142–44, 154–55,
    156, 157
Swope, Gerard, 331
Swope, Herbert Bayard, 174–75, 188,
    202, 209, 210, 211, 218, 219, 234,
    239, 331
Symington, Stuart, 673, 720

Tablet, 744
Taft, Robert A., 604–5, 638–39, 660,
    666
Talbot, Father Ted, 563
taxes, 229, 231–32, 237, 606, 608,
    625, 660
  JPK and, 157, 194, 588, 611, 612,
    625
Taylor, Henry, 66
Taylor, Myron, 308, 322, 329, 365,
    393, 632, 633
Teamsters, 710
Thayer, Eugene, 38, 39, 49, 59, 71–72,
    73–74, 78
Thompson, Dorothy, 357, 519
Thomson, Fred, 96–98, 100, 102, 106,
    107, 116
Tilden, Bill, 325
Time, 122, 174, 236, 244, 256, 268,
    278, 279, 409, 433, 519, 592, 703,
    713, 720, 738, 739
Times (London), 565

Timilty, Joe ("the Commish"), 595,
    610, 618, 621, 645, 680, 736
Tinkham, George, 500
Tito, Josip Broz, 636, 639
Tobin, Maurice, 591, 592, 593, 598,
    604
Todd, Mike, 572
Todd Shipbuilding, 69, 78, 168, 256
Tolson, Clyde, 559
Toscanini, Arturo, 300
Townsend, Francis, 230, 231
Townsend, Kathleen Kennedy
    (granddaughter), 654, 780
Transamerica, 159, 168
transatlantic communications, 422–23
transcontinental rail travel, 140
Travell, Janet, 773
Treaty of Versailles, 258, 368, 376
Treman, Robert, 66
Trespasser, The, 142–44, 154–55, 156,
    157
Trohan, Walter, 318, 518
Truitt, Max, 409, 490, 542
Truman, Harry, 573, 575–76, 580,
    583–84, 594, 599, 601, 606, 615,
    616, 637, 638, 640, 643, 649, 656,
    658, 659, 663, 666, 711, 736, 746
  Herbert Hoover and, 584
  JPK's meeting with, 632, 633–34,
    644
  Korean War and, 633, 635
  and sending U.S. troops to Europe,
    638–42
Truman Doctrine (aid to Greece and
    Turkey), 605, 607, 608, 616, 617,
    618, 636, 637
Tucker, Sophie, 93
Tugwell, Rexford, 249, 251
Tully, Grace, 542–43
Tunney, Gene, 100
Turkey, 600, 605
  U.S. aid to, 605, 607, 608, 616, 617,
    618, 636, 637
Turner, Ethel, 71
20th Century Limited, 141
Tyler, Tom, 97

unemployment, 229–30
  work relief program, 229–31, 232,
    237
unions, *see* labor

United Artists, 96, 108, 110, 114, 115, 137, 141, 143, 156, 157
United Nations, 593, 601
Universal Films, 66, 94, 119, 122
University of Virginia, 635–36, 658, 675–76
U.S. News & World Report, 689, 703, 741
U.S. Steel, 168, 319–20, 393
utilities industry, 274
  Public Utility Holding Company Act, 232–35, 236, 237

Valentino, Rudolph, 110
Vallee, Rudy, 221
Vandenberg, Arthur, 601, 607, 616
Vansittart, Robert, 431
Variety, 96, 116, 122, 143
Vatican, 252–53, 264, 381, 619, 632, 633, 634, 642, 679, 699–701, 712, 715, 724, 755, 771
  JFK's presidential campaign and, 734–35
Vickery, Howard, 543–44
Voice of America, 771
Von Stroheim, Erich, 118–19, 121, 136–39, 155
Voorhis, Jerry, 595–96

Wagner, Robert, 389
Wagner Act, 232, 237
Wakeman, Samuel, 52, 55
Waldorf Towers, 503, 547
Waldrop, Frank, 531, 541
Walker, Elisha, 112, 115, 117, 119–20, 123, 124, 129, 130, 159, 175, 192, 257
Walker, Frank, 180–81, 188
Walker, James, 178–79
Wallace, Bob, 726
Wallace, Henry, 504, 605
Wallace, Mike, 714
Wall Street, *see* stock market
Wall Street bombing of 1920, 69–70
Wall Street Journal, 236, 637
Walsh, David I., 215, 551, 604, 657
Walsh, Elizabeth, 615, 663
Walsh, Margaret, 160–61
Walsh, Tom, 769
Walter, Eugene, 138
Wanamaker, Rodman, 190

Warburg, James, 191, 246
Warner, Harry, 94, 101, 181
Warner, Jack, 181
Warner Brothers, 94, 129
  JPK's remarks at luncheon at, 501–2
Warren, Earl, 764
Washington News, 208
Washington Post, 364, 507, 620, 763
Washington Star, 284
Washington Times-Herald, 531, 540, 541
Watson, Edwin "Pa," 489–90
Watts, James, 534, 535
Week, The, 393
Weinberg, Sidney, 550
Weizmann, Chaim, 286, 351, 358, 359, 388, 390, 392, 393
Welles, Sumner, 273, 294, 309, 354, 367, 372, 374, 389, 400, 412, 440, 460, 465, 481–83, 489–90, 493, 496, 507, 512, 615
  and bombing of England, 478–79
  British-Italian negotiations and, 303–4
  Chamberlain's speech and, 342, 344
  on fact-finding tour of Europe, 433–34
  on Frankfurter, 508
  international conference proposed by, 288
  Jewish refugees and, 350–52. 364
  and JPK's meeting with German officials, 384–85
  and JPK's offer as liaison to the pope, 381
Wellington, Alfred, 33, 38
West Point cheating scandal, 649–50
Wheeler, Burton, 176, 234, 317, 514, 517
Wherry, Kenneth, 639, 640, 641
White, Thomas J., 254, 317, 356
White, Theodore, 744
White, William Allen, 507
Whitehead, T. North, 430
Whitney, Richard, 204, 205, 217
Why England Slept (JFK), 212, 424, 435–36, 457, 494, 514, 745
Williams, G. Mennen "Soapy," 720
Williams, Harrison, 191
Willicombe, Joe, 183, 186
Willkie, Wendell, 462, 482, 489, 491

Wilson, Horace, 342, 343, 400, 404
Wilson, Woodrow, 67, 181, 284, 335,
    736
  Britain and, 44
  Prohibition and, 79
  Selective Service System and, 50
  World War I and, 40, 49, 54
Winchell, Walter, 369, 540, 600, 675
Windsor, Duchess of, 325
Windsor, Duke of, 325, 344, 526
Wise, Rabbi Stephen, 327, 386, 389
Wohlthat, Helmuth, 383, 384–85
Wolkoff, Anna, 444–45
Wood, Henry, 468
Wood, Robert E., 506
Wood, Kingsley, 448–49
Woodin, William, 183
Woodring, Harry, 393
Woolf, S. J., 212–13
Worcester Telegram, 766
World War I, 48–57, 172, 219
  Britain in, 40, 44, 49–50
  financial panic caused by, 40–41
  France in, 40, 49
  JPK's opposition to American
    involvement in, 49–50
  JPK's Selective Service registration
    during, 50–51, 54
  JPK's shipyard management position
    during, 51–57
  neutrality and, 40, 44
  outbreak of, 40
  Selective Service System created
    during, 50
  U.S. entry into, 49, 54
  Wilson and, 40, 49, 54
World War II, 576–77
  Allied invasion of Europe, 567
  America First Committee and, 506,
    510–11, 517, 519, 525, 531
  appeasement and, *see* appeasement of
    Nazi Germany
  Athenia sinking and, 408–10
  atomic bombs in, 580
  Britain in, 408–20, 427–31, 433–34,
    438–43, 448–55, 458, 460–63,
    466, 468, 469, 473–75, 477–81,
    483, 486, 496, 516, 529–31, 568,
    579, 581, 633, 745
  Britain in buildup to, 289, 290,
    292–94, 301, 302–3, 323, 329–31,

332, 334–35, 338–47, 368, 373,
    399–407
  Britain's declaration of war against
    Germany, 406–7, 408, 410, 411,
    415, 416
  destroyers-for-bases negotiations in,
    466–67, 469–72, 493
  embassy codes and, 430, 444–46
  end of, xxii, 579–81
  espionage in, 444–47
  events leading up to, xxi–xxii, 258,
    287–91, 301, 323, 372, 394–95,
    398, 399–407
  fall of France in, 440, 441, 447–56,
    458
  France in, 289, 290, 302, 323, 329,
    334, 338, 339, 341, 368, 373,
    376, 405, 413, 414, 443, 447–56,
    633
  Germany in, *see* Nazi Germany
  and illusion of Anglo-American
    alliance, 334–35, 342
  isolationism and, 289, 292, 295, 431,
    433, 434, 486, 498–500, 503, 504,
    517, 607–8
  Italy in, 451, 479–80, 497, 529, 581
  Japan in, 479–80, 538, 577, 580,
    581
  JFK's service in, 527–28, 531, 540,
    542, 543, 549, 551, 555–59, 560,
    734
  Joe Kennedy, Jr.'s service in, 527,
    528, 540, 542, 543, 546, 549, 555,
    562, 570–71
  JPK's pessimism about outcome of,
    xxii, 373, 416–19, 427–28, 429,
    431–32, 461, 479–80, 482,
    483–84, 495, 496–97, 498, 501,
    503, 509, 515, 517, 544
  Kathleen Kennedy's Red Cross
    service during, 551, 552, 555
  lend-lease program and, 510, 511–13,
    515, 516–20, 525
  Munich Agreement and, 346–47,
    348–49, 359–60, 400, 402, 435–
    36, 485, 633, 745
  neutrality laws and, 288, 415, 418,
    443, 445, 459, 510
  Pearl Harbor, xxii, 509, 538, 567
  Roosevelt's appeals for negotiations,
    341, 342, 343, 344

World War II (*cont.*)
  Selective Service System and, 476
  transatlantic communications and,
    422–23
  Tripartite Pact in, 479–80
  U.S. aid to Allies in, 441–43,
    451–54, 458–59, 461, 466–72,
    498, 503, 510, 517, 519, 605
  U.S. entry into, 538–39
  U.S. involvement with Allies in,
    428, 429, 441–43, 454, 467,
    477–80, 485, 486, 491, 504,
    513–17
  U.S. military strength and,
    494–95, 498
World Zionist Organization, 358

Wright, Bishop John, 625, 714
Wyzanski, Charles, 702

Yellow Cab Company, 88–89, 92
Young Men's Nonpartisan League of
  Boston, 38
Yugoslavia, 529, 636

Zanuck, Darryl, 299, 502
Zanuck, Virginia Fox, 299
Ziegfeld, Florenz, 97–98
Zionism, 286–87, 351–52, 358, 359,
  385, 386, 388–93, 712
Zionist Organization of America,
  391
Zukor, Adolph, 75, 94, 100, 101, 109

PHOTOGRAPH CREDITS

ABOUT THE AUTHOR

David Nasaw is the author of *Andrew Carnegie,* which was a finalist for the Pulitzer Prize, awarded the New-York Historical Society Prize in American History, and named a *New York Times* Notable Book of the Year, and *The Chief: The Life of William Randolph Hearst,* winner of the Bancroft Prize for history and the J. Anthony Lukas Book Prize and a finalist for the National Book Critics Circle Award for biography. He is the Arthur M. Schlesinger, Jr. Professor of History at the Graduate Center of the City University of New York.